For Pat McDonough,
with gratitude for
your insights, guidance,
encouragement, support,
and friendship --- in
so many ways and
on so many levels.

Fondly,

Stuart
Biegel
April 2006

EDUCATION AND THE LAW

By

Stuart Biegel
University of California, Los Angeles

AMERICAN CASEBOOK SERIES®

THOMSON

WEST

Mat #40188792

American Casebook Series and West Group are trademarks registered in the U.S. Patent and Trademark Office.

© 2006 Thomson/West
      610 Opperman Drive
      P.O. Box 64526
      St. Paul, MN 55164–0526
      1–800–328–9352

Printed in the United States of America

ISBN–13: 978–0–314–15047–9
ISBN–10: 0–314–15047–1

 TEXT IS PRINTED ON 10% POST CONSUMER RECYCLED PAPER

To my students—past, present, and future.

*

Acknowledgments

I would like to thank the many people who have contributed—directly or indirectly—to the completion of this casebook project. The project reflects twenty years of personal involvement with Education Law issues, in an academic context and in the real world of public education. During these years, I have benefited greatly from the insights, encouragement and support of my colleagues at UCLA and from so many members of both the legal community and the education community.

In particular, I would like to express my gratitude to the following current and former colleagues: Lynn Beck, Megan Franke, Kris Gutierrez, Harry Handler, John McNeil, Ted Mitchell, Danny Solorzano, Jim Trent, Concepcion Valadez, Amy Stuart Wells, and Buzz Wilms at the UCLA Graduate School of Education & Information Studies; and Michael Asimow, Paul Bergman, David Binder, Gary Blasi, Ken Karst, Chris Littleton, Grant Nelson, Gary Rowe, Bill Rubenstein, Gary Schwartz, Kirk Stark, and Eugene Volokh at the UCLA School of Law.

I would also like to express my enduring gratitude to Kristin Crosland, Amanda Datnow, Hoover Liddell, Octavio Pescador, Eric Rofes, and Kevin Welner from the education community; and the Honorable William H. Alsup, Kelly Rozmus Barnes, David Campos, Charles Forster, Ben Fox, Robin Johansen, Bob Kim, Tom Klitgaard, David Levine, David G. Lim, Shannon Minter, Thuy Thi Nguyen, The Honorable William H. Orrick, Jason Snyder, Joe Symkowick, and Ryan Tacorda from the legal community.

****

This casebook, and the accompanying teacher's edition, could not have been completed without the invaluable efforts of six outstanding research assistants: Allen Chiu and Jennifer Gin Lee in 2004–2005, Elizabeth Oh and Arvin Tseng in the Summer and Fall of 2005, and Jacob Foster and Jonathan Kuai in 2005–2006. I would also like to acknowledge with gratitude the assistance, support, and professionalism of the Thomson/West editorial team, and in particular the two editors I have worked most closely with, Staci Herr and Kathleen Vandergon.

Finally, special thanks should go to the following people, who have contributed directly to the completion of this project on so many levels over time: Ryan Christopher Fox, Joel Handler, Michael Hersher, Daniel Javitch, Jerry Kang, Allan Keown, Patricia McDonough, Rick Mintrop, Jeannie Oakes, Brad Sears, Diane Steinberg, Richard Steinberg, Dylan Vade, and Jonathan Zasloff.

In sum, this was not a project I could have completed on my own. I have been truly fortunate to have met so many wonderful people over such an extended period of time who have given so much on both a professional and a personal level.

STUART BIEGEL

Spring 2006

Summary of Contents

*

Table of Contents

Table of Cases

The principal cases are in bold type. Cases cited or discussed in the text are roman type. References are to pages. Cases cited in principal cases and within other quoted materials are not included.

*

EDUCATION
AND THE LAW

*

Chapter I

INTRODUCTION: CONTEXT FOR EXAMINING EDUCATION-RELATED DISPUTES

Education Law has emerged today as a bona fide area of specialization, both within the legal community and within the education community. Its major topical areas, which continue to grow and change, are derived from some of the most volatile controversies of our times. The primary focus of the field is public education, with issues spanning both the K–12 and the higher education sectors.

Almost every education-related legal dispute is accompanied by important public policy considerations. These considerations include not only the general policy context for the dispute, but also the policy implications of any proposed resolution. Thus it is not surprising that a rich body of Education Law scholarship can be identified, with cutting-edge literature continuing to be published in both legal and education journals, and significant books being written about these issues on a regular basis.

Education continues to be a central area of concern for political leaders, policy makers, and of course individuals across the nation, with legal issues comprising an integral part of almost every area of education today. Given the ongoing increase in education-related litigation and legislation, it is also not surprising that the opportunities for practicing in this area continue to grow exponentially. It is an area rich with possibility, and there is great opportunity for creativity on all levels.

A. SOURCES, INTERDISCIPLINARY FEATURES, & UNIQUE CHARACTERISTICS OF EDUCATION LAW

In general, the sources of Education Law include constitutions, statutes, case law, regulations, and policies. This list does constitute a hierarchy, with the constitution, for example, superseding any inconsistent statutes, case decisions, regulations, and policies. International

1

treaties and collective bargaining agreements may also need to be factored in, depending on the nature of the particular dispute.

Education Law is an interdisciplinary field, and education-related cases can generate issues in a number of traditional legal areas simultaneously. A large percentage of the disputes fall within the category of constitutional law, and other areas that might be implicated include criminal law and procedure, torts, and remedies. In addition, particularly in the employment context, issues of contract law and civil procedure may arise. The interface between case law and statutory frameworks is often at the heart of the dispute, with questions of statutory interpretation sometimes playing a central role.

Unless a controversy is specifically covered by statute, the relevant legal principles are typically the same at both the K–12 and the higher education levels. Yet these principles are often applied in very different ways depending on the setting and the age of the students. Often the question arises as to the precedential value of a given case decision at a grade level other than the one addressed. Sometimes, for example, the courts have recognized the applicability of major K–12 decisions to higher education disputes, and sometimes higher education cases have been deemed directly applicable at the K–12 level. Other times, however, the courts distinguish cases based on which grade level was initially addressed, on the grounds that the settings are very different. Patterns are often difficult to discern in this regard.

Finally, it is important to note that while education was traditionally seen as primarily the province of the states, there has been a major shift in this regard in recent years, particularly at the K–12 level. Education is not even mentioned in the U.S. Constitution, while it is typically a central feature of individual state constitutions. There was no separate U.S. Department of Education until the late 1970's. Yet with the passage of the bipartisan "No Child Left Behind" legislation by Congress in 2001, the entire dynamic shifted. Suddenly the federal government was seeking to play a central role in public education, defining the obligations of state and local educational agencies, and establishing draconian penalties for the failure to comply. This new and dramatic story is only just beginning to unfold.

B. PATTERNS, TRENDS, AND CASEBOOK ORGANIZATION

Education Law is an evolving field, and the controversies that are being addressed today are often very different from those education-related issues that were being confronted by the legal community twenty and thirty years ago. The controversies may also be much broader in scope, embodying the range of "front-burner" disputes that are on the minds of many Americans on a day-to-day basis. The organization of this casebook is designed to reflect these emerging patterns and trends.

Each of the ten substantive chapters in the casebook is designed to stand on its own, and the inquiry in any given chapter is not necessarily dependent on having first read the material in the previous chapters. But Chapters 2–9 can be viewed as constituting three clearly defined thematic groupings that exemplify recent developments. And the ten chapters together reflect five major areas of inquiry, as follows:

- *Chapters 2, 3 & 4*
  campus safety issues and related efforts to protect student privacy and freedom of expression in that context

- *Chapters 5, 6 & 7*
  parameters of the right to equal educational opportunity and related efforts to increase educational quality for all students

- *Chapters 8 & 9*
  religion, morality, and values in public education

- *Chapter 10*
  intellectual property issues in education, as reflected in volatile disputes regarding copyright in the higher education community

- *Chapter 11*
  rights of educators in the interrelated areas of labor relations, tenure, dismissal, academic freedom, and employment discrimination

The casebook begins with a focus on campus safety, because if the schools are not safe, then arguably little else matters. Chapter 2 also introduces the range of privacy-related issues that arise in education, and the built-in tension between efforts to maximize safety and efforts to address privacy interests. Chapter 3 provides an overview of First Amendment student "freedom of expression" principles, and highlights the extent to which safety concerns are reflected in the legal frameworks that have emerged. Chapter 4 then turns to the changing nature of efforts to combat threatening behavior, peer harassment, and peer mistreatment, and notes just how much this relatively new area of the law has been fueled by such watershed events as the tragic school shootings at Columbine High School and the September 11, 2001 attacks on the nation.

Chapter 5 shifts the focus to the continuing vitality of the right to equal educational opportunity, and to the range of disputes that are being litigated in that context, including but not limited to ongoing efforts to maximize equal access and equal treatment for students on the basis of race, ethnicity, and gender. Chapter 6 turns to the related topic of educational quality, documenting an emerging area of the law that is reflected in efforts—sometimes at cross purposes—to ensure educational "adequacy" through school finance litigation, guarantee accountability through the U.S. "No Child Left Behind" Act, increase school choice through charter schools or even vouchers, and facilitate privatization across the board. Chapter 7 follows by examining the legal and policy debates regarding the unmet needs of English learners and students with disabilities, debates that encompass issues of equity *and* educational quality.

Chapter 8 provides an overview of First Amendment principles in the area of religion, and documents the central role of education-related disputes in shaping Establishment Clause jurisprudence, especially with regard to school prayer and public funding for private sectarian education. Chapter 9 then turns to recent debates relating to "morality" and values, focusing in particular on paradigmatic controversies such as the text of the flag salute, disputed access to campus forums and facilities, the context for the teaching of evolution, the nature of the values that should be taught in public schools, the extent to which certain topics should be included in the curriculum, and the parameters of sex education in general.

Chapter 10 addresses copyright issues in education, a topic that exemplifies an increasing focus on intellectual property disputes in this country generally. The chapter provides an overview of basic principles in this area, examines traditional disputes regarding ownership and fair use, and then turns to the range of unresolved controversies relating to the digitization of information that have emerged over the past ten years as the Internet became a central feature of virtually everyone's daily life in higher education.

Chapter 11 concludes with a separate inquiry into the panoply of educator rights that have been recognized through collective bargaining laws, tenure statutes, protections against arbitrary dismissal, victories in First Amendment cases, and noteworthy prohibitions against employment discrimination. Academic freedom emerges as a surprisingly complex topic in this area, with the parameters of the "freedom" neither as precise nor as sweeping as many educators believe.

Fifty hypothetical problems are included throughout the casebook, designed to help focus the inquiry and supplement the questions raised in the materials generally. While most of these are traditional legal hypotheticals, many contain related policy questions that seek to highlight important contextual issues. And in certain instances, a given hypothetical may focus directly on educational policy matters that are at the very heart of a particular controversy.

C. THE CHALLENGE OF EFFECTING CHANGE IN AN EDUCATION SETTING

The study of Education Law would be incomplete without an acknowledgment of the complexities that are often prevalent behind the scenes. Particularly when change is sought with regard to how institutions operate and how educators act on a day-to-day level, these complexities can make it very difficult to effect any sort of lasting transformation.

Thus it is important to recognize that victories in the legal arena do not necessarily translate into substantive and effective change in the education arena. Indeed, a legal victory is often the first of many steps that may be necessary before stated goals are actually accomplished.

Not only do many educators distrust attorneys and question their understanding of education issues, but the educational system—as commentators have noted—is particularly resistant to change. For example, in certain settings, so many people may need to be informed of a legal requirement and so many levels of bureaucracy may be implicated that too often the persons who have the ability to actually make the changes may not be aware of what needs to be done. In addition, education officials responsible for monitoring relevant activity and enforcing compliance may have so many other responsibilities that it may not be humanly possible to do all that is being asked of them.

For many reasons, then, an education-related law may be "on the books," but there may be no mechanism in place for its enforcement. And even if strategies are developed and implemented to address compliance with court orders, decrees, statutory mandates, and regulatory requirements, these strategies may prove ineffective. For example:

- Funding may be unavailable to fully implement the strategies.

- Accountability measures designed to facilitate monitoring may be linked to standardized tests that provide a distorted or incomplete picture of day-to-day realities.

- Self-reporting mechanisms can lead to incomplete or even incorrect depictions of what is actually taking place.

- Sanctions, if implemented, may do more harm than good.

- External monitoring, if required, may be resisted, obfuscated, or even blocked... sometimes in subtle ways that are difficult to discern.

- Independent reports documenting failure to act or even a lack of compliance may end up sitting on the proverbial shelf, gathering dust, for example, in a court clerk's office, as months and years go by.

- Motions to enforce provisions of court orders or decrees pursuant to findings in legally mandated reports may be denied by courts.

- Political forces may compromise the ability of well-meaning people to act.

- The adversarial system may lead to educational institutions bringing in highly skilled attorneys to help them resist efforts to change.

None of these examples should discourage continued efforts to use the legal system to shape educational policy and improve quality of life for those involved. Indeed, much has changed in education as a result of efforts by members of the legal community. Education-related litigation has led to noteworthy victories, and education-related statutory schemes have proliferated. The impact of the law in this setting has indeed been far-reaching.

And often the lasting changes that do actually occur are the result of attorneys and educators working together—and not at cross purposes—to make those changes happen.

D. THE RIGHT TO AN EDUCATION

Many of the legal disputes that reach the courts in this field continue to directly or indirectly implicate the right to an education. Everyone agrees that there is such a right, but there is ongoing disagreement over its parameters.

The sources of the right to an education are many and varied. While the U.S. Constitution does not specifically mention education, many U.S. Supreme Court cases have determined—particularly under the First, Fourth, and Fourteenth Amendments—that students have the right to certain protections and guarantees in an education setting. On occasion, the Court actually does speak very precisely about both the content and the quality of the education that is expected, especially at the K–12 level.

One of the most widely recognized rights in this context is the right to equal educational opportunity. Consider the following description of the parameters of this right, originally written in 1989. What, if anything, would you add to it today?

The Continuing Vitality of the Right to Equal Educational Opportunity[a]

In Brown v. Board of Education, the Court held that under the Equal Protection Clause "the opportunity of an education ... is a right which must be made available to all on equal terms." Most commentators and jurists have determined that this language validates a "right" to some form of "equal educational opportunity," with the subsequent debates centering on the definition of the term and on the extent to which a legal system can require or enforce equality of opportunity.

More than three decades later, Justice Marshall relied heavily on the language of Brown in his Kadrmas dissent, reproducing the most famous paragraph from Chief Justice Warren's opinion and concluding that the North Dakota statute authorizing the imposition of fees for transporting students infringes upon the right to equal opportunity. "In allowing a State to burden the access of poor persons to an education," he declared, "the Court denies equal opportunity and discourages hope. I do not believe the Equal Protection Clause countenances such a result." * * *

Marshall's focus on the right to equal educational opportunity as the key interest at stake in the North Dakota case reflects the continuing vitality of this right in the American legal system today. Indeed,

a. *From* Stuart Biegel, *Reassessing the Applicability of Fundamental Rights Analysis: The Fourteenth Amendment and the Shaping of Educational Policy after Kadrmas v. Dickinson Public Schools,* 74 Cornell L. Rev. 1078, 1081–1084 (1989).

the controversy regarding the parameters of the right has been at the center of many school-related disputes. Although not always mentioned explicitly, "denial of equal opportunity" is typically a central, underlying concern in fourteenth amendment litigation that involves such volatile areas as school desegregation, school finance, [the rights of students with disabilities] * * *, standardized testing, and bilingual education. * * *

The right to equal educational opportunity has become a strong and multi-faceted interest * * * When federal legislation establishing a separate Department of Education included a declaration that the new cabinet post had been set up "to strengthen the federal commitment to ensuring access to equal opportunity for every individual," Congress was simply affirming that this recognized right now occupied a position of central importance in educational policy making.

As discussed above, one of the most significant changes in this area has been the passage of the "No Child Left Behind" Act at the federal level. While this legislation has engendered great controversy, particularly with regard to its "accountability" provisions, many who join in criticism of certain provisions also believe that its focus on raising the bar for all students will serve to enhance the right to equal educational opportunity. In addition, commentators have suggested that the Act's explicit requirement that every school work toward proficiency for every student has strengthened the right to a quality education as well.

Other federal statutes, along with their accompanying regulations, continue to play an important role in guaranteeing rights for students. Civil rights statutes generally have been of central importance in guaranteeing equal access, and statutes addressing particular areas of education—including but not limited to the Individuals with Disabilities Education Act (IDEA)—have provided road maps that have led to significant improvement in many settings.

At the state court level, additional rights have been recognized under individual state constitutional provisions guaranteeing the availability of public education until a certain age. In addition, states have sometimes recognized broader protections for individual rights in this area, protections that go beyond the federal baseline. For example, while the U.S. Supreme Court, by a vote of 5–4, determined that education was not a fundamental right under the Fourteenth Amendment, a number of state courts have come to an opposite conclusion under their own constitutions.

The California Supreme Court was one of these institutions, holding in 1976 that education would be considered a fundamental right in California, at least within the context of equalizing public school finance. In 1992, the same Court was presented with the question of whether this fundamental right could be deemed to have broader applicability, beyond the narrower fact pattern of the 1970's litigation.

What might be the implications of a recognition that education is a fundamental constitutional right? Consider the following excerpt from the opinion of that Court, *Thomas K. Butt v. State of California,* 4 Cal.4th 668, 15 Cal.Rptr.2d 480, 842 P.2d 1240 (1992):

> In late April 1991, after a period of mounting deficits, the Richmond Unified School District (District) announced it lacked funds to complete the final six weeks of its 1990–1991 school term. The District proposed to close its doors on May 1, 1991.
>
> [A group of parents, represented by pro bono attorneys from the San Francisco office of Morrison Foerster and acting in concert with the California Department of Education's legal team, challenged the proposed closure as violative of the children's fundamental right to an education and obtained a preliminary injunction from Contra Costa County Superior Court. The injunction directed the State of California (State), its Controller, and its Superintendent of Public Instruction (SPI) to ensure that the District's students would receive a full school term or its equivalent.
>
> Rather than complying, the State of California, represented by the Governor and the Attorney General, chose to file an appeal.]
>
> We declined to stay implementation of the plan pending the State's appeal. However, we transferred the appeal here in order to decide an important issue of first impression: Whether the State has a constitutional duty, aside from the equal allocation of educational funds, to prevent the budgetary problems of a particular school district from depriving its students of "basic" educational equality.
>
> We affirm the trial court's determination that such a duty exists under the California Constitution.
>
> * * *
>
> Since its admission to the Union, California has assumed specific responsibility for a statewide public education system open on equal terms to all. The Constitution of 1849 directed the Legislature to "provide for a system of common schools, by which a school shall be kept up and supported in each district ...." That constitutional command, with the additional proviso that the school maintained by each district be "free," has persisted to the present day.
>
> * * * [T]he State itself has broad responsibility to ensure basic educational equality under the California Constitution. Because access to a public education is a uniquely fundamental personal interest in California, our courts have consistently found that the State charter accords broader rights against State-maintained educational discrimination than does federal law. Despite contrary federal authority, California constitutional principles require State assistance to correct basic "interdistrict" disparities in the system of common schools, even when the discriminatory effect was not produced by the purposeful conduct of the State or its agents. * * *
>
> Hence, * * * [we declared, in 1976, that] "[i]n applying our state constitutional provisions guaranteeing equal protection of the laws

we shall continue to apply strict and searching judicial scrutiny" to claims of discriminatory educational classifications. More recent cases confirm that education is a fundamental interest under the California equal protection guaranties and that the unique importance of public education in California's constitutional scheme requires careful scrutiny of state interference with basic educational rights.

* * * It therefore appears well settled that the California Constitution makes public education uniquely a fundamental concern of the State and prohibits maintenance and operation of the common public school system in a way which denies basic educational equality to the students of particular districts. The State itself bears the ultimate authority and responsibility to ensure that its district-based system of common schools provides basic equality of educational opportunity.

The State claims it need only ensure the six-month minimum term guaranteed by the free school clause. This contention, however, misconstrues the basis of the trial court's decision. Whatever the requirements of the free school guaranty, the equal protection clause precludes the State from maintaining its common school system in a manner that denies the students of one district an education basically equivalent to that provided elsewhere throughout the State. * * *

The State suggests there was no showing that the impact of the threatened closure on District students' fundamental right to basic educational equality was real and appreciable. Of course, the Constitution does not prohibit all disparities in educational quality or service. Despite extensive State regulation and standardization, the experience offered by our vast and diverse public school system undoubtedly differs to a considerable degree among districts, schools, and individual students. These distinctions arise from inevitable variances in local programs, philosophies, and conditions. "[A] requirement that [the State] provide [strictly] 'equal' educational opportunities would thus seem to present an entirely unworkable standard requiring impossible measurements and comparisons...." Moreover, principles of equal protection have never required the State to remedy all ills or eliminate all variances in service. * * *

Even unplanned truncation of the intended school term will not necessarily constitute a denial of "basic" educational equality. A finding of constitutional disparity depends on the individual facts. Unless the actual quality of the district's program, viewed as a whole, falls fundamentally below prevailing statewide standards, no constitutional violation occurs.

Here, however, plaintiffs' preliminary showing suggested that closure of the District's schools on May 1, 1991, would cause an extreme and unprecedented disparity in educational service and progress. District students faced the sudden loss of the final six weeks, or almost one-fifth, of the standard school term originally intended by the District and provided everywhere else in California. The record indicates that the decision to close early was a desperate, unplanned response to the District's impending insolvency and the impasse in negotiations for further emergency State aid. Several District teachers declared that they were operating on standard-term lesson schedules made at the beginning of the school year. These declarants outlined in detail how the proposed early closure would prevent them from completing instruction and grading essential for academic promotion, high school graduation, and college entrance. Faced with evidence of such extensive educational disruption, the trial court did not abuse its discretion by concluding that the proposed closure would have a real and appreciable impact on the affected students' fundamental California right to basic educational equality. * * *

In addition to the decisions of state courts, state legislatures have also delineated rights for students in the area of education beyond the federal baseline. These rights have included, but are not limited to, protection against discrimination and mistreatment on the basis of race, ethnicity, gender, age, disability, religion, and lesbian, gay, bisexual, and transgender (LGBT) status. State legislation and accompanying regulations also provide many specific programmatic guarantees, both in the area of curriculum generally as well as with regard to students with additional needs. The scope of state education codes, in particular, is typically very broad and wide-ranging.

Consider the following hypothetical, which takes place in the fictional state of Eldorado. Given the range of protections and guarantees that are available for students, what are your initial reactions to the questions presented?

PROBLEM 1: The Fundamental Right to an Education

The Rainbow Ridge Unified School District grants permission to the Nanotech Valley Consortium to establish five charter schools for economically disadvantaged students. As envisioned, these schools would serve as models for the integration of wireless computer technology into the daily education program. Yet once the schools are open they are not only plagued by inconsistent connections, but they are constantly in the process of repairing unreliable equipment (much of it donated and relatively outdated). In addition, the faculty appears to have abandoned the teaching of basic skills in favor of an Internet-based curriculum which emphasizes analysis, synthesis, and creative problem solving.

When the state-mandated standardized test results are released the following summer, the students in all five charter schools score—on the average—in the 35th percentile in reading and in the 38th percentile in math (based on national percentile rankings). A group of parents, infuriated by these test results and by what they perceive to be a second rate education for their students, consult you for the purpose of filing a lawsuit on the grounds that their children's *fundamental right to an education* has been violated.

What arguments might you consider setting forth? What additional factual information might you wish to obtain? What would be an appropriate remedy under the circumstances? Or would you even consider taking such a case? Why?

Chapter II

CAMPUS SAFETY AND PRIVACY

This chapter addresses basic issues of safety in the education community. We begin with safety, because if campuses are not safe, little else matters. Education is invariably ineffective in an atmosphere of fear and distrust. But an analysis of safety issues, particularly in this era, is incomplete without a concurrent examination of privacy concerns. Indeed, both under the law and as a matter of policy, a perennial ongoing tension between safety concerns and privacy concerns continues to be evident in this country.

This tension is especially apparent in school settings, and has only increased after the 1999 shootings at Columbine High School and the attacks against the nation on September 11, 2001. And privacy issues have become even more pressing with the advent of the information age and continued advances in surveillance technology.

Chapter 2 begins with an examination of negligence, which continues to be the main area of the law implicated in a school safety context. Part A addresses liability at the K–12 level, and Part B addresses liability at the higher education level. Related statutes at both the federal and the state levels are also referenced in these sections. These include zero-tolerance statutes addressing weapons on campus and safety-related requirements under the "No Child Left Behind" Act.

The second half of the chapter focuses on privacy interests that may be compromised by efforts to maintain or increase campus safety. Part D addresses search and seizure issues, including but not limited to drug testing. Part E addresses student records, focusing in particular on the scope of protections available under the Family Educational Rights and Privacy Act (FERPA). Part F then turns to technology and privacy, examining both the range of Internet-related issues that continue to arise as well as recent developments in offline surveillance that will invariably lead to novel legal disputes.

It is important to note that incidents affecting campus safety often implicate multiple areas of the law. In addition to negligence, for example, issues may arise under the First Amendment Free Speech Clause, under threat law generally, and under laws specifically addressing peer harassment and mistreatment. We examine these additional areas of the law in the two chapters that follow.

A. LIABILITY FOR INJURIES AT THE K-12 LEVEL

PROBLEM 2: Green v. Suburbia Sch. Dist.

As the Suburbia High Senior Class Cabinet assembled in Room 190 for their weekly lunchtime meeting, Class Sponsor Fred Brown realized that he had forgotten to pack a sandwich. Having left these meetings several times before, Coach Brown did not hesitate to do so now. After all, the only people in the room were the school's top student leaders.

While he was in the cafeteria purchasing lunch, however, Sherry Marvin passed around a vial of cocaine and a silver spoon. Six of the eight students in the room (including Class President Amanda Green) ingested several "doses" of cocaine while Coach Brown was gone.

Amanda, who had permission to leave school to pick up supplies for the Senior Class Dance, departed before Coach Brown returned. Eight blocks from school, however, she drove her new 4Runner into a tree and suffered a variety of injuries, including a whiplash and a broken leg. She was hospitalized for three days, and missed two weeks of school.

Amanda "confessed" to her parents that she had indeed been under the influence of cocaine when the accident occurred. She also explained that this was the third time she had ingested cocaine ... all three times coming on the Suburbia campus. In September, a classmate had shared the substance with her while they were dressing in the girls locker room after P.E., and in October a fellow class officer had given her several "hits" while seated in the bleachers watching a football game.

A. What arguments would the Green family set forth under a negligence theory in a lawsuit against the Suburbia School District?

B. Would the plaintiff's case be stronger or weaker if the following happened instead? Why? If the case went to trial, what result? Discuss.

1. Students were sixth graders rather than high school seniors, and Amanda rode on roller skates instead of in her car. All other facts were the same.

2. Coach Brown actually was in the room when the cocaine was ingested. All other facts were the same.

3. Coach Brown left and an earthquake occurred; some students were injured.

4. A gun was passed around, not cocaine; Amanda was injured in her car when the gun went off while she was examining it.

5. A gun was passed around, not cocaine; a student was accidentally shot.

6. It was not lunchtime, but class time. Coach Brown left the class with a student teacher in charge. All other facts were the same.

7. Two school dropouts (former students of Coach Brown) came into the room while he was gone. A fight ensued, and several students were injured.

1. STATE NEGLIGENCE LAW PRINCIPLES

Negligence cases are typically decided in state courts, under principles that are generally similar from place to place. Negligence has been defined as the breach of a duty of care, owed to the plaintiff, that is the actual and proximate cause of plaintiff's injury.

While school districts in general are no longer immune from lawsuits in this area, both the type and the extent of "sovereign immunity" protection vary from state to state. For example, in Illinois, immunity is granted in those situations where state actors are deemed to have been in a position where they were "exercising discretion." In Mississippi, immunity is granted if educators are deemed to have been using ordinary care in controlling students. In South Carolina, a public school district is generally not liable for injuries resulting from negligent supervision unless the supervising educator is "grossly negligent."[a] In California, however, if statutory liability can be established under provisions of the state's Government Code, a successful cause of action can often be maintained. As the California Supreme Court has stated, "the rule is liability; immunity is the exception."[b]

Assuming that the doctrine of sovereign immunity does not apply, educational institutions can generally be found liable for the negligence of their employees under the traditional doctrine of *respondeat superior*.[c]

At the K–12 level, on school grounds and during school hours, duty is typically not an issue. There is both a common law duty to supervise, and—in many states—a statutory duty to supervise. In general, the standard of care in carrying out this duty is deemed to be identical to that required of school personnel in the performance of their other duties. As a general rule, adults in these settings are held to that degree of care which a person of ordinary prudence, charged with comparable duties, would exercise under the same circumstances. These cases, therefore, often turn on an analysis of breach. If one student is injured by another (the most typical fact pattern), a breach of the school district's duty of care can generally be found in one of two ways: (1) failure to exercise proper supervision, and (2) directing or permitting

a. Todd A. DeMitchell, *The Educator and Tort Liability,* 154 ED. LAW REP. 417 (2001).

b. Lopez v. Southern Cal. Rapid Transit Dist., 40 Cal.3d 780, 792, 221 Cal.Rptr. 840, 710 P.2d 907, 914 (1985). In California, all government tort liability must be based on statute, and an aggrieved party must show that the District acted in violation of at least one provision "designed to protect against the risk of . . . [that] particular kind of injury. . . ." CAL. GOV'T CODE § 815.6

(West 2005). *See generally id.* at §§ 810–895.8.

c. *See, e.g.,* Hoff v. Vacaville Unified Sch. Dist., 19 Cal.4th 925, 80 Cal.Rptr.2d 811, 968 P.2d 522 (1998) (Mosk, J., concurring) ("[A] school district may be liable for the acts or omissions of school employees within the scope of employment 'if the act or omission would, apart from this section, have given rise to a cause of action against that employee.'").

pupils to engage in activities that might reasonably be foreseen to result in injuries.

Duty can be a major issue, however, if the injuries occur before school, after school, or near school, or if the injured party is not a student. Injuries during extracurricular activities can also raise troublesome questions regarding the duty owed. And circumstances surrounding a school shooting can be particularly complex in this regard.

The cases and problems that follow wrestle with the parameters of the duty owed in these types of situations.

a.   *Extent of the Duty to Supervise*

GLASER v. EMPORIA UNIFIED SCH. DIST. NO. 253

271 Kan. 178, 21 P.3d 573 (2001).

ALLEGRUCCI, J.:

This is a personal injury action brought on behalf of Todd Glaser, a seventh-grader at Lowther Middle School in Emporia, Kansas. When he was chased by another student, he ran off school grounds into a public street. He was injured in a collision with a car driven by Patricia Gould–Lipson. Glaser settled his claims against the driver, [but prosecuted a lawsuit against the District]. * * *

* * * The only factual findings the district court determined to be necessary to its decision are the following:

1.   The plaintiff was injured when he collided with an automobile on the 22nd day of December 1993.

2.   Prior to the collision, the plaintiff was on school property that was unsupervised by Emporia Unified School District No. 253 employees.

3.   The collision between the plaintiff and an automobile driven by Patricia Gould–Lipson occurred prior to classes beginning, and the collision occurred on a public street adjacent to school property.

The district court also noted that it was undisputed that the school district "does not exercise supervision before school until a student is in the building."

On appeal, both parties supply additional facts with references to the record. The following "additional facts" are not disputed:

On December 22, 1993, Glaser was a 12-year-old seventh-grade student at Lowther South. He lived approximately a 15- to 20-minute walk from school, and he normally got to school by walking. School began at 8:10 a.m. On the day he was injured, Glaser arrived at school between 7:30 a.m. and 7:45 a.m.

A school district policy, which was approved June 22, 1993, provided: "Teachers who observe students in a potentially dangerous situation should attempt, as they are reasonably able, either to halt or prevent injury to students or property."

The sole issue on appeal is whether the school district owed a duty to Glaser under the circumstances.

* * *

Cases cited by Glaser from other jurisdictions include *Raymond v. Paradise Unified School Dist.*, 218 Cal.App.2d 1, 31 Cal.Rptr. 847 (1963); *Tymkowicz v. San Jose, Etc. Unified School Dist.*, 151 Cal.App.2d 517, 312 P.2d 388 (1957); * * * *Titus v. Lindberg*, 49 N.J. 66, 228 A.2d 65 (1967); and *Rice v. School District No. 302, Pierce Co.*, 140 Wash. 189, 248 Pac. 388 (1926). The general principle for which Glaser cites these cases is that schools and school personnel have a duty to protect the safety of students.

In the New Jersey case, a 9-year-old student named Titus was on the grounds of his school, headed for the rack to put up the bicycle that he had ridden there, when he was struck by a paper clip shot from an elastic band by 13-year-old Lindberg. The principal of Titus' school "stated flatly that he maintained 'supervision outside the building on the grounds between eight and 8:30.' " For the reason that the principal "assumed the responsibility for supervising the school grounds beginning at 8 a.m.," the New Jersey court rejected the argument that his responsibilities did not begin before 8:15. The New Jersey court gave an additional reason:

They customarily began coming at 8 a.m and that was reasonable. Smith[, the principal,] undoubtedly knew of their coming and of their 'keep away' games. When all this is coupled with the fact that Fairview was also a pickup site for the older students, the dangers and the need for reasonable supervision from 8 a.m. on were entirely apparent.

Titus could be distinguished from the present case on the ground that Lowther Middle School was not a designated pickup site for older students. * * *

In *Tymkowicz*, a 10-year-old student died from injuries sustained on the school grounds while he was engaged in a game with other students. The object of the game was to render a participant unconscious. The principal admitted knowing that the game was played, and there was no evidence of any efforts by school authorities to stop the game. The California Education Code contained a provision requiring that "[e]very teacher in the public schools shall hold pupils to a strict account for their conduct ... on the playgrounds, or during recess." The distinction with the present case is obvious. The injury occurred during recess, on school grounds, and we have no comparable statute.

* * *

In *Raymond*, a 7-year-old boy waited on the grounds of the high school for the school bus that took him to his elementary school. He was injured when he ran toward the bus before it came to a halt, placed his left hand on the side of the bus, and fell backward on the sidewalk. The jury found that the school district was negligent in failing to provide for supervision of the bus boarding area. A basis on which the appellate court affirmed the judgment were statutory provisions obliging the school district, once it furnished transportation for students, to provide a reasonably safe system. Other considerations were: (1) that supervision of the bus stop on the grounds of the high school rather than in an isolated place was a practical possibility for the school district, (2) that it was a very busy stop, with up to three busloads of students arriving and departing there at peak periods, and (3) that small children were present.

Although there are some similarities between the present case and *Raymond,* differences prevail. The injured student in the California case, Raymond, was 7, and Glaser was a seventh-grader. Raymond was injured at a school district designated bus stop, and Glaser was injured when he ran off school grounds into a public street.

In *Rice,* an 11-year-old student was severely shocked and burned on the school grounds before classes began when he pulled on a radio aerial wire, which had broken after being installed for a PTA entertainment, and the radio wire dropped on electric wires. Earlier, several teachers passed by, saw Rice and other boys tugging on the broken wire, and told them to play elsewhere. In response, Rice played football for awhile before returning to the wire. School policy provided playground supervision for one-half hour before classes, but there was no supervision at the time of the injury. There was disputed evidence about whether the injury occurred within the period that should have been supervised. The disposition of the case in the student's favor, however, did not turn on the issue of supervision. The school district was charged with the duty "from the time the defendant had knowledge that the wire was dangling down and reaching the ground where pupils might take hold of it" to put the school grounds in a reasonably safe condition.

The present case does not involve an extraordinary, dangerous condition on the school grounds such as the one that existed in *Rice.* Nonetheless, Glaser quotes Section 364 of the Restatement (Second) of Torts, Creation or Maintenance of Dangerous Artificial Conditions (1964). Generally stated, § 364 provides that a landholder is subject to liability for injuries caused by a structure or other artificial condition created by the landholder or with his permission. Proximity to the public street and the absence of a fence seem to be the conditions complained of by Glaser. Neither would seem to be a structure or other artificial condition within the meaning of § 364. With regard to this claim, the trial court stated that Glaser "provides no evidence that would meet [this] duty * * *."

* * *

Glaser asserts that his classroom was locked at the time of his injury, thus forcing him to remain outside on the unsupervised school grounds. There is nothing in the district court's findings of fact that would support the assertion. Nor does Glaser supply a reference to the record where his assertion is supported. The school district, on the other hand, furnished a reference to the record where there is evidence that Glaser had the option of waiting inside the school building where the school provided supervision before classes began. * * *

The district court found that neither the school district nor [teacher Douglas] Epp had assumed a duty to supervise Glaser. Glaser's contention that they had assumed a duty to supervise rests on written school district policies, including the following provisions: "Students shall be under the supervision of appropriate school personnel at all times when they are under the jurisdiction of the school," and "[t]eachers who observe students in a potentially dangerous situation should attempt, as they are reasonably able, either to halt or prevent injury to students or property." Glaser contends that the policies constitute "clear evidence" that the duty to prevent injury was not limited to the interior of the building or the time when classes are in session. He further contends that the policies demonstrate that the school district assumed a duty to protect students in any potentially dangerous situation. We disagree.

* * *

> Plaintiff would add that * * * [p]rior to the accident, a teacher for Lowther Middle School, Douglas Epp, observed Todd and Justin playing and running in an area not ten feet away from Congress street. Despite observing the students in a potentially dangerous situation, he took no action. He simply kept walking, even though he would later admit to Pagan Glaser that he thought "somebody was going to run out in that street and get hit by a car."

* * * [However,] the issue for this court is simply whether the school district, by adopting its written policies, assumed to protect the safety of students gathered on the school grounds before classes began. Epp's presence and conduct are not relevant to the court's review of the trial court's entry of summary judgment on the assumption of duty question.

The legal basis for Glaser's contention is Restatement (Second) of Torts § 324A (1964), and its interpretation in *Honeycutt* [*v. City of Wichita,* 251 Kan. 451, 836 P.2d 1128 (1992)] * * * .

[*Honeycutt* was a personal injury action brought on behalf of a minor in which summary judgment was granted in favor of the school district. This court affirmed. Jeremy Honeycutt attended morning kindergarten. Railroad tracks ran between his house and the school. He usually was taken or escorted to school by an adult, but on March 5, 1987, Jeremy and another student were walking home after school unaccompanied by an adult. Jeremy ran alongside a moving train and fell under the wheels.

Jeremy argued that the school district owed him three duties: "(1) to retain him until an authorized adult took custody of him, (2) to retain him on school property through a 'hold back' policy in the event of a train operating off school property, and (3) to establish a safety patrol at the railroad crossing." His bases for arguing that the school district owed him those duties were that the student-school district relationship created a duty and that the school district assumed a duty by its conduct and written policies.]

In [*rejecting plaintiff's argument*], the [*Honeycutt*] court engaged in an extensive discussion of § 324A * * * [.]

This court has accepted § 324A's theory of liability and established the following principles:

"The threshold requirement for the application of the Restatement (Second) of Torts § 324A (1964) is a showing that the defendant undertook, gratuitously or for consideration, to render services to another. In order to meet this requirement, the evidence must show the defendant did more than act, but *through affirmative action* assumed an obligation or intended to render services for the benefit of another.

"A duty is owed to third persons by one who undertakes, *by an affirmative act,* to render aid or services to another and then is negligent in the performance of that undertaking." "For a defendant to meet the threshold requirements of § 324A, the defendant must not only take affirmative action to render services to another, but the person to whom the services are directed *must accept such services* in lieu of, or in addition to, such person's obligation to perform the services."

"The extent of the undertaking should define the scope of the duty."

"[O]ne who does not assume an obligation to render services does not owe a duty to third persons."

* * *

In *Honeycutt,* the court rejected plaintiff's argument that the school district assumed a duty by its written policies.

Here, as in *Honeycutt,* the injury occurred off school premises and at a time when the student was not on school property or in school custody. Todd was injured after he ran off the school grounds, across a parking area and into a city street. The school district never undertook to render services calculated to protect or supervise Todd, either by affirmative acts or promise to act, nor was Todd under the control or in the custody of the school district. Thus, as in *Honeycutt,* there has been no showing that a student-school district duty existed.

Affirmed.

Notes

1. State courts are typically very deferential to school districts in negligence cases. As a general rule, only the most egregious set of circumstances result in school district liability. The principle that schools cannot be "insurers of safety" is articulated over and over again in case decisions.

Courts decide cases in this area on practical grounds, determining whether or not a school could reasonably be expected to prevent the particular injury under all the circumstances of the case. And implicit in these decisions is the recognition that educational institutions are almost always financially strapped, especially at the K–12 level.

2. In *Glaser,* the Kansas Court appeared to determine that the cases from other jurisdictions cited by the plaintiff were relatively easy to distinguish. Was this analysis justified? Why?

3. Would the Court have come to the same conclusion if the plaintiff had been in kindergarten rather than in seventh grade? Should it have come to the same conclusion?

4. Assume the same set of facts, except that instead of being hit by a car off school grounds, the plaintiff was hit by a car on school grounds. Would the decision have been the same? Should the decision have been the same? In light of this inquiry, should *Glaser* be characterized as a broad ruling, or a narrow and fact-specific ruling, in the end?

5. In *Hoff v. Vacaville Unified School District,* 19 Cal.4th 925, 80 Cal.Rptr.2d 811, 968 P.2d 522 (1998), the California Supreme Court considered the question of whether the school district owed a duty of care to a non-student who was walking across the street from the high school and sustained serious injuries when a 16-year-old student lost control of his car and slammed into him:

> In exiting the lot, Lozano had "floor[ed]" the accelerator, "peeled out" with the wheels "screeching," "fishtailed," and jumped the curb and hit Hoff, who was walking on the sidewalk across the street. Lozano had been driving for six months, had no history of misbehavior, and obeyed his school supervisors. *Id.* at 930.

The Court determined that neither a common law duty nor a state statutory duty ran to Hoff. Under common law, the Court analogized to the duty of parents to control their children:

> California follows the Restatement rule (Rest.2d Torts, § 316), which finds a "special relationship" between parent and child, and accordingly places upon the parent "a duty to exercise reasonable care so to control his minor child as to prevent [the child] from intentionally harming others or from so [behaving] * * * as to create an unreasonable risk of bodily harm to them, if the parent (a) knows or has reason to know that he has the ability to control his child, and (b) knows or should know of the necessity and opportunity for exercising such control." * * * Thus, knowledge of dangerous habits and ability to control the child are prerequisites to imposition of liability. * * * Only the manifestation of specific dangerous tendencies * * * triggers a parental duty to exercise reasonable care to control the minor child in order to prevent * * * harm to third persons. * * *
>
> * * * At common law, "[s]chool officials are said to stand *in loco parentis*, in the place of parents, to their students, with similar powers and responsibilities." Moreover, by statute, we measure school personnel's criminal liability for exercising physical control over students by the standard applicable to parents. Given these similarities, any duty

that school employees owe off-campus nonstudents should at least be no greater in scope than the duty that parents owe third persons. Accordingly, school personnel who neither know nor reasonably should know that a particular student has a tendency to drive recklessly owe no duty to off-campus nonstudents. *Id.* at 934–35.

Hoff was not referenced in *Glaser*. Would the decision have helped either party, or are the facts easily distinguishable?

PROBLEM 3: The Marbury Middle School Lawsuits

Over a twenty-year period, Marbury Middle School—a fictional urban campus—developed a unique relationship with the Fred Korematsu Public Library. Both the school's main office and classroom facility and the public library were situated in the same complex, and when a combination of overcrowding and budget cutbacks led to the dismantling and closing down of the school's own library collection, a close working arrangement was established between the two separate institutions. Under this informal arrangement, all Marbury students received automatic borrowing privileges, later expanded to include free and unlimited use of the 15 computer terminals. Teachers brought their classes to the library on a regular basis pursuant to a schedule worked out by Korematsu librarians. And when the library installed unrestricted Internet access on all the terminals, students were able to benefit from this additional service as well.

In early February 2006, a major incident took place at the library involving Mrs. Parks' eighth grade English class and resulting in both computer damage and injuries. Parks, a tough disciplinarian whose calm and supportive personality meshed well with the 39 high-energy students, never had any trouble in class. The incident took place, however, on a day when she was not in school, due to an unexpected family emergency linked to the high winds that were buffeting the area. At the last minute, the school office contacted Mr. Purview, a retired teacher who sometimes assisted in the reading recovery classes. Purview was not walking well, but he agreed to come in and take the class for the day, knowing that Parks always left detailed lesson plans for substitutes in the unlikely event that she could not be there.

Things went fairly well throughout the morning, but everything changed when Purview took the 5th period eighth graders to the library after lunch as scheduled. Students jostled each other as they walked over, and several yelled so loudly that two other teachers had to leave their classrooms to quiet them down. In the library, they quickly ran over to the terminals, and some pushing occurred as students vied for the best seats. But before too long things had settled down, and most students worked on their Internet research projects. Purview, however, suddenly remembered that he needed to call his son to schedule a ride home, and asked Morrie to watch the students while he went to retrieve his cell phone. Morrie—a Korematsu employee and part-time poet—was everyone's favorite librarian.

Three minutes after Purview had left the room, Janie—angry at a Web site she had come across that questioned the war policies of the Bush Administration—gestured clumsily at the computer screen and accidentally knocked it over. The monitor fell to the floor, and landed on Sally's foot. Sally and Janie, who feuded constantly over everything from boyfriends to politics, immediately began pushing and shoving each other, knocking over three other monitors in the process. Several other students joined in the melee, including five members of the junior wrestling team. According to Morrie, it was unclear how many were actually fighting and how many were simply playing. Yet numerous injuries did occur, including one broken arm (Sally), and several cuts requiring stitches. In addition, Julio—a two-year-old who was in the library with his mother while these events occurred—was knocked out of his mother's arms and fell against a broken computer monitor, suffering injuries that required an overnight stay in the local hospital.

Negligence lawsuits are filed against the school district by both Sally's family and Julio's family. What arguments would be set forth by the plaintiffs in these respective lawsuits? What result?

Assume that the Marbury Education Code provides, in pertinent part:

No school district, city or county board of education, county superintendent of schools, or any officer or employee of such district or board shall be responsible or in any way liable for the conduct or safety of any pupil of the public schools at any time when such pupil is not on school property, unless such district, board, or person has undertaken to provide transportation for such pupil to and from the school premises, has undertaken a school-sponsored activity off the premises of such school, has otherwise specifically assumed such responsibility or liability or has failed to exercise reasonable care under the circumstances.

Would the language of this statute make the plaintiff's case easier? More difficult? Explain.

b.   *Supervision During Extracurricular Activities*

CERNY v. CEDAR BLUFFS JUNIOR/SENIOR PUB. SCH.

267 Neb. 958, 679 N.W.2d 198 (2004).

MILLER-LERMAN, J.

* * *

[Cerny, a high school football player, brought this action against the school district, seeking damages for the alleged negligence of his coaches in allowing him to reenter a game after suffering a head injury, and then allowing him to participate in contact drill practice several days later.]

II.   STATEMENT OF FACTS

* * *

In the fall of 1995, Cerny was a student at the School and a member of its football team. On the evening of Friday, September 15, 1995, he participated in a football game between Cedar Bluffs and Beemer high schools. Mitchell R. Egger was the head coach of the Cedar Bluffs team, and Robert M. Bowman was the assistant coach. Both held Nebraska teaching certificates with coaching endorsements.

Cerny fell while attempting to make a tackle during the second quarter of the Beemer game, striking his head on the ground. Although he felt dizzy and disoriented after the fall, Cerny initially remained in the game but took himself out after a few plays. He returned to the game during the third quarter. Subsequently, during football practice on Tuesday, September 19, Cerny was allegedly injured again when his helmet struck that of another player during a contact tackling drill.

There was conflicting evidence at trial regarding the symptoms experienced and communicated by Cerny during and after the Beemer game. Cerny testified that when he came out of the game, he told Egger and Bowman that he felt dizzy, disoriented, and extremely weak. Egger stated that Cerny complained of dizziness when he came off the field during the Beemer game. He also noted that Cerny was short of breath and had a tingling sensation in his neck. Egger stated that Bowman continued to monitor Cerny.

Bowman testified that Cerny did not complain of a headache when he left the game, but did state that he felt fuzzy or dizzy, that he had some burning in his shoulder, and that he could not catch his breath. Bowman attributed Cerny's dizziness to hyperventilation, not a head injury. Bowman stated that when Cerny came out of the game, Cerny made normal eye contact with Bowman and Cerny's speech and movement appeared normal. After catching his breath, Cerny appeared to Bowman to be in a normal emotional state. However, Bowman did recommend to Egger that Cerny should get medical attention, but to his knowledge, no medical personnel examined Cerny that evening.

When Cerny asked to re-enter the game during the third quarter, Bowman observed that he seemed completely normal, exhibiting neither confusion, disorientation, nor abnormal speech. Bowman also noted that Cerny did not complain of a headache. Egger allowed Cerny to re-enter the game after observing that his color looked good, his eyes looked clear, and his speech was normal.

Cerny testified that he had a headache continuously from Friday night until the practice on Tuesday. However, there is conflicting evidence as to whether he reported this to his coaches. Cerny testified he told Bowman he had a headache during the bus ride home after the Beemer game. However, Bowman testified that during the bus ride, he asked Cerny how he felt, and Cerny replied "I feel good, Coach" and did not complain of a headache. . . . Cerny testified that he told his coaches before the Tuesday practice that he had a nagging headache all weekend, but on cross-examination, he admitted that he did not remember if he had told the coaches that he was feeling bad before practice. Egger testified that he did not talk to Cerny before the Tuesday practice and permitted him to participate because "I thought he was okay, just—he was okay Friday. At least in our eyes he was okay."

Dr. Thomas A. McKnight, a family practice physician who has treated Cerny since September 1995, and Dr. Richard Andrews, a neurologist to whom Cerny was referred by McKnight, both expressed opinions that Cerny suffered a concussion during the Friday night game; that he was still symptomatic at the practice on the following Tuesday; and that during the practice, he suffered a closed-head injury with second concussion syndrome. Andrews testified that the second blow to the head sustained during the practice was "the principal cause of [Cerny's] traumatic brain injury, and the sequelae as [they] exist now."

Cerny filed a personal injury action against the School under the Political Subdivisions Tort Claims Act, and in his amended petition (petition) alleged that the School, acting through its coaches, was negligent in a number of particulars, including "failing to adequately examine [Cerny] following his initial concussion ... to determine the need for immediate qualified medical attention" and "allowing [Cerny] to return to play ... without authorization from qualified medical personnel and without verifying it was safe to do so."

* * *

V. Analysis

* * *

2. District Court's Findings of Fact

* * * Cerny asserts that the district court erred (1) in its finding of fact as to what conduct was required to meet the applicable standard of care, (2) in its finding of fact that the coaches' decision to permit Cerny to reenter the game did not violate the applicable standard of care, and (3) in its resolution of the question of fact that the School was not negligent. Cerny is asserting on appeal that the evidence shows that Cerny's coaches, Mitchell Egger and Robert Bowman, acted negligently in failing to keep Cerny out of competition until after he had received clearance from a physician to play. * * *

As noted above, in *Cerny I,* we set forth the standard of care to be applied in this case. We stated that determining the standard of care to be applied in a particular case is a question of law, and we concluded that in the instant case, "[t]he applicable standard of care by which the conduct of the School's coaching staff should be judged is that of a reasonably prudent person holding a Nebraska teaching certificate with a coaching endorsement." Under the law-of-the-case doctrine, the applicable standard of care that the School's coaches were required to meet in this case has been conclusively established.

* * *

(a) Conduct Required to Meet Standard of Care

As noted above, on remand, after reviewing the evidence, the district court found that the conduct required of a reasonably prudent person holding a Nebraska teaching certificate with a coaching endorsement in

1995, when a player has sustained a possible head injury, was (1) to be familiar with the features of a concussion; (2) to evaluate the player who appeared to have suffered a head injury for the symptoms of a concussion; (3) to repeat the evaluation at intervals before the player would be permitted to reenter the game; and (4) to determine, based upon the evaluation, the seriousness of the injury and whether it was appropriate to let the player reenter the game or to remove the player from all contact pending a medical examination.

* * *

(b) Conformance With Standard of Care

In its evaluation of whether the coaches' conduct conformed to the standard of care, we note that the district court found that the evidence in the case showed that Bowman was familiar with the signs of a concussion. The district court found additional facts that showed that the coaches met the standard of care regarding evaluating Cerny at intervals and making their determination whether to permit Cerny to reenter the game.

The facts found by the district court include the following: The district court found that when Cerny removed himself from the game, he told Bowman that he was fuzzy and had tingling in his neck. The district court found that Bowman talked to Cerny continuously for 5 to 6 minutes and observed that Cerny did not have a vacant stare, responded normally to conversation, did not appear to be disoriented or confused, and did not complain of nausea, headache, or blurred vision. The district court also found that the record demonstrated that Bowman observed and talked to Cerny approximately 15 minutes after his initial evaluation and that during this second observation, Bowman noted that Cerny was oriented, breathing normally, speaking coherently, and not complaining of headache, dizziness, vision problems, or nausea. The district court also found that Bowman observed Cerny on the sidelines during the third quarter and that Bowman noted that Cerny appeared to be "100% normal"; that his responses were appropriate; that he did not seem confused or disoriented; that his speech was not incoherent or slurred; that his emotions were appropriate; that he did not complain of dizziness, unsteadiness, nausea, or headache; and that he told the coach he felt "fine." Based upon the foregoing, the district court found that Bowman evaluated Cerny for symptoms of a concussion and that Cerny was evaluated at intervals. Further, the district court found that Cerny was properly allowed to reenter the game.

With regard to whether the conduct of the coaches met the standard of care, we note that the record contains Stineman's testimony, in which he stated that the evaluations and actions taken by Egger and Bowman regarding Cerny were reasonable for Nebraska endorsed coaches on September 15, 1995. According to Stineman, Bowman's evaluation of Cerny during the Beemer football game and Egger's decision to permit Cerny to reenter the game were the actions that would have been taken by a reasonable Nebraska endorsed football coach under similar circumstances in 1995.

Given its findings of fact summarized above, the district court determined, inter alia, that "the conduct of the coaches in this matter comported with the standard of care required of reasonable [sic] prudent persons holding a Nebraska teaching certificate with a coach's endorsement. The court finds no negligence on the part of [the School]."

Although we recognize that the record contains evidence that could controvert the district court's findings of fact, we are required to consider the evidence in a light most favorable to the School. The district court's findings that the coaches' conduct met the standard of care and that the School was not negligent are supported by evidence and are not clearly wrong. Pursuant to our standard of review, we determine that there is sufficient evidence to sustain the district court's judgment.

Cerny's second, third, and fourth arguments are without merit. Further, we have considered all of Cerny's remaining arguments on appeal and determine that they are without merit.

VI. CONCLUSION

For the reasons stated above, the decision of the district court finding in favor of the School and dismissing Cerny's petition is affirmed.

AFFIRMED.

Notes

1. Not only have courts been much more likely to rule in favor of school districts generally in negligence cases, but they have also shown great deference to coaches, athletic directors, and sports programs ... unless the actions in question vary dramatically from common practice. In a sense, it can be argued that the courts have deferred to the will of the majority in this context, given that so many Americans—particularly in certain parts of the country—love athletic competition and follow the exploits of individuals and teams with great interest on a regular basis. Yet an argument can be made that the legislatures and the courts need to dissociate themselves from the majority in this area and provide greater protection for young people whose sports-related injuries too often lead to devastating disabilities when they reach middle age. *See, e.g.*, Matthew J. Mitten, *Emerging Legal Issues in Sports Medicine,* 76 ST. JOHN'S L. REV. 5, 48–57 (2002).

2. In *Kahn v. East Side Union High School District,* 31 Cal.4th 990, 4 Cal.Rptr.3d 103, 75 P.3d 30 (2003), the California Supreme Court considered the case of a 14-year-old plaintiff who, while participating in a competitive swim meet as a member of the junior varsity team, executed a practice dive into a shallow racing pool and broke her neck. Plaintiff "alleged that the injury was caused in part by the failure of her coach, a district employee, to provide her with any instruction in how to safely dive into a shallow racing pool. She also alleged lack of adequate supervision and further that the coach breached the duty of care owed to her by insisting that she dive at the

swim meet despite her objections, her lack of expertise, her fear of diving, and the coach's previous promise to exempt her from diving." *Id.* at 995.

Showing the traditional deference to coaches and school sports programs, the Court explained that "because a significant part of an instructor's or coach's role is to challenge or 'push' a student or athlete to advance in his or her skill level and to undertake more difficult tasks, and because the fulfillment of such a role could be improperly chilled by too stringent a standard of potential legal liability, we conclude that the same general standard should apply in cases in which an instructor's alleged liability rests primarily on a claim that he or she challenged the player to perform beyond his or her capacity or failed to provide adequate instruction or supervision before directing or permitting a student to perform a particular maneuver that has resulted in injury to the student. A sports instructor may be found to have breached a duty of care to a student or athlete only if the instructor intentionally injures the student or engages in conduct that is reckless in the sense that it is 'totally outside the range of the ordinary activity' involved in teaching or coaching the sport." *Id.* at 996.

Even under this stringent standard, however, the Court concluded that "the totality of the circumstances precludes the grant of defendants' motion for summary judgment. Specifically, we refer to evidence of defendant coach's failure to provide plaintiff with training in shallow-water diving, his awareness of plaintiff's intense fear of diving into shallow water, his conduct in lulling plaintiff into a false sense of security by promising that she would not be required to dive at competitions, his last-minute breach of this promise in the heat of a competition, and his threat to remove her from competition or at least from the meet if she refused to dive. Plaintiff's evidence supports the conclusion that the maneuver of diving into a shallow racing pool, if not done correctly, poses a significant risk of extremely serious injury, and that there is a well-established mode of instruction for teaching a student to perform this maneuver safely." *Id.*

3. In *Curtis v. Board of Education of Sayre Public Schools*, 914 P.2d 656 (1995), the Oklahoma Supreme Court considered whether that state's very forgiving rules regarding immunity applied to protect the school district in a sports-related negligence lawsuit. Plaintiff parents sought damages against the school district after their twelve-year-old son was "severely injured when he was hit in the mouth with a baseball bat." *Id.* at 657. Apparently the student was instructed by his teacher to play the position of catcher, but was not supplied with a catcher's mask.

Ruling in favor of the school district, the Court—by a 5–4 vote—found that § 155(20) of the Oklahoma Governmental Tort Claims Act did in fact protect the District in this instance. § 155(20) provides:

A political subdivision shall not be liable if a loss or claim results from: 20. Participation in or practice for any interscholastic *or other athletic contest* sponsored or conducted by or on the property of the state. * * *

The Court determined that "[a] physical education class softball game, sponsored by a public school and conducted on school property falls within the parameters of § 155(20), and the school is shielded from liability for losses resulting therefrom." *Id.* at 660.

4. For a discussion of sports-related negligence issues within the context of higher education, *see infra,* Liability for Injuries at the Higher Education Level.

c. *School Shootings*

PROBLEM 4: The Tragic Events at Columbine High School

On April 20, 1999, at Columbine High School in Littleton, Colorado, two seniors—Eric Harris and Dylan Klebold—fatally shot fourteen fellow students and one teacher and wounded at least twenty-three others before taking their own lives.

According to news reports, the young men, armed with guns and explosives, entered the school from the back parking lot at about 11:30 a.m. Wearing ski masks, they first went upstairs to the library, firing semiautomatic weapons at students and teachers and throwing explosives. Then they went back downstairs to the cafeteria, still shooting. Finally they returned to the library, where they later killed themselves. During these events, which together comprised a five-hour siege, students reported hiding throughout the school.

At least 13 bombs were found in the school, and one, set with a timer, exploded at night. Three automobiles were also found rigged with bombs, one of which exploded. The bodies of the gunmen and some of their victims also appear to have been wired with explosives. *See, e.g.,* James Brooke, *Terror in Littleton: The Overview,* New York Times, April 21, 1999.

Extensive details emerged regarding the extent to which Harris and Klebold had themselves been victims of bullying by fellow students. They apparently banded together with a small group of others, calling themselves the "trench coat mafia" and wearing dark gothic-style clothing. From all evidence, it appears that during the attacks they specifically targeted athletes and those who had bullied or otherwise mistreated them in the past.

Not long after the attacks, it also became clear that many signs of the violence to come had been evident, or should have been evident, to school officials and members of the community for some time. CNN reported, for example, that "Harris' and Klebold's interest in Hitler and World War II was well-known around school. They played war games and bragged about their guns. The two sometimes spoke German in the hallways and made references to '4–20,' Hitler's birthday. * * * The massacre took place on the anniversary of Hitler's birthday." CNN, *Harris Hinted at Violence to Come,* Apr. 21, 1999. The *Washington Post* reported "[c]onfrontations with kids they disdained. A fascination with Nazism and automatic weapons. A video made for a class project months ago in which the real-life shooters play trench-coated triggermen who mow down athletes in a school hallway." Kevin Merida, *Not Telling Anymore: Fearful Kids Keep a Code of Silence,* Wash. Post, Apr. 27, 1999.

All the lawsuits that followed were ultimately settled. But had a negligence lawsuit against school officials proceeded to trial, given these facts and the additional evidence presented in the Castaldo Complaint that follows, would the school district officials have been found liable for negligence? What are the arguments that would be set forth by the respective sides?

FROM COLUMBINE HIGH SCHOOL COMPLAINT

Plaintiff Richard R. Castaldo.
DISTRICT COURT, COUNTY OF JEFFERSON, STATE OF COLORADO.
Civil Action No. 2000CV921, Division 6.

General Allegations

1. Plaintiff Richard R. Castaldo was a student at Columbine High School in Jefferson County, Colorado on April 20, 1999, when he was shot and seriously injured. At the time of his injuries, Richard R. Castaldo was a minor, aged 17.

* * *

9. Defendant Frank DeAngelis was, at all material times, Principal of Columbine High School.

* * *

11. Defendant Garrett Talocco was, at all material times, a teacher at Columbine High School. In one of Defendant Talocco's classes, Eric Harris (Harris) presented a videotape depicting himself and Dylan Klebold (Klebold) enacting revenge shootings of other Columbine High School students. This video depicted Harris and Klebold in possession of guns enacting the killing of other Columbine students.

12. Defendant Judy Kelly was, at all material times, a teacher at Columbine High School who taught Eric Harris and Dylan Klebold in a creative writing class.

13. Defendant Tom Johnson was, at all material times, a teacher at Columbine High School who taught Eric Harris and Dylan Klebold in a psychology class.

14. John or Jane Does 11 through 30 were, at all material times, deans, administrators, counselors, teachers or staff members at Columbine High School who knew of the Eric Harris Web site described elsewhere in this Complaint, or of any of the violent videotapes made by or depicting Harris and Klebold, or of the violent writings and discussions of Harris and Klebold which depicted themes of murder, suicide, possession and use of firearms, and desire and intent to kill and injure others, including fellow Columbine students.

* * *

20. On the morning of April 20, 1999, at approximately 11:20 a.m. local time, at Columbine High School in Jefferson County, Colorado, at a location outside near the rear door to the cafeteria, the Plaintiff Richard R. Castaldo was shot approximately nine times by one Dylan Klebold and/or Eric Harris with a 9 millimeter weapon or weapons.

21. At the said time and place, Dylan Klebold and Eric Harris were students at Columbine High School and were co-conspirators in a plot

and scheme to assault, terrorize and kill fellow students at Columbine High School. Their plot and its execution included multiple random killings and infliction of severe injuries by gunshots and placement of multiple explosive devices inside the school building.

22.   The plot and scheme of Harris and Klebold was planned for more than a year and involved meticulous planning and extensive preparation, including selection of a date, design of a scheme, surveillance of school activities, acquisition of bomb-making supplies, construction and testing of bombs, acquisition of firearms, modification of firearms, shooting practice, transportation and delivery of bombs to Columbine High School, and numerous other steps.

23.   The lengthy preparation for the April 20, 1999 attack was accompanied by multiple disclosures and announcements by Harris and Klebold of their evil desires and intent, in the form of a Web site, videotapes, writings and verbal statements.

24.   The plot and scheme carried out by Harris and Klebold resulted in the deaths of 12 students and one teacher, and in physical injuries to at least 26 others, many of which were life-threatening, catastrophic, or serious.

25.   The plot and scheme created by Harris and Klebold and which they attempted to execute, was calculated to cause hundreds of deaths and serious injuries. Hundreds of deaths and serious injuries were averted because large explosive devices planted in the cafeteria malfunctioned.

First Claim for Relief
(Willful and wanton conduct against the Sheriff Defendants)

* * *

45.   In approximately February of 1998, the Jefferson County Sheriff's Department acquired knowledge that, on or about January 30, 1998, Harris and Klebold broke into a van to steal tools. Thereafter, Harris and Klebold were defendants in the Jefferson County justice system and, commencing approximately March 25, 1998, were placed in a Jefferson County juvenile offender diversion program.

46.   On or about March 18, 1998, Defendant Mark M. Miller, while acting within the course and scope of his employment, was notified by one Randall P. Brown, a citizen of Jefferson County, that Harris had repeatedly threatened to kill Mr. Brown's son, that Harris often talked about making pipe bombs and using them to kill numerous people, and that Klebold knew of Harris' bomb-making activity. Mr. Brown also told Defendant Miller that Harris maintained an Internet Web site, a hard copy of which was printed out by Mr. Brown and provided to Defendant Miller. The Web site contained death threats and statements that Harris and Klebold were planning to use pipe bombs to kill numerous people. The Web site included: description of a pipe bomb detonation by Harris and Klebold; detailed descriptions of multiple pipe bombs that were built

by Harris and Klebold; explicit threats to shoot and kill people; reference to killing using a sawed-off shotgun; threatening to "go to some downtown area in some big . . . city and blow up and shoot everything I can"; threatening to rig up and detonate explosives and shoot numerous people; and similar threats and statements of intent. The Web site printout was attached to Defendant Miller's Report of his contact with Mr. Brown and became part of the Jefferson County Sheriff Department's records available thereafter to any Jefferson County Sheriff's deputy charged with investigating Harris and Klebold. [A copy of Deputy Miller's Report and the printed Web site are attached to the original Complaint as Exhibit A.]

47.   The existence and address of the Web site was disclosed to Brooks Brown by Dylan Klebold.

* * *

50.   Defendant Neil Gardner also knew, or in the exercise of reasonable care should have known information available to Columbine teachers and school officials about the bizarre, hate-filled and threatening behavior of Harris and Klebold. Upon information and belief, this information included, but was not limited to, video tapes made by Harris and Klebold showing: Harris and Klebold in possession of firearms; Harris and Klebold in a mock attack on Columbine High School students; an enactment portraying Harris and Klebold killing Columbine students. The said information known to school personnel also included hateful, threatening writings and similar verbal statements by Harris and Klebold. * * *

Second Claim for Relief
(Willful and wanton conduct against the School Defendants)

* * *

80.   The videotapes produced by Eric Harris for Defendant Talocco's class were violent, threatening, and a representation and foreshadowing of the assault of April 20, 1999.

81.   In the creative writing class taught by Defendant Judy Kelly, Eric Harris and Dylan Klebold produced writings and other presentations which also described or demonstrated some or all of the following: their hatred, anger, possession and use of firearms, and desire and intent to kill and injure others, including fellow Columbine students.

82.   In the psychology class taught by Defendant Tom Johnson, Harris and Klebold produced writings and other presentations which also described or demonstrated some or all of the following: their hatred, anger, possession and use of firearms, and desire and intent to kill and injure others, including fellow Columbine students.

83.   Harris and/or Klebold produced or appeared in, and presented in classes at Columbine High School, other videotapes depicting them-

selves in possession of firearms enacting violence on others including fellow Columbine students.

84.   Harris and Klebold at various times and on multiple occasions in classes not specifically known to these Plaintiffs writings and verbal statements describing irrational hatred, obsession with guns, bombs and violence, and their desire and intent to harm or kill others, including fellow Columbine students.

85.   Taken together, and in many instances taken separately, the Web site, videotapes, writings and verbal statements of Harris and Klebold demonstrated, revealed and conveyed to the School Defendants information which any reasonable person would perceive and understand as serious threats to the safety of students at Columbine High School.

86.   Other malevolent writings of Harris and Klebold were stored on the school's network server.

87.   The School Defendants, and each of them, at all material times, by virtue of their positions in a public school, had a relationship with all Columbine students, including Eric Harris, Dylan Klebold, and Richard R. Castaldo, in the nature of an *in loco parentis* relationship.

88.   By virtue of the relationship in the nature of *in loco parentis*, the School Defendants, and each of them, owed a duty to all Columbine students to discipline those students who presented a threat of harm to other students and to provide a safe learning environment for all students while on school premises.

89.   The duty of the School Defendants included a duty not to act in a willful and wanton manner in reckless disregard of the rights of Columbine High School students.

90.   This duty included a responsibility to confer and consult with each other, other school personnel including teachers involved with Harris and Klebold, counselors, administrators, deans and the school resource officer and security personnel about the disturbing behavior of Harris and Klebold and to report the disturbing videotapes, writings and Statements of Harris and Klebold to other teachers, counselors, administrators, deans, the school resource officer and security personnel.

91.   The School Defendants' duty also included a responsibility to initiate, investigate, and implement contact with the parents of Harris and Klebold and other intervention, including law enforcement intervention concerning the behavior of Harris and Klebold.

92.   The School Defendants, and each of them, made a conscious decision not to report, consult, confer, or intervene at all or any further concerning the behavior of Harris and Klebold.

93.   The decisions of the School Defendants, and each of them, in view of the nature and seriousness of the threats and magnitude of the harm threatened by Klebold and Harris to other Columbine students, was willful, wanton and reckless.

94. To an extent not specifically known to Plaintiffs at this time, the School Defendants consciously conspired in their decision to decline to pursue reports or intervention concerning the behavior of Harris and Klebold.

95. The said Web site, videotapes, writings and verbal statements of Harris and Klebold announced predicted, foretold and made foreseeable the events of April 20, 1999. Between the time the School Defendants became aware of the disturbing behavior of Harris and Klebold and April 20, 1999, the School Defendants, acting independently or in conjunction with law enforcement authorities, had ample opportunity to intervene and interrupt the nefarious plans of Harris and Klebold.

96. Had the School Defendants, or any of them, acted in a manner that was not reckless, willful and wanton and pursued further reporting or intervention concerning Harris and Klebold's behavior, the attack at Columbine High School on April 20, 1999 would have been prevented.

97. Therefore, the injuries and damages to Plaintiffs as more fully described in paragraph 74, above, are a direct and proximate result of the reckless, willful and wanton conduct of the School Defendants and each of them.

* * *

Sixth Claim for Relief
(42 U.S.C. § 1983 against School Defendants)

* * *

128. The School Defendants had a duty to Richard R. Castaldo which included, but is not limited to, obligations to:

a) Contact the parents of Harris and Klebold concerning the contents of videotapes, writings and verbal statements known to the School Defendants;

b) To refer these matters to higher level administrators or directly intervene, or both;

c) To report these matters to the School Resource Officer or other law enforcement personnel;

d) To initiate or conduct disciplinary proceedings against Harris and Klebold;

e) To elicit information from the School Resource Officer concerning his knowledge of Harris and Klebold;

f) To otherwise intervene or set in motion a process that would result in effective intervention to interrupt the plan and scheme of Harris and Klebold;

g) To take whatever reasonable measures necessary to protect the safety and security of Columbine High School students.

129.   The School Defendants breached their duty, and in so doing violated the United States Constitution depriving Plaintiffs of their Federal Rights and subjecting the School Defendants to liability pursuant to 42 U.S.C. § 1983.

130.   The practical manifestation of the rights of Richard R. Castaldo that were violated as a result of the Sheriff Defendants' breach, i.e. the right to be physically safe at his public school, was a well known right clearly protected by the Constitution.

131.   The savagery and seriousness of the threats by Harris and Klebold, and the extreme potential for harm, demanded serious attention and investigation.

132.   The School Defendants made deliberate and conscious decisions not to further investigate or intervene as to Harris and Klebold and not to take any of the measures outlined in paragraphs 90 and 128, above.

133.   These deliberate and conscious decisions were in reckless indifference and disregard of the safety of Columbine students, including Richard R. Castaldo.

134.   The School Defendants' deliberate indifference, reckless, willful and callous disregard to their duties, which created a substantial risk of injury to Plaintiffs, deprived Plaintiff of his Constitutional Rights in a manner which shocks the conscience. The failure to address the threatening behavior of Harris and Klebold in any meaningful way showed a conscious and unreasonable disregard of the substantial risk of serious immediate and proximate harm to students at Columbine including Plaintiff and the failure to take action by the School Defendants shock the conscience.

135.   For the foregoing deprivations of Richard R. Castaldo's constitutional rights to life, liberty and personal security, the School Defendants are liable in their individual capacities for compensatory and punitive damages as well as reasonable attorney's fees and costs under 28 U.S.C. § 1988 in an amount to be proven at trial.

136.   As a direct and proximate result of the violations of his Civil Rights, Richard R. Castaldo and his parents suffered the injuries and damages described in paragraph 74, above.

Notes

1.   While Problem 4 raises the question of negligence, the complaint actually sought damages for "willful, wanton, and reckless conduct." The rules and the terminology may vary slightly from state to state, but in general negligence is viewed as synonymous with inadvertent or unintentional action, with a failure to take precautions, and/or as reflecting a certain level of incompetence. Willful and wanton conduct, on the other hand, is more egregious, going far beyond mere inadvertence. It is typically characterized as reflecting a conscious choice of a course of action with a knowledge of the serious danger to others.

Some state courts have recognized a sliding scale in this context. In Illinois, for example, the distinction between negligence and willful and wanton conduct is sometimes seen as only slight, and in other instances willful and wanton acts may be only degrees less than intentional wrongdoing.

A key question, then, in Problem 4 is whether the acts of the school officials even constituted basic negligence. If so, then an additional question is whether the actions went beyond negligence and rose to the level of willful and wanton conduct.

In the end, the Columbine cases all settled, and the questions remain hypothetical from a legal perspective.

2. The tragic events at Columbine High School, however, continue to remain very compelling from both a legal and a policy perspective all these years later, for so many reasons, and on so many fronts.

Among other things, the events at Columbine have raised issues regarding: (a) race (racial epithets were reportedly shouted by at least one of the white perpetrators when an African American football player was shot and killed), (b) gender (a videotape recorded by the perpetrators the night before the killings and subsequently transcribed in Time Magazine included highly offensive comments about women), (c) bullying (the perpetrators and their friends had apparently been victimized repeatedly by campus bullies), (d) Neo–Nazism (the perpetrators dressed in black trench coats, often greeted each other and their friends with the expression "heil Hitler," and planned the killings to take place on Hitler's birthday), (e) parenting (many have wondered how the perpetrators could have stockpiled so many weapons and communicated so extensively regarding their plans without their parents finding out or intervening), (f) side effects of anti-depressant drugs (Eric Harris had apparently been taking anti-depressant drugs, and experts were ready to testify in a lawsuit against drug companies that these drugs sometimes amplify suicidal tendencies), and (g) gun control (the young perpetrators in suburban Denver appear to have been able to obtain an arsenal of weapons all too easily).

d. Issues Relating to Race and Ethnicity

No discussion of campus safety issues in the public schools at the K–12 level would be complete without addressing the dynamic of race and the role that relationships between and among students of different races and ethnicities can and does play in this context.

Consider the following excerpts from a piece published in 1995 by Education Professor Pedro Noguera. In it, Dr. Noguera reflects on his experiences as the only African American person on the Berkeley School Board during a time of significant racial tension at Berkeley High School. In light of more recent events in cities across the country, what conclusions can be drawn regarding prospective legal and policy initiatives that might be implemented in this context?

TIES THAT BIND, FORCES THAT DIVIDE: BERKELEY HIGH SCHOOL AND THE CHALLENGE OF INTEGRATION

Pedro A. Noguera.
29 U.S.F. L. Rev. 719 (1995).

* * *

Left on their own to figure out how to create an educational environment where respect and tolerance for difference supersedes racial antagonisms and hostilities, many schools have settled for a less ambitious goal: minimizing racial conflict. In several schools this has meant allowing students to resegregate themselves within the school in order to create social harmony. * * *

Despite the adverse consequences that often accompany segregation within schools, many administrators have tacitly supported this development out of fear that forcing greater interaction might increase the likelihood of interracial conflict. For this reason, instead of being truly integrated, many desegregated schools continue to be racially fragmented and polarized.

* * * This Essay presents a case study analysis of the challenges encountered by a school that has been called "the most integrated high school in America." Berkeley High School ("BHS") has attained this distinction because its student population is racially, ethnically and socio-economically diverse. Drawing many of its white students from middle and upper-middle class neighborhoods in the Berkeley hills, and many of its minority students from low income flatland neighborhoods, BHS has served as the single public institution that attempts to meet Berkeley's divergent needs. * * *

* * *

III.   * * * The Suppression of Discourse about Race

* * *

On issues like school violence, * * * [m]y experience has led me to conclude that all groups at BHS are engaged in an ongoing struggle for ownership of the victim mantle, because with it comes sympathy, understanding and, occasionally, resources. Labeling themselves as victims allows minority students to avoid taking responsibility for failing a class or starting a fight. This victimization also makes it possible for white students to ignore the privileges of attending a school where most teachers and administrators are white, and the cultural bias of the school curriculum clearly favors the white middle class. Moreover, racial conflicts at BHS more frequently take a political, not physical, form. Because of the school's paralysis in addressing racial issues, competition over who the true victims and villains really are tends to become the primary focus of discourse about race.

The school's inability to deal effectively with racial issues negatively affects many aspects of its daily operations. The difficulties BHS has experienced in responding to the growing problem of violence provides a prime example of this paralysis. Over the last four years, there have been shootings, stabbings and some evidence of gang violence at the school. Although most violence among students occurs within racial groups, the occurrence of racially motivated assaults upon white students has generated the greatest degree of concern.

In response to demands from parents and teachers for tough action, the BHS administration adopted a fairly traditional approach to the problem in 1991. Police officers were hired to patrol the campus, fences were built to secure the perimeter from outsiders and hidden security cameras were installed in an attempt to identify some of the perpetrators. The school board's adoption of these measures was no small feat, given the existence of considerable opposition within some segments of the community to any tactic which could be construed as a violation of students' civil liberties. However, given the depth of concern about school safety and the consequences that continued negative publicity might have on future white student enrollment, the security measures were adopted with minimal opposition.

Interestingly, during the many public meetings that were held on the subject of school violence, there was never any discussion on the causes of violent conflicts between minority and white students. There were indirect references to race, such as a comment by one black parent that white teachers at the school were "unable to deal with this problem because they lacked moral authority in their relations with black students." However, the question of why students who had attended integrated schools all of their lives would engage in unprovoked attacks that appeared to be racially motivated was not discussed. The merits of metal detectors and strategies for graffiti removal were hotly debated, but the cause of racial violence went largely unexplored, at least during the public meetings.

IV. Creating Space for Discussions About Race

While most adults connected to BHS have been unwilling or afraid to discuss racial issues openly in racially mixed groups, students generally have not. Left to interpret and give meaning to the reality of race which confronts them on a daily basis, students have devised their own means to add fuel to racial conflict, and occasionally to create space for productive dialogue.

An example of the former can be seen in the publication and distribution of *The God Knows Truth* and student reaction to it on the campus. During the spring of 1992, a newsletter began appearing at BHS with an explicit focus on racial issues. Clandestinely published and distributed, the paper contained personal attacks on individuals the authors accused of racism or "selling out." Topics covered in the first issue of *The God Knows Truth* included the following: 1) an article on how the spread of homosexuality was sterilizing the black population; 2) an article which argued that black women who perm their hair deserve to be burned and; 3) an article which suggested that the Rodney King beating was understandable "because police were created to brutalize, capture, and lynch black people."

Another article directly addressed the issue of racial violence at BHS. * * *

While administrators attempted to downplay the newsletter's significance and dismiss it as the rantings of a few extremists, other students reacted with anger and put forward arguments that matched the hostility of the first issue. * * * [All this] * * * prompted the publishers of *The God Knows Truth* to become even more provocative and extreme. * * *

As the attacks increased, the administration began to take the newsletter more seriously and attempted to identify the authors by offering rewards to anyone who would provide information. Although none of the individuals behind the publication was ever apprehended, outrage over the newsletter created the opportunity for heated discussion among students. In mixed groups, students began discussing what it meant to act white or black. They argued about why racial violence at BHS had increased and what could be done to curtail it. They also debated how their racial identities influenced their options and opportunities for the future. These discussions took place in classrooms, hallways and on school grounds. While the tenor of debate was often intense, for the first time in many years students of different races were openly communicating with one another about issues that had previously been treated as taboo in public conversation.

Reactions to clandestine publications have not been the only cause for dialogue about racial issues among BHS students. In the spring of 1990, a group calling itself STOP (Students Together Opposing Prejudice) called upon the School Board to establish a mandatory ethnic studies course that would compel students to learn about different racial and ethnic groups. In a presentation before the School Board, STOP argued:

> At Berkeley High there are tremendous barriers that separate the students, one of the most pervasive being tracking.... Required history courses at BHS fail to do a thorough job of educating students about non-Whites as well as working class Euro–Americans. We would like to see a course that gives us a chance to learn about each other, not just historical events, but learning about culture.

The School Board responded favorably to the students' demand and, despite opposition from teachers, established a mandatory ethnic studies class for ninth grade students. However, the fact that the course had been imposed upon the school made its implementation initially difficult. Most teachers refused to teach the new classes, so new teachers, most of whom lacked experience, were assigned. Furthermore, only a small amount of funding was allocated to support curriculum development for the course, and the new teachers were not hired until September, making prior planning impossible.

Given the obstacles encountered at the inception of the course, it is not surprising that the first year was anything but successful. Teachers complained about the lack of materials and the absence of a coherent curriculum. Students complained that the course, rather than a means of reducing prejudice, actually served as a forum for students to vent racist opinions. Parents also became concerned that poor management of the course was fueling hostility between students, and some petitioned the School Board to eliminate the course so that students could enroll "in more important elective courses like a foreign language or vocational class."

Despite growing opposition, the School Board refused to rescind the course and in the spring of 1993 directed the newly hired principal to take measures to insure that past mistakes were not repeated. Taking advantage of the summer, the principal was able to hire teachers who had the experience and desire to teach the ethnic studies class. Together, they were able to use part of the summer to develop a common approach to teaching the class and began to devise an appropriate curriculum.

Now that it is in its fourth year of existence, opposition to the ethnic studies course has subsided and many regard it as a major success. Despite continued opposition from some teachers and parents, many students enrolled in the course have expressed support for its continued existence. Student responses to an anonymous survey revealed that eighty-two percent of those enrolled in the spring of 1994 believed the course was a "worthwhile and valuable learning experience." Similarly, sixty-eight percent of those polled claimed that "the course had substantially changed the way [they] think about other racial groups." Commenting on what he had gained from taking the course, ninth grader Peter Graham claimed the class helped him "communicate with people that [he] thought [he] couldn't talk to." In an attempt to explain why the class had made such a change possible, classmate Jose Perez explained that "[o]ne of the best ways for us to break through the stereotypes and generalizations about other people is for us to get to know each other ... then all the labels you have on them have to fall away."

Conclusion

The experience of integrated schools like BHS provide a valuable source of information on race relations in schools and in society. Left on their own to figure out how to make integration work, such schools have been forced to grapple with difficult issues with minimal support. Particularly as support for the goal of integration in public education diminishes, the successes and failures of schools like BHS will be seen by others as evidence for abandoning the effort or pressing on toward integration.

It is easy to point out the many ways in which integration is not working at BHS. The producers of *School Colors* did so dramatically through their PBS documentary on the school. Although the drop-out rates for all students are relatively low, black and Latino students leave the school in large numbers prior to graduation. Moreover, despite the school's proclaimed commitment to equality, many white and Asian students graduate with honors and attend elite colleges and universities, while few black and Latino students follow a similar path. As is true in many other schools across the country, racial tensions among students, between students and teachers, and between parents and school personnel, continue to be a major problem plaguing BHS.

While these issues are by no means minor, over the years BHS has demonstrated a commitment to confronting them. Too often however, reforms that have been initiated to address the educational needs of minority students have not been well thought out or well planned. Berkeley's willingness to embrace innovation and to concede quickly to the demands of organized groups has at times exacerbated the school's educational problems. Still, no one can claim that efforts have not been undertaken to reform educational inequality at BHS and to improve race relations among its students.

Given its many problems, how do we explain the school's popularity among students? Each year, hundreds of students of all races from communities throughout the Bay Area petition the Berkeley Unified School District for admission to BHS. Perhaps the attraction is the reputation BHS has developed as a liberal school with lax discipline policies. However, the security measures that were adopted in 1991 have led to much stricter enforcement of school discipline policies and substantially reduced the degree of freedom enjoyed by students at the school. Perhaps it is the outstanding academic programs and extracurricular activities that have brought numerous awards to the school. While this is also likely, it seems that the school's diversity adds to its appeal and is perceived as an advantage by prospective students.

Undoubtedly, some of those students admitted to BHS on intradistrict transfers are quickly disappointed by the reality of race relations at the school. BHS is not one big happy family. Conflicts and tensions are a real and ever present part of the school. But where do we find schools or communities in the United States that have created alternatives to the conflicts that abound at BHS? Again, this is not simply a matter of racial diversity, but of diversity based upon socioeconomic status as well as race. Most demographic indicators point to greater racial separation in the United States, not only in public schools, but also in communities, churches and social organizations. Fear of difference, distrust of the "other" and plain old-fashioned bigotry, continue to drive ethnic groups apart.

Schools like BHS, which struggle to make diversity an asset rather than a weakness, need support. They are engaging in an effort that most of the nation has abandoned. These schools are swimming against the tide and their failure will represent more than just another example of public school incompetence; it may serve as further evidence that the promise of racial equality in the United States cannot be fulfilled.

Notes

1. Not only are racial tensions still at the heart of campus disputes in many parts of the country from time to time, but a lack of cultural sensitivity and the concurrent prevalence of low expectations and negative stereotyping in both classroom placement and the discipline process only serve to exacerbate these tensions.

2. In the Spring of 2005, racially charged altercations broke out at several high school campuses in the Los Angeles Unified School District. These incidents appeared to be part of a longstanding pattern, according to the Associated Press, which reported that "[c]ampus hate crimes rose more than 300 percent in the past decade in the nation's second-largest school district[.] * * * Nearly all of the 52 hate crimes in the 2003–04 school year were racially motivated, up from 12 in 1995–96. Besides recent fights at Jefferson and Taft High Schools, an e-mailed threat of race-related gang violence raised tensions and kept hundreds of students out of dozens of schools."

Addressing these developments, the publication *Black Issues in Higher Education* reported the following on June 30, 2005:

> Actor Louis Gossett Jr. joined community activists last month in calling for an end to violence between Blacks and Hispanics after a series of racially charged brawls at public schools.

> At South Los Angeles' Leimert Park, about one hundred people held hands and bowed their heads in prayer for a summer without youth and gang violence. Spoken word artists delivered anti-gang messages, a Hispanic rap group performed and activists made speeches calling for peace. * * *

> "Those of use who are responsible have to take our children and our streets back," Gossett said before the prayer. "We've got to stop our children from killing each other."

> The latest student fracas came earlier this month at Jefferson High School and involved several dozen Black and Hispanic teens, the third brawl on campus in six weeks. There were no major injuries, though 22 students were suspended, officials say.

> Mayor-elect Antonio Villaraigosa went to the inner-city school to appeal for an end to the racially motivated violence. Villaraigosa united Black and Hispanic voters recently to become the city's first Hispanic mayor in a century. * * *

3. On the other hand, it is important to note just how well things are working in most places most of the time, and how the day-to-day realities of public education fly in the face of the negative stereotypes that too many families develop regarding campus climate in diverse urban settings.

4. Is it possible for you to posit a hypothetical fact situation where school officials might be deemed negligent for not taking affirmative, proac-

tive steps to address racial/ethnic issues in particular settings? How would this fact pattern look?

2. THE "RIGHT TO SAFE SCHOOLS" UNDER STATE LAW

A handful of states have added explicit "right to safe schools" provisions to their own bodies of law. In California, Article I, Section 28 (c) was added to the Constitution by the voters in 1982. Originally a little-noticed portion of a high-profile ballot initiative entitled "The Victim's Bill of Rights," the provision soon became the subject of extended controversy, as the legal and education communities wrestled with its prospective applicability.

California Constitution, Article I, Section 28 (c) provides:

All students and staff of public primary, elementary, junior high and senior high schools have the inalienable right to attend campuses which are safe, secure, and peaceful.

While some commentators and legal activists sought to use this "safe schools" provision to make it easier to find school districts liable for injuries, in the end the California Courts of Appeal determined that Article I, Section 28 (c) was not self-executing, and that unless the Legislature identified specific additional requirements, there would be no change in the liability laws.

Article I, Section 28 (c) is often referenced by attorneys and jurists in a school safety context, but it is questionable, all these years later, whether it has had any impact whatsoever. At best, it remains an important mission statement.

Recently, the Rhode Island State Legislature voted to include a version of the California provision in its General Laws. Section 16–2–17 of the Rhode Island General Laws now provides that "[e]ach student, staff member, teacher, and administrator has a right to attend and/or work at a school which is safe and secure."

For an overview of the Rhode Island legislation and its prospective implications, as well as a retrospective on the California "safe schools" provision twenty years down the road, see Kyle Zambarano, *Rhode Island's Right to a Safe School: A Means to an End, or an End Without Means?*, 8 WILLIAMS U. L. REV. 383 (2003).

3. RELEVANT FEDERAL STATUTES AND CASE LAW

a. *Federal Gun–Free Requirements in Elementary & Secondary Schools, 20 U.S.C. § 7151*

(a) Short title.

This subpart [this section] may be cited as the "Gun–Free Schools Act".

(b) Requirements.

(1) In general. Each State receiving Federal funds under any title of this Act [20 USC §§ 6301 et seq.] shall have in effect a State law

requiring local educational agencies to expel from school for a period of not less than 1 year a student who is determined to have brought a firearm to a school, or to have possessed a firearm at a school, under the jurisdiction of local educational agencies in that State, except that such State law shall allow the chief administering officer of a local educational agency to modify such expulsion requirement for a student on a case-by-case basis if such modification is in writing.

(2) Construction. Nothing in this subpart [this section] shall be construed to prevent a State from allowing a local educational agency that has expelled a student from such a student's regular school setting from providing educational services to such student in an alternative setting.

* * *

(g) Exception.

Nothing in this section shall apply to a firearm that is lawfully stored inside a locked vehicle on school property, or if it is for activities approved and authorized by the local educational agency and the local educational agency adopts appropriate safeguards to ensure student safety.

(h) Policy regarding criminal justice system referral.

(1) In general. No funds shall be made available under any title of this Act [20 USC §§ 6301 et seq.] to any local educational agency unless such agency has a policy requiring referral to the criminal justice or juvenile delinquency system of any student who brings a firearm or weapon to a school served by such agency.

Notes

1. The U.S. "Gun–Free Schools Act" is a prime example of the zero tolerance statutes that have been added to federal and state codes in recent decades. Many of the initial statutes of this type focused on drug abuse. But as weapons-related incidents became more prevalent in the early 1990's, guns became a greater concern in K–12 schools nationwide. Zero tolerance statutes remain controversial, however, as they significantly limit the ability of school site administrators to address particular problems in a manner that might best meet the needs of both the students and the community. *See, e.g.,* Avarita L. Hanson, *Have Zero Tolerance School Discipline Policies Turned into a Nightmare?* 9 U.C. DAVIS J. JUV. L. & POL'Y 289 (2005).

2. Two major U.S. Supreme Court decisions addressed the interrelated areas of discipline and punishment in the 1970s: *Goss v. Lopez,* 419 U.S. 565, 95 S.Ct. 729 (1975), and *Ingraham v. Wright,* 430 U.S. 651, 97 S.Ct. 1401 (1977).

In *Goss,* the Court determined that the procedural due process rights of K–12 students would be violated if they were suspended from school without notice and an opportunity to be heard. As a result of this decision, states found themselves obligated to revise their education codes and provide extensive guidance for school officials regarding the suspension and expulsion process.

In *Ingraham,* the Court ruled that the Cruel and Unusual Punishment Clause of the Eighth Amendment did not apply to disciplinary corporal punishment. Many states have thus been able to continue some level of corporal punishment, although many others have moved to end the practice since that time. *See, e.g.,* Deana Pollard, *Banning Child Corporal Punishment,* 77 TULANE L. REV. 575, 586 (2003) (documenting the change from 1986, when only five states had banned corporal punishment, to 2003, when this number had grown to 27 states and the District of Columbia).

3. It should be noted in this context that school districts may be liable for excessive corporal punishment, even in states where the practice has not been prohibited by statute.

b. The "Unsafe School Choice Option" Under the "No Child Left Behind Act" (2001), 20 U.S.C. § 7912

(a) Unsafe School Choice Policy

Each State receiving funds under this Act shall establish and implement a statewide policy requiring that a student attending a persistently dangerous public elementary school or secondary school, as determined by the State in consultation with a representative sample of local educational agencies, or who becomes a victim of a violent criminal offense, as determined by State law, while in or on the grounds of a public elementary school or secondary school that the student attends, be allowed to attend a safe public elementary school or secondary school within the local educational agency, including a public charter school.

(b) Certification

As a condition of receiving funds under this Act, a State shall certify in writing to the Secretary that the State is in compliance with this section.

Notes

1. It is important to recognize that, consistent with the structure of the "No Child Left Behind" Act (NCLB) generally, each state gets to determine its own definition of "persistently dangerous." And not only do these definitions vary significantly from state to state, but in most cases the definitions have been criticized for being far too lax.

For example, the following guidelines were adopted in selected states for determining whether a school should be labeled "persistently dangerous":[d]

Illinois: For two consecutive years, violence-related expulsions greater than 3% of enrollment; one or more students expelled for firearm possession.

Minnesota: During previous fiscal year: a student expelled for possessing a firearm; a student expelled for weapons, drugs or sexual assault.

---

d. Greg Toppo, *"Persistently dangerous": Label will lead schools to hide crime,* *not fight it, critics say,* USA TODAY, Mar. 10, 2003.

Mississippi: For two consecutive years, 20 or more violent criminal offenses per 1000 students.

Missouri: For three consecutive years, one or more gun violations or violent criminal offenses, plus five to more than 15 expulsions in any two of those years, depending on number of students.

Montana: For three consecutive years, one or more gun violations or violent criminal offenses, plus five to more than 15 expulsions in any two of those years, depending on number of students.

Nevada: For three consecutive years, one or more gun violations or violent criminal offenses; suspensions or expulsions related to assaults, drug dealing or firearms possession. Plus a 1:100 student ratio of related expulsions.

North Carolina: Two consecutive years of five or more violent criminal offenses per 100 students, and if the state school board decides the conditions that contributed to these crimes are likely to continue into a third year.

Ohio: Two or more violent criminal offenses per 100 students in each of two consecutive years.

Utah: At least one gun violation and more than two violent criminal offenses for each 200 students; for schools with less than 200 students, two violent offenses.

Wyoming: For two consecutive years, one or more gun violations or violent criminal offenses; five to more than 15 expulsions in any two of those years, depending on number of students.

Arguably, in most of these states, few—if any—schools will ultimately be labeled "persistently dangerous." What might be done to change this, if in fact it is true? Or should anything be changed?

2.   The "Unsafe School Choice Option" is one of several key NCLB provisions that set forth school choice as a remedy for parents whose children attend "unacceptable" schools. It is indeed striking to note just how central school choice principles (underlying the school voucher movement) were to this legislation. For an extensive overview and analysis of the NCLB, *see infra,* Chapter 6.

3.   The question of parental "notice" also arises in this context. What requirements exist, if any, regarding the notification of parents under the statute? Or are things left completely to the discretion of individual states and local districts?

4.   The entire question of notice in Education Law is arguably highly significant but often relatively unexplored. It arises not only in a NCLB context, but in other education-related settings as well ... including, but not limited to, "failure to warn" disputes, the right to opt out of bilingual education programs, the choices available to parents under District-wide student assignment plans, and issues relating to opt-out provisions in the sex education curriculum. In this context, it should be noted that there is also a requirement of notice and opportunity to be heard for suspended students under the procedural due process requirements of the Fourteenth Amendment.

5.   If school districts fail to provide adequate notice/warning under the NCLB, might liability be found if someone gets hurt? Might this constitute an argument for expanding the "duty to warn" in a school setting. *See* Melissa L. Gilbert, *Time-Out for Student Threats: Imposing a Duty to Protect on School Officials,* 49 UCLA L. REV. 917 (2002).

6.   While issues relating to liability for injuries at the K–12 level continue to arise primarily within the context of state law, several federal courts of appeal have considered the question of whether school districts should be held liable under a Fourteenth Amendment Due Process Clause theory. *See, e.g., Doe v. Hillsboro Indep. Sch. Dist.,* 113 F.3d 1412 (5th Cir. 1997), *Morse v. Lower Merion Sch. Dist.,* 132 F.3d 902 (3d Cir. 1997)

B.   LIABILITY FOR INJURIES AT THE COLLEGE & UNIVERSITY LEVEL

In cases involving injuries at colleges and universities, courts look to the same basic negligence principles discussed above. Given the difference in setting, age, and circumstances, however, the application of these principles may be very different.

Duty is almost always an issue at the higher education level. And injuries in these cases are often much more egregious. Disputes relating to alcohol abuse, hazing, suicide, and sexual assault continue to recur with troubling regularity in this setting.

The typical legal analysis in this context is derived from the special relationship doctrine, with state courts engaging in a case-by-case determination of whether the facts give rise to a higher duty of care. Factors to be considered in this analysis depend on an individual state's case law, and on the type of relationship that is identified. Some disputes may be decided under the rubric of the university-student relationship, for example, while others may look to a *dangerous condition* analysis under rules pertaining to landowner and invitee. *See, e.g.,* Peter F. Lake, *The Special Relationship(s) Between a College and a Student: Law and Policy Ramifications for the Post In Loco Parentis College,* 37 Idaho L. Rev. 531 (2001). *See generally Joseph Beckham & Douglas Pearson, Negligent Liability Issues Involving Colleges and Students: Does a Holistic Learning Environment Heighten Institutional Liability?* 175 ED. LAW REP. 379 (2003).

1.   HIGHER EDUCATION NEGLIGENCE–RELATED CONTROVERSIES GENERALLY

PROBLEM 5: *Perot v. Univ. of Eldorado at Emerald City*

On March 21st, Maria (a former student who had recently withdrawn from the University of Eldorado at Emerald City in good standing) attended UEEC's "Spring Fling." She was accompanied by three of her former high school friends who were currently in the United States Marine Corps. The annual event, organized by the university's fraternities and sororities, was designed to help raise money for various UEEC programs. As usual, the festivities took place adjacent to the rural campus in a privately owned meadow that was made available to the students at no cost. The only access to the meadow was through a gate at the northern edge of the campus.

The group of four (two men and two women) soon began drinking heavily. They each purchased several beers at the refreshment stand, and then proceeded to consume the hard liquor that they had brought with them.

Later that evening, one of Maria's friends observed his former fiancée walking arm-in-arm with Fraternity President Lance Perot III, accompanied by several other fraternity members who had also been drinking heavily. Words were exchanged, and a fight soon broke out. One of the students was so badly injured that he required surgery on his shoulder and could not return to school until the following fall. After finally recovering, the student filed a negligence lawsuit against the university in Eldorado state court.

What legal arguments will the injured fraternity member set forth? What result? Discuss. (Assume that no affirmative defenses will be raised by the university.)

PROBLEM 6: The East Platte Lawsuits

This hypothetical takes place in East Platte City, a college town in the fictional State of Continental Divide. The town is the home of the University of Continental Divide (UCD), a large public university and a perennial national football powerhouse. At the K–12 level, it is served by the East Platte Unified School District (EPUSD), which includes five elementary schools, two middle schools, and one high school.

Four months after the U.S. Supreme Court's 5–4 ruling in *Boy Scouts of America v. James Dale*, East Platte City was engulfed in controversy. Almost all the young people in the town join the Boy Scouts or the Girl Scouts, and the residents had paid close attention to the New Jersey case. Indeed, a great percentage of the residents were thrilled with the result. But the town also included many college students who disagreed strongly with the Boy Scouts' stance and were disappointed by the recent court decision.

In Late August, the East Platte City Gay–Straight Alliance was formed. Composed primarily of local high school and college students, but also including several local politicians and members of the state's legal community, the Alliance joined forces with persons and groups across the country who were developing an activist agenda in this regard. Alliance members sought to convince local scout chapters to disavow the national charter, but they announced that if such a disavowal were not forthcoming, they would seek (1) to ban local Scout troops from using public facilities and (2) to persuade local businesses to cut the Boy Scouts out of United Way donations.

When school started up again in the Fall of 2000, tensions were high on both the high school and college campuses, and shouting matches often erupted on school grounds. In town, fistfights related to the controversy broke out with troubling regularity, particularly at bars frequented by football fans after games. Student government representatives counseled restraint, but no strong adult leader emerged to calm things down. Indeed, the city's "power brokers"—which included the Mayor (Charlene Smith), the high school principal (Todd Jones), and the university president (Larry Maines)—all spoke out bitterly against the new Gay–Straight Alliance and defended the right of the Boy Scouts to determine its own membership rules. Jones and Maines, former Scouts themselves, were particularly outspoken.

The following events subsequently transpired.

1.   Harold Jackson, an openly gay senior at UCD, posted an open letter to Todd Jones on a university-sponsored online discussion forum. The letter castigated the principal for "stirring up the forces of fascism and repression," and included the following quotes: "I'll meet you, one-on-one, any time and any place. Your words are fighting words, and you need to be prepared to pay. Don't think, for example, that you can ever set foot on this campus and hope to leave in one piece." Many people were taken aback by these highly publicized comments, especially given the fact that Jackson was a soft-spoken, slightly built young man known mostly for his roles in school dramatic productions, while Jones was a former nose guard for the UCD football team.

2.   Tammy Jones, daughter of Todd Jones and a junior at UCD, exchanged e-mails with several friends in which she set forth explicit and highly offensive scenarios involving the kidnapping, rape, mutilation, and violent murder of specifically named members of the local Gay–Straight Alliance. "What happened to Matthew Shepard in Wyoming is too good for these people," she insisted at the end of one message. Tammy had no criminal record, and had never been in trouble for any reason, although she was known to be as outspoken as her father on a variety of local issues and concerns.

3.   On December 3, 2000, a community meeting was held on the UCD campus, sponsored jointly by the school district and the university. Principal Todd Jones and University President Larry Maines issued a joint statement prior to the meeting in which they said, in part, that "it's time to settle this once and for all." At the meeting, which was held in an overcrowded room with a faulty ventilation system that was clearly too small for the anticipated crowd, a brawl broke out between opposing sides. Several people were so badly injured that they required hospitalization. Among the injured were Todd Jones, whose nose and front teeth were broken by Harold Jackson. Jackson himself, and his 16-year-old brother Darin (a student at East Platte High), were badly beaten by Tammy Jones and a group of her friends. Harold's right leg was badly fractured, and Darin suffered three broken ribs and a black eye.

As a result of these events, the Jackson family filed a negligence lawsuit against the school district, and Harold Jackson filed a negligence lawsuit against the university. Both seek large monetary awards for the respective injuries sustained by the two young men. (Assume that no affirmative defenses will be raised by defendants.) What arguments will be set forth by the respective parties? What result? Discuss.

PETERSON v. SAN FRANCISCO CMTY. COLL. DIST.

36 Cal.3d 799, 205 Cal.Rptr. 842, 685 P.2d 1193 (1984).

Broussard, Justice.

This case presents the question whether a community college district and its agents have a duty to exercise due care to protect students from reasonably foreseeable assaults on the campus. We conclude that the district does owe such a duty to its students. As we shall explain, we also conclude that while the district is immune from liability for failure to provide adequate police protection, it is not immune for failure to warn its students of known dangers posed by criminals on the campus.

Plaintiff Kathleen Peterson brought this action for damages under California's Tort Claims Act (Gov. Code, § 810 et seq.)[1] against the San Francisco Community College District, a state agency, and its agents. The plaintiff, a student, sustained injuries as a result of an attempted daylight rape in the parking lot area of the City College of San Francisco campus. * * *

The complaint consists of two causes of action. In the first cause of action plaintiff alleges that by virtue of a special relationship between the defendant district and herself, the defendants had a duty to protect her and/or to warn her of danger. In her second cause of action plaintiff alleges that defendants are liable under section 835 for maintaining a dangerous condition of property which together with the criminal act of a third party caused her injuries.

FACTS

* * *

On April 25, 1978, plaintiff, a student at City College of San Francisco, was assaulted while ascending a stairway in the school's parking lot. An unidentified male jumped from behind "unreasonably thick and untrimmed foliage and trees" which adjoined the stairway and attempted to rape her. The assailant used a modus operandi which was similar to that used in previous attacks on the same stairway. The defendants were aware that other assaults of a similar nature had occurred in that area and had taken steps to protect students who used the parking lot and stairway. Plaintiff relied upon this increased protection.

Plaintiff had been issued a parking permit by the college in return for a fee. Defendants did not publicize the prior incidents or in any way warn the plaintiff that she was in danger of being attacked in that area of campus. Plaintiff sustained physical and emotional injuries and economic loss as a result of the assault.

Although plaintiff has chosen to proceed under two different theories, the primary question before us is whether under the facts as alleged the defendants owed her a duty of care. The question then becomes whether this duty is affected by the fact that the defendants here are a public entity and its agents. Accordingly, we proceed to consider the

1. All further statutory references are to the Government Code unless specified otherwise.

nature of the relationship between plaintiff and defendants and the duty, if any, which the defendants owed her.

DUTY

Plaintiff alleges that the following circumstances placed upon the defendants an affirmative duty to exercise due care for her protection: "Having invited [her] onto the campus property, having enrolled her as a student, having issued to [her] a permit to park and use the parking lot and stairway in question in exchange for ... payment of a fee, having undertaken to patrol the parking lot and stairway in question in the light of the prior incidents of violence in the area, and having induced [her] to rely and depend upon this protection, a special relationship existed between Plaintiff and Defendants pursuant to which Defendants were obliged to take reasonable protective measures to ensure Plaintiff's safety against violent attacks and otherwise protect her from foreseeable criminal conduct and/or to warn her as to the location of prior violent assaults in the vicinity of the subject parking lot and stairway."

We have observed that the question of a duty " '... is a shorthand statement of a conclusion, rather than an aid to analysis in itself ... [b]ut it should be recognized that 'duty' is not sacrosanct in itself, but only an expression of the sum total of those considerations of policy which lead the law to say that a particular plaintiff is entitled to protection.' " In considering whether one owes another a duty of care, several factors must be weighed including among others: " '[T]he foreseeability of harm to the plaintiff, the degree of certainty that the plaintiff suffered injury, the closeness of the connection between the defendant's conduct and the injury suffered, the moral blame attached to the defendant's conduct, the policy of preventing future harm, the extent of the burden to the defendant and consequences to the community of imposing a duty to exercise care with resulting liability for breach, and the availability, cost, and prevalence of insurance for the risk involved.' " When public agencies are involved, additional elements include 'the extent of [the agency's] powers, the role imposed upon it by law and the limitations imposed upon it by budget; ...' * * *

As a general rule one has no duty to control the conduct of another, and no duty to warn those who may be endangered by such conduct. * * * A duty may arise, however, where "(a) a special relation exists between the actor and the third person which imposes a duty upon the actor to control the third person's conduct, or (b) a special relation exists between the actor and the other which gives the other a right to protection." Among the commonly recognized special relationships are that between a common carrier and its passengers, that between an innkeeper and his or her guests, and that between a possessor of land and members of the public who enter in response to the landowner's invitation.[3]

---

3. We have also observed that in some instances the relationship of a school district to its students gives rise to a duty of care. In *Dailey v. Los Angeles Unified*

There is no question that if the defendant district here were a private landowner operating a parking lot on its premises it would owe plaintiff a duty to exercise due care for her protection. * * * It has long been recognized that "a possessor of land who holds it open to the public for entry for business purposes is subject to liability to members of the public while they are upon the land for such a purpose, for physical harm caused by the accidental, negligent or intentionally harmful acts of third persons ... and by the failure of the possessor to exercise reasonable care to (a) discover that such acts are being done or are likely to be done, or (b) give a warning adequate to enable the visitors to avoid the harm, or otherwise to protect them against it." Liability will normally be imposed in circumstances where the possessor has reasonable cause to anticipate the misconduct of third persons.

* * *

Under the circumstances of this case, plaintiff, an enrolled student using the parking lot in exchange for a fee, was an invitee to whom the possessor of the premises would ordinarily owe a duty of due care.[6] * * * The question remains whether the provisions of the Tort Claims Act preclude the imposition of such a duty on the defendants under the circumstances of this case.

The Tort Claims Act

Turning to the Tort Claims Act, we note initially that public entity liability is statutory in nature. (§ 815.)[7] Its provisions, however, are to be

School District (1970) 2 Cal.3d 741, 87 Cal. Rptr. 376, 470 P.2d 360, we stated: "While school districts and their employees have never been considered insurers of the physical safety of students, California law has long imposed on school authorities a duty to 'supervise at all times the conduct of the children on the school grounds and to enforce those rules and regulations necessary to their protection. [Citations.]' " (Taylor v. Oakland Scavenger Co. (1941) 17 Cal.2d 594, 600 [110 P.2d 1044]; Ed.Code, § 13557.) [Citations.] The standard of care imposed upon school personnel in carrying out this duty to supervise is identical to that required in the performance of their other duties. This uniform standard to which they are held is that degree of care 'which a person of ordinary prudence, charged with [comparable] duties, would exercise under the same circumstances.' [Citations.] Either a total lack of supervision [citation] or ineffective supervision [citation] may constitute a lack of ordinary care on the part of those responsible for student supervision...." (Id., at p. 747, 87 Cal. Rptr. 376, 470 P.2d 360.)

Dailey arose in the context of a secondary school where a 16-year-old was killed while engaging in a "slap boxing match." We

observed that children of that age "should not be expected to exhibit that degree of discretion, judgment, and concern for the safety of themselves and others which we associate with full maturity." Id., at p. 748, 87 Cal.Rptr. 376, 470 P.2d 360. The present case, by contrast, does not implicate the duty to supervise the activities of students who are too immature to exercise judgment for their personal safety. Rather, the issue here is the extent of the school's duty to provide safe premises.

6.   The characterization of students as invitees is not a novel proposition. In Vreeland v. State Board of Regents (1969) 9 Ariz. App. 61 [449 P.2d 78], Jesik v. Maricopa County Community College Dist. (1980) 125 Ariz. 543 [611 P.2d 547] and Relyea v. State (Fla. 1980) 385 So.2d 1378, students were characterized as invitees to whom a duty was owed to make the premises reasonably safe. In both Jesik and Relyea the danger to the students arose because of criminal conduct by a third party.

7.   Section 815 provides in relevant part: "Except as otherwise provided by statute: [#] (a) A public entity is not liable for an injury, whether such injury arises out of an act or omission of the public entity or a public employee or any other person."

read against the background of general tort law. "The conceptual theory of statutory liability under the act is keyed to the common law of negligence and damages. . . ." * * *

Section 835 is the principal provision addressing the circumstances under which the government may be held liable for maintaining a dangerous condition of public property. It provides in relevant part: "Except as provided by statute, a public entity is liable for injury caused by a dangerous condition of its property if the plaintiff establishes that the property was in a dangerous condition at the time of the injury, that the injury was proximately caused by the dangerous condition, that the dangerous condition created a reasonably foreseeable risk of the kind of injury which was incurred, and that either:

"(a) A negligent or wrongful act or omission of an employee of the public entity within the scope of his employment created the dangerous condition; or

"(b) The public entity had actual or constructive notice of the dangerous condition under Section 835.2 a sufficient time prior to the injury to have taken measures to protect against the dangerous condition." Section 830 defines a "dangerous condition" as: ". . . a condition of property that creates a substantial (as distinguished from a minor, trivial or insignificant) risk of injury when such property or adjacent property is used with due care in a manner in which it is reasonably foreseeable that it will be used."

* * *

The majority of cases which have construed these provisions have concluded that third party conduct by itself, unrelated to the condition of the property, does not constitute a "dangerous condition" for which a public entity may be held liable. * * * The cases so holding have relied primarily on policy considerations and the definition of dangerous condition as a "condition of *property*" for the conclusion that a defect in property is necessary in order to state a cause of action based on the wrongful conduct of third parties. Nothing in the provisions of section 835, however, specifically precludes a finding that a public entity may be under a duty, given special circumstances, to protect against harmful criminal conduct on its property.

* * *

* * * [I]ntervening criminal conduct cannot absolve the defendant of liability where as here the plaintiff alleges that defendants maintained the property in such a way so as to increase the risk of criminal activity. In *Slapin v. Los Angeles International Airport*, 65 Cal.App.3d 484, plaintiff was attacked in a parking lot. Plaintiff alleged that prior to the incident, defendants were aware that the parking lot was unsafe unless properly supervised and maintained. Moreover, plaintiff alleged that defendants " 'carelessly, negligently, and improperly owned, operated, managed, maintained, supervised, controlled, lighted, and secured [the] parking area . . . so as to maintain a dangerous condition of proper-

ty...' " The Court of Appeal held that the trial court erred in sustaining defendant's demurrer to the dangerous condition theory. "That a mugger thrives in dark public places is a matter of common knowledge. If defendant so poorly lighted the parking lot as to create a substantial risk of muggings, plaintiffs may be able to establish the elements of a cause of action under section 835."

The instant case is indistinguishable from *Slapin*. The court in *Slapin* recognized that a defendant may not escape liability by claiming that plaintiff's injuries were caused by a criminal agency when the basis of plaintiff's cause of action is that the defendant created a reasonably foreseeable risk of that criminal conduct.

Plaintiff alleges here that the property was in a dangerous condition because the thick and untrimmed foliage and trees around the parking lot and stairway permitted the assailant to perpetrate his crime; she further alleges that defendants were aware of the condition and failed to take reasonable protective measures, including trimming the foliage or warning her of the danger. Defendant's inaction she alleges, created a reasonably foreseeable risk that she and others using the stairway would be injured. In light of the relationship between plaintiff and defendants as well as the facts known to the defendants, we conclude that plaintiff has stated a cause of action under the provisions of the Tort Claims Act.

* * *

An examination of the policies discussed in *Rowland v. Christian*, 69 Cal.2d 108, and other cases compels the conclusion that the defendants did in fact owe the plaintiff a duty of care. First, the allegations, if proved, suggest that harm to the plaintiff was clearly foreseeable. In light of the alleged prior similar incidents in the same area, the defendants were on notice that any woman who might use the stairs or the parking lot would be a potential target. Secondly, it is undisputed that plaintiff suffered injury. Third, given that the defendants were in control of the premises and that they were aware of the prior assaults, it is clear that failure to apprise students of those incidents, to trim the foliage, or to take other protective measures closely connects the defendants' conduct with plaintiff's injury. These factors, if established, also indicate that there is moral blame attached to the defendants' failure to take steps to avert the foreseeable harm. Imposing a duty under these circumstances also furthers the policy of preventing future harm. Finally, the duty here does not place an intolerable burden on the defendants.

The fact that the defendants are a public entity and its agents also does not preclude the imposition of a duty of care. As we have often noted, the policy of compensating injured parties is an important one. "Unless the Legislature has clearly provided for immunity, the important societal goal of compensating injured parties for damages caused by wilful or negligent acts must prevail." As a community college district responsible for overseeing the campus, the defendant and its agents are in a superior position to know about the incidences of crime and to protect against any recurrences.

* * *

* * * [W]e conclude that plaintiff is entitled to prove that the failure to warn, to trim the foliage, or to take other reasonable measures to protect her was the proximate cause of her injuries.

Plaintiff's first cause of action alleges facts which are sufficient to establish a common law duty of care but which are inadequate to state a cause of action against a public entity. Plaintiff's second cause of action, by incorporating by reference the allegations in the first cause of action and by pleading the elements of section 835, states a cause of action against defendants. Thus the judgment of dismissal was entered erroneously. The judgment is reversed.

Notes

1. The *Peterson* case ultimately stands for the proposition that there is a duty (under a dangerous condition theory) to exercise due care to protect students from reasonably foreseeable assaults on the campus, and that public policy considerations are central to a determination of whether such a duty exists in a given situation.

It is clear from the facts of this case that the San Francisco Community College District "did not publicize the prior incidents or in any way warn the plaintiff that she was in danger of being attacked in that area of campus." Indeed, "plaintiff's complaint . . . alleges not only inadequate police protection but failure to warn her of the known danger and failure to trim the foliage growing by the parking lot stairway."

Arguably, however, the case does not actually rule that a duty to protect would include a duty to warn, but it certainly says that "plaintiff is entitled to prove that the failure to warn, to trim the foliage, or to take other reasonable measures to protect her was the proximate cause of her injuries."

The "duty to warn" issue is directly relevant to our examination of threats, *infra*, Chapter 4, since negligence law is implicated when a threat arises and school officials with knowledge of alleged threats fail to warn. It is important to note, however, that school officials must proceed carefully in this context. Generalized warnings may do nothing more than foster an atmosphere of fear and paranoia, leading to an environment where productive learning cannot easily take place.

2. *Peterson* is different, however, from the more typical negligence cases in this area, in that both the level of foreseeability and the apparent ability of the educational institution to take reasonable steps to address the problem led to a clear decision in favor of the plaintiff. In most cases, particularly where one student is injured by another, courts continue to be very deferential to institutions of higher education in this context. Indeed, even in the prototypical situation where excessive alcohol in consumed and students may be seriously injured or even killed, colleges and universities are often found not liable, absent additional facts.

3.   For example, in *Tanja H. v. Regents of Univ. of Cal.*, 228 Cal.App.3d 434, 278 Cal.Rptr. 918 (Cal. App. 1991) the apparent victim of a highly publicized gang rape by male football players in a UC Berkeley dormitory argued that the university should be found negligent for failing to protect her against this activity. The California Court of Appeal, however, citing well-established case law in this area, ruled against her and in favor of the university:

> Relevant authority indicates universities are not generally liable for the sometimes disastrous consequences which result from combining young students, alcohol, and dangerous or violent impulses. * * *

> We agree with the assessment of [the university] that it could 'not have prevented this [violent] incident from taking place except *possibly* by posting guards in each dorm room on a 24–hour, 365–day per year basis.' * * *

> As campuses have * * * moved away from their former role as semi-monastic environments subject to intensive regulation of student lives by college authorities, they have become microcosms of society; and unfortunately, sexually degrading conduct or violence in general—and violence against women in particular—are all too common within society at large. College administrators have a moral duty to help educate students in this respect, but they do not have a legal duty to respond in damages for student crimes.

> We agree with appellant that it may be—in some sense not relevant here—foreseeable that a group of football players could rape a fellow student after a party where alcohol was served. The problem of gang rape, rape by acquaintances, and alcohol abuse on campuses is heinous. It is also foreseeable that there will always be criminals among us. The relevant issue here, however, is the one posed by the courts in [other recent cases]: Should a duty be imposed which would make colleges liable for damages caused by third parties, unless colleges impose onerous conditions on the freedom and privacy of resident students—which restrictions are incompatible with a recognition that students are now generally responsible for their own actions and welfare? * * * In these circumstances, the courts can establish the criminal and civil liability of the perpetrators of crimes; but the courts with good reason have been unwilling to shift moral and legal responsibility away from student perpetrators and onto the heads of college administrators. *Id.* at 437–39.

4.   Sexual assault cases such as *Tanja H.* are not the only examples of decisions by the courts that even in the most tragic of circumstances liability for injuries will not necessarily be found. In *Jain v. State,* the Iowa Supreme Court held that the University was not liable for the death of a freshman student who had committed suicide in his dormitory room. The family had sued the university for wrongful death, claiming it "negligently failed to exercise reasonable care and caution for the student's safety." In particular, plaintiffs claimed "that if the university had followed its policy of notifying parents of a student's self-destructive behavior, the suicide could have been prevented."

On the university's motion for summary judgment, the district court had dismissed the suit. It concluded the university owed no legal duty to Sanjay Jain to prevent him from harming himself, nor did it breach any legally recognized duty of care by failing to notify his parents of an earlier suicide attempt. The state supreme court affirmed:

* * * [T]he crux of Plaintiff's claim [was] that the university [had] voluntarily adopted a policy * * * of notifying parents when a student engages in self-destructive behavior but * * * negligently failed to act on that policy in the case of Sanjay Jain. By not following its own policy, plaintiff argues, the "university deprived Sanjay of the medical intervention he so desperately needed."

The argument implicates section 323 of the Restatement (Second) of Torts. In *Power v. Boles,* the Ohio Court of Appeals neatly summarized what a plaintiff must prove to show assumption of a duty under section 323:

* * * [Section] 323(a) applies only when the defendant's actions increased the risk of harm to plaintiff relative to the risk that would have existed had the defendant never provided the services initially. Put another way, the defendant's negligent performance must somehow put the plaintiff in a worse situation than if the defendant had never begun performance.... [T]o prevail under a theory of increased harm a plaintiff must "identify the sins of commission rather than sins of omission."

Likewise with respect to the "reliance" prong of section 323(b), the *Power* court noted the general requirement that the plaintiff show "actual or affirmative reliance, i.e., reliance 'based on specific actions or representations which cause a person to forego other alternatives of protecting themselves.'"

Plaintiff argues, in essence, that once university employees discovered Sanjay and Roopa fighting over the moped keys, elicited comments suggestive of a suicide threat and referred Sanjay to counseling, they were bound under section 323 to follow through with their undertaking. In this case, plaintiff argues, that meant bringing the matter to the attention of the dean of students for the purpose of notifying Sanjay's parents.

Although, in hindsight, plaintiff's contention carries considerable appeal, the duty he seeks to impose upon the university cannot be squared with section 323(a) or (b). The record, read in the light most favorable to the plaintiff, reveals that Sanjay may have been at risk of harming himself. No affirmative action by the defendant's employees, however, increased that risk of self-harm. To the contrary, it is undisputed that the RAs appropriately intervened in an emotionally-charged situation, offered Sanjay support and encouragement, and referred him to counseling. Beth Merritt likewise counseled Sanjay to talk things over with his parents, seek professional help, and call her at any time, even when she was not at work. She sought Sanjay's permission to contact his parents but he refused. In short, no action by university personnel prevented Sanjay from taking advantage of the help and encouragement being offered, nor did they do anything to prevent him from seeking help on his own accord.

The record is similarly devoid of any proof that Sanjay relied, to his detriment, on the services gratuitously offered by these same personnel. To the contrary, it appears by all accounts that he failed to follow up on recommended counseling or seek the guidance of his parents, as he assured the staff he would do.

* * * [T]he record before us reveals that the university's limited intervention in this case neither increased the risk that Sanjay would commit suicide nor led him to abandon other avenues of relief from his distress. Thus no legal duty on the part of the university arose under Restatement section 323 as a matter of law. The district court was correct in so ruling. Jain v. State, 617 N.W.2d 293 (Iowa 2000).

5. The ongoing prevalence of sexual assault issues on college and university campuses continues to disproportionately impact female students. In late 2003, for example, a civilian commission report documented the existence of frequent and unpunished sexual assaults on female cadets at the Air Force Academy over time. It charged that "since at least 1993, the highest levels of Air Force leadership have known of serious sexual misconduct problems at the academy," but failed to take effective action. *See* Diana Jean Schemo, *Air Force Ignored Sex Abuse At Academy, Inquiry Reports,* N.Y. TIMES, Sept. 23, 2003.

6. In August 2005, a Pentagon task force focusing on the U.S. Military Academy at West Point and at the Naval Academy in Annapolis concluded that hostile attitudes and inappropriate treatment of women persist on these campuses. *See* John J. Lumpkin, *Sexual Harassment, Assault, Not Adequately Addressed by Military Academies,* ASS. PRESS, Aug. 26, 2005:

The "Report of the Defense Task Force on Sexual Harassment and Violence and the Military Service Academies" is the latest to deal with sexual issues and cultural attitudes at those academies. * * *

The new study credited both academies with making progress in addressing some sexual harassment and assault issues, particularly in improving services to victims. But it called for putting more women in leadership roles at the two academies and said more women should be admitted as cadets and midshipmen.

"Some research shows that a 'critical mass' can make a difference in creating an environment that has a markedly positive effect on the acceptance and integration of women in a mostly male community, resulting in decreased incidence of sexual harassment and assault," the report said. * * *

The task force also called for new military law aimed at protecting the confidentiality of cadets and midshipmen who are victims of sexual misconduct when they speak with medical personnel or victims' advocates. Task force members also said allegations of sexual misconduct were only rarely prosecuted to the maximum extent.

7. *Peterson* is not only noteworthy as an exception to the rule that colleges and universities are not typically found liable for sexual assault or attempted sexual assault absent additional facts, but it also is an example of a negligence case that had an impact on policy decisions throughout the state. After the decision, colleges and universities statewide trimmed back bushes and foliage, increased lighting, and implemented campus escort services. In addition, the momentum of these actions and the concurrent efforts of the women's rights movement led to the establishment of women's resource centers and women's studies departments on campuses. All of these efforts together have had an important and often-significant impact, although there is still agreement that much work remains to be done.

8. While negligence law in and of itself may not require colleges and universities to do any more than they have been doing today, emerging legal principles under threat law and harassment law arguably require a higher baseline of protection for students today.

BRUECKNER v. NORWICH UNIV.

169 Vt. 118, 730 A.2d 1086 (1999).

AMESTOY, C.J.

Norwich University appeals from the denial of its post-trial motions for judgment as a matter of law, or in the alternative, for a new trial, following a jury verdict finding it liable and awarding compensatory and punitive damages on several tort claims arising from incidents of hazing suffered by plaintiff while a freshman. * * * We affirm the court's rulings on liability and lost earnings damages, but reverse the award of punitive damages because there was an insufficient showing of malice to support the award.

* * * In August 1990, plaintiff William C. Brueckner, Jr. arrived as an incoming freshman, or "rook," at the Military College of Vermont of Norwich University (Norwich). At the time, he was a twenty-four year old, five-year veteran of the United States Navy, having been awarded a four-year naval ROTC scholarship in the amount of $80,000 to attend Norwich. Under the authority and training of Norwich and its leadership, certain upperclassmen were appointed by the university to indoctrinate and orient the incoming rooks, including plaintiff. These upperclassmen were known as the "cadre."

Plaintiff attended Norwich for only sixteen days as a result of his subjection to, and observation of, numerous incidents of hazing. In those sixteen days, plaintiff withstood a regular barrage of obscene, offensive and harassing language. He was interrogated at meals and thereby prevented from eating. He was ordered to disrobe in front of a female student, although he did not follow the order. He was prevented from studying during some of the assigned study periods and, on several occasions, cadre members destroyed his academic work with water. Members of the cadre also forced him to squat in the hall as they squirted him with water. He was forced to participate in unauthorized calisthenic sessions, despite an injured shoulder. He was slammed into a wall by a cadre member riding a skateboard in the hall. After cadre members vandalized his room by dumping water in it, plaintiff was ordered to clean up the mess. On two occasions, plaintiff was prevented from attending mandatory ROTC study hall on time, leading him to believe his scholarship status was endangered. One morning, as plaintiff walked along the corridor in the dormitory, he encountered two cadre members, one of whom asked plaintiff where plaintiff's name tag was. When plaintiff responded that he had forgotten it, one cadre member hit plaintiff hard in the shoulder, which was injured and in a sling. After the other cadre member told the hitter to stop, the hitter struck plaintiff again in the same shoulder, causing pain and bruises. After reporting the hazing problems to Norwich officials, plaintiff left the campus, believing that his situation would not improve. He returned briefly once more, then withdrew from Norwich, his scholarship terminated. Norwich investigated plaintiff's complaints and, as a result, several cadets were disciplined.

Plaintiff brought this action against Norwich for assault and battery, negligent infliction of emotional distress, intentional infliction of emotional distress and negligent supervision. * * *

A.   Vicarious Liability * * *

Norwich claims error in the court's entry of judgment on the claims of assault and battery, as well as negligent and intentional infliction of emotional distress, because those claims are premised on acts of the cadre members that were not authorized and did not occur within the scope of their employment. Norwich claims it should not be held vicariously liable for the cadre's hazing.

Under the settled doctrine of respondeat superior, an employer or master is held vicariously liable for the tortious acts of an employee or servant committed during, or incidental to, the scope of employment. Norwich concedes that cadre members acted as its agents in "indoctrinating and orienting" rooks such as plaintiff. Norwich claims, however, that the tortious acts complained of were not committed within the cadre members' "scope of employment." Whether a given act is committed within the scope of employment is properly determined by the finder of fact after consideration of the attendant facts and circumstances of the particular case.

To be within the scope of employment, conduct must be of the same general nature as, or incidental to, the authorized conduct. Conduct of the servant falls within the scope of employment if: (a) it is of the kind the servant is employed to perform; (b) it occurs substantially within the authorized time and space limits; (c) it is actuated, at least in part, by a purpose to serve the master; and (d) in a case in which the force is intentionally used by the servant against another, it is not unexpectable by the master. Conduct of a servant is not within the scope of employment if it is different in kind from that authorized, far beyond the authorized time and space limits, or too little actuated by a purpose to serve the master.

Here, the cadre were authorized by Norwich to indoctrinate and orient rooks through activities performed at various times of the day and night. A jury could reasonably find members of the cadre were acting in furtherance of their general duties to indoctrinate and orient the rooks and thus within their "scope of employment" at the time of the hazing incidents of which plaintiff complains.

Norwich argues that, because it had adopted policies against hazing and had instructed the cadre to refrain from mistreating the rooks, the tortious conduct was outside the scope of employment. Norwich contends that *McHugh v. University of Vermont* supports this result. In *McHugh*, the Second Circuit Court of Appeals, applying Vermont law, concluded that an employee who sexually and religiously harassed a fellow employee was not acting within the scope of employment. There, a major in the United States Army and an employee at the University of Vermont's Department of Military Studies told plaintiff, a female secretary, that his definition of a "secretary" was a "paid whore." The employee repeatedly joked about plaintiff contracting AIDS, stating that he hoped she would be able to avoid infection. The employee also told plaintiff that it was "a good day to watch Catholic babies burn." *Id.* at 68–69. The court rejected the argument that the employee's conduct was within his scope of employment because it was within that scope for him to talk with the plaintiff, either to give instructions or to avoid the awkwardness of silence at work. It held: "It can hardly be contended that [the employee's] alleged conduct furthered the business" of his employer.

The same cannot be said of this case, where the actions involved in hazing rooks may fairly be seen as qualitatively similar to the indoctrination and orientation with which the cadre members were charged. Indeed, Norwich described some of the acts of which plaintiff complained, such as forced calisthenics and questioning at mealtime, as not far removed from the official system of military discipline and training which recruits are expected to endure. The evidence supported the jury's conclusion that the cadre members were acting within the scope of employment.

* * *

III. NEGLIGENT INFLICTION OF EMOTIONAL DISTRESS

Norwich claims that it was error for the court to uphold the jury's finding of liability for the claim of negligent infliction of emotional distress. To establish a claim for negligent infliction of emotional distress, a plaintiff must make a threshold showing that he or someone close to him faced physical peril. The prerequisites for establishing a claim differ according to whether plaintiff suffered a physical impact from an external force. If there has been an impact, plaintiff may recover for emotional distress stemming from the incident during which the impact occurred. If plaintiff has not suffered an impact, plaintiff must show that: (1) he was within the "zone of danger" of an act negligently directed at him by defendant, (2) he was subjected to a reasonable fear of immediate personal injury, and (3) he in fact suffered substantial bodily injury or illness as a result.

In this case, plaintiff withstood at least two incidents of physical impact by a cadre member. Plaintiff testified about the fear of personal injury he felt in connection with a cadre member's careening down the dormitory hallway on a skateboard and "plowing" into rooks. On one such occasion, the cadre member ran into plaintiff. Plaintiff also testified as to the fear and apprehension he felt when struck twice in the shoulder he had previously injured. Plaintiff's doctor testified that plaintiff suffered from post-traumatic-stress disorder and a major depressive disorder as a result of his perception that he was at risk of serious physical injury during the incidents just described. The evidence at trial fairly and reasonably supported the jury's verdict on negligent infliction of emotional distress.

B.   Direct Liability—Negligent Supervision

Norwich argues it was not liable to plaintiff for negligent supervision of the students in the cadre because it owed no duty of care to plaintiff. Norwich's claim is premised on the fact that the hazing in question came at the hands of fellow students. It cites *Smith v. Day* for the proposition that Norwich owed no duty to control the actions of Norwich students for the protection of plaintiff. We disagree because, unlike the *Smith* case, Norwich specifically charged cadre members with "indoctrinating and orienting" plaintiff.

A principal may, in addition to being found *vicariously* liable for tortious conduct of its agents, be found *directly* liable for damages resulting from negligent supervision of its agents' activities. Norwich's claim that it owed no duty to plaintiff under the circumstances of this case fails under these established principles. Under the Restatement, "[a] person conducting an activity through servants or other agents is subject to liability for harm resulting from his conduct if he is negligent or reckless ... in the supervision of the activity." According to the Restatement's drafters, § 213 "is a special application of the general rules stated in the Restatement of Torts.... Liability exists only if all the requirements of an action of tort for negligence exist." In this instance, the cadre members, and by extension Norwich, owed plaintiff at minimum the duty to use reasonable care to avoid harming him. "One who engages in an enterprise is under a duty to anticipate and to guard against the human traits of his employees which unless regulated are likely to harm others. He is likewise required to make such reasonable regulations as the size or complexity of his business may require." Norwich, therefore, owed plaintiff a duty of reasonable care in the control and supervision of the cadre.

In the instant case, the court correctly instructed the jury that Norwich owed plaintiff a duty to use reasonable care in avoiding harm to plaintiff, and the evidence in the record fairly and reasonably supports the jury's finding of liability.

* * *

The judgment of punitive damages is reversed. The judgment is affirmed in all other respects.

Notes

1. At the higher education level, hazing injuries often occur in a fraternity context, as they have for a very long time, raising issues of university jurisdiction over such extracurricular (and sometimes off-campus) events.

2. In *Furek v. University of Delaware,* 594 A.2d 506 (Del. 1991), a student who had entered the university on a full football scholarship suffered permanent injuries during "Hell Night," "an extended period of hazing during which [he and other pledges to the local chapter of Sig Ep were] physically and emotionally abused." As part of the ritual, the pledges were "escorted into the kitchen blindfolded, and pancake batter, ketchup and other foodstuffs were poured on their heads. During this process, [a fraternity member] poured a container containing a lye-based liquid oven cleaner over the back and neck" of the plaintiff, who was "permanently scarred, subsequently withdrew from the University and forfeited his football scholarship."

"Although official policy directives from the University and the National Fraternity forbade hazing, Sig Ep and other fraternities on the Newark campus had engaged in various forms of hazing for at least five years previous to the incident in question."

Plaintiff brought a negligence action in state court, seeking to hold the university liable for the failure to protect him from the hazing activities of Sig Ep and its members. The Delaware Supreme Court ruled in his favor:

> Certain established principles of tort law provide a sufficient basis for the imposition of a duty on the University to use reasonable care to protect resident students against the dangerous acts of third parties. * * * [W]here there is direct university involvement in, and knowledge of, certain dangerous practices of its students, the university cannot abandon its residual duty of control. * * *

> While Furek may be deemed an invitee, the University's duty to protect him from dangerous conditions * * * is not absolute. The duty extends only to the acts of third persons which are both foreseeable and subject to university control. * * *

> Premises control is not determined in absolute terms. A landowner may exercise control in certain areas while relinquishing it in others. * * * If control includes authority to direct, restrict and regulate, the University with its significant involvement in the regulation of fraternity life, particularly in the area of hazing, may be deemed to have exercised supervision over the use of its property to permit "at least the inference of control." For the purpose of testing the sufficiency of the evidence to

withstand the granting of a directed verdict, Furek was entitled to the benefit of that inference.

In sum, although the University no longer stands *in loco parentis* to its students, the relationship is sufficiently close and direct to impose a duty * * * . The university is not an insurer of the safety of its students nor a policeman of student morality, nonetheless, it has a duty to regulate and supervise foreseeable dangerous activities occurring on its property. That duty extends to the negligent or intentional activities of third persons. * * *

3. In *Lloyd v. Alpha Phi Alpha Fraternity,* 1999 WL 47153 (N.D.N.Y. 1999), plaintiff student sought to hold Cornell University liable for "various forms of physical beatings and torture, psychological coercion and embarrassment" suffered during hazing activities. In that case, however, the federal court in a diversity action found neither actual nor constructive knowledge of the events, and ruled for the university.

4. Knowledge of the specific fraternity hazing activities appears to have been a central factor in both *Furek* & *Lloyd.* The University of Delaware apparently had knowledge that these specific activities were taking place, while Cornell apparently did not. But location also appeared to play a major role in the Delaware case. What if the Delaware fraternity had been located off-campus, on private property, but all other facts were the same? Would the legal result have been different? Should the legal result have been different?

5. Colleges and universities nationwide often voluntarily "exercise" their jurisdiction over off-campus events and activities that pertain to students. This is typically done formally, with guidelines included in written campus policies. And it may also involve the establishment of a relationship between campus police and the local community police department.

A 2003 University of North Carolina policy, for example, provides the following broad, general, guiding principles:

Conduct by students on University premises or the premises of groups affiliated with the University, as well as conduct that occurs elsewhere, may give rise to offenses prohibited by this Instrument if University interests are implicated. Determinations of whether such conduct should be addressed pursuant to this Instrument in instances in which University interests are implicated is reserved to the discretion of the Student Attorney General and campus authorities with associated responsibilities.

The 2005–2006 UC Riverside Student Conduct Policy, on the other hand, provides a much greater degree of specificity:

3.30 Off Campus Jurisdiction. Student conduct that occurs off University property is subject to UCR Standards of Conduct where it 1) adversely affects the health, safety, or security of any member of the University community, or the mission of the University, or 2) involves academic work or any records, or documents of the University. In determining whether or not to exercise jurisdiction over such conduct, the University shall consider the seriousness of the alleged offense, the risk of harm involved, whether the victim(s) are members of the campus community and/or whether the off-campus conduct is part of a series of actions, which occurred both on and off University property. Recommendations to extend jurisdiction will be reviewed by the Assistant Vice Chancellor for Student Affairs.

The University may also exercise jurisdiction over student conduct that occurs off campus where, the conduct compromises University neighbor relations.

For examples of such policies nationwide, *see* Information on Off–Campus Behavior Policies, National Association of State Universities and Land Grant Colleges (NASULGC), http://www.nasulgc.org/CSA/Off-campus.pdf (last visited Sept. 2, 2005).

6. Disciplinary action against students at public institutions of higher education is, of course, subject to the Due Process Clause. And similar protections are granted to students at many private colleges and universities as a matter of policy. Other legal issues may also arise in this context, some similar to those that have arisen at the K–12 level, but many others very different. For an example of a safety-related suspension/expulsion case with parallels to K–12, *see Gorman v. Univ. of Rhode Island,* 837 F.2d 7 (1st Cir. 1988). For an example a degree-revocation case that is more uniquely higher education, see *Crook v. Baker,* 813 F.2d 88 (6th Cir. 1987).

7. A distinction has been identified at the higher education level between academic discipline and non-academic discipline. *See Board of Curators, Univ. of Miss. v. Horowitz,* 435 U.S. 78, 98 S.Ct. 948 (1978) (actions of public university under the Fourteenth Amendment); *Corso v. Creighton University,* 731 F.2d 529 (8th Cir. 1984) (actions of private university under policies set forth in the student handbook). *See generally* Jayme L. Butcher, MIT v. Yoo: *Revocation of Academic Degrees for Non–Academic Reasons,* 51 Case W. L. Rev. 749 (2001).

2. NEGLIGENCE AND INTERCOLLEGIATE ATHLETICS

KAVANAGH v. TRUSTEES OF BOSTON UNIV.

440 Mass. 195, 795 N.E.2d 1170 (2003).

Sosman, J.

Having been punched by an opposing Boston University player during an intercollegiate basketball game, the plaintiff brought suit against the trustees of Boston University (university) and the coach of the university's team, contending that the university was vicariously liable for the conduct of its "scholarship athlete," and that the university and its coach were negligent in that they "took no steps to prevent this act." Against the coach, Kavanagh also alleged both negligent and intentional infliction of emotional distress. * * *

1. *Facts.* On December 22, 1998, the university hosted a men's intercollegiate basketball game against Manhattan College. The plaintiff, Kenneth Kavanagh, was a member of the Manhattan College team. Following a contested rebound during the second half, the referee blew his whistle to signal a foul, and some elbowing and shoving ensued

among a few of the competing players. When Kavanagh intervened to break up a developing scuffle between one of his teammates and a university player, he was punched in the nose by another university player, Levar Folk. Folk was immediately ejected from the game. Kavanagh was treated for what turned out to be a broken nose and returned to play later in the same game.

* * * Until the incident involving Kavanagh, Folk had not been involved in any physical altercation during a game and had never been ejected from a game. He had no prior history of physical confrontations or fights with either his own teammates or opposing players.

[However, i]n his junior year, one year prior to the assault on Kavanagh, Folk had had an argument with Coach Wolff about his manner of play (Wolff believed that Folk was taking too many shots) and about an academic issue (Wolff was concerned that Folk had missed an examination and had tried to secure an excuse for having done so). The argument was heated, but involved no physical contact. Wolff suspended Folk for a period of several games, and Folk resumed team play thereafter without incident until the December, 1998, game against Manhattan College.

Folk's disciplinary history with the university included the imposition of two periods of "residence probation" for violation of the university's policies on noise and alcohol. Neither infraction involved any act of violence or threatened violence.

Although Kavanagh characterizes the December 22, 1998, game as "the most physical" he ever played, the number of penalties called by the referees was within a normal range. Up until the time he struck Kavanagh during the second half, no technical fouls had been called on Folk, and no university players had been ejected. Kavanagh describes the university team's play as follows: "with reckless abandon," "elbows to people's faces, trying to steal the ball," "after plays, bumping people," "holding you with both their hands, walking by, getting the elbow." He also claimed that Coach Wolff incited the team's aggressiveness by yelling encouragement from the sideline, not substituting for players who were allegedly elbowing opposing players, and calling out praise for his players, despite the fact that they were, in Kavanagh's view, committing fouls. Wolff denied that he had ever instructed Folk (or any other player) to hit or fight with any opposing player, and Kavanagh presented no contrary evidence.

* * * When Wolff talked to Folk about the incident sometime after the game, Folk's explanation for his misconduct was that he "lost it."

2. *Discussion.* a. *Vicarious liability.* Kavanagh contends that Folk's status as a scholarship athlete playing for the university made him an agent of the university and that the university is therefore vicariously liable for any torts committed by Folk while playing for the university's basketball team. We reject the proposition that the doctrine of responde-at superior renders schools liable for the acts of their students, and

decline to treat scholarship students any differently from paying students for these purposes.

* * *

b. *Negligence.* Kavanagh also claims that the university breached a duty to protect him from the allegedly foreseeable assault and battery by Folk. He acknowledges that, as a general rule, there is no duty to protect another from the criminal conduct of a third party. However, such a duty arises when there is a "special relationship" between the defendant and the injured victim. "[S]pecial relationships exist in several situations, based either on responsibilities imposed by statute or common law (or both). A special relationship, when derived from common law, is predicated on a plaintiff's reasonable expectations and reliance that a defendant will anticipate harmful acts of third persons and take appropriate measures to protect the plaintiff from harm." * * * Kavanagh contends that his status as a student athlete on an opposing team created such a special relationship between himself and the university.

In recent years, courts and commentators have taken differing views as to what duties schools have to the scholarship athletes that they have recruited. Some are of the view that the unequal bargaining power in the recruitment process, the degree of influence that a school and its coaches have over a student athlete's daily life, the pressures placed on student athletes to win at all costs (which may cause some students to risk their own health and safety), and the enormous sums of money schools now reap from their successful teams, are such that schools should be deemed to have a "special relationship" with their own scholarship athletes and a corresponding duty to protect those athletes from injury. * * * Others have rejected that theory on the ground that there is "nothing different about a student athlete's relationship with a university which would justify the conclusion that a student athlete is a custodial ward of the university while the non-athlete student is an emancipated adult." * * *

For purposes of this case, we need not enter that debate, as none of the authorities favoring such a "special relationship" has opined that that relationship extends to athletes from another school. Here, the university did not recruit Kavanagh; Kavanagh did not depend on the university nor the university on him for any benefit; and the university did not exert any form of control or influence over Kavanagh, or affect his ability or motive to protect himself. In short, Kavanagh had no relationship with the university, special or otherwise, and the sources he cites would, if accepted as law here in Massachusetts, place a duty on his own school, Manhattan College, not on the university.

Kavanagh's negligence claim also fails on the ground that any duty to protect him from the harm of another's criminal acts extends only to those acts that are reasonably foreseeable. However, "where there has been a showing that the risk of a criminal assault is foreseeable, the exact nature and source of the assault need not be shown in order for liability to attach." In a general sense, one can always foresee that, in the thrill of competition and the heat of battle inherent in a contact sport, any player might some day lose his or her temper and strike an opposing player. If that possibility alone sufficed to make an assault on the field of play reasonably "foreseeable," schools and coaches would face liability every time they allowed their enthusiastic players to take the field against an opposing team. For these purposes, foreseeability must mean something more than awareness of the ever-present possibility that an athlete may become overly excited and engage in physical contact beyond the precise boundaries of acceptably aggressive play. Rather, a defendant would have to have specific information about a player suggesting a propensity to engage in violent conduct, or some warning that a player or players appeared headed toward such conduct as the game progressed.

No such evidence has been presented here. On the undisputed facts, neither the university nor its coach had any reason to foresee that Folk would engage in violent behavior. He had never done so before, he had no history suggestive of potential violence on or off the basketball court,[7] and nothing in his conduct during the earlier part of the game provided any warning signal that Folk was on the verge of a violent outburst. Neither the university nor its coach had any duty to protect Kavanagh from a harm that they could not have reasonably foreseen.

Kavanagh's final theory of negligence alleges that Folk's attack was incited by Coach Wolff's own aggressive demeanor on the sidelines. Kavanagh has no evidence that Wolff instructed or expressly encouraged Folk to hit an opposing player. Rather, he contends that Wolff's animated style of coaching effectively pushed Folk beyond the boundaries of aggressive physical play into criminal violence. We agree with the motion judge that the record fails to support Kavanagh's theory.

We must first address what standard is to be applied to claims that coaches are liable for causing their players to injure other players. Recognizing that, by their nature, competitive sports involve physical contact between opposing players, and that some degree of aggressiveness in play is essential to athletic competition, we have held that mere negligence on the part of a player does not suffice to impose liability for injuries inflicted by that player during competition. Rather, an injured player must show that the other player's conduct amounted to recklessness before the law will impose liability. Utilizing a standard of recklessness, as opposed to mere negligence, "furthers the policy that '[v]igorous and active participation in sporting events should not be chilled by the threat of litigation.'" Just as players are entitled to play aggressively without fear of liability, a coach properly may encourage players to play aggressively. Indeed, a coach's ability to inspire players to compete aggressively is one of a coach's important attributes. The mere possibility that some players might overreact to such inspiration or encouragement should not, by itself, suffice to impose liability on a coach. As we do

---

7. While Kavanagh makes much of the fact that Folk had previously been suspended from the team, and had been disciplined by university authorities, none of those prior incidents had anything to do with violence or threats of violence.

with the players themselves, we must impose liability only where a coach's behavior amounts to at least recklessness.

Here, Kavanagh cannot demonstrate any recklessness on the part of Coach Wolff. To the extent that Wolff's demeanor was excited and aggressive, that is demeanor appropriate for a coach during a game. As to Kavanagh's contention that Wolff encouraged violence by failing to send in substitute players for players who were allegedly committing fouls, that contention would effectively require Wolff to be more sensitive to possible fouls than the referees. Under the rules of any sport, fouls or other violations carry their own penalties, and it is up to the officials refereeing the competition to enforce those rules and impose those penalties. It is not up to a coach to remove a player who may, conformably with the rules of the sport and the judgment of the referees, remain in the game despite the infractions allegedly committed. Finally, Kavanagh contends that Wolff yelled encouragement to aggressive players, praising their play when those same players were, in Kavanagh's judgment, committing fouls. Again, the policing of fouls is up to the referees, and the mere fact that a player has committed a foul, or even multiple fouls, does not preclude a coach from encouraging that player to play aggressively. Coach Wolff's behavior, viewed in the light most favorable to the plaintiff, amounted to nothing more than aggressive coaching. It did not amount to reckless conduct.

Judgments affirmed.

Notes

1. Perhaps the most highly publicized incident involving injury to a college athlete in this era was the tragic death of Hank Gathers, star basketball player for an outstanding Loyola Marymount team (LMU) that was headed for a top seed in the men's NCAA playoffs. Gathers, a high scoring and inspirational forward, would have been one of the top draft picks in the National Basketball Association. As described in the following law journal excerpt, a series of interrelated and troubling issues were raised by the death:

> On the afternoon of March 4, 1990, * * * Hank Gathers * * * collapsed after scoring a basket. Less than two hours later he was dead, a victim of idiopathic cardiomyopathy, a heart disorder. As a result of Gather's death, a $32.5 million lawsuit [was] filed by his family * * *.

> Defendants in the suit include Loyola Marymount University, Loyola Marymount's athletic director, its team trainer, and the former coach. Also named as defendants [were] several physicians who were treating Gathers for an irregular heartbeat discovered after he collapsed during a game on December 9, 1989. Among the allegations raised by the Gathers family [were] that the team coach induced the physicians into lowering the dosage of medication Gathers was taking to control his heart condition; that the physicians failed to adequately monitor the effects of the changed dosage; and that they failed to fully disclose the nature, extent, and effects of Gathers' heart disease and the consequences of his

returning to play basketball with such a condition. The complaint also [raised] the issue of whether Gathers should have been allowed to continue his basketball career at all after the heart condition was discovered months before his death.

On its face, *Gathers* appears to be another case of alleged medical malpractice raising concerns about the treatment provided to a heart patient. However, because Hank Gathers was a major college basketball star playing for a school that allegedly hoped to parlay his athletic abilities into millions of dollars and national exposure for itself, *Gathers* raises deeper, and indeed more troubling, questions concerning relationships among athletic teams, their players, and the team physicians who must serve them both. A reexamination of the relationship of the team physician to both the team and the athletes he or she serves is one of the most important issues raised by Gathers' death. A team physician's professional obligations are confronted by both the triangular nature of the relationships and the pressures raised by the competition and money involved in high-stakes sports. Craig A. Isaacs, *Conflicts of Interest for Team Physicians: A Retrospective in Light of* Gathers v. LMU, 2 ALBANY L.J. SCI. & TECH. 147, 148–49 (1992).

While the case ultimately settled, many believe that the alleged conduct of the treating physicians, if proven, would have constituted actionable negligence.

What are the lessons that might be drawn from this incident today, legally and as a matter of policy?

C. SEARCH AND SEIZURE, DRUG TESTING, AND RELATED FOURTH AMENDMENT CONCERNS

1. THE DOCTRINE OF *IN LOCO PARENTIS*

As referenced above under a negligence law analysis, the doctrine of *in loco parentis* has had a significant impact on the laws relating to campus activity. The doctrine is predicated on the idea that educators should be viewed as standing *in loco parentis* (in the place of parents) in a school setting, and should therefore have the same rights and responsibilities as parents. This reasoning has not only impacted the scope of the duty of care under negligence law, but has been used to justify limiting student rights under the First and Fourth Amendments. Just as parents are legally entitled to silence their children at the dinner table, for example, educators were once able to silence their students in a similarly arbitrary fashion. And just as parents are able under the law to search their children's rooms and belongings without permission, so too were educators able to search their students indiscriminately.

It is unclear today just exactly where the doctrine stands, and the picture may be different depending on the area of the law impacted, the geographical location, and of course the age of the students. For the youngest students, few would argue that the school does not stand in the place of the parent today for all intents and purposes. For graduate students, few would argue the opposite.

As a general rule, however, the doctrine has arguably gained renewed force in recent decades, after having been all but completely abrogated by the courts in the 1960's, 1970's, and 1980's. Even at the higher education level, both legislators and jurists have shown an increasing tendency to place additional responsibilities on the educational institutions, particularly with regard to campus safety.

Consider the materials in the second half of this chapter in light of the meaning, rationale, and arguably renewed vigor of the *in loco parentis* doctrine. What are the implications for student privacy rights, particularly in an era of increasing electronic and digital surveillance across the board? What can or should be done to address these trends?

2. K–12 SEARCH & SEIZURE CASE LAW GENERALLY: THE CONTINUING VITALITY OF *NEW JERSEY v. TLO*

PROBLEM 7: The Suburbia Lawsuits (continued)

SUBURBIA HIGH, NOVEMBER 4th: Senior Class Sponsor Fred Brown, on his way to the teacher's cafeteria, realized that he had forgotten his wallet and returned to his room to retrieve it. As he walked into the room, where several Senior Class officers were participating in a lively impromptu debate, he saw Sherry Marvin dip a key into a small vial of white powder and bring it up to her nose.

There were various interpretations as to what happened next. All agreed that "Coach" Brown yelled "What is going on here?" and that in the ensuing commotion the vial disappeared from view. The students had been sitting in somewhat of a semicircle, with several backpacks and purses lying around (some open, the others closed). It appeared to Brown that at least three students reached for backpacks, and it seemed to him that one or two packs or purses (he could not be sure) were either exchanged or at least shuffled around under the desks. Then the room became silent. Coach Brown explained that he had to take Sherry to the Assistant Principal.

As Sherry and Coach Brown began walking out of the classroom, Senior Class President Amanda Green suddenly became visibly agitated. "Sherry," she yelled, "you don't need to go with him." A large crowd of students gathered, and followed Amanda, Sherry, and Brown to the office building. Just before they entered the building, Amanda shouted: "Sherry, would you please give me back my purse!" The action was so dramatic that not only did everyone hear Amanda, but everyone saw Sherry hand over the purse.

Once inside the office building, Assistant Principal Margie Cole asked Amanda to leave, but she insisted on waiting to see what would happen to Sherry (who seemed to have disappeared). Cole hesitated, then asked Amanda and Brown to come into her private office. After repeated unsuccessful attempts to convince Amanda to hand over the purse, Ms. Cole forcefully took it and opened it up. Inside was a plastic bag containing white powder, and three small, empty vials. The police were called, Amanda was arrested, and lab tests later revealed that the white powder was in fact 7.5 grams of high quality cocaine.

NOVEMBER 5th: While all the students were in their Period 2 classes, Principal Arthur Ramsey ordered a search of the lockers of all Suburbia High Senior Class officers. Although no additional cocaine was found, two marijuana cigarettes were found in one locker, and one "wine cooler" in another. The police were called, and the students whose lockers had been searched were arrested. (When students were assigned lockers in September, no notice of any kind was provided regarding the possibility of locker searches. In fact, this was the first time in the history of Suburbia High that student lockers had been "searched.")

NOVEMBER 6th: Sherry Marvin, after two sleepless nights, contacted the local newspaper and in a shocking interview, admitted that she was in fact a Suburbia Police Officer who was only posing as a student. She also announced that she was checking herself into a drug rehabilitation center.

What arguments should be set forth in the following lawsuits? What result? Discuss.

Amanda Green v. Suburbia School District (alleging that the search of Amanda's purse violated her constitutional rights)

Suzukida v. Suburbia School District (alleging that the locker search violated the students' constitutional rights)

NEW JERSEY v. T.L.O.
469 U.S. 325, 105 S.Ct. 733 (1985).

JUSTICE WHITE delivered the opinion of the Court.

* * *

I

On March 7, 1980, a teacher at Piscataway High School in Middlesex County, N.J., discovered two girls smoking in a lavatory. One of the two girls was the respondent T.L.O., who at that time was a 14-year-old high school freshman. Because smoking in the lavatory was a violation of a school rule, the teacher took the two girls to the Principal's office, where they met with Assistant Vice Principal Theodore Choplick. In response to questioning by Mr. Choplick, T.L.O.'s companion admitted that she had violated the rule. T.L.O., however, denied that she had been smoking in the lavatory and claimed that she did not smoke at all.

Mr. Choplick asked T.L.O. to come into his private office and demanded to see her purse. Opening the purse, he found a pack of cigarettes, which he removed from the purse and held before T.L.O. as he accused her of having lied to him. As he reached into the purse for the cigarettes, Mr. Choplick also noticed a package of cigarette rolling papers. In his experience, possession of rolling papers by high school students was closely associated with the use of marihuana. Suspecting that a closer examination of the purse might yield further evidence of drug use, Mr. Choplick proceeded to search the purse thoroughly. The search revealed a small amount of marihuana, a pipe, a number of empty plastic bags, a substantial quantity of money in one-dollar bills, an index card that appeared to be a list of students who owed T.L.O. money, and two letters that implicated T.L.O. in marihuana dealing.

Mr. Choplick notified T.L.O.'s mother and the police, and turned the evidence of drug dealing over to the police. At the request of the police, T.L.O.'s mother took her daughter to police headquarters, where T.L.O. confessed that she had been selling marihuana at the high school. On the basis of the confession and the evidence seized by Mr. Choplick, the State brought delinquency charges against T.L.O. in the Juvenile and Domestic Relations Court of Middlesex County. Contending that Mr. Choplick's search of her purse violated the Fourth Amendment, T.L.O. moved to suppress the evidence found in her purse as well as her confession, which, she argued, was tainted by the allegedly unlawful search.

* * *

II

In determining whether the search at issue in this case violated the Fourth Amendment, we are faced initially with the question whether that Amendment's prohibition on unreasonable searches and seizures applies to searches conducted by public school officials. We hold that it does.

It is now beyond dispute that "the Federal Constitution, by virtue of the Fourteenth Amendment, prohibits unreasonable searches and seizures by state officers." Equally indisputable is the proposition that the Fourteenth Amendment protects the rights of students against encroachment by public school officials * * * .

* * *

III

To hold that the Fourth Amendment applies to searches conducted by school authorities is only to begin the inquiry into the standards governing such searches. Although the underlying command of the Fourth Amendment is always that searches and seizures be reasonable, what is reasonable depends on the context within which a search takes place. The determination of the standard of reasonableness governing any specific class of searches requires "balancing the need to search against the invasion which the search entails." On one side of the balance are arrayed the individual's legitimate expectations of privacy and personal security; on the other, the government's need for effective methods to deal with breaches of public order.

We have recognized that even a limited search of the person is a substantial invasion of privacy. We have also recognized that searches of closed items of personal luggage are intrusions on protected privacy interests, for "the Fourth Amendment provides protection to the owner of every container that conceals its contents from plain view." A search of a child's person or of a closed purse or other bag carried on her person,[5] no less than a similar search carried out on an adult, is undoubtedly a severe violation of subjective expectations of privacy.

Of course, the Fourth Amendment does not protect subjective expectations of privacy that are unreasonable or otherwise "illegitimate." To receive the protection of the Fourth Amendment, an expectation of privacy must be one that society is "prepared to recognize as legitimate." * * *

Although this Court may take notice of the difficulty of maintaining discipline in the public schools today, the situation is not so dire that students in the schools may claim no legitimate expectations of privacy. * * * We are not yet ready to hold that the schools and the prisons need be equated for purposes of the Fourth Amendment.

Nor does the State's suggestion that children have no legitimate need to bring personal property into the schools seem well anchored in reality. Students at a minimum must bring to school not only the supplies needed for their studies, but also keys, money, and the necessaries of personal hygiene and grooming. In addition, students may carry on their persons or in purses or wallets such nondisruptive yet highly personal items as photographs, letters, and diaries. Finally, students may have perfectly legitimate reasons to carry with them articles of property needed in connection with extracurricular or recreational activities. In short, schoolchildren may find it necessary to carry with them a variety of legitimate, noncontraband items, and there is no reason to conclude that they have necessarily waived all rights to privacy in such items merely by bringing them onto school grounds.

Against the child's interest in privacy must be set the substantial interest of teachers and administrators in maintaining discipline in the classroom and on school grounds. Maintaining order in the classroom has never been easy, but in recent years, school disorder has often taken particularly ugly forms: drug use and violent crime in the schools have become major social problems. Even in schools that have been spared the most severe disciplinary problems, the preservation of order and a proper educational environment requires close supervision of schoolchildren, as well as the enforcement of rules against conduct that would be perfectly permissible if undertaken by an adult. "Events calling for

---

5. We do not address the question, not presented by this case, whether a schoolchild has a legitimate expectation of privacy in lockers, desks, or other school property provided for the storage of school supplies. Nor do we express any opinion on the standards (if any) governing searches of such areas by school officials or by other public authorities acting at the request of school officials. Compare *Zamora v. Pomeroy,* 639 F.2d 662, 670 (CA10 1981) ("Inasmuch as the school had assumed joint control of the locker it cannot be successfully maintained that the school did not have a right to inspect it."), and *People v. Overton,* 24 N.Y.2d 522, 249 N.E.2d 366, 301 N.Y.S.2d 479 (1969) (holding that school administrators have power to consent to search of a student's locker), with *State v. Engerud,* 94 N.J. 331, 348, 463 A.2d 934, 943 (1983) ("We are satisfied that in the context of this case the student had an expectation of privacy in the contents of his locker.... For the four years of high school, the school locker is a home away from home. In it the student stores the kind of personal 'effects' protected by the Fourth Amendment.").

discipline are frequent occurrences and sometimes require immediate, effective action." Accordingly, we have recognized that maintaining security and order in the schools requires a certain degree of flexibility in school disciplinary procedures, and we have respected the value of preserving the informality of the student-teacher relationship.

How, then, should we strike the balance between the schoolchild's legitimate expectations of privacy and the school's equally legitimate need to maintain an environment in which learning can take place? It is evident that the school setting requires some easing of the restrictions to which searches by public authorities are ordinarily subject. The warrant requirement, in particular, is unsuited to the school environment: requiring a teacher to obtain a warrant before searching a child suspected of an infraction of school rules (or of the criminal law) would unduly interfere with the maintenance of the swift and informal disciplinary procedures needed in the schools. Just as we have in other cases dispensed with the warrant requirement when "the burden of obtaining a warrant is likely to frustrate the governmental purpose behind the search," we hold today that school officials need not obtain a warrant before searching a student who is under their authority.

The school setting also requires some modification of the level of suspicion of illicit activity needed to justify a search. Ordinarily, a search—even one that may permissibly be carried out without a warrant—must be based upon "probable cause" to believe that a violation of the law has occurred. However, "probable cause" is not an irreducible requirement of a valid search. The fundamental command of the Fourth Amendment is that searches and seizures be reasonable, and although "both the concept of probable cause and the requirement of a warrant bear on the reasonableness of a search, . . . in certain limited circumstances neither is required." Thus, we have in a number of cases recognized the legality of searches and seizures based on suspicions that, although "reasonable," do not rise to the level of probable cause. Where a careful balancing of governmental and private interests suggests that the public interest is best served by a Fourth Amendment standard of reasonableness that stops short of probable cause, we have not hesitated to adopt such a standard.

We join the majority of courts that have examined this issue in concluding that the accommodation of the privacy interests of schoolchildren with the substantial need of teachers and administrators for freedom to maintain order in the schools does not require strict adherence to the requirement that searches be based on probable cause to believe that the subject of the search has violated or is violating the law. Rather, the legality of a search of a student should depend simply on the reasonableness, under all the circumstances, of the search. Determining the reasonableness of any search involves a twofold inquiry: first, one must consider "whether the . . . action was justified at its inception,"; second, one must determine whether the search as actually conducted "was reasonably related in scope to the circumstances which justified the interference in the first place." Under ordinary circumstances, a search of a student by a teacher or other school official will be "justified at its inception" when there are reasonable grounds for suspecting that the search will turn up evidence that the student has violated or is violating either the law or the rules of the school.[8] Such a search will be permissible in its scope when the measures adopted are reasonably related to the objectives of the search and not excessively intrusive in light of the age and sex of the student and the nature of the infraction.

This standard will, we trust, neither unduly burden the efforts of school authorities to maintain order in their schools nor authorize unrestrained intrusions upon the privacy of schoolchildren. By focusing attention on the question of reasonableness, the standard will spare teachers and school administrators the necessity of schooling themselves in the niceties of probable cause and permit them to regulate their conduct according to the dictates of reason and common sense. At the same time, the reasonableness standard should ensure that the interests of students will be invaded no more than is necessary to achieve the legitimate end of preserving order in the schools.

IV

* * * Our review of the facts surrounding the search leads us to conclude that the search was in no sense unreasonable for Fourth Amendment purposes.[10]

The incident that gave rise to this case actually involved two separate searches, with the first—the search for cigarettes—providing the suspicion that gave rise to the second the search for marihuana. Although it is the fruits of the second search that are at issue here, the validity of the search for marihuana must depend on the reasonableness of the initial search for cigarettes, as there would have been no reason to suspect that T.L.O. possessed marihuana had the first search not taken place. Accordingly, it is to the search for cigarettes that we first turn our attention.

* * * T.L.O. had been accused of smoking, and had denied the accusation in the strongest possible terms when she stated that she did not smoke at all. Surely it cannot be said that under these circumstances, T.L.O.'s possession of cigarettes would be irrelevant to the

---

8. We do not decide whether individualized suspicion is an essential element of the reasonableness standard we adopt for searches by school authorities. In other contexts, however, we have held that although "some quantum of individualized suspicion is usually a prerequisite to a constitutional search or seizure[,] . . . the Fourth Amendment imposes no irreducible requirement of such suspicion." Exceptions to the requirement of individualized suspicion are generally appropriate only where the privacy interests implicated by a search are minimal and where "other safeguards" are available "to assure that the individual's reasonable expectation of privacy is not 'subject to the

discretion of the official in the field.' " Because the search of T.L.O.'s purse was based upon an individualized suspicion that she had violated school rules, *see infra,* at 745–46, we need not consider the circumstances that might justify school authorities in conducting searches unsupported by individualized suspicion.

10. Of course, New Jersey may insist on a more demanding standard under its own Constitution or statutes. In that case, its courts would not purport to be applying the Fourth Amendment when they invalidate a search.

charges against her or to her response to those charges. T.L.O.'s possession of cigarettes, once it was discovered, would both corroborate the report that she had been smoking and undermine the credibility of her defense to the charge of smoking. To be sure, the discovery of the cigarettes would not prove that T.L.O. had been smoking in the lavatory; nor would it, strictly speaking, necessarily be inconsistent with her claim that she did not smoke at all. But it is universally recognized that evidence, to be relevant to an inquiry, need not conclusively prove the ultimate fact in issue, but only have "any tendency to make the existence of any fact that is of consequence to the determination of the action more probable or less probable than it would be without the evidence." The relevance of T.L.O.'s possession of cigarettes to the question whether she had been smoking and to the credibility of her denial that she smoked supplied the necessary "nexus" between the item searched for and the infraction under investigation. * * *

* * * Mr. Choplick's suspicion that there were cigarettes in the purse was not an "inchoate and unparticularized suspicion or 'hunch,'" [R]ather, it was the sort of "common-sense conclusio[n] about human behavior" upon which "practical people"—including government officials—are entitled to rely. Of course, even if the teacher's report were true, T.L.O. *might* not have had a pack of cigarettes with her; she might have borrowed a cigarette from someone else or have been sharing a cigarette with another student. But the requirement of reasonable suspicion is not a requirement of absolute certainty: "sufficient probability, not certainty, is the touchstone of reasonableness under the Fourth Amendment...." Because the hypothesis that T.L.O. was carrying cigarettes in her purse was itself not unreasonable, it is irrelevant that other hypotheses were also consistent with the teacher's accusation. Accordingly, it cannot be said that Mr. Choplick acted unreasonably when he examined T.L.O.'s purse to see if it contained cigarettes.

Our conclusion that Mr. Choplick's decision to open T.L.O.'s purse was reasonable brings us to the question of the further search for marihuana once the pack of cigarettes was located. The suspicion upon which the search for marihuana was founded was provided when Mr. Choplick observed a package of rolling papers in the purse as he removed the pack of cigarettes. Although T.L.O. does not dispute the reasonableness of Mr. Choplick's belief that the rolling papers indicated the presence of marihuana, she does contend that the scope of the search Mr. Choplick conducted exceeded permissible bounds when he seized and read certain letters that implicated T.L.O. in drug dealing. This argument, too, is unpersuasive. The discovery of the rolling papers concededly gave rise to a reasonable suspicion that T.L.O. was carrying marihuana as well as cigarettes in her purse. This suspicion justified further exploration of T.L.O.'s purse, which turned up more evidence of drug-related activities: a pipe, a number of plastic bags of the type commonly used to store marihuana, a small quantity of marihuana, and a fairly substantial amount of money. Under these circumstances, it was not unreasonable to extend the search to a separate zippered compartment of the purse; and when a search of that compartment revealed an index card containing a list of "people who owe me money" as well as two letters, the inference that T.L.O. was involved in marihuana trafficking was substantial enough to justify Mr. Choplick in examining the letters to determine whether they contained any further evidence. In short, we cannot conclude that the search for marihuana was unreasonable in any respect.

Because the search resulting in the discovery of the evidence of marihuana dealing by T.L.O. was reasonable, the New Jersey Supreme Court's decision to exclude that evidence from T.L.O.'s juvenile delinquency proceedings on Fourth Amendment grounds was erroneous. Accordingly, the judgment of the Supreme Court of New Jersey is

Reversed.

JUSTICE POWELL, with whom JUSTICE O'CONNOR joins, concurring.

I agree with the Court's decision, and generally with its opinion. I would place greater emphasis, however, on the special characteristics of elementary and secondary schools that make it unnecessary to afford students the same constitutional protections granted adults and juveniles in a nonschool setting.

In any realistic sense, students within the school environment have a lesser expectation of privacy than members of the population generally. They spend the school hours in close association with each other, both in the classroom and during recreation periods. The students in a particular class often know each other and their teachers quite well. Of necessity, teachers have a degree of familiarity with, and authority over, their students that is unparalleled except perhaps in the relationship between parent and child. It is simply unrealistic to think that students have the same subjective expectation of privacy as the population generally. But for purposes of deciding this case, I can assume that children in school—no less than adults—have privacy interests that society is prepared to recognize as legitimate.

* * *

The special relationship between teacher and student also distinguishes the setting within which schoolchildren operate. Law enforcement officers function as adversaries of criminal suspects. These officers have the responsibility to investigate criminal activity, to locate and arrest those who violate our laws, and to facilitate the charging and bringing of such persons to trial. Rarely does this type of adversarial relationship exist between school authorities and pupils. Instead, there is a commonality of interests between teachers and their pupils. The attitude of the typical teacher is one of personal responsibility for the student's welfare as well as for his education.

The primary duty of school officials and teachers, as the Court states, is the education and training of young people. A State has a compelling interest in assuring that the schools meet this responsibility. Without first establishing discipline and maintaining order, teachers cannot begin to educate their students. And apart from education, the school has the obligation to protect pupils from mistreatment by other children, and also to protect teachers themselves from violence by the few students whose conduct in recent years has prompted national concern. For me, it would be unreasonable and at odds with history to argue that the full panoply of constitutional rules applies with the same force and effect in the schoolhouse as it does in the enforcement of criminal laws.

In sum, although I join the Court's opinion and its holding, my emphasis is somewhat different.

JUSTICE BLACKMUN, concurring in the judgment.

I join the judgment of the Court and agree with much that is said in its opinion. I write separately, however, because I believe the Court omits a crucial step in its analysis of whether a school search must be based upon probable-cause. The Court correctly states that we have recognized limited exceptions to the probable-cause requirement "[w]here a careful balancing of governmental and private interests suggests that the public interest is best served" by a lesser standard. I believe that we have used such a balancing test, rather than strictly applying the Fourth Amendment's Warrant and Probable–Cause Clause, only when we were confronted with "a special law enforcement need for greater flexibility." I pointed out in *United States v. Place*:

> While the Fourth Amendment speaks in terms of freedom from unreasonable [searches], the Amendment does not leave the reasonableness of most [searches] to the judgment of courts or government officers; the Framers of the Amendment balanced the interests involved and decided that a [search] is reasonable only if supported by a judicial warrant based on probable cause.

Only in those exceptional circumstances in which special needs, beyond the normal need for law enforcement, make the warrant and probable-cause requirement impracticable, is a court entitled to substitute its balancing of interests for that of the Framers.

* * *

The Court's implication that the balancing test is the rule rather than the exception is troubling for me because it is unnecessary in this case. The elementary and secondary school setting presents a special need for flexibility justifying a departure from the balance struck by the Framers. As Justice POWELL notes, "[w]ithout first establishing discipline and maintaining order, teachers cannot begin to educate their students." Maintaining order in the classroom can be a difficult task. A single teacher often must watch over a large number of students, and, as any parent knows, children at certain ages are inclined to test the outer boundaries of acceptable conduct and to imitate the misbehavior of a peer if that misbehavior is not dealt with quickly. Every adult remembers from his own schooldays the havoc a water pistol or peashooter can wreak until it is taken away. Thus, the Court has recognized that "[e]vents calling for discipline are frequent occurrences and sometimes require immediate, effective action." Indeed, because drug use and possession of weapons have become increasingly common among young people, an immediate response frequently is required not just to maintain an environment conducive to learning, but to protect the very safety of students and school personnel.

Such immediate action obviously would not be possible if a teacher were required to secure a warrant before searching a student. Nor would it be possible if a teacher could not conduct a necessary search until the teacher thought there was probable cause for the search. A teacher has neither the training nor the day-to-day experience in the complexities of probable cause that a law enforcement officer possesses, and is ill-equipped to make a quick judgment about the existence of probable cause. The time required for a teacher to ask the questions or make the observations that are necessary to turn reasonable grounds into probable cause is time during which the teacher, and other students, are diverted from the essential task of education. A teacher's focus is, and should be, on teaching and helping students, rather than on developing evidence against a particular troublemaker.

Education "is perhaps the most important function" of government, *Brown v. Board of Education,* 347 U.S. 483, 493, 74 S. Ct. 686, 691 (1954), and government has a heightened obligation to safeguard students whom it compels to attend school. The special need for an immediate response to behavior that threatens either the safety of schoolchildren and teachers or the educational process itself justifies the Court in excepting school searches from the warrant and probable-cause requirement, and in applying a standard determined by balancing the relevant interests. I agree with the standard the Court has announced, and with its application of the standard to the facts of this case. I therefore concur in its judgment.

JUSTICE BRENNAN, with whom JUSTICE MARSHALL joins, concurring in part and dissenting in part.

I fully agree with Part II of the Court's opinion. Teachers, like all other government officials, must conform their conduct to the Fourth Amendment's protections of personal privacy and personal security. * * *

I do not, however, otherwise join the Court's opinion. Today's decision sanctions school officials to conduct full-scale searches on a "reasonableness" standard whose only definite content is that it is *not* the same test as the "probable cause" standard found in the text of the Fourth Amendment. In adopting this unclear, unprecedented, and unnecessary departure from generally applicable Fourth Amendment standards, the Court carves out a broad exception to standards that this Court has developed over years of considering Fourth Amendment problems. Its decision is supported neither by precedent nor even by a fair application of the "balancing test" it proclaims in this very opinion.

* * *

On my view, the presence of the word "unreasonable" in the text of the Fourth Amendment does not grant a shifting majority of this Court the authority to answer *all* Fourth Amendment questions by consulting its momentary vision of the social good. Full-scale searches unaccompanied by probable cause violate the Fourth Amendment. I do not pretend that our traditional Fourth Amendment doctrine automatically answers all of the difficult legal questions that occasionally arise. I do contend, however, that this Court has an obligation to provide some coherent framework to resolve such questions on the basis of more than a conclusory recitation of the results of a "balancing test." The Fourth Amendment itself supplies that framework and, because the Court today fails to heed its message, I must respectfully dissent.

JUSTICE STEVENS, with whom JUSTICE MARSHALL joins, and with whom JUSTICE BRENNAN joins as to Part I, concurring in part and dissenting in part.

* * *

The State of New Jersey sought review in this Court, first arguing that the exclusionary rule is wholly inapplicable to searches conducted by school officials, and then contending that the Fourth Amendment itself provides no protection at all to the student's privacy. The Court has accepted neither of these frontal assaults on the Fourth Amendment. It has, however, seized upon this "no smoking" case to announce "the proper standard" that should govern searches by school officials who are confronted with disciplinary problems far more severe than smoking in the restroom. Although I join Part II of the Court's opinion, I continue to believe that the Court has unnecessarily and inappropriately reached out to decide a constitutional question. More importantly, I fear that the concerns that motivated the Court's activism have produced a holding that will permit school administrators to search students suspected of violating only the most trivial school regulations and guidelines for behavior.

* * *

Justice Brandeis was both a great student and a great teacher. It was he who wrote:

"Our Government is the potent, the omnipresent teacher. For good or for ill, it teaches the whole people by its example. Crime is contagious. If the Government becomes a lawbreaker, it breeds contempt for law; it invites every man to become a law unto himself; it invites anarchy." Those of us who revere the flag and the ideals for which it stands believe in the power of symbols. We cannot ignore that rules of law also have a symbolic power that may vastly exceed their utility.

Schools are places where we inculcate the values essential to the meaningful exercise of rights and responsibilities by a self-governing citizenry. If the Nation's students can be convicted through the use of arbitrary methods destructive of personal liberty, they cannot help but feel that they have been dealt with unfairly. The application of the exclusionary rule in criminal proceedings arising from illegal school searches makes an important statement to young people that "our society attaches serious consequences to a violation of constitutional rights," and that this is a principle of "liberty and justice for all."

* * *

In arguing that teachers and school administrators need the power to search students based on a lessened standard, the United States as *amicus curiae* relies heavily on empirical evidence of a contemporary crisis of violence and unlawful behavior that is seriously undermining the process of education in American schools. A standard better attuned to this concern would permit teachers and school administrators to search a student when they have reason to believe that the search will uncover *evidence that the student is violating the law or engaging in conduct that is seriously disruptive of school order, or the educational process.*

* * *

Like the New Jersey Supreme Court, I would view this case differently if the Assistant Vice Principal had reason to believe T.L.O.'s purse contained evidence of criminal activity, or of an activity that would seriously disrupt school discipline. There was, however, absolutely no basis for any such assumption—not even a "hunch."

In this case, Mr. Choplick overreacted to what appeared to be nothing more than a minor infraction—a rule prohibiting smoking in the bathroom of the freshmen's and sophomores' building. It is, of course, true that he actually found evidence of serious wrongdoing by T.L.O., but no one claims that the prior search may be justified by his unexpected discovery. As far as the smoking infraction is concerned, the search for cigarettes merely tended to corroborate a teacher's eyewitness account of T.L.O.'s violation of a minor regulation designed to channel student smoking behavior into designated locations. Because this conduct was neither unlawful nor significantly disruptive of school order or the educational process, the invasion of privacy associated with the forcible opening of T.L.O.'s purse was entirely unjustified at its inception.

A review of the sampling of school search cases relied on by the Court demonstrates how different this case is from those in which there was indeed a valid justification for intruding on a student's privacy. In most of them the student was suspected of a criminal violation; in the remainder either violence or substantial disruption of school order or the integrity of the academic process was at stake. Few involved matters as trivial as the no-smoking rule violated by T.L.O. The rule the Court adopts today is so open-ended that it may make the Fourth Amendment virtually meaningless in the school context. Although I agree that school administrators must have broad latitude to maintain order and discipline in our classrooms, that authority is not unlimited.

IV

The schoolroom is the first opportunity most citizens have to experience the power of government. Through it passes every citizen and public official, from schoolteachers to policemen and prison guards. The values they learn there, they take with them in life. One of our most cherished ideals is the one contained in the Fourth Amendment: that the government may not intrude on the personal privacy of its citizens without a warrant or compelling circumstance. The Court's decision today is a curious moral for the Nation's youth. Although the search of T.L.O.'s purse does not trouble today's majority, I submit that we are not dealing with "matters relatively trivial to the welfare of the Nation. There are village tyrants as well as village Hampdens, but none who acts under color of law is beyond reach of the Constitution." *West Virginia State Board of Education v. Barnette,* 319 U.S. 624, 638, 63 S. Ct. 1178, 1185 (1943).

I respectfully dissent.

Notes

1. The numerous opinions filed by the justices in *T.L.O.* reflect the multi-dimensional and highly nuanced nature of the issues raised. As discussed below, Justice Blackmun's concurrence arguably has had the greatest impact on the development of the law (with regard to the special needs doctrine) over time; but the respective dissenting opinions of Justices Brennan and Stevens highlight the dilemmas educators face in trying to teach values, dilemmas that are equally compelling today. *Cf infra,* Ch. 9. And the Powell/O'Connor concurrence raises important privacy issues that remain very much unresolved.

2. It is important to note the changing nature of the law in the area of criminal procedure generally, with the pendulum swinging from the 1960s and 1970s—where many Americans fought for greater protection from searches and seizures—to a willingness of the same Americans to retain less rights in the 1980s and 1990s as concerns regarding safety, on campus and in society as a whole, increased.

3. Footnote 8 of the majority opinion raises the important question of whether and to what extent a requirement of individualized suspicion must be met before individual students can be searched under the Fourth Amendment. For an overview of developments in this area in the aftermath of *T.L.O.,* and a summary of issues that remained unresolved 15 years down the road, see Jason E. Yearout, *Individualized School Searches and the Fourth Amendment: What's a School District to Do?,* 10 WM. & MARY BILL RTS. J. 489 (2002).

3. DRUG TESTING OF STUDENTS

PROBLEM 8: Drug Testing and Nirvana Macro Systems

The following hypothetical is set in the fictional state of Nirvana.

In response to the increasing demand for distance education programs linked to the interrelated areas of home schooling, charter schooling, and the

"No Child Left Behind" Act, Nirvana Macro Systems (NMS, a private, entrepreneurial company) develops a full-featured program that can lead to the attainment of a high school diploma online. NMS educational materials, accessible only after registration and the payment of a fee, range from text and picture files to MP3 files, streaming video, and webcasting. In addition, registrants can benefit from personal feedback regarding their work, feedback provided by NMS "educational advisers" via e-mail.

A highly effective marketing team succeeds in getting the NMS program endorsed by a significant number of educators and political leaders, and before too long it is serving a significant student population. But noted policymakers are quick to criticize the quality of the program, questioning in particular the loose nature of the registration system, the professional background of the educational advisers, and the boilerplate materials that focus primarily on basic skills ... to the exclusion of inquiry, analysis, problem solving, and other higher level cognitive abilities.

After a series of reports in local newspapers documenting allegations that a significant percentage of NMS students are using recreational drugs before, during, and after participating in the online activities. NMS, in conjunction with participating local school districts, implements a requirement that all NMS students residing in the relevant geographical areas served by these districts be randomly drug tested.

The district-mandated and publicly funded drug testing program is challenged by the local branch of the ACLU, on behalf of several students who refuse to be tested.

What arguments will be set forth by the ACLU? What result? Discuss.

BOARD OF EDUC. OF INDEP. SCH. DIST. NO. 92 v. EARLS

536 U.S. 822, 122 S.Ct. 2559 (2002).

JUSTICE THOMAS delivered the opinion of the Court.

* * *

I

The city of Tecumseh, Oklahoma, is a rural community located approximately 40 miles southeast of Oklahoma City. The School District administers all Tecumseh public schools. In the fall of 1998, the School District adopted the Student Activities Drug Testing Policy (Policy), which requires all middle and high school students to consent to drug testing in order to participate in any extracurricular activity. In practice, the Policy has been applied only to competitive extracurricular activities sanctioned by the Oklahoma Secondary Schools Activities Association, such as the Academic Team, Future Farmers of America, Future Homemakers of America, band, choir, pom-pom, cheerleading, and athletics. Under the Policy, students are required to take a drug test before participating in an extracurricular activity, must submit to random drug testing while participating in that activity, and must agree to be tested at any time upon reasonable suspicion. The urinalysis tests are designed to detect only the use of illegal drugs, including amphetamines, marijuana, cocaine, opiates, and barbituates, not medical conditions or the presence of authorized prescription medications.

At the time of their suit, both respondents attended Tecumseh High School. Respondent Lindsay Earls was a member of the show choir, the marching band, the Academic Team, and the National Honor Society. Respondent Daniel James sought to participate in the Academic Team. Together with their parents, Earls and James brought a Rev. Stat. § 1979, 42 U.S.C. § 1983, action against the School District, challenging the Policy both on its face and as applied to their participation in extracurricular activities. They alleged that the Policy violates the Fourth Amendment as incorporated by the Fourteenth Amendment and requested injunctive and declarative relief. They also argued that the School District failed to identify a special need for testing students who participate in extracurricular activities, and that the "Drug Testing Policy neither addresses a proven problem nor promises to bring any benefit to students or the school."

* * *

II

The Fourth Amendment to the United States Constitution protects "[t]he right of the people to be secure in their persons, houses, papers, and effects, against unreasonable searches and seizures." Searches by public school officials, such as the collection of urine samples, implicate Fourth Amendment interests. We must therefore review the School District's Policy for "reasonableness," which is the touchstone of the constitutionality of a governmental search.

In the criminal context, reasonableness usually requires a showing of probable cause. * * * [However,] [t]he Court has * * * held that a warrant and finding of probable cause are unnecessary in the public school context because such requirements " 'would unduly interfere with the maintenance of the swift and informal disciplinary procedures [that are] needed.' "

Given that the School District's Policy is not in any way related to the conduct of criminal investigations, * * * respondents do not contend that the School District requires probable cause before testing students for drug use. Respondents instead argue that drug testing must be based at least on some level of individualized suspicion. It is true that we generally determine the reasonableness of a search by balancing the nature of the intrusion on the individual's privacy against the promotion of legitimate governmental interests. But we have long held that "the Fourth Amendment imposes no irreducible requirement of [individualized] suspicion." "[I]n certain limited circumstances, the Government's need to discover such latent or hidden conditions, or to prevent their development, is sufficiently compelling to justify the intrusion on privacy entailed by conducting such searches without any measure of individualized suspicion." Therefore, in the context of safety and administrative regulations, a search unsupported by probable cause may be reasonable "when 'special needs, beyond the normal need for law enforcement, make the warrant and probable-cause requirement impracticable.' "

Significantly, this Court has previously held that "special needs" inhere in the public school context. While schoolchildren do not shed their constitutional rights when they enter the schoolhouse, see *Tinker v. Des Moines Independent Community School Dist.,* 393 U.S. 503, 506, 89 S. Ct. 733 (1969), "Fourth Amendment rights ... are different in public schools than elsewhere; the 'reasonableness' inquiry cannot disregard the schools' custodial and tutelary responsibility for children." In particular, a finding of individualized suspicion may not be necessary when a school conducts drug testing.

In *Vernonia,* this Court held that the suspicionless drug testing of athletes was constitutional. The Court, however, did not simply authorize all school drug testing, but rather conducted a fact-specific balancing of the intrusion on the children's Fourth Amendment rights against the promotion of legitimate governmental interests. Applying the principles of *Vernonia* to the somewhat different facts of this case, we conclude that Tecumseh's Policy is also constitutional.

A

We first consider the nature of the privacy interest allegedly compromised by the drug testing. As in *Vernonia,* the context of the public school environment serves as the backdrop for the analysis of the privacy interest at stake and the reasonableness of the drug testing policy in general. * * *

A student's privacy interest is limited in a public school environment where the State is responsible for maintaining discipline, health, and safety. Schoolchildren are routinely required to submit to physical examinations and vaccinations against disease. Securing order in the school environment sometimes requires that students be subjected to greater controls than those appropriate for adults.

Respondents argue that because children participating in nonathletic extracurricular activities are not subject to regular physicals and communal undress, they have a stronger expectation of privacy than the athletes tested in *Vernonia.* This distinction, however, was not essential to our decision in *Vernonia,* which depended primarily upon the school's custodial responsibility and authority.

In any event, students who participate in competitive extracurricular activities voluntarily subject themselves to many of the same intrusions on their privacy as do athletes. Some of these clubs and activities require occasional off-campus travel and communal undress. All of them have their own rules and requirements for participating students that do not apply to the student body as a whole. For example, each of the competitive extracurricular activities governed by the Policy must abide by the rules of the Oklahoma Secondary Schools Activities Association, and a faculty sponsor monitors the students for compliance with the various rules dictated by the clubs and activities. This regulation of extracurricular activities further diminishes the expectation of privacy among schoolchildren. * * * We therefore conclude that the students affected by this Policy have a limited expectation of privacy.

B

Next, we consider the character of the intrusion imposed by the Policy. Urination is "an excretory function traditionally shielded by great privacy." But the "degree of intrusion" on one's privacy caused by collecting a urine sample "depends upon the manner in which production of the urine sample is monitored."

Under the Policy, a faculty monitor waits outside the closed restroom stall for the student to produce a sample and must "listen for the normal sounds of urination in order to guard against tampered specimens and to insure an accurate chain of custody." The monitor then pours the sample into two bottles that are sealed and placed into a mailing pouch along with a consent form signed by the student. This procedure is virtually identical to that reviewed in *Vernonia,* except that it additionally protects privacy by allowing male students to produce their samples behind a closed stall. Given that we considered the method of collection in *Vernonia* a "negligible" intrusion, the method here is even less problematic.

In addition, the Policy clearly requires that the test results be kept in confidential files separate from a student's other educational records and released to school personnel only on a "need to know" basis. Respondents nonetheless contend that the intrusion on students' privacy is significant because the Policy fails to protect effectively against the disclosure of confidential information and, specifically, that the school "has been careless in protecting that information: for example, the Choir teacher looked at students' prescription drug lists and left them where other students could see them." But the choir teacher is someone with a "need to know," because during off-campus trips she needs to know what medications are taken by her students. Even before the Policy was enacted the choir teacher had access to this information. In any event, there is no allegation that any other student did see such information. This one example of alleged carelessness hardly increases the character of the intrusion.

Moreover, the test results are not turned over to any law enforcement authority. Nor do the test results here lead to the imposition of discipline or have any academic consequences. Rather, the only consequence of a failed drug test is to limit the student's privilege of participating in extracurricular activities. Indeed, a student may test positive for drugs twice and still be allowed to participate in extracurricular activities. After the first positive test, the school contacts the student's parent or guardian for a meeting. The student may continue to participate in the activity if within five days of the meeting the student shows proof of receiving drug counseling and submits to a second drug test in two weeks. For the second positive test, the student is suspended from participation in all extracurricular activities for 14 days, must complete four hours of substance abuse counseling, and must submit to monthly drug tests. Only after a third positive test will the student be suspended from participating in any extracurricular activity for the remainder of the school year, or 88 school days, whichever is longer.

Given the minimally intrusive nature of the sample collection and the limited uses to which the test results are put, we conclude that the invasion of students' privacy is not significant.

C

Finally, this Court must consider the nature and immediacy of the government's concerns and the efficacy of the Policy in meeting them. This Court has already articulated in detail the importance of the governmental concern in preventing drug use by schoolchildren. The drug abuse problem among our Nation's youth has hardly abated since *Vernonia* was decided in 1995. In fact, evidence suggests that it has only grown worse.[5] As in *Vernonia,* "the necessity for the State to act is magnified by the fact that this evil is being visited not just upon individuals at large, but upon children for whom it has undertaken a special responsibility of care and direction." The health and safety risks identified in *Vernonia* apply with equal force to Tecumseh's children. Indeed, the nationwide drug epidemic makes the war against drugs a pressing concern in every school.

Additionally, the School District in this case has presented specific evidence of drug use at Tecumseh schools. Teachers testified that they had seen students who appeared to be under the influence of drugs and that they had heard students speaking openly about using drugs. A drug dog found marijuana cigarettes near the school parking lot. Police officers once found drugs or drug paraphernalia in a car driven by a Future Farmers of America member. And the school board president reported that people in the community were calling the board to discuss the "drug situation." We decline to second-guess the finding of the District Court that "[v]iewing the evidence as a whole, it cannot be reasonably disputed that the [School District] was faced with a 'drug problem' when it adopted the Policy."

Respondents consider the proffered evidence insufficient and argue that there is no "real and immediate interest" to justify a policy of drug testing nonathletes. We have recognized, however, that "[a] demonstrated problem of drug abuse ... [is] not in all cases necessary to the validity of a testing regime," but that some showing does "shore up an

---

5. For instance, the number of 12th graders using any illicit drug increased from 48.4 percent in 1995 to 53.9 percent in 2001. The number of 12th graders reporting they had used marijuana jumped from 41.7 percent to 49.0 percent during that same period. *See* DEP'T OF HEALTH & HUMAN SERVICES, MONITORING THE FUTURE: NATIONAL RESULTS ON ADOLESCENT DRUG USE, OVERVIEW OF KEY FINDINGS (2001) (Table 1).

assertion of special need for a suspicionless general search program." The School District has provided sufficient evidence to shore up the need for its drug testing program.

Furthermore, this Court has not required a particularized or pervasive drug problem before allowing the government to conduct suspicionless drug testing. For instance, in *Von Raab,* the Court upheld the drug testing of customs officials on a purely preventive basis, without any documented history of drug use by such officials. In response to the lack of evidence relating to drug use, the Court noted generally that "drug abuse is one of the most serious problems confronting our society today," and that programs to prevent and detect drug use among customs officials could not be deemed unreasonable. Likewise, the need to prevent and deter the substantial harm of childhood drug use provides the necessary immediacy for a school testing policy. Indeed, it would make little sense to require a school district to wait for a substantial portion of its students to begin using drugs before it was allowed to institute a drug testing program designed to deter drug use.

Given the nationwide epidemic of drug use, and the evidence of increased drug use in Tecumseh schools, it was entirely reasonable for the School District to enact this particular drug testing policy.

* * *

Respondents also argue that the testing of nonathletes does not implicate any safety concerns, and that safety is a "crucial factor" in applying the special needs framework. They contend that there must be "surpassing safety interests," or "extraordinary safety and national security hazards," in order to override the usual protections of the Fourth Amendment. Respondents are correct that safety factors into the special needs analysis, but the safety interest furthered by drug testing is undoubtedly substantial for all children, athletes and nonathletes alike. We know all too well that drug use carries a variety of health risks for children, including death from overdose.

We also reject respondents' argument that drug testing must presumptively be based upon an individualized reasonable suspicion of wrongdoing because such a testing regime would be less intrusive. In this context, the Fourth Amendment does not require a finding of individualized suspicion, and we decline to impose such a requirement on schools attempting to prevent and detect drug use by students. Moreover, we question whether testing based on individualized suspicion in fact would be less intrusive. Such a regime would place an additional burden on public school teachers who are already tasked with the difficult job of maintaining order and discipline. A program of individualized suspicion might unfairly target members of unpopular groups. The fear of lawsuits resulting from such targeted searches may chill enforcement of the program, rendering it ineffective in combating drug use.
* * *

Finally, we find that testing students who participate in extracurricular activities is a reasonably effective means of addressing the School

District's legitimate concerns in preventing, deterring, and detecting drug use. While in *Vernonia* there might have been a closer fit between the testing of athletes and the trial court's finding that the drug problem was "fueled by the 'role model' effect of athletes' drug use," such a finding was not essential to the holding. *Vernonia* did not require the school to test the group of students most likely to use drugs, but rather considered the constitutionality of the program in the context of the public school's custodial responsibilities. Evaluating the Policy in this context, we conclude that the drug testing of Tecumseh students who participate in extracurricular activities effectively serves the School District's interest in protecting the safety and health of its students.

III

Within the limits of the Fourth Amendment, local school boards must assess the desirability of drug testing schoolchildren. In upholding the constitutionality of the Policy, we express no opinion as to its wisdom. Rather, we hold only that Tecumseh's Policy is a reasonable means of furthering the School District's important interest in preventing and deterring drug use among its schoolchildren. Accordingly, we reverse the judgment of the Court of Appeals.

It is so ordered.

* * *

JUSTICE O'CONNOR, with whom JUSTICE SOUTER joins, dissenting.

I dissented in *Vernonia School Dist. 47J v. Acton*, and continue to believe that case was wrongly decided. Because *Vernonia* is now this Court's precedent, and because I agree that petitioners' program fails even under the balancing approach adopted in that case, I join Justice GINSBURG's dissent.

JUSTICE GINSBURG, with whom JUSTICE STEVENS, JUSTICE O'CCONNOR, and JUSTICE SOUTER join, dissenting.

Seven years ago, in *Vernonia School Dist. 47J v. Acton*, this Court determined that a school district's policy of randomly testing the urine of its student athletes for illicit drugs did not violate the Fourth Amendment. In so ruling, the Court emphasized that drug use "increase[d] the risk of sports-related injury" and that Vernonia's athletes were the "leaders" of an aggressive local "drug culture" that had reached " 'epidemic proportions.' " Today, the Court relies upon *Vernonia* to permit a school district with a drug problem its superintendent repeatedly described as "not ... major," to test the urine of an academic team member solely by reason of her participation in a nonathletic, competitive extracurricular activity—participation associated with neither special dangers from, nor particular predilections for, drug use.

"[T]he legality of a search of a student," this Court has instructed, "should depend simply on the reasonableness, under all the circumstances, of the search." *New Jersey v. T.L.O.*, 469 U.S. 325, 341, 105 S. Ct. 733 (1985). Although " 'special needs' inhere in the public school context," those needs are not so expansive or malleable as to render reasonable any program of student drug testing a school district elects to install. The particular testing program upheld today is not reasonable; it is capricious, even perverse: Petitioners' policy targets for testing a student population least likely to be at risk from illicit drugs and their damaging effects. I therefore dissent.

* * *

Notes

1. It is instructive to trace the development of the "special needs" doctrine from Justice Blackmun's concurrence in *New Jersey v. TLO,* to the *Earls* decision, seventeen years later. *See, e.g.,* Fabio Arcila, Jr., *Special Needs and Special Deference: Suspicionless Civil Searches in the Modern Regulatory State,* 56 ADMIN. L. REV. 1223, 1228 (2004):

> From the Court's perspective, the special needs principle has proved wonderfully flexible. For example, the Court has applied it to civil searches that were premised on individualized suspicion, as well as to suspicionless civil searches.

> The special needs principle provides that, when a special need beyond the normal need of law enforcement exists, courts will determine Fourth Amendment reasonableness by balancing the competing governmental and private interests at stake. Justice Blackmun first formulated the special needs test in *New Jersey v. T.L.O.,* writing that "[o]nly in those exceptional circumstances in which special needs, beyond the normal need for law enforcement, make the warrant and probable-cause requirement impracticable, is a court entitled to substitute its balancing of interests for that of the Framers." As this formulation indicates, the special needs principle requires consideration of three factors. Under the first factor, special need, courts ask whether a legitimate governmental interest apart from crime detection exists. Under the second factor, impracticability, courts determine whether a warrant or individualized suspicion requirement would frustrate the non-criminal governmental interest. Under the third factor, balancing, courts inquire whether the governmental interests at stake outweigh the private interests in order to decide the ultimate issue of whether the search was reasonable under the Fourth Amendment. A negative answer to any of these three factors renders a civil search unconstitutional under the Reasonableness Clause.

> In the years since *New Jersey v. T.L.O.,* the Supreme Court has decided a series of suspicionless civil search cases using the special needs principle, the most recent of which all involved suspicionless drug testing of individuals. In the first three of these drug testing cases, the Court approved suspicionless drug testing of some railroad employees in *Skinner v. Railway Labor Executives' Ass'n,* certain customs officials in *National Treasury Employees Union v. Von Raab,* as well as precollegiate student athletes in *Vernonia School District 47J v. Acton.* Not until the fourth such case, *Chandler v. Miller,* which involved candidates for public office in Georgia, did the Court strike down a suspicionless drug

testing regime that had come before it. Most recently, the Court expanded Vernonia's scope through its decision in *Board of Education of Independent School District No. 92 of Pottawatomie County v. Earls*, in which it held constitutional the suspicionless drug testing of all pre-collegiate students who participate in extracurricular activities. Apart from border cases, these drug testing cases constitute the only instances in which the Court has held constitutional state-sponsored suspicionless civil searches of individuals.

2. Drug testing of student athletes at the higher education level—particularly the testing program mandated by the NCAA—was challenged by plaintiffs in the late 1980s and early 1990s. *See University of Colorado v. Derdeyn*, 863 P.2d 929 (Colo. 1993), *Hill v. NCAA*, 7 Cal.4th 1, 865 P.2d 633, 26 Cal.Rptr.2d 834 (1994). After the NCAA prevailed in the *Hill* case, drug testing became standard procedure for intercollegiate athletics, not only under NCAA mandates, but under programs implemented by individual colleges and universities.

Today, these higher education programs are generally accepted as legal, and little debate regarding their efficacy is evident. Yet it must be noted that even with extensive testing of student athletes, abuses of steroids and related substances continue to be a major problem in organized athletic competition, at both the amateur and the professional level. Many believe that the prototypical drug testing programs at colleges and universities are not focusing in on the heart of the problem in this context, and that they are not having the sort of deterrent effect that many might have hoped.

D.   STUDENT RECORDS

1.   THE FAMILY EDUCATIONAL RIGHTS AND PRIVACY ACT (FERPA) AND RELATED FEDERAL STATUTES

From Electronic Privacy Information Center, *Student Privacy,*
at http://www.epic.org/privacy/student/ (2005)

[Federal Statutes Relating to Privacy of Student Records Generally]

* * * The most prominent of the federal protections for student privacy is the Family Educational Rights and Privacy Act (FERPA), also known as the "Buckley Amendment," "FERPA protects the confidentiality of student records to some extent, while also giving students the right to review their own records."

Students' personal information is often collected through in-school surveys, sometimes for commercial use. Congress most recently addressed such surveys in the No Child Left Behind Act, a broad federal educational act. The Act provides parents and students the right to be notified of, and consent to, the collection of student information. However, the Act includes many exceptions to this right.

* * * Another provision of No Child Left Behind mandates that high schools turn over student contact information to military recruiters, unless parents or students explicitly opt out of such disclosure. And in 2002, Congress amended FERPA, via the USA Patriot Act, to require schools to transmit information about immigrant students to the INS. Under this program, the Student and Exchange Visitor Information System, schools had to begin in 2003 reporting immigrants' academic information, such as disciplinary actions or changes in programs of study.

Family Educational Rights and Privacy Act

The FERPA protects the confidentiality of student educational records. The Act applies to any public or private elementary, secondary, or post-secondary school and any state or local education agency that receives federal funds. All public schools and virtually all private schools are covered by FERPA because they receive some sort of federal funding.

The Act has two parts. First, it gives students the right to inspect and review their own education records, request corrections, halt the release of personally identifiable information, and obtain a copy of their institution's policy concerning access to educational records. (20 U.S.C.S. § 1232g(a)). Second, it prohibits educational institutions from disclosing "personally identifiable information in education records" without the written consent of the student, or if the student is a minor, the student's parents. (20 U.S.C.S. § 1232g(b)). Schools that fail to comply with FERPA risk losing federal funding.

However, there are several exceptions that allow the release of student records to certain parties or under certain conditions. Records may be released without the student's consent: (1) to school officials with a legitimate educational interest; (2) to other schools to which a student seeks or intends to enroll; (3) to education officials for audit and evaluation purposes; (4) to accrediting organizations; (5) to parties in connection with financial aid to a student; (6) to organizations conducting certain studies for or on behalf of a school; (7) to comply with a judicial order or lawfully issued subpoena; (8) in the case of health and safety emergencies; and (9) to state and local authorities within a juvenile justice system. (20 U.S.C.S. § 1232g(b)(1)).

In addition, some records maintained by schools are exempt from FERPA, including: (1) records in the sole possession of school officials; (2) records maintained by a law enforcement unit of the educational institution; (3) records of an educational institution's non-student employees; and (4) records on a student who is 18 years of age or older or who attends a post-secondary institution that are maintained by a health professional. (20 U.S.C.S. § 1232g(a)(4)(B)). In addition, FERPA allows, but does not require, schools to release "directory information," including students' names and addresses, to the public. (20 U.S.C.S. § 1232g(a)(5)(A)). However, this exception was modified in 2002, and high schools are now required to provide students' names, addresses and telephone numbers to military recruiters, unless a student or parent opts out of such disclosure.

Note

1. A related issue that has moved to the proverbial "front burner" in recent years is the responsibility of educational institutions regarding data flow and data protection. As the country moves increasingly toward the digitization of all records, the difficulties inherent in trying to secure these records and protect the privacy of all those involved has moved to the forefront. When institutional records were all on paper, stored in locked file cabinets, securing those documents was generally a much simpler operation than it has become today. This is an area that will undoubtedly be the focus of greater attention on the part of both the legal and the educational policy communities. In light of the principles identified in this portion of Chapter 2, and the interrelated issues that have emerged, what might an appropriate response entail? Are there additional legal protections that can or should be put in place? What technological challenges must be faced in this context?

2. DETERMINING THE PARAMETERS OF FERPA IN THE U.S. SUPREME COURT

OWASSO INDEP. SCH. DIST. NO. I–011 v. FALVO

534 U.S. 426, 122 S.Ct. 934 (2002).

Justice Kennedy delivered the opinion of the Court.

Justice KENNEDY delivered the opinion of the Court.

Teachers sometimes ask students to score each other's tests, papers, and assignments as the teacher explains the correct answers to the entire class. Respondent contends this practice, which the parties refer to as peer grading, violates the Family Educational Rights and Privacy Act of 1974 (FERPA or Act), 88 Stat. 571, 20 U.S.C. § 1232g. We took this case to resolve the issue.

I

Under FERPA, schools and educational agencies receiving federal financial assistance must comply with certain conditions. § 1232g(a)(3). One condition specified in the Act is that sensitive information about students may not be released without parental consent. The Act states that federal funds are to be withheld from school districts that have "a policy or practice of permitting the release of education records (or personally identifiable information contained therein ...) of students without the written consent of their parents." The phrase "education records" is defined, under the Act, as "records, files, documents, and other materials" containing information directly related to a student, which "are maintained by an educational agency or institution or by a person acting for such agency or institution." The definition of education records contains an exception for "records of instructional, supervisory, and administrative personnel ... which are in the sole possession of the maker thereof and which are not accessible or revealed to any other person except a substitute." The precise question for us is whether peer graded classroom work and assignments are education records.

Three of respondent Kristja J. Falvo's children are enrolled in Owasso Independent School District No. I–011, in a suburb of Tulsa, Oklahoma. The children's teachers, like many teachers in this country, use peer grading. In a typical case the students exchange papers with each other and score them according to the teacher's instructions, then return the work to the student who prepared it. The teacher may ask the students to report their own scores. In this case it appears the student could either call out the score or walk to the teacher's desk and reveal it in confidence, though by that stage, of course, the score was known at least to the one other student who did the grading. Both the grading and the system of calling out the scores are in contention here.

Respondent claimed the peer grading embarrassed her children. She asked the school district to adopt a uniform policy banning peer grading and requiring teachers either to grade assignments themselves or at least to forbid students from grading papers other than their own. The school district declined to do so, and respondent brought [this] class action * * * .

      *   *   *

We granted certiorari to decide whether peer grading violates FER-PA. Finding no violation of the Act, we reverse.

II

At the outset, we note it is an open question whether FERPA provides private parties, like respondent, with a cause of action enforceable under § 1983. We have granted certiorari on this issue in another case. See *Gonzaga Univ. v. Doe*, [534 U.S.] 1103, 122 S. Ct. 865 [(2002)]. * * * In these circumstances we assume, but without so deciding or expressing an opinion on the question, that private parties may sue an educational agency under § 1983 to enforce the provisions of FERPA here at issue. * * *

The parties appear to agree that if an assignment becomes an education record the moment a peer grades it, then the grading, or at least the practice of asking students to call out their grades in class, would be an impermissible release of the records under § 1232g(b)(1). Without deciding the point, we assume for the purposes of our analysis that they are correct. The parties disagree, however, whether peer graded assignments constitute education records at all. The papers do contain information directly related to a student, but they are records under the Act only when and if they "are maintained by an educational agency or institution or by a person acting for such agency or institution."

Petitioners, supported by the United States as *amicus curiae*, contend the definition covers only institutional records—namely, those materials retained in a permanent file as a matter of course. They argue that records "maintained by an educational agency or institution" generally would include final course grades, student grade point averages, standardized test scores, attendance records, counseling records, and records of disciplinary actions—but not student homework or classroom work.

Respondent, adopting the reasoning of the Court of Appeals, contends student graded assignments fall within the definition of education records. That definition contains an exception for "records of instructional, supervisory, and administrative personnel . . . which are in the sole possession of the maker thereof and which are not accessible or revealed to any other person except a substitute." The Court of Appeals reasoned that if grade books are not education records, then it would have been unnecessary for Congress to enact the exception. Grade books and the grades within, the court concluded, are "maintained" 939 by a teacher and so are covered by FERPA. The court recognized that teachers do not maintain the grades on individual student assignments until they have recorded the result in the grade books. It reasoned, however, that if Congress forbids teachers to disclose students' grades once written in a grade book, it makes no sense to permit the disclosure immediately beforehand. The court thus held that student graders maintain the grades until they are reported to the teacher.

The Court of Appeals' logic does not withstand scrutiny. Its interpretation, furthermore, would effect a drastic alteration of the existing allocation of responsibilities between States and the National Government in the operation of the Nation's schools. We would hesitate before interpreting the statute to effect such a substantial change in the balance of federalism unless that is the manifest purpose of the legislation. This principle guides our decision.

Two statutory indicators tell us that the Court of Appeals erred in concluding that an assignment satisfies the definition of education records as soon as it is graded by another student. First, the student papers are not, at that stage, "maintained" within the meaning of § 1232g(a)(4)(A). The ordinary meaning of the word "maintain" is "to keep in existence or continuance; preserve; retain." Even assuming the teacher's grade book is an education record—a point the parties contest and one we do not decide here—the score on a student graded assignment is not "contained therein," until the teacher records it. The teacher does not maintain the grade while students correct their peers' assignments or call out their own marks. Nor do the student graders maintain the grades within the meaning of § 1232g(a)(4)(A). The word "maintain" suggests FERPA records will be kept in a filing cabinet in a records room at the school or on a permanent secure database, perhaps even after the student is no longer enrolled. The student graders only handle assignments for a few moments as the teacher calls out the answers. It is fanciful to say they maintain the papers in the same way the registrar maintains a student's folder in a permanent file.

The Court of Appeals was further mistaken in concluding that each student grader is "a person acting for" an educational institution for purposes of § 1232g(a)(4)(A). The phrase "acting for" connotes agents of the school, such as teachers, administrators, and other school employees. Just as it does not accord with our usual understanding to say students are "acting for" an educational institution when they follow their teacher's direction to take a quiz, it is equally awkward to say students are "acting for" an educational institution when they follow their teacher's direction to score it. Correcting a classmate's work can be as much a part of the assignment as taking the test itself. It is a way to teach material again in a new context, and it helps show students how to assist and respect fellow pupils. By explaining the answers to the class as the students correct the papers, the teacher not only reinforces the lesson but also discovers whether the students have understood the material and are ready to move on. We do not think FERPA prohibits these educational techniques. We also must not lose sight of the fact that the phrase "by a person acting for [an educational] institution" modifies "maintain." Even if one were to agree students are acting for the teacher when they correct the assignment, that is different from saying they are acting for the educational institution in maintaining it.

Other sections of the statute support our interpretation. FERPA, for example, requires educational institutions to "maintain a record, kept with the education records of each student." This record must list those who have requested access to a student's education records and their reasons for doing so. The record of access "shall be available only to parents, [and] to the school official and his assistants who are responsible for the custody of such records."

Under the Court of Appeals' broad interpretation of education records, every teacher would have an obligation to keep a separate record of access for each student's assignments. Indeed, by that court's logic, even students who grade their own papers would bear the burden of maintaining records of access until they turned in the assignments. We doubt Congress would have imposed such a weighty administrative burden on every teacher, and certainly it would not have extended the mandate to students.

Also, FERPA requires "a record" of access for each pupil. This single record must be kept "with the education records." This suggests Congress contemplated that education records would be kept in one place with a single record of access. By describing a "school official" and "his assistants" as the personnel responsible for the custody of the records, FERPA implies that education records are institutional records kept by a single central custodian, such as a registrar, not individual assignments handled by many student graders in their separate classrooms.

FERPA also requires recipients of federal funds to provide parents with a hearing at which they may contest the accuracy of their child's education records. The hearings must be conducted "in accordance with regulations of the Secretary," which in turn require adjudication by a disinterested official and the opportunity for parents to be represented by an attorney. It is doubtful Congress would have provided parents with this elaborate procedural machinery to challenge the accuracy of the grade on every spelling test and art project the child completes.

Respondent's construction of the term "education records" to cover student homework or classroom work would impose substantial burdens on teachers across the country. It would force all instructors to take time, which otherwise could be spent teaching and in preparation, to correct an assortment of daily student assignments. Respondent's view would make it much more difficult for teachers to give students immediate guidance. The interpretation respondent urges would force teachers to abandon other customary practices, such as group grading of team assignments. Indeed, the logical consequences of respondent's view are all but unbounded. At argument, counsel for respondent seemed to agree that if a teacher in any of the thousands of covered classrooms in the Nation puts a happy face, a gold star, or a disapproving remark on a classroom assignment, federal law does not allow other students to see it.

We doubt Congress meant to intervene in this drastic fashion with traditional state functions. Under the Court of Appeals' interpretation of FERPA, the federal power would exercise minute control over specific teaching methods and instructional dynamics in classrooms throughout the country. The Congress is not likely to have mandated this result, and we do not interpret the statute to require it.

For these reasons, even assuming a teacher's grade book is an education record, the Court of Appeals erred, for in all events the grades on students' papers would not be covered under FERPA at least until the teacher has collected them and recorded them in his or her grade book. We limit our holding to this narrow point, and do not decide the broader question whether the grades on individual student assignments, once they are turned in to teachers, are protected by the Act.

The judgment of the Court of Appeals is reversed, and the case is remanded for further proceedings consistent with this opinion.

It is so ordered.

GONZAGA UNIV. v. DOE

536 U.S. 273, 122 S.Ct. 2268 (2002).

CHIEF JUSTICE REHNQUIST delivered the opinion of the Court.

The question presented is whether a student may sue a private university for damages under Rev. Stat. § 1979, 42 U.S.C. § 1983 (1994 ed., Supp. V), to enforce provisions of the Family Educational Rights and Privacy Act of 1974 (FERPA or Act), 88 Stat. 571, 20 U.S.C. § 1232g, which prohibit the federal funding of educational institutions that have a policy or practice of releasing education records to unauthorized persons. We hold such an action foreclosed because the relevant provisions of FERPA create no personal rights to enforce under 42 U.S.C. § 1983 (1994 ed., Supp. V).

Respondent John Doe is a former undergraduate in the School of Education at Gonzaga University, a private university in Spokane, Washington. He planned to graduate and teach at a Washington public elementary school. Washington at the time required all of its new teachers to obtain an affidavit of good moral character from a dean of their graduating college or university. In October 1993, Roberta League, Gonzaga's "teacher certification specialist," overheard one student tell another that respondent engaged in acts of sexual misconduct against Jane Doe, a female undergraduate. League launched an investigation and contacted the state agency responsible for teacher certification, identifying respondent by name and discussing the allegations against him. Respondent did not learn of the investigation, or that information about him had been disclosed, until March 1994, when he was told by League and others that he would not receive the affidavit required for certification as a Washington schoolteacher.

Respondent then sued Gonzaga and League (petitioners) in state court. He alleged violations of Washington tort and contract law, as well as a pendent violation of § 1983 for the release of personal information to an "unauthorized person" in violation of FERPA. * * *

      * * *

Like the Washington Supreme Court and the State Court of Appeals below, other state and federal courts have divided on the question of FERPA's enforceability under § 1983. The fact that all of these courts have relied on the same set of opinions from this Court suggests that our opinions in this area may not be models of clarity. We therefore granted certiorari, to resolve the conflict among the lower courts and in the process resolve any ambiguity in our own opinions.

Congress enacted FERPA under its spending power to condition the receipt of federal funds on certain requirements relating to the access and disclosure of student educational records. The Act directs the Secretary of Education to withhold federal funds from any public or private "educational agency or institution" that fails to comply with these conditions. As relevant here, the Act provides:

> No funds shall be made available under any applicable program to any educational agency or institution which has a policy or practice of permitting the release of education records (or personally identifiable information contained therein ...) of students without the written consent of their parents to any individual, agency, or organization.

The Act directs the Secretary of Education to enforce this and other of the Act's spending conditions. The Secretary is required to establish an office and review board within the Department of Education for "investigating, processing, reviewing, and adjudicating violations of [the Act]." Funds may be terminated only if the Secretary determines that a recipient institution "is failing to comply substantially with any requirement of [the Act]" and that such compliance "cannot be secured by voluntary means."

Respondent contends that this statutory regime confers upon any student enrolled at a covered school or institution a federal right, enforceable in suits for damages under § 1983, not to have "education records" disclosed to unauthorized persons without the student's express written consent. But we have never before held, and decline to do so here, that spending legislation drafted in terms resembling those of FERPA can confer enforceable rights.

      *   *   *

[T]here is no question that FERPA's nondisclosure provisions fail to confer enforceable rights. To begin with, the provisions entirely lack the sort of "rights creating" language critical to showing the requisite congressional intent to create new rights. Unlike the individually focused terminology of Titles VI and IX ("No person . . . shall . . . be subjected to discrimination"), FERPA's provisions speak only to the Secretary of Education, directing that "[n]o funds shall be made available" to any "educational agency or institution" which has a prohibited "policy or practice." This focus is two steps removed from the interests of individual students and parents and clearly does not confer the sort of "individual entitlement" that is enforceable under § 1983. *   *   *

FERPA's nondisclosure provisions further speak only in terms of institutional policy and practice, not individual instances of disclosure. Therefore, as in *Blessing*, they have an "aggregate" focus, they are not concerned with "whether the needs of any particular person have been satisfied," and they cannot "give rise to individual rights." Recipient institutions can further avoid termination of funding so long as they "comply substantially" with the Act's requirements. This, too, is not unlike *Blessing*, which found that Title IV D failed to support a § 1983 suit in part because it only required "substantial compliance" with federal regulations. Respondent directs our attention to subsection (b)(2), but the text and structure of subsections (b)(1) and (b)(2) are essentially the same.[6] In each provision the reference to individual

---

6. Subsection (b)(2) provides in relevant part:

"No funds shall be made available under any applicable program to any educational agency or institution which has a policy or practice of releasing, or providing access to, any personally identifiable information in education records other than directory information . . . unless—"

"(A) there is written consent from the student's parents specifying records to be released, the reasons for such release, and to whom, and with a copy of the records to be released to the student's parents and the student if desired by the parents." 20 U.S.C. § 1232g(b)(2)(A).

Respondent invokes this provision to assert the very awkward "individualized right to withhold consent and prevent the unauthorized release of personally identifiable information in education records by an educational institution that has a policy or practice of releasing, or providing access to, consent is in the context of describing the type of "policy or practice" that triggers a funding prohibition. For reasons expressed repeatedly in our prior cases, however, such provisions cannot make out the requisite congressional intent to confer individual rights enforceable by § 1983.

Our conclusion that FERPA's nondisclosure provisions fail to confer enforceable rights is buttressed by the mechanism that Congress chose to provide for enforcing those provisions. Congress expressly authorized the Secretary of Education to *"deal with violations"* of the Act, § 1232g(f) (emphasis added), and required the Secretary to "establish or designate [a] review board" for investigating and adjudicating such violations, § 1232g(g). Pursuant to these provisions, the Secretary created the Family Policy Compliance Office (FPCO) "to act as the Review Board required under the Act [and] to enforce the Act with respect to all applicable programs." The FPCO permits students and parents who suspect a violation of the Act to file individual written complaints. If a complaint is timely and contains required information, the FPCO will initiate an investigation, notify the educational institution of the charge, and request a written response. If a violation is found, the FPCO distributes a notice of factual findings and a "statement of the specific steps that the agency or institution must take to comply" with FERPA. These administrative procedures squarely distinguish this case from *Wright* and *Wilder*, where an aggrieved individual lacked any federal review mechanism, and further counsel against our finding a congressional intent to create individually enforceable private rights.[8]

Congress finally provided that "[e]xcept for the conduct of hearings, none of the functions of the Secretary under this section shall be carried out in any of the regional offices" of the Department of Education. This centralized review provision was added just four months after FERPA's enactment due to "concern that regionalizing the enforcement of [FERPA] may lead to multiple interpretations of it, and possibly work a hardship on parents, students, and institutions." It is implausible to presume that the same Congress nonetheless intended private suits to be brought before thousands of federal-and state-court judges, which could only result in the sort of "multiple interpretations" the Act explicitly sought to avoid.

In sum, if Congress wishes to create new rights enforceable under § 1983, it must do so in clear and unambiguous terms—no less and no more than what is required for Congress to create new rights enforceable under an implied private right of action. FERPA's nondisclosure provisions contain no-rights creating language, they have an aggregate, not individual, focus, and they serve primarily to direct the Secretary of Education's distribution of public funds to educational institutions. They

such information." That is a far cry from the sort of individualized, concrete monetary entitlement found enforceable in *Maine v. Thiboutot, Wright,* and *Wilder v. Virginia Hospital Assn.*

8. We need not determine whether FERPA's procedures are "sufficiently comprehensive" to offer an independent basis for precluding private enforcement, due to our finding that FERPA creates no private right to enforce.

therefore create no rights enforceable under § 1983. Accordingly, the judgment of the Supreme Court of Washington is reversed, and the case is remanded for further proceedings not inconsistent with this opinion.

It is so ordered.

E.　PRIVACY AND TECHNOLOGY IN THE INFORMATION AGE

The rapid growth of digital and electronic surveillance technology over the past two decades, and the proliferating use of this technology in both the public and the private sector, have led many people to focus on privacy issues in both a legal and a public policy context.

What people are finding when they do focus on this area is that not only are individual privacy interests arguably being compromised as they never had been before, but that the legal system affords much less protection than Americans might have thought. There is an illusion of privacy, for example, on the Internet, but in actuality online communication and digital footsteps are being more closely monitored than most off-line activity had ever been. And in the off-line world, the growing presence of tiny, unobtrusive, and often-hidden cameras in public locations, privately owned settings, and of course in the cell phones that people carry with them is leading increasingly to an entirely different set of realities than might have existed even as recently as a decade ago.

Not only does the legal system afford less protection for individual privacy interests than most people imagine, but recent federal statutes have actually increased the ability of public and private agencies to monitor the activities of the American people. Most notably, the U.S. Patriot Act, passed in the aftermath of the 9/11/01 attacks, has enabled the government to engage in surveillance that might previously have been found unconstitutional. And in the private sector, the Digital Millennium Copyright Act has paved the way for private monitoring of Internet activity, silently and with little protest.

While the alarms that have been sounded in this regard have focused mainly on society as a whole, it is inevitable that many of these same concerns will find their way into the education community. Regulations and policies will need to be promulgated, and inevitable disputes are certain to be litigated. Areas that may be particularly ripe for prospective litigation include online monitoring generally, surveillance cameras in public schools, colleges, and universities, tracking devices that can monitor student whereabouts, high tech search devices, and technology that can serve as the functional equivalent of checkpoints or metal detectors.

Consider the materials in this section in light of recent privacy-related developments. Given the perspectives presented by the commentators, and the relevant legal principles that are identified, what predictions might you make regarding how all this will look in 5–10 years?

How will educational institutions be impacted? What can or should be done in this area at the present time?

PROBLEM 9: Driver's Licenses for the Information Superhighway

Consider the efficacy of the following proposed federal legislation, designed to implement a hypothetical international treaty.

To increase online safety, protect online users, & enhance Internet commerce, the legislation would mandate the creation of a National Internet Clearinghouse (akin to a national DMV) which would issue driver's licenses for the Information Superhighway. Access to the Internet in the U.S. would be limited to those who do not have a criminal record and who pass a written test regarding a new, international "acceptable use policy." The license must be renewed every four years, and can be revoked if an Internet-related crime is committed. The latest in biometric technology will be used to make sure that when a person logs on, his or her license number will be correctly identified.

1.   In light of your analysis of (a) the regulatory design and (b) whether the plan is likely to achieve its purpose, would you recommend passage of such a bill? Why? Alternatively, could you support a modified version of this bill? If so, what modifications might be appropriate?

2.   Instead, might you support a more limited version of this legislation that would impact only students?

3.   Alternatively, assuming the existence of the technology, could you support the creation of a private Internet for educational institutions only, where students would be required to comply with the above guidelines and obtain "driver's licenses" before they could access this private Internet? Or might there be a better way to accomplish the same safety-related purposes and goals?

4.   Assume that a version of this bill passes that impacts only students, and that it is challenged as violative of their right to privacy. What arguments might be set forth? What result? Discuss.

RECONSTRUCTING ELECTRONIC SURVEILLANCE LAW

Daniel J. Solove.
72 GEO. WASH. L. REV. 1264 (2004).

* * *

Today, technology has given the government an unprecedented ability to engage in surveillance. New X-ray devices can see through people's clothing, amounting to what some call a "virtual strip-search." Thermal sensors can detect movement and activity via heat patterns. Telephone calls can be wiretapped; places can be "bugged" with hidden recording devices; and parabolic microphones can record conversations at long distances. A device known as Carnivore developed by the Federal

Bureau of Investigation ("FBI") can scan through all of the e-mail traffic of an internet service provider ("ISP"). Keystroke logger devices can record every keystroke typed on one's computer, and these devices can be installed into a person's computer by e-mailing a computer virus called "Magic Lantern." Tracking devices can relay information about a person's whereabouts. One can trace cell phone calls to a person's particular location.

Surveillance cameras have become ubiquitous. Britain has erected an elaborate system of video cameras which enable officials to monitor city streets through closed circuit television. Called CCTV, this system has grown rapidly ever since it was first used in 1994 in response to terrorist bombings. By 2001, according to estimates, Britain had one half million surveillance cameras, one for every 120 people. The United States has begun moving toward the British model. In 2002, the U.S. National Park Service installed surveillance cameras around national monuments in Washington, D.C.

Surveillance technology can be a useful law enforcement tool, for it provides the government with the power to watch people's activities and listen to their conversations. These profound powers, however, raise difficult problems. As with many countries throughout the world, the United States has enacted a series of laws to balance the benefits and dangers of surveillance.

* * *

I. THE PURPOSE AND HISTORY OF ELECTRONIC SURVEILLANCE LAW

In order to examine the effectiveness of electronic surveillance law and the methods by which to improve it, we must first articulate the goals that we want the law to achieve. At a very general level, the law of electronic surveillance recognizes two things: that government surveillance is good and that it is bad. Surveillance is an important law enforcement tool, and it can be highly effective at solving and preventing crimes. Thus, we want the government to be able to engage in certain forms of surveillance. But surveillance is also a very dangerous tool, with profound implications for our freedom and democracy. Hence, we also want government surveillance to be tightly controlled.

Our electronic surveillance law was created in response to specific problems. It was thus borne out of experience, and it is designed to redress these problems. In this Part, I discuss the animating problems and concerns of surveillance law. I examine the costs and benefits of electronic surveillance as well as the history of how and why surveillance law developed the way it did.

A. SURVEILLANCE: THE GOOD AND THE BAD

Electronic surveillance is one of the central tools of modern law enforcement. It can aid significantly in the investigations of crimes, for it allows the government to watch and listen to people during their unguarded moments, when they may speak about their criminal activity.

Video cameras may capture criminals in the act and aid in their identification and arrest. Surveillance can also assist in preventing crimes because it enables the government to learn about criminal activity that is afoot and to halt it before it happens. Few would argue that these are not significant benefits.

Surveillance can also prevent crime in another way. In 1791, Jeremy Bentham imagined a new architectural design for a prison which he called the Panopticon. As Michel Foucault describes it:

> [A]t the periphery, an annular building; at the centre, a tower; this tower is pierced with wide windows that open onto the inner side of the ring; the peripheric building is divided into cells, each of which extends the whole width of the building. . . . All that is needed, then, is to place a supervisor in a central tower and to shut up in each cell a madman, a patient, a condemned man, a worker or a schoolboy. By the effect of backlighting, one can observe from the tower, standing out precisely against the light, the small captive shadows in the cells of the periphery. They are like so many cages, so many small theatres, in which each actor is alone, perfectly individualized and constantly visible.

The Panopticon achieves obedience and discipline by having all prisoners believe they could be watched at any moment. Their fear of being watched inhibits transgression. Surveillance can thus prevent crime by making people decide not to engage in it at all. More generally, surveillance is good because it is a highly effective tool for maintaining social order. We want to foster a society where people are secure from theft, vandalism, assault, murder, rape, and terrorism. We thus desire social control, and surveillance can help achieve that end.

But surveillance is bad for the very same reason. George Orwell's Nineteen Eighty–Four chronicles a totalitarian government called "Big Brother" that aims for total social control. Everyone is under constant fear of being watched or overheard, and everything that people do is rigidly controlled by the government. In contrast to the society depicted in Orwell's novel, our society aims to be free and democratic, and our government is a far cry from Big Brother. The goal is not to suppress all individuality, to force everybody to think and act alike. Our government, however, has some of the same surveillance capabilities as Big Brother. And even when the government does not aim for total social control, surveillance can still impair freedom and democracy.

Surveillance has negative side effects that affect both the observed and the observers. For the observed, surveillance can lead to self-censorship and inhibition. According to Julie Cohen: "Pervasive monitoring of every first move or false start will, at the margin, incline choices toward the bland and the mainstream." Monitoring constrains the "acceptable spectrum of belief and behavior," and it results in "a subtle yet fundamental shift in the content of our character, a blunting and blurring of rough edges and sharp lines." Surveillance "threatens not only to chill the expression of eccentric individuality, but also, gradually, to dampen the force of our aspirations to it." Paul Schwartz argues that surveillance inhibits freedom of choice, impinging upon self-determination. Surveillance rigidifies one's past; it is a means of creating a trail of information about a person. Christopher Slobogin argues that being placed under surveillance impedes one's anonymity, inhibits one's freedom to associate with others, makes one's behavior less spontaneous, and alters one's freedom of movement. Surveillance's inhibitory effects are especially potent when people are engaging in political protest or dissent. People can face persecution, public sanction, and blacklisting for their unpopular political beliefs. Surveillance can make associating with disfavored groups and causes all the more difficult and precarious.

For the observers, surveillance presents a profound array of powers that are susceptible to abuse. As Raymond Ku notes, the Framers of the Constitution were concerned about "unfettered governmental power and discretion." The Framers were deeply opposed to general warrants and writs of assistance. General warrants "resulted in 'ransacking' and seizure of the personal papers of political dissidents, authors, and printers of seditious libel." Writs of assistance authorized "sweeping searches and seizures without any evidentiary basis." As Patrick Henry declared: "They may, unless the general government be restrained by a bill of rights, or some similar restrictions, go into your cellars and rooms, and search, ransack, and measure, every thing you eat, drink, and wear. They ought to be restrained within proper bounds." The problem, in short, is with the government having too much power.

Electronic surveillance presents additional problems. It is a sweeping form of investigatory power. It extends beyond a search, for it records behavior, social interaction, and everything that a person says and does. Rather than a targeted query for information, surveillance is often akin to casting a giant net, which can ensnare a significant amount of data beyond that which was originally sought. As James Dempsey notes, electronic surveillance captures a wide range of communications, "whether they are relevant to the investigation or not, raising concerns about compliance with the particularity requirement in the Fourth Amendment and posing the risk of general searches." Moreover, unlike a typical search, which is often performed in a short once-and-done-fashion, electronic surveillance "continues around-the-clock for days or months." Additionally, in a regular search, the government comes to a suspect's house and often searches while the suspect is present; on the other hand, "the usefulness of electronic surveillance depends on lack of notice to the suspect." As Justice Douglas observed, wiretapping can become "a dragnet, sweeping in all conversations within its scope."

Dissenting from *Lopez v. United States*, where the Court upheld the use of a pocket wire recorder to record a conversation, Justice Brennan observed that surveillance "makes the police omniscient; and police omniscience is one of the most effective tools of tyranny." As Justice Brandeis observed:

Whenever a telephone line is tapped, the privacy of the persons at both ends of the line is invaded and all conversations between them upon any subject, although proper, confidential and privileged, may be overheard. Moreover, the tapping of one man's telephone line involves the tapping of the telephone of every other person whom he may call or who may call him. As a means of espionage, writs of assistance and general warrants are but puny instruments of tyranny and oppression when compared with wire tapping.

Furthermore, information collected by electronic surveillance can potentially be abused. Even if abuses are rare or the risk of abuse is low, the existence of legal protection is comforting and freedom-enhancing. People need a degree of control over the government in order to feel free. Freedom is not just the absence of restraints; it is a mental state, a felt reality in both structure and sentiment. Like insurance, protections against surveillance provide a sense of security.

Surveillance gives significant power to the watchers. Part of the harm is not simply in being watched, but in the lack of control that people have over the watchers. Surveillance creates the need to worry about the judgment of the watchers. Will our e-mail be misunderstood? Will our confidential information be revealed? What will be done with the information gleaned from surveillance?

Thus, the goal of surveillance law is to ameliorate these problems while at the same time allowing for effective law enforcement. This can be accomplished by providing for the oversight of government surveillance, accountability for abuses and errors, and limits against generalized forms of surveillance.

    * * *

1. MONITORING OF STUDENT ONLINE ACTIVITY GENERALLY

PRIVACY v. PIRACY

Sonia K. Kaytal.
7 Yale J. L. & Tech. 222 (2005).

* * * Today, the Recording Industry Association of America (RIAA) and other copyright owners maintain automated Web crawlers that regularly survey and record the Internet Protocol addresses of computers that trade files on peer to peer networks. After the RIAA's initial victories, hundreds of subpoenas were issued—sometimes numbering seventy-five per day—each unveiling the digital identities of various Internet subscribers. Schools, responding to threats from the recording industry, have implemented programs that track and report the exchange of copyrighted files. A few have even decided to audit and actively monitor files traded by their students, at the RIAA's request. * * *

This outcome is not solely attributable to the development of peer-to-peer technologies, or the explosion of piracy in cyberspace, as some might suggest. Rather, the outcome involves the comparatively more subtle failure of law to resolve the troubling and often rivalrous relationship between the protection of intellectual property and privacy in cyberspace. The irony, of course, is that both areas of law are facing enormous challenges because of technology's ever-expanding pace of development. * * *

B. SPECTERS OF PIRACY SURVEILLANCE

In August 2001, the Ninth Circuit, in a debate of unprecedented visibility, refused to install certain software that would enable monitoring of their computers to detect the downloading of music, streaming video, and pornography. The software was a filtering device ostensibly designed to prevent overloading the network system—but the judges believed that the alleged purpose behind its installation was broader. They feared that third parties would use such "content-detection" monitoring policies to identify individuals who engaged in file sharing or other potentially nefarious activities at work. A firestorm of controversy ensued. The judges ultimately defied the administrative order, disabled the software, and issued a host of statements publicly criticizing the administrative decision. As Judge Alex Kozinski put it:

> At the heart of the policy is a warning—very much like that given to federal prisoners—that every employee must surrender privacy as a condition of using common office equipment. Like prisoners, judicial employees must acknowledge that, by using this equipment, their "consent to monitoring and recording is implied with or without cause." ... The proposed policy tells our 30,000 dedicated employees that we trust them so little that we must monitor all their communications just to make sure they are not wasting their work day cruising the Internet.

Even though the larger policymaking body of the federal court system, the Judicial Conference, disagreed with the Ninth Circuit, and chose to continue using the monitoring software, its decision angered some federal workers, highlighting the tradeoffs that many universities and employers have made in order to prevent being saddled with a lawsuit for contributory liability.

As this example demonstrates, the problem of piracy has led some private entities to respond even more forcefully than necessary, seeking to destroy not only the peer-to-peer networks that have sprouted across the Internet, but the very boundaries of privacy, anonymity, and autonomy in cyberspace. * * * [F]ear of suits for contributory infringement has led to regimes of institutional monitoring from ISPs, colleges, and private entities. Some schools have utilized monitoring regimes that bar students from sharing certain types of files; others undertake less invasive bandwidth monitoring practices; and still others continue to closely monitor students' and employees' activity out of fear of suits for contributory liability.

The result is a protracted, and largely invisible, web of surveillance[.]

* * *

Notes

1. Preventing copyright infringement and any prospective liability (under the DMCA and related statutes) is only one of many purposes articulated by those who argue for increased monitoring of student online activity. Other purposes may include protecting students from Internet predators, protecting students from inappropriate content (such as violence or obscenity), protecting students from each other (*cf* Columbine), protecting everyone from terrorism (*cf* the Patriot Act), and law enforcement generally.

2. Issues relating to the monitoring of student online activity interface with the materials in several other chapters of this book, including Chapter 3 (student "freedom of expression" rights), Chapter 4 (combating threatening activity and peer mistreatment), Chapter 9 (morality and values), and Chapter 10 (copyright issues in education).

3. The Children's Online Privacy Protection Act (COPPA) was passed by the U.S. Congress in 1998 for the purpose of protecting against the disclosure of personal information by children under the age of 13. The Act became effective in 2000, and the Federal Trade Commission ("FTC") was given the power to enforce it. As was the case with just about every piece of Internet-related legislation adopted by the federal government in that era, the Act engendered much debate. *See, e.g,* Danielle J. Garber, *COPPA: Protecting Children's Personal Information on the Internet,* 10 J. L. & Pol'y 129 (2001)(arguing that "although the COPPA presents some enforcement problems, such as the inability to detect whether children are truthfully disclosing their age, it will likely prove to be effective in making the Internet a more private and safe place for children"); *see also* Melanie A. Hersh, *Is COPPA a Cop Out? The Child Online Privacy Protection Act as Proof That Parents, Not Government, Should Be Protecting Children's Interests on the Internet* (asserting that "in light of COPPA's shortcomings and faulty attempts to emulate regulations of other media, the government should step back and allow parents to maintain the bulk of regulatory responsibility").

4. A survey commissioned by a non-profit marketing research board in New York and reported in Education Week in early 2005 found that about 75 percent of the parents of children under 18 who have home Internet access remain in the room while their children use the Internet. The survey also found more than a third of the parents surveyed check the Web-browser history after their children have been online to track their activity. The results were based on a quarterly survey of 10,000 households, conducted in the third quarter of 2004. *See* Jessica L. Tonn, *Online Monitoring,* ED. WEEK, Jan. 19, 2005.

2. MONITORING OF E–MAIL BY EDUCATIONAL INSTITUTIONS

Consider the following article, written at the beginning of the era when educational institutions were beginning to move much of their daily communication to the Internet. In light of the fact that virtually all educational institutions have retained the ability to access back-up copies of e-mail sent and received through their servers, what are the implications of this activity today, legally and as a matter of policy?

EASY ACCESS: LEGAL PROTECTION FOR E–MAIL LAGS BEHIND THE LAW COVERING ITS NONTECHNICAL COUNTERPARTS

Stuart Biegel.
New Directions in Cyberspace Law.
L.A. Daily Journal.
April 25, 1996.

U.S. residents have come to expect a certain basic level of protection from intrusion in all their personal communications, and they are likely to assume that this protection extends to their electronic mail. Yet from a technological perspective e-mail today is significantly less secure than either the U.S. Postal Service or the typical telephone conversation.

It is generally accepted by e-mail users that their messages are at least somewhat vulnerable at some level if they are stored by either the sender or the receiver. People understand that law enforcement personnel may seek legal access to files, and that offices can have stated policies regarding e-mail privacy.

But the vulnerability of e-mail messages goes far beyond access to stored files. Apart from potential problems with hackers or prying systems operators, some e-mail systems actually copy messages as they pass through the system. Other systems may automatically create back-up copies of new e-mail as it arrives on system "servers." Thus even erasing messages from in-boxes and out-boxes may not actually delete e-mail from system files. Local attorneys have been amazed to discover that they can actually obtain access to electronic communication by relying on such automatic "storage" devices.

From a legal perspective, too, e-mail users have substantially less protection in most jurisdictions today than those who converse on the telephone or send traditional mail through the U.S. Postal Service. And for most users of either the Internet or private electronic mail systems, determining the parameters of this protection is a complex inquiry that is likely to trigger an analysis of a wide-ranging and often contradictory body of law.

To begin with, some privacy protections are available under the U.S. Constitution. These protections are typically rooted in the Fourth Amendment's guarantee against unreasonable searches and seizures and in the Fourteenth Amendment's implied right of privacy in the areas of marriage, procreation, contraception, and abortion.

In California, Article I, Section 1 of the State Constitution provides an express right to privacy, which has been held to protect state residents in both the public and the private sector. The scope of this protection has arguably been limited to at least some degree by the California Supreme Court's recent decision in a Stanford drug testing case, *Hill v. NCAA.* In *Hill,* the court analyzed the claim by student athletes that the NCAA's mandatory post-season and championship tournament drug testing program violated the California Constitution, and ruled that a compelling state interest need not be shown to justify a privacy-right infringement under Article I, Section 1.

Under federal statutory law, the Electronic Communications Privacy Act (ECPA), which originally served as an anti-wiretapping act, has now been expanded to include electronic communication. But commentators have pointed out that this statute is filled with exceptions and provides a significantly lower level of protection for e-mail users than it does for others employing electronic transmission devices. For example, if there is no agreement on privacy between a systems operator and an e-mail user, the operator can generally review all e-mail that is stored in the system . . . even messages that have not yet been retrieved by the user. And, as a general rule, the ECPA provides a significantly lower level of protection for e-mail users in the private sector.

Under common law tort doctrine, a plaintiff in this context might be able to rely on the protections against unreasonable intrusion that are deemed to be part of the right of privacy. But this protection has only been deemed applicable if a plaintiff is entitled to privacy in the first place.

Given the sketchy and uneven protections outlined above, it is understandable that commentators continue to argue that new legislation is needed to provide e-mail with the same protection as other forms of personal communication.

Lawsuits regarding the nature and extent of e-mail privacy are beginning to make their way into the courts. Two recent California cases are particularly instructive in this regard. For example, in a class action lawsuit brought against Epson under California Penal Code Section 631—which provides a private cause of action for illegal interceptions of private wire communications—seven hundred employees argued that the company was illegally intercepting and reading e-mail messages on the office system. The trial court ruled in favor of Epson, however, declaring (1) that it was not clear that these employees had a reasonable expectation of privacy in their e-mail messages, and (2) that even if plaintiffs had such an expectation, Section 631 did not apply to e-mail.

In a similar lawsuit filed under tort law by employees who argued that the Nissan Motor Company was tortiously intercepting many of their personal e-mail messages, the California Court of Appeal affirmed the trial court's decision that Nissan was well within its rights to do so. The court reasoned in an unpublished opinion that plaintiffs had no reasonable expectation of privacy because they had signed a waiver form which stated that "it is company policy that employees . . . restrict their use of company-owned computer hardware and software to company business."

A very interesting and related hypothetical might be set at a California public university, where so many employees, students, and faculty members have dial-in capabilities and are able to use the university e-mail systems at home for a variety of personal reasons. Suppose, for example, that a local reporter seeks access to a professor's e-mail under the California Public Records Act, which provides that "any person may receive a copy of any identifiable public record." Public record is defined in the Act as including "any writing containing information relating to the conduct of the public's business."

Although the professor might challenge such a disclosure under both the California Constitution and the ECPA, her case would be a lot stronger if her e-mail had been student-related. If the e-mail had been sent to or from a student, or if it had addressed a student-related issue, it could then be construed as a student record. And student records are given extensive privacy protection under the Family Educational Rights and Privacy Act (FERPA).

Finally, it should be noted that if the e-mail in question was in fact private communication with family and friends, it might not even constitute "public business" within the meaning of the Public Records Act.

E-mail privacy is a complex and multi-faceted area, and disputes that reach the courts will clearly require an exploration of the interplay between a wide variety of legal principles under both federal and state law. It will be some time before the rights and responsibilities in this area can be sorted out by the legislatures and the courts.

3. THE PROSPECTIVE APPLICABILITY OF THE RIGHT TO ANONYMITY

A related legal principle in the area of privacy in the right to anonymity. This limited right, recognized by the U.S. Supreme Court within the context of political speech, has been referenced subsequently in a variety of online disputes.

Particularly in an education setting, the parameters of the right remain unclear. And it must be recognized that students are not generally expected to anonymous in educational institutions. In fact, educators are invariably urged to do all they can to fight against anonymity in such settings. On the other hand, students do have privacy rights, and the right to anonymity has been recognized in the highest courts of the land.

Consider the following opinion in the *McIntyre* case. While not an education law case per se, *McIntyre* sets forth basic principles regarding the relative right to anonymity under First Amendment law. To what extent might this case be applicable in an education setting? To what extent might it be distinguishable? Why?

McINTYRE v. OHIO ELECTIONS COMM'N

514 U.S. 334, 115 S.Ct. 1511 (1995).

JUSTICE STEVENS delivered the opinion of the Court.

The question presented is whether an Ohio statute that prohibits the distribution of anonymous campaign literature is a "law ... abridging the freedom of speech" within the meaning of the First Amendment.

I

On April 27, 1988, Margaret McIntyre distributed leaflets to persons attending a public meeting at the Blendon Middle School in Westerville, Ohio. At this meeting, the superintendent of schools planned to discuss an imminent referendum on a proposed school tax levy. The leaflets expressed Mrs. McIntyre's opposition to the levy. There is no suggestion that the text of her message was false, misleading, or libelous. She had composed and printed it on her home computer and had paid a professional printer to make additional copies. Some of the handbills identified her as the author; others merely purported to express the views of "CONCERNED PARENTS AND TAX PAYERS." Except for the help provided by her son and a friend, who placed some of the leaflets on car windshields in the school parking lot, Mrs. McIntyre acted independently.

While Mrs. McIntyre distributed her handbills, an official of the school district, who supported the tax proposal, advised her that the unsigned leaflets did not conform to the Ohio election laws. Undeterred, Mrs. McIntyre appeared at another meeting on the next evening and handed out more of the handbills.

The proposed school levy was defeated at the next two elections, but it finally passed on its third try in November 1988. Five months later, the same school official filed a complaint with the Ohio Elections Commission charging that Mrs. McIntyre's distribution of unsigned leaflets violated § 3599.09(A) of the Ohio Code. The commission agreed and imposed a fine of $100.

* * *

Mrs. McIntyre passed away during the pendency of this litigation. Even though the amount in controversy is only $100, petitioner, as the executor of her estate, has pursued her claim in this Court. Our grant of certiorari reflects our agreement with his appraisal of the importance of the question presented.

II

Ohio maintains that the statute under review is a reasonable regulation of the electoral process. The State does not suggest that all anonymous publications are pernicious or that a statute totally excluding them from the marketplace of ideas would be valid. This is a wise (albeit implicit) concession, for the anonymity of an author is not ordinarily a sufficient reason to exclude her work product from the protections of the First Amendment.

"Anonymous pamphlets, leaflets, brochures and even books have played an important role in the progress of mankind." Great works of literature have frequently been produced by authors writing under assumed names.[4] Despite readers' curiosity and the public's interest in identifying the creator of a work of art, an author generally is free to decide whether or not to disclose his or her true identity. The decision in favor of anonymity may be motivated by fear of economic or official retaliation, by concern about social ostracism, or merely by a desire to preserve as much of one's privacy as possible. Whatever the motivation may be, at least in the field of literary endeavor, the interest in having anonymous works enter the marketplace of ideas unquestionably outweighs any public interest in requiring disclosure as a condition of entry.[5] Accordingly, an author's decision to remain anonymous, like other decisions concerning omissions or additions to the content of a publication, is an aspect of the freedom of speech protected by the First Amendment.

The freedom to publish anonymously extends beyond the literary realm. In *Talley*, the Court held that the First Amendment protects the distribution of unsigned handbills urging readers to boycott certain Los Angeles merchants who were allegedly engaging in discriminatory employment practices. Writing for the Court, Justice Black noted that "[p]ersecuted groups and sects from time to time throughout history have been able to criticize oppressive practices and laws either anonymously or not at all." Justice Black recalled England's abusive press licensing laws and seditious libel prosecutions, and he reminded us that even the arguments favoring the ratification of the Constitution advanced in the Federalist Papers were published under fictitious names. On occasion, quite apart from any threat of persecution, an advocate may believe her ideas will be more persuasive if her readers are unaware

---

4. American names such as Mark Twain (Samuel Langhorne Clemens) and O. Henry (William Sydney Porter) come readily to mind. Benjamin Franklin employed numerous different pseudonyms. *See* 2 W. Bruce, Benjamin Franklin Self Revealed: A Biographical and Critical Study Based Mainly on His Own Writings, ch. 5 (2d ed. 1923). Distinguished French authors such as Voltaire (Francois Marie Arouet) and George Sand (Amandine Aurore Lucie Dupin), and British authors such as George Eliot (Mary Ann Evans), Charles Lamb (sometimes wrote as "Elia"), and Charles Dickens (sometimes wrote as "Boz"), also published under assumed names. Indeed, some believe the works of Shakespeare were actually written by the Earl of Oxford rather than by William Shaksper of Stratford on Avon. *See* C. Ogburn, The Mysterious William Shake-

speare: The Myth & the Reality (2d ed. 1992); *but see* S. Schoenbaum, Shakespeare's Lives (2d ed. 1991) (adhering to the traditional view that Shakespeare was in fact the author). *See also Stevens, The Shakespeare Canon of Statutory Construction*, 140 U. Pa. L. Rev. 1373 (1992) (commenting on the competing theories).

5. Though such a requirement might provide assistance to critics in evaluating the quality and significance of the writing, it is not indispensable. To draw an analogy from a nonliterary context, the now pervasive practice of grading law school examination papers "blindly" (i.e., under a system in which the professor does not know whose paper she is grading) indicates that such evaluations are possible—indeed, perhaps more reliable—when any bias associated with the author's identity is prescinded.

of her identity. Anonymity thereby provides a way for a writer who may be personally unpopular to ensure that readers will not prejudge her message simply because they do not like its proponent. Thus, even in the field of political rhetoric, where "the identity of the speaker is an important component of many attempts to persuade," the most effective advocates have sometimes opted for anonymity. The specific holding in *Talley* related to advocacy of an economic boycott, but the Court's reasoning embraced a respected tradition of anonymity in the advocacy of political causes.[6] This tradition is perhaps best exemplified by the secret ballot, the hard won right to vote one's conscience without fear of retaliation.

III

California had defended the Los Angeles ordinance at issue in *Talley* as a law "aimed at providing a way to identify those responsible for fraud, false advertising and libel." We rejected that argument because nothing in the text or legislative history of the ordinance limited its application to those evils. We then made clear that we did "not pass on the validity of an ordinance limited to prevent these or any other supposed evils." The Ohio statute likewise contains no language limiting its application to fraudulent, false, or libelous statements; to the extent, therefore, that Ohio seeks to justify § 3599.09(A) as a means to prevent the dissemination of untruths, its defense must fail for the same reason given in *Talley*. As the facts of this case demonstrate, the ordinance plainly applies even when there is no hint of falsity or libel.

Ohio's statute does, however, contain a different limitation: It applies only to unsigned documents designed to influence voters in an election. In contrast, the Los Angeles ordinance prohibited all anonymous handbilling "in any place under any circumstances." For that reason, Ohio correctly argues that *Talley* does not necessarily control the disposition of this case. We must, therefore, decide whether and to what extent the First Amendment's protection of anonymity encompasses documents intended to influence the electoral process.

* * *

6. That tradition is most famously embodied in the *Federalist Papers*, authored by James Madison, Alexander Hamilton, and John Jay, but signed "Publius." Publius' opponents, the Anti–Federalists, also tended to publish under pseudonyms: prominent among them were "Cato," believed to be New York Governor George Clinton; "Centinel," probably Samuel Bryan or his father, Pennsylvania judge and legislator George Bryan; "The Federal Farmer," who may have been Richard Henry Lee, a Virginia member of the Continental Congress and a signer of the Declaration of Independence; and "Brutus," who may have been Robert Yates, a New York Supreme Court justice who walked out on the Constitutional Convention. 2 THE COMPLETE ANTI FEDER-ALIST (H. Storing ed. 1981). A forerunner of all of these writers was the pre-Revolutionary War English pamphleteer "Junius," whose true identity remains a mystery. *See* ENCYCLOPEDIA OF COLONIAL AND REVOLUTIONARY AMERICA 220 (J. Faragher ed. 1990) (positing that "Junius" may have been Sir Phillip Francis). The "*Letters of Junius*" were "widely reprinted in colonial newspapers and lent considerable support to the revolutionary cause."

* * * [A]s we have explained on many prior occasions, the category of speech regulated by the Ohio statute occupies the core of the protection afforded by the First Amendment[.] * * *

* * * Indeed, the speech in which Mrs. McIntyre engaged—handing out leaflets in the advocacy of a politically controversial viewpoint—is the essence of First Amendment expression. * * * No form of speech is entitled to greater constitutional protection than Mrs. McIntyre's.

When a law burdens core political speech, we apply "exacting scrutiny," and we uphold the restriction only if it is narrowly tailored to serve an overriding state interest. * * *

   * * *

VI

Under our Constitution, anonymous pamphleteering is not a pernicious, fraudulent practice, but an honorable tradition of advocacy and of dissent. Anonymity is a shield from the tyranny of the majority. It thus exemplifies the purpose behind the Bill of Rights, and of the First Amendment in particular: to protect unpopular individuals from retaliation—and their ideas from suppression—at the hand of an intolerant society. The right to remain anonymous may be abused when it shields fraudulent conduct. But political speech by its nature will sometimes have unpalatable consequences, and, in general, our society accords greater weight to the value of free speech than to the dangers of its misuse. Ohio has not shown that its interest in preventing the misuse of anonymous election related speech justifies a prohibition of all uses of that speech. The State may, and does, punish fraud directly. But it cannot seek to punish fraud indirectly by indiscriminately outlawing a category of speech, based on its content, with no necessary relationship to the danger sought to be prevented. One would be hard pressed to think of a better example of the pitfalls of Ohio's blunderbuss approach than the facts of the case before us.

The judgment of the Ohio Supreme Court is reversed.

It is so ordered.

Chapter III

STUDENT FREEDOM OF EXPRESSION

The nature and extent of student "free speech" rights under the First Amendment is both one of the most vibrant and one of the most difficult areas of constitutional law. Not necessarily difficult doctrinally, since clear rules have been articulated to address a wide range of fact patterns, but difficult in that the disputes often involve rights in conflict and gut-wrenching compromises. In addition, as a matter of policy, the correct course of action in these disputes is often unclear.

In the 1960s and 1970s, free speech issues were at the forefront of education-related debates, with students asserting themselves in ways they never had before. After a period of relative calm in the 1980s and early 1990s, free speech disputes flared up again, and by the early twenty-first century, they had once again become among the most compelling of all the controversies in the education community.

It is often impossible to separate free speech issues from campus safety concerns, and students accused of threatening or harassing behavior often seek to rely on the protections of the First Amendment. In addition, freedom of expression principles are often at the center of controversies in areas relating to curriculum, religion, morality, and values.

This chapter is designed to serve as an introduction to the large and arguably well-settled body of law that has emerged in this area. It highlights the major U.S. Supreme Court decisions that first recognized broad protections for student freedom of expression at both the K–12 and higher education levels, and provides examples of cases over the next several decades that clarified the parameters of those protections. In this manner, it points toward a further examination of complex First Amendment disputes in Chapter 4 (combating threats and peer harassment) and Chapter 9 (morality and values).

It can be argued, in this regard, that a key principle implicit in Education Law—and especially in First Amendment speech and religion cases—is the principle of *respect*. Although rarely stated explicitly, U.S.

116

law appears to require that every person attending public schools be treated with respect. Factoring in the equal protection guarantees, the principle can be expanded to embody a requirement that all persons be treated with equal respect and equal dignity.

Consider the materials in this chapter in light of this argument. What evidence can you find that a *respect principle* does in fact exist? What evidence is there that this may not necessarily be the case, at least at the present time, and at least in certain instances? If a *respect principle* is indeed evident, what are its parameters? What guidelines are people expected to follow? What are the accompanying rights and responsibilities?

A.   BASIC FIRST AMENDMENT PRINCIPLES APPLICABLE IN ALL SETTINGS

HIGHLIGHTS OF U.S. FIRST AMENDMENT LAW: BASIC PRINCIPLES AND MAJOR EXCEPTIONS

From Beyond Our Control? Confronting
the Limits of Our Legal System
In the Age of Cyberspace
Stuart Biegel.
MIT Press (2001).

Two basic principles of U.S. free speech law as interpreted by the courts under the Constitution are particularly relevant [in an education-related context]. * * * The first is that statutes and policies designed by public entities to regulate speech are unconstitutional if vague or overbroad.[1] The second is that speech cannot generally be regulated on the basis of its content, unless the regulation falls within some recognized exception or some other related rule of law.

Under well-settled constitutional law, a statute or policy is unconstitutionally *vague* "when men of common intelligence must necessarily guess at its meaning.... [It] must give adequate warning of the conduct which is to be prohibited and must set out explicit standards for those who apply it."[2] A statute or policy regulating speech will be deemed *overbroad* "if it sweeps within its ambit a substantial amount of protected speech along with that which it may legitimately regulate."[3] * * *

Any attempt by a governmental entity to restrict speech on the basis of its * * * content would be deemed *content-based regulation,* a type of regulation that is disfavored and presumed unconstitutional under First Amendment law.[4] Yet speech can indeed be regulated on the basis of its

---

1. *See, e.g.,* UWM Post v. Bd. of Regents of the Univ. of Wis. Sys., 774 F. Supp. 1163 (E.D. Wis. 1991); Doe v. Univ. of Mich., 721 F. Supp. 852 (E.D. Mich. 1989).

2. *See Doe,* 721 F. Supp. at 866–67.

3. *Id.* at 864; *see also UWM Post,* 774 F. Supp. at 1169.

4. Under First Amendment case law, it is often useful to identify two types of speech regulation: content-based regulation and content-neutral regulation. Content-neutral regulation can generally be regulated under reasonable time, place, and manner restrictions. But content-based regulacontent if it is found to be (1) obscene, (2) child pornography, (3) fighting words, (4) incitement to imminent lawless conduct, (5) defamation (libel or slander), (6) an invasion of privacy under tort law, (7) harassment, (8) a true threat, (9) copyright infringement, or (10) another recognized tort or crime. * * *

1/ Obscenity—While Justice Potter Stewart's famous line "I know it when I see it" is still quoted in this context, the U.S. Supreme Court in the 1973 case of *Miller v. California*[5] developed a three-part test for obscenity that is still being used today. A Court will inquire whether:

(a) " 'the average person applying contemporary community standards' would find that the work, taken as a whole appeals to the prurient interest";

(b) it "depicts or describes, in a patently offensive way, sexual conduct specifically defined by applicable state law"; *and*

(c) "the work, taken as a whole, lacks serious literary, artistic, political, or scientific value."

2/ Child Pornography—The definition of child pornography, as set forth by the U.S. Congress, was originally limited to visual depictions of real children. It was expanded in 1996, however, to include both "computer-generated images" and pictures of people who only appear to be under 18. Under Title 18 of the U.S. Code, § 2256, child pornography is defined as "any visual depiction, including any photograph, film, video, picture, or computer or computer generated image or picture, whether made or produced by electronic, mechanical, or other means, of sexually explicit conduct, where

(a) the production of such visual depiction involves the use of a minor engaging in sexually explicit conduct;

(b) such visual depiction is, or appears to be, of a minor engaging in sexually explicit conduct;

(c) such visual depiction has been created, adapted, or modified to appear that an identifiable minor is engaging in sexually explicit conduct; or

(d) such visual depiction is advertised, promoted, presented, described, or distributed in such a manner that conveys the impression that the material is or contains a visual depiction of a minor engaging in sexually explicit conduct."

In [2002, however, the U.S. Supreme Court in *Ashcroft v. The Free Speech Coalition,* held that "the prohibitions of §§ 2256(8)(B) and 2256(8)(D) are overbroad and unconstitutional.[6]"]

tion can only be regulated if the speech falls within one or more recognized exceptions or can be prohibited under other relevant laws. *See, e.g.,* LAURENCE H. TRIBE, *AMERICAN CONSTITUTIONAL LAW,* Chapter 12, *Rights of Communication and Expression* (2d ed. 1988).

5.   413 U.S. 15 (1973).

6.   535 U.S. 234 (2002).

3/ Fighting Words—The U.S. Supreme Court in the 1942 case of *Chaplinsky v. New Hampshire* set out a two-part definition for fighting words:

(a) words which by their very utterance inflict injury and

(b) words which by their very utterance tend to incite an immediate breach of the peace.[7]

Since *Chaplinsky,* the Supreme Court has narrowed and clarified the scope of the fighting words doctrine in at least three ways. First, the Court has arguably limited the fighting words definition so that it now only includes its second half. Second, the Court has stated that in order for words to meet the second half of the definition they must "naturally tend to provoke violent resentment." Finally, the Court has held that fighting words must be "directed at the person of the hearer."[8]

Chaplinsky himself was distributing religious literature on public sidewalk and was led away by the City Marshal because of fear that his acts were causing or would cause a public disturbance. As he was led away, he called the Marshal a "G-damned racketeer and a damned fascist." His breach of peace conviction was upheld because of the danger that listener of his words would be incited to violence. The test was whether or not men of common intelligence would understand the words as likely to cause the average addressee to fight. For speech to be restricted under this doctrine, it had to be "words and expressions which by general consent are fighting words when said without a disarming smile." And the Court referred to words that would produce an "uncontrollable impulse."

It must be noted that since *Chaplinsky* not one conviction under the fighting words exception has been upheld by the U.S. Supreme Court.[9] And after the Court's decision in the 1992 case of *R.A.V. v. City of St. Paul,*[10] many commentators argued that the fighting words doctrine had become a relic of another age. Yet the doctrine has not been explicitly overruled, and it remains on the books as a recognized exception to the rule that speech cannot be regulated on the basis of its content.

4/ Incitement to Imminent Lawless Conduct—Under the rule set forth by the U.S. Supreme Court in *Brandenburg v. Ohio,* speech can be restricted on the basis of its content if it is "directed to inciting or producing imminent lawless action and is likely to incite or produce such action."[11] As the Court further explained in a subsequent case, "we have not permitted the government to assume that every expression of a provocative idea will incite a riot, but have instead required careful

---

7.   315 U.S. 568, 571–72 (1942).

8.   *See also UWM Post,* 774 F. Supp. at 1169–72.

9.   *See* Nadine Strossen, *Regulating Racist Speech On Campus: A Modest Proposal,* 1990 Duke L.J. 484, 508–14.

10.   505 U.S. 377 (1992).

11.   395 U.S. 444, 447 (1969).

consideration of the actual circumstances surrounding such expression."[12]

Brandenburg focused on circumstances surrounding a rally and speeches by members of the Ku Klux Klan. During the rally, "revengeance" was threatened, and the defendant—who had organized the event—added that "the n——r should be returned to Africa" and "the Jew returned to Israel." Defendant was convicted under a 1919 Ohio statute which forbid "advocating . . . the duty, necessity, or propriety of crime, sabotage, violence, or unlawful methods of terrorism as a means of accomplishing industrial or political reform." In a relatively short opinion, the Court found in favor of the defendant, holding that the statute was unconstitutional because the First Amendment does not permit a state "to forbid or proscribe advocacy of the use of force or of law violation except where such advocacy is directed to inciting or producing *imminent* lawless action and is likely to incite or produce such action."[13]

Commentators have noted that the distinction drawn between "mere advocacy" and "incitement to imminent lawless action" parallels the reasoning in *Chaplinsky* and indicates that in the U.S. the "public peace" can only be protected against speech which is likely to produce immediate violence.[14]

5/ Defamation—In general, defamatory statements—which include libel (the written word) and slander (the spoken word)—are not protected by the First Amendment. Rules of defamation have evolved under the common law and vary from state to state, but typically, to qualify as defamation, a statement must be

(a) a defamatory communication about the plaintiff,

(b) published to third persons,

(c) which was false at the time it was made.[15]

A *defamatory communication* has been defined as one which "tends so to harm the reputation of another as to lower him in the estimation of the community or to deter third persons from associating or dealing with

---

12. *Texas v. Johnson*, 491 U.S. 397 (1989).

13. *Brandenburg*, 395 U.S. at 447 (emphasis added).

14. *See generally* Friedrich Kubler, *How Much Freedom for Racist Speech? Transnational Aspects of a Conflict of Human Rights*, 27 HOFSTRA L. REV. 335 (1998).

15. John Faucher explains that, according to the general rule,

[T]o prevail in a defamation action, the plaintiff must show that: (1) the defendant published the statement by showing or saying it to a third party, (2) the statement identified the plaintiff, (3) the statement put the plaintiff in a bad light,

and (4) it was false at the time that it was made.

Though law schools teach the same defamation law from Hawaii to Maine, state laws vary widely. In particular, state laws vary on standards of fault, distinctions between fact and opinion, application of rules of libel per se and per quod, availability of punitive damages, and statutes of limitations. Any of these laws could affect the outcome of a case.

John D. Faucher, *Let the Chips Fall Where They May: Choice of Law in Computer Bulletin Board Defamation Cases*, 26 U.C. DAVIS L. REV. 1045, 1052–54 (1993).

him."[16] *Published to third persons* means that the communication (oral or written) must be to someone other than the person allegedly defamed. As to the *falsity* requirement, virtually all states today require that the communication be untrue before a defamation action can proceed.

[While at one time the U.S. courts recognized a cause of action for "group defamation," this doctrine has been discredited over time, and is generally not viewed as either a viable avenue of litigation today or a valid justification for the restriction of speech on the basis of its content.]

Over the years, the law of defamation has been bolstered by many special rules. For example, under the First Amendment, if the subject of the communication is a public figure, defendant can be held liable for defamation only if the statement was made with actual malice or reckless disregard for the truth.[17] Even if the subject is a private figure, media defendants focusing on matters of *public concern* must also have acted with actual malice or reckless disregard for the truth to be found liable.[18]

In addition, a statement that is only an opinion—and not fact—cannot be considered defamatory under the First Amendment if it

(a) addresses matters of public concern,

(b) is expressed in a manner that is not provably false, and

(c) cannot be reasonably interpreted as stating actual facts about a person.[19]

Finally, it should be noted that a "republisher" of defamatory statements is also liable under the basic framework outlined here. *Republishers* are "those who participate in distributing a libel," and can include, for example, newspapers that print op-ed pieces or even letters to the editor. As a general rule, if the original author is liable for defamation, republishers can also be found liable for defamation for the same defamation.[20]

6/ *Invasion of Privacy*—Statements that constitute an invasion of privacy under tort law are also not protected by the First Amendment. Four separate torts (or civil wrongs) have actually emerged in this

---

16. RESTATEMENT (SECOND) OF TORTS, § 559 (1977).

17. New York Times v. Sullivan, 376 U.S. 254 (1964).

18. Gertz v. Robert Welch, 418 U.S. 323 (1974).

19. Milkovich v. Lorain Journal Co., 497 U.S. 1, 17–21 (1990). In determining whether a statement is intended to convey an actual fact about a person, the Court will look at (1) whether the language loose, figurative, or hyperbolic, which would negate the impression that the speaker was seriously maintaining the truth of the underlying facts, (2) whether the general tenor of the article negate the impression that the

speaker was seriously maintaining the truth of the underlying fact, and (3) whether the connotation sufficiently factual to be susceptible of being proved true or false. *Id.* at 21.

20. *See generally* Eugene Volokh, *Freedom of Speech in Cyberspace from the Listener's Perspective: Private Speech Restrictions, Libel, State Action, Harassment, and Sex*, 1996 U. CHI. LEGAL F. 377. Other rules under the law of defamation include certain "privileges" that defendants may invoke against claims of defamation in certain circumstances.

context over the past 100 years. They include *appropriation* of a person's picture or name, *intrusion* upon a person's private affairs or seclusion, publication of facts placing a person in a *false light,* and public disclosure of *private facts*. Each tort has its own basic requirements.[21]

An *appropriation* is an unauthorized use by defendant of plaintiff's picture or name for commercial advantage. Plaintiff can be a celebrity or a private person, but a celebrity typically stands a better chance of winning a large monetary award by suing not under this right of privacy but under the related "right of publicity."[22]

An *intrusion* is an intentional or negligent act of prying or intruding by the defendant into a private area of plaintiff's life. The intrusion must be something that would be objectionable to a reasonable person. It can be physical (such as entering private property uninvited), or nonphysical (such as repeatedly calling a person late at night). In any case, plaintiff cannot prevail in such a lawsuit unless it can be shown that a person could reasonably expect that he or she would not be intruded upon in this manner by someone in defendant's position.

False light invasion of privacy is the publication of facts about the plaintiff placing him or her in a false light in the public eye. As with an intrusion, it must be objectionable to a reasonable person under the circumstances. False light invasion of privacy may include views that a person does not hold, or a description of actions that he or she did not take. It should be noted that such behavior may also constitute defamation if the falsity affects a person's reputation.

Public disclosure of private facts is the disclosure of private information about the plaintiff. Disclosure must be highly offensive, such that a reasonable person of ordinary sensibilities would object to having it made public. Private facts under this tort must involve those aspects of plaintiff's private life that have not already received some publicity and are not left open to public observation. Thus a magazine selling mailing lists of subscribers has been held not to have publicly disclosed private facts within the meaning of this rule.[23]

Any statements that fall within the definitions of one or more of these four torts can be restricted by governmental entities without violating the First Amendment.

7/ *Harassment*—Rules prohibiting racial, religious, or sexual harassment evolved in the workplace under Title VII of the U.S. Civil Rights Act of 1964. At this point in time, sexual harassment laws are arguably the most highly developed,[24] and they include prohibitions

---

21. In addition, like defamation, certain arguments have been recognized as providing valid defenses to invasion of privacy claims.

22. *See generally* Cristina Fernandez, *The Right of Publicity on the Internet,* 8 MARQ. SPORTS L.J. 289 (1998).

23. Shibley v. Time, Inc., 40 Ohio Misc. 51 (1974).

24. In *Faragher v. Boca Raton,* 524 U.S. 775 (1998), the U.S. Supreme Court noted that hostile environment sexual harassment claims had actually developed from the earlier racial and national origin harassment cases.

against both *quid pro quo* harassment and *hostile environment* harassment.

Hostile environment claims were first recognized by the U.S. Supreme Court in 1986,[25] and over the next 10–15 years the rules were fine tuned by subsequent judicial opinions. 1998 proved to be a turning point, with the Court deciding four sexual harassment cases in one year.[26] Commentators have raised questions in recent years regarding the extent to which the First Amendment can or should be employed to limit the scope of harassment law,[27] but as of the Year 2000—as long as certain expression falls within the definitions outlined by the Court—it is not protected speech and can be restricted accordingly.

The basic hostile environment claim under Title VII can only be filed by a person who alleges harassment in the workplace. Sexual harassment is not a crime, but an act or a series of acts that can lead to large monetary awards for aggrieved employees who have sued their employers under Title VII. * * *

To establish actionable hostile environment harassment, plaintiffs must prove that the activity in question was unwelcome and that it constituted "a sexually objectionable environment" which was

(a) objectively offensive and

(b) subjectively offensive.

An environment is deemed *objectively offensive* if a "reasonable person" would find it to be hostile or abusive, and it will be found *subjectively offensive* if the victim in fact perceived it to be so.

A version of this framework has recently been applied by the Courts in federally funded education programs under Title IX of the Education Amendments of 1972 to the Civil Rights Act of 1964. In *Davis v. Monroe County Board of Education,* the Court held that educational institutions can be held liable for peer-to-peer hostile environment sexual harassment "that is so severe, pervasive, and objectively offensive that it effectively bars the victim's access to an educational opportunity or benefit." But even if plaintiff can meet the requirements of this stringent test for actionable harassment, he or she can only prevail if the education officials in charge acted "with deliberate indifference to known acts of harassment."[28]

8/ True Threats—As discussed in earlier chapters, threatening speech can be restricted by governmental entities only if it constitutes a "true threat." The U.S. courts have disagreed over the years regarding the exact contours of an appropriate test to determine whether words

---

25. *See* Meritor Savings Bank v. Vinson, 477 U.S. 57 (1986).

26. The four cases were *Oncale v. Sundowner Offshore Services,* 523 U.S. 75 (1998), *Gebser v. Lago Vista Independent School District,* 524 U.S. 274 (1998), *Faragher v. City of Boca Raton,* 524 U.S. 775

(1998), and *Ellerth v. Burlington Industries,* 524 U.S. 951 (1998).

27. *See, e.g.,* Eugene Volokh, *Freedom of Speech and Workplace Harassment,* 39 UCLA L. REV. 1791 (1992).

28. *See* Davis v. Monroe County Bd. of Educ., 526 U.S. 629, 633 (1999).

amount to a *true* threat, but there is general agreement in most jurisdictions regarding certain basic principles.

(a) The threat must be "against the physical safety or freedom of some individual or class of persons,"[29] and

(b) The communication * * * would lead a reasonable, objective recipient to believe that the person expressing the threat "was serious about his threat ... regardless of the subjective intent of the speaker to make an actual threat or whether anyone actually felt frightened, intimidated, or coerced by the threat."[30]

As with many other legal tests, then, the Courts here inquire into the state of mind of a hypothetical objective reasonable person. The key question is whether such a hypothetical person would feel threatened, regardless of whether the real-life recipient of the threat actually did. If the communication is objectively threatening, it is deemed to be a true threat.

9/ Copyright Infringement—On some level, copyright laws act to restrict freedom of expression on the basis of content, because limitations on expressive activity that infringes one or more of the five exclusive rights of a copyright owner have of course been deemed acceptable if they reflect the balance of interests required by the U.S. Constitution.

There has been a significant amount of scholarship over the years addressing the interface between First Amendment law and copyright law. Certain disputes have been characterized as pitting one body of law against the other, and commentators have set out a range of very interesting positions in these debates * * * some favoring the primacy of the free speech guarantees and others favoring the primacy of intellectual property protection. While interpretations still vary, most believe that the U.S. Supreme Court decision in *Harper & Row v. Nation Enterprises*[31] ended this debate, or at least significantly limited the impact of any future arguments in favor of loosening copyright restrictions on free speech grounds.

In *Harper,* defendants—who had reproduced excerpts of President Ford's biography in their magazine prior to the biography's formal publication—invoked First Amendment principles in an effort to excuse their actions.[32] The Court rejected their argument, finding that current copyright law "strikes a definitional balance" in this context "by permitting free communications of facts while still protecting an author's expression."

An early cyberlaw case, *Religious Technology Center v. Netcom,*[33] also addressed the viability of First Amendment arguments by defendants accused of copyright infringement. Netcom—an Internet Service Provider—had been charged by the Church of Scientology with contribu-

29. U.S. v. Alkhabaz, 104 F.3d 1492, 1506 (6th Cir. 1997) (Krupansky, J., dissenting). This requirement is generally satisfied "irrespective of the identity of the person or group threatened, the originator's motivation for issuing the threat, or the existence or nonexistence of any goal pursued by the threat."

30. *Id.*

31. 471 U.S. 539 (1985).

32. *See id.* at 555–56.

33. 907 F. Supp. 1361 (N.D. Cal. 1995).

tory copyright infringement for the posting of protected church documents via its server. * * *

Netcom argued in part that if it were found liable for copyright infringement, First Amendment principles would be contravened * * * "as it would chill the use of the Internet because every access provider or user would be subject to liability when a user posts an infringing work to a Usenet newsgroup." The court, however, disagreed, declaring that "while an overbroad injunction might implicate the First Amendment ... imposing liability for infringement where it is otherwise appropriate does not necessarily raise a First Amendment issue."[34] * * *

[In general, then] * * * words constituting copyright infringement can still be restricted as they have been in the past despite the imperatives of recent free speech law.

10/ Another Recognized Tort or Crime—Other expressive activity can also be regulated on the basis of its content if it is a crime and/or a tort under U.S. law. The crimes and torts discussed in this section are typically among the most prominent examples, but different circumstances may trigger the application of other legal principles in this area.

Beyond these ten categories, additional restrictions on freedom of expression may be implemented in certain special circumstances, such as on K–12 public school campuses. While the U.S. Supreme Court has indeed recognized that students do not "shed their constitutional rights to freedom of speech or expression at the schoolhouse gate," student speech may be regulated if it materially and substantially interferes with schoolwork, discipline, or the rights of others.[35] * * *

Finally, it must be noted again that all these First Amendment rules and exceptions generally apply only in the public sector. Non-public entities such as private universities, corporations, and [Internet Service Providers] are not typically under any obligation to comply with the limits imposed by case law in this context. As a matter of policy, however, most private institutions of higher education and a good number of ISPs do in fact choose to follow these same rules and regulations.

B. "FREEDOM OF EXPRESSION" AT THE K–12 LEVEL: THE *MATERIAL & SUBSTANTIAL DISRUPTION* RULE AND CAMPUS SAFETY

PROBLEM 10: The Coalition to Resist Political and Social Indoctrination

Assume that all the events in this hypothetical take place in a publicly funded education setting.

In response to the announcement of the new "Groundhog Day" humanities unit (as it came to be called),[a] Jamie—an eleventh grader who has

---

34. *See id.* at 1377.   **35.** Tinker v. Des Moines Indep. Cmty. Sch. Dist., 393 U.S. 503 (1969).

consistently been an outspoken student activist on a range of political and social issues since entering Southern Valley High in the ninth grade—organizes the Coalition to Resist Political and Social Indoctrination (CRI). Meetings of the CRI attract significant numbers of students, many of whom dress differently and have been consistent victims of bullying perpetrated by apolitical students showing off for their friends. Jamie himself takes pride in defying the culture of the school, dressing flamboyantly, and being perennially provocative.

An activist agenda is developed at the CRI meetings to protest what the organization believes to be "one-sided" education. The protest activities are slated to include the distribution of fliers on and off campus, the creation of a Web site, and plans for picketing the school. But before any of these activities can be implemented, Principal Madeline Arthur announces that the organization will be prohibited from meeting on campus or distributing any materials online or offline relating to the announced agenda, and that any picketing will result in the immediate suspension of all those participating. At the next faculty meeting, Dr. Arthur asserts that there were two reasons behind the decision to restrict this expression "Not only am I concerned," she said, "that many of the CRI students—who have been victims of peer harassment and mistreatment in the past—would be vulnerable to further bullying as a result of their protest activities, but I simply do not believe that students have the right to question the curricular decisions of the faculty on a high school campus."

Represented by the ACLU, Jamie and two fellow CRI members file a lawsuit challenging the principal's restrictions as violative of their free speech rights. In addition, Jamie and several of his peers choose to defy the principal by wearing CRI buttons. As the four are walking down the hall one day, dressed flamboyantly and wearing the buttons, they are accosted by six well-known and aggressive seniors, whose trademark "practical jokes" include "going bowling" with fellow students. A teacher assigned to "hall duty" views the interaction from a distance, but she is simultaneously involved in a discussion with two other students about an upcoming trip to the Mediterranean and chooses not to intercede. Events move quickly, and before Jamie and his friends can respond or leave, the seniors squirt baby oil on the hallway floor and send Jamie and his friends sliding into other

a. As envisioned, the new four-week unit would be taught once a year to all students in the humanities program. Designed by the English and social studies teachers of Southern Valley High's award-winning humanities program, the unit is built around a study of "the central importance of morality, truth, justice, and patriotism in literature and history."

The unit would begin each year with a showing of the popular 1993 film, *Ground-* *hog Day*. Discussions and activities would flow from the viewing of that film, and appropriate readings would be assigned. These readings would include, but would not be limited to, primary religious texts. Every year, students in the program would be expected to spend 3–5 days reading from a different primary religious text, until they had been exposed to the holy books of Judaism, Christianity, Islam, Hinduism and Buddhism.

students and crashing into lockers. Three adults hear the crashing and rush to the scene, but it is too late. Several students suffer injuries requiring significant medical treatment.

What arguments should the respective parties set forth in the free speech lawsuit filed by the ACLU on behalf of the students in the CRI?

TINKER v. DES MOINES INDEP. CMTY. SCH. DIST.

393 U.S. 503, 89 S.Ct. 733 (1969).

MR. JUSTICE FORTAS delivered the opinion of the Court.

Petitioner John F. Tinker, 15 years old, and petitioner Christopher Eckhardt, 16 years old, attended high schools in Des Moines, Iowa. Petitioner Mary Beth Tinker, John's sister, was a 13-year-old student in junior high school.

In December 1965, a group of adults and students in Des Moines held a meeting at the Eckhardt home. The group determined to publicize their objections to the hostilities in Vietnam and their support for a truce by wearing black armbands during the holiday season and by fasting on December 16 and New Year's Eve. Petitioners and their parents had previously engaged in similar activities, and they decided to participate in the program.

The principals of the Des Moines schools became aware of the plan to wear armbands. On December 14, 1965, they met and adopted a policy that any student wearing an armband to school would be asked to remove it, and if he refused he would be suspended until he returned without the armband. Petitioners were aware of the regulation that the school authorities adopted.

On December 16, Mary Beth and Christopher wore black armbands to their schools. John Tinker wore his armband the next day. They were all sent home and suspended from school until they would come back without their armbands. They did not return to school until after the planned period for wearing armbands had expired—that is, until after New Year's Day.

This complaint was filed in the United States District Court by petitioners, through their fathers, under § 1983 of Title 42 of the United States Code. It prayed for an injunction restraining the respondent school officials and the respondent members of the board of directors of the school district from disciplining the petitioners, and it sought nominal damages. After an evidentiary hearing the District Court dismissed the complaint. It upheld the constitutionality of the school authorities' action on the ground that it was reasonable in order to prevent disturbance of school discipline. The court referred to but expressly declined to follow the Fifth Circuit's holding in a similar case that the wearing of symbols like the armbands cannot be prohibited unless it "materially and substantially interfere(s) with the requirements of appropriate discipline in the operation of the school."

On appeal, the Court of Appeals for the Eighth Circuit considered the case *en banc*. The court was equally divided, and the District Court's decision was accordingly affirmed, without opinion. We granted certiorari.

* * *

First Amendment rights, applied in light of the special characteristics of the school environment, are available to teachers and students. It can hardly be argued that either students or teachers shed their constitutional rights to freedom of speech or expression at the schoolhouse gate. This has been the unmistakable holding of this Court for almost 50 years. * * *

In *West Virginia State Board of Education v. Barnette*, this Court held that under the First Amendment, the student in public school may not be compelled to salute the flag. Speaking through Mr. Justice Jackson, the Court said:

> The Fourteenth Amendment, as now applied to the States, protects the citizen against the State itself and all of its creatures—Boards of Education not excepted. These have, of course, important, delicate, and highly discretionary functions, but none that they may not perform within the limits of the Bill of Rights. That they are educating the young for citizenship is reason for scrupulous protection of Constitutional freedoms of the individual, if we are not to strangle the free mind at its source and teach youth to discount important principles of our government as mere platitudes. 319 U.S. at 637.

On the other hand, the Court has repeatedly emphasized the need for affirming the comprehensive authority of the States and of school officials, consistent with fundamental constitutional safeguards, to prescribe and control conduct in the schools. Our problem lies in the area where students in the exercise of First Amendment rights collide with the rules of the school authorities.

II.

The problem posed by the present case does not relate to regulation of the length of skirts or the type of clothing, to hair style, or deportment. It does not concern aggressive, disruptive action or even group demonstrations. Our problem involves direct, primary First Amendment rights akin to "pure speech."

The school officials banned and sought to punish petitioners for a silent, passive expression of opinion, unaccompanied by any disorder or disturbance on the part of petitioners. There is here no evidence whatever of petitioners' interference, actual or nascent, with the schools' work or of collision with the rights of other students to be secure and to be let alone. Accordingly, this case does not concern speech or action that intrudes upon the work of the schools or the rights of other students.

Only a few of the 18,000 students in the school system wore the black armbands. Only five students were suspended for wearing them. There is no indication that the work of the schools or any class was disrupted. Outside the classrooms, a few students made hostile remarks to the children wearing armbands, but there were no threats or acts of violence on school premises.

The District Court concluded that the action of the school authorities was reasonable because it was based upon their fear of a disturbance from the wearing of the armbands. But, in our system, undifferentiated fear or apprehension of disturbance is not enough to overcome the right to freedom of expression. Any departure from absolute regimentation may cause trouble. Any variation from the majority's opinion may inspire fear. Any word spoken, in class, in the lunchroom, or on the campus, that deviates from the views of another person may start an argument or cause a disturbance. But our Constitution says we must take this risk; and our history says that it is this sort of hazardous freedom—this kind of openness—that is the basis of our national strength and of the independence and vigor of Americans who grow up and live in this relatively permissive, often disputatious, society.

In order for the State in the person of school officials to justify prohibition of a particular expression of opinion, it must be able to show that its action was caused by something more than a mere desire to avoid the discomfort and unpleasantness that always accompany an unpopular viewpoint. Certainly where there is no finding and no showing that engaging in the forbidden conduct would "materially and substantially interfere with the requirements of appropriate discipline in the operation of the school," the prohibition cannot be sustained.

In the present case, the District Court made no such finding, and our independent examination of the record fails to yield evidence that the school authorities had reason to anticipate that the wearing of the armbands would substantially interfere with the work of the school or impinge upon the rights of other students. Even an official memorandum prepared after the suspension that listed the reasons for the ban on wearing the armbands made no reference to the anticipation of such disruption.

On the contrary, the action of the school authorities appears to have been based upon an urgent wish to avoid the controversy which might result from the expression, even by the silent symbol of armbands, of opposition to this Nation's part in the conflagration in Vietnam.[4] It is revealing, in this respect, that the meeting at which the school principals

4. The District Court found that the school authorities, in prohibiting black armbands, were influenced by the fact that "(t)he Viet Nam war and the involvement of the United States therein has been the subject of a major controversy for some time. When the arm band regulation involved herein was promulgated, debate over the Viet Nam war had become vehement in many localities. A protest march against the war had been recently held in Washington, D.C. A wave of draft card burning incidents protesting the war had swept the country. At that time two highly publicized draft card burning cases were pending in this Court. Both individuals supporting the war and those opposing it were quite vocal in expressing their views."

decided to issue the contested regulation was called in response to a student's statement to the journalism teacher in one of the schools that he wanted to write an article on Vietnam and have it published in the school paper. (The student was dissuaded.)

It is also relevant that the school authorities did not purport to prohibit the wearing of all symbols of political or controversial significance. The record shows that students in some of the schools wore buttons relating to national political campaigns, and some even wore the Iron Cross, traditionally a symbol of Nazism. The order prohibiting the wearing of armbands did not extend to these. Instead, a particular symbol—black armbands worn to exhibit opposition to this Nation's involvement in Vietnam—was singled out for prohibition. Clearly, the prohibition of expression of one particular opinion, at least without evidence that it is necessary to avoid material and substantial interference with schoolwork or discipline, is not constitutionally permissible.

In our system, state-operated schools may not be enclaves of totalitarianism. School officials do not possess absolute authority over their students. Students in school as well as out of school are "persons" under our Constitution. They are possessed of fundamental rights which the State must respect, just as they themselves must respect their obligations to the State. In our system, students may not be regarded as closed-circuit recipients of only that which the State chooses to communicate. They may not be confined to the expression of those sentiments that are officially approved. In the absence of a specific showing of constitutionally valid reasons to regulate their speech, students are entitled to freedom of expression of their views. As Judge Gewin, speaking for the Fifth Circuit, said, school officials cannot suppress "expressions of feelings with which they do not wish to contend."

In *Meyer v. Nebraska*, Mr. Justice McReynolds expressed this Nation's repudiation of the principle that a State might so conduct its schools as to "foster a homogeneous people." He said:

> In order to submerge the individual and develop ideal citizens, Sparta assembled the males at seven into barracks and intrusted their subsequent education and training to official guardians. Although such measures have been deliberately approved by men of great genius, their ideas touching the relation between individual and State were wholly different from those upon which our institutions rest; and it hardly will be affirmed that any Legislature could impose such restrictions upon the people of a state without doing violence to both letter and spirit of the Constitution.

This principle has been repeated by this Court of numerous occasions during the intervening years. In *Keyishian v. Board of Regents*, Mr. Justice Brennan, speaking for the Court, said:

> The vigilant protection of constitutional freedoms is nowhere more vital than in the community of American schools. The classroom is peculiarly the "marketplace of ideas." The Nation's future depends upon leaders trained through wide exposure to that robust exchange

of ideas which discovers truth 'out of a multitude of tongues, [rather] than through any kind of authoritative selection.

The principle of these cases is not confined to the supervised and ordained discussion which takes place in the classroom. The principal use to which the schools are dedicated is to accommodate students during prescribed hours for the purpose of certain types of activities. Among those activities is personal intercommunication among the students. This is not only an inevitable part of the process of attending school; it is also an important part of the educational process. A student's rights, therefore, do not embrace merely the classroom hours. When he is in the cafeteria, or on the playing field, or on the campus during the authorized hours, he may express his opinions, even on controversial subjects like the conflict in Vietnam, if he does so without 'materially and substantially interfere[ing] with the requirements of appropriate discipline in the operation of the school' and without colliding with the rights of others. But conduct by the student, in class or out of it, which for any reason—whether it stems from time, place, or type of behavior—materially disrupts classwork or involves substantial disorder or invasion of the rights of others is, of course, not immunized by the constitutional guarantee of freedom of speech.

Under our Constitution, free speech is not a right that is given only to be so circumscribed that it exists in principle but not in fact. Freedom of expression would not truly exist if the right could be exercised only in an area that a benevolent government has provided as a safe haven for crackpots. The Constitution says that Congress (and the States) may not abridge the right to free speech. This provision means what it says. We properly read it to permit reasonable regulation of speech-connected activities in carefully restricted circumstances. But we do not confine the permissible exercise of First Amendment rights to a telephone booth or the four corners of a pamphlet, or to supervised and ordained discussion in a school classroom.

If a regulation were adopted by school officials forbidding discussion of the Vietnam conflict, or the expression by any student of opposition to it anywhere on school property except as part of a prescribed classroom exercise, it would be obvious that the regulation would violate the constitutional rights of students, at least if it could not be justified by a showing that the students' activities would materially and substantially disrupt the work and discipline of the school. In the circumstances of the present case, the prohibition of the silent, passive "witness of the armbands," as one of the children called it, is no less offensive to the constitution's guarantees.

As we have discussed, the record does not demonstrate any facts which might reasonably have led school authorities to forecast substantial disruption of or material interference with school activities, and no disturbances or disorders on the school premises in fact occurred. These petitioners merely went about their ordained rounds in school. Their deviation consisted only in wearing on their sleeve a band of black cloth, not more than two inches wide. They wore it to exhibit their disapproval of the Vietnam hostilities and their advocacy of a truce, to make their views known, and, by their example, to influence others to adopt them. They neither interrupted school activities nor sought to intrude in the school affairs or the lives of others. They caused discussion outside of the classrooms, but no interference with work and no disorder. In the circumstances, our Constitution does not permit officials of the State to deny their form of expression.

We express no opinion as to the form of relief which should be granted, this being a matter for the lower courts to determine. We reverse and remand for further proceedings consistent with this opinion.

Reversed and remanded.

Notes

1. Subsequent cases have clarified the parameters of the *Tinker* rule, and how it might play out on a day-to-day level at individual school sites. The basic principle is that educators do not have to wait for the "disruption" to happen before the expressive activity can be restricted,[a] but at the same time "undifferentiated fear" of disruption is not sufficient.[b]

Recent Ninth Circuit decisions, for example, provide relevant guidelines for school site administrators seeking to ascertain the nature and extent of the prospective disruption. In a 2001 case addressing a dispute over a student poem that the school believed might constitute a threat in the highly charged aftermath of the tragic shootings at Columbine, the court synthesized the set of rules that govern the application of *Tinker*.[c] Judge Fisher explained that if school officials wish to "suppress speech" in anticipation of disruption that has not yet occurred, they must "justify their decision by showing facts which might reasonably have led school authorities to forecast substantial disruption of or material interference with school activities." He noted that this standard "does not require certainty that disruption will occur," and that it contemplates an analysis based on the "totality of the facts."[d]

On the other hand, it is clear from *Tinker* and its progeny that "undifferentiated fear or apprehension of disturbance is not enough to overcome the right to freedom of expression."[e] In a 2001 decision addressing the constitutionality of a "campus speech code" at the high school level, the Third Circuit summarized the applicable case law in this regard.[f] It cau-

---

a. Chandler v. McMinnville Sch. Dist., 978 F.2d 524, 529 (9th Cir. 1992); Karp v. Becken, 477 F.2d 171, 175 (9th Cir. 1973).

b. Tinker v. Des Moines Indep. Cmty. Sch. Dist., 393 U.S. 503, 508, 89 S.Ct. 733 (1969).

c. LaVine v. Blaine School District, 257 F.3d 981 (9th Cir. 2001). In synthesizing these principles, the Ninth Circuit also looked to its 1992 decision, *Chandler v. McMinnville Sch. Dist.*, 978 F.2d 524, where middle school students had been disciplined for wearing provocative political buttons that supported striking teachers and criticized "scabs" during a bitter school strike.

d. "In applying *Tinker*, we look to the totality of the relevant facts. We look not only to James' actions, but to all of the circumstances confronting the school officials that might reasonably portend disruption." *LaVine*, 257 F.3d at 989.

e. *Tinker*, 393 U.S. at 508.

f. Saxe v. State College Area Sch. Dist., 240 F.3d 200 (3d Cir. 2001).

tioned that, "[a]s subsequent federal cases have made clear, *Tinker* requires a specific and significant fear of disruption, not just some remote apprehension of disturbance."[g] And the court cited numerous examples of fact patterns where administrators acted incorrectly under this standard to restrict student expression when in fact the fear was indeterminate and the perceived danger was remote. These examples included the failure of an Oregon school district "to present any evidence" that the wearing of buttons supporting striking teachers were "inherently disruptive" to school activities,[h] the finding of both "insufficient evidence of actual disruption" and the lack of "substantial reason to anticipate a disruption" when a Texas high school prohibited a devoutly religious student from wearing a rosary to school on the ground that some gangs had adopted the rosary as their identifying symbol,[i] and the insufficient nature of the Dallas Independent School District's attempt to rely on "the objection of several other students" to justify its prohibition of the distribution of religious tracts on school grounds.[j]

And even when the Tenth Circuit did in fact rule on behalf of a school district in this context, such a ruling—according to the 2001 Third Circuit panel—only "confirms *Tinker's* requirements of specificity and concreteness." The Tenth Circuit panel had determined that the suspension of a middle school student "for drawing a Confederate flag in math class" was justified by the district's demonstration of "a concrete threat of substantial disruption"—the fact that the district had already experienced "a series of racial incidents [including 'hostile confrontations' and at least one fight] that year, some of which were related to the Confederate flag."[k]

In sum, all the recent cases in this area have made clear that

the mere desire to avoid "discomfort" or "unpleasantness" is not enough to justify restricting student speech under *Tinker*. However, if a school can point to a well-founded expectation of disruption—especially one based on past incidents arising out of similar speech—the restriction may pass constitutional muster.[l]

C.   THE EVOLUTION AND REFINEMENT OF K–12 "FREEDOM OF EXPRESSION" RULES: ADDRESSING *APPROPRIATENESS* AND *LEGITIMATE PEDAGOGICAL CONCERNS*

BETHEL SCH. DIST. NO. 403 v. FRASER
478 U.S. 675, 106 S.Ct. 3159 (1986).

CHIEF JUSTICE BURGER delivered the opinion of the Court.

We granted certiorari to decide whether the First Amendment prevents a school district from disciplining a high school student for giving a lewd speech at a school assembly.

g. *Id.* at 211.

h. *Chandler*, 978 F.2d at 530.

i. Chalifoux v. New Caney Indep. Sch. Dist., 976 F.Supp. 659, 667 (S.D.Tex.1997).

j. Clark v. Dallas Indep. Sch. Dist., 806 F.Supp. 116, 120 (N.D.Tex.1992).

k. West v. Derby Unif. Sch. Dist. No. 260, 206 F.3d 1358, 1366 (10th Cir. 2000) ("The history of racial tension in the district made administrators' and parents' concerns about future substantial disruptions from possession of Confederate flag symbols at school reasonable.").

l. *Saxe*, 240 F.3d at 212.

I.

A.

On April 26, 1983, respondent Matthew N. Fraser, a student at Bethel High School in Pierce County, Washington, delivered a speech[2] nominating a fellow student for student elective office. Approximately 600 high school students, many of whom were 14–year-olds, attended the assembly. Students were required to attend the assembly or to report to the study hall. * * * Students who elected not to attend the assembly were required to report to study hall. During the entire speech, Fraser referred to his candidate in terms of an elaborate, graphic, and explicit sexual metaphor.

Two of Fraser's teachers, with whom he discussed the contents of his speech in advance, informed him that the speech was "inappropriate and that he probably should not deliver it," and that his delivery of the speech might have "severe consequences."

During Fraser's delivery of the speech, a school counselor observed the reaction of students to the speech. Some students hooted and yelled; some by gestures graphically simulated the sexual activities pointedly alluded to in respondent's speech. Other students appeared to be bewildered and embarrassed by the speech. One teacher reported that on the day following the speech, she found it necessary to forgo a portion of the scheduled class lesson in order to discuss the speech with the class.

* * *

The morning after the assembly * * * Fraser was * * * suspended for three days, and * * * his name [was] removed from the list of candidates for graduation speaker at the school's commencement exercises.

* * *

II.

* * * The marked distinction between the political "message" of the armbands in *Tinker* and the sexual content of respondent's speech in

---

2. The Court speculates that the speech was "insulting" to female students, and "seriously damaging" to 14-year-olds, so that school officials could legitimately suppress such expression in order to protect these groups. There is no evidence in the record that any students, male or female, found the speech "insulting." And while it was not unreasonable for school officials to conclude that respondent's remarks were inappropriate for school-sponsored assembly, the language respondent used does not even approach the sexually explicit speech regulated in *Ginsberg v. New Yorl*, or the indecent speech banned in *FCC v. Pacifica Foundation*. Indeed, to my mind, respondent's speech was no more "obscene," "lewd," or "sexually explicit" than the bulk of programs currently appearing on prime time television or in the local cinema. Thus, I disagree with the Court's suggestion that school officials could punish respondent's speech out of a need to protect younger students.

this case seems to have been given little weight by the Court of Appeals.
* * *

III.

The role and purpose of the American public school system were well described by two historians, who stated: "[P]ublic education must prepare pupils for citizenship in the Republic.... It must inculcate the habits and manners of civility as values in themselves conducive to happiness and as indispensable to the practice of self-government in the community and the nation." In *Ambach v. Norwick,* we echoed the essence of this statement of the objectives of public education as the "inculcat[ion of] fundamental values necessary to the maintenance of a democratic political system."

These fundamental values of "habits and manners of civility" essential to a democratic society must, of course, include tolerance of divergent political and religious views, even when the views expressed may be unpopular. But these "fundamental values" must also take into account consideration of the sensibilities of others, and, in the case of a school, the sensibilities of fellow students. The undoubted freedom to advocate unpopular and controversial views in schools and classrooms must be balanced against the society's countervailing interest in teaching students the boundaries of socially appropriate behavior. Even the most heated political discourse in a democratic society requires consideration for the personal sensibilities of the other participants and audiences.

In our Nation's legislative halls, where some of the most vigorous political debates in our society are carried on, there are rules prohibiting the use of expressions offensive to other participants in the debate. The Manual of Parliamentary Practice, drafted by Thomas Jefferson and adopted by the House of Representatives to govern the proceedings in that body, prohibits the use of "impertinent" speech during debate and likewise provides that "[n]o person is to use indecent language against the proceedings of the House." The Rules of Debate applicable in the Senate likewise provide that a Senator may be called to order for imputing improper motives to another Senator or for referring offensively to any state. Senators have been censured for abusive language directed at other Senators. Can it be that what is proscribed in the halls of Congress is beyond the reach of school officials to regulate?

The First Amendment guarantees wide freedom in matters of adult public discourse. A sharply divided Court upheld the right to express an antidraft viewpoint in a public place, albeit in terms highly offensive to most citizens. It does not follow, however, that simply because the use of an offensive form of expression may not be prohibited to adults making what the speaker considers a political point, the same latitude must be permitted to children in a public school. In *New Jersey v. T.L.O.,* we reaffirmed that the constitutional rights of students in public school are not automatically coextensive with the rights of adults in other settings. As cogently expressed by Judge Newman, "the First Amendment gives a high school student the classroom right to wear Tinker's armband, but not Cohen's jacket."

Surely it is a highly appropriate function of public school education to prohibit the use of vulgar and offensive terms in public discourse. Indeed, the "fundamental values necessary to the maintenance of a democratic political system" disfavor the use of terms of debate highly offensive or highly threatening to others. Nothing in the Constitution prohibits the states from insisting that certain modes of expression are inappropriate and subject to sanctions. The inculcation of these values is truly the "work of the schools." *Tinker,* 393 U.S. at 508. The determination of what manner of speech in the classroom or in school assembly is inappropriate properly rests with the school board.

The process of educating our youth for citizenship in public schools is not confined to books, the curriculum, and the civics class; schools must teach by example the shared values of a civilized social order. Consciously or otherwise, teachers—and indeed the older students—demonstrate the appropriate form of civil discourse and political expression by their conduct and deportment in and out of class. Inescapably, like parents, they are role models. The schools, as instruments of the state, may determine that the essential lessons of civil, mature conduct cannot be conveyed in a school that tolerates lewd, indecent, or offensive speech and conduct such as that indulged in by this confused boy.

The pervasive sexual innuendo in Fraser's speech was plainly offensive to both teachers and students—indeed to any mature person. By glorifying male sexuality, and in its verbal content, the speech was acutely insulting to teenage girl students. The speech could well be seriously damaging to its less mature audience, many of whom were only 14 years old and on the threshold of awareness of human sexuality. Some students were reported as bewildered by the speech and the reaction of mimicry it provoked.

This Court's First Amendment jurisprudence has acknowledged limitations on the otherwise absolute interest of the speaker in reaching an unlimited audience where the speech is sexually explicit and the audience may include children * * * These cases recognize the obvious concern on the part of parents, and school authorities acting *in loco parentis,* to protect children—especially in a captive audience—from exposure to sexually explicit, indecent, or lewd speech.

We have also recognized an interest in protecting minors from exposure to vulgar and offensive spoken language. * * *

We hold that petitioner School District acted entirely within its permissible authority in imposing sanctions upon Fraser in response to his offensively lewd and indecent speech. Unlike the sanctions imposed on the students wearing armbands in *Tinker,* the penalties imposed in this case were unrelated to any political viewpoint. The First Amendment does not prevent the school officials from determining that to permit a vulgar and lewd speech such as respondent's would undermine the school's basic educational mission. A high school assembly or classroom is no place for a sexually explicit monologue directed towards an unsuspecting audience of teenage students. Accordingly, it was perfectly appropriate for the school to disassociate itself to make the point to the pupils that vulgar speech and lewd conduct is wholly inconsistent with the "fundamental values" of public school education. Justice Black, dissenting in *Tinker,* made a point that is especially relevant in this case:

I wish therefore * * * to disclaim any purpose * * * to hold that the Federal Constitution compels the teachers, parents, and elected school officials to surrender control of the American public school system to public school students. 393 U.S. at 526.

* * *

The judgment of the Court of Appeals for the Ninth Circuit is

Reversed.

* * *

JUSTICE BRENNAN, concurring in the judgment.

Respondent gave the following speech at a high school assembly in support of a candidate for student government office:

I know a man who is firm—he's firm in his pants, he's firm in his shirt, his character is firm—but most ... of all, his belief in you, the students of Bethel, is firm. Jeff Kuhlman is a man who takes his point and pounds it in. If necessary, he'll take an issue and nail it to the wall. He doesn't attack things in spurts—he drives hard, pushing and pushing until finally—he succeeds.

Jeff is a man who will go to the very end—even the climax, for each and every one of you.

So vote for Jeff for A.S.B. vice-president—he'll never come between you and the best our high school can be.'

The Court, referring to these remarks as "obscene," "vulgar," "lewd," and "offensively lewd," concludes that school officials properly punished respondent for uttering the speech. Having read the full text of respondent's remarks, I find it difficult to believe that it is the same speech the Court describes. To my mind, the most that can be said about respondent's speech—and all that need be said—is that in light of the discretion school officials have to teach high school students how to conduct civil and effective public discourse, and to prevent disruption of school educational activities, it was not unconstitutional for school officials to conclude, under the circumstances of this case, that respondent's remarks exceeded permissible limits. Thus, while I concur in the Court's judgment, I write separately to express my understanding of the breadth of the Court's holding.

The Court today reaffirms the unimpeachable proposition that students do not "shed their constitutional rights to freedom of speech or expression at the schoolhouse gate.'' If respondent had given the same speech outside of the school environment, he could not have been penalized simply because government officials considered his language to be inappropriate; the Court's opinion does not suggest otherwise. Moreover, despite the Court's characterizations, the language respondent used is far removed from the very narrow class of ''obscene'' speech which the Court has held is not protected by the First Amendment. It is true, however, that the State has interests in teaching high school students how to conduct civil and effective public discourse and in avoiding disruption of educational school activities. Thus, the Court holds that under certain circumstances, high school students may properly be reprimanded for giving a speech at a high school assembly which school officials conclude disrupted the school's educational mission. Respondent's speech may well have been protected had he given it in school but under different circumstances, where the school's legitimate interests in teaching and maintaining civil public discourse were less weighty.

In the present case, school officials sought only to ensure that a high school assembly proceed in an orderly manner. There is no suggestion that school officials attempted to regulate respondent's speech because they disagreed with the views he sought to express. *Cf. Tinker.* Nor does this case involve an attempt by school officials to ban written materials they consider ''inappropriate'' for high school students, cf. *Board of Education v. Pico,* 457 U.S. 853 (1982), or to limit what students should hear, read, or learn about. Thus, the Court's holding concerns only the authority that school officials have to restrict a high school student's use of disruptive language in a speech given to a high school assembly.

* * *

* * * Under the circumstances of this case * * * I believe that school officials did not violate the First Amendment in determining that respondent should be disciplined for the disruptive language he used while addressing a high school assembly. Thus, I concur in the judgment reversing the decision of the Court of Appeals.

HAZELWOOD v. KUHLMEIER

484 U.S. 260, 108 S.Ct. 562 (1988).

JUSTICE WHITE delivered the opinion of the Court.

This case concerns the extent to which educators may exercise editorial control over the contents of a high school newspaper produced as part of the school's journalism curriculum.

I.

Petitioners are the Hazelwood School District in St. Louis County, Missouri; various school officials; Robert Eugene Reynolds, the principal of Hazelwood East High School; and Howard Emerson, a teacher in the school district. Respondents are three former Hazelwood East students who were staff members of Spectrum, the school newspaper. They contend that school officials violated their First Amendment rights by deleting two pages of articles from the May 13, 1983, issue of Spectrum.

Spectrum was written and edited by the Journalism II class at Hazelwood East. The newspaper was published every three weeks or so during the 1982–1983 school year. More than 4,500 copies of the newspaper were distributed during that year to students, school personnel, and members of the community.

* * *

The practice at Hazelwood East during the spring 1983 semester was for the journalism teacher to submit page proofs of each Spectrum issue to Principal Reynolds for his review prior to publication. On May 10, Emerson delivered the proofs of the May 13 edition to Reynolds, who objected to two of the articles scheduled to appear in that edition. One of the stories described three Hazelwood East students' experiences with pregnancy; the other discussed the impact of divorce on students at the school.

Reynolds was concerned that, although the pregnancy story used false names "to keep the identity of these girls a secret," the pregnant students still might be identifiable from the text. He also believed that the article's references to sexual activity and birth control were inappropriate for some of the younger students at the school. In addition, Reynolds was concerned that a student identified by name in the divorce story had complained that her father "wasn't spending enough time with my mom, my sister and I" prior to the divorce, "was always out of town on business or out late playing cards with the guys," and "always argued about everything" with her mother. Reynolds believed that the student's parents should have been given an opportunity to respond to these remarks or to consent to their publication. He was unaware that Emerson had deleted the student's name from the final version of the article.

Reynolds believed that there was no time to make the necessary changes in the stories before the scheduled press run and that the newspaper would not appear before the end of the school year if printing were delayed to any significant extent. He concluded that his only options under the circumstances were to publish a four-page newspaper instead of the planned six-page newspaper, eliminating the two pages on which the offending stories appeared, or to publish no newspaper at all. Accordingly, he directed Emerson to withhold from publication the two pages containing the stories on pregnancy and divorce.[1] He informed his superiors of the decision, and they concurred.

* * *

1. The two pages deleted from the newspaper also contained articles on teenage marriage, runaways, and juvenile delinquents, as well as a general article on teen-

II.

Students in the public schools do not "shed their constitutional rights to freedom of speech or expression at the schoolhouse gate." *Tinker*, 393 U.S. at 506. They cannot be punished merely for expressing their personal views on the school premises—whether "in the cafeteria, or on the playing field, or on the campus during the authorized hours," 393 U.S. at 512–513—unless school authorities have reason to believe that such expression will "substantially interfere with the work of the school or impinge upon the rights of other students."

We have nonetheless recognized that the First Amendment rights of students in the public schools "are not automatically coextensive with the rights of adults in other settings," *Bethel School District No. 403 v. Fraser*, 478 U.S. 675, 682 (1986) and must be "applied in light of the special characteristics of the school environment." *Tinker*, 393 U,S, at 506. A school need not tolerate student speech that is inconsistent with its "basic educational mission," *Fraser*, 478 U.S. at 685, even though the government could not censor similar speech outside the school. Accordingly, we held in *Fraser* that a student could be disciplined for having delivered a speech that was "sexually explicit" but not legally obscene at an official school assembly, because the school was entitled to "disassociate itself" from the speech in a manner that would demonstrate to others that such vulgarity is "wholly inconsistent with the 'fundamental values' of public school education." * * *

A.

We deal first with the question whether Spectrum may appropriately be characterized as a forum for public expression. The public schools do not possess all of the attributes of streets, parks, and other traditional public forums that "time out of mind, have been used for purposes of assembly, communicating thoughts between citizens, and discussing public questions." Hence, school facilities may be deemed to be public forums only if school authorities have "by policy or by practice" opened those facilities "for indiscriminate use by the general public," or by some segment of the public, such as student organizations. If the facilities have instead been reserved for other intended purposes, "communicative or otherwise," then no public forum has been created, and school officials may impose reasonable restrictions on the speech of students, teachers, and other members of the school community. "The government does not create a public forum by inaction or by permitting limited discourse, but only by intentionally opening a nontraditional forum for public discourse."

The policy of school officials toward Spectrum was reflected in Hazelwood School Board Policy 348.51 and the Hazelwood East Curriculum Guide. Board Policy 348.51 provided that "[s]chool sponsored publi-

---

age pregnancy. Reynolds testified that he had no objection to these articles and that they were deleted only because they ap-

peared on the same pages as the two objectionable articles.

cations are developed within the adopted curriculum and its educational implications in regular classroom activities." * * *

School officials did not deviate in practice from their policy that production of *Spectrum* was to be part of the educational curriculum and a "regular classroom activit[y]." * * *

* * * School officials did not evince either "by policy or by practice," any intent to open the pages of Spectrum to "indiscriminate use," by its student reporters and editors, or by the student body generally. Instead, they "reserve[d] the forum for its intended purpos[e]," as a supervised learning experience for journalism students. Accordingly, school officials were entitled to regulate the contents of *Spectrum* in any reasonable manner. It is this standard, rather than our decision in *Tinker,* that governs this case.

B.

The question whether the First Amendment requires a school to tolerate particular student speech—the question that we addressed in *Tinker*—is different from the question whether the First Amendment requires a school affirmatively to promote particular student speech. The former question addresses educators' ability to silence a student's personal expression that happens to occur on the school premises. The latter question concerns educators' authority over school-sponsored publications, theatrical productions, and other expressive activities that students, parents, and members of the public might reasonably perceive to bear the imprimatur of the school. These activities may fairly be characterized as part of the school curriculum, whether or not they occur in a traditional classroom setting, so long as they are supervised by faculty members and designed to impart particular knowledge or skills to student participants and audiences.

Educators are entitled to exercise greater control over this second form of student expression to assure that participants learn whatever lessons the activity is designed to teach, that readers or listeners are not exposed to material that may be inappropriate for their level of maturity, and that the views of the individual speaker are not erroneously attributed to the school. Hence, a school may in its capacity as publisher of a school newspaper or producer of a school play "disassociate itself," *Fraser,* 478 U.S. at 685, not only from speech that would "substantially interfere with [its] work ... or impinge upon the rights of other students," *Tinker,* 393 U.S. at 509, but also from speech that is, for example, ungrammatical, poorly written, inadequately researched, biased or prejudiced, vulgar or profane, or unsuitable for immature audiences. A school must be able to set high standards for the student speech that is disseminated under its auspices—standards that may be higher than those demanded by some newspaper publishers or theatrical producers in the "real" world—and may refuse to disseminate student speech that does not meet those standards. In addition, a school must be able to take into account the emotional maturity of the intended audience in determining whether to disseminate student speech on potentially sensitive topics, which might range from the existence of Santa Claus in an elementary school setting to the particulars of teenage sexual activity in a high school setting. A school must also retain the authority to refuse to sponsor student speech that might reasonably be perceived to advocate drug or alcohol use, irresponsible sex, or conduct otherwise inconsistent with "the shared values of a civilized social order," *Fraser, 478* U.S. at 683, or to associate the school with any position other than neutrality on matters of political controversy. Otherwise, the schools would be unduly constrained from fulfilling their role as "a principal instrument in awakening the child to cultural values, in preparing him for later professional training, and in helping him to adjust normally to his environment." *Brown v. Board of Education,* 347 U.S. 483 (1954).

Accordingly, we conclude that the standard articulated in *Tinker* for determining when a school may punish student expression need not also be the standard for determining when a school may refuse to lend its name and resources to the dissemination of student expression. Instead, we hold that educators do not offend the First Amendment by exercising editorial control over the style and content of student speech in school-sponsored expressive activities so long as their actions are reasonably related to legitimate pedagogical concerns.

This standard is consistent with our oft-expressed view that the education of the Nation's youth is primarily the responsibility of parents, teachers, and state and local school officials, and not of federal judges. It is only when the decision to censor a school-sponsored publication, theatrical production, or other vehicle of student expression has no valid educational purpose that the First Amendment is so "directly and sharply implicate[d]," as to require judicial intervention to protect students' constitutional rights.

III.

We also conclude that Principal Reynolds acted reasonably in requiring the deletion from the May 13 issue of Spectrum of the pregnancy article, the divorce article, and the remaining articles that were to appear on the same pages of the newspaper.

* * *

The judgment of the Court of Appeals for the Eighth Circuit is therefore

Reversed.

Notes

1. In the First Amendment area, individual states are able to go beyond the federal "baseline" and grant their students additional free speech rights. California, for example, provides its students with more free speech protection than the *Tinker-Fraser-Hazelwood* line of cases. *See, e.g.,* CAL. EDUC. CODE § 48907 (2005), which provides, in pertinent part:

Students of the public schools shall have the right to exercise freedom of speech and of the press including, but not limited to, the use of bulletin boards, the distribution of printed material or petitions, the wearing of buttons, badges, and other insignia, and the right of expression in official publications, whether or not such publications or other means of expression are supported financially by the school or by use of school facilities, except that expression shall be prohibited which is obscene, libelous, or slanderous. Also prohibited shall be material which so incites students as to create a clear and present danger of the commission of unlawful acts on school premises or the violation of lawful school regulations, or the substantial disruption of the orderly operation of the school.

Student editors ... shall be responsible for assigning and editing the news, editorial, and feature content of their publications subject to the limitations of this section. However, it shall be the responsibility of a journalism adviser ... to maintain professional standards of English and journalism....

Id.; see also CAL. EDUC. CODE § 48950, which provides in pertinent part that "[s]chool districts * * * shall not make or enforce any rule subjecting any high school pupil to disciplinary sanctions solely on the basis of conduct that is speech or other communication that, when engaged in outside of the campus, is protected * * * by the First Amendment."

On the other hand, individual states may mandate dress codes and uniforms without violating First Amendment rights.

BOROFF v. VAN WERT CITY BOARD OF EDUC.

220 F.3d 465, 146 Ed. Law Rep. 629 (6th Cir. 2000).

WELLFORD, CIRCUIT JUDGE.

After Van Wert (Ohio) High School administrators told Nicholas Boroff that he was not allowed to wear "Marilyn Manson" T-shirts to school, Boroff's mother initiated this action on his behalf pursuant to 42 U.S.C. § 1983, alleging that the administrators' refusal to let him wear the T-shirts violated his rights under the First and Fourteenth Amendments. The district court entered summary judgment in favor of the Van Wert City Board of Education and each of the school administrators who were named as defendants. We **AFFIRM** the decision of the district court.

I. BACKGROUND

* * * Marilyn Manson is the stage name of "goth" rock performer Brian Warner, and also the name of the band in which he is the lead singer. *See* Encarta World English Dictionary (2000) * * * (defining "goth" as "a style of popular music that combines elements of heavy metal with punk" and also "a style of fashion ... characterized by black clothes, heavy silver jewelry, black eye make-up and lipstick, and often pale face make-up"). Band members take the first part of their stage names from a famous model or celebrity, such as Marilyn Monroe,

Madonna, or Twiggy, and the second part from a notorious serial killer, such as Charles Manson, John Wayne Gacy, or Richard Ramirez. Marilyn Manson (the individual) is popularly regarded as a worshiper of Satan, which he has denied. * * * He is also widely regarded as a user of illegal drugs, which he has not denied. * * *

On August 29, 1997, Boroff, then a senior at Van Wert High School, went to school wearing a "Marilyn Manson" T-shirt. The front of the T-shirt depicted a three-faced Jesus, accompanied by the words "See No Truth. Hear No Truth. Speak No Truth." On the back of the shirt, the word "BELIEVE" was spelled out in capital letters, with the letters "LIE" highlighted. Marilyn Manson's name (although not his picture) was displayed prominently on the front of the shirt. At the time, Van Wert High School had in effect a "Dress and Grooming" policy that provided that "clothing with offensive illustrations, drug, alcohol, or tobacco slogans ... are not acceptable." Chief Principal's Aide David Froelich told Boroff that his shirt was offensive and gave him the choice of turning the shirt inside-out, going home and changing, or leaving and being considered truant. Boroff left school.

On September 4, 1997, which was the next school day, Boroff wore another Marilyn Manson T-shirt to school. Boroff and his mother met that day with Froelich, Principal William Clifton, and Superintendent John Basinger. Basinger told the Boroffs that students would not be permitted to wear Marilyn Manson T-shirts on school grounds. Undaunted, Boroff wore different Marilyn Manson T-shirts on each of the next three school days, September 5, 8, and 9, 1997. The shirts featured pictures of Marilyn Manson, whose appearance can fairly be described as ghoulish and creepy. Each day, Boroff was told that he would not be permitted to attend school while wearing the T-shirts.

* * *

On * * * September 16, 1997, his mother initiated the present suit * * *.

II. ANALYSIS

* * *

B. First Amendment Claim

"It is a highly appropriate function of public school education to prohibit the use of vulgar and offensive terms in public discourse." *Bethel School District No. 403 v. Fraser*, 478 U.S. 675, 683 (1986). While students do not "shed their constitutional rights to freedom of speech or expression at the schoolhouse gate," *Tinker v. Des Moines Independent Community School District*, 393 U.S. 503, 506, 89 S. Ct. 733 (1969), the First Amendment rights of students in the public schools must be "applied in light of the special characteristics of the school environment." *Hazelwood School District v. Kuhlmeier*, 484 U.S. 260, 266, 108

S. Ct. 562 (1988). With those precepts in mind, we apply the *Tinker-Fraser–Kuhlmeier* trilogy to the facts of this case.

      * * *

    * * * [I]n *Bethel School District No. 403 v. Fraser,* 478 U.S. 675, 106 S. Ct. 3159 (1986), the Court "cast some doubt on the extent to which students retain free speech rights in the school setting." In *Fraser,* the Court held that a school district acted within its permissible authority in disciplining a student who gave an offensively lewd and indecent speech at a school assembly. In reaching its conclusion, the Court noted "[t]he marked distinction between the political 'message' of the armbands in *Tinker* and the sexual content of respondent's speech in this case." *Fraser,* 478 U.S. at 680, 106 S. Ct. 3159. The Court recognized "that the constitutional rights of students in public schools are not automatically coextensive with the rights of adults in other settings." *Id.* at 682, 106 S. Ct. 3159. It distinguished *Tinker* because the vulgar and offensive speech at issue was "unrelated to any political viewpoint." *Id.* at 685, 106 S. Ct. 3159. The Court ultimately held that the school district had the authority to determine that the vulgar and lewd speech at issue would undermine the school's basic educational mission.

    In *Hazelwood School District v. Kuhlmeier,* 484 U.S. 260, 108 S. Ct. 562 (1988), the Court echoed its position in *Fraser* that "[a] school need not tolerate student speech that is inconsistent with its 'basic educational mission ... even though the government could not censor similar speech outside the school.' " * * * The Court distinguished between the First Amendment analysis applied in *Tinker* and the analysis applied in *Fraser,* noting that the decision in *Fraser* rested on the vulgar and offensive character of the speech, whereas *Tinker* rested on the propensity of the speech materially to disrupt classwork or involve substantial disorder. * * *

    The district court below determined that the rule in *Fraser* applied to this case, concluding that "[a] school may prohibit a student from wearing a T-shirt that is offensive, but not obscene, on school grounds, even if the T-shirt has not been shown to cause a substantial disruption of the academic program." The court then held that the School did not act in a manifestly unreasonable manner in finding the T-shirts offensive and in enforcing its dress code.

    In this appeal, Boroff argues that the district court erred in granting summary judgment to the School. In his appellate brief he maintains:

> The way to analyze this is to first determine whether the speech is "vulgar or offensive". If it is, then *Fraser* allows banning it, and the analysis is complete. Otherwise, apply *Tinker* and examine if there is a threat of substantial disruption such that would allow the school to ban the speech.

    Boroff claims that the administrators' decision that the T-shirts are offensive was manifestly unreasonable and unsupported by the evidence. Boroff relies to a great extent on evidence that similar T-shirts promoting other bands, such as Slayer and Megadeth, were not prohibited, and also on evidence that one other student was not prohibited from carrying a backpack that donned three "Marilyn Manson" patches. Because the T-shirts were not "offensive," Boroff reasons, and because there is no evidence that a substantial disruption would arise from his wearing the T-shirts, then the School violated his First Amendment rights. We disagree.

The standard for reviewing the suppression of vulgar or plainly offensive speech is governed by *Fraser*. The School in this case, according to the affidavit of Principal Clifton, found the Marilyn Manson T-shirts to be offensive because the band promotes destructive conduct and demoralizing values that are contrary to the educational mission of the school. Specifically, Clifton found the "three-headed Jesus" T-shirt to be offensive because of the "See No Truth. Hear No Truth. Speak No Truth." mantra on the front, and because of the obvious implication of the word "BELIEVE" with "LIE" highlighted on the back. The principal specifically stated that the distorted Jesus figure was offensive, because "[m]ocking any religious figure is contrary to our educational mission which is to be respectful of others and others' beliefs." The other T-shirts were treated with equal disapproval. Clifton went on to explain the reasoning behind the School's prohibition of the T-shirts generally:

> 17. Although I do not know if [Boroff] intends to communicate anything when wearing the Marilyn Manson t-shirts, I believe that the Marilyn Manson t-shirts can reasonably be considered a communication agreeing with or approving of the views espoused by Marilyn Manson in its lyrics and those views which have been associated to Marilyn Manson through articles in the press. I find some of the Marilyn Manson lyrics and some of the views associated with Marilyn Manson as reported in articles in the news and entertainment press offensive to our basic educational mission at Van Wert High School. Therefore, I believe that all of the Marilyn Manson t-shirts ... are offensive to and inconsistent with our educational mission at Van Wert High School.

Furthermore, Clifton quotes some of the lyrics from Marilyn Manson songs that the School finds offensive, which include (but certainly are not limited to) lines such as, "you can kill yourself now because you're dead in my mind," "let's jump upon the sharp swords/and cut away our smiles/without the threat of death/there's no reason to live at all," and "Let's just kill everyone and let your god sort them out/Fuck it/Everybody's someone else's nigger/I know you are so am I/I wasn't born with enough middle fingers." The principal attested that those types of lyrics were contrary to the school mission and goal of establishing "a common core of values that include ... human dignity and worth ... self respect, and responsibility," and also the goal of instilling "into the students, an understanding and appreciation of the ideals of democracy and help them to be diligent and competent in the performance of their obligations as citizens."

Clifton also submitted to the district court magazine articles that portray Marilyn Manson as having a "pro-drug persona" and articles wherein Marilyn Manson himself admits that he is a drug user and promotes drug use. Clifton concludes from his fourteen years of experience that children are genuinely influenced by the rock group and such propaganda.

Affidavits of other School officials support the administration's position that the Marilyn Manson T-shirts, generally speaking, were prohibited because they were "counter-productive and go against the educational mission of the Van Wert City School District community." * * * The record is devoid of any evidence that the T-shirts, the "three-headed Jesus" T-shirt particularly, were perceived to express any particular political or religious viewpoint.

Under these circumstances, we find that the district court was correct in finding that the School did not act in a manifestly unreasonable manner in prohibiting the Marilyn Manson T-shirts pursuant to its dress code. The Supreme Court has held that the school board has the authority to determine "what manner of speech in the classroom or in school is inappropriate." *Fraser*, 478 U.S. at 682, 106 S. Ct. 3159. The Court has determined that "[a] school need not tolerate student speech that is inconsistent with its 'basic educational mission ... even though the government could not censor similar speech outside the school.'" *Kuhlmeier*, 484 U.S. at 266, 108 S. Ct. 562. In this case, where Boroff's T-shirts contain symbols and words that promote values that are so patently contrary to the school's educational mission, the School has the authority, under the circumstances of this case, to prohibit those T-shirts.

The dissent would find that the evidence was sufficient for a reasonable jury to infer that the School has engaged in "viewpoint discrimination" by prohibiting the T-shirts, similar to the armband prohibition in *Tinker*. The dissent primarily relies on one sentence in Principal Clifton's affidavit, in which Clifton stated that he found the "three-headed Jesus" T-shirt to be offensive because "it mocks a major religious figure." Under that reasoning, if a jury finds that the School has prohibited the T-shirts because of any viewpoint expressed on the shirts, then the School must show that it reasonably predicted that allowing the T-shirts would have caused a substantial disruption of, or material interference with, school activities. *See Tinker*, 393 U.S. at 509, 89 S. Ct. 733.

In our view, however, the evidence does not support an inference that the School intended to suppress the expression of Boroff's viewpoint, because of its religious implications. Rather, the record demonstrates that the School prohibited Boroff's Marilyn Manson T-shirts generally because this particular rock group promotes disruptive and demoralizing values which are inconsistent with and counter-productive to education. The dissenting judge agrees that "[i]f the only T-shirts at issue in this case were the ones that simply displayed illustrations of

Marilyn Manson largely unadorned by text, the judgment of the district court might be sustainable." He reasons, however, that the one T-shirt featuring the distorted Jesus figure may have been prohibited because of the School's disagreement with its religious message. In our view, the School's treatment of the "three-headed Jesus" T-shirt and the others is not distinguishable. The record establishes that all of the T-shirts were banned in the same manner for the same reasons—they were determined to be vulgar, offensive, and contrary to the educational mission of the school.

In sum, we are of the view that the School has the authority to prohibit Marilyn Manson T-shirts under these circumstances. * * *

III. CONCLUSION

For the foregoing reasons and for the reasons stated in its opinion, we **AFFIRM** the decision of the district court.

GILMAN, CIRCUIT JUDGE, dissenting.

* * * Unlike the majority, I believe that a jury could reasonably find that the reason why School officials declared Boroff's Marilyn Manson T-shirts "offensive" was because the first Marilyn Manson T-shirt he wore contained a message about religion that they considered obnoxious. Accordingly, I believe that summary judgment in favor of the Board on Boroff's First Amendment claim was inappropriate, and therefore respectfully dissent.

I.

I have little doubt that school administrators may reasonably decide that certain rock performers are so closely identified with illegal drug use or other unlawful activities that T-shirts bearing their images are unacceptable for high school students to wear in school. In fact, after the Supreme Court's decisions in *Bethel School District No. 403 v. Fraser,* 478 U.S. 675, 106 S. Ct. 3159 (1986) and *Hazelwood School District v. Kuhlmeier,* 484 U.S. 260, 108 S. Ct. 562 (1988) I suspect that forbidding a student from wearing a T-shirt simply because it makes a statement with which school administrators disagree is one of a very few decisions about student dress that school administrators are *not* allowed to make. Nevertheless, from the record presented, a reasonable jury could easily conclude that this was exactly what the School did.

I believe that the School in this case came perilously close to admitting that its decision to prohibit Boroff from wearing the three-headed Jesus T-shirt was made precisely because the School found the T-shirt's viewpoint repugnant. Principal Clifton explained in an affidavit that

> I have found the t-shirt which contains the three-faced Jesus to be offensive.... This t-shirt is offensive because it mocks a major religious figure. Mocking any religious figure is contrary to our

educational missions which is to be respectful of others and others' beliefs. Second, mocking this particular religious figure is particularly offensive to a significant portion of our school community, including students, teachers, staff members and parents.

In view of this explanation, I am at a loss to understand how the majority can say that "[t]he record is devoid of any evidence that the T-shirts, the 'three-headed Jesus' T-shirt particularly, were perceived to express any particular political or religious viewpoint." Of course the three-headed Jesus T-shirt was perceived to express a political or religious viewpoint. Principal Clifton said so himself. It appears unmistakable that the reason why the three-headed Jesus T-shirt was deemed "offensive" was because it said something about a venerated religious figure, and because many people in Van Wert (presumably including Principal Clifton) happen to disagree vehemently with what they perceived the T-shirt as saying. Indeed, from Principal Clifton's explanation, it would not be unreasonable to presume that if the T-shirt had depicted Jesus in a positive light, it would not have been considered "offensive."

Consistent with the Supreme Court's First Amendment jurisprudence, taking sides in that manner would be considered viewpoint discrimination, which is accompanied by an all-but-irrebuttable presumption of unconstitutionality. *See, e.g., Rosenberger v. Rector & Visitors of Univ. of Virginia*, 515 U.S. 819, 828–29, 115 S. Ct. 2510 (1995) (describing viewpoint discrimination as "an egregious form of content discrimination" and observing that "[w]hen the government targets not subject matter, but particular views taken by speakers on a subject, the violation of the First Amendment is all the more blatant.") * * *.

II.

I also believe that the majority misapprehends the meaning of the terms "vulgar" and "offensive." In First Amendment cases, those terms refer to words and phrases that are themselves coarse and crude, regardless of whether one disagrees with the overall message that the speaker is trying to convey. Roughly speaking, they are the words and phrases that might have appeared on comedian George Carlin's list of words that one cannot say on the radio. That is why the high school administrators in *Pyle v. South Hadley School Committee* were allowed to prohibit a student from wearing a T-shirt proclaiming "See Dick Drink. See Dick die. Don't Be a Dick." The school administrators in *Pyle* were obviously not objecting to the message that drunk driving is bad and should be discouraged.

If Boroff had worn a T-shirt featuring Marilyn Manson's name and the song lyrics contained in the majority's opinion, this would be a very easy case. A number of those words are vulgar, regardless of whether one likes or dislikes Marilyn Manson's music or agrees or disagrees with whatever message Boroff would be trying to convey by wearing the shirt. But that sort of vulgarity is absent from the three-headed Jesus T-shirt that Boroff wore. This particular T-shirt was found "offensive" because it expresses a viewpoint that many people personally find repellent, not because it is vulgar.

Censorship on that basis is simply not permitted in the absence of a reasonable prediction by school officials of substantial disruption of, or material interference with, school activities. Indeed, that was the holding of *Tinker*. * * *

The majority asserts that "the School prohibited the Marilyn Manson T-shirts," including the three-headed Jesus T-shirt that precipitated this case, "because this particular rock group promotes disruptive and demoralizing values which are inconsistent with and counter-productive to education." It is not clear, however, what "disruptive and demoralizing values" the majority is referring to. If the majority is suggesting that the School could have concluded that Marilyn Manson's apparent endorsement of, say, illegal drug use, makes his picture an unacceptable image for students to wear in high school, I would agree. A fair reading of the record, however, suggests that the "disruptive and demoralizing values" that the School was really concerned about was disrespect for a specific venerated religious figure.

Or so a reasonable jury could have found. As noted above, however, school officials are not free to decide that only one side of a topic is open for discussion because the other side is too repugnant or demoralizing to listen to. * * *

I also believe that the majority dropped its guard much too quickly at the School's conclusory invocation of "disruptive and demoralizing values." I am quite confident that the school officials in *Tinker* thought it would be highly disruptive and demoralizing—not to mention downright unpatriotic—for students to wear black armbands in order to protest a war in which thousands of American soldiers were fighting and dying. The Supreme Court nevertheless concluded that the officials could not prohibit the students from wearing the armbands in the absence of evidence that a ban would be necessary to prevent "material and substantial interference with schoolwork or discipline."

III.

This brings me to the last, but certainly not least important, matter on which I disagree with the majority. The majority apparently reads the Supreme Court's opinions in *Fraser* and *Kuhlmeier* as essentially overruling *Tinker*, concluding that after *Fraser* and *Kuhlmeier*, school officials can forbid whatever student speech they consider "offensive" (in the sense of promoting "disruptive and demoralizing values"), as long as their decision does not appear "manifestly unreasonable."

That, however, is not what the Supreme Court held in either *Fraser* or *Kuhlmeier*. *Fraser* concluded that school officials could temporarily suspend a high school student who persisted in giving a speech permeated with obvious sexual metaphors during a school assembly, despite being warned that the speech was "inappropriate" and that delivering it might result in "severe consequences." *Kuhlmeier* concluded that high school administrators do not offend the First Amendment by exercising editorial control over the style and content of school-sponsored publications as long as their actions are reasonably related to legitimate pedagogical concerns.

Because nothing in either *Fraser* or *Kuhlmeier* purports to overrule *Tinker* (indeed, *Tinker* was recently cited with approval by the Supreme Court in *United States v. Playboy Entertainment Group, Inc.*), * * * I believe that it should be left to the Supreme Court to determine whether and when *Tinker* should be cast by the wayside.

Instead, in both *Fraser* and *Kuhlmeier,* the Supreme Court distinguished *Tinker* by noting that the school officials in the latter cases might reasonably have been thought to be endorsing or condoning the student expression at issue had they taken no action. In *Fraser,* the student campaign speech at issue occurred at an assembly during school hours that students were expected to attend. *See Fraser*, 478 U.S. at 677, 106 S. Ct. 3159 * * *. *Kuhlmeier* involved a student newspaper that was funded and sponsored by the school itself. *See Kuhlmeier*, 484 U.S. at 271, 108 S. Ct. 562 * * *. This distinction was critical to both the *Fraser* and *Kuhlmeier* decisions.

In contrast, I do not believe that school officials can reasonably be thought to endorse or condone a message worn on a student's T-shirt simply because they do not prohibit the student from wearing the T-shirt to school.

IV.

In sum, the Supreme Court's First Amendment jurisprudence prohibits school officials from telling a student that he cannot wear a particular T-shirt simply because they perceive that the T-shirt is communicating a message with which they disagree. Because I believe that a reasonable jury could conclude that this is exactly what the School did in the present case, I respectfully dissent from the majority's decision to affirm the grant of summary judgment in favor of the School on Boroff's First Amendment claim, I would therefore reverse the judgment of the district court to the extent that it entered summary judgment for the School on this claim, and remand the case for trial.

Notes

1. How important are the prospective rights of religious students in this context? Did the Court pay less attention to this aspect of the dispute than it should have?

PROBLEM 11: Variations on the *Boroff* Case

Assume the following changes in the facts of the *Boroff* case: (a) the specific t-shirt in question was originally one of many sold on campus by the student council as part of a fund-raiser to help raise money for athletic equipment; (b) the t-shirt was worn on several occasions by Boroff and numerous other students over time before any action was taken by the administration; (c) a delegation of local clergy met with the principal to register their complaints regarding the t-shirt and indicate that it was not only disturbing to the religious community and to the highly religious students on campus but was distracting the students from their schoolwork; and (d) several scuffles had broken out between goth students and religious students on campus for a variety of reasons over the past half year. Would the District's case then be stronger? Why or why not?

D. CONCEPTUALIZING THE PARAMETERS OF THE RIGHT TO BE "OUT"

In the public sector today, every individual has a right to be "out" regarding fundamental aspects of identity, personhood, and group affiliation. Reflecting a classic combination of First Amendment and Fourteenth Amendment principles, it is both a right to express an identity and a right to be treated equally as a result of expressing this identity.

Emerging under both case law and a range of relevant federal and state statutes, the right to be "out" encompasses—but is not limited to—disclosure of one's race, ethnicity, religion, sexual orientation, gender identity, political views, medical conditions, past experiences, present involvement, and future plans.[a]

Within the lesbian, gay, bisexual, and transgender (LGBT) communities, nothing is more central than the right to be out. To the extent that it is in fact recognized in the U.S. today, it encompasses the right to identify openly as an LGBT person and the right to live openly as an LGBT person ... without experiencing any negative consequences as a result.

The centrality of this right for LGBT persons can be linked to the fact that not only is there still so much pressure, in so many settings, not to come out, but that as recently as 30–40 years ago the U.S. legal system had set forth such imposing hurdles to living openly that being out was typically not an option. Public school teachers, for example, could lose their jobs if they were openly gay. Bars were actually prohibited from serving drinks to persons who were known homosexuals or openly homosexual. Dancing with same sex partners in public was restricted. And propositioning another person of the same gender was not only a crime but an act that could lead to "sex offender" status and the accompanying loss of employment, legal rights, and social standing in the community.[b]

---

a. It must be noted, of course, that just as there is a concurrent right, under the First Amendment Free Speech Clause, not to speak, there is also a concurrent right in this context not to be out. Indeed, the right not to be out is an important component of the right to privacy.

b. *See, e.g.,* WILLIAM N. ESKRIDGE, JR., GAYLAW 98, Harvard University Press (1999):

The homosexual in 1961 was smothered by law. She or he risked arrest and possible police brutalization for dancing with someone of the same sex, cross-dressing, propositioning another adult homosexual,

It is generally agreed that we are currently undergoing a significant transition with regard to issues impacting LGBT persons in this country. The legal terrain is changing dramatically, and the accompanying public policy issues reflect a society that is wrestling openly for the first time in U.S. history with high-profile controversies concerning the role that LGBT persons can and should be playing in daily life. Underlying every one of these controversies is an implicit but not-often-stated tension regarding the nature and extent of the right to be out.

Nowhere is this tension more evident than in our nation's educational institutions. Indeed, particularly at the K–12 level, LGBT students, teachers, and school site administrators have found themselves at the eye of the proverbial storm as school communities confront the rapidly changing realities in this area. The intensive and ongoing level of personal contact in a setting where certain values are expected to be instilled can and often does lead to high emotions and volatile confrontations. Litigation and legislation addressing these issues has increased substantially in recent years, and a growing body of relevant law has developed as a result.[c]

The material in this section includes decisions that, when taken together, comprise the First Amendment component of the right to be out for LGBT students in the public schools. It also reflects an initial inquiry into the parameters of this emerging right. Additional aspects of the inquiry appear in the Chapter 4 section on peer harassment and mistreatment (addressing the equal protection component of the right to be out), the gender equity section of Chapter 5 (addressing transgender issues in a gender equity context), the *religion, morality, and values* chapters (addressing the debates regarding competing visions of "morality" and the contours of the "wall of separation" between church and state), and the overview of the rights of educators in Chapter 11 (addressing both academic freedom issues and employment discrimination concerns).

possessing a homophile publication, writing about homosexuality without disapproval, displaying pictures of two people of the same sex in intimate positions, [or]... operating a lesbian or gay bar... Misdemeanor arrests for sex-related vagrancy or disorderly conduct offenses meant that the homosexual might have her or his name published in the local newspaper, would probably lose her or his job, and in several states would have to register as a sex offender. If the homosexual were not a citizen, she or he would likely be deported. If the homosexual were a professional—teacher, lawyer, doctor, mortician, beautician—she or he could lose the certification needed to practice that profession.

LGBT persons of color have often faced additional challenges above and beyond those described above. *See, e.g.,* JOHN D'EMI-LIO, LOST PROPHET: THE LIFE AND TIMES OF BAYARD RUSTIN, Free Press (2003); BLACK LIKE US: A CENTURY OF LESBIAN, GAY, AND BISEXUAL AFRICAN AMERICAN FICTION, Cleis Press (Devon W. Carbado et al. eds., 2002); *see also* REINALDO ARENAS, ANTES QUE ANO-CHEZCA (BEFORE NIGHT FALLS), Penguin Books (1992); RUSSELL LEONG, ASIAN AMERICAN SEXUALITIES: DIMENSIONS OF THE GAY AND LESBIAN EXPERIENCE, Routledge (1995).

c. For examples of an early identification of relevant principles in this area, see, for example, Kenneth L. Karst, *Myths of Identity: Individual and Group Portraits of Race and Sexual Orientation,* 43 UCLA L. REV. 263, 360 (1995); Kenji Yoshino, *Covering,* 111 YALE L.J. 769 (2002). For an in-depth examination of these developments and their implications, see STUART BIEGEL, The Right to Be Out, STANFORD UNIVERSITY PRESS (forthcoming 2007).

FRICKE v. LYNCH

491 F. Supp. 381 (D. R.I. 1980).

PETTINE, CHIEF JUDGE.

Most of the time, a young man's choice of a date for the senior prom is of no great interest to anyone other than the student, his companion, and, perhaps, a few of their classmates. But in Aaron Fricke's case, the school authorities actively disapprove of his choice, the other students are upset, the community is abuzz, and out-of-state newspapers consider the matter newsworthy. All this fuss arises because Aaron Fricke's intended escort is another young man. Claiming that the school's refusal to allow him to bring a male escort violates his first and fourteenth amendment rights, Fricke seeks a preliminary injunction ordering the school officials to allow him to attend with a male escort.

Two days of testimony have revealed the following facts. The senior reception at Cumberland High School is a formal dinner–dance sponsored and run by the senior class. It is held shortly before graduation but is not a part of the graduation ceremonies. This year the students have decided to hold the dance at the Pleasant Valley Country Club in Sutton, Massachusetts on Friday, May 30. All seniors except those on suspension are eligible to attend the dance; no one is required to go. All students who attend must bring an escort, although their dates need not be seniors or even Cumberland High School students. Each student is asked the name of his date at the time he buys the tickets.

* * *

The seeds of the present conflict were planted a year ago when Paul Guilbert, then a junior at Cumberland High School, sought permission to bring a male escort to the junior prom. The principal, Richard Lynch (the defendant here), denied the request, fearing that student reaction could lead to a disruption at the dance and possibly to physical harm to Guilbert. The request and its denial were widely publicized and led to widespread community and student reaction adverse to Paul. Some students taunted and spit at him, and once someone slapped him; in response, principal Lynch arranged an escort system, in which Lynch or an assistant principal accompanied Paul as he went from one class to the next. No other incidents or violence occurred. Paul did not attend the prom. At that time Aaron Fricke (plaintiff here) was a friend of Paul's and supported his position regarding the dance.

This year, during or after an assembly in April in which senior class events were discussed, Aaron Fricke, a senior at Cumberland High School, decided that he wanted to attend the senior reception with a male companion. Aaron considers himself a homosexual, and has never dated girls, although he does socialize with female friends. He has never taken a girl to a school dance. Until this April, he had not "come out of the closet" by publicly acknowledging his sexual orientation.

Aaron asked principal Lynch for permission to bring a male escort, which Lynch denied. * * * Lynch gave Aaron written reasons for his action; his prime concern was the fear that a disruption would occur and Aaron or, especially, Paul would be hurt. He indicated in court that he would allow Aaron to bring a male escort if there were no threat of violence.

After Aaron filed suit in this Court, an event reported by the Rhode Island and Boston papers, a student shoved and, the next day, punched Aaron. The unprovoked, surprise assault necessitated five stitches under Aaron's right eye. The assailant was suspended for nine days. After this, Aaron was given a special parking space closer to the school doors and has been provided with an escort (principal or assistant principal) between classes. No further incidents have occurred.

This necessarily brief account does not convey the obvious concern and good faith Lynch has displayed in his handling of the matter. Lynch sincerely believes that there is a significant possibility that some students will attempt to injure Aaron and Paul if they attend the dance. Moreover, Lynch's actions in school have displayed a concern for Aaron's safety while at school. Perhaps—one cannot be at all sure—a totally different approach by Lynch might have kept the matter from reaching its present proportions, but I am convinced that Lynch's actions have stemmed—in significant part—from a concern for disruption.

Aaron contends that the school's action violates his first amendment right of association, his first amendment right to free speech, and his fourteenth amendment right to equal protection of the laws. (The equal protection claim is a "hybrid" one—that he has been treated differently than others because of the content of his communication.)

* * *

* * * [T]he proposed activity has significant expressive content. Aaron testified that he wants to go because he feels he has a right to attend and participate just like all the other students and that it would be dishonest to his own sexual identity to take a girl to the dance. He went on to acknowledge that he feels his attendance would have a certain political element and would be a statement for equal rights and human rights. * * *

Accordingly, the school's action must be judged by the standards articulated in *United States v. O'Brien* and applied in *Bonner*: (1) was the regulation within the constitutional power of the government; (2) did it further an important or substantial governmental interest; (3) was the governmental interest unrelated to the suppression of free expression; and (4) was the incidental restriction on alleged first amendment freedoms no greater than essential to the furtherance of that interest?

I need not dwell on the first two *O'Brien* requirements: the school unquestionably has an important interest in student safety and has the power to regulate students' conduct to ensure safety. As to the suppression of free expression, Lynch's testimony indicated that his personal views on homosexuality did not affect his decision, and that but for the threat of violence he would let the two young men go together. Thus the government's interest here is not in squelching a particular message because it objects to its content as such. On the other hand, the school's interest is in suppressing certain speech activity because of the reaction its message may engender. Surely this is still suppression of free expression.

It is also clear that the school's action fails to meet the last criterion set out in *O'Brien*, the requirement that the government employ the "least restrictive alternative" before curtailing speech. * * * It is, of course, impossible to guarantee that no harm will occur, no matter what measures are taken. But only one student so far has attempted to harm Aaron, and no evidence was introduced of other threats. The measures taken already, especially the escort system, have been highly effective in preventing any further problems at school. Appropriate security measures coupled with a firm, clearly communicated attitude by the administration that any disturbance will not be tolerated appear to be a realistic, and less restrictive, alternative to prohibiting Aaron from attending the dance with the date of his choice.

The analysis so far has been along traditional first amendment lines, making no real allowance for the fact that this case arises in a high school setting. The most difficult problem this controversy presents is how this setting should affect the result. *Tinker v. Des Moines Independent Community School District*, 393 U.S. 503, 89 S. Ct. 733 (1969), makes clear that high school students do not "shed their constitutional rights to freedom of speech or expression at the schoolhouse gate." * * *

It seems to me that here, not unlike in *Tinker*, the school administrators were acting on "an undifferentiated fear or apprehension of disturbance." True, Aaron was punched and then security measures were taken, but since that incident he has not been threatened with violence nor has he been attacked. There has been no disruption at the school; classes have not been cancelled, suspended, or interrupted. In short, while the defendants have perhaps shown more of a basis for fear of harm than in *Tinker*, they have failed to make a "showing" that Aaron's conduct would "materially and substantially interfere" with school discipline. *See Tinker* at 509, 89 S. Ct. at 737. However, even if the Court assumes that there is justifiable fear and that Aaron's peaceful speech leads, or may lead, to a violent reaction from others, the question remains: may the school prohibit the speech, or must it protect the speaker?

It is certainly clear that outside of the classroom the fear—however justified—of a violent reaction is not sufficient reason to restrain such speech in advance, and an actual hostile reaction is rarely an adequate basis for curtailing free speech. * * * Thus, the question here is whether the interest in school discipline and order, recognized in *Tinker*, requires a different approach.

After considerable thought and research, I have concluded that even a legitimate interest in school discipline does not outweigh a student's right to peacefully express his views in an appropriate time, place, and manner. To rule otherwise would completely subvert free speech in the schools by granting other students a "heckler's veto," allowing them to decide—through prohibited and violent methods—what speech will be heard. The first amendment does not tolerate mob rule by unruly school children. This conclusion is bolstered by the fact that any disturbance here, however great, would not interfere with the main business of school—education. No classes or school work would be affected; at the very worst an optional social event, conducted by the students for their own enjoyment, would be marred. In such a context, the school does have an obligation to take reasonable measures to protect and foster free speech, not to stand helpless before unauthorized student violence.

* * *

The present case is so difficult because the Court is keenly sensitive to the testimony regarding the concerns of a possible disturbance, and of physical harm to Aaron or Paul. However, I am convinced that meaningful security measures are possible, and the first amendment requires that such steps be taken to protect—rather than to stifle—free expression. Some may feel that Aaron's attendance at the reception and the message he will thereby convey is trivial compared to other social debates, but to engage in this kind of a weighing in process is to make the content-based evaluation forbidden by the first amendment.

As to the other concern raised by *Tinker*, some people might say that Aaron Fricke's conduct would infringe the rights of the other students, and is thus unprotected by *Tinker*. This view is misguided, however. Aaron's conduct is quiet and peaceful; it demands no response from others and—in a crowd of some five hundred people—can be easily ignored. Any disturbance that might interfere with the rights of others would be caused by those students who resort to violence, not by Aaron and his companion, who do not want a fight.

Because the free speech claim is dispositive, I find it unnecessary to reach the plaintiff's right of association argument or to deal at length with his equal protection claim. I find that the plaintiff has established a probability of success on the merits and has shown irreparable harm; accordingly his request for a preliminary injunction is hereby granted.

* * *

COLIN v. ORANGE UNIFIED SCH. DIST.

83 F. Supp. 2d 1135 (C.D. Cal. 2000).

CARTER, DISTRICT JUDGE.

* * *

In late August 1999, Anthony Colin ("Colin") and his friend Shannon MacMillan ("MacMillan") decided to form a "Gay–Straight Alliance

Club" ("GSA") at their school, El Modena High School in Orange, California. Colin, a tenth-grade student, had the idea after Matthew Shepherd, a young man from Wyoming, died after being brutally assaulted due to his homosexuality. Colin testified that he wanted to form the club to promote acceptance among and for gay and straight students at the school. After discussing the idea with friends and family, Colin submitted a club constitution in compliance with school policy during the week of September 7, 1999, the first week of the school year.[a] * * *

* * * Colin asked Mrs. Maryina Herde, a drama and English teacher at the school, to serve as the faculty advisor and she accepted. * * *

Colin and the other founders of the Gay–Straight Alliance had reason to believe that their application would be accepted. Consistent with the policy of the Orange Unified School District's Board of Education ("the Board"), their high school had a policy of allowing student-initiated groups to meet on school grounds during lunch period and to use school facilities to publicize their meetings and activities[b] * * *

[The application was denied, however, and Plaintiffs brought this action alleging violations of the Equal Access Act, 20 U.S.C. §§ 4071–4074, the Civil Rights Act of 1871, 42 U.S.C. § 1983, and the Fourteenth Amendment to the United States Constitution. Plaintiffs sought declaratory relief under 28 U.S.C. §§ 2201–2202.]

II. Analysis

A. The Equal Access Act

* * * Under the [U.S. Equal Access Act of 1984], schools that allow student groups whose purpose is not directly related to the curriculum to meet on school grounds during lunch or after school cannot deny other student groups access to the school due to the content of the students' proposed discussions. * * *

* * * As Justice Kennedy pointed out, "one of the consequences of the statute, as we now interpret it, is that clubs of a most controversial character might have access to the student life of high schools that in the past have given official recognition only to clubs of a more conventional

---

a. The mission statement for the club, written by MacMillan, a twelfth grade student, stated the following:

Public schools have an obligation to provide an equal opportunity for all students to receive an education in a safe, nonhostile, nondiscriminatory environment. Our goal in this organization is to raise public awareness and promote tolerance by providing a safe forum for discussion of issues related to sexual orientation and homophobia. We wish to stress the need for people to put aside their personal prejudice and agree to treat everyone with respect when the situation calls for it. We invite ALL students, gay or straight, to join us in discussions, field trips, lectures, and social activities that

will counterattack unfair treatment and prejudice. We respect privacy and require NO one to make disclosures regarding his or her own sexual orientation. This is not a sexual issue, it is about gaining support and promoting tolerance and respect for all students.

b. A recent list of the clubs on campus, of which there were 38 in total, included the following noncurriculum related student groups: the Asian Club, Black Student Union, Christian Club, Gentlemen's Club, Girls' League, Koinonia (for Catholic students), MECHA (Movimiento Estudiantil Chicano de Aztlan), and Red Cross/Key Club.

kind." * * * Due to the First Amendment, Congress passed an "Equal Access Act" when it wanted to permit religious speech on school campuses. It did not pass a "Religious Speech Access Act" or an "Access for All Students Except Gay Students Act" because to do so would be unconstitutional.[c]

It is against the backdrop of this federal law that this Court must decide whether the locally elected Orange Unified School District Board of Education can vote to deny recognition by the school to one club out of many that have sought to meet on campus.

* * *

C. Plaintiffs Have a Strong Likelihood of Succeeding on the Merits of their Claim for Violation of the Equal Access Act

In order for Plaintiffs to show a likely violation of the Equal Access Act, they must show that El Modena High School accepts federal funds, has a "limited open forum," and has discriminated against students wishing to conduct a meeting within the open forum due to the content of speech that will take place at the proposed meetings. * * * It is undisputed that the Board accepts federal funding.

* * *

[In addition, the Court found that the Board had established a "limited open forum" at El Modena High because it had granted "an offering to or opportunity for one or more noncurriculum related student groups to meet on school premises during noninstructional time." 20 U.S.C. § 4071(b). Modena "is therefore precluded from discriminating against student groups seeking access to that open forum."]

2. The Gay–Straight Alliance is a "Noncurriculum Related Student Group"

Defendants contend that the Gay–Straight Alliance is not protected by the Act because it is related to the curriculum. Specifically, Board Member Kathy Ward stated in her motion that "the District has a curriculum on sex education, which deals with human sexuality, sexual behavior and consequences, and prevention of sexually transmitted diseases. To the extent that the proposed GSA club intends to discuss these issues related to sexual orientation, the club is a 'curriculum related' club, not covered by the Equal Access Act." * * *

According to Colin, Zetin, and the Mission Statement of the Gay–Straight Alliance, however, they do not intend to discuss topics that are covered under the sex education curriculum. According to the Mission Statement, their goal was to talk about "tolerance," "issues related to sexual orientation and homophobia," the need to "treat everyone with

---

c. *See* Bd. of Educ. v. Mergens, 496 U.S. 226 (1990), where the U.S. Supreme Court agreed with the plaintiff that the Equal Access Act, 20 U.S.C. §§ 4071–4074 (2000), prohibits a high school "from denying a student religious group permission to meet on school premises during noninstructional time," and that the Act, so construed, does not violate the Establishment Clause of the First Amendment. In so doing, the Court set forth guidelines for schools to follow pursuant to the Act.

respect," and counterattacking "unfair treatment and prejudice." The Mission Statement emphasizes, in a one-sentence paragraph at the end, that "[t]his is not a sexual issue, it is about gaining support and promoting tolerance and respect for all students." Both Colin and Zetin state in their declarations that the club did not propose to talk about the things that were covered in sex education. Furthermore, none of the classes at El Modena covered discrimination and harassment based on sexual orientation. Zetin testified that "the word homosexual is never even mentioned in our classes." Colin testified that the club was about "acceptance" for gay and straight people, and about helping people deal with being called "fag" or "dyke." Both Colin and Zetin laughed on the stand at the thought of the group discussing the "physiology of the reproductive system" and the other issues covered in Health class. What the students *did* want to talk about is best expressed in their own words. Echoing the Mission Statement, Zetin testified "I want us to talk about the experiences that gay, lesbian and bisexual kids go through in their everyday lives such as harassment, coming out of the closet or telling people that they are gay: the fear and the emotions such as self-hatred or denial that a lot of kids go through and the harassment they get and how to deal with that."

    * * *

    * * * A curriculum-related student group is "one that has more than just a tangential or attenuated relationship to courses offered by the school" and "must at least have a more direct relationship to the curriculum than a religious or political club would have." Thus, if a Christian Club prays for abstinence, it is still "noncurriculum related" even though abstinence is a topic covered in the curriculum. Indeed, Zetin testified that she believed in abstinence. Just as with the Christian Club, if discussion of abstinence were to arise at one of the meetings of the Gay–Straight Alliance, the club would still be "noncurriculum related."

    * * *

Finally, even if the Court were to find at trial that the subject matter of the Gay–Straight Alliance was actually taught in a regularly offered course at El Modena, the Equal Access Act does not then allow the Board to withhold official recognition of the group. Whether or not a school recognizes a "noncurriculum related student group" merely determines whether or not the Act's obligations are triggered. Once a school recognizes any such group, it has created a "limited open forum" and the school is prohibited "from denying equal access to *any* other student group on the basis of the content of that group's speech." Contrary to the Board's interpretation of the Act, the Board may not foreclose access to the "limited open forum" merely by labeling a group curriculum-related. The only meetings that schools subject to the Act can prohibit are those that would "materially and substantially interfere with the orderly conduct of educational activities within the school." So long as the Board has a "limited open forum" at El Modena and allows any "noncurriculum related" student groups to meet, it can not prohibit the Gay–Straight Alliance even if its meetings directly relate to the curriculum. Instead, the Board will have to show that meetings will "materially and substantially interfere with the orderly" instruction of students. The Board will not likely be able to show that groups of students discussing homophobia and acceptance of all students regardless of sexual orientation somehow serves as a major disruption to the education of students. Indeed, this club is actually being formed to avoid the disruptions to education that can take place when students are harassed based on sexual orientation.

* * *

The Board Members may be uncomfortable about students discussing sexual orientation and how all students need to accept each other, whether gay or straight. As in *Tinker,* however, when the school administration was uncomfortable with students wearing symbols of protest against the Vietnam War, Defendants can not censor the students' speech to avoid discussions on campus that cause them discomfort or represent an unpopular viewpoint. In order to comply with the Equal Access Act, Anthony Colin, Heather Zetin, and the members of the Gay–Straight Alliance must be permitted access to the school campus in the same way that the District provides access to all clubs, including the Christian Club and the Red Cross/Key Club. Plaintiffs have shown a strong likelihood of succeeding on their claim that Defendants have violated their rights under the Equal Access Act.

D. First Amendment Claim

In finding that the District has likely violated the Equal Access Act, the Court need not reach Plaintiffs' First Amendment claim.

E. Plaintiffs Will Be Irreparably Injured Absent Preliminary Relief

"The loss of First Amendment freedoms, for even minimal periods of time unquestionably constitutes irreparable injury." * * *

Plaintiffs have been injured not only by the Board's excessive delay, but also by the inability to effectively address the hardships they encounter at school every day. Some students at El Modena do not even feel safe using the school's restrooms. Zetin is often harassed by students calling her a "dyke." While such harms may not be cured by a preliminary injunction, "gay-straight alliance clubs provide a safe place for students ... [and] create a respectful environment where students realize that they have a place at the table ..." * * *

Granting a preliminary injunction would also be in the public interest. Recent California legislation confirms that it is state public policy to prevent discrimination on the basis of sexual orientation. In passing the California Student Safety and Violence Prevention Act of 2000, the California Legislature found that "[v]iolence is the number one cause of death for young people in California and has become a public health problem of epidemic proportion" and "[t]he fastest growing, violent crime in California is hate crime." The Legislature felt that "it is incumbent upon us to ensure that all students attending public school in California are protected from potentially violent discrimination." The California Penal Code already contained a prohibition on hate crimes based on sexual orientation. In passing ch. 587, however, the Legislature added sexual orientation to the list of prohibited forms of discrimination in public schools. In addition to protecting students from hate crimes, the Legislature was also concerned about suicide. * * *

By adding sexual orientation to the list of prohibited forms of in-school discrimination, the Legislature could specifically target the teen suicide rate. According to a Center for Disease Control and Prevention analysis of Massachusetts statistics in 1997, gay students were more than six times as likely to have tried suicide as straight students. This injunction therefore is not just about student pursuit of ideas and tolerance for diverse viewpoints. As any concerned parent would understand, this case may involve the protection of life itself. Since the Gay–Straight Alliance seeks to end discrimination on the basis of sexual orientation, a preliminary injunction requiring the Board to recognize the club would be consistent with state public policy and in the public interest.

In addition to demonstrating a strong likelihood that Defendants have violated the Equal Access Act, Plaintiffs have also shown a significant threat of irreparable injury, greater hardship to Plaintiffs than Defendants, and that the public interest favors granting the injunction. The Court finds that a preliminary injunction is warranted under these circumstances.

BOYD COUNTY HIGH SCH. GAY STRAIGHT ALLIANCE v. BOARD OF ED.

258 F. Supp. 2d 667 (E.D. Ky. 2003).

BUNNING, DISTRICT JUDGE.

I. INTRODUCTION

* * * Plaintiffs claim that Defendants violated their rights under the Equal Access Act, 20 U.S.C. § 4071, *et seq.,* and their First Amendment rights of expression and association by denying the Boyd County High School Gay Straight Alliance the same access to school facilities given to other student groups. * * *

Plaintiffs seek a preliminary injunction requiring Defendants to offer them the same opportunities given to other student groups at Boyd County High School. Plaintiffs assert that affording them the same opportunities includes authorization to meet at school during noninstructional time, to use the school hallways and bulletin boards for posters, and to use the intercom to make club announcements during home room.

* * *

II. FINDINGS OF FACT

* * *

3.   In January or February of 2002, students at BCHS circulated a petition to create a GSA Club. * * * The purpose of the GSA Club is to provide students with a safe haven to talk about anti-gay harassment and to work together to promote tolerance, understanding and acceptance of one another regardless of sexual orientation. * * *

4.   Anti-gay harassment, homophobia, and use of anti-gay epithets have been and continue to be serious problems at BCHS.[1] One student dropped out of BCHS because of harassment based on sexual orientation and another student dropped out because of both anti-gay harassment at school as well as problems at home. * * *

III. ANALYSIS

* * *

A. *Plaintiffs' Likelihood of Success on the Merits*

* * *

Although the majority of cases defining and interpreting the Equal Access Act involve requests by religious groups to meet on school property during noninstructional time, several district courts have specifically addressed the more contentious issue of permitting gay rights groups to meet during noninstructional time. For example, in *Colin v. Orange Unified School District,* 83 F. Supp. 2d 1135, 1147 (C.D. Cal. 2000) the court * * * ruled that the GSA Club had been denied access to the school's limited open forum, holding this denial is "exactly the type of content-based restriction that is forbidden by the Equal Access Act." The court granted the injunction, ordering the school district to provide equal access to the GSA Club.

[Also,] * * * [i]n *East High Gay/Straight Alliance v. Board of Education of Salt Lake City School Disrict,* a GSA club was granted injunctive relief, thereby permitting it to meet at the defendant high school. * * *

* * * [H]aving found that the Defendants [in the case at hand] are subject to the EAA by virtue of permitting at least one noncurriculum-related group to meet or use the facilities at BCHS, in order to properly exclude the GSA from having equal access as required by the EAA, Defendants must show that the GSA Club will "materially and substantially interfere with the orderly conduct of educational opportunities

---

1. One example of the harassment includes students in Plaintiff Fugett's English class stating that they needed to take all the fucking faggots out in the back woods and kill them. This occurred in October, 2002. During a basketball game in January 2003, students with megaphones chanted at Plaintiff Reese: "faggot-kisser," "GSA" and "fag-lover." On a regular basis, students call out "homo," "fag," and "queer" behind Plaintiff McClelland's back as he walks in the hallway between classes. On April 10, 2002, during an observance of National Day of Silence, about 25 participants sat in a circle in the front lobby of BCHS. During the lunch hour observance, protesters used anti-gay epithets and threw things at them.

within the school," 20 U.S.C. § 4071(c)(4), or will limit the school's ability "to maintain order and discipline on school premises, to protect the well-being of students and faculty . . . "

* * *

In this case, it is obvious that the proposed creation of a GSA Club at BCHS has caused some level of uproar within the local community. It is equally apparent that several school administrators and board members received numerous complaints and questions from parents who were concerned about the approval of the GSA Club and how that approval might affect the safety of their children. Additionally, there were two student protests regarding the approval of the GSA Club, one on October 30, 2002, and the other on November 4, 2002. In short, the disruption to which Defendants were responding when they voted to ban all clubs was caused by GSA opponents, not GSA Club members themselves.

Although there is a relative paucity of case law interpreting what level of disruption is necessary before a school, subject to the obligations of the EAA can deny equal access without violating the Act, a review of what little case law does exist is helpful. The leading case on attempts to suppress speech within the high school setting is *Tinker v. Des Moines Independent Community School Dist.*, 393 U.S. 503, 89 S. Ct. 733 (1969).

* * *

Refusing to allow a "heckler's veto" to justify suppression of student speech, the Court in *Tinker* was careful to focus on whether "*engaging in the forbidden conduct* would materially and substantially interfere with the requirements of appropriate discipline," *id.* at 538, 89 S. Ct. 733 (emphasis added), and concluded that the protesting students' speech was protected because it was "entirely divorced from actually or potentially disruptive conduct *by those participating in it.*"

* * *

Incorporation of the *Tinker* rule into 20 U.S.C. § 4071(f) means that a school may not deny equal access to a student group because student and community opposition to the group substantially interferes with the school's ability to maintain order and discipline, even though equal access is not required if the student group itself substantially interferes with the school's ability to maintain order and discipline. * * * [T]he Equal Access Act permits Defendants to prohibit Plaintiffs from meeting on equal terms with the noncurriculum-related student groups that have been permitted to meet * * * only upon a showing that Plaintiffs' *own* disruptive activities have interfered with Defendants ability to maintain order and discipline. * * * As addressed herein, Defendants have made no such showing in this case.

* * *

While Defendants argue that these protests and the public uproar surrounding the GSA Club have materially and substantially interfered with the orderly conduct of educational activities at BCHS, limited their authority to maintain order and discipline, and limited their ability to protect the well-being of students and faculty, the facts simply do not support such a conclusion. Other than one incident, there have been no documented instances of disruptions caused by GSA members or GSA supporters. * * *

As the district court stated in *Colin, supra:*

The Board Members may be uncomfortable about students discussing sexual orientation and how all students need to accept each other, whether gay or straight. As in *Tinker,* however, when the school administration was uncomfortable with students wearing symbols of protest against the Vietnam War, Defendants cannot censor the students' speech to avoid discussions on campus that cause them discomfort or represent an unpopular viewpoint. 83 F. Supp. 2d. at 1149.

For these reasons, the Court finds that Plaintiffs have shown a strong likelihood of succeeding on their claim that Defendants violated their rights under the Equal Access Act.

* * *

[The motion for a preliminary injunction was granted.]

Notes

1. Plaintiffs challenging their school district's decision to ban gay-straight alliances tend to prevail under the Equal Access Act. In addition to *Colin* and *Boyd, see, e.g., East High Gay/Straight Alliance v. Board of Education of Salt Lake City Sch. Dist.,* 81 F. Supp. 2d 1166 (D. Utah 1999); *East High School Prism Club v. Seidel,* 95 F. Supp. 2d 1239 (D. Utah 2000); *Gay-Straight Alliance Network v. Visalia Unified School District,* 262 F.Supp.2d 1088 (E.D. Cal. 2001); *Franklin Cent. Gay/Straight Alliance v. Franklin Township Community School Corporation,* 2002 WL 32097530 (S.D. Ind. 2002). *But see Caudillo v. Lubbock Independent School District,* 311 F. Supp. 2d 550 (N.D. Tex. 2004), a recent exception to this trend. The *Caudillo* court found the other cases to be distinguishable, in part, because it was "unable to find that any of the cases involved a school that maintained an abstinence-only policy and banned any discussion of sexual activity on its campuses."

2. LGBT students in many of the gay-straight alliance cases have benefited from prior efforts by religious students and their affiliated organizations, who lobbied for a federal Equal Access Act and then prevailed in *Board of Education v. Mergens,* the major case construing the parameters of the Act. These prior efforts played a major role in establishing precedent that gay plaintiffs could rely upon in *Colin.*

3. The reasoning in many of these cases also parallels the reasoning found in the higher education cases of the 1970s and 1980s, where the federal courts ruled, consistently, in favor of gay and lesbian students who were prohibited from starting gay student clubs on campus.

HENKLE v. GREGORY

150 F. Supp. 2d 1067 (D. Nev. 2001).

McQUAID, UNITED STATES MAGISTRATE JUDGE.

BACKGROUND

Plaintiff, Derek R. Henkle, began his freshman year, in 1994, at Galena High School ("Galena") after skipping the eighth grade. In Fall 1995, Plaintiff appeared on the local access channel's program "Set Free" where he participated in a discussion about gay high school students and their experiences. From this point on, the alleged harassment began. Plaintiff alleges that, during school hours and on school property, he endured constant harassment, assaults, intimidation, and discrimination by other students because he is gay and male and school officials, after being notified of the continuous harassment, failed to take any action.

One incident of alleged harassment occurred in Fall 1995. Several students approached Plaintiff, on Galena property, calling him "fag," "butt pirate," "fairy," and "homo." They lassoed him around the neck and suggested dragging him behind a truck. Plaintiff escaped to a classroom and used an internal phone to report the incident to Defendant, Assistant Vice Principal Hausauer. After waiting nearly two hours, Defendant Hausauer arrived and responded with laughter. Defendant, Principal Gregory, was also made aware of the incident, but they took no action against the alleged harassers despite knowing their identities.

Another alleged incident occurred in Plaintiff's English class. Students in the class continuously wrote the word "fag" on the whiteboard and sent him notes calling him "fag." Students also drew sexually explicit pictures and called Plaintiff's attention to them. Defendant Rende, Plaintiff's English teacher, was allegedly aware of the harassment and identity of the harassers. Despite this knowledge, Defendant Rende chose to tell Plaintiff that his sexuality was a private matter that should be kept to himself, rather than end the harassment or discipline the harassers. Plaintiff alleges that Defendants Gregory and Hausauer also knew of this incident, yet did nothing to remedy the situation.

Plaintiff also faced harassment when reporting the incidents to Galena's discipline office. Several students, running by the office and shouting anti-gay epithets, threw a metal object at the Plaintiff that missed him and stuck in the wall. A school administrator witnessed this incident and a report was filed. Again, it is alleged that no investigation was made or discipline taken, despite the fact that school administrators were aware of the incident. Plaintiff suffered an emotional breakdown because of this episode.

At the end of the Fall 1995 semester, Plaintiff asked to leave Galena because he feared further harassment and assaults. Defendant Anastasio decided to transfer Plaintiff to Washoe High School ("Washoe"), an alternative high school. Plaintiff's transfer allegedly was conditioned on the fact that he keep his sexuality to himself. During Plaintiff's time at Galena, he wore buttons on his backpack that said "We are everywhere" and "Out," however, upon his transfer to Washoe, he removed the buttons.

Defendant Floyd was the Principal at Washoe during Plaintiff's tenure from January 1996 to May 1996. Defendant Floyd, on several occasions, allegedly told Plaintiff to keep quiet about his sexual orientation and during one meeting with Plaintiff, Floyd told him to "stop acting like a fag." On some occasions, Plaintiff expressed his viewpoints and identity, but for the most part kept them to himself. Finally, Plaintiff requested a transfer because of the lack of educational opportunities at Washoe. Plaintiff alleges that Floyd initially told him the transfer was not possible because Plaintiff was openly gay and a traditional high school would not be appropriate.

Plaintiff was subsequently transferred to Wooster High School ("Wooster") and, once again, prior to the transfer, was told by Floyd to keep his sexuality to himself. When Plaintiff's classmates, at Wooster, learned his identity and the fact that he was gay, they allegedly harassed and intimidated him during school hours and on school property. Plaintiff reported the incidents several times, however, he alleges the administration took no action.

One particular incident of inaction occurred when Plaintiff was assaulted at Wooster. Several students approached him shouting gay epithets, and one student punched him in the face, calling him "bitch." The other students encouraged the attack. School police, Defendants Ramilo and Selby, allegedly witnessed the attack, but did nothing. In fact, Plaintiff alleges Defendants Ramilo and Selby discouraged him from calling the assault a hate crime and from reporting it to the Reno Police Department. Furthermore, Defendants refused to arrest the attacker despite knowing the identity.

After this incident, Defendants Floyd and Anastasio agreed that Plaintiff should be transferred back to Washoe. However, Floyd later decided not to accept Plaintiff at Washoe despite having room for him. Instead, Defendants placed Plaintiff in an adult education program at Truckee Meadows Community College, thus making Plaintiff ineligible for a high school diploma because he was no longer enrolled in a public high school.

* * *

II. Violation of Plaintiff's First Amendment Rights

Plaintiff's Third and Fourth Claims for Relief allege Defendants violated his First Amendment rights by censoring, chilling, and deterring him from exercising his right to freedom of speech and by retaliating against him when he did exercise his rights.

* * *

In examining a First Amendment retaliation claim, courts engage in [a] three part inquiry. For the first two prongs of the inquiry, plaintiff must demonstrate: (1) the speech at issue was constitutionally protected; and (2) the speech was a substantial or motivating factor in the adverse action. If plaintiff satisfies this burden, the burden shifts to the defendants to demonstrate they would have taken the same actions against plaintiff, even in the absence of his protected conduct.

In light of the previous discussion, Plaintiff satisfied element one by alleging that his speech was constitutionally protected [under *Tinker*]. Thus, we will turn our attention to element two.

Plaintiff alleges several actions and/or inactions by Defendants that warrant the inference that the actions and/or inactions were retaliatory in nature. He alleges that after his appearance on "Set Free" where he participated in a discussion about gay high school students and their experiences, the harassment began at Galena and, ultimately, resulted in his transfer to Washoe, an alternative high school. Plaintiff also alleges, rather than disciplining the harassers, Defendants treated him as the problem and told him numerous times to keep his sexuality to himself. Plaintiff further alleges, his first transfer from Galena to Washoe was conditioned on the fact that he keep his sexuality to himself. In an effort to comply with this request, he removed buttons, pertaining to his sexuality, from his backpack. Moreover, Defendants transferred Plaintiff, a gifted and talented student, to Washoe, and alternative education program. Furthermore, when he asked for a transfer from Washoe because of lack of educational opportunities, Defendant Floyd told him the transfer was not possible because he was openly gay and a traditional high school was not appropriate, but was eventually transferred to Wooster. And finally, after Plaintiff continued to express his sexuality at Wooster, he was denied a transfer back to Washoe, and instead was transferred to an adult education program where he could not receive a high school diploma because he was no longer enrolled in a public high school.

Thus, at this stage of the proceedings, Plaintiff has made sufficient allegations, that his constitutionally protected speech was a substantial motivating factor in adverse action directed at him. Therefore, this court cannot say as a matter of law that Plaintiff failed to state a claim for retaliation for exercising his First Amendment rights.

　　　　* * *

In *Tinker,* the Supreme Court clearly established that students in public schools have the right to freedom of speech and expression. This is a broad right that would encompass the right of a high school student to express his sexuality. * * *

PROBLEM 12: Jamie and the Coalition Revisited

Assume the same facts and circumstances that were set forth in Problem 10, above, except that Jamie is openly gay and the organization is not the CRI but the GSCRI (the Gay–Straight Coalition to Resist Social Indoctri-nation). What additional arguments might plaintiffs consider putting forth under the circumstances? Would their chances of success improve as a result? Why or why not?

PROBLEM 13: The Right to Be Out and Its Implications

A.   Parameters of the Right to Be Out

Under recent rulings addressing the rights of LGBT students, what examples of student expressive activity are now permitted that may not have been permitted 5–10 years ago? What are the obligations of school site educators, at a minimum, in this regard?

B.   Responsibilities of LGBT Students under the Right to Be Out

Every right has its accompanying responsibilities. What responsibilities of LGBT students, if any, can be discerned under the law in this context? What responsibilities exist, or should exist, as a matter of policy?

C.   Limits on the Right to Be Out

How far does the right to be out go? What examples of expressive activity might reasonably be prohibited? Are there concrete rules that can be identified in this regard?

D.   Curriculum and Professional Development Which Would Address the Mistreatment of LGBT Students and Also Remain Sensitive to the Religious Views of Many Americans

In *Lawrence v. Texas*, 539 U.S. 558, 123 S.Ct. 2472 (2003), Justice Kennedy notes that many people still have "profound and deep" convictions based on interpretations of "ethical and moral principles" that lead them to disapprove in some way of LGBT persons, their respective "lifestyles," etc. But, Kennedy explains, "[t]he issue is whether the majority may use the power of the State to enforce these views on the whole society. . . . Our obligation is to define the liberty of all, not to mandate our own moral code." Justice O'Connor, concurring in the decision, adds even stronger language in this context. "Moral disapproval of this group," she writes, "is . . . insuffi-cient. . . . we have never held that moral disapproval, without any other asserted state interest, is a sufficient rationale to justify a law that discrimi-nates among groups of persons." This conclusion in a Supreme Court decision is in many ways unprecedented.

Still, *Lawrence* does not prohibit efforts of educators to factor in the religious views of the community—as long as existing rights under the law are not violated. In light of this, is there some way that school districts can address the mistreatment of LGBT students in the schools through curricu-lum changes and teacher/administrator professional development and at the same time remain sensitive to the religious views of many Americans? *See infra,* Chapter 9, for additional material relating to this inquiry.

E. HIGHER EDUCATION "FREEDOM OF EXPRESSION" CONTROVERSIES GENERALLY

PROBLEM 14: The Alistaire & Georgina Jones Cases

This hypothetical takes place (basically) at public educational institutions in the fictional State of Eldorado.

Early in the fall semester, Alistaire Jones—who had covered campus religious issues at the University of Golden Galleon (UGG) as a freshman cub reporter the previous year—began writing a weekly column on world events. Almost immediately, he chose to focus on the events in Abscella and the interrelated, often-violent disputes regarding land, culture, and religion.

(Abscella is a fictional region that had been controlled by an authoritarian Communist government from 1945 to 1989. At the end of the Cold War, five separate countries had been formed in the region, but three of these countries contained combinations of two ethnic groups (Group A & Group B) that had been at war on and off for eight centuries. While most of the people in Group A were nominal followers of Religion A, 5–10 percent were highly religious and followed fundamentalist teachings which—among other things—promised the entire region of Abscella to them. Most of the people in Group B followed Religion B, but 10–15 percent were highly religious and followed fundamentalist teachings which, among other things, promised eternal paradise to anyone who was killed defending Abscella from "infidels.")

Alistaire, whose mother had been born in Abscella and had been raised as a devout member of Religion B, began to take up the cause of Group B in his columns. Many letters soon appeared in response to Alistaire's writings, some laudatory, but many others angry and emotional. (UGG was home to the largest percentage of students of Abscellan descent in the entire USA).

In response to the letters, Alistaire's columns took on an even more strident tone, and also became more religious in nature. He urged fellow members of Religion B to stand up for their land and their religion, and referred to members of Religion A as infidels. After several of these columns, the faculty journalism advisor called Alistaire into his office and asked him to tone down the columns. Alistaire sat quietly and listened, but then went out and wrote another column that was even more strident. In the column, dated November 8th, he wrote that all self-respecting citizens of the world—upon learning the truth—will learn why members of Group B grow to hate members of Group A and view them as "the animals that they are." He urged student members of Group B to stand up to student members of Religion A, and to use "whatever means might be necessary" to uphold the honor of Religion B.

The next day, Alistaire was informed that his column would be discontinued. He resigned from the *Daily Explorer* staff and proceeded to post all his Abscella-related columns on a new Web site, which was situated on the university server. He was determined to continue writing articles, and planned to "publish" them on the Web.

Two days later, a fundamentalist member of Religion A shot at a group of western tourists in Abscella, killing 25 and injuring 32 others. On November 12th, three fundamentalist members of Religion B strapped explosives to their bodies and entered a shopping mall in a crowded commercial area of Abscella populated almost exclusively by members of Religion A. The explosives were detonated, and hundreds of people were killed. On campus, several fights broke out among students from the two groups, and a number of students were arrested.

On November 14th, Alistaire's cousin Georgina—who attended Sir Francis Drake High School—was caught downloading and printing Alistaire's November 8th article. She was suspended for three days under a school policy that prohibited "the possession and/or dissemination of hate-related literature in school."

On November 15th, Alistaire wrote a new "column," which was clearly his most strident and emotional piece to date. In powerful and highly articulate prose, he wrote approvingly of the suicide bombers and called their actions "an integral part of our holy war against a people of unacceptable moral character who practice a religion of depravity." He urged members of Religion B "wherever in the world they might be located, to fight ceaselessly until our land has been ethnically and religiously cleansed and our temple is rebuilt."

After receiving numerous complaints, the campus network administrator notified Alistaire that—pursuant to the university's acceptable use policy—his Internet access privileges would be suspended for the year and his Web site would be taken down. But before it could be taken down, self-styled "computer commandos" from Group A—infuriated after finding Alistaire's columns posted online—hacked into the university computer system and disrupted operations for several hours before all systems could be restored. During the time that the system was down, previous records for three student patients at the campus medical center were unobtainable, and incorrect medication was administered to all three. As a result, one of the students lapsed into a coma.

Predictably, numerous lawsuits were filed as a result of these events, under a variety of legal principles and theories.

A.   In the free speech area, assume that Alistaire and Georgina—represented by the ACLU—file separate lawsuits against their respective educational institutions. Alistaire is prepared to argue that the university unconstitutionally restricted his speech on the basis of its content, and that no recognized exceptions apply. Georgina is prepared to argue that her First Amendment rights were violated, and further, that the district's hate speech policy is in and of itself unconstitutional. What contentions should be set forth by the respective parties? What result?

B.   What if Alistare was a K–12 student and all these events (minus campus medical center incidents) took place at the high school level instead of at the university? Would the legal result be the same? Should the legal result be the same?

HEALY v. JAMES

408 U.S. 169, 92 S.Ct. 2338 (1972).

MR. JUSTICE POWELL delivered the opinion of the Court.

This case [arises] out of a denial by a state college of official recognition to a group of students who desired to form a local chapter of Students for a Democratic Society (SDS) * * *.

I.

We mention briefly at the outset the setting in 1969–1970. A climate of unrest prevailed on many college campuses in this country. There had been widespread civil disobedience on some campuses, accompanied by the seizure of buildings, vandalism, and arson. Some colleges had been shut down altogether, while at others files were looted and manuscripts destroyed. SDS chapters on some of those campuses had been a catalytic force during this period. Although the causes of campus disruption were many and complex, one of the prime consequences of such activities was the denial of the lawful exercise of First Amendment rights to the majority of students by the few. Indeed, many of the most cherished characteristics long associated with institutions of higher learning appeared to be endangered. Fortunately, with the passage of time, a calmer atmosphere and greater maturity now pervade our campuses. Yet, it was in this climate of earlier unrest that this case arose.

Petitioners are students attending Central Connecticut State College (CCSC), a state-supported institution of higher learning * * *.

II.

At the outset we note that state colleges and universities are not enclaves immune from the sweep of the First Amendment. "It can hardly be argued that either students or teachers shed their constitutional rights to freedom of speech or expression at the schoolhouse gate." *Tinker v. Des Moines Independent School District*, 393 U.S. 503, 506 (1969). Of course, as Mr. Justice Fortas made clear in *Tinker*, First Amendment rights must always be applied "in light of the special characteristics of the ... environment" in the particular case. And, where state-operated educational institutions are involved, this Court has long recognized "the need for affirming the comprehensive authority of the States and of school officials, consistent with fundamental constitutional safeguards, to prescribe and control conduct in the schools." Yet, the precedents of this Court leave no room for the view that, because of the acknowledged need for order, First Amendment protections should apply with less force on college compuses than in the community at large. Quite to the contrary, "[t]he vigilant protection of constitutional freedoms is nowhere more vital than in the community of American schools." The college classroom with its surrounding environs is peculiarly the "marketplace of ideas," and we break no new constitutional ground in reaffirming this Nation's dedication to safeguarding academic freedom.

Among the rights protected by the First Amendment is the right of individuals to associate to further their personal beliefs. While the freedom of association is not explicitly set out in the Amendment, it has long been held to be implicit in the freedoms of speech, assembly, and petition. There can be no doubt that denial of official recognition, without justification, to college organizations burdens or abridges that associational right. The primary impediment to free association flowing from nonrecognition is the denial of use of campus facilities for meetings and other appropriate purposes. The practical effect of nonrecognition was demonstrated in this case when, several days after the President's decision was announced, petitioners were not allowed to hold a meeting in the campus coffee shop because they were not an approved group.

Petitioners' associational interests also were circumscribed by the denial of the use of campus bulletin boards and the school newspaper. If an organization is to remain a viable entity in a campus community in which new students enter on a regular basis, it must possess the means of communicating with these students. Moreover, the organization's ability to participate in the intellectual give and take of campus debate, and to pursue its stated purposes, is limited by denial of access to the customary media for communicating with the administration, faculty members, and other students. Such impediments cannot be viewed as insubstantial.

Respondents and the courts below appear to have taken the view that denial of official recognition in this case abridged no constitutional rights. * * *

We do not agree with the characterization by the courts below of the consequences of nonrecognition.

* * * [Also, i]t is to be remembered that the effect of the College's denial of recognition was a form of prior restraint, denying to petitioners' organization the range of associational activities described above. While a college has a legitimate interest in preventing disruption on the campus, which under circumstances requiring the safeguarding of that interest may justify such restraint, a "heavy burden" rests on the college to demonstrate the appropriateness of that action.

III.

* * * [D]iscounting the existence of a cognizable First Amendment interest and misplacing the burden of proof—require that the judgments below be reversed. But we are unable to conclude that no basis exists upon which nonrecognition might be appropriate. Indeed, based on a reasonable reading of the ambiguous facts of this case, there appears to be at least one potentially acceptable ground for a denial of recognition. Because of this ambiguous state of the record we conclude that the case should be remanded and, in an effort to provide guidance to the lower

courts upon reconsideration, it is appropriate to discuss the several bases of President James' decision. Four possible justifications for nonrecognition, all closely related, might be derived from the record and his statements. Three of those grounds are inadequate to substantiate his decision: a fourth, however, has merit.

A.

From the outset the controversy in this case has centered in large measure around the relationship, if any, between petitioners' group and the National SDS. * * *

Although this precise issue has not come before the Court heretofore, the Court has consistently disapproved governmental action imposing criminal sanctions or denying rights and privileges solely because of a citizen's association with an unpopular organization. * * *

Students for a Democratic Society, as conceded by the College and the lower courts, is loosely organized, having various factions and promoting a number of diverse social and political views only some of which call for unlawful action. Not only did petitioners proclaim their complete independence from this organization, but they also indicated that they shared only some of the beliefs its leaders have expressed. On this record it is clear that the relationship was not an adequate ground for the denial of recognition.

B.

Having concluded that petitioners were affiliated with, or at least retained an affinity for, National SDS, President James attributed what he believed to be the philosophy of that organization to the local group. He characterized the petitioning group as adhering to "some of the major tenets of the national organization," including a philosophy of violence and disruption. Understandably, he found that philosophy abhorrent. In an article signed by President James in an alumni periodical, and made a part of the record below, he announced his unwillingness to "sanction an organization that openly advocates the destruction of the very ideals and freedoms upon which the academic life is founded." He further emphasized that the petitioners' "philosophies" were "counter to the official policy of the college."

The mere disagreement of the President with the group's philosophy affords no reason to deny it recognition. As repugnant as these views may have been, especially to one with President James' responsibility, the mere expression of them would not justify the denial of First Amendment rights. Whether petitioners did in fact advocate a philosophy of 'destruction' thus becomes immaterial. The College, acting here as the instrumentality of the State, may not restrict speech or association simply because it finds the views expressed by any group to be abhorrent. * * *

C.

As the litigation progressed in the District Court, a third rationale for President James' decision—beyond the questions of affiliation and philosophy—began to emerge. His second statement, issued after the court-ordered hearing, indicates that he based rejection on a conclusion that this particular group would be a "disruptive influence at CCSC." This language was underscored in the second District Court opinion. In fact, the court concluded that the President had determined that CCSC—SDS' "prospective campus activities were likely to cause a disruptive influence at CCSC."

If this reason, directed at the organization's activities rather than its philosophy, were factually supported by the record, this Court's prior decisions would provide a basis for considering the propriety of nonrecognition. The critical line heretofore drawn for determining the permissibility of regulation is the line between mere advocacy and advocacy "directed to inciting or producing imminent lawless action and ... likely to incite or produce such action." In the context of the "special characteristics of the school environment," the power of the government to prohibit "lawless action" is not limited to acts of a criminal nature. Also prohibitable are actions which "materially and substantially disrupt the work and discipline of the school." *Tinker v. Des Moines Independent School District*, 393 U.S. at 513. Associational activities need not be tolerated where they infringe reasonable campus rules, interrupt classes, or substantially interfere with the opportunity of other students to obtain an education.

The "Student Bill of Rights" at CCSC, upon which great emphasis was placed by the President, draws precisely this distinction between advocacy and action. * * *

* * * [T]here was no substantial evidence that these particular individuals acting together would constitute a disruptive force on campus. Therefore, insofar as nonrecognition flowed from such fears, it constituted little more than the sort of "undifferentiated fear or apprehension of disturbance [which] is not enough to overcome the right to freedom of expression." *Tinker v. Des Moines Independent School District*, 393 U.S. at 508.

D.

These same references in the record to the group's equivocation regarding how it might respond to "issues of violence" and whether it could ever "envision ... interrupting a class," suggest a fourth possible reason why recognition might have been denied to these petitioners. These remarks might well have been read as announcing petitioners' unwillingness to be bound by reasonable school rules governing conduct. The College's Statement of Rights, Freedoms, and Responsibilities of Students contains, as we have seen, an explicit statement with respect to campus disruption. The regulation, carefully differentiating between advocacy and action, is a reasonable one, and petitioners have not questioned it directly. Yet their statements raise considerable question whether they intend to abide by the prohibitions contained therein.

As we have already stated in Parts B and C, the critical line for First Amendment purposes must be drawn between advocacy, which is entitled to full protection, and action, which is not. Petitioners may, if they so choose, preach the propriety of amending or even doing away with any or all campus regulations. They may not, however, undertake to flout these rules. * * *

Just as in the community at large, reasonable regulations with respect to the time, the place, and the manner in which student groups conduct their speech-related activities must be respected. A college administration may impose a requirement, such as may have been imposed in this case, that a group seeking official recognition affirm in advance its willingness to adhere to reasonable campus law. Such a requirement does not impose an impermissible condition on the students' associational rights. Their freedom to speak out, to assemble, or to petition for changes in school rules is in no sense infringed. It merely constitutes an agreement to conform with reasonable standards respecting conduct. This is a minimal requirement, in the interest of the entire academic community, of any group seeking the privilege of official recognition.

* * *

IV.

We think the above discussion establishes the appropriate framework for consideration of petitioners' request for campus recognition. Because respondents failed to accord due recognition to First Amendment principles, the judgments below approving respondents' denial of recognition must be reversed. Since we cannot conclude from this record that petitioners were willing to abide by reasonable campus rules and regulations, we order the case remanded for reconsideration. We note, in so holding, that the wide latitude accorded by the Constitution to the freedoms of expression and association is not without its costs in terms of the risk to the maintenance of civility and an ordered society. Indeed, this latitude often has resulted, on the campus and elsewhere, in the infringement of the rights of others. Though we deplore the tendency of some to abuse the very constitutional privileges they invoke, and although the infringement of rights of others certainly should not be tolerated, we reaffirm this Court's dedication to the principles of the Bill of Rights upon which our vigorous and free society is founded.

Reversed and remanded.

Mr. Chief Justice Burger, concurring.

I am in agreement with what is said in the Court's opinion and I join in it. I do so because I read the basis of the remand as recognizing that student organizations seeking the privilege of official campus recognition must be willing to abide by valid rules of the institution applicable to all such organizations. This is a reasonable condition insofar as it calls for the disavowal of resort to force, disruption, and interference with the rights of others.

* * *

Notes

1.   It is important to note the references by the Court to the decision in *Tinker*, delivered only three years earlier, in 1969. Many have come to view *Healy* as the higher education version of the *Tinker* decision.

2.   It can be argued that *Healy,* and the higher education freedom of the press case decided the following year, *Papish v. Board of Curators, Univ. of Missouri,* 410 U.S. 667, 93 S.Ct. 1197 (1973), together constitute a culmination of the Berkeley Free Speech Movement of 1964.

> The Free Speech Movement (FSM) Digital Archives document the role of Mario Savio and other participants in the Free Speech Movement (University of California, Berkeley, September–December 1964), as well as its origins in political protest and civil rights movements and its legacy of political activism and educational reform that can be traced throughout the country and the world down to the present. UC Berkeley Free Speech Movement Digital Archive, http://bancroft.berkeley.edu/FSM/.

3.   As has been the case at the K–12 level, the most controversial student groups at the higher education level over time have not been the political student groups per se, but the religious student groups and the gay student groups. The U.S. Supreme Court addressed the nature and extent of the rights of religious student groups on college and university campuses in the two major decisions that follow, *Widmar* and *Rosenberger*.

WIDMAR v. VINCENT
454 U.S. 263, 102 S.Ct. 269 (1981).

JUSTICE POWELL delivered the opinion of the court.

This case presents the question whether a state university, which makes its facilities generally available for the activities of registered student groups, may close its facilities to a registered student group desiring to use the facilities for religious worship and religious discussion.

I.

It is the stated policy of the University of Missouri at Kansas City[1] to encourage the activities of student organizations. The University officially recognizes over 100 student groups. It routinely provides University facilities for the meetings of registered organizations. Students pay an activity fee of $41 per semester (1978–1979) to help defray the costs to the University.

---

1.   The University of Missouri at Kansas City (UMKC) is one of four campuses of the University of Missouri, an institution of the State of Missouri.

From 1973 until 1977 a registered religious group named Cornerstone regularly sought and received permission to conduct its meetings in University facilities.[2] In 1977, however, the University informed the group that it could no longer meet in University buildings. The exclusion was based on a regulation, adopted by the Board of Curators in 1972, that prohibits the use of University buildings or grounds "for purposes of religious worship or religious teaching."

* * *

II.

Through its policy of accommodating their meetings, the University has created a forum generally open for use by student groups. Having done so, the University has assumed an obligation to justify its discriminations and exclusions under applicable constitutional norms. The Constitution forbids a State to enforce certain exclusions from a forum generally open to the public, even if it was not required to create the forum in the first place. * * *

The University's institutional mission, which it describes as providing a "secular education" to its students, does not exempt its actions from constitutional scrutiny. With respect to persons entitled to be there, our cases leave no doubt that the First Amendment rights of speech and association extend to the campuses of state universities.

Here UMKC has discriminated against student groups and speakers based on their desire to use a generally open forum to engage in religious worship and discussion. These are forms of speech and association protected by the First Amendment. In order to justify discriminatory exclusion from a public forum based on the religious content of a group's intended speech, the University must therefore satisfy the standard of review appropriate to content-based exclusions. It must show that its regulation is necessary to serve a compelling state interest and that it is narrowly drawn to achieve that end.

III.

In this case the University claims a compelling interest in maintaining strict separation of church and State. It derives this interest from the "Establishment Clauses" of both the Federal and Missouri Constitutions.

A.

The University first argues that it cannot offer its facilities to religious groups and speakers on the terms available to other groups

2. Cornerstone is an organization of evangelical Christian students from various denominational backgrounds. According to an affidavit filed in 1977, "perhaps twenty students . . . participate actively in Cornerstone and form the backbone of the campus organization." Cornerstone held its on-campus meetings in classrooms and in the student center. These meetings were open to the public and attracted up to 125 students. A typical Cornerstone meeting included prayer, hymns, Bible commentary, and discussion of religious views and experiences.

without violating the Establishment Clause of the Constitution of the United States. * * *

The University's argument misconceives the nature of this case. The question is not whether the creation of a religious forum would violate the Establishment Clause. The University has opened its facilities for use by student groups, and the question is whether it can now exclude groups because of the content of their speech. In this context we are unpersuaded that the primary effect of the public forum, open to all forms of discourse, would be to advance religion.

* * *

B.

Arguing that the State of Missouri has gone further than the Federal Constitution in proscribing indirect state support for religion, the University claims a compelling interest in complying with the applicable provisions of the Missouri Constitution.

* * *

* * * [However,] the state interest asserted here—in achieving greater separation of church and State than is already ensured under the Establishment Clause of the Federal Constitution—is limited by the Free Exercise Clause and in this case by the Free Speech Clause as well. In this constitutional context, we are unable to recognize the State's interest as sufficiently "compelling" to justify content-based discrimination against respondents' religious speech.

IV.

Our holding in this case in no way undermines the capacity of the University to establish reasonable time, place, and manner regulations. Nor do we question the right of the University to make academic judgments as to how best to allocate scarce resources or "to determine for itself on academic grounds who may teach, what may be taught, how it shall be taught, and who may be admitted to study." Finally, we affirm the continuing validity of cases, that recognize a University's right to exclude even First Amendment activities that violate reasonable campus rules or substantially interfere with the opportunity of other students to obtain an education.

The basis for our decision is narrow. Having created a forum generally open to student groups, the University seeks to enforce a content-based exclusion of religious speech. Its exclusionary policy violates the fundamental principle that a state regulation of speech should be content-neutral, and the University is unable to justify this violation under applicable constitutional standards.

For this reason, the decision of the Court of Appeals is

Affirmed.

ROSENBERGER v. RECTOR & VISITORS OF UNIV. OF VA.

515 U.S. 819, 115 S.Ct. 2510 (1995).

JUSTICE KENNEDY delivered the opinion of the Court.

The University of Virginia, an instrumentality of the Commonwealth for which it is named and thus bound by the First and Fourteenth Amendments, authorizes the payment of outside contractors for the printing costs of a variety of student publications. It withheld any authorization for payments on behalf of petitioners for the sole reason that their student paper "primarily promotes or manifests a particular belie[f] in or about a deity or an ultimate reality." That the paper did promote or manifest views within the defined exclusion seems plain enough. The challenge is to the University's regulation and its denial of authorization, the case raising issues under the Speech and Establishment Clauses of the First Amendment.

I.

* * *

Before a student group is eligible to submit bills from its outside contractors for payment by the fund described below, it must become a "Contracted Independent Organization" (CIO). * * *

Petitioners' organization, Wide Awake Productions (WAP), qualified as a CIO. Formed by petitioner Ronald Rosenberger and other undergraduates in 1990, WAP was established "[t]o publish a magazine of philosophical and religious expression," "[t]o facilitate discussion which fosters an atmosphere of sensitivity to and tolerance of Christian viewpoints," and "[t]o provide a unifying focus for Christians of multicultural backgrounds." WAP publishes Wide Awake: A Christian Perspective at the University of Virginia. The paper's Christian viewpoint was evident from the first issue, in which its editors wrote that the journal "offers a Christian perspective on both personal and community issues, especially those relevant to college students at the University of Virginia." The editors committed the paper to a two-fold mission: "to challenge Christians to live, in word and deed, according to the faith they proclaim and to encourage students to consider what a personal relationship with Jesus Christ means." The first issue had articles about racism, crisis pregnancy, stress, prayer, C.S. Lewis' ideas about evil and free will, and reviews of religious music. In the next two issues, Wide Awake featured stories about homosexuality, Christian missionary work, and eating disorders, as well as music reviews and interviews with University professors. Each page of Wide Awake, and the end of each article or review, is marked by a cross. The advertisements carried in Wide Awake also reveal the Christian perspective of the journal. For the most part, the advertisers are churches, centers for Christian study, or Christian bookstores. By June 1992, WAP had distributed about 5,000 copies of Wide Awake to University students, free of charge.

* * *

A few months after being given CIO status, WAP requested the SAF to pay its printer $5,862 for the costs of printing its newspaper. The Appropriations Committee of the Student Council denied WAP's request on the ground that Wide Awake was a "religious activity" within the meaning of the Guidelines, *i.e.*, that the newspaper "promote[d] or manifest[ed] a particular belie[f] in or about a deity or an ultimate reality." It made its determination after examining the first issue. WAP appealed the denial to the full Student Council, contending that WAP met all the applicable Guidelines and that denial of SAF support on the basis of the magazine's religious perspective violated the Constitution. The appeal was denied without further comment, and WAP appealed to the next level, the Student Activities Committee. In a letter signed by the Dean of Students, the committee sustained the denial of funding.

Having no further recourse within the University structure, WAP, Wide Awake, and three of its editors and members filed suit in the United States District Court for the Western District of Virginia * * *.

* * * They alleged that refusal to authorize payment of the printing costs of the publication, solely on the basis of its religious editorial viewpoint, violated their rights to freedom of speech and press, to the free exercise of religion, and to equal protection of the law. * * *

II.

It is axiomatic that the government may not regulate speech based on its substantive content or the message it conveys. Other principles follow from this precept. In the realm of private speech or expression, government regulation may not favor one speaker over another. Discrimination against speech because of its message is presumed to be unconstitutional. These rules informed our determination that the government offends the First Amendment when it imposes financial burdens on certain speakers based on the content of their expression. When the government targets not subject matter, but particular views taken by speakers on a subject, the violation of the First Amendment is all the more blatant. Viewpoint discrimination is thus an egregious form of content discrimination. The government must abstain from regulating speech when the specific motivating ideology or the opinion or perspective of the speaker is the rationale for the restriction.

These principles provide the framework forbidding the State to exercise viewpoint discrimination, even when the limited public forum is one of its own creation. * * * The necessities of confining a forum to the limited and legitimate purposes for which it was created may justify the State in reserving it for certain groups or for the discussion of certain topics. Once it has opened a limited forum, however, the State must respect the lawful boundaries it has itself set. The State may not exclude speech where its distinction is not "reasonable in light of the purpose served by the forum," nor may it discriminate against speech on the basis of its viewpoint. Thus, in determining whether the State is acting to preserve the limits of the forum it has created so that the exclusion of a class of speech is legitimate, we have observed a distinction between, on the one hand, content discrimination, which may be permissible if it preserves the purposes of that limited forum, and, on the other hand, viewpoint discrimination, which is presumed impermissible when directed against speech otherwise within the forum's limitations.

The SAF is a forum more in a metaphysical than in a spatial or geographic sense, but the same principles are applicable. The most recent and most apposite case is our decision in *Lamb's Chapel*. There, a school district had opened school facilities for use after school hours by community groups for a wide variety of social, civic, and recreational purposes. The district, however, had enacted a formal policy against opening facilities to groups for religious purposes. Invoking its policy, the district rejected a request from a group desiring to show a film series addressing various child-rearing questions from a "Christian perspective." There was no indication in the record in *Lamb's Chapel* that the request to use the school facilities was "denied, for any reason other than the fact that the presentation would have been from a religious perspective." Our conclusion was unanimous: "[I]t discriminates on the basis of viewpoint to permit school property to be used for the presentation of all views about family issues and childrearing except those dealing with the subject matter from a religious standpoint."

The University does acknowledge (as it must in light of our precedents) that "ideologically driven attempts to suppress a particular point of view are presumptively unconstitutional in funding, as in other contexts," but insists that this case does not present that issue because the Guidelines draw lines based on content, not viewpoint. As we have noted, discrimination against one set of views or ideas is but a subset or particular instance of the more general phenomenon of content discrimination. And, it must be acknowledged, the distinction is not a precise one. It is, in a sense, something of an understatement to speak of religious thought and discussion as just a viewpoint, as distinct from a comprehensive body of thought. The nature of our origins and destiny and their dependence upon the existence of a divine being have been subjects of philosophic inquiry throughout human history. We conclude, nonetheless, that here, as in *Lamb's Chapel,* viewpoint discrimination is the proper way to interpret the University's objections to Wide Awake. By the very terms of the SAF prohibition, the University does not exclude religion as a subject matter but selects for disfavored treatment those student journalistic efforts with religious editorial viewpoints. Religion may be a vast area of inquiry, but it also provides, as it did here, a specific premise, a perspective, a standpoint from which a variety of subjects may be discussed and considered. The prohibited perspective, not the general subject matter, resulted in the refusal to make third-party payments, for the subjects discussed were otherwise within the approved category of publications.

The dissent's assertion that no viewpoint discrimination occurs because the Guidelines discriminate against an entire class of viewpoints reflects an insupportable assumption that all debate is bipolar and that antireligious speech is the only response to religious speech. Our understanding of the complex and multifaceted nature of public discourse has not embraced such a contrived description of the marketplace of ideas. If the topic of debate is, for example, racism, then exclusion of several views on that problem is just as offensive to the First Amendment as exclusion of only one. It is as objectionable to exclude both a theistic and an atheistic perspective on the debate as it is to exclude one, the other, or yet another political, economic, or social viewpoint. The dissent's declaration that debate is not skewed so long as multiple voices are silenced is simply wrong; the debate is skewed in multiple ways.

* * *

Vital First Amendment speech principles are at stake here. The first danger to liberty lies in granting the State the power to examine publications to determine whether or not they are based on some ultimate idea and, if so, for the State to classify them. The second, and corollary, danger is to speech from the chilling of individual thought and expression. That danger is especially real in the University setting, where the State acts against a background and tradition of thought and experiment that is at the center of our intellectual and philosophic tradition. See *Healy v. James*, 408 U.S. 169, 180–181 (1972). In ancient Athens, and, as Europe entered into a new period of intellectual awakening, in places like Bologna, Oxford, and Paris, universities began as voluntary and spontaneous assemblages or concourses for students to speak and to write and to learn. The quality and creative power of student intellectual life to this day remains a vital measure of a school's influence and attainment. For the University, by regulation, to cast disapproval on particular viewpoints of its students risks the suppression of free speech and creative inquiry in one of the vital centers for the Nation's intellectual life, its college and university campuses.

The Guideline invoked by the University to deny third-party contractor payments on behalf of WAP effects a sweeping restriction on student thought and student inquiry in the context of University sponsored publications. The prohibition on funding on behalf of publications that "primarily promot[e] or manifes[t] a particular belie[f] in or about a deity or an ultimate reality," in its ordinary and commonsense meaning, has a vast potential reach. The term "promotes" as used here would comprehend any writing advocating a philosophic position that rests upon a belief in a deity or ultimate reality. And the term "manifests" would bring within the scope of the prohibition any writing that is explicable as resting upon a premise that presupposes the existence of a deity or ultimate reality. Were the prohibition applied with much vigor at all, it would bar funding of essays by hypothetical student contributors named Plato, Spinoza, and Descartes. And if the regulation covers, as the University says it does, those student journalistic efforts that primarily manifest or promote a belief that there is no deity and no ultimate reality, then under-graduates named Karl Marx, Bertrand Russell, and Jean–Paul Sartre would likewise have some of their major essays excluded from student publications. If any manifestation of beliefs in first principles disqualifies the writing, as seems to be the case, it is indeed difficult to name renowned thinkers whose writings would be accepted, save perhaps for articles disclaiming all connection to their ultimate philosophy. Plato could contrive perhaps to submit an acceptable essay on making pasta or peanut butter cookies, provided he did not point out their (necessary) imperfections.

Based on the principles we have discussed, we hold that the regulation invoked to deny SAF support, both in its terms and in its application to these petitioners, is a denial of their right of free speech guaranteed by the First Amendment. It remains to be considered whether the violation following from the University's action is excused by the necessity of complying with the Constitution's prohibition against state establishment of religion. * * *

To obey the Establishment Clause, it was not necessary for the University to deny eligibility to student publications because of their viewpoint. The neutrality commanded of the State by the separate Clauses of the First Amendment was compromised by the University's course of action. The viewpoint discrimination inherent in the University's regulation required public officials to scan and interpret student publications to discern their underlying philosophic assumptions respecting religious theory and belief. That course of action was a denial of the right of free speech and would risk fostering a pervasive bias or hostility to religion, which could undermine the very neutrality the Establishment Clause requires. There is no Establishment Clause violation in the University's honoring its duties under the Free Speech Clause.

The judgment of the Court of Appeals must be, and is, reversed.

It is so ordered.

F. HATE–RELATED SPEECH CONTROVERSIES AT THE HIGHER EDUCATION LEVEL

PROBLEM 15: Hate-Related Web Site Activity

Consider the efficacy of the following hypothetical policy, designed to be implemented at a major public university. In light of your legal analysis, would you recommend such a policy? Why? Alternatively, could you support a modified version of this bill? If so, what modifications might be appropriate?

A. The Regents of the University are concerned about the corrosive effects of hate-related Web sites and believe that such expression in public settings is another form of obscenity, equally offensive and inappropriate.

B. The purpose of this policy is to prohibit Web-based expression—created and fostered by Web site owners—that (a) includes slurs based on the race, ethnicity, religion, gender, gender identity, and/or sexual orientation of persons or groups; and (b) contains extensive deprecatory remarks and/or highly offensive visual imagery regarding the alleged inferiority of such persons or groups.

C. In determining whether online expression constitutes *hate-related Web site activity* within the meaning of this policy, campus officials will inquire whether:

1. the average person applying contemporary community standards would find that the site, taken as a whole, appeals to the bigoted and malevolent interest;

2. the site embraces, encourages, or sets forth—in an aggressive and patently offensive way—propaganda, invective, and/or activity designed to intimidate others and subject them to hatred; and

3. taken as a whole, the site lacks serious literary, artistic, political, or scientific value.

DOE v. UNIVERSITY OF MICH.

721 F.Supp. 852 (E.D. Mich. 1989).

COHN, UNITED STATES DISTRICT JUDGE.

* * * Recently, the University of Michigan at Ann Arbor (the University), a state-chartered university, adopted a Policy on Discrimination and Discriminatory Harassment of Students in the University Environment (the Policy) in an attempt to curb what the University's governing Board of Regents (Regents) viewed as a rising tide of racial intolerance and harassment on campus. The Policy prohibited individuals, under the penalty of sanctions, from "stigmatizing or victimizing" individuals or groups on the basis of race, ethnicity, religion, sex, sexual orientation, creed, national origin, ancestry, age, marital status, handicap or Vietnam-era veteran status. However laudable or appropriate an effort this may have been, the Court found that the Policy swept within its scope a significant amount of "verbal conduct" or "verbal behavior" which is unquestionably protected speech under the First Amendment. Accordingly, the Court granted plaintiff John Doe's (Doe) prayer for a permanent injunction as to those parts of the Policy restricting speech activity, but denied the injunction as to the Policy's regulation of physical conduct. The reasons follow.

II. FACTS GENERALLY

According to the University, in the last three years incidents of racism and racial harassment appeared to become increasingly frequent at the University. * * *

Following discussions with a national civil rights leader in March of 1987, the University adopted a six-point action plan to remedy the racial problems on campus. This included the adoption of "an anti-racial harassment policy ... as a component of the University's rules and regulations with appropriate sanctions specified."

* * *

III. THE UNIVERSITY OF MICHIGAN POLICY ON DISCRIMINATION AND DISCRIMINATORY HARASSMENT

A. *The Terms of the Policy*

The Policy established a three-tiered system whereby the degree of regulation was dependent on the location of the conduct at issue. The broadest range of speech and dialogue was "tolerated" in variously described public parts of the campus. Only an act of physical violence or destruction of property was considered sanctionable in these settings. Publications sponsored by the University such as the *Michigan Daily* and the *Michigan Review* were not subject to regulation. The conduct of students living in University housing is primarily governed by the standard provisions of individual leases, however the Policy appeared to apply in this setting as well. The Policy by its terms applied specifically to "[e]ducational and academic centers, such as classroom buildings, libraries, research laboratories, recreation and study centers[.]" In these areas, persons were subject to discipline for:

1. Any behavior, verbal or physical, that stigmatizes or victimizes an individual on the basis of race, ethnicity, religion, sex, sexual orientation, creed, national origin, ancestry, age, marital status, handicap or Vietnam-era veteran status, and that

>   a. Involves an express or implied threat to an individual's academic efforts, employment, participation in University sponsored extra-curricular activities or personal safety; or

>   b. Has the purpose or reasonably foreseeable effect of interfering with an individual's academic efforts, employment, participation in University sponsored extra-curricular activities or personal safety; or

>   c. Creates an intimidating, hostile, or demeaning environment for educational pursuits, employment or participation in University sponsored extra-curricular activities.

2. Sexual advances, requests for sexual favors, and verbal or physical conduct that stigmatizes or victimizes an individual on the basis of sex or sexual orientation where such behavior:

>   a. Involves an express or implied threat to an individual's academic efforts, employment, participation in University sponsored extra-curricular activities or personal safety; or

>   b. Has the purpose or reasonably foreseeable effect of interfering with an individual's academic efforts, employment, participation in University sponsored extra-curricular activities or personal safety; or

>   c. Creates an intimidating, hostile, or demeaning environment for educational pursuits, employment or participation in University sponsored extra-curricular activities.

On August 22, 1989, the University publicly announced, without prior notice to the Court or Doe, that it was withdrawing section 1(c) on the grounds that "a need exists for further explanation and clarification of [that section] of the policy." No reason was given why the analogous provision in paragraph 2(c) was allowed to stand.

The Policy by its terms recognizes that certain speech which might be considered in violation may not be sanctionable by stating: "The Office of the General Counsel will rule on any claim that conduct which is the subject of a formal hearing is constitutionally protected by the first amendment."

B.   *Hearing Procedures*

Any member of the University community could initiate the process leading to sanctions by either filing a formal complaint with an appropriate University office or by seeking informal counseling with described University officials and support centers. * * *

C.   *Sanctions*

The Policy provided for progressive discipline based on the severity of the violation. It stated that the University encouraged hearing panels to impose sanctions that include an educational element in order to sensitize the perpetrator to the harmfulness of his or her conduct. The Policy provided, however, that compulsory class attendance should not be imposed "in an attempt to change deeply held religious or moral convictions." Depending on the intent of the accused student, the effect of the conduct, and whether the accused student is a repeat offender, one or more of the following sanctions may be imposed: (1) formal reprimand; (2) community service; (3) class attendance; (4) restitution; (5) removal from University housing; (6) suspension from specific courses and activities; (7) suspension; (8) expulsion. The sanctions of suspension and expulsion could only be imposed for violent or dangerous acts, repeated offenses, or a willful failure to comply with a lesser sanction. The University President could set aside or lessen any sanction.

D.   *Interpretive Guide*

Shortly after the promulgation of the policy in the fall of 1988, the University Office of Affirmative Action issued an interpretive guide (Guide) entitled *What Students Should Know about Discrimination and Discriminatory Harassment by Students in the University Environment.* The Guide purported to be an authoritative interpretation of the Policy and provided examples of sanctionable conduct. These included:

A flyer containing racist threats distributed in a residence hall.

Racist graffiti written on the door of an Asian student's study carrel.

A male student makes remarks in class like "Women just aren't as good in this field as men," thus creating a hostile learning atmosphere for female classmates.

Students in a residence hall have a floor party and invite everyone on their floor except one person because they think she might be a lesbian.

A black student is confronted and racially insulted by two white students in a cafeteria.

Male students leave pornographic pictures and jokes on the desk of a female graduate student.

Two men demand that their roommate in the residence hall move out and be tested for AIDS.

In addition, the Guide contained a separate section entitled "You are a harasser when" which contains the following examples of discriminatory conduct:

You exclude someone from a study group because that person is of a different race, sex, or ethnic origin than you are.

You tell jokes about gay men and lesbians.

Your student organization sponsors entertainment that includes a comedian who slurs Hispanics.

You display a confederate flag on the door of your room in the residence hall.

You laugh at a joke about someone in your class who stutters.

You make obscene telephone calls or send racist notes or computer messages.

You comment in a derogatory way about a particular person or group's physical appearance or sexual orientation, or their cultural origins, or religious beliefs.

It was not clear whether each of these actions would subject a student to sanctions, although the title of the section suggests that they would. It was also unclear why these additional examples were listed separately from those in the section entitled "What is Discriminatory Harassment."

According to the University, the Guide was withdrawn at an unknown date in the winter of 1989, because "the information in it was not accurate." The withdrawal had not been announced publicly as of the date this case was filed.

IV. STANDING

Doe is a psychology graduate student. His specialty is the field of biopsychology, which he describes as the interdisciplinary study of the biological bases of individual differences in personality traits and mental abilities. Doe said that certain controversial theories positing biologically-based differences between sexes and races might be perceived as "sexist" and "racist" by some students, and he feared that discussion of such theories might be sanctionable under the Policy. He asserted that his right to freely and openly discuss these theories was impermissibly chilled, and he requested that the Policy be declared unconstitutional and enjoined on the grounds of vagueness and overbreadth.

* * *

V.   VAGUENESS AND OVERBREADTH

* * *

B.   *Overbreadth*

1.

Doe claimed that the Policy was invalid because it was facially overbroad. It is fundamental that statutes regulating First Amendment activities must be narrowly drawn to address only the specific evil at hand. "Because First Amendment freedoms need breathing space to survive, government may regulate in the area only with narrow specificity." A law regulating speech will be deemed overbroad if it sweeps within its ambit a substantial amount of protected speech along with that which it may legitimately regulate.

The Supreme Court has consistently held that statutes punishing speech or conduct solely on the grounds that they are unseemly or offensive are unconstitutionally overbroad. * * * These cases stand generally for the proposition that the state may not prohibit broad classes of speech, some of which may indeed be legitimately regulable, if in so doing a substantial amount of constitutionally protected conduct is also prohibited. This was the fundamental infirmity of the Policy.

2.

The University repeatedly argued that the Policy did not apply to speech that is protected by the First Amendment. It urged the Court to disregard the Guide as "inaccurate" and look instead to "the manner in which the Policy has been interpreted and applied by those charged with its enforcement." However, as applied by the University over the past year, the Policy was consistently applied to reach protected speech.

On December 7, 1988, a complaint was filed against a graduate student in the School of Social Work alleging that he harassed students based on sexual orientation and sex. The basis for the sexual orientation charge was apparently that in a research class, the student openly stated his belief that homosexuality was a disease and that he intended to develop a counseling plan for changing gay clients to straight. He also related to other students that he had been counseling several of his gay patients accordingly. The student apparently had several heated discussions with his classmates over the validity and morality of his theory and program. On January 11, 1989, the Interim Policy Administrator wrote to the student informing him that following an investigation of the complaints, there was sufficient evidence to warrant a formal hearing on the charges of sex and sexual orientation harassment. A formal hearing on the charges was held on January 28, 1989. The hearing panel

unanimously found that the student was guilty of sexual harassment but refused to convict him of harassment on the basis of sexual orientation.
* * *

Although the student was not sanctioned over the allegations of sexual orientation harassment, the fact remains that the Policy Administrator—the authoritative voice of the University on these matters—saw no First Amendment problem in forcing the student to a hearing to answer for allegedly harassing statements made in the course of academic discussion and research. Moreover, there is no indication that had the hearing panel convicted rather than acquitted the student, the University would have interceded to protect the interests of academic freedom and freedom of speech.

A second case, which was informally resolved, also demonstrated that the University did not exempt statements made in the course of classroom academic discussions from the sanctions of the policy. On September 28, 1988, a complaint was filed against a student in an entrepreneurship class in the School of Business Administration for reading an allegedly homophobic limerick during a scheduled class public-speaking exercise which ridiculed a well known athlete for his presumed sexual orientation. The Policy Administrator was able to persuade the perpetrator to attend an educational "gay rap" session, write a letter of apology to the *Michigan Daily*, and apologize to his class and the matter was dropped. No discussion of the possibility that the limerick was protected speech appears in the file or in the Administrator's notes.

A third incident involved a comment made in the orientation session of a preclinical dentistry class. The class was widely regarded as one of the most difficult for second year dentistry students. To allay fears and concerns at the outset, the class was broken up into small sections to informally discuss anticipated problems. During the ensuing discussion, a student stated that "he had heard that minorities had a difficult time in the course and that he had heard that they were not treated fairly." A minority professor teaching the class filed a complaint on the grounds that the comment was unfair and hurt her chances for tenure. Following the filing of the complaint, the student was "counseled" about the existence of the policy and agreed to write a letter apologizing for making the comment without adequately verifying the allegation, which he said he had heard from his roommate, a black former dentistry student.
* * *

The manner in which these three complaints were handled demonstrated that the University considered serious comments made in the context of classroom discussion to be sanctionable under the Policy. The innocent intent of the speaker was apparently immaterial to whether a complaint would be pursued. Moreover, the Administrator generally failed to consider whether a comment was protected by the First Amendment before informing the accused student that a complaint had been filed. The Administrator instead attempted to persuade the accused student to accept "voluntary" sanctions. Behind this persuasion was, of course, the subtle threat that failure to accept such sanctions might result in a formal hearing. There is no evidence in the record that the Administrator ever declined to pursue a complaint through attempted mediation because the alleged harassing conduct was protected by the First Amendment. Nor is there evidence that the Administrator ever informed an accused harasser during mediation negotiations that the complained of conduct might be protected. The Administrator's manner of enforcing the Policy was constitutionally indistinguishable from a full blown prosecution. The University could not seriously argue that the policy was never interpreted to reach protected conduct. It is clear that the policy was overbroad both on its face and as applied.

C. *Vagueness*

Doe also urges that the policy be struck down on the grounds that it is impermissibly vague. A statute is unconstitutionally vague when "men of common intelligence must necessarily guess at its meaning." A statute must give adequate warning of the conduct which is to be prohibited and must set out explicit standards for those who apply it. "No one may be required at the peril of life, liberty or property to speculate as to the meaning of penal statutes. All are entitled to be informed as to what the State commands or forbids." These considerations apply with particular force where the challenged statute acts to inhibit freedoms affirmatively protected by the constitution. * * *

Looking at the plain language of the Policy, it was simply impossible to discern any limitation on its scope or any conceptual distinction between protected and unprotected conduct. The structure of the Policy was in two parts; one relates to cause and the other to effect. Both cause and effect must be present to state a prima facie violation of the Policy. The operative words in the cause section required that language must "stigmatize" or "victimize" an individual. However, both of these terms are general and elude precise definition. Moreover, it is clear that the fact that a statement may victimize or stigmatize an individual does not, in and of itself, strip it of protection under the accepted First Amendment tests.

The first of the "effects clauses" stated that in order to be sanctionable, the stigmatizing and victimizing statements had to "involve an express or implied threat to an individual's academic efforts, employment, participation in University sponsored extra-curricular activities or personal safety." It is not clear what kind of conduct would constitute a "threat" to an individual's academic efforts. It might refer to an unspecified threat of future retaliation by the speaker. Or it might equally plausibly refer to the threat to a victim's academic success because the stigmatizing and victimizing speech is so inherently distracting. Certainly the former would be unprotected speech. However, it is not clear whether the latter would.

Moving to the second "effect clause," a stigmatizing or victimizing comment is sanctionable if it has the purpose or reasonably foreseeable effect of interfering with an individual's academic efforts, etc. Again, the question is what conduct will be held to "interfere" with an individual's academic efforts. The language of the policy alone gives no inherent guidance. The one interpretive resource the University provided was withdrawn as "inaccurate," an implicit admission that even the University itself was unsure of the precise scope and meaning of the Policy.

During the oral argument, the Court asked the University's counsel how he would distinguish between speech which was merely offensive, which he conceded was protected, and speech which "stigmatizes or victimizes" on the basis of an invidious factor. Counsel replied "very carefully." The response, while refreshingly candid, illustrated the plain fact that the University never articulated any principled way to distinguish sanctionable from protected speech. Students of common understanding were necessarily forced to guess at whether a comment about a controversial issue would later be found to be sanctionable under the Policy. * * *

VI. CONCLUSION

* * *

While the Court is sympathetic to the University's obligation to ensure equal educational opportunities for all of its students, such efforts must not be at the expense of free speech. Unfortunately, this was precisely what the University did. * * * [T]here is no evidence in the record that anyone at the University ever seriously attempted to reconcile their efforts to combat discrimination with the requirements of the First Amendment. * * *

RIGHTS IN CONFLICT: THE FIRST AMENDMENT'S THIRD CENTURY

Robert M. O'Neil.
65 LAW & CONTEMP. PROBS. 7 (2002).

* * *

III.   Civility and Free Speech in an Increasingly Uncivil Society

* * * [M]uch confusion surrounds the constitutional boundaries in the quest for civility. On one hand, the Supreme Court has said that a person can be punished for uttering "fighting words" in a public place.[65] On the other hand, the same person could not be charged for the public display of a taboo or vulgar four-letter word.[66] The tension between two such rulings, and the consequent difficulty of defining the line between protected speech and unprotected epithets, is apparent. The lack of clarity in this area has created much confusion and has led to the

65. Chaplinsky v. New Hampshire, 315 U.S. 568 (1942).

66. Cohen v. California, 203 U.S. 15 (1971).

adoption of various measures (campus speech codes, for example) that have fared poorly in the courts.[67]

It all began one Saturday afternoon in the town center of Rochester, New Hampshire, shortly before the outbreak of World War II.[68] A Jehovah's Witness named Chaplinsky had unsettled spectators by loudly denouncing mainstream religious faiths.[69] The local constabulary, without making an arrest, escorted him toward the police station.[70] Chaplinsky then turned on the officer and uttered the words which became the basis for an immediate criminal charge and an eventual Supreme Court ruling.[71] The precise words remain in doubt to this day. The arresting officer insisted that he had been called, to his face, "a damned fascist" and "a God-damned racketeer."[72] Chaplinsky, however, maintained that he had firmly but politely informed the officer that "You, sir, are damned in the eyes of God" and "no better than a racketeer."[73] Whatever he actually said, Chaplinsky was convicted of violating a state law which made it a crime to "address any offensive, derisive, or annoying word to any person who is lawfully in any street or other public place, nor call him by any offensive or derisive name . . . ."[74]

The New Hampshire Supreme Court affirmed the conviction, finding the statute properly limited to "face to face words plainly likely to cause a breach of the peace … classical fighting words."[75] A unanimous Supreme Court affirmed, including several Justices who had consistently supported free expression in the past.[76] Justice Murphy wrote for the Court, and Justices Black and Douglas joined without comment, a brief opinion that allowed states to punish the utterance of mere words, albeit under unusual conditions.[77] The key to the ruling was the Court's view that "such utterances are no essential part of any exposition of ideas, and are of such slight social value as a step to truth that any benefit that may be derived from them is clearly outweighed by the social interest in order and morality."[78]

So dismissive a view of expression that was both provocative and substantive now seems remarkable; it is even more so given the deeply religious context in which Chaplinsky voiced his disdain for the police.[79] But the Court was convinced that such words lost any claim to First Amendment protection when they were uttered face to face in a manner that was "likely to cause a breach of the peace," even though no disorder

---

67. *See, e.g.,* ROBERT M. O'NEIL, FREE SPEECH IN THE COLLEGE COMMUNITY (1997) [hereinafter O'NEIL, FREE SPEECH].

68. *Chaplinsky,* 315 U.S. at 569.

69. *Id.* at 569–70.

70. *Id.* at 570.

71. *Id.*

72. *Id.* at 569.

73. This alternative version of Chaplinsky's words, advanced in the trial court by the defendant himself, was rejected in the absence of any third-party corroboration. The judge understandably favored the ac-

count given by the arresting officer, which provided the record and, in substantial part, the rationale for successive affirmance of Chaplinsky's conviction.

74. *Id.* at 569.

75. *Id.* at 573.

76. *Id.* at 574.

77. *Id.*

78. *Id.* at 572.

79. *Id.* at 570.

actually ensued.[80] The New Hampshire law was deemed "a statute punishing verbal acts," which, through interpretation, had been "limited to define and punish specific conduct lying within the domain of state power."[81] Under such conditions, the words Chaplinsky was charged with speaking seemed provocative enough not to merit any First Amendment protection.[82] Commentators have rightly observed that the decision had two prongs or elements: First, there was an assumption that utterance of epithets under such conditions inherently inflicts injury on a person who is their target.[83] Second, when such verbal hostility creates an imminent breach of the peace, government may intercede even though only words are involved.[84] Justice Murphy's cryptic opinion offered little guidance to those—law enforcement officers and judges—who would seek after *Chaplinsky* to resolve the inherent tension between the "damaging words" and "breach of peace" theories which the judgment blended.[85]

The *Chaplinsky* decision has caused no end of confusion during the ensuing six decades. This case has been cited with sufficient deference to imply that uttering "fighting words" remains a recognized exception to First Amendment freedoms.[86] As recently as the "hate speech" decision in 1992, the majority assumed *Chaplinsky*'s continuing vitality, stressing only that fighting words which were used to convey particular messages could not be selectively disfavored on a subject-matter basis.[87] Moreover, in that ruling Justice Scalia expressly declined an invitation to "modify the scope of the *Chaplinsky* formulation," a step he deemed unnecessary to the majority's disposition of the case.[88] Rumors of *Chaplinsky*'s demise are, therefore, greatly exaggerated and quite premature.[89]

When it comes to factually similar cases, however, the Justices have consistently distinguished *Chaplinsky*. Even when based on verbal affronts and assaults at least as provocative as the events of that long-ago New Hampshire Saturday afternoon, convictions have been set aside.[90] The lower courts have been understandably confused, however, and have been less reticent to invoke *Chaplinsky* as the basis for affirming the convictions of "in your face" verbal assailants—believing, quite understandably, that the precedent for doing so remained alive, if not in perfect health.[91]

The paradox of civility is not limited to fighting words. At the height of the Vietnam War, Paul Cohen walked about the lobby of the Los

---

80. *Id.* at 573–74.

81. *Id.* at 574.

82. *Id.*

83. Note, *The Demise of the Chaplinsky Fighting Words Doctrine: An Argument for Its Interment*, 106 HARV. L. REV. 1111, 1129, 1130–31 (1993) [hereinafter *Demise*].

84. *Id.*

85. *Id.*

86. *See, e.g.*, Martin Redish, *The Value of Free Speech*, 130 U. PA. L. REV. 591, 626 (1982).

87. R.A.V. v. City of St. Paul, 505 U.S. 377, 387 (1992).

88. *Id.* at 381.

89. *Id.* at 399.

90. Lewis v. New Orleans, 415 U.S. 130 (1974); Gooding v. Wilson, 405 U.S. 518 (1972).

91. *E.g.*, Mercer v. Winston, 199 S.E.2d 724 (Va. 1973), *cert. denied*, 416 U.S. 988 (1974).

Angeles County courthouse wearing a jacket which bore in prominent lettering the words "Fuck the Draft."[92] He was arrested, and charged with violating a California breach of the peace law.[93] The state courts affirmed the conviction, one of several at the time involving the arrest of protestors who had used the same taboo word in public places, including one at the center of the Berkeley campus during the Free Speech Movement.[94] To the surprise of most observers, the U.S. Supreme Court agreed to review the conviction. Even greater was the surprise at the outcome—a six-to-three reversal of Cohen's conviction, with a ringing defense of free speech in a majority opinion by Justice John Marshall Harlan.[95] * * *

Justice Harlan [made] almost a virtue of the defendant's choice of language when he noted: "[I]t is often true, that one man's vulgarity is another's lyric."[103] If government could ban the public utterance of disfavored language, he warned, those in power "might soon seize upon the censorship of particular words as a convenient guise for banning the expression of unpopular views."[104] Thus it would be unwise and even dangerous for the high Court to assume "that one can forbid particular words without also running a substantial risk of suppressing ideas in the process."[105]

Herein lies the paradox of *Cohen* and its uneasy coexistence with *Chaplinsky* as an arbiter of civility in public discourse. The most persistent question, which the Justices had no occasion to address in *Cohen* and have managed to avoid ever since, is how far this judgment reflects the political context of Cohen's statement and the "unpopular view" whose expression was enhanced by the use of a taboo four-letter word. A few simple variants will suggest how soon we enter a realm of uncertainty. * * * [S]uppose Mr. Cohen had returned to the courthouse to flaunt his Supreme Court triumph, sporting the very same jacket, but having removed "the draft" to leave the offending word in splendid isolation. While charging him with a breach of the peace would still be problematic on the original facts, the gathering of a crowd angered by such language might change the circumstances. Any charge based on the isolated use of a vulgar and taboo word would require some assessment of the anti-war context of the actual *Cohen* case. While there is ample support in Justice Harlan's opinion for a non-contextual view—"one man's vulgarity is another's lyric," most notably—there are also grounds in the opinion for confining its protection of public incivility to the use of a taboo or vulgar term in order to, as the Court put it, "express unpopular views."[106]

The latter, context-driven and narrower, reading of *Cohen* seems recently to have gained favor. The lower federal courts have reviewed a growing number of charges brought against faculty members on the

92. *Cohen*, 403 U.S. at 16.

93. *Id.* at 17.

94. *Id.*

95. *Id.* at 26.

103. *Id.* at 25.

104. *Id.* at 26.

105. *Id.*

106. *Id.*

basis of their classroom use of vulgar and taboo language, usually designed to revive flagging student interest in arcane subject matter.[107] The legal fortunes of professors so charged have varied, more on the basis of particular institutional policies invoked than on broad academic freedom or free speech grounds.[108] The latest such ruling does, however, reopen the larger issue of incivility. John Bonnell, a long-time faculty member at a Michigan community college, was suspended for the occasional use of taboo and sexually offensive words in his classroom.[109] The particular choice of language was deemed to violate the college's sexual harassment policy.[110] Bonnell sought redress in federal court and persuaded a district judge that his free speech had been abridged.[111] The Sixth Circuit, however, took a much less sympathetic view than that of the district court, or of other federal courts that have recently assessed such claims.[112] The Sixth Circuit invoked a recent Supreme Court ruling which had sustained curbs on unwelcome approaches to clinic visitors by anti-abortion protestors.[113] In that case, the Supreme Court, in support of a patient's right to be free of unwanted entreaties while seeking clinic access, recalled *Cohen* in this way: "Even in a public forum, one of the reasons we tolerate a protestor's right to wear a jacket expressing his opposition to government policy in vulgar language is because offended viewers can effectively avoid further bombardment of their sensibilities simply by averting their eyes."[114] For the Sixth Circuit, this rather cautious use of *Cohen* buttressed its view that "the context in which a message is delivered is often the pivotal factor when determining whether the speech will be protected"—and held that, in Bonnell's case, the speech was protected.[115]

One citation does not, of course, reflect a trend. Nothing in *Bonnell* necessarily impairs or qualifies *Cohen*'s broad protection for public incivility. On the other hand, there may be some risk in continuing to assume that the unadorned utterance of taboo or vulgar words enjoys full First Amendment protection. That seems to be the premise on which the appellate courts of several states recently relied in the cases noted at the opening of this section.[116] The facts in none of those cases would have met *Chaplinsky*'s test for "fighting words," much less the more stringent test the Supreme Court later imposed on such outbursts.[117] Yet the holdings in these cases have caused uncertainty over the current balance between the contending interests in civility and free expression.[118]

107. *E.g.*, Cohen v. San Bernardino Valley College, 92 F.3d 968 (9th Cir. 1996).

108. 1 Silva v. Univ. of N.H., 888 F. Supp. 293 (D.N.H. 1994).

109. Bonnell v. Lorenzo, 241 F.3d 800, 803 (6th Cir. 2001).

110. *Id.*

111. *Id.* at 806–07.

112. *Id.* at 826–27.

113. *Id.* at 819.

114. Hill v. Colorado, 530 U.S. 703, 716 (2000).

115. *Bonnell*, 214 F.3d at 819.

116. *E.g.*, Minnesota v. Clay, No. CX–99–343, 1999 Minn. App. LEXIS 1059 (Minn. Ct. App. Sept. 14, 1999); Hamilton v. Johnson, No. CA99–02–025, 1999 Ohio App. LEXIS 5623 (Ohio Ct. App. Nov. 29, 1999).

117. *Id.*

118. *See, e.g.*, Melody L. Hurdle, R.A.V. v. City of St. Paul: *The Continuing Confusion of the Fighting Words Doctrine*, 47 Vand. L. Rev. 1143 (1994); E. Kenly Ames,

* * * *Cohen* and *Chaplinsky* cannot coexist indefinitely, because one declares that offensive epithets are "no essential part of any exposition of ideas" while the other insists with equal conviction that "one man's vulgarity is another's lyric."

IV. Equality and Free Expression

Patrick Suiter is not the only Idaho resident whose public utterances have incurred legal action. Not many months before Mr. Suiter's outburst, Lonnie Rae had been in the stands at a high school football game in Boise.[120] His wife Kim, a newspaper photographer, tried to photograph the referees in order to illustrate an article.[121] The referees objected, and one of them, an African–American named Ken Manley, tried to take Mrs. Rae's camera.[122] The husband then shouted at Manley, using a racially derogatory and offensive epithet.[123] He was promptly arrested and charged with violating a state hate-crime law, aimed specifically at "malicious harassment," conviction for which could bring a five-year prison sentence.[124] Although no further proceedings have yet been pursued, the Raes' attorney has maintained, and the facts confirm, that "the charge is based solely on the language [my client] used."[125]

Whether such abusive language, uttered at a football game or in any other public place, warrants a criminal sanction poses [another] of our persistent tensions. Here, too, we find continuing ambivalence among our own views and those of the courts—hardly a surprise since we greatly esteem both equality and free expression. For most of the past century, protecting vulnerable religious, ethnic, and other groups from extreme verbal assaults has been a high priority.[126] It has also been a source of much litigation, the results of which are as confusing as our national ambivalence toward the underlying values of equality and expression.[127] On one hand, the Supreme Court a half-century ago held that states may enact and enforce "group libel" laws against purveyors of hostile and demeaning racist tracts and the like.[128] Much more recently, a unanimous Court rendered a remarkable and not easily compatible pair of judgments striking down "hate speech" laws while upholding laws that impose harsher sentences on those who commit "hate crimes."[129] A journey along this tortuous path of First Amendment law concludes our review of persistent tensions between free expression and other transcendent societal values.

Note, *The Fighting Words Doctrine*, 93 Co-
LUM. L. REV. 1473 (1993); *Demise, supra* note
83 at 1111, 1129.

120. Aarika Mack, Hate–Crimes Bill
Raise First Amendment Concerns for Some,
Freedom Forum, *at* http://www.freedomfo-
rum.org/templates/document.asp? documen-
tID=13756 (Apr. 23, 2001).

121. *Id.*

122. *Id.*

123. *Id.*

124. *Id.*

125. *Id.*

126. 1 O'NEIL, FREE SPEECH, *supra* note
67 at 5–7.

127. 1 *Compare* Wisconsin v. Mitchell,
508 U.S. 476 (1993) *with* R.A.V. v. City of
St. Paul, 505 U.S. 377 (1992).

128. Beauharnais v. Illinois, 343 U.S.
250 (1952).

129. *R.A.V.*, 505 U.S. at 398.

We tend to assume that laws which protect vulnerable groups from verbal assault and abuse have recent origins. In fact, however, the first statute clearly aimed at curbing racist speech was adopted by the New York legislature in 1913.[130] This earliest version of what would come to be known as group libel laws specifically forbade hotels from discriminatory advertising—that is, publicly announcing a refusal to accommodate guests on the basis of race, color, or religion.[131] No concern about free expression was raised at the time; the only opposition came from those who feared hotels might be unable under the law to refuse rooms to persons infected with tuberculosis.[132]

By the mid 1920s, at least seven states had adopted similar anti-discrimination laws that targeted hostile words as well as acts.[133] Concern for the legal protection of minorities was further heightened in the post-war period by anti-Semitic publications, notably Henry Ford's Dearborn Independent and its focus on the allegedly subversive Protocols of Zion. Specific efforts were made by a number of cities, with mixed success, to ban distribution of Ford's newspaper.[134] For the first time, free speech and free press concerns were raised in opposition to such proposals.

The Michigan legislature declined to adopt such a measure largely because of challenge by the state's mainstream media and the fledgling American Civil Liberties Union.[135] A Cleveland, Ohio, ordinance aimed at the Independent was successfully challenged in federal court, producing what is undoubtedly the first judgment invalidating government efforts to suppress racist or ethnically offensive expression.[136] The American Jewish Committee viewed the events which led to such legislation with intense ambivalence, and the prospects for protection from verbal assaults of the Dearborn Independent variety with frustration.[137] The president of the Anti–Defamation League of B'Nai B'rith lamented in 1935 that, although the First Amendment "was never intended as a protection against group libel any more than as an obstacle individual libel," it had nonetheless posed "an insurmountable obstacle in bringing before the bar of justice one of the lowest forms of malefactors."[138]

Events in Europe leading up to World War II would intensify such concerns. The most direct response to the world-wide threat of Nazi propaganda was a two-part article written in 1942 by the young David Reisman, who was a law teacher well before his metamorphosis into the eminent sociologist he became a decade later.[139] Reisman's plea was for the wider enactment and enforcement of group libel laws, which he saw

---

130. Evan P. Schulz, *Group Rights, American Jews, and the Failure of Group Libel Laws, 1913–1952*, 66 Brooklyn L. Rev. 71, 92 (2000).

131. *Id.* at 91.

132. *Id.* at 92.

133. *Id.* at 98–99.

134. *Id.* at 102–03.

135. *Id.* at 105.

136. Dearborn Pub. Co. v. Fitzgerald, 271 Fed. 479 (N.D. Ohio 1921).

137. Schultz, *supra* note 130 at 110–11.

138. *Id.* at 111.

139. David Reisman, *Democracy and Defamation: Control of Group Libel*, 42 Colum. L. Rev. 727 (1942).

as the most effective antidote to Nazi propaganda.[140] Though he could hardly overlook the potential conflict with free speech and press that such laws would present, he insisted that, in perilous /times, even Bill of Rights guarantees must yield to national exigency: "[I]t is no longer tenable to continue a negative policy of protection from the state ... [which] plays directly into the hands of the groups whom supporters of democracy need most to fear."[141]

In substantial part as a response to Reisman's plea, a number of states did enact laws that specifically targeted racist, anti-religious, and otherwise ethnically demeaning publications.[142] The validity of such laws was bound to reach the Supreme Court, and, in 1951, it did.[143] The specific context was an Illinois law applied to the publications of a racist group known as the White Circle League.[144] The statute imposed penalties on those who published or exhibited material that "portrays depravity, criminality, unchastity, or lack of virtue of a class of citizens, of any race, color, creed, or religion which said publication or exhibition exposes the citizens of any race, color, creed, or religion to contempt, derision, or obloquy or which is productive of breach of the peace or riots."[145]

The officers of the White Circle League were charged with organizing the distribution of a provocative leaflet that urged the Chicago city government to "halt the further encroachment, harassment and invasion of white people, their property, neighborhoods and persons by the Negro" and called upon "one million self respecting white people in Chicago to unite."[146] The leaflet also warned of ominous prospects—" the rapes, robberies, knives, guns, and marijuana of the Negro"—should such pleas not be heeded by the white community.[147]

The Illinois courts sustained the convictions, rejecting First Amendment and due process claims, noting that the statute provided a defense only for publication "with good motives and for justifiable ends."[148] The state courts also rejected the defendants' plea that a "clear and present danger" must exist before such a sanction could be imposed on expression, however hateful.[149] A sharply divided U.S. Supreme Court in *Beauharnais v. Illinois* upheld the convictions and the validity of group libel laws.[150] The majority found persuasive an analogy to individual civil redress for defamation, and also by recent and earlier racial tensions in Chicago area: "We would deny experience," wrote Justice Frankfurter for the Court, "to say that the Illinois legislature was without reason in seeking ways to curb false or malicious defamation of racial and religious groups, made in public places and calculated to have a powerful emotion-

---

140. *Id.* at 777–78.

141. *Id.* at 779–80.

142. *E.g.*, the Illinois statute which the Supreme Court sustained in *Beauharnais*, 343 U.S. at 251.

143. *Beauharnais*, 343 U.S. at 251.

144. *Id.* at 252–53.

145. *Id.* at 251.

146. *Id.* at 252.

147. *Id.*

148. *Id.* at 254.

149. *Id.*

150. *Id.* at 267.

al impact on those to whom it was presented."[151] Since libel at that time claimed no First Amendment protection, there was no constitutional imperative for a clear and present danger standard.[152]

The dissenters were dismayed by such a ruling; Justice Black (who often cited *Beauharnais* as the Court's very worst judgment during his three and one-half decades) insisted that the majority "acts on the bland assumption that the First Amendment is wholly irrelevant."[153] Even Justice Stanley Reed, seldom counted among champions of free speech, dissented here, albeit more on due process than First Amendment grounds.[154] Justice Robert Jackson, usually found on the other side of such issues after his experience as chief War Crimes prosecutor at Nuremberg, also dissented from what he deemed an unsupportable inference of danger or threat from a misguided racist tract.[155]

Despite universal condemnation in later years[156] and ample opportunity, the Court has never overruled *Beauharnais*. Though one would today rely upon it at very considerable peril, as recently as a decade ago the Court cited *Beauharnais* as illustrative of categories of speech that had been denied First Amendment protection.[157] The central premise of *Beauharnais* may survive in a different and more ominous form. To what extent persistent efforts to curb racist, sexist, anti-religious, and homophobic rhetoric may have taken comfort from the survival of this precedent, albeit without honor, is impossible to tell. The fact remains that the past half-century has been a time of pervasive and recurrent effort to protect vulnerable groups in our society from words that may wound or offend because of racial, religious, ethnic or other differences.[158] This question has taken several forms beyond the criminal sanctions against "group libel" that were theoretically validated in *Beauharnais*.

In the late 1970s, a dozen or so states, including New York and California, did enact laws that imposed civil sanctions on those who uttered racially or religiously hostile words.[159] It was on the basis of such statutes, for example, that an upstate New York gift shop was ordered to remove from its window an abacus device jokingly labeled "Polish calculator"[160] and that a downstate restaurant owner was ordered to apologize in writing to a waitress whom he had denounced publicly as a "Jewish Broad" because she allegedly sought special treatment.[161] While

---

151. *Id.* at 261.

152. *Id.* at 267.

153. *Id.*

154. *Id.* at 277.

155. *Id.* at 287.

156. *See, e.g.,* HARRY KALVEN, JR., THE NEGRO AND THE FIRST AMENDMENT 15–16, 50–51 (1965).

157. New York v. Ferber, 458 U.S. 747, 763 (1982).

158. *See, e.g.,* O'NEIL, FREE SPEECH, *supra* note 67, at Chapter 1.

159. *E.g.,* N.Y. EXEC. LAW § 296 (1980).

160. The order was reversed by the Appellate Division, and the reversal was sustained by a sharply divided Court of Appeals. State Div. of Human Rights *ex rel.* Gladwin v. McHarris Gift Center, 419 N.Y.S.2d 405, *aff'd,* 418 N.E.2d 393 (N.Y. 1980).

161. Imperial Diner, Inc. v. State Human Rights Appeals Bd., 417 N.E.2d 525 (N.Y. 1980).

such laws were occasionally challenged, they seem to have remained on the books, largely forgotten and apparently seldom, if ever, enforced.[162]

The ensuing decade saw renewed focus on the protection of vulnerable groups in a very different form. Several hundred colleges and universities, responding both to minority student pressure and to an institutional quest for civility, adopted restrictive speech codes.[163] The precise approach varied substantially from campus to campus. Some such constraints were added to existing harassment codes,[164] while others buttressed anti-bias rules,[165] and a few targeted racially or religiously oriented "fighting words."[166] Legal challenges by civil liberties groups were not far behind.

By the mid 1990s, every speech code challenged in court was found wanting, chiefly because of imprecise language, often drafted in haste, that left the campus community genuinely uncertain about what language was prohibited.[167] Moreover, there was little evidence that the existence of such speech codes genuinely made a difference—either in the sensitivity of the campus racial climate, or in the civility of discourse.[168] Occasionally, even today, a university may consider adopting a speech code in response to racial or other campus tensions despite the dismal record of such regulations in the courts and the meager proof of positive impact.[169]

It is the latest attempt to balance free speech and equality that has produced the Supreme Court's conundrum. Even as speech codes were being challenged, some communities adopted "hate speech" laws.[170] The St. Paul, Minnesota, ordinance, which brought the issue to the high Court, was representative. That law made it a crime to place on public or private property "a symbol, object . . . or graffiti including, but not limited to, a burning cross or Nazi swastika, which one knows or has reasonable grounds to know arouses anger, alarm or resentment in others on the basis of race, color, creed, religion or gender."[171] One of the first persons so charged was a juvenile who had burned a cross on the lawn of an African–American family.[172] Although charges for trespass, arson, and other clearly unlawful conduct would have been in order, the prosecutor opted to use the newly enacted ordinance.[173]

---

162. *See* Robert M. O'Neil, *Second Thoughts on the First Amendment*, 13 N.M.L. Rev. 577, 588–89 (1983).

163. *See* O'Neil, Free Speech, *supra* note 67, at Chapter 1.

164. *Id.* at 8.

165. *Id.* at 8–9.

166. *Id.* at 9.

167. *E.g.*, Doe v. University of Michigan, 721 F. Supp. 852 (E.D. Mich. 1989).

168. *See* O'Neil, Free Speech, *supra* note 67, at 12–13.

169. For a relatively recent revival of such interest at Rutgers University, see John Carlin, *Racial Slur Sparks Student Revolt Against "PC" Notions*, The Independent, Feb. 19, 1995, at 16.

170. *E.g.*, St. Paul, Minn. Legis. Code § 292.012 (1990).

171. R.A.V. v. City of St. Paul, 505 U.S. 377, 379 (1992).

172. *Id.*

173. *Id.* at 380.

Minnesota's courts rejected First Amendment challenges to the law, and the Supreme Court granted certiorari.[174] The unanimity of the Justices in reversing the conviction in *R.A.V. v. St. Paul* masked a deep philosophical division within the Court.[175] For Justice Scalia, writing for the new majority, the fatal flaw of the ordinance was its reliance on content differentiation.[176] Even though the expression involved in such a case might well be less than fully protected—as fighting words, for example—its status did not empower government to "regulate [its] use based on hostility—or favoritism—towards the underlying message expressed."[177] While the City might well have forbidden all expression of a certain type, it could not selectively target only regulable speech which evoked tension or hostility "on the basis of race, color, creed, religion or gender" and not for other reasons or in other realms of advocacy.[178]

For the four Justices who concurred only in the result, such a novel approach departed sharply from familiar First Amendment jurisprudence, and potentially created far more problems than it solved–indeed, for one of these Justices, potentially "an aberration."[179] They were "puzzled" by the notion that otherwise unprotected speech, such as fighting words, might gain protection if targeted because of specific content.[180] For them, the same result should have been reached, and the conviction overturned, because of the overbreadth of the ordinance.[181] Under a narrower and more precise prohibition aimed at such activity, three of the concurring Justices strongly implied they would have been ready to recognize state power to proscribe such hateful activity, even if it incidentally included some expression.[182]

That suggestion soon proved prophetic. In the very next term, again with unanimity, the Court held in *Wisconsin v. Mitchell* that states might decree harsher sentences for those who commit certain criminal acts on the basis of the race of the victim.[183] Many states had, even while rejecting hate speech laws and codes, enacted versions of a model law which required a stiffer sentence if it were proved that the defendant had "select[ed] the person against whom the crime is committed because of the race, religion, color, disability, sexual orientation, national origin or ancestry of that person."[184]

Distinguishing hate crimes from hate speech might have proved an impossible task. The defendant in Mitchell had insisted that a racially hostile motive or animus could be established only by evidence of the very type of speech that *R.A.V.* seemed to protect from direct criminal sanctions.[185] Thus, the precise words that could not be reached directly because of the Court's concern about content selectivity now seemed

---

174. *Id.* at 380–81.

175. *Id.* at 379.

176. *Id.* at 381.

177. *Id.* at 386.

178. *Id.* at 391.

179. *Id.* at 415.

180. *Id.* at 402.

181. *Id.*

182. *Id.* at 417.

183. 508 U.S. 476, 490 (1993).

184. *Id.* at 483.

185. *Id.* at 488.

vulnerable to collateral use for the purpose of justifying a substantially harsher penalty.

The Mitchell Justices were not deterred. The Court reasoned that to the extent that a sentence-enhancement law targeted motive, it was not markedly different from reliance on motive for a host of other purposes.[186] Here the Court invoked two recent rulings that had allowed trial judges to take account of racial animus in the sentencing process and overlooked the difference between what was in those cases a discretionary use of words that revealed bias, and the mandatory use of such evidence under the Wisconsin law.[187] *R.A.V.* was distinguished in a few sentences as an ipse dixit. Although the law struck down the year before "was explicitly directed at expression (i.e., 'speech' or 'messages'), the statute in this case," declared the *Mitchell* opinion, "is aimed at conduct unprotected by the First Amendment."[188] Such a distinction was not satisfying at the time and, though the Court has not revisited the hate speech/hate crime distinction, it remains troubling a decade later.

If perfect consistency in so complex and contentious a field as First Amendment law is unrealistic, the current tension between free expression and equality leaves much to be desired. As though to illustrate, one of the Supreme Court's most recent rulings compounds the confusion. A divided Court ruled that the Boy Scouts of America could not, as a First Amendment matter, be compelled to accept a gay person as a scoutmaster in violation of longstanding policy and its declared mission.[189] In several previous encounters with comparable conflicts between freedom of association and anti-bias laws, the First Amendment claim had been forced to yield to a compelling state interest in equal access to places of public accommodation.[190] Thus, service organizations and even private social clubs had been required to admit women despite long traditions as all-male entities.[191] Now, however, the balance tipped the other way. What the Chief Justice found crucial was that compelled acceptance of a gay scoutmaster would "force the organization to send a message" abhorrent to its mission and its traditions.[192] In that respect, the majority found guidance in an earlier judgment which declined to force the organizers of a St. Patrick's Day parade to accept a gay and lesbian contingent, even though state law defined the parade as a "place of public accommodation" for such purposes.[193] In the parade case, the anti-bias law had been stretched well beyond its customary reading, and there was little doubt that having to include an unwelcome group in a two-hour event would have conveyed, if not compelled, an abhorrent message.[194]

---

186. *Id.* at 485.

187. *Id.* at 486–87.

188. *Id.* at 487.

189. Boy Scouts of Am. v. Dale, 530 U.S. 640, 661 (2000).

190. *E.g.*, Roberts v. United States Jaycees, 468 U.S. 609 (1984).

191. *E.g.*, New York State Club Ass'n v. New York, 487 U.S. 1 (1988).

192. *Id.* at 653.

193. *Id.* at 653–54.

194. Hurley v. Irish–Am. Gay, Lesbian & Bisexual Group, 515 U.S. 557, 574–75 (1995).

Such concerns were substantially muted, however, in the Boy Scout case. To the four dissenters, the private club precedents were dispositive, save for one implicit distinction.[195] "The only apparent explanation for the majority's holding," concluded Justice Stevens, "is that homosexuals are simply so different from the rest of society that their presence alone—unlike any other individual's—should be singled out for special First Amendment treatment."[196] Such a critique seems both harsh and warranted–though no harsher than the claim of Justices Scalia, Thomas, and Kennedy that, in sustaining curbs against anti-abortion protest, the Court has acted "in stark contradiction of the constitutional principles we apply in all other contexts."[197]

The culprit, in the Boy Scout case at least, is in substantial part our deep and persistent ambivalence about equality and expression.[198] Under the First Amendment, we highly value all speech. Almost alone among nations, we extend such protection fully to material that is racist, sexist, anti-Semitic, and homophobic.[199] Even Canada, whose values are remarkably similar to ours in virtually all respects, imprisons virulent anti-Semites and racists.[200] We still insist, at least in theory, that we do not recognize different levels of protection on the basis of favored and disfavored messages. Indeed, the teaching of *R.A.V.* is that even material which normally deserves less than full protection may somehow acquire such protection if it is targeted on the basis of its treatment of race, gender, religion, or sexual orientation.

Somehow our view of the relationship between equality and speech remains confused, and the tension unresolved. *Beauharnais*, to the extent it survives, suggests that certain sanctions may be appropriate for such expression where they would not (even a half century ago) have been acceptable for less volatile material. The Court's seemingly clear aversion to hate speech laws was sharply tempered by its readiness to embrace not easily distinguishable hate crime or sentence enhancement provisions. So it has been for well over a half century. Easy answers are not a ready prospect.

195. *Dale*, 530 U.S. at 696.

196. *Id.*

197. Hill v. Colorado, 730 U.S. 703, 742 (2000).

198. *See, e.g.*, Steven Shiffrin, *Racist Speech, Outsider Jurisprudence, and the Meaning of America*, 80 CORNELL L. REV. 43 (1994).

199. *See*, ROBERT M. O'NEIL, THE FIRST AMENDMENT AND CIVIL LIABILITY 14–15 (2001).

200. *E.g.*, R. v. Keegstra, [1990] 3 S.C.R. 697. The Canadian Human Rights Commission recently ruled that Holocaust denier Ernst Zundel must close down his Internet Web site because of the hateful messages it contained and disseminated. Noting that, on the Zundelsite, as it is often cited, "Jews are vilified in the most rabid and extreme manner," the Commission answered Zundel's free speech claims by observing that material such as that which he regularly posted "can erode an individual's personal dignity and self worth." See Kirk Makin, *Rights Group Orders Zundel to Kill Hate Site*, TORONTO GLOBE & MAIL, Jan. 19, 2002, at A7 (summarizing a sixty-nine page opinion rendered by the Commission the previous day).

Chapter IV

COMBATING THREATENING BE-HAVIOR, PEER HARASSMENT, AND PEER MISTREATMENT

In recent decades, relevant legal doctrine in the area of campus safety has expanded far beyond the traditional negligence inquiry. A large number of highly publicized campus shootings in the 1990s led to an increasing focus on threatening activity at the K–12 level, and this focus was ramped up considerably in the aftermath of the September 11, 2001 attacks. New developments in Title VII "hostile environment" law, combined with watershed national events such as the Anita Hill testimony at the confirmation hearings of Justice Clarence Thomas, led to an increasing awareness of peer-to-peer sexual harassment in the schools and widespread litigation seeking to hold educational institutions liable under Title IX. And litigation focusing on the mistreatment of LGBT students by their peers led to greater awareness in this area as well, and to notable rulings under the Equal Protection Clause.

As referenced above in Chapter 2, legal principles impacting campus safety often span a range of interrelated areas. It is not unusual, in this context, for on-campus injuries to raise questions relating to negligence, privacy, freedom of expression, threat law, harassment law, and/or equal protection.

The materials in this chapter reflect these developments and interrelationships. The chapter begins with an inquiry into threatening activity generally, examining relevant statutory language, and exploring examples of threat-related disputes that have arisen under both negligence law and criminal law. It then turns to freedom of expression issues, focusing on how courts have sought to determine whether speech that some find threatening might still be protected under the First Amendment.

In the last section of the chapter, the focus shifts to peer harassment and mistreatment, documenting the significant changes in relevant legal doctrine and the prospects for continued positive change in the future.

A.   THREATENING ACTIVITY GENERALLY

PROBLEM 16: Zero Tolerance for Threats I

Belinda—an eleventh grade student at a large public high school in the fictional state of Riverview—sends an e-mail from a school computer to a friend in the fictional state of Floral Valley, which reads in part: "I can't wait until I can kill the people in my class. I'll just go to the entrance of the school on a clear, sunny day and blow up and shoot everything I can." She also sends copies to five friends, one of whom shares it with her parents. The parents report the details to the school, which suspends Belinda for ten days under a new "zero tolerance for threats" policy enacted in the aftermath of the events at Columbine. Belinda is not only suspended from school, she is also arrested by the local police and charged with a violation of Riverview General Law Ch. 275, Section 2, which provides, in pertinent part:

> If complaint is made to any such court or justice that a person has threatened to commit a crime against the person or property of another, such court or justice shall examine the complainant and any witnesses who may be produced, on oath, reduce the complaint to writing and cause it to be subscribed by the complainant.

A.   The state is prepared to argue that Belinda is guilty of "threaten[ing] to commit a crime against the person or property of another," and should be adjudicated juvenile delinquent. What arguments might Belinda set forth in her defense? What result? Discuss.

B.   Assume that Belinda actually attempts to blow up and shoot everything she can, but is thwarted before any major damage occurs. However, three students are in fact shot, and spend months recovering from their injuries. If a negligence lawsuit is brought against the District, what arguments would be set forth? What result? Discuss.

1.   ADDRESSING THREATS UNDER NEGLIGENCE LAW

TARASOFF v. REGENTS OF UNIV. OF CAL.

17 Cal.3d 425, 131 Cal.Rptr. 14, 551 P.2d 334 (1976).

Tobriner, Justice.

On October 27, 1969, Prosenjit Poddar killed Tatiana Tarasoff. Plaintiffs, Tatiana's parents, allege that two months earlier Poddar confided his intention to kill Tatiana to Dr. Lawrence Moore, a psychologist employed by the Cowell Memorial Hospital at the University of California at Berkeley. They allege that on Moore's request, the campus police briefly detained Poddar, but released him when he appeared rational. They further claim that Dr. Harvey Powelson, Moore's superior, then directed that no further action be taken to detain Poddar. No one warned plaintiffs of Tatiana's peril.

* * *[2]

We shall explain that defendant therapists cannot escape liability merely because Tatiana herself was not their patient. When a therapist determines, or pursuant to the standards of his profession should determine, that his patient presents a serious danger of violence to another, he incurs an obligation to use reasonable care to protect the intended victim against such danger. The discharge of this duty may require the therapist to take one or more of various steps, depending upon the nature of the case. Thus it may call for him to warn the intended victim or others likely to apprise the victim of the danger, to notify the police, or to take whatever other steps are reasonably necessary under the circumstances.

* * *

2. *Plaintiffs can state a cause of action against defendant therapists for negligent failure to protect Tatiana.*

The second cause of action can be amended to allege that Tatiana's death proximately resulted from defendants' negligent failure to warn Tatiana or others likely to apprise her of her danger. Plaintiffs contend that as amended, such allegations of negligence and proximate causation, with resulting damages, establish a cause of action. Defendants, however, contend that in the circumstances of the present case they owed no duty of care to Tatiana or her parents and that, in the absence of such duty, they were free to act in careless disregard of Tatiana's life and safety.

In analyzing this issue, we bear in mind that legal duties are not discoverable facts of nature, but merely conclusory expressions that, in cases of a particular type, liability should be imposed for damage done. As stated in *Dillon v. Legg*, 68 Cal. 2d 728, 734 (1968): "The assertion that liability must ... be denied because defendant bears no 'duty' to plaintiff 'begs the essential question—whether the plaintiff's interests are entitled to legal protection against the defendant's conduct.... [Duty] is not sacrosanct in itself, but only an expression of the sum total of those considerations of policy which lead the law to say that the particular plaintiff is entitled to protection.' "

In the landmark case of *Rowland v. Christian*, 69 Cal. 2d 108 (1968), Justice Peters recognized that liability should be imposed "for injury occasioned to another by his want of ordinary care or skill" as expressed in section 1714 of the Civil Code. Thus, Justice Peters quoting from *Heaven* v. *Pender*, 11 Q.B.D. 503, 509 (1883) stated: "whenever one person is by circumstances placed in such a position with regard to another ... that if he did not use ordinary care and skill in his own conduct ... he would cause danger of injury to the person or property of

---

2. The therapist defendants include Dr. Moore, the psychologist who examined Poddar and decided that Poddar should be committed; Dr. Gold and Dr. Yandell, psychiatrists at Cowell Memorial Hospital who concurred in Moore's decision; and Dr. Powelson, chief of the department of psychiatry, who countermanded Moore's decision and directed that the staff take no action to confine Poddar.

the other, a duty arises to use ordinary care and skill to avoid such danger."

We depart from "this fundamental principle" only upon the "balancing of a number of considerations"; major ones "are the foreseeability of harm to the plaintiff, the degree of certainty that the plaintiff suffered injury, the closeness of the connection between the defendant's conduct and the injury suffered, the moral blame attached to the defendant's conduct, the policy of preventing future harm, the extent of the burden to the defendant and consequences to the community of imposing a duty to exercise care with resulting liability for breach, and the availability, cost and prevalence of insurance for the risk involved."

The most important of these considerations in establishing duty is foreseeability. As a general principle, a "defendant owes a duty of care to all persons who are foreseeably endangered by his conduct, with respect to all risks which make the conduct unreasonably dangerous." As we shall explain, however, when the avoidance of foreseeable harm requires a defendant to control the conduct of another person, or to warn of such conduct, the common law has traditionally imposed liability only if the defendant bears some special relationship to the dangerous person or to the potential victim. Since the relationship between a therapist and his patient satisfies this requirement, we need not here decide whether foreseeability alone is sufficient to create a duty to exercise reasonable care to protect a potential victim of another's conduct.

Although, as we have stated above, under the common law, as a general rule, one person owed no duty to control the conduct of another,[5] nor to warn those endangered by such conduct, the courts have carved out an exception to this rule in cases in which the defendant stands in some special relationship to either the person whose conduct needs to be controlled or in a relationship to the foreseeable victim of that conduct. Applying this exception to the present case, we note that a relationship of defendant therapists to either Tatiana or Poddar will suffice to establish a duty of care; as explained in section 315 of the Restatement Second of Torts, a duty of care may arise from either "(a) a special relation ... between the actor and the third person which imposes a duty upon the actor to control the third person's conduct, or (b) a special relation ... between the actor and the other which gives to the other a right of protection."

Although plaintiffs' pleadings assert no special relation between Tatiana and defendant therapists, they establish as between Poddar and defendant therapists the special relation that arises between a patient

---

5. This rule derives from the common law's distinction between misfeasance and nonfeasance, and its reluctance to impose liability for the latter.... Morally questionable, the rule owes its survival to "the difficulties of setting any standards of unselfish service to fellow men, and of making any workable rule to cover possible situations where fifty people might fail to rescue...." WILLIAM PROSSER, TORTS § 56, at 341 (4th ed. 1971). Because of these practical difficulties, the courts have increased the number of instances in which affirmative duties are imposed not by direct rejection of the common law rule, but by expanding the list of special relationships which will justify departure from that rule. See PROSSER, supra, § 56, at 348–50.

and his doctor or psychotherapist.[6] Such a relationship may support affirmative duties for the benefit of third persons. Thus, for example, a hospital must exercise reasonable care to control the behavior of a patient which may endanger other persons.[7] A doctor must also warn a patient if the patient's condition or medication renders certain conduct, such as driving a car, dangerous to others.

Although the California decisions that recognize this duty have involved cases in which the defendant stood in a special relationship *both* to the victim and to the person whose conduct created the danger,[9] we do not think that the duty should logically be constricted to such situations. Decisions of other jurisdictions hold that the single relationship of a doctor to his patient is sufficient to support the duty to exercise reasonable care to protect others against dangers emanating from the patient's illness. The courts hold that a doctor is liable to persons infected by his patient if he negligently fails to diagnose a contagious disease, or, having diagnosed the illness, fails to warn members of the patient's family.

Since it involved a dangerous mental patient, the decision in *Merchants Nat. Bank & Trust Co. of Fargo v. United States*, 272 F. Supp. 409 (D.N.D. 1967) comes closer to the issue. The Veterans Administration arranged for the patient to work on a local farm, but did not inform the farmer of the man's background. The farmer consequently permitted the patient to come and go freely during nonworking hours; the patient borrowed a car, drove to his wife's residence and killed her. Notwithstanding the lack of any "special relationship" between the Veterans Administration and the wife, the court found the Veterans Administration liable for the wrongful death of the wife.

In their summary of the relevant rulings Fleming and Maximov conclude that the "case law should dispel any notion that to impose on the therapists a duty to take precautions for the safety of persons threatened by a patient, where due care so requires, is in any way opposed to contemporary ground rules on the duty relationship. On the

---

6. The pleadings establish the requisite relationship between Poddar and both Dr. Moore, the therapist who treated Poddar, and Dr. Powelson, who supervised that treatment. Plaintiffs also allege that Dr. Gold personally examined Poddar, and that Dr. Yandell, as Powelson's assistant, approved the decision to arrange Poddar's commitment. These allegations are sufficient to raise the issue whether a doctor-patient or therapist-patient relationship, giving rise to a possible duty by the doctor or therapist to exercise reasonable care to protect a threatened person of danger arising from the patient's mental illness, existed between Gold or Yandell and Poddar. *See* DAVID M. HARNEY, MEDICAL MALPRACTICE 7 (1973).

7. When a "hospital has notice or knowledge of facts from which it might

reasonably be concluded that a patient would be likely to harm himself *or others* unless preclusive measures were taken, then the hospital must use reasonable care in the circumstances to prevent such harm."

9. *Ellis v. D'Angelo*, 116 Cal. App. 2d 310 (1953), upheld a cause of action against parents who failed to warn a babysitter of the violent proclivities of their child; *Johnson v. California*, 69 Cal. 2d 782 (1968), upheld a suit against the state for failure to warn foster parents of the dangerous tendencies of their ward; *Morgan v. County of Yuba*, 230 Cal. App. 2d 938 (1964), sustained a cause of action against a sheriff who had promised to warn decedent before releasing a dangerous prisoner, but failed to do so.

contrary, there now seems to be sufficient authority to support the conclusion that by entering into a doctor-patient relationship the therapist becomes sufficiently involved to assume some responsibility for the safety, not only of the patient himself, but also of any third person whom the doctor knows to be threatened by the patient.''

Defendants contend, however, that imposition of a duty to exercise reasonable care to protect third persons is unworkable because therapists cannot accurately predict whether or not a patient will resort to violence. In support of this argument amicus representing the American Psychiatric Association and other professional societies cites numerous articles which indicate that therapists, in the present state of the art, are unable reliably to predict violent acts; their forecasts, amicus claims, tend consistently to overpredict violence, and indeed are more often wrong than right. Since predictions of violence are often erroneous, amicus concludes, the courts should not render rulings that predicate the liability of therapists upon the validity of such predictions.

The role of the psychiatrist, who is indeed a practitioner of medicine, and that of the psychologist who performs an allied function, are like that of the physician who must conform to the standards of the profession and who must often make diagnoses and predictions based upon such evaluations. Thus the judgment of the therapist in diagnosing emotional disorders and in predicting whether a patient presents a serious danger of violence is comparable to the judgment which doctors and professionals must regularly render under accepted rules of responsibility.

We recognize the difficulty that a therapist encounters in attempting to forecast whether a patient presents a serious danger of violence. Obviously, we do not require that the therapist, in making that determination, render a perfect performance; the therapist need only exercise "that reasonable degree of skill, knowledge, and care ordinarily possessed and exercised by members of [that professional specialty] under similar circumstances." Within the broad range of reasonable practice and treatment in which professional opinion and judgment may differ, the therapist is free to exercise his or her own best judgment without liability; proof, aided by hindsight, that he or she judged wrongly is insufficient to establish negligence.

In the instant case, however, the pleadings do not raise any question as to failure of defendant therapists to predict that Poddar presented a serious danger of violence. On the contrary, the present complaints allege that defendant therapists did in fact predict that Poddar would kill, but were negligent in failing to warn.

Amicus contends, however, that even when a therapist does in fact predict that a patient poses a serious danger of violence to others, the therapist should be absolved of any responsibility for failing to act to protect the potential victim. In our view, however, once a therapist does in fact determine, or under applicable professional standards reasonably should have determined, that a patient poses a serious danger of violence to others, he bears a duty to exercise reasonable care to protect the foreseeable victim of that danger. While the discharge of this duty of due care will necessarily vary with the facts of each case,[11] in each instance the adequacy of the therapist's conduct must be measured against the traditional negligence standard of the rendition of reasonable care under the circumstances. As explained in Fleming and Maximov, *The Patient or His Victim: The Therapist's Dilemma*, 62 Cal. L. Rev. 1025, 1067 (1974): "... the ultimate question of resolving the tension between the conflicting interests of patient and potential victim is one of social policy, not professional expertise.... In sum, the therapist owes a legal duty not only to his patient, but also to his patient's would-be victim and is subject in both respects to scrutiny by judge and jury."

* * * Weighing the uncertain and conjectural character of the alleged damage done the patient by such a warning against the peril to the victim's life, we conclude that professional inaccuracy in predicting violence cannot negate the therapist's duty to protect the threatened victim.

The risk that unnecessary warnings may be given is a reasonable price to pay for the lives of possible victims that may be saved. We would hesitate to hold that the therapist who is aware that his patient expects to attempt to assassinate the President of the United States would not be obligated to warn the authorities because the therapist cannot predict with accuracy that his patient will commit the crime.

* * *

Notes

1. While *Tarasoff* is a state court ruling, it has increasingly taken on the trappings of a national decision, as one court after another adopted its principles and built on its conclusions. Issues continue to arise in this context, as commentators and jurists debate its prospective applicability to new and different fact patterns at both the higher education and the K–12 levels.

2. How relevant is the *Tarasoff* ruling to threat-related issues in the aftermath of Columbine and 9/11/01? Should the courts be applying *Tarasoff* to expand an educational institution's duties? *See* Melissa L. Gilbert, *Time-Out for Student Threats: Imposing a Duty to Protect on School Officials,* 49 UCLA L. Rev. 917 (2002).

3. Recall the *Peterson* decision from Chapter 2, *supra*, where several attempted rapes had occurred in the exact spot that plaintiff had been injured. The Court determined that—under the facts of the case—there was

---

11. Defendant therapists and amicus also argue that warnings must be given only in those cases in which the therapist knows the identity of the victim. We recognize that in some cases it would be unreasonable to require the therapist to interrogate his patient to discover the victim's identity, or to conduct an independent investigation. But there may also be cases in which a moment's reflection will reveal the victim's identity. The matter thus is one which depends upon the circumstances of each case, and should not be governed by any hard and fast rule.

a duty to exercise due care to protect students from reasonably foreseeable assaults on the campus. While the case, arguably, does not actually rule that a duty to protect would include a duty to warn, it certainly says that "plaintiff is entitled to prove that the failure to warn, to trim the foliage, or to take other reasonable measures to protect her was the proximate cause of her injuries."

Read together in light of current realities, *Tarasoff* and *Peterson* might very well stand for the proposition that in threat-related situations, a higher duty of care is more likely to be found, and that this obligation might often include a duty to warn. This may be particularly true in circumstances similar to those at Columbine, where students communicate through word and deed a desire or propensity to commit violent acts on campus.

4. A duty to warn may also be applicable in other education contexts. For example, an ongoing debate continues to rage in the area of sex education, with advocates of a more explicit curriculum—particularly relating to the threat of HIV—beginning to argue that educators have a legal obligation to warn students of the foreseeable dangers that may await them, and to communicate to them what precautions they could reasonably take to prevent irreversible injuries. *See infra*, Chapter 9.

2. RELEVANT STATUTORY PROHIBITIONS ADDRESSING THREATS UNDER FEDERAL & STATE LAW

At the K–12 level, state education codes generally permit all school districts to suspend students for threatening behavior on campus. Some statutes do not actually define the word *threat,* leaving it to local districts and individual educators to come up with workable descriptions of threatening activity. Others include either an actual definition or at least describe the type of threatening behavior that would be punishable. In certain circumstances—such as threats accompanied by possession of a weapon—suspensions or expulsions may be mandatory.

At the higher education level, threats are generally prohibited in student codes of conduct, and may be the basis for disciplinary action or even dismissal.

In general, both federal law and state law also include broad prohibitions against threatening behavior. These prohibitions are often found in the criminal law, and may sometimes be accompanied by precise definitions. At other times, the prohibitions are very general, leaving it to the courts to articulate tests for determining whether a person's words or actions, in a particular situation, might constitute a threat within the meaning of the statute.

With the increasing focus on hate-related violence in the U.S. over the past several decades, some state legislatures have made an effort to address threatening behavior in this context as well. California, for example, is one of a small but growing number of states that has sought to provide broad protection for all its citizens against threats and related activity on the basis of a person's actual or perceived group affiliation.

Consider the parameters of California Penal Code Section 422.6. Is such a statute important primarily for its symbolic value, or can it truly have a real-life impact?

CALIFORNIA PENAL CODE § 422.6

(Injury or Threat to Person or Damage to Property
because of Specified Beliefs or Characteristics).

(a) No person, whether or not acting under color of law, shall by force or threat of force, willfully injure, intimidate, interfere with, oppress, or threaten any other person in the free exercise or enjoyment of any right or privilege secured to him or her by the Constitution or laws of this state or by the Constitution or laws of the United States because of the other person's race, color, religion, ancestry, national origin, disability, gender, or sexual orientation, or because he or she perceives that the other person has one or more of those characteristics.

(b) No person, whether or not acting under color of law, shall knowingly deface, damage, or destroy the real or personal property of any other person for the purpose of intimidating or interfering with the free exercise or enjoyment of any right or privilege secured to the other person by the Constitution or laws of this state or by the Constitution or laws of the United States, because of the other person's race, color, religion, ancestry, national origin, disability, gender, or sexual orientation, or because he or she perceives that the other person has one or more of those characteristics.

(c) Any person convicted of violating subdivision (a) or (b) shall be punished by imprisonment in a county jail not to exceed one year, or by a fine not to exceed five thousand dollars ($5,000), or by both that imprisonment and fine, and the court shall order the defendant to perform a minimum of community service, not to exceed 400 hours, to be performed over a period not to exceed 350 days, during a time other than his or her hours of employment or school attendance. However, no person shall be convicted of violating subdivision (a) based upon speech alone, except upon a showing that the speech itself threatened violence against a specific person or group of persons and that the defendant had the apparent ability to carry out the threat.

Especially in the aftermath of Columbine, many people turned their attention to the Internet, seeking to identify ways to combat threatening behavior that may originate online. One particular area of focus was bomb-making activity, since so much information has been made available online regarding weapons, explosives, how to obtain them, and indeed how to make them.

A federal ban on "bomb-making instructions" was indeed passed by Congress as a result of these concerns, but its provisions were significantly limited by First Amendment considerations.

Consider the language of Section 842, which follows. Given the limiting language regarding knowledge and intent, can such a law play any sort of significant role in combating the very type of threatening behavior that its proponents were hoping to address?

Federal Ban on "Bomb–Making Instructions"
from **18 U.S.C. § 842 (2000)**

(p) Distribution of information relating to explosives, destructive devices, and weapons of mass destruction.

(1) Definitions. In this subsection—

(A) the term "destructive device" has the same meaning as in section 921(a)(4);[1]

(B) the term "explosive" has the same meaning as in section 844(j);[2]

(C) the term "weapon of mass destruction" has the same meaning as in section 2332a(c)(2).[3]

---

1. 18 U.S.C. § 921(a)(4) provides:

(4) The term "destructive device" means—

(A) any explosive, incendiary, or poison gas—

   (i) bomb,

   (ii) grenade,

   (iii) rocket having a propellant charge of more than four ounces,

   (iv) missile having an explosive or incendiary charge of more than one-quarter ounce,

   (v) mine, or

   (vi) device similar to any of the devices described in the preceding clauses;

(B) any type of weapon (other than a shotgun or a shotgun shell which the Secretary finds is generally recognized as particularly suitable for sporting purposes) by whatever name known which will, or which may be readily converted to, expel a projectile by the action of an explosive or other propellant, and which has any barrel with a bore of more than one-half inch in diameter; and

(C) any combination of parts either designed or intended for use in converting any device into any destructive device described in subparagraph (A) or (B) and from which a destructive device may be readily assembled.

The term "destructive device" shall not include any device which is neither designed nor redesigned for use as a weapon; any device, although originally designed for use as a weapon, which is redesigned for use as a signaling, pyrotechnic, line throw-ing, safety, or similar device; surplus ordinance sold, loaned, or given by the Secretary of the Army pursuant to the provisions of section 4684(2), 4685, or 4686 of title 10; or any other device which the Secretary of the Treasury finds is not likely to be used as a weapon, is an antique, or is a rifle which the owner intends to use solely for sporting, recreational or cultural purposes.

2. 18 U.S.C. § 844(j) provides:

the term "explosive" means gunpowders, powders used for blasting, all forms of high explosives, blasting materials, fuzes (other than electric circuit breakers), detonators, and other detonating agents, smokeless powders, other explosive or incendiary devices within the meaning of paragraph (5) of section 232 of this title, and any chemical compounds, mechanical mixture, or device that contains any oxidizing and combustible units, or other ingredients, in such proportions, quantities, or packing that ignition by fire, by friction, by concussion, by percussion, or by detonation of the compound, mixture, or device or any part thereof may cause an explosion.

3. 18 U.S.C. § 2332a(c)(2) provides:

(2) the term "weapon of mass destruction" means—

   (A) any destructive device as defined in section 921 of this title;

   (B) any weapon that is designed or intended to cause death or serious bodily injury through the release; dissemination, or impact of toxic or poisonous chemicals, or their precursors;

   (C) any weapon involving a disease organism; or

(2) Prohibition. It shall be unlawful for any person—

(A) to teach or demonstrate the making or use of an explosive, a destructive device, or a weapon of mass destruction, or to distribute by any means information pertaining to, in whole or in part, the manufacture or use of an explosive, destructive device, or weapon of mass destruction, with the intent that the teaching, demonstration, or information be used for, or in furtherance of, an activity that constitutes a Federal crime of violence; or

(B) to teach or demonstrate to any person the making or use of an explosive, a destructive device, or a weapon of mass destruction, or to distribute to any person, by any means, information pertaining to, in whole or in part, the manufacture or use of an explosive, destructive device, or weapon of mass destruction, knowing that such person intends to use the teaching, demonstration, or information for, or in furtherance of, an activity that constitutes a Federal crime of violence.

3. RECENT CRIMINAL LAW CASES ADDRESSING THREATENING ACTIVITY

COMMONWEALTH v. MILO M., A JUVENILE

433 Mass. 149, 740 N.E.2d 967 (2001).

IRELAND, J.

Milo M., a juvenile defendant, appeals from the Juvenile Court's adjudication of him as delinquent by reason of threatening his teacher in violation of G.L. c.275, § 2.[a] While public schools remain very safe places for children to be, with respect to this appeal, we face the important and troubling question whether, given recent, highly publicized incidents of school violence, a drawing that depicts a student pointing a gun at his teacher constitutes a threat. We conclude that it does, and thus, affirm the adjudication of delinquency.

1. *Facts and procedural history*

On October 27, 1998, the twelve year old juvenile sat at a desk in the hall directly outside of his classroom and drew a picture. While the juvenile was awaiting the principal's arrival to address with him "some issues from the previous day," a teacher at the school confiscated the drawing and showed it to the juvenile's teacher, Mrs. F. The drawing depicted a violent scene of the juvenile shooting Mrs. F. See Appendix A.

(D) any weapon that is designed to release radiation or radioactivity at a level dangerous to human life

a. Mass. Gen. Law ch. 275, § 2, provides:

If complaint is made to any such court or justice that a person has threatened to commit a crime against the person or property of another, such court or justice shall examine the complainant and any witnesses who may be produced, on oath, reduce the complaint to writing and cause it to be subscribed by the complainant.

Meanwhile, the juvenile left the desk, entered the classroom, took a piece of paper, returned to the desk in the hall and "proceeded to draw another picture." Moments later, the juvenile reentered the classroom and stood near the doorway. He held up the second picture, which depicted the juvenile pointing a gun at Mrs. F. See Appendix B. He looked at Mrs. F and in a defiant tone said, "[D]o you want this one too?" From where she was standing, Mrs. F could not see the drawing. However, after seeing the first drawing, and "[f]rom his posture, [and] the look on his face," Mrs. F realized that the juvenile was very upset and very angry. Because she did not want the juvenile to approach her, she instructed him to give the drawing to another student, who then gave it to Mrs. F. The juvenile returned to his desk in the hall without further comment. Mrs. F testified that, after seeing the second drawing, she became "apprehensive" and "[a]fraid for [her] safety." Apparently, as a result of these incidents, the juvenile was suspended immediately for three days and sent home. However, at the end of that same school day, both Mrs. F and the teacher who confiscated the first drawing witnessed the juvenile at the school, loitering very near Mrs. F's car.

Subsequently, the Worcester Division of the Juvenile Court Department issued a complaint, charging the juvenile with threatening Mrs. F in violation of G.L. c. 275, § 2. At trial, the judge adjudicated the juvenile delinquent by reason of threatening his teacher, on the basis of the second drawing.[2] The juvenile appealed, and we transferred the case on our own motion.

2. *The standard applied*

The word "threatened" is not defined in the Massachusetts threat statute, G.L. c. 275, § 2. However, "[t]he elements of threatening a crime include an expression of intention to inflict a crime on another and an ability to do so in circumstances that would justify apprehension on the part of the recipient of the threat."

* * *

There was sufficient evidence to support the judge's finding that the juvenile expressed an intent to commit the threatened crime and an ability to do so in circumstances that would justify apprehension on Mrs. F's part. In making this determination, we consider "the context in which the allegedly threatening [drawing was given to Mrs. F] and all of the surrounding circumstances." The juvenile's intention to carry out the threat may be inferred from several facts. First, the content of each drawing separately evidences his intent.[6] The first drawing portrays a figure, labeled with the juvenile's name, pointing what appears to be a

---

2. The judge found that the first drawing could not have constituted a threat because the juvenile himself did not communicate it to Mrs. F.

6. In finding that the second drawing constituted a threat, the judge considered the first drawing, which he found to "por-

tray[ ] an act of violence being perpetrated upon the teacher." The fact that the judge ruled that the first drawing was not a separate threat because the juvenile did not communicate it to Mrs. F, did not diminish its evidentiary value and he could have inferred the juvenile's intent from it.

gun at another figure, labeled with Mrs. F's name. The Mrs. F figure has her hands clasped in front of her and is crying and pleading, "Please don't kill me." Drawn directly next to the Mrs. F figure is another unlabeled figure, whose head is falling off to the right. At the bottom of the drawing is the word "Blood," written in large letters. The second drawing depicts a figure labeled with the juvenile's name, aiming a gun at another figure, labeled with Mrs. F's name. Directly above the Mrs. F figure are the words "Pissy Pants." The Mrs. F figure is kneeling with her hands clasped in front of her, and appears to have urinated on herself, suggesting her extreme fear of being shot. Some words are written inside a box drawn under the barrel of the gun; one of the words appears to be "Bang." The content of both drawings makes the juvenile's intent to harm Mrs. F clear.[7] Second, the juvenile made not just one, but two drawings, both of which depicted images of himself perpetrating violence upon Mrs. F. The judge could have inferred the juvenile's intent from the number of drawings. Third, the juvenile's intent may be inferred from his very angry demeanor and defiant manner toward Mrs. F when he held out the drawing to her. Thus, there was sufficient evidence to support the judge's finding that the drawing was "an expression of an intention to harm...."

As to the juvenile's present ability to carry out the threat, the juvenile contends that "there was no direct evidence that the [juvenile] had the ability to commit this crime." There was, however, sufficient circumstantial evidence to support this finding. This is not a case where the finding of ability "rest[s] on surmise, conjecture, or guesswork." Indeed, as discussed above, the juvenile held the second of two very violent drawings out to Mrs. F in an angry and defiant manner. Moreover, prior to the incident, the juvenile was sitting out in the hall, awaiting the principal's arrival. Although it is not clear exactly what, if anything, the juvenile had done to warrant this discipline, the teacher who confiscated the first drawing testified that "[u]sually, if a student is outside the room, [the student] had done something to cause that situation...." Thus, the judge could have reasonably inferred that the juvenile was already being disciplined, and that Mrs. F, as his teacher, "was familiar with the [juvenile's] history" at school and in her classroom.

Moreover, although there is no evidence that the juvenile possessed an immediate ability to carry out the threat at the time he communicated the drawing to Mrs. F, this does "not mean that [the juvenile] could not have carried out his threat at a later time." Indeed, the juvenile's ability to carry out the threat in the future could have been inferred from the fact that the juvenile was seen loitering near Mrs. F's car later the same day.

---

7. The intent that must be expressed is an intent to commit a crime. We note that both drawings depict extreme fear on the part of Mrs. F and express the juvenile's desire to instill such fear on her part. As-suming that the drawings should not be interpreted as an intent to actually shoot Mrs. F, an intent to assault her by means of a dangerous weapon would still constitute an intent to commit a crime.

Finally, given the recent highly publicized, school-related shootings by students, we take judicial notice of the actual and potential violence in public schools. Although we note that schools remain very safe places for children to be, such violent episodes are matters of common knowledge, particularly within the teaching community, and thus, are "indisputably true."[8] Recently, "[o]ther children of like age [have] made similar threats . . . and [have] carried them out with tragic consequences for both juveniles and their victims."

These factors, when considered in light of the "climate of apprehension" concerning school violence in which this incident occurred, make Mrs. F's fear that the juvenile could carry out the threat quite reasonable and justifiable.

Finally, we conclude that the record supports the finding that the juvenile communicated the threat, vis-a-vis the second drawing, to Mrs. F. Indeed, the obviously angry juvenile entered Mrs. F's classroom, held out the second violent picture—the content of which was directed at Mrs. F—to her and defiantly asked, "[D]o you want this one too?" Although Mrs. F testified that initially, she could not "really see" the picture, she was able to once she received it from the other student shortly thereafter. From these facts, the judge could have found that the drawing itself, when held out to Mrs. F, communicated the threat. Viewed in the light most favorable to the Commonwealth, the combina-

---

8. We take judicial notice of the fact that, prior to this incident, the following highly publicized school shootings had occurred: On February 2, 1996, in Moses Lake, Washington, a fourteen year old fatally shot a teacher and two students and wounded another student; on February 19, 1997, in Bethel, Alaska, a sixteen year old shot and killed his principal and a student, and wounded two other students; on October 1, 1997, in Pearl, Mississippi, a sixteen year old boy shot his mother, and then went to school and shot nine students, two fatally; on December 1, 1997, in West Paducah, Kentucky, a fourteen year old student shot and killed three students and wounded five others; on March 24, 1998, in Jonesboro, Arkansas, two boys, aged eleven and thirteen years, shot to death four girls and a teacher, and wounded ten others during a false fire alarm; on April 24, 1998, in Edinboro, Pennsylvania, a fourteen year old student was charged with fatally shooting his science teacher at an eighth grade dance; on May 19, 1998, in Fayetteville, Tennessee, an eighteen year old honor student allegedly shot his classmate to death in the parking lot of their high school; on May 21, 1998, in Springfield, Oregon, a fifteen year old boy allegedly shot and killed two of his classmates and wounded more than twenty other students; on June 15, 1998, in Richmond, Virginia, a fourteen year old allegedly wounded one teacher and one guidance counselor in a high school. This tragic trend regrettably continued after the incident at issue in this case occurred. On April 20, 1999, at Columbine High School in Littleton, Colorado, two young men fatally shot fourteen students and one teacher and wounded at least twenty-three others, before taking their own lives. *See 25 Feared Dead, 20 Hurt in High School Shooting: Colorado Rampage Ends When 2 Commit Suicide*, COURIER JOURNAL (Louisville, Kentucky), Apr. 21, 1999 at 1A; *Haney, A Timeline of Recent School Shootings* (Apr. 27, 2000); *ABC News, An Explosion of Violence* (Mar. 28, 2000). We also note that, in 1985, the United States Supreme Court noted that "in recent years, school disorder has often taken particularly ugly forms: drug use and violent crime in the schools have become major social problems." New Jersey v. T.L.O., 469 U.S. 325, 339, 105 S.Ct. 733 (1985). Additionally, in 1995, the United States Supreme Court in a dissent by Justice Breyer noted that "reports, hearings, and other readily available literature make clear that the problem of guns in and around schools is widespread and extremely serious." United States v. Lopez, 514 U.S. 549, 619, 115 S.Ct. 1624, 1657 (1995) (Breyer, J., dissenting).

tion of these factors sufficiently supports the finding that the juvenile communicated the threat to Mrs. F.

This evidence, when viewed as a whole "may constitute the requisite expression [of intention to do bodily harm], and may indicate additionally, in these circumstances, ability and apprehension." Thus, we find that sufficient evidence supports the judge's decision that the drawing constituted a threat.

"[T]he First Amendment [to the United States Constitution] does not protect conduct that threatens another." Because we find there was sufficient evidence to support the judge's conclusion that the juvenile's drawing constituted a threat, there is no violation of the juvenile's First Amendment rights.

The adjudication of delinquency is affirmed.

So ordered.

Appendices to *Milo M.*

APPENDIX A

APPENDIX B

IN RE GEORGE T.

33 Cal.4th 620, 16 Cal.Rptr.3d 61, 93 P.3d 1007 (2004).

MORENO, J.

We consider in this case whether a high school student made a criminal threat by giving two classmates a poem labeled "Dark Poetry," which recites in part, "I am Dark, Destructive, & Dangerous. I slap on my face of happiness but inside I am evil!! For I can be the next kid to bring guns to kill students at school. So parents watch your children cuz I'm BACK!!" For the reasons below, we conclude that the ambiguous nature of the poem, along with the circumstances surrounding its dissemination, fail to establish that the poem constituted a criminal threat.

I. FACTS AND PROCEDURAL HISTORY

Fifteen-year-old George T. (minor) had been a student at Santa Teresa High School in Santa Clara County for approximately two weeks when on Friday, March 16, 2001, toward the end of his honors English class, he approached fellow student Mary S. and asked her, "Is there a poetry class here?" Minor then handed Mary three sheets of paper and told her, "[r]ead these." Mary did so. The first sheet of paper contained a note stating, "These poems describe me and my feelings. Tell me if they describe you and your feelings." The two other sheets of paper contained poems. Mary read only one of the poems, which was labeled "Dark Poetry" and entitled "Faces":

> Who are these faces around me? Where did they come from? They would probably become the next doctors or loirs or something. All really intelligent and ahead in their game. I wish I had a choice on what I want to be like they do. All so happy and vagrant. Each origonal in their own way. They make me want to puke. For I am Dark, Destructive, & Dangerous. I slap on my face of happiness but inside I am evil!! For I can be the next kid to bring guns to kill students at school. So parents watch your children cuz I'm BACK!!
>
> by: Julius AKA Angel[1]

Minor had a "straight face," not "show[ing] any emotion, neither happy or sad or angry or upset," when he handed the poems to Mary.

Upon reading the "Faces" poem, Mary became frightened, handed the poems back to minor, and immediately left the campus in fear. After she informed her parents about the poem, her father called the school, but it was closed. Mary testified she did not know minor well, but they were on "friendly terms." When asked why she felt minor gave her the poem to read, she responded: "I thought maybe because the first day he came into our class, I approached him because that's the right thing to do" and because she continued to be nice to him.

After Mary handed the poems back to minor, minor approached Erin S. and Natalie P., students minor had met during his two weeks at Santa Teresa High School. Erin had been introduced to minor a week prior and had subsequently spoken with him on only three or four occasions,

---

1. Minor went by the name "Julius"; misspelled words are in original.

whereas Natalie considered herself minor's friend and had come to know him well during their long after-school conversations, which generally lasted between an hour to an hour and a half and included discussions of poetry. Minor handed Erin a "folded up" piece of paper and asked her to read it. He also handed a similarly folded piece of paper to Natalie, who was standing with Erin. Because Erin was late for class, she only pretended to read the poem to be polite, but did not actually read it. She placed the unread poem in the pocket of her jacket.

* * * Mary remained in fear throughout the weekend because she understood the poem to be personally threatening to her, as a student. Asked why she felt the poem was a threat, Mary responded: "It's obvious he thought of himself as a dark, destructive, and dangerous person. And if he was willing to admit that about himself and then also state that he could be the next person to bring guns and kill students, then I'd say that he was threatening." She understood the term "dark poetry" to mean "angry threats; any thoughts that aren't positive."

* * *

Police officers went to the school the following Monday to investigate the dissemination of the poem. Erin was summoned to the vice-principal's office and asked whether minor had given her any notes. She responded in the affirmative, realized that the poem was still in the pocket of her jacket, and retrieved it. The paper contained a poem entitled "Faces," which was the same poem given to Mary. Upon reading the poem for the first time in the vice-principal's office, Erin became terrified and broke down in tears, finding the poem to be a personal threat to her life. She testified that she was not in the poetry club and had no interest in the subject.

* * *

Natalie did not feel threatened by the poem, rather it made her "feel sad" because "[i]t was kind of lonely." She testified that "dark poetry is * * * relevant to like pure emotions, like sadness, loneliness, hate or just like pure emotions. Sometimes it tells a story, like a dark story." Based on her extended conversations with minor, Natalie found him to be "mild and calm and very serene" and did not consider him to be violent.

Minor testified the poem "Faces" was not intended to be a threat and, because Erin and Natalie were his friends, he did not think they would have taken his poems as such. He thought of poetry as art and stated that he was very much interested in the subject, particularly as a medium to describe "emotions instead of acting them out." He wrote "Faces" during his honors English class on the day he showed it to Mary and Erin. Minor was having a bad day as a consequence of having forgotten to ask his parents for lunch money and having to forgo lunch that day, and because he was unable to locate something in his backpack. He had many thoughts going through his head, so he decided to write them down as a way of getting them out. The poem "Who Am I," which was given to Natalie, was written the same day as "Faces," but was written during the lunch period. Neither poem was intended to be a threat. Instead they were "just creativity."

Minor and his friends frequently joked about the school shootings in Littleton, Colorado.[3] They would jokingly say, "I'm going to be the next Columbine kid." Minor testified that Natalie and Erin had been present when he and some of his friends had joked about Columbine, with someone stating that "I'll probably be the next Columbine killer," and indicating who would be killed and who would be spared. Given this past history, minor believed Natalie and Erin would understand the poems as jokes.

The poems were labeled "dark poetry" to inform readers that they were exactly that and, minor testified, "if anybody was supposed to read this poem, or let's say if my mom ever found my poem or something of that nature, I would like them to know that it was dark poetry. Dark poetry is usually just an expression. It's creativity. It is not like you're actually going to do something like that, basically."

* * *

On cross-examination, minor conceded that he had had difficulties in his two previous schools, including being disciplined for urinating on a wall at his first school and had been asked to leave his second school for plagiarizing from the Internet. He explained that the urination incident was caused by a doctor-verified bladder problem. He denied having any ill will toward the school district, but conceded when pressed by the prosecutor that he felt the schools "had it in for me."

An amended petition under Welfare and Institutions Code section 602 was filed against minor, alleging minor made three criminal threats in violation of Penal Code section 422.[4] * * *

Following a contested jurisdictional hearing, * * * the court adjudicated minor a ward of the court and ordered a 100–day commitment in juvenile hall. Minor appealed, challenging the sufficiency of the evidence to support the juvenile court's finding that he made criminal threats. Over a dissent, the Court of Appeal affirmed the juvenile court. * * * We granted review and now reverse.

II. DISCUSSION

* * * [We have made it clear] ... that not all threats are criminal and enumerated the elements necessary to prove the offense of making criminal threats under section 422. The prosecution must prove "(1)

---

3. This reference is to the 1999 school shooting at Columbine High School in Colorado involving two student shooters that resulted in the death of 12 fellow students and one faculty member.

4. Section 422 provides in relevant part:

Any person who willfully threatens to commit a crime which will result in death or great bodily injury to another person, with the specific intent that the statement, made verbally [or] in writing ... is to be taken as a threat, even if there is no intent of actually carrying it out, which,

on its face and under the circumstances in which it was made, is so unequivocal, unconditional, immediate, and specific as to convey to the person threatened, a gravity of purpose and an immediate prospect of execution of the threat, and thereby causes that person reasonably to be in sustained fear for his or her own safety, shall be punished by imprisonment in the county jail not to exceed one year, or by imprisonment in the state prison.

that the defendant 'willfully threaten[ed] to commit a crime which will result in death or great bodily injury to another person,' (2) that the defendant made the threat 'with the specific intent that the statement * * * is to be taken as a threat, even if there is no intent of actually carrying it out,' (3) that the threat—which may be 'made verbally, in writing, or by means of an electronic communication device'—was 'on its face and under the circumstances in which it [was] made, * * * so unequivocal, unconditional, immediate, and specific as to convey to the person threatened, a gravity of purpose and an immediate prospect of execution of the threat,' (4) that the threat actually caused the person threatened 'to be in sustained fear for his or her own safety or for his or her immediate family's safety,' and (5) that the threatened person's fear was 'reasonabl[e]' under the circumstances.''

    * * *

* * * Minor challenges the findings with respect to two of the five elements, contending that the poem "was [not] 'on its face and under the circumstances in which it [was disseminated] so unequivocal, unconditional, immediate, and specific as to convey to [Mary and Erin] a gravity of purpose and an immediate prospect of execution of the threat' '' and that the facts fail to establish he harbored the specific intent to threaten Mary and Erin.

With respect to the requirement that a threat be "so unequivocal, unconditional, immediate, and specific as to convey to the person threatened a gravity of purpose and an immediate prospect of execution of the threat," we ... [have] ... explained that the word "so" in section 422 meant that " 'unequivocality, unconditionality, immediacy and specificity are not absolutely mandated, but must be sufficiently present in the threat and surrounding circumstances....' '' "The four qualities are simply the factors to be considered in determining whether a threat, considered together with its surrounding circumstances, conveys those impressions to the victim." A communication that is ambiguous on its face may nonetheless be found to be a criminal threat if the surrounding circumstances clarify the communication's meaning.

With the above considerations in mind, we examine the poem at issue—"Faces." What is readily apparent is that much of the poem plainly does not constitute a threat. "Faces" begins by describing the protagonist's feelings about the "faces" that surround him: "Where did they come from? They would probably become the next doctors or loirs or something. All really intelligent and ahead in their game. I wish I had a choice on what I want to be like they do. All so happy and vagrant. Each origonal in their own way. They make me want to puke." These lines convey the protagonist's feelings about the students around him and describe his envy over how happy and intelligent they appear to be, with opportunities he does not have. There is no doubt this portion of the poem fails to convey a criminal threat as no violent conduct whatsoever is expressed or intimated. Neither do the next two lines of the poem convey a threat: "For I am Dark, Destructive, & Dangerous. I slap on my face of happiness but inside I am evil!!'' These lines amount to an introspective description of the protagonist, disclosing that he is "destructive," "dangerous," and "evil." But again, such divulgence threatens no action.

Only the final two lines of the poem could arguably be construed to be a criminal threat: "For I can be the next kid to bring guns to kill students at school. So parents watch your children cuz I'm BACK!!" Mary believed this was a threat, but her testimony reveals that her conclusion rested upon a considerable amount of interpretation: "I feel that when he said, 'I can be the next person,' that he meant that he will be, because also he says that he's dark, destructive, and dangerous person. And I'd describe a dangerous person as someone who has something in mind of killing someone or multiple people." The juvenile court's finding that minor threatened to kill Mary and Erin likewise turned primarily on its interpretation of the words, "For I *can* be the next kid to bring guns to kill students at school" (italics added) to mean not only that minor could do so, but that he would do so. In other words, the court construed the word "can" to mean "will." But that is not what the poem recites. However the poem was interpreted by Mary and Erin, and the court, the fact remains that "can" does not mean "will." While the protagonist in "Faces" declares that he has the potential or capacity to kill students given his dark and hidden feelings, he does not actually threaten to do so. While perhaps discomforting and unsettling, in this unique context this disclosure simply does not constitute an actual threat to kill or inflict harm.

As is evident, the poem "Faces" is ambiguous and plainly equivocal. It does not describe or threaten future conduct since it does not state that the protagonist plans to kill students, or even that any potential victims would include Mary or Erin. Such ambiguity aside, it appears that Mary actually misread the text of the poem. In her e-mail to Rasmussen, she stated that the poem read, "he's *going* to be the next person to bring a gun to school and kill random people.'" (Italics added.) She did not tell Rasmussen that this was her interpretation of the poem, but asserted that those were the words used by minor. Given the student killings in Columbine and Santee, this may have been an understandable mistake, but it does not alter the requirement that the words actually used must constitute a threat in light of the surrounding circumstances.

* * * [In this regard, the note given to Mary] . . . is consistent with the contention that the poem did nothing more than describe certain dark feelings. The note asked whether Mary had the same feelings; it did not state or imply something to the effect of, "this is what I plan to do, are you with me."

Of course, exactly what the poem means is open to varying interpretations because a poem may mean different things to different readers. As a medium of expression, a poem is inherently ambiguous. In general, "[r]easonable persons understand musical lyrics and poetic conventions as the figurative expressions which they are," which means they "are not intended to be and should not be read literally on their face, nor judged by a standard of prose oratory." Ambiguity in poetry is sometimes intended: " 'Ambiguity' itself can mean an indecision as to what you mean, an intention to mean several things, a probability that one or the other or both of two things has been meant, and the fact that a statement has several meanings." * * *

In short, viewed in isolation the poem is not "so unequivocal" as to have conveyed to Mary and Erin a gravity of purpose and an immediate prospect that minor would bring guns to school and kill them. Ambiguity, however, is not necessarily sufficient to immunize the poem from being deemed a criminal threat because the surrounding circumstances may clarify facial ambiguity. * * *

[However,] [u]nlike some cases that have turned on an examination of the surrounding circumstances given a communication's vagueness, incriminating circumstances in this case are noticeably lacking: there was no history of animosity or conflict between the students.... Thus the circumstances surrounding the poem's dissemination fail to show that, as a threat, it was sufficiently unequivocal to convey to Mary and Erin an immediate prospect that minor would bring guns to school and shoot students.

The themes and feelings expressed in "Faces" are not unusual in literature * * * "Faces" was in the style of a relatively new genre of literature called "dark poetry" that amici curiae J.M. Coetzee et al. explain is an extension of the poetry of Sylvia Plath, John Berryman, Robert Lowell, and other confessional poets who depict "extraordinarily mean, ugly, violent, or harrowing experiences." Consistent with that genre, "Faces" invokes images of darkness, violence, discontentment, envy, and alienation. The protagonist describes his duplicitous nature—malevolent on the inside, felicitous on the outside.

For the foregoing reasons, we hold the poem entitled "Faces" and the circumstances surrounding its dissemination fail to establish that it was a criminal threat because the text of the poem, understood in light of the surrounding circumstances, was not "so unequivocal, unconditional, immediate, and specific as to convey to [the two students] a gravity of purpose and an immediate prospect of execution of the threat."

Our conclusion that the poem was not an unequivocal threat disposes of the matter and we need not, and do not, discuss minor's contention that he did not harbor the specific intent to threaten the students as required by section 422.

This case implicates two apparently competing interests: a school administration's interest in ensuring the safety of its students and faculty versus students' right to engage in creative expression. Following Columbine, Santee, and other notorious school shootings, there is a heightened sensitivity on school campuses to latent signs that a student may undertake to bring guns to school and embark on a shooting rampage. Such signs may include violence-laden student writings. For example, the two student killers in Columbine had written poems for their English classes containing "extremely violent imagery." Ensuring a safe school environment and protecting freedom of expression, however, are not necessarily antagonistic goals.

Minor's reference to school shootings and his dissemination of his poem in close proximity to the Santee school shooting no doubt reasonably heightened the school's concern that minor might emulate the actions of previous school shooters. Certainly, school personnel were amply justified in taking action following Mary's e-mail and telephone conversation with her English teacher, but that is not the issue before us. We decide here only that minor's poem did not constitute a criminal threat.

* * *

Notes

1. There are many parallels between the *Milo M.* case and the *George T.* case. In particular, both reflect the efforts of state supreme court justices to wrestle with threat-related issues within a national context in the aftermath of Columbine and related events.

2. Given the parallels and the broad similarities, why did the decisions come out differently? Why did the Massachusetts court rule against the student, while the California court ruled in the student's favor? Can the two opinions be reconciled, or do they ultimately stand as examples of different state courts coming to different conclusions regarding the same issue?

3. It is interesting to note that in *Milo M.*, had it not been for the teacher who came upon the student after he had completed the first drawing, none of the subsequent events would have happened and arguably no threatening behavior would have taken place. Was the court wrong in its decision to apparently pay no attention to the fact that had this other teacher left things alone, the situation would not have careened out of control?

4. In the late 1990s, a series of hate-related e-mail cases led to highly publicized prosecutions of persons at the higher education level. Perhaps the most prominent of these cases was *United States v. Machado,* No. SACR 96–142–AHS (S.D. Cal. 1998). Richard Machado—a former UC Irvine student—was found guilty of violating federal civil rights laws after sending a hateful and threatening e-mail message to 59 UCI students with Asian surnames. The message, signed "Asian Hater," warned that all Asians should leave UC Irvine or the sender would "hunt all of you down and kill your stupid asses." He also wrote: "I personally will make it my life's work to find and kill every one of you personally. OK? That's how determined I am. Do you hear me?" At trial, the defense attempted to portray Machado's actions as "a classic flame," and argued that no reasonable person should have felt threatened by it. But the federal court did not agree. *See also* Davan Maharaj, *Anti-Asian E–Mail Was Hate Crime, Jury Finds*, L.A. TIMES, Feb. 11, 1998, at A1.

A case with many similarities was resolved without a trial in 1999 when Kingman Quon—a Cal Poly Pomona student—pled guilty to seven misdemeanor counts of interfering with federally protected activities. Quon had sent his message to persons with Hispanic surnames across the U.S., including 42 professors at California State University, Los Angeles, 25 students at MIT, and employees of Indiana University, Xerox Corp., the Texas Hispanic Journal, the Internal Revenue Service, and NASA's Ames Research Center. The message was two pages long, strewn with profanity, and began with the words "I hate your race. I want you all to die." It also included such phrases as "kill all wetbacks." David Rosenzweig, *Man Charged in Sending Hate E–Mail to Latinos Across U.S.*, L.A. TIMES, Jan. 29, 1999, at B1.

B. FIRST AMENDMENT ISSUES IN A THREAT–RELATED CONTEXT

Case law regarding threats in an education setting—and indeed threat-related case law in general—remains relatively unsettled at this point in time. Different courts may approach the issues in different ways, and different circuits have set forth different tests for deciding the First Amendment questions.

In sorting through this material, it is useful to divide the cases into two general categories: those that involve actual criminal prosecutions, and those that only involve some sort of administrative/ disciplinary action taken against the student.

In the criminal cases, some courts simply base the inquiry on whether the elements of the criminal statute were violated. This is true for the *Milo M.* and *George T.* cases, above, and for the Sixth Circuit majority in *United States v. Alkhabaz,* below. Other courts link the criminal analysis to whether there was a "true threat" as defined by First Amendment case law. Examples of this are the Sixth Circuit dissent by Judge Krupansky in *Alkhabaz,* and the Wisconsin Supreme Court's opinion in *Douglas D., infra.*

The *Douglas D.* analysis is a particularly good example of how First Amendment doctrine fits into a criminal prosecution:

> [F]or purposes of First Amendment analysis, a "threat" is very different from a "true threat." "Threat" is a nebulous term that can describe anything from "[a]n expression of an intention to inflict pain, injury, evil, or punishment" to any generalized "menace." Under such a broad definition, "threats" include protected and unprotected speech. Thus, states cannot enact general laws prohibiting all "threats" without infringing on some speech protected by the First Amendment. By contrast, "true threat" is a constitutional term of art used to describe a specific category of unprotected speech. This category, although often inclusive of speech or acts that fall within the broader definition of "threat," does not include protected speech. Therefore, states may, consistent with the First Amendment, prohibit all "true threats." *In re* Douglas D., 243 Wis.2d 204, 230–31, 626 N.W.2d 725, 739 (2001).

In the disciplinary action cases, First Amendment rights of students are typically *the* central issue. Some courts, such as the Eighth Circuit in *Doe v. Pulaski*, address the question under the true threat doctrine. Others, like the Ninth Circuit in *Lavine v. Blaine Sch. Dist.*, analyze the facts under the *Tinker* rule alone.

1. CONSTRUING THE "TRUE THREAT" DOCTRINE IN A HIGHER EDUCATION SETTING

PROBLEM 17: The Alistaire Jones Litigation, Part II

The following hypothetical is based on the facts set forth in Problem 14, *supra*, Chapter 3.

Assume that a Joseph, a member of Group A, upon reading Alistaire's November 8th column, posted an open letter to Alistaire on a university-sponsored online discussion forum which castigated him for "stirring up the forces of fascism and repression," and included the following quotes: "I'll meet you, one-on-one, any time and any place. Your words are fighting words, and you need to be prepared to pay. Don't think, for example, that you can ever set foot on this campus again and hope to leave in one piece." Many people were taken aback by these highly publicized comments, especially given the fact that Joseph was a soft-spoken, slightly built young man known mostly for his roles in school dramatic productions, while Alistaire was a former nose guard on his high school football team. Joseph is prosecuted by the local U.S. Attorney under Title 18, Section 875(c) of the U.S. Code. Would the U.S. prevail? Why?

(Assume that this jurisdiction follows Judge Krupansky's view of threat law set forth in the *Alkhabaz* dissent.)

UNITED STATES v. ALKHABAZ, ALSO KNOWN AS JAKE BAKER

104 F.3d 1492 (6th Cir. 1997).

BOYCE F. MARTIN, JR., CHIEF JUDGE.

Claiming that the district court erred in determining that certain electronic mail messages between Abraham Jacob Alkhabaz, a.k.a. Jake Baker, and Arthur Gonda did not constitute "true threats," the government appeals the dismissal of the indictment charging Baker with violations of 18 U.S.C. § 875(c).

From November 1994 until approximately January 1995, Baker and Gonda exchanged e-mail messages over the Internet, the content of which expressed a sexual interest in violence against women and girls. Baker sent and received messages through a computer in Ann Arbor, Michigan, while Gonda—whose true identity and whereabouts are still unknown—used a computer in Ontario, Canada.

Prior to this time, Baker had posted a number of fictional stories to "alt.sex.stories," a popular interactive Usenet news group. Using such shorthand references as "B & D," "snuff," "pedo," "mf," and "nc,"

Baker's fictional stories generally involved the abduction, rape, torture, mutilation, and murder of women and young girls. On January 9, Baker posted a story describing the torture, rape, and murder of a young woman who shared the name of one of Baker's classmates at the University of Michigan.

On February 9, Baker was arrested and appeared before a United States Magistrate Judge on a criminal complaint alleging violations of 18 U.S.C. § 875(c), which prohibits interstate communications containing threats to kidnap or injure another person. The Magistrate Judge ordered Baker detained as a danger to the community and a United States District Court affirmed his detention. Upon Baker's motion to be released on bond, this Court ordered a psychological evaluation. When the evaluation concluded that Baker posed no threat to the community, this Court ordered Baker's release.

* * * On March 15, 1995, citing several e-mail messages between Gonda and Baker, a federal grand jury returned a[n] * * * indictment, charging Baker and Gonda with five counts of violations of 18 U.S.C. § 875(c). The e-mail messages supporting the superseding indictment were not available in any publicly accessible portion of the Internet.

* * * [T]he district court dismissed the indictment against Baker, reasoning that the e-mail messages sent and received by Baker and Gonda did not constitute "true threats" under the First Amendment and, as such, were protected speech. The government argues that the district court erred in dismissing the indictment because the communications between Gonda and Baker do constitute "true threats" and, as such, do not implicate First Amendment free speech protections. * * *

* * * For the reasons stated below, we conclude that the indictment failed, as a matter of law, to allege violations of Section 875(c). Accordingly, we decline to address the First Amendment issues raised by the parties.

* * * Because Congress's intent is essentially a question of statutory interpretation, we review the district court's decision *de novo*.

Title 18, United States Code, Section 875(c) states:

Whoever transmits in interstate or foreign commerce any communication containing any threat to kidnap any person or any threat to injure the person of another, shall be fined under this title or imprisoned not more than five years, or both.

The government must allege and prove three elements to support a conviction under Section 875(c): "(1) a transmission in interstate [or foreign] commerce; (2) a communication containing a threat; and (3) the threat must be a threat to injure [or kidnap] the person of another." In this case, the first and third elements cannot be seriously challenged by the defendant. However, the second element raises several issues that this Court must address. * * *

Although its language does not specifically contain a mens rea element, this Court has interpreted Section 875(c) as requiring only general intent. Accordingly, Section 875(c) requires proof that a reasonable person would have taken the defendant's statement as "a serious expression of an intention to inflict bodily harm."

Additionally, Section 875(c) does not clearly define an actus reus. * * *

        * * *

To determine what type of action Congress intended to prohibit, it is necessary to consider the nature of a threat. At their core, threats are tools that are employed when one wishes to have some effect, or achieve some goal, through intimidation. This is true regardless of whether the goal is highly reprehensible or seemingly innocuous.

For example, the goal may be extortionate or coercive. * * *

Additionally, the goal, although not rising to the level of extortion, may be the furtherance of a political objective. * * *

Finally, a threat may be communicated for a seemingly innocuous purpose. For example, one may communicate a bomb threat, even if the bomb does not exist, for the sole purpose of creating a prank. However, such a communication would still constitute a threat because the threatening party is attempting to create levity (at least in his or her own mind) through the use of intimidation.

The above examples illustrate threats because they demonstrate a combination of the mens rea with the actus reus. Although it may offend our sensibilities, a communication objectively indicating a serious expression of an intention to inflict bodily harm cannot constitute a threat unless the communication also is conveyed for the purpose of furthering some goal through the use of intimidation.

Accordingly, to achieve the intent of Congress, we hold that, to constitute "a communication containing a threat" under Section 875(c), a communication must be such that a reasonable person (1) would take the statement as a serious expression of an intention to inflict bodily harm (the mens rea), and (2) would perceive such expression as being communicated to effect some change or achieve some goal through intimidation (the actus reus).

The dissent argues that Congress did not intend to include as an element of the crime the furthering of some goal through the use of intimidation. Emphasizing the term "any" in the language of the statute, the dissent maintains that Congress did not limit the scope of communications that constitutes criminal threats. While we agree that Congress chose inclusive language to identify the types of threats that it intended to prohibit, we cannot ignore the fact that Congress intended to forbid only those communications that in fact constitute a "threat." The conclusion that we reach here is one that the term "threat" necessarily implies. * * *

It is important to note that we are not expressing a subjective standard. * * * [T]he actus reus element of a Section 875(c) violation must be determined objectively, from the perspective of the receiver.

Our interpretation of the actus reus requirement of Section 875(c) conforms not only to the nature of a threat, but also to the purpose of prohibiting threats. Several other circuits have recognized that statutes prohibiting threats are designed to protect the recipient's sense of personal safety and well being. If an otherwise threatening communication is not, from an objective standpoint, transmitted for the purpose of intimidation, then it is unlikely that the recipient will be intimidated or that the recipient's peace of mind will be disturbed.

* * *

Applying our interpretation of the statute to the facts before us, we conclude that the communications between Baker and Gonda do not constitute "communication[s] containing a threat" under Section 875(c). Even if a reasonable person would take the communications between Baker and Gonda as serious expressions of an intention to inflict bodily harm, no reasonable person would perceive such communications as being conveyed to effect some change or achieve some goal through intimidation. Quite the opposite, Baker and Gonda apparently sent e-mail messages to each other in an attempt to foster a friendship based on shared sexual fantasies.

Ultimately, the indictment against Baker fails to "set forth ... all the elements necessary to constitute the offense intended to be punished" and must be dismissed as a matter of law. We agree with the district court, that "[w]hatever Baker's faults, and he is to be faulted, he did not violate 18 U.S.C. § 875(c)."

For the foregoing reasons, the judgment of the district court is affirmed.

Krupansky, Circuit Judge, dissenting.

The panel majority has ruled that an interstate or international "communication containing any threat" to kidnap or injure another person is criminalized by 18 U.S.C. § 875(c) only when the subject communication was conveyed with the general intent "to effect some change or achieve some goal through intimidation." The majority concludes that because the instant indictment alleges only communications purportedly intended to foster a perverse camaraderie between the correspondents, rather than "to effect some change or realize some goal through intimidation," the indictment must be dismissed because each count fails to allege an essential element of a section 875(c) charge. Because the majority has intruded upon Congressional prerogatives by judicially legislating an exogenous element into section 875(c) that materially alters the plain language and purpose of that section and ignores the prevailing precedents of the Supreme Court and this circuit, I respectfully dissent from the majority's decision.

Jake Baker (also known as Abraham Jacob Alkhabaz), an undergraduate student attending the University of Michigan in Ann Arbor, for some time prior to November 1994 and continuing until February 1995 was a regular contributor of sadistic fictional "short stories" intended for public dissemination and comment via a Usenet electronic bulletin board. The appellate record contains a substantial anthology of Baker's efforts. Overall, these misogynistic articles evince an extreme and morbid fascination with the concept of the physical and psychological abuse and torment of women and young girls, described in lurid detail, and often culminating in murder.[1]

By November 1994, Baker's sadistic stories attracted the attention of an individual who called himself "Arthur Gonda,"[2] a Usenet service subscriber residing in Ontario, Canada, who apparently shared similarly misdirected proclivities. Baker and Gonda subsequently exchanged at least 41 private computerized electronic mail ("e-mail") communications between November 29, 1994 and January 25, 1995. Concurrently, Baker continued to distribute violent sordid tales on the electronic bulletin board. On January 9, 1995, Baker brazenly disseminated publicly, via the electronic bulletin board, a depraved torture-and-snuff story in which the victim shared the name of a female classmate of Baker's referred to below as "Jane Doe."[3] This imprudent act triggered notification of the University of Michigan authorities by an alarmed citizen on January 18, 1995. On the following day, Baker admitted to a University of Michigan investigator that he had authored the story and published it on the Internet.

Later that month, pursuant to Baker's written consent, university security personnel searched the defendant's dormitory room, personal papers, and computer files including his unique e-mail compartment. This investigation surfaced a second violent and reprehensible tale featuring Jane Doe's actual name, as well as her accurate residential address. The search of Baker's electronic mailbox disclosed a chilling correspondence between the defendant and Gonda chronicling the two

---

1. The "Jane Doe story," which he named after an actual female classmate and which in fact is a relatively mild exemplar of the bestial genre of Baker's fiction, follows:

[LAST NAME OF A SPECIFIC FEMALE CLASSMATE OF BAKER'S OMITTED]

Prologue: The following story start [sic] in media res. The premise is that my friend Jerry and I have broken into the apartment of this girl, [FULL NAME OMITTED], whom I know from call [sic], and are porceeding [sic] to have a little fun with her. ('I' = the protagonist).

[Judge Krupansky then proceeded to quote further from the defendant's exact words, in which he describes in highly graphic detail how he and his friend Jerry will rape, torture, humiliate, and mutilate

this woman. This extreme violence culminates with the pouring of gasoline over the woman and setting both her and her apartment on fire.]

2. The true identity and current whereabouts of "Arthur Gonda" are unknown.

3. Although the true name of "Jane Doe" was known to the district court and to this appellate forum, her identity has been concealed to spare this young woman any additional and unnecessary fear, emotional trauma, or embarrassment. The record reflected that during an interview concerning Baker's Jane Doe publication conducted by a University of Michigan investigator, Jane Doe "appeared to be controlling herself with great difficulty[,]" resulting in a recommendation for psychological counseling by University of Michigan personnel.

men's plans of abduction, bondage, torture, humiliation, mutilation, rape, sodomy, murder, and necrophilia. Most ominously, these messages cumulated in a conspiracy between the two men to realize their aberrant e-mail discussions and exchanges by implementing an actual abduction, rape, and murder of a female person.

* * *

[Judge Krupansky then proceeded to reproduce extensive portions of the highly offensive e-mail exchange, which focused in great part on what Baker and Gonda wanted to do sexually to young teenage girls. In one exchange, for example, Gonda wrote that "their young bodies would really be fun to hurt." Baker replied: "Oh. They'd scream nicely too!"

Recent "sex slayings" in Canada were also referenced in this context.

On several occasions, specific locations and/or persons were referenced. For example, in one exchange, Baker wrote: "As I said before, my room is right across from the girl's bathroom. Wiat until late at night. grab her when she goes to unlock the door. Knock her unconscious. and put her into one of those portable lockers (forget the word for it). or even a duffle bag. Then hurry her out to the car and take her away * * * What do you think?"

In another exchange, Gonda wrote: "I had a great orgasm today thinking of how you and I would torture this very very petite and cute, south american girl in one of my classes." To which Baker replied: "Just thinking about it anymore doesn't do the trick * * * I need TO DO IT."

Gonda then wrote back, stating: "My feelings exactly! We have to get together * * * I will give you more details as soon as I find out my situation. . . ."]

* * *

On April 25, 1995, Baker moved to quash the superseding indictment, averring that the charged communications were not "true threats" as that term has been defined by the Supreme Court and federal appellate courts and hence constituted innocuous speech protected by the First Amendment. The lower court agreed, dismissing all five counts of the superseding indictment. Although the majority of this panel now affirms the judgment of the district court, it has avoided addressing the First Amendment issue. Instead it mandates, by judicial license, that the communications charged in the superseding indictment did not constitute "threats" of *any* kind because the panel majority interprets section 875(c) to require, as a matter of law, that a "threatening" communication must be accompanied by an intent to intimidate or coerce someone to attain some "change" or "goal." It is obvious, however, from the concise language of 18 U.S.C. § 875(c) that Congress refused to include an "intent to intimidate or coerce someone to attain some change or goal" as an element of the criminal act addressed therein:

Whoever transmits in interstate or foreign commerce any communication containing *ANY* threat *to kidnap ANY person* or *ANY threat to injure the person of another,* shall be fined under this title or imprisoned not more than five years, or both.

18 U.S.C. § 875(c) (emphases added).

The words in section 875(c) are simple, clear, concise, and unambiguous. The plain, expressed statutory language commands only that the alleged communication must contain *any threat* to kidnap or physically injure *any person,* made for *any reason* or no reason. Section 875(c) by its terms does *not* confine the scope of criminalized communications to those directed to identified individuals and intended to effect some particular change or goal. This circuit has already considered and decided the meaning of section 875(c) in ... a decision in which a member of this panel concurred, wherein it defined, to the exclusion of "intimidation," the three essential elements under 18 U.S.C. § 875(c). * * *

By contrast to section 875(c), a companion statutory provision, 18 U.S.C. § 875(b), *criminalizes similar communications made with the intent to extort money or other value,* coupled with more severe penalties than those appertaining to a threat illegalized by section 875(c). * * *

Patently, Congress sought to punish *all* interstate or international communications containing a threat to kidnap or injure any person; such communications accompanied by an intent to extort value (section 875(b)) could be punished more severely than those which are not coupled with the intent to extort (section 875(c)). * * *

The panel majority attempts to justify its improper fusion of an extra-legislative element re the "intent to intimidate some change or goal" upon section 875(c) by embracing an artificially narrow legal definition of the term "threat." The panel majority posits, "[a]t their core, threats are tools that are employed when one wishes to have some effect, or achieve some goal, through intimidation." However, this interpretation does not comprise the *exclusive* ordinary or legal meaning of the word "threat." Undeniably, a simple, credible declaration of an intention to cause injury to some person, made for any reason, or for no reason whatsoever, may *also* constitute a "threat." For instance, *Black's Law Dictionary* 1480–81 (6th ed. 1990) adopts, among other definitions, the following:

> **Threat**. *A communicated intent to inflict physical or other harm on any person or on property. A declaration of an intention to injure another or his property by some unlawful act. A declaration of intention or determination to inflict punishment, loss, or pain on another, or to injure another or his property by the commission of some unlawful act....*
>
> *The term, "threat" [sic] means an avowed present determination or intent to injure presently or in the future.* A statement may constitute a threat even though it is subject to a possible contingency in the maker's control. The prosecution must establish a "true threat,"

which means a serious threat as distinguished from words uttered as mere political argument, idle talk or jest. In determining whether words were uttered as a threat the context in which they were spoken must be considered.

(Emphases added & citations omitted).

Although some reported threat convictions have embraced a form or degree of intimidation, this circuit has not previously adopted that element as an essential component of a prosecution under 18 U.S.C. § 875(c). * * *

Thus, the plain language of 18 U.S.C. § 875(c), together with its interpretive precedents, compels the conclusion that "threats" within the scope of the statute in controversy include all reasonably credible communications which express the speaker's objective intent to kidnap or physically injure another person. Whether the originator of the message intended to intimidate or coerce anyone thereby is irrelevant. Rather, the pertinent inquiry is whether a jury could find that a reasonable recipient of the communication would objectively tend to believe that the speaker was serious about his stated intention. * * * There can be no doubt that a rational jury could find that some or all of the minacious communications charged in the superseding indictment against Baker constituted threats by the defendant to harm a female human being, which a reasonable objective recipient of the transmissions could find credible.[11]

Because the communications charged against Baker could be found by a rational jury to constitute "threats" within the ambit of 18 U.S.C. § 875(c), the district court's resolution that a rational jury could not find that any of these communications comprised constitutionally unprotected "true threats" is ripe for review.[12] The Supreme Court has recognized that, while the First Amendment extends varying degrees of protection against government censure to most forms of expression (with political speech receiving the most stringent safeguards), certain forms of speech are deemed unworthy of any constitutional protection and consequently may be criminalized. A "threat" is a recognized category of expression which warrants no First Amendment protection. * * * However, only communications which convey "true threats" (as opposed to, for exam-

---

11. The majority's concern that interpreting 18 U.S.C. § 875(c) to encompass threatening messages sent by persons who did not intend to achieve some coercive result would effectively criminalize the legitimate and innocent reiteration, such as by news reporters, trial watchers, or publishers of judicial opinions, of communications initiated by another, is misplaced. To constitute a threat under section 875(c), the communication at issue must be accompanied by the perpetrator's general intent to kidnap or harm someone. Stated differently, by promulgating the menacing verbiage, the speaker must be expressing a credible intention to perform, or cause to be performed, the forbidden actions. Typically, only the originator of the minatorial communication, or a confederate, could possess or express this intent. By contrast, a person who republishes the threatening language for legitimate or otherwise innocuous purposes cannot reasonably be deemed to have articulated an intent to kidnap or injure any person.

12. The determination whether a communication embodies a "true threat" resides in the fact finder.

ple, inadvertent statements, mistakes, jests, hyperbole, innocuous talk, or political commentary not objectively intended to express a real threat) are "threats" outside the embrace of the First Amendment's guarantees.

In *Watts,* the Court announced that "threats" against the President were obviously proscribable, but also recognized that, as "pure speech" which may be imbued with protected political commentary, such ostensibly minatory speech must be assessed for its true nature—that is, whether it constituted mere political commentary or hyperbole, which was protected, or constituted a *"true threat"* which is not protected. Watts had stated at a public rally that he would not willingly submit to the draft but, if forced to carry a rifle, "the first man I want to get in my sights is L.B.J." The Court instructed that this statement, in its factual context, was not a "true threat" which could be constitutionally prosecuted, but instead was mere "political hyperbole" immunized by the First Amendment.[13]

* * *

The majority's disposition leads to absurd results where, as in the case at bench, minacious communications have been made which may satisfy the constitutional "true threat" standard because a reasonable jury could find that those communications contained believable expressions of an intention to injure a person, yet those same communications are nonetheless deemed beyond the reach of 18 U.S.C. § 875(c) as not constituting "threats" as a matter of law, merely because the subject communications were not made with the intent to realize a specific purpose through intimidation. Although Congress, via section 875(c), clearly intended to punish *every* credible interstate or transnational expression of an intent to kidnap or injure another person, the majority's legally erroneous unduly restrictive interpretation of the word "threat" as used in section 875(c) effectively divests Congress of its constitutional lawmaking authority by artificially confining the intended scope of section 875(c) to a degree not compelled by the First Amendment.

Accordingly, in order to prove a "true threat" proscribed by 18 U.S.C. § 875(c) and unprotected by the First Amendment, the prosecution must evidence to a rational jury's satisfaction *only* the following: (1) that the defendant transmitted the subject communication in interstate or foreign commerce, (2) that the communication contained a threat, (3) that the threat was one against the physical safety or freedom of some individual or class of persons (irrespective of the identity of the person or group threatened, the originator's motivation for issuing the threat, or the existence or nonexistence of any goal pursued by the threat), and (4) that the subject communication in its factual context would lead a reasonable, objective recipient to believe that the publisher of the communication was serious about his threat (regardless of the subjective

---

13. The Supreme Court has recognized that the considerations which remove threats of violence outside the reach of the First Amendment apply with "special force" to threats which menace the President. By contrast, threats against private individuals are typically devoid of political content and hence should be accorded less stringent First Amendment protection.

intent of the speaker to make an actual threat or whether anyone actually felt frightened, intimidated, or coerced by the threat).

Finally, the facts of the instant case justify reversal and remand because they even satisfy the judicially legislated edict articulated in the majority opinion. Assuming *arguendo* that a threat under 18 U.S.C. § 875(c) requires a general intent by the speaker to attain some result or change through intimidation (which it does not), a rational jury could conclude that this element was proved in this case. By publishing his sadistic Jane Doe story on the Internet, Baker could reasonably foresee that his threats to harm Jane Doe would ultimately be communicated to her (as they were), and would cause her fear and intimidation, which in fact ultimately occurred. The panel majority may casually conclude within the security of chambers that Baker's threats conveyed to Jane Doe in his articles published on the Internet were nonintimidating. However, Jane Doe's reaction to those threats when brought to her attention evinces a contrary conclusion of a shattering traumatic reaction that resulted in recommended psychological counseling.

A jury in the instant case could reasonably infer, in the light of all the evidence, that Baker intended the foreseeable, natural, and ordinary consequences of his voluntary actions. Indeed, a rational jury could infer that the reason Baker published his Jane Doe story featuring the actual name of a young woman was the probability that its threats would be communicated to her and cause her to suffer fear, anxiety, and intimidation. Moreover, the e-mail correspondence between Baker and Gonda evidenced overt acts of a conspiracy to violate 18 U.S.C. § 875(c) in that the two men clearly agreed *at the least* to threaten, and otherwise implement their conspiracy by intimidating, one or more women or young girls with physical harm as discussed in their plans.

Accordingly, I would reverse the district court's judgment which dismissed the superseding indictment as purportedly not alleging "true threats," and remand the cause to the lower court. **I DISSENT.**

Notes

1.   The Sixth Circuit majority's analysis, including its determination that an "intimidation" element is built into the federal criminal statute, is not reflective of the general trend in this area. In fact, Judge Krupansky's dissent would be considered the more typical, more "mainstream" analysis of these issues in most parts of the country. In your view, which approach is more consistent with the implicit goals of the federal statute? Which approach might be more appropriate as a matter of policy?

2.   It is important to note that while both the newsgroup post by Jake Baker and the e-mail exchange between him and Arthur Gonda were referenced in the opinions—and while the newsgroup post, because of its particularly offensive and notorious character—garnered the most publicity in the national media—the U.S. Attorney's Office ultimately prosecuted the defendant only for the e-mail exchange. *See* United States v. Baker, 890 F.Supp. 1375, 1380 n.6 (1995) ("At oral argument on May 26, 1995, the

government stated that it abandoned the story as a basis of prosecution because it did not constitute a threat."). Yet for Judge Krupansky, the post provided important context, particularly since the law in this area typically calls for an analysis of context within the totality of the circumstances. Thus, he reproduces this post in its entirety, in Footnote 1 of the dissent.

3. The widely publicized *Alkhabaz* case not only left everyone unsatisfied but also left the larger issue unresolved. Free speech advocates criticized the "persecution" of Jake Baker, who ultimately left the university after undergoing what amounted to a public humiliation. And university officials—justifiably concerned that expressions of intent to commit violent acts are often translated into reality—felt let down by the legal system. In light of this disappointment on all sides, might there have been a better way to handle the dispute?

4. Threats in cyberspace are a particular challenge for public officials, both in education and in society as a whole. Unlike the real-time, offline world, for example, there are no visual cues and few contextual cues that would help a person to determine whether a particular communication does in fact constitute a threat. In light of the result in *Alkhabaz*, would you conclude that threat law in need of substantial revision? Is greater precision possible, for example? Or, particularly given the complexities of cyberspace, is this an example of a situation where the limits of the legal system might have been reached?

2. CONSTRUING THE "TRUE THREAT" DOCTRINE IN A K–12 SETTING

PROBLEM 18: Zero Tolerance for Threats II

Belinda—an eleventh grade student at a large public high school in the fictional state of Riverview—sends an e-mail from a school computer to a friend in the fictional state of Floral Valley, which reads in part: "I can't wait until I can kill the people in my class. I'll just go to the entrance of the school on a clear, sunny day and blow up and shoot everything I can." She also sends copies to five friends, one of whom shares it with her parents. The parents report the details to the school, which expels Belinda under a new "zero tolerance for threats" policy enacted in the aftermath of the events at Columbine.

Legal Inquiry

A. Belinda, represented by the ACLU, challenges her expulsion on the grounds that her free speech rights have been violated. The ACLU is prepared to argue that her actions did not constitute true threats. What arguments should the ACLU set forth on her behalf? What result? Discuss.

B. If this case had taken place at a public university instead of at the high school level, would the ACLU make any additional or different arguments? Would the result be any different? Explain.

Policy Inquiry

A. Does the problem of online and offline threats in U.S. high schools today (after Columbine and after 9/11) justify a "zero tolerance for threats" policy in public high schools? Just how bad are things in that regard nationwide? Is "zero tolerance" the answer? Why? If not, what other strategies from both a legal and a policy perspective would you recommend? Why?

B. In light of the fact that there have already been several "online threats" cases at the higher education level in recent years, does this problem justify a "zero tolerance for threats" policy at major public universities? Just how bad are things in this regard nationwide after 9/11? Is "zero tolerance" the answer? Why? If not, what other strategies from both a legal and a policy perspective would you recommend? Why?

WISCONSIN v. DOUGLAS D.

243 Wis.2d 204, 626 N.W.2d 725 (2001).

JON P. WILCOX, J.

* * * The circuit court found that the content of an eighth-grade creative writing assignment authored by the petitioner, Douglas D. (Douglas), a minor, constituted a threat against Douglas's English teacher. Based on this finding, the court adjudicated Douglas delinquent for violating the . . . [Wisconsin] . . . disorderly conduct statute.

* * *

We conclude that purely written speech, even written speech that fails to cause an actual disturbance, can constitute disorderly conduct as defined by § 947.01; however, because Douglas's speech falls within the protection of the First Amendment, the State nonetheless is barred from prosecuting Douglas for disorderly conduct. Accordingly, we reverse the decision of the court of appeals.

I.

This case arises from events that occurred while Douglas was an eighth-grade student at an Oconto County public school. On October 7, 1998, Douglas's English teacher, who commonly referred to herself in class as "Mrs. C," gave Douglas a creative writing assignment to complete during class. Mrs. C instructed Douglas to begin writing a story, which later would be passed on to a series of three other students, each adding to Douglas's work. But other than entitling the assignment "Top Secret," Mrs. C provided no limit regarding the topic on which Douglas was to write.

Rather than beginning his assignment, Douglas visited with some friends and disrupted the class. Therefore, Mrs. C sent Douglas into the hall to complete his assignment.

At the end of the period, Douglas returned to class and handed his work to Mrs. C. A few minutes later, Mrs. C read what Douglas had written:

There one lived an old ugly woman her name was Mrs. C that stood for crab. She was a mean old woman that would beat children sencless. I guess that's why she became a teacher.

Well one day she kick a student out of her class & he din't like it. That student was named Dick.

The next morning Dick came to class & in his coat he conseled a machedy. When the teacher told him to shut up he whiped it out & cut her head off.

When the sub came 2 days later she needed a paperclipp so she opened the droor. Ahh she screamed as she found Mrs. C.'s head in the droor.

Mrs. C believed this story to be a threat that if she disciplined Douglas again, Douglas intended to harm her. As a result, she became frightened and, after dismissing Douglas's class as scheduled, notified the school assistant principal of the incident.

Upon learning of the incident and observing that Mrs. C was very upset, the assistant principal called Douglas into his office. Douglas apologized for the story, stating that he did not intend it to be interpreted as a threat. The assistant principal then imposed on Douglas an in-school suspension.

After Douglas served his suspension, the school readmitted him to class—albeit with a different English teacher. However, on November 19, 1998, the police filed a delinquency petition against Douglas, alleging that by submitting a "death threat" to Mrs. C, Douglas had engaged in "abusive conduct under circumstances in which the conduct tends to cause a disturbance," thus violating the disorderly conduct statute, § 947.01.

* * *

We * * * must consider whether Douglas's story is protected by the First Amendment, thus falling outside the bounds of conduct prosecutable under § 947.01. * * *

Contrary to the court of appeals holding, for purposes of First Amendment analysis, a "threat" is very different from a "true threat." "Threat" is a nebulous term that can describe anything from "[a]n expression of an intention to inflict pain, injury, evil, or punishment" to any generalized "menace." Under such a broad definition, "threats" include protected and unprotected speech. Thus, states cannot enact general laws prohibiting all "threats" without infringing on some speech protected by the First Amendment. By contrast, "true threat" is a constitutional term of art used to describe a specific category of unprotected speech. This category, although often inclusive of speech or acts that fall within the broader definition of "threat," does not include protected speech. Therefore, states may, consistent with the First Amendment, prohibit all "true threats."

* * *

We thus must determine whether Douglas's story constitutes a true threat. The question of whether particular conduct constitutes a true threat is an issue of fact, typically best left for the finder of fact.

However, if the conduct unquestionably is protected by the First Amendment, a court may dismiss the charge as a matter of law.

As this court explained in *Perkins,* a true threat is a statement that, in light of all the surrounding circumstances,

> a speaker would reasonably foresee that a listener would reasonably interpret as a serious expression of a purpose to inflict harm, as distinguished from hyperbole, jest, innocuous talk, expressions of political views, or other similarly protected speech.[12] It is not necessary that the speaker have the ability to carry out the threat.

Some factors that courts and juries should consider when applying this test include, but are not limited to:

> how the recipient and other listeners reacted to the alleged threat, whether the threat was conditional, whether [the threat] was communicated directly to its victim, whether the maker of the threat had made similar statements to the victim on other occasions, and whether the victim had reason to believe that the maker of the threat had a propensity to engage in violence.

In the present case, Douglas argues that his story was not a true threat because it did not express an "unequivocal, unconditional and specific expression [ ] of intention immediately to inflict injury." He contends that his story is a fictional, third-person creative writing assignment, which should receive full protection under the First Amendment.

Conversely, the State contends that Douglas's story is a true threat. According to the State's argument, the first two paragraphs of Douglas's story closely parallel the events that had taken place immediately before Douglas began his assignment: a teacher named Mrs. C removed a male student from her class. The next two paragraphs, the State contends, convey the threat: when the teacher disciplined the student the following day, the student used a machete to cut off the teacher's head. Further, the State attributes great weight to the fact that Douglas handed his story directly to Mrs. C—the subject of his threat—rather than, for example, reading it in jest to his friends. In light of these circumstances, the State argues that Douglas's threat to Mrs. C is direct and clear: If she disciplines him again, he intends to injure her. Thus, the State argues that Douglas's story expresses a true threat.

* * * [W]hile we believe that Douglas's story is crude and repugnant, we nonetheless must reject the State's argument. To be sure, Mrs. C testified that Douglas's story frightened her. Further, Douglas con-

---

12.   We recognize that there may be instances where true threats are conveyed by means other than pure speech. For this reason, the terms "speaker" and "listener" should be broadly construed to encompass all conveyors and recipients of true threats.

We further note that the "reasonable speaker" and "reasonable listener" are not to be misconstrued as omniscient persons, aware of every fact potentially existing at the time of the speech. The "reasonable speaker" and "reasonable listener" are limited in knowledge to the facts readily available to the actual speaker and/or the actual listener at the time of the speech at issue.

veyed his message directly to Mrs. C, the alleged victim of the threat. However, there is no evidence that Douglas had threatened Mrs. C in the past or that Mrs. C believed Douglas had a propensity to engage in violence.

Moreover, Douglas wrote his story, pursuant to Mrs. C's request, in the context of a creative writing class. In such a class, teachers and students alike should expect and allow more creative license—be it for better or, as in this case, for worse—than in other circumstances. Had Douglas penned the same story in a math class, for example, where such a tale likely would be grossly outside the scope of his assigned work, we would have a different case before us.

But in the context of a creative writing class, Douglas's story does not amount to a true threat. First, the story does not contain any language directly addressed from Douglas to Mrs. C. Rather, it is written in the third person, with no mention of Douglas. Second, Douglas's story contains hyperbole and attempts at jest. It jokes that the "C" in "Mrs. C" is short for "crab." In addition, it suggests that Mrs. C is so mean that she beats children and speculates that, for this reason, she became a teacher. Third, Mrs. C explained to Douglas that in this particular assignment, he merely was to begin writing a story that other children would complete. Thus, Douglas could have expected another student to end his grisly tale as a dream or otherwise imagined event. Under these specific circumstances, Douglas's story is protected by the First Amendment.[15]

We do not doubt that the story was a result of Douglas's anger at having been removed from class. Further, we sympathize with Mrs. C; she was justified in feeling offended. And we firmly believe that the school took appropriate disciplinary action against Douglas.

However, a thirteen-year-old boy's impetuous writings do not necessarily fall from First Amendment protection due to their offensive nature. * * * With this in mind, we conclude that Douglas's story, although we find it to be offensive and distasteful, unquestionably is protected by the First Amendment. Our feelings of offense and distaste do not allow us to set aside the Constitution. We therefore hold as a matter of law that Douglas's story cannot be prosecuted under § 947.01. * * *

By no means should schools interpret this holding as undermining their authority to utilize their internal disciplinary procedures to punish speech such as Douglas's story. Although the First Amendment prohibits law enforcement officials from prosecuting protected speech, it does not necessarily follow that schools may not discipline students for such speech.

* * *

---

15. * * * [T]he dissent suggests that numerous other "facts" support its conclusion that Douglas's story was a true threat. Whatever these facts may be, there is no evidence that Mrs. C or any other person was aware of any of these purported facts at the time of Douglas's alleged threat.

Under the circumstances in the present case, we hold that the school had more than enough reason to discipline Douglas for the content of his story. Although the story is not a true threat, it is an offensive, crass insult to Mrs. C. Schools need not tolerate this type of assault to the sensibilities of their educators or students. * * * [The court cites *Tinker* and the *Tinker* line of cases in support of this conclusion.] * * *

This case reinforces our belief that while some student conduct may warrant punishment by both law enforcement officials and school authorities, school discipline generally should remain the prerogative of our schools, not our juvenile justice system. Accordingly, we reverse the decision of the court of appeals.

The decision of the court of appeals is reversed.

* * *

DOE v. PULASKI COUNTY SPECIAL SCH. DIST.

306 F.3d 616 (8th Cir. 2002).

HANSEN, CIRCUIT JUDGE.

We granted en banc review to determine whether a school board ran afoul of a student's free speech rights when it expelled him for an offensive and vulgar letter that the student had prepared at home. The expelled student described in the letter how he would rape, sodomize, and murder a female classmate who had previously broken up with him. After a bench trial, the district court ordered the expelled student reinstated, concluding that the letter was not a "true threat" and that it therefore was protected speech under the First Amendment. A divided panel of our court affirmed the district court's decision. We vacated the panel decision, ordered en banc rehearing, and now hold that the school board did not violate the student's First Amendment rights when it expelled him.

I. BACKGROUND AND FACTS

J.M., a male, and K.G., a female, began "going together" during their seventh-grade year at Northwood Junior High School. As one would expect from typical junior high students, the two primarily saw each other at school and church, and their relationship was marked by multiple breakups during the school year. Sometime during the summer vacation after the end of the seventh-grade year, K.G. "broke up" with J.M. for the final time because she was interested in another boy.

Frustrated by the breakup and upset that K.G. would not go out with him again, J.M. drafted two violent, misogynic, and obscenity-laden rants expressing a desire to molest, rape, and murder K.G. According to J.M., he intended to write a rap song with lyrics similar in theme to the more vulgar and violent rap songs performed by controversial "rappers" such as Eminem, Juvenile, and Kid Rock, but found that his "song" fit no particular beat or rhythm. J.M. ultimately penned the documents as letters, signing them at their conclusion. J.M. prepared both letters at his home, where they remained until J.M.'s best friend, D.M., discovered one of them approximately a month before the youths were to begin their eighth-grade year at Northwood.

D.M. found the letter in J.M.'s bedroom while he was searching for something on top of a dresser. Before D.M. had a chance to read the letter, J.M. snatched it from his hand. D.M. asked to read the letter, and J.M. handed it back to him and gave D.M. permission to read the letter. D.M. asked for a copy of the letter, but J.M. refused to give him one.

K.G. also learned about the existence and contents of the letter, but it was not made clear during the trial when or how she learned about it. K.G. testified that she first learned about *a* letter during a telephone conversation with J.M. She claimed that J.M. told her that another boy had written a letter that stated she would be killed. J.M. claimed instead that K.G. learned about the letter from D.M. Either way, the testimony clearly established that J.M. voluntarily discussed the letter with K.G. during two or three telephone conversations and that J.M. admitted to K.G. in their final telephone conversation that he, not another boy, had written the letter.

Concerned about the letter, K.G. enlisted D.M.'s help in obtaining it from J.M. About a week before the start of school, D.M. spent the night at J.M.'s house and took the letter from J.M.'s room on the following morning. D.M. did so without J.M.'s knowledge or permission. D.M. delivered the letter to K.G. on the second day back from summer vacation, and K.G. read it in gym class in the presence of some other students. One of those students went immediately to the school resource officer, Officer James Kesterson, and reported that threats had been made against K.G. Officer Kesterson accompanied the student back to the gym where he found K.G. frightened and crying. * * *

Bob Allison, the principal, conducted his own investigation and learned that D.M. had taken the letter from J.M. and delivered it to K.G. at school. After the investigation, Principal Allison recommended that J.M. be expelled from Northwood for the remainder of his eighth-grade year. Allison based his recommendation on Rule 36 of the district's Handbook for Student Conduct and Discipline, which prohibits students from making terrorizing threats against others. The rule requires that a violator be recommended for expulsion.

     * * *

Upset with the school board's decision ... [expelling J.M. from both Northwood and the alternative school for the remainder of his eighth-grade year] ... , J.M.'s mother filed this lawsuit on her son's behalf. J.M. sought reinstatement at Northwood on the ground that the school board violated his free speech rights when it disciplined him for the letter. * * *

II. DISCUSSION AND ANALYSIS

     * * *

B. The True Threat Inquiry

* * *

In *Watts v. United States,* 394 U.S. 705, 89 S.Ct. 1399, (1969), the Supreme Court recognized that threats of violence * * * fall within the realm of speech that the government can proscribe without offending the First Amendment. Although there may be some political or social value associated with threatening words in some circumstances, the government has an overriding interest in "protecting individuals from the fear of violence, from the disruption that fear engenders, and from the possibility that the threatened violence will occur." Our task, therefore, is to determine "[w]hat is a threat ... from what is constitutionally protected speech." The Court in *Watts,* however, set forth no particular definition or description of a true threat that distinguishes an unprotected threat from protected speech. Thus, the lower courts have been left to ascertain for themselves when a statement triggers the government's interest in preventing the disruption and fear of violence associated with a threat.

The federal courts of appeals that have announced a test to parse true threats from protected speech essentially fall into two camps * * *. All the courts to have reached the issue have consistently adopted an objective test that focuses on whether a reasonable person would interpret the purported threat as a serious expression of an intent to cause a present or future harm. The views among the courts diverge, however, in determining from whose viewpoint the statement should be interpreted. * * *

Our court is in the camp that views the nature of the alleged threat from the viewpoint of a reasonable recipient. ... [W]e ... [have] ... emphasized the fact intensive nature of the true threat inquiry and held that a court must view the relevant facts to determine "whether the recipient of the alleged threat could reasonably conclude that it expresses 'a determination or intent to injure presently or in the future.' " * * * We ... [have] ... also set forth ... a nonexhaustive list of factors relevant to how a reasonable recipient would view the purported threat. Those factors include: 1) the reaction of those who heard the alleged threat; 2) whether the threat was conditional; 3) whether the person who made the alleged threat communicated it directly to the object of the threat; 4) whether the speaker had a history of making threats against the person purportedly threatened; and 5) whether the recipient had a reason to believe that the speaker had a propensity to engage in violence.

* * * [W]e adhere to ... [this] ... inquiry and hold that a true threat is a statement that a reasonable recipient would have interpreted as a serious expression of an intent to harm or cause injury to another.

C. Intent to Communicate

Before we address whether a reasonable recipient would view the letter as a threat, we are faced with a threshold question of whether J.M.

intended to communicate the purported threat. The district court's conclusion that the letter was protected speech turned on its finding that J.M. never intended to deliver the letter to K.G.; in other words, that J.M. never intended to communicate the purported threat to K.G. In determining whether a statement amounts to an unprotected threat, there is no requirement that the speaker intended to carry out the threat, nor is there any requirement that the speaker was capable of carrying out the purported threat of violence. However, the speaker must have intentionally or knowingly communicated the statement in question to someone before he or she may be punished or disciplined for it. The requirement is satisfied if the speaker communicates the statement to the object of the purported threat *or* to a third party. * * *

Requiring less than an intent to communicate the purported threat would run afoul of the notion that an individual's most protected right is to be free from governmental interference in the sanctity of his home and in the sanctity of his own personal thoughts. * * * It is only when a threatening idea or thought is communicated that the government's interest in alleviating the fear of violence and disruption associated with a threat engages.

We conclude here that J.M. intended to communicate the letter and is therefore accountable if a reasonable recipient would have viewed the letter as a threat. Although J.M. snatched the letter out of D.M.'s hands when D.M. first found it, J.M. handed the letter back to D.M. and *permitted* D.M. to read it. J.M.'s decision to let D.M. read the letter is even more problematic for J.M. given his testimony that he knew there was a good possibility that D.M. would tell K.G. about the letter because D.M. and K.G. were friends. J.M. also discussed the letter in more than one phone conversation with K.G., and J.M. admitted to K.G. that he wrote the letter and that it talked of killing her. J.M. made similar admissions to K.G.'s best friend who would be likely to convey the information to K.G. One can hardly say, based on J.M.'s willingness to let D.M. read the letter and his overt discussion of the letter and its contents with K.G. and K.G.'s best friend, that J.M. intended to keep the letter, and the message it contained, within his own lockbox of personal privacy.

D.   Reasonable Recipient's Perception of the Letter

We turn next to the question of whether a reasonable recipient would have perceived the letter as a threat. There is no question that the contents of the letter itself expressed an intent to harm K.G., and we disagree entirely, but respectfully, with the district court's assessment that the words contained in it were only "arguably" threatening. The letter exhibited J.M.'s pronounced, contemptuous and depraved hate for K.G. J.M. referred to or described K.G. as a "bitch," "slut," "ass," and a "whore" over 80 times in only four pages. He used the f-word no fewer than ninety times and spoke frequently in the letter of his wish to sodomize, rape, and kill K.G. The most disturbing aspect of the letter, however, is J.M.'s warning in two passages, expressed in unconditional terms, that K.G. should not go to sleep because he would be lying under her bed waiting to kill her with a knife.[3] Most, if not all, normal thirteen-year-old girls (and probably most reasonable adults) would be frightened by the message and tone of J.M.'s letter and would fear for their physical well-being if they received the same letter.

The fact that J.M. did not personally deliver the letter to K.G. did not dispel its threatening nature. Although J.M. did not personally hand the letter to K.G., J.M. titled the letter "F____ that bitch [K.G.]," and he wrote the letter as though he was speaking directly to her. As a consequence, the letter was extremely intimate and personal, and the violence described in it was directed unequivocally at K.G.

There is also no indication that J.M. ever attempted to alleviate K.G.'s concerns about the letter during the period between when he told her about the letter and when she received it at school. Prior to K.G. obtaining the letter, J.M. had discussed its contents with her in phone conversations, and he testified at trial that he knew K.G. might have taken the threat as being truthful. It readily appears that J.M. wanted K.G. to be scared as retribution for her treatment of him. In fact, K.G.'s best friend testified at trial that J.M. told her, before D.M. obtained the letter and delivered it, that J.M. wanted to hide under K.G.'s bed and kill her. J.M. told this to K.G.'s best friend knowing the friend would likely pass the message along to K.G. J.M. also shared the letter with D.M. suspecting that D.M. would pass the information it contained to K.G. J.M. ultimately apologized to K.G., but his apology came only after he was expelled by the school board and during the pendency of the district court proceeding. The crescendoing events that presaged K.G.'s receipt of the actual letter would not have given a reasonable person in K.G.'s shoes much solace that J.M. did not want or intend to harm her.

Based on the tone of the letter, and the situation surrounding its communication, we are not surprised that those who read it interpreted it as a threat. D.M. was concerned enough by the letter that he purloined it from his friend's home because he "felt that something should be done about it." A girl present when K.G. first read the letter immediately went to Officer Kesterson because she thought someone needed to know about the letter and the threats contained therein. * * *[4]

J.M.'s previous portrayal of himself as a tough guy with a propensity for aggression made his threat more credible and contributed to K.G.'s reaction. Before the breakup, J.M. had told K.G., as well as K.G.'s best friend and D.M., that he was a member of the "Bloods" gang. K.G. also testified at trial that J.M. once shot a cat while she was speaking to him

---

3. J.M. argues it would have been improbable for him to harm K.G. in the manner he described because K.G. resided with her parents. However, a threat does not need to be logical or based in reality before the government may punish someone for making it. . . . It seems quite probable that the threat to hide under a person's bed with a knife would induce fear and apprehension.

4. We find it untenable in the wake of Columbine and Jonesboro that any reasonable school official who came into possession of J.M.'s letter would not have taken some action based on its violent and disturbing content.

on the phone and that J.M.'s penchant for violence towards animals heightened her concern over the letter. The district court excluded the district's evidence of J.M.'s violent propensities on the ground that the evidence was not considered by the school board. We conclude, however, that the evidence is relevant to an understanding of K.G.'s response to the threat and our determination of whether her response was a reasonable one. * * *

Viewing the entire factual circumstances surrounding the letter, we conclude that a reasonable recipient would have perceived J.M.'s letter as a serious expression of an intent to harm K.G. As such, the letter amounted to a true threat, and the school's administrators and the school board did not violate J.M.'s First Amendment rights by initiating disciplinary action based on the letter's threatening content. The district court's contrary conclusion was erroneous. Had we been sitting as the school board, we might very well have approached the situation differently, for it appears to us that the board's action taken against J.M. was unnecessarily harsh. Other options have occurred to us that could have furthered the district's interest in protecting its students, as well as have punished J.M., but also have aided him in understanding the severity and inappropriateness of his conduct. However, "[i]t is not the role of the federal courts to set aside decisions of school administrators which the court may view as lacking a basis in wisdom or compassion." Those judgments are best left to the voters who elect the school board.

III. CONCLUSION

We reverse the judgment of the district court and remand the case to the district court with instructions to dissolve the injunctive relief afforded J.M. and to dismiss J.M.'s First Amendment claim against the school district.

HEANEY, Circuit Judge, with whom McMILLIAN, MORRIS SHEPPARD ARNOLD, and BYE, Circuit Judges, join, dissenting.

Because I believe the majority has undermined the scope of the First Amendment by failing to consider the unique circumstances of speech in a school setting, I respectfully dissent. I believe the proper inquiry before us is 1) whether J.M.'s written expression is protected speech or a true threat; and 2) if it is protected speech, as I believe it is, whether it is subject to regulation because it may cause substantial disruption or interfere with the rights of other students. The majority ignores the school context analysis and creates dangerously broad precedent by holding that *any* private utterance of an intent to injure another person is not entitled to First Amendment protection. I reject this reasoning because it violates the fundamental principles of the First Amendment. I would hold instead that J.M.'s written expression is constitutionally protected speech, but can be *reasonably* regulated by school administrators to prevent substantial disruption in the school setting.

I. True Threat Analysis

I agree with the majority that in the Eighth Circuit, a true threat is a statement that a reasonable recipient would interpret as a serious expression of an intent to harm or cause injury to another. I disagree, however, with the majority's rejection of the district court's determination that J.M. had not communicated a true threat to K.G. The district court's factual findings do not constitute "a forbidden intrusion on the field of free expression," nor are they clearly erroneous. The majority ignores the district court's findings to conclude that J.M. intended to communicate a threat to D.M., and that a reasonable recipient of J.M.'s letter understood the letter to be a threat. This holding cannot be independently supported by the record. I would therefore affirm the district court.

    * * *

Had J.M. had a criminal record, or handed the letter to her directly, or previously expressed an intent to hurt her, it would be far easier to conclude that K.G. reasonably believed that J.M. intended to impose harm. Those are not the facts of this case. K.G. and her friends had to work hard to obtain a copy of the letter, indicating J.M.'s reluctance to make it a public issue. * * *

Finally, the majority relies on J.M.'s reputation in concluding that a reasonable recipient could conclude that he had issued a threat. K.G. testified that she thought J.M. had killed a cat and remembered that J.M. had boasted that he, a white kid from rural Arkansas, was a member of the Bloods. This amounts to teenage bravado at best, and does not warrant serious consideration by this court.

A comparison of this case and others in which our circuit has found a true threat demonstrates how far the majority stretches the law today. In concluding that J.M.'s letter constitutes a true threat, the majority has placed this boy in the company of the following cast of characters: a pro-life advocate who physically assaulted an employee at Planned Parenthood and, over a period of a year, warned a doctor with the aid of a blow horn nearly fifty times that he should remember Dr. Gunn, the doctor who was murdered because he performed abortions; three teenage boys who burned three crosses in the yards of African American families; a convicted murderer who sent a judge a letter informing him that he will "see you in hell before I permit you to [revoke custody of my son],"; an anti-abortion activist who parked and left unattended two Ryder trucks in the entrance driveways of two Little Rock abortion clinics after the Oklahoma City bombing, causing the evacuation of the area and the call for a bomb squad investigation; a man charged with bombing a building and who sent twenty-three letters to the home and work addresses of judges and government workers, threatening to kill them. J.M.'s conduct does not resemble the acts of these criminals. He wrote a disturbing but private letter that was not intended to be viewed by anyone. It would be a great injustice to conclude that his writings rise to the level of a true threat: there was no communication of a true threat, nor could there have been a reasonable belief that he intended to carry out the actions in the letter.

* * *

IV. School Board Action

Because I would find that J.M.'s letter is not a true threat and is entitled to First Amendment protection, I next examine whether the school board acted reasonably in regulating J.M.'s speech. * * *

The board's draconian punishment is unprecedented among the school threat cases across the nation. Consider these: a fifteen year old student who exclaimed to a counselor that she was so angry she "could just shoot someone," or "[i]f you don't give me this schedule change, I'm going to shoot you," was suspended for three days; an adjudicated delinquent who wrote a rap song that threatened his female friend's life and which he handed to her at school, was sentenced to 24 months supervised probation and seven days in a juvenile detention facility, but was allowed to attend school; a seventh-grader who was placed on nine months probation and ordered to complete forty hours of community service for writing a "hit list" at school, discovered by his teacher, but whose case was dismissed and order vacated by appellate court because there was insufficient evidence to find a true threat.

There is something fundamentally wrong with our system of justice if we willingly revoke a non-offending teenager's privilege to attend public school, particularly where an alternative school is available, and where the responsible school authority recommended the alternative school as a constructive way to handle the matter. J.M., of all people, belongs in school. It does not pass unnoticed by this court that teachers and administrators in today's world are expected to undertake greater responsibilities than what the one-room schoolhouse teacher shouldered. Educators serve as surrogate parents, psychologists, social workers, and security guards, above and beyond their normal teaching responsibilities. They are charged with the duties of creating a safe learning environment, teaching clear communication, and protecting students' constitutional rights. It is clear that we as parents, neighbors, members of religious communities, political leaders, and members of the court cannot alienate teachers and administrators as they grapple with issues of violence in the classroom. It is not acceptable, however, to lower the bar for what constitutes a true threat and expel a "good kid" with a good scholastic record when other remedies are available. * * *

Because I believe that J.M.'s written expression was protected speech, I would affirm the district court's holding that J.M. had not issued a true threat. Although I agree that J.M.'s conduct required disciplinary action, the school board's response was an abuse of discretion. I would therefore affirm the district court.

McMILLIAN, CIRCUIT JUDGE, dissenting.

I join Judge Heaney's dissenting opinion and also write separately because I believe, first, that J.M.'s statement made in the privacy of his home was protected speech. That statement was not a true threat.

In addition, and of equal importance, I question whether the school had any legitimate authority over such a statement, made in the privacy of his home, not at school or during school hours or using school equipment, which was stolen from his home by one of his friends, at the request of another, and then turned over to school officials. If anything, the statement was arguably a police matter, for which, I note, the local prosecuting attorney refused to issue any charges.

3. APPLYING *TINKER* & ITS PROGENY TO K–12 THREAT-RELATED SITUATIONS

LaVINE v. BLAINE SCH. DIST.

257 F.3d 981 (9th Cir. 2001).

FISHER, CIRCUIT JUDGE:

This case has its genesis in a high school student's poem, which led to his temporary, emergency expulsion from school. * * * Although this is a close case in retrospect, we conclude that when the school officials expelled James LaVine they acted with sufficient justification and within constitutional limits, not to punish James for the content of his poem, but to avert perceived potential harm.

FACTUAL AND PROCEDURAL BACKGROUND

In the fall of 1998, James LaVine was in eleventh grade and a student in Vivian Bleecker's sixth period English class at Blaine High School. One evening in June or July 1998, James wrote the first draft of a poem he entitled "Last Words." The final version reads:

> As each day passed, I watched, love sprout, from the most, unlikely places, wich reminds, me that, beauty is in the eye's, of the beholder.
>
> As I remember, I start to cry, for I, had leared, this to late, and now, I must spend, each day, alone, alone for supper, alone at night, alone at death.
>
> Death I feel, crawlling down, my neck at, every turn, and so, now I know, what I must do.
>
> I pulled my gun, from its case, and began to load it.
>
> I remember, thinking at least I won't, go alone, as I, jumpped in, the car, all I could think about, was I would not, go alone.
>
> As I walked, through the, now empty halls, I could feel, my hart pounding.
>
> As I approached, the classroom door, I drew my gun and, threw open the door, **Bang, Bang, Bang–Bang**.

When it all was over, 28 were, dead, and all I remember, was not felling, any remorce, for I felt, I was, clensing my soul,

I quickly, turned and ran, as the bell rang, all I could here, were screams, screams of friends, screams of co workers, and just plain, screams of shear horor, as the students, found their, slayen classmates,

2 years have passed, and now I lay, 29 roses, down upon, these stairs, as now, I feel, I may, strike again.

No tears, shall be shead, in sarrow, for I am, alone, and now, I hope, I can feel, remorce, for what I did, without a shed, of tears, for no tear, shall fall, from your face, but from mine, as I try, to rest in peace, **Bang**!

Around that time, several school shootings had occurred—including the tragedy at Thurston High School in nearby Springfield, Oregon—and were frequent topics in the news. The morning after James wrote the poem, he showed it to his mother. She warned James not to turn the poem in to his teachers at school, because "with everything that was on the news . . . whoever read it might overreact."

James forgot about the poem until he rediscovered it in his living room on September 30, 1998. He made some editorial changes and brought it to school on Friday, October 2. He showed the poem to several of his friends, some of whom liked it and some of whom did not. At that point, he decided to ask his English teacher, Ms. Bleecker, her opinion of "Last Words."

James had not been in school for the three days prior to October 2. At the end of his sixth period English class, he turned in several assignments and the poem. James asked Bleecker if she would read the poem and tell him what she thought. Bleecker thanked James for the poem and said she looked forward to reading it. The poem was not an assignment or an "extra credit" project, but James had turned in other poems to his previous English teachers at Blaine High School and appreciated their feedback.

That evening, Bleecker read "Last Words" and became concerned. Her impression of James up to that time was that he was a very quiet student. She thought the poem might be "James' way of letting somebody know that * * * maybe something's hurting him, maybe he's upset about something, maybe he's afraid." The next morning (Saturday), Bleecker contacted Karen Mulholland, James' school counselor, to discuss the contents of the poem. Mulholland was similarly concerned and set up a meeting that evening with Bleecker and Tim Haney, the school's vice principal.

During his time at Blaine High School, James had frequently confided in Mulholland, who is also a school psychologist. In 1996, James told her that he thought about suicide. Mulholland made James promise her that he would talk to her before he tried to kill himself. Thereafter, Mulholland kept an eye out for James and tried to make time to help him when he needed it. In fall 1998, James told her about several incidents that had occurred in his home. In particular, on September 12, James and his father had had an argument about James' car. James' father, Bruce, had thrown a rock in the direction of James and his car. James called the police, who filed charges against Bruce. As a result of the charges, a court issued a no-contact order that led to James moving out of his home temporarily to live with his sister. James had also missed school on September 17, 1998 to participate in the resulting legal proceedings. In addition, in the preceding weeks, James had broken up with his girlfriend. The school authorities had become aware of this because the ex-girlfriend's mother had called the school to report that James was stalking her daughter.

Mulholland disclosed these events to Haney and Bleecker. Haney also reviewed James' disciplinary file, which recorded several additional incidents, including a fight in February 1998 and an episode of insubordination with a teacher in March 1997. Moreover, Haney said that a few weeks before October 2, 1998, he had personally disciplined James for wearing to school a T-shirt emblazoned with the words "eat shit and die." Haney's impression of James at that time was that he was a "good kid, but . . . somewhat of a 'loner.' "

* * * [B]ased upon the information he had, [Principal]. . . Newell decided to "emergency expel" James under Washington Administrative Code § 180–40–295. Haney left a message with James' parents that day telling them to attend a meeting the next morning at the school. At 8:00 a.m. on Monday, Newell told James and his father that James was being emergency expelled from school. This expulsion was formally expressed in a letter of the same date. That letter in relevant part states:

> This letter is to inform you of the following violations of the Blaine High School Discipline Policy by your son James:

> On October 2, 1998 at 2:50 p.m., your son James presented a paper to his English teacher, which implied extreme violence to our student body. This violation of [sic] was of a nature significant enough to be classified as dangerous to your son and/or a threat to other students and/or a threat of serious disruption to the education process. Therefore I impose the sanction of emergency expulsion.

> * * *

After James was expelled, his parents hired an attorney, Breean Beggs, and appealed James' expulsion to the Blaine School Board. * * * Shortly thereafter, the school district rescinded its expulsion and James was allowed to return to school after missing 17 days. He completed the school year without incident.

Even though James was allowed to return to school, James and his parents continued with their appeal of the expulsion to the School Board. Concerned that the October 5 letter would hurt James' chances of entering the military, they requested that it be removed from James' file. After a hearing on December 15, 1998, the Board affirmed the expulsion, but agreed to rewrite the letter. A new, back-dated letter was substituted emphasizing that James was expelled for safety as opposed to disciplinary reasons; the revised letter did not refer to events that had transpired subsequent to October 5, 1998.

James and his father filed suit in federal court on July 6, 1999, claiming the Blaine School District, Tim Haney, Dan Newell and Karen Mulholland (collectively "the school" or "defendants") violated James' constitutional rights by expelling him and maintaining documentation in his school file. The suit asked for general and specific damages and for an order permanently enjoining defendants from maintaining any letters in James' file regarding his expulsion. * * * The district court * * * entered an injunction preventing the school district from placing or maintaining any negative documentation in James LaVine's school file.

* * *

DISCUSSION

As we noted at the outset, we live in a time when school violence is an unfortunate reality that educators must confront on an all too frequent basis. The recent spate of school shootings have put our nation on edge and have focused attention on what school officials, law enforcement and others can do or could have done to prevent these kinds of tragedies. After Columbine, Thurston, Santee and other school shootings, questions have been asked about how teachers or administrators could have missed telltale "warning signs," why something was not done earlier and what should be done to prevent such tragedies from happening again.

Although schools are being asked to do more to prevent violence, the Constitution sets limits as to how far they can go. Just as the Constitution does not allow the police to imprison all suspicious characters, schools cannot expel students just because they are "loners," wear black and play video games. * * * Schools must achieve a balance between protecting the safety and well-being of their students and respecting those same students' constitutional rights * * *.

The LaVines, in this lawsuit, argue that the school failed to reach the proper balance when it expelled James. They contend that James' poem is protected by the First Amendment and that he was unconstitutionally disciplined for the content of his speech. The school argues that James was not disciplined because of the poem, but was expelled based upon a confluence of factors, including the poem, that indicated he was a danger to the safety of the school and to himself.

To determine whether the school violated James' First Amendment rights, we must consider what those rights are. Public school students are protected by the First Amendment and do not "shed their constitutional rights to freedom of speech or expression at the schoolhouse gate." Tinker v. Des Moines Indep. Cmty. Sch. Dist., 393 U.S. 503, 506, 89 S. Ct. 733 (1969) (upholding students' right to wear black armbands in protest against the Vietnam War). The First Amendment rights of public school students, however, "are not automatically coextensive with the rights of adults in other settings" and must be "applied in light of the special characteristics of the school environment." Hazelwood Sch. Dist. v. Kuhlmeier, 484 U.S. 260, 266, 108 S.Ct. 562 (1988) (holding school principal could censor the student newspaper) (quoting *Bethel Sch. Dist. No. 403 v. Fraser,* 478 U.S. 675, 682, 106 S.Ct. 3159 (1986) (holding school could punish students for making lewd remarks at school assembly), and *Tinker,* 393 U.S. at 506, 89 S.Ct. 733, respectively). For example, a school need not tolerate student speech that is inconsistent with its basic educational mission. *Hazelwood,* 484 U.S. at 266, 108 S.Ct. 562.

In the school context, we have granted educators substantial deference as to what speech is appropriate. * * * With that said, deference does not mean abdication; there are situations where school officials overstep their bounds and violate the Constitution. In deciding whether school officials have infringed a student's First Amendment rights, we must first determine what type of student speech is at issue. [W]e . . . [have] . . . "discerned three distinct areas of student speech," each of which is governed by different Supreme Court precedent:

(1) vulgar, lewd, obscene and plainly offensive speech is governed by *Fraser;*

(2) school-sponsored speech is governed by *Hazelwood;* and

(3) speech that falls into neither of these categories is governed by *Tinker.*

James' poem clearly falls within the third category.[5]

* * *

To suppress speech falling within * * * [the] "all other speech" category, school officials must justify their decision by showing "facts which might reasonably have led school authorities to forecast substantial disruption of or material interference with school activities." *Tinker* does not require school officials to wait until disruption actually occurs before they may act. "In fact, they have a duty to prevent the occurrence of disturbances." Forecasting disruption is unmistakably difficult to do. *Tinker* does not require certainty that disruption will occur, "but rather the existence of facts which might reasonably lead school officials to forecast substantial disruption."

In applying *Tinker,* we look to the totality of the relevant facts. We look not only to James' actions, but to all of the circumstances confronting the school officials that might reasonably portend disruption. When we look to all of the relevant facts here, we conclude that the school did not violate the First Amendment when it emergency expelled James.

The school had a duty to prevent any potential violence on campus to James or to other students. When the school officials made their

5. The school argues that James' poem was a "true threat" and not protected by the First Amendment at all. Because we conclude that even if the poem was protected speech, the school's actions were justified, we need not resolve this issue.

decision not to allow James to attend class on Monday morning, they were aware of a substantial number of facts that in isolation would probably not have warranted their response, but in combination gave them a reasonable basis for their actions. The school was aware that James previously had suicidal ideations that he had shared with school officials. The officials were aware that James was involved in a domestic dispute where he was forced to move out of his family home. James told Mulholland that his filing charges against his father caused financial pressure on his family because of the legal costs associated with his father's defense, and that in turn his family placed pressure upon him to rescind his allegations. The school was also aware that in the past weeks James had broken up with his girlfriend and he was reportedly stalking her. Moreover, James had had several disciplinary problems in the past, at least one of which involved some violence. Further, in the three days prior to turning in the poem, James had been absent from school, a cause of concern.

Last, and maybe most importantly, there was the poem itself. "Last Words" is filled with imagery of violent death and suicide. At its extreme it can be interpreted as a portent of future violence, of the shooting of James' fellow students. Even in its most mild interpretation, the poem appears to be a "cry for help" from a troubled teenager contemplating suicide. Taken together and given the backdrop of actual school shootings, we hold that these circumstances were sufficient to have led school authorities reasonably to forecast substantial disruption of or material interference with school activities—specifically, that James was intending to inflict injury upon himself or others.

It is true that the Whatcom Sheriff's Department and Dr. Dewitt did not believe James should be involuntarily committed, but the standard for involuntary commitment is not the same as that for school officials to take action. To commit a minor 13 years of age or older involuntarily in Washington State, a mental health professional must conclude that the minor is suffering from a mental disorder and presents a likelihood of serious harm. Under *Tinker*, there is no requirement that the student be mentally ill and likely to cause serious harm. Indeed, because of the special circumstances of the school environment, the level of disturbance required to justify official intervention is lower inside a public school than it is outside the school.

Given the potential for substantial disruption, we cannot fault the school's response. In Washington, if school officials want to immediately bar a student from coming to school for safety purposes, they have only one option—emergency expulsion under Washington Administrative Code § 180–40–295. Under § 180 40–295, if school officials have "good and sufficient reason to believe that the student's presence poses an immediate and continuing danger to the student, other students, or school personnel or an immediate and continuing threat of substantial disruption of the educational process," they can emergency expel the student until they deem it safe for the student to return. Here, after emergency expelling James, the school allowed him to return to classes as soon as he was evaluated by a psychiatrist who determined in his professional opinion that James was not a threat to himself or others. Considering all of the relevant facts and the totality of the circumstances, we hold that the school's emergency expulsion was reasonable and did not violate the First Amendment.

* * *

The record is * * * clear that in addition to any potential disciplinary violation James may or may not have committed by writing the poem, the school was foremost concerned about student safety. * * * Their first concern was the homecoming dance scheduled for that night. Haney decided to call James' home to see if he planned to attend the dance. Even though James said he would not be attending, Haney decided to warn security at the dance to be on the look-out for James. The three school officials then decided to call the police for help in this situation and were referred to a crisis hotline and eventually a psychiatrist. After discussing the situation with the psychiatrist, they decided that James should be evaluated by a mental health professional. Deputy sheriffs went to James' home for that purpose but, after James refused to be voluntarily examined, concluded that they lacked probable cause under Washington law to commit him. Taken together, the school's actions on the weekend before they emergency expelled him substantiate that it was not trying to discipline James for his speech, but was trying to protect its students from potential violence.

In retrospect, it may appear that, as James' mother predicted, the school overreacted. James very well may have been using his poetry to explore the disturbing topic of school violence and chose to do so through the perspective of a suicidal mass murderer. In fact, James strongly contends this was all he was doing and that he had no intention of hurting himself or others. We have no reason now to disbelieve James, as he did return to Blaine High School without further incident. We review, however, with deference, schools' decisions in connection with the safety of their students even when freedom of expression is involved. At the time the school officials made their determination to emergency expel James, they had facts which might reasonably have led them to forecast a substantial disruption of or material interference with school activities. *See Tinker,* 393 U.S. at 514, 89 S. Ct. 733. School officials have a difficult task in balancing safety concerns against chilling free expression. This case demonstrates how difficult that task can be.

That said, even though we conclude that emergency expelling James did not violate the First Amendment, the same cannot be said for the school's placement and maintenance in James' file of what the district court characterized as "negative documentation." The school need not permanently blemish James' record and harm his ability to secure future employment. We recognize that the school may have had justification to document contemporaneously the reasons for its emergency expulsion, but the revised October 5, 1998 letter was written and maintained in James' file after the perceived threat had subsided, the school had allowed James to return to classes and had satisfied itself that James was not a threat to himself or others. As such, it created a permanent indictment of James without reference to the later, ameliorating events and thus went beyond the school's legitimate documentation needs. Accordingly, we affirm the district court's injunction prohibiting the placement or maintenance of any such negative documentation in James' file.

For the foregoing reasons we AFFIRM in part and REVERSE in part the district court's grant of partial summary judgment in favor of the plaintiffs and AFFIRM the injunction entered prohibiting the placement or maintenance of negative documentation in James' file. Because we conclude that even viewing the evidence in the light most favorable to the plaintiffs there is no genuine issue of material fact in dispute with regard to the expulsion claim, we also REVERSE in part the denial of partial summary judgment in favor of the defendants on this limited issue. REMANDED for further proceedings consistent with this opinion. Each side to bear its own costs.

LaVINE v. BLAINE SCH. DIST.

279 F.3d 719 (9th Cir. 2002).

Dissent from Denial of Rehearing En Banc

KLEINFELD, CIRCUIT JUDGE, with whom KOZINSKI, CIRCUIT JUDGE, joins and REINHARDT, CIRCUIT JUDGE, joins except as set forth in his separate dissent, dissenting from denial of rehearing en banc:

After today, members of the black trench coat clique in high schools in the western United States will have to hide their art work. They have lost their free speech rights. If a teacher, administrator, or student finds their art disturbing, they can be punished, even though they say nothing disruptive, defamatory or indecent and do not intend to threaten or harm anyone. School officials may now subordinate students' freedom of expression to a policy of making high schools cozy places, like daycare centers, where no one may be made uncomfortable by the knowledge that others have dark thoughts, and all the art is of hearts and smiley faces. The court has adopted a new doctrine in First Amendment law, that high school students may be punished for non-threatening speech that administrators believe may indicate that the speaker is emotionally disturbed and therefore dangerous.

* * *

The issue in this case is whether the school could *punish* James for what he said in his poem. The expulsion mechanism used against James is, as is set out below, a form of punishment. It is not unusual to hear some troubled person say things that give rise to the thought, "That person may be mentally ill or emotionally disturbed," and sometimes, "That person ought to be examined to determine whether he poses a danger to himself or others." Those conclusions, even assuming that they are well taken, do not justify *punishing* the speaker.

This case does not put at issue whether the school could, consistently with the Constitution, remove James pending psychiatric examination to ensure that he did not pose an unreasonable risk to the safety of other students. The district court only addressed whether the school could punish James with "emergency expulsion" for writing his poem. James's poem is disturbing. Reasonable school officials could have reasonably been concerned, based on his poem, and considering that he had once thought about suicide and experienced various disturbing events in his life, that James was a troubled and depressed boy. And they might have reasonably concluded that he ought to be examined by a psychiatrist before being allowed back into the school or into school events. The school administrators did not read the poem carefully enough to notice when it used the past tense and when it used the future tense, so they misread a dramatic monologue about a crime two years before as a statement that the monologuist intended to commit the crime in the future. Nevertheless, it is of legitimate concern when a boy in high school is preoccupied with thoughts about murder and suicide. Neither the LaVines, nor the district court, nor I, have taken issue with the proposition that James could properly be excluded from the school so that a psychiatrist could examine him and communicate a judgment about when it was safe to readmit him.

Punishment has meaning and consequences distinct from examination, counseling, and exclusion for health or safety reasons based on predictions about future conduct. As the district court proceedings on the injunction make clear, James and his father brought this case in part because the disciplinary expulsion in his school record has kept James from enlisting in the armed services. People are often asked on job and other applications whether they were ever "disciplined" in school, but not whether they were ever removed from school for medical reasons. School nurses commonly send children home when they appear to have communicable or dangerous medical conditions, such as impetigo, lice, measles, German measles, and chicken pox, and do not allow them to return until a doctor confirms that they are no longer dangerous to others. The Constitution does not permit the government to punish an individual for being ill, regardless of whether his illness is dangerous to others. And the Constitution does not permit the government to punish people for the content of their speech, if it is not a "true threat," where the punishment is grounded on a prediction based on the speech that the individuals may commit crimes against others. James, though, was not treated like a child with measles, who would likely be referred by his teacher to the school nurse and then sent home until he was better. He was punished, by expulsion, as having broken the rules.

The panel decision creates a new First Amendment rule: where school officials perceive a major social concern about school safety, they may punish school children whose speech gives rise to a concern that they may be dangerous to themselves or others, even though the speech is not a threat, disruptive, defamatory, sexual, or otherwise within any previously recognized category of constitutionally unprotected speech.

* * *

The applicable state law governing emergency expulsion establishes that it is punitive. School officials must show that a student poses an "immediate and continuing danger" to himself or others to justify immediate expulsion with a hearing afterwards. * * *

The panel consigns high schools to a constitutional black hole, where freedom of speech exists only to the extent that administrators are comfortable with it. That is not the law. *Tinker v. Des Moines Independent Community School District* holds that students "do not shed their constitutional rights to freedom of speech or expression at the schoolhouse gate." Regulations that directly interfere with speech, such as laws against libel, incitement to violence, threats, and obscenity, must fit within narrowly defined exceptions to otherwise absolute First Amendment protection. The nature and purposes of schools, and the fact that their students are generally minors, allows for restraints that do not apply in other contexts, but the general rule remains supportive of freedom of speech.

* * *

The panel's errors on *Tinker* are these: (1) *Tinker* does not hold that a mere prediction that speech may interfere with discipline justifies suppression, it holds only the converse, that suppression is not justified in the absence of such a finding and showing; (2) *Tinker* does not hold that a student may be punished for speech that, without intentional wrongdoing by the student, may disrupt discipline, but at most implies that, had the armbands been disruptive, the students could have been punished for refusing to obey an order to take them off, that is, to cease engaging in the prohibited expression; (3) *Tinker* requires a "showing," not a mere prediction based on amorphous concern.

* * *

In the absence of any viewpoint discrimination or other disqualifier, perhaps a school could constitutionally punish student personal expression within the school if (1) as in *Tinker, Bethel* and *Hazelwood*, the student had clear notice that the speech was prohibited and would be punished, and (2) "disturbances or disorders on the school premises in fact occurred" or the record demonstrated "facts which might reasonably have led school authorities to forecast substantial disruption of or material interference with school activities." I have no doubt that the school could prohibit discussion of poetry in calculus class under such a rule, but am considerably less confident that it could prohibit students from talking to each other during recesses about sex, religion or politics, on the ground that such discussions were likely to lead to hard feelings and disruption. But even under such a rule, James could not be punished, because he did not have notice that his poem would expose him to punishment. At most, the school could, under *Tinker, Bethel,* and *Hazel-*

wood, tell him not to circulate it any more in school, and then punish him if he did.

* * *

The panel describes this case as arising "against the backdrop of tragic school shootings" and school officials' knowledge of "shootings at Columbine, Thurston, and Santee high schools." Constitutional law ought to be based on neutral principles, and should not easily sway in the winds of popular concerns, for that would make our liberty a weak reed that swayed in the winds. Nevertheless we do not perform our work in isolation from the society we live in, and there is a notion that permeates the record in this case that because of increased violence in the schools, free speech ought to give way to increased security. Both the diagnosis and the cure are probably wrong, and such constitutional law ought not to be based on this vague popular sociology. There may well be, not an increase in school violence, but rather an increase in newspaper, magazine, and television stories about school violence, which has in fact been declining or steady in its frequency. As for the cure, there is no particular reason to think that punishing speech about school violence will reduce the amount of school violence. Though we judges have traditionally explained the value of freedom of speech in terms of the value of having a free marketplace of ideas, those whose profession is psychology and psychiatry rather than law traditionally explain it in terms of what they can learn about a patient if the patient communicates openly. An article in *American Psychologist* explains that (1) rates of criminal victimization in schools have apparently not risen in the past decade; (2) prediction of violent behavior is exceedingly difficult, because "for every killer youth, there are many others with the same behaviors or attitudes who never come close to killing their classmates"; (3) "the ratio of false positives to false negatives matters greatly if all identified individuals are stigmatized or if their opportunities are limited"; (4) youths who engage in violent behavior "are not usually loners"; (5) both diagnosis and interventions for violence-prone adolescents are not well developed; (6) for risk assessment, "the best source of information about the activities of students in a school is other students"; (7) expulsion dries up information, because "students will withhold information from the administration to avoid such disproportionate punishments."

I do not cite this article to suggest that constitutional law ought to be based on this sociological and psychological basis instead of the basis to which the panel gave some deference, that expulsion for speech not amounting to a "true threat" will reduce school violence. My purpose is to show that there is not necessarily any trade-off between speech and security. Suppression of speech may reduce security as well as liberty. Allowing the school to punish a student for writing a poem about a school killer may foster school killings, by drying up information from students about their own and other students' emotional troubles. If the students don't talk, the administrators and medical professionals won't find out about problems that speech might reveal. Punishment based on prediction rather than misconduct tends to be unjust, and where the predicted event is extremely rare, as in-school murders are, predictive punishment such as the school imposed is likely to punish vast numbers of innocent people for every one who would have engaged in the feared misconduct.

What was threatening about James's poem was not the words but the writer. The fact that he wrote the poem, given his background, might have indicated that he was so emotionally distraught that he might hurt himself and others. The fact that James wrote the poem might reasonably have justified a temporary suspension for mental examination, which was done, and which ascertained after three psychiatric visits that he could safely return to school. But the fact that James's poem might have revealed his emotional condition did not constitutionally justify punishing him.

Not everyone who writes about murder and evil is an incipient murderer. There is a lot of art about homicide (*e.g.*, the folk songs "On the Banks of the Ohio" and "Tom Dooley," Dostoevski's *Crime and Punishment*) and about homicidal maniacs who commit mass murder (*e.g.*, *Taxi Driver*). This art sometimes inspires crime (*e.g.*, John Hinckley shooting President Reagan to impress Jodie Foster's character in *Taxi Driver*). But the government could not properly punish Robert DeNiro for acting in *Taxi Driver*, nor the Kingston Trio for performing "Tom Dooley," no matter how many people found these artworks disturbing or threatening. We do not, under our constitution, allow the government to punish artists for making art, whether the art is good or bad, whether it makes people feel good or bad, unless the expression falls within a well established category of unprotected speech. This right too does not end at the schoolhouse gate.

C. PEER HARASSMENT AND MISTREATMENT

1. LIABILITY FOR PEER-TO-PEER SEXUAL HARASSMENT

PROBLEM 19: Maxwell v. Valhalla Unified School District

This problem is based on the following hypothetical, which focuses on the high school journalism class at Nirvana High, in the Valhalla Unified School District (a public school district located in the fictional state of Columbia).

At the beginning of his third semester in Nirvana High's award-winning journalism program, Joey—a quiet 15–year-old with an interest in pursuing a writing career—was promoted to the position of reporter for the *Nirvana News*, the official school newspaper. The Nirvana News was produced by students who were enrolled in the journalism production class and were graded by the faculty advisor.

Joey was assigned to work under the supervision of Sheree, a gregarious 17–year-old who served as the paper's front page editor. Sheree followed recent developments nationwide as a matter of course, and she soon became fascinated by the emerging news stories focusing on the Clinton–Lewinsky affair and the investigation by Kenneth Starr.

One day in early February 1998, when they were alone in the production room, Sheree asked Joey what he thought about the alleged events in the Paula Jones lawsuit. "If you came into the room and I was there and started taking off my clothes, what would you do?" she asked him. Embarrassed, Joey did not respond.

As time passed, Sheree began sharing stories and pictures of the Lewinsky affair with all four of her reporters. Yet Joey began to feel that she was sending him more e-mail attachments than she had sent the others. In addition, on several occasions when they were alone in the production room, Sheree brushed up against Joey, and on two occasions patted him on his backside (as coaches often do to their players) to congratulate him on his latest stories for the *Nirvana News*.

Joey, a highly religious young man who lived a very simple life with his foster parents, began to feel that he was being sexually harassed. For weeks he told no one, but finally he confided in his foster father, Mr. Maxwell, a highly respected elder in a local church. Unbeknownst to Joey, Maxwell then scheduled an appointment with the school principal, and demanded that the school do something to stop this "harassment" of his foster son. The principal listened, and then shook his head. "This sounds like normal behavior to me," the principal said. "Sheree is a great kid, and Joey is pretty lucky to be getting this attention, if you ask me."

A week later, Joey and Sheree were working after school, and everybody else had gone home. Joey walked into the back room, and there was Sheree, unbuttoning her shirt and smiling at him. "OK," she said, "I'll be Clinton. Here's the role play come true." Joey bolted out the door, and immediately went to his foster father's office in the church, where he told Mr. Maxwell about the latest incident. Outraged, Maxwell went back to see the principal, insisting that something be done. "At least talk to this girl, and to the journalism advisor," Maxwell exclaimed. "I'm sorry," the principal responded, "but in situations like this it's always one student's word against the other. I just don't see that I can or should get involved."

The next day, Joey withdrew from the journalism program, and Mr. Maxwell visited the local office of the Columbia Legal Foundation, a conservative public interest law firm. A widely publicized lawsuit was filed against the district on Joey's behalf, seeking monetary damages under Title VII principles applicable to the schools through Title IX. A key component of the foundation's argument was that the school would have responded very differently had the alleged harasser been a boy and had the alleged victim been a girl.

What arguments might be set forth by the respective sides? What result?

PROBLEM 20: Student Teaching at McKinley High

This hypothetical is set in the fictional state of Valhalla.

Sarah Jackson, a graduate student at the University of Northern Valhalla (a large public university located in an urban setting), was ready to begin the student teaching component of her one-year teacher preparation program. After considerable pressure from friends and family, she decided to carry a small handgun with her when she reported to McKinley High School for her first day of student teaching.

(McKinley High had been in the news often over the previous few months. Not only had there been a shooting incident at a football game, but nine current and former male students had been accused of raping or molesting young girls and keeping an account of their sexual conquests. The boys had all been members of the "Hornets' Nest," a clique of teen-agers who readily acknowledge their desire to have sex with large numbers of young girls.)

As Sarah walked down the hall to her assigned classroom on her first morning, she was greeted by catcalls from several male students, and one student shouted out: "There's number fifty-nine for you, Carl." She soon learned that one of these boys, Carl Haley, was actually in the class that she would be teaching. In addition, she found out that he was the star of the football team . . . *and* that he was a member of the Hornets' Nest.

The rest of the day, and indeed the next two weeks, passed without incident. Sarah worked on the observation/participation component of her assignment, and continued to bring the gun with her every day. Two other people found out that she had a gun in her purse: a fellow student teacher (Jamal) whom she had taken into confidence, and Jamal's supervising teacher (Ms. Kelly) (whom Jamal had told). Ms. Kelly kept several weapons at home, and told Jamal that she had considered bringing a gun to school herself.

Finally the time came for Sarah to teach her first lesson. After introductory remarks and a brief discussion, she put the students to work on a written assignment. Things were going just fine until she observed Carl and several of his friends snickering and passing papers in the back of the room. Walking over to them, she discovered that Carl had drawn a lewd and suggestive caricature of her—accompanied by a caption describing all the sexual acts she was allegedly ready to participate in with members of the Hornets' Nest.

Sarah turned back toward her supervising teacher's desk, but Mr. Gonzales had left the room for a few minutes to give Sarah the experience of being alone with the students. Embarrassed and increasingly flustered, she literally ran over to the desk to get Mr. Gonzales' referral slips so that she could send Carl to the office. As she did so, she knocked over her purse, and her gun fell out onto the ground. The room fell silent, but then Carl slowly stood up and began walking toward the desk area—where Sarah was standing next to the fallen purse. Julio, a quiet student who respected and admired Sarah, suddenly got up, pushed Carl aside, and picked up the gun. In the ensuing commotion, the gun went off, seriously wounding Latrice Elliot—who was hospitalized and missed three months of school.

The following events subsequently transpired:

A. After being apprised of all the facts leading up to the shooting incident, Dr. Lisa Caunca (the principal) decided to punish Carl by suspending him for harassing Sarah Jackson within the meaning of

Education Code sections 212.5 and 48900.2. The football coach protested, but to no avail. Carl missed the last two games of the season, and the quarterback at arch-rival Harding High won the league's most valuable player award (an award that everyone had expected Carl to win).

B.   The Elliot family filed a lawsuit against the school district, arguing under a variety of legal theories that the district was responsible for the injury to Latrice.

C.   Carl Haley filed a lawsuit against the school district, arguing that the district had violated his rights by suspending him.

* * *

A.   What arguments would the Elliot family be expected to raise in their lawsuit against the district? What result? Discuss.

B.   Carl Haley is prepared to argue that he did not commit sexual harassment within the meaning of Education Code sections 212.5 and 48900.2. What contentions would the district be likely to set forth in this regard? What result? Discuss.

Relevant portions of the Valhalla Education Code are reproduced below for reference:

Valhalla Education Code Section 48900.2

[A] pupil may be suspended from school or recommended for expulsion if the superintendent or the principal of the school in which the pupil is enrolled determines that the pupil has committed sexual harassment as defined in Section 212.5.

For the purposes of this chapter, the conduct described in Section 212.5 must be considered by a reasonable person of the same gender as the victim to be sufficiently severe or pervasive to have a negative impact upon the individual's academic performance or to create an intimidating, hostile, or offensive educational environment. This section shall not apply to pupils enrolled in kindergarten and grades 1 to 3, inclusive.

Valhalla Education Code Section 212.5

"Sexual harassment" means unwelcome sexual advances, requests for sexual favors, and other verbal, visual, or physical conduct of a sexual nature, made by someone from or in the work or educational setting, under any of the following conditions:

(a) Submission to the conduct is explicitly or implicitly made a term or a condition of an individual's employment, academic status, or progress.

(b) Submission to, or rejection of, the conduct by the individual is used as the basis of employment or academic decisions affecting the individual.

(c) The conduct has the purpose or effect of having a negative impact upon the individual's work or academic performance, or of creating an intimidating, hostile, or offensive work or educational environment.

(d) Submission to, or rejection of, the conduct by the individual is used as the basis for any decision affecting the individual regarding benefits and services, honors, programs, or activities available at or through the educational institution.

HOSTILE ENVIRONMENT
SEXUAL HARASSMENT LAW*

Hostile environment claims were first recognized by the U.S. Supreme Court in 1986,[5] and over the next 10–15 years the rules were fine tuned by subsequent judicial opinions. 1998 proved to be a turning point, with the Court deciding four sexual harassment cases in one year.[6]

The basic hostile environment claim under Title VII can only be filed by a person who alleges harassment in the workplace. Sexual harassment is not a crime, but an act or a series of acts that can lead to large monetary awards for aggrieved employees who have sued their employers under Title VII. To win such lawsuits, plaintiffs must follow a two-step process. First, they must establish actionable harassment. Second, they must show that the employer should be held liable for this harassment.[7]

To establish actionable hostile environment harassment, plaintiffs must prove that the activity in question was unwelcome and that it constituted "a sexually objectionable environment" which was (a) objectively offensive and (b) subjectively offensive. An environment is deemed *objectively offensive* if a "reasonable person" would find it to be hostile or abusive, and it will be found *subjectively offensive* if the victim in fact perceived it to be so.

The objectively offensive inquiry is inevitably the most complex. Courts must look at

> all the circumstances, including the frequency of the discriminatory conduct; its severity; whether it is physically threatening or humiliating, or a mere offensive utterance; and whether it unreasonably interferes with an employee's work performance.[8]

---

* Adapted from Stuart Biegel, Beyond Our Control? Confronting the Limits of Our Legal System in the Age of Cyberspace, MIT Press (2001).

5. *See* Meritor Savings Bank v. Vinson, 477 U.S. 57 (1986).

6. The four cases were *Oncale v. Sundowner Offshore Services*, 523 U.S. 75 (1998), *Gebser v. Lago Vista Indep. Sch. Dist.*, 524 U.S. 274 (1998), *Faragher v. City of Boca Raton*, 524 U.S. 775 (1998), & *Ellerth v. Burlington Indus.*, 524 U.S. 951 (1998).

7. Once actionable harassment is shown, plaintiff still needs to prove that employer's actions should give rise to liabil-

ity. Such proof is not necessary if there was a "tangible employment action" as a result of the events in question (such as retaliatory firing after plaintiff complained). However, if there was no tangible employment action, the employer can prevail if it can be shown that:

  1. Employer exercised reasonable care to prevent and correct promptly any sexually harassing behavior, and

  2. Plaintiff employee unreasonably failed to take advantage of any preventive or corrective opportunities provided by employer or to avoid harm otherwise. *Faragher*, 524 U.S. at 807.

8. *Id.* at 787–88.

Increasingly, the Court has worked very hard to try to distinguish between simple teasing on the one hand and hostile environment sexual harassment on the other. "A recurring point" in recent court opinions, Justice Souter noted in *Faragher,* is that "simple teasing, offhand comments, and isolated incidents (unless extremely serious) will not amount to discriminatory changes in the terms and conditions of employment. These standards for judging hostility," he continued, "are sufficiently demanding to ensure that Title VII does not become a 'general civility code.' "[9]

A version of this framework has recently been applied by the Courts in federally funded education programs under Title IX of the Education Amendments of 1972 to the Civil Rights Act of 1964. In *Davis v. Monroe County Board of Education,* 526 U.S. 629 (1999) the Court held that educational institutions can be held liable for peer-to-peer hostile environment sexual harassment "that is so severe, pervasive, and objectively offensive that it effectively bars the victim's access to an educational opportunity or benefit." But even if plaintiff can meet the requirements of this stringent test for actionable harassment, he or she can only prevail if the education officials in charge acted "with deliberate indifference to known acts of harassment."[10]

DAVIS v. MONROE COUNTY BD. OF ED.

526 U.S. 629, 119 S.Ct. 1661 (1999).

JUSTICE O'CONNOR delivered the opinion of the Court.

Petitioner brought suit against the Monroe County Board of Education and other defendants, alleging that her fifth-grade daughter had been the victim of sexual harassment by another student in her class. Among petitioner's claims was a claim for monetary and injunctive relief under Title IX of the Education Amendments of 1972 (Title IX), 86 Stat. 373, as amended, 20 U.S.C. § 1681 *et seq.* The District Court dismissed petitioner's Title IX claim on the ground that "student-on-student," or peer, harassment provides no ground for a private cause of action under the statute. The Court of Appeals for the Eleventh Circuit, sitting en banc, affirmed. We consider here whether a private damages action may lie against the school board in cases of student-on-student harassment. We conclude that it may, but only where the funding recipient acts with deliberate indifference to known acts of harassment in its programs or activities. Moreover, we conclude that such an action will lie only for harassment that is so severe, pervasive, and objectively offensive that it effectively bars the victim's access to an educational opportunity or benefit.

I

* * *

9. *Id.*

10. *See* Davis v. Monroe County Board of Education, 526 U.S. 629, 633 (1999).

A

Petitioner's minor daughter, LaShonda, was allegedly the victim of a prolonged pattern of sexual harassment by one of her fifth-grade classmates at Hubbard Elementary School, a public school in Monroe County, Georgia. According to petitioner's complaint, the harassment began in December 1992, when the classmate, G.F., attempted to touch LaShonda's breasts and genital area and made vulgar statements such as " 'I want to get in bed with you' " and " 'I want to feel your boobs.' " Similar conduct allegedly occurred on or about January 4 and January 20, 1993. LaShonda reported each of these incidents to her mother and to her classroom teacher, Diane Fort. Petitioner, in turn, also contacted Fort, who allegedly assured petitioner that the school principal, Bill Querry, had been informed of the incidents. Petitioner contends that, notwithstanding these reports, no disciplinary action was taken against G.F.

G.F.'s conduct allegedly continued for many months. In early February, G.F. purportedly placed a door stop in his pants and proceeded to act in a sexually suggestive manner toward LaShonda during physical education class. LaShonda reported G.F.'s behavior to her physical education teacher, Whit Maples. Approximately one week later, G.F. again allegedly engaged in harassing behavior, this time while under the supervision of another classroom teacher, Joyce Pippin. Again, LaShonda allegedly reported the incident to the teacher, and again petitioner contacted the teacher to follow up.

Petitioner alleges that G.F. once more directed sexually harassing conduct toward LaShonda in physical education class in early March, and that LaShonda reported the incident to both Maples and Pippen. In mid-April 1993, G.F. allegedly rubbed his body against LaShonda in the school hallway in what LaShonda considered a sexually suggestive manner, and LaShonda again reported the matter to Fort.

The string of incidents finally ended in mid-May, when G.F. was charged with, and pleaded guilty to, sexual battery for his misconduct. The complaint alleges that LaShonda had suffered during the months of harassment, however; specifically, her previously high grades allegedly dropped as she became unable to concentrate on her studies, and, in April 1993, her father discovered that she had written a suicide note. The complaint further alleges that, at one point, LaShonda told petitioner that she " 'didn't know how much longer she could keep [G.F.] off her.' "

Nor was LaShonda G.F.'s only victim; it is alleged that other girls in the class fell prey to G.F.'s conduct. At one point, in fact, a group composed of LaShonda and other female students tried to speak with Principal Querry about G.F.'s behavior. According to the complaint, however, a teacher denied the students' request with the statement, " 'If [Querry] wants you, he'll call you.' "

Petitioner alleges that no disciplinary action was taken in response to G.F.'s behavior toward LaShonda. In addition to her conversations with Fort and Pippen, petitioner alleges that she spoke with Principal Querry in mid-May 1993. When petitioner inquired as to what action the school intended to take against G.F., Querry simply stated, " 'I guess I'll have to threaten him a little bit harder.' " Yet, petitioner alleges, at no point during the many months of his reported misconduct was G.F. disciplined for harassment. Indeed, Querry allegedly asked petitioner why LaShonda " 'was the only one complaining.' "

Nor, according to the complaint, was any effort made to separate G.F. and LaShonda. On the contrary, notwithstanding LaShonda's frequent complaints, only after more than three months of reported harassment was she even permitted to change her classroom seat so that she was no longer seated next to G.F. Moreover, petitioner alleges that, at the time of the events in question, the Monroe County Board of Education (Board) had not instructed its personnel on how to respond to peer sexual harassment and had not established a policy on the issue.

B

On May 4, 1994, petitioner filed suit in the United States District Court for the Middle District of Georgia against the Board, Charles Dumas, the school district's superintendent, and Principal Querry. The complaint alleged that the Board is a recipient of federal funding for purposes of Title IX, that "[t]he persistent sexual advances and harassment by the student G.F. upon [LaShonda] interfered with her ability to attend school and perform her studies and activities," and that "[t]he deliberate indifference by Defendants to the unwelcome sexual advances of a student upon LaShonda created an intimidating, hostile, offensive and abus[ive] school environment in violation of Title IX." The complaint sought compensatory and punitive damages, attorney's fees, and injunctive relief.

* * *

II

Title IX provides, with certain exceptions not at issue here, that

[n]o person in the United States shall, on the basis of sex, be excluded from participation in, be denied the benefits of, or be subjected to discrimination under any education program or activity receiving Federal financial assistance.

20 U.S.C. § 1681(a).

* * *

There is no dispute here that the Board is a recipient of federal education funding for Title IX purposes. Nor do respondents support an argument that student-on-student harassment cannot rise to the level of "discrimination" for purposes of Title IX. Rather, at issue here is the question whether a recipient of federal education funding may be liable for damages under Title IX under any circumstances for discrimination in the form of student-on-student sexual harassment.

A

* * * [W]e are asked to do more than define the scope of the behavior that Title IX proscribes. We must determine whether a district's failure to respond to student-on-student harassment in its schools can support a private suit for money damages. This Court has indeed recognized an implied private right of action under Title IX, and we have held that money damages are available in such suits.

* * *

Gebser thus established that a recipient intentionally violates Title IX, and is subject to a private damages action, where the recipient is deliberately indifferent to known acts of teacher-student discrimination. Indeed, whether viewed as "discrimination" or "subject[ing]" students to discrimination, Title IX "[u]nquestionably * * * placed on [the Board] the duty not" to permit teacher-student harassment in its schools, and recipients violate Title IX's plain terms when they remain deliberately indifferent to this form of misconduct.

We consider here whether the misconduct identified in *Gebser*— deliberate indifference to known acts of harassment—amounts to an intentional violation of Title IX, capable of supporting a private damages action, when the harasser is a student rather than a teacher. We conclude that, in certain limited circumstances, it does. * * *

* * * [A] recipient's damages liability . . . [is limited] . . . to circumstances wherein the recipient exercises substantial control over both the harasser and the context in which the known harassment occurs. Only then can the recipient be said to "expose" its students to harassment or "cause" them to undergo it "under" the recipient's programs. * * *

Where, as here, the misconduct occurs during school hours and on school grounds—the bulk of G.F.'s misconduct, in fact, took place in the classroom—he misconduct is taking place "under" an "operation" of the funding recipient. In these circumstances, the recipient retains substantial control over the context in which the harassment occurs. More importantly, however, in this setting the Board exercises significant control over the harasser. We have observed, for example, "that the nature of [the State's] power [over public schoolchildren] is custodial and tutelary, permitting a degree of supervision and control that could not be exercised over free adults." On more than one occasion, this Court has recognized the importance of school officials' "comprehensive authority * * * consistent with fundamental constitutional safeguards, to prescribe and control conduct in the schools." *Tinker* v. *Des Moines Independent Community School Dist.*, 393 U.S. 503, 507, 89 S. Ct. 733, (1969). The common law, too, recognizes the school's disciplinary authority. We thus conclude that recipients of federal funding may be liable for "subject[ing]" their students to discrimination where the recipient is deliberately indifferent to known acts of student-on-student sexual harassment and the harasser is under the school's disciplinary authority.

* * *

We stress that our conclusion here—that recipients may be liable for their deliberate indifference to known acts of peer sexual harassment—does not mean that recipients can avoid liability only by purging their schools of actionable peer harassment or that administrators must engage in particular disciplinary action. We thus disagree with respondents' contention that, if Title IX provides a cause of action for student-on-student harassment, "nothing short of expulsion of every student accused of misconduct involving sexual overtones would protect school systems from liability or damages." Likewise, the dissent erroneously imagines that victims of peer harassment now have a Title IX right to make particular remedial demands. In fact, as we have previously noted, courts should refrain from second-guessing the disciplinary decisions made by school administrators.

School administrators will continue to enjoy the flexibility they require so long as funding recipients are deemed "deliberately indifferent" to acts of student-on-student harassment only where the recipient's response to the harassment or lack thereof is clearly unreasonable in light of the known circumstances. The dissent consistently mischaracterizes this standard to require funding recipients to "remedy" peer harassment, and to "ensur[e] that ... students conform their conduct to" certain rules. Title IX imposes no such requirements. On the contrary, the recipient must merely respond to known peer harassment in a manner that is not clearly unreasonable. This is not a mere "reasonableness" standard, as the dissent assumes. In an appropriate case, there is no reason why courts, on a motion to dismiss, for summary judgment, or for a directed verdict, could not identify a response as not "clearly unreasonable" as a matter of law.

Like the dissent, we acknowledge that school administrators shoulder substantial burdens as a result of legal constraints on their disciplinary authority. To the extent that these restrictions arise from federal statutes, Congress can review these burdens with attention to the difficult position in which such legislation may place our Nation's schools. We believe, however, that the standard set out here is sufficiently flexible to account both for the level of disciplinary authority available to the school and for the potential liability arising from certain forms of disciplinary action. A university might not, for example, be expected to exercise the same degree of control over its students that a grade school would enjoy, and it would be entirely reasonable for a school to refrain from a form of disciplinary action that would expose it to constitutional or statutory claims.

* * *

C

Applying this standard to the facts at issue here, we conclude that the Eleventh Circuit erred in dismissing petitioner's complaint. Petitioner alleges that her daughter was the victim of repeated acts of sexual harassment by G.F. over a 5–month period, and there are allegations in support of the conclusion that G.F.'s misconduct was severe, pervasive, and objectively offensive. The harassment was not only verbal; it included numerous acts of objectively offensive touching, and, indeed, G.F. ultimately pleaded guilty to criminal sexual misconduct. Moreover, the complaint alleges that there were multiple victims who were sufficiently disturbed by G.F.'s misconduct to seek an audience with the school principal. Further, petitioner contends that the harassment had a concrete, negative effect on her daughter's ability to receive an education. The complaint also suggests that petitioner may be able to show both actual knowledge and deliberate indifference on the part of the Board, which made no effort whatsoever either to investigate or to put an end to the harassment.

* * * Accordingly, the judgment of the United States Court of Appeals for the Eleventh Circuit is reversed, and the case is remanded for further proceedings consistent with this opinion.

It is so ordered.

Justice Kennedy, with whom The Chief Justice, Justice Scalia, and Justice Thomas join, dissenting.

* * * The remedial scheme the majority creates today is neither sensible nor faithful to Spending Clause principles. In order to make its case for school liability for peer sexual harassment, the majority must establish that Congress gave grant recipients clear and unambiguous notice that they would be liable in money damages for failure to remedy discriminatory acts of their students. The majority must also demonstrate that the statute gives schools clear notice that one child's harassment of another constitutes "discrimination" on the basis of sex within the meaning of Title IX, and that—as applied to individual cases—the standard for liability will enable the grant recipient to distinguish inappropriate childish behavior from actionable gender discrimination. The majority does not carry these burdens.

Instead, the majority finds statutory clarity where there is none and discovers indicia of congressional notice to the States in the most unusual of places. It treats the issue as one of routine statutory construction alone, and it errs even in this regard. In the end, the majority not only imposes on States liability that was unexpected and unknown, but the contours of which are, as yet, unknowable. The majority's opinion purports to be narrow, but the limiting principles it proposes are illusory. The fence the Court has built is made of little sticks, and it cannot contain the avalanche of liability now set in motion. The potential costs to our schools of today's decision are difficult to estimate, but they are so great that it is most unlikely Congress intended to inflict them.

The only certainty flowing from the majority's decision is that scarce resources will be diverted from educating our children and that many school districts, desperate to avoid Title IX peer harassment suits, will adopt whatever federal code of student conduct and discipline the Department of Education sees fit to impose upon them. The Nation's schoolchildren will learn their first lessons about federalism in class-rooms where the Federal Government is the ever-present regulator. The Federal Government will have insinuated itself not only into one of the most traditional areas of state concern but also into one of the most sensitive areas of human affairs. This federal control of the discipline of our Nation's schoolchildren is contrary to our traditions and inconsistent with the sensible administration of our schools. * * *

I

B

* * *

2

* * *

The practical obstacles schools encounter in ensuring that thousands of immature students conform their conduct to acceptable norms may be even more significant than the legal obstacles. School districts cannot exercise the same measure of control over thousands of students that they do over a few hundred adult employees. The limited resources of our schools must be conserved for basic educational services. Some schools lack the resources even to deal with serious problems of violence and are already overwhelmed with disciplinary problems of all kinds.

Perhaps even more startling than its broad assumptions about school control over primary and secondary school students is the majority's failure to grapple in any meaningful way with the distinction between elementary and secondary schools, on the one hand, and universities on the other. The majority bolsters its argument that schools can control their students' actions by quoting our decision in for the proposition that "the nature of [the State's] power [over public school children] is custodial and tutelary, permitting a degree of supervision and control that could not be exercised over free adults." Yet the majority's holding would appear to apply with equal force to universities, which do not exercise custodial and tutelary power over their adult students.

A university's power to discipline its students for speech that may constitute sexual harassment is also circumscribed by the First Amendment. A number of federal courts have already confronted difficult problems raised by university speech codes designed to deal with peer sexual and racial harassment.

The difficulties associated with speech codes simply underscore the limited nature of a university's control over student behavior that may be viewed as sexual harassment. Despite the fact that the majority relies on the assumption that schools exercise a great deal of control over their students to justify creating the private cause of action in the first instance, it does not recognize the obvious limits on a university's ability to control its students as a reason to doubt the propriety of a private cause of action for peer harassment. It simply uses them as a factor in determining whether the university's response was reasonable.

* * *

II

* * * The majority * * * imposes on schools potentially crushing financial liability for student conduct that is not prohibited in clear terms by Title IX and that cannot, even after today's opinion, be identified by either schools or courts with any precision.

The law recognizes that children—particularly young children—are not fully accountable for their actions because they lack the capacity to exercise mature judgment. It should surprise no one, then, that the schools that are the primary locus of most children's social development are rife with inappropriate behavior by children who are just learning to interact with their peers. The *amici* on the front lines of our schools describe the situation best:

> Unlike adults in the workplace, juveniles have limited life experiences or familial influences upon which to establish an understanding of appropriate behavior. The real world of school discipline is a rough-and-tumble place where students practice newly learned vulgarities, erupt with anger, tease and embarrass each other, share offensive notes, flirt, push and shove in the halls, grab and offend.

No one contests that much of this "dizzying array of immature or uncontrollable behaviors by students," is inappropriate, even "objectively offensive" at times, and that parents and schools have a moral and ethical responsibility to help students learn to interact with their peers in an appropriate manner. It is doubtless the case, moreover, that much of this inappropriate behavior is directed toward members of the opposite sex, as children in the throes of adolescence struggle to express their emerging sexual identities.

It is a far different question, however, whether it is either proper or useful to label this immature, childish behavior gender discrimination. Nothing in Title IX suggests that Congress even contemplated this question, much less answered it in the affirmative in unambiguous terms.

The majority, nevertheless, has no problem labeling the conduct of fifth graders "sexual harassment" and "gender discrimination." * * *

Contrary to the majority's assertion, however, respondents have made a cogent and persuasive argument that the type of student conduct alleged by petitioner should not be considered "sexual harassment," much less gender discrimination actionable under Title IX:

> [A]t the time Petitioner filed her complaint, no court, including this Court had recognized the concept of sexual harassment in any context other than the employment context. Nor had any Court extended the concept of sexual harassment to the misconduct of emotionally and socially immature children. The type of conduct

alleged by Petitioner in her complaint is not new. However, in past years it was properly identified as misconduct which was addressed within the context of student discipline. The Petitioner now asks this Court to create out of whole cloth a cause of action by labeling childish misconduct as "sexual harassment," to stigmatize children as sexual harassers, and have the federal court system take on the additional burden of second guessing the disciplinary actions taken by school administrators in addressing misconduct, something this Court has consistently refused to do.

* * *

III

The majority's inability to provide any workable definition of actionable peer harassment simply underscores the myriad ways in which an opinion that purports to be narrow is, in fact, so broad that it will support untold numbers of lawyers who will prove adept at presenting cases that will withstand the defendant school districts' pretrial motions. Each of the barriers to runaway litigation the majority offers us crumbles under the weight of even casual scrutiny.

For example, the majority establishes what sounds like a relatively high threshold for liability—"denial of equal access" to education—and, almost in the same breath, makes clear that alleging a decline in grades is enough to survive Federal Rule of Civil Procedure 12(b)(6) and, it follows, to state a winning claim. The majority seems oblivious to the fact that almost every child, at some point, has trouble in school because he or she is being teased by his or her peers. The girl who wants to skip recess because she is teased by the boys is no different from the overweight child who skips gym class because the other children tease her about her size in the locker room; or the child who risks flunking out because he refuses to wear glasses to avoid the taunts of "four-eyes"; or the child who refuses to go to school because the school bully calls him a "scaredy-cat" at recess. Most children respond to teasing in ways that detract from their ability to learn. The majority's test for actionable harassment will, as a result, sweep in almost all of the more innocuous conduct it acknowledges as a ubiquitous part of school life.

The string of adjectives the majority attaches to the word "harassment"—"severe, pervasive, and objectively offensive"—likewise fails to narrow the class of conduct that can trigger liability, since the touchstone for determining whether there is Title IX liability is the effect on the child's ability to get an education. Indeed, the Court's reliance on the impact on the child's educational experience suggests that the "objective offensiveness" of a comment is to be judged by reference to a reasonable child at whom the comments were aimed. Not only is that standard likely to be quite expansive, it also gives schools—and juries—little guidance, requiring them to attempt to gauge the sensitivities of, for instance, the average seven-year-old.

* * *

The majority's limitations on peer sexual harassment suits cannot hope to contain the flood of liability the Court today begins. The elements of the Title IX claim created by the majority will be easy not only to allege but also to prove. A female plaintiff who pleads only that a boy called her offensive names, that she told a teacher, that the teacher's response was unreasonable, and that her school performance suffered as a result, appears to state a successful claim.

There will be no shortage of plaintiffs to bring such complaints. Our schools are charged each day with educating millions of children. Of those millions of students, a large percentage will, at some point during their school careers, experience something they consider sexual harassment. A 1993 study by the American Association of University Women Educational Foundation, for instance, found that "fully 4 out of 5 students (81%) report that they have been the target of some form of sexual harassment during their school lives." The number of potential lawsuits against our schools is staggering.

The cost of defending against peer sexual harassment suits alone could overwhelm many school districts. * * *

The prospect of unlimited Title IX liability will, in all likelihood, breed a climate of fear that encourages school administrators to label even the most innocuous of childish conduct sexual harassment. * * *

At the college level, the majority's holding is sure to add fuel to the debate over campus speech codes that, in the name of preventing a hostile educational environment, may infringe students' First Amendment rights. Indeed, under the majority's control principle, schools presumably will be responsible for remedying conduct that occurs even in student dormitory rooms. As a result, schools may well be forced to apply workplace norms in the most private of domains.

Even schools that resist overzealous enforcement may find that the most careful and reasoned response to a sexual harassment complaint nonetheless provokes litigation. Speaking with the voice of experience, the school *amici* remind us, "[h]istory shows that, no matter what a school official chooses to do, someone will be unhappy. Student offenders almost always view their punishment as too strict, and student complainants almost always view an offender's punishment as too lax."

A school faced with a peer sexual harassment complaint in the wake of the majority's decision may well be beset with litigation from every side. One student's demand for a quick response to her harassment complaint will conflict with the alleged harasser's demand for due process. Another student's demand for a harassment-free classroom will conflict with the alleged harasser's claim to a mainstream placement under the IDEA or with his state constitutional right to a continuing, free public education. On college campuses, and even in secondary schools, a student's claim that the school should remedy a sexually hostile environment will conflict with the alleged harasser's claim that his speech, even if offensive, is protected by the First Amendment. In each of these situations, the school faces the risk of suit, and maybe even multiple suits, regardless of its response.

> * * *

The complaint of this fifth grader survives and the school will be compelled to answer in federal court. We can be assured that like suits will follow—suits, which in cost and number, will impose serious financial burdens on local school districts, the taxpayers who support them, and the children they serve. Federalism and our struggling school systems deserve better from this Court. I dissent.

Notes

1. The *Davis* case was a closely fought, 5–4 decision, with the two female justices voting with the majority in favor of the plaintiff. It is important to note that *Davis* sets forth a much higher bar for plaintiffs in an education setting under Title IX than the courts have done for plaintiffs in a workplace setting under Title VII. Is such a higher bar appropriate? Why or why not?

2. The dissent's warnings regarding the likelihood of this decision opening the floodgates of litigation do not appear to have panned out ... perhaps because the bar has been set so high.

3. While *Davis* is a K–12 ruling, it can be argued that its two-part test for liability is equally applicable in higher education settings, given the fact that Title IX also applies at colleges and universities. Indeed, Justice Kennedy appears to presume its applicability at the higher education level, warning of negative consequences that could flow in that setting from this decision. *But see* Benefield v. Board of Trustees, 214 F. Supp. 2d 1212 (S.D. Ala. 2002), questioning the applicability of *Davis* in a higher education setting.

At colleges and universities, most claims of peer harassment are handled internally, through student conduct committees.

2. LIABILITY FOR MISTREATMENT OF LESBIAN, GAY, BISEXUAL, & TRANSGENDER (LGBT) STUDENTS

There are numerous parallels that can be identified between peer-to-peer sexual harassment and peer mistreatment of LGBT students. In both instances, for example, such behavior was generally viewed as acceptable for a very long time by a very large percentage of people. In both instances, the phrase "boys will be boys" continues to be used to justify the behavior. And both types of "harassment" have often been accompanied by allegations that the victim is to blame for what happened.

For both types of behavior, it has only been in recent decades that concrete legal protection has begun to emerge, including but not limited to frameworks whereby school officials can be found liable. In the sexual harassment area, a test has evolved under Title IX. In the LGBT mistreatment area, although cases have been brought under Title IX and the OCR has developed guidelines that apply Title IX to this area, the major victories in federal court have been under the Equal Protection Clause of the Fourteenth Amendment.

Two of the most prominent opinions in this context are *Nabozny v. Podlesny* and *Flores v. Morgan Hill USD*, both of which are set forth below.

NABOZNY v. PODLESNY

92 F.3d 446 (7th Cir. 1996).

ESCHBACH, CIRCUIT JUDGE.

Jamie Nabozny was a student in the Ashland Public School District (hereinafter "the District") in Ashland, Wisconsin throughout his middle school and high school years. During that time, Nabozny was continually harassed and physically abused by fellow students because he is homosexual. Both in middle school and high school Nabozny reported the harassment to school administrators. Nabozny asked the school officials to protect him and to punish his assailants. Despite the fact that the school administrators had a policy of investigating and punishing student-on-student battery and sexual harassment, they allegedly turned a deaf ear to Nabozny's requests. Indeed, there is evidence to suggest that some of the administrators themselves mocked Nabozny's predicament.
* * *

* * * Around the time that Nabozny entered the seventh grade, Nabozny realized that he is gay. Many of Nabozny's fellow classmates soon realized it too. Nabozny decided not to "closet" his sexuality, and considerable harassment from his fellow students ensued. Nabozny's classmates regularly referred to him as "faggot," and subjected him to various forms of physical abuse, including striking and spitting on him. Nabozny spoke to the school's guidance counselor, Ms. Peterson, about the abuse, informing Peterson that he is gay. Peterson took action, ordering the offending students to stop the harassment and placing two of them in detention. However, the students' abusive behavior toward Nabozny stopped only briefly. Meanwhile, Peterson was replaced as guidance counselor by Mr. Nowakowski. Nabozny similarly informed Nowakowski that he is gay, and asked for protection from the student harassment. Nowakowski, in turn, referred the matter to school Principal Mary Podlesny; Podlesny was responsible for school discipline.

Just before the 1988 Winter holiday, Nabozny met with Nowakowski and Podlesny to discuss the harassment. During the meeting, Nabozny explained the nature of the harassment and again revealed his homosexuality. Podlesny promised to protect Nabozny, but took no action. Following the holiday season, student harassment of Nabozny worsened, especially at the hands of students Jason Welty and Roy Grande. Nabozny complained to Nowakowski, and school administrators spoke to the students. The harassment, however, only intensified. A short time later, in a science classroom, Welty grabbed Nabozny and pushed him to the floor. Welty and Grande held Nabozny down and performed a mock rape on Nabozny, exclaiming that Nabozny should enjoy it. The boys carried out the mock rape as twenty other students looked on and laughed. Nabozny escaped and fled to Podlesny's office. Podlesny's alleged response is somewhat astonishing; she said that "boys will be boys" and told Nabozny that if he was "going to be so openly gay," he should "expect" such behavior from his fellow students. In the wake of Podlesny's comments, Nabozny ran home. The next day Nabozny was forced to speak with a counselor, not because he was subjected to a mock rape in a classroom, but because he left the school without obtaining the proper permission. No action was taken against the students involved. Nabozny was forced to return to his regular schedule. Understandably, Nabozny was "petrified" to attend school; he was subjected to abuse throughout the duration of the school year.

The situation hardly improved when Nabozny entered the eighth grade. Shortly after the school year began, several boys attacked Nabozny in a school bathroom, hitting him and pushing his books from his hands. This time Nabozny's parents met with Podlesny and the alleged perpetrators. The offending boys denied that the incident occurred, and no action was taken. Podlesny told both Nabozny and his parents that Nabozny should expect such incidents because he is "openly" gay. Several similar meetings between Nabozny's parents and Podlesny followed subsequent incidents involving Nabozny. Each time perpetrators were identified to Podlesny. Each time Podlesny pledged to take action. And, each time nothing was done. Toward the end of the school year, the harassment against Nabozny intensified to the point that a district attorney purportedly advised Nabozny to take time off from school. Nabozny took one and a half weeks off from school. When he returned, the harassment resumed, driving Nabozny to attempt suicide. After a stint in a hospital, Nabozny finished his eighth grade year in a Catholic school.

The Catholic school attended by Nabozny did not offer classes beyond the eighth grade. Therefore, to attend the ninth grade, Nabozny enrolled in Ashland High School. Almost immediately Nabozny's fellow students sang an all too familiar tune. Early in the year, while Nabozny was using a urinal in the restroom, Nabozny was assaulted. Student Stephen Huntley struck Nabozny in the back of the knee, forcing him to fall into the urinal. Roy Grande then urinated on Nabozny. Nabozny immediately reported the incident to the principal's office. Nabozny recounted the incident to the office secretary, who in turn relayed the story to Principal William Davis. Davis ordered Nabozny to go home and change clothes. Nabozny's parents scheduled a meeting with Davis and Assistant Principal Thomas Blauert. At the meeting, the parties discussed numerous instances of harassment against Nabozny, including the restroom incident.

Rather than taking action against the perpetrators, Davis and Blauert referred Nabozny to Mr. Reeder, a school guidance counselor. Reeder was supposed to change Nabozny's schedule so as to minimize

Nabozny's exposure to the offending students. Eventually the school placed Nabozny in a special education class; Stephen Huntley and Roy Grande were special education students. Nabozny's parents continued to insist that the school take action, repeatedly meeting with Davis and Blauert among others. Nabozny's parents' efforts were futile; no action was taken. In the middle of his ninth grade year, Nabozny again attempted suicide. Following another hospital stay and a period living with relatives, Nabozny ran away to Minneapolis. His parents convinced him to return to Ashland by promising that Nabozny would not have to attend Ashland High. Because Nabozny's parents were unable to afford private schooling, however, the Department of Social Services ordered Nabozny to return to Ashland High.

In tenth grade, Nabozny fared no better. Nabozny's parents moved, forcing Nabozny to rely on the school bus to take him to school. Students on the bus regularly used epithets, such as "fag" and "queer," to refer to Nabozny. Some students even pelted Nabozny with dangerous objects such as steel nuts and bolts. When Nabozny's parents complained to the school, school officials changed Nabozny's assigned seat and moved him to the front of the bus. The harassment continued. Ms. Hanson, a school guidance counselor, lobbied the school's administration to take more aggressive action to no avail. The worst was yet to come, however. One morning when Nabozny arrived early to school, he went to the library to study. The library was not yet open, so Nabozny sat down in the hallway. Minutes later he was met by a group of eight boys led by Stephen Huntley. Huntley began kicking Nabozny in the stomach, and continued to do so for five to ten minutes while the other students looked on laughing. Nabozny reported the incident to Hanson, who referred him to the school's "police liaison" Dan Crawford. Nabozny told Crawford that he wanted to press charges, but Crawford dissuaded him. Crawford promised to speak to the offending boys instead. Meanwhile, at Crawford's behest, Nabozny reported the incident to Blauert. Blauert, the school official supposedly in charge of disciplining, laughed and told Nabozny that Nabozny deserved such treatment because he is gay. Weeks later Nabozny collapsed from internal bleeding that resulted from Huntley's beating. Nabozny's parents and counselor Hanson repeatedly urged Davis and Blauert to take action to protect Nabozny. Each time aggressive action was promised. And, each time nothing was done.

Finally, in his eleventh grade year, Nabozny withdrew from Ashland High School. Hanson told Nabozny and his parents that school administrators were unwilling to help him and that he should seek educational opportunities elsewhere. Nabozny left Ashland and moved to Minneapolis where he was diagnosed with Post Traumatic Stress Disorder. In addition to seeking medical help, Nabozny sought legal advice.

On February 6, 1995, Nabozny filed the instant suit pursuant to 42 U.S.C. § 1983...alleging, among other things, that the defendants violated his Fourteenth Amendment rights to equal protection and due process. * * *

The district court ruled in favor of the defendants. * * * Nabozny now brings this timely appeal. * * *

* * *

Since at least 1988, in compliance with * * * state statute, the Ashland Public School District has had a policy of prohibiting discrimination against students on the basis of gender or sexual orientation. The District's policy and practice includes protecting students from student-on-student sexual harassment and battery. Nabozny maintains that the defendants denied him the equal protection of the law by denying him the protection extended to other students, based on his gender and sexual orientation.

* * *

The gravamen of equal protection lies not in the fact of deprivation of a right but in the invidious classification of persons aggrieved by the state's action. A plaintiff must demonstrate intentional or purposeful discrimination to show an equal protection violation. Discriminatory purpose, however, implies more than intent as volition or intent as awareness of consequences. It implies that a decisionmaker singled out a particular group for disparate treatment and selected his course of action at least in part for the purpose of causing its adverse effects on the identifiable group.

A showing that the defendants were negligent will not suffice. Nabozny must show that the defendants acted either intentionally or with deliberate indifference. To escape liability, the defendants either must prove that they did not discriminate against Nabozny, or at a bare minimum, the defendants' discriminatory conduct must satisfy one of two well-established standards of review: heightened scrutiny in the case of gender discrimination, or rational basis in the case of sexual orientation.

The district court found that Nabozny had proffered no evidence to support his equal protection claims. In the alternative, the court granted to the defendants qualified immunity. Considering the facts in the light most favorable to Nabozny, we respectfully disagree with the district court's conclusions.

A. Gender and Equal Protection.

The district court disposed of Nabozny's equal protection claims in two brief paragraphs. Regarding the merits of Nabozny's gender claim, the court concluded that "[t]here is absolutely nothing in the record to indicate that plaintiff was treated differently because of his gender." The district court's conclusion affords two interpretations: 1) there is no evidence that the defendants treated Nabozny differently from other students; or, 2) there is no evidence that the discriminatory treatment was based on Nabozny's gender. We will examine each in turn.

The record viewed in the light most favorable to Nabozny, combined with the defendants' own admissions, suggests that Nabozny was treated differently from other students. The defendants stipulate that they had a commendable record of enforcing their anti-harassment policies. Yet Nabozny has presented evidence that his classmates harassed and battered him for years and that school administrators failed to enforce their anti-harassment policies, despite his repeated pleas for them to do so. If the defendants otherwise enforced their anti-harassment policies, as they contend, then Nabozny's evidence strongly suggests that they made an exception to their normal practice in Nabozny's case.

Therefore, the question becomes whether Nabozny can show that he received different treatment because of his gender. Nabozny's evidence regarding the defendants' punishment of male-on-female battery and harassment is not overwhelming. Nabozny contends that a male student that struck his girlfriend was immediately expelled, that males were reprimanded for striking girls, and that when pregnant girls were called "slut" or "whore," the school took action. Nabozny's evidence does not include specific facts, such as the names and dates of the individuals involved. Nabozny does allege, however, that when he was subjected to a mock rape Podlesny responded by saying "boys will be boys," apparently dismissing the incident because both the perpetrators and the victim were males. We find it impossible to believe that a female lodging a similar complaint would have received the same response.

* * * If Nabozny's evidence is considered credible, the record taken in conjunction with the defendants' admissions demonstrates that the defendants treated male and female victims differently.

The defendants also argue that there is no evidence that they either intentionally discriminated against Nabozny, or were deliberately indifferent to his complaints. The defendants concede that they had a policy and practice of punishing perpetrators of battery and harassment. It is well settled law that departures from established practices may evince discriminatory intent. Moreover, Nabozny introduced evidence to suggest that the defendants literally laughed at Nabozny's pleas for help. The defendants' argument, considered against Nabozny's evidence, is simply indefensible.

* * *

B. Sexual Orientation and Equal Protection.

* * *

Our discussion of equal protection analysis thus far has revealed a well established principle: the Constitution prohibits intentional invidious discrimination between otherwise similarly situated persons based on one's membership in a definable minority, absent at least a rational basis for the discrimination. There can be little doubt that homosexuals are an identifiable minority[10] subjected to discrimination in our society.

---

10. The Sixth Circuit has ruled that:
[T]he reality remains that no law can successfully be drafted that is calculated to penalize, or to benefit, or to protect, an unidentifiable group or class of individuals whose identity is defined by subjective

Given the legislation across the country both positing and prohibiting homosexual rights, that proposition was as self-evident in 1988 as it is today. In addition, the Wisconsin statute expressly prohibits discrimination on the basis of sexual orientation. Obviously that language was included because the Wisconsin legislature both recognized that homosexuals are discriminated against, and sought to prohibit such discrimination in Wisconsin schools. The defendants stipulate that they knew about the Wisconsin law, and enforced it to protect homosexuals. Therefore, it appears that the defendants concede that they knew that homosexuals are a definable minority and treated them as such.

In this case we need not consider whether homosexuals are a suspect or quasi-suspect class, which would subject the defendants' conduct to either strict or heightened scrutiny. * * * The rational basis standard is sufficient for our purposes herein.

Under rational basis review there is no constitutional violation if "there is any reasonably conceivable state of facts" that would provide a rational basis for the government's conduct. We are unable to garner any rational basis for permitting one student to assault another based on the victim's sexual orientation, and the defendants do not offer us one.

* * *

FLORES v. MORGAN HILL UNIFIED SCH. DIST.

324 F.3d 1130 (9th Cir. 2003).

SCHROEDER, CHIEF JUDGE:

Plaintiffs are former students in the Morgan Hill Unified School District who have sued the school district, administrators, and school board members. * * *

We affirm because we find sufficient evidence for a jury to infer that defendants acted with deliberate indifference. We also hold that the law was clearly established and that the evidence would support a finding that the administrators' actions were unreasonable.

I. BACKGROUND

The plaintiffs allege that during their time as students in public schools within the Morgan Hill Unified School District ("the District"), they suffered anti-gay harassment by their classmates. The alleged harassment took place between 1991 and 1998. All of the plaintiffs were, or were perceived by other students to be, lesbian, gay, or bisexual.

and unapparent characteristics such as innate desires, drives, and thoughts. Those persons having a homosexual "orientation" simply do not, as such, comprise an identifiable class.... Because homosexuals generally are not identifiable "on sight" ... they cannot constitute a suspect class or a quasi-suspect class....

* * * We express no opinion on whether sexual orientation is an "obvious, immutable, or distinguishing" characteristic. However, it does seem dubious to suggest that someone would choose to be homosexual, absent some genetic predisposition, given the considerable discrimination leveled against homosexuals.

The plaintiffs recount incidents in which the named defendants and their agents, subordinates, and employees allegedly responded to the plaintiffs' complaints in a discriminatory fashion. Flores and the other plaintiffs allege that teachers and administrators failed to stop name-calling and anti-gay remarks, and that the administrators responded with inadequate disciplinary action to physical abuse.

The following is a sampling of incidents that the plaintiffs have described in affidavits or depositions. On several occasions, plaintiff Alana Flores found pornography and notes to the effect of "Die, dyke bitch" inside her locker. Similar messages were scrawled on the outside of her locker. When Flores showed one note to an assistant principal, defendant Delia Schizzano, and asked to be reassigned to a new locker, Schizzano allegedly replied, "Yes, sure, sure, later. You need to go back to class. Don't bring me this trash any more. This is disgusting." During the conversation, the assistant principal allegedly asked Flores, "Are you gay?" When Flores answered, "No, no. I'm not gay," she was asked, "Why are you crying, then?" Flores alleges that she continued to receive notes and pornography in her locker, and continued to bring these materials to Schizzano's attention, but that school officials took no action.

The complaint alleges that during plaintiff FF's time at Martin Murphy Middle School, he was beaten by six other students who said, "Faggot, you don't belong here." He was hospitalized and treated for "severely bruised ribs." The incident was reported to Principal Don Schaefer and Assistant Principal Frank Nucci. Schaefer and Nucci punished only one of the six students involved in the incident, and FF was transferred to another school.

Plaintiffs CL and HA, two female students, allege that other students began making anti-gay comments and sexual gestures at them when they began dating during their senior year at Live Oak High School. On one occasion, a group of boys in the school parking lot shouted anti-gay slurs and threw a plastic cup at the girls. CL and HA reported the incident to defendant Assistant Principal Maxine Bartschi. Bartschi told the girls to report the incident to a campus police officer, and did not follow-up with them or conduct her own investigation of the incident.

JD alleges that she was subjected to name-calling and food throwing. She complained to a campus monitor, with no effect. One campus monitor would not take action to stop the harassment, even when it repeatedly occurred in her presence. On one occasion, that campus monitor initiated a rumor among the students that JD and another female student were having oral sex in the bathroom. JD alleges that she also complained to a teacher that her classmates in physical education class called her "dyke" and "queer," and made comments such as "Oh, I don't want [JD] to touch me. I don't want her to look at me. I don't want to be her [weight training] partner." According to JD, the teacher failed to take action against the harassers, and instead suggested that JD change clothes away from the locker room so that her classmates would not feel uncomfortable.

The plaintiffs brought suit under 42 U.S.C. § 1983, Title IX of the Education Amendments of 1972(20 U.S.C. §§ 1681–88), the California Constitution, and California statutes. This interlocutory appeal relates only to the plaintiffs' § 1983 claim that the defendants denied the plaintiffs' Fourteenth Amendment right to equal protection on the basis of their actual or perceived sexual orientation.

* * *

III. QUALIFIED IMMUNITY

We must decide whether the defendant school administrators enjoy qualified immunity from suit for the actions they are alleged to have taken. Government officials who perform discretionary functions generally are entitled to qualified immunity from liability for civil damages "insofar as their conduct does not violate clearly established statutory or constitutional rights of which a reasonable person would have known."

A. Constitutional Violation

The initial inquiry is whether the defendants violated the plaintiffs' constitutional rights. To establish a § 1983 equal protection violation, the plaintiffs must show that the defendants, acting under color of state law, discriminated against them as members of an identifiable class and that the discrimination was intentional. The plaintiffs are members of an identifiable class for equal protection purposes because they allege discrimination on the basis of sexual orientation.

In their complaint, the plaintiffs alleged that the defendants failed to enforce the District's disciplinary, anti-harassment and anti-discrimination policies to prevent physical and emotional harm to the plaintiffs. * * * The record suggests that the defendants treated plaintiffs' complaints of harassment differently from other types of harassment. The record contains evidence that the defendants believed that, under District policies, harassment of any kind would not be tolerated. The plaintiffs presented evidence, however, that they were harassed for years and that the defendants failed to enforce these policies to protect them. When viewed in the context of the other evidence plaintiffs presented and their interactions with the defendants, there is sufficient evidence for a jury to reasonably find that plaintiffs were treated differently.

The record also contains sufficient evidence for a jury to find that the defendants acted with an unconstitutional motive. We agree with the other circuits that have considered similar issues that the plaintiffs must show either that the defendants intentionally discriminated or acted with deliberate indifference. * * *

1. Defendant Bartschi

The record contains evidence that Assistant Principal Maxine Bartschi failed to follow-up or conduct an independent investigation after two of the plaintiffs reported to her that they were assaulted by a group of students in the Live Oak High School parking lot. Bartschi's sole response was to tell the students to report the incident to a campus police officer. According to the plaintiffs, Bartschi took no action to locate or discipline the harassing students. The jury may find deliberate indifference despite Bartschi referring the girls to the campus police.

2. *Defendant Davis*

The record contains sufficient evidence for a jury to infer that Principal Bob Davis was deliberately indifferent in responding to plaintiff Flores' and FF's report of an incident in the quad area where a student handed them a pornographic depiction of heterosexual sex acts. Although there were several students involved in the incident, Davis disciplined only one of them. He also failed to take any further action after Flores and FF complained that the atmosphere in the school was hostile and that the student was bragging that his punishment was light. Davis' failure to take any further steps once he knew his remedial measures were inadequate supports a finding of deliberate indifference.

3. *Defendant Gaston*

When two students reported harassment by other students and a campus monitor to Assistant Principal Rick Gaston, he acknowledged that the students had a hard time on campus because they were gay. The extent of his response, however, was to refrain from disciplining the two students for being in the hall without a hall pass. Gaston's failure to take any steps to investigate and stop the harassment would support a finding of deliberate indifference.

4. *Defendants Schaefer and Nucci*

Principal Don Schaefer and Assistant Principal Frank Nucci disciplined only one of the six students who physically assaulted FF at the bus stop while he attended Martin Murphy Middle School. Although Schaefer recommended expulsion for one student, the failure to take any disciplinary action against the other five students is sufficient to infer deliberate indifference.

5. *Defendant Schizzano*

The record contains evidence that Schizzano took no action to stop the harassment Flores reported, including the defacing of her locker and the placing of notes and pornography inside it. Schizzano promised more than once to change Flores' locker, but failed to follow through, and instead told Flores not to bring her the pornography that she found in her locker again. Schizzano's failure to do anything about the ongoing harassment supports an inference of deliberate indifference.

6. *Failure to Train*

The plaintiffs have also produced sufficient evidence that the defendants failed to adequately train teachers, students, and campus monitors about the District's policies prohibiting harassment on the basis of sexual orientation. The record contains evidence that training regarding sexual harassment was limited and did not specifically deal with sexual orientation discrimination. The defendants also inadequately communicated District anti-harassment policies to students despite defendants' awareness of hostility toward homosexual students at the schools, and in some cases despite plaintiffs' requests to do so. A jury may conclude, based on this evidence, that there was an obvious need for training and that the discrimination the plaintiffs faced was a highly predictable consequence of the defendants not providing that training.

B. Clearly Established Law

Defendants are entitled to qualified immunity only if the law at the time of the alleged constitutional violation was not clearly established. * * * In order to find that the law was clearly established, however, we need not find a prior case with identical, or even "materially similar," facts.

The Seventh Circuit has expressly held that school administrators are not immune from an equal protection claim involving peer sexual orientation harassment. *Nabozny,* 92 F.3d at 460–61. * * *

The Seventh Circuit in *Nabozny,* however, went out of its way to point out that the unconstitutionality of the defendants' conduct did not turn on the existence of the statute. *Nabozny,* 92 F.3d at 457 n.11. Rather, it held that the decisional law was sufficiently established to put defendants on notice of their obligations to gay and lesbian students, regardless of the existence of the statute. Here, our 1990 decision in *High Tech Gays* established that homosexuals were a definable minority prior to the period of the alleged discrimination in this case. The absence of a state statute, therefore, does not point us to a conclusion that differs from that of the Seventh Circuit.

         * * *

The defendants do not advance any reason to justify the alleged differential enforcement of District policies. Here, as in *Nabozny,* "[w]e are unable to garner any rational basis for permitting one student to assault another based on the victim's sexual orientation, and the defendants do not offer us one." *Nabozny,* 92 F.3d at 458.

CONCLUSION

For the foregoing reasons, we affirm the district court's denial of summary judgment on qualified immunity grounds. The record contains sufficient evidence for a jury to conclude that the defendants intentionally discriminated against the plaintiffs in violation of the Equal Protection Clause. At the time of the harassment, the plaintiffs' right to be free from intentional discrimination on the basis of sexual orientation was clearly established.

AFFIRMED.

Notes

1. The Seventh Circuit's *Nabozny* decision has proven to be a significant turning point. Since 1996, LGBT students who have been mistreated in this manner have won consistent victories in court and have achieved landmark settlements. These settlements often include both money and mandatory professional development. *Flores* was ultimately settled for $1.1 million in January 2004.

2. Although progress has been evident in this area across a wide variety of fronts, the raw numbers continue to be shocking. LGBT runaways may comprise up to 40 percent of the entire teen homeless population in certain places, and the suicide rate for LGBT students continues to be 3–4 times higher than the numbers for their straight counterparts.

A 2003 National Mental Health Association survey found that not only had over 75 percent of all teenagers witnessed bullying of classmates who are gay or thought to be gay, but that LGBT's as a group were bullied twice as much as any other group that had been identified. In a survey of 12 to 17–year-olds asking "who gets bullied all the time," the groups ranking highest on the list were students with disabilities (6%), overweight students (11%), students "who dress differently" (12%), and students "who are gay or are thought to be gay" (24%). *See* Robert Tomsho, *Schools' Efforts to Protect Gays Face Opposition*, WALL STREET J., Feb. 20, 2003.

A 2002 Report of the National Education Association (NEA) Task Force on Sexual Orientation found that "the majority" of LGBT students "feel unsafe at school," and that this forces them "to concentrate on survival rather than on education, . . . destroy[ing] . . . [their] . . . self-esteem during a critical developmental period." NEA, REPORT OF THE NEA TASK FORCE ON SEXUAL ORIENTATION (Feb. 2002), *available at* http://www.nea.org/nr/02taskforce.html#25 (last visited Sept. 22, 2005).

The National Mental Health Association has classified LGBT students as an at-risk population. "Gay and lesbian teens are at high risk," the NMHA reports, "because 'their distress is a direct result of the hatred and prejudice that surround them,' not because of their inherently gay or lesbian identity orientation." NMHA, BULLYING IN SCHOOLS: HARASSMENT PUTS GAY YOUTH AT RISK, *at* http://www.nmha.org/pbedu/backtoschool/bullyingGay Youth.cfm (last visited Sept. 22, 2005).

3. As discussed *supra*, in Chapter 1, legal victories in an education context are often only the first step in effecting change. Given the fact that peer mistreatment continues to be a problem, what more might be done in this area as a matter of policy?

PROBLEM 21: *Nabozny* and *Flores* as Hypotheticals

Assume that you have been retained to represent Jamie Nabozny and Alana Flores in their respective cases. In addition to the equal protection arguments set forth in their actual briefs, assume that you have decided to also argue that the school districts should be held liable for negligence, and that the respective student perpetrators should be held to have violated relevant laws prohibiting threats. What arguments would you set forth in this context? What result? Discuss.

Chapter V

THE CONTINUING VITALITY OF
THE RIGHT TO EQUAL
EDUCATIONAL OPPORTUNITY

Recognized explicitly by the U.S. Supreme Court in *Brown v. Board of Education,* the venerable right to equal educational opportunity has become a strong and multi-faceted interest, buttressed by an extensive statutory scheme and well-settled judicial precedent.

The right to equal educational opportunity has appeared in many different guises, typically in the form of judicially recognized rights or state statutory entitlements. At the K–12 level, for example, major cases have pinpointed a right to acquire knowledge, a right to a free and suitable "publicly supported education," a right of "advancement on the basis of individual merit," and a right to "direct the education of children by selecting reputable teachers and places." State and federal entitlements provide public school students and their parents with additional, specific protection against the denial of opportunity, such as the right to procedural safeguards when a student is suspended or expelled, the right to a free and appropriate public education for students with disabilities, and the right to a safe school environment.

Typical statutory guidelines also give citizens the right to an education that "meets the needs" of all pupils, within the framework of specific subject matter that the state deems essential. Many provisions spell out clear educational goals, specifying particular skills that parents have a right to expect their children to attain in a public school system.

At the higher education level, the parameters of the right may sometimes be more difficult to discern, since access to higher education is not always explicitly guaranteed. However, many statutory mandates and protections do exist, and no one doubts that equal educational opportunity principles continue to be applicable at public colleges and universities.

Contextually, it is important to note that the right to equal educational opportunity has expanded beyond issues of race and ethnicity over time. The right is now generally recognized as a broad protection for students against the denial of equal access and equal opportunity on the basis of such group delineations as gender, disability, language status, sexual orientation, gender identity, and religion. As referenced in Chapter 3, all students in public education settings are generally expected to be treated with equal respect and equal dignity, consistent with the mandate of the Fourteenth Amendment.

This chapter begins with a detailed examination of paradigmatic issues relating to admissions, placement, and race. It continues with a related inquiry into the persistence of the standardized testing controversy, and follows with an exploration of equal opportunity issues in the area of school sports. The chapter then turns to an examination of ongoing disputes relating to gender equity in education. It concludes with a brief overview of litigation relating to the rights of undocumented students.

* * *

Consider the following perspectives on the right to equal educational opportunity. What additional comments or quotes would you add to this collection today?

• 1954

Today, education is perhaps the most important function of state and local governments. Compulsory school attendance laws and the great expenditures for education both demonstrate our recognition of the importance of education to our democratic society. * * * In these days, it is doubtful that any child may reasonably be expected to succeed in life if he is denied the opportunity of an education. Such an opportunity, where the state has undertaken to provide it, is a right which must be made available to all on equal terms.

—Chief Justice Earl Warren
for a Unanimous Supreme Court
Brown v. Board of Education
347 U.S. 483, 493, 74 S.Ct. 686 (1954)

• 1968

* * *

[T]he present awakening of the American conscience in the matter of equal rights and equal opportunity ... is a hopeful phenomenon in our national life. Never before as a nation have we committed ourselves so directly to the hard, practical tasks of defining equality in a way that embraces millions of citizens who have heretofore been cheated in access to education, jobs, housing, medical care, and the other necessities of American life.

—Harold Howe II
U.S. Commissioner of Education
Preface to Special Issue of Harvard Educational Review
Vol. 38, Pgs. 3–4

● **1973**

It is typically American that the most significant modern attempt to achieve racial equality, *Brown v. Board of Education,* involved the schools. Americans insist that education offered on some equitable basis will permit the economically and culturally deprived to improve their lot and to claim their fair share of society's status and income rewards.
* * *

Accompanying the exalted status of education in this society is a more or less general consensus that equal educational opportunity is of paramount importance. As an abstract principle, equal educational opportunity occupies a position in the pantheon of widely share values equal to monopoly regulation, monogamy, and peace.

—Mark G. Yudof
University of Texas
Equal Educational Opportunity and the Courts
51 TEX. L. REV. 411–12 (1973)

● **1984**

Assumptions about biological difference and destiny provided the prime justification for creating a separate, inferior legal status for women. The law denied women equal opportunity for wage work and participation in public life. * * * Women were required, by law and custom, to care for men and children. * * *

Legal structures that support the dominance of men and subservience of women are fundamentally inconsistent with constitutional ideals of individual worth and equality of opportunity.

—Sylvia Law
NYU Law School
Rethinking Sex and the Constitution
132 U. Pa. L. Rev. 955

For women, then, poetry is not a luxury. It is a vital necessity of our existence. It forms the quality of the light within which we predicate our hopes and dreams toward survival and change, first made into language, then into idea, then into more tangible action. Poetry is the way we help give name to the nameless so it can be thought. The farthest horizons of our hopes and fears are cobbled by our poems, carved from the rock experiences of our daily lives.

—Audre Lorde
Poetry Is Not a Luxury
Sister Outsider: Essays & Speeches

● **1994**

It is not enough to win court rulings, as in *Brown,* or stirring legislative victories, like the Civil Rights Act of 1964. * * * Such victories, while sweet, are not ends in themselves. They are opportunities, tools to be used in the next phase of the struggle for liberty and equal opportunity.

—Bob Herbert
After Brown, What?, N.Y. TIMES, May 1994

● **2004**

Over the past fifty years we have learned and relearned that *Brown v. Board of Education* was not a victory over institutional and structural biases and racism, but one battle in a long and continuing struggle. *Brown* remains a seminal civil rights and constitutional moment. And yet, as the case recedes into the past, we can picture the promise of educational opportunities "made available to all on equal terms" on one side of a scale of justice, balancing—but not outweighing—lingering sentiments and practices of "separate and equal."

—Jeannie Oakes
UCLA Graduate School of
Education & Information Studies
Schools That Shock the Conscience
15 Berkeley La Raza L.J. 25 (2004)

Looking beyond our borders * * * we are not in the lead. The Chief Justice of the Supreme Court of Canada is a woman, as are two of that Court's eight other Justices. The Chief Justice of New Zealand is a woman. Five of the sixteen judges on Germany's Federal Constitutional Court are women, and a woman served as president of that court from 1994 until 2002. Currently, five women are members of the European Court of Justice, three as judges and two as advocates general. Women account for seven out of eighteen Judges recently placed on the International Criminal Court; two of them serve as that court's vice-presidents.

True, as Jeanne Coyne of Minnesota's Supreme Court famously said: At the end of the day, 'a wise old man and a wise old woman will reach the same decision.' But it is also true that women, like persons of different racial groups and ethnic origins, contribute what a fine jurist, the late Fifth Circuit Judge Alvin Rubin, described as 'a distinctive medley of views influenced by differences in biology, cultural impact, and life experience.' Our system of justice is surely richer for the diversity of background and experience of its judges. It was poorer, in relation to the society law exists to serve, when nearly all of its participants were cut from the same mold.

—Justice Ruth Bader Ginsburg
Remarks on Women's Progress at the Bar and on the Bench
89 Cornell L. Rev. 801

A.   ADMISSIONS, PLACEMENT, AND RACE

1.   THE EVOLUTION OF BASIC FOURTEENTH AMENDMENT DOCTRINE

BROWN v. BOARD OF EDUC.

347 U.S. 483, 74 S.Ct. 686 (1954).

MR. CHIEF JUSTICE WARREN delivered the opinion of the Court.

These cases come to us from the States of Kansas, South Carolina, Virginia, and Delaware. They are premised on different facts and different local conditions, but a common legal question justifies their consideration together in this consolidated opinion.

In each of the cases, minors of the Negro race, through their legal representatives, seek the aid of the courts in obtaining admission to the public schools of their community on a nonsegregated basis. In each instance, they have been denied admission to schools attended by white children under laws requiring or permitting segregation according to race. This segregation was alleged to deprive the plaintiffs of the equal protection of the laws under the Fourteenth Amendment. In each of the cases other than the Delaware case, a three-judge federal district court denied relief to the plaintiffs on the so-called "separate but equal" doctrine announced by this Court in *Plessy v. Ferguson*. Under that doctrine, equality of treatment is accorded when the races are provided substantially equal facilities, even though these facilities be separate. In the Delaware case, the Supreme Court of Delaware adhered to that doctrine, but ordered that the plaintiffs be admitted to the white schools because of their superiority to the Negro schools.

The plaintiffs contend that segregated public schools are not "equal" and cannot be made "equal," and that hence they are deprived of the equal protection of the laws. Because of the obvious importance of the question presented, the Court took jurisdiction. * * *

In the first cases in this Court construing the Fourteenth Amendment, decided shortly after its adoption, the Court interpreted it as proscribing all state-imposed discriminations against the Negro race. The doctrine of "separate but equal" did not make its appearance in this court until 1896 in the case of *Plessy v. Ferguson*, involving not education but transportation. American courts have since labored with the doctrine for over half a century. In this Court, there have been six cases involving the "separate but equal" doctrine in the field of public education. In *Cumming v. Board of Education of Richmond County* and *Gong Lum v. Rice*, the validity of the doctrine itself was not challenged. In more recent cases, all on the graduate school level, inequality was found in that specific benefits enjoyed by white students were denied to Negro students of the same educational qualifications. In none of these cases was it necessary to re-examine the doctrine to grant relief to the Negro plaintiff. And in *Sweatt v. Painter*, the Court expressly reserved decision on the question whether *Plessy v. Ferguson* should be held inapplicable to public education.

In the instant cases, that question is directly presented. Here, unlike *Sweatt v. Painter*, there are findings below that the Negro and white schools involved have been equalized, or are being equalized, with respect to buildings, curricula, qualifications and salaries of teachers, and other "tangible" factors. Our decision, therefore, cannot turn on merely a comparison of these tangible factors in the Negro and white schools involved in each of the cases. We must look instead to the effect of segregation itself on public education.

In approaching this problem, we cannot turn the clock back to 1868 when the Amendment was adopted, or even to 1896 when *Plessy v. Ferguson* was written. We must consider public education in the light of its full development and its present place in American life throughout the Nation. Only in this way can it be determined if segregation in public schools deprives these plaintiffs of the equal protection of the laws.

Today, education is perhaps the most important function of state and local governments. Compulsory school attendance laws and the great expenditures for education both demonstrate our recognition of the importance of education to our democratic society. It is required in the performance of our most basic public responsibilities, even service in the armed forces. It is the very foundation of good citizenship. Today it is a principal instrument in awakening the child to cultural values, in preparing him for later professional training, and in helping him to adjust normally to his environment. In these days, it is doubtful that any child may reasonably be expected to succeed in life if he is denied the opportunity of an education. Such an opportunity, where the state has undertaken to provide it, is a right which must be made available to all on equal terms.

We come then to the question presented: Does segregation of children in public schools solely on the basis of race, even though the physical facilities and other "tangible" factors may be equal, deprive the children of the minority group of equal educational opportunities? We believe that it does.

In *Sweatt v. Painter*, in finding that a segregated law school for Negroes could not provide them equal educational opportunities, this Court relied in large part on "those qualities which are incapable of objective measurement but which make for greatness in a law school." In *McLaurin v. Oklahoma State Regents*, the Court, in requiring that a Negro admitted to a white graduate school be treated like all other students, again resorted to intangible considerations: " * * * his ability to study, to engage in discussions and exchange views with other students, and, in general, to learn his profession." Such considerations apply with added force to children in grade and high schools. To separate them from others of similar age and qualifications solely because of their race generates a feeling of inferiority as to their status in the community that may affect their hearts and minds in a way unlikely ever to be undone. The effect of this separation on their educational opportunities was well stated by a finding in the Kansas case by a court which nevertheless felt compelled to rule against the Negro plaintiffs:

> Segregation of white and colored children in public schools has a detrimental effect upon the colored children. The impact is greater when it has the sanction of the law; for the policy of separating the races is usually interpreted as denoting the inferiority of the negro group. A sense of inferiority affects the motivation of a child to learn. Segregation with the sanction of law, therefore, has a tendency to [retard] the educational and mental development of Negro children and to deprive them of some of the benefits they would receive in a racial[ly] integrated school system.

Whatever may have been the extent of psychological knowledge at the time of *Plessy v. Ferguson*, this finding is amply supported by modern authority.[11] Any language in *Plessy v. Ferguson* contrary to this finding is rejected.

We conclude that in the field of public education the doctrine of "separate but equal" has no place. Separate educational facilities are inherently unequal. Therefore, we hold that the plaintiffs and others similarly situated for whom the actions have been brought are, by reason of the segregation complained of, deprived of the equal protection of the laws guaranteed by the Fourteenth Amendment. * * *

SAN ANTONIO INDEP. SCH. DIST. v. RODRIGUEZ
411 U.S. 1, 93 S.Ct. 1278 (1973).

Mr. Justice Powell delivered the opinion of the Court.

This suit attacking the Texas system of financing public education was initiated by Mexican–American parents whose children attend the

---

11. K. B. Clark, *Effect of Prejudice and Discrimination on Personality Development* (Midcentury White House Conference on Children and Youth, 1950); [Helen] Witmer & [Ruth] Kotinsky, Personality in the Making c. 6 (1952); Deutscher and Chein, *The Psychological Effects of Enforced Segregation: A Survey of Social Science Opinion*, 26 J. Psychol. 259 (1948); Chein, *What are the Psychological Effects of Segregation Under Conditions of Equal Facilities?*, 3 Int. J. Opinion & Attitude Res. 229 (1949); Brameld, Educational Costs, in Discrimination and National Welfare 44–48 (MacIver, ed., 1949); [E. Franklin] Frazier, The Negro in the United States 674–81 (1949). *See generally* [Gunnar] Myrdal, An American Dilemma (1944).

elementary and secondary schools in the Edgewood Independent School District, an urban school district in San Antonio, Texas. They brought a class action on behalf of schoolchildren throughout the State who are members of minority groups or who are poor and reside in school districts having a low property tax base. * * *

I

The first Texas State Constitution, promulgated upon Texas' entry into the Union in 1845, provided for the establishment of a system of free schools. Early in its history, Texas adopted a dual approach to the financing of its schools, relying on mutual participation by the local school districts and the State. As early as 1883, the state constitution was amended to provide for the creation of local school districts empowered to levy ad valorem taxes with the consent of local taxpayers for the "erection ... of school buildings" and for the "further maintenance of public free schools." Such local funds as were raised were supplemented by funds distributed to each district from the State's Permanent and Available School Funds. * * *

Until recent times, Texas was a predominantly rural State and its population and property wealth were spread relatively evenly across the State. Sizable differences in the value of assessable property between local school districts became increasingly evident as the State became more industrialized and as rural-to-urban population shifts became more pronounced. The location of commercial and industrial property began to play a significant role in determining the amount of tax resources available to each school district. These growing disparities in population and taxable property between districts were responsible in part for increasingly notable differences in levels of local expenditure for education.

In due time it became apparent to those concerned with financing public education that contributions from the Available School Fund were not sufficient to ameliorate these disparities. * * *

The school district in which appellees reside, the Edgewood Independent School District, has been compared throughout this litigation with the Alamo Heights Independent School District. This comparison between the least and most affluent districts in the San Antonio area serves to illustrate the manner in which the dual system of finance operates and to indicate the extent to which substantial disparities exist despite the State's impressive progress in recent years. Edgewood is one of seven public school districts in the metropolitan area. Approximately 22,000 students are enrolled in its 25 elementary and secondary schools. The district is situated in the core-city sector of San Antonio in a residential neighborhood that has little commercial or industrial property. The residents are predominantly of Mexican–American descent: approximately 90% of the student population is Mexican–American and over 6% is Negro. The average assessed property value per pupil is $5,960—the lowest in the metropolitan area—and the median family income ($4,686) is also the lowest. At an equalized tax rate of $1.05 per $100 of assessed property—the highest in the metropolitan area—the district contributed $26 to the education of each child for the 1967–1968 school year above its Local Fund Assignment for the Minimum Foundation Program. The Foundation Program contributed $222 per pupil for a state-local total of $248. Federal funds added another $108 for a total of $356 per pupil.

Alamo Heights is the most affluent school district in San Antonio. Its six schools, housing approximately 5,000 students, are situated in a residential community quite unlike the Edgewood District. The school population is predominantly "Anglo," having only 18% Mexican–Americans and less than 1% Negroes. The assessed property value per pupil exceeds $49,000, and the median family income is $8,001. In 1967–1968 the local tax rate of $.85 per $100 of valuation yielded $333 per pupil over and above its contribution to the Foundation Program. Coupled with the $225 provided from that Program, the district was able to supply $558 per student. Supplemented by a $36 per-pupil grant from federal sources, Alamo Heights spent $594 per pupil.

* * *

* * * [S]ubstantial interdistrict disparities in school expenditures found by the District Court to prevail in San Antonio and in varying degrees throughout the State still exist. And it was these disparities, largely attributable to differences in the amounts of money collected through local property taxation, that led the District Court to conclude that Texas' dual system of public school financing violated the Equal Protection Clause. The District Court held that the Texas system discriminates on the basis of wealth in the manner in which education is provided for its people. Finding that wealth is a "suspect" classification and that education is a "fundamental" interest, the District Court held that the Texas system could be sustained only if the State could show that it was premised upon some compelling state interest. On this issue the court concluded that "[n]ot only are defendants unable to demonstrate compelling state interests ... they fail even to establish a reasonable basis for these classifications."

* * *

We must decide, first, whether the Texas system of financing public education operates to the disadvantage of some suspect class or impinges upon a fundamental right explicitly or implicitly protected by the Constitution, thereby requiring strict judicial scrutiny. If so, the judgment of the District Court should be affirmed. If not, the Texas scheme must still be examined to determine whether it rationally furthers some legitimate, articulated state purpose and therefore does not constitute an invidious discrimination in violation of the Equal Protection Clause of the Fourteenth Amendment.

II

The District Court's opinion does not reflect the novelty and complexity of the constitutional questions posed by appellees' challenge to Texas' system of school financing. In concluding that strict judicial scrutiny was required, that court relied on decisions dealing with the rights of indigents to equal treatment in the criminal trial and appellate processes, and on cases disapproving wealth restrictions on the right to vote. Those cases, the District Court concluded, established wealth as a suspect classification. Finding that the local property tax system discriminated on the basis of wealth, it regarded those precedents as controlling. It then reasoned, based on decisions of this Court affirming the undeniable importance of education, that there is a fundamental right to education and that, absent some compelling state justification, the Texas system could not stand.

We are unable to agree that this case, which in significant aspects is *sui generis*, may be so neatly fitted into the conventional mosaic of constitutional analysis under the Equal Protection Clause. Indeed, for the several reasons that follow, we find neither the suspect-classification not the fundamental-interest analysis persuasive.

A

The wealth discrimination discovered by the District Court in this case, and by several other courts that have recently struck down school-financing laws in other States, is quite unlike any of the forms of wealth discrimination heretofore reviewed by this Court. * * *

The case comes to us with no definitive description of the classifying facts or delineation of the disfavored class. Examination of the District Court's opinion and of appellees' complaint, briefs, and contentions at oral argument suggests, however, at least three ways in which the discrimination claimed here might be described. The Texas system of school financing might be regarded as discriminating (1) against "poor" persons whose incomes fall below some identifiable level of poverty or who might be characterized as functionally "indigent," or (2) against those who are relatively poorer than others, or (3) against all those who, irrespective of their personal incomes, happen to reside in relatively poorer school districts. Our task must be to ascertain whether, in fact, the Texas system has been shown to discriminate on any of these possible bases and, if so, whether the resulting classification may be regarded as suspect.

* * *

[The Court then found that "[In] the absence of any evidence that the financing system discriminates against any definable category of 'poor' people or that it results in the absolute deprivation of education— the disadvantaged class is not susceptible of identification in traditional terms." It discerned "no factual basis exists upon which to found a claim of comparative wealth discrimination."]

* * *

This brings us, then, to the third way in which the classification scheme might be defined—*district* wealth discrimination. * * *

However described, it is clear that appellees' suit asks this Court to extend its most exacting scrutiny to review a system that allegedly discriminates against a large, diverse, and amorphous class, unified only by the common factor of residence in districts that happen to have less taxable wealth than other districts. The system of alleged discrimination and the class it defines have none of the traditional indicia of suspectness: the class is not saddled with such disabilities, or subjected to such a history of purposeful unequal treatment, or relegated to such a position of political powerlessness as to command extraordinary protection from the majoritarian political process.

We thus conclude that the Texas system does not operate to the peculiar disadvantage of any suspect class. But in recognition of the fact that this Court has never heretofore held that wealth discrimination alone provides an adequate basis for invoking strict scrutiny, appellees have not relied solely on this contention. They also assert that the State's system impermissibly interferes with the exercise of a "fundamental" right and that accordingly the prior decisions of this Court require the application of the strict standard of judicial review. It is this question—whether education is a fundamental right, in the sense that it is among the rights and liberties protected by the Constitution—which has so consumed the attention of courts and commentators in recent years.

B

In *Brown v. Board of Education*, 347 U.S. 483, 74 S. Ct. 686 (1954), a unanimous Court recognized that "education is perhaps the most important function of state and local governments." *Id.* at 493, 74 S. Ct. at 691. What was said there in the context of racial discrimination has lost none of its vitality with the passage of time * * * .

This theme, expressing an abiding respect for the vital role of education in a free society, may be found in numerous opinions of Justices of this Court writing both before and after *Brown* was decided.

Nothing this Court holds today in any way detracts from our historic dedication to public education. We are in complete agreement with the conclusion of the three-judge panel below that "the grave significance of education both to the individual and to our society" cannot be doubted. But the importance of a service performed by the State does not determine whether it must be regarded as fundamental for purposes of examination under the Equal Protection Clause. * * *

The lesson of these cases in addressing the question now before the Court is plain. It is not the province of this Court to create substantive constitutional rights in the name of guaranteeing equal protection of the laws. Thus, the key to discovering whether education is "fundamental" is not to be found in comparisons of the relative societal significance of education as opposed to subsistence or housing. Nor is it to be found by weighing whether education is as important as the right to travel. Rather, the answer lies in assessing whether there is a right to education explicitly or implicitly guaranteed by the Constitution.

Education, of course, is not among the rights afforded explicit protection under our Federal Constitution. Nor do we find any basis for saying it is implicitly so protected. As we have said, the undisputed importance of education will not alone cause this Court to depart from the usual standard for reviewing a State's social and economic legislation. It is appellees' contention, however, that education is distinguishable from other services and benefits provided by the State because it bears a peculiarly close relationship to other rights and liberties accorded protection under the Constitution. Specifically, they insist that education is itself a fundamental personal right because it is essential to the effective exercise of First Amendment freedoms and to intelligent utilization of the right to vote. In asserting a nexus between speech and education, appellees urge that the right to speak is meaningless unless the speaker is capable of articulating his thoughts intelligently and persuasively. The "marketplace of ideas" is an empty forum for those lacking basic communicative tools. Likewise, they argue that the corollary right to receive information becomes little more than a hollow privilege when the recipient has not been taught to read, assimilate, and utilize available knowledge.

A similar line of reasoning is pursued with respect to the right to vote. Exercise of the franchise, it is contended, cannot be divorced from the educational foundation of the voter. The electoral process, if reality is to conform to the democratic ideal, depends on an informed electorate: a voter cannot cast his ballot intelligently unless his reading skills and thought processes have been adequately developed.

We need not dispute any of these propositions. The Court has long afforded zealous protection against unjustifiable governmental interference with the individual's rights to speak and to vote. Yet we have never presumed to possess either the ability or the authority to guarantee to the citizenry the most *effective* speech or the most *informed* electoral choice. That these may be desirable goals of a system of freedom of expression and of a representative form of government is not to be doubted. These are indeed goals to be pursued by a people whose thoughts and beliefs are freed from governmental interference. But they are not values to be implemented by judicial instruction into otherwise legitimate state activities.

Even if it were conceded that some identifiable quantum of education is a constitutionally protected prerequisite to the meaningful exercise of either right, we have no indication that the present levels of educational expenditures in Texas provide an education that falls short.

Whatever merit appellees' argument might have if a State's financing system occasioned an absolute denial of educational opportunities to any of its children, that argument provides no basis for finding an interference with fundamental rights where only relative differences in spending levels are involved and where—as is true in the present case—no charge fairly could be made that the system fails to provide each child with an opportunity to acquire the basic minimal skills necessary for the enjoyment of the rights of speech and of full participation in the political process.

* * *

We have carefully considered each of the arguments supportive of the District Court's finding that education is a fundamental right or liberty and have found those arguments unpersuasive. In one further respect we find this a particularly inappropriate case in which to subject state action to strict judicial scrutiny. The present case, in another basic sense, is significantly different from any of the cases in which the Court has applied strict scrutiny to state or federal legislation touching upon constitutionally protected rights. Each of our prior cases involved legislation which "deprived," "infringed," or "interfered" with the free exercise of some such fundamental personal right or liberty. A critical distinction between those cases and the one now before us lies in what Texas is endeavoring to do with respect to education. * * *

* * * Every step leading to the establishment of the system Texas utilizes today—including the decisions permitting localities to tax and expend locally, and creating and continuously expanding the state aid— was implemented in an effort to extend public education and to improve its quality. Of course, every reform that benefits some more than others may be criticized for what it fails to accomplish. But we think it plain that, in substance, the thrust of the Texas system is affirmative and reformatory and, therefore, should be scrutinized under judicial principles sensitive to the nature of the State's efforts and to the rights reserved to the States under the Constitution.

C

* * *

[The Court then found that the finance system survived rational basis analysis.]

* * *

IV

* * *

* * * The consideration and initiation of fundamental reforms with respect to state taxation and education are matters reserved for the legislative processes of the various States, and we do no violence to the values of federalism and separation of powers by staying our hand. We hardly need add that this Court's action today is not to be viewed as placing its judicial imprimatur on the status quo. The need is apparent for reform in tax systems which may well have relied too long and too heavily on the local property tax. And certainly innovative thinking as to public education, its methods, and its funding is necessary to assure both a higher level of quality and greater uniformity of opportunity. These matters merit the continued attention of the scholars who already have contributed much by their challenges. But the ultimate solutions must come from the lawmakers and from the democratic pressures of those who elect them.

Reversed.

Notes

1. Justice Marshall, writing on behalf of four justices, issued a highly influential 67-page dissent in the *Rodriguez* case, significantly longer than the majority opinion itself, and containing the most elaborate statement of Marshall's position regarding equal protection jurisprudence. Indeed, both Marshall's contention regarding the parameters of equal protection jurisprudence at the time and his articulation of the reasons behind the push to recognize education as a fundamental right arguably anticipate future directions in law and public policy. Certainly, as a matter of law, commentators have argued that the Court, in subsequent opinions, actually adopted Marshall's "sliding scale" approach, with "variations in the degree of care with which the Court will scrutinize particular classifications depending * * * on the constitutional and societal importance of the interest adversely affected and the recognized invidiousness of the basis upon which the particular classification is drawn." *Rodriguez*, 411 U.S. at 98–99 (Marshall, J., dissenting).

2. How different, if at all, might things have been in public education today had Justice Marshall been able to garner a fifth vote recognizing education as a fundamental right and wealth as a suspect classification under the Fourteenth Amendment in 1973?

3. Three years after *Rodriguez,* the Court in *Washington v. Davis* cast doubt on the continuing viability of the Fourteenth Amendment as a vehicle for the protection of individual rights in the public school setting.

Davis addressed the elements of discrimination under the Equal Protection Clause. Until 1976, it was arguably unclear whether plaintiffs in certain cases were able to trigger strict scrutiny on the basis of racial or ethnic discrimination by demonstrating a discriminatory impact alone. The *Davis* Court held that plaintiffs challenging facially neutral state action in this context must prove discriminatory purpose and cannot prevail simply by showing discriminatory effects.

The *Davis* doctrine of discriminatory purpose was particularly troubling for activists in this area. With many of the inequities in public school programs occurring as a result of facially neutral practices that could not be linked to any overt discriminatory intent, commentators generally concluded that *Davis* significantly limited the ability of education plaintiffs to prevail under the traditional Fourteenth Amendment Equal Protection framework.

However, it can be argued that at least on some level concerns in many quarters regarding the impact of the *Rodriguez* and *Davis* rulings are no longer relevant, because legislatures and courts have provided—and continue to provide—so many other vehicles for addressing education-related "deprivations" that are neither purposeful nor less-than-absolute. In fact, it can be argued that in the "No Child Left Behind" Act, Congress has in fact recognized education to be a fundamental right at the federal level, without specifically using the same terminology. *See* 20 U.S.C. § 6301, which provides in pertinent part that "The purpose of [the Act] is to ensure that all children have a fair, equal, and significant opportunity to obtain a high-quality education." *See generally infra,* Chapter 6 of this casebook.

2. AFFIRMATIVE ACTION IN HIGHER EDUCATION ADMISSIONS: THE PARADIGMATIC EQUAL EDUCATIONAL OPPORTUNITY CONTROVERSY OF OUR ERA

During the 1990s, the push to end racial preferences in the public sector—and particularly at the higher education level—resulted in significant changes. Not only had Fourteenth Amendment jurisprudence at the Supreme Court level evolved to a point where many commentators and jurists could reasonably conclude that *no* use of race as a factor in admissions decisions would be constitutional, but a growing number of states actually banned race-based affirmative action at their public colleges and universities. By 2003, when *Grutter* and *Gratz*—the University of Michigan affirmative action cases—came before the Court, the list had grown to include California (under Proposition 209), Texas (under the Fifth Circuit's *Hopwood* decision), Louisiana (under *Hopwood*), Mississippi (under *Hopwood*), Georgia (under the Eleventh Circuit's *Johnson* decision), Florida (under Governor Jeb Bush's Executive Order), and Washington (under I–200).

The *Grutter* case, decided in favor of the law school by a vote of 5–4, was therefore seen as a major turning point in the battle over affirmative action. Had the plaintiffs succeeded in garnering one more vote in *Grutter,* and had the justices then explicitly banned the use of racial preferences in affirmative action programs, as they were being asked to do, the above list would have immediately grown to include all 50 states. Instead, it was pared down to only three, California, Washington, and Florida.

The controversy regarding affirmative action has not subsided in the aftermath of *Grutter*. However, the parameters of the debate regarding public sector admissions programs have changed. *Grutter* made it clear that under the Fourteenth Amendment, while race could be used as a factor in admissions decisions, it could not be the only factor. Indeed, this principle had been a central component of Justice Powell's opinion in *Regents of UC v. Bakke,* 25 years earlier, although no other justice had joined in. Now, a Supreme Court majority had confirmed that only multi-faceted diversity, determined pursuant to a policy that met a rigorous *narrow tailoring* test, would be constitutional.

Thus the affirmative action debate in the public sector today is clearly and unequivocally about whether race can or should be employed as one of many factors—including but not limited to preferential status on the basis of bilingualism, athletic ability, unique life experiences, having overcome unique challenges generally, age, socioeconomic status, veteran status, and legacy. Colleges and universities generally can and often do grant preferential status based on most, if not all, of these other factors. The question now is whether and to what extent race can also be included in such a list. It is a very different debate than it would be if the only determining factor was race alone.

PROBLEM 22: Meglino v. Regents of Atlantis State Teachers College

The following hypothetical takes place in the fictional State of Atlantis.

Concerned about the shortage of qualified teachers in urban settings, the Atlantis state legislature approved funds for the construction of a new, unique and prestigious state teachers college devoted to training students for leadership roles in urban education. Five years later the high-tech campus— located in the heart of Capital City (a major urban center)—was finally completed. Faculty and staff were hired, an admissions committee was formed, and applications for the fall were accepted.

The following is a quote from the application bulletin:

Atlantis State Teachers College (ASTC) is an innovative institution designed to prepare students for leadership roles in urban education. The college offers an undergraduate liberal arts program, a two-year master's in urban schooling (which includes training for a K–12 teacher credential), and a doctorate in educational leadership. The college is committed to the eventual training of 1,000 urban school teachers per year, and to the dissemination of research relating to the needs of urban youth.

As per our legislative mandate, the college is designed to serve a diverse urban community, and to that end it seeks applicants from diverse backgrounds. Priority will be given to applicants who (1) have attended urban schools, (2) are fluent in Spanish, Cantonese, Mandarin, or Korean, and/or (3) can contribute to the diversity of the cohort.

To take advantage of the latest technology and to assure fairness in the application process, all applicants will initially be processed by computer. The computer will rank students based on both the traditional indicators (grades and test scores) and the priority categories.

With regard to the diversity category, the computer will be programmed to rank the applicant's potential contribution to the diversity of the cohort by employing the following objective factors: (a) socioeconomic status (SES) of the student's parents, (b) amount of work with economically disadvantaged young people (e.g. tutoring, serving as a teacher's aide, other forms of public service), and (c) race or ethnicity.

Members of the admissions committee will make final decisions regarding applicants based on computer rankings and on other relevant factors such as exceptional personal talents, unique work or service experience, leadership potential, maturity, demonstrated compassion, and a history of overcoming disadvantage.

After the first year, the computer will generate a diversity index for the entire student population at ASTC, based on the three factors identified above. Applicants will then be ranked in the diversity category based on how well they contribute to the diversity of the college's population. Thus, for example, if the college in a given year has a small number of students from a low SES background, then low SES applicants will have greater priority during that year.

The college proved very popular, and students from all over the country sought admission.

One of these applicants—Maria Meglino—sought to be admitted to the teacher education/master's program but was denied admission. Maria was an Italian American from a middle class family who had worked extensively with young people in an urban setting and was strongly committed to helping the community. However, even though she had a 3.85 undergraduate GPA and scored 1450 on the GRE, she only spoke English, and did not herself attend an urban school. Faculty gave her additional points for demonstrated compassion, but this was not enough to compensate for her lack of priority points in other areas. Bitterly disappointed, she consulted the local office of the Institute for Justice for the purpose of filing a lawsuit in federal court.

A.   What arguments would Maria be expected to set forth under the Equal Protection Clause of the Fourteenth Amendment? What result in light of the Michigan decisions? Discuss.

B.   If you were asked to recommend any changes in this admissions policy, would you do so? Why? If you would, what would you recommend?

GRUTTER v. BOLLINGER

539 U.S. 306, 123 S.Ct. 2325 (2003).

JUSTICE O'CONNOR delivered the opinion of the Court.

This case requires us to decide whether the use of race as a factor in student admissions by the University of Michigan Law School (Law School) is unlawful.

I

A

The Law School ranks among the Nation's top law schools. It receives more than 3,500 applications each year for a class of around 350 students. Seeking to "admit a group of students who individually and collectively are among the most capable," the Law School looks for individuals with "substantial promise for success in law school" and "a strong likelihood of succeeding in the practice of law and contributing in diverse ways to the well-being of others." More broadly, the Law School seeks "a mix of students with varying backgrounds and experiences who will respect and learn from each other." In 1992, the dean of the Law School charged a faculty committee with crafting a written admissions policy to implement these goals. In particular, the Law School sought to ensure that its efforts to achieve student body diversity complied with this Court's most recent ruling on the use of race in university admissions. Upon the unanimous adoption of the committee's report by the Law School faculty, it became the Law School's official admissions policy.

The hallmark of that policy is its focus on academic ability coupled with a flexible assessment of applicants' talents, experiences, and potential "to contribute to the learning of those around them." The policy requires admissions officials to evaluate each applicant based on all the information available in the file, including a personal statement, letters of recommendation, and an essay describing the ways in which the applicant will contribute to the life and diversity of the Law School. In reviewing an applicant's file, admissions officials must consider the applicant's undergraduate grade point average (GPA) and Law School Admissions Test (LSAT) score because they are important (if imperfect) predictors of academic success in law school. The policy stresses that "no applicant should be admitted unless we expect that applicant to do well enough to graduate with no serious academic problems."

The policy makes clear, however, that even the highest possible score does not guarantee admission to the Law School. Nor does a low score automatically disqualify an applicant. Rather, the policy requires admissions officials to look beyond grades and test scores to other criteria that are important to the Law School's educational objectives. So-called " 'soft' variables' such as 'the enthusiasm of recommenders, the quality of the undergraduate institution, the quality of the applicant's essay, and the areas and difficulty of undergraduate course selection" are all brought to bear in assessing an "applicant's likely contributions to the intellectual and social life of the institution."

The policy aspires to "achieve that diversity which has the potential to enrich everyone's education and thus make a law school class stronger than the sum of its parts." The policy does not restrict the types of diversity contributions eligible for "substantial weight" in the admissions process, but instead recognizes "many possible bases for diversity admissions." The policy does, however, reaffirm the Law School's longstanding commitment to "one particular type of diversity," that is, "racial and ethnic diversity with special reference to the inclusion of students from groups which have been historically discriminated against, like African–Americans, Hispanics and Native Americans, who without this commitment might not be represented in our student body in meaningful numbers." By enrolling a " 'critical mass' of [underrepresented] minority students," the Law School seeks to "ensur[e] their ability to make unique contributions to the character of the Law School."

The policy does not define diversity "solely in terms of racial and ethnic status." Nor is the policy "insensitive to the competition among all students for admission to the [L]aw [S]chool." Rather, the policy seeks to guide admissions officers in "producing classes both diverse and academically outstanding, classes made up of students who promise to continue the tradition of outstanding contribution by Michigan Graduates to the legal profession."

B

Petitioner Barbara Grutter is a white Michigan resident who applied to the Law School in 1996 with a 3.8 grade point average and 161 LSAT score. The Law School initially placed petitioner on a waiting list, but subsequently rejected her application. In December 1997, petitioner filed suit in the United States District Court for the Eastern District of Michigan against the Law School, the Regents of the University of Michigan, Lee Bollinger (Dean of the Law School from 1987 to 1994, and President of the University of Michigan from 1996 to 2002), Jeffrey Lehman (Dean of the Law School), and Dennis Shields (Director of Admissions at the Law School from 1991 until 1998). Petitioner alleged that respondents discriminated against her on the basis of race in violation of the Fourteenth Amendment; Title VI of the Civil Rights Act of 1964, 42 U. S. C. § 2000d; and 42 U. S. C. § 1981.

Petitioner further alleged that her application was rejected because the Law School uses race as a "predominant" factor, giving applicants who belong to certain minority groups "a significantly greater chance of admission than students with similar credentials from disfavored racial groups." Petitioner also alleged that respondents "had no compelling interest to justify their use of race in the admissions process." * * *

During the 15–day bench trial, the parties introduced extensive evidence concerning the Law School's use of race in the admissions process. Dennis Shields, Director of Admissions when petitioner applied to the Law School, testified that he did not direct his staff to admit a particular percentage or number of minority students, but rather to consider an applicant's race along with all other factors. Shields testified that at the height of the admissions season, he would frequently consult the so-called "daily reports" that kept track of the racial and ethnic composition of the class (along with other information such as residency status and gender). This was done, Shields testified, to ensure that a critical mass of underrepresented minority students would be reached so as to realize the educational benefits of a diverse student body. Shields stressed, however, that he did not seek to admit any particular number or percentage of underrepresented minority students.

Erica Munzel, who succeeded Shields as Director of Admissions, testified that "critical mass" means "meaningful numbers" or "meaningful representation," which she understood to mean a number that encourages underrepresented minority students to participate in the classroom and not feel isolated. Munzel stated there is no number, percentage, or range of numbers or percentages that constitute critical mass. Munzel also asserted that she must consider the race of applicants because a critical mass of underrepresented minority students could not be enrolled if admissions decisions were based primarily on undergraduate GPAs and LSAT scores.

The current Dean of the Law School, Jeffrey Lehman, also testified. Like the other Law School witnesses, Lehman did not quantify critical mass in terms of numbers or percentages. He indicated that critical mass means numbers such that underrepresented minority students do not feel isolated or like spokespersons for their race. When asked about the extent to which race is considered in admissions, Lehman testified that it varies from one applicant to another. In some cases, according to Lehman's testimony, an applicant's race may play no role, while in others it may be a "determinative" factor.

The District Court heard extensive testimony from Professor Richard Lempert, who chaired the faculty committee that drafted the 1992 policy. Lempert emphasized that the Law School seeks students with diverse interests and backgrounds to enhance classroom discussion and the educational experience both inside and outside the classroom. When asked about the policy's "commitment to racial and ethnic diversity with special reference to the inclusion of students from groups which have been historically discriminated against," Lempert explained that this language did not purport to remedy past discrimination, but rather to include students who may bring to the Law School a perspective different from that of members of groups which have not been the victims of such discrimination. Lempert acknowledged that other groups, such as Asians and Jews, have experienced discrimination, but explained they were not mentioned in the policy because individuals who are members of those groups were already being admitted to the Law School in significant numbers.

Kent Syverud was the final witness to testify about the Law School's use of race in admissions decisions. Syverud was a professor at the Law School when the 1992 admissions policy was adopted and is now Dean of Vanderbilt Law School. In addition to his testimony at trial, Syverud submitted several expert reports on the educational benefits of diversity. Syverud's testimony indicated that when a critical mass of underrepresented minority students is present, racial stereotypes lose their force because nonminority students learn there is no "minority viewpoint" but rather a variety of viewpoints among minority students.

* * *

We granted certiorari, to resolve the disagreement among the Courts of Appeals on a question of national importance: Whether diversity is a compelling interest that can justify the narrowly tailored use of race in selecting applicants for admission to public universities.

II

A

We last addressed the use of race in public higher education over 25 years ago. In the landmark *Bakke* case, we reviewed a racial set-aside program that reserved 16 out of 100 seats in a medical school class for members of certain minority groups. The decision produced six separate opinions, none of which commanded a majority of the Court. * * *

The only holding for the Court in *Bakke* was that a "State has a substantial interest that legitimately may be served by a properly devised admissions program involving the competitive consideration of race and ethnic origin." Thus, we reversed that part of the lower court's judgment that enjoined the university "from any consideration of the race of any applicant."

Since this Court's splintered decision in *Bakke*, Justice Powell's opinion announcing the judgment of the Court has served as the touchstone for constitutional analysis of race-conscious admissions policies. Public and private universities across the Nation have modeled their own admissions programs on Justice Powell's views on permissible race-conscious policies. * * *

* * * [F]or the reasons set out below, today we endorse Justice Powell's view that student body diversity is a compelling state interest that can justify the use of race in university admissions.

* * *

We first wish to dispel the notion that the Law School's argument has been foreclosed, either expressly or implicitly, by our affirmative-action cases decided since *Bakke*. It is true that some language in those opinions might be read to suggest that remedying past discrimination is the only permissible justification for race-based governmental action. But we have never held that the only governmental use of race that can survive strict scrutiny is remedying past discrimination. Nor, since *Bakke*, have we directly addressed the use of race in the context of public higher education. Today, we hold that the Law School has a compelling interest in attaining a diverse student body.

The Law School's educational judgment that such diversity is essential to its educational mission is one to which we defer. The Law School's assessment that diversity will, in fact, yield educational benefits is substantiated by respondents and their *amici*. Our scrutiny of the interest asserted by the Law School is no less strict for taking into account complex educational judgments in an area that lies primarily within the expertise of the university. Our holding today is in keeping with our tradition of giving a degree of deference to a university's academic decisions, within constitutionally prescribed limits.

We have long recognized that, given the important purpose of public education and the expansive freedoms of speech and thought associated with the university environment, universities occupy a special niche in our constitutional tradition. In announcing the principle of student body diversity as a compelling state interest, Justice Powell invoked our cases recognizing a constitutional dimension, grounded in the First Amendment, of educational autonomy: "The freedom of a university to make its own judgments as to education includes the selection of its student body." From this premise, Justice Powell reasoned that by claiming "the right to select those students who will contribute the most to the 'robust exchange of ideas,' " a university "seek[s] to achieve a goal that is of paramount importance in the fulfillment of its mission." Our conclusion that the Law School has a compelling interest in a diverse student body is informed by our view that attaining a diverse student body is at the heart of the Law School's proper institutional mission, and that "good faith" on the part of a university is "presumed" absent "a showing to the contrary."

As part of its goal of "assembling a class that is both exceptionally academically qualified and broadly diverse," the Law School seeks to "enroll a 'critical mass' of minority students." The Law School's interest is not simply "to assure within its student body some specified percentage of a particular group merely because of its race or ethnic origin." That would amount to outright racial balancing, which is patently unconstitutional. Rather, the Law School's concept of critical mass is defined by reference to the educational benefits that diversity is designed to produce.

These benefits are substantial. As the District Court emphasized, the Law School's admissions policy promotes "cross-racial understanding," helps to break down racial stereotypes, and "enables [students] to better understand persons of different races." These benefits are "important and laudable," because "classroom discussion is livelier, more spirited, and simply more enlightening and interesting' when the students have 'the greatest possible variety of backgrounds."

The Law School's claim of a compelling interest is further bolstered by its *amici*, who point to the educational benefits that flow from student body diversity. In addition to the expert studies and reports entered into evidence at trial, numerous studies show that student body diversity promotes learning outcomes, and "better prepares students for an increasingly diverse workforce and society, and better prepares them as professionals."

These benefits are not theoretical but real, as major American businesses have made clear that the skills needed in today's increasingly global marketplace can only be developed through exposure to widely diverse people, cultures, ideas, and viewpoints. What is more, high-ranking retired officers and civilian leaders of the United States military assert that, "[b]ased on [their] decades of experience," a "highly qualified, racially diverse officer corps ... is essential to the military's ability to fulfill its principle mission to provide national security." The primary sources for the Nation's officer corps are the service academies and the Reserve Officers Training Corps (ROTC), the latter comprising students already admitted to participating colleges and universities. At present, "the military cannot achieve an officer corps that is *both* highly qualified *and* racially diverse unless the service academies and the ROTC used limited race-conscious recruiting and admissions policies." To fulfill its mission, the military "must be selective in admissions for training and education for the officer corps, *and* it must train and educate a highly qualified, racially diverse officer corps in a racially diverse setting." We agree that "[i]t requires only a small step from this analysis to conclude that our country's other most selective institutions must remain both diverse and selective."

We have repeatedly acknowledged the overriding importance of preparing students for work and citizenship, describing education as pivotal to "sustaining our political and cultural heritage" with a fundamental role in maintaining the fabric of society. *Plyler v. Doe.* This Court has long recognized that "education ... is the very foundation of good citizenship." *Brown v. Board of Education,* 347 U. S. 483, 493 (1954). For this reason, the diffusion of knowledge and opportunity through public institutions of higher education must be accessible to all individuals regardless of race or ethnicity. The United States, as *amicus curiae,* affirms that "[e]nsuring that public institutions are open and available to all segments of American society, including people of all races and ethnicities, represents a paramount government objective." And, "[n]owhere is the importance of such openness more acute than in the context of higher education." Effective participation by members of all racial and ethnic groups in the civic life of our Nation is essential if the dream of one Nation, indivisible, is to be realized.

Moreover, universities, and in particular, law schools, represent the training ground for a large number of our Nation's leaders. Individuals with law degrees occupy roughly half the state governorships, more than half the seats in the United States Senate, and more than a third of the seats in the United States House of Representatives. The pattern is even more striking when it comes to highly selective law schools. A handful of these schools accounts for 25 of the 100 United States Senators, 74 United States Courts of Appeals judges, and nearly 200 of the more than 600 United States District Court judges.

In order to cultivate a set of leaders with legitimacy in the eyes of the citizenry, it is necessary that the path to leadership be visibly open to talented and qualified individuals of every race and ethnicity. All members of our heterogeneous society must have confidence in the openness and integrity of the educational institutions that provide this training. As we have recognized, law schools "cannot be effective in isolation from the individuals and institutions with which the law interacts." Access to legal education (and thus the legal profession) must be inclusive of talented and qualified individuals of every race and ethnicity, so that all members of our heterogeneous society may participate in the educational institutions that provide the training and education necessary to succeed in America.

The Law School does not premise its need for critical mass on "any belief that minority students always (or even consistently) express some characteristic minority viewpoint on any issue." To the contrary, diminishing the force of such stereotypes is both a crucial part of the Law School's mission, and one that it cannot accomplish with only token numbers of minority students. Just as growing up in a particular region or having particular professional experiences is likely to affect an individual's views, so too is one's own, unique experience of being a racial minority in a society, like our own, in which race unfortunately still matters. The Law School has determined, based on its experience and expertise, that a "critical mass" of underrepresented minorities is necessary to further its compelling interest in securing the educational benefits of a diverse student body.

B

Even in the limited circumstance when drawing racial distinctions is permissible to further a compelling state interest, government is still "constrained in how it may pursue that end: [T]he means chosen to accomplish the [government's] asserted purpose must be specifically and narrowly framed to accomplish that purpose." * * *

Since *Bakke*, we have had no occasion to define the contours of the narrow-tailoring inquiry with respect to race-conscious university admissions programs. That inquiry must be calibrated to fit the distinct issues raised by the use of race to achieve student body diversity in public higher education. * * *

To be narrowly tailored, a race-conscious admissions program cannot use a quota system—it cannot "insulat[e] each category of applicants with certain desired qualifications from competition with all other applicants." Instead, a university may consider race or ethnicity only as a " 'plus' in a particular applicant's file," without "insulat[ing] the individual from comparison with all other candidates for the available seats." In other words, an admissions program must be "flexible enough to consider all pertinent elements of diversity in light of the particular qualifications of each applicant, and to place them on the same footing for consideration, although not necessarily according them the same weight."

We find that the Law School's admissions program bears the hallmarks of a narrowly tailored plan. As Justice Powell made clear in *Bakke*, truly individualized consideration demands that race be used in a flexible, nonmechanical way. It follows from this mandate that universities cannot establish quotas for members of certain racial groups or put members of those groups on separate admissions tracks. Nor can universities insulate applicants who belong to certain racial or ethnic groups from the competition for admission. Universities can, however, consider race or ethnicity more flexibly as a "plus" factor in the context of individualized consideration of each and every applicant.

We are satisfied that the Law School's admissions program, like the Harvard plan described by Justice Powell, does not operate as a quota. Properly understood, a "quota" is a program in which a certain fixed number or proportion of opportunities are "reserved exclusively for certain minority groups." Quotas " 'impose a fixed number or percentage which must be attained, or which cannot be exceeded,' " and "insulate the individual from comparison with all other candidates for the available seats." In contrast, "a permissible goal ... require[s] only a good-faith effort ... to come within a range demarcated by the goal itself," and permits consideration of race as a "plus" factor in any given case while still ensuring that each candidate "compete[s] with all other qualified applicants."

Justice Powell's distinction between the medical school's rigid 16–seat quota and Harvard's flexible use of race as a "plus" factor is instructive. Harvard certainly had minimum *goals* for minority enrollment, even if it had no specific number firmly in mind. What is more, Justice Powell flatly rejected the argument that Harvard's program was "the functional equivalent of a quota" merely because it had some "plus" for race, or gave greater "weight" to race than to some other factors, in order to achieve student body diversity.

The Law School's goal of attaining a critical mass of underrepresented minority students does not transform its program into a quota. As the Harvard plan described by Justice Powell recognized, there is of course "some relationship between numbers and achieving the benefits to be derived from a diverse student body, and between numbers and providing a reasonable environment for those students admitted." "[S]ome attention to numbers," without more, does not transform a flexible admissions system into a rigid quota. * * *

That a race-conscious admissions program does not operate as a quota does not, by itself, satisfy the requirement of individualized consideration. When using race as a "plus" factor in university admissions, a university's admissions program must remain flexible enough to ensure that each applicant is evaluated as an individual and not in a way that makes an applicant's race or ethnicity the defining feature of his or her application. The importance of this individualized consideration in the context of a race-conscious admissions program is paramount.

Here, the Law School engages in a highly individualized, holistic review of each applicant's file, giving serious consideration to all the ways an applicant might contribute to a diverse educational environment. The Law School affords this individualized consideration to applicants of all races. There is no policy, either *de jure* or *de facto*, of automatic acceptance or rejection based on any single "soft" variable. Unlike the program at issue in *Gratz v. Bollinger*, the Law School awards no mechanical, predetermined diversity "bonuses" based on race or ethnicity. Like the Harvard plan, the Law School's admissions policy "is flexible enough to consider all pertinent elements of diversity in light of the particular qualifications of each applicant, and to place them on the same footing for consideration, although not necessarily according them the same weight."

We also find that, like the Harvard plan Justice Powell referenced in *Bakke*, the Law School's race-conscious admissions program adequately ensures that all factors that may contribute to student body diversity are meaningfully considered alongside race in admissions decisions. With respect to the use of race itself, all underrepresented minority students admitted by the Law School have been deemed qualified. By virtue of our Nation's struggle with racial inequality, such students are both likely to have experiences of particular importance to the Law School's mission, and less likely to be admitted in meaningful numbers on criteria that ignore those experiences.

The Law School does not, however, limit in any way the broad range of qualities and experiences that may be considered valuable contributions to student body diversity. To the contrary, the 1992 policy makes clear "[t]here are many possible bases for diversity admissions," and provides examples of admittees who have lived or traveled widely abroad, are fluent in several languages, have overcome personal adversity and family hardship, have exceptional records of extensive community service, and have had successful careers in other fields. The Law School seriously considers each "applicant's promise of making a notable contribution to the class by way of a particular strength, attainment, or characteristic—*e.g.*, an unusual intellectual achievement, employment experience, nonacademic performance, or personal background." All applicants have the opportunity to highlight their own potential diversity contributions through the submission of a personal statement, letters of recommendation, and an essay describing the ways in which the applicant will contribute to the life and diversity of the Law School.

What is more, the Law School actually gives substantial weight to diversity factors besides race. The Law School frequently accepts nonminority applicants with grades and test scores lower than underrepresented minority applicants (and other nonminority applicants) who are rejected. This shows that the Law School seriously weighs many other diversity factors besides race that can make a real and dispositive difference for nonminority applicants as well. By this flexible approach, the Law School sufficiently takes into account, in practice as well as in theory, a wide variety of characteristics besides race and ethnicity that contribute to a diverse student body. JUSTICE KENNEDY speculates that "race is likely outcome determinative for many members of minority groups" who do not fall within the upper range of LSAT scores and grades. But the same could be said of the Harvard plan discussed approvingly by Justice Powell in *Bakke*, and indeed of any plan that uses race as one of many factors.

Petitioner and the United States argue that the Law School's plan is not narrowly tailored because race-neutral means exist to obtain the educational benefits of student body diversity that the Law School seeks. We disagree. Narrow tailoring does not require exhaustion of every conceivable race-neutral alternative. Nor does it require a university to choose between maintaining a reputation for excellence or fulfilling a commitment to provide educational opportunities to members of all racial groups. Narrow tailoring does, however, require serious, good faith consideration of workable race-neutral alternatives that will achieve the diversity the university seeks.

We agree with the Court of Appeals that the Law School sufficiently considered workable race-neutral alternatives. The District Court took the Law School to task for failing to consider race-neutral alternatives such as "using a lottery system" or "decreasing the emphasis for all applicants on undergraduate GPA and LSAT scores." But these alternatives would require a dramatic sacrifice of diversity, the academic quality of all admitted students, or both.

The Law School's current admissions program considers race as one factor among many, in an effort to assemble a student body that is diverse in ways broader than race. Because a lottery would make that kind of nuanced judgment impossible, it would effectively sacrifice all other educational values, not to mention every other kind of diversity. So too with the suggestion that the Law School simply lower admissions standards for all students, a drastic remedy that would require the Law School to become a much different institution and sacrifice a vital component of its educational mission. The United States advocates "percentage plans," recently adopted by public undergraduate institutions in Texas, Florida, and California to guarantee admission to all students above a certain class-rank threshold in every high school in the State. The United States does not, however, explain how such plans could work for graduate and professional schools. More-over, even assuming such plans are race-neutral, they may preclude the university from conducting the individualized assessments necessary to assemble a student body that is not just racially diverse, but diverse along all the qualities valued by the university. We are satisfied that the Law School adequately considered race-neutral alternatives currently capable of producing a critical mass without forcing the Law School to abandon the academic selectivity that is the cornerstone of its educational mission.

We acknowledge that "there are serious problems of justice connected with the idea of preference itself." Narrow tailoring, therefore, requires that a race-conscious admissions program not unduly harm members of any racial group. Even remedial race-based governmental action generally "remains subject to continuing oversight to assure that it will work the least harm possible to other innocent persons competing for the benefit." To be narrowly tailored, a race-conscious admissions program must not "unduly burden individuals who are not members of the favored racial and ethnic groups."

We are satisfied that the Law School's admissions program does not. Because the Law School considers "all pertinent elements of diversity," it can (and does) select nonminority applicants who have greater potential to enhance student body diversity over underrepresented minority applicants. As Justice Powell recognized in *Bakke*, so long as a race-conscious admissions program uses race as a "plus" factor in the context of individualized consideration, a rejected applicant "will not have been foreclosed from all consideration for that seat simply because he was not the right color or had the wrong surname.... His qualifications would have been weighed fairly and competitively, and he would have no basis to complain of unequal treatment under the Fourteenth Amendment."

We agree that, in the context of its individualized inquiry into the possible diversity contributions of all applicants, the Law School's race-conscious admissions program does not unduly harm nonminority applicants.

We are mindful, however, that "[a] core purpose of the Fourteenth Amendment was to do away with all governmentally imposed discrimination based on race." Accordingly, race-conscious admissions policies must be limited in time. This requirement reflects that racial classifications, however compelling their goals, are potentially so dangerous that they may be employed no more broadly than the interest demands. Enshrining a permanent justification for racial preferences would offend this fundamental equal protection principle. We see no reason to exempt race-conscious admissions programs from the requirement that all governmental use of race must have a logical end point. The Law School, too, concedes that all "race-conscious programs must have reasonable durational limits."

In the context of higher education, the durational requirement can be met by sunset provisions in race-conscious admissions policies and periodic reviews to determine whether racial preferences are still necessary to achieve student body diversity. Universities in California, Florida, and Washington State, where racial preferences in admissions are prohibited by state law, are currently engaged in experimenting with a wide variety of alternative approaches. Universities in other States can and should draw on the most promising aspects of these race-neutral alternatives as they develop.

The requirement that all race-conscious admissions programs have a termination point "assure[s] all citizens that the deviation from the norm of equal treatment of all racial and ethnic groups is a temporary matter, a measure taken in the service of the goal of equality itself."

We take the Law School at its word that it would "like nothing better than to find a race-neutral admissions formula" and will terminate its race-conscious admissions program as soon as practicable. It has been 25 years since Justice Powell first approved the use of race to further an interest in student body diversity in the context of public higher education. Since that time, the number of minority applicants with high grades and test scores has indeed increased. We expect that 25 years from now, the use of racial preferences will no longer be necessary to further the interest approved today.

IV

In summary, the Equal Protection Clause does not prohibit the Law School's narrowly tailored use of race in admissions decisions to further a compelling interest in obtaining the educational benefits that flow from a diverse student body. * * * The judgment of the Court of Appeals for the Sixth Circuit, accordingly, is affirmed.

It is so ordered.

* * *

Justice Thomas, with whom Justice Scalia joins as to Parts I–VII, concurring in part and dissenting in part.

Frederick Douglass, speaking to a group of abolitionists almost 140 years ago, delivered a message lost on today's majority:

> [I]n regard to the colored people, there is always more that is benevolent, I perceive, than just, manifested towards us. What I ask for the negro is not benevolence, not pity, not sympathy, but simply *justice*. The American people have always been anxious to know what they shall do with us.... I have had but one answer from the beginning. Do nothing with us! Your doing with us has already played the mischief with us. Do nothing with us! If the apples will not remain on the tree of their own strength, if they are worm-eaten at the core, if they are early ripe and disposed to fall, let them fall! ... And if the negro cannot stand on his own legs, let him fall also. All I ask is, give him a chance to stand on his own legs! Let him alone! ... [Y]our interference is doing him positive injury.

Like Douglass, I believe blacks can achieve in every avenue of American life without the meddling of university administrators. Because I wish to see all students succeed whatever their color, I share, in some respect, the sympathies of those who sponsor the type of discrimination advanced by the University of Michigan Law School (Law School). The Constitution does not, however, tolerate institutional devotion to the status quo in admissions policies when such devotion ripens into racial discrimination. Nor does the Constitution countenance the unprecedented deference the Court gives to the Law School, an approach inconsistent with the very concept of "strict scrutiny."

No one would argue that a university could set up a lower general admission standard and then impose heightened requirements only on black applicants. Similarly, a university may not maintain a high admission standard and grant exemptions to favored races. The Law School, of its own choosing, and for its own purposes, maintains an exclusionary admissions system that it knows produces racially disproportionate results. Racial discrimination is not a permissible solution to the self-inflicted wounds of this elitist admissions policy.

The majority upholds the Law School's racial discrimination not by interpreting the people's Constitution, but by responding to a faddish slogan of the cognoscenti. Nevertheless, I concur in part in the Court's opinion. First, I agree with the Court insofar as its decision, which approves of only one racial classification, confirms that further use of race in admissions remains unlawful. Second, I agree with the Court's holding that racial discrimination in higher education admissions will be illegal in 25 years. I respectfully dissent from the remainder of the Court's opinion and the judgment, however, because I believe that the Law School's current use of race violates the Equal Protection Clause and that the Constitution means the same thing today as it will in 300 months.

* * *

CHIEF JUSTICE REHNQUIST, with whom JUSTICE SCALIA, JUSTICE KENNEDY, and JUSTICE THOMAS join, dissenting.

I agree with the Court that, "in the limited circumstance when drawing racial distinctions is permissible," the government must ensure that its means are narrowly tailored to achieve a compelling state interest. I do not believe, however, that the University of Michigan Law School's (Law School) means are narrowly tailored to the interest it asserts. The Law School claims it must take the steps it does to achieve a " 'critical mass' " of underrepresented minority students. But its actual program bears no relation to this asserted goal. Stripped of its "critical mass" veil, the Law School's program is revealed as a naked effort to achieve racial balancing.

* * *

Notes

1. In *Grutter,* the Court set forth, for the first time, a series of guidelines for determining whether the use of race in public education admissions programs was narrowly tailored to further the compelling state interest in "student body diversity." While subsequent court of appeals decisions applying these principles at the K–12 level differed slightly in their conclusions as to the number of factors to consider and which factors would be more directly applicable to desegregation programs, the following check-list is arguably an appropriate characterization of the questions that a Court should ask in determining under Fourteenth Amendment Equal Protection Clause jurisprudence whether *a university admissions policy that includes race as a factor* is in fact narrowly tailored:

I. Was it clear that the policy did not operate as a quota (i.e. that it was not "a program in which a certain fixed number or proportion of opportunities were reserved exclusively for certain minority groups")?

II. Did the policy satisfy the requirement of "individualized consideration"?

A. No mechanical, predetermined diversity "bonuses" based on race/ethnicity.

B. Adequate assurance that "all factors that may contribute to student body diversity are meaningfully considered alongside race."

1. Not limiting in any way the broad range of qualities and experiences that may be considered valuable contributions to student body diversity.

2. Giving substantial weight to diversity factors besides race.

    3. Establishing "a flexible approach, taking into account, in practice as well as in theory, a wide variety of characteristics besides race and ethnicity that contribute to a diverse student body."

III. Did the university in good faith consider workable, race-neutral alternatives that would achieve the diversity it seeks?

IV. Did the race-conscious admissions program "not unduly burden individuals who are not members of the favored racial and ethnic groups"?

V. Was the admissions policy "limited in time"?

Finding that *all* the above factors were satisfied by the Michigan law school admissions policy, the Court upheld its constitutionality (*Grutter*).

Not finding that all the above factors were satisfied by the Michigan undergraduate admissions policy, the Court struck that policy down as unconstitutional (*Gratz*).

Is it reasonable to conclude that all these requirements must in fact be met for a policy to be found constitutional under *Grutter*?

    2. *Grutter* and *Gratz* were companion cases, decided on the same day. In *Gratz v. Bollinger,* 539 U.S. 244, 123 S.Ct. 2411 (2003), the Court addressed an admissions policy for undergraduates that had changed several times during the course of the litigation. Beginning with the 1998 academic year, the university had set up a "selection index," on which an applicant could score a maximum of 150 points. Those scoring 100 or above were definitely admitted, and those scoring below 75 were delayed or rejected.

> Each application received points based on high school grade point average, standardized test scores, academic quality of an applicant's high school, strength or weakness of high school curriculum, in-state residency, alumni relationship, personal essay, and personal achievement or leadership. Of particular significance here, under a "miscellaneous" category, an applicant was entitled to 20 points based upon his or her membership in an underrepresented racial or ethnic minority group. *Id.* at 255.

The Court found that this practice did not satisfy the individualized consideration requirement of the narrow tailoring guidelines articulated in *Grutter* that day:

> The current LSA policy does not provide such individualized consideration. The LSA's policy automatically distributes 20 points to every single applicant from an "underrepresented minority" group, as defined by the University. The only consideration that accompanies this distribution of points is a factual review of an application to determine whether an individual is a member of one of these minority groups. Moreover, * * * the LSA's automatic distribution of 20 points has the effect of making "the factor of race ... decisive" for virtually every minimally qualified underrepresented minority applicant. *Id.* at 271–72.

While the admissions policy had features and nuances that made it much more complex than simply an automatic distribution of numbers, six justices found the fixed 20–point bonus to be violative of the Fourteenth Amendment.

As a result of the two decisions, Michigan—committed to an affirmative action program—adjusted its undergraduate policy to comply with the guidelines set forth by the Court. For other public colleges and universities, the law school's "critical mass" policy became an example of a plan that would meet the requirements of the Constitution, while the undergraduate numerical bonus policy became an example of a plan that should not be replicated.

3. In *Grutter,* the Court ruled that affirmative action could be implemented, and that race could be employed as a factor in admissions decision, if the policy was narrowly tailored to further the compelling interest in student body diversity. But it is important to emphasize that the Court was not requiring affirmative action. States were still free to "experiment" with race neutral programs, should they so desire. California, Washington, and Florida were therefore able to continue their respective prohibitions on affirmative action.

4. In her discussion regarding the narrow tailoring requirement that the policy be "limited in time," Justice O'Connor wrote: "We expect that 25 years from now, the use of racial preferences will no longer be necessary to further the interest approved today." This language has been the subject of much debate. Some have argued, as Justice Thomas appears to have done, that this means that any use of race in admissions programs will automatically be unconstitutional in 2028. Others have argued that this statement is dicta, or, at best, a broad goal with no legal impact and no precedential value.

Is it now time to target a specific end-date for the use of racial preferences in affirmative action programs? Would you personally support such an approach? Why or why not?

Similar questions have been asked regarding school desegregation. These questions are addressed below, in the pages that follow.

THE CALIFORNIA CIVIL RIGHTS INITIATIVE (PROPOSITION 209) (1996)

Approved by the Voters (54 percent to 46 percent).

California became the first state in the country to ban race-based affirmative action programs in admissions and hiring when the Regents of the University of California—at the urging of then-Governor Pete Wilson—approved SP–1 and SP–2. The following year, these resolutions were superseded by Proposition 209, a ballot initiative that applied statewide throughout the public sector.

The proposition also banned "preferential treatment" on the basis of "sex, color, or national origin." But it was soon clear that preferential treatment could still be granted in public education—as discussed above—based upon a myriad of other factors.[a] In addition, questions

---

a. *See generally* Eugene Volokh, *The California Civil Rights Initiative: An Inter-* *pretive Guide,* 44 UCLA L. Rev. 1335 (1997).

remained regarding the scope of 209. And while some of these questions were addressed by subsequent court decisions, others—such as 209's applicability at the K–12 level—remained unanswered.

Early on, many believed that 209 was a harbinger of things to come, and that it would only be a matter of time before all states had similar restrictions in place. Yet by 2006 not only had this not happened, but the entire "anti-preferences movement" had arguably stalled as a result of the rulings in *Grutter* and its progeny.

Of course, these issues have not gone away. Indeed, ten years after the initiative became law, it continued to engender great controversy and emotion, particularly on California's public college and university campuses. Many have come to view the state as "cutting edge" in this regard. For many others, however—especially after the U.S. Supreme Court ruling in *Grutter*—it made no sense for a handful of educational institutions to be prohibiting only these preferences when the overwhelming majority of colleges and universities throughout the country were able and willing to act otherwise.

Consider the text of California Proposition 209. What are the arguments today for not only keeping 209 in place, but for adding similar provisions to other state constitutions? What are the arguments for modifying or overturning 209?

Assume that you have been asked to advise a coalition of public interest groups regarding possible modifications to 209 consistent with recent federal court jurisprudence? What suggestions might you provide? How do you think the voters would react if your proposed revisions were placed on the ballot? Why?

Article I, Section 31 of the California Constitution (Proposition 209) provides:

a) The state shall not discriminate against, or grant preferential treatment to, any individual or group on the basis of race, sex, color, ethnicity, or national origin in the operation of public employment, public education, or public contracting.

b) This section shall apply only to action taken after this section's effective date.

c) Nothing in this section shall be interpreted as prohibiting bona fide qualifications based on sex which are reasonably necessary to the normal operation of public employment, public education, or public contracting.

d) Nothing in this section shall be interpreted as invalidating any court order or consent decree which is in force as of the effective date of this section.

e) Nothing in this section shall be interpreted as prohibiting action which must be taken to establish or maintain any federal program, where ineligibility would result in a loss of federal funds to the state.

f) For the purposes of this section, 'state' shall include, but not necessarily be limited to, the state itself, any city, county, city and county, public university system, including the University of California, community college district, school district, special district, or any other political subdivision or governmental instrumentality of or within the state.

g) The remedies available for violations of this section shall be the same, regardless of the injured party's race, sex, color, ethnicity, or national origin, as are otherwise available for violations of then-existing California and discrimination law.

h) This section shall be self-executing. If any part or parts of this section are found to be in conflict with federal law or the United States Constitution, the section shall be implemented to the maximum extent that federal law and the United States Constitution permit. Any provision held invalid shall be severable from the remaining portions of this section.

PROBLEM 23: The New Mendocino Professional Development Program

The following hypothetical takes place in the fictional state of New Mendocino.

Concerned about the quality of public education in New Mendocino, and in particular about the low test scores of language minority students, wealthy entrepreneur Manuel Rodriguez establishes a new foundation for the sole purpose of focusing on bilingual education reform issues. After consulting with a task force of educators and community leaders, Rodriguez announces an ambitious plan composed of three interrelated parts: (1) substantial grants to private schools that volunteer to "adopt" public schools with high percentages of English learners; (2) the development of model gifted programs for bilingual students; and (3) extensive professional development for bilingual teachers linked to a career ladder that would double the current salaries of bilingual educators so that the top teachers in the field would actually earn the same amount of money as first-year associates at major law firms.

The adoption process would be limited to public schools with English learner populations of 50% or greater. As envisioned, substantial interaction—both online and, if possible, in real time—would occur between and among the faculty and students of both schools. Courses would be team taught, interactive projects would bring students together, and a range of extracurricular activities would cement the bonds.

The professional development/career ladder program, also funded with substantial grant money from the Rodriguez Foundation and administered jointly by the public and private schools involved in the adoption partnerships, would be limited to teachers in the high need language areas of Spanish, Cantonese, and Vietnamese (reflecting an English learner population in New Mendocino that is approximately 35% Spanish-speaking, 20% Cantonese-speaking, and 15% Vietnamese-speaking). Teachers applying to the program would need to be fully credentialed under state law, and would need to present evidence of proficiency in one of the three high need languages. They would be admitted by language skill in direct proportion to the percentages of students in the three targeted groups. A numerical rating system for applicants would include bonus points based on the amount of work they have done with economically disadvantaged young people, their years of experience as bilingual teachers, and other relevant factors such as exceptional personal talents, unique work or service experience, and a history of overcoming disadvantage. In the event that two applicants earn the same score, those applicants who are Latino, Chinese American, or Vietnamese American (in that order) would receive priority.

The Rodriguez Foundation programs receive highly positive feedback from all relevant stakeholders, and many low performing public schools with large English learner populations are adopted by private schools throughout the state. In addition, teachers rush to participate in the professional development/career ladder program, seeing it as a unique opportunity to improve the quality of public education while at the same time increasing their salaries. By the second year, 1,934 qualified teachers had submitted applications for 500 spaces.

Assume that you are representing the defendants in the following cases arising out of the above facts, and that no state action issues will be raised.

A. A federal Equal Protection Clause lawsuit filed on behalf of two Filipino American teachers, both veteran bilingual educators who were fluent in English, Spanish, and Tagalog but were denied admission to the professional development program based on the tie-breaker process. What arguments should defendants expect plaintiffs to set forth, and how should they be countered? What result? Discuss.

B. Assume that New Mendocino has a state constitutional provision identical to CA Prop. 209, and that plaintiffs bring this action under that provision. What result? Discuss.

C. Assume instead that there is a state statute identical to Washington's I–200, and that the litigation is brought under that provision. What result?

3. SORTING OUT THE PARAMETERS OF K–12 DESEGREGA-
   TION LAW IN THE AFTERMATH OF *GRUTTER* AND 50
   YEARS AFTER *BROWN*

Desegregation issues are very different during this era than they were in the decades immediately following *Brown,* but they are no less compelling.

Major legal disputes in this context can be divided into two broad areas: guidelines for determining when court supervision should end, and the legality of using race as a factor in voluntary plans.

As a matter of policy, the debate regarding the efficacy of desegregation programs continues in many communities. While many contend that desegregation is an outmoded strategy that "did not work," others insist that many people have benefited greatly from desegregation programs over time, particularly when these programs also addressed within-school segregation issues and were linked to carefully thought-out education plans.

This section of the chapter begins by documenting U.S. Supreme Court decisions regarding the guidelines for ending court-supervised desegregation programs, and identifies unresolved legal issues in that context. It then turns to the legal battle regarding the use of race as a factor in voluntary programs, a battle that has become very prevalent in the years following *Grutter.* The subsequent section continues the inquiry with a case study regarding the San Francisco's unique desegregation consent decree and the implications of that experience. And the materials that follow in other sections, addressing such issues as within-school segregation and standardized testing, all interrelate as well.

a. Terminating Court Supervision: the Green Factors, Vestiges, and Related Questions

ACKNOWLEDGING THOSE STUBBORN FACTS OF HISTORY: THE VESTIGES OF SEGREGATION

Ryan Tacorda.
50 UCLA L. REV. 1547 (2003).

Introduction

"[T]he [Supreme] Court has never explicitly defined what constitutes a 'vestige' of state-enforced segregation," Thurgood Marshall wrote in his dissent to *Board of Education v. Dowell.* The *Dowell* decision currently serves as the instruction manual for school districts seeking to free themselves from court-ordered desegregation programs. According to Justice Marshall, the "majority sa[id] very little" about the "scope or meaning" of the term "vestiges." Some scholars have recognized this curious silence as a noteworthy omission, given the significance of the concept in the determining the continued existence of court-ordered desegregation decrees. *Dowell* orders courts to examine "whether the vestiges of past discrimination ha[ve] been eliminated to the extent practicable." With this mandate, the Court partially hinges the fate of desegregation programs on the interpretation of the term vestiges, and in doing so, makes vestiges more than a mere term of art. As a result of the recent dismantling of several desegregation programs and the increasing number of court challenges involving more than four hundred desegregation decrees throughout the country, the definition of the term vestiges is central and critical to the future existence of desegregation programs.

Customarily, the Court's interpretation of an undefined term is a standard practice that does not stir alarm. However, in interpreting vestiges, the consequences are far-reaching. A party's ability to demonstrate that a school district has eliminated the vestiges of discrimination to the extent practicable may signal the death of a desegregation decree. Alternatively, proving that vestiges of segregation continue to linger may result in a decree's affirmation, and perhaps even its extension. Viewed more broadly, the absence or existence of vestiges implicates more than a court order. Our inability to locate vestiges of segregation in present day school systems that are as segregated as ever signals that the vision of an integrated United States, first endorsed in *Brown v. Board of Education*, is perhaps unattainable. On the other hand, recognizing vestiges around us not only acknowledges the hard-to-remove stain of hundreds of years of discrimination, but also allows for the possibility that *Brown's* aspirations still carry value. The consequences are too great for the term to remain undefined or misdefined, which is precisely why I contend that it has not yet been defined. Absent a clear definition, lower courts have developed a functional meaning for vestiges. Subsequently, appellate courts in various circuits have amended these definitions, establishing an entirely new phase in desegregation jurisprudence worthy of close examination.

* * *

I.   Desegregation and the U.S. Supreme Court

The story of vestiges begins with *Brown v. Board of Education*. In *Brown*, the Court declared that the "separate but equal" doctrine has no place in public education and paved the way for court-ordered and court-supervised desegregation decrees throughout the United States. *Brown v. Board of Education II* assigned these orders to district court judges, who were instructed to retain jurisdiction over the litigation and "enter such orders and decrees ... as are necessary and proper to admit to public schools on a racially nondiscriminatory basis with all deliberate speed the parties to the cases." The intention of issuing the decrees was to provide a "prompt and reasonable" start toward full compliance with *Brown*. However, these instructions provided little guidance to the district courts retaining jurisdiction over the daily operations necessary to implement school desegregation—and even less guidance for recognizing when the task was complete.

Some direction arrived with the Court's opinion in *Green v. County School Board*, in which the plaintiffs sued the New Kent County School Board for maintaining a segregated school system through its "freedom-of-choice" desegregation program. Under this plan, students retained the ability to choose any public school in the district. Evaluating the plan, the Court examined six areas, later known as the "Green factors," to measure the school district's level of desegregation: faculty, staff, transportation, extracurricular activities, facilities, and student assignment. Given that no white student ever chose to attend New Kent County's traditionally African American school, the school district remained a dual system, segregated for two races. Therefore, the Court ruled that New Kent County's freedom-of-choice plan was not sufficient to meet *Brown* II's mandate. While the six Green factors easily pointed to this result based on the simple, unambiguous facts of Green, they would later prove less helpful in determining exactly when a dual system transitioned into a unitary one. Green instructed lower courts where to look for signs of desegregation, but provided less guidance on specifically what to look for once there.

Nearly a quarter of a century later, the final days of some desegregation programs arrived, putting the *Green* factors to the test. These challenges were instigated by families frustrated with student assignment plans imposing racial caps at particular schools, local school districts tired of federal government supervision, and parents weary of having their children bused far distances. The latter describes the sentiments that pressed the Oklahoma City School Board to abolish the provisions of its 1972 desegregation decree in 1985. Oklahoma City's unilateral abolition of its desegregation program, which eliminated federal oversight without approval by the district court supervising the decree, eventually required the Supreme Court's involvement. Oklahoma City's actions provided the Court with the opportunity to finally set down a standard for determining when a school district had successfully achieved unitary status. In 1991, in *Board of Education v. Dowell*, district courts were finally given a roadmap that enabled them to bring desegregation decrees to a halt.

Prior to arriving at its conclusion in *Dowell*, the Court established that remedial decrees were not "intended to operate in perpetuity" and that local control of public school systems was valued highly. In this context, the Court advanced a test for identifying the achievement of unitary status. First, courts should assess whether the moving party "complied in good faith with [its] desegregation decree since it was entered." Secondly, courts should evaluate "whether the vestiges of past discrimination had been eliminated to the extent practicable." Affirmative responses to these two inquiries would result in a declaration of unitary status for a school district. These are the instructions the Court sent down to the district court upon remand.

However, the inquiries themselves were problematic because of their vagueness and susceptibility to competing interpretations. What is "good faith" compliance? What are "practicable" measures for a school district to adopt? What constitutes a "vestige" of segregation? Elaborating on this latter question, the Court articulated additional instructions to shed light on the ambiguous "vestiges" prong: "In considering whether the vestiges of de jure segregation had been eliminated as far as practicable the District Court should look not only at student assignments, but 'to every facet of school operations—faculty, staff, transportation, extracurricular activities and facilities.' " By thus invoking the *Green* factors, the Court left the district court with the same inadequate instructions for determining the end point of a desegregation decree as it had for determining when to order one in the first place.

The *Dowell* mandate to assess whether "vestiges of discrimination had been eliminated to the extent practicable" assumed a district court knew how to clearly identify such a vestige. Although the term regularly appeared in desegregation litigation and court opinions, no uniform definition prevailed. Moreover, the term was far from self-explanatory, as Justice Marshall explained in his *Dowell* dissent. Identifying the absence of a definition, Marshall proposed his own: "[T]he function that this concept [of vestiges] has performed in our jurisprudence suggests that it extends to any condition that is likely to convey the message of inferiority implicit in a policy of segregation." Marshall insisted that the "effects of past discrimination remain chargeable to . . . school district[s] regardless of [their] lack of continued enforcement of segregation." For Marshall, therefore, an obvious vestige of discrimination remained the racial identification of separate schools for whites and African Americans because these institutions still had the capacity of tainting African American students with the stigma of inferiority. Justice Marshall believed that the Court should have never invited the possibility of Oklahoma City's unitary status. Such a determination paved the way for a reversion of Oklahoma City's schools back to the segregated system that had originally warranted the decree.

Despite Marshall's indignation that vestige was undefined, the majority did not reconsider its opinion. Marshall's dissent provides the *Dowell* Court's only substantial discussion on vestiges, and further, illuminates the term's meaning in a way the majority fails to accomplish. His definition provides a useful starting point for unraveling the application of the vestiges test. The *Dowell* majority makes clear that the racial identification of a school is not a vestige. Hence, a majority African American school is not a vestige of segregation solely by virtue of its demographics. Dowell leaves a positive definition of the term an open question, which Marshall attempted to respond to through his own characterization of the majority's interpretation. According to Marshall, the majority believed a school district's present and future compliance with the Equal Protection Clause was sufficient to eliminate past vestiges. Hence, if the contemporary practices and policies of the Oklahoma City School Board comported with the constitutional requirements of the Fourteenth and Fifth Amendments, any of the lingering effects of segregation-era regulations would be healed. In articulating the majority position in this fashion, Marshall recognized both the narrow frame through which the majority sought to explain the term, as well as the increasing irrelevance of the past to explain the present-day realities of school systems.

One year later, the Supreme Court further elaborated on its definition of vestiges in *Freeman v. Pitts*, the case challenging the DeKalb County, Georgia desegregation program that had governed the school district since 1969. The *Freeman* Court decided that a district court could relinquish control over a school district in incremental stages—meaning it could withdraw supervision from those *Green* factors in which the school achieved compliance with the court-ordered desegregation plan. Therefore, a school district did not need to achieve unitary status in all six *Green* factors simultaneously before a district court terminated its consent decree as to one of them. For my purposes, the importance of *Freeman* lies in the majority's fuller discussion of vestiges, a concept that *Green* left vague:

In one sense of the term, vestiges of past segregation by state decree do remain in our society and in our schools. Past wrongs to the black race, wrongs committed by the State and in its name, are a stubborn fact of history. And stubborn facts of history linger and persist. But though we cannot escape our history, neither must we overstate its consequences in fixing legal responsibilities. The vestiges of segregation that are the concern of the law ... may be subtle and intangible but nonetheless they must be so real that they have a causal link to the de jure violation being remedied. In stating this, the Court extended the breadth of vestiges beyond the six *Green* factors. Now, vestiges could be "subtle and intangible," in addition to being present in the various, more conspicuous facets of school operation established by *Green*. Subsequently, lower courts used the formulation offered by both *Green* and *Freeman* to determine the fates of their own desegregation programs.

* * *

III.   Advocating a Broader Definition

Although [recent circuit court decisions] never explicitly defined vestiges for themselves, they consistently refused to recognize vestiges proposed by plaintiffs seeking to preserve school district desegregation programs. Courts simply followed the Dowell Court and approached these cases with the confidence that they would be able to identify what a vestige was, or was not, when presented with suggestions. What a vestige was, based on the circuit court opinions discussed, was never established systematically. Moreover, no circuit court acknowledged even one vestige in any of the proposals argued before them. However, the courts were able to compile an extensive list of what did not constitute a vestige: racially imbalanced schools, lower course placement of African American students, lower academic achievement levels of African American students, different expectations of minority students based on their race, targeting of African Americans in student discipline practices, declining numbers of minority teachers, racially imbalanced school staff, outdated curricula and teacher training, less experienced teachers in minority schools, differing quality in school facilities, racially identifiable extracurricular activities, previous court orders that had implicitly recognized racial segregation, busing burdens that fell predominantly on African American students, and new school sitings in mostly non-African American areas. Apparently, the school districts had been completely cured of segregation's consequences.

The circuit courts approached any suggestion that vestiges still lingered in the various school districts with great caution and skepticism. Any vestige, they believed, needed to be clearly and causally linked to the former system of de jure segregation that the offending school district had perpetrated. No party presented any evidence of vestiges that met this standard. By mandating this causation requirement, the circuit courts required smoking guns that directly connected the school system's present ills to the segregation of the past. In doing so, the circuit courts advanced a rather narrow definition of vestiges that parties seeking to preserve desegregation decrees could not meet. This narrow interpretation facilitated the easy removal of desegregation programs and the achievement of unitary status in school districts. However, these were not the inevitable outcomes for courts to reach, for another reading of the Supreme Court's desegregation jurisprudence could encompass an alternative view of vestiges applicable to the various school districts.

    * * *

b. *The Use of Race in Voluntary Desegregation Plans*

Many school districts have chosen to implement some type of desegregation plan even when they may not be required to do so under the law. These plans are often put in place soon after judicial supervision ends.

While at one time desegregation cases and affirmative action cases were analyzed under legal principles that may have differed in significant ways, the two areas of law have converged in recent decades. By the mid to late 1990s, federal courts determining the constitutionality of using race in voluntary desegregation plans looked to principles identified in the most recent affirmative action opinions. Thus, for example, in the late 1990s, several decisions limiting or even forbidding the use of race in K–12 student assignment plans relied on the Court's 1995 opinion in *Adarand Constructors v. Pena.*

After June 2003, a new debate emerged regarding the parameters of Fourteenth Amendment jurisprudence in this area, fueled by the *Grutter v. Bollinger* decision and subsequent questions regarding its prospective applicability. For noteworthy examples of the differing perspectives on the applicability of *Grutter* at the K–12 level, *see* Goodwin Liu, *Brown, Bollinger, and Beyond,* 47 How. L.J. 705 (2004) (asserting that Grutter provides a crucial pivot for a return of the law to the imperative of equal opportunity expressed in Brown); David I. Levine, *Public School Assignment Methods After Grutter and Gratz: The View from San Francisco,* 30 Hastings Const. L.Q. 511 (2003) (arguing that the cases draw a "blurry line" between the permissible and the impermissible).

In mid-to-late 2005, three different circuits—two sitting en banc— determined that principles in *Grutter* were directly applicable to K–12 settings, and that under a *Grutter* analysis the use of race in a narrowly tailored fashion would be constitutional. *See Comfort v. Lynn School Committee,* 418 F.3d 1 (1st Cir. 2005); *McFarland v. Jefferson County Public Schools,* 416 F.3d 513 (6th Cir. 2005); *Parents Involved in Community Schools v. Seattle School Dist.,* 426 F.3d 1162 (9th Cir. 2005). In addition, all three courts employed broad and unequivocal language regarding the importance of policies designed to further desegregation efforts.

At the same time, there were signs during this time period that the courts may be moving away from the convergence of desegregation law and affirmative action law and toward a determination that these may be very different types of programs that operate in very different ways.

Thus state courts considering challenges to voluntary desegregation plans under I–200 in Washington and Proposition 209 in California have found that these initiatives, while clearly designed to prohibit race-based affirmative action in the public sector, should not be construed to also prohibit the use of race in a desegregation context.[a]

Ninth Circuit Judge Alex Kozinski's concurring opinion in the October 2005 Seattle decision is consistent with this trend. Judge Kozinski makes the case for adopting a less stringent standard of review for desegregation plans than might be required in an affirmative action context. He proposes "robust and realistic" rational basis review rather than strict scrutiny review.[b]

a. *See Parents Involved in Community Schools v. Seattle School Dist. No.1,* 72 P.3d 151 (Wash. 2003), the Washington Supreme Court's analysis of the applicability of I–200 to the Seattle plan at issue in the subsequent Ninth Circuit opinion. *See also* Avila v. Berkeley USD, No. RG03–110397, 2004 WL 793295 (Cal. Super. Ct. 2004):

[Plaintiff has alleged that] * * * the Voluntary Racial Desegregation Plan violates Proposition 209[.] * * * The Court is not persuaded. * * *

[R]ace and/or ethnicity is but one of several factors BUSD applies to assign students to its elementary schools. In some instances, the other factors may already result in balanced enrollment of different racial and ethnic groups in each school. If the implementation of the Plan might not result in a single pupil's school assignment being changed based on the pupil's race, the Plan cannot be unconstitutional on its face. * * * In sum, the Plan does not on its face discriminate against, or grant preferential treatment to, any individual or group on the basis of race, color, ethnicity, or national origin. The Court cannot conclude that any consideration of race—one several criteria—makes the Plan unconstitutional.

Such a conclusion is buttressed by the well settled mandate that, whenever possible, the Court is required to harmonize new and previously existing constitutional provisions: "So strong is the presumption against implied repeals that when a new enactment conflicts with an existing provision, 'In order for the second law to repeal or supersede the first, the former must constitute a revision of the entire subject, so that the court may say that it was intended to be a substitute for the first' "

Applying this rule, Defendants argue that Plaintiff's interpretation of Proposition 209 would conflict with California Constitution, Art. I, § 7(a), the Equal

Protection Clause of the Constitution, which, not incidentally, has been held to make education a "fundamental interest." As Justice Tobriner there noted: "Given the fundamental importance of education, particularly to minority children, and the distinctive racial hand traditionally inflicted by segregated education, a school board bears an obligation, under article 1, section 7, subdivision (a) of the California Constitution, mandating the equal protection of the laws, to attempt to alleviate segregated education and its harmful consequences, even if such segregation results from the application of a facially neutral state policy." The Court agrees with Defendants. Although Proposition 209 specifically applies to public education, its text does not mention voluntary desegregation plans or otherwise indicate that prohibited discrimination or preferential treatment includes a race-conscious school assignment plan that seeks to provide all students with the same benefit of desegregated schools. * * *

In sum, the Voluntary Racial Desegregation Plan passes constitutional muster. It is not a quota. It does not provide for special notice. And it does not show favoritism. It provides for race or ethnicity as one of many criteria for the placement of children in elementary schools, to "strive" to have each school's demographics within plus or minus 5% of the district-wide demographics. The Plan does not on its face violate the California Constitution.

b. *See also Coalition for Economic Equity v. Wilson,* 122 F.3d 692, 708 n.16 (9th Cir.1997):

We have recognized ... that 'stacked deck' programs trench on Fourteenth Amendment values in ways that 'reshuffle' programs do not. Unlike racial preference programs, school desegregation pro-

Major excerpts from the Louisville case, representative of the decisions handed down in mid to late 2005, are reproduced below.

McFARLAND v. JEFFERSON COUNTY PUB. SCHS.

416 F.3d 513 (6th Cir. 2005).

Before: NORRIS and DAUGHTREY, CIRCUIT JUDGES; JORDAN, DISTRICT JUDGE.

OPINION

PER CURIAM.

Plaintiff Crystal Meredith, on behalf of her son Joshua Ryan McDonald, appeals the decision of the district court to uphold the student assignment plan of the Jefferson County Public Schools, which includes racial guidelines. The district court concluded that the assignment plan met the constraints of the Equal Protection Clause of the Fourteenth Amendment because the school board had a compelling interest to use the racial guidelines and applied them in a manner that was narrowly tailored to realize its goals. *McFarland v. Jefferson County Public Schs.*, 330 F. Supp. 2d 834 (W.D. Ky. 2004).

Because the reasoning which supports summary judgment for defendants has been articulated in the well-reasoned opinion of the district court, the issuance of a detailed written opinion by this court would serve no useful purpose.

The judgment of the district court is affirmed.

Excerpts from the lower court opinion follow below...

MEMORANDUM OPINION

HEYBURN, CHIEF JUDGE.

For twenty-five years, the Jefferson County Public Schools ("JCPS" or "the Board") maintained an integrated school system under a 1975 federal court decree. After release from that decree four years ago, the JCPS elected to continue its integrated schools through a managed choice plan that includes broad racial guidelines ("the 2001 Plan"). This case arises because some students and their parents say that the Board's student assignment plan violates their rights under the Equal Protection Clause of the United States Constitution.

* * *

II.

FACTUAL BACKGROUND

* * *

grams are not inherently invidious, do not work wholly to the benefit of certain members of one group and correspondingly to the harm of certain members of another group, and do not deprive citizens of rights.

A.

JCPS is the 28th largest public school system in the United States. Its district boundaries mirror those of the new Metropolitan Louisville which is now the 16th largest city in the nation. * * * The racial profile of students subject to the 2001 Plan is about 34% Black and 66% White.[6]

* * *

III.

THE 2001 STUDENT ASSIGNMENT PLAN

Notwithstanding many changes and refinements to its assignment plans over the past twenty-five years, the Board's primary objective has remained constant: to maintain a fully integrated countywide system of schools. The 2001 Plan contains three basic organizing principles: (1) management of broad racial guidelines, (2) creation of school boundaries or "resides" areas and elementary school clusters, and (3) maximization of student choice through magnet schools, magnet traditional schools, magnet and optional programs, open enrollment and transfers. Using these principles, JCPS provides a form of managed choice in student assignment for its students individually and for the system as a whole.

A.

The racial guidelines broadly influence the overall student assignment plan. This is not surprising since one of the Board's current stated goals under the 2001 Plan is to provide "substantially uniform educational resources to all students" and to teach basic skills and critical thinking skills "in a racially integrated environment." To accomplish these objectives, the 2001 Plan requires each school to seek a Black student enrollment of at least 15% and no more than 50%. This reflects a broad range equally above and below Black student enrollment system-wide.

Prior to any consideration of a student's race, a myriad of other factors, such as place of residence, school capacity, program popularity, random draw and the nature of the student's choices, will have a more significant effect on school assignment. The guidelines mostly influence student assignment in subtle and indirect ways. For instance, where the racial composition of an entire school lies near either end of the racial guidelines, the application of any student for open enrollment, transfer or even to a magnet program could be affected. In a specific case, a

---

6. The JCPS student assignment plan records the race of each student as Black or African–American and Other, which this Court will denote as "White." This particular practice of distinguishing only Black and non-Black students and referencing non-Black students as "Others" was discussed rather extensively during the hearing. As several witnesses testified, JCPS is a school district almost entirely populated by only Black and White students. Students of other races and backgrounds, such as Latino and Asian students, are represented only in very small numbers, e.g., less than five percent of the total student population is neither non-Hispanic Black nor White. The Court believes that it is more accurate to refer to the two groups as "Black" and "White."

student's race, whether Black or White, could determine whether that student receives his or her first, second, third or fourth choice of school.

For the most part, the guidelines provide administrators with the authority to facilitate, negotiate and collaborate with principals and staff to maintain schools within the 15–50% range. * * *

B.

Geographic boundaries greatly influence student assignments. Each JCPS school, except Central, duPont Manual and YPAS, Male and Butler high schools, the Brown School, Brandeis Elementary, and the traditional programs at Foster and Maupin, has a designated geographic attendance area, which is called its "resides area." Each student is assigned a "resides school" based upon the residence address of his or her parent(s) or guardian. In 2002–2003, 57.5% of all students attended their resides school.

At the elementary school level, all non-magnet elementary schools are grouped into twelve clusters. The elementary schools in a cluster, which includes a student's resides school, are designated as "cluster resides schools" for that student. Racial demographics have influenced the boundaries for contiguous and non-contiguous resides areas and the composition of some elementary school clusters. Elementary schools are clustered so that combined attendance zones, assuming normal voluntary choices, will produce at each school student populations somewhere within the racial guidelines.

Each non-magnet middle and high school has its own resides area. There are no clusters at those levels. Apart from age, graduation from previous grade and residence, no selection criteria govern admission of any student to his or her resides school or a school within his or her cluster. The geographic boundaries of resides areas and cluster schools determine most school assignments.

C.

Student choice may be the most significant element of the 2001 Plan. In addition to a choice of geographic location, JCPS offers students the choice of numerous and varied specialized schools and programs. The basic settings of specialized curriculum are: (1) magnet schools, (2) magnet and optional programs, and (3) magnet career academies. Differences abound, even within these broad groupings. Virtually all age appropriate students may apply for admission to any of these specialized programs. * * *

D.

School geographic boundaries and student choice interact to create a huge array of choices and flexibility within the assignment process.

At the Primary 1 (or kindergarten) level, a student is assigned to his or her resides school unless that school lacks capacity or the student applies for another school. The racial guidelines do not apply to kindergarten.

* * *

At the middle school level, students have three choices. Most students choose to attend their resides school, for which the only selection criteria are graduation from an elementary school and place of residence. A student may also apply for a first and second choice magnet middle school or magnet or optional program. Regardless of acceptance to a magnet program, a student may choose to attend either his or her resides school or select a third option, which is to apply for a transfer to another middle school.

At the high school level, students have the same basic three choices. Most high school students choose to attend their resides school for which the only selection criteria are middle school graduation and place of residence. Students may also apply for a first and second choice magnet high school or optional or magnet program.

* * *

V.

JCPS HAS ESTABLISHED A COMPELLING INTEREST IN MAINTAINING INTEGRATED SCHOOLS

Strict scrutiny means that racial classifications must further a compelling governmental interest and must be narrowly tailored to meet that interest. * * *

The Supreme Court has said that universities and graduate schools may state a compelling interest in obtaining "the educational benefits of a diverse student body." [*Grutter*, 539 U.S.] at 328. The Board's interests articulated here overlap with those of the Michigan Law School at the individual student level. In addition, in its statement of interests, the Board has articulated broader concerns in the different context of public elementary and secondary education. The different context "matters" because, under the Equal Protection Clause, "[n]ot every decision influenced by race is equally objectionable and strict scrutiny is designed to provide a framework for carefully examining the importance and the sincerity of the reasons advanced by the governmental decisionmaker for the use of race in that particular context." *Id.* at 327. No particular interest, however, is categorically compelling. The interest asserted must be examined and approved in each case in light of the particular context in which it is asserted.

Whether an asserted interest is truly compelling is revealed only by assessing the objective validity of the goal, its importance to JCPS and the sincerity of JCPS's interest. For the reasons that follow, the Court has no doubt that Defendants have proven that their interest in having integrated schools is compelling by any definition.

* * *

B.

* * *

Integrated schools, better academic performance, appreciation for our diverse heritage and stronger, more competitive public schools are consistent with central values and themes of American culture. Access to equal and integrated schools has been an important national ethic ever since *Brown v. Board of Education* established what Richard Kluger described as "nothing short of a reconsecration of American ideals."[33] What Kluger and others have articulated is that *Brown*'s symbolic, moral and now historic significance may now far exceed its strictly legal importance. Alluding to that very point, this Court has said that *"Brown* and its progeny established a moral imperative to eradicate racial injustice in the public schools." Congress recently affirmed the value of racial integration and interaction by its enactment of the No Child Left Behind Act and by the statements contained in that legislation.[34] Likewise, the Supreme Court has reiterated that "education . . . is the very foundation of good citizenship." *Grutter*, 539 U.S. at 331 (quoting *Brown*, 347 U.S. at 493).

Neither Congress's statements nor Supreme Court references are proof that a policy of school integration is a compelling goal. They do reinforce, however, the notion that *Brown*'s original moral and constitutional declaration has survived to become a mainstream value of American education and that the Board's interests are entirely consistent with these traditional American values. They reinforce our intuitive sense that education is about a lot more than just the "three-R's."

For the majority in *Grutter*, cross-racial understanding and racial tolerance, preparation for a diverse workplace and training of the nation's future leaders were "substantial" benefits of diversity in higher education. *Id.* at 330–32. Like institutions of higher education, elementary and secondary schools are "pivotal to 'sustaining our political and cultural heritage' with a fundamental role in maintaining the fabric of society." *Id.* at 331 (quoting *Plyler v. Doe*, 457 U.S. 202, 221 (1982)). For

---

33. Richard Kluger, Simple Justice: The History of *Brown v. Board of Education* and Black America's Struggle for Equality 710 (1975).

34. In offering assistance to local educational agencies in setting up magnet schools, Congress specifically noted that:

[i]t is in the best interests of the United States . . . to continue the Federal Government's support of local educational agencies that are implementing court-ordered desegregation plans and local educational agencies that are voluntarily seeking to foster meaningful interaction among students of different racial and ethnic backgrounds . . . [;] to ensure that all students have equitable access to a high quality education that will prepare all students to function well in . . . a

highly competitive economy comprised of people from many different racial and ethnic backgrounds; and . . . to continue to desegregate and diversify schools by supporting magnet schools. . . .

20 U.S.C. § 7231(a)(4). Congress further noted that the purpose of this particular section of the bill was "to assist in the desegregation of schools . . . by providing financial assistance to eligible local educational agencies for . . . the elimination, reduction, or prevention of minority group isolation in elementary schools and secondary schools with substantial proportions of minority students" and for "the development and design of innovative educational methods and practices that promote diversity." *Id.* § 7231(b)(1), (3).

that reason, these same benefits accrue to students in racially integrated public schools.[35] Several JCPS witnesses testified that, in a racially integrated learning environment, students learn tolerance towards others from different races, develop relationships across racial lines and relinquish racial stereotypes. These values transcend their experiences in public school and carry over to their relationships in college and in the workplace. As a result, these students are better prepared for jobs in a diverse workplace and exhibit greater social and intellectual maturity with their peers in the classroom and at their job. These benefits that the Board seeks from an integrated school system are precisely those articulated and approved of in *Grutter*. The Court finds that the benefits of racial tolerance and understanding are equally as "important and laudable" in public elementary and secondary education as in higher education.[36] *Id.* at 330.

Other benefits the Board seeks are quite different from those articulated in *Grutter*. Nevertheless, they seem equally compelling. The Board believes that integration has produced educational benefits for students of all races. Over the past twenty-five years, White and Black students in JCPS have progressed by every measure. In *Hampton II*, this Court found that "the Board is convinced that integrated schools provide a better educational setting for all its students; [and] that concentrations of poverty which may arise in neighborhood schools are much more likely to adversely affect black students than whites." 102 F. Supp. 2d at 371 n.30. The evidence presented in this and earlier cases "seems to suggest that African–American student achievement has improved substantially" during the past twenty-five years. Indeed, one of Defendants' experts testified that racial integration benefits Black students substantially in terms of academic achievement. The Court cannot be certain to what extent the policy of an integrated school system has contributed to these successes. Opinions surely vary on this issue. The Court certainly need not resolve this ongoing debate. But, the Fourteenth Amendment does not enact any particular preference of educational policy. As a matter of evidence, however, this Court can find that the Board has valid reasons for believing that its student assignment policies may aid student performance.

The Board also believes that school integration benefits the system as a whole by creating a system of roughly equal components, not one urban system and another suburban system, not one rich and another poor, not one Black and another White. It creates a perception, as well as the potential reality, of one community of roughly equal schools. Student

---

35. Justice Scalia calls these benefits merely "a lesson of life" as opposed to an "educational benefit." *Grutter*, 539 U.S. at 347 (Scalia, J., dissenting). Such lessons are pretty important for most people who are fortunate enough to learn them early in life. These are precisely the lessons that JCPS hopes its students will absorb. JCPS is not attempting to cure "general societal ills" but, rather, to prepare its students for dealing with them. *Id.* at 371 (Thomas, J., dissenting).

36. Purely as a matter of evidence, JCPS more than carried its burden on this issue. Numerous witnesses testified about the value of these benefits. Plaintiffs offered nothing to the contrary.

choice and integrated schools, the Board believes, invest parents and students alike with a sense of participation and a positive stake in their schools and the school system as a whole. This is vital to JCPS because, in a very real sense, it competes for students with many types of private and parochial schools throughout Jefferson County. In recent years, it has competed very successfully. One of the ways JCPS meets the competition is by offering quality education in an integrated setting at every school. Every measure of student and public attitudes on the value of integration completely supports the conclusion that an integrated school system is an advantage for many parents and students.

The evidence on each of these points demonstrates that maintaining an integrated system may help the Board to achieve its goals for individual students and the system as a whole. The Court concludes, therefore, that the Board's policy of integrated schools is both important and valid.

C.

The final factor of the compelling interest analysis is whether the Board's motives are sincere and not aimed at some improper or illegitimate purpose, or are merely for the purpose of racial balancing.

* * *

Considering all the evidence presented in this and other cases, the Court is convinced that the Board's policy of maintaining an integrated school system is sincerely held and not intended to disadvantage any race. Based on the strong evidence of the Board's sincerity and the importance and validity of its goals, the Court concludes that the Board has met its burden of establishing a compelling interest in maintaining racially integrated schools.

VI.

THE 2001 PLAN IS NARROWLY TAILORED
IN MOST RESPECTS

* * *

[I]n order to determine whether the 2001 Plan is narrowly tailored, the Court will evaluate the four primary factors that the Supreme Court considered in *Grutter*: (1) whether the 2001 Plan amounts to a quota that seeks a fixed number of desirable minority students and insulates one group of applicants from another, *id.* at 334–35; (2) whether the applicant is afforded individualized review, *id.* at 336; (3) whether the 2001 Plan "unduly harm[s] members of any racial group," *id.* at 341; and (4) whether JCPS has given "serious, good faith consideration of workable race-neutral alternatives" to achieve its goals, *id.* at 339. Together, these factors constitute the "fit" that is so important to the narrow tailoring analysis. *Id.* at 333. * * *

The Court now considers each of these factors in turn.

A.

The most important narrow tailoring issue, and Plaintiffs' primary argument, concerns whether the 2001 Plan operates as a racial quota. "Properly understood, a 'quota' is a program in which a certain fixed number or proportion of opportunities are 'reserved exclusively for certain minority groups.'" *Id.* at 335. The Supreme Court said that a race-conscious admissions program cannot use a quota system because it would almost always violate the narrow tailoring requirement. *Id.* at 334–35. As the Supreme Court also wisely noted, however, "'[s]ome attention to numbers,' without more, does not transform a flexible admissions system into a rigid quota." *Id.* at 336 (quoting *Bakke*, 438 U.S. at 323). Common sense and the Supreme Court suggest that any strict or *de facto* racial quota has a couple of known characteristics: it has a precise target, and it insulates some applicants from competition with other applicants. The Court concludes that, for the most part, the 2001 Plan's use of the racial guidelines lacks these attributes.

1.

By definition, a quota must present a relatively precise target.[45] While this would appear clear enough, everyone appears to have different ways of applying this definition to a given set of facts.

The 2001 Plan's racial guidelines for all schools present a quite flexible and broad target range. The Board's goal is to achieve a racial mix of between 15% and 50% Black students at each school. That the actual percentage of Black students at individual schools ranges between 20.1% and 50.4% demonstrates the extent of the Board's flexibility in achieving its goals. Even within this broad range, the Court finds a wide dispersal among the percentages of Black students in JCPS schools. For instance, 62 out of 87 elementary schools, 17 of 23 middle schools, and 15 of 20 high schools have a racial mix of over 40% or under 30% Black students. In other words, only about 30% of all schools show a racial mix within even five percent of either side of the systemwide average. This represents a widely dispersed range in Black students among JCPS schools rather than a precise target. * * *

2.

A quota also insulates "each category of applicants with certain desired qualifications from competition with all other applicants." *Id.* at 334. In other words, it "put[s] members of those groups on separate admissions tracks." *Id.* Except for traditional school assignment, all JCPS students are subject to the same criteria within the 2001 Plan. Criteria such as residence, student choice and random lottery are significant assignment factors for every student. No JCPS student is insulated

---

45. A quota is "the share or proportional part of a total that is required" or "the number or percentage of persons of a specified kind permitted to enroll in a college, join a club, immigrate to a country, etc." RANDOM HOUSE UNABRIDGED DICTIONARY 1588 (2d ed. 1993).

from competition with all other students, and no student is placed on a separate admissions track.

It is constitutionally permissible to set racial goals to achieve truly compelling interests. It is impermissible, however, to seek that racial goal so assiduously and precisely that it amounts to a quota. JCPS's conduct resembles the former because it has set "a permissible goal ... requir[ing] only a good-faith effort ... to come within a range demarcated by the goal itself." *Id.* at 335. The broad range in the guidelines shows that the Board does not operate a *de facto* quota that imposes or arrives at a "fixed number or percentage which must be attained." *Id.* Thus, the evidence simply does not support the conclusion that the broad racial guidelines actually mask a tighter range, create a *de facto* quota or insulate one group of applicants from competition with another group.

B.

In *Grutter*, Justice O'Connor noted that the law school's "highly individualized" review of applications meant that the admissions process did not contain "mechanical" or "predetermined diversity bonuses." *Id.* at 337. * * *

"[H]ighly individualized, holistic review" of each applicant ensures that "each applicant is evaluated as an individual and not in a way that makes an applicant's race or ethnicity the defining feature of his or her application." *Grutter*, 539 U.S. at 337. All relevant factors for assignment must be placed "on the same footing for consideration" even though one factor may be accorded more weight in the end. *Id.* Likewise, the process must ensure that "all factors that may contribute to student body diversity are meaningfully considered alongside race in admissions decisions." *Id.* Under those circumstances, race is "one of many factors" to consider and may be used as a permissible "tipping" factor in deciding a particular student's placement. *Id.* at 339.

One must analyze the 2001 Plan in its totally different context. Unlike the law school, JCPS does not deny anyone the benefits of an education. Unlike the law school, JCPS does not have the goal of creating elite and highly selective school communities. Unlike the law school's admissions process, the JCPS assignment process does not involve weighing comparative criteria in a competitive manner. Rather than excluding applicants, the Board's goal is to create more equal school communities for educating all students. But, like the law school, the JCPS assignment process focuses a great deal of attention upon the individual characteristics of a student's application, such as place of residence and student choice of school or program. It is individualized attention of a different kind in a different context than the Supreme Court found in *Grutter*.

In significant ways, the 2001 Plan actually operates like the "plus" system of which the Supreme Court has spoken so approvingly. *Id.* at 335. Many factors determine student assignment, including address, student choice, lottery placement, and, at the margins, the racial guidelines. But, race is simply one possible factor among many, acting only occasionally as a permissible "tipping" factor in most of the JCPS assignment process. The Supreme Court has said this narrow use of race is permissible given a compelling reason. Specifically, Justice Powell stated in *Bakke* that "[w]hen the [Harvard] Committee on Admissions reviews the large middle group of applicants who are 'admissible' and deemed capable of doing good work in their courses, the race of an applicant may tip the balance in his favor...." In *Grutter*, the Supreme Court echoed these sentiments, stating that situations where race makes a difference in admissions could happen in "any plan that uses race as one of many factors," including the Michigan Law School plan. 539 U.S. at 339.

In light of the foregoing analysis, the Court concludes that the 2001 Plan allows for the consideration of several factors, including race. Moreover, except as to traditional schools, the appropriate consideration of individual factors within the assignment context ensures that race does not become "the defining feature" of a student's application.

C.

Another factor in the narrow tailoring analysis is that the Board's use of race does not "unduly harm members of any racial group." *Grutter*, 539 U.S. at 341. This is neither a new nor surprising concept. Some twenty-six years ago, Justice Powell referenced the same distinction between denial of admission to a selective graduate school and the assignment of a student to an alternative but appropriate public school.[47] His observation seems applicable here.

Justice Powell's observation is consistent with the now well established concept that a student has no constitutional right to attend a particular school. As this Court explained in *Hampton II*, the consequences of assigning students to various public schools are quite different from denying an applicant admission to a selective college or job placement[.]

     * * *

The difference between the use of race in graduate school admissions and the JCPS student assignment plan results from the vastly different concept of each system. The law school admissions program excludes many applicants because of its goal of creating an elite community. The JCPS policy of creating communities of equal and integrated schools for everyone excludes no one from those communities. Consequently, when the Board makes a student assignment among its equal

---

47. Justice Powell contrasted the situation of the applicant in *Bakke* rejected by his preferred medical school against that of a public school student sent away from his neighborhood school: "[The applicant's] position is wholly dissimilar to that of a pupil bused from his neighborhood school to a comparable school in another neighborhood in compliance with a desegregation decree. [The medical school] did not arrange for [Allan Bakke] to attend a different medical school in order to desegregate Davis Medical School; instead, it denied him admission and may have deprived him altogether of a medical education."

and integrated schools, it neither denies anyone a benefit nor imposes a wrongful burden.

The Court concludes that the 2001 Plan uses race in a manner calculated not to harm any particular person because of his or her race. Certainly, no student is directly denied a benefit because of race so that another of a different race can receive that benefit. Rather, the Board uses race in a limited way to achieve benefits for all students through its integrated schools.

D.

Finally, narrow tailoring requires "serious, good faith consideration of workable race-neutral alternatives that will achieve" the Board's goals. *Grutter*, 539 U.S. at 339. It is apparent that, with the notable exception of the traditional schools, the Board not only considered, but actually implemented, a variety of race-neutral strategies to achieve its goals.

* * *

"Narrow tailoring does not require exhaustion of every conceivable race-neutral alternative." *Id*. * * *

E.

In summary, except for the traditional school assignment process, which will be discussed separately, the 2001 Plan is a proper "fit" because it is sufficiently flexible to determine school assignments for all students by a host of factors, such as residence, student choice, capacity, school and program popularity, pure chance and race. *Id*. at 337. Data showing that the majority of students attend their resides schools and that only a very small percentage of students are not assigned to one of the schools they preferred suggest the minimal impact of race on this process. Even for those students assigned to a school they did not select, race is not necessarily "a defining feature" in those assignments. Students may also be enrolled in a particular school because, for instance, (a) they did not make any choices at all or stated only a preference for one particular magnet program that did not accept them, or (b) their preferred or resides school or program was already filled to capacity. Even where race does "tip" the balance in some cases, it does so only at the end of the process, *after* residence, choice and all the other factors have played their part.

The 2001 Plan also "fits" its intended objectives because it does not unduly harm other students. The Plan works so that most students attend a school of their choice. Because all schools have similar funding, offer similar academic programs and comprise more similar ranges of students than possible in neighborhood schools, an assignment to one school over another does not cause constitutional harm to any student.

Except as to traditional schools, the Court cannot see that JCPS has any other workable race-neutral alternatives for accomplishing its compelling objective.

VII.

THE TRADITIONAL SCHOOL ASSIGNMENT PROCESS IS NOT NARROWLY TAILORED

The sole exception to the Court's narrow tailoring inquiry concerns the traditional school assignment process. Traditional school enrollment amounts to a small portion of the overall student census. The assignment process for those schools has features that make it distinct from other aspects of the 2001 Plan and present particularly difficult constitutional questions. In the end, the Court finds that the use of race in the traditional school assignment process is not narrowly tailored.

* * *

The Court will enter an order consistent with this Memorandum Opinion.

* * *

4. THE SFUSD CONSENT DECREE (1983–2005): A CASE STUDY

The 1983 *SFNAACP v. SFUSD* Consent Decree has been recognized as unique in many ways. Unlike most desegregation orders and decrees, it did not rely on desegregation efforts alone, but also focused explicitly on academic achievement. In addition, the desegregation mandate was not limited to school-by-school numbers, but also required a focus on within-school segregation by program and classroom. Interrelated strategies designed to maximize access to a quality education for students of all races and ethnicities were set forth in great detail, and a collaborative relationship between the parties led to enduring results over time.

At the same time, however, the Decree led to one of the most volatile and excruciatingly difficult lawsuits of the era, *Brian Ho v. SFUSD*. Filed by Chinese–American plaintiffs who argued that the Decree and its racial caps discriminated against them in violation of the Fourteenth Amendment, the *Ho* litigation led to the removal of race as a factor from the student assignment plan and to the establishment of a termination date for the Decree.

The *SFNAACP* Decree involved many high-profile members of the education community, including but not limited to Harold Howe (education adviser to President Lyndon B. Johnson), Gary Orfield (Harvard professor and longtime desegregation expert), Robert L. Green (education adviser to Martin Luther King), Ramon Cortines (Superintendent of Schools, 1986–1992), Bill Rojas (Superintendent of Schools, 1992–1999), Arlene Ackerman (Superintendent of Schools, 2000–2006), Henry Der (Founder of Chinese for Affirmative Action), Hoover Liddell (longtime educator, activist, and community leader in San Francisco), and Eugene Garcia (bilingual education expert and Dean of the UC Berkeley Graduate School of Education). The Decree was supervised by the Honorable William H. Orrick, legendary federal judge, from its inception until his retirement in 2001. In addition, some of the most well-known attorneys in the country participated in the various negotiations, hearings, and court appearances.

The author of this casebook served as the State Monitor for this Decree during its final nine years. All the reports filed by the Monitoring Team with the federal court from 1997 through 2005 are available at http://www.gseis.ucla.edu/courses/edlaw/sfrepts.htm.

Consider the materials that follow in light of the cases and developments documented in this chapter and the two chapters that follow. What are the implications of the San Francisco experience for educators, attorneys, and policy makers seeking to address unresolved issues in urban education today?

SAN FRANCISCO NAACP v. SAN FRANCISCO UNIFIED SCH. DIST.

59 F.Supp.2d 1021 (N.D. Cal. 1999).

ORRICK, DISTRICT JUDGE.

* * *

I.

In 1978, the San Francisco National Association for the Advancement of Colored People ("NAACP") filed the *NAACP* action, seeking desegregation of the San Francisco Unified School District ("SFUSD") on behalf of a class of all children of school age who are or may in the future become eligible to attend the public schools of the SFUSD. The suit was brought against the SFUSD, its Board Members, and its Superintendent (collectively the "Local Defendants"), and the California State Board of Education, the State Superintendent of Public Instruction, and the State Department of Education (collectively the "State Defendants").

In 1983, the Court approved a Consent Decree to resolve the *NAACP* action. Paragraph 13 of the Consent Decree, as amended, sets forth racial and ethnic guidelines for the assignment of San Francisco schoolchildren to the schools of the SFUSD. Pursuant to paragraph 13, no school may have fewer than four racial/ethnic groups represented in its student body, and no racial/ethnic group may constitute more than forty-five percent of the student enrollment at any regular school, or more than forty percent at any alternative school. Paragraph 12 of the Consent Decree identifies nine racial/ethnic groups for the purpose of defining the racial/ethnic composition of each school: Spanish-surname, Other White, African–American, Chinese, Japanese, Korean, Filipino, American Indian, and Other Non–White.

In 1994, several schoolchildren of Chinese descent filed the *Ho* action against the State and Local Defendants, alleging that paragraph 13's student assignment plan constitutes race discrimination in violation of the Equal Protection Clause of the Fourteenth Amendment of the

United States Constitution. In January 1995, the *Ho* plaintiffs filed a first amended complaint adding the NAACP as a defendant. In March 1996, the Court certified the *Ho* action as a class action on behalf of all children of Chinese descent of school age who are current residents of San Francisco and who are eligible to attend the public school system.

In May 1997, the Court denied the *Ho* plaintiffs' motion for summary judgment. The *Ho* plaintiffs appealed the Court's summary judgment ruling * * * . In an Opinion filed June 4, 1998, the Ninth Circuit dismissed the appeal for lack of jurisdiction * * * , but provided substantial guidance to the parties and the Court on the issues remaining for trial, and on the law governing those issues. *Ho v. San Francisco Unified Sch. Dist.*, 147 F.3d 854, 861 (9th Cir.1998).

The Ninth Circuit affirmed this Court's finding that the assignment of students by race subjects the students to a race-based classification by a state actor. *Id.* at 862. Such racial classifications are subject to strict scrutiny, and may be used by the government only if necessary to correct the effects of government action of a racist character. * * * It described the issues remaining for trial as follows:

> As race may permissibly be used by government in the very limited way described, two issues remain for trial: Do vestiges remain of the racism that justified paragraph 13 of the consent decree in 1983? Is paragraph 13 necessary to remove the vestiges if they do remain? *Id.* at 865.

* * * The Ninth Circuit stressed that defendants' evidence must tie the current vestiges of segregation to the discriminating practices and policies that justified the adoption of the Consent Decree in 1983. * * *

* * *

On February 16, 1999, the day trial was to begin, * * * the parties reached a settlement and submitted it to the Court. * * *

II.

The terms of the settlement [include the following]:

A. The Consent Decree entered in [the *NAACP* action] shall be modified to provide (a) that it will terminate no later than December 31, 2002, subject to Court approval; and (b) that any party may move for unitary status prior to that date. The parties anticipate that no later than such time, the state and local governmental defendants will have taken all reasonably practical measures to remedy any vestiges of segregation.

B. Pursuant to paragraph 50 of the Consent Decree, the SFUSD and the State Superintendent of Public Instruction shall develop a new student assignment plan consistent with the criteria contained in this agreement. The SFUSD and the State Superintendent shall submit the proposed modifications to the San Francisco NAACP and the *Ho* plaintiffs for review and comment.

C. The parties acknowledge that SFUSD officials have the duty and authority to determine lawful criteria for admission to all schools in the SFUSD. The parties further acknowledge that in setting those criteria, state and federal law provide that district officials may consider many factors, including the desire to promote residential, geographic, economic, racial and ethnic diversity in all SFUSD schools. However, race or ethnicity may not be the primary or predominant consideration in determining such admission criteria. Further, the SFUSD will not assign or admit any student to a particular school, class or program on the basis of the race or ethnicity of that student, except as related to the language needs of the student or otherwise to assure compliance with controlling federal or state law. * * *

III.

* * *

C.

In determining whether the settlement is fair, reasonable, and adequate, the Court is required to balance [a range of factors] * * * . The issue is not whether the settlement could be better, but whether it is fair, reasonable, and adequate and free from collusion. There is a strong judicial policy in favor of settlements in complex class actions. * * *

1.

The first factor is the strength of plaintiffs' case. Based on the evidence submitted to the Court before trial, plaintiffs were likely to succeed on their claim that the race-based student assignment plan is no longer constitutional.

The Supreme Court has placed severe restrictions on the use of racial classifications by governmental entities. Such classifications are subject to the strictest judicial scrutiny, and are constitutional only if they are narrowly tailored measures that further compelling governmental interests. In the *Ho* action, the Ninth Circuit held that "[r]acial balancing cannot be the objective of a federal court unless the balancing is shown to be necessary to correct the effects of government action of a racist character." *Ho*, 147 F.3d at 865 (citing *Freeman*, 503 U.S. at 494, 112 S. Ct. 1430). The Ninth Circuit found that the [defendants] had the burden of proving that vestiges still exist of the discriminatory policies and practices that justified the Consent Decree in 1983, and that the race-based student assignment plan in the Consent Decree is necessary to address the problems caused by the vestiges of the earlier segregation. *Id.*

* * *

It is * * * clear to the Court that defendants had very little chance of prevailing at trial. There was little likelihood that defendants would be able to prove that the race-based student assignment plan was still constitutional today in light of the very strict burdens of proof imposed by the Supreme Court and the Ninth Circuit.

* * *

e.

The immediate effect of the proposed settlement is to eliminate race-based student assignments. * * *

The Consent Decree can exist only as long as it is needed to remedy the original constitutional violations that justified its adoption in 1983. *See Freeman,* 503 U.S. at 489, 112 S. Ct. 1430 ("A remedy is justifiable only insofar as it advances the ultimate objective of alleviating the initial constitutional violation."); *id.* at 496, 112 S. Ct. 1430 ("The vestiges of segregation that are the concern of the law in a school case may be subtle and intangible but nonetheless they must be so real that they have a causal link to the *de jure* violation being remedied.") By the terms of the proposed settlement, the Consent Decree will terminate by December 31, 2002, subject to approval of the Court. The Supreme Court has held that the party moving to terminate a desegregation consent decree must demonstrate good-faith compliance with the Consent Decree since it was entered, and that the vestiges of past discrimination have been eliminated to the extent practicable. [S]*ee also Rufo v. Inmates of Suffolk County Jail,* 502 U.S. 367, 383, 112 S. Ct. 748 (1992)(the party seeking to modify a consent decree bears the burden of establishing that a significant change in circumstances warrants revision of the decree.). The Consent Decree will remain in effect as long as there is evidence that vestiges of segregation remain to be remedied. * * *

f.

Dr. Orfield recommends that if the Court approves the proposed settlement, it should increase its oversight of the Consent Decree by directing all parties to respond to the recommendations in the recent reports by the Consent Decree Advisory Committee and the State Consent Decree Monitor, and by holding regular hearings on the progress of the parties. The Court will adopt this suggestion. As the parties move toward the goal of remedying all remaining vestiges of segregation to the extent reasonably practicable, the Court will assist the parties by requiring them to (1) respond to the recent reports submitted to the Court by the Advisory Committee and Consent Decree Monitor Stuart Biegel, and (2) submit a plan for addressing the issues raised in those reports. The Court will also hold yearly hearings specifically to require the parties to address the findings in the yearly Consent Decree Monitor Reports and to create a detailed record for the final determination of whether the goals of the Consent Decree have been fulfilled to the extent reasonably practicable. * * *

Notes

1. After the *Ho* Settlement of 1999, the District was still required to desegregate on the basis of race, but was not allowed to use race as a factor

in doing so. In this regard, as well, the *SFNAACP* Consent Decree was unique.

2. In 1999, the District simply removed race from the equation, and otherwise continued with the same student assignment plan it had been using, a plan that had been based on a combination of parental choice, attendance areas for particular schools, alternative schools that anyone could attend, and a lottery system. By 2000, however, District leaders put forth a plan for a computerized diversity index, designed to maximize equal access and equal opportunity in the spirit of the Decree.

The first version of the diversity index was based on four factors, one of which was race. However, the *Ho* Plaintiffs resisted the plan, and Judge Orrick ruled that it violated the 1999 Settlement Agreement.

The second version of the diversity index was based on seven factors other than race, and was included in the District's 2001 proposal for a Comprehensive Five–Year Plan to meet the goals of the Decree. The index at that point included socioeconomic status, home language, and academic performance indicators. It also included geography as a factor. However, agreement could not be reached on either the inclusion or the parameters of the geography factor, and in the end it was dropped. The final version of the diversity index, then, included six factors.

3. Unfortunately, the new student assignment plan—adopted pursuant to a new Settlement Agreement in 2001 (and an extension of the Decree through 2005)—failed to stem the resegregation that had begun in the District after the *Ho* Settlement of 1999. Indeed, the resegregation only increased after 2001. By 2004, the Monitoring Team had reported that

> [W]hile the plan was a good faith effort by the District to comply with the terms of the 99 and 01 Settlement Agreements, it has clearly not furthered either the racial and ethnic desegregation goals or the academic achievement goals of [the Decree]. Under the current plan, * * * resegregation has continued unabated, and a dramatic achievement gap has persisted in spite of the programs put in place to improve educational quality and student performance. Indeed, we have found that the efforts of SFUSD educators to address this gap continue to be impeded by the resegregation that has emerged.

4. In retrospect, it is ironic that during an era when the federal courts recognized the constitutionality of using race as a factor in a narrowly tailored fashion to maximize diversity, counter de facto housing segregation, and maintain integrated schools, the parties to the formerly cutting-edge San Francisco Consent Decree were blocked from using race as a factor because of agreements reached during an era when everyone thought that Fourteenth Amendment jurisprudence prohibited any use of race at all.

5. As As referenced in other chapters, a Consent Decree of this type can be a great opportunity to create lasting change. And the balance sheet below indicates that such change was indeed forthcoming. However, many unresolved issues remained.

The Decree's high-profile focus on academic achievement, and on interrelated goals of equity and excellence, remains an important example of a viable strategy for effecting change in this context. Many children benefited greatly from this Decree and its enduring achievements, but its effectiveness was sometimes limited by complex political forces, conflicting personal agendas, and a less-than-enthusiastic commitment on the part of certain District leaders to the Decree's mandates and goals.

SFNAACP v. SFUSD Consent Decree Balance Sheet

Report #22, the Independent Review of the Consent Decree Monitoring Team
Filed August 1, 2005

Key SFUSD Achievements Pursuant to the Requirements & Mandates of the Consent Decree

1. Innovative strategies for education reform that have resulted in higher quality education for a very large number of students of all races/ethnicities and socioeconomic status groups over time.

2. Desegregation efforts that have led to greater access and more equality of opportunity for a very large number of students of all races/ethnicities—and particularly for socioeconomically disadvantaged and traditionally marginalized students—over time.

3. Additional resources at the school site level that have led in numerous instances to stronger learning programs and richer, more diverse educational environments.

4. Concrete success in "turning around" entire low-performing schools.

5. The creation of new, higher performing schools in low income areas.

6. Changes in the District culture generally, at the beginning of the Decree and at various other points in time, rooted in the Philosophical Tenets and leading to higher standards throughout SFUSD. These changes have resulted in greater expectations for all students in many of the District's schools.[2]

7. The closing of the achievement gap at certain noteworthy schools.

8. A more diverse faculty and staff in many of the District's schools.

9. A system of public school choice that includes a large number of high performing schools throughout the City.

10. The emergence of certain schools that can serve as models of the best features and most noteworthy accomplishments of the Decree. These schools and their achievements are documented below in a special section of this Annual Report.

---

2. As documented in many of our past reports, "the Philosophical Tenets ... [of the Special Plan for Bayview–Hunters Point] ... explicitly address the issue of expectations and focus on changing the prevalent view that only some students can achieve...." *See, e.g.,* Report #16, at page 8.

Key Unresolved Issues under the Terms
and Conditions of the Decree

1. Low academic achievement at certain chronically low performing schools.

2. The inability of certain other schools to sustain gains that were originally achieved under the Decree.

3. A pattern of continuing resegregation at close to half of the District schools since 1999, and an inability to identify and implement adjustments in the student assignment plan that could address this resegregation to the extent practicable.[3]

4. A persistent gap between the academic performance of African American and Latino students overall and the performance of the District as a whole, and an inability to define a vision and reach goals that could address this gap to the extent practicable.[4]

5. An inability to confront the crisis that is evident within the African American community in San Francisco, a crisis that is reflected in highly troubling numbers on a range of traditional objective indicators and shows little sign of dissipating.[5]

3. Paragraph 12 of the Consent Decree requires the District "to eliminate racial/ethnic segregation or identifiability in any SFUSD school, program, or classroom and to achieve the broadest *practicable* distribution throughout the system of students from the racial and ethnic groups which comprise the enrollment." In many of the recent Monitoring Team reports, we have highlighted numerous instances and provided numerous examples of areas where more could have been done in this context. We have also noted where more still can be done, but has not been done, to the extent practicable. *See generally* March 2004 Supplemental Report at Part V, pages 9–15 (Addressing Problems of Equity and Educational Quality "To The Extent Practicable").

4. *See, e.g.,* March 2004 Supplemental Report at pages 9–15; July 2004 Response to District's Offer of Proof, at pages 13–14. *See generally* Report #21 at pages 9–10:

We continue to emphasize the fact that none of these realities should be viewed in a vacuum, and that all of these issues are interrelated. Consent Decree guidelines have been developed for this very purpose. They include, but are not limited to, desegregation by school, program, and classroom; an explicit focus on academic achievement; a continued effort to increase expectations; an emphasis on increasing the quality of programs and practices, particularly with regard to English Learners and Students with Dis-

abilities; increasing both Advanced Placement (AP) course offerings and access; building more after school program offerings and increasing access to these programs; addressing attendance issues; adjusting bus transportation routes and options; improving discipline practices; linking professional development to Consent Decree goals; and allocating Consent Decree money in a manner that would best further the attainment of these goals.

5. *See, e.g.,* Report #19 at pages 23, 93, 126–29; Report #21 at pages 6–8; March 2004 Supplemental Report at pages 9–15; April 2005 Supplemental Report at pages 12–16 (documenting the parameters of the multi-faceted achievement gap—based on test scores, GPA, AP enrollment, and graduation rates—between African American students and the District's student population as a whole, as well as the continued rock-bottom performance of the African American students in San Francisco when compared with their counterparts in other major urban districts).

See also the April 2005 Supplemental Report and the annual Paragraph 12, Paragraph 38, and Paragraph 39 documentation (1999–2005) ... showing a persistent disproportionate representation of African American students in separate special education classes generally, the overwhelmingly disproportionate representation of African American students in the highly subjective "emotionally disturbed"

6. An ongoing lack of compliance with the Paragraph 12 within-school desegregation mandate of the Decree, resulting in a persistently different, less challenging curriculum for students in certain racially identifiable and socioeconomic-status-identifiable programs and classrooms.

7. Continuing issues regarding inequitable distribution of Consent Decree funds, with many schools that evidence the greatest needs in this context still receiving significantly less money than other, higher performing schools. Also, continued evidence of inappropriate allocation of these funds by administrators at certain school sites.

8. An inability to develop and maintain District-wide professional development programs that address the basic requirements of Paragraph 36 and convey basic Consent Decree principles and Philosophical Tenets to teachers and school site administrators.

9. Substantially different approaches and ineffective efforts regarding school discipline from school site to school site, resulting in a continuing lack of compliance with the mandate of Paragraph 38.

10. Vestiges of segregation, present in the District prior to 1978, that are reflected in both the continuing existence of low expectations for low income students of color and in the segregative nature of many District programs, particularly in the area of special education.[6]

* * *

In our analysis of [schools that have achieved success under the Decree], we have identified a number of factors that have enabled them to achieve their successes. These factors include maintaining a diverse student body, awareness of the individual learning differences and personal needs of every student, a school-wide commitment to improving

and "severe learning disabled" categories of special education, the substantial ongoing disparities in suspension and expulsion rates by race/ethnicity, as well as a pervasive and unrelenting attendance gap between African American students and the District as a whole. *See generally* March 2004 Supplemental Report, at pages 20–21: "A large number of students in this city are not succeeding, their very lives are on the line, and in too many instances their schools are failing them."

6. In Report #16, we documented the existence of vestiges of segregation as reflected in the low expectations of many District educators, particularly with regard to African American and Latino students, over time. See Report #16 at pages 37–40:

As time goes by, the monitoring team continues to uncover evidence of low ex-

pectations for student achievement throughout SFUSD.... [T]here are still a substantial number of classroom teachers, school site administrators, and district-level administrators whose actions reflect continuing low expectations for certain students and student groups. Such low expectations are vestiges of segregation that have not been eliminated to the extent practicable. *Id.* at 37.

In our June 2004 Response to the Parties' Joint Response, we confirmed the ongoing existence of these same realities. *See* June 2004 Response to the Parties' Joint Response, at page 13, n.11c. In this Report, *infra,* Paragraph 12 Section, we provide additional documentation, particularly as it relates to the interrelationship between special education placement and low expectations for African American students over time. *See* Appendix 2, *infra,* at pages 4–8.

African American and Latino student performance, strong intervention programs, school culture that promotes academic excellence for all students, qualified and caring faculty who understand the tenets of the Consent Decree, communication and collaboration between the administration and faculty, strong parent involvement in the school community, and effective site-based professional development programs that specifically address issues relating to the narrowing of the achievement gap.

As we have done many times in the past when we have documented District successes, we urge the community to build on these successes and seek to publicize, disseminate, and replicate the noteworthy steps taken by these educators to achieve their goals.

5. WITHIN–SCHOOL SEGREGATION, TRACKING, & HOMO-GENEOUS ABILITY GROUPING

One of the most significant unresolved issues in education from an equal opportunity perspective is within-school segregation. In the public schools today, a large percentage of students continue to be separated out from their peers either for programmatic reasons or on the basis of perceived ability. As a result of this separation, many receive a lower quality curriculum, are unable to complete the coursework required for college admission, or are otherwise disadvantaged in a variety of troubling ways.

Legal challenges to these types of practices have had mixed success. *See, e.g.,* KEVIN G. WELNER, LEGAL RIGHTS, LOCAL WRONGS: WHEN COMMUNITY CONTROL COLLIDES WITH EDUCATIONAL EQUITY, SUNY Press (2001). The 1967 case of *Hobson v. Hansen* represents a landmark victory that achieved great results, yet to the extent that this pre-*Washington v. Davis* case was decided on the basis of discriminatory effects alone, the decision may no longer be good law. On the other hand, *Hobson* remains an important touchstone in this context, since the District's approach to tracking and its justification for tracking are now, in light of almost four decades of additional research, clearly unacceptable. *See generally* JEANNIE OAKES, KEEPING TRACK: HOW SCHOOLS STRUCTURE INEQUALITY, Yale University Press (2d ed. 2005).

HOBSON v. HANSEN

269 F.Supp. 401 (D.D.C. 1967).

J. SKELLY WRIGHT, CIRCUIT JUDGE:

SUMMARY

In *Bolling v. Sharpe*, the Supreme Court held that the District of Columbia's racially segregated public school system violated the due process clause of the Fifth Amendment. The present litigation, brought in behalf of Negro as well as poor children generally in the District's public schools, tests the current compliance of those schools with the principles announced in *Bolling*, its companion case, *Brown v. Board of*

Education, 347 U.S. 483, 74 S. Ct. 686 (1954), and their progeny. The basic question presented is whether the defendants, the Superintendent of Schools and the members of the Board of Education, in the operation of the public school system here, unconstitutionally deprive the District's Negro and poor public school children of their right to equal educational opportunity with the District's white and more affluent public school children. This court concludes that they do.

In support of this conclusion the court makes the following principal findings of fact:

* * *

9.   The track system as used in the District's public schools is a form of ability grouping in which students are divided in separate, self-contained curricula or tracks ranging from "Basic" for the slow student to "Honors" for the gifted.

10.   The aptitude tests used to assign children to the various tracks are standardized primarily on white middle class children. Since these tests do not relate to the Negro and disadvantaged child, track assignment based on such tests relegates Negro and disadvantaged children to the lower tracks from which, because of the reduced curricula and the absence of adequate remedial and compensatory education, as well as continued inappropriate testing, the chance of escape is remote.

11.   Education in the lower tracks is geared to what Dr. Hansen, the creator of the track system, calls the "blue collar" student. Thus such children, so stigmatized by inappropriate aptitude testing procedures, are denied equal opportunity to obtain the white collar education available to the white and more affluent children.

* * *

In sum, all of the evidence in this case tends to show that the Washington school system is a monument to the cynicism of the power structure which governs the voteless capital of the greatest country on earth.

Remedy

To correct the racial and economic discrimination found in the operation of the District of Columbia public school system, the court has issued a decree attached to its opinion ordering: 1. An injunction against racial and economic discrimination in the public school system here. 2. Abolition of the track system. * * *

FINDINGS OF FACT

* * *

IV. THE TRACK SYSTEM

The District of Columbia school system employs a form of ability grouping commonly known as the track system, by which students at the elementary and secondary level are placed in tracks or curriculum levels according to the school's assessment of each student's ability to learn. * * *

A. *Origin.*

The track system was approved for introduction into the Washington school system by the Board of Education in 1956, just two years after the desegregation decision in *Bolling v. Sharpe.* * * * The court is persuaded that [Superintendent] Hansen personally was then and is now motivated by a desire to respond—according to his own philosophy—to an educational crisis in the District school system. On the other hand, the court cannot ignore the fact that until 1954 the District schools were by direction of law operated on a segregated basis. It cannot ignore the fact that of all the possible forms of ability grouping, the one that won acceptance in the District was the one that—with the exception of completely separate schools—involves the greatest amount of physical separation by grouping students in wholly distinct, homogeneous curriculum levels. It cannot ignore that the immediate and known effect of this separation would be to insulate the more academically developed white student from his less fortunate black schoolmate, thus minimizing the impact of integration; nor can the court ignore the fact that this same cushioning effect remains evident even today. Therefore, although the track system cannot be dismissed as nothing more than a subterfuge by which defendants are attempting to avoid the mandate of *Bolling v. Sharpe,* neither can it be said that the evidence shows racial considerations to be absolutely irrelevant to its adoption and absolutely irrelevant in its continued administration. To this extent the track system is tainted.

The court does not, however, rest its decision on a finding of intended racial discrimination. Apart from such intentional aspects, the effects of the track system must be held to be a violation of plaintiffs' constitutional rights. As the evidence in this case makes painfully clear, ability grouping as presently practiced in the District of Columbia school system is a denial of equal educational opportunity to the poor and a majority of the Negroes attending school in the nation's capital, a denial that contravenes not only the guarantees of the Fifth Amendment but also the fundamental premise of the track system itself. * * *

B. *Track Theory.*

Basic to an understanding of the conflict between the parties in this lawsuit is an appreciation of the theory that motivates the track system as it operates in the District school system. The most comprehensive statement of that theory can be found in Dr. Hansen's book, FOUR TRACK CURRICULUM FOR TODAY'S HIGH SCHOOLS, published in 1964. Although Dr. Hansen disclaims full responsibility for creating the track system, a reading of his book leaves no doubt that it was his firm guiding hand that shaped that system in its essential characteristics. Thus, as principal architect of the track system and as Superintendent of Schools, Dr. Hansen presumably can be looked to as the authoritative spokesman on the subject.

Purpose and philosophy. Dr. Hansen believes that the comprehensive high school (and the school system generally) must be systematically organized and structured to provide differing levels of education for students with widely differing levels of academic ability. This is the purpose of the track system. In expressing the track system's philosophy Dr. Hansen has said, "Every pupil in the school system must have the maximum opportunity for self-development and this can best be brought about by adjusting curriculum offerings to different levels of need and ability as the pupil moves through the stages of education and growth in our schools." And he has identified as the two objectives on which the track system is founded: "(1) The realization of the doctrine of equality of education and (2) The attainment of quality education."

Student types. Within the student body Dr. Hansen sees generally four types of students: the intellectually gifted, the above-average, the average, and the retarded. He assumes that each of these types of students has a maximum level of academic capability and, most importantly, that that level of ability can be accurately ascertained. The duty of the school is to identify these students and provide a curriculum commensurate with their respective abilities. Dr. Hansen contends that the traditional school curriculum—including the usual two-level method of ability grouping—does a disservice to those at either end of the ability spectrum.

The gifted student is not challenged, so that he becomes bored, lazy, and perhaps performs far below his academic potential; his intellectual talents are a wasted resource. The remedy lies in discovering the gifted student, placing him with others of his own kind, thereby stimulating him through this select association as well as a rigorous, demanding curriculum to develop his intellectual talent. Indeed, "the academically capable student should be required as a public necessity to take the academically challenging honors curriculum."

On the other hand, continues Dr. Hansen, the retarded or "stupid" student typically has been forced to struggle through a curriculum he cannot possibly master and only imperfectly comprehends. Typically he is slow to learn and soon falls behind in class; he repeatedly fails, sometimes repeating a grade again and again; he becomes isolated, frustrated, depressed, and—if he does not drop out before graduation— graduates with a virtually useless education. Here the remedy is seen as separating out the retarded student, directing him into a special curriculum geared to his limited abilities and designed to give him a useful "basic" education—one which makes no pretense of equalling traditionally taught curricula.

In short, Hansen views the traditional school curriculum as doing too little for some students and expecting too much of others. As for the latter type, whom Dr. Hansen characterizes as "the blue-collar student," going to school—a "white-collar occupation"—can be an artificial experience.

"Twelve years of white-collar experience is unrealistic preparation for the young man or woman who will suddenly make the change into work clothes for jobs in kitchens, stockrooms, street maintenance or building construction.

* * *

"One reason (for education's failure to meet the needs of the blue collar student) * * * is that it is at best an environment artificially created for the education of the young. From the beginning of his career in school, the child enjoys the comforts of a protected and unrealistic environment. Most of the Nation's classrooms are insulated from reality. To many students what happens in the classroom has little connection with what happens outside the classroom.

"Another reason * * * is that the school environment excludes most of the sterner discipline of the work-a-day world * * *."

Tracking. In order to tailor the educational process to the level appropriate to each student, Dr. Hansen adopted the track system. Each track is intended to be a separate and self-contained curriculum, with the educational content ranging from the very basic to the very advanced according to the track level. In the elementary and junior high schools three levels are used: Basic or Special Academic (retarded students), General (average and above-average), and Honors (gifted). In the senior high school a fourth level is added: the Regular Track, a college-preparatory track intended to accommodate the above-average student.

The significant feature of the track system in this regard is its emphasis on the ability of the student. A student's course of instruction depends upon what the school system decides he is capable of handling. * * *

OPINION OF LAW

* * *

VI. THE TRACK SYSTEM

* * *

As the court's findings have shown, the track system is undeniably an extreme form of ability grouping. Students are early in elementary school sorted into homogeneous groups or tracks (and often into subgroups within a track), thereby being physically separated into different classrooms. Not only is there homogeneity, in terms of supposed levels of ability—the intended result—but as a practical matter there is a distinct sameness in terms of socio-economic status as well. More importantly, each track offers a substantially different kind of education, both in pace of learning and in scope of subject matter. At the bottom there is the slow-paced, basic (and eventually almost purely low-skill vocational) Special Academic Track; at the top is the intense and challenging Honors program for the gifted student. For a student locked into one of the lower tracks, physical separation from those in other tracks is of course complete insofar as classroom relationships are concerned; and the limits on his academic progress, and ultimately the kind of life work he can hope to attain after graduation, are set by the orientation of the lower curricula. Thus those in the lower tracks are, for the most part, molded for various levels of vocational assignments; those in the upper tracks, on the other hand, are given the opportunity to prepare for the higher ranking jobs and, most significantly, for college.

In theory, since tracking is supposed to be kept flexible, relatively few students should actually ever be locked into a single track or curriculum. Yet, in violation of one of its principal tenets, the track system is not flexible at all. Not only are assignments permanent for 90% or more of the students but the vast majority do not even take courses outside their own curriculum. Moreover, another significant failure to implement track theory—and in major part responsible for the inflexibility just noted—is the lack of adequate remedial and compensatory education programs for the students assigned to or left in the lower tracks because of cultural handicaps. Although one of the express reasons for placing such students in these tracks is to facilitate remediation, little is being done to accomplish the task. Consequently, the lower track student, rather than obtaining an enriched educational experience, gets what is essentially a limited or watered-down curriculum.

These are, then, the significant features of the track system: separation of students into rigid curricula, which entails both physical segregation and a disparity of educational opportunity; and, for those consigned to the lower tracks, opportunities decidedly inferior to those available in the higher tracks.

A precipitating cause of the constitutional inquiry in this case is the fact that those who are being consigned to the lower tracks are the poor and the Negroes, whereas the upper tracks are the provinces of the more affluent and the whites. Defendants have not, and indeed could not have, denied that the pattern of grouping correlates remarkably with a student's status, although defendants would have it that the equation is to be stated in terms of income, not race. However, as discussed elsewhere, to focus solely on economics is to oversimplify the matter in the District of Columbia where so many of the poor are in fact the Negroes. And even if race could be ruled out, which it cannot, defendants surely "can no more discriminate on account of poverty than on account of religion, race, or color." As noted before, the law has a special concern for minority groups for whom the judicial branch of government is often the only hope for redressing their legitimate grievances; and a court will not treat lightly a showing that educational opportunities are being allocated according to a pattern that has unmistakable signs of invidious discrimination. Defendants, therefore, have a weighty burden of explaining why the poor and the Negro should be those who populate the lower ranks of the track system.

Since by definition the basis of the track system is to classify students according to their ability to learn, the only explanation defendants can legitimately give for the pattern of classification found in the District schools is that it does reflect students' abilities. If the discriminations being made are founded on anything other than that, then the whole premise of tracking collapses and with it any justification for relegating certain students to curricula designed for those of limited abilities. While government may classify persons and thereby effect disparities in treatment, those included within or excluded from the respective classes should be those for whom the inclusion or exclusion is appropriate; otherwise the classification risks becoming wholly irrational and thus unconstitutionally discriminatory. It is in this regard that the track system is fatally defective, because for many students placement is based on traits other than those on which the classification purports to be based.

The evidence shows that the method by which track assignments are made depends essentially on standardized aptitude tests which, although given on a system-wide basis, are completely inappropriate for use with a large segment of the student body. Because these tests are standardized primarily on and are relevant to a white middle class group of students, they produce inaccurate and misleading test scores when given to lower class and Negro students. As a result, rather than being classified according to ability to learn, these students are in reality being classified according to their socio-economic or racial status, or—more precisely— according to environmental and psychological factors which have nothing to do with innate ability.

Compounding and reinforcing the inaccuracies inherent in test measurements are a host of circumstances which further obscure the true abilities of the poor and the Negro. For example, teachers acting under false assumptions because of low test scores will treat the disadvantaged student in such a way as to make him conform to their low expectations; this acting out process—the self-fulfilling prophecy—makes it appear that the false assumptions were correct, and the student's real talent is wasted. Moreover, almost cynically, many Negro students are either denied or have limited access to the very kinds of programs the track system makes a virtual necessity: kindergartens; Honors programs for the fast-developing Negro student; and remedial and compensatory education programs that will bring the disadvantaged student back into the mainstream of education. Lacking these facilities, the student continues hampered by his cultural handicaps and continues to appear to be of lower ability than he really is. Finally, the track system as an institution cannot escape blame for the error in placements, for it is tracking that places such an emphasis on defining ability, elevating its importance to the point where the whole of a student's education and future are made to turn on his facility in demonstrating his qualifications for the higher levels of opportunity. Aside from the fact that this makes the consequences of misjudgments so much the worse, it also tends to alienate the disadvantaged student who feels unequal to the task of competing in an ethnocentric school system dominated by white middle class values; and alienated students inevitably do not reveal their true abilities—either in school or on tests.

All of these circumstances, and more, destroy the rationality of the class structure that characterizes the track system. Rather than reflecting classifications according to ability, track assignments are for many students placements based on status. Being, therefore, in violation of its own premise, the track system amounts to an unlawful discrimination against those students whose educational opportunities are being limited on the erroneous assumption that they are capable of accepting no more.

* * *

CLOSING THE ACHIEVEMENT GAP BY DETRACKING

Carol Corbett Burris & Kevin G. Welner.
4/1/05 Phi Delta Kappan 594
2005 WLNR 5373631.

* * *

Because African American and Hispanic students are consistently overrepresented in low-track classes, the effects of tracking greatly concern educators who are interested in closing the achievement gap. Detracking reforms are grounded in the established ideas that higher achievement follows from a more rigorous curriculum and that low-track classes with unchallenging curricula result in lower student achievement.[4] Yet, notwithstanding the wide acceptance of these ideas, we lack concrete case studies of mature detracking reforms and their effects. This article responds to that shortage, describing how the school district in which Carol Burris serves as a high school principal was able to close the gap by offering its high-track curriculum to all students, in detracked classes.

* * *

PROVIDING 'HIGH–TRACK' CURRICULUM TO ALL STUDENTS

The Rockville Centre School District is a diverse suburban school district located on Long Island. In the late 1990s, it embarked on a multiyear detracking reform that increased learning expectations for all

---

4. CLIFFORD ADELMAN, ANSWERS IN THE TOOL BOX: ACADEMIC INTENSITY, ATTENDANCE PATTERNS, AND BACHELOR'S DEGREE ATTAINMENT (Washington, D.C.: Office of Educational Research, U.S. Department of Education, 1999), available on the Web at http://www.ed.gov/pubs/Toolbox; HENRY LEVIN, ACCELERATED SCHOOLS FOR AT RISK STUDENTS (New Brunswick, N.J.: Rutgers University, Center for Policy Research in Education, Report No. 142, 1988); Mano Singham, *The Achievement Gap: Myths and Realities*, PHI DELTA KAPPAN, April 2003, pp. 586 91; and JAY P. HEUBERT AND ROBERT M. HAUSER, HIGH STAKES: TESTING FOR TRACKING, PROMOTION, AND GRADUATION (Washington, D.C.: National Research Council, 1999).

students. The district began replacing its tracked classes with heterogeneously grouped classes in which the curriculum formerly reserved for the district's high-track students was taught.

This reform began as a response to an ambitious goal set by the * * * [District]: By the year 2000, 75% of all graduates will earn a New York State Regents diploma. At that time, the district and state rates of earning Regents diplomas were 58% and 38% respectively.

To qualify for a New York State Regents diploma, students must pass, at a minimum, eight end-of-course Regents examinations, including two in mathematics, two in laboratory sciences, two in social studies, one in English language arts, and one in a foreign language. * * *

Regents exams are linked with coursework; therefore, the district gradually eliminated low-track courses. The high school eased the transition by offering students instructional support classes and carefully monitoring the progress of struggling students. * * *

ACCELERATED MATHEMATICS IN HETEROGENEOUS CLASSES

* * * In order to provide all students with ample opportunity to pass the needed courses and to study calculus prior to graduation, [the superintendent] decided that all students would study the accelerated math curriculum formerly reserved for the district's highest achievers. * * * [M]iddle school math teachers revised and condensed the curriculum. The new curriculum was taught to all students, in heterogeneously grouped classes. To support struggling learners, the school initiated support classes called math workshops and provided after-school help four afternoons a week.

The results were remarkable. Over 90% of incoming freshmen entered the high school having passed the first Regents math examination. The achievement gap dramatically narrowed. Between the years of 1995 and 1997, only 23% of regular education African American or Hispanic students had passed this algebra-based Regents exam before entering high school. After universally accelerating all students in heterogeneously grouped classes, the percentage more than tripled—up to 75%. The percentage of white or Asian American regular education students who passed the exam also greatly increased—from 54% to 98%.

DETRACKING THE HIGH SCHOOL

* * *

The entire 1999 cohort also studied science in heterogeneous classes throughout middle school, and it became the first cohort to be heterogeneously grouped in ninth-grade English and social studies classes.

Ninth-grade teachers were pleased with the results. The tone, activities, and discussions in the heterogeneously grouped classes were academic, focused, and enriched. Science teachers reported that the heterogeneously grouped middle school science program prepared students well for ninth-grade biology.

Detracking at the high school level continued, paralleling the introduction of revised New York State curricula. Students in the 2000 cohort studied the state's new biology curriculum, "The Living Environment," in heterogeneously grouped classes. This combination of new curriculum and heterogeneous grouping resulted in a dramatic increase in the passing rate on the first science Regents exam, especially for minority students who were previously overrepresented in the low-track biology class. After just one year of heterogeneous grouping, the passing rate for African American and Hispanic students increased from 48% to 77%, while the passing rate for white and Asian American students increased from 85% to 94%.

The following September, the 2001 cohort became the first class to be heterogeneously grouped in all subjects in the ninth grade. The state's new multiyear "Math A" curriculum was taught to this cohort in heterogeneously grouped classes in both the eighth and ninth grades.

In 2003, some 10th-grade classes detracked. Students in the 2002 cohort became the first to study a heterogeneously grouped pre–International Baccalaureate (IB) 10th-grade curriculum in English and social studies. To help all students meet the demands of an advanced curriculum, the district provides every-other-day support classes in math, science, and English language arts. These classes are linked to the curriculum and allow teachers to pre–and post-teach topics to students needing additional reinforcement.

CLOSING THE GAP ON OTHER MEASURES THAT MATTER

New York's statewide achievement gap in the earning of Regents diplomas has persisted. In 2000, only 19.3% of all African American or Hispanic 12th–graders and 58.7% of all white or Asian American 12th–graders graduated with Regents diplomas. By 2003, while the percentage of students in both groups earning the Regents diploma increased (26.4% of African American or Hispanic students, 66.3% of white or Asian American students), the gap did not close.

In contrast, Rockville Centre has seen both an increase in students' rates of earning Regents diplomas and a decrease in the gap between groups. For those students who began South Side High School in 1996 (the graduating class of 2000), 32% of all African American or Hispanic and 88% of all white or Asian American graduates earned Regents diplomas. By the time the cohort of 1999 graduated in 2003, the gap had closed dramatically—82% of all African American or Hispanic and 97% of all white or Asian American graduates earned Regents diplomas. In fact, * * * for this 1999 cohort (the first to experience detracking in all middle school and most ninth-grade subjects), the Regents diploma rate for the district's minority students surpassed New York State's rate for white or Asian American students.

In order to ensure that the narrowing of the gap was not attributable to a changing population, we used binary logistic regression analyses to compare the probability of earning a Regents diploma before and after detracking. In addition to membership in a detracked cohort, the model included socioeconomic and special education status as covariates. Those students who were members of the 1996 and 1997 cohorts were compared with members of the 1998–2000 cohorts. We found that membership in a cohort subsequent to the detracking of middle school math was a significant contributor to earning a Regents diploma ($p < .0001$). In addition, low-SES students and special education students in the 2001 cohort also showed sharp improvement.

These same three cohorts (1998–2000) showed significant increases in the probability of minority students' studying advanced math courses. Controlling for prior achievement and SES, minority students' enrollment in trigonometry, precalculus, and Advanced Placement calculus all grew.[15] And as more students from those cohorts studied AP calculus, the enrollment gap decreased from 38% to 18% in five years, and the AP calculus scores significantly increased ($p < .01$).

Finally, detracking in the 10th grade, combined with teaching all students the pre-IB curriculum, appears to be closing the gap in the study of the IB curriculum. This year 50% of all minority students will study IB English and "History of the Americas" in the 11th grade. In the fall of 2003, only 31% chose to do so.

Achievement follows from opportunities—opportunities that tracking denies. The results of detracking in Rockville Centre are clear and compelling. When all students were taught the high-track curriculum, achievement rose for all groups of students—majority, minority, special education, low-SES, and high-SES. This evidence can now be added to the larger body of tracking research that has convinced the Carnegie Council for Adolescent Development, the National Governors' Association, and most recently the National Research Council to call for the reduction or elimination of tracking.[16] The Rockville Centre reform confirms common sense: closing the "curriculum gap" is an effective way to close the "achievement gap."

PROBLEM 24: Tracking & Ability Grouping

For each of these examples, as a matter of law, would the practices be upheld? As a matter of policy, should the practices be upheld? In light of the findings by the Hobson court and the recent developments documented in the Burris–Welner piece, what viable alternatives might be appropriate? Why?

A.   After a court order mandating the desegregation of the Seminole County School District, students were placed in tracks based primarily on

15.   Carol Corbett Burris, Jay P. Heubert, and Henry M. Levin, Math Acceleration for All, Educational Leadership, February 2004, pp. 68–71.

16.   Carnegie Council on Adolescent Development, Turning Points: Preparing American Youth for the 21st Century (New York: Carnegie Corporation, 1989); Ability Grouping and Tracking: Current Issues and Concerns (Washington, D.C.: National Governors Association, 1993); and National Research Council, Engaging Schools: Fostering High School Students' Motivation to Learn (Washington, D.C.: National Academies Press, 2004).

group intelligence test scores. Three tracks in elementary and junior high grades (special academic (retarded), general (average), and honors (gifted)), with a fourth track added in high school for above-average college-bound students. Movement between tracks bordered on the non-existent. Each track was provided with a different curriculum, commensurate with the students' perceived abilities. Low-income and black students were placed disproportionately in the low tracks. Key underlying assumptions, according to the district, were that each type of student had a maximum level of academic capability, and that this ability could be accurately ascertained.

B. After a court order mandating the desegregation of the Orchard School District, students in grades 4–12 were to be assigned to one of the two schools in the district on the basis of their California Achievement Test scores.

C. The Eldorado County School District set aside one of its eleven high schools as a "preferred," college-preparatory school which admitted students on the basis of past academic achievement. The percentage of students who qualified for admission was substantially disproportionate to the percentage of black, Hispanic, and low-income students in the district at large.

D. Several school districts in the State of Freedonia instituted ability grouping practices in the elementary grades, typically for reading and math only. Such practices were neither mandated nor prohibited by state law. Grouping decisions were predicated on a variety of factors, including subject-specific standardized tests and teacher evaluations. Movement between groups occurred regularly, based on continuous progress rating systems and formalized, periodic reevaluations of achievement.

B. THE PERSISTENCE OF THE STANDARDIZED TESTING CONTROVERSY

Legal challenges to standardized testing have mirrored the major public policy questions facing educators in this area today: what type of tests to use, and how to use them. Litigation has therefore focused on either the test instrument itself and/or the alleged misuse of these instruments.

Few people question the need for accountability measures that could help determine what is going on in the schools and how children are doing. The key questions that are raised in this context, however, focus on whether and to what extent current practices most appropriately and most effectively accomplish the task.

In this regard, it is especially important to note a basic principle of educational assessment and evaluation. Experts in the field are nearly unanimous in their findings that multiple measures yield the most precise and the most complete results. The prototypical multiple choice test only tells part of the story.

Yet multiple choice tests predominate in education today. U.S. public school students must take a very large number of these tests in the course of a given year (perhaps more than in any other country), and major life-changing decisions are often made based on the results of just one of them.

This section provides an introduction to these issues, which correlate directly with much of the material in the chapter. It focuses in particular on the *Debra P.* case, a landmark decision regarding the constitutionality of basing of such life-changing decisions on tests of questionable validity.

Issues raised in this section re-occur in Chapters 6 & 7, particularly in the educational quality inquiry, and notably under the "No Child Left Behind" Act.

DEBRA P. v. TURLINGTON

644 F.2d 397 (5th Cir. 1981).

FAY, CIRCUIT JUDGE:

The State of Florida, concerned about the quality of its public educational system, enacted statutory provisions leading to the giving of a competency examination covering certain basic skills. Many students passed the examination but a significant number failed. The failing group included a disparate number of blacks. This class action, brought on their behalf, challenges the right of the state to impose the passing of the examination as a condition precedent to the receipt of a high school diploma. The overriding legal issue of this appeal is whether the State of Florida can constitutionally deprive public school students of their high school diplomas on the basis of an examination which *may* cover matters not taught through the curriculum. We hold that the State may not constitutionally so deprive its students unless it has submitted proof of the curricular validity of the test. Accordingly, we vacate the judgment of the district court and remand for further findings of fact.

I.

* * *

We find, based upon stipulated facts, that because the state had not made any effort to make certain whether the test covered material actually studied in the classrooms of the state and because the record is insufficient in proof on that issue, the case must be remanded for further findings. If the test covers material not taught the students, it is unfair and violates the Equal Protection and Due Process clauses of the United States Constitution.

II.

At the outset, we wish to stress that neither the district court nor we are in a position to determine educational policy in the State of Florida. The state has determined that minimum standards must be met and that the quality of education must be improved. We have nothing but praise for these efforts. The state's plenary powers over education come from the powers reserved to the states through the Tenth Amendment, and usually they are defined in the state constitution. As long as it does so in a manner consistent with the mandates of the United States Constitution, a state may determine the length, manner, and content of any education it provides.

The United States courts have interfered with state educational directives only when necessary to protect freedoms and privileges guaranteed by the United States Constitution. In 1899, for example, in the case of *Cumming v. Board of Education*, the Court upheld the decision of a local board to close a black school while keeping a white school open. Finding that the decision was based on economic reasons, the Court said:

> [T]he education of the people in schools maintained by state taxation is a matter belonging to the respective States, and any interference on the part of Federal authority with the management of such schools cannot be justified except in the case of a clear and unmistakable disregard of the rights secured by the supreme law of the land.

While the outcome of the *Cumming* case might be questioned in this post *Brown* era, it must be remembered that it was not until just before the First World War that compulsory school attendance laws were in force in all states.[7] Public education was virtually unknown at the time of the adoption of the Constitution. In 1647 Colonial Massachusetts directed its towns to establish schools, and in 1749, Franklin proposed the Philadelphia academy. Until after the turn of the century, education was primarily private and usually sectarian. Once part of the government, however, education became a significant governmental responsibility. As the Court noted in *Brown v. Board of Education*, 347 U.S. 483, 493, 74 S. Ct. 686, 691, (1954):

> Today, education is perhaps the most important function of State and local governments. Compulsory school attendance laws and the great expenditures for education both demonstrate our recognition of the importance of education to our democratic society.

Stating that the provision of education ranks at the apex of the functions of a state, the Court in *Wisconsin v. Yoder*, 406 U.S. 205, 92 S. Ct. 1526 (1971) was required to balance the state's need for its citizens to be educated against the citizens' hallowed right to free exercise of religion. "There is no doubt," the Court said, "as to the power of a state, having a high responsibility for education of its citizens, to impose reasonable regulations for the control and duration of basic education."

Though the state has plenary power, it cannot exercise that power without reason and without regard to the United States Constitution. Although the Court has never labeled education as a "fundamental right" automatically triggering strict scrutiny of state actions, see *San*

7. Brown v. Board of Education, 347 U.S. 483, 489–90 n.4, 74 S. Ct. 686, 691, n.4 (1954).

Antonio School District v. Rodriguez, 411 U.S. 1, 93 S. Ct. 1278 (1972), it is clear that if the state does provide an educational system, it must do so in a non-discriminatory fashion. "Among other things, the State is constrained to recognize a student's legitimate entitlement to a public education as a property interest which may be protected by the Due Process Clause...."

III.

It is in the light of the foregoing discussion of the relationship between the state and federal governments that we must analyze the plaintiffs' claims that [the Florida State Assessment Test (SSAT II)] violates the equal protection and due process clauses of the Fourteenth Amendment. It is clear that in establishing a system of free public education and in making school attendance mandatory,[8] the state has created an expectation in the students. From the students' point of view, the expectation is that if a student attends school during those required years, and indeed more, and if he takes and passes the required courses, he will receive a diploma. This is a property interest as that term is used constitutionally. Although the state of Florida constitutionally may not be obligated to establish and maintain a school system, it has done so, required attendance and created a mutual expectation that the student who is successful will graduate with a diploma. This expectation can be viewed as a state-created "understanding" that secures certain benefits and that supports claims of entitlement to those benefits. As the trial court noted, "graduation is the logical extension of successful attendance," and as appellees note in brief, before SSAT II, a student completing the necessary number of credits would graduate with a diploma.

Based upon this implied property right, we find that the trial court was correct in holding that the implementation schedule for the test violated due process of law.

* * *

The due process violation potentially goes deeper than deprivation of property rights without adequate notice. When it encroaches upon concepts of justice lying at the basis of our civil and political institutions, the state is obligated to avoid action which is arbitrary and capricious, does not achieve or even frustrates a legitimate state interest, or is fundamentally unfair. We believe that the state administered a test that was, at least on the record before us, fundamentally unfair in that it may have covered matters not taught in the schools of the state.

Testimony at trial by experts for both plaintiffs and defendants indicated that several types of studies were done before and after the administration of the test. The experts agreed that of the several types of validity studies,[10] a content validity study would be most important for a

---

8. Fla.Stat.Ann. § 232.01 (West Supp. 1981) mandates that children between the ages of 6 and 16 attend school.

10. Basic types of validity as defined by the American Psychological Association, *Standards for Educational and Psychological Tests* (1974) are as follows:

competency examination such as SSAT II. The trial court apparently found that the test had adequate content validity, but we find that holding upon the record before us to be clearly erroneous. In the field of competency testing, an important component of content validity is curricular validity, defined by defendants' expert Dr. Foster, as "things that are currently taught." This record is simply insufficient in proof that the test administered measures what was actually taught in the schools of Florida.

* * *

Dr. Thomas H. Fisher, Administrator of the Student Assessment Section, Department of Education, testified that the DOE merely assumed that things were being taught. Dr. John E. Hills, professor of Educational Research at Florida State University, testified that the test reliably and validly assessed applications of basic communications and math skills to everyday situations, but he agreed that everything on the test might not have been taught. Appellants placed into evidence some math books and communications teaching materials, but at least one teacher, Mr. Crihfield, testified that he did not cover the whole book in class.

We acknowledge that in composing items for a test, the writer is dealing with applications of knowledge, and therefore the form of the test question would not necessarily be the same as the form of the information taught in class. We think, however, that fundamental fairness requires that the state be put to test on the issue of whether the students were tested on material they were or were not taught.

We note that in requiring the state to prove on remand that the material was covered in class, we are not substituting our judgment for that of the state legislature on a matter of state policy. We do not question the right of the state to condition the receipt of a diploma upon the passing of a test so long as it is a fair test of that which was taught. Nor do we seek to dictate what subjects are to be taught or in what manner. We do not share appellants' fear that our decision would prevent new items from being added to the curriculum. * * *

Just as a teacher in a particular class gives the final exam on what he or she has taught, so should the state give its final exam on what has been taught in its classrooms.

Criterion—related validity—measurements of how well the test items predict the future performance of the test takers and how well the test results correlate with other criteria which might provide the same type of information.

content validity—measurements of how well a test measures a representative sample of behaviors in the universe of situations the test is intended to represent.

construct validity—how well the test measures the construct (defined as the theoretical idea developed to explain and organize some aspects of existing knowledge) for which it was designed.

For an excellent discussion of the APA Standards as they relate to competency testing, see M.S. McClung, *Competency Testing Programs: Legal and Educational Issues*, 47 Fordham L. Rev. 651, 683 (1979).

It follows that if the test is found to be invalid for the reason that it tests matters outside the curriculum, its continued use would violate the Equal Protection Clause. In analyzing the constitutionality of the examination under the Equal Protection Clause, the trial court stated, "[i]f the test by dividing students into two categories, passers and failers, did so without a rational relation to the purpose for which it was designed, then the Court would be compelled to find the test unconstitutional." Analyzing the test from the viewpoint of its objectives, the court found that it does have adequate construct validity, that is, it does test functional literacy as defined by the Board.[13] We accept this finding and affirm that part of the trial court's opinion holding that having a functional literacy examination bears a rational relation to a valid state interest. That finding is, however, subject to a further finding on remand that the test is a fair test of that which was taught. If the test is not fair, it cannot be said to be rationally related to a state interest.

* * *

CONCLUSION

* * * We hold * * *that the State may not deprive its high school seniors of the economic and educational benefits of a high school diploma until it has demonstrated that the SSAT II is a fair test of that which is taught in its classrooms and that the racially discriminatory impact is not due to the educational deprivation in the "dual school" years.

* * *

Notes

1. In general, testing instruments and practices have been successfully challenged under one or more of the following theories: perpetuating racial segregation, lack of test validity, cultural/linguistic bias; and gender bias.

Perpetuating Segregation. Several cases have discussed the relationship between ability grouping, standardized testing, tracking, and racial segregation. In determining whether tracking and ability grouping practices are constitutional, the courts have looked at several key factors:

(1) the methods of assessment and evaluation that the schools rely upon when making placement decisions;

(2) the extent to which these placement decisions are reassessed on a regular basis;

(3) how often the students actually change groups or move into different tracks if such changes are warranted; and

(4) whether a disproportionate number of minority students are placed in the lower groups or tracks. *Georgia State Conference of Branches of NAACP v. Georgia,* 775 F.2d 1403, 1409–1412, 1417–1420 (11th

---

13. Functional literacy is defined as "the ability to apply basic skills in reading, writing, and arithmetic to problems and tasks of a practical nature as encountered in everyday life."

Cir. 1985). *See generally* Note, *Teaching Inequality: The Problem of Public School Tracking* 102 Harv. L. Rev. 1318, 1323–1326 (1989).

The critical message from tracking cases is that the courts will not allow educators to perpetuate or promote racial segregation. A disproportionate number of minority students in the lower groups is not, in and of itself, unconstitutional. However, if this disproportionate placement is the result of questionable assessment techniques, if student performance is not carefully monitored, and if movement between groups does not occur on a regular basis, educators will have difficulty justifying their actions. Assessment practices, then, must not exclude or segregate children because of race, ethnicity, or national origin.

Test Validity. A fundamental educational principle in the area of testing is that a test should measure what it is supposed to measure: i.e., that the test should be "valid." It follows, then, that tests of educational progress should be accurate measures of what a child is actually learning. Where test validity is shown to be lacking, and where the result of failing to pass the test has major implications for the student's life, the test is subject to being challenged on due process grounds. Where the test has a disproportionate impact upon a particular racial or ethnic group, the test can be challenged on equal protection grounds as well.

In *Debra P. v. Turlington,* plaintiffs successfully challenged the Florida minimum competency testing program by focusing on the validity of the test instrument itself. An injunction was issued prohibiting further use of the exam until the state could show that the schools were teaching the material that was included in the exam.

Cultural/Linguistic Bias. Latino students in many school districts in California were overrepresented in special education classes in the 1960s. This led to a class action lawsuit in 1970 by nine elementary school pupils against the State of California—*Diana v. State Board of Education.* They alleged that they had been misdiagnosed as mentally retarded on the basis of biased and invalid intelligence tests (the Stanford–Binet and Wechsler Intelligence Scale for Children–Revised [WISC–R]). These misdiagnoses, they claimed, resulted in adverse stigma and irreparable educational harm.

The bias charge was based upon two contentions. First, the tests were not administered in the children's first language (Spanish). Second, the tests were culturally biased because they did not take into account the students' Mexican, rural, and migrant background. Apparently recognizing the validity of at least a portion of these assertions, the State Board settled out of court in 1974. *Diana v. State Board of Education, et al.,* No. C–70–37.

A year later, the Education for All Handicapped Children Act, Public Law 94–142, was passed by Congress. Consistent with the *Diana* settlement, the Act provides that testing and evaluation materials must 1) be racially and culturally nondiscriminatory and 2) be "administered in the child's native language or mode of communication, unless it is clearly not feasible to do so."

In another case, *Larry P. v. Riles,* African–American students successfully challenged the use of intelligence tests for the purpose of special education placements. After concluding that these tests were indeed culturally biased, the court ruled that school districts are prohibited from administering standardized intelligence tests to African–American students with regard to special education eligibility or placement in special day classes for the educable mentally retarded (E.M.R.).

In situations where students of racial and ethnic diversity are inappropriately placed or overrepresented in special education, a successful challenge to current testing practices could be based upon the *Diana* and *Larry P.* cases. Expert testimony would be used to demonstrate that a particular test was culturally biased. A court would then be asked to conclude that, under the rationale of the *Diana* settlement and *Larry P.* decision, any administration of a culturally-biased test to a racial or ethnic minority group for the purposes of educational placement would violate the law.

Gender Bias. In 1989, a federal district court in New York State found that the Scholastic Aptitude Test (SAT) was biased on the basis of gender. It held that New York may not determine the winners of its Empire & Regents Scholarship Awards by relying solely on SAT scores. "After a careful review of the evidence," the court declared in *Sharif v. N.Y. State Education Department,* "SAT scores capture a student's academic achievement no more than a student's yearbook photograph captures the full range of her experiences in high school."

Adapted from Allan H. Keown & Stuart Biegel, *General Legal Principles Involving Challenges to Standardized Tests,* Ca. State Dep't of Ed. Legal Advisory LO: 2–92 (Nov. 30, 1992).

C. INTERSCHOLASTIC AND INTERCOL-LEGIATE ATHLETICS GENERALLY

PROBLEM 25: School Sports, Testing, and Related Academic Issues

Consider the following hypotheticals, all taking place at public educational institutions in the fictional state of Columbia.

A. The Marine Valley Interscholastic Federation adopts a policy whereby no student in any Marine Valley school is eligible to participate in interscholastic athletics unless he or she scores in the "basic" or above category in every subject on the Columbia Standards Test. Plaintiff, after obtaining proof that much of the material on the test is not covered in class, files a lawsuit challenging the policy under principles articulated in *Debra P. v. Turlington.*

B. The University of Catalina Ridge adopts a policy whereby no student may participate in intercollegiate athletics unless he or she scores at least 1000 on the SAT. A group of female students file a lawsuit challenging the policy under principles articulated in gender equity cases, statutes, and regulations.

C. A student athlete at the University of Vernal Falls becomes ineligible to participate after failing introductory psychology. After obtaining proof that 7 of the 100 questions on the multiple choice final tested material that was neither in the readings nor covered in class, he files a lawsuit seeking relief under a variety of legal theories.

What arguments will plaintiffs set forth? What result? Discuss.

1. EQUAL EDUCATIONAL OPPORTUNITY ISSUES IN SCHOOL SPORTS

STEFFES v. CALIFORNIA INTERSCHOLASTIC FED'N

176 Cal.App.3d 739, 222 Cal.Rptr. 355 (1986).

ARABIAN, ASSOCIATE JUSTICE.

INTRODUCTION

The principal question in this case of first impression is whether, under the California Constitution, the right to participate in interscholastic athletics is a "fundamental right."

FACTS

Plaintiff and appellant, Kent Conrad Steffes * * * appeals from an order of the trial court denying his petition for a preliminary injunction to restrain defendants * * * from enforcing a California Interscholastic Federation (CIF) rule under which Steffes was declared ineligible to participate in varsity level competition in basketball and volleyball at Palisades High School (Pali High) during the 1984–1985 academic year.

Defendant CIF is a statewide organization that was established to enact and enforce rules and regulations governing secondary school interscholastic athletics in the state of California. Defendant CIF, Los Angeles City Section, is a division of CIF with responsibility for administering interscholastic athletics in the Los Angeles City School District. * * *

Steffes spent his freshman and sophomore years at Brentwood School. During his sophomore year (the 1983–1984 academic year), Steffes participated in junior varsity cross-country and varsity basketball and volleyball. At the end of his sophomore year, Steffes' parents decided to transfer him to Pali High, the public high school for the area in which the Steffes' family home is located. Steffes was not encouraged nor recruited for athletics by any of the personnel at Pali High.

Since Steffes transferred from Brentwood School to Pali High without a change of his parents' residence, CIF rule 214 (Rule 214) rendered him ineligible to participate in varsity athletics for one calendar year after his transfer.

* * *

According to Thomas E. Byrnes, Commissioner of the CIF, the purpose of Rule 214 is to "eliminate or minimize recruiting and school shopping."

Steffes filed an "Application for Residential Eligibility Form 214" with the CIF Los Angeles City Section to obtain a waiver of his ineligibility to participate in varsity level athletics at Pali High. In the application, Steffes stated that he had not been influenced to transfer schools for recruitment reasons. Despite this fact, the principal at Brentwood, Hunter M. Temple, declined to approve unrestricted athletic eligibility for Steffes. In a letter to Jim Cheffers, the Los Angeles City Section Director of Athletics for CIF, Mr. Temple stated that he supported the Rule 214 restriction because "a coherent athletic program can only be achieved if students complete [their] program here [at Brentwood School]."

* * *

CONTENTIONS

1. The trial court erred in applying the "rational basis" test, rather than the "strict scrutiny" test, to review Rule 214 because, under the California Constitution, the fundamental right to a public school education includes the right to participate in interscholastic athletics.

a. Rule 214 impermissibly deprives Steffes of his fundamental right to participate in extracurricular activities offered by a public school.

* * *

DISCUSSION

* * *

II. *The trial court did not err in applying the "rational basis" test to determine whether Rule 214 violates the equal protection guarantee of the California Constitution, because the right to participate in interscholastic athletics is not a fundamental right requiring "strict scrutiny."*

Steffes contends the trial court erred in denying his request for a preliminary injunction because it applied the "rational basis" test to determine whether Rule 214 violates the equal protection guarantee of the California Constitution. He argues the trial court should have applied the "strict scrutiny" standard of review, because the fundamental right to a public school education, which is guaranteed by the California Constitution, includes the right to participate in interscholastic athletics.

We note initially that, inasmuch as CIF is an organization with responsibility for administering interscholastic athletics in all California secondary schools the enforcement of its rules constitutes "state action" for purposes of constitutional analysis.

* * *

* * * The strict scrutiny test for which Steffes argues applies only in cases involving "suspect classifications" or touching on "fundamental rights."

The right to public education is a fundamental right under the California Constitution. In *Hartzell v. Connell*, the California Supreme Court had the opportunity to address the question whether extracurricular activities are encompassed within the *Serrano* concept of education as a fundamental right but, it did not do so.[3] Instead, the Court simply held that "all educational activities—curricular or 'extracurricular'—offered to students by school districts fall within the free school guarantee of article IX, section 5 [of the California Constitution]."

The *Hartzell* Court recognized that extracurricular activities (which would include interscholastic sports) constitute "an integral component of public education" and are " 'generally recognized as a fundamental ingredient of the educational process.' " However, the *Hartzell* majority never concluded that extracurricular activities are encompassed within the *Serrano* concept of education as a "fundamental right."

Therefore, the question whether participation in interscholastic athletics involves a fundamental right requiring strict judicial scrutiny is an issue of first impression in California. However, other state and federal courts have recently addressed the issue.

In a number of these decisions, the courts have concluded that the right to participate in interscholastic athletics is not a fundamental right because, under the *federal constitution*, even the right to education itself is not a "fundamental right" which requires strict judicial scrutiny. (*See, e.g., San Antonio Independent School District v. Rodriguez* (1973) 411 U.S. 1, 29–39, 93 S. Ct. 1278, 1295–1300, * * *.) Other courts, based on a procedural due process analysis, have rejected the notion that participation in interscholastic athletics is a property right.

To the extent these other courts rely for their rationale on the federal constitution (or state constitutions which provide education is not a fundamental right), they are not directly in point. That is so because, under the California Constitution, public education is itself a fundamental right requiring strict judicial scrutiny, while public education is not a fundamental right under the federal constitution (see *San Antonio Independent School District v. Rodriguez, supra,* 411 U.S. 1, 29–39, 93 S. Ct. 1278, 1295–1300).

However, the fact that public education is a fundamental right under the California Constitution does not compel a finding that in California the right to participate in interscholastic athletics is also a fundamental right entitled to the highest degree of constitutional protection. Therefore, we hold that an equal protection challenge involving

3. However, Chief Justice Bird, the author of the majority opinion, in a separate concurring opinion, stated: "[E]xtracurricular activities—like their credit-generating counterparts—promote the constitutionally recognized purposes of public education. Accordingly, they are encompassed within the concept of *education as a fundamental interest.*" (emphasis added).

that right is properly tested by the rational basis standard, rather than by the strict scrutiny standard of judicial review.

* * *

CONCLUSION

The rules, regulations and procedures discussed herein, as they relate to the interscholastic athletic transfer rule, are prophylactic in nature, reasonable in scope and rationally based. As such, they neither trammel upon fundamental rights nor occasion unnecessary burdens.

Curtailment or reduction of the abuses and transgressions which threaten to undermine student athletics are salutory goals which preserve equity between schools and protect the integrity of extracurricular programs.

DISPOSITION

The order of the trial court denying the preliminary injunction is affirmed.

Note

1. In *Young v. Montgomery County Board of Education,* 922 F.Supp. 544 (M.D. Ala. 1996), plaintiffs challenged a 1995 policy requiring student athletes to sit out a year of eligibility if they transfer to "a school for which they are not otherwise zoned" under a special "Majority-to-Minority Transfer Program." Plaintiffs, all of whom were black students negatively impacted by the policy, argued that they were discriminated against under both the Fourteenth Amendment Equal Protection Clause and Title VI of the Civil Rights Act of 1964. While the court acknowledged that the school board members knew that the policy "would disparately impact black student athletes, their knowledge of the disparate impact is not enough to prove that they intended to discriminate based on race, especially in light of their clear intent to benefit the predominantly black schools of W. Montgomery." The court held for the defendants.

WASHINGTON v. INDIANA HIGH SCH. ATHLETIC ASS'N, INC.

181 F.3d 840 (7th Cir. 1999).

RIPPLE, CIRCUIT JUDGE.

Eric Washington and Central Catholic High School obtained a preliminary injunction in the district court enjoining the Indiana High School Athletic Association ("IHSAA") from denying Mr. Washington athletic eligibility for the second semester of the 1998–99 school year. The IHSAA appeals. We affirm the district court's decision to grant the preliminary injunction.

I

BACKGROUND

A. Facts

Mr. Washington is a learning disabled student at Central Catholic High School ("Central Catholic") in Lafayette, Indiana. Throughout elementary school, he had been allowed to advance to the next grade despite academic insufficiency. He was held back, however, in the eighth grade. During the first semester of the 1994–95 academic year, while he was repeating the eighth grade, he continued to receive failing grades. School officials then decided that he might do better if he stayed with his class, and they therefore advanced him to the ninth grade at Lafayette Jefferson High School at the beginning of the second semester during the 1994–95 academic year. In this new environment, Mr. Washington continued to fail during that semester and throughout the following academic year. Early in the 1996–97 academic year, a school counselor suggested that Mr. Washington drop out of high school. Mr. Washington took that advice.

In the summer of 1997, Mr. Washington * * * met the coach of the Central Catholic basketball team, Chad Dunwoody * * * and decided to attend Central Catholic * * * and play basketball. Mr. Dunwoody, who also became Mr. Washington's academic mentor at Central Catholic, suggested that Mr. Washington be tested for learning disabilities. Although Mr. Washington had previously been tested and found not to be learning disabled, a January 1998 test indicated that he was in fact learning disabled.

The IHSAA has a rule that limits a student's athletic eligibility to the first eight semesters following the student's commencement of the ninth grade ("the eight semester rule"). The purposes of that rule, according to the IHSAA, include discouraging redshirting, promoting competitive equality, protecting students' safety, creating opportunities for younger students and promoting the idea that academics are more important than athletics. Under the rule in question, because Mr. Washington entered the ninth grade during the second semester of the 1994–95 academic year, he would no longer be eligible to play basketball in the second semester of the 1998–99 year (nine semesters after he began the ninth grade).

Central Catholic applied for a waiver of the eight semester rule for Mr. Washington. It requested that the IHSAA not count the semesters that he was not enrolled in any high school for purposes of eligibility under the eight semester rule. It requested a waiver under IHSAA Rule C12–3, which allows an exemption "if a student is injured which necessitates the student's complete withdrawal from the school or prohibits enrollment in the school for that semester, and the student does not receive any academic credit for that semester." Central Catholic also requested a waiver under IHSAA Rule 17–8, referred to by the parties as "the hardship rule." That rule allows the IHSAA not to enforce a rule if strict enforcement in the particular case would not serve to accomplish the purpose of the rule, the spirit of the rule would not be violated, and there is a showing of undue hardship in the particular case. Even though it had granted waivers for physical injuries in the past, the IHSAA denied Mr. Washington's application. Mr. Washington appealed the denial to the IHSAA Executive Committee, which denied the appeal.

* * * [Our] focus is exclusively on the eight semester rule; it is challenged on the ground that failure to grant a waiver of the eight semester rule in this case violates Title II of the Americans with Disabilities Act, 42 U.S.C. § 12132.

* * *

II

DISCUSSION

* * *

To receive protection under Title II of the ADA, the plaintiffs must establish that the IHSAA rendered Mr. Washington ineligible to play "by reason of" his disability.[8] The IHSAA contends that Mr. Washington has not presented any evidence that the IHSAA discriminated intentionally on the basis of disability. It further submits that Mr. Washington's ineligibility stems not from his disability but from the application of a facially neutral eight semester rule and the passage of time. In reply, the plaintiffs contend that they need not prove intentional discrimination. They further submit that they must show only that, but for Mr. Washington's disability, he would be eligible.

We cannot accept the suggestion that liability under Title II of the Discrimination Act must be premised on an intent to discriminate on the basis of disability. This court previously has recognized that a plaintiff making a claim under the Rehabilitation Act need not prove an impermissible intent. As we have noted, this and other circuits interpret § 504 of the Rehabilitation Act and Title II of the ADA as coextensive, except for differences not relevant here. Although the Supreme Court has not held squarely that a plaintiff need not prove discriminatory intent, it has implied that requiring such proof would be contrary to the intent of Congress. In *Choate,* the Court indicated that there is strong support in the legislative history for the proposition that the Rehabilitation Act was not intended to prohibit solely intentional discrimination. "Discrimination against the handicapped was perceived by Congress to be most often the product, not of invidious animus, but rather of thoughtlessness and indifference—of benign neglect." The Court also noted that "much of the conduct that Congress sought to alter in passing the Rehabilitation Act would be difficult if not impossible to reach were the Act construed

---

8. Title II of the ADA provides: Subject to the provisions of this subchapter, no qualified individual with a disability shall, by reason of such disability, be excluded from participation in or be denied the bene-fits of the services, programs, or activities of a public entity, or be subjected to discrimination by any such entity. 42 U.S.C. § 12132 (1999).

to proscribe only conduct fueled by a discriminatory intent." Moreover, the other circuits that have considered the issue have taken the view that a plaintiff need not prove an impermissible intent under § 504 of the Rehabilitation Act and Title II of the ADA.

* * *

The approach the Sixth Circuit has taken, and the approach we take, does not completely do away with a discrimination requirement. We simply hold that it is possible to demonstrate discrimination on the basis of disability by a defendant's refusal to make a reasonable accommodation. Therefore, we conclude that the plaintiffs need not prove that the IHSAA intended to discriminate on the basis of disability. The statute simply requires that the plaintiffs establish that the defendant's refusal to grant Mr. Washington a waiver was a failure to make a reasonable accommodation. * * *

We believe * * * that Mr. Washington has met the causation requirement for his claims. The "by reason of" language merely indicates that he must establish that, but for his learning disability, he would have been eligible to play sports in his junior year. Simply stated, Mr. Washington claims that his disability caused him to drop out of school; otherwise he would have been able to play high school basketball. In the absence of his disability, the passage of time would not have made him ineligible. There is ample record evidence to support Mr. Washington's claim. Mark Zello, a school psychologist, testified at the preliminary injunction hearing. He stated that Mr. Washington's learning disability caused him to fail at school, and that students with learning disabilities like Mr. Washington's have a high drop-out rate. Moreover, Zello testified that Mr. Washington has above average intelligence and, without the learning disability, would be fully capable of performing in high school. Under these circumstances, the district court was justified in concluding that, but for Mr. Washington's learning disability, he would not have dropped out of school.

* * *

* * * [W]aiver of the rule in Mr. Washington's case does not indicate that athletics is valued over education. Indeed, waiver of the rule in Mr. Washington's case has promoted his education. Mr. Washington has reentered school because of basketball, has improved his grades in part due to the influence of basketball and his coach, and is even considering going to college.

* * *

[W]e affirm the judgment of the district court.

PROBLEM 26: Cooper v. Clarion Unified School District (CUSD)

The following events take place in the fictional state of Valhalla.

By the time he was in kindergarten, it was apparent to all who knew him that Kevin Cooper would be a gifted athlete. Basketball soon became his favorite sport, particularly since he was always so much taller than most of his peers.

Kevin, an African–American student, grew up in the city of Clarion, which was served by a large urban public school district. All the CUSD secondary schools grouped students by ability in two subject areas: English and Mathematics.

Throughout his elementary and junior high years, Kevin was encouraged by the educators in his life to build his athletic skills. Basketball was seen as his future livelihood, his "ticket out of the ghetto." Thus, although Kevin was a bright young man, he put very little effort into his academic subjects.

Indeed, at Clarion High, the coaching staff had identified a "preferred program" for top student athletes. With the help of school counselors and administrators, many athletes were typically kept in the "remedial" English and math classes. For social studies and science, these same athletes were channeled into classes that were either taught by coaches or by teachers who were "supporters" of the athletic program and would help the students "get by."

Kevin had been placed in the remedial English and math classes when he entered middle school, and remained there until he graduated from Clarion High. He continued to receive passing grades in all his classes, typically by expending very little effort. On the basketball court, as a muscular power forward, Kevin started for the varsity team three years in a row. In his senior year, having grown to an agile 6–10, he led the school to the state championship . . . averaging 31 points and 17 rebounds a game. He was rated the top high school basketball player in the entire state of Valhalla.

Three weeks after graduation, however, Kevin was badly injured in a tragic automobile accident. His left knee was crushed, and although a series of miraculous operations enabled him to walk (albeit with a bad limp), his basketball career had ended.

Kevin enrolled in a junior college, but found that even the basic subjects were too difficult for him, and soon dropped out. With few job prospects, he faced a future that was uncertain at best.

     * * *

One day, while attending a local college basketball game, Kevin happened to be sitting next to an attorney who recognized him and remembered reading about his high school exploits. Kevin told the attorney that he was only working on an irregular basis, and spoke bitterly about his lack of preparation for junior college. During the conversation, it became apparent that Kevin knew of many other former black athletes who had pursued a similar "academic program" in the Clarion schools and had graduated with a similar level of skills.

Eventually, a class action suit was filed against the district in federal court. Not only did the former black athletes seek a mandatory injunction for themselves (i.e. additional training in basic skills), but they sought wide-ranging injunctive and declaratory relief for current black athletes in the Clarion School District.

What legal theories, identified in this chapter, might be employed on behalf of the plaintiffs? What additional facts might need to be identified before plaintiffs might have a chance of prevailing? What changes in existing law might be necessary before they could, in fact, prevail?

2. TITLE IX ISSUES IN SCHOOL SPORTS

NEAL v. BOARD OF TRUSTEES OF THE CAL. STATE UNIVS.

198 F.3d 763 (9th Cir. 1999).

CYNTHIA HOLCOMB HALL, CIRCUIT JUDGE:

The instant case requires us to consider whether Title IX prevents a university in which male students occupy a disproportionately high percentage of athletic roster spots from making gender-conscious decisions to reduce the proportion of roster spots assigned to men. We hold that Title IX does not bar such remedial actions.

* * * Neal's suit alleged that the decision of California State University, Bakersfield ("CSUB") to reduce the number of spots on its men's wrestling team, undertaken as part of a university-wide program to achieve "substantial proportionality" between each gender's participation in varsity sports and its composition in the campus's student body, violated Title IX and the Equal Protection Clause of the United States Constitution. * * *

I.

Defendant/Appellant CSUB is a large public university where female students outnumbered male students by roughly 64% to 36% in 1996. The composition of CSUB's varsity athletic rosters, however, was quite different. In the 1992–93 academic year, male students took 61% of the university's spots on athletic rosters and received 68% of CSUB's available athletic scholarship money.

This imbalance helped prompt a lawsuit by the California chapter of the National Organization for Women, alleging that the California State University system was violating a state law that is similar to the federal government's Title IX. That lawsuit eventually settled, resulting in a consent decree mandating, inter alia, that each Cal State campus have a proportion of female athletes that was within five percentage points of the proportion of female undergraduate students at that school. This portion of the consent decree was patterned after the first part of the three-part Title IX compliance test promulgated by the Department of Education's Office for Civil Rights ("OCR").

When the university agreed to the consent decree, * * * CSUB administrators were seriously constrained in what they could spend on athletic programs. The university chose to adopt squad size targets, which would encourage the expansion of the women's teams while limiting the size of the men's teams. In order to comply with the consent decree, CSUB opted for smaller men's teams across the board, rejecting the alternative of eliminating some men's teams entirely. CSUB's plan was designed to bring it into compliance with the consent decree by the 1997–98 academic year, meaning that female students would fill at least 55% of the spaces on the school's athletic teams.[1]

As part of this across-the-board reduction in the number of slots available to men's athletic teams, the size of the men's wrestling team was capped at 27. Although the reduction was protested vigorously by wrestling coach Terry Kerr, and team captain Stephen Neal expressed concerns that a smaller squad would prove less competitive, the smaller CSUB team performed exceptionally well, winning the Pac–10 Conference title and finishing third in the nation in 1996. In 1996–97, the men's wrestling roster was capped at 25, and four of these spots went unused. Nevertheless, in response to the rumored elimination of the men's wrestling team, on January 10, 1997, the team filed the instant lawsuit, alleging that the university's policy capping the size of the men's team constituted discrimination on the basis of gender in violation of Title IX and the Equal Protection Clause of the Federal Constitution.

* * *

III.

This case has its origins in Congress's passage of Title IX in 1972. Title IX was Congress's response to significant concerns about discrimination against women in education. In the words of the legislation's primary sponsor, Senator Birch Bayh, Title IX was enacted to "provide for the women of America something that is rightfully theirs—an equal chance to attend the schools of their choice, to develop the skills they want, and to apply those skills with the knowledge that they will have a fair chance to secure the jobs of their choice with equal pay for equal work."

The regulations promulgated pursuant to Title IX require schools receiving federal funding to "provide equal athletic opportunity for members of both sexes." In evaluating schools' compliance with that provision, one factor that will be considered is "whether the selection of sports and levels of competition effectively accommodate the interests and abilities of members of both sexes." At the same time, "it would require blinders to ignore that the motivation for promulgation of the regulation on athletics was the historic emphasis on boys' athletic programs to the exclusion of girls' athletic programs in ... colleges." The drafters of these regulations recognized a situation that Congress well understood: Male athletes had been given an enormous head start in the race against their female counterparts for athletic resources, and Title IX would prompt universities to level the proverbial playing field.

Appellees recognize that, given this backdrop, it would be imprudent to argue that Title IX prohibits the use of all gender-conscious remedies. Appellees therefore suggest that gender-conscious remedies are appropri-

---

1. This figure assumed 60% female enrollment for that year.

ate only when necessary to ensure that schools provide opportunities to males and females in proportion to their relative levels of interest in sports participation. By contrast, Appellants contend that schools may make gender-conscious decisions about sports-funding levels to correct for an imbalance between the composition of the undergraduate student body and the composition of the undergraduate student athletic participants pool. This disagreement has real significance: Men's expressed interest in participating in varsity sports is apparently higher than women's at the present time—although the "interest gap" continues to narrow—so permitting gender-conscious remedies until the proportions of students and athletes are roughly proportional gives universities more remedial freedom than permitting remedies only until expressed interest and varsity roster spots correspond.

Appellees' argument that equal opportunity is achieved when each gender's athletic participation roughly matches its interest in participating is hardly novel. Several courts of appeals have considered and rejected Appellees' approach as fundamentally inconsistent with the purpose of Title IX.

Cohen v. Brown University ("*Cohen I*")[2], was the first case to rule on the issues raised in the instant appeal. In *Cohen I*, female members of Brown's volleyball and gymnastics teams brought suit under Title IX after the university eliminated their teams. Women comprised 48% of the school's student body, but less than 37% of the athletes on campus.

The *Cohen I* court interpreted Title IX's requirements in light of the three-part test set forth in the Policy Interpretation promulgated by the Department of Health, Education, and Welfare in 1979.[3] That test is used to assess whether a school's athletic program is in compliance with Title IX. A university's athletics program is Title IX-compliant if it satisfies *one* of the following conditions:

(1) ... [I]ntercollegiate level participation opportunities for male and female students are provided in numbers substantially proportionate to their respective enrollments; or

(2) Where the members of one sex have been and are underrepresented among intercollegiate athletes, ... the institution can show a history and continuing practice of program expansion which is demonstrably responsive to the developing interest and abilities of the members of that sex; or

(3) Where the members of one sex are underrepresented among intercollegiate athletes, and the institution cannot show a continuing practice of program expansion such as that cited above, ... it can be demonstrated that the interests and abilities of the members of that sex have been fully and effectively accommodated by the present program.

2. The First Circuit numbers the *Cohen* decisions differently. Because we discuss only two opinions, we refer to them as *Cohen I* and *Cohen II*.

3. The OCR later was authorized by Congress to issue Title IX's regulations with respect to athletic opportunities.

Appellees attack only the first part of this test, which declares a university Title IX-compliant if participation levels for each gender are "substantially proportionate" to their representation in the student body.

The *Cohen I* court explicitly rejected Brown's argument that, because male athletes were more interested in athletics, the school could bring itself into Title IX compliance by providing females with fewer athletic roster spots "as long as the school's response is in direct proportion to the comparative levels of interest." In *Cohen II*, the rejection of Brown's argument was even more emphatic: "Brown's relative interests approach cannot withstand scrutiny on either legal or policy grounds, because it disadvantages women and undermines the remedial purposes of Title IX by limiting required program expansion for the underrepresented sex to the status quo level of relative interests."

Under *Cohen I*, if a university wanted to comply with the first part of the three-part test, it had to provide "athletics opportunities in proportion to the gender composition of the student body," not in proportion to the expressed interests of men and women.

* * *

Title IX is a dynamic statute, not a static one. It envisions continuing progress toward the goal of equal opportunity for all athletes and recognizes that, where society has conditioned women to expect less than their fair share of the athletic opportunities, women's interest in participating in sports will not rise to a par with men's overnight. The percentage of college athletes who are women rose from 15% in 1972 to 37% in 1998, and Title IX is at least partially responsible for this trend of increased participation by women. Title IX has altered women's preferences, making them more interested in sports, and more likely to become student athletes. Adopting Appellees' interest-based test for Title IX compliance would hinder, and quite possibly reverse, the steady increases in women's participation and interest in sports that have followed Title IX's enactment.

A number of courts of appeals have addressed another potentially dispositive issue in this appeal—namely, whether Title IX permits a university to diminish athletic opportunities available to men so as to bring them into line with the lower athletic opportunities available to women. Every court, in construing the Policy Interpretation and the text of Title IX, has held that a university may bring itself into Title IX compliance by increasing athletic opportunities for the underrepresented gender (women in this case) *or* by decreasing athletic opportunities for the overrepresented gender (men in this case). An extensive survey of Title IX's legislative history and the regulations promulgated to apply its provisions to college athletics concluded that boosters of male sports argued vociferously before Congress that the proposed regulations would require schools to shift resources from men's programs to women's programs, but that Congress nevertheless sided "with women's advocates" by deciding not to repeal the HEW's athletics-related Title IX regulations. Congress thus appears to have believed that Title IX would result in funding reductions to male athletic programs. If a university wishes to comply with Title IX by leveling down programs instead of ratcheting them up, as Appellant has done here, Title IX is not offended.

* * *

Finally, the district court below rejected the interpretation of Title IX advocated by the OCR and Appellants on the ground that such a reading of the statute might violate the Constitution. * * *

The First and Seventh Circuits both have considered at length the constitutionality of the first prong of the OCR's test. In *Cohen I*; *Cohen II*; and *Kelley*, the courts emphatically rejected the claim that the Policy Interpretation was unconstitutional under the Fourteenth Amendment. The separate reasoning in the two *Cohen* opinions is particularly well-developed. It applied intermediate scrutiny, which we would also do were we addressing the constitutional merits. *Cohen II* noted that the Policy Interpretation furthered the "clearly important" objectives of "avoid[ing] the use of federal resources to support discriminatory practices, and provid[ing] individual citizens effective protection against those practices." Moreover, it found that "judicial enforcement of federal anti-discrimination statutes is at least an important governmental objective." And *Cohen II* held that the district court's relief, which was essentially identical to what the OCR Policy Interpretation calls for, was "clearly substantially related" to these objectives. Along the same lines, the Seventh Circuit has held that "the remedial scheme established by Title IX and the applicable regulation and policy interpretation are clearly substantially related to" the objective of prohibiting "educational institutions from discriminating on the basis of sex." We adopt the reasoning of *Cohen I, Cohen II,* and *Kelley,* and hold that the constitutional analysis contained therein persuasively disposes of any serious constitutional concerns that might be raised in relation to the OCR Policy Interpretation. The district court's final basis for rejecting the OCR's interpretation of Title IX was therefore erroneous.

IV.

This past summer, 90,185 enthusiastic fans crowded into Pasadena's historic Rose Bowl for the finals of the Women's World Cup soccer match. An estimated 40 million television viewers also tuned in to watch a thrilling battle between the American and Chinese teams. The match ended when American defender Brandi Chastain fired the ball past Chinese goalkeeper Gao Hong, breaking a 4–4 shootout tie. The victory sparked a national celebration and a realization by many that women's sports could be just as exciting, competitive, and lucrative as men's sports. And the victorious athletes understood as well as anyone the connection between a 27–year-old statute and tangible progress in women's athletics. Title IX has enhanced, and will continue to enhance, women's opportunities to enjoy the thrill of victory, the agony of defeat, and the many tangible benefits that flow from just being given a chance to participate in intercollegiate athletics. Today we join our sister circuits in holding that Title IX does not bar universities from taking steps to ensure that women are approximately as well represented in sports programs as they are in student bodies. We REVERSE, and VACATE the preliminary injunction.

D. GENDER EQUITY IN THE EDUCATION PROCESS

As documented in the rich body of literature addressing women's issues over the past fifty years, great progress has been achieved in this area. This progress has been due, in no small part, to the tireless efforts of many members of the education community.

Yet many gender-related concerns still remain unresolved, both within educational institutions and in society as a whole.

Gender equity issues arise in many places throughout this casebook, including but not limited to the campus safety and privacy chapter, the peer harassment and mistreatment section, earlier portions of this chapter, and the religion, morality and values materials that follow in Chapters 8 and 9.

This section highlights the range of controversies in this area that relate directly to the education process. It begins with an examination of disputes regarding the separation of students on the basis of gender, focusing in particular on the landmark decision in the 1996 VMI case, *U.S. v. Virginia.* It continues by highlighting research documenting differential treatment of boys and girls in day-to-day K–12 settings, and identifying what might be done to change these realities. The section concludes by addressing transgender issues in a gender equity context.

1. SEPARATING STUDENTS ON THE BASIS OF GENDER

PROBLEM 27: Admissions and Gender

Assume that the following practices have taken place in public educational institutions, and that lawsuits are filed challenging these practices. For each hypothetical, please address two questions: (a) In general, should plaintiffs prevail? and (b) If plaintiffs allege gender discrimination under the Equal Protection Clause, would plaintiffs prevail?

A. The Eldorado County School District sets aside one of its eleven high schools as a "preferred," college-preparatory school which admits students on the basis of past academic achievement. However, female applicants are subject to more stringent admission requirements. The district argues that this practice is necessary to maintain equal numbers of boys and girls in the special school. A lawsuit is filed on behalf of female applicants who have been denied admission.

B. The Emerald City Board of Education establishes three new male academies designed to meet the special needs of the city's African American boys. These academies are designed to include an enriched educational setting, an African-centered curriculum, a "rites of passage" program to emphasize male responsibility, the use of mentors, a Saturday program, school uniforms, and special counseling. The board's decision is heavily influenced by the writings of Spencer H. Holland, director of the Center for Educating African American Males at Morgan State University in Baltimore. Mr. Holland is an originator of the concept of separate classes for minority boys taught by a man who can serve as a role model. A lawsuit is filed on behalf of two women who want to enroll their daughters in the all male academies.

C.   Responding to the concerns of community members regarding the quality of education in their public schools, the Eldorado School District turns all of the district's twenty high schools into "schools of choice." Major portions of three schools, including eighteen out of fifty-four classrooms at Susan B. Anthony High, are set aside for girls only. The decision to establish these "schools within schools" is informed by recent research. No classes are set aside for boys only, however, because similar research has revealed that although single sex high school classes benefit girls, they are not particularly advantageous for boys. Mr. and Mrs. Saticoy file a lawsuit seeking to have their two teenage sons placed in the all girls "school within a school" at Susan B. Anthony High. Among other things, the parents claim (and the district stipulates) that (a) their sons' best friends are in these classes, (b) the two boys do better in school when placed in classes with students that are primarily female, and (c) most of Anthony High's most popular teachers are now teaching in the "school within a school."

D.   In the aftermath of Proposition 209, the faculty admissions committee for the Graduate School of Computer Sciences at UC San Joaquin sets forth a revised policy for reviewing applicants. The policy focuses on only three objective indicators: GRE scores in math, undergraduate GPA in math and science courses, and overall undergraduate GPA. Plaintiffs seeking to modify the new policy contend that such an undue and inappropriate emphasis on math and science performance inevitably favors male applicants.

UNITED STATES v. VIRGINIA

518 U.S. 515, 116 S.Ct. 2264 (1996).

JUSTICE GINSBURG delivered the opinion of the Court.

Virginia's public institutions of higher learning include an incomparable military college, Virginia Military Institute (VMI). The United States maintains that the Constitution's equal protection guarantee precludes Virginia from reserving exclusively to men the unique educational opportunities VMI affords. We agree.

I

Founded in 1839, VMI is today the sole single-sex school among Virginia's 15 public institutions of higher learning. VMI's distinctive mission is to produce "citizen-soldiers," men prepared for leadership in civilian life and in military service. VMI pursues this mission through pervasive training of a kind not available anywhere else in Virginia. Assigning prime place to character development, VMI uses an "adversative method" modeled on English public schools and once characteristic of military instruction. VMI constantly endeavors to instill physical and mental discipline in its cadets and impart to them a strong moral code. The school's graduates leave VMI with heightened comprehension of their capacity to deal with duress and stress, and a large sense of accomplishment for completing the hazardous course.

VMI has notably succeeded in its mission to produce leaders; among its alumni are military generals, Members of Congress, and business executives. The school's alumni overwhelmingly perceive that their VMI training helped them to realize their personal goals. VMI's endowment reflects the loyalty of its graduates; VMI has the largest per-student endowment of all public undergraduate institutions in the Nation.

Neither the goal of producing citizen-soldiers nor VMI's implementing methodology is inherently unsuitable to women. And the school's impressive record in producing leaders has made admission desirable to some women. Nevertheless, Virginia has elected to preserve exclusively for men the advantages and opportunities a VMI education affords.

II

* * *[2]

VMI attracts some applicants because of its reputation as an extraordinarily challenging military school, and "because its alumni are exceptionally close to the school." "[W]omen have no opportunity anywhere to gain the benefits of [the system of education at VMI]."

B

In 1990, prompted by a complaint filed with the Attorney General by a female high-school student seeking admission to VMI, the United States sued the Commonwealth of Virginia and VMI, alleging that VMI's exclusively male admission policy violated the Equal Protection Clause of the Fourteenth Amendment. * * *

The District Court ruled in favor of VMI, however, and rejected the equal protection challenge pressed by the United States. That court correctly recognized that *Mississippi Univ. for Women v. Hogan* was the closest guide. There, this Court underscored that a party seeking to uphold government action based on sex must establish an "exceedingly persuasive justification" for the classification. To succeed, the defender of the challenged action must show "at least that the classification serves important governmental objectives and that the discriminatory means employed are substantially related to the achievement of those objectives."

2. Historically, most of Virginia's public colleges and universities were single sex; by the mid–1970's, however, all except VMI had become coeducational.

The District Court reasoned that education in "a single-gender environment, be it male or female," yields substantial benefits. VMI's school for men brought diversity to an otherwise coeducational Virginia system, and that diversity was "enhanced by VMI's unique method of instruction." If single-gender education for males ranks as an important governmental objective, it becomes obvious, the District Court concluded, that the *only* means of achieving the objective "is to exclude women from the all-male institution—VMI."

* * *

The Court of Appeals for the Fourth Circuit disagreed and vacated the District Court's judgment. The appellate court held: "The Commonwealth of Virginia has not . . . advanced any state policy by which it can justify its determination, under an announced policy of diversity, to afford VMI's unique type of program to men and not to women."

* * *

* * * The Court of Appeals, however, accepted the District Court's finding that "at least these three aspects of VMI's program—physical training, the absence of privacy, and the adversative approach—would be materially affected by coeducation." Remanding the case, the appeals court assigned to Virginia, in the first instance, responsibility for selecting a remedial course. The court suggested these options for the Commonwealth: Admit women to VMI; establish parallel institutions or programs; or abandon state support, leaving VMI free to pursue its policies as a private institution.

C

In response to the Fourth Circuit's ruling, Virginia proposed a parallel program for women: Virginia Women's Institute for Leadership (VWIL). The 4–year, state-sponsored undergraduate program would be located at Mary Baldwin College, a private liberal arts school for women, and would be open, initially, to about 25 to 30 students. Although VWIL would share VMI's mission—to produce "citizen-soldiers"—the VWIL program would differ, as does Mary Baldwin College, from VMI in academic offerings, methods of education, and financial resources.

The average combined SAT score of entrants at Mary Baldwin is about 100 points lower than the score for VMI freshmen. Mary Baldwin's faculty holds "significantly fewer Ph.D.'s than the faculty at VMI," and receives significantly lower salaries. While VMI offers degrees in liberal arts, the sciences, and engineering, Mary Baldwin, at the time of trial, offered only bachelor of arts degrees. A VWIL student seeking to earn an engineering degree could gain one, without public support, by attending Washington University in St. Louis, Missouri, for two years, paying the required private tuition.

Experts in educating women at the college level composed the Task Force charged with designing the VWIL program; Task Force members were drawn from Mary Baldwin's own faculty and staff. Training its attention on methods of instruction appropriate for "most women," the Task Force determined that a military model would be "wholly inappropriate" for VWIL.

VWIL students would participate in ROTC programs and a newly established, "largely ceremonial" Virginia Corps of Cadets, but the VWIL House would not have a military format, and VWIL would not require its students to eat meals together or to wear uniforms during the schoolday. In lieu of VMI's adversative method, the VWIL Task Force favored "a cooperative method which reinforces self-esteem." In addition to the standard bachelor of arts program offered at Mary Baldwin, VWIL students would take courses in leadership, complete an off-campus leadership externship, participate in community service projects, and assist in arranging a speaker series.

* * *

D

Virginia returned to the District Court seeking approval of its proposed remedial plan, and the court decided the plan met the requirements of the Equal Protection Clause. The District Court again acknowledged evidentiary support for these determinations: "[T]he VMI methodology could be used to educate women and, in fact, some women ... may prefer the VMI methodology to the VWIL methodology." But the "controlling legal principles," the District Court decided, "do not require the Commonwealth to provide a mirror image VMI for women." The court anticipated that the two schools would "achieve substantially similar outcomes." It concluded: "If VMI marches to the beat of a drum, then Mary Baldwin marches to the melody of a fife and when the march is over, both will have arrived at the same destination."

A divided Court of Appeals affirmed the District Court's judgment.

* * *

III

The cross-petitions in this suit present two ultimate issues. First, does Virginia's exclusion of women from the educational opportunities provided by VMI—extraordinary opportunities for military training and civilian leadership development—deny to women "capable of all of the individual activities required of VMI cadets," the equal protection of the laws guaranteed by the Fourteenth Amendment? Second, if VMI's "unique" situation,—as Virginia's sole single-sex public institution of higher education—offends the Constitution's equal protection principle, what is the remedial requirement?

IV

We note, once again, the core instruction of this Court's pathmarking decisions in *J.E.B. v. Alabama ex rel. T. B.* and *Mississippi Univ. for Women*: Parties who seek to defend gender-based government action must demonstrate an "exceedingly persuasive justification" for that action.

Today's skeptical scrutiny of official action denying rights or opportunities based on sex responds to volumes of history. As a plurality of this Court acknowledged a generation ago, "our Nation has had a long and unfortunate history of sex discrimination." Through a century plus three decades and more of that history, women did not count among voters composing "We the People"; not until 1920 did women gain a constitutional right to the franchise. And for a half century thereafter, it remained the prevailing doctrine that government, both federal and state, could withhold from women opportunities accorded men so long as any "basis in reason" could be conceived for the discrimination. * * *

In 1971, for the first time in our Nation's history, this Court ruled in favor of a woman who complained that her State had denied her the equal protection of its laws. Since *Reed,* the Court has repeatedly recognized that neither federal nor state government acts compatibly with the equal protection principle when a law or official policy denies to women, simply because they are women, full citizenship stature—equal opportunity to aspire, achieve, participate in and contribute to society based on their individual talents and capacities.

Without equating gender classifications, for all purposes, to classifications based on race or national origin, the Court, in post-*Reed* decisions, has carefully inspected official action that closes a door or denies opportunity to women (or to men). To summarize the Court's current directions for cases of official classification based on gender: Focusing on the differential treatment or denial of opportunity for which relief is sought, the reviewing court must determine whether the proffered justification is "exceedingly persuasive." The burden of justification is demanding and it rests entirely on the State. The State must show "at least that the [challenged] classification serves 'important governmental objectives and that the discriminatory means employed' are 'substantially related to the achievement of those objectives.' " The justification must be genuine, not hypothesized or invented *post hoc* in response to litigation. And it must not rely on overbroad generalizations about the different talents, capacities, or preferences of males and females.

The heightened review standard our precedent establishes does not make sex a proscribed classification. Supposed "inherent differences" are no longer accepted as a ground for race or national origin classifications. Physical differences between men and women, however, are enduring: "[T]he two sexes are not fungible; a community made up exclusively of one [sex] is different from a community composed of both."

"Inherent differences" between men and women, we have come to appreciate, remain cause for celebration, but not for denigration of the members of either sex or for artificial constraints on an individual's opportunity. Sex classifications may be used to compensate women "for particular economic disabilities [they have] suffered," to "promot[e] equal employment opportunity," to advance full development of the talent and capacities of our Nation's people.[7] But such classifications may not be used, as they once were, to create or perpetuate the legal, social, and economic inferiority of women.

Measuring the record in this case against the review standard just described, we conclude that Virginia has shown no "exceedingly persuasive justification" for excluding all women from the citizen-soldier training afforded by VMI. We therefore affirm the Fourth Circuit's initial judgment, which held that Virginia had violated the Fourteenth Amendment's Equal Protection Clause. Because the remedy proffered by Virginia—the Mary Baldwin VWIL program—does not cure the constitutional violation, *i.e.,* it does not provide equal opportunity, we reverse the Fourth Circuit's final judgment in this case.

* * *

2. DIFFERENTIAL TREATMENT IN K–12 SETTINGS

GENDER EQUITY IN THE CLASSROOM

Lynn Kepford.
NCSC News, Vol. 1, No. 6 (2002),
http://www.ncsc.info/newsletter/June_2002/gender.htm.

An equal opportunity to participate in the educational system is being denied to half of America's school-age population. Gender bias subtlety, insidiously, but indisputably denies girls equal access to instruction. This article explores the reasons underlying the problem and suggests strategies to promote gender equity.

The fact that females receive an inferior education is significant in today's society. An increase in the employment of women in all areas has been documented and this trend is expected to continue. Women will hold professional positions in ever increasing numbers. Education must prepare women for these careers. American Association of University Women (AAUW) and the Women's Education Equity Act (WEEA) Resource Center studies indicate that females continue to be shortchanged in the academic arena. Unsurprisingly, their professional and economic growth lags behind that of their male counterparts. The foundations for solutions begin in our schools.

Title IX of the Educational Amendments Act in 1972 and the reauthorization of the Elementary and Secondary Education Act have

7. Several *amici* have urged that diversity in educational opportunities is an altogether appropriate governmental pursuit and that single-sex schools can contribute importantly to such diversity. Indeed, it is the mission of some single-sex schools "to dissipate, rather than perpetuate, traditional gender classifications." We do not question the Commonwealth's prerogative evenhandedly to support diverse educational opportunities. We address specifically and only an educational opportunity recog- nized by the District Court and the Court of Appeals as "unique," an opportunity available only at Virginia's premier military institute, the Commonwealth's sole single-sex public university or college. *Cf. Mississippi Univ. for Women v. Hogan* ("Mississippi maintains no other single-sex public university or college. Thus, we are not faced with the question of whether States can provide 'separate but equal' undergraduate institutions for males and females.").

been touted as panacea to the problem of gender bias. Legislation made sexual discrimination unlawful in schools receiving government funding. Unfortunately, the laws did little to provide gender equity within the confines of the classroom. Gender bias, built upon unconscious acceptance of stereotypes and gender role expectations is still evident in today's classrooms. Sadker & Sadker in *Failing at Fairness* assert "girls enter school at a higher achievement level and leave it with a lower achievement level" [than their male counterparts]. Girls appear to be the ideal students in elementary school. They seem to be doing well. They receive better grades and are disciplined less frequently. The unfortunate result is that girls receive less—time, attention, help, encouragement, challenges, and feedback. "When female students are offered the leftovers of teacher time and attention ... they achieve less ... girls and women learn to speak softly or not at all; to submerge honest feelings, withhold opinions, and defer to boys; to avoid math and science as male domains; to value neatness and quiet more than assertiveness and creativity; to emphasize appearance and hide intelligence ... they are turned into educational spectators instead of players; but education is not a spectator sport" (Sadker & Sadker). As a result, their self-esteem, independence, motivation and academic opportunities suffer.

THE DISPARITIES

Teacher Attention

AAUW studies indicate that girls are less assertive in the classroom. They need more time to think when responding to questions. Sadly, they receive less time. Boys, on the other hand, call out 8 times more frequently than girls and are more often called upon to respond. Boys are allowed to call out answers while girls must raise their hands and be recognized before speaking. Accordingly, boys participate more in class and secure more teacher attention and feedback than their female counterparts. This need not occur. Research conducted by the AAUW and the WEEA indicates that girls become almost as assertive as boys in class when teachers receive training in gender equity.

Differential Feedback

When providing feedback educators are more likely to praise, correct, help, and criticize boys—all of which foster achievement. Boys are more likely to receive comments on the content of their work and suggestions for improvement. Conversely, girls receive more superficial communication, frequently focusing on the appearance rather than the academic content of their work. The message portrayed is that a higher level of performance is possible and expected of boys than girls. Accordingly, girls receive less valuable feedback impeding their ability to correct mistakes and leaving them unprepared for future real-life situations.

Classroom Assistance

A difference also exists when students request assistance. Boys are led through the exercise and given suggestions. They are encouraged to work through problems and finish projects. When girls need help, teachers are likely to tell them the answer or complete the project for them depriving them of active learning experiences. Teacher interaction of this type fosters dependence in girls and independence in boys. As a consequence, girls get less practice at problem solving skills than boys.

Belief Systems

Girls attribute the cause of academic failure to an internal locus of control. In other words, their failure is due to internal factors such as lack of ability or intelligence. Boys, on the other hand attribute academic failure to an external locus of control-teacher bias, illness, poor instruction, etc. When children internalize success and externalize failure (the male approach), they are able to tackle new and challenging tasks with a mastery orientation, one that perseveres in the face of difficulty and leads to future achievement. Children who attribute success to effort and failure to lack of ability (the female approach) exhibit "learned helplessness." Girls frequently downplay academic achievement or attribute it to luck. Boys take credit. Sadly, many teachers unconsciously support these erroneous beliefs.

Predictions for Success

A positive correlation exists between professional position, economic success, and success in math, science, and technology. Although males and females enter junior high school on equal footing in these areas, boys' performance begins to surpass that of their female classmates at this stage. This outcome appears to be largely a result of attitude and expectation, rather than of innate ability and can be attributed to:

- Expectations of parents and teachers.
- Science and math teachers are primarily male.
- Few women role models are furnished.
- Boys have higher expectations for themselves.

Most devastating of all is the fact that teachers are unaware of this inadvertent discrimination. They try to and honestly believe that they do treat all of their students equally regardless of sex. Research however indicates an entirely different reality. Incidents of discrimination are so subtle, that frequently, girls themselves cannot pinpoint it. The result is that females feel less intelligent and less valued and receive an inferior education than that of their male counterparts.

After reviewing the research, it is evident that half of the school-age population is receiving less than equal education. "Denied their history, discouraged from taking crucial courses that lead to key careers, concluding that the appearance of their bodies may be worth more than the quality of their minds, realizing they are not the gender of choice, and doubting their intelligence and ability ... girls make the journey from adolescence to womanhood. They pay a steep price." declare Sadker and Sadker. Females in the American educational system are achieving at levels far below their potential. This has very negative implications not only for their future, but for society's as well.

Solutions

Although this problem is sociologically based, the structures are already in place to implement solutions within the educational system. Teacher training is an ideal place to begin as research indicates that educators teach the way they were taught and they most strongly model the styles of their most recent instructors.

- Wait a few seconds after asking a question before calling on students. Girls, more than boys formulate their response prior to raising their hands.

- Assign more team projects as girls learn better through collaboration.

- Facilitate a cooperative, rather than a competitive environment, by conducting some classes with students sitting in a circle. (Girls will be more comfortable and learn better in this type of setting.)

- Provide coaching to develop problem-solving skills.

- Incorporate interdisciplinary teaching using real-world problems and hands-on projects to demonstrate the value of the learning being acquired.

- Create an environment that reduces stereotyping and helps students relate to each other as individuals.

- Praise students equally for achievement, creativity and effort.

- Attribute cause for poor performance accurately.

- Attend equally to the misbehavior of both sexes.

- Provide numerous opportunities for girls to experience science, math, and technology.

- Examine the rules (both implicit and explicit) set for girls and the underlying assumptions.

- Provide girls with more opportunities to be leaders.

- Create an environment that is safe for mistakes, not safe from mistakes.

- Encourage more outdoor and physical opportunities for girls.

- Teach girls how to assess the risk and how to insure their own safety. Offer more access to machinery and equipment.

- Let girls know that they are capable of learning math, science, and technology; and encourage them to choose these courses in high school.

- Expect females to pursue higher education.

- Select curriculum materials that equally and realistically represent both sexes.

Teachers having participated in gender-biased education throughout their academic careers, unknowingly perpetuate the cycle. It is unrealized that "little, by little, lesson by lesson, day by day [girls] are being robbed. * * * Every day in America little girls lose independence, achievement, and self-esteem * * *. Subtle and insidious, the gender biased lessons result in quiet catastrophes—tomorrow's women—are very real" according to Sadker and Sadker. Educators hold the key to the future in their hands. Tomorrow's society sits in their classrooms. Teachers must begin to consciously monitor their interactions with children to ensure that all students receive the education guaranteed them by law—*a free, appropriate, and equitable education for all*.

REFERENCES

AMERICAN ASS'N OF UNIVERSITY WOMEN, BEYOND THE "GENDER WARS": A CONVERSATION ABOUT GIRLS, BOYS, AND EDUCATION (Washington, D.C. 2001).

AMERICAN ASS'N OF UNIVERSITY WOMEN, SHORTCHANGING GIRLS, SHORT-CHANGING AMERICA: EXECUTIVE SUMMARY (Washington, D.C., 2d ed. 1994).

MYRA & DAVID SADKER, FAILING AT FAIRNESS 1–135, 251–80 (1994).

WEEA EQUITY RESOURCE CENTER, RESOURCES TO INFUSE EQUITY, http://www.edc.org/WomensEquity/equity.htm (last visited Oct. 2002).

3. LEGAL AND POLICY PERSPECTIVES ON TRANSGENDER ISSUES

DOE v. YUNITS

2000 WL 33162199 (Mass. Super. Ct. 2000).

Plaintiff Pat Doe ("plaintiff"), a fifteen-year-old student, has brought this action by her next friend, Jane Doe, requesting that this court prohibit defendants from excluding the plaintiff from South Junior High School ("South Junior High"), Brockton, Massachusetts, on the basis of the plaintiff's sex, disability, or gender identity and expression. * * * [A]lthough plaintiff was born biologically male, she has a female gender identity.[4] Plaintiff seeks to attend school wearing clothes and fashion accouterments that are consistent with her gender identity. Defendants have informed plaintiff that she could not enroll in school this academic year if she wore girls' clothes or accessories. After a hearing, and for the reasons stated below, plaintiff's motion for preliminary injunction is *ALLOWED*.

BACKGROUND

Plaintiff began attending South Junior High, a Brockton public school, in September 1998, as a 7th grader. In early 1999, plaintiff first began to express her female gender identity by wearing girls' make-up,

---

4. This court will use female pronouns to refer to plaintiff: a practice which is consistent with the plaintiff's gender identity and which is common among mental health and other professionals who work with transgender clients.

shirts, and fashion accessories to school. South Junior High has a dress code which prohibits, among other things, "clothing which could be disruptive or distractive to the educational process or which could affect the safety of students." In early 1999, the principal, Kenneth Cardone ("Cardone"), would often send the plaintiff home to change if she arrived at school wearing girls' apparel. On some occasions, plaintiff would change and return to school; other times, she would remain home, too upset to return. * * *

Plaintiff returned to school in September 1999, as an 8th grader, and was instructed by Cardone to come to his office every day so that he could approve the plaintiff's appearance. Some days the plaintiff would be sent home to change, sometimes returning to school dressed different-ly and sometimes remaining home. During the 1999–2000 school year, plaintiff stopped attending school, citing the hostile environment created by Cardone. Because of plaintiff's many absences during the 1999–2000 school year, plaintiff was required to repeat the 8th grade this year.

Over the course of the 1998–1999 and 1999–2000 school years, plaintiff sometimes arrived at school wearing such items as skirts and dresses, wigs, high-heeled shoes, and padded bras with tight shirts. The school faculty and administration became concerned because the plaintiff was experiencing trouble with some of her classmates. Defendants cite one occasion when the school adjustment counselor had to restrain a male student because he was threatening to punch the plaintiff for allegedly spreading rumors that the two had engaged in oral sex. Defendants also point to an instance when a school official had to break up a confrontation between the plaintiff and a male student to whom plaintiff persistently blew kisses. At another time, plaintiff grabbed the buttock of a male student in the school cafeteria. Plaintiff also has been known to primp, pose, apply make up, and flirt with other students in class. Defendants also advance that the plaintiff sometimes called atten-tion to herself by yelling and dancing in the halls. Plaintiff has been suspended at least three times for using the ladies' restroom after being warned not to.

On Friday, September 1, 2000, Cardone and Dr. Kenneth Sennett ("Sennett"), Senior Director for Pupil Personnel Services, met with the plaintiff relative to repeating the 8th grade. At that meeting, Cardone and Sennett informed the plaintiff that she would not be allowed to attend South Junior High if she were to wear any outfits disruptive to the educational process, specifically padded bras, skirts or dresses, or wigs. On September 21, 2000, plaintiff's grandmother tried to enroll plaintiff in school and was told by Cardone and Sennett that plaintiff would not be permitted to enroll if she wore any girls' clothing or accessories. Defendants allege that they have not barred the plaintiff from school but have merely provided limits on the type of dress the plaintiff may wear. Defendants claim it is the plaintiff's own choice not to attend school because of the guidelines they have placed on her attire. Plaintiff is not currently attending school, but the school has provided a home tutor for her to allow her to keep pace with her classmates.

On September 26, 2000, the plaintiff filed a complaint in this court claiming a denial of her right to freedom of expression in the public schools * * *.

* * * According to federal analysis, this court must first determine whether the plaintiff's symbolic acts constitute expressive speech which is protected, in this case, by Article VXI of the Massachusetts Declaration of Rights. If the speech is expressive, the court must next determine if the defendants' conduct was impermissible because it was meant to suppress that speech. If the defendants' conduct is not related to the suppression of speech, furthers an important or substantial governmental interest, and is within the constitutional powers of the government, and if the incidental restriction on speech is no greater than necessary, the government's conduct is permissible. In addition, because this case involves public school students, suppression of speech that "materially and substantially interferes with the work of the school" is permissible.

1. The Plaintiff's Conduct is Expressive Speech Which is Understood by Those Perceiving It

Symbolic acts constitute expression if the actor's intent to convey a particularized message is likely to be understood by those perceiving the message.

Plaintiff in this case is likely to establish that, by dressing in clothing and accessories traditionally associated with the female gender, she is expressing her identification with that gender. In addition, plaintiff's ability to express herself and her gender identity through dress is important to her health and well-being, as attested to by her treating therapist. Therefore, plaintiff's expression is not merely a personal preference but a necessary symbol of her very identity. Contrast *Olesen v. Board of Education of School District No. 228* (school's anti-gang policy of prohibiting males from wearing earrings, passed for safety reasons, was upheld because plaintiff's desire to wear an earring as an expression of his individuality and attractiveness to girls was a message not within the scope of the First Amendment).

This court must next determine if the plaintiff's message was understood by those perceiving it, i.e., the school faculty and plaintiff's fellow students. * * * [P]laintiff is likely to establish, through testimony, that her fellow students are well aware of the fact that she is a biological male more comfortable wearing traditionally "female"-type clothing because of her identification with that gender.

2. The Defendants' Conduct Was a Suppression of the Plaintiff's Speech

Plaintiff also will probably prevail on the merits of the second prong of the *Texas v. Johnson* test, that is, the defendants' conduct was meant to suppress plaintiff's speech. Defendants in this case have prohibited the plaintiff from wearing items of clothing that are traditionally labeled girls' clothing, such as dresses and skirts, padded bras, and wigs. This constitutes direct suppression of speech because biological females who wear items such as tight skirts to school are unlikely to be disciplined by school officials, as admitted by defendants' counsel at oral argument. * * *

3.   Plaintiff's Conduct is not Disruptive

This court also must consider if the plaintiff's speech "materially and substantially interferes with the work of the school." *Tinker v. Des Moines Community School Dist.* Defendants argue that they are merely preventing disruptive conduct on the part of the plaintiff by restricting her attire at school. Their argument is unpersuasive. Given the state of the record thus far, the plaintiff has demonstrated a likelihood of proving that defendants, rather than attempting to restrict plaintiff's wearing of distracting items of clothing, are seeking to ban her from donning apparel that can be labeled "girls' clothes" and to encourage more conventional, male-oriented attire. Defendants argue that any other student who came to school dressed in distracting clothing would be disciplined as the plaintiff was. However, defendants overlook the fact that, if a female student came to school in a frilly dress or blouse, make-up, or padded bra, she would go, and presumably has gone, unnoticed by school officials. Defendants do not find plaintiff's clothing distracting *per se,* but, essentially, distracting simply because plaintiff is a biological male.

In addition to the expression of her female gender identity through dress, however, plaintiff has engaged in behavior in class and towards other students that can be seen as detrimental to the learning process. This deportment, however, is separate from plaintiff's dress. Defendants vaguely cite instances when the principal became aware of threats by students to beat up the "boy who dressed like a girl" to support the notion that plaintiff's dress alone is disruptive. To rule in defendants' favor in this regard, however, would grant those contentious students a "heckler's veto." The majority of defendants' evidence of plaintiff's disruption is based on plaintiff's actions as distinct from her mode of dress. Some of these acts may be a further expression of gender identity, such as applying make-up in class; but many are instances of misconduct for which any student would be punished. Regardless of plaintiff's gender identity, any student should be punished for engaging in harassing behavior towards classmates. Plaintiff is not immune from such punishment but, by the same token, should not be punished on the basis of dress alone.

    * * *

III.   The Balance of the Equities

The balance of the equities tips in favor of plaintiff in his case. * * * [T]he harm to the school in readmitting plaintiff is minimal. On the other hand, if plaintiff is barred from school, the potential harm to plaintiff's sense of self-worth and social development is irreparable. Defendants cite cases that stand for the proposition that a school's interest in disciplining students by barring them from school outweigh the harm to the student. In this case, however, the school is not disciplining the plaintiff for certain conduct. The school is barring her from school on account of the expression of her very identity. Defendants maintain that plaintiff is free to enroll in school as long as she complies with the stated dress code. This is not entirely true because the defendants have placed specific restrictions on plaintiff's dress that may not be placed on other female students. This court does take note of the fact that defendants made efforts to accommodate the plaintiff's desire to dress in girl's clothes for over a year. However, their proscription of the items of clothing that can be worn by plaintiff is likely to be impermissible. Therefore, the harm to plaintiff by the actions of the defendants outweigh the harm to the defendants in granting this injunction.

IV.   The Harm to the Public Interest

Defendants have not made a showing that the granting of this injunction will harm the public interest. Although defendants contend that plaintiff's dress is disruptive to the learning process, the workings of the school will not be disrupted if they are permitted to discipline plaintiff according to normal procedures for truly disruptive attire and inappropriate behavior. Furthermore, this court trusts that exposing children to diversity at an early age serves the important social goals of increasing their ability to tolerate such differences and teaching them respect for everyone's unique personal experience in that "Brave New World" out there.

* * *

For all the foregoing reasons, plaintiff's motion for preliminary injunction is *ALLOWED* * * *.

Notes

1.   For a noteworthy overview of challenges facing transgender youth, and indeed transgender persons in general, when they seek protection via the legal system, *see generally* Paisley Currah & Shannon Minter, *Unprincipled Exclusions: The Struggle to Achieve Judicial and Legislative Equality for Transgender People,* 7 Wm. & Mary J. Women & L. 37 (2000).

2.   In May 2001, the plaintiff in the *Yunits* case reached a settlement agreement with the school department which would allow her to wear "girls clothing" to school the following fall. Brockton, Massachusetts Mayor John Yunits was quoted as saying that "I think in the end there was a certain realization that the continued litigation wasn't in the student's best interests." Associated Press, *School, Transgender Student Reach Agreement,* May 17, 2001.

3.   California law requires that all public school districts develop and implement policies to protect transgender youth. The San Francisco Unified School District, in early 2004, became the first District in the state to comply.

Consider the parameters of the San Francisco policy, set forth below. What additional steps might be taken at the individual school site level to maximize its effectiveness? What changes in the policy, if any, might you suggest?

The SFUSD Policy on Transgender Youth (2004)

ARTICLE 5: STUDENTS

SECTION: Non–Discrimination for Students and Employees

This regulation is meant to advise school site staff and administration regarding transgender and gender non-conforming student concerns in order to create a safe learning environment for all students, and to ensure that every student has equal access to all components of their educational program.

California Law Prohibits Gender–Based Discrimination in Public Schools

The California Education Code states that "all pupils have the right to participate fully in the educational process, free from discrimination and harassment." Cal. Ed. Code § 201(a). Section 220 of the Education Code provides that no person shall be subject to discrimination on the basis of gender in any program or activity conducted by an educational institution that receives or benefits from state financial assistance. The Code further provides that public schools have an affirmative obligation to combat sexism and other forms of bias, and a responsibility to provide equal educational opportunity to all pupils. Cal. Ed. Code § 201(b).

The California Code of Regulations similarly provides that "No person shall be excluded from participation in or denied the benefits of any local agency's program or activity on the basis of sex, sexual orientation, gender, ethnic group identification, race, ancestry, national origin, religion, color, or mental or physical disability in any program or activity conducted by an 'educational institution' or any other 'local agency' . . . that receives or benefits from any state financial assistance." 5 CCR § 4900(a).

The California Code of Regulations defines "gender" as: "a person's actual sex or perceived sex and includes a person's perceived identity, appearance or behavior, whether or not that identity, appearance, or behavior is different from that traditionally associated with a person's sex at birth." 5 CCR § 4910(k).

SFUSD Board Policy Prohibits Gender–Based Harassment

SFUSD Board Policy 5163 requires that "All educational programs, activities and employment practices shall be conducted without discrimination based on . . . sex, sexual orientation, [or] gender identity. . . ." Board Policy 5162 requires that "students should treat all persons equally and respectfully and refrain from the willful or negligent use of slurs against any person" based on sex or sexual orientation.

Therefore, transgender and gender non-conforming students must be protected from discrimination and harassment in the public school system. Staff must respond appropriately to ensure that schools are free from any such discrimination or harassment.

Names/Pronouns

Students shall have the right to be addressed by a name and pronoun corresponding to their gender identity that is exclusively and consistently asserted at school. Students are not required to obtain a court ordered name and/or gender change or to change their official records as a prerequisite to being addressed by the name and pronoun that corresponds to their gender identity. This directive does not prohibit inadvertent slips or honest mistakes, but it does apply to an intentional and persistent refusal to respect a student's gender identity. The requested name shall be included in the SIS system in addition to the student's legal name, in order to inform teachers of the name and pronoun to use when addressing the student.

Official Records

The District is required to maintain a mandatory permanent pupil record which includes the legal name of the pupil, as well as the pupil's gender. 5 Cal. Code Reg. 432(b)(1)(A), (D). The District shall change a student's official records to reflect a change in legal name or gender upon receipt of documentation that such legal name and/or gender have been changed pursuant to California legal requirements.

Restroom Accessibility

Students shall have access to the restroom that corresponds to their gender identity exclusively and consistently asserted at school. Where available, a single stall bathroom may be used by any student who desires increased privacy, regardless of the underlying reason. The use of such a single stall bathroom shall be a matter of choice for a student, and no student shall be compelled to use such bathroom.

Locker Room Accessibility

Transgender students shall not be forced to use the locker room corresponding to their gender assigned at birth. In locker rooms that involve undressing in front of others, transgender students who want to use the locker room corresponding to their gender identity exclusively and consistently asserted at school will be provided with the available accommodation that best meets the needs and privacy concerns of all students involved. Based on availability and appropriateness to address privacy concerns, such accommodations could include, but are not limited to:

- Use of a private area in the public area (i.e., a bathroom stall with a door, an area separated by a curtain, a PE instructor's office in the locker room);
- A separate changing schedule (either utilizing the locker room before or after the other students); or

- Use of a nearby private area (i.e., a nearby restroom, a nurse's office).

Sports and Gym Class

Transgender students shall not be denied the opportunity to participate in physical education, nor shall they be forced to have physical education outside of the assigned class time. Generally, students should be permitted to participate in gender-segregated recreational gym class activities and sports in accordance with the student's gender identity that is exclusively and consistently asserted at school. Participation in competitive athletic activities and contact sports will be resolved on a case by case basis.

Dress Codes

School sites can enforce dress codes that are adopted pursuant to Education Code 35291. Students shall have the right to dress in accordance with their gender identity that is exclusively and consistently asserted at school, within the constraints of the dress codes adopted at their school site. This regulation does not limit a student's right to dress in accordance with the Dress/Appearance standards articulated in the Student and Parent/Guardian Handbook, page 23.

Gender Segregation in Other Areas

As a general rule, in any other circumstances where students are separated by gender in school activities (i.e., class discussions, field trips), students shall be permitted to participate in accordance with their gender identity exclusively and consistently asserted at school. Activities that may involve the need for accommodations to address student privacy concerns will be addressed on a case by case basis. In such circumstances, staff shall make a reasonable effort to provide an available accommodation that can address any such concerns.

EXPANDING GENDER AND EXPANDING THE LAW: TOWARD A SOCIAL AND LEGAL CONCEPTUALIZATION OF GENDER THAT IS MORE INCLUSIVE OF TRANSGENDER PEOPLE

Dylan Vade.
11 MICH. J. GENDER & L. 253 (2005).

Dylan Vade is a transgender attorney and activist who co-founded and co-directed the Transgender Law Center in San Francisco. He has a J.D. from Stanford University and a Ph.D. in Philosophy from the State University of New York at Stony Brook

* * *

I. A Conceptualization of Gender that Is Inclusive and Respectful of Transgender People

A. A Description of Transgender Communities

In order to be protective of transgender people, we have to know who transgender people are. This article begins to describe the infinite gender diversity within the transgender communities.

Transgender people span all communities, cultures, races, ages, sexual orientations, and genders. This statement is fairly self-evident and clear, except perhaps the last part of the sentence: Transgender people have all genders.

1. Gender Diversity

Transgender people have all genders. Some transgender people are male; some transgender people are female. Among non-transgender people, there are feminine women, masculine women, androgynous women, feminine men, androgynous men, masculine men, to name just a few. Among transgender people as well, there are feminine women, masculine women, androgynous women, feminine men, androgynous men, masculine men, and many more. Some FTMs do drag in slinky dresses, wear sparkly clothes while hiking in the woods, and host nail polish parties. Some MTFs identify as butch dykes, play soccer, and cringe at having to wear a skirt. There is infinite variation in the world. We are all limited by imposing socialized binary gender norms on our complex real life experiences. There are infinitely different women and infinitely different men.

And there are those who are neither. Some transgender people identify as trans, tranny, trannyboy, trannygirl, transsexual, transgender, shinjuku boy, boi, grrl, boy-girl, girl-boy-girl, papi, third gender, fourth gender, no gender, bi-spirit, butch, dyke-fag, fairy, elf girl, glitterboy, transman, transwoman—just to name a few. On a San Francisco Human Rights Commission Survey one person described their gender as "[h]ormonally enhanced, pre-op, trans, genderqueer, butch-dyke with recurring femme moments! I'm just your average boy-girl-boy, really." In conversations and community discussions, there are transgender people who identify as both FTM and dyke. Some see themselves as combining aspects of female and male. Some see themselves as falling between female and male. Some see themselves as falling completely outside of the binary gender system. Some who do not identify as strictly female or strictly male identify as "genderqueer." Some do not identify with that term.

I know I'm not a man—about that I'm very clear, and I've come to the conclusion that I'm probably not a woman either. . . .

Author Leslie Feinberg "faces almost insurmountable difficulty when instructed to check an 'F' or an 'M' box on identification papers," and refers to hirself as sie.

2. Change and Fluidity

Some transgender people knew their true gender from the day they were born. Some transgender people realize their genders later in life, when they first meet another transgender person, through reading about transgender people, or through a series of experiences. Just as there is no one age at which gay or bisexual or queer people recognize and acknowledge their sexual orientation, there is also no one age at which transgender people recognize and acknowledge their gender identity. Some transgender people know their gender at the age of three, some at the age of fifteen years, some at the age of eighty-five years.

Further, a recognition of one's gender identity at one point in time does not negate a different identification at a different point in time. Some transgender people have the same gender throughout their lives. Some have different genders at different times. Some FTMs identified as women, and then identified as men. Some FTMs have always identified as men. Some transgender people identify as male for part of their life, as female for another part of their life, and later again as male. That does not mean that there was a mistake. It simply means there was change. Like so many things in life, and in fact, like every moment of life, gender can change, and it can change more than once.

For some transgender people, gender identification varies frequently. Some people's gender is situational. For instance, I identify in the "male" region of the gender galaxy, but not really as female or male. Once, a law school exercise required that students divide into groups of women and men. I looked at the side of the room with the feminine women. I looked at the side of the room with the masculine men. At that point, I strongly identified as neither female nor male. That identification was both visceral and political. I needed more space. In that gender normative space, I needed to create an opening. In contrast, at one transgender meeting in San Francisco I was told that I was welcome only if I did not identify as female or male. Here as well, I had a visceral and political reaction. Again, I needed more space. In that space, the male parts of my identity felt erased, so I needed to assert them. In that space, I identified as male. My gender is situational.

Many transgender people's genders are situational. For instance, some transgender people identify both as dyke and as FTM, more dyke or more FTM depending on the situation. Some people wake up on different days with slightly different genders. For some, gender is fixed, and for some it is fluid.

3. Body Diversity

In addition to the enormous variety of identifications, there is an equally impressive variety of bodies. Some women have wombs, some do not. Some men have facial hair, some do not. Some transgender women identify as one hundred percent female and never take hormones or have any surgeries. Transgender women define for themselves what it means to be female and to have a female body. Many transgender people name and reclaim their body parts. Some FTM transgender people take male hormones and have mastectomies and yet do not identify as men. Some do. Some mix and match to best express their gender. Some take hormones but have no surgery or vice versa. Some take low-doses or go on and off of hormones. Some female to male transgender men choose to become pregnant and bear and raise children.

When talking about bodies, I cannot leave out genitalia. Often when I tell people that I am transgender, the first question I am asked is: "Have you had THE surgery?" There is no such thing as THE surgery. There are many different possible types of surgeries. Further, many transgender people do not want any surgery whatsoever. For some, altering genitalia surgically is important. For others, it is critical to keep their parts just the way they are. Some transgender people do want surgical intervention, genital or otherwise, but cannot afford it, since there is virtually no insurance coverage for transgender surgeries. Many transgender people are excluded categorically from having health insurance and many are unemployed or underemployed.

Further, some transgender people of color want surgical procedures and/or hormones but choose to forgo those medical interventions because to date there are no studies on the effects of hormones or transgender surgeries on people of color.

In sum, transgender people make many different choices for their bodies. Some of the choices are for gender reasons; the person chooses for themselves how best to express their gender identity physically. Some choices are for economic reasons. Some choices are because the medical system does not have adequate data on transgender procedures, particularly relating to transgender people of color. Thus, to assume that transgender people all have, want, or are able to have the same type of body is incorrect.

4. Sexual Orientations

Gender identity is who one is. Sexual orientation is to whom one is attracted. Transgender people have all sexual orientations: some transgender people are straight, some are gay, some are bisexual, and some are queer. Yet, such a statement is problematic. As soon as we recognize that there are more than two genders, the terms "homosexual," "heterosexual," and "bisexual" no longer make sense. For instance, I am someone who identifies as somewhat male, but not completely, as mostly trans, perhaps as trannyfag. So, am I "homosexual" only if I am attracted to others who have the exact identification that I do? Am I heterosexual if I'm attracted to anyone who does not have my exact identification? The terms "homo-", "hetero-", and "bi-sexual" presume a world with only two genders.

5. Diversity of Experiences and Narratives

Transgender people have different identities, bodies, levels of fluidity, sexual orientations, and ways of mixing and matching all of the above. For instance, there is no one-to-one correlation between body modification and identity. It is not necessarily those who take low doses of hormones who identify as between male and female. It is not necessarily those who take hormones who identify as transsexual. It is not necessarily those who have genital surgery who identify as 100% male or 100% female. Some queer-identified transgender people modify their bodies, and some do not. Some transgender people who alter their bodies medically have static identities, and some do not.

There is no one way to be transgender. I want to highlight this statement: there is no prototypical transgender experience.

In many disciplines, including law, medicine, and psychiatry, there exists a narrative that one has to fit to be a "real" transgender person. Only if one fits this narrative does one become a bona fide transgender person, one who can receive services and legal rights. The narrative goes something like this: transgender men are very masculine, played with trucks when they were little, always have known from day one that they were men, want to be heterosexual married men, are men trapped in women's bodies, have hated their bodies all their lives, and most definitely want genital surgery. The same goes for transgender women, substituting dolls for trucks. Transgender people are held to even higher sexist standards than are non-transgender people.

Transgender people have to tell this story to their doctors to get care, and to courts and agencies to get legal rights. But for many transgender people this story is not true, or only partially true (as described above). Further, there are endless ways both to arrive at being transgender and to be transgender. Some transgender people feel and always felt at home in their bodies. Some transgender people who alter their bodies never felt trapped in their bodies. I know many transgender people who have lived happy and productive lives before coming out as transgender.

There are many different transgender experiences, as well as many different ways to conceptualize those experiences. Each person has their own narrative.

Moreover, each person has several different narratives. For instance, I can describe my past in several ways. I can pick out pieces of my past in such a way that my narrative fits more or less closely with the tranny-proto-narrative. I can try to make my past be more or less continuous and consistent. Part of me is drawn to having a narrative that fits in with a standard, or is at least consistent. But that narrative would leave out parts of my life.

I would like to let go of the need to have a cohesive linear narrative, and the need to have just one narrative. My life is complex. All our lives are complex. I would like to see us use our narratives in ways that empower us and that allow us to freely explore, and become, ourselves. For this to become a possibility, we have to tell and share many more narratives, the complicated and the simple, and to be very careful not to reify or institutionalize any particular one.

B.   A Non–Linear View of Gender—The Gender Galaxy

Often when people get past the myth of two genders and attempt to describe gender diversity, they paint a line and see a spectrum running from female to male. This article explains why the linear conception of a line or spectrum is not adequate and offers a non-linear conceptualization of gender.

To illustrate the limitation of a linear view of gender, here are a few of my friends: a butch transwoman; an FTM transperson who does not identify as male and, for that matter, is not very masculine or butch—he likes to wear nail polish; a butch woman who was assigned female at birth and who identifies as a woman; a woman who was assigned female at birth and who is viewed as "high femme," but who actually identifies as a fierce drag queen and does femininity with irony. How would my friends be ordered on a line from female to male? Where would we put a sissy FTM compared to a butch woman? Would the feminine FTM be more toward the female end of the spectrum because he is more feminine? Would the butch woman be more toward the female end of the spectrum because she identifies as a woman? Where does a fierce femme fall on this line? It is impossible to order us on a line. The linear conception of gender is a logical impossibility. The line falls apart.

Gender is much bigger than a line. It is at least a three-dimensional space, but not a Cartesian one, not a space created by three lines. There are no lines, no ordering. There is just space—an infinite space, a space that allows motion. I have gender claustrophobia and need a big space. I do not like it when people tell me that I have to identify as female or male. I also do not like it when people tell me that, because it is not radical enough, I cannot identify as female or male. I need a big space in which everyone's gender has a space, and in which our genders are not hierarchically ordered. Thus, a conception that works for me is a galaxy. A gender galaxy. It is big, and it moves.

1.   Each Person Has a Gender, a Place in the Gender Galaxy

One of my transgender friends gets annoyed when she is invited to speak on every gender panel. She asks the person who is inviting her why that person cannot be on the panel themselves—after all, that person has a gender, too. Each person has a space in the galaxy. Each person has a gender. Trannygrrrl/boy with drag queen tendencies is a location in the gender galaxy. Fierce femme is a location in the gender galaxy. Girl with a hot glue gun is a location in the gender galaxy. Female and male are locations in the gender galaxy.

Gender is one's own specific way of interacting with and presenting oneself to the world. Gender is expression—physical, mental, spiritual, sexual, inter-relational, connective expression. Gender is how we relate to each other and to the world. Gender is how we move through the world. Gender is a sense of self and a relationship to the world. One's sense of self is organic and inter-relational. Gender is that expressive, relational, embodied self.

And we all have a gender. None of us can be anything but ourselves or have a gender other than our own. Gender is complex. There are many different gender expressions. Ideally, each of our genders is our own as defined by ourselves.

2.   The Multiplicity in the Gender Galaxy Is Not a Void

I recently saw a postcard by Mollie Biewald from 1999 that said "things you can do to eradicate gender or to multiply it exponentially" followed by many trans-positive suggestions. Also, I often hear and read suggestions that all of gender is bad and we should just get rid of gender altogether—or that not having a gender is the best gender to have. Gender is seen as that which allows sexism and restrictive gender norms to exist. Gender is seen as a hindrance without which there would be no gender oppression. I often hear that the ideal world would be one in which gender does not matter, in which everyone is seen simply as themselves, is seen simply as a human being, a gender-less human being—a gender-blind world.

Sometimes, the gender galaxy with its infinite genders is conflated with having no genders and with being gender-blind. I want to be clear that this is not what I mean.

First, I do not think that it is possible to have a world without gender. What would that world look like? Does that mean that we are all androgynous? Androgynous is a gender, a specific location in the galaxy. By saying that we want to eradicate gender, are we really replacing one norm with another?

Second, I like my gender. I am rather attached to my tranny gender. It took me thirty-four years to get here. I like gendered people. Gender can be playful and fun. Gender is part of who we are. I do not want to rid myself of my gender; I want to reclaim it.

Third, I cannot erase how my gender is perceived by others and the ramifications of those perceptions. Gender-blind politics is harmful to those who are most discriminated against because of gender norms. Right now, we have sexism. Right now, we have transphobia. Right now, though we are all harmed by gender norms, some of us are harmed more than others. To move toward a world in which sexism and transphobia do not exist, we have to address issues that affect women and transgender people. If we act as if gender does not exist, then we act as if sexism and transphobia do not exist and so reinforce the privilege of gender-normal genders and, in particular, male genders.

Again, I propose a gender galaxy, a space with many genders, not no genders. The gender galaxy is a space with infinite gender options that can move and are not hierarchically related—a space in which each of us has a location, a space in which each of us can choose that location and where all locations are equally supported and respected.

The gender galaxy already exists. There are infinite genders, and they are not linearly related. The people I see every day exist. Our genders exist. We exist. The gender galaxy already exists. But, we do still have to work toward a world in which everyone can freely choose their location in the gender galaxy. We do still have to work toward a world in which all people and all gender locations are supported, recognized, and protected by the law, without threat of harm, and, ideally, celebrated.

E. THE RIGHTS OF UNDOCUMENTED STUDENTS

PLYLER v. DOE

457 U.S. 202, 102 S.Ct. 2382 (1982).

JUSTICE BRENNAN delivered the opinion of the Court.

The question presented by these cases is whether, consistent with the Equal Protection Clause of the Fourteenth Amendment, Texas may deny to undocumented school-age children the free public education that it provides to children who are citizens of the United States or legally admitted aliens.

I

* * *

In May 1975, the Texas Legislature revised its education laws to withhold from local school districts any state funds for the education of children who were not "legally admitted" into the United States. The 1975 revision also authorized local school districts to deny enrollment in their public schools to children not "legally admitted" to the country. These cases involve constitutional challenges to those provisions.

* * *

This is a class action, filed in the United States District Court for the Eastern District of Texas in September 1977, on behalf of certain school-age children of Mexican origin residing in Smith County, Tex., who could not establish that they had been legally admitted into the United States. * * *

* * *

II

* * *

The Fourteenth Amendment to the Constitution is not confined to the protection of citizens. It says: "Nor shall any state deprive any person of life, liberty, or property without due process of law; nor deny to any person within its jurisdiction the equal protection of the laws." *These provisions are universal in their application, to all persons within the territorial jurisdiction*, without regard to any differences of race, of color, or of nationality; and the protection of the laws is a pledge of the protection of equal laws.

* * *

Our conclusion that the illegal aliens who are plaintiffs in these cases may claim the benefit of the Fourteenth Amendment's guarantee of equal protection only begins the inquiry. The more difficult question is whether the Equal Protection Clause has been violated by the refusal of the State of Texas to reimburse local school boards for the education of children who cannot demonstrate that their presence within the United States is lawful, or by the imposition by those school boards of the burden of tuition on those children. It is to this question that we now turn.

III

* * *

Public education is not a "right" granted to individuals by the Constitution. *San Antonio Independent School Dist. v. Rodriguez*, 411 U.S. 1, 35, 93 S. Ct. 1278 (1973). But neither is it merely some governmental "benefit" indistinguishable from other forms of social welfare legislation. Both the importance of education in maintaining our basic institutions, and the lasting impact of its deprivation on the life of the child, mark the distinction. The "American people have always regarded education and [the] acquisition of knowledge as matters of supreme importance." We have recognized "the public schools as a most vital civic institution for the preservation of a democratic system of government," and as the primary vehicle for transmitting "the values on which our society rests." "[A]s ... pointed out early in our history, ... some degree of education is necessary to prepare citizens to participate effectively and intelligently in our open political system if we are to preserve freedom and independence." And these historic "perceptions of the public schools as inculcating fundamental values necessary to the maintenance of a democratic political system have been confirmed by the observations of social scientists." In addition, education provides the basic tools by which individuals might lead economically productive lives to the benefit of us all. In sum, education has a fundamental role in maintaining the fabric of our society. We cannot ignore the significant social costs borne by our Nation when select groups are denied the means to absorb the values and skills upon which our social order rests.

In addition to the pivotal role of education in sustaining our political and cultural heritage, denial of education to some isolated group of children poses an affront to one of the goals of the Equal Protection Clause: the abolition of governmental barriers presenting unreasonable obstacles to advancement on the basis of individual merit. Paradoxically, by depriving the children of any disfavored group of an education, we foreclose the means by which that group might raise the level of esteem in which it is held by the majority. But more directly, "education prepares individuals to be self-reliant and self-sufficient participants in society." Illiteracy is an enduring disability. The inability to read and write will handicap the individual deprived of a basic education each and every day of his life. The inestimable toll of that deprivation on the social economic, intellectual, and psychological well-being of the individual, and the obstacle it poses to individual achievement, make it most difficult to reconcile the cost or the principle of a status-based denial of basic education with the framework of equality embodied in the Equal Protection Clause. What we said 28 years ago in *Brown v. Board of Education*, 347 U.S. 483, 74 S. Ct. 686 (1954), still holds true:

> Today, education is perhaps the most important function of state and local governments. Compulsory school attendance laws and the great expenditures for education both demonstrate our recognition of the importance of education to our democratic society. It is required in the performance of our most basic public responsibilities, even service in the armed forces. It is the very foundation of good citizenship. Today it is a principal instrument in awakening the child to cultural values, in preparing him for later professional training, and in helping him to adjust normally to his environment. In these days, it is doubtful that any child may reasonably be expected to succeed in life if he is denied the opportunity of an education. Such an opportunity, where the state has undertaken to provide it, is a right which must be made available to all on equal terms. *Id.*, at 493, 74 S. Ct., at 691.

B

These well-settled principles allow us to determine the proper level of deference to be afforded § 21.031. Undocumented aliens cannot be treated as a suspect class because their presence in this country in violation of federal law is not a "constitutional irrelevancy." Nor is education a fundamental right; a State need not justify by compelling necessity every variation in the manner in which education is provided to its population. See *San Antonio Independent School Dist. v. Rodriguez, supra*, at 28–39, 93 S. Ct., at 1293–1300. But more is involved in these cases than the abstract question whether § 21.031 discriminates against a suspect class, or whether education is a fundamental right. Section 21.031 imposes a lifetime hardship on a discrete class of children not accountable for their disabling status. The stigma of illiteracy will mark them for the rest of their lives. By denying these children a basic education, we deny them the ability to live within the structure of our civic institutions, and foreclose any realistic possibility that they will contribute in even the smallest way to the progress of our Nation. In determining the rationality of § 21.031, we may appropriately take into account its costs to the Nation and to the innocent children who are its victims. In light of these countervailing costs, the discrimination contained in § 21.031 can hardly be considered rational unless it furthers some substantial goal of the State.

IV

It is the State's principal argument, and apparently the view of the dissenting Justices, that the undocumented status of these children *vel non* establishes a sufficient rational basis for denying them benefits that a State might choose to afford other residents. The State notes that while other aliens are admitted "on an equality of legal privileges with all citizens under non-discriminatory laws," the asserted right of these children to an education can claim no implicit congressional imprimatur. Indeed, in the State's view, Congress' apparent disapproval of the presence of these children within the United States, and the evasion of the federal regulatory program that is the mark of undocumented status, provides authority for its decision to impose upon them special disabilities. Faced with an equal protection challenge respecting the treatment of aliens, we agree that the courts must be attentive to congressional policy; the exercise of congressional power might well affect the State's prerogatives to afford differential treatment to a particular class of aliens. But we are unable to find in the congressional immigration scheme any statement of policy that might weigh significantly in arriving at an equal protection balance concerning the State's authority to deprive these children of an education.

   * * *

VI

If the State is to deny a discrete group of innocent children the free public education that it offers to other children residing within its borders, that denial must be justified by a showing that it furthers some substantial state interest. No such showing was made here. Accordingly, the judgment of the Court of Appeals in each of these cases is

Affirmed.

JUSTICE MARSHALL, concurring.

While I join the Court's opinion, I do so without in any way retreating from my opinion in *San Antonio Independent School District v. Rodriguez*, 411 U.S. 1, 70–133, 93 S. Ct. 1278, 1315–48 (1973) (dissenting opinion). I continue to believe that an individual's interest in education is fundamental, and that this view is amply supported "by the unique status accorded public education by our society, and by the close relationship between education and some of our most basic constitutional values." *Id.* at 111, 93 S. Ct. at 1336. Furthermore, I believe that the facts of these cases demonstrate the wisdom of rejecting a rigidified approach to equal protection analysis, and of employing an approach that allows for varying levels of scrutiny depending upon "the constitutional and societal importance of the interest adversely affected and the recognized invidiousness of the basis upon which the particular classification is drawn." *Id.* at 99, 93 S. Ct. at 1330. It continues to be my view that a class-based denial of public education is utterly incompatible with the Equal Protection Clause of the Fourteenth Amendment.

   * * *

CHIEF JUSTICE BURGER, with whom JUSTICE WHITE, JUSTICE REHNQUIST, and JUSTICE O'CONNOR join, dissenting.

Were it our business to set the Nation's social policy, I would agree without hesitation that it is senseless for an enlightened society to deprive any children—including illegal aliens—of an elementary education. I fully agree that it would be folly—and wrong—to tolerate creation of a segment of society made up of illiterate persons, many having a limited or no command of our language. However, the Constitution does not constitute us as "Platonic Guardians" nor does it vest in this Court the authority to strike down laws because they do not meet our standards of desirable social policy, "wisdom," or "common sense." We trespass on the assigned function of the political branches under our structure of limited and separated powers when we assume a policymaking role as the Court does today.

The Court makes no attempt to disguise that it is acting to make up for Congress' lack of "effective leadership" in dealing with the serious national problems caused by the influx of uncountable millions of illegal aliens across our borders. The failure of enforcement of the immigration laws over more than a decade and the inherent difficulty and expense of sealing our vast borders have combined to create a grave socioeconomic dilemma. It is a dilemma that has not yet even been fully assessed, let alone addressed. However, it is not the function of the Judiciary to provide "effective leadership" simply because the political branches of government fail to do so.

The Court's holding today manifests the justly criticized judicial tendency to attempt speedy and wholesale formulation of "remedies" for the failures—or simply the laggard pace—of the political processes of our system of government. The Court employs, and in my view abuses, the Fourteenth Amendment in an effort to become an omnipotent and omniscient problem solver. That the motives for doing so are noble and compassionate does not alter the fact that the Court distorts our constitutional function to make amends for the defaults of others.

I

In a sense, the Court's opinion rests on such a unique confluence of theories and rationales that it will likely stand for little beyond the results in these particular cases. Yet the extent to which the Court departs from principled constitutional adjudication is nonetheless disturbing.

* * *

LEAGUE OF UNITED LATIN AM. CITIZENS v. WILSON

908 F.Supp. 755 (C.D. Cal. 1995).

Pfaelzer, District Judge

Proposition 187 is an initiative measure which was submitted to the voters of the State of California in the November 8, 1994 general election. It was passed by a vote of 59% to 41% and became effective the following day. The stated purpose of Proposition 187 is to "provide for cooperation between [the] agencies of state and local government with the federal government, and to establish a system of required notification by and between such agencies to prevent illegal aliens in the United States from receiving benefits or public services in the State of California." The initiative's provisions require law enforcement, social services, health care and public education personnel to (i) verify the immigration status of persons with whom they come in contact; (ii) notify certain defined persons of their immigration status; (iii) report those persons to state and federal officials; and (iv) deny those persons social services, health care, and education.

After the initiative was passed, several actions challenging the constitutionality of Proposition 187 were commenced in state and federal courts in California. Ultimately, five actions filed in the United States District Court were consolidated in this Court for purposes of motions, hearings, petitions and trial (collectively, the "consolidated actions").

The plaintiffs in the consolidated actions have brought suit for declaratory and injunctive relief seeking to bar California Governor Pete Wilson ("Wilson"), Attorney General Dan Lungren ("Lungren"), and other state actors (collectively, defendants) from enforcing the provisions of Proposition 187.

On November 16, 1994, the Court entered a temporary restraining order enjoining the implementation of sections 4, 5, 6, 7 and 9 of the initiative. On December 14, 1995, the Court granted plaintiffs' motions for preliminary injunction, enjoining the implementation and enforcement of those sections.

* * *

III. *Whether Proposition 187 is Preempted Under Federal Law*

The question of whether provisions of Proposition 187 are preempted by federal law is governed by the Supreme Court's decision in *De Canas v. Bica* (California statute prohibiting an employer from knowingly employing an alien who is not entitled to lawful residence in the United States held not preempted under federal law). In *De Canas,* the Supreme Court set forth three tests to be used in determining whether a state statute related to immigration is preempted. Pursuant to *De Canas,* if a statute fails any one of the three tests, it is preempted by federal law.

Under the first test, the Court must determine whether a state statute is a "regulation of immigration." * * * Under the second test, even if the state law is not an impermissible regulation of immigration, it may still be preempted * * * where Congress intended to "occupy the field" which the statute attempts to regulate. * * * Under the third test, a state law is preempted if it * * * conflicts with federal law making compliance with both state and federal law impossible.

A. *Whether Proposition 187 Constitutes an Impermissible Regulation of Immigration.*

The federal government possesses the exclusive power to regulate immigration. That power derives from the Constitution's grant to the federal government of the power to "establish a uniform Rule of Naturalization," and to "regulate Commerce with foreign Nations." In addition, the Supreme Court has held that the federal government's power to control immigration is inherent in the nation's sovereignty.

* * *

3. Section 7

Section 7 is entitled "Exclusion of Illegal Aliens From Public Elementary and Secondary Schools." Like sections 5 and 6, section 7 contains classification, notification and cooperation/reporting requirements that, taken together, serve only to further the scheme to regulate immigration and are unnecessary to the denial of public education.

In section 7, subsections (a) through (c) require schools to verify the immigration status of children for the purposes of denying access to public elementary and secondary education. Subsection (d) requires verification of the immigration status of *parents* of school children. Subsection (e) requires school districts to report the "illegal" status of any parent, guardian, enrollee or pupil to state agencies and the INS. Subsection (f) requires school districts to "fully cooperate" in "accomplish[ing] an orderly transition to a school in the child's country of origin."

Subsections (a), (b) and (c), together, assure that undocumented children will be denied access to public education. Subsection (d) is wholly unnecessary to implementing the denial of education mandated by section 7, because the state has no need to know the immigration status of *parents* in order to deny benefits to *children*. * * * [T]he only purpose and effect of subsections (d), (e), and (f) is to ensure that persons determined by the state to be in the United States unlawfully are "transitioned" to the "country of their origin." Subsections (d), (e) and (f) are part of an impermissible scheme to regulate immigration and are therefore preempted under the first *De Canas* test.

In any event, an analysis of section 7 under the rigors of the first *De Canas* test is not necessary to sustain the Court's ruling on these motions. In light of the United States Supreme Court's decision in *Plyler v. Doe,* 457 U.S. 202, 102 S. Ct. 2382 (1982), in which the Court held that the Equal Protection Clause of the Fourteenth Amendment prohibits states from excluding undocumented alien children from public schools, section 7 in its entirety conflicts with and is therefore preempted by federal law.

* * *

IV. *Conclusion*

The California voters' overwhelming approval of Proposition 187 reflects their justifiable frustration with the federal government's inability to enforce the immigration laws effectively. No matter how serious the problem may be, however, the authority to regulate immigration belongs exclusively to the federal government and state agencies are not permitted to assume that authority. The State is powerless to enact its own scheme to regulate immigration or to devise immigration regulations which run parallel to or purport to supplement the federal immigration laws.

The classification, notification and cooperation/reporting provisions in sections 4 through 9 of the initiative, taken together, constitute a regulatory scheme (1) to detect persons present in California in violation of state-created categories of lawful immigration status; (2) to notify state and federal officials of their purportedly unlawful status; and (3) to effect their removal from the United States. These provisions create an impermissible state scheme to regulate immigration and are preempted under the first and second *De Canas* tests. Plaintiffs' motions for summary judgment are granted with respect to these provisions.

The benefits denial provisions of the initiative—if implemented by state regulations which would require verification of immigration status by reference to federal determinations of status—have only an incidental impact on immigration and thus do not violate the first *De Canas* test. Nor do those provisions violate the second *De Canas* test. Plaintiffs have failed to direct the Court to any authority for the proposition that Congress intended to completely oust state authority to legislate in the area of benefits denial. Consequently, the Court must conclude that those provisions are preempted only if their operation conflicts with or impedes the objectives of federal laws.

Section 7's denial of primary and secondary education conflicts with federal law as announced by the Supreme Court in *Plyler v. Doe* and is therefore preempted. Section 8's denial of postsecondary education does not appear to conflict with any federal law and thus is not preempted.
* * *

The preliminary injunction entered by the Court on December 14, 1994, shall remain in effect until further order of the Court.

Chapter VI

EDUCATIONAL QUALITY
AND THE LAW

This chapter focuses on the education process and examines attempts to use the legal system to improve the quality of education in the public schools. At this point in time, there is a relatively limited amount of case law in this area, with legal issues and strands of relevant law still in relatively early stages of development. Indeed, few cases focusing primarily on educational quality have reached the highest courts. But quality-related issues are appearing increasingly in education cases over the past twenty years, and foundational principles are beginning to emerge.

Policy context is particularly important in this area, since the issues that arise not only require an understanding of educational systems themselves, but also call for an assessment of the complex interaction between and among educators, students, parents, the community, and the political process.

For many years, when litigators and legislators looked at the education process and related matters, issues of equality—as referenced in Chapter 5—were a natural starting point. But by the 1980s it had become clear to many people that victories in those cases were not going to be enough to turn things around for many of the country's students.

A major impetus for this gradual change in thinking was the Education Reform Movement, which "officially" began in 1983 with *A Nation at Risk,* a report by the National Commission on Excellence in Education. The report documented in great detail the extensive "mediocrity" that existed in America's public schools, and played a primary role in leading many to conclude that the status quo in our educational system was no longer acceptable. Educators and elected officials on both sides of the political spectrum sought to forge a consensus, united in a new "commitment to excellence," even as they continued to disagree on the relative importance and inherent workability of the various reform proposals.

In the late 1980s and throughout the 1990s, a school choice movement emerged, and many began pushing for vouchers that could be used by parents at either public schools or private schools. In response, many school districts, cities, and states began offering parents much more choice than they had before. The charter school movement also emerged within this context, and the growing popularity of these creative alternatives added to the options that had become available.

At the same time, a new round of school finance litigation was being brought in state courts under state constitutional law, focusing less on equity-related issues and more on educational "adequacy." In retrospect, the combination of the school choice movement and the new wave of school finance litigation had the effect of putting many educational quality issues on the table in courtrooms, state legislatures, and public policy settings. By the turn of the century, the U.S. Congress was heavily involved in these debates, and the "No Child Left Behind" Act emerged as a major bipartisan statement by the federal government in this area.

At the earlier stages of the Education Reform Movement, there was much discussion about the alleged tension between "equity" and "excellence," with many arguing that schools needed to choose between one or the other, but could not have both. A classic example in this regard was the issue of tracking and homogeneous ability grouping. Some argued that a focus on equity should be primary, and that heterogeneous grouping should be employed to keep students from being locked into low level classes that condemned generations of young people to a second rate education. Others argued that ability grouping was necessary to maximize excellence and enable students who were already achieving to move farther and faster and accomplish even more.

By the end of the 1990s, however, it became clear to most people that education reform need not focus on *either* equity or excellence, but that there can and should be a focus on *both*. Indeed, an examination of the anti-tracking movement, the educational finance litigation of that era, the school choice movement, the "No Child Left Behind" Act, and recent efforts to improve the quality of programs for English learners and students with disabilities reveals that all these efforts embody attempts to both maximize equal educational opportunities and improve educational quality for all students.

This chapter begins with an examination of how litigators, legislators, jurists, and commentators have sought to define and identify educational quality. It then turns to the "No Child Left Behind" Act, focusing in particular on the controversial accountability provisions and on interrelated issues of equity and excellence under the Act's mandate. Finally, it explores issues and trends relating to school choice, under the law and as a matter of policy.

A. DEFINING AND IDENTIFYING QUALITY EDUCATION

Members of the legal and public policy communities have wrestled with issues of educational quality in different ways, and in so doing have begun to set forth relevant definitions and guiding principles. Examples of these developments include "educational malpractice" lawsuits, efforts to raise issues of quality in desegregation and school finance contexts, and attempts to construe educational quality under an individual state's fundamental right to an education.

1. EDUCATIONAL MALPRACTICE LITIGATION

In the 1970s, an era when additional new torts were being recognized by many state courts, litigators sought to bring lawsuits under an educational malpractice theory. The *Peter W.* case is a prime example of this litigation, which proved unsuccessful throughout the country.

Consider the scope of the arguments and the parameters of the legal theories raised in *Peter W.* What might be learned about educational quality and the law from this litigation, and from the arguments that were set forth?

PETER W. v. SAN FRANCISCO UNIFIED SCH. DIST.

60 Cal.App.3d 814, 131 Cal.Rptr. 854 (1976).

RATTIGAN, JUDGE

The novel—and troublesome—question on this appeal is whether a person who claims to have been inadequately educated, while a student in a public school system, may state a cause of action in tort against the public authorities who operate and administer the system.

* * * The [complaint's] first count, which is the prototype of the others (each of which incorporates all of its allegations by reference), sounds in negligence. Its opening allegations may be summarized, and quoted in part, as follows:

> XI.   Defendant school district, its agents and employees, negligently and carelessly failed to provide plaintiff with adequate instruction, guidance, counseling and/or supervision in basic academic skills such as reading and writing, although said school district had the authority, responsibility and ability [to do so]. Defendant school district, its agents and employees, negligently failed to use reasonable care in the discharge of its duties to provide plaintiff with adequate instruction * * * in basic academic skills[,] and failed to exercise that degree of professional skill required of an ordinary prudent educator under the same circumstances[,] as exemplified, but not limited to[,] the following acts:

In five enumerated subsections which follow in the same paragraph ("XI."), plaintiff alleges that the school district and its agents and employees, "negligently and carelessly" in each instance, (1) failed to apprehend his reading disabilities, (2) assigned him to classes in which he could not read "the books and other materials," (3) allowed him "to pass and advance from a course or grade level" with knowledge that he had not achieved either its completion or the skills "necessary for him to succeed or benefit from subsequent courses" (4) assigned him to classes in which the instructors were unqualified or which were not "geared" to his reading level, and (5) permitted him to graduate from high school although he was "unable to read above the eighth grade level, as required by Education Code section 8573, . . . thereby depriving him of additional instruction in reading and other academic skills."

The first count continues with allegations of proximate cause and injury:

> XII.   * * * [As] a direct and proximate result of the negligent acts and omissions by the defendant school district, its agents and employees, plaintiff graduated from high school with a reading ability of only the fifth grade [sic]. As a further proximate result [thereof], plaintiff has suffered a loss of earning capacity by his limited ability to read and write and is unqualified for any employment other than * * * labor which requires little or no ability to read or write. * * *

In the closing paragraphs of the first count, plaintiff alleges general damages based upon his "permanent disability and inability to gain meaningful employment"; special damages incurred as the cost of compensatory tutoring allegedly required by reason of the "negligence, acts and omissions of defendants"; that he had presented to the school district an appropriate and timely claim for such damages; and that the claim had been rejected in its entirety.

We proceed to assess the first count for the cause of action in negligence which it purports to plead; the others are separately treated below. * * *

According to the familiar California formula, the allegations requisite to a cause of action for negligence are (1) facts showing a duty of care in the defendant, (2) negligence constituting a breach of the duty, and (3) injury to the plaintiff as a proximate result. The present parties do not debate the adequacy of plaintiff's first count with respect to the elements of negligence, proximate cause, and injury; they focus exclusively upon the issue (which we find dispositive, as will appear) of whether it alleges facts sufficient to show that defendants owed him a "duty of care."

The facts which it shows in this respect—or not—appear in its allegations that he had been a student undergoing academic instruction in the public school system operated and administered by defendants. He argues that these facts alone show the requisite "duty of care." * * * Of course, no reasonable observer would be heard to say that these facts did not impose upon defendants a "duty of care" within any common meaning of the term; given the commanding importance of public education in society, we state a truism in remarking that the public authorities who are duty-bound to educate are also bound to do it with "care." But the truism does not answer the present inquiry, in which "duty of care" is not a term of common parlance; it is instead a legalistic concept of "duty" which will sustain liability for negligence in its breach, and it must be analyzed in that light. * * *

On occasions when the Supreme Court has opened or sanctioned new areas of tort liability, it has noted that the wrongs and injuries involved were both comprehensible and assessable within the existing judicial framework. This is simply not true of wrongful conduct and injuries allegedly involved in educational malfeasance. Unlike the activity of the highway or the marketplace, classroom methodology affords no readily acceptable standards of care, or cause, or injury. The science of pedagogy itself is fraught with different and conflicting theories of how or what a child should be taught, and any layman might—and commonly does—have his own emphatic views on the subject. The "injury" claimed here is plaintiff's inability to read and write. Substantial professional authority attests that the achievement of literacy in the schools, or its failure, are influenced by a host of factors which affect the pupil subjectively, from outside the formal teaching process, and beyond the control of its ministers. They may be physical, neurological, emotional, cultural, environmental; they may be present but not perceived, recognized but not identified.

We find in this situation no conceivable "workability of a rule of care" against which defendants; alleged conduct may be measured, no reasonable "degree of certainty that ... plaintiff suffered injury" within the meaning of the law of negligence, and no such perceptible "connection between the defendant's conduct and the injury suffered," as alleged, which would establish a causal link between them within the same meaning.

These recognized policy considerations alone negate an actionable "duty of care" in persons and agencies who administer the academic phases of the public educational process. Others, which are even more important in practical terms, command the same result. Few of our institutions, if any, have aroused the controversies, or incurred the public dissatisfaction, which have attended the operation of the public schools during the last few decades. Rightly or wrongly, but widely, they are charged with outright failure in the achievement of their educational objectives; according to some critics, they bear responsibility for many of the social and moral problems of our society at large. Their public plight in these respects is attested in the daily media, in bitter governing board elections, in wholesale rejections of school bond proposals, and in survey upon survey. To hold them to an actionable "duty of care," in the discharge of their academic functions, would expose them to the tort claims—real or imagined—of disaffected students and parents in countless numbers. They are already beset by social and financial problems which have gone to major litigation, but for which no permanent solution has yet appeared. The ultimate consequences, in terms of public

time and money, would burden them—and society—beyond calculation.
* * *

The judgment of dismissal is affirmed.

Notes

1.   The *SFNAACP v. SFUSD* litigation that led to a high-profile, widely publicized 1983 Consent Decree was filed only two years after the *Peter W.* decision. It can be argued that the *SFNAACP* litigation represents an alternative approach to addressing the same range of issues that were raised by the plaintiffs in the *Peter W.* case. *See SFNAACP v. SFUSD,* 576 F.Supp. 34 (N.D. Cal. 1983) (opinion and order setting forth the Consent Decree).

While the *SFNAACP* case never went to trial, it resulted in a unique and long-lasting Decree that focused explicitly on both desegregation and educational quality, and led to significant progress on both fronts for a very large number of students. *See* The SFUSD Consent Decree: A Case Study, *supra,* Ch. 5. *See generally* Independent Reports of the SF Consent Decree Monitoring Team, submitted to the U.S. District Court, Northern District of California (1997–2005), *at* http://www.gseis.ucla.edu/courses/edlaw/ sfrepts.htm (last visited February 3, 2006).

2.   Twenty-five years after the decision in *Peter W. v. SFUSD*, the Independent Consent Decree Monitoring Team, in its annual report for the federal court on the District's progress under the mandates of the Decree, identified forty-eight factors that it considered in assessing educational quality.

Which of the following forty-eight factors, in your view, are the most important? Why? What additions, deletions, or modifications might you suggest?

REPORT 18:
THE ANNUAL REPORT OF THE SAN FRANCISCO CONSENT DECREE MONITORING TEAM

(July 2001).

Our monitoring team has compiled a checklist of both traditional objective indicators and supplementary objective and subjective indicators of educational quality in K–12 schools. We employ these 48 indicators to assess the quality of a school as part of our systematic monitoring efforts.

Traditional objective indicators of educational quality include the following items:[1]

---

1.   We note that these 48 factors can be divided into those factors which the school site has the primary ability to change and those which the district's central office has the primary ability to change.

Also, it should be noted that research has shown a direct correlation between the "performance" of a school and the "poverty factor"—how low the socioeconomic status level of the students might be. However, these 48 factors only address what district

1. Test scores (on a range of tests)
2. Average GPA's (secondary level)
3. Average SAT scores (high school)
4. Attendance
5. Drop-out rate (secondary level)
6. AP courses offered, and number of students taking AP exams (high school)
7. AP exam passage rate (high school)
8. Percentage of students graduating "UC eligible"
9. Percentage of students going on to college

Other objective and subjective indicators of educational quality include:

1. The direction the school is heading generally (history, trends, patterns, etc.)
2. Level of engagement between educators and students
3. Level of engagement of students generally
4. Enthusiasm level of students
5. Energy and enthusiasm level of teachers & school site administrators
6. Quality of student work
7. Organization & management of school site programs, activities, and day-to-day affairs
8. Leadership skills of school site administrators
9. Pedagogical skills of teachers
10. Stability of faculty and administration
11. Percentage of credentialed teachers
12. School culture (includes mood, degree to which people get along, respect for differences, motivation, pride, vision)
13. Awards to educators
14. Awards to students
15. Awards to school
16. Record in inter-district and intra-district competitions
17. Condition of physical plant
18. Classroom environment
19. Availability of instructional materials
20. Availability of research tools

administrators and school site educators can do to improve a school, whatever the poverty level of the student population might be.

21. Quality of instructional materials & research tools

22. Quality of computer technology generally

23. Extent to which computer technology has been integrated into the instructional program

24. Degree to which school is meeting the needs of its students (can include special programs)

25. Level of teacher and school site administrator expectations

26. Quality and relevance of on-site staff development

27. Richness of the curriculum generally

28. Extent to which curriculum challenges the students

29. Curriculum for LEP students

30. Curriculum for Special Education students

31. Curriculum for low achieving students

32. Curriculum for high achieving students

33. Discipline practices generally

34. Suspension and expulsion rates

35. Diversity or lack thereof

36. Within school desegregation

37. Redesignation practices

38. Mainstreaming practices

39. School-family-community partnerships

2. FEDERAL COURT EFFORTS TO DEFINE EDUCATIONAL QUALITY IN A DESEGREGATION CONTEXT

Consider the language in the opinions that follow regarding the interface between desegregation and "educational quality." What lessons can be learned from the respective courts' efforts to wrestle with these interrelated concepts?

Freeman is one of the few examples of a decision where a federal judge in a desegregation case mentions educational quality directly. Indeed, it might be argued that the federal courts in the language below have identified a number of factors that might together comprise educational quality under the law—both in desegregation cases and in future lawsuits addressing educational quality in other contexts. (These factors have been highlighted in bold.)

from **PITTS v. FREEMAN**, 887 F.2d 1438 (11th Cir. 1989)

* * * The district court considered six factors set forth in Green: student assignment, **faculty, staff,** transportation, **extracurricular activities,** and **facilities**.[8] Green, 391 U.S. at 435, 88 S.Ct. at 1692. A

---

8. The district court also considered a seventh factor: "quality of education." We

conclude that the Green Court intended quality of education to be considered in review of these six factors constitutes the best approach for determining whether a school system has eliminated the vestiges of a dual system. Therefore, we hold that district courts should review the six Green factors to determine whether a school system has achieved unitary status. If the school system fulfills all six factors at the same time for several years, the court should declare that the school system has achieved unitary status. If the school system fails to fulfill all six factors at the same time for several years, the district court should retain jurisdiction.

from **FREEMAN v. PITTS**, 503 U.S. 467, 112 S.Ct. 1430 (1992)

[In this excerpt from the U.S. Supreme Court opinion, Justice Kennedy—in referencing the district court findings—is attempting to justify a finding of unitary status and thus an end to mandatory desegregation.]

* * * The District Court approached the question whether DCSS had achieved unitary status by asking whether DCSS was unitary with respect to each of the factors identified in Green. The court considered an additional factor that is not named in Green: the quality of education being offered to the white and black student populations. * * *

* * * Addressing the more ineffable category of quality of education, the District Court rejected most of respondents' contentions that there was racial disparity in the **provision of certain educational resources (e.g., teachers with advanced degrees, teachers with more experience, library books)**, contentions made to show that black students were not being given equal educational opportunity. The District Court went further, however, and examined the **evidence concerning achievement** of black students in DCSS. It cited expert testimony praising the overall educational program in the district, as well as objective evidence of black achievement: Black students at DCSS made greater gains on the Iowa Tests of Basic Skills than white students, and black students at DCSS are more successful than black students nationwide on the Scholastic Aptitude Test. It made the following finding:

> While there will always be something more that the DCSS can do to improve the chances for black students to achieve academic success, the court cannot find, as plaintiffs urge, that the DCSS has been negligent in its duties to implement programs to assist black students. The DCSS is a very **innovative** school system. It has implemented a number of **programs to enrich the lives and enhance the academic potential of all students**, both blacks and whites. Many **remedial programs** are targeted in the majority black schools. Programs have been implemented to **involve the parents**

conjunction with each of its six enumerated factors. See Green, 391 U.S. at 435, 88 S.Ct. at 1692 (describing the six factors as comprising "every facet of school operations").

In this case, the district court should consider the distribution of educational resources in relation to the area in which the school system applies the resource.

and **offset negative socio-economic factors**. If the DCSS has failed in any way in this regard, it is not because the school system has been negligent in its duties.

* * * Despite its finding that there was no intentional violation, the District Court found that DCSS had not achieved unitary status with respect to quality of education because teachers in schools with disproportionately high percentages of white students tended to be better educated and have more experience than their counterparts in schools with disproportionately high percentages of black students, and because per-pupil expenditures in majority white schools exceeded per-pupil expenditures in majority black schools. From these findings, the District Court ordered DCSS to equalize spending and remedy the other problems. * * *

In contrast to the circumstances in [other cases] the District Court in this case stated that throughout the period of judicial supervision it has been impressed by the **successes** DCSS has achieved and its **dedication to providing a quality education** for all students, and that DCSS "has travelled the often long road to unitary status almost to its end." [emphasis added].

3. CONCEPTUALIZING EDUCATIONAL QUALITY IN A SCHOOL FINANCE CONTEXT

EDUCATIONAL ADEQUACY: A THEORY AND ITS REMEDIES

William H. Clune.
28 U. MICH. J.L. REF. 481 (1995).

* * * School finance litigation typically has been based on one of two theories: equity or adequacy. "Equity" in school finance means equal resources across a state; for example, equal spending per pupil or equal taxable resources. "Adequacy" refers to resources that are sufficient (or adequate) to achieve some educational result, such as a minimum passing grade on a state achievement test. The two theories are not always clearly distinguishable in practice. Adequacy theory may be used as the legal basis for reaching equity when courts have rejected traditional equity theories, such as equal protection. Conversely, equity litigation may produce adequacy as a by-product. State legislatures that are required to equalize school funding often allocate large amounts of minimum-level funding in order to achieve equality without excessive budget cutting.

In at least three circumstances, adequacy may dictate results or remedies that are different from those required by equity: (1) where practically all schools in a state are inadequate and the remedy must guarantee new resources for education; (2) where certain groups of students, schools, or districts need extra resources to meet minimum achievement standards, and the remedy must include some kind of compensatory aid, such as for children in poverty; and (3) where reaching minimum achievement levels requires schools to become more effective and efficient, forcing the remedy to include elements of educational reform and accountability. * * *

II.   Judicial Remedies in School Finance Litigation

* * * At its heart, adequacy refers to a shift in the emphasis of school finance from inputs to outcomes, e.g. from dollars to student achievement as measured by standardized tests and avoidance of dropping out. Courts deciding school finance litigation cases are beginning to mirror the rest of society by seeing the present time as the age of information and efficiency. * * * [E]arlier cases viewed the "opportunity" in "equality of educational opportunity" as referring to equal access to educational resources for all students—or for their school districts. The central problem confronting courts and school finance plaintiffs was large variations in property tax bases and spending per pupil among districts within a state. Questions of how effectively and efficiently resources were used were left for local communities and educational experts to resolve. Courts deemed consideration of educational outcomes as "unmanageable," a virtual kiss of death for any case that required it. In contrast, dollar equality of tax base or spending offered a measurable standard.

The United States Supreme Court expressed early concern about outcomes in *San Antonio Independent School District v. Rodriguez*. Under the Equal Protection Clause of the United States Constitution, a guarantee of any level of resources would be possible only if tied to a fundamental right. This right would have to be a right to some minimum level of adequate education or, in other words, a right to minimum outcomes. * * * [S]chool finance litigation then shifted to the states, because the "common school ideal" was reflected through both state equal protection requirements and so-called "education clauses" in state constitutions. Some cases continued to find a guarantee of equal resources under state constitutions. Many more recent cases, however, remarkably have invoked all types of clauses and constitutional language to speak—and speak at length—of a student's right to function fully in society.

* * *

The most common and critical facet [in this area] is a method of measuring student achievement against minimum state standards. In Kentucky, despite the availability of existing standardized tests, the legislature was asked to create a new test to meet a new vision of education. In other words, "adequate" might refer to minimum achievement either on an old-style test of educational basics or on a cutting-edge test aimed at world-class standards. * * *

Accountability policies also typically include some kind of state monitoring and sanctions in the form of rewards and punishments for districts and schools that make acceptable or unacceptable progress. In other words, the state test is likely to be high stakes in some sense—

potentially leading to important consequences for either the student's graduation, the school's independence, or the school's eligibility for cash rewards.

The combination of state testing, with its implied guidance of curriculum in every school, and high-stakes monitoring means that adequacy litigation assumes a strong central role for government. This strong accountability contrasts with the old equality-based litigation, which was indifferent to the ways in which extra resources were spent and thus tolerated unmonitored local control.

* * *

[A]dequacy remedies explicitly or implicitly assume a protracted period of educational change. While equal resources, especially money, can be made available in a short period of time, improved student achievement assumes a learning process for teachers and students. For example, in a full cycle, students will need to begin and sustain higher levels of achievement from the early grades. Teachers must learn such skills as teaching new subjects and providing accelerated education for disadvantaged students. * * *

STATE EDUCATION ARTICLES

Virtually every state constitution contains provisions guaranteeing some form of public education for its residents. While education is not mentioned at all in the U.S. Constitution, it has traditionally been viewed as an integral component of state constitutional law. *See, e.g.,* Allen W. Hubsch, *Education and Self–Government: The Right to Education Under State Constitutional Law,* 18 J.L. & Educ. 93, 134–40 (1989). Some of these education provisions contain broad general language setting forth the minimum requirements of a school system. Others include specific guarantees of "thoroughness," "efficiency," or both. *See* William E. Thro, *To Render Them Safe: The Analysis of State Constitutional Provisions in Public School Finance Reform Litigation,* 75 Va. L. Rev. 1639, 1661–63 (1989).

The following are selected examples of education articles from state constitutions.

California
Article IX, Section 1

A general diffusion of knowledge and intelligence being essential to the preservation of the rights and liberties of the people, the Legislature shall encourage by all suitable means the promotion of intellectual, scientific, moral, and agricultural improvement.

Kentucky
Section 183

The General Assembly shall, by appropriate legislation, provide for an efficient system of common schools throughout the State.

Maryland
Article VIII, Section 1

The General Assembly, at its First Session after the adoption of this Constitution, shall by Law establish throughout the State a thorough and efficient System of Free Public Schools; and shall provide by taxation, or otherwise, for their maintenance.

Massachusetts
Chapter V, Section 2

Wisdom, and knowledge, as well as virtue, diffused generally among the body of the people, being necessary for the preservation of their rights and liberties; and as these depend on spreading the opportunities and advantages of education in the various parts of the country, and among the different orders of the people, it shall be the duty of legislatures and magistrates, in all future periods of this commonwealth, to cherish the interests of literature and the sciences, and all seminaries of them; especially the university at Cambridge, public schools and grammar schools in the towns; to encourage private societies and public institutions, rewards and immunities, for the promotion of agriculture, arts, sciences, commerce, trades, manufactures, and a natural history of the country; to countenance and inculcate the principles of humanity and general benevolence, public and private charity, industry and frugality, honesty and punctuality in their dealings; sincerity, good humor, and all social affections, and generous sentiments among the people.

Litigants in the area of school finance have relied upon key words in state education articles to win major victories. Plaintiffs in the *Rose* case, *infra,* for example, focused entirely on the word *efficient* in the Kentucky Constitution. And in an unprecedented ruling, the *Rose* Court determined not only that the Kentucky school finance system was inefficient, but found the entire state school system unconstitutional. Significant education reforms were implemented as a result, and many things changed for the better.

In *McDuffy v. Secretary of the Executive Office of Educ.,* 615 N.E.2d 516, 527 (Mass. 1993), Massachusetts plaintiffs won a similar victory. The Supreme Judicial Court based its decision to overturn school funding laws solely on the constitutional duty of "legislatures and magistrates" to "cherish . . . the public schools." Parallel lawsuits in Alabama and Maryland resulted in remedial orders and settlement agreements mandating changes both in funding structures and in the education process.

State constitutional provisions have become increasingly more important for litigants over the past two decades. *See* Stanley Mosk, *State Constitutionalism: Both Liberal and Conservative,* 63 Tex. L. Rev. 1081, 1081 (1985) (noting that "state constitutionalism has something to offer both liberals and conservatives"). Under these provisions, states can provide greater protection for individual rights than the federal government has provided. The protections provided by Congress and the federal courts typically constitute a baseline. State legislatures and state courts may not fall below this baseline, but they can, and often do, go much further. *See generally* William J. Brennan, Jr., *State Constitutions and the Protection of Individual Rights,* 90 HARV. L. REV. 489, 495 (1977) (noting that "of late * * * more and more state courts are construing state constitutional counterparts of provisions of the Bill of Rights as guaranteeing citizens of their states even more protection than the federal provisions, even those identically phrased."). In addition, state courts typically feel more comfortable with broad interpretations of state constitutional provisions because these documents, unlike the federal constitution, are relatively easy to amend. Many states actually allow their constitutions to be amended by ballot initiative. *See* Julian N. Eule, *Judicial Review of Direct Democracy,* 99 YALE L.J. 1503, 1509 n.22 (1990).

ROSE v. COUNCIL FOR BETTER ED., INC.

790 S.W.2d 186 (Ky.1989).

STEPHENS, CHIEF JUSTICE

The issue we decide on this appeal is whether the Kentucky General Assembly has complied with its constitutional mandate to "provide an efficient system of common schools throughout the state."

In deciding that it has not, we intend no criticism of the substantial efforts made by the present General Assembly and by its predecessors, nor do we intend to substitute our judicial authority for the authority and discretion of the General Assembly. We are, rather, exercising our constitutional duty in declaring that, when we consider the evidence in the record, and when we apply the constitutional requirement of Section 183 to that evidence, it is crystal clear that the General Assembly has fallen short of its duty to enact legislation to provide for an efficient system of common schools throughout the state. In a word, the present system of common schools in Kentucky is not an "efficient" one in our view of the clear mandate of Section 183. The common school system in Kentucky is constitutionally deficient.

In reaching this decision, we are ever mindful of the immeasurable worth of education to our state and its citizens, especially to its young people. The framers of our constitution intended that each and every child in this state should receive a proper and an adequate education, *to be provided for by the General Assembly.* This opinion dutifully applies the constitutional test of Section 183 to the existing system of common schools. We do no more, nor may we do any less.

The goal of the framers of our constitution, and the polestar of this opinion, is eloquently and movingly stated in the landmark case of *Brown v. Board of Education:* "education is perhaps the most important function of state and local governments. . . . Such an opportunity, where the state has undertaken to provide it, is a right which must be made available to all on equal terms."

These thoughts were as applicable in 1891 when Section 183 was adopted as they are today and the goals they express reflect the goals set out by the framers of our Kentucky Constitution.

* * * The complaint included allegations that the system of school financing provided for by the General Assembly is inadequate; places too much emphasis on local school board resources; and results in inadequacies, inequities and inequalities throughout the state so as to result in an inefficient system of common school education in violation of Kentucky Constitution, Sections 1, 3 and 183 and the equal protection clause and the due process of law clause of the 14th Amendment to the United States Constitution. Additionally the complaint maintains the entire system is not efficient under the mandate of Section 183.

The relief sought by the plaintiffs was a declaration of rights to the effect that the system be declared unconstitutional; that the funding of schools also be determined to be unconstitutional and inadequate; that the defendant, Superintendent of Public Instruction be enjoined from further implementing said school statutes; that a mandamus be issued, directing the Governor to recommend to the General Assembly the enactment of appropriate legislation which would be in compliance with the aforementioned constitutional provisions; that a mandamus be issued, directing the President *Pro Tempore* of the Senate and the Speaker of the House of Representatives to place before the General Assembly appropriate legislation which is constitutionally valid; and that a mandamus be issued, directing the General Assembly to provide for an "equitable and adequate funding program for all school children so as to establish an 'efficient system of common schools.' " * * *

If one were to summarize the history of school funding in Kentucky, one might well say that every forward step taken to provide funds to local districts and to equalize money spent for the poor districts has been countered by one backward step. * * *

The overall effect of appellants' evidence is a virtual concession that Kentucky's system of common schools is underfunded and inadequate; is fraught with inequalities and inequities throughout the 177 local school districts; is ranked nationally in the lower 20–25% in virtually every category that is used to evaluate educational performance; and is not uniform among the districts in educational opportunities. * * *

In a few simple, but direct words, the framers of our present Constitution, set forth the will of the people with regard to the importance of providing public education in the Commonwealth. "General Assembly to provide for school system—The General Assembly shall, by appropriate legislation, provide for an efficient system of common schools throughout the State." Ky. Const. Sec. 183.

* * * A brief sojourn into the Constitutional debates will give some idea—a contemporaneous view—of the depth of the delegates' intention when Section 183 was drafted. * * * It will provide a background for our definition of "efficient."

* * * Delegates Beckner and Moore told their fellow delegates and have told us, what this section means.

— The providing of public education through a system of common schools by the General Assembly is the most "vital question" presented to them.

— Education of children must not be minimized to the "slightest degree."

— Education must be provided to the children of the rich and poor alike.

— Education of children is essential to the prosperity of our state.

— Education of children should be supervised by the State.

— There must be a constant and continuing effort to make our schools more efficient.

— We must not finance our schools in a *de minimis* fashion.

— All schools and children stand upon one level in their entitlement to equal state support.

This Court, in defining efficiency must, at least in part, be guided by these clearly expressed purposes. The framers of Section 183 emphasized that education is essential to the welfare of the citizens of the Commonwealth. By this animus to Section 183, we recognize that education is a fundamental right in Kentucky. * * *

In our sister and adjoining state of West Virginia, the state Constitution requires that "The legislature shall provide, by general law, for a thorough and efficient system of free schools." W.Va. Const, Art. XII, Sec. 1.

In the landmark case of *Pauley v. Kelly,* 162 W.Va. 672, 255 S.E.2d 859 (1979), the West Virginia Supreme Court faced a lawsuit similar to the one before us. * * * The Court engaged in extensive historical analysis, in which it carefully interpreted other states' constitutional mandates with regard to public education. The Court rejected the contention that legislative discretion in public school system matters is determinative. * * *

In turning to the definition of "efficient" the Court, began with definition which was "lexically" founded. "(T)he mandate ... becomes a command that the education system be absolutely complete, attentive to every detail, extending beyond ordinary parameters, and further, it must produce results without waste."

Following an analysis of the admitted plethora of legal precedent, the West Virginia Supreme Court adopted a definition of "thorough and efficient." "We may now define a thorough and efficient system of schools: It develops, as best the state of education expertise allows, the minds, bodies and social morality of its charges to prepare them for useful and happy occupations, recreation and citizenship, and does so economically."

The court continued by recognizing areas in which each child educated in the system should develop to full capacity: 1) literacy; 2) mathematical ability; 3) knowledge of government sufficient to equip the individual to make informed choices as a citizen; 4) self-knowledge sufficient to intelligently choose life work; 5) vocational or advanced academic training; 6) recreational pursuits; 7) creative interests; 8) social ethics. Support services, such as good physical facilities and instructional resources, and state and local monitoring for waste and incompetency were considered to be implicit in the definition of "a thorough and efficient system."

We cite *Pauley,* and quote from it at some length to show that Courts may, should and have involved themselves in defining the standards of a constitutionally mandated educational system. * * *

We consider foreign cases, along with our constitutional debates, Kentucky precedents and the opinion of experts in formulating the definition of "efficient" as it appears in our Constitution.

OPINIONS OF EXPERTS

Numerous well-qualified experts testified in this case. They were all well educated, experienced teachers, educators, or administrators; and all were familiar with the Kentucky system of common schools and with other states' and national school issues.

Dr. Richard Salmon testified that the concept of efficiency was a three part concept. First, the system should impose no financial hardship or advantage on any group of citizens. Further, local school districts must make comparable tax efforts. Second, resources provided by the system must be adequate and uniform throughout the state. Third, the system must not waste resources.

Dr. Kern Alexander opined that an efficient system is one which is unitary. It is one in which there is uniformity throughout the state. It is one in which equality is a hallmark and one in which students must be given equal educational opportunities, regardless of economic status, or place of residence. He also testified that "efficient" involves pay and training of teachers, school buildings, other teaching staff, materials, and adequacy of all educational resources. Moreover, he, like Dr. Salmon, believed that "efficient" also applies to the quality of management of schools. Summarizing Dr. Alexander's opinion, an efficient system is unitary, uniform, adequate and properly managed.

The definitions of "efficient" were documented and supported by numerous national and local studies, prepared and authorized by many of the giants of the education profession.

The primary expert for the appellees was a local school superintendent who felt that an efficient system is one which is operated as best as can be with the money that was provided. We reject such a definition which could result in a system of common schools, efficient only in the uniformly deplorable conditions it provides throughout the state.

In summary the experts in this case believed that an "efficient" system of common schools should have several elements:

1. The system is the sole responsibility of the General Assembly.

2. The tax effort should be evenly spread.

3. The system must provide the necessary resources throughout the state—they must be uniform.

4. The system must provide an adequate education.

5. The system must be properly managed.

DEFINITION OF "EFFICIENT"

We now hone in on the heart of this litigation. In defining "efficient," we use all the tools that are made available to us. In spite of any protestations to the contrary, we do not engage in judicial legislating. We do not make policy. We do not substitute our judgment for that of the General Assembly. We simply take the plain directive of the Constitution, and, armed with its purpose, we decide what our General Assembly must achieve in complying with its solemn constitutional duty.

Any system of common schools must be created and maintained with the premise that education is absolutely vital to the present and to the future of our Commonwealth. As Herbert Spencer observed, "Education has for its object the formation of character." No tax proceeds have a more important position or purpose than those for education in the grand scheme of our government. The importance of common schools and the education they provide Kentucky's children cannot be overemphasized or overstated.

The sole responsibility for providing the system of common schools is that of our General Assembly. It is a duty—it is a constitutional mandate placed by the people on the 138 members of that body who represent those selfsame people.

The General Assembly must not only establish the system, but it must monitor it on a continuing basis so that it will always be maintained in a constitutional manner. The General Assembly must carefully supervise it, so that there is no waste, no duplication, no mismanagement, at any level.

The system of common schools must be adequately funded to achieve its goals. The system of common schools must be substantially uniform throughout the state. Each child, *every child,* in this Commonwealth must be provided with an equal opportunity to have an adequate education. Equality is the key word here. The children of the poor and the children of the rich, the children who live in the poor districts and the children who live in the rich districts must be given the same opportunity and access to an adequate education. This obligation cannot be shifted to local counties and local school districts. * * *

We do not instruct the General Assembly to enact any specific legislation. We do not direct the members of the General Assembly to raise taxes. It is their decision how best to achieve efficiency. We only decide the nature of the constitutional mandate. We only determine the intent of the framers. Carrying-out that intent is the duty of the General Assembly.

A child's right to an adequate education is a fundamental one under our Constitution. The General Assembly must protect and advance that right. We concur with the trial court that an efficient system of education must have as its goal to provide each and every child with at least the seven following capacities: (i) sufficient oral and written communication skills to enable students to function in a complex and rapidly changing civilization; (ii) sufficient knowledge of economic, social, and political systems to enable the student to make informed choices; (iii) sufficient understanding of governmental processes to enable the student to understand the issues that affect his or her community, state, and nation; (iv) sufficient self-knowledge and knowledge of his or her mental and physical wellness; (v) sufficient grounding in the arts to enable each student to appreciate his or her cultural and historical heritage; (vi) sufficient training or preparation for advanced training in either academic or vocational fields so as to enable each child to choose and pursue life work intelligently; and (vii) sufficient levels of academic or vocational skills to enable public school students to compete favorably with their counterparts in surrounding states, in academics or in the job market.[22]

The essential, and minimal, characteristics of an "efficient" system of common schools, may be summarized as follows:

1. The establishment, maintenance and funding of common schools in Kentucky is the sole responsibility of the General Assembly.

2. Common schools shall be free to all.

3. Common schools shall be available to all Kentucky children.

4. Common schools shall be substantially uniform throughout the state.

5. Common schools shall provide equal educational opportunities to all Kentucky children, regardless of place of residence or economic circumstances.

6. Common schools shall be monitored by the General Assembly to assure that they are operated with no waste, no duplication, no mismanagement, and with no political influence.

7. The premise for the existence of common schools is that all children in Kentucky have a constitutional right to an adequate education.

22. In recreating and redesigning the Kentucky system of common schools, these seven characteristics should be considered as *minimum* goals in providing an adequate education. Certainly, there is no prohibition against higher goals—whether such are implemented statewide by the General Assembly or through the efforts of any local education entities that the General Assembly may establish—so long as the General Assembly meets the standards set out in this Opinion.

8. The General Assembly shall provide funding which is sufficient to provide each child in Kentucky an adequate education.

9. An adequate education is one which has as its goal the development of the seven capacities recited previously.

* * *

SUMMARY/CONCLUSION

We have decided this case solely on the basis of our Kentucky Constitution, Section 183. We find it unnecessary to inject any issues raised under the United States Constitution or the United States Bill of Rights in this matter. We decline to issue any injunctions, restraining orders, writs of prohibition or writs of mandamus.

We have decided one legal issue—and one legal issue only—viz., that the General Assembly of the Commonwealth has failed to establish an efficient system of common schools throughout the Commonwealth.

Lest there be any doubt, the result of our decision is that Kentucky's *entire system* of common schools is unconstitutional. There is no allegation that only part of the common school system is invalid, and we find no such circumstance. This decision applies to the entire sweep of the system—all its parts and parcels. * * *

While individual statutes are not herein addressed specifically or considered and declared to be facially unconstitutional, the statutory system as a whole and the interrelationship of the parts therein are hereby declared to be in violation of Section 183 of the Kentucky Constitution. Just as the bricks and mortar used in the construction of a schoolhouse, while contributing to the building's facade, do not ensure the overall structural adequacy of the schoolhouse, particular statutes drafted by the legislature in crafting and designing the current school system are not unconstitutional in and of themselves. Like the crumbling schoolhouse which must be redesigned and revitalized for more efficient use, with some component parts found to be adequate, some found to be less than adequate, statutes relating to education may be reenacted as components of a constitutional system if they combine with other component statutes to form an efficient and thereby constitutional system.

Since we have, by this decision, declared the system of common schools in Kentucky to be unconstitutional, Section 183 places an absolute duty on the General Assembly to re-create, re-establish a new system of common schools in the Commonwealth. As we have said, the premise of this opinion is that education is a basic, fundamental constitutional right that is available to all children within this Commonwealth. The General Assembly should begin with the same premise as it goes about its duty. The system, as we have said, must be efficient, and the criteria we have set out are binding on the General Assembly as it develops Kentucky's new system of common schools.

As we have previously emphasized, the *sole responsibility* for providing the system of common schools lies with the General Assembly. If they choose to delegate any of this duty to institutions such as the local boards of education, the General Assembly must provide a mechanism to assure that the ultimate control remains with the General Assembly, and assure that those local school districts also exercise the delegated duties in an efficient manner.

The General Assembly must provide adequate funding for the system. How they do this is their decision. * * *

This decision has not been reached without much thought and consideration. We do not take our responsibilities lightly, and we have decided this case based on our perception and interpretation of the Kentucky Constitution. We intend no criticism of any person, persons or institutions. We view this decision as an opportunity for the General Assembly to launch the Commonwealth into a new era of educational opportunity which will ensure a strong economic, cultural and political future.

Notes

1.   Education-related lawsuits in this area have relied upon state education articles, state equal protection guarantees, or some combination thereof. Noteworthy school finance lawsuits brought under the state's education articles include: *Rose v. Council for Better Educ., Inc.*, 790 S.W.2d 186 (Ky. 1989); *McDuffy v. Secretary of the Executive Office of Educ.*, 415 Mass. 545, 615 N.E.2d 516 (1993); *Helena Elementary Sch. Dist. Number One v. State*, 236 Mont. 44, 769 P.2d 684 (1989); *Edgewood Indep. Sch. Dist. v. Kirby*, 777 S.W.2d 391 (Tex. 1989). Lawsuits relying on state equal protection guarantees include *Serrano v. Priest*, 18 Cal.3d 728, 135 Cal.Rptr. 345, 557 P.2d 929 (1976), *cert. denied*, 432 U.S. 907, 97 S.Ct. 2951 (1977); *Horton v. Meskill*, 172 Conn. 615, 376 A.2d 359 (1977); and *Washakie County Sch. Dist. Number One v. Herschler*, 606 P.2d 310 (Wyo. 1980), *cert. denied*, 449 U.S. 824, 101 S.Ct. 86 (1980). Lawsuits relying on both the education clauses and the equal protection provisions include *Robinson v. Cahill*, 62 N.J. 473, 303 A.2d 273 (1973), *cert. denied*, 414 U.S. 976, 94 S.Ct. 292 (1973); *Pauley v. Kelly*, 162 W.Va. 672, 255 S.E.2d 859 (1979).

2.   Plaintiffs in the Education Articles cases of the past 15–20 years have prevailed within the context of school finance. What are the prospects for applying the principles and the reasoning of these cases to a wider range of educational quality issues? Consider the following framework for prospective litigation under a broader "right to an education." The framework contemplates an extension of this framework beyond school finance, and could be employed to either seek relief for a violation of the right to an education in specific situations, or to mandate quality education generally under the right. Might plaintiffs be successful employing such an approach? What types of fact patterns might lead to greater chances of success?

Alternatively, or in addition, might such a framework interface successfully with the requirements and mandates of the "No Child Left Behind" Act, *infra*?

a. Planning the Litigation

Step 1—Identify relevant words in the state's education articles.

Step 2—Identify lists of *quality standards, guidelines, or requirements* from published education articles cases, other court orders, relevant consent decrees, expert testimony, and/or relevant literature.

Step 3—Determine whether to seek relief for a violation of the right to an education in specific situations, or to mandate quality education generally under the right. (Other approaches may be available as well.)

b. If Seeking Declaratory and/or Injunctive Relief for a Violation of the Right to an Education in Specific Situations

Step 1—Attempt to establish a consensus on what constitutes a "Right to an Education" in a particular situation. This consensus may include excerpts from the lists of *quality standards, guidelines, or requirements*.

Step 2—Argue that a school district's actions in particular instances constitute a violation of this right under the state's education articles as reflected in key words (such as "efficient") because they run counter to the standards, guidelines, or requirements that have been identified.

c. If Seeking a Court Order to Mandate Quality Education Generally

Step 1—In the complaint, set forth quality standards, guidelines, requirements, etc.

Step 2—Argue that these standards should be implemented to give effect to the language in the education articles.

PROBLEM 28: The *Peter W.* Education Articles Lawsuit

Assume facts virtually identical to those set forth in the *Peter W.* case, *supra,* for several plaintiffs in a hypothetical school district today. Assume, also, that the district is located in the State of Maryland. If plaintiffs seek to bring a lawsuit under the prospective framework outlined in the above note, what arguments might they set forth? What result? Discuss.

4. CONSTRUING EDUCATIONAL QUALITY UNDER AN INDIVIDUAL STATE'S FUNDAMENTAL RIGHT TO AN EDUCATION

T. K. BUTT v. CALIFORNIA

4 Cal.4th 668, 15 Cal.Rptr.2d 480, 842 P.2d 1240 (1992).

BAXTER, JUDGE.

In late April 1991, after a period of mounting deficits, the Richmond Unified School District (District) announced it lacked funds to complete the final six weeks of its 1990–1991 school term. The District proposed to close its doors on May 1, 1991. The Superior Court of Contra Costa County issued a preliminary injunction directing the State of California (State), its Controller, and its Superintendent of Public Instruction (SPI) to ensure that the District's students would receive a full school term or its equivalent. The court approved the SPI's plan for an emergency State loan, and for appointment by the SPI of an administrator to take temporary charge of the District's operation.

We declined to stay implementation of the plan pending the State's appeal. However, we transferred the appeal here in order to decide an important issue of first impression: Whether the State has a constitutional duty, aside from the equal allocation of educational funds, to prevent the budgetary problems of a particular school district from depriving its students of "basic" educational equality.

We affirm the trial court's determination that such a duty exists under the California Constitution. Further, the court did not err in concluding, on the basis of the plaintiffs' preliminary showing, that the particular circumstances of this case demanded immediate State intervention. However, the court exceeded its judicial powers by approving the diversion of emergency loan funds from appropriations clearly intended by the Legislature for other purposes.

FACTS AND PROCEDURAL HISTORY

On April 17, 1991, Thomas K. Butt and other named District parents filed a class action for temporary and permanent injunctive relief against the State and the District's board of education (Board). The complaint alleged as follows: The State is responsible for educating all California children, and the Board is the State's agent for carrying out this responsibility in the District. The scheduled final day of the District's 1990–1991 school term was June 14, 1991, but the District had announced that its 44 elementary, secondary, and adult schools would close on May 1, 1991. The resulting loss of six weeks of instruction would cause serious, irreparable harm to the District's 31,500 students and would deny them their "fundamental right to an effective public education" under the California Constitution. Moreover, as an unjustified discrimination against District students compared to those elsewhere in California, the closure would violate equal protection guarantees of the California and United States Constitutions. Therefore, defendants should be enjoined from closing the District's schools before the scheduled end of the scholastic term.

> * * * Plaintiffs' motion papers also included declarations by District teachers, academicians in the field of education, and members of the Contra Costa County board of education. These statements detailed the serious disruptive effect the proposed closure would have upon the educational process in the District and upon the quality of education afforded its students. * * * The motion was heard on April 29, 1991. The Attorney General represented the State in opposition.

At the conclusion of the hearing, the trial court ruled orally that under the California Constitution, the State itself is responsible for the "fundamental" educational rights of California students and must remedy a local district's inability to provide its students an education "basically equivalent" to that provided elsewhere in the State. Concluding that the threatened closure would deny the District's students a "constitutionally [equal] education," the court ordered the State and the SPI to act as "they deem appropriate" to ensure that District schools remained open until June 14, 1991, or to provide District students a "substantially equivalent educational opportunity" within the statutory school year ending June 30, 1991.

This oral decision was followed by two written orders filed May 2. One of these, drafted by plaintiffs' counsel, purported to formalize the April 29 ruling. It made findings that closure of District schools by May 1 would cause District students irreparable harm, that the balance of harm favored a preliminary injunction, that education is a "fundamental right" in California, that no "compelling interest" justified denying District students six weeks of instruction available to "every other child in the State," and that plaintiffs' ultimate success on the merits was reasonably probable. The State and its agents again were directed to act "as . . . appropriate" to ensure District students, within the school year ending June 30, 1991, an education "equivalent basically" to that provided elsewhere in California for a full school term.

* * *

2. Merits Of Plaintiffs' Claims

* * * At the outset, the State does not claim it lacks any and all constitutional role in local educational affairs. Instead, its reasoning proceeds as follows: The State fulfills its financial responsibility for educational equality by subjecting all local districts, rich and poor, to an equalized statewide revenue base.[11] Unless a district fails to provide the minimum six-month school term set forth in the "free school" clause,[12] the State has no duty to ensure prudent use of the equalized funds by local administrators. Even if local mismanagement causes one district's services to fall seriously below prevailing statewide standards, the resulting educational inequality is not grounded in district wealth, nor does it involve a "suspect classification" such as race. Thus, "strict scrutiny" of the disparity is not required, and the State's refusal to intervene must be upheld as rationally related to its policy of local control and accountabili-

11. The funding scheme for public education is complex, but no party disputes the summary description provided in the State's brief: "The Legislature has attempted to equalize school district funding . . . by the use of a 'base revenue limit' for each district. Each district is classified by size and type. Based upon this classification scheme, each district has a 'base revenue limit' per unit of average daily attendance. The base revenue limit for any district includes the amount of property tax revenues a district can raise, with other specific local revenues, coupled with an equalization payment by the State, thus bringing each district into a rough equivalency of revenues.

Because the student population is so diverse, the Legislature had to supplement the base revenue limit with specific augmentations targeted for categories of children with needs that require special attention. These supplements are designated as 'categorical' aid. . . ."

12. Article IX, section 5 provides: "The Legislature shall provide for a system of common schools by which a free school shall be kept up and supported in each district at least six months in every year, after the first year in which a school has been established."

ty. Even if strict scrutiny is appropriate, the local-control policy is "compelling" enough to justify the State's inaction.

Under the unprecedented circumstances of this case, we cannot accept the State's contentions. We set forth our reasons in detail.

Since its admission to the Union, California has assumed specific responsibility for a statewide public education system open on equal terms to all. The Constitution of 1849 directed the Legislature to "provide for a system of common schools, by which a school shall be kept up and supported in each district. . . ." That constitutional command, with the additional proviso that the school maintained by each district be "free," has persisted to the present day.

* * * [T]he State itself has broad responsibility to ensure basic educational equality under the California Constitution. Because access to a public education is a uniquely fundamental personal interest in California, our courts have consistently found that the State charter accords broader rights against State-maintained educational discrimination than does federal law. Despite contrary federal authority, California constitutional principles require State assistance to correct basic "interdistrict" disparities in the system of common schools, even when the discriminatory effect was not produced by the purposeful conduct of the State or its agents.

In *Serrano v. Priest* (1971) 5 Cal.3d 584 (*Serrano I*), this court struck down the existing State public school financing scheme, which caused the amount of basic revenues per pupil to vary substantially among the respective districts depending on their taxable property values. *Serrano I* concluded at length that such a scheme violated both state and federal equal protection guaranties because it discriminated against a fundamental interest—education—on the basis of a suspect classification—district wealth—and could not be justified by a compelling state interest under the strict scrutiny test thus applicable. As the court concluded, "where fundamental rights or suspect classifications are at stake, a state's general freedom to discriminate on a geographical basis will be significantly curtailed by the equal protection clause."

Among other things, *Serrano I* rejected a claim that the wealth-based financing scheme was immune from challenge because the interdistrict revenue disparities it produced were not de jure, but merely de facto. Our opinion detailed the purposeful state legislative action which had produced the geographically based wealth classifications. It also made clear, however, that under California principles developed in cases involving school racial segregation, the absence of purposeful conduct by the State would not prevent a finding that the State system for funding public education had produced unconstitutional results.

Serrano I also discussed two groups of federal cases suggesting that place of residence was an impermissible basis for State discrimination in the quality of education. *Serrano I* cited with approval *Hall v. St. Helena Parish School Board*, 197 F.Supp. 649 (E.D. La. 1961). This federal decision struck down a Louisiana statute permitting local parishes to close their schools rather than integrate them. As *Serrano I* noted, *Hall v. St. Helena Parish* found an equal protection violation not only because of the statute's racial consequences, but also " 'because its application in one parish, while the state provides public schools elsewhere, would unfairly discriminate against the residents of that parish, irrespective of race. . . . [A]bsent a reasonable basis for so classifying, a state cannot close the public schools in one area while, at the same time, it maintains schools elsewhere with public funds.' "

Serrano I further noted a "second group of cases, dealing with apportionment [of votes], [in which] the high court has held that accidents of geography and arbitrary boundary lines of local government can afford no ground for discrimination among a state's citizens. If a voter's address may not determine the weight to which his ballot is entitledsurely it should not determine the quality of his child's education."

In *San Antonio School District v. Rodriguez* 411 U.S. 1 (1973), decided after S*errano I*, the United States Supreme Court declined to subject Texas's similar local-property-tax based school financing scheme to heightened scrutiny under the Fourteenth Amendment. The *Rodriguez* majority concluded that a school finance scheme dependent on district tax values does not discriminate against the poor as a distinct class; in any event, the majority observed, wealth alone had never been deemed a suspect classification for federal purposes. Moreover, the majority reasoned, education is not a fundamental interest protected by the federal Constitution. Therefore finding the strict scrutiny standard of review inapplicable, the majority upheld Texas's system as rationally related to that state's policy of local control of schools.

Nonetheless, in *Serrano v. Priest* (1976) 18 Cal.3d 728, this court reaffirmed the reasoning and result of *Serrano I* as required by the separate equal protection guaranties of the California Constitution. Among other things, *Serrano II* reiterated that for California purposes, education remains a fundamental interest "which [lies] at the core of our free and representative form of government. . . ."

Hence, *Serrano II* declared, "[i]n applying our state constitutional provisions guaranteeing equal protection of the laws we shall continue to apply strict and searching judicial scrutiny" to claims of discriminatory educational classifications. More recent cases confirm that education is a fundamental interest under the California equal protection guaranties and that the unique importance of public education in California's constitutional scheme requires careful scrutiny of state interference with basic educational rights.

* * * It therefore appears well settled that the California Constitution makes public education uniquely a fundamental concern of the State and prohibits maintenance and operation of the common public school system in a way which denies basic educational equality to the students of particular districts. The State itself bears the ultimate authority and

responsibility to ensure that its district-based system of common schools provides basic equality of educational opportunity.

The State claims it need only ensure the six-month minimum term guaranteed by the free school clause. This contention, however, misconstrues the basis of the trial court's decision. Whatever the requirements of the free school guaranty, the equal protection clause precludes the State from maintaining its common school system in a manner that denies the students of one district an education basically equivalent to that provided elsewhere throughout the State.

The State argues that even if the District's fiscal problems threatened its students' basic educational equality, any State duty to redress the discrimination must be judged under the most lenient standard of equal protection review. The State reasons as follows: Plaintiffs do not claim discrimination on the suspect basis of race. Nor is wealth-based discrimination at issue; as all parties concede, the District received the full benefit of the equalized funding system mandated by our *Serrano* decisions. At most, plaintiffs assert that a misuse of equalized funds by the District's officials caused a geographical disparity in service. Because residence and geography are not suspect classifications, the State's failure to prevent educational discrimination on those grounds is not subject to strict scrutiny. Rather, State inaction must be accepted as rationally related to the legitimate State policy of local control of schools.

However, both federal and California decisions make clear that heightened scrutiny applies to State-maintained discrimination whenever the disfavored class is suspect or the disparate treatment has a real and appreciable impact on a fundamental right or interest. As we have seen, education is such a fundamental interest for purposes of equal protection analysis under the California Constitution.

The State suggests there was no showing that the impact of the threatened closure on District students' fundamental right to basic educational equality was real and appreciable. Of course, the Constitution does not prohibit all disparities in educational quality or service. Despite extensive State regulation and standardization, the experience offered by our vast and diverse public school system undoubtedly differs to a considerable degree among districts, schools, and individual students. These distinctions arise from inevitable variances in local programs, philosophies, and conditions. "[A] requirement that [the State] provide [strictly] 'equal' educational opportunities would thus seem to present an entirely unworkable standard requiring impossible measurements and comparisons...." Moreover, principles of equal protection have never required the State to remedy all ills or eliminate all variances in service.

Accordingly, the California Constitution does not guarantee uniformity of term length for its own sake. While the current statutory system for allocating State educational funds strongly encourages a term of at least 175 days, that system is not constitutionally based and is subject to change. In an uncertain future, local districts, faced with mounting fiscal pressures, may be forced to seek creative ways to gain maximum educational benefit from limited resources. In such circumstances, a planned reduction of overall term length might be compensated by other means, such as extended daily hours, more intensive lesson plans, summer sessions, volunteer programs, and the like. An individual district's efforts in this regard are entitled to considerable deference.

Even unplanned truncation of the intended school term will not necessarily constitute a denial of "basic" educational equality. A finding of constitutional disparity depends on the individual facts. Unless the actual quality of the district's program, viewed as a whole, falls fundamentally below prevailing statewide standards, no constitutional violation occurs.

Here, however, plaintiffs' preliminary showing suggested that closure of the District's schools on May 1, 1991, would cause an extreme and unprecedented disparity in educational service and progress. District students faced the sudden loss of the final six weeks, or almost one-fifth, of the standard school term originally intended by the District and provided everywhere else in California. The record indicates that the decision to close early was a desperate, unplanned response to the District's impending insolvency and the impasse in negotiations for further emergency State aid. Several District teachers declared that they were operating on standard-term lesson schedules made at the beginning of the school year. These declarants outlined in detail how the proposed early closure would prevent them from completing instruction and grading essential for academic promotion, high school graduation, and college entrance. Faced with evidence of such extensive educational disruption, the trial court did not abuse its discretion by concluding that the proposed closure would have a real and appreciable impact on the affected students' fundamental California right to basic educational equality.

* * * Nothing in the *Serrano* cases themselves, or in other California decisions, supports the State's argument. On the contrary, the cases suggest that the State's responsibility for basic equality in its system of common schools extends beyond the detached role of fair funder or fair legislator. In extreme circumstances at least, the State "has a duty to intervene to prevent unconstitutional discrimination" at the local level.

CONCLUSION AND DISPOSITION

The District's financial inability to complete the final six weeks of its 1990–1991 school term threatened to deprive District students of their California constitutional right to basic educational equality with other public school students in this State. As the court further concluded, discrimination of this nature against education, a fundamental interest, could only be justified as necessary to serve a compelling interest. The State itself, as the entity with plenary constitutional responsibility for operation of the common school system, had a duty to protect District students against loss of their right to basic educational equality. Local control of public schools was not a compelling interest which would justify the State's failure to intervene.

The trial court thus properly ordered the State and its officials to protect the students' rights. The court also acted within its remedial powers by authorizing the SPI to assume control of the District's affairs, relieve the Board of its duties, and supervise the District's financial recovery. However, the court invaded the exclusive legislative power of appropriation by approving the diversion of appropriations for GAIN and the OUSD to an emergency loan for the District.

Accordingly, we reverse the trial court's remedial order of May 2, 1991, insofar as it approves funding of an emergency loan to the District from appropriations for the Oakland Unified School District and the Greater Avenues for Independence program. In all other respects, the court's orders of April 29 and May 2, 1991, are affirmed. The Court of Appeal is directed to remand the cause to the trial court for such further proceedings as may be appropriate under the views expressed in this opinion.

Notes

1. Recall the references to the *T. K. Butt* decision and the inclusion of relevant quotes in the Chapter 1 introductory section on the right to an education, *supra. T. K. Butt* is arguably a watershed case that clarifies and expands this right under state constitutional law.

2. State constitutions contain a variety of equal protection guarantees ranging from explicit equal protection clauses to provisions that attempt to guarantee equality in certain specific instances. *See* Robert F. Williams, *Equality Guarantees in State Constitutional Law,* 63 TEX. L. REV. 1195, 1196–97 (1985). When asked to interpret these provisions, some state courts follow federal constitutional jurisprudence without deviation. *Id.* at 1219–20. Other courts employ the federal equal protection framework but reserve the right to make their own decisions as to what constitutes a fundamental right or a suspect classification. For example, in *Serrano v. Priest*, 18 Cal.3d 728, 135 Cal.Rptr. 345, 557 P.2d 929, 950–51 (1976) (*Serrano II*), the California Supreme Court rejected the U.S. Supreme Court's approach to Fourteenth Amendment jurisprudence as set forth in *San Antonio Independent School District v. Rodriguez,* 411 U.S. 1, 93 S.Ct. 1278 (1973). The California court declared that, under California's independent jurisprudence, education would indeed be recognized as a fundamental right and wealth would be added to the list of suspect classifications triggering strict scrutiny. *Serrano,* 557 P.2d at 950–52.

A small number of state courts reject the federal approach entirely and seek to develop their own independent jurisprudence.

WILLIAMS v. STATE

Cal. Super. Ct. No. 312236.
Filed May 2000.
Settled August 2004.

One of the highest profile cases of its era, garnering national attention and generating substantial ongoing inquiry at both the political level and within the legal and education communities, *Williams* was an example of litigation in this area that was able to have an impact even though it never went to trial.

In this regard, *Williams* exemplifies the principle that—particularly in cases focusing on the education process and seeking to maximize equal opportunity and improve educational quality—a lawsuit need not lead to a written opinion to achieve results. The *SFNAACP v. SFUSD* litigation referenced above is another example of this type of approach.

Settlement agreements in these cases may vary in both form and content. Some include consent decrees, and are accompanied by judicial supervision and independent monitoring. In the case of *Williams,* the agreement led to state legislation, and to the explicit adoption of basic principles in California law regarding student rights of equal access to a quality education.

I. The Legal Complaint

The *Williams* complaint relied to a great extent on the holding in *T.K. Butt, supra,* regarding the parameters of the fundamental right to an education under state constitutional law. It also sought to fill in the gaps remaining from the *Serrano* litigation of the 1960s and 1970s, which had resulted in the equalization of per-pupil expenditures from the general fund across all school districts, but had not addressed inequities in school facilities, instructional materials, and teacher quality.

The following is a representative excerpt from the complaint, filed in May 2000:

1. Tens of thousands of children attending public schools located throughout the State of California are being deprived of basic educational opportunities available to more privileged children attending the majority of the State's public schools. State law requires students to attend school. Yet all too many California school children must go to school without trained teachers, necessary educational supplies, classrooms, or seats in classrooms. Students attempt to learn in schools that lack functioning heating or air conditioning systems, that lack sufficient numbers of functioning toilets, and that are infested with vermin, including rats, mice, and cockroaches. These appalling conditions in California public schools have persisted for years and have worsened over time. The Plaintiffs bring this suit in an effort to ensure that their schools meet basic minimal educational standards.

2. The schools at which these manifestly substandard conditions exist are overwhelmingly populated by low-income and nonwhite students and students who are still learning the English language. In all but three of the schools the Plaintiffs attend, more than half the student body is eligible for free or reduced-price meals at school. Nearly all the Plaintiffs in this action are black, Latino or Latina, or Asian Pacific American, and in each of the schools the Plaintiffs attend, nonwhite students constitute far more than half the student body. In all but one of the schools, nonwhite students constitute more than 90 percent of the student body. And in all but four of the schools, more than 30 percent of the students are still learning the English language.

3. Plaintiffs are children whose education the State cannot afford to ignore or impede. These children have dreams of college and professional careers. These children have hopes to vote and participate in their communities. These children have desires to challenge themselves and to learn. But those dreams and hopes and desires will be forever frustrated if California continues to relegate these children to learning conditions that should shock the conscience of any reasonable person. The State currently denies these children the basic tools necessary for them to have educational opportunities. Without those tools, children have no option to realize their dreams as fully educated, considered members of their State community.

4. The Constitution and laws of California require the State to ensure the delivery of basic educational opportunities for every child in California and vest the State with ultimate responsibility for the State's public elementary and secondary school system. Accordingly, the State, and not local districts, has taken the primary role in governance of the public school system. For example, the State provides approximately 60 percent of the money local school districts use to operate the public secondary and elementary schools. The State specifies how approximately 48 percent of that State money is to be spent, leaving school districts no discretion about its use. The State plays the principal role in determining how much money every school district in the State will receive. Moreover, the State has recently adopted a system of statewide education standards, a rigorous system of mandatory testing to monitor whether students satisfy those standards, and a system to bar students who fail to meet those standards from graduating or being promoted within their schools.

5. State officials charged with carrying out the State's critical education obligations have failed to develop or implement appropriate procedures to identify and correct the substandard conditions at the schools the Plaintiffs attend. Although the State has established academic standards that students must meet, the State has failed to meet its responsibility to ensure that schools provide teachers who are adequately trained to prepare students to satisfy those standards, has failed to provide sufficient materials to enable students to have a reasonable chance to pass tests that measure their performance, and has failed to provide facilities in which students can safely learn the materials they

need to meet the State-mandated standards. In other words, the State has established a system for education but has abdicated its responsibility to oversee and superintend that system to ensure it functions. This lawsuit seeks to require the State and State officials charged with affording basic educational opportunity to fulfill their obligation to all California public school children. Without relief, these children will continue to be denied their constitutional right to a free, common, and equal public school education.

II. Supporting Evidence from Expert's Reports

The *Williams* plaintiffs were able to generate substantial expert testimony in support of the complaint. The following excerpt summarizes a synthesis of expert reports, prepared by UCLA Education Professor Jeannie Oakes.

The following findings stand out:

• Qualified teachers, relevant instructional materials that students may use in school and at home, and clean, safe, and educationally appropriate facilities are fundamentally important to students' education. They enable students to learn the knowledge and skills that the state has specified as important. They promote students' chances to compete for good jobs and economic security. They provide students with the tools to engage in civic life as adults. The consequences of not having access to such teachers, materials, and facilities are particularly harsh in California's current high-stakes, standards-based education system.

• Many California students do not have the teachers, materials, and facilities that are fundamental to their learning and that are enjoyed by the majority of California students. The burdens of these serious shortfalls are borne most heavily in high-poverty schools, disproportionately attended by children of color and students still learning English. Such students are often housed in overcrowded, deteriorating facilities. Their schools frequently lack critical instructional resources. Often these are also schools with the fewest qualified teachers and the schools in which student achievement and college-going rates remain very low. The insufficient supply and poor quality of these educational basics create significant obstacles for students as they attempt to meet the content standards the State has set, pass State tests that are required for grade-to-grade promotion and high school graduation, and qualify for competitive opportunities in college and the workforce. In some schools, these poor conditions breed social alienation and pose real threats to students' health and wellbeing.

• Actions (and inaction) by the State have either contributed to or failed to prevent students' lack of access to qualified teachers, appropriate instructional materials, and adequate school facilities. These actions include a) the failure to specify and/or enforce standards for adequate and equitable resources and conditions that could prevent inadequacies and inequities; b) the failure to build the capacity of districts and schools to provide these resources and conditions; c) the failure to collect and/or analyze data in ways that would permit the State to know the extent of needs and problems regarding basic educational necessities; and d) insufficient interventions and assistance to address inadequacies and disparities when they occur.

• The inadequacies and disparities in access to teachers, instructional materials, and facilities are symptomatic of deeper, systemic flaws in California's education system. These flaws include a) a fragmented and incoherent approach to state policymaking; b) a system of school finance constructed in the absence of an overall plan for providing equitable and adequate resources and conditions, let alone ensuring education of the highest quality to all students; and c) a reluctance to invest in ways that ensure an equitable distribution of adequate resources and conditions; d) the delegation of responsibility for providing adequate and equitable education to local districts in the absence of State will or capacity to prevent the occurrence of serious inadequacies and disparities or to detect and correct them, should they arise. These flaws grow out of California's peculiar education policy history since the 1960s, and they have been exacerbated by the State's recent decision to rely on test-based accountability to drive educational improvement.

These findings make clear that the State must alter its policies and practices if it is to ensure that all students have access to the basics of educational quality and opportunity. Specific policies must be created that correct specific inadequacies and inequalities in the distribution of qualified teachers, textbooks and materials, and facilities. However, given the State's policy history, we caution that when recommendations are translated into specific policies, they can easily become temporary, if well-meant "spot-fixes." To be effective, however, these specific remedies must be framed in ways that recognize the deeper structural impediments in the State's current approach to governance and funding that underlie the current inadequacies and inequities and could give rise to them again. To rectify the more systemic problems, systemic reforms are required. Those reforms should modify the State's governance of the educational system in the following ways:

• Set State standards that specify the resources and conditions that are essential for teaching and learning, in addition to content and performance standards;

• Base the school funding system on what providing essential resources and conditions actually costs, with adjustments for cost differences in schools serving different communities and students;

• Expand the State accountability system to accurately and fairly measure and report learning resources and conditions, as well as achievement test scores;

• Establish unambiguous lines of State, regional, and district responsibility for ensuring that all students have these learning resources and conditions, and develop mechanisms that hold the appropriate officials at each of these levels accountable;

- Ensure that the accountability system is reciprocal—i.e., that it includes a two-way flow of accountability information and provides legitimate roles for local communities, parents, and students in holding the system accountable.

Only with these systemic changes will the State be able to prevent, or detect and correct, the specific problems that are the focus of this litigation. * * *

In many ways, this paper goes to great lengths to demonstrate what is patently obvious to great numbers of California school children and their parents as well as uncontested by nearly all observers of California's education system. For children to be educated, they require basic educational tools—teachers, books, and safe, healthy, and uncrowded schools. Teachers, books, and adequate school buildings are the staples of American teaching and learning. They are not usually thought of as educational resources or conditions whose availability varies significantly among schools, or whose centrality to education requires examination, documentation, and defense. The state has failed to provide these basic educational tools to many, many school children. Most often these are children who are poor, non-English speaking, African American, and Latino. It is unacceptable that the educational system would deprive any California child of these basics. It is reprehensible that those children most deprived educationally are also those who society neglects most in other ways.

Jeannie Oakes, *Education Inadequacy, Inequality, and Failed State Policy: A Synthesis of Expert Reports Prepared for* Williams v. State of California, *at* http://www.idea.gseis.ucla.edu/publications/williams/reports/wws16.html (Aug. 2002).

III. The Settlement Agreement

The following excerpt is from an April 2005 overview of the *Williams* settlement agreement, available at http://www.decent-schools.org, the Web site that has been established as a guide to the *Williams* implementation process:

The *Williams* settlement requires that all students have instructional materials and that their schools be clean and safe. It also takes steps toward assuring they have qualified teachers. The settlement holds schools accountable for delivering these fundamental elements, and provides nearly $1 billion to accomplish these goals. * * *

The parties announced a Settlement Agreement on August 13, 2004, and approximately six weeks later, on September 29, 2004, five bills implementing the legislative proposals set forth in the Settlement Agreement were signed into law by Governor Schwarzenegger. The Court approved the Settlement Agreement at a hearing on March 23, 2005.

The five bills implementing the Settlement Agreement were:

 • **SB 550 & AB 2727** (establishing minimum standards regarding school facilities, teacher quality, and instructional materials and accountability systems to enforce these standards);

 • **AB 1550** (phasing out the use of the Concept 6 [limited number of school days] calendar by July 1, 2012, and setting benchmarks for districts to reach this goal);

 • **AB 3001** (encouraging placement of qualified teachers in low performing schools; enhancing an existing oversight mechanism to ensure that teachers are qualified to teach the subject matter to which they have been assigned and to ensure that teachers of English learners are properly trained; and streamlining the process for highly qualified teachers from out-of-state to teach in California schools); and

 • **SB 6** (providing up to $800 million beginning in the 2005–06 fiscal year for districts to repair facility conditions that threaten health and safety and approximately $25 million in 2004–05 for a one-time comprehensive facilities needs assessment of schools ranked in the bottom 3 deciles under the 2003 statewide Academic Performance Index (API)).

Schools Affected by the Settlement

All California public schools are affected by the settlement because the new minimum standards and most of the related accountability systems apply to all schools and districts.

For example, every school district must now provide a uniform complaint process for complaints regarding insufficient instructional materials, unsafe or unhealthy facility conditions, and teacher vacancies and misassignments. Schools ranked in deciles one to three, inclusive, on the 2003 base Academic Performance Index (API) receive additional funds and oversight.

New Standards

 • **Facilities**: The new statutory definition of "good repair" for school facilities requires that "the facility is maintained in a manner that assures that it is clean, safe, and functional as determined pursuant to an interim evaluation instrument developed by the Office of Public School Construction [OPSC]." (SB 550; Education Code Section ("ECS") 17002(d)). * * *

 • **Instructional Materials**: SB 550 defines "sufficient textbooks or instructional materials" to mean that "each pupil, including English learners, has a textbook or instructional materials, or both, to use in class and to take home to complete required homework assignments." (SB 550, § 18; ECS 60119(c)).

 • **Teachers**: SB 550 created new standards in teacher quality, establishing definitions for teacher "misassignments" (i.e., where a teacher lacks subject matter, English Learner ("EL") or other required training or authorization) and "teacher vacancies" (i.e., where a classroom has no single, designated full-time teacher, but is staffed by a series of substitutes). (SB 550, § § 10, 12; ECS 33126, 35186.) The State also reaffirmed its commitment to comply with the teacher quality provisions of the federal No Child Left Behind Act, which require that there be a "highly qualified teacher" teaching every core academic class in all schools by the 2005–2006 school year. (20 U.S.C. § 6319(a)(2)).

• **Concept 6 Calendar (providing 163 days of classroom instruction, instead of the normal 180 days)**: AB 1550 prohibits the operation of a Concept 6 program after July 1, 2012, prohibits districts from starting new Concept 6 programs, and requires each district using Concept 6 currently to develop a comprehensive action plan to eliminate it and to comply with benchmarks toward doing so in the meantime. (AB 1550; ECS 37670, 37680–37695).

Accountability Systems

• **Uniform Complaint Process**: The uniform complaint process now allows students, parents, teachers, and others to complain about insufficient instructional materials, teacher vacancies and misassignments, and unsafe or unhealthy facilities conditions. * * * A complainant can appeal a decision regarding a facilities condition that poses an emergency or urgent threat to health or safety directly to the Superintendent of Public Instruction. School districts must report summarized data on the nature and resolution of all complaints on a quarterly basis to the County Superintendent and the district governing board. (SB 550, § 12 and AB 2727, § 1; ECS 35186.)

• **County Superintendent Visits**: County Superintendents are now required to annually inspect each of the schools in deciles one to three, inclusive, on the 2003 base API in their counties to determine compliance with the new instructional materials and facilities standards and whether the schools' School Accountability Report Cards (SARCs) accurately report this data. * * * (SB 550, § 1; ECS 1240.) If a County Superintendent determines that a school lacks sufficient standards-aligned instructional materials, the legislation provides a series of steps for corrective action, culminating in the actual purchase and distribution of books. (SB 550, § 1; ECS 1240.)

• **County Superintendent Reviews of Teacher Misassignments**: Building on the existing monitoring system, County Superintendents are now required to *annually* review and correct teacher misassignments in schools ranked in deciles one to three, inclusive, on the 2003 base API and schools with that are likely to have problems with teacher misassignment and teacher vacancies based on past experience or other available information. As part of this system, County Superintendents shall review and correct assignments of teachers who are assigned to teach English Language Learners but lack the proper training. (AB 3001, § 3; ECS 44258.9.)

• **District-level Facilities Inspection Systems**: By July 1, 2005, each district or county office of education participating in the School

Facility Program or the Deferred Maintenance Program must establish a facilities inspection system to ensure that each of its schools are maintained in good repair (using the new "good repair" standard). (SB 550, § 7; ECS 17070.75(e)).

• **District Textbook and Instructional Materials Resolutions**: Each school district governing board must now hold a public hearing no later than the eighth week of the school year to determine, through a resolution, whether each pupil in the district has sufficient textbooks or instructional materials. If the governing board determines there are insufficient textbooks or instructional materials, or both, the board shall provide information to teachers and the public explaining the insufficiency and take action to ensure that each pupil has sufficient textbooks or instructional materials, or both, within two months of the beginning of the school year in which the determination is made. (SB 550, § 18; ECS 60119.)

• **School Accountability Report Cards (SARCs)**: Each school must now include in its annual School Accountability Report Card, which is published on the Internet and is made available in paper form to parents who request it, accurate and current information regarding sufficiency of instructional materials, the number of teacher misassignments and vacancies, and the condition of school facilities, including any needed maintenance to ensure "good repair." (SB 550, § 10–11; ECS 33126, 33128.1.) * * *

IV. Legal Benchmarks: "a floor, rather than a ceiling, and a beginning, not an end"

Consider the following language, included in Section 25 of SB 550 as a result of the *Williams* litigation. What additional steps, above and beyond what has been documented above, are contemplated by this language? What additional steps would maximize the prospective effectiveness of the agreement?

How might this language be employed in future, education-related litigation that could become necessary?

> The Legislature finds and the Governor agrees that these minimum thresholds [for teacher quality, instructional materials, and school facilities] are essential in order to ensure that all of California's public school pupils have access to the basic elements of a quality public education. However, these minimum thresholds in no way reflect the full extent of the Legislature's and the Governor's expectations of what California's public schools are capable of achieving. Instead, these thresholds for teacher quality, instructional materials, and school facilities are intended by the Legislature and by the Governor to be a floor, rather than a ceiling, and a beginning, not an end, to the State of California's commitment and effort to ensure that all California school pupils have access to the basic elements of a quality public education.

It is the intent of the Legislature and of the Governor that teachers, school administrators, trustees and staff, parents, and pupils all recommit themselves to the pursuit of academic excellence in California public schools.

PROBLEM 29: Amending the U.S. Constitution

Consider the text of the following proposed amendment to the U.S. Constitution, set forth in House Joint Resolution 29 (2003). If such an amendment were actually to pass, how if at all might things change?

HOUSE JOINT RESOLUTION 29 (JACKSON)

The Right to a Public Education of Equal High Quality.
2003 CONG US HJ 29 (March 2003).

H.J. RES. 29

Proposing an amendment to the Constitution of the United States regarding the right of all citizens of the United States to a public education of equal high quality.

JOINT RESOLUTION

Proposing an amendment to the Constitution of the United States regarding the right of all citizens of the United States to a public education of equal high quality.

Resolved by the Senate and House of Representatives of the United States of America in Congress assembled (two-thirds of each House concurring therein), That the following article is proposed as an amendment to the Constitution of the United States, which shall be valid to all intents and purposes as part of the Constitution when ratified by the legislatures of three-fourths of the several States:

> SECTION 1. All citizens of the United States shall enjoy the right to a public education of equal high quality.

> SECTION 2. The Congress shall have power to implement this article by appropriate legislation.

PROBLEM 30: Educational Quality Issues
in the State of Ocean Wave

The following hypothetical takes place in the State of Ocean Wave, and focuses in particular on the fictional public school district of Shell Beach Unified, where approximately one third of the students are "English learners" (EL).

April 2003: In a shocking decision, the Shell Beach Unified school board voted unanimously (and with no prior warning) to reconstitute its three lowest performing schools. All adults working at the school were told that their positions were being terminated, that they could reapply for their former jobs should they choose to do so, but that no positions would be guaranteed. Tenured teachers were guaranteed a job in the District, but not necessarily at a school of their choice.

While reconstitution continued to spread across the country, and indeed was included as a potential "corrective action" under the U.S. "No Child Left Behind" Act, this was the first time it had been used in Ocean Wave.

At a press conference, School Board President Alicia Johnson declared: "We can no longer afford to operate schools where the average scores on tests of basic skills continue to be in the lowest quartile. Neither can we afford the luxury of placing schools in one or two-year "reconstitution-eligible" programs, as San Francisco did in the 1990s. We must take action now."

In addition to the reconstitution bombshell, the Board announced that it would immediately end the district policy of offering instruction in a student's primary language to the extent possible under the law. "We have informed all the bilingual aides in the District that their services will no longer be needed," Johnson explained. "Our education of English learners will be in English only. Students will be grouped together in a heterogeneous manner, with no instruction in a student's primary language. Special assistance, however, will be provided to EL students. This special assistance will include volunteer tutors from the local colleges and universities, and special after-school programs for interested families, taught by volunteer parents."

June 2005: New norm-referenced test scores for all students in the District were released. The District scored, overall, at the 46th percentile in reading (compared with the 46th percentile in 2003 and the 45th in 2004) and at the 51st percentile in math (compared with the 49th percentile in 2003 and the 53rd percentile in 2004), based on national norms. Students at the three reconstituted schools (which had been scoring in the bottom quartile in both reading and math) showed no overall improvement, and in fact the eleventh grade students at one of the three schools scored lower in both reading and math than they had during the previous year. The EL students tested in Spanish and Cantonese District-wide showed no overall improvement either. While EL students at some schools did better, EL students at other schools did worse. At the reconstituted schools, which had hired a large percentage of new and "partially credentialed" teachers, the EL student test scores actually dropped slightly.

A. In late June 2005, a lawsuit was filed by a group of concerned parents determined to stop the District from reconstituting any more schools, and seeking additional assistance to "clean up the mess" that they argue had been made at the three reconstituted schools. What arguments might plaintiffs set forth under state constitutional law? Under other viable legal frameworks? What result? Discuss.

B. Assume that, pursuant to House Joint Resolution 29, the U.S. Constitution was amended, and now includes the following language: "All citizens of the United States shall enjoy the right to a public education of equal high quality." If a group of parents of English learners in Shell Beach Unified file a lawsuit under this provision, seeking declaratory and injunctive relief, what arguments might they set forth? What result?

B.   THE U.S. "NO CHILD LEFT BEHIND" ACT

The "No Child Left Behind" Act (NCLB) represents a giant shift in the role of federal officials with regard to K–12 education governance. While individual states retain substantial autonomy and significant decision-making authority, they no longer have the final say in shaping educational policy across the board.

As referenced above, the NCLB is a wide-ranging, bipartisan statutory framework with requirements that extend across a broad spectrum. Indeed, most of the K–12 issues addressed in this casebook are touched on in some fashion by provisions of this Act.

While many of these provisions are controversial, none have generated more emotion than those relating to accountability. Critics have focused in particular on the heavy price that teachers, administrators, individual schools, and in fact entire districts might have to pay if certain benchmarks are not reached. People can lose their jobs, schools can be closed, and entire districts can be dis-established.

Many who question the structure and content of the accountability provisions do not typically quarrel with the importance of accountability, but wonder instead how so many important decisions can be made based on test scores alone. They also wonder how loosely defined phrases such as "relevant to the failure to make adequate yearly progress" can be applied on a day-to-day level in the real world of public schooling.

The legal terrain in this context is changing rapidly, with an ongoing effort in many parts of the country to push for changes in the statutory and regulatory requirements. In addition, a growing number of lawsuits have been filed in the courts, focusing mostly on a range of procedural issues. And it is likely that once the "corrective action" provisions are applied, substantive challenges will be brought contesting the sanctions themselves.

Yet it must be emphasized that many people from all walks of life and every spot on the political spectrum favor the type of aggressive approach that the NCLB exemplifies. Not only do people see great value in the higher standards and the more ambitious goals, but few would disagree with the efforts to close the dramatic achievement gap on the basis of race that still exists in this country.

Finally, as referenced above, many in the "civil rights" community have begun to identify legal strategies for actually employing the explicit mandates of the NCLB to challenge a range of questionable policies and practices that arguably have a negative impact on student rights of equal access to a quality education. *See, e.g.,* James S. Leibman & Charles F. Sabel, *The Federal No Child Left Behind Act and the Post–Desegregation Civil Rights Agenda,* 81 N.C. L. REV. 1703 (2003).

CHALLENGING RACIAL DISPARITIES:
THE PROMISE AND PITFALLS OF THE
NO CHILD LEFT BEHIND ACT'S
RACE–CONSCIOUS ACCOUNTABILITY

Daniel J. Losen.
47 HOWARD L.J. 243 (2004).

INTRODUCTION

* * * One new step toward fulfilling Brown's promise might be found in the principle of race-conscious accountability embedded within the No Child Left Behind Act of 2001 (NCLB). The No Child Left Behind Act is the short title for the reauthorization of the Elementary and Secondary Education Act (ESEA), which first passed in 1965. Title I of NCLB provides the largest single source of federal education funding targeted to help the states meet the needs of socioeconomically disadvantaged students.[9] Each state is required to use Title I funds to supplement its own educational spending and is prohibited from supplanting its expenditures.[10] Nearly every school district in the nation receives some of the approximately $10 billion appropriated each year. To achieve its goal, however, Title I also contains numerous monitoring and enforcement requirements that accompany state, district and school level spending.

In passing NCLB, a bipartisan Congress added explicitly race-conscious accountability requirements to Title I in order to redress severe racial disparities in educational achievement. The Act's Statement of Purpose includes the following, "[c]losing the achievement gap between high and low-performing children, especially the achievement gaps between minority and nonminority students, and between disadvantaged and their more advantaged peers. . . ." The new accountability system

---

9. Title I accounts for more than $12 billion of federal education spending each year. *See* 20 U.S.C.A. § 6302 (West 2000 & Supp. 2003). More than $18 billion dollars is scheduled for budget year 2004 and funding is scheduled to rise to $25 billion by fiscal year 2007. *Id.* The authorized amount, however, is expected to fall short of what the President approved in an appropriations bill before Congress. *See, e.g.*, TITLE I REPORT, EDUCATION SPENDING BILLS ADVANCE 13 (2003) [hereinafter TITLE I REPORT] (reporting "Democrats continued to criticize the administration for not providing enough funding to help states and school districts meet the mandates in the No Child Left Behind Act, noting that the law authorizes far more spending"). Moreover, under Title I, Part A, the Bush administration proposed a budget of $12.35 billion, which was more than $6 billion less than what the Act authorized when President Bush signed it into law. *Id.*

10. Early in Title I's history, investigations by advocacy groups revealed hundreds of schools spending the money inappropriately. *See* UNITED STATES COMM'N ON CIVIL RIGHTS, EQUAL EDUCATIONAL OPPORTUNITY PROJECT SERIES VOLUME I 218 (1996) [hereinafter EQUAL EDUCATIONAL OPPORTUNITY]. As recently as 1999, the Citizens' Commission on Civil Rights criticized Alabama for supplanting rather than supplementing state education funds with federal dollars. *See* CITIZENS' COMM'N ON CIVIL RIGHTS, TITLE I IN ALABAMA: THE STRUGGLE TO MEET BASIC NEEDS 46–47 (Corrine M. Yu & William L. Taylor eds., 1999), *available at* http://www.civilrights.org/issues/education/action.cfm?CurrentPage=3&content_type_id=6&selected_issues=5_ALL&action=search. The report concluded that federal money is being used in place of state and local funds to employ non-Title I teachers, make renovations, and provide basic operating expenses. *Id.*

includes technical assistance, and increasingly severe sanctions at the school and district level. The emphasis is on improving the academic proficiency of all students with an additional layer of subgroup accountability to prevent glossing over disparities in achievement that might be hidden when achievement data is analyzed in the aggregate. Therefore, the persistent failure of any major racial or ethnic group; of students with disabilities; of socio-economically disadvantaged students; or of students with limited English proficiency, at the school or district level, can trigger intervention and possibly sanctions.[16]

Despite serious shortcomings with its implementation, and what many educators argue is an inappropriately test-driven accountability design,[18] Title I's new accountability system is among the most race-conscious legislative remedies to racial inequity in K–12 education since Title VI of the Civil Rights Act of 1964 (Title VI).

Pursuant to Title VI, the Department of Education promulgated regulations that, similar to NCLB, result in intervening in public schools on the basis of trends in racial and ethnic data that are regarded as unacceptable. Neither the Title VI regulations nor NCLB requires proof that intentional discrimination caused the unacceptable trends as a prerequisite for intervention. One of the most significant differences may be that Title VI interventions are designed to protect minority students from policies or practices that have an unjustifiable racially disparate and negative impact—regarded as a form of unintentional discrimination. NCLB interventions, on the other hand, never raise the possibility of unlawful discrimination, but instead seek to ensure that all students meet state standards of proficiency. * * *

II. BACKGROUND OF NCLB AND RACE–BASED ACCOUNTABILITY

* * * As its name suggests, the No Child Left Behind Act of 2001 has accountability provisions intended to at least ensure racially equitable outcomes at a basic level of educational achievement. As noted earlier, the law requires that all major racial and ethnic groups achieve 100% proficiency in reading and math in twelve years while meeting specified benchmarks of "adequate yearly progress" along the way. Failure by any racial or ethnic group to meet the benchmarks (over two or more consecutive years) mandates increasingly harsh interventions.

---

16. 20 U.S.C.A. § 6311(b)(2)(C)(v)(II) (West Supp. 2003). Each subgroup is held to the same standards for accountability purposes and no matter what percent are proficient in reading and math, each group must reach 100% proficiency in these areas over the next twelve years to avoid intervention. *Id.* at (b)(1).

18. *See, e.g.,* Tamar Levin, *City to Track Why Students Leave School,* N.Y. TIMES, Sept. 15, 2003, at B1 (describing how school officials are intending to crack down on "push outs" by school personnel). It is criti-

cally important that readers distinguish the concept of setting outcome goals for accountability using racially disaggregated data from the specific mechanisms, sanctions and incentive structures as set forth in NCLB. This Article is highly critical of many of the specific mechanisms and details how some of the more promising requirements are not being properly implemented. *See infra* Parts III and IV. This Article should not be construed as endorsing or supporting the NCLB.

These actions can include firing staff, taking over school boards, or closing schools completely.

A.   The General Accountability Scheme

The broader accountability principle in NCLB is based on the concept of ensuring adequacy, for both progress and educational outcomes, over time. This broader scheme was made part of the ESEA in 1994. Thus far, proficiency in reading and mathematics as indicated by scores on statewide achievement tests has been the yardstick for adequacy. This test-driven accountability system was maintained and modified when NCLB Title I provisions were drafted.

Under NCLB, the federal government oversees the state educational agencies (SEA), the states oversee the local educational agencies (LEA) and the LEA oversee the individual schools. Accountability in this context consists of monitoring, enforcement, and due process. States are obligated to create a plan to ensure that all students meet the state's "challenging academic ... achievement standards." Each plan must have benchmarks to determine whether each school and district that received Title I funding is making "adequate yearly progress" (AYP). NCLB is notable in that it requires that all (100%) students be proficient in reading and math by the 2013–2014 school year.

Each state sets its own benchmarks for "proficiency." Under the Act's AYP provisions, each state must calibrate the acceptable yearly rate of progress necessary to meet the ultimate twelve-year goal of 100% proficiency. The state then annually assesses all schools and districts for their progress toward this goal under the rubric developed by that state. Schools and districts whose students persistently fail to fulfill AYP's progress benchmarks are flagged for technical assistance and labeled as "needing improvement."

If a school or district consistently fails to make adequate yearly progress, and cannot improve by utilizing technical assistance provided by the overseeing agency, that agency must intervene. NCLB provides for a wide range of choices, from closing schools, withdrawing federal funds, and firing staff at the harsh end, to requiring the school or district to hire a consultant and submit a school improvement plan at the gentler end. This flexibility with regard to interventions must be considered in understanding what passes for accountability under NCLB. Decisions about interventions are made by the agency responsible for oversight. While the public receives information and can apply pressure, it is unlikely that parents or advocates have standing to bring a private action in court pursuant to NCLB.

Since 1994, the ESEA has required districts and states to publicly report disaggregated test scores and other accountability data by race, ethnicity, gender, migrant status, disability, LEP status, and socioeconomic status. Public reporting is designed to trigger local pressure and involvement from parents and community members at the school and district level. To effectuate this parental involvement goal, the statute requires an extensive system of school district and state report cards that are widely disseminated to the public as well as distributed to every family. There are also requirements that school improvement plans be created with the input from parents, and that governance of schools needing improvement or interested in school-wide reforms using Title I funds include parents as part of the school governance structure.

B.   Race–Conscious Accountability Under NCLB

It is important to know that racially disaggregated data collection and reporting were required under the ESEA at least as far back as 1994, but the requirements were never enforced in the face of widespread noncompliance. It is also true, however, that under the ESEA before NCLB, if a school or district's aggregate test scores met the state's standards, that entity could make adequate yearly progress and no further information was required. It is reasonable to assume that without pressure from the federal government to report racially disaggregated data to the public, as required, and with no requirement that technical assistance or sanctions follow persistent failure of a given racial group, the lack of enforced requirements contributed to the lax attention to lower performing minority groups.

Additional components to NCLB's race-conscious provisions allow a school or district to escape the consequences of its failure to generate adequate yearly progress for one particular subgroup. The "safe harbor" provision in the Act stays otherwise required intervention for a school or district if the subgroup in question reduced it's failure rate significantly (by 10%) and improved on at least one other academic measure, such as graduation rates.

NCLB modified the ESEA further to require that students attending a school "needing improvement" be provided with an opportunity to transfer to another public school within the district.[109] A specified percentage of Title I funds may be used to transport these children to adequately performing schools. If a school has failed for three consecutive years, all the "eligible" students in that school must also be offered supplemental educational services.

In addition to the accountability scheme for adequate yearly progress, NCLB also added a requirement that state plans include a system to ensure that poor and minority students are not taught at higher rates by unqualified teachers and that states publicly report their progress toward this goal each year. While some regard the public reporting of specific data and its progress as a form of accountability, there are no other federal interventions or sanctions triggered by non-compliance. Unlike the other accountability provisions of the Act, the teacher quality provisions concern resource "inputs" more directly than achievement

---

109. In regulations, the Department of Education added language requiring transfers be made available, even if there was no existing capacity to receive the transfers in adequately performing schools within the district. *See* 20 U.S.C.A. § 6316(E) (West 2000 & Supp. 2003). "An LEA may not use lack of capacity to deny students the option to transfer under paragraph (a)(1) of this section." *Id.*

outcomes. It is well established, however, that teacher quality is a leading predictor of academic success, including for minority and low-income students.

* * * [T]he Department of Education did make explicit in the regulations that all state plans must address how the state will ensure poor and minority students' equitable access to highly qualified teachers. If successfully implemented, this provision could be among the most effective in the entire Act. Yet the required student access to highly qualified teachers has no real statutory enforcement consequences for non-compliance and pales in comparison to the test-based accountability under the adequate yearly progress provisions.

A closer look at the statute, however, reveals that the relatively concrete accountability requirements for AYP actually have a great deal of flexibility built into them. For example, each state is expected to create its own standards for proficiency. Despite the appearance that the new requirement of 100% proficiency for each major racial and ethnic subgroup in twelve-years creates a clear federal standard, the law only requires that standards be "high," with no definition of the term. NCLB also requires that the statewide achievement tests that are used for determining AYP must be "aligned" with the state's high standards and that the curriculum and instruction are aligned as well. While the standards, tests and benchmarks a state selects must pass review of the U.S. Secretary of Education, the approval process is not a rigorous one. As a result, what passes for high standards from one state to the next varies considerably.

States with higher "world class" standards have changed what they deem to be proficient depending on the consequences that flow with the label. Specifically, between 2001–2003, Louisiana, Colorado, and Connecticut each lowered their required score for "proficient" in response to new NCLB requirements.

One promising development is that NCLB added graduation rates and other academic indicators to the definition of adequate yearly progress. While AYP must be based primarily on test scores, failure on other academic indicators selected by the state can also send a school or district into "school improvement status." Given that Black and Latino minority youth are failing to earn diplomas at rates often exceeding 50% of their projected enrollment, accountability for graduation rates could prove critically important for driving more effective education reforms. In a controversial decision, however, Secretary Paige, in issuing regulations, decided that in the first analysis, graduation rates did not have to be disaggregated by minority subgroups for accountability purposes unless the "safe harbor" provision is being used. Therefore, given the limitations created by the U.S. Department of Education, the only thing that could be considered part of accountability is that districts' graduation rates must be "adequate," for all students, in the aggregate. Thus, based on the Department's disputed interpretation of the statute, graduation rates, unlike test scores, could be very low for any given racial subgroup without triggering any accountability interventions.

One critical aspect of NCLB's race-based accountability is the race-neutrality of the required enforcement actions triggered by the failure of any major racial or ethnic group within a school or district to meet the achievement standards. To correct a failing school or district, the overseeing authority chooses at least one intervention among those required.

However, even if a school or district is driven into "needs improvement status" based on the lackluster performance of a single racial or ethnic group, the proscribed interventions make no explicit reference to even a possibility that racial discrimination, via stereotypes or racial or ethnic bias, contributed to the academic failure of the subgroup in question. In other words, education authorities will look at racial equality and opportunity pursuant to NCLB only where a racial or ethnic subgroup is not performing at a level the state has defined as "proficient." So long as these "proficiency" benchmarks are met, and are the same ostensibly "high" standards for all children, NCLB's requirements are satisfied.

KEY STATUTORY PROVISIONS: THE "NO CHILD LEFT BEHIND" ACT

20 U.S.C. § 6301—Statement of purpose

The purpose of this subchapter is to ensure that all children have a fair, equal, and significant opportunity to obtain a high-quality education and reach, at a minimum, proficiency on challenging state academic achievement standards and state academic assessments. This purpose can be accomplished by—

(1) ensuring that high-quality academic assessments, accountability systems, teacher preparation and training, curriculum, and instructional materials are aligned with challenging State academic standards so that students, teachers, parents, and administrators can measure progress against common expectations for student academic achievement;

(2) meeting the educational needs of low-achieving children in our Nation's highest-poverty schools, limited English proficient children, migratory children, children with disabilities, Indian children, neglected or delinquent children, and young children in need of reading assistance;

(3) closing the achievement gap between high and low-performing children, especially the achievement gaps between minority and nonminority students, and between disadvantaged children and their more advantaged peers;

(4) holding schools, local educational agencies, and States accountable for improving the academic achievement of all students, and

identifying and turning around low-performing schools that have failed to provide a high-quality education to their students, while providing alternatives to students in such schools to enable the students to receive a high-quality education;

(5) distributing and targeting resources sufficiently to make a difference to local educational agencies and schools where needs are greatest;

(6) improving and strengthening accountability, teaching, and learning by using State assessment systems designed to ensure that students are meeting challenging State academic achievement and content standards and increasing achievement overall, but especially for the disadvantaged;

(7) providing greater decisionmaking authority and flexibility to schools and teachers in exchange for greater responsibility for student performance;

(8) providing children an enriched and accelerated educational program, including the use of schoolwide programs or additional services that increase the amount and quality of instructional time;

(9) promoting schoolwide reform and ensuring the access of children to effective, scientifically based instructional strategies and challenging academic content;

(10) significantly elevating the quality of instruction by providing staff in participating schools with substantial opportunities for professional development;

(11) coordinating services under all parts of this title with each other, with other educational services, and, to the extent feasible, with other agencies providing services to youth, children, and families; and

(12) affording parents substantial and meaningful opportunities to participate in the education of their children.

Basic SCHOOL Accountability Provisions
Under the "No Child Left Behind" Act

20 U.S.C. § 6316(b)—School improvement[a]

(1) General requirements

(A) Identification

* * * a local educational agency shall identify for school improvement any elementary school or secondary school served under this part that fails, for 2 consecutive years, to make adequate yearly progress as defined in the State's plan under section 6311(b)(2) of this title * * *

(7) Corrective action

(A) In general

a. *See also* 34 C.F.R. §§ 200.30, 200.31, 200.32, 200.36–200.38.

In this subsection, the term "corrective action" means action, consistent with State law, that—

(i) substantially and directly responds to—

(I) the consistent academic failure of a school that caused the local educational agency to take such action; and

(II) any underlying staffing, curriculum, or other problems in the school; and

(ii) is designed to increase substantially the likelihood that each group of students described in 6311(b)(2)(C) of this title[b] enrolled in the school identified for corrective action will meet or exceed the State's proficient levels of achievement on the State academic assessments described in section 6311(b)(3) of this title.

(B) System

In order to help students served under this part meet challenging State student academic achievement standards, each local educational agency shall implement a system of corrective action in accordance with subparagraphs (C) through (E).

(C) Role of local educational agency

b. 20 U.S.C. 6311(b)(2)(C) provides:

"Adequate yearly progress" shall be defined by the State in a manner that—

(i) applies the same high standards of academic achievement to all public elementary school and secondary school students in the State;

(ii) is statistically valid and reliable;

(iii) results in continuous and substantial academic improvement for all students;

(iv) measures the progress of public elementary schools, secondary schools and local educational agencies and the State based primarily on the academic assessments described in paragraph (3);

(v) includes separate measurable annual objectives for continuous and substantial improvement for each of the following:

(I) The achievement of all public elementary school and secondary school students.

(II) The achievement of—

(aa) economically disadvantaged students;

(bb) students from major racial and ethnic groups;

(cc) students with disabilities; and

(dd) students with limited English proficiency;

except that disaggregation of data under subclause (II) shall not be required in a case in which the number of students in a category is insufficient to yield statistically reliable information or the results would reveal personally identifiable information about an individual student;

(vi) in accordance with subparagraph (D), includes graduation rates for public secondary school students (defined as the percentage of students who graduate from secondary school with a regular diploma in the standard number of years) and at least one other academic indicator, as determined by the State for all public elementary school students; and

(vii) in accordance with subparagraph (D), at the State's discretion, may also include other academic indicators, as determined by the State for all public school students, measured separately for each group described in clause (v), such as achievement on additional State or locally administered assessments, decreases in grade-to-grade retention rates, attendance rates, and changes in the percentages of students completing gifted and talented, advanced placement, and college preparatory courses.

In the case of any school served by a local educational agency under this part that fails to make adequate yearly progress, as defined by the State under section 6311(b)(2) of this title, by the end of the second full school year after the identification under paragraph (1), the local educational agency shall—

(i) continue to provide all students enrolled in the school with the option to transfer to another public school served by the local educational agency, in accordance with paragraph (1)(E) and (F);

(ii) continue to provide technical assistance consistent with paragraph (4) while instituting any corrective action under clause (iv);

(iii) continue to make supplemental educational services available, in accordance with subsection (e) of this section, to children who remain in the school; and

(iv) identify the school for corrective action and take at least one of the following corrective actions:

(I) Replace the school staff who are relevant to the failure to make adequate yearly progress.

(II) Institute and fully implement a new curriculum, including providing appropriate professional development for all relevant staff, that is based on scientifically based research and offers substantial promise of improving educational achievement for low-achieving students and enabling the school to make adequate yearly progress.

(III) Significantly decrease management authority at the school level.

(IV) Appoint an outside expert to advise the school on its progress toward making adequate yearly progress, based on its school plan under paragraph (3).

(V) Extend the school year or school day for the school.

(VI) Restructure the internal organizational structure of the school.

(D) Delay

Notwithstanding any other provision of this paragraph, the local educational agency may delay, for a period not to exceed 1 year, implementation of the requirements under paragraph (5), corrective action under this paragraph, or restructuring under paragraph (8) if the school makes adequate yearly progress for 1 year or if its failure to make adequate yearly progress is due to exceptional or uncontrollable circumstances, such as a natural disaster or a precipitous and unforeseen decline in the financial resources of the local educational agency or school. No such period shall be taken into account in determining the number of consecutive years of failure to make adequate yearly progress.

(E) Publication and dissemination

The local educational agency shall publish and disseminate information regarding any corrective action the local educational agency takes under this paragraph at a school—

(i) to the public and to the parents of each student enrolled in the school subject to corrective action;

(ii) in an understandable and uniform format and, to the extent practicable, provided in a language that the parents can understand; and

(iii) through such means as the Internet, the media, and public agencies.

(8) Restructuring

(A) Failure to make adequate yearly progress

If, after 1 full school year of corrective action under paragraph (7), a school subject to such corrective action continues to fail to make adequate yearly progress, then the local educational agency shall—

(i) continue to provide all students enrolled in the school with the option to transfer to another public school served by the local educational agency, in accordance with paragraph (1)(E) and (F);

(ii) continue to make supplemental educational services available, in accordance with subsection (e) of this section, to children who remain in the school; and

(iii) prepare a plan and make necessary arrangements to carry out subparagraph (B).

(B) Alternative governance

Not later than the beginning of the school year following the year in which the local educational agency implements subparagraph (A), the local educational agency shall implement one of the following alternative governance arrangements for the school consistent with State law:

(i) Reopening the school as a public charter school.

(ii) Replacing all or most of the school staff (which may include the principal) who are relevant to the failure to make adequate yearly progress.

(iii) Entering into a contract with an entity, such as a private management company, with a demonstrated record of effectiveness, to operate the public school.

(iv) Turning the operation of the school over to the State educational agency, if permitted under State law and agreed to by the State.

(v) Any other major restructuring of the school's governance arrangement that makes fundamental reforms, such as significant changes in the school's staffing and governance, to improve student academic achievement in the school and that has substantial promise of enabling the school to make adequate yearly progress as defined in the State plan under section 6311(b)(2) of this title. In the case of a rural local educational agency with a total of less than 600 students in average daily attendance at the schools that are served by the agency and all of whose schools have a School Locale Code of 7 or 8, as determined by the Secretary, the Secretary shall, at such agency's request, provide technical assistance to such agency for the purpose of implementing this clause.

(C) Prompt notice

The local educational agency shall—

(i) provide prompt notice to teachers and parents whenever subparagraph (A) or (B) applies; and

(ii) provide the teachers and parents with an adequate opportunity to—

    (I) comment before taking any action under those subparagraphs; and

    (II) participate in developing any plan under subparagraph (A)(iii).

* * *

(12) Duration

If any school identified for school improvement, corrective action, or restructuring makes adequate yearly progress for two consecutive school years, the local educational agency shall no longer subject the school to the requirements of school improvement, corrective action, or restructuring or identify the school for school improvement for the succeeding school year.

Basic SCHOOL DISTRICT Accountability Provisions Under the "No Child Left Behind" Act

20 U.S.C. § 6316(c)—State review and local educational agency improvement

* * *

(3) Identification of local educational agency for improvement

A State shall identify for improvement any local educational agency that, for 2 consecutive years, including the period immediately prior to January 8, 2002, failed to make adequate yearly progress as defined in the State's plan under section 6311(b)(2) of this title.

* * *

(10) Corrective action

In order to help students served under this part meet challenging State student academic achievement standards, each State shall implement a system of corrective action in accordance with the following:

(A) Definition

As used in this paragraph, the term "corrective action" means action, consistent with State law, that—

    (i) substantially and directly responds to the consistent academic failure that caused the State to take such action and to any underlying staffing, curricular, or other problems in the agency; and

    (ii) is designed to meet the goal of having all students served under this part achieve at the proficient and advanced student academic achievement levels.

(B) General requirements

After providing technical assistance under paragraph (9) and subject to subparagraph (E), the State—

    (i) may take corrective action at any time with respect to a local educational agency that has been identified under paragraph (3);

    (ii) shall take corrective action with respect to any local educational agency that fails to make adequate yearly progress, as defined by the State, by the end of the second full school year after the identification of the agency under paragraph (3); and

    (iii) shall continue to provide technical assistance while instituting any corrective action under clause (i) or (ii).

(C) Certain corrective actions required

In the case of a local educational agency identified for corrective action, the State educational agency shall take at least one of the following corrective actions:

    (i) Deferring programmatic funds or reducing administrative funds.

    (ii) Instituting and fully implementing a new curriculum that is based on State and local academic content and achievement standards, including providing appropriate professional development based on scientifically based research for all relevant staff, that offers substantial promise of improving educational achievement for low-achieving students.

    (iii) Replacing the local educational agency personnel who are relevant to the failure to make adequate yearly progress.

    (iv) Removing particular schools from the jurisdiction of the local educational agency and establishing alternative arrangements for public governance and supervision of such schools.

    (v) Appointing, through the State educational agency, a receiver or trustee to administer the affairs of the local educational agency in place of the superintendent and school board.

    (vi) Abolishing or restructuring the local educational agency.

    (vii) Authorizing students to transfer from a school operated by the local educational agency to a higher-performing public school operated by another local educational agency in accordance with subsections (b)(1)(E) and (F) of this section, and providing to such students transportation (or the costs of transportation) to such schools consistent with subsection (b)(9) of this section, in conjunction with carrying out not less than one additional action described under this subparagraph.

(D) Hearing

Prior to implementing any corrective action under this paragraph, the State educational agency shall provide notice and a hearing to the affected local educational agency, if State law provides for such notice and hearing. The hearing shall take place not later than 45 days following the decision to implement corrective action.

(E) Notice to parents

The State educational agency shall publish, and disseminate to parents and the public, information on any corrective action the State educational agency takes under this paragraph through such means as the Internet, the media, and public agencies.

(F) Delay

Notwithstanding subparagraph (B)(ii), a State educational agency may delay, for a period not to exceed 1 year, implementation of corrective action under this paragraph if the local educational agency makes adequate yearly progress for 1 year or its failure to make adequate yearly progress is due to exceptional or uncontrollable circumstances, such as a natural disaster or a precipitous and unforeseen decline in the financial resources of the local educational agency. No such period shall be taken into account in determining the number of consecutive years of failure to make adequate yearly progress.

PROBLEM 31: Challenging the Implementation of the NCLB in Ocean Wave

Assume the same set of facts set forth in Problem 31, *supra*. Assume, also, that the Shell Beach schools continue their pattern of lackluster performance on standardized tests, and that the District therefore fails to meet its designated Adequate Yearly Progress goals as required under the terms of the NCLB. Assume that the State, acting pursuant to 20 U.S.C. Section 6316 (c), chooses the "corrective action" of "[d]eferring programmatic funds or reducing administrative funds" for the entire District. Assume that you have been consulted by a group of angry parents for the purpose of filing a challenge to the implementation of NCLB in this regard. In particular, the parents are prepared to argue that school funding decisions based on only one of many possible indicators of educational quality violate the rights of the students under federal and state law. What legal theories might be set forth on their behalf? What result? Discuss.

Qualifications For Educators Under the "No Child Left Behind" Act

20 U.S.C. Section 6319(a).

(a) Teacher qualifications and measurable objectives

(1) In general

Beginning with the first day of the first school year after January 8, 2002, each local educational agency receiving assistance under this part shall ensure that all teachers hired after such day and teaching in a program supported with funds under this part are highly qualified.

(2) State plan

As part of the plan described in section 6311 of this title, each State educational agency receiving assistance under this part shall develop a plan to ensure that all teachers teaching in core academic subjects within the State are highly qualified not later than the end of the 2005–2006 school year. Such plan shall establish annual measurable objectives for each local educational agency and school that, at a minimum—

(A) shall include an annual increase in the percentage of highly qualified teachers at each local educational agency and school, to ensure that all teachers teaching in core academic subjects in each public elementary school and secondary school are highly qualified not later than the end of the 2005–2006 school year;

(B) shall include an annual increase in the percentage of teachers who are receiving high-quality professional development to enable such teachers to become highly qualified and successful classroom teachers; and

(C) may include such other measures as the State educational agency determines to be appropriate to increase teacher qualifications.

(3) Local plan

As part of the plan described in section 6312 of this title, each local educational agency receiving assistance under this part shall develop a plan to ensure that all teachers teaching within the school district served by the local educational agency are highly qualified not later than the end of the 2005–2006 school year.

from 34 C.F.R. §§ 200.55–.57

§ 200.55   Qualifications of teachers.

(a) Newly hired teachers in Title I programs.

(1) An LEA must ensure that all teachers hired after the first day of the 2002–2003 school year who teach core academic subjects in a program supported with funds under subpart A of this part are highly qualified as defined in § 200.56.

(2) For the purpose of paragraph (a)(1) of this section, a teacher teaching in a program supported with funds under subpart A of this part is—

(i) A teacher in a targeted assisted school who is paid with funds under subpart A of this part;

(ii) A teacher in a schoolwide program school; or

(iii) A teacher employed by an LEA with funds under subpart A of this part to provide services to eligible private school students under § 200.62.

(b) All teachers of core academic subjects.

(1) Not later than the end of the 2005–2006 school year, each State that receives funds under subpart A of this part, and each LEA in that State, must ensure that all public elementary and secondary school teachers in the State who teach core academic subjects, including teachers employed by an LEA to provide services to eligible private school students under § 200.62, are highly qualified as defined in § 200.56.

(2) A teacher who does not teach a core academic subject—such as some vocational education teachers—is not required to meet the requirements in § 200.56.

(c) Definition. The term "core academic subjects" means English, reading or language arts, mathematics, science, foreign languages, civics and government, economics, arts, history, and geography.

(d) Private school teachers. The requirements in this section do not apply to teachers hired by private elementary and secondary schools.

§ 200.56 Definition of "highly qualified teacher."

To be a "highly qualified teacher," a teacher covered under § 200.55 must meet the requirements in paragraph (a) and either paragraph (b) or (c) of this section.

(a) In general.

(1) Except as provided in paragraph (a)(3) of this section, a teacher covered under § 200.55 must—

(i) Have obtained full State certification as a teacher, which may include certification obtained through alternative routes to certification; or

(ii)(A) Have passed the State teacher licensing examination; and

(B) Hold a license to teach in the State.

(2) A teacher meets the requirement in paragraph (a)(1) of this section if the teacher—

(i) Has fulfilled the State's certification and licensure require-ments applicable to the years of experience the teacher possesses; or

(ii) Is participating in an alternative route to certification pro-gram under which—

    (A) The teacher—

        (1) Receives high-quality professional development that is sustained, intensive, and classroom-focused in order to have a positive and lasting impact on classroom instruction, before and while teaching;

        (2) Participates in a program of intensive supervision that consists of structured guidance and regular ongoing support for teachers or a teacher mentor-ing program;

        (3) Assumes functions as a teacher only for a specified period of time not to exceed three years; and

        (4) Demonstrates satisfactory progress toward full cer-tification as prescribed by the State; and

    (B) The State ensures, through its certification and licen-sure process, that the provisions in paragraph (a)(2)(ii) of this section are met.

(3) A teacher teaching in a public charter school in a State must meet the certification and licensure requirements, if any, con-tained in the State's charter school law.

(4) If a teacher has had certification or licensure requirements waived on an emergency, temporary, or provisional basis, the teacher is not highly qualified.

(b) Teachers new to the profession. A teacher covered under § 200.55 who is new to the profession also must—

(1) Hold at least a bachelor's degree; and

(2) At the public elementary school level, demonstrate, by passing a rigorous State test (which may consist of passing a State certifi-cation or licensing test), subject knowledge and teaching skills in reading/language arts, writing, mathematics, and other areas of the basic elementary school curriculum; or

(3) At the public middle and high school levels, demonstrate a high level of competency by—

(i) Passing a rigorous State test in each academic subject in which the teacher teaches (which may consist of passing a State certification or licensing test in each of these subjects); or

(ii) Successfully completing in each academic subject in which the teacher teaches—

    (A) An undergraduate major;

    (B) A graduate degree;

    (C) Coursework equivalent to an undergraduate major; or

    (D) Advanced certification or credentialing.

(c) Teachers not new to the profession. A teacher covered under § 200.55 who is not new to the profession also must—

    (1) Hold at least a bachelor's degree; and

    (2)(i) Meet the applicable requirements in paragraph (b)(2) or (3) of this section; or

    (ii) Based on a high, objective, uniform State standard of evaluation in accordance with section 9101(23)(C)(ii) of the ESEA, demonstrate competency in each academic subject in which the teacher teaches.

§ 200.57 Plans to increase teacher quality.

(a) State plan.

    (1) A State that receives funds under subpart A of this part must develop, as part of its State plan under section 1111 of the ESEA, a plan to ensure that all public elementary and secondary school teachers in the State who teach core academic subjects are highly qualified not later than the end of the 2005–2006 school year.

    (2) The State's plan must—

        (i) Establish annual measurable objectives for each LEA and school that include, at a minimum, an annual increase in the percentage o—

            (A) Highly qualified teachers at each LEA and school; and

            (B) Teachers who are receiving high-quality professional development to enable them to become highly qualified and effective classroom teachers;

        (ii) Describe the strategies the State will use to—

            (A) Help LEAs and schools meet the requirements in paragraph (a)(1) of this section; and

            (B) Monitor the progress of LEAs and schools in meeting these requirements; and

        (iii) Until the SEA fully complies with paragraph (a)(1) of this section, describe the specific steps the SEA will take to—

            (A) Ensure that Title I schools provide instruction by highly qualified teachers, including steps that the SEA will take to ensure that minority children and children from low-income families are not taught at higher rates than other children by inexperienced, unqualified, or out-of-field teachers; and

(B) Evaluate and publicly report the progress of the SEA with respect to these steps.

(3) The State's plan may include other measures that the State determines are appropriate to increase teacher qualifications.

(b) Local plan. An LEA that receives funds under subpart A of this part must develop, as part of its local plan under section 1112 of the ESEA, a plan to ensure that—

(1) All public elementary and secondary school teachers in the LEA who teach core academic subjects, including teachers employed by the LEA to provide services to eligible private school students under § 200.62, are highly qualified not later than the end of the 2005–2006 school year; and

(2) Through incentives for voluntary transfers, professional development, recruitment programs, or other effective strategies, minority students and students from low-income families are not taught at higher rates than other students by unqualified, out-of-field, or inexperienced teachers.

Note

1. Inevitably, given how fast events have been moving in this area, there have been developments subsequent to the publication of this volume that could alter the nature and extent of the inquiry. In your view, what have been the most significant recent changes in this area, legally and as a matter of policy? What do these developments tell you about where the accountability movement might be headed in the U.S.?

C.   SCHOOL CHOICE, VOUCHERS, AND PRIVATIZATION

PROBLEM 32: Choice for Literacy in the 21st Century

The following hypothetical takes place in the State of Columbia in 2006.

Concerned about the lack of viable educational alternatives for language minority students, the Columbia legislature approved a bill establishing an innovative school choice program for English learners. The passage of this "Choice for Literacy in the Twenty-first Century" Act reflected a highly unusual alliance between prominent Republicans and prominent Democrats statewide.

Under the Act, families of students identified as "English learners" would be given vouchers which could then be redeemed at any public or private school in the state. These vouchers, which would be equivalent to the average per-pupil expenditure in Columbia *plus* the average expenditure per EL student in 2005, would guarantee families of EL students a free education. Private schools would not be required to accept these vouchers, but if they did, they would be precluded from charging the families any additional money.

Publicity surrounding the passage of the Act was highly positive, and the governor did not hesitate to sign it immediately. Leaders from business, education, and politics hailed the public interest nature of this choice program and the importance of addressing language acquisition issues in a free-market context. Trustees of most major private schools in the state announced that they would be establishing programs for language minority students to further the public good.

All schools accepting vouchers would be required to submit a curriculum plan to the State Department of English Language Instruction, a new agency established by the Act. No one approach to language acquisition would be required. However, the Act specified that *private* schools would be free to provide as much primary language instruction as they desired.

To guarantee a uniform system of measurement and accountability, the Educational Testing Service (ETS) was commissioned to set up tests (entry-level and exit-level) which would measure English Language Proficiency. All students entering a California public or private school for the first time would be required to take the entry-level test, and only students whose test results identified them as EL would be eligible for vouchers. At the end of every subsequent year, these same students would be required to take the exit-level test to ascertain continued eligibility. A three-year limit, however, was placed on the acquisition of vouchers under this program.

In the Winter of 2007, you are consulted by a group of parents who seek to block the implementation of this statutory scheme. The prospective plaintiffs would like to challenge the Act under principles of equity and educational quality. What legal and policy arguments might you set forth in such a case? What result? Discuss.

1. SCHOOL CHOICE GENERALLY

REFORMING SCHOOL REFORM

Martha Minow.
68 FORDHAM L. REV. 257 (1999).

* * * American public schools are commonly described as "in crisis," or failing to generate adequate levels of achievement. Another persistent charge addresses the disparate quality of educational opportunities between cities and suburbs, between public and private, and across other familiar social divisions. The contemporary push for reforms thus mirrors longstanding, potentially conflicting aspirations for American schooling: quality and equality. Universally available inadequate schooling would offer a tragic sort of equality; thus far, however, society has had far more success generating individual schools of high quality rather than widespread high quality schooling.

* * *[R]eforms [in the mid to late 1990s have gathered] under the banner of "choice." Rather than assigning students to public schools based on the location of their residence or some other characteristic, choice proposals would let parents and guardians select a school. In so doing, they seek to generate competitive pressures to promote higher quality schooling overall. In addition, choice proposals are said to afford some measure of equality. Voucher plans are meant to grant to poor and low-income families some of the latitude for selecting schools already enjoyed by families with enough resources to move to high quality suburban districts or to opt for private schools. Charter plans, offering resources to entrepreneurial groups interested in running innovative public schools, are intended to offer high quality options within the public system.

Vouchers and charters also risk perpetuating inequality by excluding and segregating children with special needs, skimming from public schools those families motivated enough to take advantage of voucher and charter programs, and diverting resources from the project of improving the entire public school system.

In some respects, choice reforms try to redress failures of the last wave of school reform, the law-driven equality movement. Starting with racial desegregation, the push for equality expanded to gender equity, education rights for children with disabilities, bilingual and bi-cultural programs for English-language-learners, school finance reform, and even equal access for religious as well as non-religious student activities in public school settings. Each of these efforts reflects an underlying impetus to ensure equal opportunities for individual students, regardless of their race, gender, disability, linguistic and national background, economic class, or religion. Another way to perceive these reforms is to see them as extensions into our schools of the deep social struggles over group status and equality that pervade other sectors of the society. Under either formulation, these equality-based reforms absorbed enormous energy and dramatically reshaped schools and school practices around the country—with results both admirable and less than admirable.

Specific critiques of versions of school desegregation, special education for children with disabilities, school finance plans, bilingual education, and other equality reforms repeatedly appear in contemporary debates over reform. Yet the choice movement most immediately affects the equality reforms by rejecting their central features: centralized student assignment and bureaucratic compliance mechanisms. It may be coincidence, but the choice movement urges greater parental and guardian control over where and with whom each child will be educated after decades of desegregation orders and following more recent efforts to include children with disabilities in mainstream classrooms. Voucher and charter programs do not focus on either specific equality initiatives or their categorical approaches. Racial desegregation, school finance litigation, special education, and bilingual education may be once proud names of prior school reforms, but now they often are blamed, directly or indirectly, for the bureaucratization, fragmentation, and misallocation that needs redress.

Will today's reforms themselves generate the pressing need for future reforms twenty or thirty years hence? I worry that the choice movement will accelerate the already zany tendency noted by Linda Darling–Hammond, a wise observer of schools, who commented, "[s]chools chew up and spit out undigested reforms on a regular basis. This creates a sense within schools that whatever the innovation, 'this too will pass'—and that it probably should." Often it is difficult to evaluate education reforms because they come fast and furiously, with teachers and administrators sometimes participating and sometimes resisting. Schools are littered with the carcasses of partially or wholly abandoned school reforms. We have had school-based budgeting, computer-based learning, whole language reading, and back-to-basics. More recently, the standards movement has called for high expectations and the frequent use of standardized evaluations. It oversimplifies matters to suggest that new school reforms simply react to old ones. Yet the new reforms both implicitly and explicitly reject the older methods. In simple terms, the new reforms emphasize competition and standards, choice and incentives. The older efforts, framed by rights and remedies, focused on equality and fairness. The new reforms include valuable strategies but also faulty assumptions and dangers. The old reforms generated cumbersome bureaucracies and sometimes counterproductive court orders, but also provided fundamental values and protections.

Can we construct reform not by reacting against a prior wave, but instead by building upon it? Can we challenge what it means to reform schools by reforming reform? The very phrase, "reforming reform," is gaining currency. It appears in contemporary efforts to fix what seems to have gone wrong with campaign finance reforms, Eastern European democratization, welfare reform, juvenile justice reform, bankruptcy reform, as well as school reform. Yet to be more than just another round of change, reformed reforms must anticipate what are usually the unanticipated consequences of the fresh turn of reforms. This can be done without waiting until current initiatives prompt still another demand for starting anew. It means starting with a sober evaluation of the claims and assumptions of the new reform movement. At the very least, this will reduce a new round of false promises and disappointments. It also means resisting the temptation to neglect goals that remain important because of the underrealization of other goals. Reforming reform involves learning to build constructively on the past while putting in place the capacity to learn from new initiatives.

For school reform, the relationship between equality and quality deserves sustained and simultaneous attention. Equality reforms hit the barriers of reaction, such as "white flight" in the face of desegregation orders and English-only referenda that have halted bilingual education in some communities. In trying to create remedies for unequal education along the lines of race, gender, language, disability, and financial inputs, the equality reforms also confronted the basic difficulties in elevating the quality of instruction and educational experiences. It makes sense, therefore, for current reforms to embrace the goal of quality through a combination of competition through choice mechanisms, and high expectations through standards. Yet the new reforms expose children to new risks of inequality by leaving some students in dismal existing schools and by making crucial to the selection of children's schools the parents' and guardians' motivation and knowledge—qualities that are most certainly not equally distributed.

In hopes of preventing yet another reform movement's demise and facile replacement by a similar successor, I here explore the limitations of both the choice and equality reforms. I identify potential common ground and synergies of present and past school improvement struggles. I will end by suggesting ways that legislators and other public bodies can craft choice reforms that sustain the commitments to both equality and quality.

I. The Choice Movement

School choice is a broad phrase which can encompass many kinds of proposals and programs, some of which are quite inconsistent with one another. One cluster of programs works exclusively within the public system. Here, choice could refer to modest opportunities for parents and guardians to seek to enroll a child in one of a handful of specialized, or "magnet," schools within a public school system. It could refer to more ambitious efforts to de-link residence from school assignment, such as the system-wide controlled choice plan of Cambridge, Massachusetts. In this approach, parents rank desired schools throughout the system, and a complex algorithm produces school assignments by combining private preferences with targets for racial and gender mixing, along with special weights for families seeking to keep siblings in the same school or seeking to enroll in the neighborhood school. Choice within public school systems also might involve limited cross-district enrollments, such as the Metco Program offered in Boston to enable inner city residents to enroll in participating suburban schools on a limited basis.

The newest element of choice within the public system is the charter school idea. Established by a chartering agency, such as a legislature or municipality, these independent schools are intended to operate with public funds but outside the regulations of the public system. Actually, authorizing legislation in different jurisdictions varies considerably in the degree of autonomy charter schools are granted. Some governmental units exempt these schools from otherwise prevailing collective bargaining agreements, curricular requirements, and spending requirements, while others impose some or all of these obligations. Typically awarded on a competitive basis to entrepreneurial groups, charters for such schools usually have a limited term before which they must be either renewed or else terminated by the authorizing authority. Charter school arrangements also vary in the degree to which they specify how school admissions are to be governed. Some authorizing legislation does not address whether charter schools may select among applicants and, if so, on what bases.

A different set of choice initiatives cross the border between public and private systems. Typically using the device of vouchers, these initiatives offer public monetary payments to enable families to enroll their children in private schools. One kind of program extends only to secular, non-parochial private schools. Another, considerably more controversial kind allows the vouchers to be used in any approved private school, including parochial schools. More than 3700 students in Cleveland—about five percent of the public school enrollment—use public vouchers to pay for private schooling. The vast majority of these students attend religious schools. However, the usual amount set for a voucher is insufficient to cover the costs of the most elite, selective private schools. Instead, the voucher total approximates the tuition level set by parochial schools, a tuition level that reflects subsidies from other sources. Some parents, of course, gladly choose parochial schools precisely for the instruction in religion and values, or because they hope that the school will offer discipline and social mobility. But for others, the religious schools are simply the one available option to get out of failing public schools. Voucher programs could vary the degree to which they target low-income families as recipients as opposed to all families.

The movement for educational choice may seem modest or almost marginal because it often involves small-scale experiments. Yet actually, the choice movement involves a radical challenge to the common school ideal that generated public schools and compulsory schooling from the nineteenth through the early part of the twentieth century. As Seymour Sarason recently observed, "charter schools rest on a devastating critique of the present system because it implies that for a school meaningfully to innovate to achieve more desirable outcomes, it must be free of the usual rules, regulations, and traditions of a school system." If real innovation and desirable results are possible only for schools that diverge from the public school system, then the system itself is the problem. The choice movement thus represents a dramatic departure from almost all prior school reforms. Rather than aspiring to create the "one best system" of public schooling that is run by experts for all children, charter, magnet, and voucher-based education proposals seek to multiply options, promote competition, and concentrate the mechanisms for evaluation and accountability in the hands of individual parents. In theory, some measure of comparability and public accountability would then be sought through general, even legislated, standards to set expectations and methods for assessment.

The public school system itself is seen as the main source of obstacles to innovation and good outcomes. Injecting private choice, coupled with public standards, into the schooling business is supposed to bypass the bureaucracies of mediocrity to produce higher quality schooling. Indeed, eight distinct assumptions underlie the pursuit of quality by those who advance choice:

(1) Competition will produce accountability. Schools that successfully secure student enrollments and waiting lists will do so because they offer desirable educational programming. Successful

schools will attract students and unsuccessful schools will lose theirs.

(2) Successful schools will grow and unsuccessful schools will shut down or change. Growth will occur as managers expand the number of seats they control or they will generate copycats; bad schools will fail to attract enrollments, and will lose sufficient funding to stay open and/or lose their public charters. Successful schools will spread their methods; charter schools, in particular, will develop innovative methods and will then export them to remaining public schools. In these ways, competition will generate an increasing, and ultimately sufficient, supply of quality options.

(3) Competition among schools will generate sufficient, relevant, and comparable information for assessing the quality of each school.

(4) Parents and guardians will seek out or otherwise obtain sufficient, relevant, and comparable information to enable them to make informed, responsive, and responsible choices. At best, a sufficient number will do so to signal to others how to choose or to trigger the appropriate signals to competing schools.

(5) Competition will cut through burdensome bureaucracy that stunts educational innovation and responsiveness to parents and students.

(6) Competition will permit desirable pluralism in teaching methods and in the kinds of values and traditions to be emphasized. Pluralism of this sort is compatible with American commitments to the free exercise of religion and multiculturalism. Educational research suggests that quite different teaching philosophies can each sustain successful schools.

(7) Competition structured in these ways is well suited to the enterprise of educating children and youth.

(8) Other reform efforts have not worked, so more radical change is necessary, even if it involves abandoning features of the common school ideal.

These assumptions converge around confidence in market-style mechanisms to generate quality. They are anchored in faith in consumer sovereignty, skepticism about experts, and the turn to plural solutions to any dispute about substantive good. These themes may characterize what is distinctive in the American political and economic traditions, as well as the beliefs that appear globally triumphant at the close of the twentieth century.

There are significant problems with the fit between many of the particular assumptions and the context of schooling because with start-up schools, either granted charters or created to take advantage of vouchers, basic structural issues involved in setting-up effective organizations and programs interfere with the assumption that competition readily will generate a range of successful options. One of the few reports on charter schools, which are so new that there is not yet much of a track record, reviewed five charter schools one year after they started. It identified barriers to success and implementation problems in six areas. The newly founded charter schools had difficulties developing effective school governance, particularly in defining roles and processes for decision-making. Because teachers and parents often perform unfamiliar tasks in a charter school context, role definition problems were intense. The start-up schools had problems creating a school climate and culture of trust and respect, and devising manageable work loads for teachers and principals. They had trouble gaining a stable financial base to cover fixed and variable costs, overcoming isolation, and producing a believable and attractive public image to communities outside the school. Student diversity was either absent or a source of tension for the schools.

An experienced school researcher who reviewed this report concluded, "the creators, the state [education] department, and the political leadership simply did not appreciate the predictable problems the new settings would or may encounter." Ironically, perhaps, the very faith and excitement in newness that helps to animate the charter school movement works from indifference to well-documented problems faced by other reform efforts. Rather than trying to learn from prior school experiments, the new entrepreneurs seize the chance to make their own mistakes.

Aside from predictable start-up problems, most of the other fundamental assumptions behind choice proposals also are at best problematic. For example, the assumption that competition will produce accountability is flawed. Competition may produce schools that offer superficial attractions but little actual accountability. Unless admissions practices are regulated, schools may skim for students based on their ability to perform on standardized tests; schools may simply "teach to the test" rather than provide deep education; schools may opt for glitzy appearance, such as gleaming computers, rather than quality instruction, which is more difficult to establish and to parade before potential customers. Many vocational and technical schools have sprung up in response to college-level loan and grant programs; they offer overpromise and still survive, though students leave, because they draw in the next generation of gullible students.

Further, there are key analytic problems with the claim that successful schools and programs will expand and that failing ones will shut down or change. Growth, or scaling up, of successful schools or schooling methods is the single most notable gap in prior effective school reforms. There is abundant knowledge about how to build one good school, yet we have poor or at best mixed results in spreading that knowledge to other school buildings. Schools do not operate with the kind of economies of scale that generate expansion in the private sector. Schooling is a retail, not wholesale business. For-profit schools are inclined to expand without waiting for demonstrated success or developing a sensible strategy precisely because short-term expansion may look like success.

Market-style failures may significantly injure children caught in schools that shut down. In Milwaukee, Juanita Hill School, one of the schools receiving vouchers, closed its doors in the middle of its first year. Its students were dumped back into public schools. The choice advocates simply assure that the schools that will close are the inadequate public schools. But public bureaucracies are notoriously poor at closing down bad schools. Inertia, pressure by teachers, unions, and parents, and the inadequacy of alternatives (in terms of quantity, quality, transportation, and other resources) contribute to the maintenance of inadequate schools. Thus, the assumption that failing schools will close or change is faulty. Even if such schools close, delays will most likely persist, costing particular children valuable years of schooling opportunities. Experts predict the emergence of a two-tiered system: elite schools benefiting from competition and other schools declining—but not shutting down—as their student enrollments shrink and resources accordingly diminish. Further, diffusion of successful methods is not well practiced and competition between charter schools and other public schools, and between private and public schools, if anything presses against sharing information about what works.

A central problem is likely to remain the absence of reliable, comparable information about schools eligible for election. Competition among schools elevates the significance of standardized test scores, which are in fact more influenced by parents' background and income than by the quality of school instruction offered to children. If standardized tests are the chief source of information about school success, individual schools have powerful incentives to screen students at the admissions stage, to skim for the best test-takers, and to push out those who do not perform. Prevalent use of standardized tests pressures competing schools to teach to the test rather than to develop inquiring, problem-solving minds capable of approaching issues with a healthy skepticism. Deeper measures of instructional quality are costly, complex, and nonstandardized. They also take several years to develop. Thus, adequate information is not likely to be available in the short term to identify quality instruction in new and expanding schools. In public systems that adopt high-stakes testing, which links student promotion and graduation to test performance, students will pay the price directly for failures by teachers and parents.

Comparable data are often difficult or impossible to obtain for evaluations across public and private schools. Schools often administer different tests; the private schools have no obligation and instead actually have disincentives to share their results; and, once again, richer measures of the quality of school programs are either absent or not comparable across schools. Even if adequate information begins to emerge, not all parents and guardians are likely to get it, understand it, or act upon it. Interest in becoming and capacity to be an informed advocate for one's children is not evenly distributed across all parents and guardians, to put it mildly. While motivated and competent parents will seek out information (to the extent that it exists) about quality programs, other parents will not do so, or they will be more influenced by matters of convenience (transportation, availability of after-school programs) or familiarity. Rather than having a sufficient number of informed and motivated parents making choices to generate the kinds of signaling necessary to reform all schools, the choice reforms may instead remove from existing public schools the motivated parents who make those schools as adequate or good as they currently are. The remaining students then will face risks even worse than they do now. Engaged and active parents will remove their children from schools where their interest in their own children benefited other children in the past.

One of the most emphatic claims by advocates for choice is the benefit of bypassing central bureaucracies. Whether through charters or vouchers, or simply as adopted within existing public schools, school-based management offenders bypass some features of centralized bureaucracy, but sometimes at the cost of fraud. Arizona, for example, adopted vouchers to bypass public school bureaucracies and ended up with a full-fledged fraud scandal, requiring the state to shut down schools mid-term. In addition, new inefficiencies are likely to emerge as each school has to make expenditure and managerial decisions. There are also obvious risks of misallocation of funds into public relations and marketing rather than programming. And there is the loss of economies of scale in the provision of specialized services, such as education for students with disabilities. Each individual school will have more difficulty spreading the costs of educating students with particular disabilities than the entire system would and thus, each individual school will have strong incentives to exclude students with disabilities.

Independent of academic quality, at least in theory, choice programs enhance pluralism. Absent some external regulation, having unregulated pluralism in the educational world may produce its own problems. Rather than generating a desirable pluralism of methods and values, vouchers and charters could instead produce self-segregation that exacerbates intergroup misunderstandings along the familiar fault-lines of race, class, gender, religion, disability, and national origin.

The most basic assumption behind the choice programs is that competition mechanisms are at least sufficiently suited to the educational task to warrant their use. It seems difficult to disagree that some degree of competition and some additional efforts to promote accountability could improve school systems that notoriously have been plagued by laborious top-down managerial bureaucracies. Yet, a full-fledged market approach to schooling seems a mismatch between means and ends. Schooling has crucial features that depart from privately consumed goods and services. The fit between market models and schooling is awkward and partial. The choosers are parents and guardians, who are not themselves the consumers, or children, who are not usually empowered to make crucial choices about such important matters. The consequences of these choices are not the same as the consequences of choices about what kind of bicycle or dishwasher to buy.

Education has dimensions of a public good, with crucial externalities affecting the entire population. Ensuring a good education for members of the next generation is important to the entire society; to our economic, cultural, and political well-being, as well as to the life prospects for the individual students involved. Cultivating capacities to act as informed and responsible citizens and as productive workers matters to everyone else. Our political fortunes, retirement benefits, and tax dollars are all at stake.

In addition, public education has distinct purposes in a democratic society. Philosophers and pundits have debated the purposes of education through the centuries. Historians still dispute the core motivations behind America's public school movement. But a basic statement of public school purposes would include forging commonality, promoting civic engagement in a diverse and democratic nation, and offering quality opportunities on an equal basis.

Further, the capacity of schools to reach all children pose special public concerns because so many children risk remaining in or falling into poverty, failing to obtain needed skills, never getting connected to the political process, and drifting into crime, drugs, and violence. Students with disabilities who do not learn well may become dependent on the state for support. The assumptions at work in market competition to produce better products for private consumption are not mirrored in the school context. Although the particular taxpayer may not see the direct benefits of public education today, failure to invest and to provide universal education will affect national economic, political, and social conditions for decades. Have we become so captivated by free market rhetoric that it is our answer to everything? It is often said that everything looks like a nail if you only have a hammer. But who will be helped, and who will be hammered, if market mechanisms pervade schooling? The classic economic rationales for regulation—inadequacy of information, large externalities, collective action problem—are particularly acute in the educational context.

The final assumption behind current choice proposals is that radical change is necessary because prior reform efforts have failed to remedy chronic school crises. This assumption is overstated, yet, in my view, it is the most compelling of the entire set. It is overstated in part because measuring the success and failure of past educational reforms is complex and highly politicized. Using some calipers, contemporary education in the United States has never been better. More kinds of students are taught more equitably in American schools today than thirty years ago, and there are higher graduation and literacy rates today. Students who would have dropped out in the past are now often helped by special programs.

On other measures, however, there are real signs of failure. American schools are more racially segregated today than thirty years ago. They also are marked by extreme disparities in expenditures and quality within and between states. For example, the state in which a student lives has a profound impact on math achievement. Student performance in the United States on many measures (notably math) falls below student performance elsewhere (notably Taiwan, Korea, and Russia), although U.S. students perform better on reading comprehension. Even ostensibly good schools widely underestimate their students' capacities. Urban and rural children are at serious risk of stultifying years in nearly futile classrooms.

We must do better. If we cared only about economic competitiveness in a global environment, we would have to improve the educational opportunities and achievement of all students because there are no students we can afford to waste. And surely we should care about equality and individual opportunity as values in and of themselves, as expressions of deep national and constitutional commitments, and as minimal necessities for the dignity of each person.

The assumption that American schools are in crisis neglects the real achievement of what appears to be the most inclusive school system in the world. The assumption that the common school project should be abandoned neglects promising results with recent efforts to improve public school systems. For example, Texas moved from forty-sixth among all states in math instruction to fourth after giving incentives to principals whose schools had the lowest test scores. It turns out to make a real difference if we focus on bringing up those with trouble learning, if we teach for mastery, and if we reject the view that some kids just cannot learn.

American schools overall do not hold young people to the same high expectations prevailing in schools in many other countries. American schools reflect gross disparities in expectations and resources across state lines, between cities and suburbs, and between social classes and races. Some of these disparities are the legacy of inequalities not redressed in the last wave of school reform. Some, to be frank, were exacerbated by that wave. The flight of middle-class and largely white families from cities to suburbs has a large place in the decline in the quality of urban schools and the striking contrast with many public suburban school systems.

Whether the choice initiatives merely neglect equality goals or directly abandon them, they are flawed. Unless choice initiatives try to address the goal of equality along with quality, they will become illegitimate in the eyes of those still committed to the prior wave of reform. And they will likely generate yet another round of reforms precisely to remedy the new inequalities. If the new wave of reforms helps to generate drastic changes, to jump-start more profound efforts to raise educational opportunities for the least advantaged, and to raise expectations for all students, it could help to realize the still-unattained goal of equal opportunity and high quality schooling. But to get there, we need to consider both why those goals are as yet unachieved and what it would take for choice initiatives to help reach them. * * *

III.   EQUALITY AND QUALITY: PRIVATE CHOICE AND PUBLIC COMMITMENTS

Choice reforms, notably vouchers and charters, could undermine equality goals unless there are direct efforts to maintain and enforce them. Offering vouchers and creating charters would exacerbate existing problems for the most disadvantaged students. Either there will be only a limited number of exit tickets or, if there are universally available vouchers and charter school places, they will not offer quality instruction for everyone. Not enough slots exist in demonstrably good schools, not enough is known about how to start up quality programs quickly and effectively, and there are not enough qualified and competent teachers.

African–American and Latino students in impoverished areas disproportionately attend inadequate schools that will lose out in any real competition. Anyone able to move or afford transportation would select other schools. Those unable to move or pay for transportation "will be trapped in inferior institutions providing inferior educations...." The loss of motivated students and families from those inferior institutions will cause them to decline further.

Indeed, the most vulnerable children are those who are not only poor and members of historically disadvantaged groups, but who also have parents lacking the skills, motivation, or ability to be engaged advocates for their children. Taking advantage of a choice system requires knowledge and initiative, which not all parents have. Children have no choice about who their parents are. A system that makes the content and form of schooling turn on parental choice makes the differences in parents matter even more than they already do in shaping educational opportunities. A choice system will make the inequalities among parents directly cost the children currently enrolled in public schools.

Inequalities along these fault-lines already deeply affect children's chances, to be sure. Wealthier, more educated, and more motivated parents already choose to live in districts with better schools, to pay for private schools, or to press for scholarships or slots in magnet schools, Metco programs, or a particularly effective teacher's classroom. Expanding choice options through vouchers and charter schools initially may seem to advance equality by opening up more options for more children. In practice, however, at least for a considerable time to come, such choice schemes will also put the most vulnerable children at an even greater disadvantage by simply abandoning them to failing schools.

With vouchers, practically speaking and given the existing institutions and the levels at which vouchers are set, the most likely option is parochial schools. Advocates of vouchers trumpet the ability of Catholic schools to generate higher test scores and more successful graduates than neighboring public schools, although the mutual selection process involved renders the comparison much less than scientific. Ironically, Catholic schools started originally in reaction to the curriculum devised for public schools, which Catholic leaders at the turn of the century feared imposed a dominant Protestant ideology. Catholic schools today already reflect the diversity of their communities in many urban areas and often educate more non-Catholics than Catholics. Many take on the goals of promoting tolerance across groups and civic engagement even more avidly than do the public schools, although from the vantage point of Catholic teachings. If they took on the task of educating not ten or twenty percent of the student cohort, but instead fifty or sixty percent, not only the mission of the Catholic schools but also the public education mission could be put in serious jeopardy. Catholic schools are private schools and do not, and probably should not, embrace the mission of public education.

What is or should be the mission of public education? The equality reformers fundamentally pursued the public missions of forging commonality, promoting civic engagement in a diverse and democratic nation, and offering quality opportunities on an equal basis. Such goals may seem lost at times in the conflicts and disappointments surrounding racial desegregation, bilingual education, gender equity struggles, school finance fights, and special education reform. Yet, the equality focus articulates the understanding that the entire society is affected by the educational opportunities and achievements of each new generation, and that no one can be wasted.

Choice initiatives advance equality only indirectly: if schools must compete for students, then more opportunities for high quality education could be generated and each individual might then seek out those opportunities. In addition to the worries already discussed about the obstacles to producing sufficient information about success and sufficient effective schools, the choice initiatives jeopardize the primary public education mission of promoting commonality and civic preparation. Schools inculcate and express values never more profoundly than when they model and enact in microcosm what could be imagined for the entire society. Taken to an extreme, choice reforms abandon the ideal of common, public institutions. They are premised on self-segregation and sorting, and they encourage competitors to slice off sectors, to skim for excellence, to celebrate competition over dialogue, and exit over debate. One school may offer military-style discipline; another could specialize in Western Civilization; a third in an Afro-centric curriculum. Others might be framed for Orthodox Judaism, Islam, or Baptist Revival. School choice tells us to treat schooling as a matter of private consumption rather than shared time that is formative of community and nation. Vouchers and charters risk abandoning our longstanding commitment to a common future. They therefore may pose the greatest jeopardy to equality and democracy that schools have seen in decades.

Choice programs also could exacerbate inequalities unless we establish systemic safeguards against exclusions and segregation. Without vigorous, creative regulatory efforts, vouchers and charter schools will increase the growing racial and ethnic segregation in American schools. Initial reports indicate that charter schools generally serve a lower percentage of disabled students and limited English proficiency students than do ordinary public schools. Charter schools could avoid the stratification that vouchers to private schools are likely to produce by maintaining the same per-pupil expenditure and the same tuition rate at each school. But what about students who actually cost more to educate due to disabilities or limited English proficiency? Dollars for their special needs should follow those students so that charter schools will seek, or at least, accept them. Here, too, market pressures and economies of scale push for specialty niche schools rather than schools that mainstream and integrate. Although national data indicate that charter schools serve more than their proportional share of students of color, charter schools in both Georgia and Colorado serve about half as many black students, in percentage terms, as do traditional public schools.

Voucher programs risk enlarging class-based divisions in schooling options. Wealthier people will continue to be able and willing to pay a premium above the level set by vouchers and to enroll their children in more expensive schools. People able to move to wealthier districts will have better-endowed charter school options unless charter programs cut across district lines. A market niche may develop for schools specializing in difficult youth, such as dropouts. Yet, such schools do not promote access to higher quality education, advanced placement classes, or integration with other kinds of students.

With these risks of worsening existing inequalities and divisions, charter and voucher schools face challenges from those still committed to equality in schooling. Such challenges will directly pose the question of whether freedom from bureaucratic requirements that accompanies charters and vouchers includes freedom from public obligations to combat discrimination and to promote equality across groups identified in terms of race, class, gender, disability, language, and religion. This raises knotty problems customarily gathered by lawyers under the state-action doctrines: when do obligations attached to public entities or actors also attach to private entities or actors? It is easier to craft arguments applying constitutional and statutory obligations to charter schools, which receive public authorization, than to voucher programs, which essentially direct public funds to private families who in turn select private schools. Different answers also could emerge depending upon the particular kind of category at issue (courts are more likely to find state action involved where racial exclusions occur than in other circumstances with some important exceptions). On many matters other than racial exclusiveness, courts will be reluctant to attach public obligations to private actors. The Supreme Court has ruled that even when ninety percent of the revenues funding a private school are from the public, that school is not bound by federal statutory and constitutional restrictions in employment decisions.

Judicial decisions are too remote and indirect for addressing the policy judgments today about how much should public dollars for schooling also entail public norms and obligations. Rather than pursue the arguments that could be mounted through litigation surrounding state-action issues or legal restrictions on private school conduct, those concerned with the direct consequences for equality of choice proposals should work to ensure that the governing legislation includes appropriate restrictions and guidelines.

These are the most obvious, basic questions that must be tackled:

(1) Can a participating charter or voucher school exclude students on the basis of race, class, or religion?

(2) Can a participating school reserve places for students of one race or gender in order to produce a desired balance or mix?

(3) Under what, if any, conditions can a participating school restrict enrollment to students of one gender, or students with or without particular disabilities, or students with or without English language proficiency?

(4) Can participating schools mitigate the tendency toward segregation along the many lines of difference among students by joining in system-wide programs or activities?

(5) How will participating schools be evaluated and how can analysis be generated to permit parents, school administrators, governmental and non-governmental leaders, as well as other community members, to assess choice experiments seriously as well as to assess particular schools?

More crucial than my own answers is the basic proposition that authorizing legislation, backed by enforcement possibilities, address each of these issues with specificity.

I offer my own initial responses simply to begin to sketch possible legislative guidelines. First, no school receiving public dollars through charter or voucher programs should be permitted to exclude applicants on the basis of race, class, or religion; but schools should be allowed to seek racial and gender balance by reserving spots until a brief period (such as one month) before each fall starting date, at which time unreserved spots should open on a random basis. Second, no school should be allowed to accept a voucher and then demand additional tuition payments from the family; the voucher should cover the entire tuition expense. Third, no school should be allowed to exclude persons of one sex, persons with (or without) particular disabilities, or persons based on their degree of English proficiency unless the school is part of a cooperative plan with other school(s) or systems ensuring comparable opportunities for those excluded from that school. If an all-boy charter school is permitted, for example, there must be comparable educational programs available in all-girl settings and also in co-ed settings. If students with mental retardation are excluded from a school, there must be integrated educational programs designed for those students available elsewhere. Fourth, segregation that occurs either by design or through patterns of self-selection must be mitigated by requiring each school to participate in city or region-wide programs to mix students enrolled in different schools and programs in joint projects such as journalism, drama, music, and sports (on cross-school teams). Only such programs have been shown to have success in reducing stereotypes and mistrust among students across group lines. Finally, participating schools must join in gathering data with uniform guidelines to permit evaluations of each school; the data should include standardized tests, but also richer measures of school programming, implementation, and results.

These recommendations balance the current law governing public schools with respect for innovation and experimentation that choice initiatives can bring. They also embody cautions about choice initiatives, cautions anchored in the hopes and the disappointments of the equality reforms of the recent past.

IV. STEERING THE WAVES

Much analysis proceeds by puncturing balloons of optimism. I do something like that here in the hope of reducing the hot air, but not the pressure, for change. The biggest problem with the current phase of reforms is the familiar one of exaggeration. Exaggeration and simplification seem to have become simply part of the territory you have to know of mass democratic politics both in the statement of the problem—most schools are NOT in great or increasing crisis—and in the promise of solutions—quick, easy, and painless. We should know better than to believe recycled themes that can be discerned in almost all the waves of past school reform. Excessive claims seem necessary to get the lift and buoyancy needed for movement. But puffed up claims are waiting to be punctured.

More than two decades ago, I evaluated a then-new small federal program termed "career education." Its supporters claimed that the program would solve student apathy, curricular irrelevance, tension between generations, and that it also would ease the transition between school and adult work—all this by introducing students through brief and simple lectures to various kinds of adult career options. I am sure I do not need to state in detail how far short the results fell from these high aims. But I will hum a few bars: I concluded that the program should have been called the "76 Trombones of Career Education." Like the Music Man, the program promised to create enormous changes simply by modeling some thinking about them. Fancy talk, and even fancy uniforms, do not make students into a well-tuned marching band.

What if we tried to mobilize around reforming school reform? Then we would talk of the costs of trying and discarding reforms that litter the lives of children. We would criticize new and prior reforms not as part of the perpetual puncture game, but as part of a demand for honest assessments of the mixed picture of the present and the mixed promises of any given initiative. School choice proposals admirably generate energy, initiative, creativity, and resources. Let us solicit new entrepreneurs to schools and substantial donations to end business as usual; let's build high expectations for all children, and demand accountability of parents as well as school administrators. We also should acknowledge the limitations of past equality reforms. But we must not abandon either equality or the commitment to free, high quality education for all children. The challenge is not to shift schools into the private frame of markets, but to build the benefits of choice and competition into the public frame. The goal is not to get every kid into a private school, but to make all schools the kinds of places that give every kid the best possible fighting chance. The goal is to steer the wave rather than watch it crash across and inundate prior dreams.

In my view, building on the best of the past and the most promising features of school choice means expanding charter schools rather than vouchers for private schools. Charter schools remain within the public system. Therefore, they remain more likely to be tied to the mission of the public schools. They also can be encouraged to share information about successes and failures. Technical assistance can and should be available so that each individual school does not have to invent its own solutions to predictable start-up problems.

Additionally, charter schools can be directed not to set tuition higher than the public stipend accompanying each student. Even charter schools have incentives, however, to skim talented students who have active parents while abandoning others to less desirable schools. Charter schools can and should be bound by the same admissions guidelines applicable to any other public school; preferably, charter schools should select randomly from the pool of those students who apply. Guidelines mean regulation, bureaucracy, and administration, but the entrepreneurship stimulated through charter schools can assist the development of better guidelines and more effective regulation. Just as industries now participate in negotiating over the specific details of environmental and safety regulations to produce more effective but less onerous rules, individual schools could participate in designing the means, but not the ends, of school regulations promoting equality and quality. Voucher plans also could be brought within this regulatory process to promote equality, although many private schools then would likely decline to participate.

The excitement and radical reconsideration opened by choice initiatives should be tapped to enlarge the range of good choices available to the most disadvantaged families. If residential segregation by race and class produces patterns of increasing school segregation, then genuine choice programs must transcend geographic and district borders. Cross-district choice programs and incentives to help suburban schools make room for urban students could make the promises of choice more genuine. So would college and university direct engagement in the tasks of supporting and mentoring classroom teachers, generating rich educational experiences for young children, and aiding in the collating and dissemination of crucial data.

School reform is always a symbolic as well as a practical fight. Schools afford an arena for fighting about what kind of society we should be, how the old and new generations should relate, whether commerce should govern democracy or democracy shall govern commerce, and how individual freedoms should be rendered compatible with the common good. It is imperative that the new round of school fights center as much on the symbols of inclusion and equality as upon the rhetoric of individualism and quality. These values need one another so that the whole is at least as worthy as the sum of the parts, if not perhaps more so.

School reform traditionally chews up and spits out undigested initiatives. What if school choice reforms afforded the occasion for building on the past while undertaking bold experiments? What if we recognized, as Audre Lorde put it, that "[w]e have the power those who came before us have given us, to move beyond the place where they were standing." We must keep our commitments, if not quite our heads.

2. THE SCHOOL CHOICE PROVISIONS OF NCLB

School choice, as referenced above, is a key component of the 2001 U.S. "No Child Left Behind" Act. Under the legislation, parents have gained the right to choose additional educational options for their children if—among other things—their child's current school either fails to meet "performance" requirements or is deemed "persistently dangerous." Indeed, both proponents and critics of NCLB have alluded to the fact that this Act continues the push toward more school choice that has been a central policy imperative for many who favor a free-market approach and greater privatization in the nation's educational system.

In addition to the choice options built into other provisions, the Act includes a separate section that directly addresses school choice.

School Choice Provisions Under the "No Child Left Behind" Act and Relevant Federal Regulations

20 U.S.C. § 6316(b)—School improvement * * *

(9) Transportation

In any case described in paragraph (1)(E) for schools described in paragraphs (1)(A), (5), (7)(C)(i), and (8)(A), and subsection (c)(10)(C)(vii) of this section, the local educational agency shall provide, or shall pay for the provision of, transportation for the student to the public school the student attends. * * *

(13) Special rule

A local educational agency shall permit a child who transferred to another school under this subsection to remain in that school until the child has completed the highest grade in that school. The obligation of the local educational agency to provide, or to provide for, transportation for the child ends at the end of a school year if the local educational agency determines that the school from which the child transferred is no longer identified for school improvement or subject to corrective action or restructuring.

from 34 C.F.R. § 200.44 Public school choice

(a) Requirements.

(1) In the case of a school identified for school improvement under § 200.32, for corrective action under § 200.33, or for restructuring under § 200.34, the LEA must provide all students enrolled in the school with the option to transfer to another public school served by the LEA.

(2) The LEA must offer this option not later than the first day of the school year following the year in which the LEA administered the assessments that resulted in its identification of the school for improvement, corrective action, or restructuring.

(3) The schools to which students may transfer under paragraph (a)(1) of this section—

    (i) May not include schools that—

        (A) The LEA has identified for improvement under § 200.32, corrective action under § 200.33, or restructuring under § 200.34; or

        (B) Are persistently dangerous as determined by the State; and

    (ii) May include one or more public charter schools.

(4) If more than one school meets the requirements of paragraph (a)(3) of this section, the LEA must—

    (i) Provide to parents of students eligible to transfer under paragraph (a)(1) of this section a choice of more than one such school; and

    (ii) Take into account the parents' preferences among the choices offered under paragraph (a)(4)(i) of this section.

(5) The LEA must offer the option to transfer described in this section unless it is prohibited by State law in accordance with paragraph (b) of this section.

(6) Except as described in §§ 200.32(d) and 200.33(c), if a school was in school improvement or subject to corrective action before January 8, 2002, the State must ensure that the LEA provides a public school choice option in accordance with paragraph (a)(1) of this section not later than the first day of the 2002–2003 school year.

(b) Limitation on State law prohibition. An LEA may invoke the State law prohibition on choice described in paragraph (a)(5) of this section only if the State law prohibits choice through restrictions on public school assignments or the transfer of students from one public school to another public school.

(c) Desegregation plans.

(1) If an LEA is subject to a desegregation plan, whether that plan is voluntary, court-ordered, or required by a Federal or State administrative agency, the LEA is not exempt from the requirement in paragraph (a)(1) of this section.

(2) In determining how to provide students with the option to transfer to another school, the LEA may take into account the requirements of the desegregation plan.

(3) If the desegregation plan forbids the LEA from offering the transfer option required under paragraph (a)(1) of this section, the LEA must secure appropriate changes to the plan to permit compliance with paragraph (a)(1) of this section.

(d) Capacity. An LEA may not use lack of capacity to deny students the option to transfer under paragraph (a)(1) of this section.

(e) Priority.

(1) In providing students the option to transfer to another public school in accordance with paragraph (a)(1) of this section, the LEA must give priority to the lowest-achieving students from low-income families.

(2) The LEA must determine family income on the same basis that the LEA uses to make allocations to schools under subpart A of this part.

(f) Status. Any public school to which a student transfers under paragraph (a)(1) of this section must ensure that the student is enrolled in classes and other activities in the school in the same manner as all other students in the school.

(g) Duration of transfer.

(1) If a student exercises the option under paragraph (a)(1) of this section to transfer to another public school, the LEA must permit the student to remain in that school until the student has completed the highest grade in the school.

(2) The LEA's obligation to provide transportation for the student may be limited under the circumstances described in paragraph (i) of this section and in § 200.48.

(h) No eligible schools within an LEA. If all public schools to which a student may transfer within an LEA are identified for school improvement, corrective action, or restructuring, the LEA—

(1) Must, to the extent practicable, establish a cooperative agreement for a transfer with one or more other LEAs in the area; and

(2) May offer supplemental educational services to eligible students under § 200.45 in schools in their first year of school improvement under § 200.39.

(i) Transportation.

(1) If a student exercises the option under paragraph (a)(1) of this section to transfer to another public school, the LEA must, consistent with § 200.48, provide or pay for the student's transportation to the school.

(2) The limitation on funding in § 200.48 applies only to the provision of choice-related transportation, and does not affect in any way the basic obligation to provide an option to transfer as required by paragraph (a) of this section.

(3) The LEA's obligation to provide transportation for the student ends at the end of the school year in which the school from which the student transferred is no longer identified by the LEA for school improvement, corrective action, or restructuring.

(j) Students with disabilities and students covered under Section 504 of the Rehabilitation Act of 1973 (Section 504). For students with disabilities under the IDEA and students covered under Section 504, the public school choice option must provide a free appropriate public education as that term is defined in section 602(8) of the IDEA or 34 CFR 104.33, respectively.

3. OBLIGATIONS OF PRIVATE INSTITUTIONS UNDER PUBLIC LAW IF THEY ACCEPT PUBLIC FUNDING

Would private schools that accept vouchers be subject to greater regulation as a result? Some have argued that school choice may actually result in a larger and more unwieldy educational bureaucracy than currently exists.

Consider the following quotation from Frank R. Kemerer, *The Constitutionality of School Vouchers*, 101 ED. L. REP. 17 n.51 (1995):

Government regulation of private schools creates problems for institutional autonomy. In an important but often overlooked passage, Justice McReynolds noted in *Pierce v. Society of Sisters*, that "No question is raised concerning the power of the State reasonably to regulate all schools, to inspect, supervise and examine them, their teachers and pupils; to require that all children of proper age attend some school, that teachers shall be of good moral character and patriotic disposition, that certain studies plainly essential to good citizenship must be taught, and that nothing be taught which is manifestly inimical to the public welfare." In the years since Pierce, there have many challenges to state regulation of private schools. For the most part, these challenges have been unsuccessful.

State regulation at issue in most of the decisions has been relatively limited and has occurred in the absence of any substantial flow of public funds to private schools. The case for regulation of private schools is enhanced under a publicly-funded voucher program because of the potential increase in the number of students educated in the private sector, the state's traditional role in overseeing its educational system, and the need to assure accountability for the expenditure of public money. The types of regulation public policymakers are likely to consider are multifarious, ranging from the constitutional and statutory rights of students and teachers to teacher qualifications, curriculum, student admissions, health and safety, tuition and fees, and information and transportation. Many of these regulatory features will have cost implications.

The more regulation, the greater the threat to institutional autonomy. At the extreme, substantial regulation could conceivably convert some private action to state action, thus requiring institutional adherence to Fourteenth Amendment liberty and property rights.

Notes

1.   For an earlier discussion of state regulation of private schools and how a state funded voucher program encompassing sectarian private schools might affect such regulation, see Frank R. Kemerer, et al., *Vouchers and Private School Autonomy,* 21 J.L. & EDUC. 601 (1992). *See also* ARNOLD FEGE, *Private School Vouchers: Separate and Unequal, in* WHY WE STILL NEED PUBLIC SCHOOLS 233, (Art Must, Jr. ed., 1992) (asserting that if vouchers were implemented, private schools "would come under mounting pressure for public regulation.").

2.   In 1995, Republican presidential candidate Patrick Buchanan argued that vouchers "are 'wolves in sheep's clothing' that could open the way to federal control of private and religious education." Ralph Z. Hallow, *Buchanan Hits School Vouchers,* WASH. TIMES, Sept. 14, 1995, at A4. However, a pro-school voucher platform continues to be central to Republican Party doctrine over a decade later.

3.   In light of recent developments and the current state of the law, what are the chances that private schools voluntarily choosing to accept publicly funded vouchers would be subject to increasing regulation under current federal and state laws impacting public education? As a matter of policy, what should be the parameters of the regulatory approach in this context? Does the charter school model offer any guidance here?

D.   CHARTER SCHOOLS

CHARTER SCHOOLS AS POSTMODERN PARADOX: RETHINKING SOCIAL STRATIFICATION IN AN AGE OF DEREGULATED SCHOOL CHOICE

Amy Stuart Wells, Alejandra Lopez; Janelle Scott & Jennifer Jellison Holme.
69 HARVARD ED. REV. (1999).

* * *

Charter school laws, now passed in thirty-four states and the District of Columbia, allow groups of people to come together to start autonomous schools that are free of much of the governmental oversight that exists within the public educational system yet still receive public funds. While state charter school laws vary, the central ideal of the reform is to grant groups of school founders a charter that spells out what they hope to accomplish in their schools. Once a charter is granted—either by a local school board, a state board of education, or other entity—the schools operate with much less oversight and regulation than traditional public schools. In exchange for their freedom they are, in theory, supposed to meet the goals stated in their charters. If they fail to do so, they can lose their charter. In this way, charter school reform offers an alternative to the bureaucratic and regulated public education system, opening the door for more variation in the delivery of educational services, greater local community input into how schools are run, and, in theory, more market-based competition between schools. Also, because charter schools in most states do not receive funding for their capital costs, the reform leads to an increased reliance on private resources to pay rent or a mortgage for the school facilities. The main political attraction of these popular schools is that they give people of various political, social, cultural, and philosophical persuasions who are discontented with the educational system an alternative to regular public schools. Demand for such options has led to the creation of more than one thousand charter schools nationwide in just eight years.

Charter schools embody many of the contradictions of the so-called postmodern paradox. According to Hargreaves, the major paradox of postmodernity is that the complexity and uncertainty wrought by globalization has led to a simultaneous search for meaning in locally defined identities. Thus charter schools are, on the one hand, fragmented and decentered localized projects that celebrate difference over uniformity and fight for cultural recognition, and, on the other, are conceptualized within and connected to larger global trends of less redistribution and more privatization, greater inequality between the rich and the poor, and of increased commodification of culture via images of mass marketing.

In this way, we see charter schools as being caught between the politics of modernity, in which the liberal project promised—often unsuccessfully to provide more equal distribution of material resources along with universal rights and freedoms, and the politics of postmodernity, which are punctuated by fragmented social movements, identity politics, and the struggle for recognition. Because charter schools shape and are shaped by these complex social shifts, our study of this reform movement had to take into account these political shifts and the ways in which they change the meaning of "success" in education reform. In other words, the goals and purposes of education in some communities may be more about creating schools that reflect a particular cultural heritage than about improved test scores. Education policy research often fails to acknowledge these distinctions. Through our in-depth research on charter schools in California, we learned that modern definitions of "social stratification," "segregation," and "equal education opportunity" are not as useful as they once were. For instance, groups of parents, students, educators, and community activists in low-income communities of color are using charter school reform to gain freedom from state-mandated curricula in order to embrace their own cultural heritage. After forty years of unsatisfactory progress with reforms designed to improve the unequal distribution of resources across schools or help marginalized groups gain access to mainstream institutions, members of these communities now seek to create schools of their own. Reforms such as charter schools help them redefine educational opportunities as the creation of separate spaces.

Yet these emancipatory efforts in local communities are circumscribed by highly unequal economic, social, and political conditions—vestiges of modernity that are in many ways exacerbated in postmodernity. In other words, the unfulfilled promises of equality that defined the modern era are still with us and are, in fact, becoming more pronounced in this postmodern era of global economic development.

At the same time that disenfranchised communities are creating sites of resistance to the traditional state-run education system through charter school reform, more powerful and privileged communities are also breaking off from the public system via charter schools. Even in low-income neighborhoods, charter schools tend to serve students who are better off in terms of having parents who are actively engaged in their education.

* * *

After two-and-a-half years of traveling, listening, observing, and reading, we emerged from our study with a deeper understanding of the range of diverse localized social movements that have started different charter schools across the state. Based on this knowledge, as well as information * * * from other sources (for example, SRI International, 1997), we created a set of six composite sketches of idealized charter schools that capture the most prevalent themes, issues, and phenomena of this reform—for example, why people start charter schools, who becomes part of their school communities, and what they hope to accomplish through this particular reform.

These composites are by no means representative of every charter school in existence, nor is each composite necessarily mutually exclusive—some charter schools have characteristics of more than one of these composites. Thus, each composite is conceptual and fluid. They help to illustrate the major categories of charter schools we have found, as well as the diversity of charter schools within the movement. Additionally, they help illustrate the emancipatory possibilities that some charter schools offer, as well as the threats to equal student access and resources that some charter schools pose.

Urban, Ethnocentric, and Grassroots Charter Schools

These are charter schools founded by groups of parents, educators, and community members who wish to create a "safe space" or "home-place" for students of a particular racial or ethnic group who live in the surrounding community. Many of these schools are Afrocentric, Chicano-centric, or Native American-centric in their curricular foci and orientations. But whether or not they have such a focus, they are started by people within the local communities and thus represent localized social movements, people of color fighting for greater independence from what they see as a hegemonic state-run system.

These urban schools in low-income communities are seen by the parents and educators as safe havens from the nearby public schools, which they often perceive to be dangerous. They are also concerned with serving the specific needs of their student population in ways that large, impersonal public schools frequently are not. These charter schools are born of the frustration that parents and educators in marginalized communities often feel toward an educational system that has failed to take their knowledge, their history, and their experiences seriously.

Three of the charter schools—all of which were start-up charters located in urban areas—in our study were created in part to serve students of a particular racial/ethnic group who the founders or operators thought were not being well served in the public system. In one of these schools, which is also a back-to-basics school, some of the educators said that part of their mission was to provide students with greater knowledge and appreciation of their own history. In the other two schools the central focus went beyond infusing more history of the ethnic group served and included an emphasis on the ethnic culture, heritage, and identity of the students.

For instance, a founder of one of these schools told us that in the early planning stages she met with several people from her community who were hopeful that the curriculum and instruction at the charter school would be different—that the school would present history and culture from the point of view of the people in that community, not from the perspective of mainstream public school textbooks and curriculum.

A teacher at this school noted that she has seen improvements in her students over the school year: "We know our own history, nobody has to tell us, we know it. And they're developing a sense of pride. And I can see it's taken a long time, but it's happening slowly." She added that, while the school does try to fulfill the minimum standard graduation requirements set by the district, "we have to meet the culture part, the spiritual part, and here what's nice is that we can touch the spiritual part and it's OK."

Many of these types of charter schools require parents to be involved in the school; often the schools have a parent contract that must be signed before students are enrolled. Thus, while parents and students associated with these schools are "disadvantaged" within their larger social context, they may well be less disadvantaged when compared to other families within their poor and segregated urban districts. For instance, these charter schools enroll the students with the most involved parents and with parents who are able to drive them to and from school each day.

Meanwhile, there is ample evidence that the charter school law has done little to redistribute material resources in this global economic era. Many of these charter schools are housed in poor and makeshift facilities, such as those of one school we studied that consisted of a cluster of portable classrooms on a dirt and asphalt parking lot. The long-term survival of these schools usually depends on their ability to garner corporate sponsors to help make up for the lack of private resources in their poor communities. Often there is an overlap between these schools and two of those described below—charter schools founded by charismatic educational leaders and teacher-led charter schools.

Home Schooling/Independent Study Programs

These charter schools span wide geographic distances and often use technology for distance learning in order to expand the "attendance zone" of their schools. It is not unusual for them to draw together, under one charter umbrella, clusters of parents and families who had already been home schooling their children before the charter school was created. These families participate in home schooling for a variety of religious, practical (e.g., a handicapped or bed-ridden student), pedagogical, and/or philosophical reasons that cause them to withdraw from the public school system. In this way, the families associated with these charter schools often run the political gamut from extremely conservative to libertarian to more progressive, yet they are united under one loosely organized charter school. This type of school does not ask families to adopt one method of home schooling; rather, it accommodates their diversity by allowing each family to make its own pedagogical decisions about what is valued knowledge and whose culture is reflected in the curriculum. Thus, home-schooling charter schools tend to attract a wide range of families, from very conservative "fundamentalist" Christian families to more liberal "Birkenstock and tie-dye" parents who are more like the flower children of the 1960s. For example, in one home-schooling charter school we studied, we interviewed parents ranging from those who were extremely religious and had taken their children out of public schools in protest of the secular nature of the curriculum to those who wanted to home school their children as they toured the country in a camper selling motorcycle helmets at trade shows.

Generally, most of the students and parents enrolled in these programs are White and, for the most part, middle class. In our study, we found it was generally non-working mothers who teach their children at home. In this way, these charter schools are a localized social movement, engaged by those who have the time and resources to take advantage of the freedom from the traditional public system. Yet, at the same time, they illustrate the characteristics of a post-industrial economy. For instance, many of the schools' teachers or facilitators are part-time workers who are paid by the hour or by the number of students they serve and who travel from house to house to provide parents with assistance, help them order school-bought materials, and give students formal credit for their work. These teachers often are also parents of students enrolled in the school. When the students reach high school age, they are more likely to be doing more teacher-directed or independent study work.

Through independent study programs, many of these same charter schools also serve older students, often from lower socioeconomic status families, who either dropped out or were pushed out of regular public schools. Such programs enable these students to earn high school diplomas instead of GEDs, but they also vary greatly in terms of the level of support and the quality of the instructional materials students receive. For instance, at one of the home-schooling/independent study schools we studied, the instructors, some of whom did not have bachelor's degrees, would spend very little time with each student enrolled in the program. Instructor-student interaction consisted mainly of brief, half-hour (if that) visits by the instructors to the students' homes to drop off mass-produced, standardized curriculum packets and the corresponding multiple-choice tests, and to pick up completed assignments and tests. Students were left on their own to read and work through the assignments and tests. During one visit, an independent study student—a woman in her mid-twenties who was a high school dropout had several questions and attempted to engage the instructor in a conversation on the Articles of Confederation and other topics she had read about in the U.S. history material. But the instructor, who was paid on a per pupil basis and had to drive long distances between her students' rural homes, did not have much time to talk.

Yet at another home-schooling/independent study charter school we studied, the independent study students came into the school's storefront facility on a regular basis—usually two or three times a week—to work with instructors, many of whom were certified teachers. Thus, the range of student experiences across various independent study programs was wide.

These independent study programs are also sometimes seen by charter school founders and district administrators as a way to make money because of the limited expense involved in serving students for only a few hours a week. There is often an overlap between these schools and the entrepreneur-initiated charter schools described below.

Charter Schools Founded by Charismatic Educational Leaders

This type of charter school is found in different settings, from suburban to large urban school districts. What seems to connect them is that they generally arise out of the hard work and vision of an educational leader surrounded by a core of committed teachers. This type of school is often driven toward charter status by the educational leader's desire for more curricular, pedagogical, and/or fiscal autonomy from the local school district. These leaders tend to see the need for greater fiscal autonomy to accomplish the kind of pedagogical, organizational, or facility and maintenance changes they envision. For example, one charismatic charter school principal in our study wanted to convert her school into a charter so that she could adopt a different math program than the one the district had adopted. Another charismatic charter school leader wanted to implement a schedule that varied from the one his district had mandated. Some charismatic charter school leaders focused on using their funding in different ways, such as constructing a new building or hiring non-union maintenance staff.

Such educational leaders are often mavericks within the public system and are generally charismatic people who may have an entrepreneurial bent but who generally value the professional knowledge of educators. These schools are often, but not always, "converted" public schools—that is, schools that existed in the public system before becoming charter schools. Thus, these are schools with an institutional history of employing credentialed teachers who are members of a union and who are paid full salaries and benefits. The extent to which the charismatic leaders will maintain these standards for teachers varies, and depends on whether he or she chooses to shift the expenditures or resources from salaries to facilities or other areas. These leaders frequently choose to save money by contracting out certain services, such as maintenance and cafeteria services, to competitive bidders and bypass the salaried classified employees hired by the district. In this way, their schools begin to reflect the post-industrial service sector economy of part-time workers and flexible staffing that is becoming the norm in postmodernity.

Furthermore, the charismatic leaders often maintain an extremely high profile within their local communities (and often beyond). Thus, they tend to wield a great deal of political power and symbolic capital that helps them get what they need for their schools—from their local school districts, their state departments of education, or private foundations and corporations. The major question hanging over many of these schools is what will happen to them when the charismatic leader is gone.

Teacher-Led Charter Schools

Similar in some ways to schools that fit the description of schools founded by charismatic educational leaders above, charter schools led by groups of teachers tend to be even more focused on the instructional program of the school as the primary reason for going charter. These schools, like those above, also tend to be existing public schools that were reforming and taking risks even before becoming charters. They can, however, run the gamut in terms of their particular pedagogical foci—from progressive, multi-age, and open classroom schools to more traditional and rigid college-prep or "classic" curricula. They also vary greatly in terms of their location and student population. Some of these teacher-led charter schools serve at-risk students who have dropped out of regular schools, while others are suburban neighborhood elementary schools. Still others, as were two in our study, are converted urban public schools serving low-income students. Whether they were schools in our study or schools we heard about at a conference, these teacher-led charters share an ethos that teachers know what is best for the students they serve. In this way, these schools resemble a grassroots localized social movement of teachers attempting to gain control of their pedagogy and curriculum.

Some of these teacher-led schools are being started with the help of local teacher union affiliates. Teachers in these schools are generally credentialed and often still part of a collective bargaining unit, which means they receive the same pay and benefits as other teachers in their districts. Like employee-owned companies, these teacher-led charter schools are generally vested in maintaining the honor of the teaching profession and are supportive of public education in general, as long as the teachers are given the latitude to use their professional judgment to determine what type of instruction will best meet the students' needs.

Parent-Led Charter Schools

Schools that resemble this composite can also be found in various types of communities, but we believe that they are most likely to be found in wealthy suburban areas or in exclusive urban neighborhoods where well-educated parents have the money and connections to place their children in private schools. At this type of charter school, a core of extremely involved parents generally works with educators to move toward charter school status, and often these parents are intricately involved in writing the policies and procedures for the charters. For instance, in one charter school in our study, the most involved parents were those from the nearby wealthy community. At this school, these parents helped write the charter and were involved in the governance of the school. These are also parents who are able to muster incredible private resources—cash, in-kind services, and materials—for their schools. These schools are likely to have many parent professionals, especially lawyers and accountants, who play major roles in helping the schools define the terms of their financial and legal agreements with their charter-granting agencies, and to work through the difficult budgeting process that autonomous charter schools face. In addition, it is not unusual for these parents to play a part in deciding who will ultimately enroll in the charter school; thus they can control with whom their own children will associate. For instance, in one charter school we studied, parents sit on a student review board that decides which students have violated the student behavior code and thus who should be expelled from the school. In many cases, therefore, these parent-led charter schools provide examples of the communities and families that have the greatest advantages under policies that foster localized social movements to create or reinvent publicly funded schools.

The working conditions at these charter schools can vary, but the educators are generally fairly well-paid professionals. The pedagogical foci of these schools may also vary incredibly from a back-to-basics curriculum to a more progressive, open classroom approach, depending on the philosophical and political orientation of the parents and teachers involved. In some settings there is an overlap between schools with strong leaders and those with powerful parents, especially when the parents are involved in bringing in a leader to run their charter school.

Entrepreneur–Initiated Charter Schools

This type of charter school is generally, but not always, found in urban areas and often, but not exclusively, serves so-called "at risk" poor students of color who have dropped out or been kicked out of regular public schools. These schools are less likely to be "grassroots" or community based and are more likely to be founded by people from outside the communities they serve, people with a strong entrepreneurial philosophy of how schools should operate. This composite would include charter schools run by for-profit management firms. These charter school founders often, but not always, place little value on the professional knowledge of educators. They generally have little or no background in education and tend to believe that what is wrong with the public school system is that educators lack the business skills and wherewithal to run schools efficiently and effectively. They often represent a neoliberal or free enterprise ideology that calls for market solutions to all social ills. For instance, the founder and director of one of the charter schools in our study regularly espoused his belief that his background in business made him a better charter school director than any educator. He argued, as do many people within the charter school movement, that the public education system is a failure and that it ought to be privatized and run by entrepreneurs like himself.

The curriculum in these schools is often driven by textbook publishers or GED test-preparation guidelines, and the educational goal is generally a high school diploma or its equivalent. Thus, this composite often overlaps with the independent study programs described in the "Home Schooling/Independent Study Programs" composite above. Compared to the other charter school composites, there is often far less parental involvement in these more entrepreneurial schools, and students spend relatively little time with their teachers—maybe a few hours a week. The remainder of the time they are presumed to be working independently on their schoolwork. Teachers in these schools, as with the home schools, are often part-time workers with few or no benefits and are paid hourly or based on student load. These entrepreneurial independent study schools also are likely to use technology to provide distance learning opportunities to students. Other than the less expensive teachers and perhaps the more innovative use of technology, it is not entirely clear how these schools differ from continuation schools currently operating in most schools districts—except that the entrepreneurial founders have much more control over how and when they spend public money on the students than do regular school administrators.

CHARTING THE COURT CHALLENGES TO CHARTER SCHOOLS

Robert J. Martin.
109 Penn St. L. Rev. 43 (2004).

I. Introduction

One of the most controversial developments in public education during the past decade has been the establishment of charter schools. By their establishment, charter schools provide families an opportunity to choose an education for their children in public schools that are individually chartered and separated from the local public school system. This type of choice is especially geared for families who believe that the traditional public schools are not well suited for their children but who lack the means to afford private schools or the ability to relocate to more highly regarded school districts. If families are dissatisfied with the assignment of their children within the traditional public schools of their local school district, they may seek placement of their children in available public charter schools, space permitting.

Because the establishment of charter schools constitutes an implicit criticism of and challenge to the existing public school system, however, charter school proponents have often encountered fierce resistance from organized groups associated with traditional public schools. These charter school adversaries have frequently resorted to proactive countermeasures to prevent charter schools from opening and continuing operations. In doing so, they have repeatedly turned to the legal system for assistance. Among the principal means they have employed to prevent charter schools from opening and operating have been the filing of court challenges predicated on alleged violations of state and federal law. As one legal commentator has aptly noted, "[b]ecause the stakeholders in the traditional public school system find themselves under siege to improve the quality of public education, the legal battles surrounding charter schools are certain to be acrimonious."

In pursuing their struggle against charter schools, adversaries have utilized both state and federal court systems. After typically first exhausting state administrative forums, many dissatisfied adversaries have pursued claims in state appellate courts and, in some instances, have then taken an appeal to their state's supreme court. In other cases, adversaries have bypassed their state legal system and have filed claims in federal district court and, sometimes, have then taken an appeal to their respective federal circuit court of appeals.

In so doing, adversaries have raised a wide variety of legal claims. Such claims have included state constitutional challenges based on requirements to provide a thorough and efficient education and prohibition of an unlawful delegation of power; state statutory challenges based on eligibility qualifications for the issuance of charters and the criteria of funding formula for distribution of state aid; federal constitutional challenges based on the First Amendment and the Equal Protection Clause of the Fourteenth Amendment; and federal statutory challenges based on Title VI of the Individuals with Disabilities in Education Act. Moreover, the adversaries' proposed remedies for alleged violations have included orders declaring that state charter school programs be abolished on grounds that their enabling acts are unconstitutional, that funding for charter schools be terminated because the methods for obtaining revenue are impermissible, and that individual charter schools be suspended or closed for failure to comply with mandatory statutes.

* * *

PREVIOUS COMMENTARY ON LEGAL CHALLENGES BASED ON FEDERAL LAW

Numerous legal observers have * * * produced commentary that analyzes how federal law has or could affect the expansion and direction of the charter school movement. A review of the commentary pertaining to constitutional law indicates that most of the attention has focused on the First and Fourteenth Amendments.

As a preliminary step in addressing the impact of either amendment on charter schools, several commentators, including Jason Wren, Robert O'Neill, and Karla Turekian have raised the threshold issue as to how the "state action doctrine" may come into play. They emphasize that, without state action (a legal determination as to whether schools are "sufficiently imbued with a government quality or nexus"), the force of these constitutional safeguards may not extend to non-traditional public schools such as charter schools. Observers have acknowledged, however, that most charter school programs do fall within the scope of state action, since most states have specifically designated their charters schools to be public in that they must remain open to all students and be non-sectarian, tuition-free, and paid for by public financing.

One reason that states have decided to restrict their charter school programs in this manner is because of conditions that the federal government has imposed. In order to obtain available federal funding for charter schools, states must comply with the federal "definition" of a charter school. A primary component of that definition is that a charter school be "nonsectarian in its programs, admissions policies, employment practices, and all other operations, and [not] affiliated with a sectarian school or religious institution."

To the extent that states maintain charter school programs that are strictly non-sectarian, their charter schools must not conflict with First Amendment religious restrictions. Jesse Choper and other scholars have explained that the major source of First Amendment controversy has centered on the extent to which church-related schools can be included in school choice programs. In recent years there has been increased litigation as to whether the inclusion of sectarian schools would violate the Establishment Clause and its affiliated doctrine pertaining to the separation of church and state. Such litigation has focused primarily on programs associated with vouchers and does not appear to affect directly the operation of charter schools in most states, since they have previously consented to comply with the federal requirement of non-sectarianism.

Legal commentators have also indicated that the Fourteenth Amendment does not appear to provide a profitable means by which adversaries may succeed in challenging charter school practices. At least one has suggested that courts are likely to accord charter schools the same deferential treatment as they do to traditional public schools. In those challenges alleging violations of the Fourteenth Amendment's Equal Protection Clause, courts presumably would apply a "rational relationship" analysis. The Supreme Court has previously determined that most educational challenges deserve only this minimal level of scrutiny because the Court has not deemed education to be a fundamental right embodied in the United States Constitution. Moreover, the Supreme Court has also ruled that plaintiffs must establish that an alleged act of discrimination was intentional, as opposed to having caused simply a disproportionate impact on a suspect class of historically disadvantaged persons. With such difficult obstacles placed on potential plaintiffs, charter school programs should probably be able to survive most Equal Protection challenges.

Alternatively, several commentators have suggested that challengers may have more success in discriminatory claims against charter schools by utilizing federal statutory provisions, particularly Title VI of the Civil Right Act of 1964 and Title IX (20 U.S.C.A., § 1681). Title VI outlaws discrimination on the basis of race, color or nationality in any federally funded programs, and Title IX provides similar protection on the basis of gender. To establish such a claim, plaintiffs do not have to prove intentional discrimination in order to prevail, but can establish a prima facie case by demonstrating a discriminatory effect on their ability to participate in programs offered by public institutions such as charter schools. Nevertheless, the relatively recent Supreme Court holding in *Alexander v. Sandoval* appears to have eliminated the right of private individuals—such as charter school adversaries—to bring Title VI claims based on alleged disparate impact. Thus, unless Congress overturns the Court's statutory interpretation (which appears unlikely in the foreseeable future given the current make-up of Congress), there presumably will not be successful litigation based on the "effects" theory pertaining to Title VI and the similar theory pertaining to Title IX.

Because the choices of legal remedies may be severely restricted for those alleging discriminatory practices on the part of charter schools, several legal scholars have strongly urged state policymakers to ensure that issues affecting equal educational opportunities for historically disadvantaged students be specifically addressed within the framework of their charter school programs. Martha Minow has voiced concern that recently enacted charter school initiatives may otherwise foster neglect or abandonment of the goals that were the cornerstone of the "last wave" of school reforms emanating from *Brown v. Board of Education* and subsequent federal civil rights litigation and legislation.

* * *

Another noted legal scholar, Betsy Levin, has in essence taken the same position as Minow, expressing concern that school choice options such as charter schools "will lead to increased racial and economic isolation." Like Minow, she has suggested that the best means of minimizing this potential problem is through carefully crafted legislation.

Several additional commentators have emphasized in particular that charter school programs may violate federal laws providing protections for students with disabilities. These commentators appear in agreement that charter schools are obliged to adhere to all of the rules and procedures of federal disability law. Although a state may choose to absolve charter schools from meeting certain state regulations, the state cannot absolve them from federal regulations. Thus charter schools must comply with such mandates, even if federal and state funding proves insufficient to cover the cost of administering those services.

Moreover, for those charter schools that operate independently of local school districts (as do most charter schools), they may actually incur greater obligations than most traditional schools for servicing the needs of students with disabilities. This increased burden occurs because independent public charter schools must assume the responsibilities of a local education agency (LEA) and, as such, must make appropriate services to all students who fall within the scope of federal disabilities law. Thus an independent charter school is "obligated to provide special education services and funding to students with disabilities in the same manner that the [school district] provides support to its other public school programs." Unless they are able to make agreements with other charter schools or LEAs, the charter schools must provide these services themselves. Their obligation to do so stems from the fact that each of the fifty states accepts federal funding to assist in covering the cost of educating students with disabilities. Their receipt of federal funding is conditioned on an agreement by the states, through their state education agency (SEA), mandating that all of their LEAs comply with the three primary federal disabilities statutes: the IDEA, Section 504, and Title II.

Heubert provides a comprehensive analysis of the various obligations imposed on charter schools by each of these three federal disabilities statutes. He points out that the IDEA contains five major requirements: (1) that each LEA attempt to achieve nondiscrimination "to the maximum extent appropriate" in any program in which non-disabled children participate; (2) that each LEA provide students with disabilities a "free and appropriate public education" (FAPE), including appropriate special education and related services; (3) that each child with disabilities receive assessments by means of an "individualized educational program" (IEP); (4) that students with disabilities obtain placement in the "least restrictive environment" (LRE) to "the maximum extent appropriate;" and (5) that teachers who instruct students with disabilities possess the highest standards of special education certification within their respective states.

Although Heubert further notes that Section 504 and Title II in many respects also mirror and incorporate IDEA requirements, he demonstrates that the two provisions also provide enhanced protections for students with disabilities. The first area of enhanced protections involves the scope of coverage. Section 504 and Title II "are more extensive . . . in the types of disabilities they cover, the class of individuals they protect, and the safeguards they provide against coercion and retaliation." The second area involves the duty to provide and pay for FAPE. Heubert suggests that LEAs may find the FAPE requirement within Section 504 and Title II harder to meet because the two provisions contain an "equality" definition of FAPE. The third area derives from the terminology of Section 504 and Title II as applied to K–12 students and employees with disabilities. Unlike many public institutions such as colleges, K–12 schools may not exclude certain individuals who cannot meet essential eligibility requirements despite the institution's willingness to make "reasonable accommodations." The fourth area of enhanced protection derives from the nondiscrimination provisions of Section 504 and Title II that extend beyond the requirements of the IDEA. The focus of these provisions is on denoting what policies and actions may constitute unlawful discrimination. Charter schools are especially vulnerable to potential violations because they typically offer innovative and unique programs but often possess limited means to pool resources and activities.

Heubert indicates that the general standards imposed by Section 504 and Title II may be difficult for a charter school to satisfy. Charter schools must bear the burden of proof in order to receive an exemption. In many instances they would not be entitled to an exemption for their academic, language or physical fitness programs because they could probably overcome most obstacles confronting students with disabilities simply through the granting of waivers.

Summary of Cases Decided by State Courts

My review and analysis of the of challenges to charter schools in state courts during the first decade of their existence demonstrates that such challenges have not proven to be a significant impediment to the growth of the charter school movement. None of the state court decisions—including five state supreme court decisions—held that their respective states' charter school enabling acts was unconstitutional. The courts held that such acts provided reasonable safeguards, including sufficient public accountability (MI–1), appropriate allocation of control (CO–1) and adequate state supervision (UT–1 and CA–1), to withstand challenges alleging an improper delegation of authority. Thus, so far, these courts have determined that one of the central characteristics of charter schools, their relative freedom from traditional regulations, is not problematic from a legal perspective.

Most of the state cases that involved the interpretation and application of charter school enabling acts construed the acts in favor of charter school applicants. * * *

In those cases that included federal issues, the state courts have again tended to be protective of their legislatively enacted charter school programs. In one case, *Salt River* (AZ–1), the state court ruled that Native American charter schools did not suffer a violation of equal protection in the amount of state funding provided by the charter school enabling act, even though it amounted to less than that provided to other schools, since those schools had received comparable funding from the federal government. In another Arizona case, *Shelby School* (AZ–2), the court found that the state could conduct financial background checks on charter school officials without violating their rights of equal protection and privacy.

In the case with the most significant national implications, *Lighthouse Charter School* (SC–1), the South Carolina Supreme Court ruled that a county school board had grounds to deny a charter school application based, in part, on a provision in the charter school act prohibiting the student body of the proposed school from deviating significantly from the racial composition of the school district. In its decision, the court acknowledged that an equal protection challenge raised by the state attorney general contesting the racial composition provision might have merit, but avoided ruling on the issue. Such a challenge, which eventually led to a statutory amendment in South Carolina, could trigger potentially serious repercussions for charter school programs throughout the country. Like South Carolina, many states—such as New Jersey—have requirements aimed at thwarting segregation in charter student enrollment. As of now, it is uncertain whether such requirements can survive future equal protection challenges. The answer may depend largely on the extent to which courts construe them as mandatory quotas predicated on race.

Because most of the state court cases have involved decisions based on their own state constitutions or interpretation and application of their own charter school enabling acts, most of these cases should not have a substantial legal impact on other states. With few exceptions, none of them has seemed particularly surprising and, for purposes of potential guidance to other states, seemed particularly persuasive. In a large majority of the states in which litigation has occurred, the state courts have consistently held that charter schools programs constitute a legitimate manifestation of public policy and have thus tended to rule in favor of charter schools. Nevertheless, there definitely have been a few cases in other states, such as the *Lighthouse Charter School* case (SC–1), to which educational policymakers and school law practitioners should pay close attention.

SUMMARY OF CASES DECIDED BY FEDERAL COURTS

As with the charter school cases decided by state courts prior to 2002, most of the cases decided by federal courts involving charter schools found in favor of charter schools, and none of the decisions has apparently had a detrimental impact on the expansion of the charter school movement. To date, the United States Supreme Court has not made any rulings pertaining to the operation of charter schools, and the three cases that circuit courts have decided have not produced major consequences. None of the federal circuit court or district court cases has proven to be a landmark decision that has or would necessarily persuade other jurisdictions to subscribe to the rationale of its decision-making.

In these federal cases plaintiffs have consistently failed in their attempts to establish that state charter school programs have violated constitutional provisions or other federal law. In *Villanueva*, for example, the circuit court held that that the plaintiffs could not establish an equal protection or Title VI claim against a school district, which the court found had not intended to nor caused discrimination to Latino students through the opening of a charter school. The results in these cases suggest that future broad-based federal challenges to charter schools are not likely to succeed, and therefore they will not likely alter the status quo of charter school programs in sister states.

That is not to imply, of course, that plaintiffs may never ever be able to prevail in challenges directed at the practices of individual charter schools. Although, so far, the federal courts have deemed almost all such cases without merit (e.g., Perry, Omegbu, Jones, Daugherty, and Porta), plaintiffs should be able to succeed if they can prove specific violations of constitutional or other federal provisions. As have other public schools, charter schools may occasionally engage in various discriminatory or other unlawful practices. If that occurs, plaintiffs may legitimately seek remedies in federal court. To the extent that plaintiffs remain aggressive in pursuing such relief, they may cause charter schools in all states to be more mindful of ensuring that they do not infringe on federal rights. Should charter schools fail to take precautionary measures, they may simply become more vulnerable to needless litigation and exposure to greater liability.

VI. Conclusion

It seems clear that the outcome of charter school cases decided in state and federal courts have not served as a significant derailment to the growth of the charter school movement. The state and federal courts have shown almost unwavering constancy in rejecting the challenges brought by school boards and other adversaries against the opening or continued operation of charter schools. Most of the cases have involved issues pertaining to specific state constitutions and the interpretation and application of specific statewide enabling acts. Hence these cases have afforded no precedence and only limited persuasive value outside of their own jurisdictions.

In general, the decisions of state courts have demonstrated two tendencies: (1) the state courts' inclination to uphold prior decisions of their state boards of education; and (2) the state courts' inclination to uphold their charter school enabling acts. By their actions, the state courts have thus helped to sustain and promote the development of the charter school movement and to lend support to the view that charter schools represent a legitimate means of pursuing improvement in public school systems.

As with the state court cases, the charter school cases decided by federal courts have followed similar tendencies. In federal cases plaintiffs have consistently proven unsuccessful in their attempts to establish that state charter school programs have violated constitutional provisions or other federal laws. The results of these cases suggest that future broad-based federal challenges to charter schools will not have a high likelihood of success and, therefore, will probably not alter the status quo of most states' charter school programs.

Thus, apparently, the charter school movement has successfully survived the initial legal challenges to its right of operation and continued expansion during the first decade of its existence. The legal battles, however, may be far from over. To the extent that the movement continues to grow and leads to the creation of still more charter schools, especially in districts with high concentrations of historically disadvantaged students, the concern regarding the movement's fiscal impact on traditional public schools will probably increase in significance. This may likely produce further court challenges, regarding fundamental issues of public school financing that the courts up to now have tended to avoid. Failure on the part of individual charter schools to comply with federal laws specifically designed to assist historically disadvantaged students may also lead to additional court challenges, especially students with disabilities.

Yet, during their brief history, charter schools have obtained the consistent backing of state and federal court systems in their legal battles to open and remain in operation. Whether they provide the rich learning environments for students that their proponents have predicted, of course, is well beyond the scope of this article. Nevertheless, charter schools have at least proven overwhelmingly successful in overcoming court cases challenging their status as a legitimate component within the public school framework.

Note

1. Consider, again, the hypothetical fact situation in Problem 1, Chapter 1. In light of the relevant legal frameworks and accompanying policy considerations introduced in Chapters 5 and 6, what additional arguments might plaintiffs set forth? What result? Discuss.

Chapter VII

THE RIGHTS OF STUDENTS WITH PARTICULAR NEEDS: ENGLISH LEARNERS & STUDENTS WITH DISABILITIES

Issues relating to English learners and students with disabilities come up often in both an equal opportunity context and an educational quality context. This chapter turns to a detailed examination of these issues, focusing on efforts to secure legal rights for students with particular needs and on attempts to translate those rights into positive change on a day-to-day level.

Effecting such change at the individual school sites is often the most difficult challenge. Many see bilingual education and special education as highly specialized areas, appropriately delegated to *other* people and appropriately relegated to *separate* offices, *separate* inquiries, and *separate* programs. In many instances, it is assumed by educators that once students are identified as participating in such programs, they no longer need to be the focus of the basic educational planning that takes place in the central office and at local school sites, since they are under the purview of a separate program office. Such a mindset too often results in the marginalizing of these students.

Indeed, in many settings, very few discussions regarding educational policy even appear to acknowledge the fact that in many urban districts—particularly at the elementary grades and especially in states such as California, Illinois, New York, and Texas—at least 50 percent of all the students are either English learners and/or students with disabilities. And it can be argued that a failure to improve educational outcomes in such settings can be traced directly to the inability of education leaders to place the needs of these students at the forefront of reform efforts and strategies for change.

In recent years, such programs and practices have been reexamined, and renewed efforts by advocates are focusing on what might be done to

513

build on the legal successes of the recent past while addressing the many unresolved issues that still remain.

A. BILINGUAL EDUCATION AND OTHER PROGRAMS FOR ENGLISH LEARNERS

The legal and policy debates regarding appropriate curricular and pedagogical approaches for educating students who are in the process of learning English have raised issues that continue to reverberate throughout the nation. At the heart of the debate has been the question of whether and to what extent instruction should be delivered, if possible, in the student's primary language.

A range of "bilingual" models have been identified, and they include *transitional* programs that begin with instruction and materials almost entirely in a student's primary language, gradually introducing English into the classroom until the instruction and materials are almost entirely in English. Transitional programs may also include "maintenance" of proficiency in the primary language, and indeed many programs seek to build strength in both languages with the stated goal that the students will exit the program or graduate from the K–12 schools completely bilingual.

Another model of bilingual education that has grown in popularity in many places over time is dual immersion. Under that model, English learners are grouped together in the same classroom with English speakers whose parents want them to become proficient in a language other than English. Thus, for example, a class may be comprised of English learners whose primary language is Spanish, and English speakers whose parents want them to learn Spanish. Students may remain together in this configuration for their entire elementary school careers, with instruction and materials in both English and Spanish. The stated goal is that all the students will exit the program completely fluent in both.

Other research-based models contemplate instruction that is primarily if not exclusively in English from the beginning. These include, but are not limited to, English as a Second Language (ESL), English Language Development (ELD), and Specially Designed Academic Instruction in English (SDAIE). Often such programs are necessary, particularly if no teacher is fluent in the child's primary language, and/or if only a small number of students speak a particular language.

While conflicting studies abound, there is a broad consensus within the education community that bilingual education, if done right, is the most effective approach to maximizing equal access to a quality education for English learners (EL's).

Literature in this field consistently emphasizes that language proficiency is not just a matter of conversational fluency. It ranges across four interrelated areas: reading, writing, speaking, and listening. And it cannot easily be picked up in a short period of time. In this respect, some scholars distinguish between Basic Interpersonal Conversation Skill (BICS) and Cognitive Academic Language Proficiency (CALP). BICS is necessary to communicate in everyday settings, while CALP is needed to perform academic tasks successfully. Conversational skills have been found to approach native-like levels within two years of exposure to English, but 5–12 years may be required to match native speakers in academic English. *See* LYNNE T. DÍAZ-RICO & KATHRYN Z. WEED, THE CROSSCULTURAL, LANGUAGE, AND ACADEMIC DEVELOPMENT (CLAD) HANDBOOK 29 (1995).

A highly acclaimed study by Stanford University scholars in January 2000 found that even in schools that are considered the most successful in teaching English to EL students, oral proficiency takes 3 to 5 years to develop, and academic English proficiency can take 4 to 7 years. The study, by UC Merced Professor Kenji Hakuta, reveals a continuing and widening gap between EL and native English speakers, and concludes:

> The gap illustrates the daunting task facing these students, who not only have to acquire oral and academic English, but also have to keep pace with native English speakers, who continue to develop their language skills. It may simply not be possible, within the constraints of the time available in regular formal school hours, to offer efficient instruction that would enable the EL students to catch up with the rest. Alternatives such as special summer and after-school programs may be needed. The results suggest that policies that assume rapid acquisition of English * * * are wildly unrealistic. A much more sensible policy would be one that sets aside the entire spectrum of the elementary grades as the realistic range within which English acquisition is accomplished, and plans a balanced curriculum that pays attention not just to English, but to the full array of academic needs of the students. Kenji Hakuta et al., *How Long Does it Take English Learners to Attain Proficiency?* 1 (The University of California Linguistic Minority Research Institute Policy Report, January 2000).

This section of the casebook provides an overview of the legal and public policy issues that have arisen in this area over the past 40–50 years. It begins with *Lau v. Nichols,* the one U.S. Supreme Court case that addresses bilingual education issues and in so doing sets forth foundational federal guidelines. It also highlights the portion of the U.S. Equal Educational Opportunity Act that codified *Lau,* and the Fifth Circuit's test for compliance with the Act that is generally accepted as the law of the land.

The section then turns to state issues, focusing in particular on California, which has the largest number of English learners in the country and has been the site of so many high profile disputes in this context. The state has seen a pendulum shift with regard to these issues, requiring bilingual education in the public schools from 1976–1987 but then seeking to end bilingual education instruction in the 1990s.

In conclusion, the section examines specialized inquiries relating to English learners. It focuses on the perceived conflict between bilingual education mandates and desegregation, and on the prospective impact of the "No Child Left Behind" Act in this area.

PROBLEM 33: The Community Language Academy

The following hypothetical takes place in the fictional state of Eldorado.

Assume for the purposes of this hypothetical that you have been retained by the founders and directors of a new charter school—the Community Language Academy—to advise them on their policies with regard to language programs for the forthcoming academic year. Charter schools, by definition, are generally exempt from state education code requirements, and pursuant to a recent legal advisory issued by the Eldorado State Department of Education, charter schools have been notified that they only need to comply with basic *federal* law in this area.

The Community Language Academy has been formed by educators who believe that English learners have been subjected to a "dumbed-down" curriculum in too many classrooms throughout the state for too long a period of time. One of the founders' stated goals is "to provide innovative learning opportunities for English learners," and 50 percent of the slots at the school will be reserved for students who have been identified EL. The directors anticipate, however, that the percentage of English learners at the school may very well be much higher than 50 percent.

Your consulting contract specifies that you will be asked to focus on four questions:

A. What basic legal principles should the founders and directors of the Community Language Academy have at their fingertips and keep in mind as they put together programs and plan curriculum for this charter school?

B. What educational methods and models of instruction do you recommend for the students of this school? Why? Could these methods and models vary depending on the language background and proficiency of the students enrolled?

C. What specific curricular programs would you put in place to ensure that English learners at this school do not receive a "dumbed-down" curriculum?

D. How would your recommended methods, models, and programs be consistent with current legal requirements outside of the state's education code? What legal challenges might be anticipated, and how might you recommend responding?

1. BASIC FEDERAL DOCTRINE

LAU v. NICHOLS

414 U.S. 563, 94 S.Ct. 786 (1974).

MR. JUSTICE DOUGLAS delivered the opinion of the Court.

The San Francisco, California, school system was integrated in 1971 as a result of a federal court decree. The District Court found that there are 2,856 students of Chinese ancestry in the school system who do not speak English. Of those who have that language deficiency, about 1,000 are given supplemental courses in the English language.[1] About 1,800, however, do not receive that instruction.

This class suit brought by non-English-speaking Chinese students against officials responsible for the operation of the San Francisco Unified School District seeks relief against the unequal educational opportunities, which are alleged to violate, inter alia, the Fourteenth Amendment. No specific remedy is urged upon us. Teaching English to the students of Chinese ancestry who do not speak the language is one choice. Giving instructions to this group in Chinese is another. There may be others. Petitioners ask only that the Board of Education be directed to apply its expertise to the problem and rectify the situation.

The District Court denied relief. The Court of Appeals affirmed, holding that there was no violation of the Equal Protection Clause of the Fourteenth Amendment or of § 601 of the Civil Rights Act of 1964, which excludes from participation in federal financial assistance, recipients of aid which discriminate against racial groups. One judge dissented. A hearing en banc was denied, two judges dissenting.

We granted the petition for certiorari because of the public importance of the question presented.

The Court of Appeals reasoned that "[e]very student brings to the starting line of his educational career different advantages and disadvantages caused in part by social, economic and cultural background, created and continued completely apart from any contribution by the school system." Yet in our view the case may not be so easily decided. This is a public school system of California and § 71 of the California Education Code states that "English shall be the basic language of instruction in all schools." That section permits a school district to determine "when and under what circumstances instruction may be given bilingually." That section also states as "the policy of the state" to insure "the mastery of English by all pupils in the schools." And bilingual instruction is authorized "to the extent that it does not interfere with the systematic,

---

1. A report adopted by the Human Rights Commission of San Francisco and submitted to the Court by respondents after oral argument shows that, as of April 1973, there were 3,457 Chinese students in the school system who spoke little or no English. The document further showed 2,136 students enrolled in Chinese special instruction classes, but at least 429 of the enrollees were not Chinese but were included for ethnic balance. Thus, as of April 1973, no more than 1,707 of the 3,457 Chinese students needing special English instruction were receiving it.

sequential, and regular instruction of all pupils in the English language."

Moreover, § 8573 of the Education Code provides that no pupil shall receive a diploma of graduation from grade 12 who has not met the standards of proficiency in English, as well as other prescribed subjects. Moreover, by § 12101 of the Education Code (Supp. 1973) children between the ages of six and 16 years are (with exceptions not material here) "subject to compulsory full-time education."

Under these state-imposed standards there is no equality of treatment merely by providing students with the same facilities, textbooks, teachers, and curriculum; for students who do not understand English are effectively foreclosed from any meaningful education.

Basic English skills are at the very core of what these public schools teach. Imposition of a requirement that, before a child can effectively participate in the educational program, he must already have acquired those basic skills is to make a mockery of public education. We know that those who do not understand English are certain to find their classroom experiences wholly incomprehensible and in no way meaningful.

We do not reach the Equal Protection Clause argument which has been advanced but rely solely on § 601 of the Civil Rights Act of 1964, to reverse the Court of Appeals.

That section bans discrimination based "on the ground of race, color, or national origin," in "any program or activity receiving Federal financial assistance." The school district involved in this litigation receives large amounts of federal financial assistance. The Department of Health, Education, and Welfare (HEW), which has authority to promulgate regulations prohibiting discrimination in federally assisted school systems in 1968 issued one guideline that "[s]chool systems are responsible for assuring that students of a particular race, color, or national origin are not denied the opportunity to obtain the education generally obtained by other students in the system." In 1970 HEW made the guidelines more specific, requiring school districts that were federally funded "to rectify the language deficiency in order to open" the instruction to students who had "linguistic deficiencies."

By § 602 of the Act HEW is authorized to issue rules, regulations, and orders[2] to make sure that recipients of federal aid under its jurisdiction conduct any federally financed projects consistently with § 601. HEW's regulations specify that the recipients may not

---

2. Section 602 provides:

Each Federal department and agency which is empowered to extend Federal financial assistance to any program or activity, by way of grant, loan, or contract other than a contract of insurance or guaranty, is authorized and directed to effectuate the provisions of section 2000d of this title with respect to such program or activity by issuing rules, regulations, or orders of general applicability which shall be consistent with achievement of the objectives of the statute authorizing the financial assistance in connection with which the action is taken....

42 U.S.C. § 2000d–1.

(ii) Provide any service, financial aid, or other benefit to an individual which is different, or is provided in a different manner, from that provided to others under the program;

* * *

(iv) Restrict an individual in any way in the enjoyment of any advantage or privilege enjoyed by others receiving any service, financial aid, or other benefit under the program.

Discrimination among students on account of race or national origin that is prohibited includes "discrimination . . . in the availability or use of any academic . . . or other facilities of the grantee or other recipient."

Discrimination is barred which has that *effect* even though no purposeful design is present: a recipient "may not . . . utilize criteria or methods of administration which have the effect of subjecting individuals to discrimination" or have "the effect of defeating or substantially impairing accomplishment of the objectives of the program as respect individuals of a particular race, color, or national origin."

It seems obvious that the Chinese-speaking minority receive fewer benefits than the English-speaking majority from respondents' school system which denies them a meaningful opportunity to participate in the educational program—all earmarks of the discrimination banned by the regulations. In 1970 HEW issued clarifying guidelines, which include the following:

"Where inability to speak and understand the English language excludes national origin-minority group children from effective participation in the educational program offered by a school district, the district must take affirmative steps to rectify the language deficiency in order to open its instructional program to these students."

"Any ability grouping or tracking system employed by the school system to deal with the special language skill needs of national origin-minority group children must be designed to meet such language skill needs as soon as possible and must not operate as an educational dead end or permanent track."

Respondent school district contractually agreed to "comply with title VI of the Civil Rights Act of 1964 . . . and all requirements imposed by or pursuant to the Regulation" of HEW which are "issued pursuant to that title . . . " and also immediately to "take any measures necessary to effectuate this agreement." The Federal Government has power to fix the terms on which its money allotments to the States shall be disbursed. Whatever may be the limits of that power, they have not been reached here. Senator Humphrey, during the floor debates on the Civil Rights Act of 1964, said:

"Simple justice requires that public funds, to which all taxpayers of all races contribute, not be spent in any fashion which encourages, entrenches, subsidizes, or results in racial discrimination."

We accordingly reverse the judgment of the Court of Appeals and remand the case for the fashioning of appropriate relief.

Reversed and remanded.

* * *

MR. JUSTICE BLACKMUN, with whom THE CHIEF JUSTICE joins, concurring in the result.

I join Mr. Justice STEWART'S opinion and thus I, too, concur in the result. Against the possibility that the Court's judgment may be interpreted too broadly, I stress the fact that the children with whom we are concerned here number about 1,800. This is a very substantial group that is being deprived of any meaningful schooling because the children cannot understand the language of the classroom. We may only guess as to why they have had no exposure to English in their preschool years. Earlier generations of American ethnic groups have overcome the language barrier by earnest parental endeavor or by the hard fact of being pushed out of the family or community nest and into the realities of broader experience.

I merely wish to make plain that when, in another case, we are concerned with a very few youngsters, or with just a single child who speaks only German or Polish or Spanish or any language other than English, I would not regard today's decision, or the separate concurrence, as conclusive upon the issue whether the statute and the guidelines require the funded school district to provide special instruction. For me, numbers are at the heart of this case and my concurrence is to be understood accordingly.

THE PARAMETERS OF THE BILINGUAL EDUCATION DEBATE IN CALIFORNIA TWENTY YEARS AFTER *LAU v. NICHOLS*

Stuart Biegel.
14 CHICANO-LATINO L. REV. 48 (1994).

INTRODUCTION

Twenty years ago, the U.S. Supreme Court recognized the equal educational opportunity rights of limited-English proficient (LEP) and non-English proficient (NEP) children in *Lau v. Nichols*.[1] During these past two decades, the multi-faceted debate regarding bilingual education has continued unabated. While new statutes have been implemented and a growing body of case law has evolved, many legal and policy issues in this area remain unresolved. * * *

A.   The Federal Track

In *Lau*, non-English-speaking Chinese students brought a class action suit in which they argued that the San Francisco Unified School

---

1.   414 U.S. 563 (1974).

District's failure to provide equal educational opportunities for children who did not speak English amounted to a violation of the Fourteenth Amendment.[3] The Supreme Court ruled in favor of the students, but declined to decide the Fourteenth Amendment challenge relying solely on Title VI of the Civil Rights Act of 1964.[4]

Writing for the Court, Justice Douglas explained that no specific remedy would be granted because none had been requested.[5] While he did identify some possible "choices" in this regard[6], Douglas made it clear that any remedy designed by local district officials would have to be consistent with the Office of Civil Rights' (OCR) interpretation of Title VI, including the following guideline:

> Where an inability to speak and understand the English language excludes national-origin minority group children from effective participation in the educational program offered by a school district, the district must take affirmative steps to rectify the language deficiency in order to open its instructional program to these students.[7] By providing school districts with little more than these general guiding principles, *Lau* crystallized the volatile dispute in both educational and legal circles that continues unabated today.

* * *

3. *Lau*, 414 U.S. at 564. Judge Hufstedler, dissenting from the denial of hearing en banc by the Ninth Circuit, outlined the plaintiffs' arguments:

> The majority opinion correctly identifies the two groups of children who brought this action: (1) 1,790 Chinese school children who speak no English and are taught none, and (2) 1,066 Chinese children who speak no English and who receive some kind of remedial instruction in English. The majority's characterization of the relief sought as "bilingual education" is misleading. The children do not seek to have their classes taught in both English and Chinese. All they ask is that they receive instruction in the English language. Access to education offered by the public schools is completely foreclosed to these children who cannot comprehend any of it. They are functionally deaf and mute. . . .
>
> These Chinese children are not separated from their English speaking classmates by state-erected walls of brick and mortar but the language barrier, which the state helps to maintain, insulates the children from their classmates as effectively as any physical bulwarks. Indeed, these children are more isolated from equal educational opportunity than were those physically segregated blacks in *Brown*;

these children cannot communicate at all with their classmates or their teachers.

Id. (citing Lau v. Nichols, 483 F.2d 791, 805–06 (9th Cir. 1973) (Hufstedler, J., dissenting)).

4. *Id.* at 566. Title VI of the Civil Rights Act of 1964, 42 U.S.C. § 2000(d), has been relied upon by plaintiffs in a number of key education cases. It provides: "No person in the United States shall, on the ground of race, color or national origin, be excluded from participation in, be denied the benefits of, or be subjected to discrimination under any program or activity receiving Federal financial assistance."

5. *Lau*, 414 U.S. at 564, 569.

6. *Id.* at 565 (stating that "teaching English" or "giving instructions in Chinese" were two options available).

7. *Id.* at 568. Key words and phrases in this passage triggered an ongoing debate and remain subject to varying interpretations. Educators and policymakers have focused particularly on the relative nature of the following: "effective participation," "affirmative steps," "rectify the language deficiency," and "open its instructional program." *See generally* MARK YUDOF ET AL., EDUCATIONAL POLICY AND THE LAW 793–809 (3d ed. 1992).

In late 1974, Congress passed the Equal Educational Opportunity Act (EEOA) and included a key provision that appears to have explicitly adopted the *Lau* decision's approach.[20] Section 204 of the Act provides:

No State shall deny equal educational opportunity to an individual on account of his or her race, color, sex, or national origin, by . . . (f) the failure by an educational agency to take appropriate action to overcome language barriers that impede equal participation by its students in the instructional programs.[21]

The broad, general mandate of the EEOA triggered many questions of statutory interpretation, including an inquiry into what groups are covered, what kinds of programs are called for, and whether "equal participation" is synonymous with "effective participation."[22] While the *Lau* guidelines attempted to answer many of these questions,[23] it was the Fifth Circuit in *Castaneda v. Pickard*[24] that ultimately determined the Act's current applicability and scope.

In *Castaneda*, a group of Mexican–American children and their parents challenged the practices of a Texas school district that allegedly resulted in a deprivation of equal educational opportunity. Among plaintiffs' allegations was the charge that the district failed "to implement adequate bilingual education to overcome the linguistic barriers that impede the plaintiffs' equal participation in the educational program of the district."[25]

Applying the EEOA, the court decided the bilingual education issue in favor of the plaintiffs. Judge Randall considered the meaning of "appropriate action" in the Act, and concluded that the phrase was not intended to be synonymous with "bilingual education."[26] Randall stated:

Congress . . . did not specify that a state must provide a program of bilingual education. . . . We think Congress' use of the less specific term, "appropriate action," rather than "bilingual education," indicates that Congress intended to leave state and local educational authorities a substantial amount of latitude in choosing the programs and techniques they would use to meet their obligations under the EEOA.[27]

In the end, Castaneda set forth a three-prong analysis that federal courts continue to follow today when evaluating a school district's language remediation program. First, a court must determine whether the district is pursuing a program "informed by an educational theory recognized as sound by some experts in the field or, at least, deemed a

---

20. *See* Rachel F. Moran, *Bilingual Education as a Status Conflict*, 75 Cal. L. Rev. 321, 329 (1987).

21. 20 U.S.C. § 1703(f).

22. *See, e.g.*, Yudof , *supra* note 7, at 793.

23. *See supra* note 8.

24. 2 648 F.2d 989 (5th Cir. 1981).

25. *Id.* at 992. Plaintiffs brought this suit under the Fourteenth Amendment, Title VI, and the EEOA. In addition to the bilingual education component of the lawsuit, plaintiffs' charges included an allegation that the district "unlawfully discriminated against them by using an ability grouping system for classroom assignments . . . based on racially and ethnically discriminatory criteria and resulted in impermissible classroom segregation." *Id.*

26. *Id.* at 1009.

27. *Id.*

legitimate experimental strategy."[28] Second, the court must establish whether "the programs and practices actually used . . . are reasonably calculated to implement effectively the educational theory adopted by the school."[29] Finally, the court must determine whether the school's program, even if premised on sound educational theory and effectively implemented, produces "results indicating that the language barriers confronting students are actually being overcome."[30]

Today, most bilingual education litigation is decided under the EEOA and the *Castaneda* three-part test. Professor Rachel Moran explains that such an analysis "looks only at whether a program has the effect of excluding NEP and LEP students from the educational program and does not require proof of discriminatory intent."[31] In a sense, recognition of this analysis constituted a victory for those who favored at least some education in a student's primary language. However, the remedial consequences of an EEOA victory are far different than they might have been under the OCR's *Lau* guidelines, since the Act's "appropriate action" requirement appears broad enough to encompass educational programs taught entirely in English.[32]

B. The State Track [California as a Case Study]

In the aftermath of *Lau*, the California Legislature passed the Chacon–Moscone Bilingual–Bicultural Education Act of 1976.[33] The aggressive, far-reaching Chacon–Moscone Act mandated bilingual education in California and established the state as a leader in this volatile area.

The Act recognized that a lack of English language communication skills presented "an obstacle" to the equal educational opportunity rights of LEP students which could be "removed by instruction and training in the pupils' primary languages while such pupils are learning English."[34] In its central provision, the Act (as amended in 1980) required: "Each pupil of limited-English proficiency enrolled in the California public school system in kindergarten through grade 12 shall receive instruction in a language understandable to the pupil which

---

28. *Id.*

29. *Id.* at 1010.

30. *Id.* For a representative example of how this three-part analysis has been applied by the federal courts in recent years, see Teresa P. v. Berkeley Unified School District, 724 F. Supp. 698 (N.D. Cal. 1989).

31. Moran, *supra* note 20, at 331.

32. For additional analysis regarding the applicability of federal law in this area, see Michael A. Rebell & Anne W. Murdaugh, *National Values and Community Values: Part II: Equal Educational Opportunity for Limited English Proficient Students*, 21 J. L. & EDUC. 335, 356–73 (1992).

33. CAL. EDUC. CODE §§ 52160–52178 (Deering 1987).

34. *Id.* at § 52161 (emphasis added). The Legislature also found that "the dropout rate is excessive among limited-English-speaking pupils," and that "this represents a tremendous loss in human resources." *Id.*; *Id.* at § 52163 (m) defines "pupils with limited-English proficiency" as those "who do not have the clearly developed English language skills of comprehension, speaking, reading and writing necessary to receive instruction only in English at a level substantially equivalent to pupils of the same age or grade whose primary language is English." *Id.*

recognizes the pupil's primary language and teaches the pupil English."[35] In grades K–6, school districts with at least fifteen LEP students speaking the same primary language in the same grade level had to "offer" these students "full bilingual instruction" and "bilingual-bicultural education."[36] At the junior high and high school levels, districts were required to evaluate individually all LEP students not receiving at least "partial bilingual education" and provide educational services "in a manner consistent" with *Lau*, the EEOA, and applicable federal regulations.[37]

In 1987, legislation was enacted to continue the Chacon–Moscone Act,[38] but the legislation was vetoed by Governor George Deukmejian, who declared that local school districts should be free to "fashion their own programs."[39] However, while the mandatory bilingual education program ceased to be operative, the "Sunset Statutes" became applicable.[40]

The Sunset Statutes of the California Education Code provide continuing funds for specific programs that may cease to be mandatory. If a program is not renewed, school districts may still choose to continue offering the specialized services to their students, and money will remain available from the state for the purpose of providing these services.[41] The statutes designate the State Department of Education as the government body in charge of disbursing these funds.[42]

Thus, in 1987, the State Department of Education was faced with an important policy decision—what sort of "bilingual education" programs would be required before school districts could receive state funds. Section 62002 provides in part:

> If the Legislature does not enact legislation to continue a program
> . . . the funding of that program shall continue for the general

---

35. *Id.* at § 52165 (emphasis added).

36. *Id.* at § 52165(a) (exact language prior to 1980 amendment). School districts with at least ten K–6 LEP students speaking the same primary language at the same grade level had to offer at least "partial bilingual education." *Id.* Section 52163 (exact language prior to 1980 amendment) of the Chacon–Moscone Act provided the following pertinent definitions:

(a) "Partial bilingual instruction" means listening, speaking, reading and writing skills developed in both languages. Material related to culture and history is taught in the language the pupil understands better.

(b) "Full bilingual instruction" means basic language skills developed and maintained in both languages. Instruction in required subject matter or classes is provided in both languages in addition to culture and history.

(c) "Bilingual-bicultural education" is a system of instruction which uses two

languages, one of which is English, as a means of instruction. It is a means of instruction which builds upon and expands the existing language skills of each participating pupil, which will enable the pupil to achieve competency in both languages.

37. CAL. EDUC. CODE § 52163(f) (1977) (prior to 1980 amendment).

38. *Id.* at §§ 62000, 62006 (Deering 1987 & Supp. 1993) (regarding the mandatory review prescribed by the legislature before the mandatory bilingual education program could be continued).

39. *See Governor Buries Bilingual Education Bill and 6 Other Education Proposals*, L.A. DAILY JOURNAL , July 27, 1987, at 2.

40. CAL. EDUC. CODE §§ 62000–62002.5.

41. *Id.*

42. *Id.* at § 62003.

purposes of that program as specified in the provisions relating to the establishment and operation of the program. . . . The funds shall be used for the intended purposes of the program. . . .[43]

Superintendent of Public Instruction Bill Honig took an aggressive position based upon a facial reading of section 62002. In a program advisory distributed to all the school districts in the state, Honig noted that the "purposes" language of the education code was quite broad and included many of the basic requirements of the Chacon–Moscone Act. Thus, California school districts were no longer required to comply with the Act, but if they wished to continue receiving money for bilingual education programs they had to continue providing services that were consistent with the general purposes of the old bilingual-bicultural requirements.[44]

* * *

2. CALIFORNIA PROPOSITION 227

Perhaps the most volatile turning point in the recent history of bilingual education has been California Proposition 227, approved overwhelmingly by the voters in 1998. This ballot initiative generated tremendous emotion, and reverberated throughout the country, particularly in states with substantial numbers of English learners.

The new law significantly limited the type of instruction that could be offered to English learners in the public schools. It must be emphasized, however, that Proposition 227 did not succeed in ending bilingual education in California, and the aftermath of that campaign is still playing out in interesting and unpredictable ways.

The situation nationwide remains very fluid. Other states have since considered legislation similar to Proposition 227, adopting a parallel approach in some instances but rejecting such an approach in others. And there has been a renewed interest in identifying innovative new directions that build on well-settled principles regarding curriculum and pedagogy identified by educators in this area.

Consider the following excerpts from 227 in light of these developments. What opportunities are available under the statutory scheme for those who seek greater flexibility in providing at least some instruction in a student's primary language?

CALIFORNIA EDUCATION CODE, TITLE 1, DIVISION 1, PART 1, CHAPTER 3

(as approved by the voters in 1998, 61 percent to 39 percent).

305: Subject to the exceptions provided in Article 3 (commencing with section 310), all children in California public schools shall be taught

---

43. *Id.* at § 62002.

44. *See* Bill Honig, Program Advisory to County and District Superintendents and Selected Program Directors, regarding Options Available to Districts for Achieving Compliance with the Staffing and Instructional Requirements of the State Program for Students of Limited English Proficiency, California State Dep't of Educ., May 20, 1988, at 1.

English by being taught in English. In particular, this shall require that all children be placed in English language classrooms. Children who are English learners shall be educated through sheltered English immersion during a temporary transition period not normally intended to exceed one year. Local schools shall be permitted to place in the same classroom English learners of different ages but whose degree of English proficiency is similar. Local schools shall be encouraged to mix together in the same classroom English learners from different native-language groups but with the same degree of English fluency. Once English learners have acquired a good working knowledge of English, they shall be transferred to English language mainstream classrooms. As much as possible, current supplemental funding for English learners shall be maintained, subject to possible modification under Article 8 (commencing with section 335) below.

306: The definitions of the terms used in this article and in Article 3 (commencing with section 310) are as follows: (a) "**English learner**" means a child who does not speak English or whose native language is not English and who is not currently able to perform ordinary classroom work in English, also known as a Limited English Proficiency or LEP child; (b) "**English language classroom**" means a classroom in which the language of instruction used by the teaching personnel is overwhelmingly the English language, and in which such teaching personnel possess a good knowledge of the English language; (c) "**English language mainstream classroom**" means a classroom in which the pupils either are native English language speakers or already have acquired reasonable fluency in English; (d) "**Sheltered English immersion**" or "structured English immersion" means an English language acquisition process for young children in which nearly all classroom instruction is in English but with the curriculum and presentation designed for children who are learning the language; (e) "**Bilingual education/native language instruction**" means a language acquisition process for pupils in which much or all instruction, textbooks, and teaching materials are in the child's native language.

310: The requirements of section 305 may be waived with the prior written informed consent, to be provided annually, of the child's parents or legal guardian under the circumstances specified below and in section 311. Such informed consent shall require that said parents or legal guardian personally visit the school to apply for the waiver and that they there be provided a full description of the educational materials to be used in the different educational program choices and all the educational opportunities available to the child. Under such parental waiver conditions, children may be transferred to classes where they are taught English and other subjects through bilingual education techniques or other generally recognized educational methodologies permitted by law. Individual schools in which 20 pupils or more of a given grade level receive a waiver shall be required to offer such a class; otherwise, they must allow the pupils to transfer to a public school in which such a class is offered.

311: The circumstances in which a parental exception waiver may be granted under section 310 are as follows:

(a) Children who already know English: the child already possesses good English language skills, as measured by standardized tests of English vocabulary comprehension, reading, and writing, in which the child scores at or above the state average for his or her grade level or at or above the 5th grade average, whichever is lower; or

(b) Older children: the child is age 10 years or older, and it is the informed belief of the school principal and educational staff that an alternate course of educational study would be better suited to the child's rapid acquisition of basic English language skills; or

(c) Children with special needs: the child already has been placed for a period of not less than thirty days during that school year in an English language classroom and it is subsequently the informed belief of the school principal and educational staff that the child has such special physical, emotional, psychological, or educational needs that an alternate course of educational study would be better suited to the child's overall educational development. A written description of these special needs must be provided and any such decision is to be made subject to the examination and approval of the local school superintendent, under guidelines established by and subject to the review of the local Board of Education and ultimately the State Board of Education. The existence of such special needs shall not compel issuance of a waiver, and the parents shall be fully informed of their right to refuse to agree to a waiver.

320: As detailed in Article 2 (commencing with section 305) and Article 3 (commencing with section 310), all California school children have the right to be provided with an English language public education. If a California school child has been denied the option of an English language instructional curriculum in public school, the child's parent or legal guardian shall have legal standing to sue for enforcement of the provisions of this statute, and if successful shall be awarded normal and customary attorney's fees and actual damages, but not punitive or consequential damages. Any school board member or other elected official or public school teacher or administrator who willfully and repeatedly refuses to implement the terms of this statute by providing such an English language educational option at an available public school to a California school child may be held personally liable for fees and actual damages by the child's parents or legal guardian.

Notes

1. A Fourteenth Amendment lawsuit challenging the constitutionality of Proposition 227 after its passage was defeated in U.S. District Court, and the decision was upheld by the Ninth Circuit. In *Valeria v. Davis*, 307 F.3d 1036, 1042 (9th Cir. 2002), the Court stated:

> Given Proposition 227's facial neutrality, and the lack of evidence that it was motivated by racial considerations, we hold that Proposition 227's reallocation of political authority over bilingual education does not offend the Equal Protection Clause.

But note Judge Pregerson's dissent from the denial of rehearing *en banc,* Valeria v. Davis, 320 F.3d 1014, 1018–20 (9th Cir. 2003):

> Proposition 227 generates the type of restructuring of the political process that runs afoul of the equal protection guarantees of the Fourteenth Amendment. Proposition 227 siphons power away from those minorities who are directly affected by bilingual education policy and transfers the power to influence that area of educational policy to the general electorate. While public school students and parents could influence policy at the local level before the passage of Proposition 227, they must now launch a successful statewide ballot initiative to bring about any meaningful change. Requiring the affected minority to navigate this remote and amorphous level of governmental decision-making to effect any change in bilingual education policy undoubtedly "mak[es] it more difficult for certain racial ... minorities ... to achieve legislation that is in their interest." * * * Proposition 227 creates a political structure that has the consequence of making it substantially more difficult to effect change with respect to an issue with a racial focus. Therefore, because Proposition 227: (1) restructures the political process and (2) only with respect to an area of educational policy that has a racial focus, the statute violates the Equal Protection Clause * * *.

2. The *Valeria* Court ruled against the plaintiffs in a facial challenge to the constitutionality of the statutory scheme, but might there be a set of circumstances that could lead to an "as applied" challenge? Would plaintiffs stand a chance of prevailing in such a challenge? Under what arguments?

3. At the district court level, in addition to the Fourteenth Amendment, plaintiffs alleged violations under the First Amendment, the Equal Educational Opportunity Act (EEOA), the Supremacy Clause, and international charters. With regard to the EEOA, the Court appeared to suggest that a challenge under the third prong of *Castaneda* might become relevant over time. Consider the requirements of *Castaneda,* as set forth below in *Cortez.* Might a challenge to Proposition 227 under the EEOA have a chance of succeeding today?

PROBLEM 34: The New Mendocino Education Code Litigation

The following hypothetical takes place in the fictional state of New Mendocino.

Concerned about the quality of public education in New Mendocino, and in particular about the low test scores of language minority students years after they enter the school system with limited proficiency in English, wealthy entrepreneur Manuel Rodriguez establishes a new foundation for the sole purpose of focusing on bilingual education reform issues. After consulting with a task force of educators and community leaders, Rodriguez announces an ambitious plan composed of three interrelated parts: (1) substantial grants to private schools that volunteer to "adopt" public schools with high percentages of English learners; (2) the development of model gifted programs for bilingual students; and (3) extensive professional development for bilingual teachers linked to a career ladder that would double the current salaries of bilingual educators so that the top teachers in the field would actually earn the same amount of money as first-year associates at major law firms.

The adoption process would be limited to public schools with English Learner populations of 50 percent or greater. As envisioned, substantial interaction—both online and, if possible, in real time—would occur between and among the faculty and students of both schools. Courses would be team taught, interactive projects would bring students together, and a range of extracurricular activities would cement the bonds.

The Rodriguez Foundation programs receive highly positive feedback from all relevant stakeholders, and many low performing public schools with large English Learner populations are adopted by private schools throughout the state. In addition, teachers rush to participate in the professional development/career ladder program, seeing it as a unique opportunity to improve the quality of public education while at the same time increasing their salaries.

Assume that a lawsuit brought by the New Mendocino English First Coalition. The group is prepared to argue that a separate gifted program for English learners violates the requirements set forth in New Mendocino Education Code § 305. (Assume that New Mendocino has adopted an exact version of CA Prop. 227, and that their Education Codes in this area are identical.) What arguments should defendants expect plaintiffs to set forth, and how should they be countered? What result? Discuss.

3. RECENT DEVELOPMENTS: THE CONTINUING VITALITY OF THE EQUAL EDUCATIONAL OPPORTUNITY ACT AND THE *CASTANEDA* TEST

CORTEZ v. CALUMET PUB. SCH. DIST. #132

2002 WL 31177378 (N.D.Ill. 2002).

LEFKOW, J.

Plaintiffs, Latino students attending school in Calumet Public School District #132 (the "School District"), filed this putative class action * * * alleging that the state defendants violated the Equal Education Opportunities Act ("EEOA"), 20 U.S.C. §§ 1701 *et seq.* Before the court is the state defendants' motion to dismiss under Rules 12(b)(1) and 12(b)(6). For the reasons set forth below, the court denies the motion.

* * *

BACKGROUND

Plaintiffs, Latino students with limited English proficiency ("LEP"),[2] presently attend Burr Oak Academy, Burr Oak Elementary or Calumet Elementary School located within the School District. By and through their parents, plaintiffs bring this action individually and on behalf of a putative class of other present and future similarly situated Latino students.

According to plaintiffs, for several years parents of Latino LEP students in the School District contacted school administrators and the School District's Board of Education attempting to resolve the deficiencies in the School District's bilingual education programs. After these attempts to resolve the matter at the local level were unsuccessful, the parents filed complaints with the [Illinois State Board of Education (ISBE)] and the United States Department of Education, Office of Civil Rights ("OCR").[3]

Responding to the parents' complaints, the ISBE conducted a compliance review of the School District in March 2000, finding that the school district was not in compliance with state requirements for transitional bilingual education programs. Plaintiffs allege that the state defendants provide and administer federal and state funding for local school districts and have the power to deny a school district's claim for funding. If a school district is found to be non-compliant with the bilingual education requirements, the state defendants have the power to place a school district on probation when it "fails or refuses to serve students according to relevant legal and/or regulatory requirements" and "prolongs or repeats instances of non-compliance to a degree that indicates an intention not to comply." Plaintiffs also point out that a school or district that fails to correct its deficiencies within the time set forth in its plan may be "nonrecognized" by the ISBE, at which point the school or district would be ineligible to file any claim upon the common school fund or collect tuition from another school district. The ISBE threatened to cut district funding, and the School District responded initially by not applying for funds for its bilingual program for the 2000–2001 school year. Despite ISBE's threats, the district has continually failed to implement an appropriate transitional bilingual program.

Plaintiffs allege that despite the School District's failure to correct the deficiencies in its transitional bilingual education program, the state defendants have not yet declared the School District "nonrecognized" or

2. LEP students are students either (1) not born in the United States whose native language is other than English and are incapable of performing ordinary classwork in English, or (2) were born in the United States of parents possessing no or limited English-speaking ability and are incapable of performing ordinary classwork in English. 105 ILCS 5/14C–2(d).

3. OCR conducted its own investigation and found that the School District's failure to inform and involve parents through communication in their native language violated federal law. Consequently, OCR issued a Corrective Action Agreement establishing a time line of compliance for the School District (Amd.Compl.¶ 52). According to plaintiffs, the School District has not yet complied with the Corrective Action Agreement (Amd.Compl.¶ 53).

ineligible to file a claim upon the common school fund as they are empowered to do under state law. Plaintiffs argue that the state defendants have failed to take "appropriate action" to enforce the statutory and regulatory requirements of the Illinois Transitional Bilingual Education Program, and as a result, plaintiffs have been denied equal access to educational opportunities in violation of the EEOA.

Discussion

Under the EEOA, a state is prohibited from denying equal educational opportunities to an individual "on account of his or her race, color, sex, or national origin, by-(f) the failure of an educational agency to take *appropriate action* to overcome the language barriers that impede equal participation by its students in its instructional programs." Plaintiffs allege that because the state defendants have failed to enforce the Illinois Transitional Bilingual Education Program's statutory and regulatory requirements against the School District, the state defendants have not taken "appropriate action" as the EEOA requires. Specifically, plaintiffs argue that the state defendants have not taken "appropriate action" because they have not found the School District to be "nonrecognized" and thus ineligible to file a claim on the common school fund despite the School District's continued deficiencies in transitional bilingual education programs.

The state defendants argue that this claim cannot survive a motion to dismiss because: * * * (3) the state defendants have not violated federal law; (4) the plaintiffs have not pled the appropriate standard to hold the state defendants liable; * * * [and] (5) Congress' use of the term "appropriate action" confers discretionary authority on the state defendants.

* * *

C. State Defendants' Violation of Federal Law

The state defendants * * * assert that they have not violated federal law because they have taken appropriate action to remedy the situation in the School District. Defendants point out, and plaintiffs admit, that the state defendants have taken some steps to remedy the situation in the School District. The state defendants assert that the court should defer to the expert knowledge of the educators, who may not wish to implement the remedy of "non-recognition" of the School District, which would result in measures that "[punish] the innocent as well as the guilty."

Clearly, a state board of education can be held liable under the EEOA for not taking "appropriate action." Accepting plaintiffs' well-pleaded allegations as true and drawing all reasonable inferences in the plaintiffs' favor, a claim upon which relief can be granted exists based on the plaintiffs' allegations that the state defendants failed to properly supervise the School District, that the School District was clearly unwilling to comply with federal and state law requirements, and that the state defendants' enforcement efforts were lax. As such, the state defendants' motion to dismiss on this ground is denied.

D. Appropriate Pleading Standard

The state defendants next argue that because the EEOA does not define "appropriate action," the court should examine other cases where federal courts have determined that a school district or municipality becomes liable in damages for failure to enforce regulations against third parties. After examining these cases, the state defendants assert that a school board must be deliberately indifferent before being held liable for the acts of third parties. According to the state defendants, because this standard has not been pled, the complaint should be dismissed.

This argument is unavailing. The cases that the state defendants point to were not brought under the EEOA. The EEOA provides that no state shall discriminate against an individual by the failure of an educational agency to take "appropriate action" to overcome language barriers that impede equal participation by students. All that the plaintiffs are required to plead is that the state defendants did not take "appropriate action." The plaintiffs are not required to plead a deliberate indifference standard. Therefore, the state defendants' motion to dismiss for plaintiffs' failure to plead deliberate indifference is denied.

E. Appropriate Action and Discretionary Authority

The state defendants next assert that Congress' use of the term "appropriate action" in the EEOA confers discretionary authority on the state defendants. The state defendants cite *Heckler v. Chaney*, 470 U.S. 821, 831 (1985), for the proposition that an agency's decision not to exercise its enforcement authority is committed to its absolute discretion.

The Seventh Circuit in *Gomez* grappled with the issue of deference given to state and local education authorities under the EEOA, recognizing that "[t]he term 'appropriate action' used ... indicates that the federal legislature did not mandate a specific program for language instruction, but rather conferred substantial latitude on state and local educational authorities in choosing their programs to meet the obligations imposed by federal law." While state and local educators were entitled to substantial deference, the court further reasoned that "[t]he duty remains [on the courts] to interpret and enforce congressional enactments, and [courts] cannot accord such sweeping deference to state and local agencies that judicial review becomes in practice judicial abdication." The *Gomez* court concluded that courts should "review a state's implementation of § 1703(f) in a manner similar to that which [courts] employ in reviewing an administrative agency's interpretation and implementation of a legislative mandate.".

The court[, pursuant to the test articulated in *Castaneda v. Pickard*,] set out a three-step framework. First, courts should "examine carefully the evidence of record regarding the soundness of the educational theory or principles upon which the challenged program is based." Second, courts "must determine whether the programs actually used by a school system are reasonably calculated to implement effectively the educational theory adopted by the system." Finally, courts must decide if the school's program "although ostensibly premised on a legitimate educational theory and adequately implemented initially, fails, after a period of time sufficient to give the plan a legitimate trial, to obtain results that would indicate that the language barriers confronting students are actually being overcome." With regard to the final step, the court explicitly noted that "[j]udicial deference to the school system is unwarranted if over a certain period the system has failed to make substantial progress in correcting the language deficiencies of its students."

The state defendants argue that they have implemented appropriate regulations, established guidelines, monitored the LEP program at the School District, and have placed the School District on probation. Any further punitive measures, according to the state defendants, should be committed to the ISBE's absolute discretion.

Although the court should give the state defendants deference for their decision not to implement more stringent punishment against the School District, *Gomez* recognizes that at some point this deference is no longer warranted. Plaintiffs have alleged that they have complained to the ISBE, and that no progress has been made to correct the deficiencies in the school programs over a period of time. Throughout this time, plaintiffs allege, they have been without access to transitional bilingual education programs. Therefore, the ISBE's decision not to punish the School District more stringently may not be "appropriate action" because of the failure to make substantial progress in correcting the School District's deficiencies. As such, the state defendants' motion to dismiss based on its discretionary authority is denied.

* * *

4. SPECIALIZED INQUIRIES RELATING TO ENGLISH LEARNERS: DESEGREGATION & THE NCLB ACT

BILINGUAL EDUCATION AND RESEGREGATION: RECONCILING THE APPARENT PARADOX BETWEEN BILINGUAL EDUCATION PROGRAMS AND DESEGREGATION GOALS

Edward W. Lew.
7 ASIAN PAC. AM. L.J. 88 (2001).

INTRODUCTION

During the last half of the twentieth century, racial minorities have won significant legal battles in the context of primary and secondary public education. On more than one occasion, the federal courts have rendered decisions that have increased both the accessibility and quality of public education for people of color. In 1954, the Supreme Court held in *Brown v. Board of Education* that a state could not permit or require the segregation of white and black students in public schools solely on the basis of race. Nearly twenty years after *Brown*, the Court added that a state school system must also take affirmative steps to provide students who could not speak English with a meaningful opportunity to participate in public education. In *Lau v. Nichols*, the Court held that a state school system's failure to take such affirmative steps violated federal statutory law prohibiting discrimination based on race, color, or national origin.

While the two decisions are generally considered to be victories for the rights of racial minorities, a dilemma arises as to how a state school system can simultaneously achieve both goals. A paradox appears to exist in trying to promote certain types of bilingual education programs while maintaining racially-integrated classrooms. The maintenance of certain bilingual education programs has often resulted in the classroom segregation of minority students in school classrooms.

Generally, the term "bilingual education" describes a wide range of programs designed to provide a meaningful education for non-English and limited-English speaking students. Bilingual education programs include basic bilingual classes, also called English-as-a-second language ("ESL") classes, and bilingual-bicultural classes. The primary purpose of ESL classes is to teach non-English proficient ("NEP") and limited-English proficient ("LEP") students the English language by using English language instruction. In contrast, bilingual-bicultural classes have multiple purposes. Bilingual classes are designed to teach students to be "bilingual and bi-literate, in English and at least one other language." Bilingualism and bi-literacy are usually achieved by teaching students core subjects in their native languages.

Of the two bilingual education programs, bilingual-bicultural classes have been more controversial. Bilingual-bicultural classes have often undermined the process of racial integration. Students in bilingual-bicultural classes are typically placed in classrooms with other students of the same race or ethnicity, where they spend their entire school day. Students often remain in bilingual-bicultural classes for several years and in some cases, will remain in bilingual-bicultural classes indefinitely. Many of these students never develop the English-language proficiency required to transfer from the bilingual-bicultural classes. As a result, students in bilingual-bicultural classes often lack any exposure to students outside of their particular programs.

In this Comment, I [set forth] * * * a framework to reconcile the apparent paradox between bilingual education programs and desegregation goals. I conclude that bilingual education programs do not inherently contradict the principles of desegregation. * * * [And] I suggest modifications to the existing bilingual education programs in each school that may help reduce the harms created by segregation.

I. ESTABLISHED LEGAL PRINCIPLES REGARDING DESEGREGATION
AND LANGUAGE RIGHTS IN EDUCATION

A.   Paving the Road for Desegregation—Brown v. Board of Education

In *Brown v. Board of Education*, the Supreme Court rejected the doctrine of "separate but equal" in public education and held that the segregation of students in separate educational facilities solely on the basis of race violated the Equal Protection Clause of the Fourteenth Amendment. The Court announced its unanimous decision in response to four cases from different jurisdictions that asked for resolution of the same legal question. In each case, black children were "denied admission to schools attended by white children under laws requiring or permitting segregation according to race."

The Court dismissed the relevance of findings that the black and white schools were equalized "with respect to buildings, curricula, qualifications and salaries of teachers, and other 'tangible' factors." Instead, the Court was more concerned with "the effect of segregation itself on public education." Based on the intangible effects of segregation, the Court expressly rejected the 1896 "separate but equal" doctrine from *Plessy v. Ferguson*:

> Segregation of white and colored children in public schools has a detrimental effect upon the colored children. The impact is greater when it has the sanction of the law; for the policy of separating the races is usually interpreted as denoting the inferiority of the Negro group. A sense of inferiority affects the motivation of a child to learn. Segregation with the sanction of law, therefore, has a tendency to [retard] the educational and mental development of Negro children and to deprive them of some of the benefits they would receive in a racial[ly] integrated society.... We conclude that in the field of public education the doctrine of "separate but equal" has no place. Separate educational facilities are inherently unequal.

Although the school districts were allowed to fashion their own desegregation plans, the Court clearly announced that state-sanctioned segregation no longer comported with contemporary equal protection jurisprudence.

*B.   Providing Language Minorities with a Meaningful
Education—Lau v. Nichols*

In *Lau v. Nichols*, the Supreme Court held that a school district that received federal funds was required to "take affirmative steps" to ensure that non-English speaking students could effectively participate in the school system's educational program. In *Lau*, students brought a class action suit against the SFUSD for failing to provide any type of English language instruction to nearly 1,800 of the 2,856 non-English speaking Chinese American students in violation of the Equal Protection Clause of the Fourteenth Amendment. The Court did not reach the equal protection claim but held for the students under section 601 of the Federal Civil Rights Act of 1964. Section 601 "excludes from participation in federal financial assistance, recipients of aid which discriminate against racial groups."

The Court relied on two federal guidelines promulgated by the Department of Health, Education, and Welfare ("HEW") to hold that SFUSD's failure to provide English language instruction to non-English speaking students constituted impermissible discrimination based on race, color, or national origin. The first HEW guideline was issued in 1968 and required that "school systems are responsible for assuring that students of a particular race, color, or national origin are not denied the opportunity to obtain the education generally obtained by other students in the system." In 1970, HEW elaborated on the first guideline by issuing a second guideline that required federally-funded school districts "to rectify the language deficiency in order to open the instruction to students who had 'linguistic' deficiencies."

The Court reasoned that the students of Chinese ancestry who could not speak English were "effectively foreclosed from any meaningful education." The Court found it "obvious" that these non-English speaking students would receive "fewer benefits [from SFUSD] than the English speaking majority." Thus, the Court held that SFUSD's failure to provide English language instruction constituted either a form of "discrimination" or at least had "the effect of defeating or substantially impairing accomplishment of the objectives of the [educational] program [with respect to] individuals of a particular race, color, or national origin." Because either result violated federal regulations, the Court held, "Where inability to speak and understand the English language excludes national origin-minority group children from effective participation in the educational program offered by a school district, the district must take affirmative steps to rectify the language deficiency in order to open its instructional program to these."

Although the Court did not specify what types of programs should be implemented to satisfy the "affirmative step requirement," it became clear that schools districts had to do something to comply with the federal mandate to create a meaningful opportunity for linguistic minorities to participate in the public educational system.

C. The Apparent Paradox Between Bilingual Education and Desegregation

In *Brown*, the Court held that racially-segregated schools are unconstitutional under the Equal Protection Clause. In *Lau*, the Court held that federally-funded school districts are required under section 601 of the Civil Rights Act of 1964 to take affirmative steps to provide non-English speaking students with a meaningful education. To date, the Court has not spoken directly as to which of the two goals should take precedence when they conflict. Two federal circuit courts, however, have addressed the issue in the cases of *Keyes v. School District Number 1*, and *Bradley v. Milliken*. Although the circuit court decisions arose in distinct contexts, the analytical frameworks contained within them help explain the contours of the debate.

1. *Keyes v. School District Number 1*

Keyes culminated in a long battle against racial segregation in the Denver School District. In 1969, plaintiffs raised a claim in federal court that the school board had intentionally created racially segregated schools within the district throughout the decade. The district court considered evidence that the board had purposefully contained racial minority students within particular schools and prevented their movement into predominantly white schools through three mechanisms: 1) manipulating school boundaries to contain racial minority students; 2) establishing a new school with conscious knowledge that it would be a one-race school; and 3) increasing the number of classrooms in a one-race minority school with the intent of preventing overflow into predominantly white schools.

The court held for the plaintiffs, finding that the board's intentional acts of segregation created a "dual school system." To execute a remedy, the court ordered the parties to submit desegregation plans. After considering each of the plans during a separate trial and determining that each one was inadequate, the court then conducted its own independent study and adopted the desegregation plan submitted by the court consultant, Dr. John A. Finger, which led to the creation of the "Finger Plan."

Under the "Finger Plan," five elementary schools were each left with Latino enrollments between seventy-seven and eighty-eight percent. The court justified the continued segregation of students in four of the schools partially on grounds of "the institution of bilingual-bicultural programs." The Tenth Circuit subsequently reviewed the court's desegregation order and considered whether it was permissible to leave certain schools predominantly one-race. The Tenth Circuit applied the rule from *Swann v. Charlotte–Mecklenburg Board of Education* and prescribed a strict limitation on when the school district would be able to maintain segregated schools: "In a system with a history of segregation the need for remedial criteria of sufficient specificity to assure a school authority's compliance with its constitutional duty warrants a presumption against schools that are substantially disproportionate in their racial composition."

Given the Denver School District's history of segregation, the Tenth Circuit held that continued segregation would only be allowable: 1) "where practical or legitimate considerations render[ed] desegregation unwise," or 2) "on the basis of proof that the racial compositions of [the] schools [was] not the result of past discriminatory action on the part of the Board." In keeping with the heavy presumption against the school district, the Tenth Circuit held that bilingual education was insufficient to justify the continued segregation: "Bilingual education ... is not a substitute for desegregation. Although bilingual instruction may be required to prevent isolation of minority students in a predominantly Anglo school system, such instruction must be subordinate to a plan of desegregation." The court then remanded the case to the district judge with instructions to "make every effort to achieve the greatest possible degree of actual desegregation and . . . necessarily be concerned with the elimination of one-race schools."

2.   *Bradley v. Milliken*

In *Bradley v. Milliken*, the Sixth Circuit again confronted the conflict between bilingual education and segregation while reviewing a desegregation plan. The district court had adopted the plan, on remand from the Supreme Court, under the order to promptly formulate "a decree to eliminat[e] the segregation found to exist in Detroit city schools. . . ." The district court had found at trial that the defendants, the state of Michigan and the Detroit school board, had created acts and policies that resulted in impermissible de jure segregation. The state and the school board did not challenge these findings.

The district court's plan to desegregate included the reassignment of Latinos between school district Region 2, where they were heavily concentrated in bilingual education programs, and district Region 1, where Latino representation was lacking. The school board challenged that part of the plan by arguing that the reassignment would "disrupt state required bilingual educational programs while achieving only token integration." Specifically, "the Director of the Bilingual Education for the School Board testified that reassigning Spanish speaking students . . . enrolled in Region 2 bilingual programs would impede the Board's ability to develop a model program and train bilingual teachers; produce fear and anxiety for students; limit community participation and interest in the schools; produce shortages of qualified bilingual teachers and necessary resource materials; and require the Board to adopt less efficient and effective methods of instruction."

The Sixth Circuit rejected the school board's challenge and agreed "with the district court that when the choice is between maintaining optimal conditions in a bilingual education program and desegregating all-black schools, desegregation must prevail." However, the Sixth Circuit's decision was subject to many caveats. Prior to the holding, the court observed that "[c]ircumstances permitting, we might well agree that the desegregative benefits would not justify the disruption created by reassigning Spanish-dominant students. Circumstances, however, do not so permit." Moreover, the district court's finding that "desegregation must prevail," was followed by a supplemental order to the school board "to develop a plan for reassigning pupils between Regions 1 and 2 which would provide for bilingual education in receiving schools."

II.   RECONCILING THE APPARENT PARADOX BETWEEN BILINGUAL EDUCATION AND DESEGREGATION

A.   *The Difference Between Effects of Segregation Resulting from Bilingual Education Programs and Effects Prohibited by the Supreme Court in Brown v. Board of Education*

Segregation resulting from bilingual education programs differs in purpose and effect from the segregation that the Court expressly rejected in *Brown*. In *Brown*, the Court held for the black children in order to protect them from the "detrimental effects" that resulted from state-imposed segregation. The Court's holding thus focused on two problematic aspects of the segregation: 1) the segregation had detrimental effects on the black students, and 2) the segregation was state-imposed.

With respect to the purpose analysis, the Court challenged the constitutional validity of any legislation that was unfriendly to racial minorities because they were racial minorities, finding no other reason to explain the reason for segregation than prejudice and discrimination. The Court viewed such legislation as being repugnant to the Equal Protection Clause of the Fourteenth Amendment, which declared "that the law in the States shall be the same for the black as for the white; that all persons, whether colored or white, shall stand equal before the laws of the States...." It recognized that the Equal Protection Clause was primarily designed to prohibit states from discriminating against racial minorities because of their color and to provide a positive immunity for them from such discriminatory laws. Moreover, the Court found the Equal Protection Clause to be grounded in the belief that legal discrimination "impl[ied] inferiority in civil society, lessen[ed] the security of their enjoyment of the rights which others enjoy, and ... are steps towards reducing them to the condition of a subject race."

With respect to the effects analysis, the Court was concerned about the social, psychological, and educational harms resulting from the "segregation of white and colored children in public schools." The Court cited to social science studies and literature that discussed these detrimental effects. It found a nexus between the prejudice and discrimination underlying the state sanction of segregation in public schools and the resulting detrimental effects of the sanction. Observing that "the policy of separating the races is usually interpreted as denoting the inferiority of the [N]egro group," the Court reasoned state-imposed segregation affected "the motivation of a child to learn."

The Court held that "[s]egregation, with the sanction of law, therefore, has a tendency to [retard] the educational and mental development of Negro children and to deprive them of the benefits they would receive in a racial[ly] integrated school system." This holding clearly indicates the Court's foremost concern with the diminished educational and learning opportunities for segregated black students that resulted from a state policy of segregation. Thus, the Court took great care to emphasize the importance of education.

> Today, education is perhaps the most important function of state and local governments. [Education is important] to our democratic society. It is required in the performance of our most basic public responsibilities.... It is the very foundation of good citizenship.... Today, it is a principal instrument in awakening the child to cultural values, in preparing him for later professional training, and in helping him to adjust normally to his environment. In these days, it is doubtful that any child may reasonably be expected to succeed in

life if he is denied the opportunity of an education. Such an opportunity, where the state has undertaken to provide it, is a right which must be made available to all on equal terms.

The Court had decided an earlier case, *McLaurin v. Oklahoma State Regents*, based on similar "intangible considerations." In *McLaurin*, the Court required that a black student admitted to a white graduate school be treated like all other students in his ability to study, engage in discussions, exchange views with other students, and in general, learn his profession. The Court in *Brown* found the *McLaurin* reasoning to be even more compelling when dealing with elementary and high school children, where "[t]o separate [children] from others of similar age and qualifications solely because of their race generates a feeling of inferiority as to their status in the community that may affect their hearts and minds in a way unlikely to ever be undone." The appropriate remedy to address the constitutional violation in Brown, therefore, was to end segregation.

Any segregation that arises from bilingual education programs are distinguishable in purpose and effect from the segregation that was rejected in *Brown*. With respect to purpose, bilingual education programs differ from the *Brown*-type segregation because they do not invidiously discriminate against children based on race. Bilingual education programs serve a distinct educational purpose and are not grounded on prejudice and discrimination. Although students in bilingual education programs may ultimately be grouped with others of the same race, such segregation is not based on racial classifications. The students' native language and proficiency with English, are the factors which determine their placement.

The bilingual education programs do not result in the detrimental effects prohibited by *Brown*. In fact, it appears that bilingual education helps to achieve the results that *Brown* championed. The Court in *Brown* argued that state-imposed segregation violated the Equal Protection Clause because it denied racial minorities an education equal to that which was available to white students. Bilingual education programs are designed to allow non-and limited-English speaking students meaningful participation in the school's educational program. In the absence of programs implemented to affirmatively rectify language deficiencies, these students would otherwise receive "fewer benefits ... than the English-speaking majority."

B. The Difference Between Segregated Bilingual Classrooms and Segregated Schools

The form of segregation that results from bilingual education programs is predominantly within-school, as opposed to within-district. Schools create bilingual education classrooms by grouping LEP and NEP students together according to native languages. Because a student's native language is usually related to his race or ethnicity, bilingual education classrooms each assume an identifiable racial or ethnic character. For example, Spanish bilingual classrooms are usually comprised entirely of Latino students, while Cantonese bilingual classrooms are usually comprised entirely of Cantonese students.

The courts in *Keyes* and *Bradley* were concerned with the elimination of one-race schools and not one-race classrooms. Moreover, the circuit courts found no inherent problems with bilingual education programs. Although both the Tenth and Sixth Circuits chose desegregation goals over bilingual education, their holdings were limited by the following factors: 1) both the Denver and Detroit school systems had histories of de jure segregation resulting in one-race schools, and 2) desegregation goals were undermined by bilingual education programs when bilingual education goals were being used to justify the continuation of one-race schools. The Sixth Circuit defended the goal of bilingual education and noted that "[t]he Board's concern for the continued viability of its bilingual educational programs is commendable. Circumstances permitting, we might well agree that the desegregative benefits would not justify the disruption created by reassigning Spanish-dominant students. Circumstances, however, do not so permit." Moreover, the Sixth Circuit did not indicate that there was any question of the legality of the district court's supplemental order requiring the Board to "provide for bilingual education in receiving schools." The Tenth Circuit also spoke in defense of bilingual education when it noted that "bilingual instruction may be required to prevent the isolation of minority students . . . ." One-race classrooms resulting from bilingual education under normal circumstances, therefore, seemingly do not contradict the decisions nor reasoning from *Keyes* and *Bradley*.

Nevertheless, many critics contend that the one-race classroom is equally as harmful as one-race schools. One-race classrooms resulting from bilingual education programs are defensible, however, because bilingual education programs: are intended to separate students only temporarily, and do not foreclose the opportunity to meaningfully interact with students of other races and ethnicities.

With respect to the ephemerality of bilingual education programs, Lau requires schools that adopt bilingual education programs as a method to rectify language deficiencies to tailor the programs to be educational and transitory. "Any ability grouping or tracking system employed by the school system to deal with the special language skill needs of national origin-minority children must be designed to meet such language skill needs as soon as possible and must not operate as an educational dead-end or permanent track." In defense of ephemeral segregation, therefore, bilingual education is premised on the notion that students should and will eventually integrate with students of other races. This differs from the case of one-race schools, where ultimate integration is not even possible. Where bilingual education has been criticized as resulting in a "dead-end or permanent track," the problem of segregation lies in the execution of the particular bilingual education program and not in the concept of bilingual education per se.

Moreover, students are not foreclosed from integrating with students of other races even during the time that they are enrolled in bilingual education programs. Such integration can occur both informally and formally. Informally, integration can occur on the playground, in extracurricular activities, and during all the various social activities that occur in schools on a daily basis. Formally, integration can result by mixing bilingual education students with other students during classes such as art and physical education, and during school-sponsored activities such as assemblies.

When students are racially segregated by school, however, the students within the segregated school are foreclosed from any integration with students of other races. They are unable to mix with students of different races because the school lacks racial diversity among the student body.

* * *

B. Principles for School Districts to Minimize the Detrimental Effects of Segregation Resulting from Bilingual Education Programs

With a better understanding of the legal and policy considerations that establish the parameters of the conflict between desegregation and bilingual education, I now offer three strategies to minimize concerns that segregation resulting from bilingual education programs creates detrimental effects: 1) maximizing and monitoring integration time; 2) involving students in the integration process; and 3) making an ideological commitment to both desegregation and bilingual education. Throughout this section, I incorporate observations from my visits at Starr King, Golden Gate, Sherman, and Commodore Stockton elementary schools in San Francisco.

1. Maximizing and Monitoring Integration Time

The most practical solution to the problem of segregation arising from bilingual education programs is to integrate the students. While full classroom integration during the entire day will likely undermine the effectiveness of most bilingual pedagogical approaches, bilingual education students should be integrated with non-bilingual students in a controlled learning environment for at least some substantial portion of the day. Principal Chin of Commodore Stockton seems to think that the twenty-percent standard is a good minimum to balance the goal of desegregation with bilingual education.

Moreover, a school should try to integrate students in substantive courses, beyond simply art, drama, music, and physical education. Often, those courses do not require any verbal participation. A primary purpose of integrated classes should be to encourage discourse in topics such as culture or poetry. The purpose of integration should thus extend beyond encouraging mere facial recognition of students of other races. A dual immersion program that emphasizes the acquisition of two languages could also succeed in completely integrating students.

A school must also monitor the success of integration efforts. Although Superintendent Rojas indicated that the district is keeping abreast of within-school segregation, Sherman was the only school I visited that suggested they had a structured system to evaluate how well students were integrating. Sherman surveys its students using a standard form. Nevertheless, the survey merely touches upon the students' comfort levels with one another while addressing a wide range of other issues. Schools should be required to prepare formal integration plans to administrators and to compile detailed reports specifying the time and substance of integration time.

2. Student Involvement in the Integration Process

A school should also encourage students to integrate with students outside of the classroom. A school could form a student council, for example, comprised of student leaders who initiate activities including bilingual education students and non-bilingual education students. The student council at Commodore Stockton succeeds in integrating students that actually serve on the council but does not do much to facilitate integration among its peers.

The student council should include at least one student from every classroom in the school, including bilingual education classrooms. This group of student leaders could also help to monitor integration efforts. They could serve as members of focus groups, expressing views on behalf of their peers as to feelings about race, culture, and integration.

A school cannot rely on the expectation that students will naturally integrate with one another under informal conditions, such as recess or lunchtime. For example, although Golden Gate has implemented "Friday Funtime," in hopes of encouraging student interaction, I witnessed that most students only interacted with other students whom they already knew. A reporter from the *San Francisco Examiner* made a similar observation when she wrote that "on a recent visit, it was clear that at recess students rarely ventured beyond their classroom cliques." A school must be aware of the fact that students may be shy or influenced by the same cultural prejudices that permeate throughout our society. To the extent that schools can promote tolerance and acceptance early in life, they should certainly do so.

3. Ideological Commitment to Both Bilingual Education and Integration

An overarching principle to my previous suggestions is that administrators and teachers should maintain an ideological commitment to both bilingual education and integration. The mutual goal underlying both bilingual education and desegregation is the notion that discrete and insular minorities should be afforded some special scrutiny under law and policy. Most of society shares the common desire to eliminate unfair barriers to the enjoyment of life to which we are all fundamentally entitled. The most revealing part of my visit was speaking to Principal Cleveland at Golden Gate and hearing about the overt racism that existed among the pre-reconstitution faculty. Those faculty members seemed to be oblivious to the inherent contradiction of supporting either desegregation or bilingual education, but not both. In order to move forward in finding a solution to the apparent paradox between desegregation and bilingual education, we must be able to comprehend and internalize the ideals that they embody and the promise they can offer to our society. Without such comprehension and internalization, our efforts to resolve the paradox will be in vain.

* * *

BILINGUAL EDUCATION UNDER THE NO CHILD LEFT BEHIND ACT OF 2001: ¿SE QUEDARÁ ATRÁS?

Barbara J. Brunner, Ph.D.
169 ED. LAW REP. 505 (2002).

* * *

Although there are provisions relating to Limited English Proficiency (LEP) students in various sections of NCLB, the education of LEP and immigrant children is primarily addressed in Title III of the Act. Title III consolidates and revises all former bilingual education and immigrant programs that had been endorsed previously in Title VII of the ESEA under the Bilingual Education Act of 1968 (BEA) and the Emergency Immigrant Education Program.

II.   BRIEF HISTORY OF FEDERAL BILINGUAL EDUCATION LEGISLATION

The new Title III reflects recent fundamental shifts in U.S. educational and political attitudes toward bilingual education. Bilingual instruction was initially viewed as an integral part of the Civil Rights Act of 1964's remedy for historical civil rights violations. Throughout the 1960s and 70s, bilingual education was believed to be an essential tool for U.S. Hispanics to gain a sense of ethnic pride, in a country where Spanish culture traditionally has suffered from low regard. The importance of bilingual instruction continued to grow as new waves of immigrants from Central America, Southeast Asia, and Eastern Europe rapidly increased the number of children in American public schools who were unable to speak or understand English.

The BEA of 1968 represented the first official federal legislative recognition of the unique educational needs of LEPs. The most significant feature of BEA was its official endorsement of instruction for LEPs in their native language. The 1968 version of BEA stopped short, however, of requiring bilingual education and offered few concrete guidelines to local educational agencies (LEAs) for the instruction of LEP students.

Official support for bilingual education was strengthened in 1974, when the Supreme Court held in *Lau v. Nichols* that LEP students who were being taught exclusively in English were "foreclosed from any meaningful education.'' The *Lau* Court did not, however, mandate a specific remedy. Instead, the Court suggested that bilingual and native language education were two of the various possible ways schools could provide adequate instruction to non-English speaking children. In the same year as *Lau*, Congress amended BEA to show a clear preference for bilingual instruction, indicating that English as a Second Language (ESL) programs were not sufficient by themselves to provide adequate education to LEPs.

To help school districts comply with the amended BEA and the *Lau* mandate requiring schools to respond to the educational needs of LEPs, the Office for Civil Rights (OCR) prepared a set of guidelines. Known as the *Lau* Remedies, the guidelines called for the use of bilingual instruction as the remedy of choice when school districts were found in violation of the civil rights of LEP students. From 1975 to 1981, as OCR aggressively enforced the *Lau* Remedies, bilingual education programs were imposed on nearly 500 school districts through consent agreements known as *Lau* Plans. In time, however, the *Lau* Plans became a point of conflict between federal and local education authorities, as courts began to refuse to accept schools' excuses, including a lack of funds, for delaying the implementation of bilingual education programs. Moreover, districts complained that the Remedies had been implemented without opportunity for public comment. Critics of bilingual education observe in retrospect that even LEP parents never enthusiastically embraced federally imposed bilingual programs, and some posit that bilingual education might have remained little more than a marginal experiment had it not been institutionalized through OCR's interpretation of Lau.

Congress began to retreat from endorsing bilingual education as the favored solution for LEP students' needs as LEAs increasingly complained of financial and practical difficulties, such as finding enough qualified teachers and specialized materials, in implementing programs under the federal guidelines. Moreover, persistently high failure and drop-out rates among Hispanic students led critics to charge that however well-intentioned, the *Lau* Remedies were failing to fulfill their promise as a form of civil rights relief. As an initial step away from official endorsement of bilingual instruction, Congress made clear in the 1978 Educational Amendments that bilingual educational programs were intended as transitional and should be designed to prepare LEP students to enter the regular classroom as quickly as possible. The 1978 Amendments eliminated funding for any program designed primarily to maintain native languages and mandated that LEPs' native languages be used in instruction only to the extent necessary for students to become proficient in English.

In 1981, DOE officially abandoned the *Lau* Remedies, which had never been granted formal regulatory authority. Although bilingual education continued to receive federal funding, the amount reserved for such programs was reduced in that year by 25%. A further step away from endorsement of bilingual instruction occurred a few years later, when in the 1984 Educational Amendments Congress officially encouraged the establishment of "special alternative instructional programs" for LEPs in school districts where bilingual programs were "not practicable, or [could not be implemented] for other appropriate reasons." The 1984 legislation reserved up to 4% of federal funds for "special alternative instructional programs" not involving native language instruction, and allowed LEAs to apply for funds for any LEP program that best fit their needs.

In the following year, Secretary of Education William Bennett introduced the Bilingual Education Initiative (BEI), which clearly stated that the goal of programs for LEP students was the rapid acquisition of fluency in English. BEI also increased LEAs' discretion in identifying the instructional methods most appropriate for their individual needs. In 1988, Congress' revision to BEA authorized up to 25% of federal funds to be given to LEAs for "special alternative instructional programs" and placed a three-year limitation on a student's participation in a transitional bilingual education program. The 1988 BEA, under which LEAs were still required to spend a minimum of 75% of federal aid on programs (such as bilingual education) that used native language instruction, remained essentially intact until NCLB.

III.   RECENT STATE BILINGUAL EDUCATION LEGISLATION

The movement away from official support of bilingual education programs in some states has been much more aggressive—and the resulting statutes more restrictive—than at the federal level. The strongest state movements opposing bilingual education, founded on the conviction that those programs have failed miserably in educating LEPs, call for the complete elimination of all instruction in any language other than English.

In 1998, voters in California approved a ballot initiative entitled English Language in Public Schools, popularly known as Proposition 227 (Cal. Educ. Code §§ 300–340). Proposition 227 mandates that all children in California public schools be taught English "by being taught in English." Specifically, the statute requires that all children receive classroom instruction "overwhelmingly" in the English language. Under Proposition 227, LEP students, particularly young children, may still be placed in sheltered English immersion classrooms designed for language learners, in which "nearly all" instruction is in English, but such placement may only be for "a temporary transition period." Although under limited circumstances individual parents may exercise a waiver to have a child placed in a bilingual or native language instructional setting, no general waiver of the mandates of Proposition 227 is available to school districts, regardless of the number or the characteristics of the LEP students they service. As a result, the initiative, which has survived constitutional challenge, has effectively dismantled California's previously extensive bilingual education system.

Section 320 provides a means for parents to enforce the English instruction requirements of Proposition 227. If a student is denied the option of English language instruction, the child's parents are granted standing to sue for enforcement of the statute's provisions, attorney's fees, and actual damages. This provision allows parents to hold personally liable any educator who "willfully and repeatedly refuses to implement the statute" by speaking to children in their native language during instructional activities. Section 320 has itself survived a recent constitutional challenge alleging vagueness and violation of the First and Fourteenth Amendments.

Legislation similar to California's Proposition 227 has recently been passed in Arizona, despite the fact that in 1998 that state's Supreme Court declared unconstitutional Arizona's ten-year-old "English Only" state language amendment. In 2000, a large majority of Arizona voters approved Proposition 203, which replaces bilingual education programs with intensive English immersion instruction for the state's large LEP student population. Notably, the Arizona legislation contains no parental waiver option comparable to California's § 310, which would have allowed some bilingual instruction to continue.

* * *

Other states have reformed their bilingual programs in other ways, without proposing complete elimination of the methodology. Connecticut, for example, has imposed a 30–month limit on the time students may remain in transitional language programs. Some individual urban school districts with large LEP populations have implemented similar reforms. The Denver and Chicago public school systems, for example, have imposed a three-year limit on students' participation in transitional language programs, and in 2001, the New York City Board of Education created new English language immersion classes designed to offer students a "rapid transition to English fluency."

IV. THE CURRENT STATUS OF BILINGUAL EDUCATION UNDER NCLB

As shown above, at the federal level there has been an increasing shift away from endorsement of bilingual education as the best approach for meeting the needs of all LEP children in all U.S. public schools, in favor of allowing individual educational agencies to employ the methods they identify as best suited for their specific LEP populations. At the same time, one of the bases for maintaining bilingual education programs—fear of strong political backlash from Hispanic voters if the programs ended—has begun to erode, as increasing numbers of Hispanic voters express their preference for English language instruction. Until NCLB, however, Congress continued to favor bilingual education as the best way to address the needs of most LEP students.

According to DOE's Overview of NCLB's Title III, "[e]nsuring that all children, regardless of background, have the chance to succeed is a central purpose of the federal role in education." The Overview affirms that all parents want their children to graduate from the public school system with "the basic tools needed to succeed in today's global marketplace," and recognizes that for millions of LEP students, "this means learning English in school." Under Title III, native language instruction is still permitted (although no longer officially favored), and no limit is imposed on the number of years a child may be enrolled in a bilingual program. Indeed, bilingual educators are quick to note that bilingual education is not "dead" under NCLB. However, for the first time, the statute mandates that LEP students demonstrate measurable yearly progress in acquiring English language skills. Chairman John Boehner (R–OH) of the House Education and the Workforce Committee summarizes the statute's new focus by affirming that LEPs have been "too long trapped" in classes taught in their native language and acknowledges that "federal education policy has helped keep them there."

Many advocates nonetheless view NCLB as a victory for bilingual education. Spokespersons for the National Association of Bilingual Education (NABE), for example, note that during the two-year reauthorization drafting process there was, for the first time, "no debate as to whether there is a federal role for providing services to help LEPs succeed. [A federal role] was just assumed." NABE leaders also point with satisfaction to the large increase in federal funding for the education of LEP children under Title III, from $265 million under the previous BEA to $665 million allocated for 2002 (resulting in an average increase to state and local educational agencies of 10–17% this year). Additionally, NABE celebrates the continuation of all current federal grants for professional development of LEP teachers and instructional services to LEPs, noting Title III's specific mandate that the new funds be used to "supplement, not supplant" existing programs servicing LEP children.

Title III opens with the assertion that "English is the common language of the U.S." The "Findings and Purposes" section then declares that " ... every citizen and other person residing in the U.S. should have a command of the English language in order to develop to their full potential." This assertion, which is in line with NCLB supporters' affirmation that all children should be given the tools needed to succeed in the global marketplace, clearly reflects the statute's focus on economic empowerment. Although Title III does not define the term "full potential," it is difficult to imagine that Congress could have meant to suggest that a person cannot achieve full artistic, spiritual, physical or other human potential except in English. Rather, the purpose statement implies that developing to one's full potential involves achieving economic success, and indicates that in the U.S. such success is possible only for those who are proficient in English.

Title III thus reflects the spirit of state initiatives such as California's Proposition 227 to the extent that it contends that bilingual education has largely failed to accomplish its goals and that English proficiency is the key to success in American society. While not openly endorsing the creation of an official national language, NCLB proposes that English is the de facto national language of success. Under the statute, bilingual education, although not prohibited, is no longer seen as an effective way of ensuring that LEP children are not "left behind" along the road to success. NCLB's message is that academic achievement alone is no longer officially good enough to keep all children in step with their peers; that achievement must occur in English.

NCLB sweeps much more broadly than the state movements, which are limited to insisting that schools help children to become proficient in English by teaching them in English. The overall focus of NCLB is to ensure that all children are equally able to meet rigorous achievement standards in academic content areas. NCLB's requirements for LEP programs therefore derive from the overarching goal of helping LEPs "meet the same challenging State academic content and student academic achievement standards as all children are expected to meet" and "achieve at high levels in the core academic subjects."

    * * *

CONCLUSION

There is no question that NCLB permits bilingual instruction options to exist where LEAs are committed to them. The statute contains provisions that assist LEAs in "legitimizing" the decision to create or maintain bilingual education programs, increase the potential for those programs to be staffed by highly qualified personnel, encourage parental involvement in their implementation, and guarantee that schools are held accountable for the academic achievement of the LEP children participating in them. Nonetheless, it is also clear that NCLB does little to encourage the development of new bilingual education programs or the improvement of those already in existence. Permeating the provisions throughout NCLB that relate to the education of LEP children is the message that American schools must ensure students' achievement in English and that bilingual education programs have consistently not done so. NCLB declares, therefore, that past instructional practices with respect to LEP students (i.e., bilingual education programs) have failed.

Despite the statute's prohibition on official preclusion of any particular methodology, the inevitable conclusion that must be drawn is that bilingual education under NCLB, if not "dead," is certainly now disfavored. * * *

B. SPECIAL EDUCATION AND OTHER PROGRAMS FOR STUDENTS WITH DISABILITIES

Over the past 30–40 years, major federal statutes have dramatically expanded the rights of persons with disabilities and in so doing have literally transformed the educational landscape for students in this area. Section 504 of the Rehabilitation Act of 1973, amounting to nothing less than a federal civil rights act for persons with disabilities in the public sector, provided broad protection for students of all ages in all public educational settings. The Individuals with Disabilities Education Act (IDEA)—formerly Pub. Law No. 94–142, the 1975 Education of All

Handicapped Children Act—created a structure whereby K–12 students with special needs could have an Individualized Education Plan (IEP) prepared that would qualify them for a wide range of support services under the umbrella of special education. And the Americans with Disabilities Act (ADA) of 1990 not only extended Section 504 rights to the private sector, but added additional protections for persons with disabilities in the public sphere.

This section focuses primarily on K–12 issues, but also provides an overview of key legal principles applicable to students with disabilities in higher education. As a general rule, progress under these statutes has been much more consistent at colleges and universities. At the K–12 level, many students have benefited greatly from changes in the law and the accompanying efforts of dedicated educators in this context, but many others have arguably been deprived of equal access to quality education under the unwieldy principles and inconsistent practices of special education. Indeed, commentators are increasingly voicing concerns with regard to both educational quality (under the "free appropriate public education" requirement of the IDEA) and equal educational opportunity (under the "least restrictive environment" component of the Act).

Analyzing the quality of special education curriculum and pedagogy, some have looked back at *Board of Education v. Rowley,* 458 U.S. 176, 102 S.Ct. 3034 (1982), the first U.S. Supreme Court decision to address special education, and have argued that the decision should now be reassessed. The *Rowley* Court concluded that schools were not required to maximize potential for students with disabilities, but only to provide a basic floor of opportunity. Arguably, in light of related developments in the law in the years since *Rowley,* this holding is no longer consistent with either federal or state mandates.

With regard to the "least restrictive environment" requirement of the law, commentators have noted that a range of options and organizational structures exist, including but not limited to inclusion (where students are generally placed in heterogeneous settings but are provided with additional support in those settings) and resource specialist programs (RSP, where students are grouped together with everyone else for part of the time, and in separate settings with additional support for the remainder of the time). But reports documenting special education practices nationwide have found that too often, arguably in violation of express provisions of the IDEA—which require that students with disabilities be segregated "only when the nature or severity of the disability of a child is such that education in regular classes with the use of supplementary aids and services cannot be achieved satisfactorily"— many students are separated out into "special day classes" (SDC) for the entire day and often for their entire public school careers. Compounding the problem, many schools group students with a wide range of disabilities together in one classroom.

Perhaps the most volatile of all the issues in this context is the disproportionate representation of African American students, not only in the separate special education classes, but also in the highly subjective categories of "emotionally disturbed" (ED) and "learning disabled," (LD). These two categories are the most controversial of all the special education classifications.

While no one doubts the importance of providing additional support services for students with special needs, researchers and policy makers nationwide have highlighted problematic aspects of these categories, both in theory and in practice. A review of relevant literature reveals that (a) these categories, unlike other "disabilities" such as physical impairments, are often very imprecise, and classification by its very nature can be quite subjective, (b) they are based on school identification rather than some organicity, (c) the nebulous criteria that may be employed to identify students in this area have been compared in recent studies with substantially discredited categories of the past, such as "educable mentally retarded" (EMR), (d) red flags have been raised with regard to the fact that it is in these categories that students who may be viewed as "discipline problems" or "low performing" end up being placed, when it may be that a more adept classroom teacher can effectively work with these students in a non-special education setting, and (e) in this context, educators have been taken to task for placing a disproportionate percentage of students of color in separate classes as a result of classifying them as ED or LD. *See, e.g.,* Matthew Ladner & Christopher Hammons, *Special But Unequal: Race and Special Education, in* RETHINKING SPECIAL EDUCATION FOR A NEW CENTURY (Chester E. Finn, Jr. et al. eds., 2001); NAT'L RESEARCH COUNCIL, MINORITY STUDENTS IN SPECIAL AND GIFTED EDUCATION (2002). *See generally* DANIEL J. LOSEN & GARY ORFIELD, RACIAL INEQUITY IN SPECIAL EDUCATION (2002).

This section begins with an overview of special education law as it relates to K–12 education. It then focuses on the "appropriateness" of the education, analyzing the *Rowley* decision and its aftermath. Within-school segregation issues are then addressed, followed by ongoing issues relating to standardized testing. The chapter concludes with an examination of how these issues are playing out at the higher education level.

1. FEDERAL SPECIAL EDUCATION LAW GENERALLY

ADEQUATE SPECIAL EDUCATION: DO CALIFORNIA SCHOOLS MEET THE TEST?

Jane K. Babin.
37 SAN DIEGO L. REV. 211 (2000).

* * *2

2. The definition of disability and the relationship between impairment, disability, and handicap has been set forth as:

Impairment is a medical term for anatomical loss or a loss of bodily function. Disability is the measurable, functional

II. The History of Special Education Reform in the United States

In the wake of civil rights successes of the 1960s and sparked by Equal Protection promises of *Brown v. Board of Education*, parents of [students with disabilities][a] began to demand access to education during the 1970s. The initial forum for these demands was the courts. In 1972, two pivotal cases led the way: *Pennsylvania Ass'n for Retarded Children (PARC) v. Pennsylvania*[22] and *Mills v. Board of Education*.[23]

A. Early Case Law in Special Education

In PARC, parents of students [identified "mentally retarded"] challenged Pennsylvania statutes that excluded them from public education.[24] PARC alleged that these statutes violated Fourteenth Amendment Equal Protection and Due Process guarantees. The federal district court agreed, noting expert testimony that stated "[a]ll mentally retarded persons are capable of benefiting from a program of education and training." The consent decree that settled PARC established Pennsylvania's obligation to educate mentally retarded children, while an accompanying stipulation detailed procedural safeguards protecting the right to education for all students.

loss resulting from an impairment. Handicap is the social consequence caused by environmental and social conditions which prevent a person achieving the maximum potential a person seeks. Disabilities are what people cannot do....
Gillian Fulcher, Disabling Policies? A Comparative Approach to Education Policy and Disability 22 (1989) (citation omitted). The legal definition of disability and handicap depend on the particular statute or constitutional principle asserted. The Individuals with Disabilities Education Act defines the handicapping conditions covered under the Act as "mental retardation, hearing impairments including deafness, speech or language impairments, visual impairments including blindness, serious emotional disturbance, orthopedic impairments, autism, traumatic brain injury, other health impairments, or specific learning disabilities." 20 U.S.C. § 1401(3)(A) (1994 & Supp. III 1997). Section 504 of the Rehabilitation Act of 1973 applies a functional definition of handicap to include "any person who (i) has a physical or mental impairment which substantially limits one or more major life activities, (ii) has a record of such an impairment, or (iii) is regarded as having such an impairment." 34 C.F.R. § 104.3 (1998) (implementing the Rehabilitation Act of 1973, Pub. L. No. 93–112, § 504, 87 Stat. 355, 394 (codified as amended at 29 U.S.C. § 794 (1994))). For a comparison of these definitions, see H. Rutherford Turnbull III,

Free Appropriate Public Education: The Law and Children with Disabilities 20–22 (3d ed. 1990). It is important to note, however, that many children who qualify as educationally handicapped would not otherwise be thought of as disabled. *See* Donna L. Terman et al., *Special Education for Students with Disabilities: Analysis and Recommendations*, Future Children, Spring 1996, at 4, 5. Children with specific learning disabilities, for example, are unlikely to be considered disabled outside the education system. *See id.*

a. Throughout this chapter, the term "handicapped children" has been changed to "students with disabilities," unless the term is included in a direct quote or title.

22. 343 F.Supp. 279 (E.D. Pa. 1972).

23. 348 F.Supp. 866 (D.D.C. 1972).

24. *See PARC*, 343 F.Supp. at 281–82. Section 13–1375 of the Pennsylvania law provided for the establishment of standards to certify children as "uneducable and untrainable" and relieved the State Board of Education from educating or training such children. *Id.* at 282 & n.3. Children could also be denied education based on section 13–1304 of the law, which excluded children who had not reached a mental age of five (effectively excluding children with an I.Q. of 35 or below). *See id.* at 282 & n.4. A determination that a child was unable to profit from school attendance also justified denying education. *See id.* at 282 & nn.5–6.

Similar Due Process and Equal Protection violations were asserted in *Mills* by a plaintiff class comprised of children with behavioral and emotional problems, as well as mental retardation. The defendant school district did not dispute its affirmative duty to provide public education or constitutionally adequate Due Process, admitting failure to discharge both obligations. The school district asserted that it was unable to provide the required educational services given available funds, for to do so would be "inequitable" to other children in the school district. However, the *Mills* court rejected these claims, stating that the financial inadequacies of the district "cannot be permitted to bear more heavily on the 'exceptional' or handicapped child than on the normal child." The court ruled that "available funds must be expended equitably in such a manner that no child is entirely excluded from a publicly supported education."

Taken together, these cases defined the contours of education for [students with disabilities] for the next quarter century. Three basic principles established in *PARC* and *Mills* formed the essential foundation for subsequent litigation and legislative reforms. First, Equal Protection and substantive Due Process prevent states that choose to provide public education from excluding children solely on the basis of disability. Second, parents of the disabled are entitled to procedural Due Process in order to assert their children's right to receive public education.[36] Third, the additional costs of providing appropriate educational services to disabled students cannot be used to justify categorical exclusion of disabled children from public school.[37]

* * *

B. *Congressional Actions to Advance Education of Disabled Children*

Beginning in 1958, Congress expressed support for the education of students with disabilities through various grant programs. In 1970, Congress replaced and expanded existing programs by enacting the Education of the Handicapped Act. Subsequent amendments conditioned federal assistance on state assurances of educational opportunity for all students with disabilities, and due process protections should services be denied. By 1975, however, less than half the estimated eight million students with disabilities in the United States were receiving appropriate

---

36. Procedural Due Process was initially envisioned as a check on the State's ability to exclude disabled students from education or to label them as special needs, but has evolved to encompass parental rights to challenge an array of school district decisions regarding their children's education. *See generally* Turnbull, *supra* note 2, at 192–211.

37. Under the "zero reject" policy, all children must be served by state-supported education. *See id.* at 27–79, 172–79. Subsequent development of special education law has permitted the consideration of cost in determining the level of services provided to

an individual student. *See id.* at 172–79. Most recently, however, the U.S. Supreme Court reiterated its interpretation of the IDEA as requiring the provision of services necessary for a child to attend school without consideration of the cost or magnitude of those services. *See* Cedar Rapids Community Sch. Dist. v. Garret F., 119 S.Ct. 992 (1999); *see also infra* note 138 (providing details of this case in greater depth). In order to be able to attend school, Garret requires extensive support in the form of health-related services that can be performed by a non-physician caregiver. *See id.*

education while 1.75 million were not receiving any educational services at all.

A 1975 report of the Senate Labor and Public Welfare Committee acknowledged the rights of students with disabilities to appropriate education which, by that time, had been repeated in more than thirty-six state and federal court decisions. Lack of financial resources, the Committee concluded, prevented states from implementing the law. The report stressed the need for legislation to address this issue, on economic as well as constitutional grounds, asserting that proper education would permit the handicapped to "become productive citizens, contributing to society instead of being forced to remain burdens." Accordingly, Congress concluded that it was in the "national interest that the Federal Government assist [s]tate and local efforts to provide programs to meet the educational needs of handicapped children in order to assure equal protection of the law." With this patina of intent, Congress enacted the Education for All Handicapped Children Act (EAHCA) in 1975 for the purpose of ensuring that all handicapped children have available . . . a free appropriate public education which emphasizes special education and related services designed to meet their unique needs, to assure that the rights of handicapped children and their parents or guardians are protected, to assist [s]tates and localities to provide for the education of all handicapped children, and to assess and assure the effectiveness of efforts to educate handicapped children. Although case law and other federal statutes arguably imposed substantially similar requirements on states,[47] the EAHCA provided incentives in the form of grants rather than a federal mandate to follow its provisions. States would be entitled to receive federal funds upon a showing of compliance, but were not precluded by federal law from eschewing such support and meeting a lesser standard.

47. *See* Turnbull, *supra* note 2, at 18–22. Section 504 of the Rehabilitation Act of 1973 prohibits federally-funded programs from discriminating on the basis of handicap. *See* Rehabilitation Act of 1973, Pub. L. No. 93–112, § 504, 87 Stat. 355, 394 (codified as amended at 29 U.S.C. § 794 (1994)). Section 504 is broader in scope than the EAHCA (IDEA), which prescribes that only specific handicapping conditions are eligible for assistance. *Cf.* 20 U.S.C. § 1401(3)(A) (1994 & Supp. III 1997). But section 504's requirement for reasonable accommodation of disabled students has frequently been ignored and is often misinterpreted by courts and school districts. *See* Goldman, *supra* note 5, at 249. *See generally* Kristine L. Lingren, Comment, *The Demise of Reasonable Accommodation Under Section 504: Special Education, the Public Schools, and an Unfunded Mandate*, 1996 Wisc. L. Rev. 633 (discussing the uncertainty in interpreting section 504 and its implementing regulations promulgated by the U.S. Department of Education's Office for Civil Rights). Lingren suggests that section 504 may hold a higher standard for educating children than that under IDEA. *See id.* at 636. Title II of the Americans with Disabilities Act of 1990 (ADA) now provides protections similar to section 504. *See* 42 U.S.C. § 12132 (1994). It has infrequently been invoked in education litigation. *See* William D. Goren, *Individuals with Disabilities Education Act: The Interrelationship to the ADA and Preventive Law*, Fla. B.J., July–Aug. 1997, at 76, 78; *see also* Michael L. Williams, Assistant Secretary for Civil Rights, OCR Senior Staff Memorandum, U.S. Dept. of Educ., Office for Civil Rights (Nov. 19, 1992), *reprinted in* 19 Individuals with Disabilities Educ. L. Rep. 859 (providing guidance on issues of coverage and comparing application of Title II of the ADA and section 504).

The chief tenet of the EAHCA (and its successor, the IDEA) is the provision of a free appropriate public education (FAPE) for all children in the least restrictive environment (LRE). The mechanism for providing an appropriate education is the individualized education program (IEP). The IEP details educational and related services designed by a team of local educators, service providers, and the child's parents, to meet the unique needs of that particular child. LRE is a term of art providing that students with disabilities should be educated with children who are not handicapped "[t]o the maximum extent appropriate" and should be segregated "only when the nature or severity of the disability of a child is such that education in regular classes with the use of supplementary aids and services cannot be achieved satisfactorily."

These seemingly straightforward provisions have become the basis for significant controversy since the EAHCA was first enacted.[54] As detailed below, the questions of what defines an appropriate education and least restrictive environment remain central issues in special education policy and law.

Another key element of the EAHCA was a high level of parental involvement. Parents would share in decisions regarding the placement of their children, the development of IEP goals, and the services to be provided to achieve these goals. To ensure parental involvement and protect the rights established for students with disabilities, the EAHCA incorporated procedural safeguards modeled after the stipulation in *PARC*. If parents disagreed with the local education agency, these safeguards provided a variety of mechanisms for resolving the conflict, including informal negotiations, administrative hearings, and ultimately civil action in federal or state courts.

In reality, however, special education due process[59] has become a complicated, burdensome, and expensive endeavor of which both parents and local school districts complain. School districts complain of the cost in both time and money, which could be better spent on providing educational services. Parents, although envisioned as partners in a non-adversarial process, are frequently intimidated by the educational bureaucracy into acquiescence with school district recommendations, which all too often, are motivated by fiscal and political incentives rather than the true needs of the child. When a dispute does arise, only the most sophisticated and affluent are able to mount a successful challenge, and it may take years to reach a judicially enforceable decision. Those who succeed in due process may secure educational opportunities for their children entirely unavailable to most. But even for these fortunate

---

54. Special education litigation has steadily increased in the past 20 years with the number of published decisions approaching 50 per year. *See* Perry A. Zirkel, *Tuition Reimbursement for Special Education Students*, Future Children, Winter 1997, at 122, 123.

59. In the context of special education, due process is frequently used as a term of

art, referring specifically to the detailed administrative procedures for asserting a child's right to special education and for disputing local education agency decisions regarding its provision. *See generally* Community Alliance for Special Educ. & Protection and Advocacy, Special Education Rights and Responsibilities (7th ed. 1998).

children, the cost in time spent disputing an educational program may be time irretrievably lost. Thus, the system designed to eliminate inequities in education may actually create a two-class system of discrimination based on the assertiveness and resources of the parents.

Another significant goal of the EAHCA was to assess and assure the effectiveness of education for students with disabilities. Congress assumed that by specifying procedures for providing education and the process by which its objectives would be implemented, the substantive content of that education would be assured. Until 1997, however, issues of educational quality and positive outcomes for students with disabilities had not been directly addressed by the Act. This Comment asserts that Congress's inattention to these issues and its assumption that states would detail the requisite substantive components of educating disabled students, if given financial assistance, has resulted in great disappointment and confusion in special education. Describing only the manner in which education is to be provided has not guaranteed that its content is of high quality. Providing only the mechanism for students to enter the gates of the schoolhouse has proven a hollow victory for millions of disabled students who are not ensured meaningful education before leaving.

The EAHCA, however, is not static. Within the limits of their authority, Congress continues to improve upon and refine the EAHCA through amendment and reauthorization. In 1986, assistance for the development of early intervention services for infants and toddlers was added. The 1986 amendments also authorized attorneys' fees for parents who prevail in due process proceedings and judicial actions against school districts. In 1990, the act was renamed the Individuals with Disabilities Education Act (IDEA). * * *

C.   Judicial Interpretation

Since its enactment, courts have been called upon to interpret the full range of the EAHCA and IDEA provisions. However, two particularly relevant aspects of the statute have become the focus of significant judicial scrutiny: FAPE and LRE.

1.   Free Appropriate Public Education

In 1982, the U.S. Supreme Court was asked to interpret "appropriate" education under the Act.[73] Amy Rowley, an intelligent deaf child, claimed that she had been denied an appropriate education because the Hendrick Hudson Central School District refused to provide a sign-language interpreter in her first grade classes.[74] Because Amy had been performing well in the regular education environment with the additional supports of speech therapy, tutoring, and a hearing aid, the school

---

73.   Board of Educ. v. Rowley, 458 U.S. 176, 186 (1982). *Rowley* was the first case to come before the U.S. Supreme Court under the EAHCA. *See id.* at 187.

74.   *See id.* at 184–85.

district determined that she did not need an interpreter.[75] However, she was "not learning as much, or performing as well academically, as she would without her handicap."[76] Her parents asserted that sign-language interpretation would permit her to understand more of what was said in the classroom and thereby achieve more of her potential.[77] The district court agreed, holding that an appropriate education must provide each child "an opportunity to achieve his full potential commensurate with the opportunity provided to other children."[78] The United States Court of Appeals for the Second Circuit affirmed.[79]

The U.S. Supreme Court, however, ruled that since Amy had been making satisfactory progress and had been provided personalized instruction and related services as required by the EAHCA, Amy's education was appropriate. * * * The Court construed the EAHCA to give deference to states in determining the substantive content of education, noting that "courts must be careful to avoid imposing their view of preferable educational methods." Instead, compliance with extensive procedural requirements was emphasized as the means Congress had intended to assure much, if not all, in the way of substantive educational content.

* * *

2. *Least Restrictive Environment*

Superimposed on the requirement for appropriate education is an equally elusive requirement for educating children in the least restrictive environment. The EAHCA called for students with disabilities to be educated with children who are not handicapped "to the maximum extent appropriate." They should be segregated "only when the nature or severity of the handicap is such that education in regular classes with the use of supplementary aids and services cannot be achieved satisfactorily." As with FAPE, LRE could be interpreted to require a potentially limitless number of supplemental services to achieve satisfactory edu-

---

75. *See id.* A sign-language interpreter had been provided for a trial period in kindergarten, but he concluded that Amy did not need his services at that time. *See id.* The school district had also consulted experts, Amy's teacher, and visited a class for the deaf before reaching its decision. *See id.*

76. *Id.* at 185 (quoting Rowley v. Board of Educ., 483 F.Supp. 528, 532 (S.D.N.Y. 1980)).

77. *See id.* at 184–85.

78. *Rowley*, 483 F.Supp. at 534. It should be noted that the district court did not attempt to establish a higher standard for educating handicapped students than for non-handicapped students. The court was careful to point out that "even the best public schools lack the resources to enable every child to achieve his full potential." *Id.*

The qualification that a child's potential should be maximized "commensurate with the opportunity provided other children," was intended to impose a similar standard of education for both the handicapped and the non-handicapped. *Id.* at 534. The court suggested that an "appropriate" education standard should compare Amy Rowley's "performance to that of non-handicapped students of similar intellectual caliber and comparable energy and initiative" in determining the level of services that should be provided. *Id.* Under this standard, a handicapped child would be given the opportunity to achieve as much of his or her potential as a non-handicapped child in the same environment.

79. *See* Rowley v. Board of Educ., 632 F.2d 945 (2d Cir. 1980).

cation in the regular classroom. As with FAPE, LRE embraces both Equal Protection and substantive educational components.

In the early years of special education, school districts found it convenient and cost-effective to centralize instruction of disabled students in separate classrooms or buildings. Segregation of disabled children, however, evokes concepts of discrimination rejected in *Brown v. Board of Education*. Inclusion[127] advocates argue that students with disabilities have a right to associate with non-handicapped peers. Since "separate but equal" is inherently unequal under *Brown*, segregation violates the spirit if not the letter of Fourteenth Amendment constitutional protection. Furthermore, increasing evidence suggests that inclusion confers independent educational and social benefits to the child. Children model other children's behavior and benefit from interaction with appropriate non-disabled peer models. This concept is intuitively appealing: if one goal of education is to promote the ability to participate productively in society, then children must have the opportunity to practice social participation in school.

Courts grappling with this issue have devised various balancing tests to weigh the benefits of inclusion or mainstreaming with the burdens imposed. In general, courts have placed the burden on school officials to justify removal of children from the general education environment, especially when the disability is mild to moderate. Schools must make more than a token effort to provide supplemental aids and services. However, costs and resource allocation can be considered. For example, the Eighth Circuit's test does not require costs so great as to "significantly impact upon the education of other children in the district."[138]

---

127. Although the terms "inclusion" and "mainstreaming" are sometimes used interchangeably, for the purpose of this Comment, inclusion refers to situations in which a disabled child's primary educational placement is in a regular classroom. Mainstreaming refers to placing a child whose primary placement is in a segregated environment into the general education population for part of the school day. *See* Anne M. Hocutt, *Effectiveness of Special Education: Is Placement a Critical Factor?*, FUTURE CHILDREN, Spring 1996, at 77, 78–79.

138. *Greer*, 950 F.2d at 697. Note, however, that cost can only be considered when choosing between two appropriate placements (i.e., a more restrictive, but appropriate, placement and a less restrictive alternative). The threshold question is whether there is more than one appropriate placement; if only one placement is deemed appropriate, school districts cannot deny FAPE to a child because of cost. Compare, for example, the recent U.S. Supreme Court decision in *Cedar Rapids Community School District v. Garret F.*, 119 S.Ct. 992 (1999). In that case, the school district argued that it should be allowed to consider

cost-based factors in deciding whether to provide necessary health-related services to a disabled child (such as ventilator support, urinary catheterization, suctioning of tracheotomy tubes, and other services). *See id.* at 995–99. The Court held that the school district could not consider such costs. *See id.* at 999–1000. The fundamental difference between *Garret F.* and LRE cases is that the disputed services in *Garret F.* were not optional—Garret would require them to participate in any placement. *See id.* at 1000. Thus, the narrow statutory issue the Court considered was whether the services Garret required fell under the medical care exception of IDEA. *See id.* at 997. The Court affirmed its earlier unanimous ruling in *Irving Independent School District v. Tatro*, 468 U.S. 883 (1984), in which it drew a bright line between related health services (that a district is required to provide) and medical services (not required). *See Garret F.*, 119 S.Ct. at 997–98. Medical services, the Court concluded, are those which must be delivered by a physician. *See Garret F.*, 119 S.Ct. at 997–98; *Tatro*, 468 U.S. at 892–94. Since Garret's needs could be addressed by a nurse or other staff, the school district

Thus, LRE reflects a preference that, although strong, is subordinate to the provision of FAPE and can be limited by the burdens it imposes on schools.

D. The Move Toward Quality of Education and the 1997 IDEA Amendments

* * *

The 1997 amendments to IDEA (IDEA 97) provide[d] a myriad of improvements to increase the quality of education for disabled children. Of great significance are congressional requirements that students with disabilities be included in statewide achievement tests. States must establish performance goals and indicators to judge progress of children with disabilities. Disabled students' scores must now be reported to parents and the public, and beginning July 1, 2000, alternative testing must be in place for students unable to participate in standardized assessments. These provisions will enable parents and educators to begin measuring and assessing the effectiveness of education for disabled children, and track the progress individual students make. They demonstrate renewed congressional commitment to improving the quality of education for disabled students and improving outcomes. However, they [were] only a first step toward making actual improvements and holding schools accountable for educational quality.

In addition, Congress * * * re-emphasized its preference for the inclusion of disabled students with non-disabled peers. IEPs must now provide a statement of reasons when students are not educated in the regular classroom. This requirement shifts the burden to schools to demonstrate that they have considered all supports and services available to enable a child to be educated in the regular classroom. General education teachers must now participate in IEP teams for mainstreamed or included students, reenforcing the cooperative nature of general and special education. States must now make assurances that special education funding mechanisms are placement-neutral, consistent with educating disabled children in the least restrictive environment. Furthermore, language permitting general education students to receive incidental benefits from special education services has been added. Previously, schools were strictly prohibited from using IDEA funds for general education purposes, and school districts were often reluctant to place a disabled child in the regular education classroom for fear of losing funding.

Nevertheless, the IDEA 97 amendments still [fell] short of establishing definitive educational standards for disabled children.

* * *

was responsible for their provision, regardless of the cost. *See Garret F.*, 119 S.Ct. at 999–1000.

ALIGNING OR MALIGNING? GETTING INSIDE A NEW IDEA, GETTING BEHIND NO CHILD LEFT BEHIND AND GETTING OUTSIDE OF IT ALL

Stephen A. Rosenbaum.
15 Hastings Women's L.J. 1, 27–30 (2004).

* * *

How does NCLB benefit disabled students? First, it sets high achievement standards for all students, including those with a physical or mental impairment. The 1997 amendments to IDEA began the shift from "access to education" to "improving results," although the reality does not necessarily match the rhetoric. NCLB has the potential to prove a stronger incentive than the IDEA amendments to align student IEP goals and objectives with the content standards of the state's general education content. * * *

NCLB also bolsters the right of special needs students to participate in the general curriculum by requiring that the same grade-level academic content standards apply to all students. This reinforces IDEA's requirement that students with disabilities be involved, and make progress, in the general education curriculum. The potential is great for improving the integration of disabled students in regular classrooms, beyond social opportunities. As one advocacy organization observed, the "[i]nclusive classrooms are designed to facilitate every student's active participation in learning...." Advocates must be vigilant, however, against moves to re-segregate students through tracking or assigning independent seatwork, rather than attempting multi-level curriculum and instruction in heterogeneous classrooms.

Advocates must also ensure that students with disabilities are being provided the testing accommodations and adaptations that are required by NCLB. Some students will take the same tests as their non-disabled peers, with or without accommodations or modifications. Others will take an alternative assessment that measures the same grade-level achievement standards as their peers. Those who meet the definition of a student with a "significant cognitive disability" will take an alternative assessment based on alternative achievement standards. For IDEA-eligible students, each student's IEP determines the necessary accommodations and adaptations.

Under certain circumstances, students with disabilities are eligible for "supplemental educational services." Beginning in school year 2003–04, low-income students in schools that fail to demonstrate AYP for three consecutive years must be provided supplemental services, with specific achievement goals and a timeline for reaching those goals. Even with the restriction that this category of service is available only after a school's demonstrated academic failure, and only to children from poorer families, it will undoubtedly reach a number of children enrolled in special education. These students could use these services to augment their IEPs—or compensate for IEPs that have not been fully implemented. While supplemental service providers need not adhere to a student's IEP or § 504 plan per se, they must enter into agreements with the school district and parents that describe the student's specific achievement goals, how progress will be measured and the timeline for improving achievement. Furthermore, they are subject to ADA requirements to make reasonable modifications to their policies, practices and procedures for students with disabilities.

Also beginning with the 2003–04 school year, those schools failing to demonstrate adequate yearly progress must develop school improvement plans. This must be done in consultation with parents, among others. It is important that parents of disabled students participate in the development of these plans. Lastly, NCLB sets standards for teachers and paraprofessionals that could be an improvement over current state standards for special education teachers and aides. By 2005–06, all teachers teaching core academic standards must be "highly qualified"—i.e., have at least a bachelor's degree and meet other requirements. Paraprofessionals who teach in Title I programs are also subject to new qualifications. Moreover, parents are entitled to obtain the information regarding the instructional staff's professional qualifications—something that is routinely sought by parents of disabled students, and frequently withheld.

PROBLEM 35: Johnson v. Eldorado Unified School District

This hypothetical focuses on Sutter Springs Unified, a large and diverse urban district located in the fictional state of Eldorado.

A coalition of civil rights organizations, determined to establish case precedent that would "blow the top off of the many abuses" that they believe are taking place within the special education system in the public schools, files a highly publicized lawsuit against the Sutter Springs Unified School District (SSUSD).

The lawsuit is filed on behalf of African American, Cambodian, Filipino, Latino, and Samoan families. All plaintiff families have annual incomes significantly below the poverty line, and all have children in the District who have been identified "emotionally disturbed" or "learning disabled" by their local school sites pursuant to the provisions of the IDEA. In addition, all these children have been placed in separate "special day classes," many of which include students with diverse disabilities ... ranging from students who are hearing impaired and visually impaired to paraplegics, quadriplegics, students who are autistic, and students with Down Syndrome.

All the children of the plaintiff families score "below basic" or "far below basic" on every section of the Eldorado Standards Test. And over 50 percent of their teachers in this setting have either been long-term substitutes and/or persons who have not completed the requirements necessary to be fully credentialed by the State.

Plaintiffs allege in their complaint that "the District has misused the special education system," citing to reports of the independent reviewer that document "a widespread pattern of classroom activities amounting to babysitting rather than education." They declare that "not only are the low-income students from these five racial/ethnic groups often incorrectly identified as eligible for special education, but once they are identified and placed, they are often relegated to a separate and unequal education that locks them into third-rate programs, prevents them from meeting the basic requirements for admission to the state universities, and generally serves to limit their life chances in significant ways."

In further support of these allegations, plaintiffs plan to rely in particular on the following data available to the public on the Eldorado Department of Education Web site:

- Low-income SSUSD students from these five racial/ethnic groups together comprise 23% of the District's overall student population, yet they comprise over 80% of all the students in District special education programs.

- 79 percent of all the low-income students from these racial/ethnic groups who are in SSUSD special education programs are classified as either "emotionally disturbed" or as having a "specific learning disability." This compares with 43 percent of the low-SES Whites, 32 percent of the low-income Chinese Americans, and 24 percent of the low-income Korean Americans who are in SSUSD special education programs.

At a press conference held in response to plaintiffs' filing, the Superintendent declares that the District is complying fully with the IDEA and that it is not discriminating against any of these children, but is doing all that is practicable to provide the level of education and support that is due under relevant federal and state law. With regard to the identification issues, she emphasizes that all children labeled "emotionally disturbed" or "learning disabled" have been identified pursuant to the recommendations of teachers and school site administrators, as well as the evaluations of licensed school psychologists.

What arguments should the plaintiffs set forth under the IDEA as interpreted by the federal courts? Under state constitutional law? How might provisions of the U.S. "No Child Left Behind" Act be employed to provide additional support for plaintiff's arguments? What result? Discuss.

2.   "APPROPRIATENESS" OF THE SPECIAL EDUCATION: AN INCREASING FOCUS ON EDUCATIONAL QUALITY

BOARD OF EDUCATION v. ROWLEY

458 U.S. 176, 102 S.Ct. 3034 (1982).

JUSTICE REHNQUIST delivered the opinion of the Court.

This case presents a question of statutory interpretation. Petitioners contend that the Court of Appeals and the District Court misconstrued the requirements imposed by Congress upon States which receive federal funds under the Education of the Handicapped Act. We agree and reverse the judgment of the Court of Appeals.

I

The Education of the Handicapped Act (Act), 84 Stat. 175, as amended, 20 U.S.C. § 1401 *et seq.* (1976 ed. and Supp. IV), provides federal money to assist state and local agencies in educating handicapped children, and conditions such funding upon a State's compliance with extensive goals and procedures. The Act represents an ambitious federal effort to promote the education of handicapped children, and was passed in response to Congress' perception that a majority of handicapped children in the United States "were either totally excluded from schools or [were] sitting idly in regular classrooms awaiting the time when they were old enough to 'drop out.' " * * *

In order to qualify for federal financial assistance under the Act, a State must demonstrate that it "has in effect a policy that assures all handicapped children the right to a free appropriate public education." That policy must be reflected in a state plan submitted to and approved by the Secretary of Education, § 1413, which describes in detail the goals, programs, and timetables under which the State intends to educate handicapped children within its borders. States receiving money under the Act must provide education to the handicapped by priority, first "to handicapped children who are not receiving an education" and second "to handicapped children . . . with the most severe handicaps who are receiving an inadequate education," § 1412(3), and "to the maximum extent appropriate" must educate handicapped children "with children who are not handicapped." The Act broadly defines "handicapped children" to include "mentally retarded, hard of hearing, deaf, speech impaired, visually handicapped, seriously emotionally disturbed, orthopedically impaired, [and] other health impaired children, [and] children with specific learning disabilities."[5]

The "free appropriate public education" required by the Act is tailored to the unique needs of the handicapped child by means of an "individualized educational program" (IEP)[,] * * * which is prepared at a meeting between a qualified representative of the local educational agency, the child's teacher, the child's parents or guardian, and, where appropriate, the child[.] * * *

In addition to the state plan and the IEP already described, the Act imposes extensive procedural requirements upon States receiving federal funds under its provisions.

* * *

5. In addition to covering a wide variety of handicapping conditions, the Act requires special educational services for children "regardless of the severity of their handicap." §§ 1412(2)(C), 1414(a)(1)(A).

II

This case arose in connection with the education of Amy Rowley, a deaf student at the Furnace Woods School in the Hendrick Hudson Central School District, Peekskill, N.Y. Amy has minimal residual hearing and is an excellent lipreader. During the year before she began attending Furnace Woods, a meeting between her parents and school administrators resulted in a decision to place her in a regular kindergarten class in order to determine what supplemental services would be necessary to her education. Several members of the school administration prepared for Amy's arrival by attending a course in sign-language interpretation, and a teletype machine was installed in the principal's office to facilitate communication with her parents who are also deaf. At the end of the trial period it was determined that Amy should remain in the kindergarten class, but that she should be provided with an FM hearing aid which would amplify words spoken into a wireless receiver by the teacher or fellow students during certain classroom activities. Amy successfully completed her kindergarten year.

As required by the Act, an IEP was prepared for Amy during the fall of her first-grade year. The IEP provided that Amy should be educated in a regular classroom at Furnace Woods, should continue to use the FM hearing aid, and should receive instruction from a tutor for the deaf for one hour each day and from a speech therapist for three hours each week. The Rowleys agreed with parts of the IEP, but insisted that Amy also be provided a qualified sign-language interpreter in all her academic classes in lieu of the assistance proposed in other parts of the IEP. Such an interpreter had been placed in Amy's kindergarten class for a 2–week experimental period, but the interpreter had reported that Amy did not need his services at that time. The school administrators likewise concluded that Amy did not need such an interpreter in her first-grade classroom. They reached this conclusion after consulting the school district's Committee on the Handicapped, which had received expert evidence from Amy's parents on the importance of a sign-language interpreter, received testimony from Amy's teacher and other persons familiar with her academic and social progress, and visited a class for the deaf.

When their request for an interpreter was denied, the Rowleys demanded and received a hearing before an independent examiner. After receiving evidence from both sides, the examiner agreed with the administrators' determination that an interpreter was not necessary because "Amy was achieving educationally, academically, and socially" without such assistance. The examiner's decision was affirmed on appeal by the New York Commissioner of Education on the basis of substantial evidence in the record. Pursuant to the Act's provision for judicial review, the Rowleys then brought an action in the United States District Court for the Southern District of New York, claiming that the administrators' denial of the sign-language interpreter constituted a denial of the "free appropriate public education" guaranteed by the Act.

The District Court found that Amy "is a remarkably well-adjusted child" who interacts and communicates well with her classmates and has "developed an extraordinary rapport" with her teachers. It also found that "she performs better than the average child in her class and is advancing easily from grade to grade," but "that she understands considerably less of what goes on in class than she could if she were not deaf" and thus "is not learning as much, or performing as well academically, as she would without her handicap." This disparity between Amy's achievement and her potential led the court to decide that she was not receiving a "free appropriate public education," which the court defined as "an opportunity to achieve [her] full potential commensurate with the opportunity provided to other children." According to the District Court, such a standard "requires that the potential of the handicapped child be measured and compared to his or her performance, and that the resulting differential or 'shortfall' be compared to the shortfall experienced by nonhandicapped children." The District Court's definition arose from its assumption that the responsibility for "giv[ing] content to the requirement of an 'appropriate education'" had "been left entirely to the [federal] courts and the hearing officers."

A divided panel of the United States Court of Appeals for the Second Circuit affirmed. The Court of Appeals "agree[d] with the [D]istrict [C]ourt's conclusions of law," and held that its "findings of fact [were] not clearly erroneous."

We granted certiorari to review the lower courts' interpretation of the Act. * * *

III

A

This is the first case in which this Court has been called upon to interpret any provision of the Act. As noted previously, the District Court and the Court of Appeals concluded that "[t]he Act itself does not define 'appropriate education,'" but leaves "to the courts and the hearing officers" the responsibility of "giv[ing] content to the requirement of an 'appropriate education.'" Petitioners contend that the definition of the phrase "free appropriate public education" used by the courts below overlooks the definition of that phrase actually found in the Act. Respondents agree that the Act defines "free appropriate public education," but contend that the statutory definition is not "functional" and thus "offers judges no guidance in their consideration of controversies involving 'the identification, evaluation, or educational placement of the child or the provision of a free appropriate public education.'" The United States, appearing as *amicus curiae* on behalf of respondents, states that "[a]lthough the Act includes definitions of a 'free appropriate public education' and other related terms, the statutory definitions do not adequately explain what is meant by 'appropriate.'"

We are loath to conclude that Congress failed to offer any assistance in defining the meaning of the principal substantive phrase used in the

Act. It is beyond dispute that, contrary to the conclusions of the courts below, the Act does expressly define "free appropriate public education":

> The term 'free appropriate public education' means *special education* and *related services* which (A) have been provided at public expense, under public supervision and direction, and without charge, (B) meet the standards of the State educational agency, (C) include an appropriate preschool, elementary, or secondary school education in the State involved, and (D) are provided in conformity with the individualized education program required under section 1414(a)(5) of this title.

"Special education," as referred to in this definition, means "specially designed instruction, at no cost to parents or guardians, to meet the unique needs of a handicapped child, including classroom instruction, instruction in physical education, home instruction, and instruction in hospitals and institutions." "Related services" are defined as "transportation, and such developmental, corrective, and other supportive services . . . as may be required to assist a handicapped child to benefit from special education."[10]

Like many statutory definitions, this one tends toward the cryptic rather than the comprehensive, but that is scarcely a reason for abandoning the quest for legislative intent. Whether or not the definition is a "functional" one, as respondents contend it is not, it is the principal tool which Congress has given us for parsing the critical phrase of the Act. We think more must be made of it than either respondents or the United States seems willing to admit.

According to the definitions contained in the Act, a "free appropriate public education" consists of educational instruction specially designed to meet the unique needs of the handicapped child, supported by such services as are necessary to permit the child "to benefit" from the instruction. Almost as a checklist for adequacy under the Act, the definition also requires that such instruction and services be provided at public expense and under public supervision, meet the State's educational standards, approximate the grade levels used in the State's regular education, and comport with the child's IEP. Thus, if personalized instruction is being provided with sufficient supportive services to permit the child to benefit from the instruction, and the other items on the definitional checklist are satisfied, the child is receiving a "free appropriate public education" as defined by the Act.

Other portions of the statute also shed light upon congressional intent. Congress found that of the roughly eight million handicapped children in the United States at the time of enactment, one million were "excluded entirely from the public school system" and more than half were receiving an inappropriate education. In addition, as mentioned in

---

10. Examples of "related services" identified in the Act are "speech pathology and audiology, psychological services, physical and occupational therapy, recreation, and medical and counseling services, except that such medical services shall be for diagnostic and evaluation purposes only." § 1401(17).

Part I, the Act requires States to extend educational services first to those children who are receiving no education and second to those children who are receiving an "inadequate education." When these express statutory findings and priorities are read together with the Act's extensive procedural requirements and its definition of "free appropriate public education," the face of the statute evinces a congressional intent to bring previously excluded handicapped children into the public education systems of the States and to require the States to adopt *procedures* which would result in individualized consideration of and instruction for each child.

Noticeably absent from the language of the statute is any substantive standard prescribing the level of education to be accorded handicapped children. Certainly the language of the statute contains no requirement like the one imposed by the lower courts—that States maximize the potential of handicapped children "commensurate with the opportunity provided to other children."

* * *

By passing the Act, Congress sought primarily to make public education available to handicapped children. But in seeking to provide such access to public education, Congress did not impose upon the States any greater substantive educational standard than would be necessary to make such access meaningful.

* * *

That the Act imposes no clear obligation upon recipient States beyond the requirement that handicapped children receive some form of specialized education is perhaps best demonstrated by the fact that Congress, in explaining the need for the Act, equated an "appropriate education" to the receipt of some specialized educational services. * * *

(ii)

Respondents contend that "the goal of the Act is to provide each handicapped child with an equal educational opportunity." We think, however, that the requirement that a State provide specialized educational services to handicapped children generates no additional requirement that the services so provided be sufficient to maximize each child's potential "commensurate with the opportunity provided other children." Respondents and the United States correctly note that Congress sought "to provide assistance to the States in carrying out their responsibilities under ... the Constitution of the United States to provide equal protection of the laws." But we do not think that such statements imply a congressional intent to achieve strict equality of opportunity or services.

The educational opportunities provided by our public school systems undoubtedly differ from student to student, depending upon a myriad of factors that might affect a particular student's ability to assimilate information presented in the classroom. The requirement that States provide "equal" educational opportunities would thus seem to present an entirely unworkable standard requiring impossible measurements and comparisons. Similarly, furnishing handicapped children with only such services as are available to nonhandicapped children would in all probability fall short of the statutory requirement of "free appropriate public education"; to require, on the other hand, the furnishing of every special service necessary to maximize each handicapped child's potential is, we think, further than Congress intended to go. Thus to speak in terms of "equal" services in one instance gives less than what is required by the Act and in another instance more. The theme of the Act is "free appropriate public education," a phrase which is too complex to be captured by the word "equal" whether one is speaking of opportunities or services.

The legislative conception of the requirements of equal protection was undoubtedly informed by the two District Court decisions referred to above. But cases such as *Mills* and *PARC* held simply that handicapped children may not be excluded entirely from public education. * * *

The District Court and the Court of Appeals thus erred when they held that the Act requires New York to maximize the potential of each handicapped child commensurate with the opportunity provided nonhandicapped children. Desirable though that goal might be, it is not the standard that Congress imposed upon States which receive funding under the Act. Rather, Congress sought primarily to identify and evaluate handicapped children, and to provide them with access to a free public education.

(iii)

Implicit in the congressional purpose of providing access to a "free appropriate public education" is the requirement that the education to which access is provided be sufficient to confer some educational benefit upon the handicapped child. It would do little good for Congress to spend millions of dollars in providing access to a public education only to have the handicapped child receive no benefit from that education. The statutory definition of "free appropriate public education," in addition to requiring that States provide each child with "specially designed instruction," expressly requires the provision of "such ... supportive services ... as may be required to assist a handicapped child *to benefit* from special education." We therefore conclude that the "basic floor of opportunity" provided by the Act consists of access to specialized instruction and related services which are individually designed to provide educational benefit to the handicapped child.

The determination of when handicapped children are receiving sufficient educational benefits to satisfy the requirements of the Act presents a more difficult problem. The Act requires participating States to educate a wide spectrum of handicapped children, from the marginally hearing-impaired to the profoundly retarded and palsied. It is clear that the benefits obtainable by children at one end of the spectrum will differ dramatically from those obtainable by children at the other end, with infinite variations in between. One child may have little difficulty competing successfully in an academic setting with nonhandicapped children while another child may encounter great difficulty in acquiring even the most basic of self-maintenance skills. We do not attempt today to establish any one test for determining the adequacy of educational benefits conferred upon all children covered by the Act. Because in this case we are presented with a handicapped child who is receiving substantial specialized instruction and related services, and who is performing above average in the regular classrooms of a public school system, we confine our analysis to that situation.

The Act requires participating States to educate handicapped children with nonhandicapped children whenever possible.[24] When that "mainstreaming" preference of the Act has been met and a child is being educated in the regular classrooms of a public school system, the system itself monitors the educational progress of the child. Regular examinations are administered, grades are awarded, and yearly advancement to higher grade levels is permitted for those children who attain an adequate knowledge of the course material. The grading and advancement system thus constitutes an important factor in determining educational benefit. Children who graduate from our public school systems are considered by our society to have been "educated" at least to the grade level they have completed, and access to an "education" for handicapped children is precisely what Congress sought to provide in the Act.[25]

C

When the language of the Act and its legislative history are considered together, the requirements imposed by Congress become tolerably clear. Insofar as a State is required to provide a handicapped child with a "free appropriate public education," we hold that it satisfies this requirement by providing personalized instruction with sufficient support services to permit the child to benefit educationally from that instruction. Such instruction and services must be provided at public expense, must meet the State's educational standards, must approximate the grade levels used in the State's regular education, and must comport with the child's IEP. In addition, the IEP, and therefore the personalized

---

24. Title 20, U.S.C. § 1412(5) requires that participating States establish "procedures to assure that, to the maximum extent appropriate, handicapped children, including children in public or private institutions or other care facilities, are educated with children who are not handicapped, and that special classes, separate schooling, or other removal of handicapped children from the regular educational environment occurs only when the nature or severity of the handicap is such that education in regular classes

with the use of supplementary aids and services cannot be achieved satisfactorily."

25. We do not hold today that every handicapped child who is advancing from grade to grade in a regular public school system is automatically receiving a "free appropriate public education." In this case, however, we find Amy's academic progress, when considered with the special services and professional consideration accorded by the Furnace Woods school administrators, to be dispositive.

instruction, should be formulated in accordance with the requirements of the Act and, if the child is being educated in the regular classrooms of the public education system, should be reasonably calculated to enable the child to achieve passing marks and advance from grade to grade.

IV

* * * [A] court's inquiry in suits brought under § 1415(e)(2) is twofold. First, has the State complied with the procedures set forth in the Act? And second, is the individualized educational program developed through the Act's procedures reasonably calculated to enable the child to receive educational benefits? If these requirements are met, the State has complied with the obligations imposed by Congress and the courts can require no more.

B

In assuring that the requirements of the Act have been met, courts must be careful to avoid imposing their view of preferable educational methods upon the States. The primary responsibility for formulating the education to be accorded a handicapped child, and for choosing the educational method most suitable to the child's needs, was left by the Act to state and local educational agencies in cooperation with the parents or guardian of the child. The Act expressly charges States with the responsibility of "acquiring and disseminating to teachers and administrators of programs for handicapped children significant information derived from educational research, demonstration, and similar projects, and [of] adopting, where appropriate, promising educational practices and materials." In the face of such a clear statutory directive, it seems highly unlikely that Congress intended courts to overturn a State's choice of appropriate educational theories in a proceeding conducted pursuant to § 1415(e)(2).

We previously have cautioned that courts lack the "specialized knowledge and experience" necessary to resolve "persistent and difficult questions of educational policy." We think that Congress shared that view when it passed the Act. As already demonstrated, Congress's intention was not that the Act displace the primacy of States in the field of education, but that States receive funds to assist them in extending their educational systems to the handicapped. Therefore, once a court determines that the requirements of the Act have been met, questions of methodology are for resolution by the States.

* * *

VI

Applying these principles to the facts of this case, we conclude that the Court of Appeals erred in affirming the decision of the District Court. Neither the District Court nor the Court of Appeals found that petitioners had failed to comply with the procedures of the Act, and the findings of neither court would support a conclusion that Amy's educational program failed to comply with the substantive requirements of the Act. On the contrary, the District Court found that the "evidence firmly establishes that Amy is receiving an 'adequate' education, since she performs better than the average child in her class and is advancing easily from grade to grade." In light of this finding, and of the fact that Amy was receiving personalized instruction and related services calculated by the Furnace Woods school administrators to meet her educational needs, the lower courts should not have concluded that the Act requires the provision of a sign-language interpreter. Accordingly, the decision of the Court of Appeals is reversed, and the case is remanded for further proceedings consistent with this opinion.

So ordered.

JUSTICE BLACKMUN, concurring in the judgment.

Although I reach the same result as the Court does today, I read the legislative history and goals of the Education of the Handicapped Act differently. Congress unambiguously stated that it intended to "take a more active role under its responsibility for equal protection of the laws to guarantee that handicapped children are provided *equal educational opportunity.*"

As I have observed before, "[i]t seems plain to me that Congress, in enacting [this statute], intended to do more than merely set out politically self-serving but essentially meaningless language about what the [handicapped] deserve at the hands of state ... authorities." The clarity of the legislative intent convinces me that the relevant question here is not, as the Court says, whether Amy Rowley's individualized education program was "reasonably calculated to enable [her] to receive educational benefits," measured in part by whether or not she "achieve[s] passing marks and advance[s] from grade to grade." Rather, the question is whether Amy's program, *viewed as a whole*, offered her an opportunity to understand and participate in the classroom that was substantially equal to that given her nonhandicapped classmates. This is a standard predicated on equal educational opportunity and equal access to the educational process, rather than upon Amy's achievement of any particular educational outcome.

In answering this question, I believe that the District Court and the Court of Appeals should have given greater deference than they did to the findings of the School District's impartial hearing officer and the State's Commissioner of Education, both of whom sustained petitioners' refusal to add a sign-language interpreter to Amy's individualized education program. I would suggest further that those courts focused too narrowly on the presence or absence of a particular service—a sign-language interpreter—rather than on the total package of services furnished to Amy by the School Board.

As the Court demonstrates, petitioner Board has provided Amy Rowley considerably more than "a teacher with a loud voice." By concentrating on whether Amy was "learning as much, or performing as well academically, as she would without her handicap," the District

Court and the Court of Appeals paid too little attention to whether, on the entire record, respondent's individualized education program offered her an educational opportunity substantially equal to that provided her nonhandicapped classmates. Because I believe that standard has been satisfied here, I agree that the judgment of the Court of Appeals should be reversed.

JUSTICE WHITE, with whom JUSTICE BRENNAN and JUSTICE MARSHALL join, dissenting.

In order to reach its result in this case, the majority opinion contradicts itself, the language of the statute, and the legislative history. Both the majority's standard for a "free appropriate education" and its standard for judicial review disregard congressional intent.

* * *

The majority reads [the] statutory language as establishing a congressional intent limited to bringing "previously excluded handicapped children into the public education systems of the States and [requiring] the States to adopt *procedures* which would result in individualized consideration of and instruction for each child." In its attempt to constrict the definition of "appropriate" and the thrust of the Act, the majority opinion states: "Noticeably absent from the language of the statute is any substantive standard prescribing the level of education to be accorded handicapped children. Certainly the language of the statute contains no requirement like the one imposed by the lower courts—that States maximize the potential of handicapped children 'commensurate with the opportunity provided to other children.' "

I agree that the language of the Act does not contain a substantive standard beyond requiring that the education offered must be "appropriate." However, if there are limits not evident from the face of the statute on what may be considered an "appropriate education," they must be found in the purpose of the statute or its legislative history. The Act itself announces it will provide a *"full* educational opportunity to all handicapped children." This goal is repeated throughout the legislative history, in statements too frequent to be " 'passing references and isolated phrases.' " These statements elucidate the meaning of "appropriate." According to the Senate Report, for example, the Act does "guarantee that handicapped children are provided *equal* educational opportunity." This promise appears throughout the legislative history. Indeed, at times the purpose of the Act was described as tailoring each handicapped child's educational plan to enable the child "to achieve his or her maximum potential." Senator Stafford, one of the sponsors of the Act, declared: "We can all agree that education [given a handicapped child] should be equivalent, at least, to the one those children who are not handicapped receive." The legislative history thus directly supports the conclusion that the Act intends to give handicapped children an educational opportunity commensurate with that given other children.

The majority opinion announces a different substantive standard, that "Congress did not impose upon the States any greater substantive educational standard than would be necessary to make such access meaningful." While "meaningful" is no more enlightening than "appropriate," the Court purports to clarify itself. Because Amy was provided with *some* specialized instruction from which she obtained *some* benefit and because she passed from grade to grade, she was receiving a meaningful and therefore appropriate education.

This falls far short of what the Act intended. The Act details as specifically as possible the kind of specialized education each handicapped child must receive. It would apparently satisfy the Court's standard of "access to specialized instruction and related services which are individually designed to provide educational benefit to the handicapped child," for a deaf child such as Amy to be given a teacher with a loud voice, for she would benefit from that service. The Act requires more. It defines "special education" to mean "specifically designed instruction, at no cost to parents or guardians, to *meet the unique needs* of a handicapped child...."[3] Providing a teacher with a loud voice would not meet Amy's needs and would not satisfy the Act. The basic floor of opportunity is instead, as the courts below recognized, intended to eliminate the effects of the handicap, at least to the extent that the child will be given an equal opportunity to learn if that is reasonably possible. Amy Rowley, without a sign-language interpreter, comprehends less than half of what is said in the classroom—less than half of what normal children comprehend. This is hardly an equal opportunity to learn, even if Amy makes passing grades.

Despite its reliance on the use of "appropriate" in the definition of the Act, the majority opinion speculates that "Congress used the word as much to describe the settings in which handicapped children should be educated as to prescribe the substantive content or supportive services of their education." Of course, the word "appropriate" can be applied in many ways; at times in the Act, Congress used it to recommend mainstreaming handicapped children; at other points, it used the word to refer to the content of the individualized education. The issue before us is what standard the word "appropriate" incorporates when it is used to modify "education." The answer given by the Court is not a satisfactory one.

II

The Court's discussion of the standard for judicial review is as flawed as its discussion of a "free appropriate public education." According to the Court, a court can ask only whether the State has "complied with the procedures set forth in the Act" and whether the individualized education program is "reasonably calculated to enable the child to receive educational benefits." Both the language of the Act and the

3. "Related services" are "transportation, and such developmental, corrective, and other supportive services . . . as may be required to assist a handicapped child to benefit from special education." § 1401(17).

legislative history, however, demonstrate that Congress intended the courts to conduct a far more searching inquiry.

* * *

Notes

1. As discussed above, in the introduction to Chapter 7, many in the legal and education communities are reassessing the *Rowley* decision and its implications. *See, e.g.*, Daniel J. Losen & Kevin G. Welner, *Disabling Discrimination in Our Public Schools: Comprehensive Legal Challenges to Inappropriate and Inadequate Special Education Services for Minority Children,* 36 HARV. C.R.-C.L. L. REV. 407 (2001).

2. Jane K. Babin explained in 2000 that "[t]he Rowley decision has been widely criticized as a setback" for students with disabilities:

> Scholars who had read great promise of bountiful rewards into the EAHCA were left with only the minimal expectation of "some benefit." Despite admonitions by the Court that Rowley should be read narrowly, it was feared that the decision would permit states to receive EAHCA funds yet provide only de minimis services.

> Indeed, many courts have relied on Rowley to deny services * * * Recent attempts to require schools to demonstrate that a child has actually benefitted from his or her education have been largely unsuccessful. Courts have interpreted the FAPE requirement as prospective, requiring that school districts devise educational plans calculated to provide some benefit rather than provide education that actually benefits the child in a meaningful way. * * *

> In a small number of cases, however, courts have departed from the general trend by applying Rowley narrowly. Such courts have either interpreted Rowley to require additional services because the disputed IEP offered no benefit or have distinguished the facts of a case to avoid applying Rowley. Babin, *supra*, 37 SAN DIEGO L. REV. 211, 227–229 (2000).

3. In 2003, Scott F. Johnson identified some of the arguments in support of the growing effort to rethink *Rowley*:

> Three important events occurred after the Rowley decision, all of which impact the validity of the "some educational benefit" standard and change the nature of educational services that schools must provide students who receive special education services under the IDEA. The first significant post-Rowley event is state litigation over the constitutional requirements of providing an "adequate" education to students * * * under state constitutional law. * * * The second event is the education standards movement that created high expectations for all students, including students with disabilities, by creating generally applicable content and proficiency standards. * * * The third event is the reauthorization of IDEA in 1997. * * * These three changes require a reevaluation of what the standard for FAPE and Rowley mean today. * * *

> Reexamining Rowley is no small undertaking. It has provided the basic framework for special education services for the last 20 years. However,

the 1997 amendments to the IDEA make clear that the foundation underlying Rowley's reasoning is no longer present. That is, the IDEA is no longer intended to simply provide students with access to educational services that provide some benefit. The IDEA is intended to go beyond that to ensure that students with disabilities receive educational services based upon the high expectations in state educational standards and in state court cases regarding an adequate education. Once these elements are incorporated into the analysis, much of Rowley seems inapplicable to questions about the contours of a free and appropriate public education. * * *

Scott F. Johnson, *Reexamining* Rowley: *A New Focus in Special Education Law,* 2003 B.Y.U. EDUC. & L.J. 561, 567, 584–585.

3. WITHIN–SCHOOL SEGREGATION ISSUES IN SPECIAL EDUCATION

a. Disputes Regarding Inclusion, Mainstreaming, and the Least Restrictive Environment Generally

SACRAMENTO CITY UNIFIED SCH. DIST. v. RACHEL H.

14 F.3d 1398 (9th Cir. 1994).

SNEED, CIRCUIT JUDGE:

The Sacramento Unified School District ("the District") timely appeals the district court's judgment in favor of Rachel Holland ("Rachel") and the California State Department of Education. The court found that the appropriate placement for Rachel under the Individuals with Disabilities Act ("IDEA") was full-time in a regular second grade classroom with some supplemental services. The District contends that the appropriate placement for Rachel is half-time in special education classes and half-time in a regular class. We affirm the judgment of the district court.

I.

FACTS AND PRIOR PROCEEDINGS

Rachel Holland is now 11 years old and is mentally retarded. She was tested with an I.Q. of 44. She attended a variety of special education programs in the District from 1985–89. Her parents sought to increase the time Rachel spent in a regular classroom, and in the fall of 1989, they requested that Rachel be placed full-time in a regular classroom for the 1989–90 school year. The District rejected their request and proposed a placement that would have divided Rachel's time between a special education class for academic subjects and a regular class for non-academic activities such as art, music, lunch, and recess. The district court found that this plan would have required moving Rachel at least six times each day between the two classrooms. The Hollands instead enrolled Rachel in a regular kindergarten class at the Shalom School, a private school. Rachel remained at the Shalom School in regular classes and at the time the district court rendered its opinion was in the second grade.

The Hollands and the District were able to agree on an Individualized Education Program ("IEP") for Rachel. Although the IEP is required to be reviewed annually, because of the dispute between the parties, Rachel's IEP has not been reviewed since January 1990.[3]

The Hollands appealed the District's placement decision to a state hearing officer pursuant to 20 U.S.C. § 1415(b)(2). They maintained that Rachel best learned social and academic skills in a regular classroom and would not benefit from being in a special education class. The District contended Rachel was too severely disabled to benefit from full-time placement in a regular class. The hearing officer concluded that the District had failed to make an adequate effort to educate Rachel in a regular class pursuant to the IDEA. The officer found that (1) Rachel had benefited from her regular kindergarten class—that she was motivated to learn and learned by imitation and modeling; (2) Rachel was not disruptive in a regular classroom; and (3) the District had overstated the cost of putting Rachel in regular education—that the cost would not be so great that it weighed against placing her in a regular classroom. The hearing officer ordered the District to place Rachel in a regular classroom with support services, including a special education consultant and a part-time aide.

The District appealed this determination to the district court. Pursuant to 20 U.S.C. § 1415(e)(2), the parties presented additional evidence at an evidentiary hearing. The court affirmed the decision of the hearing officer that Rachel should be placed full-time in a regular classroom.

In considering whether the District proposed an appropriate placement for Rachel, the district court examined the following factors: (1) the educational benefits available to Rachel in a regular classroom, supplemented with appropriate aids and services, as compared with the educational benefits of a special education classroom; (2) the non-academic benefits of interaction with children who were not disabled; (3) the effect of Rachel's presence on the teacher and other children in the classroom; and (4) the cost of mainstreaming Rachel in a regular classroom.

1. Educational Benefits

The district court found the first factor, educational benefits to Rachel, weighed in favor of placing her in a regular classroom. Each side

---

3. The 1990 IEP objectives include: speaking in 4–or 5–word sentences; repeating instructions of complex tasks; initiating and terminating conversations; stating her name, address and phone number; participating in a safety program with classmates; developing a 24–word sight vocabulary; counting to 25; printing her first and last names and the alphabet; playing cooperatively; participating in lunch without supervision; and identifying upper and lower case letters and the sounds associated with them.

presented expert testimony which is summarized in the margin. The court noted that the District's evidence focused on Rachel's limitations but did not establish that the educational opportunities available through special education were better or equal to those available in a regular classroom. Moreover, the court found that the testimony of the Hollands' experts was more credible because they had more background in evaluating children with disabilities placed in regular classrooms and that they had a greater opportunity to observe Rachel over an extended period of time in normal circumstances. The district court also gave great weight to the testimony of Rachel's current teacher, Nina Crone, whom the court found to be an experienced, skillful teacher. Ms. Crone stated that Rachel was a full member of the class and participated in all activities. Ms. Crone testified that Rachel was making progress on her IEP goals: She was learning one-to-one correspondence in counting, was able to recite the English and Hebrew alphabets, and was improving her communication abilities and sentence lengths.

The district court found that Rachel received substantial benefits in regular education and that all of her IEP goals could be implemented in a regular classroom with some modification to the curriculum and with the assistance of a part-time aide.

2. Non-academic Benefits

The district court next found that the second factor, non-academic benefits to Rachel, also weighed in favor of placing her in a regular classroom. The court noted that the Hollands' evidence indicated that Rachel had developed her social and communications skills as well as her self-confidence from placement in a regular class, while the District's evidence tended to show that Rachel was not learning from exposure to other children and that she was isolated from her classmates. The court concluded that the differing evaluations in large part reflected the predisposition of the evaluators. The court found the testimony of Rachel's mother and her current teacher to be the most credible. These witnesses testified regarding Rachel's excitement about school, learning, and her new friendships and Rachel's improved self-confidence.

3. Effect on the Teacher and Children in the Regular Class

The district court next addressed the issue of whether Rachel had a detrimental effect on others in her regular classroom. The court looked at two aspects: (1) whether there was detriment because the child was disruptive, distracting or unruly, and (2) whether the child would take up so much of the teacher's time that the other students would suffer from lack of attention. The witnesses of both parties agreed that Rachel followed directions and was well-behaved and not a distraction in class. The court found the most germane evidence on the second aspect came from Rachel's second grade teacher, Nina Crone, who testified that Rachel did not interfere with her ability to teach the other children and in the future would require only a part-time aide. Accordingly, the district court determined that the third factor, the effect of Rachel's presence on the teacher and other children in the classroom weighed in favor of placing her in a regular classroom.

4. Cost

Finally, the district court found that the District had not offered any persuasive or credible evidence to support its claim that educating Rachel in a regular classroom with appropriate services would be significantly more expensive than educating her in the District's proposed setting.

The District contended that it would cost $109,000 to educate Rachel full-time in a regular classroom. This figure was based on the cost of providing a full-time aide for Rachel plus an estimated $80,000 for school-wide sensitivity training. The court found that the District did not establish that such training was necessary. Further, the court noted that even if such training were necessary, there was evidence from the California Department of Education that the training could be had at no cost. Moreover, the court found it would be inappropriate to assign the total cost of the training to Rachel when other children with disabilities would benefit. In addition, the court concluded that the evidence did not suggest that Rachel required a full-time aide.

In addition, the court found that the District should have compared the cost of placing Rachel in a special class of approximately 12 students with a full-time special education teacher and two full-time aides and the cost of placing her in a regular class with a part-time aide. The District provided no evidence of this cost comparison.

The court also was not persuaded by the District's argument that it would lose significant funding if Rachel did not spend at least 51% of her time in a special education class. The court noted that a witness from the California Department of Education testified that waivers were available if a school district sought to adopt a program that did not fit neatly within the funding guidelines. The District had not applied for a waiver.

By inflating the cost estimates and failing to address the true comparison, the District did not meet its burden of proving that regular placement would burden the District's funds or adversely affect services available to other children. Therefore, the court found that the cost factor did not weigh against mainstreaming Rachel.

The district court concluded that the appropriate placement for Rachel was full-time in a regular second grade classroom with some supplemental services and affirmed the decision of the hearing officer.

* * *

III.

STANDARDS OF REVIEW

The appropriateness of a special education placement under the IDEA is reviewed de novo. The district court's findings of fact are reviewed for clear error. The clearly erroneous standard applies to the district court's factual determinations regarding (1) whether Rachel was receiving academic and non-academic benefits in the regular classroom; (2) whether her presence was a detriment to others in the classroom; and (3) whether the District demonstrated that the cost of placing her in a regular classroom would be significantly more expensive. * * *

IV.

DISCUSSION

* * *

B. Mainstreaming Requirements of the IDEA

1. The Statute

The IDEA provides that each state must establish:

[P]rocedures to assure that, to the maximum extent appropriate, children with disabilities ... are educated with children who are not disabled, and that special classes, separate schooling, or other removal of children with disabilities from the regular educational environment occurs only when the nature or severity of the disability is such that education in regular classes with the use of supplementary aids and services cannot be achieved satisfactorily.... 20 U.S.C. § 1412(5)(B).

This provision sets forth Congress's preference for educating children with disabilities in regular classrooms with their peers.

2. Burden of Proof

* * * [T]he District * * * [has] the burden of demonstrating in the district court that its proposed placement provided mainstreaming to "the maximum extent appropriate."

3. Test for Determining Compliance with the IDEA's Mainstreaming Requirement

We have not adopted or devised a standard for determining the presence of compliance with 20 U.S.C. § 1412(5)(B). The Third, Fifth and Eleventh Circuits use what is known as the *Daniel R.R.* test.[5] The Fourth, Sixth and Eighth Circuits apply the *Roncker* test.[6]

---

5. First, the court must determine "whether education in the regular classroom, with the use of supplemental aids and services, can be achieved satisfactorily...." *Daniel R.R.,* 874 F.2d at 1048. If the court finds that education cannot be achieved satisfactorily in the regular classroom, then it must decide "whether the school has mainstreamed the child to the maximum extent appropriate." *Id.*

Factors the courts consider in applying the first prong of this test are (1) the steps the school district has taken to accommodate the child in a regular classroom; (2) whether the child will receive an educational benefit from regular education; (3) the child's overall educational experience in regular education; and (4) the effect the

disabled child's presence has on the regular classroom. *Daniel R.R.,* 874 F.2d at 1048–49. In *Greer* the court added the factor of cost, stating that "if the cost of educating a handicapped child in a regular classroom is so great that it would significantly impact upon the education of other children in the district, then education in a regular classroom is not appropriate." 950 F.2d at 697.

Regarding the second factor, the *Oberti* and *Greer* courts compared the educational benefits received in a regular classroom with the benefits received in a special education class. *Oberti,* 995 F.2d at 1216; *Greer,* 950 F.2d at 697.

6. According to the court in *Roncker [v. Walter,* 700 F.2d 1058, 1063 (6th Cir.

Although the district court relied principally on *Daniel R.R.* and *Greer,* it did not specifically adopt the *Daniel R.R.* test over the *Roncker* test. Rather, it employed factors found in both lines of cases in its analysis. The result was a four-factor balancing test in which the court considered (1) the educational benefits of placement full-time in a regular class; (2) the non-academic benefits of such placement; (3) the effect Rachel had on the teacher and children in the regular class; and (4) the costs of mainstreaming Rachel. This analysis directly addresses the issue of the appropriate placement for a child with disabilities under the requirements of 20 U.S.C. § 1412(5)(B). Accordingly, we approve and adopt the test employed by the district court.

4. The District's Contentions on Appeal

The District strenuously disagrees with the district court's findings that Rachel was receiving academic and non-academic benefits in a regular class and did not have a detrimental effect on the teacher or other students. It argues that the court's findings were contrary to the evidence of the state Diagnostic Center and that the court should not have been persuaded by the testimony of Rachel's teacher, particularly her testimony that Rachel would need only a part-time aide in the future. The district court, however, conducted a full evidentiary hearing and made a thorough analysis. The court found the Hollands' evidence to be more persuasive. Moreover, the court asked Rachel's teacher extensive questions regarding Rachel's need for a part-time aide. We will not disturb the findings of the district court.

The District is also not persuasive on the issue of cost. The District now claims that it will lose up to $190,764 in state special education funding if Rachel is not enrolled in a special education class at least 51% of the day. However, the District has not sought a waiver pursuant to California Education Code § 56101. This section provides that (1) any school district may request a waiver of any provision of the Education Code if the waiver is necessary or beneficial to the student's IEP, and (2) the Board may grant the waiver when failure to do so would hinder compliance with federal mandates for a free appropriate education for children with disabilities.

Finally, the District, citing *Wilson v. Marana Unified Sch. Dist.,* 735 F.2d 1178 (9th Cir.1984), argues that Rachel must receive her academic and functional curriculum in special education from a specially credent-

---

1983)], "[W]here the segregated facility is considered superior, the court should determine whether the services which make that placement superior could be feasibly provided in a non-segregated setting. If they can, the placement in the segregated school would be inappropriate under the Act."

Courts are to (1) compare the benefits the child would receive in special education with those she would receive in regular education; (2) consider whether the child would be disruptive in the non-segregated setting; and (3) consider the cost of mainstreaming. *Id.*

ialed teacher. *Wilson* does not stand for this proposition. Rather, the court in *Wilson* stated:

> The school district argues that under state law a child who qualifies for special education *must* be taught by a teacher who is certificated in that child's particular area of disability. We do not agree and do not reach a decision on that broad assertion. We hold only, under our standard of review, that the school district's decision was a reasonable one under the circumstances of this case.

735 F.2d at 1180 (emphasis in original). More importantly, the District's proposition that Rachel must be taught by a special education teacher runs directly counter to the congressional preference that children with disabilities be educated in regular classes with children who are not disabled.

We affirm the judgment of the district court. While we cannot determine what the appropriate placement is for Rachel at the present time, we hold that the determination of the present and future appropriate placement for Rachel should be based on the principles set forth in this opinion and the opinion of the district court.

AFFIRMED.

BETH B. v. VAN CLAY

282 F.3d 493 (7th Cir. 2002).

FLAUM, CHIEF JUDGE.

Thirteen-year-old Beth B. and her parents appeal the district court's grant of summary judgment to the Lake Bluff School District, affirming an administrative decision that upheld the school district's recommendation to place Beth in a special education classroom. Beth is severely mentally and physically challenged. Her parents have long been fighting a battle to keep her in the regular education classroom[.] * * * For the reasons stated herein, we affirm the decision of the district court.

I. BACKGROUND

Beth has Rett Syndrome, a neurological disorder that almost exclusively affects girls. It results in severe disabilities, both cognitive and physical. Beth is nonverbal; she uses an instrument called an eye gaze, a board with various pictures and symbols that she singles out with eye contact, to communicate her wants and needs, as well as other communication devices that allow her to choose among symbols or to hear messages recorded by others. She relies on a wheelchair for mobility. She, like nearly all Rett sufferers, has an extreme lack of control over body movement. Although her mental capacity is difficult to assess precisely, due to her extreme communicative and motor impairments, some experts contend that she has the cognitive ability of a twelve-to-eighteen-month old infant. Others estimate that she has the ability of a four-to-six-year old. She is unable to read or recognize numbers.

Beth has been educated in regular classrooms at her neighborhood public school for seven years. She is currently in the seventh grade at Lake Bluff Middle School with other thirteen-year-old children. Students in the seventh grade attend six 42–minute classes a day. They have three-minute passing periods between class. Beth's aides help her travel from room to room during the passing periods, although it is extremely difficult for her to do so in such a short time frame. Since the first grade, Beth has worked with a one-on-one aide at all times and has used an individualized curriculum tied in subject matter, as much as possible, to that of the other students in the class. Beth's current curriculum is geared toward someone at a preschool level. When her peers worked on mathematics, she was exposed to various numbers. When the class studied meteorology and weather patterns, she looked at pictures of clouds. Beth cannot participate in class discussions or lectures.

The school district held an annual conference with Beth's parents, teachers, and district administrators to review Beth's individualized education program ("IEP"). After her second grade year, the school district recommended at her IEP meeting that Beth be placed in an ELS setting. No appropriate special education environment exists in the Lake Bluff District; Beth would have to attend school in a neighboring school district. The ELS program recommended by the district would be located in a public school building and would serve students between the ages of six and twenty one with mild, moderate, or severe handicaps. Generally, six to eight students comprise one ELS classroom, and the student-teacher ratio is one-to-one. ELS students in the program are mainstreamed into regular education classrooms during music, library, art, computer, and certain social studies and science classes, and join other students at the school during lunch, recess, assemblies, and field trips. Additionally, reverse mainstreaming is employed; that is, regular education students come into the ELS classroom to allow for interaction between ELS and non ELS students.

Beth's parents disagreed with Beth's placement in an ELS program, requested a due process review under the IDEA, and invoked the Act's stay-put provision, which has allowed Beth to remain in the regular classroom at her neighborhood school pending the resolution of this litigation.

II. Discussion

Beth's parents argue that the school district's placement of Beth in an ELS classroom violates the IDEA. The district court erred, they contend, in upholding the administrative decision finding otherwise. Although we review the school board's ultimate decision *de novo* because it is a mixed question of law and fact, we will reverse only if the district court's findings were clearly erroneous, absent a mistake of law.

* * *

B. The IDEA

The IDEA, enacted in 1975 as The Education of All Handicapped Children's Act, entitles all children with disabilities to access to public education. It conditions federal funding for educating disabled children on a state's compliance with certain conditions. A school district must provide such children with a free appropriate public education ("FAPE"), together, to the maximum extent appropriate, with nondisabled children ("least restrictive environment" or "LRE"). The FAPE provision and LRE provision are two sides of the same IEP coin. The first requirement is absolute and focuses on the school district's proposed placement—here, the ELS program; the second is relative and concentrates on other placement options—here, keeping Beth in the regular classroom. The LRE requirement shows Congress's strong preference in favor of mainstreaming, but does not require, or even suggest, doing so when the regular classroom setting provides an unsatisfactory education. 34 C.F.R. § 300.550(b)(2) ("[S]pecial classes, separate schooling or other removal of children with disabilities from the regular educational environment occurs only if the nature or severity of the disability is such that education in regular classes with the use of supplementary aids and services cannot be achieved satisfactorily.").

1. FAPE

We agree with the district court and the hearing officer, and find that the district's recommendation to place Beth in an ELS classroom satisfies the FAPE requirement. In determining whether the district's placement of Beth meets the standard, we must ask: "First, has the State complied with the procedures set forth in the Act? And second, is the individualized educational program developed through the Act's procedures reasonably calculated to enable the child to receive educational benefits?" No one contests that the program recommended during Beth's IEP review passes muster under this test; the FAPE mandate is, therefore, not at issue. Its discussion is required, however, because of the confusion that ensues when language from the FAPE requirement and analysis is misapplied to the LRE inquiry.

Beth's parents confuse the FAPE side of the coin with the LRE side. They contend that Beth's current placement satisfies the *Rowley* standard because she received an educational benefit at Lake Bluff Middle School. So long as the regular classroom confers "some educational benefit" to Beth, they argue, the school district cannot remove her from that setting. This language is misplaced. The *Rowley* holding applies only to the school district's responsibility to provide a FAPE—a requirement that analyzes the appropriateness of the district's placement—not the appropriateness of the ELS alternatives, including the regular education classroom. As the district court properly noted, the FAPE determination is at the threshold of the placement inquiry. Only with the subsequent LRE analysis does the question of the educational benefit to Beth in the regular classroom arise; in that context, the *Rowley* language does not apply.

2. *LRE*

The core of this dispute involves whether the school district's decision to place Beth in an ELS classroom violates the LRE provision of the IDEA. Under this clause, the district must mainstream Beth—that is, provide her an education with her nondisabled peers—to the "greatest extent appropriate." Again, Congress used the modifier "appropriate" in stating the requirements of the Act, limiting its mainstreaming mandate. The regular class room would be a less restrictive environment than the ELS classroom. That point is not at issue, however, because the Lake Bluff school district is not required to educate Beth in such an environment unless doing so would be appropriate. The Supreme Court, although it has not yet interpreted the language of the LRE provision, has stated that "[t]he Act's use of the word 'appropriate' thus seems to reflect Congress' recognition that some settings simply are not suitable environments for the participation of some handicapped children." This case turns, then, on whether educating Beth in the regular classroom (or, more appropriately in the middle school setting, classrooms) would be appropriate.

The relevant IDEA regulation provides that children may not be removed from the regular classroom unless their education there, with the use of supplementary aids and services, cannot be achieved satisfactorily. This preference for mainstreaming demands a hard look and a careful analysis of the education Beth was receiving at Lake Bluff Middle School. Beth's parents rely on misplaced language from *Rowley* to argue that so long as she was receiving *any* benefit—improvement in eye contact, or progress in responding to a request to "look" or "touch"— her removal would violate the LRE requirement. We cannot agree with this definition of satisfactory education.

Rowley requires, in its analysis of the FAPE provision, "that the education to which access is provided be sufficient to confer some educational benefit upon the handicapped child." The Court's rationale behind using this standard was "to leave the selection of educational policy and methods where they traditionally have resided—with state and local school officials." The standard is intended to give school districts "flexibility in educational planning." By applying it to the LRE directive and arguing that the school district cannot remove Beth from the regular classroom if she receives *any* benefit there, Beth's parents turn the "some educational benefit" language on its head. Instead of granting flexibility to educators and school officials, it places an extreme restriction on their policymaking authority and the deference they are owed; it essentially vitiates school districts' authority to place any disabled children in separate special education environments. Neither Congress nor the Supreme Court intended such a result. *Rowley,* 458 U.S. at 181, 102 S.Ct. 3034, fn. 4 ("Congress recognized that regular classrooms simply would not be a suitable setting for the education of many handicapped children.'').

Each student's educational situation is unique. We find it unnecessary at this point in time to adopt a formal test for district courts uniformly to apply when deciding LRE cases. The Act itself provides enough of a framework for our discussion; if Beth's education at Lake Bluff Middle School was satisfactory, the school district would be in violation of the Act by removing her. If not, if its recommended placement will mainstream her to the maximum appropriate extent, no violation occurs. In this case we can say with confidence that the Lake Bluff school district's decision to remove Beth from her regular school did not violate the IDEA's mandate to mainstream disabled children to the maximum extent appropriate. Beth was in class for about fifty percent of each day. Her academic progress was virtually nonexistent and her developmental progress was limited. Although the school district provided her with aides, communication devices, computerized books, and an individual curriculum, she was receiving very little benefit from her time there.

We agree with the school district's decision that a modicum of developmental achievement does not constitute a satisfactory education. The ELS classroom, so long as it includes reverse mainstreaming opportunities, as well as time spent with nondisabled peers in nonacademic classes, during special projects, lunch, and the like, is at an acceptable point along the "continuum of services" between total integration and complete segregation, and satisfies the requirement that Beth be mainstreamed to the maximum extent appropriate. The school officials' decision about how to best educate Beth is based on expertise that we cannot match. They relied on years of evidence that Beth was not receiving a satisfactory education in the regular classroom. The placement shows a concern both for her development and for keeping her mainstreamed, to an appropriate extent, with her nondisabled peers. We cannot hold that the Lake Bluff School District has failed to provide her with the free, appropriate public education where she is mainstreamed to the maximum extent appropriate, to which she is entitled under the IDEA. Although we respect the input Beth's parents have given regarding her placement and the their continued participation in IEP decision-making, educators "have the power to provide handicapped children with an education they consider more appropriate than that proposed by the parents." We find that the district's proposed IEP, which includes reverse mainstreaming and provides that Beth will take part in certain regular-education classes, does not violate the statutory LRE mandate.

III. CONCLUSION

For the reasons stated herein, we find that the school district's recommendation to place Beth in an ELS classroom does not violate the IDEA. We AFFIRM the decision of the district court.

b. *Disproportionate Representation of Minority Students in Separate Special Education Classrooms*

LARRY P. v. RILES

343 F.Supp. 1306 (N.D. Cal. 1972).

PECKHAM, DISTRICT JUDGE.

Plaintiffs in this case have asked the Court to issue a preliminary injunction restraining the San Francisco Unified School District from administering I.Q. tests for purposes of determining whether to place black students in classes for the educable mentally retarded. Named plaintiffs, who remain anonymous for their own protection, are black San Francisco elementary school children who have been placed in EMR (Educable Mentally Retarded) classes because, *inter alia,* they scored below 75 on the defendant School District's I.Q. tests. They claim that they are not mentally retarded, and that they have been placed in EMR classes on the basis of tests which are biased against the culture and experience of black children as a class, in violation of their fourteenth amendment rights. In fact, plaintiffs have presented evidence, in the form of affidavits from certain black psychologists, that when they were given the same I.Q. tests but with special attempts by the psychologists to establish rapport with the test takers, to overcome plaintiffs' defeatism and easy distraction, to reword items in terms more consistent with plaintiffs' cultural background, and to give credit for non-standard answers which nevertheless showed an intelligent approach to problems in the context of that background, plaintiffs scored significantly above the cutting-off point of 75.

Irreparable injury is alleged to flow from plaintiffs' placement in EMR classes because the curriculum is so minimal academically, teacher expectations are so low, and because other students subject EMR students to ridicule on account of their status. Furthermore, EMR students allegedly acquire severe feelings of inferiority. To add to this alleged irreparable harm, the fact of placement in EMR classes is noted on a student's permanent school record, for colleges, prospective employers, and the armed forces to see. Plaintiffs charge that the harm is especially great because under state law placement in EMR classes is reevaluated only once every three years; this law was recently changed, however, to require reevaluation yearly.

Defendants justify the EMR program by noting that the curriculum, pace, and increased attention available in its classes are designed to be beneficial to retarded students, and that in San Francisco the classes are labeled "ungraded" or "adjustment" in order to minimize any stigma. However, defendants do not seem to controvert plaintiffs' assertion that a student who does not belong in an EMR class is harmed by being placed there. Rather, defendants claim that since students are permitted to achieve their way out of EMR classes on the basis of yearly evaluations, plaintiffs can be suffering only negligible harm as a result of their placement in such classes, even if it is true that they are not mentally retarded. The Court finds this contention to be specious. For even if a student remains in an EMR class for only one month, that placement is noted on his permanent record, his education is retarded to some degree, and he is subjected to whatever humiliation students are exposed to for being separated into classes for the educable mentally retarded.

This Court is thus of the view that for those students who are wrongfully placed in EMR classes, irreparable harm ensues. * * *

The fact of racial imbalance is demonstrated by plaintiffs' undisputed statistics, which indicate that while blacks constitute 28.5 per cent of all students in the San Francisco Unified School District, 66 per cent of all students in San Francisco's EMR program are black. Statewide, the disproportion is similar. Blacks comprise 9.1 per cent of all school children in California, but 27.5 per cent of all school children in EMR classes. Certainly these statistics indicate that there is a significant disproportion of blacks in EMR classes in San Francisco and in California. * * *

4. STANDARDIZED TESTING AND STUDENTS WITH DISABILITIES

LARRY P. v. RILES

793 F.2d 969 (9th Cir. 1984).

POOLE, CIRCUIT JUDGE:

The State Superintendent of Public Instruction appeals a decision holding that IQ tests used by the California school system to place children into special classes for the educable mentally retarded (E.M.R.) violated federal statutes and the equal protection clauses of the United States and California Constitutions. The district court enjoined the use of non-validated IQ tests, and ordered the state to develop plans to eliminate the disproportionate enrollment of black children in E.M.R. classes. We affirm on the statutory grounds and reverse on the federal and state constitutional issues.

I. PROCEDURE BELOW

The initial complaint for declaratory and injunctive relief was filed in 1971, with six black elementary schoolchildren in the San Francisco Unified School District as named plaintiffs. Appellees challenged as unconstitutional the use of standardized intelligence tests for placement of black children in E.M.R. classes in San Francisco. The defendants were the city and state superintendents, the members of the State Board of Public Instruction and the members of the City Board of Education. The district court certified the plaintiff class as consisting "of all black San Francisco schoolchildren who have been classified as mentally retarded on the bases of IQ test results" and granted appellees' motion for a preliminary injunction.

* * * In December 1974 the district court expanded the class to include "all Black California school children who have been or may in the future be classified as mentally retarded on the basis of I.Q. tests." The terms of the preliminary injunction were correspondingly expanded. * * *

Trial began on October 11, 1977 and concluded on March 15, 1978. On October 16, 1979 the district court entered judgment for the appellees. The district court held that the plaintiffs were adequate representatives of the class of black children who had been or in the future would be wrongly placed and maintained in special classes for the educable mentally retarded. The court held that the use of IQ tests for placement of black children in E.M.R. classes violated Title VI of the Civil Rights Act of 1964, 42 U.S.C. § 2000d et seq., the Rehabilitation Act of 1973, 29 U.S.C. § 794, and the Education For All Handicapped Children Act of 1975, 20 U.S.C. §§ 1401–1461, and the equal protection clauses of the federal and state constitutions. * * *

The district court permanently enjoined the defendants from utilizing any standardized IQ test for the identification of black E.M.R. children or their placement into E.M.R. classes, without securing prior approval of the court. The court ordered the defendants to direct each school district to re-evaluate every black child currently identified as an E.M.R. pupil without using standardized intelligence tests.

Further, the defendants were "ordered to monitor and eliminate disproportionate placement of black children in California's E.M.R. classes." The district court specifically ordered the defendants to obtain an annual report from each school district on the racial proportions of E.M.R. classes, to prepare a statewide report, and to direct each school district with a black E.M.R. pupil enrollment one standard deviation above the district rate of white E.M.R. pupil enrollment to prepare a plan to correct the imbalance. The defendants were ordered to bring to the attention of the court any district imbalance if the disparity in excess of one standard deviation existed after three years.

Wilson Riles, California Superintendent of Public Instruction, filed a timely notice of appeal. The other defendants did not appeal.

II. FACTS

* * *

In the mid–60's California created programs for several categories of students with educational problems. The "educable mentally retarded" (E.M.R.) program was for schoolchildren of retarded intellectual development who are considered incapable of being educated through the regular educational program, but who could benefit from special educational facilities to make them economically useful and socially adjusted. The "trainable mentally retarded" (T.M.R.) category was for children with more severe retardation than educable mentally retarded. In addition, there were two categories for students who, with help, could be returned to a regular school program. These were the programs for "culturally disadvantaged minors," children with cultural or economic disadvantages, but with potential for successfully completing a regular educational program, and for "educationally handicapped minors" (E.H.), students with marked learning or behavioral disorders, capable of returning to a regular school program but who cannot presently benefit from the regular program.

The E.M.R. classes are for children who are considered "incapable of learning in the regular classes," and the E.M.R. curriculum "is not designed to help students learn the skills necessary to return to the regular instructional program." The E.M.R. classes are designed only to teach social adjustment and economic usefulness.

"The [E.M.R.] classes are conceived of as 'dead-end classes,'" and a misplacement in E.M.R. causes a stigma and irreparable injury to the student.

From 1968 until trial in 1977, black children have been significantly overrepresented in E.M.R. classes. For example, in 1968–69, black children were about 9% of the state school population, yet accounted for 27% of the E.M.R. population.

"These apparent overenrollments could not be the result of chance. For example, there is less than a one in a million chance that the overenrollment of black children and the underenrollment of non-black children in the E.M.R. classes in 1976–77 would have resulted under a color-blind system." *Id.* at 944. To explain this overenrollment, the defendants proffered a theory that there is a higher incidence of mental retardation among the black population. The district court found that this theory fails to account for the problem, because even "if it is assumed that black children have a 50 percent greater incidence of this type of mental retardation, there is still less than a one in 100,000 chance that the enrollment could be so skewed towards black children.... [Further,] the disproportionate E.M.R. enrollment of black children is not duplicated in the classes for the so-called 'trainable mentally retarded' children."

Since 1967 complaints and concern had been mounting about the use of IQ tests and the placement of minorities in E.M.R. classes. In 1969 the state legislature enacted a resolution calling for a study by the State Board of Education of the overenrollment of minorities in E.M.R. classes. Litigation began in 1969 that raised many of these same issues on the behalf of children from Spanish-speaking backgrounds.[2]

* * *

2. [Diana v. Board of Education, No. C–70–37 RFP (N.D. Cal.)] *Diana* made essentially the same claims as *Larry P.* with respect to Hispanic children, and also involved the issue of linguistic discrimination. The issues of that case were resolved through a stipulated settlement approved by the court on June 18, 1973. Under the terms of the settlement, the State Board of Education agreed to inquire into any school district in which there was a "significant variance" between the expected and actual percentage of Mexican–Americans in E.M.R. classes, to collect relevant data and to develop a plan to eliminate any such variances or disproportionate enrollments.

On the average, black children score fifteen points, or one standard deviation, below white children on standardized intelligence tests. Thus, utilizing the premoratorium criteria used by California for E.M.R. placement, "approximately two percent of the total population fall below the two standard deviation cut-off, while about 15 percent of black children fall below that level."

The court found that "the tests were never designed to eliminate cultural biases against black children; it was assumed in effect that black children were less 'intelligent' than whites.... The tests were standardized and developed on an all-white population, and naturally their scientific validity is questionable for culturally different groups." Since the 1920's it has been generally known that black persons perform less well than white persons on the standardized intelligence tests. IQ tests had been standardized so that they yielded no bias because of sex. For example, when sample tests yielded different scores for boys and girls, the testing experts assumed such differences were unacceptable and modified the tests so that the curve in the standardization sample for boys and girls was identical. No such modifications on racial grounds has ever been tried by the testing companies. The district court noted that "the experts have from the beginning been willing to tolerate or even encourage tests that portray minorities, especially blacks, as intellectually inferior."

The district court analyzed and rejected the defendants' arguments advanced at trial that would explain the test score differences, which theorized that the lower scores for blacks were the result of actual, relevant differences between black and white children. The first argument is the genetic argument, which states that natural selection has resulted in black persons having a "gene pool" with lower intelligence than whites. The district court found the assumptions underlying the genetic argument highly suspect, and in any event that the defendants "were unwilling to admit any reliance on [this theory] for policy-making purposes."

The second theory is the socioeconomic argument, which theorizes that because of blacks' lower socioeconomic status, they are at a greater risk for all kinds of diseases due to malnutrition and poor medical attention. The district court found that the facts did not support this theory, since it did not explain why more severe mental retardation, *e.g.* that consistent with placement into classes for the trainable mentally retarded children, does not occur in greater proportions among blacks and poorer sections of the population.

The district court found that the appellants failed to show that the IQ tests were validated for blacks with respect to the characteristics consistent with E.M.R. status and placement in E.M.R. classes, *i.e.*, that the defendants failed to establish that the IQ tests were accurate predictors that black elementary schoolchildren who scored less than 70 were indeed mentally retarded.

The district court found that alternatives to IQ testing for E.M.R. placement have been in effect since the state moratorium on IQ testing in 1975. These procedures, in which schools take more time and care with their assessments for E.M.R. classification and rely more on observational data, are less discriminatory than under the IQ-centered standard.

The district court found that defendants were guilty of intentional discrimination in the use of the IQ tests for E.M.R. placement. The court based this determination on the facts that the historical background of the IQ tests shows cultural bias; the adoption of the mandatory IQ testing requirement in 1969 was riddled with procedural and substantive irregularities, in which no outside sources were consulted by the State Board and the question of bias was never considered, even though the officials were well aware of the bias and disproportionate placement problems caused by the IQ tests (this problem having been addressed in a legislative resolution); the defendants' "complete failure to ascertain or attempt to ascertain the validity of the tests for minority children;" and the failure of the state to investigate and act on legal requirements to report significant variances in racial and ethnic composition in E.M.R. classes. The court noted that "the SDE's actions revealed a complacent acceptance of those disproportions, and that complacency was evidently built on easy but unsubstantiated assumptions about the incidence of retardation or at least low intelligence among black children."

The court found that the named plaintiffs' assignments to E.M.R. classes were based on their scores on IQ tests, and that these plaintiffs were either in E.M.R. classes or subject to reassignment at the time the class was certified. Further, the court found that "the only relevant evidence on their cases indicated that they were not retarded."

* * *

VI.   REHABILITATION ACT

The Rehabilitation Act of 1973 provides *inter alia*:

No otherwise qualified handicapped individual in the United States, as defined in section 706(7) of this Title, shall, solely by reason of his handicap, be excluded from the participation in, be denied the benefits of, or be subjected to discrimination under any program or activity receiving Federal financial assistance. 29 U.S.C. § 794.[5]

The Education For All Handicapped Children Act ("EAHCA"), provides that a state qualifying for federal assistance under the Act must establish:

procedures to assure that testing and evaluation materials and procedures utilized for the purposes of evaluation and placement of handicapped children will be selected and administered so as not to

---

5. Even though the named plaintiffs claim not to be handicapped (retarded), they are still protected by this Act. The Rehabilitation Act provides that it covers persons who are "regarded" as handicapped. 29 U.S.C. § 706(7)(B); 29 C.F.R. § 32.3.

be racially or culturally discriminatory ... [N]o single procedure shall be the sole criterion for determining an appropriate educational program for a child. 20 U.S.C. § 1412(5)(C).

Congress was clearly concerned with the misclassification of students as retarded. The Senate Report for the Rehabilitation Act states that "racial and ethnic factors may contribute to misclassification as mentally retarded." The Senate Report for the Education For All Handicapped Children Act states that "[t]he [Labor and Public Welfare] Committee is deeply concerned about practices and procedures which result in classifying children as having handicapping conditions when, in fact, they do not have such conditions."

The Department of Education adopted almost identical regulations under both of these acts. These regulations require that recipients of federal funds under the acts ensure that:

[t]ests and other evaluation materials have been validated for the specific purpose for which they are used ... [and] assess specific areas of educational need and not merely those which are designed to provide a single general intelligence quotient. 34 C.F.R. § 104.35(b)(1), (2) and 34 C.F.R. § 300.532(a)(2), (b), originally adopted as 45 C.F.R. § 121a.532(a)(2), (b).

The regulations further provide that evaluation and placement be based on "a variety of sources, including aptitude and achievement tests, teacher recommendations, physical conditions, social or cultural background, and adaptive behavior."

In summary, the Education For All Handicapped Children Act specifically requires that tests and evaluation procedures be free of racial and cultural bias. Both the EAHCA and the Rehabilitation Act require that the tests used for evaluation be validated for the specific purpose for which they are used, and that placement not be based upon a single criterion but on a variety of sources. It is undisputed that California receives substantial federal assistance under these acts, and thus is required to conform to these procedures and regulations. The regulations place the burden on the recipient to show it has complied with the requirements.

Appellant argues that the IQ tests were validated for the specific purposes for which they are used. Appellant analogizes to Title VII cases, notably *Washington v. Davis*, 426 U.S. 229, 96 S. Ct. 2040 (1976), for the proposition that tests that are valid predictors of future performance can be utilized even if they have a discriminatory impact. There are two problems with appellant's proposition. First, the employment context is quite different from the educational situation. As the district court stated, "[i]f tests can predict that a person is going to be a poor employee, the employer can legitimately deny that person a job, but if tests suggest that a young child is probably going to be a poor student, the school cannot on that basis alone deny that child the opportunity to improve and develop the academic skills necessary to success in our society." Assigning a student to an E.M.R. class denies that child the opportunity to develop the necessary academic skills, since E.M.R. classes do not teach academic subjects and are essentially a dead-end academic track. Second, and more important, the question for predictive validity in schools is not whether the standardized intelligence tests predict future school performance generally, as appellant argues, but whether the tests predict specifically that black elementary schoolchildren (as opposed to white elementary schoolchildren) who score at or below 70 on the IQ tests are mentally retarded and incapable of learning the regular school curriculum. In this case, the appellant would have to have shown that the tests are a proven tool to determine which students have characteristics consistent with E.M.R. status and placement in E.M.R. classes, *i.e.*, "whose mental capabilities make it impossible for them to profit from the regular educational programs" even with remedial instruction. The regulations place the burden of showing such validation on the defendants.

The district court found that defendants failed to show that the tests were validated for placing black students with scores of 70 or less in E.M.R. classes. The district court noted that very few studies had examined the difference of IQ predictability for black as compared to white populations, and that those studies which had examined this problem found the tests much less valid for blacks than for whites. Further, the district court found that, even assuming the tests were validated for placement of white schoolchildren in E.M.R. classes, such validation for blacks had been generally assumed but not established. For example, the tests had been adjusted to eliminate differences in the average scores between the sexes, but such adjustment was never made to adjust the scores to be equal for black and white children. The court found that the reason for this was a basic assumption of a lower level of intelligence in blacks than in whites. The fact that early test developers indeed made this assumption is borne out by the literature and testimony at trial. In addition, no studies have been made, either by the defendants or the testing companies, to investigate the reasons for the one standard deviation difference in test scores between the races or to determine whether test redesign could eliminate any bias. There was expert testimony that a much larger percentage of black than white children had been misplaced in E.M.R. classes. Based on the evidence in the record, the district court finding that the appellant had not established validation of the test is not clearly erroneous.

The district court also found that the appellant did not utilize the variety of information required by statute and regulation to make E.M.R. placements, but relied primarily on the IQ test. This finding also is not clearly erroneous. Testimony showed that school records lacked sufficient evidence of educational history, adaptive behavior, social and cultural background or health history for these factors to have been utilized in placement.

Since the appellant has not shown that these findings are clearly erroneous, we affirm the district court's holding that the defendants violated the provisions of the Rehabilitation Act and the Education For

All Handicapped Children Act (1) by not insuring that the tests were validated for the specific purpose for which they are used, and (2) by not using the variety of statutorily mandated evaluation tools.

* * *

CHAPMAN v. CA DEPT. OF EDUCATION

229 F.Supp.2d 981 (N.D. Cal. 2002).

BREYER, DISTRICT JUDGE.

Plaintiffs seek a preliminary injunction to halt the administration of the California High School Exit Exam ("CAHSEE") currently scheduled for March 5, 6, and 7, 2002. As an alternative, plaintiffs propose making the CAHSEE voluntary for all students. As set forth below, the Court concludes that plaintiffs have shown that preliminary relief is warranted. Absent a court order, the March administration of the CAHSEE is likely to violate rights guaranteed to learning disabled students under federal law. However, the scope of relief prayed for is not warranted. The Court has crafted an injunction that protects the rights of learning disabled students without derailing the State of California's efforts to improve education in the State.

BACKGROUND

The CAHSEE was administered to freshmen in the class of 2004 on a voluntary basis in March 2001. On March 5, 6, and 7 of this year, the CAHSEE will be administered on a mandatory basis to all members of the class of 2004 (sophomores) who have not already passed the exam. Under current California law, members of the class of 2004 are required to pass the CAHSEE to receive a diploma.

The plaintiff class consists of learning disabled students eligible for either an Individualized Education Program ("IEP") pursuant to the Individuals with Disabilities Education Act ("IDEA"), or a Section 504 Education Plan ("504 Plan") pursuant to the Rehabilitation Act of 1973. These plans, created by a team consisting of the student (where appropriate), parents, educators, and other professionals, are the blueprints of a learning disabled child's education. They assess the current performance of a child, set annual goals, and specify special education and related services a child is to receive.

Federal regulations require the IEP to specifically address state-wide assessments such as the CAHSEE. Where the IEP team determines that a child cannot participate in a particular state-wide assessment, even with modifications, the IEP must include a statement of why the state-wide assessment is not appropriate and how the child will be assessed. The evidence before the Court, however, suggests that, with regard to the CAHSEE, most IEP teams have not had time to comply with these provisions.

IEPs in California do address other testing situations. For example, pursuant to their IEPs, the named plaintiffs take classroom tests with certain accommodations. Chapman uses a laptop computer. Smiley uses a calculator and a laptop computer and has his tests presented orally. Lyons is permitted to use a spell checker, a calculator, a computer, a scanner, and a tape recorder. Among other matters, this order addresses the extent to which similar accommodations are appropriate for the CAHSEE.

DISCUSSION

Plaintiffs claim that a preliminary injunction is warranted on five independent grounds: 1) there is no alternate assessment to the CAHSEE, 2) required accommodations are not provided to learning disabled students taking the CAHSEE, 3) the test violates due process because it covers materials that students have had no opportunity to learn, 4) the test is invalid, and 5) the CAHSEE fails to conform to nationally recognized standards.

As set forth below, the Court concludes that a limited preliminary injunction is warranted. * * *

I. LEGAL STANDARD

Traditionally, a preliminary injunction will issue where the plaintiff shows: 1) a likelihood of success on the merits, 2) the possibility of irreparable injury, 3) a balance of hardships favoring the plaintiff, and 4) that preliminary relief is in the public interest. * * * This test has evolved into the modern test that the plaintiff must "demonstrate either (1) a combination of probable success on the merits and the possibility of irreparable injury if relief is not granted, or (2) the existence of serious questions going to the merits and that the balance of hardships tips sharply in its favor." * * *

II. EDUCATION POLICY GENERALLY

The Court notes at the outset that the State of California is afforded broad latitude in crafting public education policy and setting standards for students and educators. *See* San Antonio Independent School Dist. v. Rodriguez, 411 U.S. 1, 42–43, 93 S. Ct. 1278, 1301–03 (1973); * * * Debra P. v. Turlington, 644 F.2d 397 (5th Cir. 1981). Respecting the state's role in education policy under our system of federalism, this Court "will interfere with educational policy decisions only when necessary to protect individual statutory or constitutional rights." Accordingly any relief must be "narrowly tailored to enforce federal constitutional and statutory law only."

III. LIKELIHOOD OF SUCCESS

* * *

E. *Accommodation*

The question of accommodation on the CAHSEE is substantially confused by the tendency to conflate two separate and distinct issues.

The first issue is what accommodations and/or modifications are students entitled to when actually taking the CAHSEE. The second distinct issue is whether federal law requires the State to treat scores achieved with certain accommodations and/or modifications the same way it treats scores achieved by students without accommodation and/or modification. With the CAHSEE only days away, the Court must address the first issue now. No similar urgency requires an answer to the second issue. Any benefit to an immediate answer to the question of what the State must do with the test scores is outweighed by the benefit of extra time to brief and deliberate the issue fully.

With the understanding that the Court is focused on the issue of what accommodations must be permitted in actually taking the test, the starting point is again the language of the IDEA which provides:

> Children with disabilities are included in general State and district-wide assessment programs, with appropriate accommodations, where necessary. As appropriate, the State or local educational agency, 20 U.S.C. § 1412(a)(17)(A).

The regulations contain similar language:

> Children with disabilities are included in general State and district-wide assessment programs, with appropriate accommodations and modifications in administration, if necessary. 34 C.F.R. § 300.138.

In defining "appropriate accommodations" under the IDEA the most logical place to look would be to a student's IEP or 504 plan. However, the IDEA does not explicitly incorporate this definition, and there is some limited authority suggesting that the definitions are not identical.

* * *

The Court finds a U.S. Department of Education memorandum, from the Office of Special Education Programs, entitled "Guidance on Including Students with Disabilities in Assessment Programs," more persuasive in construing the accommodations requirement of the IDEA. In discussing design of IEP plans, the memorandum states:

> IDEA gives the IEP team the authority to determine what, if any, accommodations or modifications are needed in order for a child with a disability to participate in an assessment. However, state and local school agencies have the authority to determine how test scores are reported and used, and the may limit the use of test scores if certain accommodations or modifications are involved.

As this memo suggests, an "appropriate accommodation" under the IDEA is one necessary to access the test. In the context of the CAHSEE therefore, an "appropriate accommodation" is any accommodation necessary to render a student's score on the CAHSEE a meaningful measure of that student's academic achievement. The determination of what specific accommodations are appropriate for any specific student is ultimately best left to the IEP and Section 504 process.

The Court's preliminary judgment is that the Department of Education memorandum best reconciles a state's wide discretion to set and implement education policy with the IDEA's basic mandate that all students be accorded meaningful participation in any state-wide assessment programs. The state must permit accommodations necessary for a student to access a state-wide assessment such as the CAHSEE. This way a student's score provides a meaningful measure of achievement. This type of feedback when measured against clearly articulated standards helps hold educators accountable for teaching all students—a key goal of the IDEA. The feedback is also valuable to students and parents.

At the same time, a state may set specific standards and require any student seeking a diploma to satisfy them. Of course, federal law places some limits on a state's discretion to set educational standards. Those limits are not set today. By requiring all appropriate accommodations, the IDEA does not interfere with the state's prerogative to set these standards; it merely ensures that the state is held to account for its efforts in helping all students meet them.

    * * *

G. Conclusion

The Court concludes that plaintiffs have shown they are likely to prevail on [the claim] * * * that the IDEA requires school districts to permit students to take the CAHSEE with appropriate accommodations.

    * * *

IV. POSSIBILITY OF IRREPARABLE INJURY

As stated above, administration of the CAHSEE threatens to violate specific statutory rights of learning disabled students. Regardless of how the CAHSEE scores are used, the plaintiffs have a right to participate meaningfully in the assessment provided by the CAHSEE. As stated above, it appears that administration of the CAHSEE will violate this right. Furthermore, because the receipt of a diploma is conditioned upon passage of the CAHSEE, administration of the CAHSEE without protections plaintiffs may be entitled to under federal law could effectively deny plaintiffs an opportunity to receive a diploma.

Both of these injuries, one probable and the other possible, implicate a dignity interest in full participation in the educational process. Harm to a student's dignity and educational prospects constitutes irreparable injury.

V. BALANCE OF HARDSHIPS/SCOPE OF RELIEF

Because plaintiffs have shown a likelihood of success on the merits and the possibility of irreparable harm, preliminary relief is warranted. Having made this showing, however, the scope of relief remains to be determined. Only a small portion of students scheduled to take the CAHSEE in March are members of the plaintiff class.

As stated above, the State is afforded wide discretion in crafting education policy and setting standards. The Court will not second guess the judgment of the State of California that the CAHSEE is a vital component of a standards-based reform effort. Indeed, California is not alone in this judgment. Twenty-seven states have high school exit exams. Indeed the IDEA itself expresses the opinion that learning disabled students can benefit from higher expectations and standards.

* * *

Because education is a core state function, relief from this Court must be "narrowly tailored" and constrain a state's actions only where necessary to protect the individual rights of the class members.

CONCLUSION

Therefore, the Court ORDERS as follows:

(1) Students shall be permitted to take the CAHSEE with any accommodations or modifications[2] their IEP or Section 504 plan specifically provides for the CAHSEE. If a student's IEP or Section 504 plan does not address the CAHSEE specifically, the student shall be permitted to take the CAHSEE with any accommodations or modifications their IEP or Section 504 plan provides for standardized testing. If a student's IEP or Section 504 plan does not address either the CAHSEE specifically or standardized testing generally, the student shall be permitted to take the CAHSEE with any accommodations or modifications their IEP or Section 504 plan provides for general classroom testing.[3]

(2) A student may choose to forego any accommodation or modification to which he or she is entitled under this Order.

* * *

(6) In order for a student covered by this Order to avail himself or herself of any rights under this Order, no additional IEP or Section 504 team meeting shall be necessary.

(7) Nothing in this Order shall be interpreted to prevent the State from continuing to develop its regulations and policies regarding the CAHSEE.

* * *

(9) As stated above, the Court reserves for future consideration the issues of whether, and to what extent, the State may treat

2. California has defined an "accommodation" as a change in the CAHSEE (in format, student response, timing, or other attribute) that does not invalidate the score achieved. California has defined a "modification" as a change in the CAHSEE that invalidates the test score because it fundamentally alters what the test measures.

3. The plaintiff class consists of all students eligible for an IEP or Section 504 plan. This order, however, provides relief only to students with such a plan. The Court finds the practical difficulties of providing relief to the entire class insurmountable. Furthermore, states are already under an affirmative obligation to identify students needing special education and related services. Of course, the Court expects those efforts to continue.

students taking the CAHSEE with an unapproved modification or given an alternate assessment differently from other students with respect to the granting of a diploma.

* * *

IT IS SO ORDERED.

5. PROVIDING SUPPORT FOR STUDENTS WITH DISABILITIES IN HIGHER EDUCATION

SOUTHEASTERN CMTY. COLL. v. DAVIS
442 U.S. 397, 99 S.Ct. 2361 (1979).

MR. JUSTICE POWELL delivered the opinion of the Court.

This case presents a matter of first impression for this Court: Whether § 504 of the Rehabilitation Act of 1973, which prohibits discrimination against an "otherwise qualified handicapped individual" in federally funded programs "solely by reason of his handicap," forbids professional schools from imposing physical qualifications for admission to their clinical training programs.

I

Respondent, who suffers from a serious hearing disability, seeks to be trained as a registered nurse. During the 1973–1974 academic year she was enrolled in the College Parallel program of Southeastern Community College, a state institution that receives federal funds. Respondent hoped to progress to Southeastern's Associate Degree Nursing program, completion of which would make her eligible for state certification as a registered nurse. In the course of her application to the nursing program, she was interviewed by a member of the nursing faculty. It became apparent that respondent had difficulty understanding questions asked, and on inquiry she acknowledged a history of hearing problems and dependence on a hearing aid. She was advised to consult an audiologist.

On the basis of an examination at Duke University Medical Center, respondent was diagnosed as having a "bilateral, sensori-neural hearing loss." A change in her hearing aid was recommended, as a result of which it was expected that she would be able to detect sounds "almost as well as a person would who has normal hearing." But this improvement would not mean that she could discriminate among sounds sufficiently to understand normal spoken speech. Her lipreading skills would remain necessary for effective communication: "While wearing the hearing aid, she is well aware of gross sounds occurring in the listening environment. However, she can only be responsible for speech spoken to her, when the talker gets her attention and allows her to look directly at the talker."

Southeastern next consulted Mary McRee, Executive Director of the North Carolina Board of Nursing. On the basis of the audiologist's report, McRee recommended that respondent not be admitted to the nursing program. In McRee's view, respondent's hearing disability made it unsafe for her to practice as a nurse. In addition, it would be impossible for respondent to participate safely in the normal clinical training program, and those modifications that would be necessary to enable safe participation would prevent her from realizing the benefits of the program: "To adjust patient learning experiences in keeping with [respondent's] hearing limitations could, in fact, be the same as denying her full learning to meet the objectives of your nursing programs."

After respondent was notified that she was not qualified for nursing study because of her hearing disability, she requested reconsideration of the decision. The entire nursing staff of Southeastern was assembled, and McRee again was consulted. McRee repeated her conclusion that on the basis of the available evidence, respondent "has hearing limitations which could interfere with her safely caring for patients." Upon further deliberation, the staff voted to deny respondent admission.

Respondent then filed suit in the United States District Court for the Eastern District of North Carolina, alleging both a violation of § 504 of the Rehabilitation Act of 1973, 87 Stat. 394, as amended, 29 U.S.C. § 794 (1976 ed., Supp. II),[2] and a denial of equal protection and due process. After a bench trial, the District Court entered judgment in favor of Southeastern. It confirmed the findings of the audiologist that even with a hearing aid respondent cannot understand speech directed to her except through lipreading, and further found:

> [I]n many situations such as an operation room intensive care unit, or post-natal care unit, all doctors and nurses wear surgical masks which would make lip reading impossible. Additionally, in many situations a Registered Nurse would be required to instantly follow the physician's instructions concerning procurement of various types of instruments and drugs where the physician would be unable to get the nurse's attention by other than vocal means.

Accordingly, the court concluded:

> [Respondent's] handicap actually prevents her from safely performing in both her training program and her proposed profession. The trial testimony indicated numerous situations where [respondent's] particular disability would render her unable to function properly. Of particular concern to the court in this case is the potential of danger to future patients in such situations.

Based on these findings, the District Court concluded that respondent was not an "otherwise qualified handicapped individual" protected against discrimination by § 504. In its view, "[o]therwise qualified, can only be read to mean otherwise able to function sufficiently in the position sought in spite of the handicap, if proper training and facilities

---

2. The statute, as set forth in 29 U.S.C. § 794 (1976 ed., Supp. II), provides in full:
No otherwise qualified handicapped individual in the United States, as defined in section 706(7) of this title, shall, solely by reason of his handicap, be excluded from the participation in, be denied the benefits of, or be subjected to discrimination under any program or activity receiving Federal financial assistance * * *

are suitable and available." Because respondent's disability would prevent her from functioning "sufficiently" in Southeastern's nursing program, the court held that the decision to exclude her was not discriminatory within the meaning of § 504.[3]

On appeal, the Court of Appeals for the Fourth Circuit reversed. It did not dispute the District Court's findings of fact, but held that the court had misconstrued § 504. In light of administrative regulations that had been promulgated while the appeal was pending, the appellate court believed that § 504 required Southeastern to "reconsider plaintiff's application for admission to the nursing program without regard to her hearing ability." It concluded that the District Court had erred in taking respondent's handicap into account in determining whether she was "otherwise qualified" for the program, rather than confining its inquiry to her "academic and technical qualifications." The Court of Appeals also suggested that § 504 required "affirmative conduct" on the part of Southeastern to modify its program to accommodate the disabilities of applicants, "even when such modifications become expensive."

Because of the importance of this issue to the many institutions covered by § 504, we granted certiorari. We now reverse.

II

As previously noted, this is the first case in which this Court has been called upon to interpret § 504. It is elementary that "[t]he starting point in every case involving construction of a statute is the language itself." Section 504 by its terms does not compel educational institutions to disregard the disabilities of handicapped individuals or to make substantial modifications in their programs to allow disabled persons to participate. Instead, it requires only that an "otherwise qualified handicapped individual" not be excluded from participation in a federally funded program "solely by reason of his handicap," indicating only that mere possession of a handicap is not a permissible ground for assuming an inability to function in a particular context.[6]

---

3. The District Court also dismissed respondent's constitutional claims. The Court of Appeals affirmed that portion of the order, and respondent has not sought review of this ruling.

6. The Act defines "handicapped individual" as follows:

The term "handicapped individual" means any individual who (A) has a physical or mental disability which for such individual constitutes or results in a substantial handicap to employment and (B) can reasonably be expected to benefit in terms of employability from vocational rehabilitation services provided pursuant to subchapters I and III of this chapter. For the purposes of subchapters IV and V of this chapter, such term means any person who (A) has a physical or mental

impairment which substantially limits one or more of such person's major life activities, (B) has a record of such an impairment, or (C) is regarded as having such an impairment.

§ 7(6) of the Rehabilitation Act of 1973, 87 Stat. 361, *as amended*, 88 Stat. 1619, 89 Stat. 2–5, 29 U.S.C. § 706(6). This definition comports with our understanding of § 504. A person who has a record of, or is regarded as having, an impairment may at present have no actual incapacity at all. Such a person would be exactly the kind of individual who could be "otherwise qualified" to participate in covered programs. And a person who suffers from a limiting physical or mental impairment still may possess other abilities that permit him to meet the requirements of various programs.

* * * We think the understanding of the District Court is closer to the plain meaning of the statutory language. An otherwise qualified person is one who is able to meet all of a program's requirements in spite of his handicap.

The regulations promulgated by the Department of HEW to interpret § 504 reinforce, rather than contradict, this conclusion. * * *

III

The remaining question is whether the physical qualifications Southeastern demanded of respondent might not be necessary for participation in its nursing program. It is not open to dispute that, as Southeastern's Associate Degree Nursing program currently is constituted, the ability to understand speech without reliance on lipreading is necessary for patient safety during the clinical phase of the program. As the District Court found, this ability also is indispensable for many of the functions that a registered nurse performs.

Respondent contends nevertheless that § 504, properly interpreted, compels Southeastern to undertake affirmative action that would dispense with the need for effective oral communication. First, it is suggested that respondent can be given individual supervision by faculty members whenever she attends patients directly. Moreover, certain required courses might be dispensed with altogether for respondent. It is not necessary, she argues, that Southeastern train her to undertake all the tasks a registered nurse is licensed to perform. Rather, it is sufficient to make § 504 applicable if respondent might be able to perform satisfactorily some of the duties of a registered nurse or to hold some of the positions available to a registered nurse.[8]

Respondent finds support for this argument in portions of the HEW regulations discussed above. In particular, a provision applicable to postsecondary educational programs requires covered institutions to make "modifications" in their programs to accommodate handicapped persons, and to provide "auxiliary aids" such as sign-language interpreters. Respondent argues that this regulation imposes an obligation to

Thus, it is clear that Congress included among the class of "handicapped" persons covered by § 504 a range of individuals who could be "otherwise qualified." *See* S. Rep. No. 93–1297, at 38–39 (1974); U.S.Code Cong. & Admin.News, at 6373.

8. The court below adopted a portion of this argument:

[Respondent's] ability to read lips aids her in overcoming her hearing disability; however, it was argued that in certain situations such as in an operating room environment where surgical masks are used, this ability would be unavailing to her.

Be that as it may, in the medical community, there does appear to be a number of

settings in which the plaintiff could perform satisfactorily as an RN, such as in industry or perhaps a physician's office. Certainly [respondent] could be viewed as possessing extraordinary insight into the medical and emotional needs of those with hearing disabilities.

If [respondent] meets all the other criteria for admission in the pursuit of her RN career, under the relevant North Carolina statutes, it should not be foreclosed to her simply because she may not be able to function effectively in all the roles which registered nurses may choose for their careers.

574 F.2d 1158, 1161 n.6 (1978).

ensure full participation in covered programs by handicapped individuals and, in particular, requires Southeastern to make the kind of adjustments that would be necessary to permit her safe participation in the nursing program.

We note first that on the present record it appears unlikely respondent could benefit from any affirmative action that the regulation reasonably could be interpreted as requiring. Section 84.44(d)(2), for example, explicitly excludes "devices or services of a personal nature" from the kinds of auxiliary aids a school must provide a handicapped individual. Yet the only evidence in the record indicates that nothing less than close, individual attention by a nursing instructor would be sufficient to ensure patient safety if respondent took part in the clinical phase of the nursing program. Furthermore, it also is reasonably clear that § 84.44(a) does not encompass the kind of curricular changes that would be necessary to accommodate respondent in the nursing program. In light of respondent's inability to function in clinical courses without close supervision, Southeastern, with prudence, could allow her to take only academic classes. Whatever benefits respondent might realize from such a course of study, she would not receive even a rough equivalent of the training a nursing program normally gives. Such a fundamental alteration in the nature of a program is far more than the "modification" the regulation requires.

Moreover, an interpretation of the regulations that required the extensive modifications necessary to include respondent in the nursing program would raise grave doubts about their validity. If these regulations were to require substantial adjustments in existing programs beyond those necessary to eliminate discrimination against otherwise qualified individuals, they would do more than clarify the meaning of § 504. Instead, they would constitute an unauthorized extension of the obligations imposed by that statute.

The language and structure of the Rehabilitation Act of 1973 reflect a recognition by Congress of the distinction between the evenhanded treatment of qualified handicapped persons and affirmative efforts to overcome the disabilities caused by handicaps. Section 501(b), governing the employment of handicapped individuals by the Federal Government, requires each federal agency to submit "an affirmative action program plan for the hiring, placement, and advancement of handicapped individuals. . . ." These plans "shall include a description of the extent to which and methods whereby the special needs of handicapped employees are being met." Similarly, § 503(a), governing hiring by federal contractors, requires employers to "take affirmative action to employ and advance in employment qualified handicapped individuals. . . ." The President is required to promulgate regulations to enforce this section.

Under § 501(c) of the Act, by contrast, state agencies such as Southeastern are only "encourage[d] . . . to adopt and implement such policies and procedures." Section 504 does not refer at all to affirmative action, and except as it applies to federal employers it does not provide for implementation by administrative action. A comparison of these provisions demonstrates that Congress understood accommodation of the needs of handicapped individuals may require affirmative action and knew how to provide for it in those instances where it wished to do so.

Although an agency's interpretation of the statute under which it operates is entitled to some deference, "this deference is constrained by our obligation to honor the clear meaning of a statute, as revealed by its language, purpose, and history." Here, neither the language, purpose, nor history of § 504 reveals an intent to impose an affirmative-action obligation on all recipients of federal funds. Accordingly, we hold that even if HEW has attempted to create such an obligation itself, it lacks the authority to do so.

IV

We do not suggest that the line between a lawful refusal to extend affirmative action and illegal discrimination against handicapped persons always will be clear. It is possible to envision situations where an insistence on continuing past requirements and practices might arbitrarily deprive genuinely qualified handicapped persons of the opportunity to participate in a covered program. Technological advances can be expected to enhance opportunities to rehabilitate the handicapped or otherwise to qualify them for some useful employment. Such advances also may enable attainment of these goals without imposing undue financial and administrative burdens upon a State. Thus, situations may arise where a refusal to modify an existing program might become unreasonable and discriminatory. Identification of those instances where a refusal to accommodate the needs of a disabled person amounts to discrimination against the handicapped continues to be an important responsibility of HEW.

In this case, however, it is clear that Southeastern's unwillingness to make major adjustments in its nursing program does not constitute such discrimination. The uncontroverted testimony of several members of Southeastern's staff and faculty established that the purpose of its program was to train persons who could serve the nursing profession in all customary ways. This type of purpose, far from reflecting any animus against handicapped individuals is shared by many if not most of the institutions that train persons to render professional service. It is undisputed that respondent could not participate in Southeastern's nursing program unless the standards were substantially lowered. Section 504 imposes no requirement upon an educational institution to lower or to effect substantial modifications of standards to accommodate a handicapped person.

One may admire respondent's desire and determination to overcome her handicap, and there well may be various other types of service for which she can qualify. In this case, however, we hold that there was no violation of § 504 when Southeastern concluded that respondent did not qualify for admission to its program. Nothing in the language or history of § 504 reflects an intention to limit the freedom of an educational institution to require reasonable physical qualifications for admission to a clinical training program. Nor has there been any showing in this case that any action short of a substantial change in Southeastern's program would render unreasonable the qualifications it imposed.

V

Accordingly, we reverse the judgment of the court below, and remand for proceedings consistent with this opinion.

So ordered.

ZUKLE v. REGENTS OF THE UNIV. OF CAL.

166 F.3d 1041 (9th Cir. 1999).

O'SCANNLAIN, CIRCUIT JUDGE:

We must decide whether a medical school violated the Americans with Disabilities Act or the Rehabilitation Act when it dismissed a learning disabled student for failure to meet the school's academic standards.

I

Sherrie Lynn Zukle entered the University of California, Davis School of Medicine ("Medical School") in the fall of 1991 for a four year course of study. The first two years comprise the "basic science" or "pre-clinical" curriculum, consisting of courses in the function, design and processes of the human body. The final two years comprise the "clinical curriculum." In the third year, students take six consecutive eight-week clinical clerkships. During the fourth year, students complete clerkships of varying lengths in more advanced areas. Most clerkships involve treating patients in hospitals or clinics, and oral and written exams.

From the beginning, Zukle experienced academic difficulty. During her first quarter, she received "Y" grades in Anatomy and Biochemistry.[1] Upon reexamination, her Biochemistry grade was converted to a "D." She did not convert her Anatomy grade at that time. In her second quarter, she received a "Y" grade in Human Physiology, which she converted to a "D" upon reexamination.

In April 1992, the Medical School referred Zukle to the Student Evaluation Committee ("SEC"). Although subject to dismissal pursuant to the Medical School's bylaws, Zukle was allowed to remain in school. The SEC (1) placed Zukle on academic probation, (2) required her to retake Anatomy and Biochemistry, (3) required her to be tested for a

---

1. The Medical School assigns letter grades of A, B, C, D, F, I and Y to measure academic performance. A "Y" grade in a pre-clinical course is provisional; it means that a student has earned a failing grade but will be or has been permitted to retake the exam. However, a "Y" grade in a clinical clerkship indicates unsatisfactory performance in a major portion of that clerkship and may not be converted until the student repeats that portion of the clerkship.

learning disability, and (4) placed her on a "split curriculum," meaning that she was given three years to complete the pre-clinical program, instead of the usual two years. Zukle continued to experience academic difficulty. For the spring quarter of 1992 (while on academic probation) she received a "Y" grade in Neurobiology. In the fall, she received a "Y" grade in Medical Microbiology and in the winter she received a "Y" in Principles of Pharmacology. In total, Zukle received eight "Y" grades during the pre-clinical portion of her studies. Five were converted to "C" after reexamination, two to "D" and one to "F."

In November 1992, Zukle was tested for a learning disability. The results received in January 1993, revealed that Zukle suffered from a reading disability which "affects visual processing as it relates to reading comprehension and rate when under timed constraints." In short, it takes Zukle longer to read and to absorb information than the average person.[5] Zukle asked Christine O'Dell, Coordinator of the University's Learning Disability Resource Center, to inform the Medical School of her test results in mid-July 1993. O'Dell informed Gail Currie of the Office of Student Affairs in a letter dated July 21, 1993. O'Dell recommended that the Medical School make various accommodations for Zukle's disability and recommended various techniques for Zukle to try to increase her reading comprehension. The Medical School offered all of these accommodations to Zukle.

After completing the pre-clinical portion of Medical School, Zukle took the United States Medical Licensing Exam, Part I ("USMLE") in June 1994. Shortly thereafter, she began her first clinical clerkship, OB–GYN. During this clerkship, Zukle learned that she had failed the USLME.[6] The Medical School allowed Zukle to interrupt her OB–GYN clerkship to take a six-week review course to prepare to retake the USMLE, for which the Medical School paid.

Before leaving school to take the USMLE review course offered in southern California, Zukle asked Donal A. Walsh, the Associate Dean of Curricular Affairs, if she could rearrange her clerkship schedule. At this point, Zukle had completed the first half of her OB–GYN clerkship. She asked Dean Walsh if, instead of completing the second half of her OB–GYN clerkship upon return from retaking the USMLE, she could start the first half of a Family Practice Clerkship, and then repeat the OB–GYN clerkship in its entirety at a later date. Zukle testified that she made this request because she was concerned about how far behind she would be when she returned from the USMLE review course. She further asserted that she thought that if she started the Family Practice clerkship (which apparently requires less reading than the OB–GYN clerkship), she would be able to read for her upcoming Medicine clerkship at night. Zukle testified that Dean Walsh, and several other faculty members, including the Instructor of Record for Family Practice and the

---

5. Under timed conditions, Zukle's reading comprehension is in the 2nd percentile, whereas when untimed her comprehension is in the 83rd percentile.

6. Zukle's score placed her in the 5th percentile nationally.

Instructor of Record for OB–GYN, initially approved her request. Later, however, Dean Walsh denied Zukle's request and informed her that she had to complete the OB–GYN clerkship before beginning another clerkship.

In September 1994, Zukle took and passed the USMLE on her second attempt.[7] She returned to the Medical School and finished her OB–GYN clerkship. Without requesting any accommodations, she began her Medicine clerkship. During this clerkship, she learned that she had earned a "Y" grade in her OB–GYN clerkship. Because of this grade, Zukle was automatically placed back on academic probation.[8]

Two weeks before the Medicine written exam, Zukle contacted her advisor, Dr. Joseph Silva, and expressed concern that she had not completed the required reading. Dr. Silva offered to speak with Dr. Ruth Lawrence, the Medicine Instructor of Record, on Zukle's behalf. According to Zukle, she then spoke with Dr. Lawrence in person and requested time off from the clerkship to prepare for the exam. Dr. Lawrence denied Zukle's request. Zukle passed the written exam, but failed the Medicine clerkship because of unsatisfactory clinical performance. On Zukle's grade sheet, Dr. Lawrence rated Zukle as unsatisfactory in clinical problem solving skills; data acquisition, organization and recording; and skill/ability at oral presentations. Dr. Lawrence also reported negative comments from the people who worked with Zukle during the clerkship. Because Zukle had earned a failing grade while on academic probation, she was again subject to dismissal pursuant to the Medical School's bylaws.

On January 13, 1995, Zukle appeared before the SEC. The SEC recommended that Zukle (1) drop her current clerkship, Pediatrics; (2) start reviewing for the OB–GYN exam, and retake it; (3) repeat the Medicine clerkship in its entirety; (4) obtain the approval of the SEC before enrolling in any more clerkships; and (5) remain on academic probation for the rest of her medical school career.

On January 17, 1995, the Promotions Board met to consider Zukle's case. The Promotions Board voted to dismiss Zukle from the Medical School for "failure to meet the academic standards of the School of Medicine." According to Dr. Lewis, who was a member of the Promotions Board and was present when it reached its decision, "the Promotions Board considered Plaintiff's academic performance throughout her tenure at the medical school and determined that it demonstrated an incapacity to develop or use the skills and knowledge required to competently practice medicine."

7. Zukle's score placed her in the 9th percentile nationally.

8. The Promotions Board had voted to remove Zukle from academic probation in October 1994. At that time, it was unaware of her OB–GYN clerkship grade. The Medical School's bylaws provide that a student who receives a "Y" grade in her third or fourth years is automatically placed on academic probation at the time of receipt of the grade.

The Board on Student Dismissal voted unanimously to uphold the Promotions Board's decision of dismissal.

On January 22, 1996, Zukle filed a complaint in federal district court for damages and injunctive relief against the Regents of the University of California ("Regents"). The complaint alleged discrimination based on disability, sex and race, and sexual harassment. On June 6, 1997, the Regents filed a motion for summary judgment. The district court entered its Memorandum of Opinion and Order on August 7, 1997, granting summary judgment to The Regents on all of Zukle's claims. The court found that Zukle's "race, sex, and sexual harassment claims are unsupported by the record and do not merit discussion." On Zukle's Americans with Disabilities Act ("ADA") and Rehabilitation Act claims, the district court found that "[b]ecause the evidence before the court shows that Zukle could not meet the minimum standards of the UCD School of Medicine with reasonable accommodation, she is not an otherwise qualified individual with a disability under the Rehabilitation Act or the ADA."

Zukle timely appeals from the district court's grant of summary judgment on her ADA and Rehabilitation Act claims.

II

Zukle claims that she was dismissed from the Medical School in violation of Title II of the ADA and section 504 of the Rehabilitation Act. Title II of the ADA provides, in relevant part:

> no qualified individual with a disability shall, by reason of such disability, be excluded from participation in or be denied the benefits of the services, programs, or activities of a public entity, or be subjected to discrimination by any such entity. 42 U.S.C. § 12132.

Title II prohibits discrimination by state and local agencies, which includes publicly funded institutions of higher education.

Title II of the ADA was expressly modeled after Section 504 of the Rehabilitation Act, which provides:

> No otherwise qualified individual with a disability . . . shall, solely by reason of her or his disability, be excluded from the participation in, be denied the benefits of, or be subjected to discrimination under any program or activity receiving Federal financial assistance. . . . 29 U.S.C. § 794.

To make out a prima facie case under either the ADA or Rehabilitation Act Zukle must show that (1) she is disabled under the Act; (2) she is "otherwise qualified" to remain a student at the Medical School, i.e., she can meet the essential eligibility requirements of the school, with or without reasonable accommodation; (3) she was dismissed solely because of her disability; and (4) the Medical School receives federal financial assistance (for the Rehabilitation Act claim), or is a public entity (for the ADA claim).[11]

The Regents do not dispute that Zukle is disabled and that the Medical School receives federal financial assistance and is a public entity. The Regents argue, however, that Zukle was not "otherwise qualified" to remain at the Medical School. Zukle responds that she *was* "otherwise qualified" with the aid of reasonable accommodations and that the Medical School failed reasonably to accommodate her.

A

The ADA defines a "qualified individual with a disability" as one who "meets the essential eligibility requirements ... for participation in [a given] program[ ] provided by a public entity" *"with or without reasonable modifications* to rules, policies, or practices...." 42 U.S.C. § 12131(2) (emphasis added); *accord* Southeastern Community College v. Davis, 442 U.S. 397, 406, 99 S. Ct. 2361, (1979) (holding that under the Rehabilitation Act, an otherwise qualified individual is "one who is able to meet all of a program's requirements in spite of his handicap"). In the school context, the implementing regulations of the Rehabilitation Act define an otherwise qualified individual as an individual who, although disabled, "meets the academic and technical standards requisite to admission or participation in the [school's] education program or activity."

However, under Rehabilitation Act regulations, educational institutions are required to provide a disabled student with reasonable accommodations to ensure that the institution's requirements do not discriminate on the basis of the student's disability. Similarly, the ADA's implementing regulations require a public entity to "make reasonable modifications in policies, practices, or procedures when the modifications are necessary to avoid discrimination on the basis of disability, unless the public entity can demonstrate that making the modifications would fundamentally alter the nature of the services, program, or activity." The Supreme Court has made clear that an educational institution is not required to make fundamental or substantial modifications to its program or standards; it need only make reasonable ones.

* * *

C

* * *

We agree with the First, Second and Fifth circuits that an educational institution's academic decisions are entitled to deference. Thus, while we recognize that the ultimate determination of whether an individual is otherwise qualified must be made by the court, we will extend judicial deference "to the evaluation made by the institution

---

11. There is no significant difference in analysis of the rights and obligations created by the ADA and the Rehabilitation Act. *See* 42 U.S.C. § 12133 ("The remedies, pro- cedures, and rights set forth in [the Reha- bilitation Act] shall be the remedies, proce- dures, and rights [applicable to ADA claims].") * * *

itself, absent proof that its standards and its application of them serve no purpose other than to deny an education to handicapped persons."

Deference is also appropriately accorded an educational institution's determination that a reasonable accommodation is not available. Therefore, we agree with the First Circuit that "a court's duty is to first find the basic facts, giving due deference to the school, and then to evaluate whether those facts add up to a professional, academic judgment that reasonable accommodation is not available."

We recognize that extending deference to educational institutions must not impede our obligation to enforce the ADA and the Rehabilitation Act. Thus, we must be careful not to allow academic decisions to disguise truly discriminatory requirements. The educational institution has a "real obligation . . . to seek suitable means of reasonably accommodating a handicapped person and to submit a factual record indicating that it conscientiously carried out this statutory obligation." Once the educational institution has fulfilled this obligation, however, we will defer to its academic decisions.

III

* * * [W]e now turn to the ultimate question—did Zukle establish a prima facie case of discrimination under the ADA or the Rehabilitation Act? As noted before, only the "otherwise qualified" prong of the prima facie case requirements is disputed by the parties. Zukle argues that she was otherwise qualified to remain at the Medical School, with the aid of the three accommodations she requested. The Medical School argues that Zukle's requested accommodations were not reasonable because they would have required a fundamental or substantial modification of its program.

Zukle bears the burden of pointing to the existence of a reasonable accommodation that would enable her to meet the Medical School's essential eligibility requirements. Once she meets this burden, the Medical School must show that Zukle's requested accommodation would fundamentally alter the nature of the school's program. We must determine, viewing the evidence in the light most favorable to Zukle, if there are any genuine issues of material fact with regard to the reasonableness of Zukle's requested accommodations.

We note at this stage that "[r]easonableness is not a constant. To the contrary, what is reasonable in a particular situation may not be reasonable in a different situation-even if the situational differences are relatively slight." Thus, we must evaluate Zukle's requests in light of the totality of her circumstances.

The evidence is undisputed that the Medical School offered Zukle all of the accommodations that it normally offers learning disabled students. When the Medical School first learned of Zukle's disability she was offered double time on exams, notetaking services and textbooks on audio cassettes. Further, Zukle was allowed to retake courses, proceed on a decelerated schedule and remain at the Medical School despite being subject to dismissal under the Medical School's bylaws.

Even with these accommodations, Zukle consistently failed to achieve passing grades in her courses. Though Zukle was on a decelerated schedule, she continued to receive "Y" grades in her pre-clinical years and failed the USMLE on her first attempt. Further, although she was able to remedy some of her failing grades in her pre-clinical years, she was only able to do so by retaking exams. Moreover, she received a "Y" grade in her first clinical clerkship, automatically placing her on academic probation, and an "F" in her second. Because Zukle received a failing grade while on academic probation, she was subject to dismissal pursuant to the Medical School's bylaws. Clearly, Zukle could not meet the Medical School's essential eligibility requirements without the additional accommodations she requested.

The issue, then, is whether the ADA and Rehabilitation Act required the Medical School to provide Zukle with those additional accommodations. As noted above, the Medical School was only required to provide Zukle with *reasonable* accommodations. Accordingly, we examine the reasonableness of Zukle's requested accommodations.

A

Zukle claims that the Medical School should have granted her request to modify her schedule by beginning the first half of the Family Practice Clerkship instead of finishing the second half of her OB–GYN clerkship when she returned from retaking the USMLE. She proposed that she would then begin the Medicine clerkship, and finish Family Practice and OB–GYN at a later time.

The Regents presented evidence that granting this request would require a substantial modification of its curriculum.

* * *

The facts are undisputed that no student had been allowed to rearrange their clerkship schedule as Zukle requested. Indeed, Zukle admitted in the district court that "no student has been permitted to finish an interrupted course in the fashion [she] requested because it would require substantial curricular alteration." We defer to the Medical School's academic decision to require students to complete courses once they are begun and conclude, therefore, that this requested accommodation was not reasonable.

B

Two weeks before the scheduled written exam in her Medicine clerkship, Zukle asked Dr. Silva, her advisor, if she could have more time to prepare for the exam because she was behind in the readings. Zukle testified that she specifically requested to leave the hospital early every day so that she could spend more time preparing for the written exam in Medicine. Dr. Silva and Zukle spoke with the Instructor of Record in Zukle's Medicine clerkship, Dr. Lawrence. Dr. Lawrence told Zukle that she could not excuse her from the in-hospital part of the clerkship. Dr. Lawrence testified that she denied this request because she thought that it would be unfair to the other students.

The Medical School presented uncontradicted evidence that giving Zukle reduced clinical time would have fundamentally altered the nature of the Medical School curriculum.

* * *

We defer to the Medical School's academic decision that the in-hospital portion of a clerkship is a vital part of medical education and that allowing a student to be excused from this requirement would sacrifice the integrity of its program. Thus, we conclude that neither the ADA nor the Rehabilitation Act require the Medical School to make this accommodation.

In any event, the evidence shows that Zukle was not prejudiced by the Medical School's failure to grant this accommodation because she in fact passed the Medicine written exam. Zukle's low score on the exam did not help her Medicine grade, but Zukle failed the clerkship because of her inadequate clinical performance. Indeed, as the district court stated, because Zukle was doing so poorly in the clinical portion of the clerkship, "[g]iving [her] time off from the clinical portion to study for the test[ ] could not have helped, but could only have further damaged, her already marginal clinical skills." Thus, Zukle did not establish that she would have been able to meet the Medical School's requirements with the requested accommodation.

C

Finally, after she was dismissed, Zukle requested that the *ad hoc* Board place her on a decelerated schedule during the clinical portion of her studies. Specifically, Zukle sought eight weeks off before each clerkship to read the assigned text for that clerkship in its entirety.

Zukle presented evidence that the Medical School regularly allowed students to proceed on a decelerated schedule. Indeed, Zukle herself was allowed an extra year to complete the pre-clinical curriculum. However, no student had been provided the specific accommodation that Zukle requested, *i.e.*, taking eight weeks off between clerkships. Furthermore, simply because the Medical School had granted other students' requests to proceed on a decelerated schedule, does not mean that Zukle's request was reasonable. The reasonableness of Zukle's request must be evaluated in light of Zukle's particular circumstances.

We agree with the district court that the Board's denial of Zukle's request to proceed on a decelerated schedule was a "rationally justifiable conclusion." The Board noted that, even on a decelerated schedule during the pre-clinical phase, Zukle experienced severe academic difficulties: Zukle earned deficient grades in five courses and failed the USMLE exam on her first attempt even though she had taken several pre-clinical courses twice. The Board noted that there is "a fair amount of overlap on written exams of material from second-year courses and that the clinical work overlaps with the written." In sum, the evidence makes clear that the decelerated schedule would not have aided Zukle in meeting the Medical School's academic standards. Given Zukle's unenviable academic record, allowing her to remain in Medical School on a decelerated schedule would have lowered the Medical School's academic standards, which it was not required to do to accommodate Zukle.

IV

In conclusion, we are persuaded that Zukle failed to establish that she could meet the essential eligibility requirements of the Medical School with the aid of reasonable accommodations. Accordingly, she failed to establish a prima facie case of disability discrimination under the ADA or the Rehabilitation Act.

AFFIRMED.

Chapter VIII

RELIGION AND PUBLIC EDUCATION: DETERMINING THE SHIFTING CONTOURS OF ESTABLISHMENT CLAUSE JURISPRUDENCE

This chapter provides an introduction to the interplay between religion and public education, as reflected in the development of First Amendment Establishment Clause jurisprudence. In general, public education is expected to be secular in nature, with parents having the right to send their children to private sectarian schools if they wish to provide them with an education that is religious in nature. But cases and statutes recognize numerous instances where religion-related expression and activities can in fact take place in a public educational setting. And there is an ongoing battle over boundaries in this regard.

A basic principle that appears often in both Establishment Clause and Free Exercise Clause cases over time is that the nature and extent of the religion that can be included by public officials in public sector activities is not dependent on what percentage of people may be members of a particular religion, practitioners of a particular sect or denomination, or affiliated with organized religion at all. Justice O'Connor described this principle in her analysis of the issues in the 2005 Kentucky Ten Commandments case:

> * * * The First Amendment expresses our Nation's fundamental commitment to religious liberty by means of two provisions—one protecting the free exercise of religion, the other barring establishment of religion. They were written by the descendents of people who had come to this land precisely so that they could practice their religion freely. Together with the other First Amendment guarantees—of free speech, a free press, and the rights to assemble and petition—the Religion Clauses were designed to safeguard the freedom of conscience and belief that those immigrants had sought.

They embody an idea that was once considered radical: Free people are entitled to free and diverse thoughts, which government ought neither to constrain nor to direct.

Reasonable minds can disagree about how to apply the Religion Clauses in a given case. But the goal of the Clauses is clear: to carry out the Founders' plan of preserving religious liberty to the fullest extent possible in a pluralistic society. By enforcing the Clauses, we have kept religion a matter for the individual conscience, not for the prosecutor or bureaucrat. * * *

Our guiding principle has been James Madison's—that "[t]he Religion ... of every man must be left to the conviction and conscience of every man." To that end, we have held that the guarantees of religious freedom protect citizens from religious incursions by the States as well as by the Federal Government. Government may not coerce a person into worshiping against her will, nor prohibit her from worshiping according to it. It may not prefer one religion over another or promote religion over nonbelief. It may not entangle itself with religion. And government may not, by "endorsing religion or a religious practice," "mak[e] adherence to religion relevant to a person's standing in the political community."

When we enforce these restrictions, we do so for the same reason that guided the Framers—respect for religion's special role in society. Our Founders conceived of a Republic receptive to voluntary religious expression, and provided for the possibility of judicial intervention when government action threatens or impedes such expression. Voluntary religious belief and expression may be as threatened when government takes the mantle of religion upon itself as when government directly interferes with private religious practices. When the government associates one set of religious beliefs with the state and identifies nonadherents as outsiders, it encroaches upon the individual's decision about whether and how to worship. In the marketplace of ideas, the government has vast resources and special status. Government religious expression therefore risks crowding out private observance and distorting the natural interplay between competing beliefs. Allowing government to be a potential mouthpiece for competing religious ideas risks the sort of division that might easily spill over into suppression of rival beliefs. Tying secular and religious authority together poses risks to both. * * *

It is true that many Americans find the Commandments in accord with their personal beliefs. But we do not count heads before enforcing the First Amendment. * * * Nor can we accept the theory that Americans who do not accept the Commandments' validity are outside the First Amendment's protections. There is no list of approved and disapproved beliefs appended to the First Amendment—and the Amendment's broad terms ("free exercise," "establishment," "religion") do not admit of such a cramped reading. It is true that the Framers lived at a time when our national religious diversity was neither as robust nor as well recognized as it is now. They may not have foreseen the variety of religions for which this Nation would eventually provide a home. They surely could not have predicted new religions, some of them born in this country. But they did know that line-drawing between religions is an enterprise that, once begun, has no logical stopping point. They worried that "the same authority which can establish Christianity, in exclusion of all other Religions, may establish with the same ease any particular sect of Christians, in exclusion of all other Sects." The Religion Clauses, as a result, protect adherents of all religions, as well as those who believe in no religion at all. * * * McCreary County v. ACLU, 125 S.Ct. 2722, 2746–47 (2005) (O'Connor, J., concurring).

A significant percentage of the U.S. Supreme Court's Establishment Clause cases over the past 35 years have focused on the public schools, and the seminal case of *Lemon v. Kurtzman* was itself an education-related dispute. In *Lemon,* the Court considered the constitutionality of public aid to private sectarian schools in Pennsylvania and Rhode Island, and in so doing set forth a three-part test. Under this test, a statute or policy would be violative of the Establishment Clause if any one of the following could be proven: (1) its purpose is not secular, (2) its principal/primary effect either advances or inhibits religion, or (3) it fosters an excessive entanglement with religion.

While the inquiry in *Lemon* was limited to the constitutionality of public funding for private religious education, subsequent cases began to apply the tripartite test in virtually every Establishment Clause dispute that arose. Over time, however, many came to believe that this approach was inappropriately "hostile to religion." Not only was the *Lemon* test itself ultimately modified, but additional Establishment Clause frameworks were developed, with the justices struggling to identify guidelines that would help determine which principles and frameworks to apply in what types of situations.

The broad, general framework for all Establishment Clause disputes continues to reflect a foundational inquiry into *purpose* and *effects.* This chapter thus begins with an examination of key cases, both before *Lemon* and subsequent to *Lemon,* which show the Court wrestling with this inquiry. The chapter then goes on to document the emergence of additional inquiries focusing on endorsement, coercion, and perhaps on neutrality alone. While some commentators and jurists have viewed these as components of the broader inquiry into purpose and effects, others have insisted that they stand alone as separate and independent tests.

Establishment Clause jurisprudence remains relatively unsettled, with lower courts—unsure of which frameworks and principles to apply—sometimes taking the time to conduct as many as 3–4 separate analytical inquiries in a single case decision. But multiple inquiries are not generally found in the individual opinions at the Supreme Court level. And recognizable patterns are in fact beginning to emerge. In a school setting, for example, endorsement is typically found to be an appropriate test for displays and programs. A coercion test is applied within the context of school prayer. And neutrality is arguably a central principle underlying the inquiry into public funding for private religious education.

PROBLEM 36: United Parents of Newman County v. NCUSD

Every semester, from time to time, Ms. Mayberry reads Bible stories to her second graders. These stories are children's versions of events described in the Holy Bible. To the best of anyone's recollection, this pattern has continued for at least ten years.

In early 2001, the Newman County Unified School District agrees to provide each classroom teacher with a check for $1,000, which "may be used at the teacher's individual discretion to provide additional resources to his or her classroom." As a condition of receiving this money, teachers are required to complete a simple form, documenting their expenditures and attaching receipts. An administrator at each school site is appointed to review these forms, and this review is generally *pro forma*.

Many teachers use the funds to pay for the duplication of materials that were once paid for out of their own pockets. Others use the funds for supplies. Ms. Mayberry decides to use a portion of the funds to purchase new editions of books with children's versions of Bible stories.

Every year, Ms. Mayberry turns her room into a "World's Fair" as a culminating activity for her World Religions and Culture Unit. She decides to use a portion of her funds to purchase primary religious texts, religious objects, and religious paintings to enhance the World's Fair Pavilions depicting the world's major religions.

In June 2006, after failing in their informal attempts to restrict Ms. Mayberry's activities and expenditures in this context, a coalition of Newman County parents files a lawsuit against the District, contending that the First Amendment has been violated. What arguments might be set forth under Establishment Clause jurisprudence? What result? Discuss.

A. THE EVOLVING INQUIRY INTO PURPOSE & EFFECTS

The three cases in this section show the evolution of the Court's Establishment Clause jurisprudence in particularly stark terms. In *Engel v. Vitale,* nine years before *Lemon,* one has to look very hard to discern what may be an implicit focus on purpose and effects. In *Wallace v. Jaffree,* fourteen years after *Lemon,* an arguably splintered majority appears to feel obligated to follow the rigid strictures of the traditional *Lemon* test but is also struggling to move away from its seeming rigidity. In *Agostini v. Felton,* twelve more years down the road, the Court takes the step of explicitly modifying *Lemon,* overruling two *Lemon*-era precedents on the grounds that the jurisprudence has changed, and establishing a more forgiving inquiry.

Consider the opinions of the respective justices in this context. What lessons might be discerned regarding the parameters and viability of the inquiry into purpose and effects today?

ENGEL v. VITALE

370 U.S. 421, 82 S.Ct. 1261 (1962).

MR. JUSTICE BLACK delivered the opinion of the Court.

The respondent Board of Education of Union Free School District No. 9, New Hyde Park, New York, acting in its official capacity under state law, directed the School District's principal to cause the following prayer to be said aloud by each class in the presence of a teacher at the beginning of each school day:

> Almighty God, we acknowledge our dependence upon Thee, and we beg Thy blessings upon us, our parents, our teachers and our Country.

This daily procedure was adopted on the recommendation of the State Board of Regents, a governmental agency created by the State Constitution to which the New York Legislature has granted broad supervisory, executive, and legislative powers over the State's public school system. These state officials composed the prayer which they recommended and published as a part of their "Statement on Moral and Spiritual Training in the Schools," saying: "We believe that this Statement will be subscribed to by all men and women of good will, and we call upon all of them to aid in giving life to our program."

Shortly after the practice of reciting the Regents' prayer was adopted by the School District, the parents of ten pupils brought this action in a New York State Court insisting that use of this official prayer in the public schools was contrary to the beliefs, religions, or religious practices of both themselves and their children. Among other things, these parents challenged the constitutionality of both the state law authorizing the School District to direct the use of prayer in public schools and the School District's regulation ordering the recitation of this particular prayer on the ground that these actions of official governmental agencies violate that part of the First Amendment of the Federal Constitution which commands that "Congress shall make no law respecting an establishment of religion"—a command which was "made applicable to the State of New York by the Fourteenth Amendment of the said Constitution." The New York Court of Appeals, over the dissents of Judges Dye and Fuld, sustained an order of the lower state courts which had upheld the power of New York to use the Regents' prayer as a part of the daily procedures of its public schools so long as the schools did not compel any pupil to join in the prayer over his or his parents' objection. We granted certiorari to review this important decision involving rights protected by the First and Fourteenth Amendments.

We think that by using its public school system to encourage recitation of the Regents' prayer, the State of New York has adopted a practice wholly inconsistent with the Establishment Clause. There can, of course, be no doubt that New York's program of daily classroom invocation of God's blessings as prescribed in the Regents' prayer is a religious activity. It is a solemn avowal of divine faith and supplication for the blessings of the Almighty. The nature of such a prayer has always been religious, none of the respondents has denied this and the trial court expressly so found:

> The religious nature of prayer was recognized by Jefferson and has been concurred in by theological writers, the United States Supreme Court and state courts and administrative officials, including New York's Commissioner of Education. A committee of the New York Legislature has agreed.

> The Board of Regents as amicus curiae, the respondents and intervenors all concede the religious nature of prayer, but seek to distinguish this prayer because it is based on our spiritual heritage. * * *

The petitioners contend among other things that the state laws requiring or permitting use of the Regents' prayer must be struck down as a violation of the Establishment Clause because that prayer was composed by governmental officials as a part of a governmental program to further religious beliefs. For this reason, petitioners argue, the State's use of the Regents' prayer in its public school system breaches the constitutional wall of separation between Church and State. We agree with that contention since we think that the constitutional prohibition against laws respecting an establishment of religion must at least mean that in this country it is no part of the business of government to compose official prayers for any group of the American people to recite as a part of a religious program carried on by government.

> * * *

There can be no doubt that New York's state prayer program officially establishes the religious beliefs embodied in the Regents' prayer. The respondents' argument to the contrary, which is largely based upon the contention that the Regents' prayer is "nondenominational" and the fact that the program, as modified and approved by state courts, does not require all pupils to recite the prayer but permits those who wish to do so to remain silent or be excused from the room, ignores the essential nature of the program's constitutional defects. Neither the fact that the prayer may be denominationally neutral nor the fact that its observance on the part of the students is voluntary can serve to free it from the limitations of the Establishment Clause, as it might from the Free Exercise Clause, of the First Amendment, both of which are operative against the States by virtue of the Fourteenth Amendment. Although these two clauses may in certain instances overlap, they forbid two quite different kinds of governmental encroachment upon religious freedom. The Establishment Clause, unlike the Free Exercise Clause, does not depend upon any showing of direct governmental compulsion and is violated by the enactment of laws which establish an official religion whether those laws operate directly to coerce nonobserving individuals or not. This is not to say, of course, that laws officially prescribing a particular form of religious worship do not involve coercion of such individuals. When the power, prestige and financial support of government is placed behind a particular religious belief, the indirect coercive pressure upon religious minorities to conform to the prevailing officially approved religion is plain. But the purposes underlying the Establishment Clause go much further than that. Its first and most immediate purpose rested on the belief that a union of government and religion tends to destroy government and to degrade religion. The history of governmentally established religion, both in England and in this country, showed that whenever government had allied itself with one particular form of religion, the inevitable result had been that it had incurred the hatred, disrespect and even contempt of those who held contrary beliefs. That same history showed that many people had lost their respect for any religion that had relied upon the support for government to spread its faith. The Establishment Clause thus stands as an expression of principle on the part of the Founders of our Constitution that religion is too personal, too sacred, too holy, to permit its "unhallowed perversion" by a civil magistrate. Another purpose of the Establishment Clause rested upon an awareness of the historical fact that governmentally established religions and religious persecutions go hand in hand. * * *

It has been argued that to apply the Constitution in such a way as to prohibit state laws respecting an establishment of religious services in public schools is to indicate a hostility toward religion or toward prayer. Nothing, or course, could be more wrong. The history of man is inseparable from the history of religion. And perhaps it is not too much to say that since the beginning of that history many people have devoutly believed that "More things are wrought by prayer than this world dreams of." It was doubtless largely due to men who believed this that there grew up a sentiment that caused men to leave the cross-currents of officially established state religions and religious persecution in Europe and come to this country filled with the hope that they could find a place in which they could pray when they pleased to the God of their faith in the language they chose. And there were men of this same faith in the power of prayer who led the fight for adoption of our Constitution and also for our Bill of Rights with the very guarantees of religious freedom that forbid the sort of governmental activity which New York has attempted here. These men knew that the First Amendment, which tried to put an end to governmental control of religion and of prayer, was not written to destroy either. They knew rather that it was written to quiet well-justified fears which nearly all of them felt arising out of an awareness that governments of the past had shackled men's tongues to make them speak only the religious thoughts that government wanted them to speak and to pray only to the God that government wanted them to pray to. It is neither sacrilegious nor antireligious to say that each separate government in this country should stay out of the business of writing or sanctioning official prayers and leave that purely religious function to the people themselves and to those the people choose to look to for religious guidance.[21]

* * *

The judgment of the Court of Appeals of New York is reversed and the cause remanded for further proceedings not inconsistent with this opinion.

Reversed and remanded.

Mr. Justice Douglas, concurring.

* * * First, a word as to what this case does not involve.

Plainly, our Bill of Rights would not permit a State or the Federal Government to adopt an official prayer and penalize anyone who would not utter it. This, however, is not that case, for there is no element of compulsion or coercion in New York's regulation requiring that public schools be opened each day with the following prayer:

> Almighty God, we acknowledge our dependence upon Thee, and we beg Thy blessings upon us, our parents, our teachers and our Country.

The prayer is said upon the commencement of the school day, immediately following the pledge of allegiance to the flag. The prayer is said aloud in the presence of a teacher, who either leads the recitation or selects a student to do so. No student, however, is compelled to take part. The respondents have adopted a regulation which provides that "Neither teachers nor any school authority shall comment on participation or non-participation * * * nor suggest or request that any posture or language be used or dress be worn or be not used or not worn." Provision is also made for excusing children, upon written request of a parent or guardian, from the saying of the prayer or from the room in which the prayer is said. A letter implementing and explaining this regulation has been sent to each taxpayer and parent in the school district. As I read this regulation, a child is free to stand or not stand, to recite or not recite, without fear of reprisal or even comment by the teacher or any other school official.

In short, the only one who need utter the prayer is the teacher; and no teacher is complaining of it. Students can stand mute or even leave the classroom, if they desire.

* * *

21. There is of course nothing in the decision reached here that is inconsistent with the fact that school children and others are officially encouraged to express love for our country by reciting historical documents such as the Declaration of Independence which contain references to the Deity or by singing officially espoused anthems which include the composer's professions of faith in a Supreme Being, or with the fact that there are many manifestations in our public life of belief in God. Such patriotic or ceremonial occasions bear no true resemblance to the unquestioned religious exercise that the State of New York has sponsored in this instance.

The question presented by this case is therefore an extremely narrow one. It is whether New York oversteps the bounds when it finances a religious exercise.

What New York does on the opening of its public schools is what we do when we open court. Our Crier has from the beginning announced the convening of the Court and then added "God save the United States and this Honorable Court." That utterance is a supplication, a prayer in which we, the judges, are free to join, but which we need not recite any more than the students need recite the New York prayer.

* * *

[I] cannot say that to authorize this prayer is to establish a religion in the strictly historic meaning of those words. A religion is not established in the usual sense merely by letting those who choose to do so say the prayer that the public school teacher leads. Yet once government finances a religious exercise it inserts a divisive influence into our communities. The New York Court said that the prayer given does not conform to all of the tenets of the Jewish, Unitarian, and Ethical Culture groups. One of the petitioners is an agnostic.

"We are a religious people whose institutions presuppose a Supreme Being." Under our Bill of Rights free play is given for making religion an active force in our lives.[9] But "if a religious leaven is to be worked into the affairs of our people, it is to be done by individuals and groups, not by the Government." By reason of the First Amendment government is commanded "to have no interest in theology or ritual," for on those matters "government must be neutral." The First Amendment leaves the Government in a position not of hostility to religion but of neutrality. The philosophy is that the atheist or agnostic—the nonbeliever—is entitled to go his own way. The philosophy is that if government interferes in matters spiritual, it will be a divisive force. The First Amendment teaches that a government neutral in the field of religion better serves all religious interests.

* * *

MR. JUSTICE STEWART, dissenting.

A local school board in New York has provided that those pupils who wish to do so may join in a brief prayer at the beginning of each school day, acknowledging their dependence upon God and asking His blessing upon them and upon their parents, their teachers, and their country. The Court today decides that in permitting this brief non-denominational prayer the school board has violated the Constitution of the United States. I think this decision is wrong.

9. Religion was once deemed to be a function of the public school system. The Northwest Ordinance, which antedated the First Amendment, provided in Article III that "Religion, morality, and knowledge be-ing necessary to good government and the happiness of mankind, schools and the means of education shall forever be encouraged."

The Court does not hold, nor could it, that New York has interfered with the free exercise of anybody's religion. For the state courts have made clear that those who object to reciting the prayer must be entirely free of any compulsion to do so, including any "embarrassments and pressures." *Cf. West Virginia State Board of Education v. Barnette,* 319 U.S. 624, 63 S.Ct. 1178. But the Court says that in permitting school children to say this simple prayer, the New York authorities have established "an official religion."

With all respect, I think the Court has misapplied a great constitutional principle. I cannot see how an "official religion" is established by letting those who want to say a prayer say it. On the contrary, I think that to deny the wish of these school children to join in reciting this prayer is to deny them the opportunity of sharing in the spiritual heritage of our Nation.

The Court's historical review of the quarrels over the Book of Common Prayer in England throws no light for me on the issue before us in this case. England had then and has now an established church. Equally unenlightening, I think, is the history of the early establishment and later rejection of an official church in our own States. For we deal here not with the establishment of a state church, which would, of course, be constitutionally impermissible, but with whether school children who want to begin their day by joining in prayer must be prohibited from doing so. Moreover, I think that the Court's task, in this as in all areas of constitutional adjudication, is not responsibly aided by the uncritical invocation of metaphors like the "wall of separation," a phrase nowhere to be found in the Constitution. What is relevant to the issue here is not the history of an established church in sixteenth century England or in eighteenth century America, but the history of the religious traditions of our people, reflected in countless practices of the institutions and officials of our government.

At the opening of each day's Session of this Court we stand, while one of our officials invokes the protection of God. Since the days of John Marshall our Crier has said, "God save the United States and this Honorable Court." Both the Senate and the House of Representatives open their daily Sessions with prayer. Each of our Presidents, from George Washington to John F. Kennedy, has upon assuming his Office asked the protection and help of God.[3]

The Court today says that the state and federal governments are without constitutional power to prescribe any particular form of words to

---

3. On January 20, 1961, President John F. Kennedy said:

The world is very different now. * * * And yet the same revolutionary beliefs for which our forebears fought are still at issue around the globe—the belief that the rights of man come not from the generosity of the state but from the hand of God.

* * *

With a good conscience our only sure reward, with history the final judge of our deeds, let us go forth to lead the land we love, asking His blessing and His help, but knowing that here on earth God's work must truly be our own.

be recited by any group of the American people on any subject touching religion. One of the stanzas of "The Star–Spangled Banner," made our National Anthem by Act of Congress in 1931, contains these verses:

> Blest with victory and peace, may the heav'n rescued land
> Praise the Pow'r that hath made and preserved us a nation!
> Then conquer we must, when our cause it is just,
> And this be our motto 'In God is our Trust.'

In 1954 Congress added a phrase to the Pledge of Allegiance to the Flag so that it now contains the words "one Nation under God, indivisible, with liberty and justice for all." In 1952 Congress enacted legislation calling upon the President each year to proclaim a National Day of Prayer. Since 1865 the words "IN GOD WE TRUST" have been impressed on our coins.

Countless similar examples could be listed, but there is no need to belabor the obvious. It was all summed up by this Court just ten years ago in a single sentence: "We are a religious people whose institutions presuppose a Supreme Being."

I do not believe that this Court, or the Congress, or the President has by the actions and practices I have mentioned established an "official religion" in violation of the Constitution. And I do not believe the State of New York has done so in this case. What each has done has been to recognize and to follow the deeply entrenched and highly cherished spiritual traditions of our Nation—traditions which come down to us from those who almost two hundred years ago avowed their "firm Reliance on the Protection of divine Providence" when they proclaimed the freedom and independence of this brave new world.[10]

I dissent.

Notes

1.   What evidence can be found in both Justice Black's majority opinion and Justice Douglas' concurrence that an analysis based on purpose and effects may in fact have been conducted?

2.   It is also important to note the explicit reliance in this decision on core Establishment Clause principles prohibiting coercion and requiring neutrality.

3.   One year later, the Court decided the related case of *School District of Abington Township v. Schempp,* finding unconstitutional the requirement that schools in Pennsylvania and Maryland begin each day with readings from the Bible. It is interesting to note just how united the Court was in these two cases, with Justice Stewart casting the lone dissenting vote in each.

4.   Twenty-two years later, however, the Court was anything but united when it considered the constitutionality of Alabama's "moment of silence" laws in Wallace v. Jaffree, which follows.

---

10. The Declaration of Independence ends with this sentence: "And for the support of this Declaration, with a firm reliance on the protection of divine Providence, we mutually pledge to each other our Lives, our Fortunes and our sacred Honor."

WALLACE v. JAFFREE

472 U.S. 38, 105 S.Ct. 2479 (1985).

JUSTICE STEVENS delivered the opinion of the Court.

[The primary focus of this dispute is the constitutionality of § 16–1–20.1, enacted in 1981, which authorized a period of silence "for meditation or voluntary prayer" in Alabama.ᵃ

The statute was actually the second of three passed in Alabama between 1978 and 1982. § 16–1–20 (1978) had authorized a 1–minute period of silence in all public schools "for meditation", but § 16–1–20.1 (1981) authorized a period of silence "for meditation or voluntary prayer." Plaintiffs apparently conceded that the 1978 law was constitutional, and the dispute among the justices centered primarily on the second statute that includes "voluntary prayer" as a permitted purpose.]

* * *

III

When the Court has been called upon to construe the breadth of the Establishment Clause, it has examined the criteria developed over a period of many years. Thus, in *Lemon v. Kurtzman,* we wrote:

> Every analysis in this area must begin with consideration of the cumulative criteria developed by the Court over many years. Three such tests may be gleaned from our cases. First, the statute must have a secular legislative purpose; second, its principal or primary effect must be one that neither advances nor inhibits religion; finally, the statute must not foster "an excessive government entanglement with religion."

It is the first of these three criteria that is most plainly implicated by this case. As the District Court correctly recognized, no consideration of the second or third criteria is necessary if a statute does not have a clearly secular purpose. For even though a statute that is motivated in part by a religious purpose may satisfy the first criterion, the First Amendment requires that a statute must be invalidated if it is entirely motivated by a purpose to advance religion.

In applying the purpose test, it is appropriate to ask "whether government's actual purpose is to endorse or disapprove of religion."[42] In

---

a. Alabama Code § 16–1–20.1 (Supp. 1984) provides:

At the commencement of the first class of each day in all grades in all public schools the teacher in charge of the room in which each class is held may announce that a period of silence not to exceed one minute in duration shall be observed for meditation or voluntary prayer, and during any such period no other activities shall be engaged in.

Also at issue in the lower courts was § 16–1–20.2, enacted in 1982, which authorized teachers to lead "willing students" in a prescribed prayer to "Almighty God ... the Creator and Supreme Judge of the world."

42. *Lynch v. Donnelly,* 465 U.S. at 690, 104 S.Ct. at 1368 (O'CONNOR, J., concurring) ("The purpose prong of the *Lemon* test asks whether government's actual purpose is to endorse or disapprove of religion.

this case, the answer to that question is dispositive. For the record not only provides us with an unambiguous affirmative answer, but it also reveals that the enactment of § 16–1–20.1 was not motivated by any clearly secular purpose—indeed, the statute had *no* secular purpose.

IV

The sponsor of the bill that became § 16–1–20.1, Senator Donald Holmes, inserted into the legislative record—apparently without dissent—a statement indicating that the legislation was an "effort to return voluntary prayer" to the public schools. Later Senator Holmes confirmed this purpose before the District Court. In response to the question whether he had any purpose for the legislation other than returning voluntary prayer to public schools, he stated: "No, I did not have no other purpose in mind."[44] The State did not present evidence of *any* secular purpose.

* * *

The legislative intent to return prayer to the public schools is, of course, quite different from merely protecting every student's right to engage in voluntary prayer during an appropriate moment of silence during the school day. The 1978 statute already protected that right, containing nothing that prevented any student from engaging in voluntary prayer during a silent minute of meditation.[47] Appellants have not identified any secular purpose that was not fully served by § 16–1–20 before the enactment of § 16–1–20.1. Thus, only two conclusions are consistent with the text of § 16–1–20.1: (1) the statute was enacted to convey a message of state endorsement and promotion of prayer; or (2) the statute was enacted for no purpose. No one suggests that the statute was nothing but a meaningless or irrational act.[48]

We must, therefore, conclude that the Alabama Legislature intended to change existing law and that it was motivated by the same purpose that the Governor's answer to the second amended complaint expressly admitted; that the statement inserted in the legislative history revealed; and that Senator Holmes' testimony frankly described. The legislature enacted § 16–1–20.1, despite the existence of § 16–1–20 for the sole purpose of expressing the State's endorsement of prayer activities for one minute at the beginning of each school day. The addition of "or voluntary prayer" indicates that the State intended to characterize prayer as a favored practice. Such an endorsement is not consistent with

The effect prong asks whether, irrespective of government's actual purpose, the practice under review in fact conveys a message of endorsement or disapproval. An affirmative answer to either question should render the challenged practice invalid").

44. The District Court and the Court of Appeals agreed that the purpose of § 16–1–20.1 was "an effort on the part of the State of Alabama to encourage a religious activity." * * *

47. Indeed, for some persons meditation itself may be a form of prayer.

48. If the conclusion that the statute had no purpose were tenable, it would remain true that no purpose is not a secular purpose. But such a conclusion is inconsistent with the common sense presumption that statutes are usually enacted to change existing law. Appellants do not even suggest that the State had no purpose in enacting § 16–1–20.1.

the established principle that the government must pursue a course of complete neutrality toward religion.

The importance of that principle does not permit us to treat this as an inconsequential case involving nothing more than a few words of symbolic speech on behalf of the political majority. For whenever the State itself speaks on a religious subject, one of the questions that we must ask is "whether the government intends to convey a message of endorsement or disapproval of religion." The well-supported concurrent findings of the District Court and the Court of Appeals—that § 16–1–20.1 was intended to convey a message of state approval of prayer activities in the public schools—make it unnecessary, and indeed inappropriate, to evaluate the practical significance of the addition of the words "or voluntary prayer" to the statute. Keeping in mind, as we must, "both the fundamental place held by the Establishment Clause in our constitutional scheme and the myriad, subtle ways in which Establishment Clause values can be eroded," we conclude that § 16–1–20.1 violates the First Amendment.

The judgment of the Court of Appeals is affirmed.

It is so ordered.

JUSTICE POWELL, concurring.

I concur in the Court's opinion and judgment that Alabama Code § 16–1–20.1 violates the Establishment Clause of the First Amendment. My concurrence is prompted by Alabama's persistence in attempting to institute state-sponsored prayer in the public schools by enacting three successive statutes. I agree fully with Justice O'CONNOR's assertion that some moment-of-silence statutes may be constitutional, a suggestion set forth in the Court's opinion as well.

I write separately to express additional views and to respond to criticism of the three-pronged *Lemon* test. *Lemon v. Kurtzman* identifies standards that have proved useful in analyzing case after case both in our decisions and in those of other courts. It is the only coherent test a majority of the Court has ever adopted. Only once since our decision in *Lemon, supra,* have we addressed an Establishment Clause issue without resort to its three-pronged test. *Lemon* has not been overruled or its test modified. Yet, continued criticism of it could encourage other courts to feel free to decide Establishment Clause cases on an ad hoc basis.

The first inquiry under *Lemon* is whether the challenged statute has a "secular legislative purpose." As Justice O'CONNOR recognizes, this secular purpose must be "sincere"; a law will not pass constitutional muster if the secular purpose articulated by the legislature is merely a "sham." In *Stone v. Graham* for example, we held that a statute requiring the posting of the Ten Commandments in public schools violated the Establishment Clause, even though the Kentucky Legislature asserted that its goal was educational. We have not interpreted the first prong of *Lemon,* however, as requiring that a statute have "exclusively secular" objectives.[6] If such a requirement existed, much conduct and legislation approved by this Court in the past would have been invalidated.

The record before us, however, makes clear that Alabama's purpose was solely religious in character. Senator Donald Holmes, the sponsor of the bill that became Alabama Code § 16–1–20.1, freely acknowledged that the purpose of this statute was "to return voluntary prayer" to the public schools. I agree with Justice O'CONNOR that a single legislator's statement, particularly if made following enactment, is not necessarily sufficient to establish purpose. But, as noted in the Court's opinion, the religious purpose of § 16–1–20.1 is manifested in other evidence, including the sequence and history of the three Alabama statutes.

I also consider it of critical importance that neither the District Court nor the Court of Appeals found a secular purpose, while both agreed that the purpose was to advance religion. In its first opinion (enjoining the enforcement of § 16–1–20.1 pending a hearing on the merits), the District Court said that the statute did "not reflect a clearly secular purpose." Instead, the District Court found that the enactment of the statute was an "effort on the part of the State of Alabama to encourage a religious activity." The Court of Appeals likewise applied the *Lemon* test and found "a lack of secular purpose on the part of the Alabama Legislature." It held that the objective of § 16–1–20.1 was the "advancement of religion." When both courts below are unable to discern an arguably valid secular purpose, this Court normally should hesitate to find one.

I would vote to uphold the Alabama statute if it also had a clear secular purpose. Nothing in the record before us, however, identifies a clear secular purpose, and the State also has failed to identify any nonreligious reason for the statute's enactment. Under these circumstances, the Court is required by our precedents to hold that the statute fails the first prong of the *Lemon* test and therefore violates the Establishment Clause.

Although we do not reach the other two prongs of the *Lemon* test, I note that the "effect" of a straightforward moment-of-silence statute is unlikely to "advanc[e] or inhibi[t] religion." Nor would such a statute "foster 'an excessive government entanglement with religion.'" *Lemon v. Kurtzman*.

I join the opinion and judgment of the Court.

Justice Rehnquist, dissenting.

Thirty-eight years ago this Court, in *Everson v. Board of Education*, summarized its exegesis of Establishment Clause doctrine thus:

---

6. The Court's opinion recognizes that "a statute that is motivated in part by a religious purpose may satisfy the first criterion." The Court simply holds that "a stat- ute must be invalidated if it is *entirely motivated* by a purpose to advance religion."

"In the words of Jefferson, the clause against establishment of religion by law was intended to erect 'a wall of separation between church and State.' "

This language from *Reynolds,* a case involving the Free Exercise Clause of the First Amendment rather than the Establishment Clause, quoted from Thomas Jefferson's letter to the Danbury Baptist Association the phrase "I contemplate with sovereign reverence that act of the whole American people which declared that their legislature should 'make no law respecting an establishment of religion, or prohibiting the free exercise thereof,' thus building a wall of separation between church and State."

It is impossible to build sound constitutional doctrine upon a mistaken understanding of constitutional history, but unfortunately the Establishment Clause has been expressly freighted with Jefferson's misleading metaphor for nearly 40 years. Thomas Jefferson was of course in France at the time the constitutional Amendments known as the Bill of Rights were passed by Congress and ratified by the States. His letter to the Danbury Baptist Association was a short note of courtesy, written 14 years after the Amendments were passed by Congress. He would seem to any detached observer as a less than ideal source of contemporary history as to the meaning of the Religion Clauses of the First Amendment.

Jefferson's fellow Virginian, James Madison, with whom he was joined in the battle for the enactment of the Virginia Statute of Religious Liberty of 1786, did play as large a part as anyone in the drafting of the Bill of Rights. He had two advantages over Jefferson in this regard: he was present in the United States, and he was a leading Member of the First Congress. But when we turn to the record of the proceedings in the First Congress leading up to the adoption of the Establishment Clause of the Constitution, including Madison's significant contributions thereto, we see a far different picture of its purpose than the highly simplified "wall of separation between church and State."

* * *

The language Madison proposed for what ultimately became the Religion Clauses of the First Amendment was this:

"The civil rights of none shall be abridged on account of religious belief or worship, nor shall any national religion be established, nor shall the full and equal rights of conscience be in any manner, or on any pretext, infringed."

* * *

On the basis of the record of these proceedings in the House of Representatives, James Madison was undoubtedly the most important architect among the Members of the House of the Amendments which became the Bill of Rights, but it was James Madison speaking as an advocate of sensible legislative compromise * * *. During the ratification debate in the Virginia Convention, Madison had actually opposed the idea of any Bill of Rights. His sponsorship of the Amendments in the House was obviously not that of a zealous believer in the necessity of the Religion Clauses, but of one who felt it might do some good, could do no harm, and would satisfy those who had ratified the Constitution on the condition that Congress propose a Bill of Rights. His original language "nor shall any national religion be established" obviously does not conform to the "wall of separation" between church and State idea which latter-day commentators have ascribed to him. His explanation on the floor of the meaning of his language—"that Congress should not establish a religion, and enforce the legal observation of it by law" is of the same ilk.

* * *

None of the other Members of Congress who spoke during the August 15th debate expressed the slightest indication that they thought the language before them from the Select Committee, or the evil to be aimed at, would require that the Government be absolutely neutral as between religion and irreligion. The evil to be aimed at, so far as those who spoke were concerned, appears to have been the establishment of a national church, and perhaps the preference of one religious sect over another; but it was definitely not concerned about whether the Government might aid all religions evenhandedly. If one were to follow the advice of Justice BRENNAN, concurring in *Abington School District v. Schempp*, and construe the Amendment in the light of what particular "practices . . . challenged threaten those consequences which the Framers deeply feared; whether, in short, they tend to promote that type of interdependence between religion and state which the First Amendment was designed to prevent," one would have to say that the First Amendment Establishment Clause should be read no more broadly than to prevent the establishment of a national religion or the governmental preference of one religious sect over another.

* * *

As the United States moved from the 18th into the 19th century, Congress appropriated time and again public moneys in support of sectarian Indian education carried on by religious organizations. Typical of these was Jefferson's treaty with the Kaskaskia Indians, which provided annual cash support for the Tribe's Roman Catholic priest and church. It was not until 1897, when aid to sectarian education for Indians had reached $500,000 annually, that Congress decided thereafter to cease appropriating money for education in sectarian schools. This history shows the fallacy of the notion found in *Everson* that "no tax in any amount" may be levied for religious activities in any form.

* * *

The Establishment Clause did not require government neutrality between religion and irreligion nor did it prohibit the Federal Government from providing nondiscriminatory aid to religion. There is simply no historical foundation for the proposition that the Framers intended to build the "wall of separation" that was constitutionalized in *Everson*.

Notwithstanding the absence of a historical basis for this theory of rigid separation, the wall idea might well have served as a useful albeit misguided analytical concept, had it led this Court to unified and principled results in Establishment Clause cases. The opposite, unfortunately, has been true; in the 38 years since *Everson* our Establishment Clause cases have been neither principled nor unified. Our recent opinions, many of them hopelessly divided pluralities, have with embarrassing candor conceded that the "wall of separation" is merely a "blurred, indistinct, and variable barrier," which "is not wholly accurate" and can only be "dimly perceived."

* * *

But the greatest injury of the "wall" notion is its mischievous diversion of judges from the actual intentions of the drafters of the Bill of Rights. The "crucible of litigation," is well adapted to adjudicating factual disputes on the basis of testimony presented in court, but no amount of repetition of historical errors in judicial opinions can make the errors true. The "wall of separation between church and State" is a metaphor based on bad history, a metaphor which has proved useless as a guide to judging. It should be frankly and explicitly abandoned.

The Court has more recently attempted to add some mortar to *Everson*'s wall through the three-part test of *Lemon v. Kurtzman*, which served at first to offer a more useful test for purposes of the Establishment Clause than did the "wall" metaphor. Generally stated, the *Lemon* test proscribes state action that has a sectarian purpose or effect, or causes an impermissible governmental entanglement with religion.

Lemon cited *Board of Education v. Allen* as the source of the "purpose" and "effect" prongs of the three-part test. The *Allen* opinion explains, however, how it inherited the purpose and effect elements from *Schempp* and *Everson,* both of which contain the historical errors described above. Thus the purpose and effect prongs have the same historical deficiencies as the wall concept itself: they are in no way based on either the language or intent of the drafters.

* * *

[T]he *Lemon* test has no more grounding in the history of the First Amendment than does the wall theory upon which it rests. The three-part test represents a determined effort to craft a workable rule from a historically faulty doctrine; but the rule can only be as sound as the doctrine it attempts to service. The three-part test has simply not provided adequate standards for deciding Establishment Clause cases, as this Court has slowly come to realize. Even worse, the *Lemon* test has caused this Court to fracture into unworkable plurality opinions, depending upon how each of the three factors applies to a certain state action. The results from our school services cases show the difficulty we have encountered in making the *Lemon* test yield principled results.

* * *

If a constitutional theory has no basis in the history of the amendment it seeks to interpret, is difficult to apply and yields unprincipled results, I see little use in it. The "crucible of litigation," has produced only consistent unpredictability, and today's effort is just a continuation of "the sisyphean task of trying to patch together the 'blurred, indistinct and variable barrier' described in *Lemon v. Kurtzman*." We have done much straining since 1947, but still we admit that we can only "dimly perceive" the *Everson* wall. Our perception has been clouded not by the Constitution but by the mists of an unnecessary metaphor.

* * *

The State surely has a secular interest in regulating the manner in which public schools are conducted. Nothing in the Establishment Clause of the First Amendment, properly understood, prohibits any such generalized "endorsement" of prayer. I would therefore reverse the judgment of the Court of Appeals.

Notes

1. What evidence can be discerned in this decision that although the Court explicitly invoked the tripartite *Lemon* test, the *Wallace* case might have actually been decided under an *endorsement* inquiry? Four years later, in *Allegheny*, a non-education-related case addressing the constitutionality of a holiday display, Justice Blackmun explicitly recognized the endorsement analysis as a method of determining whether the effects prong of *Lemon* has been violated. *County of Allegheny v. ACLU*, 492 U.S. 573, 109 S.Ct. 3086 (1989).

2. A "moment of silence" in the public schools, by itself...and absent additional facts, is generally deemed to be constitutional. *See, e.g., Bown v. Gwinnett County Sch. Dist.*, 112 F.3d 1464 (11th Cir. 1997).

AGOSTINI v. FELTON

521 U.S. 203, 117 S.Ct. 1997 (1997).

Justice O'Connor delivered the opinion of the Court.

In *Aguilar v. Felton*, this Court held that the Establishment Clause of the First Amendment barred the city of New York from sending public school teachers into parochial schools to provide remedial education to disadvantaged children pursuant to a congressionally mandated program. On remand, the District Court for the Eastern District of New York entered a permanent injunction reflecting our ruling. Twelve years later, petitioners—the parties bound by that injunction—seek relief from its operation. Petitioners maintain that *Aguilar* cannot be squared with our intervening Establishment Clause jurisprudence and ask that we explicitly recognize what our more recent cases already dictate: *Aguilar* is no longer good law. We agree with petitioners that *Aguilar* is not consistent with our subsequent Establishment Clause decisions and further conclude that, on the facts presented here, petitioners are entitled * * * to relief from the operation of the District Court's prospective injunction.

* * *

III

* * *

B

Our more recent cases have undermined the assumptions upon which [previous decisions of this Court] relied. To be sure, the general principles we use to evaluate whether government aid violates the Establishment Clause have not changed since *Aguilar* was decided. For example, we continue to ask whether the government acted with the purpose of advancing or inhibiting religion, and the nature of that inquiry has remained largely unchanged. * * * Likewise, we continue to explore whether the aid has the "effect" of advancing or inhibiting religion. What has changed * * * is our understanding of the criteria used to assess whether aid to religion has an impermissible effect.

1

As we have repeatedly recognized, government inculcation of religious beliefs has the impermissible effect of advancing religion. Our cases subsequent to *Aguilar* have, however, modified in two significant respects the approach we use to assess indoctrination. First, we have abandoned the presumption erected in [previous decisions] that the placement of public employees on parochial school grounds inevitably results in the impermissible effect of state-sponsored indoctrination or constitutes a symbolic union between government and religion. * * *

Second, we have departed from the rule * * * that all government aid that directly assists the educational function of religious schools is invalid. * * * [U]nder current law, * * * New York City's Title I program in *Aguilar* will not, as a matter of law, be deemed to have the effect of advancing religion through indoctrination. Indeed, each of the premises upon which we relied in [past decisions] to reach a contrary conclusion is no longer valid. First, there is no reason to presume that, simply because she enters a parochial school classroom, a full-time public employee such as a Title I teacher will depart from her assigned duties and instructions and embark on religious indoctrination * * *. Certainly, no evidence has ever shown that any New York City Title I instructor teaching on parochial school premises attempted to inculcate religion in students. Thus, both our precedent and our experience require us to reject respondents' remarkable argument that we must presume Title I instructors to be "uncontrollable and sometimes very unprofessional."

[Recent decisions] * * * also repudiate * * * [prior] assumption[s] that the presence of Title I teachers in parochial school classrooms will, without more, create the impression of a "symbolic union" between church and state.

* * *

3

* * *

The * * * Title I program does not result in an "excessive" entanglement that advances or inhibits religion. As discussed previously, the Court's finding of "excessive" entanglement in *Aguilar* rested on three grounds: (i) the program would require "pervasive monitoring by public authorities" to ensure that Title I employees did not inculcate religion; (ii) the program required "administrative cooperation" between the Board and parochial schools; and (iii) the program might increase the dangers of "political divisiveness." Under our current understanding of the Establishment Clause, the last two considerations are insufficient by themselves to create an "excessive" entanglement. They are present no matter where Title I services are offered, and no court has held that Title I services cannot be offered off campus. * * * Further, the assumption underlying the first consideration has been undermined. In *Aguilar,* the Court presumed that full-time public employees on parochial school grounds would be tempted to inculcate religion, despite the ethical standards they were required to uphold. Because of this risk *pervasive* monitoring would be required. But * * * we no longer presume that public employees will inculcate religion simply because they happen to be in a sectarian environment. Since we have abandoned the assumption that properly instructed public employees will fail to discharge their duties faithfully, we must also discard the assumption that *pervasive* monitoring of Title I teachers is required. There is no suggestion in the record before us that unannounced monthly visits of public supervisors are insufficient to prevent or to detect inculcation of religion by public employees. Moreover, we have not found excessive entanglement in cases in which States imposed far more onerous burdens on religious institutions than the monitoring system at issue here.

To summarize, New York City's Title I program does not run afoul of any of three primary criteria we currently use to evaluate whether government aid has the effect of advancing religion: It does not result in governmental indoctrination; define its recipients by reference to religion; or create an excessive entanglement. We therefore hold that a federally funded program providing supplemental, remedial instruction to disadvantaged children on a neutral basis is not invalid under the Establishment Clause when such instruction is given on the premises of sectarian schools by government employees pursuant to a program containing safeguards such as those present here. The same considerations that justify this holding require us to conclude that this carefully constrained program also cannot reasonably be viewed as an endorsement of religion. * * * Accordingly, we must acknowledge that *Aguilar* * * * [is] no longer good law.

> * * *

IV

We therefore conclude that our Establishment Clause law has "significant[ly] change[d]" since we decided *Aguilar.* * * *

[W]e reverse the judgment of the Court of Appeals and remand the cases to the District Court with instructions to vacate its September 26, 1985, order.

It is so ordered.

B. THE ENDORSEMENT INQUIRY

In the 1980s, Justice O'Connor became the leading proponent of an argument that a separate and independent endorsement framework could be discerned as emerging under Establishment Clause jurisprudence. Declaring that a central tenet of Establishment Clause doctrine was the principle that the State must not make "adherence to a religion relevant in any way to a person's standing in the community," O'Connor asserted that "the government violates this prohibition if it endorses or disapproves of religion." Such endorsement or disapproval, she explained, sent a message of exclusion to "nonadherents that they are outsiders ... and an accompanying message to adherents that they are insiders." Lynch v. Donnelly, 465 U.S. 668, 687–88, 104 S.Ct. 1355 (1984) (O'Connor, J., concurring)

In *County of Allegheny v. ACLU,* 492 U.S. 573, 109 S.Ct. 3086 (1989), four justices joined the portion of Justice Blackmun's opinion of the Court that recognized the validity of an endorsement inquiry:

> Our * * * decisions [after *Lemon*] have refined the definition of governmental action that unconstitutionally advances religion. In recent years, we have paid particularly close attention to whether the challenged governmental practice either has the purpose or effect of "endorsing" religion, a concern that has long had a place in our Establishment Clause jurisprudence. See *Engel v. Vitale,* 370 U.S. 421, 436, 82 S.Ct. 1261, 1270 (1962). Thus, in *Wallace v. Jaffree,* 472 U.S. at 60, 105 S.Ct. at 2491, the Court held unconstitutional Alabama's moment-of-silence statute because it was "enacted ... for the sole purpose of expressing the State's endorsement of prayer activities." The Court similarly invalidated Louisiana's "Creationism Act" because it "endorses religion" in its purpose. *Edwards v. Aguillard,* [*infra,* Chapter 9]. * * *
>
> Of course, the word "endorsement" is not self-defining. Rather, it derives its meaning from other words that this Court has found useful over the years in interpreting the Establishment Clause. Thus, it has been noted that the prohibition against governmental

endorsement of religion "preclude[s] government from conveying or attempting to convey a message that religion or a particular religious belief is *favored* or *preferred.*" *Wallace v. Jaffree,* 472 U.S. at 70, 105 S.Ct. at 2497 (O'CONNOR, J., concurring in judgment) (emphasis added). Accord, * * * *Edwards v. Aguillard* ("preference" for particular religious beliefs constitutes an endorsement of religion). Moreover, the term "endorsement" is closely linked to the term "promotion," * * * and this Court long since has held that government "may not . . . promote one religion or religious theory against another or even against the militant opposite." *See also Wallace v. Jaffree,* 472 U.S. at 59–60, 105 S.Ct. at 2491 (using the concepts of endorsement, promotion, and favoritism interchangeably). * * * County of Allegheny v. ACLU, 492 U.S. 573, 592–93 (1989).

Justice O'Connor, concurring in that same case, reaffirmed the principle that the endorsement test should be conducted from the point of view of a reasonable observer. In addition, she emphasized the importance of historical context:

Under the endorsement test, * * * *the "history and ubiquity" of a practice is relevant because it provides part of the context in which a reasonable observer evaluates whether a challenged governmental practice conveys a message of endorsement of religion.* It is the combination of the longstanding existence of practices such as opening legislative sessions with legislative prayers or opening Court sessions with "God save the United States and this honorable Court," as well as their nonsectarian nature, that leads me to the conclusion that those particular practices, despite their religious roots, do not convey a message of endorsement of particular religious beliefs. *Id.* at 630–31 (emphasis added).

As referenced in the introductory material to this chapter, federal judges at the district court and appellate levels are often unable to determine from the Supreme Court's Establishment Clause cases exactly which inquiry to conduct in what circumstances. They do sometimes apply an endorsement test in education-related religion disputes, but often as one of several interrelated inquiries. The 1995 *Duncanville* decision, which follows, is an example of such an approach.

DOE v. DUNCANVILLE INDEP. SCH. DIST.

70 F.3d 402 (5th Cir. 1995).

W. EUGENE DAVIS, Circuit Judge:

Defendants (collectively, the Duncanville Independent School District or DISD) appeal the district court's permanent injunction forbidding certain religious practices in curricular and extracurricular activities at their schools as violations of the Establishment Clause of the First Amendment of the United States Constitution. * * *

I. FACTS

Plaintiffs in this case are Jane Doe, a student in the Duncanville Independent School District, and John Doe, her father.

* * *

Jane Doe * * * joined the choir program at DISD. Students in this program also receive academic credit for their participation. In the seventh and eighth grade choruses, Doe was required to sing the choir theme song *Go Ye Now in Peace,* which is based on Christian text. Upon progressing to the high school choirs, Doe was required to sing another Christian theme song, *The Lord Bless You and Keep You.* David McCullar, the director for the ninth through twelfth grade choirs, testified that *The Lord Bless You and Keep You* had been the choirs' theme song for at least 20 years; he did not know how it had originally been chosen. The choirs learn this song as part of their overall repertoire, sing it at the end of class on Fridays, at the end of some performances and during choral competitions. They also sing this song on the bus on the way home from performances. The parties stipulated that the choir's theme song is a "Christian religious song."

* * *

II. ANALYSIS

As we noted in *Doe I,* modern Establishment Clause jurisprudence is rife with confusion. This Court attempted to bring some order to the organization and application of the existing precedents * * * by identifying three tests that the Supreme Court has used to determine whether a government action or policy constitutes an establishment of religion. First, we identified the Establishment Clause test of longest lineage: the *Lemon* test. * * * We then recognized that the Court has also analyzed school-sponsored religious activity in terms of the coercive effect that the activity has on students. * * * Lastly, we found that the Court has disapproved of governmental practices that appear to endorse religion.

* * *

B. DISD Choirs' Theme Song

DISD contends that the district court erred by enjoining DISD from permitting DISD choirs to sing songs with religious content as their theme songs. The district court enjoined DISD, its employees and agents from:

> 2. initiating, leading, authorizing, encouraging, or condoning the recitation or singing of religious songs as a theme song of the Duncanville school choirs. Religious songs may be sung, however, for their artistic and historic qualities if presented objectively as part of a secular program of education.

The district court made only two findings specific to this issue: (1) that "Jane Doe is a member of the DISD choir and receives academic credit for her participation in the choir"; and (2) that "[a]s a DISD choir member, Jane Doe was required to sing a religious Christian song entitled, *The Lord Bless You and Keep You*. This song is sung at each DISD choir performance and has been adopted by school personnel and students as the choir's theme song.''

All parties recognize that the Establishment Clause does not prohibit DISD choirs from singing religious songs as part of a secular music program. * * * Thus, the Does essentially contend that the act of treating *The Lord Bless You and Keep You* as the theme song, rather than as simply one song in the repertoire, transforms the permissible practice of singing this song into an endorsement of religion. The record reveals that two practical effects flow from designating this as the theme song: it is sung often and it is carried over from year to year.

Legitimate secular reasons exist for maintaining *The Lord Bless You and Keep You* as the theme song. As the choir director, David McCullar, testified, this song is particularly useful to teach students to sight read and to sing *a capella*. In Mr. McCullar's words, it is also ''a good piece of music . . . by a reputable composer.''

Neither does utilizing *The Lord Bless You and Keep You* as a theme song advance or endorse religion. The Does do not argue that the choir sings the theme song as a religious exercise per se[7] so we do not accept the notion that repeated singing of a particular religious song amounts to an endorsement of religion. At trial, Mr. McCullar estimated that 60–75 percent of serious choral music is based on sacred themes or text. Given the dominance of religious music in this field, DISD can hardly be presumed to be advancing or endorsing religion by allowing its choirs to sing a religious theme song. As a matter of statistical probability, the song best suited to be the theme is more likely to be religious than not. Indeed, to forbid DISD from having a theme song that is religious would force DISD to disqualify the majority of appropriate choral music simply because it is religious. Within the world of choral music, such a restriction would require hostility, not neutrality, toward religion.

A position of neutrality towards religion must allow choir directors to recognize the fact that most choral music is religious. Limiting the number of times a religious piece of music can be sung is tantamount to censorship and does not send students a message of neutrality. Where, as here, singing the theme song is not a religious exercise, we will not find an endorsement of religion exists merely because a religious song with widely recognized musical value is sung more often than other songs. Such animosity towards religion is not required or condoned by the Constitution.

We conclude that the district court erred by enjoining DISD from using songs with religious content as theme songs for its choirs.

* * *

7. * * * The fact that singing these songs is not a religious exercise also means that maintaining them as theme songs does not impermissibly entangle government with religion or coerce students into participating in a religious activity.

MAHON, DISTRICT JUDGE, dissenting in part:

* * * I respectfully disagree with my colleagues that DISD's choice of religious theme songs for its choirs is consistent with the First Amendment. Viewed as a whole, the facts in this case fully support the district court's prohibition of DISD's participation, in any form, in the use by its choirs of religious theme songs. Accordingly, I dissent from the majority's decision to reverse the district court's ruling on this issue.

Although the majority opinion sets forth many of the facts in the case, it will help to recount here those facts which demonstrate the similarity between the DISD's choice of a religious theme song and its other religious practices, which the majority agree are unconstitutional.

It is undisputed that for some twenty years, DISD, through the actions of its teachers and other employees, permitted, encouraged and even sponsored the recitation of prayers during curricular and extracurricular activities. Prayers were recited during classes. Many events were begun and closed with a prayer. Sports teams recited prayers before games in the locker rooms, after games on the field and in the buses returning to school. At award ceremonies, prayers were recited and DISD teachers distributed pamphlets of religious songs for participants to sing. The prayers and songs were always Christian.

During the same twenty year period, DISD choir teachers treated as the theme song for the ninth grade and high school choirs what the parties have stipulated is a Christian religious song entitled *The Lord Bless You and Keep You.* The song is in the form of a prayer seeking God's blessings on behalf of a third party.[1] The theme song was sung at the end of each performance except when circumstances made it inappropriate, such as when members of the choir performed as a barbershop quartet. In addition, the choir sang the song on the bus on the way home from performances and at the end of class each Friday. The students were not given an opportunity to choose a new theme song each year or to determine whether to have a theme song at all. Rather, the song was passed on as an established tradition to incoming choir teachers, who in turn taught it to each new group of students. Although there apparently was no formal, written designation of the theme song, choir teachers and students were aware that the specified song was the theme song and treated it accordingly.

DISD's intermediate school choir had a different theme song, which was also a Christian religious song. Although the record is less developed as to this song, *Go Ye Now in Peace,* the evidence shows that it also was sung at the end of each performance.

 * * *

---

1. The words of the song are:
The Lord bless you and keep you, the Lord lift His countenance upon you; and give you peace, and give you peace, the Lord make his face to shine upon you, and be gracious unto you, be gracious, the Lord be gracious, gracious unto you. Amen, Amen, Amen, Amen, Amen.

This text, taken from the Old Testament, Numbers VI, 24 26, would be better characterized as Judeo–Christian.

The district court did not err in viewing DISD's choice of religious theme songs as an inseparable part of its historical pattern of encouraging and endorsing Christian religious beliefs through the activities of its teachers. This is not a case where the choice of theme songs was the only arguably religious practice involved, but one where expression of religious belief was permitted and approved at almost every level of school life. In virtually the same way that prayers were recited during classes, sports and other events, the choirs' theme songs were used to mark the close of performances and the week, and to unify participants in a common outlook. Viewed in this context, the theme songs served as yet another vehicle for inculcating a Christian attitude, and their singing constituted a religious exercise.

The majority does not disagree with the legal principles applied by the district court. Instead, by ignoring the role and effect of theme songs in general, and the connection between DISD's theme songs and its other religious practices in particular, the majority reaches the conclusion that DISD's religious theme songs had a secular purpose and did not have the effect of advancing or endorsing religion. An analysis of the majority's reasoning shows it to be faulty in several respects.

* * *

As with the question of purpose, the majority's narrow findings regarding the effects of designating a religious theme song—that the song was sung often and was carried over from year to year—disregard the characteristic role and resulting effects of a theme song. In common understanding, a theme song is a song used by a group to represent or identify itself. By choosing a particular song, the group expresses a shared emotion, experience or outlook. The theme song is played at each of the group's meetings or performances and has special significance for the group and for others who identify the group by its song.

DISD intended its choirs' religious theme songs to play this role. Though the theme songs were singled out from the overall music program by their continual singing throughout the year, thereby achieving a prominence not enjoyed by other songs, this was not the sole effect of their designation. More importantly, the theme songs were given special emphasis by their placement at the close of performances and, in the case of the high school choirs' song, its use to end class on Fridays, treatment that served to highlight the songs' sacred character.[4] Choir members were informed that the song was their theme song and a tradition at the school, thereby being directed, in effect, to at least superficially identify themselves with it. Indeed, the choir teacher testified that the theme song was supposed to give the students a sense of unity, camaraderie, belonging, and something to identify with. Since any

4. The evidence suggests that DISD choir performances were carefully arranged to give religious songs, including the theme songs, the role that prayers played in other DISD events. For example, during the time that Jane Doe was in the intermediate school choir, one performance began with the song *Before Our Lord and King* and ended with the theme song. The rest of the songs in the performance were secular in nature.

student, upon learning that a particular song is his or her group's theme song, would look to the words of the song as an important part of its special meaning, the school's designation of a theme song that consists entirely of calls for God's blessing could not help but reinforce existing religious belief and convey the impression to believers and nonbelievers alike that the school favored religion. In fact, Jane Doe indicated she felt the choirs' theme songs reflected and embodied DISD's favor for Christian beliefs. The district court did not err in determining that DISD's choice of religious theme songs had the primary effect of advancing and endorsing religion.

Adopting DISD's reasoning, the majority attempts to minimize the significance of the choice of a religious theme song by pointing to the choir teacher's estimate that 60–75 percent of serious choral music is based on sacred themes or text. Considering these figures, it suggests, statistical probability would predict that a religious song would be best suited to serve as the theme song. This apparent logic obscures the real questions at issue—the purpose and effects of DISD choosing religious theme songs. This is not a case where the students, or even the teachers, have picked a theme song each year and statistics would predict the choice of a religious song some percentage of the time. Nor has DISD directly claimed that it chose its particular theme songs because they were better suited to that purpose than any secular songs. Thus, there is no basis to conclude that the relative percentages of religious and secular music have had any bearing on DISD's purpose in choosing a religious theme song. Similarly, that religious songs may constitute the majority of serious choral music does not minimize the religious effects, discussed above, of DISD designating a religious theme song.

* * *

Because the record supports the injunction against any school involvement in the choice or use of a religious theme song, I would affirm the district court on this issue.

PROBLEM 37: Re-litigating *Doe v. Duncanville* Today

Assume the same set of facts as those set forth in *Doe v. Duncanville,* except that the case is being litigated today, and the Supreme Court ultimately agrees to hear the case.

In light of developments in the law since 1995, and particularly in light of the Court's decision in the 2005 Kentucky Ten Commandments case, how might plaintiffs case be strengthened? Would plaintiffs have a better chance of prevailing today? Why or why not?

Might the implicit *respect principle,* arguably emerging in education cases across all areas of the law, provide additional support for plaintiffs? Or would such a principle provide equal support for defendants?

As a matter of policy, what approach should schools be taking in this context, and in this era? Why?

C. THE COERCION INQUIRY

In the *Allegheny* case, *supra,* Justice Kennedy argued against the endorsement inquiry as set forth by Justices Blackmun and O'Connor. He contended that a coercion inquiry would be the more appropriate approach for deciding the dispute, and explained that it would also permit government "some latitude in recognizing and accommodating the central role religion plays in our society."

Joined by Chief Justice Rehnquist, Justice White, and Justice Scalia, Kennedy declared:

> Our cases disclose two limiting principles: government may not coerce anyone to support or participate in any religion or its exercise; and it may not, in the guise of avoiding hostility or callous indifference, give direct benefits to religion in such a degree that it in fact "establishes a [state] religion or religious faith, or tends to do so." County of Allegheny v. ACLU, 492 U.S. 573, 659 (Kennedy, J., concurring in the judgment and dissenting in part).

According to Kennedy, such an approach was a more correct characterization of Establishment Clause principles and case law than either the *Lemon* test or the endorsement test. He pointed out that James Madison, who proposed the First Amendment in Congress, "apprehended the meaning of the [Religion Clauses] to be, that Congress should not establish a religion, and *enforce* the legal observation of it by law, nor *compel* men to worship God in any manner contrary to their conscience." *See generally* Michael W. McConnell, *Coercion: the Lost Element of Establishment,* 27 WILLIAM & MARY L. REV. 933 (1986).

Three years later, Kennedy was able to apply this very coercion test to the facts of *Lee v. Weisman.* However, in a somewhat ironic turn of events, the test was not employed to justify state action, but to strike down as unconstitutional the actions of a school district in a dispute over graduation invocations and benedictions.

LEE v. WEISMAN

505 U.S. 577, 112 S.Ct. 2649 (1992).

JUSTICE KENNEDY delivered the opinion of the Court.

School principals in the public school system of the city of Providence, Rhode Island, are permitted to invite members of the clergy to offer invocation and benediction prayers as part of the formal graduation ceremonies for middle schools and for high schools. The question before us is whether including clerical members who offer prayers as part of the official school graduation ceremony is consistent with the Religion Clauses of the First Amendment, provisions the Fourteenth Amendment makes applicable with full force to the States and their school districts.

I

A

Deborah Weisman graduated from Nathan Bishop Middle School, a public school in Providence, at a formal ceremony in June 1989. She was about 14 years old. For many years it has been the policy of the Providence School Committee and the Superintendent of Schools to permit principals to invite members of the clergy to give invocations and benedictions at middle school and high school graduations. Many, but not all, of the principals elected to include prayers as part of the graduation ceremonies. Acting for himself and his daughter, Deborah's father, Daniel Weisman, objected to any prayers at Deborah's middle school graduation, but to no avail. The school principal, petitioner Robert E. Lee, invited a rabbi to deliver prayers at the graduation exercises for Deborah's class. Rabbi Leslie Gutterman, of the Temple Beth El in Providence, accepted.

It has been the custom of Providence school officials to provide invited clergy with a pamphlet entitled "Guidelines for Civic Occasions," prepared by the National Conference of Christians and Jews. The Guidelines recommend that public prayers at nonsectarian civic ceremonies be composed with "inclusiveness and sensitivity," though they acknowledge that "[p]rayer of any kind may be inappropriate on some civic occasions." The principal gave Rabbi Gutterman the pamphlet before the graduation and advised him the invocation and benediction should be nonsectarian.

Rabbi Gutterman's prayers were as follows:

INVOCATION

God of the Free, Hope of the Brave:

For the legacy of America where diversity is celebrated and the rights of minorities are protected, we thank You. May these young men and women grow up to enrich it.

For the liberty of America, we thank You. May these new graduates grow up to guard it.

For the political process of America in which all its citizens may participate, for its court system where all may seek justice we thank You. May those we honor this morning always turn to it in trust.

For the destiny of America we thank You. May the graduates of Nathan Bishop Middle School so live that they might help to share it.

May our aspirations for our country and for these young people, who are our hope for the future, be richly fulfilled.

AMEN

BENEDICTION

O God, we are grateful to You for having endowed us with the capacity for learning which we have celebrated on this joyous commencement.

Happy families give thanks for seeing their children achieve an important milestone. Send Your blessings upon the teachers and administrators who helped prepare them.

The graduates now need strength and guidance for the future, help them to understand that we are not complete with academic knowledge alone. We must each strive to fulfill what You require of us all: To do justly, to love mercy, to walk humbly.

We give thanks to You, Lord, for keeping us alive, sustaining us and allowing us to reach this special, happy occasion.

AMEN

* * *

The school board (and the United States, which supports it as *amicus curiae*) argued that these short prayers and others like them at graduation exercises are of profound meaning to many students and parents throughout this country who consider that due respect and acknowledgment for divine guidance and for the deepest spiritual aspirations of our people ought to be expressed at an event as important in life as a graduation. We assume this to be so in addressing the difficult case now before us, for the significance of the prayers lies also at the heart of Daniel and Deborah Weisman's case.

* * *

II

These dominant facts mark and control the confines of our decision: State officials direct the performance of a formal religious exercise at promotional and graduation ceremonies for secondary schools. Even for those students who object to the religious exercise, their attendance and participation in the state-sponsored religious activity are in a fair and real sense obligatory, though the school district does not require attendance as a condition for receipt of the diploma.

This case does not require us to revisit the difficult questions dividing us in recent cases, questions of the definition and full scope of the principles governing the extent of permitted accommodation by the State for the religious beliefs and practices of many of its citizens. For without reference to those principles in other contexts, the controlling precedents as they relate to prayer and religious exercise in primary and secondary public schools compel the holding here that the policy of the city of Providence is an unconstitutional one. We can decide the case without reconsidering the general constitutional framework by which public schools' efforts to accommodate religion are measured. Thus we do not accept the invitation of petitioners and *amicus* the United States to reconsider our decision in *Lemon v. Kurtzman*. The government involvement with religious activity in this case is pervasive, to the point of creating a state-sponsored and state-directed religious exercise in a public school. Conducting this formal religious observance conflicts with settled rules pertaining to prayer exercises for students, and that suffices to determine the question before us.

The principle that government may accommodate the free exercise of religion does not supersede the fundamental limitations imposed by the Establishment Clause. It is beyond dispute that, at a minimum, the Constitution guarantees that government may not coerce anyone to support or participate in religion or its exercise, or otherwise act in a way which "establishes a [state] religion or religious faith, or tends to do so." The State's involvement in the school prayers challenged today violates these central principles.

That involvement is as troubling as it is undenied. A school official, the principal, decided that an invocation and a benediction should be given; this is a choice attributable to the State, and from a constitutional perspective it is as if a state statute decreed that the prayers must occur. The principal chose the religious participant, here a rabbi, and that choice is also attributable to the State. The reason for the choice of a rabbi is not disclosed by the record, but the potential for divisiveness over the choice of a particular member of the clergy to conduct the ceremony is apparent.

Divisiveness, of course, can attend any state decision respecting religions, and neither its existence nor its potential necessarily invalidates the State's attempts to accommodate religion in all cases. The potential for divisiveness is of particular relevance here though, because it centers around an overt religious exercise in a secondary school environment where, as we discuss below, subtle coercive pressures exist and where the student had no real alternative which would have allowed her to avoid the fact or appearance of participation.

* * *

We are asked to recognize the existence of a practice of nonsectarian prayer, prayer within the embrace of what is known as the Judeo–Christian tradition, prayer which is more acceptable than one which, for example, makes explicit references to the God of Israel, or to Jesus Christ, or to a patron saint. There may be some support, as an empirical observation, to the statement of the Court of Appeals for the Sixth Circuit, picked up by Judge Campbell's dissent in the Court of Appeals in this case, that there has emerged in this country a civic religion, one which is tolerated when sectarian exercises are not. If common ground can be defined which permits once conflicting faiths to express the shared conviction that there is an ethic and a morality which transcend human invention, the sense of community and purpose sought by all decent societies might be advanced. But though the First Amendment does not allow the government to stifle prayers which aspire to these ends, neither does it permit the government to undertake that task for itself.

The First Amendment's Religion Clauses mean that religious beliefs and religious expression are too precious to be either proscribed or prescribed by the State. The design of the Constitution is that preservation and transmission of religious beliefs and worship is a responsibility and a choice committed to the private sphere, which itself is promised freedom to pursue that mission. It must not be forgotten then, that while concern must be given to define the protection granted to an objector or a dissenting nonbeliever, these same Clauses exist to protect religion from government interference. James Madison, the principal author of the Bill of Rights, did not rest his opposition to a religious establishment on the sole ground of its effect on the minority. A principal ground for his view was: "[E]xperience witnesseth that ecclesiastical establishments, instead of maintaining the purity and efficacy of Religion, have had a contrary operation."

These concerns have particular application in the case of school officials, whose effort to monitor prayer will be perceived by the students as inducing a participation they might otherwise reject. Though the efforts of the school officials in this case to find common ground appear to have been a good-faith attempt to recognize the common aspects of religions and not the divisive ones, our precedents do not permit school officials to assist in composing prayers as an incident to a formal exercise for their students. *Engel v. Vitale,* 370 U.S. 421, 425, 82 S.Ct. 1261, 1264 (1962). And these same precedents caution us to measure the idea of a civic religion against the central meaning of the Religion Clauses of the First Amendment, which is that all creeds must be tolerated and none favored. The suggestion that government may establish an official or civic religion as a means of avoiding the establishment of a religion with more specific creeds strikes us as a contradiction that cannot be accepted.

The degree of school involvement here made it clear that the graduation prayers bore the imprint of the State and thus put school-age children who objected in an untenable position. We turn our attention now to consider the position of the students, both those who desired the prayer and she who did not.

To endure the speech of false ideas or offensive content and then to counter it is part of learning how to live in a pluralistic society, a society which insists upon open discourse towards the end of a tolerant citizenry. And tolerance presupposes some mutuality of obligation. It is argued that our constitutional vision of a free society requires confidence in our own ability to accept or reject ideas of which we do not approve, and that prayer at a high school graduation does nothing more than offer a choice. By the time they are seniors, high school students no doubt have been required to attend classes and assemblies and to complete assignments exposing them to ideas they find distasteful or immoral or absurd or all of these. Against this background, students may consider it an odd measure of justice to be subjected during the course of their educations to ideas deemed offensive and irreligious, but to be denied a brief, formal prayer ceremony that the school offers in return. This argument cannot prevail, however. It overlooks a fundamental dynamic of the Constitution.

The First Amendment protects speech and religion by quite different mechanisms. Speech is protected by ensuring its full expression even when the government participates, for the very object of some of our most important speech is to persuade the government to adopt an idea as its own. The method for protecting freedom of worship and freedom of conscience in religious matters is quite the reverse. In religious debate or expression the government is not a prime participant, for the Framers deemed religious establishment antithetical to the freedom of all. The Free Exercise Clause embraces a freedom of conscience and worship that has close parallels in the speech provisions of the First Amendment, but the Establishment Clause is a specific prohibition on forms of state intervention in religious affairs with no precise counterpart in the speech provisions. The explanation lies in the lesson of history that was and is the inspiration for the Establishment Clause, the lesson that in the hands of government what might begin as a tolerant expression of religious views may end in a policy to indoctrinate and coerce. A state-created orthodoxy puts at grave risk that freedom of belief and conscience which are the sole assurance that religious faith is real, not imposed.

The lessons of the First Amendment are as urgent in the modern world as in the 18th century when it was written. One timeless lesson is that if citizens are subjected to state-sponsored religious exercises, the State disavows its own duty to guard and respect that sphere of inviolable conscience and belief which is the mark of a free people. To compromise that principle today would be to deny our own tradition and forfeit our standing to urge others to secure the protections of that tradition for themselves.

As we have observed before, there are heightened concerns with protecting freedom of conscience from subtle coercive pressure in the elementary and secondary public schools. * * * Our decisions in *Engel v. Vitale,* 370 U.S. 421, 82 S.Ct. 1261 (1962), and *School Dist. of Abington* recognize, among other things, that prayer exercises in public schools carry a particular risk of indirect coercion. The concern may not be limited to the context of schools, but it is most pronounced there. What to most believers may seem nothing more than a reasonable request that the nonbeliever respect their religious practices, in a school context may appear to the nonbeliever or dissenter to be an attempt to employ the machinery of the State to enforce a religious orthodoxy.

We need not look beyond the circumstances of this case to see the phenomenon at work. The undeniable fact is that the school district's supervision and control of a high school graduation ceremony places public pressure, as well as peer pressure, on attending students to stand as a group or, at least, maintain respectful silence during the invocation and benediction. This pressure, though subtle and indirect, can be as real as any overt compulsion. Of course, in our culture standing or remaining silent can signify adherence to a view or simple respect for the views of others. And no doubt some persons who have no desire to join a prayer have little objection to standing as a sign of respect for those who do. But for the dissenter of high school age, who has a reasonable perception that she is being forced by the State to pray in a manner her conscience will not allow, the injury is no less real. There can be no doubt that for many, if not most, of the students at the graduation, the act of standing or remaining silent was an expression of participation in the rabbi's prayer. That was the very point of the religious exercise. It is of little comfort to a dissenter, then, to be told that for her the act of standing or remaining in silence signifies mere respect, rather than participation. What matters is that, given our social conventions, a reasonable dissenter in this milieu could believe that the group exercise signified her own participation or approval of it.

Finding no violation under these circumstances would place objectors in the dilemma of participating, with all that implies, or protesting. We do not address whether that choice is acceptable if the affected citizens are mature adults, but we think the State may not, consistent with the Establishment Clause, place primary and secondary school children in this position. Research in psychology supports the common assumption that adolescents are often susceptible to pressure from their peers towards conformity, and that the influence is strongest in matters of social convention. To recognize that the choice imposed by the State constitutes an unacceptable constraint only acknowledges that the government may no more use social pressure to enforce orthodoxy than it may use more direct means.

The injury caused by the government's action, and the reason why Daniel and Deborah Weisman object to it, is that the State, in a school setting, in effect required participation in a religious exercise. It is, we concede, a brief exercise during which the individual can concentrate on joining its message, meditate on her own religion, or let her mind wander. But the embarrassment and the intrusion of the religious exercise cannot be refuted by arguing that these prayers, and similar ones to be said in the future, are of a *de minimis* character. To do so would be an affront to the rabbi who offered them and to all those for whom the prayers were an essential and profound recognition of divine authority. * * *

Attendance may not be required by official decree, yet it is apparent that a student is not free to absent herself from the graduation exercise in any real sense of the term "voluntary," for absence would require forfeiture of those intangible benefits which have motivated the student through youth and all her high school years. Graduation is a time for family and those closest to the student to celebrate success and express mutual wishes of gratitude and respect, all to the end of impressing upon the young person the role that it is his or her right and duty to assume in the community and all of its diverse parts.

* * *

The Government's argument gives insufficient recognition to the real conflict of conscience faced by the young student. The essence of the Government's position is that with regard to a civic, social occasion of this importance it is the objector, not the majority, who must take unilateral and private action to avoid compromising religious scruples, hereby electing to miss the graduation exercise. This turns conventional First Amendment analysis on its head. It is a tenet of the First Amendment that the State cannot require one of its citizens to forfeit his or her rights and benefits as the price of resisting conformance to state-sponsored religious practice. To say that a student must remain apart from the ceremony at the opening invocation and closing benediction is to risk compelling conformity in an environment analogous to the classroom setting, where we have said the risk of compulsion is especially high. Just as in *Engel v. Vitale,* 370 U.S. at 430, 82 S.Ct. at 1266, where we found that provisions within the challenged legislation permitting a student to be voluntarily excused from attendance or participation in the daily prayers did not shield those practices from invalidation, the fact that attendance at the graduation ceremonies is voluntary in a legal sense does not save the religious exercise.

* * *

Our society would be less than true to its heritage if it lacked abiding concern for the values of its young people, and we acknowledge the profound belief of adherents to many faiths that there must be a place in the student's life for precepts of a morality higher even than the law we today enforce. We express no hostility to those aspirations, nor would our oath permit us to do so. A relentless and all-pervasive attempt to exclude religion from every aspect of public life could itself become inconsistent with the Constitution. We recognize that, at graduation time and throughout the course of the educational process, there will be instances when religious values, religious practices, and religious persons will have some interaction with the public schools and their students. But these matters, often questions of accommodation of religion, are not before us. The sole question presented is whether a religious exercise may be conducted at a graduation ceremony in circumstances where, as we have found, young graduates who object are induced to conform. No holding by this Court suggests that a school can persuade or compel a student to participate in a religious exercise. That is being done here, and it is forbidden by the Establishment Clause of the First Amendment.

For the reasons we have stated, the judgment of the Court of Appeals is

Affirmed.

Note

1. *Weisman* was a closely fought, 5–4 decision. Eight years later, in *Santa Fe Independent School District v. Doe,* 530 U.S. 290, 120 S.Ct. 2266 (2000), the Court, by a vote of 6–3, applied the coercion test set forth in *Weisman* to find that a student-led prayer delivered over the public address system before each varsity football game for the entire season violated the Establishment Clause:

> Even if we regard every high school student's decision to attend a home football game as purely voluntary, we are nevertheless persuaded that the delivery of a pregame prayer has the improper effect of coercing those present to participate in an act of religious worship. For "the government may no more use social pressure to enforce orthodoxy than it may use more direct means." As in *Lee,* "[w]hat to most believers may seem nothing more than a reasonable request that the nonbeliever respect their religious practices, in a school context may appear to the nonbeliever or dissenter to be an attempt to employ the machinery of the State to enforce a religious orthodoxy." The constitutional command will not permit the District "to exact religious conformity from a student as the price" of joining her classmates at a varsity football game. Santa Fe Indep. Sch. Dist. v. Doe, 530 U.S. 290, 313 (2000).

The Court also rejected the *percentages* argument cited above in the introductory materials to this Chapter. The District had authorized an election to determine whether "invocations" should be delivered at the football games, and also to select the spokesperson to deliver them, and its attorneys argued that this election served to justify its subsequent practices. But the Court found that "while Santa Fe's majoritarian election might ensure that *most* of the students are represented, it does nothing to protect the minority; indeed, it likely serves to intensify their offense."

SCHOOL PRAYER
UNDER THE "NO CHILD LEFT BEHIND" ACT

Much to the surprise of many educators, the "No Child Left Behind" Act included specific provisions addressing school prayer. 20 U.S.C § 7904 provides:

> (a) Guidance. The Secretary shall provide and revise guidance, not later than September 1, 2002, and of every second year thereafter, to State educational agencies, local educational agencies, and the public on constitutionally protected prayer in public elementary schools and secondary schools, including making the guidance available on the Internet. The guidance shall be reviewed, prior to distribution, by the Office of Legal Counsel of the Department of Justice for verification that the guidance represents the current state of the law concerning constitutionally protected prayer in public elementary schools and secondary schools.

> (b) Certification. As a condition of receiving funds under this Act [20 USCS §§ 6301 et seq.], a local educational agency shall certify in

writing to the State educational agency involved that no policy of the local educational agency prevents, or otherwise denies participation in, constitutionally protected prayer in public elementary schools and secondary schools, as detailed in the guidance required under subsection (a). The certification shall be provided by October 1 of each year. The State educational agency shall report to the Secretary by November 1 of each year a list of those local educational agencies that have not filed the certification or against which complaints have been made to the State educational agency that the local educational agencies are not in compliance with this section.

(c) Enforcement. The Secretary is authorized and directed to effectuate subsection (b) by issuing, and securing compliance with, rules or orders with respect to a local educational agency that fails to certify, or is found to have certified in bad faith, that no policy of the local educational agency prevents, or otherwise denies participation in, constitutionally protected prayer in public elementary schools and secondary schools.

The provisions, and the subsequent "guidance" issued by the U.S. Department of Education, proved to be the subject of considerable debate ... with some members of the legal and education communities declaring that the posted document contained misleading and in some cases questionable assertions regarding the current state of Establishment Clause law.

MELLEN v. BUNTING

327 F.3d 355 (4th Cir. 2003).

KING, Circuit Judge:

General Josiah Bunting, III, the former Superintendent of the Virginia Military Institute ("VMI"), appeals the district court's award of declaratory and injunctive relief, prohibiting VMI from sponsoring a daily "supper prayer." * * *

I.

* * *

B.

All members of VMI's Corps of Cadets (the student body) are required to pay a room and board fee. This fee covers all of a cadet's meals, which are served in the Post mess hall. Although VMI serves supper to the Corps twice each evening in the mess hall, nearly all cadets attend the first seating; only those who participate in athletics or have other special circumstances can obtain authorization to attend the second seating.

The first seating begins with the "supper roll call" (the "SRC"), initiated by a bugle call summoning the Corps into formation in front of the Barracks. * * * [T]he Corps is called to attention, and the Regimental Commander—the senior cadet officer—presents the Corps to the TAC Officer. Salutes are then exchanged, and the command "REST" is given. While standing at rest, a cadet may move to a limited extent, leaving his or her right foot in place. The daily announcements are made, and the Cadet Chaplain then reads the supper prayer to the assembled Corps.[5]

The SRC ceremony is conducted every day except Saturday, and the Post Chaplain, Colonel James S. Park, has composed a separate supper prayer for each day. Depending on the day, the prayer begins with "Almighty God," "O God," "Father God," "Heavenly Father," or "Sovereign God." As the district court recognized, "[e]ach day's prayer is dedicated to giving thanks or asking for God's blessing." The court also observed that "a prayer may thank God for the Institute, ask for God's blessing on the Corps, or give thanks for the love and support of family and friends," and that "each day's prayer ends with the following invocation: 'Now O God, we receive this food and share this meal together with thanksgiving. Amen.'" The Corps must remain standing and silent while the supper prayer is read, but cadets are not obliged to recite the prayer, close their eyes, or bow their heads.

C.

On January 23, 2001, the Plaintiffs submitted a Permit Form to VMI's administration, requesting that cadets "be allowed to go about their business in the Mess Hall during the supper prayer (in a sense of not acknowledging that the prayer is occurring)." After their request was denied, the Plaintiffs wrote to General Bunting, asserting that the supper prayer was unconstitutional. The General promptly rejected this contention, advising them that "[t]he Constitution does not prohibit our saying grace before supper. And we shall continue to do so." General Bunting also informed the Plaintiffs that the supper prayer "is a precious link to our heritage and an admirable practice for a school of our provenience and culture," and that it would continue.

On May 9, 2001, Plaintiffs filed their complaint in the Western District of Virginia, seeking declaratory and injunctive relief, along with nominal damages, costs, and attorney's fees. They alleged that the supper prayer violated the Establishment Clause of the First Amendment; Article I, § 16 of the Virginia Constitution; and the Virginia Act for Religious Freedom, Va. Code Ann. § 57–1.

* * *

IV.

* * *

5. In the past, VMI sponsored a similar meal-time prayer, but the school's administration discontinued this practice in 1990 as a result of a decision to replace family-style dining with cafeteria-style dining. In 1995, General Bunting assumed control of VMI. Seeking to bring a stronger sense of unity to the Corps, he decided to return the Corps to a traditional SRC formation and family-style dining, including the supper prayer. Although now retired, General Bunting possessed the authority during his tenure at VMI over all VMI activities, including the supper prayer.

A.

* * *

As [the K–12 school prayer] decisions reflect, the Court has been unwavering in its position that the Establishment Clause prohibits public schools from sponsoring an official prayer. The Court has not, however, directly addressed whether, or to what extent, a state may sponsor prayer at an institution of higher education. Because VMI is such an institution, we briefly consider how our sister circuits have dealt with the issue of state-sponsored prayer in public colleges and universities.

B.

In a situation closely analogous to that presented here, the Court of Appeals for the District of Columbia, in *Anderson v. Laird*, addressed a federal regulation that required all cadets and midshipmen at the military academies to attend "Protestant, Catholic or Jewish chapel services on Sundays." In *Anderson,* the court ruled that this chapel attendance requirement violated the Establishment Clause. In its lead opinion, the court concluded that the "government may not require an individual to engage in religious practices or be present at religious exercises." Significantly, the court held that the regulation violated the Constitution even though: (1) attendance at the military academies was voluntary; and (2) cadets and midshipmen could be excused from the chapel attendance requirement.

More recently, in *Tanford v. Brand*, the Seventh Circuit considered whether a state university could include a religious invocation as part of its graduation ceremony. In upholding the practice, the court suggested that the invocation was not coercive, in that students were not required to attend and attendees did not feel compelled to participate in the invocation—in fact, students and their guests frequently came in and out (or remained seated) while the invocation was delivered. The court characterized the invocation as "simply a tolerable acknowledgment of beliefs widely held among the people of this country."

In *Chaudhuri v. Tennessee*, the Sixth Circuit also declined to enjoin a state university's practice of including prayer in its graduation ceremony. Evaluating the practice under the *Lemon* test, the court first held that such prayers had a secular purpose in that they "solemniz[ed] public occasions, express[ed] confidence in the future, and encourag[ed] the recognition of what is worthy of appreciation in society." Moving to *Lemon*'s second prong, the court decided that "an audience of college-educated adults could [not] be influenced unduly by prayers of the sort in question here." On *Lemon*'s final criterion, the court concluded: "[i]t does not seem to us that the practice of including nonsectarian prayers or moments of silence at [school] events creates any church-state entanglement at all."

V.

General Bunting * * * suggests that we should apply the standard employed by the Supreme Court in *Marsh v. Chambers*, where the Court—based on the unique history of the practice—upheld Nebraska's practice of opening its legislative sessions with a prayer. In support of his position, the General insists that prayer during military ceremonies and before meals is part of the fabric of our society, and that the drafters of the First Amendment did not intend to prohibit prayer before meals at a military school.[8] Independently, General Bunting maintains that, even if the traditional Establishment Clause analysis applies, the supper prayer should be upheld because the prohibition on state-sponsored prayer does not apply to a military college.

The Plaintiffs, by contrast, contend that the supper prayer is no different than the government-sponsored prayers struck down by the Supreme Court in *Engel, Schempp, Lee*, and *Santa Fe*. They emphasize that the supper prayer is composed by a state official (the VMI Post Chaplain) and that it is delivered on a daily basis at mealtime, when the Corps is assembled as a "family." Furthermore, the prayer is delivered as part of an official VMI function, entirely controlled by the school. The supper prayer, according to the Plaintiffs, bears the strong imprimatur of the state: VMI's cadets are marched in uniform and in formation to the mess hall before the state-composed prayer is delivered.

A.

We must begin our resolution of these competing positions by identifying the standard that should guide our analysis of the constitutionality of VMI's supper prayer. General Bunting first suggests that we should view the prayer as a uniquely historical practice, in an approach similar to that employed by the Supreme Court in *Marsh*. In *Marsh,* though, the Court was specifically influenced by the fact that, in September of 1789, members of the first Congress voted to submit the First Amendment to the states in the same week that they voted "to appoint and to pay a Chaplain for each House" of Congress. In upholding the Nebraska practice, Chief Justice Burger reasoned: "[t]his unique history leads us to accept the interpretation of the First Amendment draftsmen who saw no real threat to the Establishment Clause arising from a practice of prayer similar to that now challenged."

The Supreme Court has since emphasized that *Marsh* is applicable only in narrow circumstances. In *County of Allegheny v. ACLU Greater Pittsburgh Chapter*, the Court recognized that the *Marsh* decision "relied specifically on the fact that Congress authorized legislative prayer at the

---

8. General Bunting also suggests that VMI has a First Amendment interest that must be weighed in the Establishment Clause analysis. Contrary to this contention, VMI has no First Amendment interests that it can wield against the constitutional rights of its cadets. *See Hopwood v.*

Texas ("Saying that a [state] university has a First Amendment interest in this context is somewhat troubling.... The First Amendment generally protects citizens from the actions of government, not government from its citizens.").

same time that it produced the Bill of Rights." The Court expressly declined to interpret *Marsh* to mean that "all accepted practices 200 years old and their equivalents are constitutional today." Likewise, in *North Carolina Civil Liberties Union Legal Foundation v. Constangy,* we emphasized, in invalidating a judge's practice of opening court with a prayer, that *Marsh* was "predicated on the particular historical circumstances presented in that case."

Put simply, the supper prayer does not share *Marsh*'s "unique history." In fact, public universities and military colleges, such as VMI, did not exist when the Bill of Rights was adopted. We are therefore unable to apply *Marsh*'s reasoning to the evaluation of the constitutionality of the supper prayer. *See Edwards v. Aguillard,* 482 U.S. 578, 583 n.4, 107 S.Ct. 2573 (1987) (emphasizing that the *Marsh* analysis "is not useful in determining the proper roles of church and state in public schools, since free public education was virtually nonexistent at the time the Constitution was adopted").

B.

In rejecting the *Marsh* analysis, we are left to choose among the three traditional tests that the Supreme Court has used to evaluate Establishment Clause challenges. The test most often employed is that enunciated by the Court in *Lemon.* A second test, known as the "endorsement test," was first articulated by Justice O'Connor in her concurrence in *Lynch v. Donnelly,* and later adopted by a majority of the Court in *County of Allegheny.* Under the endorsement test, the government may not engage in a practice that suggests to the reasonable, informed observer that it is endorsing religion. Finally, in *Lee,* the Court formulated its "coercion test," under which "government may not coerce anyone to support or participate in religion or its exercise." 505 U.S. 577, 587, 112 S.Ct. 2649 (1992).

While the *Lemon* test dominates Establishment Clause jurisprudence, coercion has emerged as a prevailing consideration in the school prayer context. Because the Court has applied a variety of tests (in various combinations) in school prayer cases, federal appellate courts have also followed an inconsistent approach. * * *

During the past decade, we have emphasized that the *Lemon* test guides our analysis of Establishment Clause challenges. In the context of school prayer, though, we must give special consideration, under the principles discussed in *Lee* and *Santa Fe,* to whether a state has coerced religious worship. In the analysis that follows, we therefore assess the supper prayer against the principles announced in *Lee* and *Santa Fe,* and we then apply the *Lemon* criteria, treating the endorsement test as a refinement of *Lemon*'s second prong.

VI.

A.

Under the Supreme Court's decisions in *Lee* and *Santa Fe,* school officials may not, consistent with the Establishment Clause, compel students to participate in a religious activity. As the Court emphasized in *Lee,* "our precedents do not permit school officials to assist in composing prayers as an incident to a formal exercise for their students." 505 U.S. at 590, 112 S.Ct. 2649. The efforts of school officials "to monitor prayer will be perceived by the students as inducing a participation they might otherwise reject." *Id.* In defending the constitutionality of the supper prayer, General Bunting gives two reasons why the prayer should be upheld. First, he insists that VMI's cadets are mature adults, who will not feel coerced to participate in the supper prayer. Alternatively, he suggests that the members of the Corps (other than the rats) may avoid the prayer by falling out of the SRC formation before the Corps enters the mess hall.

It is undoubtedly true that grade school children are particularly "susceptible to pressure from their peers towards conformity." *Id.* at 593, 112 S.Ct. 2649. Recognizing a difference between such children and college students, certain of our sister circuits have approved the decisions of public universities to offer an invocation at graduation ceremonies. For example, in *Tanford,* the Seventh Circuit found that an invocation at a university commencement was not coercive. Similarly, in *Chaudhuri,* the Sixth Circuit allowed a state university to include a prayer at its graduation ceremonies, concluding that "here there was no coercion—real or otherwise—to participate in the nonsectarian prayers," because "an audience of college-educated adults could [not] be influenced unduly by prayers of the sort in question here."

Although VMI's cadets are not children, in VMI's educational system they are uniquely susceptible to coercion. VMI's adversative method of education emphasizes the detailed regulation of conduct and the indoctrination of a strict moral code. Entering students are exposed to the "rat line," in which upperclassmen torment and berate new students, bonding "new cadets to their fellow sufferers and, when they have completed the 7–month experience, to their former tormentors." *United States v. Virginia,* 518 U.S. 515, 522, 116 S.Ct. 2264 (1996). At VMI, even upperclassmen must submit to mandatory and ritualized activities, as obedience and conformity remain central tenets of the school's educational philosophy. In this atmosphere, General Bunting reinstituted the supper prayer in 1995 to build solidarity and bring the Corps together as a family. In this context, VMI's cadets are plainly coerced into participating in a religious exercise. Because of VMI's coercive atmosphere, the Establishment Clause precludes school officials from sponsoring an official prayer, even for mature adults.

The technical "voluntariness" of the supper prayer does not save it from its constitutional infirmities. At all relevant times, VMI's upperclass cadets could avoid the mess hall in order to shield themselves from the prayer. Nevertheless, the communal dining experience, like other official activities, is undoubtedly experienced as obligatory.[9] Through the

9. Even if dining in the mess hall was truly voluntary, the First Amendment prohibits General Bunting from requiring religious objectors to alienate themselves from hazing rituals that dominate a cadet's first year, members of the Corps are trained to participate in VMI's official activities. With this atmosphere as a background, VMI cannot avoid Establishment Clause problems by simply asserting that a cadet's attendance at supper and his or her participation in the supper prayer are "voluntary." In the words of the Supreme Court, " 'the government may no more use social pressure to enforce orthodoxy than it may use more direct means.' " *Santa Fe Indep. School Dist. v. Doe,* 530 U.S. 290, 312, 120 S.Ct. 2266 (2000) (quoting *Lee,* 505 U.S. at 594, 112 S.Ct. 2649). Put simply, VMI's supper prayer exacts an unconstitutional toll on the consciences of religious objectors. While the First Amendment does not in any way prohibit VMI's cadets from praying before, during, or after supper, the Establishment Clause prohibits VMI from sponsoring such a religious activity.

B.

We are compelled to reach the same conclusion when the supper prayer is measured against the three-part *Lemon* test. Under *Lemon,* a prayer must have a secular purpose; the primary effect of the prayer must be one that neither advances nor inhibits religion; and finally, the prayer must not foster an excessive government entanglement with religion. If we accept General Bunting's asserted purposes, the supper prayer may satisfy *Lemon*'s "secular purpose" prong. Nevertheless, in sponsoring an official prayer, VMI has plainly violated *Lemon*'s second and third prongs.

1.

The first prong of *Lemon* contemplates an inquiry into the subjective intentions of the government. "In applying the purpose test, it is appropriate to ask 'whether government's actual purpose is to endorse or disapprove of religion.' " *Wallace v. Jaffree,* 472 U.S. 38, 56, 105 S.Ct. 2479 (1985) (quoting *Lynch,* 465 U.S. at 690, 104 S.Ct. 1355 (O'Connor, J., concurring)). The secular purpose requirement presents "a fairly low hurdle" for the state, and a state-sponsored practice violates this prong of *Lemon* only "if it is *entirely* motivated by a purpose to advance religion." *Wallace,* 472 U.S. at 56, 105 S.Ct. 2479 (emphasis added). Nevertheless, a state may disingenuously profess a secular purpose for what is, in fact, a religious practice. While the state's characterization of its purpose is entitled to deference, it is our obligation to distinguish "a sham secular purpose from a sincere one." *Santa Fe,* 530 U.S. at 308, 120 S.Ct. 2266 (internal quotation marks omitted).

General Bunting has proffered several purposes (purportedly secular) for the supper prayer. First, he maintains that the prayer serves "an academic function by aiding VMI's mission of developing cadets into military and civilian leaders." Toward this end, the supper prayer supposedly promotes religious tolerance, educates cadets about religion,

the VMI community in order to avoid a religious practice. *Lee,* 505 U.S. at 596, 112 S.Ct. 2649.

and gets "students to engage with their own beliefs." According to General Bunting, the supper prayer encourages "cadets to reflect on and develop their own spiritual dimension." The prayer, in the General's words, also serves an expressive and institutional function by "providing an occasion for American's tradition of expressing thanksgiving and requesting divine guidance." Finally, General Bunting contends that the prayer "accommodate[s] the spiritual needs and free exercise rights of cadets, whose opportunities to meet those needs and exercise those rights are limited by the demands of barracks life and the highly structured nature of the VMI program."

In assessing General Bunting's asserted purposes for the supper prayer, we are concerned that he seeks to obscure the difference between educating VMI's cadets about religion, on the one hand, and forcing them to practice it, on the other. When a state-sponsored activity has an overtly religious character, courts have consistently rejected efforts to assert a secular purpose for that activity. Indeed, we have emphasized that "an act so intrinsically religious as prayer cannot meet, or at least would have difficulty meeting, the secular purpose prong of the *Lemon* test." And we have also recognized the obvious, that recitation of a prayer "is undeniably religious and has, by its nature, both a religious purpose and effect."

In an analogous situation, the Court of Appeals for the District of Columbia rejected the government's contention that a federal regulation requiring chapel attendance had a secular purpose. The federal government maintained (as VMI does here) that chapel services accommodated the free exercise rights of cadets and midshipmen, as well as sensitizing them to the religious beliefs of the soldiers and sailors they would someday lead. Rejecting the contention that these purposes justified the chapel attendance requirement, the court found that the regulation lacked a secular purpose. *See also Edwards,* 482 U.S. at 581, 586, 107 S.Ct. 2573 (concluding that statute violated *Lemon's* secular purpose prong by prohibiting "the teaching of the theory of evolution in public schools unless accompanied by instruction in 'creation science' ").

Similarly, in *Stone v. Graham*, the Supreme Court found no secular purpose for a statute that required the Ten Commandments be posted on the walls of all of a state's public schools. In that situation, the legislature of Kentucky had required that each copy of the Ten Commandments be printed with the words: "[t]he secular application of the Ten Commandments is clearly seen in its adoption as the fundamental legal code of Western Civilization and the Common Law of the United States." The Supreme Court rejected this characterization, concluding that:

> [t]he pre-eminent purpose for posting the Ten Commandments on schoolroom walls is plainly religious in nature. The Ten Commandments are undeniably a sacred text in the Jewish and Christian faiths, and no legislative recitation of a supposed secular purpose can blind us to that fact.

In invalidating the statute, the Court refused to ignore the religious purpose of this overtly religious text.

We are inclined to agree that the purpose of an official school prayer "is plainly religious in nature."[11] In evaluating the constitutionality of the supper prayer, however, we will accord General Bunting the benefit of all doubt and credit his explanation of the prayer's purposes. Assuming the supper prayer to be motivated by secular goals, we turn to the second and third prongs of *Lemon*.

2.

Regardless of the purposes motivating it, the supper prayer fails *Lemon*'s second prong. This "primary effect" prong must be assessed objectively, in order to measure whether the principal effect of government action "is to suggest government preference for a particular religious view or for religion in general." Put differently, "[t]he effect prong asks whether, irrespective of government's actual purpose, the practice under review in fact conveys a message of endorsement or disapproval [of religion]." *Wallace*, 472 U.S. at 56 n.42, 105 S.Ct. 2479 (internal quotation marks omitted).

The supper prayer has the primary effect of promoting religion, in that it sends the unequivocal message that VMI, as an institution, endorses the religious expressions embodied in the prayer. *See Engel v. Vitale*, 370 U.S. 421, 430, 82 S.Ct. 1261 (1962) ("There can be no doubt that New York's state prayer program officially establishes the religious beliefs embodied in the ... prayer."). The supper prayer is "delivered to a large audience assembled as part of a regularly scheduled, school-sponsored function conducted on school property." *Santa Fe*, 530 U.S. at 307, 120 S.Ct. 2266. In this context, "an objective observer, acquainted with the [supper prayer] would perceive it as a state endorsement of prayer in public schools." *Id.* at 308, 120 S.Ct. 2266 (internal quotation marks omitted).

As the Court has observed, "[s]uch an endorsement is not consistent with the established principle that the government must pursue a course of complete neutrality toward religion." *Wallace*, 472 U.S. at 60, 105 S.Ct. 2479. Even though VMI intended the supper prayer to be both inclusive and nondenominational, the Establishment Clause prohibits a state from promoting religion by authoring and promoting prayer for its citizens. In the words of the Court, "[t]he First Amendment was added to the Constitution to stand as a guarantee that neither the power nor the prestige of the Federal Government would be used to control, support or influence the kinds of prayer the American people can say." *Engel*, 370 U.S. at 429, 82 S.Ct. 1261. In establishing its supper prayer, VMI has done precisely what the First Amendment forbids.

11. Indeed, the district court found that the supper prayer lacked a secular purpose, stating that "[t]he only logical conclusion that can be drawn from [the asserted pur-poses] is that part of the Institute's educational mission, in the eyes of General Bunting, is religious indoctrination."

In numerous other cases, courts have struck down similar practices under *Lemon*'s "primary effect" prong. *See, e.g., Doe v. Duncanville Indep. Sch. Dist.,* 70 F.3d 402, 406 (5th Cir.1995) (striking down policy requiring participation of basketball coach in prayer after games).

With these decisions as a jurisprudential background, we are constrained to conclude that the supper prayer conflicts with *Lemon*'s second prong. Although we recognize and respect a cadet's individual desire to say grace before supper, the Establishment Clause prohibits VMI from sponsoring this religious practice.

3.

While *Lemon*'s second prong could dispose of the constitutional issue, VMI's sponsorship of the supper prayer also brings the school into conflict with *Lemon*'s third prong, excessively entangling it with religious activity. As the Eleventh Circuit recently stated, "[t]he ability to regulate the content of speech is a hallmark of state involvement." Here, VMI has composed, mandated, and monitored a daily prayer for its cadets. In this way, VMI has taken a position on what constitutes appropriate religious worship—an entanglement with religious activity that is forbidden by the Establishment Clause.

C.

Our decision today does not reflect any "hostility toward religion or toward prayer."[13] *Engel,* 370 U.S. at 434, 82 S.Ct. 1261. As we have recognized, our " 'Nation's history has not been one of entirely sanitized separation between Church and State,' and it 'has never been thought either possible or desirable to enforce a regime of total separation.' " Indeed, the Establishment Clause protects religious expression from governmental interference. "The Establishment Clause thus stands as an expression of principle on the part of the Founders of our Constitution that religion is too personal, too sacred, too holy, to permit its 'unhallowed perversion' " by government. *Engel,* 370 U.S. at 431–32, 82 S.Ct. 1261 (quoting *Memorial and Remonstrance against Religious Assessments*, II WRITINGS OF JAMES MADISON 183, 187).

While General Bunting may have instituted the supper prayer with the best of intentions, in so doing he has placed VMI at odds with the Establishment Clause. The Founding Fathers "led the fight for adoption of our Constitution and also for our Bill of Rights with the very guarantees of religious freedom that forbid [this] sort of governmental activity." *Engel,* 370 U.S. at 435, 82 S.Ct. 1261. Indeed, "one of the greatest dangers to the freedom of the individual to worship in his own way [lies] in the Government's placing its official stamp of approval upon one particular kind of prayer." *Id.* at 429, 82 S.Ct. 1261.

13. We also note that we are not called upon to address whether, or to what extent, the military may incorporate religious practices into its ceremonies. The Virginia General Assembly, not the Department of Defense, controls VMI.

VII.

Having decided that VMI's supper prayer conflicts with First Amendment principles, we turn to whether General Bunting is nevertheless entitled to qualified immunity. As a state official, General Bunting is immune from damages unless he violated "clearly established statutory or constitutional rights of which a reasonable person would have known." In this regard, a principle of constitutional law may be "clearly established" even though the precise factual situation has never been presented to a court. Accordingly, "officials can still be on notice that their conduct violates established law even in novel factual circumstances."

Although the Establishment Clause plainly forbids public schools from sponsoring an official prayer for young children, the Supreme Court has never addressed the constitutionality of state-sponsored prayer in any university setting, much less in a military college. Indeed, some of our sister circuits have approved prayer at certain university functions. In addition, the Court has not had the occasion to consider whether, or to what extent, the military may incorporate religious practices in its ceremonies. In these circumstances, General Bunting could reasonably have believed that the supper prayer was constitutional, and we must affirm the district court's decision to award him qualified immunity.

VIII.

For the foregoing reasons, we vacate the district court's judgment awarding Plaintiffs declaratory and injunctive relief. We affirm the court's decision that the Plaintiffs have alleged a violation of their rights under the Establishment Clause, but that General Bunting is nevertheless entitled to qualified immunity.

AFFIRMED IN PART AND VACATED IN PART.

D. APPLYING THE NEUTRALITY PRINCIPLE: PUBLIC FUNDING FOR PRIVATE RELIGIOUS EDUCATION

As mentioned above, neutrality has been an explicit component of Establishment Clause jurisprudence for a very long time. The question, though, has always been whether and to what extent neutrality amounts to an actual legal requirement. Can neutrality actually constitute a separate legal framework, or perhaps a test, similar in form and substance to other Establishment Clause tests? Is it a guiding principle or at least a relevant inquiry that can play a major role in the legal analysis, even if it is not actually a test? Is it, in reality, little more than a policy imperative that can assist judges in determining the contours of the debate in complex legal disputes? Does the impact of the neutrality question vary depending on the type of dispute at issue?

In the area of public funding for private religious education, recent decisions of the U.S. Supreme Court arguably give credence to the argument that—within this context—neutrality is at least a guiding principle. And for more than just 1–2 justices, it may actually amount to a framework for deciding a case itself.

Consider the treatment of the neutrality question in the *Zobrest* and *Simmons-Harris* cases, which follow? At this point in time, is there a separate and independent test for public funding of private religious education based at least in part, if not entirely, on a neutrality requirement?

PROBLEM 38: The Eldorado Teacher Education Institute

The following hypothetical takes place in the fictional state of Eldorado.

Concerned about the ongoing shortage of applicants for public school teaching positions in high-need areas, the Eldorado Department of Education and the Eldorado State University system establish a highly publicized partnership for the purpose of identifying innovative methods of teacher recruitment and training. The statewide Eldorado Teacher Education Institute (ETI) is formed, jointly administered by the partnership and funded by a combination of public and private money. An unprecedented program with no actual campus, the ETI will not only have a site-based component leading to a teacher credential, but is also expected to generate new research in this area.

The ETI will offer an alternative approach for those wishing to begin careers in K–12 education. Student teaching requirements will be expanded to comprise the equivalent of a half-time teaching position for two full years, under the supervision of trained professionals.[a] In addition, the student teachers admitted to the ETI will all receive stipends of $75,000 per year. One-half of the stipend will be in the form of a check payable to the student teacher, and this check will in essence comprise a full-time salary for the half-time teaching position. The second half of the stipend will be in the form of a voucher that the student teacher will then turn over to the participating training site to fund the on-site supervision required.

Under the terms of the ETI's policies, these training sites can be public or private, religious or sectarian. Student teachers complete a formal request sheet, specifying their preferred type of student teaching assignment and listing up to five choices of training sites. These training sites are chosen, generally, from a list of eligible schools provided by the ETI, but may also include sites where the student teacher has established personal contacts. While ETI personnel consult with the student teachers and seek to collaborate with them on the choice of assignment,

---

a. Student teaching, or "practice teaching"—as it is sometimes called—is an integral component of teacher credential programs. Students enrolled in these programs are given student teaching assignments in actual classrooms, typically at local public schools, where they teach lessons under the supervision of experienced classroom teachers who are legally responsible for the class. In the typical assignment, students eventually take over the class for a specific portion of the day (at the elementary level) or for an entire period (at the secondary level), grade papers, assign grades, etc. Each state specifies, by statute and/or regulation, the requisite number of "student teaching" hours required before the teacher education student is eligible to receive a credential. Alternate avenues of credentialing are often available as well.

in the end the final decision regarding the training sites is necessarily made by the ETI professionals.

Admission to the ETI is limited to applicants interested in becoming special education teachers for students of any language background, or those interested in becoming bilingual teachers in the high-need language areas of Spanish, Cantonese, and Vietnamese.

Volatile data regarding the first cohort, however, leads to widespread debate throughout the state regarding the efficacy of the program and its prospective implications. An independent evaluation of the ETI program had in fact revealed that approximately 40 percent of the student teachers in the first cohort used their stipends to student teach at traditional religious schools, while another 25 percent used their stipends to teach at schools with a religious affiliation but with programs that are primarily secular in nature.[b]

A lawsuit is ultimately filed by members of the Eldorado branch of Parents United for the Separation of Church and State. Plaintiffs plan to argue that both the student teacher salary provision of the stipend program and the voucher provision of the stipend program violate the Establishment Clause. They are not only prepared to argue under principles articulated by Chief Justice Rehnquist in *Zobrest* and *Simmons-Harris,* but also under the principles articulated by Justice Souter in the latter case.

What arguments will be set forth by the plaintiffs under the respective Rehnquist opinions? Under the Souter opinion in *Simmons-Harris?* What result? Discuss.

ZOBREST v. CATALINA FOOTHILLS SCH. DIST.

509 U.S. 1, 113 S.Ct. 2462 (1993).

CHIEF JUSTICE REHNQUIST delivered the opinion of the Court.

Petitioner James Zobrest, who has been deaf since birth, asked respondent school district to provide a sign-language interpreter to accompany him to classes at a Roman Catholic high school in Tucson, Arizona, pursuant to the Individuals with Disabilities Education Act (IDEA) and its Arizona counterpart. The United States Court of Appeals for the Ninth Circuit decided, however, that provision of such a publicly employed interpreter would violate the Establishment Clause of the First Amendment. We hold that the Establishment Clause does not bar the school district from providing the requested interpreter.

James Zobrest attended grades one through five in a school for the deaf, and grades six through eight in a public school operated by

---

b. "Traditional" religious schools can be defined as those with required religious instruction delivered by members of the clergy, as well as required participation in religious ceremonies and observances on campus. The more secular institutions are those with some religious affiliation but relatively limited religious activity. Harvard–

Westlake in Los Angeles, for example, is listed in the Episcopal diocese, but describes itself as "a nondenominational independent institution" that includes "a Rabbi and Episcopal Chaplain on the faculty who are available to students. Both lead religious activities for interested students and faculty."

respondent. While he attended public school, respondent furnished him with a sign-language interpreter. For religious reasons, James' parents (also petitioners here) enrolled him for the ninth grade in Salpointe Catholic High School, a sectarian institution.[1] When petitioners requested that respondent supply James with an interpreter at Salpointe, respondent referred the matter to the county attorney, who concluded that providing an interpreter on the school's premises would violate the United States Constitution. Pursuant to Ariz. Rev. Stat. Ann. § 15–253(B) (1991), the question next was referred to the Arizona attorney general, who concurred in the county attorney's opinion. Respondent accordingly declined to provide the requested interpreter.

* * *

We have never said that "religious institutions are disabled by the First Amendment from participating in publicly sponsored social welfare programs." For if the Establishment Clause did bar religious groups from receiving general government benefits, then "a church could not be protected by the police and fire departments, or have its public sidewalk kept in repair." *Widmar v. Vincent,* 454 U.S. 263, 274–75, 102 S.Ct. 269, 277 (1981) (internal quotation marks omitted). Given that a contrary rule would lead to such absurd results, we have consistently held that government programs that neutrally provide benefits to a broad class of citizens defined without reference to religion are not readily subject to an Establishment Clause challenge just because sectarian institutions may also receive an attenuated financial benefit. Nowhere have we stated this principle more clearly than in *Mueller v. Allen*, and *Witters v. Washington Dept. of Services for Blind*, two cases dealing specifically with government programs offering general educational assistance.

In *Mueller,* we rejected an Establishment Clause challenge to a Minnesota law allowing taxpayers to deduct certain educational expenses in computing their state income tax, even though the vast majority of those deductions (perhaps over 90%) went to parents whose children attended sectarian schools. Two factors, aside from States' traditionally broad taxing authority, informed our decision. We noted that the law "permits *all* parents—whether their children attend public school or private—to deduct their children's educational expenses." See *Widmar, supra,* 454 U.S. at 274, 102 S.Ct. at 277 ("The provision of benefits to so broad a spectrum of groups is an important index of secular effect"); *Board of Ed. of Westside Community Schools (Dist. 66) v. Mergens,* 496 U.S. 226, 248, 110 S.Ct. 2356, 2371 (1990) (plurality opinion) (same). We also pointed out that under Minnesota's scheme, public funds become available to sectarian schools "only as a result of numerous private choices of individual parents of school-age children," thus distinguishing *Mueller* from our other cases involving "the direct transmission of assistance from the State to the schools themselves."

1. The parties have stipulated: "The two functions of secular education and advancement of religious values or beliefs are inextricably intertwined throughout the operations of Salpointe."

Witters was premised on virtually identical reasoning. In that case, we upheld against an Establishment Clause challenge the State of Washington's extension of vocational assistance, as part of a general state program, to a blind person studying at a private Christian college to become a pastor, missionary, or youth director. Looking at the statute as a whole, we observed that "[a]ny aid provided under Washington's program that ultimately flows to religious institutions does so only as a result of the genuinely independent and private choices of aid recipients." The program, we said, "creates no financial incentive for students to undertake sectarian education." We also remarked that, much like the law in *Mueller,* "Washington's program is 'made available generally without regard to the sectarian-nonsectarian, or public-nonpublic nature of the institution benefited.'" In light of these factors, we held that Washington's program—even as applied to a student who sought state assistance so that he could become a pastor—would not advance religion in a manner inconsistent with the Establishment Clause.

That same reasoning applies with equal force here. The service at issue in this case is part of a general government program that distributes benefits neutrally to any child qualifying as "disabled" under the IDEA, without regard to the "sectarian-nonsectarian, or public-nonpublic nature" of the school the child attends. By according parents freedom to select a school of their choice, the statute ensures that a government-paid interpreter will be present in a sectarian school only as a result of the private decision of individual parents. In other words, because the IDEA creates no financial incentive for parents to choose a sectarian school, an interpreter's presence there cannot be attributed to state decisionmaking. Viewed against the backdrop of *Mueller* and *Witters,* then, the Court of Appeals erred in its decision. When the government offers a neutral service on the premises of a sectarian school as part of a general program that "is in no way skewed towards religion," it follows under our prior decisions that provision of that service does not offend the Establishment Clause. Indeed, this is an even easier case than *Mueller* and *Witters* in the sense that, under the IDEA, no funds traceable to the government ever find their way into sectarian schools' coffers. The only indirect economic benefit a sectarian school might receive by dint of the IDEA is the disabled child's tuition—and that is, of course, assuming that the school makes a profit on each student; that, without an IDEA interpreter, the child would have gone to school elsewhere; and that the school, then, would have been unable to fill that child's spot.

* * *

The IDEA creates a neutral government program dispensing aid not to schools but to individual handicapped children. If a handicapped child chooses to enroll in a sectarian school, we hold that the Establishment Clause does not prevent the school district from furnishing him with a sign-language interpreter there in order to facilitate his education. The judgment of the Court of Appeals is therefore

Reversed.

ZELMAN v. SIMMONS–HARRIS

536 U.S. 639, 122 S.Ct. 2460 (2002).

CHIEF JUSTICE REHNQUIST delivered the opinion of the Court.

The State of Ohio has established a pilot program designed to provide educational choices to families with children who reside in the Cleveland City School District. The question presented is whether this program offends the Establishment Clause of the United States Constitution. We hold that it does not.

There are more than 75,000 children enrolled in the Cleveland City School District. The majority of these children are from low-income and minority families. Few of these families enjoy the means to send their children to any school other than an inner-city public school. For more than a generation, however, Cleveland's public schools have been among the worst performing public schools in the Nation. In 1995, a Federal District Court declared a "crisis of magnitude" and placed the entire Cleveland school district under state control. Shortly thereafter, the state auditor found that Cleveland's public schools were in the midst of a "crisis that is perhaps unprecedented in the history of American education." The district had failed to meet any of the 18 state standards for minimal acceptable performance. Only 1 in 10 ninth graders could pass a basic proficiency examination, and students at all levels performed at a dismal rate compared with students in other Ohio public schools. More than two-thirds of high school students either dropped or failed out before graduation. Of those students who managed to reach their senior year, one of every four still failed to graduate. Of those students who did graduate, few could read, write, or compute at levels comparable to their counterparts in other cities.

It is against this backdrop that Ohio enacted, among other initiatives, its Pilot Project Scholarship Program. The program provides financial assistance to families in any Ohio school district that is or has been "under federal court order requiring supervision and operational management of the district by the state superintendent." Cleveland is the only Ohio school district to fall within that category.

The program provides two basic kinds of assistance to parents of children in a covered district. First, the program provides tuition aid for students in kindergarten through third grade, expanding each year through eighth grade, to attend a participating public or private school of their parent's choosing. Second, the program provides tutorial aid for students who choose to remain enrolled in public school.

The tuition aid portion of the program is designed to provide educational choices to parents who reside in a covered district. Any private school, whether religious or nonreligious, may participate in the program and accept program students so long as the school is located within the boundaries of a covered district and meets statewide educational standards. Participating private schools must agree not to discriminate on the basis of race, religion, or ethnic background, or to "advocate or foster unlawful behavior or teach hatred of any person or group on the basis of race, ethnicity, national origin, or religion." Any public school located in a school district adjacent to the covered district may also participate in the program. Adjacent public schools are eligible to receive a $2,250 tuition grant for each program student accepted in addition to the full amount of per-pupil state funding attributable to each additional student. All participating schools, whether public or private, are required to accept students in accordance with rules and procedures established by the state superintendent.

Tuition aid is distributed to parents according to financial need. Families with incomes below 200% of the poverty line are given priority and are eligible to receive 90% of private school tuition up to $2,250. For these lowest income families, participating private schools may not charge a parental copayment greater than $250. For all other families, the program pays 75% of tuition costs, up to $1,875, with no copayment cap. These families receive tuition aid only if the number of available scholarships exceeds the number of low-income children who choose to participate.[2] Where tuition aid is spent depends solely upon where parents who receive tuition aid choose to enroll their child. If parents choose a private school, checks are made payable to the parents who then endorse the checks over to the chosen school.

* * *

The program has been in operation within the Cleveland City School District since the 1996–1997 school year. In the 1999–2000 school year, 56 private schools participated in the program, 46 (or 82%) of which had a religious affiliation. None of the public schools in districts adjacent to Cleveland have elected to participate. More than 3,700 students participated in the scholarship program, most of whom (96%) enrolled in religiously affiliated schools. Sixty percent of these students were from families at or below the poverty line. In the 1998–1999 school year, approximately 1,400 Cleveland public school students received tutorial aid. This number was expected to double during the 1999–2000 school year.

The program is part of a broader undertaking by the State to enhance the educational options of Cleveland's schoolchildren in response to the 1995 takeover. That undertaking includes programs governing community and magnet schools.

* * *

In July 1999, respondents filed this action in United States District Court, seeking to enjoin the reenacted program on the ground that it violated the Establishment Clause of the United States Constitution. In August 1999, the District Court issued a preliminary injunction barring

2. The number of available scholarships per covered district is determined annually by the Ohio Superintendent for Public Instruction.

further implementation of the program, which we stayed pending review by the Court of Appeals. In December 1999, the District Court granted summary judgment for respondents. In December 2000, a divided panel of the Court of Appeals affirmed the judgment of the District Court, finding that the program had the "primary effect" of advancing religion in violation of the Establishment Clause. The Court of Appeals stayed its mandate pending disposition in this Court. We granted certiorari and now reverse the Court of Appeals.

The Establishment Clause of the First Amendment, applied to the States through the Fourteenth Amendment, prevents a State from enacting laws that have the "purpose" or "effect" of advancing or inhibiting religion. *Agostini v. Felton,* 521 U.S. 203, 222–23, 117 S.Ct. 1997 (1997) ("[W]e continue to ask whether the government acted with the purpose of advancing or inhibiting religion [and] whether the aid has the 'effect' of advancing or inhibiting religion"). There is no dispute that the program challenged here was enacted for the valid secular purpose of providing educational assistance to poor children in a demonstrably failing public school system. Thus, the question presented is whether the Ohio program nonetheless has the forbidden "effect" of advancing or inhibiting religion.

To answer that question, our decisions have drawn a consistent distinction between government programs that provide aid directly to religious schools, *Mitchell v. Helms,* 530 U.S. 793, 810–14, 120 S.Ct. 2530 (2000) (plurality opinion); *id.* at 841–44, 120 S.Ct. 2530 (O'CONNOR, J., concurring in judgment); *Agostini, supra,* at 225–27, 117 S.Ct. 1997; *Rosenberger v. Rector and Visitors of Univ. of Va.,* 515 U.S. 819, 842, 115 S.Ct. 2510 (1995) (collecting cases), and programs of true private choice, in which government aid reaches religious schools only as a result of the genuine and independent choices of private individuals, *Zobrest v. Catalina Foothills School Dist.,* 509 U.S. 1, 113 S.Ct. 2462 (1993). While our jurisprudence with respect to the constitutionality of direct aid programs has "changed significantly" over the past two decades, *Agostini, supra,* at 236, 117 S.Ct. 1997, our jurisprudence with respect to true private choice programs has remained consistent and unbroken. Three times we have confronted Establishment Clause challenges to neutral government programs that provide aid directly to a broad class of individuals, who, in turn, direct the aid to religious schools or institutions of their own choosing. Three times we have rejected such challenges.

[The Court then discusses *Mueller, Witters,* and *Zobrest* at some length.]

* * *

Mueller, Witters, and *Zobrest* * * * make clear that where a government aid program is neutral with respect to religion, and provides assistance directly to a broad class of citizens who, in turn, direct government aid to religious schools wholly as a result of their own genuine and independent private choice, the program is not readily subject to challenge under the Establishment Clause. A program that shares these features permits government aid to reach religious institutions only by way of the deliberate choices of numerous individual recipients. The incidental advancement of a religious mission, or the perceived endorsement of a religious message, is reasonably attributable to the individual recipient, not to the government, whose role ends with the disbursement of benefits. * * *

[W]e have never found a program of true private choice to offend the Establishment Clause.

We believe that the program challenged here is a program of true private choice, consistent with *Mueller, Witters,* and *Zobrest,* and thus constitutional. As was true in those cases, the Ohio program is neutral in all respects toward religion. It is part of a general and multifaceted undertaking by the State of Ohio to provide educational opportunities to the children of a failed school district. It confers educational assistance directly to a broad class of individuals defined without reference to religion, *i.e.,* any parent of a school-age child who resides in the Cleveland City School District. The program permits the participation of *all* schools within the district, religious or nonreligious. Adjacent public schools also may participate and have a financial incentive to do so. Program benefits are available to participating families on neutral terms, with no reference to religion. The only preference stated anywhere in the program is a preference for low-income families, who receive greater assistance and are given priority for admission at participating schools.

There are no "financial incentive[s]" that "ske[w]" the program toward religious schools. Such incentives "[are] not present . . . where the aid is allocated on the basis of neutral, secular criteria that neither favor nor disfavor religion, and is made available to both religious and secular beneficiaries on a nondiscriminatory basis." *Agostini, supra,* at 231, 117 S.Ct. 1997. The program here in fact creates financial *dis*incentives for religious schools, with private schools receiving only half the government assistance given to community schools and one-third the assistance given to magnet schools. Adjacent public schools, should any choose to accept program students, are also eligible to receive two to three times the state funding of a private religious school. Families too have a financial disincentive to choose a private religious school over other schools. Parents that choose to participate in the scholarship program and then to enroll their children in a private school (religious or nonreligious) must copay a portion of the school's tuition. Families that choose a community school, magnet school, or traditional public school pay nothing. Although such features of the program are not necessary to its constitutionality, they clearly dispel the claim that the program "creates . . . financial incentive[s] for parents to choose a sectarian school." *Zobrest,* 509 U.S. at 10, 113 S.Ct. at 2462.

Respondents suggest that even without a financial incentive for parents to choose a religious school, the program creates a "public perception that the State is endorsing religious practices and beliefs." But we have repeatedly recognized that no reasonable observer would think a neutral program of private choice, where state aid reaches religious schools solely as a result of the numerous independent decisions of private individuals, carries with it the *imprimatur* of government endorsement. *Zobrest, supra,* at 10–11, 113 S.Ct. 2462; *e.g., Mitchell, supra,* at 842–43, 120 S.Ct. 2530 (O'CONNOR, J., concurring in judgment) ("In terms of public perception, a government program of direct aid to religious schools . . . differs meaningfully from the government distributing aid directly to individual students who, in turn, decide to use the aid at the same religious schools"). The argument is particularly misplaced here since "the reasonable observer in the endorsement inquiry must be deemed aware" of the "history and context" underlying a challenged program. *Good News Club v. Milford Central School,* 533 U.S. 98, 119, 121 S.Ct. 2093 (2001) (internal quotation marks omitted). Any objective observer familiar with the full history and context of the Ohio program would reasonably view it as one aspect of a broader undertaking to assist poor children in failed schools, not as an endorsement of religious schooling in general.

There also is no evidence that the program fails to provide genuine opportunities for Cleveland parents to select secular educational options for their school-age children. Cleveland schoolchildren enjoy a range of educational choices: They may remain in public school as before, remain in public school with publicly funded tutoring aid, obtain a scholarship and choose a religious school, obtain a scholarship and choose a nonreligious private school, enroll in a community school, or enroll in a magnet school. That 46 of the 56 private schools now participating in the program are religious schools does not condemn it as a violation of the Establishment Clause. The Establishment Clause question is whether Ohio is coercing parents into sending their children to religious schools, and that question must be answered by evaluating *all* options Ohio provides Cleveland schoolchildren, only one of which is to obtain a program scholarship and then choose a religious school.

JUSTICE SOUTER speculates that because more private religious schools currently participate in the program, the program itself must somehow discourage the participation of private nonreligious schools. But Cleveland's preponderance of religiously affiliated private schools certainly did not arise as a result of the program; it is a phenomenon common to many American cities. * * *

Respondents and JUSTICE SOUTER claim that even if we do not focus on the number of participating schools that are religious schools, we should attach constitutional significance to the fact that 96% of scholarship recipients have enrolled in religious schools. They claim that this alone proves parents lack genuine choice, even if no parent has ever said so. We need not consider this argument in detail, since it was flatly rejected in *Mueller,* where we found it irrelevant that 96% of parents taking deductions for tuition expenses paid tuition at religious schools. Indeed, we have recently found it irrelevant even to the constitutionality of a direct aid program that a vast majority of program benefits went to religious schools. See *Agostini,* 521 U.S. at 229, 117 S.Ct. 1997 ("Nor are we willing to conclude that the constitutionality of an aid program depends on the number of sectarian school students who happen to receive the otherwise neutral aid" (citing *Mueller,* 463 U.S. at 401, 103 S.Ct. 3062)); see also *Mitchell,* 530 U.S. at 812 n.6, 120 S.Ct. 2530 (plurality opinion) ("[*Agostini*] held that the proportion of aid benefiting students at religious schools pursuant to a neutral program involving private choices was irrelevant to the constitutional inquiry"); *id.,* at 848, 120 S.Ct. 2530 (O'CONNOR, J., concurring in judgment) (same) (quoting *Agostini, supra,* at 229, 117 S.Ct. 1997). The constitutionality of a neutral educational aid program simply does not turn on whether and why, in a particular area, at a particular time, most private schools are run by religious organizations, or most recipients choose to use the aid at a religious school. As we said in *Mueller,* "[s]uch an approach would scarcely provide the certainty that this field stands in need of, nor can we perceive principled standards by which such statistical evidence might be evaluated." 463 U.S. at 401, 103 S.Ct. 3062.

This point is aptly illustrated here. The 96% figure upon which respondents and JUSTICE SOUTER rely discounts entirely (1) the more than 1,900 Cleveland children enrolled in alternative community schools, (2) the more than 13,000 children enrolled in alternative magnet schools, and (3) the more than 1,400 children enrolled in traditional public schools with tutorial assistance. Including some or all of these children in the denominator of children enrolled in nontraditional schools during the 1999–2000 school year drops the percentage enrolled in religious schools from 96% to under 20%. The 96% figure also represents but a snapshot of one particular school year. In the 1997–1998 school year, by contrast, only 78% of scholarship recipients attended religious schools. The difference was attributable to two private nonreligious schools that had accepted 15% of all scholarship students electing instead to register as community schools, in light of larger per-pupil funding for community schools and the uncertain future of the scholarship program generated by this litigation. Many of the students enrolled in these schools as scholarship students remained enrolled as community school students, thus demonstrating the arbitrariness of counting one type of school but not the other to assess primary effect. In spite of repeated questioning from the Court at oral argument, respondents offered no convincing justification for their approach, which relies entirely on such arbitrary classifications.

* * *

In sum, the Ohio program is entirely neutral with respect to religion. It provides benefits directly to a wide spectrum of individuals, defined only by financial need and residence in a particular school district. It permits such individuals to exercise genuine choice among options public and private, secular and religious. The program is therefore a program of true private choice. In keeping with an unbroken line of decisions rejecting challenges to similar programs, we hold that the program does not offend the Establishment Clause.

The judgment of the Court of Appeals is reversed.

It is so ordered.

JUSTICE O'CONNOR, concurring.

* * * While I join the Court's opinion, I write separately for two reasons. First, although the Court takes an important step, I do not believe that today's decision, when considered in light of other long-standing government programs that impact religious organizations and our prior Establishment Clause jurisprudence, marks a dramatic break from the past. Second, given the emphasis the Court places on verifying that parents of voucher students in religious schools have exercised "true private choice," I think it is worth elaborating on the Court's conclusion that this inquiry should consider all reasonable educational alternatives to religious schools that are available to parents. To do otherwise is to ignore how the educational system in Cleveland actually functions.

I

These cases are different from prior indirect aid cases in part because a significant portion of the funds appropriated for the voucher program reach religious schools without restrictions on the use of these funds. The share of public resources that reach religious schools is not, however, as significant as respondents suggest. Data from the 1999–2000 school year indicate that 82 percent of schools participating in the voucher program were religious and that 96 percent of participating students enrolled in religious schools, but these data are incomplete. These statistics do not take into account all of the reasonable educational choices that may be available to students in Cleveland public schools. When one considers the option to attend community schools, the percentage of students enrolled in religious schools falls to 62.1 percent. If magnet schools are included in the mix, this percentage falls to 16.5 percent.

* * *

II

Nor does today's decision signal a major departure from this Court's prior Establishment Clause jurisprudence. A central tool in our analysis of cases in this area has been the *Lemon* test. As originally formulated, a statute passed this test only if it had "a secular legislative purpose," if its "principal or primary effect" was one that "neither advance[d] nor inhibit[ed] religion," and if it did "not foster an excessive government entanglement with religion." In *Agostini v. Felton,* 521 U.S. 203, 218, 232–233, 117 S.Ct. 1997 (1997), we folded the entanglement inquiry into the primary effect inquiry. This made sense because both inquiries rely on the same evidence, and the degree of entanglement has implications for whether a statute advances or inhibits religion. The test today is basically the same as that set forth in *School Dist. of Abington Township v. Schempp,* over 40 years ago.

The Court's opinion in these cases focuses on a narrow question related to the *Lemon* test: how to apply the primary effects prong in indirect aid cases? Specifically, it clarifies the basic inquiry when trying to determine whether a program that distributes aid to beneficiaries, rather than directly to service providers, has the primary effect of advancing or inhibiting religion, or, as I have put it, of "endors[ing] or disapprov[ing] ... religion." Courts are instructed to consider two factors: first, whether the program administers aid in a neutral fashion, without differentiation based on the religious status of beneficiaries or providers of services; second, and more importantly, whether beneficiaries of indirect aid have a genuine choice among religious and nonreligious organizations when determining the organization to which they will direct that aid. If the answer to either query is "no," the program should be struck down under the Establishment Clause.

* * *

III

There is little question in my mind that the Cleveland voucher program is neutral as between religious schools and nonreligious schools. Justice SOUTER rejects the Court's notion of neutrality, proposing that the neutrality of a program should be gauged not by the opportunities it presents but rather by its effects. In particular, a "neutrality test ... [should] focus on a category of aid that may be directed to religious as well as secular schools, and ask whether the scheme favors a religious direction." Justice SOUTER doubts that the Cleveland program is neutral under this view. He surmises that the cap on tuition that voucher schools may charge low-income students encourages these students to attend religious rather than nonreligious private voucher schools. But Justice SOUTER's notion of neutrality is inconsistent with that in our case law. As we put it in *Agostini,* government aid must be "made available to both religious and secular beneficiaries on a nondiscriminatory basis." 521 U.S. at 231, 117 S.Ct. 1997.

* * *

In my view the more significant finding in these cases is that Cleveland parents who use vouchers to send their children to religious private schools do so as a result of true private choice. * * *

JUSTICE SOUTER, with whom JUSTICE STEVENS, JUSTICE GINSBURG, and JUSTICE BREYER join, dissenting.

The Court's majority holds that the Establishment Clause is no bar to Ohio's payment of tuition at private religious elementary and middle schools under a scheme that systematically provides tax money to support the schools' religious missions. The occasion for the legislation thus upheld is the condition of public education in the city of Cleveland. The record indicates that the schools are failing to serve their objective, and the vouchers in issue here are said to be needed to provide adequate alternatives to them. If there were an excuse for giving short shrift to the Establishment Clause, it would probably apply here. But there is no excuse. Constitutional limitations are placed on government to preserve constitutional values in hard cases, like these. "[C]onstitutional lines have to be drawn, and on one side of every one of them is an otherwise sympathetic case that provokes impatience with the Constitution and with the line. But constitutional lines are the price of constitutional government." *Agostini v. Felton,* 521 U.S. 203, 254, 117 S.Ct. 1997 (1997) (SOUTER, J., dissenting). I therefore respectfully dissent.

The applicability of the Establishment Clause to public funding of benefits to religious schools was settled in *Everson v. Board of Ed. of Ewing*, which inaugurated the modern era of establishment doctrine. The Court stated the principle in words from which there was no dissent:

> No tax in any amount, large or small, can be levied to support any religious activities or institutions, whatever they may be called, or whatever form they may adopt to teach or practice religion.

The Court has never in so many words repudiated this statement, let alone, in so many words, overruled *Everson.*

Today, however, the majority holds that the Establishment Clause is not offended by Ohio's Pilot Project Scholarship Program, under which students may be eligible to receive as much as $2,250 in the form of tuition vouchers transferable to religious schools. In the city of Cleveland the overwhelming proportion of large appropriations for voucher money must be spent on religious schools if it is to be spent at all, and will be spent in amounts that cover almost all of tuition. The money will thus pay for eligible students' instruction not only in secular subjects but in religion as well, in schools that can fairly be characterized as founded to teach religious doctrine and to imbue teaching in all subjects with a religious dimension. Public tax money will pay at a systemic level for teaching the covenant with Israel and Mosaic law in Jewish schools, the primacy of the Apostle Peter and the Papacy in Catholic schools, the truth of reformed Christianity in Protestant schools, and the revelation to the Prophet in Muslim schools, to speak only of major religious groupings in the Republic.

How can a Court consistently leave *Everson* on the books and approve the Ohio vouchers? The answer is that it cannot. It is only by ignoring *Everson* that the majority can claim to rest on traditional law in its invocation of neutral aid provisions and private choice to sanction the Ohio law. It is, moreover, only by ignoring the meaning of neutrality and private choice themselves that the majority can even pretend to rest today's decision on those criteria.

I

The majority's statements of Establishment Clause doctrine cannot be appreciated without some historical perspective on the Court's announced limitations on government aid to religious education, and its repeated repudiation of limits previously set. My object here is not to give any nuanced exposition of the cases, which I tried to classify in some detail in an earlier opinion, see *Mitchell v. Helms,* 530 U.S. 793, 873–99, 120 S.Ct. 2530 (2000) (dissenting opinion), but to set out the broad doctrinal stages covered in the modern era, and to show that doctrinal bankruptcy has been reached today.

Viewed with the necessary generality, the cases can be categorized in three groups. In the period from 1947 to 1968, the basic principle of no aid to religion through school benefits was unquestioned. Thereafter for some 15 years, the Court termed its efforts as attempts to draw a line against aid that would be divertible to support the religious, as distinct from the secular, activity of an institutional beneficiary. Then, starting in 1983, concern with divertibility was gradually lost in favor of approving aid in amounts unlikely to afford substantial benefits to religious schools, when offered evenhandedly without regard to a recipient's religious character, and when channeled to a religious institution only by the genuinely free choice of some private individual. Now, the three stages are succeeded by a fourth, in which the substantial character of government aid is held to have no constitutional significance, and the espoused criteria of neutrality in offering aid, and private choice in directing it, are shown to be nothing but examples of verbal formalism. * * *

II

Although it has taken half a century since *Everson* to reach the majority's twin standards of neutrality and free choice, the facts show that, in the majority's hands, even these criteria cannot convincingly legitimize the Ohio scheme.

A

Consider first the criterion of neutrality. As recently as two Terms ago, a majority of the Court recognized that neutrality conceived of as evenhandedness toward aid recipients had never been treated as alone sufficient to satisfy the Establishment Clause, *Mitchell,* 530 U.S. at 838–39, 120 S.Ct. 2530 (O'CONNOR, J., concurring in judgment); *id.* at 884, 120 S.Ct. 2530 (SOUTER, J., dissenting). But at least in its limited significance, formal neutrality seemed to serve some purpose. Today, however, the majority employs the neutrality criterion in a way that renders it impossible to understand.

Neutrality in this sense refers, of course, to evenhandedness in setting eligibility as between potential religious and secular recipients of public money. *Id.* at 809–10, 120 S.Ct. 2530 (plurality opinion); *id.* at 878–84, 120 S.Ct. 2530 (SOUTER, J., dissenting) (three senses of "neutrality"). Thus, for example, the aid scheme in *Witters* provided an eligible recipient with a scholarship to be used at any institution within a practically unlimited universe of schools; it did not tend to provide more or less aid depending on which one the scholarship recipient chose, and there was no indication that the maximum scholarship amount would be insufficient at secular schools. Neither did any condition of Zobrest's interpreter's subsidy favor religious education.

In order to apply the neutrality test, then, it makes sense to focus on a category of aid that may be directed to religious as well as secular schools, and ask whether the scheme favors a religious direction. Here, one would ask whether the voucher provisions, allowing for as much as $2,250 toward private school tuition (or a grant to a public school in an adjacent district), were written in a way that skewed the scheme toward benefiting religious schools.

This, however, is not what the majority asks. The majority looks not to the provisions for tuition vouchers, but to every provision for educational opportunity: "The program permits the participation of *all* schools within the district, [as well as public schools in adjacent districts], religious or nonreligious." The majority then finds confirmation that "participation of *all* schools" satisfies neutrality by noting that the better part of total state educational expenditure goes to public schools, thus showing there is no favor of religion.

The illogic is patent. If regular, public schools (which can get no voucher payments) "participate" in a voucher scheme with schools that can, and public expenditure is still predominantly on public schools, then the majority's reasoning would find neutrality in a scheme of vouchers available for private tuition in districts with no secular private schools at all. "Neutrality" as the majority employs the term is, literally, verbal and nothing more. This, indeed, is the only way the majority can gloss over the very nonneutral feature of the total scheme covering *"all* schools"*: public tutors may receive from the State no more than $324 per child to support extra tutoring (that is, the State's 90% of a total amount of $360), whereas the tuition voucher schools (which turn out to be mostly religious) can receive up to $2,250.

Why the majority does not simply accept the fact that the challenge here is to the more generous voucher scheme and judge its neutrality in relation to religious use of voucher money seems very odd. It seems odd, that is, until one recognizes that comparable schools for applying the criterion of neutrality are also the comparable schools for applying the other majority criterion, whether the immediate recipients of voucher aid have a genuinely free choice of religious and secular schools to receive the voucher money. And in applying this second criterion, the consideration of *"all* schools" is ostensibly helpful to the majority position.

B

The majority addresses the issue of choice the same way it addresses neutrality, by asking whether recipients or potential recipients of voucher aid have a choice of public schools among secular alternatives to religious schools. Again, however, the majority asks the wrong question and misapplies the criterion. The majority has confused choice in spending scholarships with choice from the entire menu of possible educational placements, most of them open to anyone willing to attend a public school. I say "confused" because the majority's new use of the choice criterion, which it frames negatively as "whether Ohio is coercing parents into sending their children to religious schools," ignores the reason for having a private choice enquiry in the first place. Cases since *Mueller* have found private choice relevant under a rule that aid to religious schools can be permissible so long as it first passes through the hands of students or parents. The majority's view that all educational choices are comparable for purposes of choice thus ignores the whole point of the choice test: it is a criterion for deciding whether indirect aid to a religious school is legitimate because it passes through private hands that can spend or use the aid in a secular school. The question is whether the private hand is genuinely free to send the money in either a secular direction or a religious one. The majority now has transformed this question about private choice in channeling aid into a question about selecting from examples of state spending (on education) including direct spending on magnet and community public schools that goes through no private hands and could never reach a religious school under any circumstance. When the choice test is transformed from where to spend the money to where to go to school, it is cut loose from its very purpose.

* * *

If, contrary to the majority, we ask the right question about genuine choice to use the vouchers, the answer shows that something is influencing choices in a way that aims the money in a religious direction: of 56 private schools in the district participating in the voucher program (only 53 of which accepted voucher students in 1999–2000), 46 of them are religious; 96.6% of all voucher recipients go to religious schools, only 3.4% to nonreligious ones. Unfortunately for the majority position, there is no explanation for this that suggests the religious direction results simply from free choices by parents. One answer to these statistics, for example, which would be consistent with the genuine choice claimed to be operating, might be that 96.6% of families choosing to avail themselves of vouchers choose to educate their children in schools of their own religion. This would not, in my view, render the scheme constitutional, but it would speak to the majority's choice criterion. Evidence shows, however, that almost two out of three families using vouchers to send their children to religious schools did not embrace the religion of those schools. The families made it clear they had not chosen the schools because they wished their children to be proselytized in a religion not their own, or in any religion, but because of educational opportunity.

* * *

There is, in any case, no way to interpret the 96.6% of current voucher money going to religious schools as reflecting a free and genuine choice by the families that apply for vouchers. The 96.6% reflects, instead, the fact that too few nonreligious school desks are available and few but religious schools can afford to accept more than a handful of voucher students. And contrary to the majority's assertion, public schools in adjacent districts hardly have a financial incentive to participate in the Ohio voucher program, and none has. For the overwhelming number of children in the voucher scheme, the only alternative to the public schools is religious. And it is entirely irrelevant that the State did not deliberately design the network of private schools for the sake of channeling money into religious institutions. The criterion is one of genuinely free choice on the part of the private individuals who choose, and a Hobson's choice is not a choice, whatever the reason for being Hobsonian.

III

* * *

If the divisiveness permitted by today's majority is to be avoided in the short term, it will be avoided only by action of the political branches at the state and national levels. Legislatures not driven to desperation by the problems of public education may be able to see the threat in vouchers negotiable in sectarian schools. Perhaps even cities with problems like Cleveland's will perceive the danger, now that they know a federal court will not save them from it.

My own course as a judge on the Court cannot, however, simply be to hope that the political branches will save us from the consequences of the majority's decision. *Everson's* statement is still the touchstone of sound law, even though the reality is that in the matter of educational aid the Establishment Clause has largely been read away. True, the majority has not approved vouchers for religious schools alone, or aid earmarked for religious instruction. But no scheme so clumsy will ever get before us, and in the cases that we may see, like these, the Establishment Clause is largely silenced. I do not have the option to leave it silent, and I hope that a future Court will reconsider today's dramatic departure from basic Establishment Clause principle.

Notes

1. *Simmons-Harris* was a long-awaited opinion by both proponents and opponents of school voucher programs. The 5–4 decision ended at least one component of the debate: channeling public funds through parents for the funding of private religious education was not a blanket violation of the Establishment Clause. What is the scope of the *Simmons–Harris* decision? Is it limited to the type of voucher program at issue in the Ohio case, or are all voucher programs now going to be constitutional under Establishment Clause jurisprudence? How important was it to Chief Justice Rehnquist and Justice O'Connor that this was a particular type of program, geared toward helping low socioeconomic status (SES) children who had been attending the lowest performing schools in a District that was clearly in crisis? How important was it that the program was part of an entire menu of options that had been made available to these students under the rubric of equal educational opportunity? How central to the legal analysis were these facts? How applicable would this decision be in determining the constitutionality of a voucher program that provided equally for all students in a given city or state, despite differences in such factors as SES and individual school performance?

2. Church-state issues continue to play either a direct or an indirect role in current and prospective legal challenges to voucher program under state constitutional law. At least ten state constitutions, in fact, appear to provide for a greater level of separation between church and state than the federal baseline. *See, e.g., Bush v. Holmes,* ___ So.2d ___, 2006 WL 20584 (Fla.), at *19, Note 17. In *Holmes,* the Florida Supreme Court held by a vote of 5–2 that the Florida voucher program–the only statewide program of its kind in the country at the time–violated its own state constitution. However, it did so under a provision that was found to indirectly bar public money for private sectarian education in this manner. Excerpts from this recent decision follow.

BUSH v. HOLMES

___ So.2d ___, 2006 WL 20584 (Fla.)

PARIENTE, C.J.

* * * The issue we decide is whether the State of Florida is prohibited by the Florida Constitution from expending public funds to allow students to obtain a private school education in kindergarten through grade twelve, as an alternative to a public school education. The law in question, now codified at section 1002 .38, Florida Statutes (2005), authorizes a system of school vouchers and is known as the Opportunity Scholarship Program (OSP).

Under the OSP, a student from a public school that fails to meet certain minimum state standards has two options. The first is to move to another public school with a satisfactory record under the state standards. The second option is to receive funds from the public treasury, which would otherwise have gone to the student's school district, to pay the student's tuition at a private school. The narrow question we address is whether the second option violates a part of the Florida Constitution requiring the state to both provide for "the education of all children residing within its borders" and provide "by law for a uniform, efficient, safe, secure, and high quality system of free public schools that allows students to obtain a high quality education." Art. IX, § 1(a), Fla. Const.

As a general rule, courts may not reweigh the competing policy concerns underlying a legislative enactment. The arguments of public policy supporting both sides in this dispute have obvious merit, and the Legislature with the Governor's assent has resolved the ensuing debate in favor of the proponents of the program. In most cases, that would be the end of the matter. However, as is equally self-evident, the usual deference given to the Legislature's resolution of public policy issues is at all times circumscribed by the Constitution. Acting within its constitutional limits, the Legislature's power to resolve issues of civic debate receives great deference. Beyond those limits, the Constitution must prevail over any enactment contrary to it.

Thus, in reviewing the issue before us, the justices emphatically are not examining whether the public policy decision made by the other branches is wise or unwise, desirable or undesirable. Nor are we examining whether the Legislature intended to supplant or replace the public school system to any greater or lesser extent. Indeed, we acknowledge, as does the dissent, that the statute at issue here is limited in the number of students it affects. * * *

Our inquiry begins with the plain language of the second and third sentences of article IX, section 1(a) of the Constitution. The relevant words are these: "It is ... a paramount duty of the state to make adequate provision for the education of all children residing within its borders." Using the same term, "adequate provision," article IX, section 1(a) further states: "Adequate provision shall be made by law for a uniform, efficient, safe, secure, and high quality system of free public schools." For reasons expressed more fully below, we find that the OSP violates this language. It diverts public dollars into separate private systems parallel to and in competition with the free public schools that are the sole means set out in the Constitution for the state to provide for the education of Florida's children. This diversion not only reduces money available to the free schools, but also funds private schools that are not "uniform" when compared with each other or the public system. Many standards imposed by law on the public schools are inapplicable to the private schools receiving public monies. * * * [T]hrough the OSP the state is fostering plural, nonuniform systems of education in direct violation of the constitutional mandate for a uniform system of free public schools.

* * *

In sum, article IX, section 1(a) provides for the manner in which the state is to fulfill its mandate to make adequate provision for the education of Florida's children—through a system of public education. The OSP contravenes this constitutional provision because it allows some children to receive a publicly funded education through an alternative system of private schools that are not subject to the uniformity requirements of the public school system. The diversion of money not only reduces public funds for a public education but also uses public funds to provide an alternative education in private schools that are not subject to the "uniformity" requirements for public schools. Thus, in two significant respects, the OSP violates the mandate set forth in article IX, section 1(a).

We do not question the basic right of parents to educate their children as they see fit. We recognize that the proponents of vouchers have a strongly held view that students should have choices. Our decision does not deny parents recourse to either public or private school alternatives to a failing school. Only when the private school option depends upon public funding is choice limited. This limit is necessitated by the constitutional mandate in article IX, section 1(a), which sets out the state's responsibilities in a manner that does not allow the use of state monies to fund a private school education. * * *

WELLS, ANSTEAD, LEWIS, and QUINCE, concur.

BELL, J., dissents with an opinion, in which CANTERO, J., concurs.

BELL, J., dissenting.

"[N]othing in article IX, section 1 clearly prohibits the Legislature from allowing the well-delineated use of public funds for private school education, particularly in circumstances where the Legislature finds such use is necessary." *Bush v. Holmes,* 767 So.2d 668, 675 (Fla. 1st DCA 2000). This conclusion, written by Judge Charles Kahn for a unanimous panel of the First District Court of Appeal, is the only answer this Court is empowered to give to the constitutional question the majority has decided to answer. Therefore, I dissent.

* * *

The majority's reading of article IX, section 1 is flawed. * * * [The] mandate is to make adequate provision *for* a public school system. The text does not provide that the government's provision for education shall be "by" or "through" a system of free public schools. Without language of exclusion or preclusion, there is no support for the majority's finding that public schools are the exclusive means by or through which the government may fulfill its duty to make adequate provision for the education of every child in Florida.

As the ultimate sovereign, if the people of Florida had wanted to mandate this exclusivity, they could have very easily written article IX to include such a proscription. Ten other states have constitutional provisions that expressly prohibit the allocation of public education funds to private schools. *Compare* art. IX, Fla. Const., *with, e.g.,* Miss. Const. art. 8, § 208 ("[N]or shall any funds be appropriated toward the support of any sectarian school, or to any school that at the time of receiving such appropriation is not conducted as a free school."), *and* S.C. Const. art. XI, § 4 ("No money shall be paid from public funds nor shall the credit of the State or any of its political subdivisions be used for the direct benefit of any religious or other private educational institution."). However, the people of Florida have not included such a proscription in article IX, section 1 of the Florida Constitution. Therefore, without any express or necessarily implied proscription in article IX, section 1 of Florida's Constitution, this Court has no authority to declare the OSP unconstitutional as violative of article IX, section 1.

* * *

Our position as justices vests us with the right and the responsibility to declare a legislative enactment invalid—but only when such a declaration is an "imperative and unavoidable necessity." *State ex rel. Crim,* 159 So. at 664. No such necessity is evident in this case. Nothing in the plain language or history of article IX requires a finding that the Opportunity Scholarship Program is unconstitutional. The clear purpose behind article IX is to ensure that every child in Florida has the opportunity to receive a high-quality education and to ensure access to such an education by requiring the Legislature to make adequate provision for a uniform system of free public schools. There is absolutely no evidence before this Court that this mandate is not being fulfilled. * * *

Chapter IX

MORALITY, VALUES, AND EDUCATIONAL POLICY

This chapter focuses on recent controversies that exemplify competing visions of "morality" and "values." Underlying many of the debates in this area is the question of whether and to what extent morality and values should be reflected in the requirements of public education. Related inquiries include volatile questions of who gets to define *morality* and *which values* might appropriately inform the day-to-day decisions and practices of educators.

Controversies in this area are often based implicitly or explicitly on religion, and they may be even more emotional than the ones addressed in the previous chapter. Indeed, not only are there continuing examples in these materials of disagreements regarding the extent to which religion should be reflected in the legal mandates, but the efficacy of religious doctrine itself may be questioned.

The U.S. is a pluralistic society, and its residents often hold widely differing views on the place of religion in the public sector. Many Americans, for example, insist that religious doctrine is the necessary basis for any decision regarding morality and values in the schools. Many other Americans hold to the view that not only does religion not necessarily equal morality, but that religious doctrine as determined by certain religious leaders and denominations may sometimes be immoral.

The disputes in this chapter often epitomize these differences of opinion. Arguably, however, the cases together reflect the emergence of a broad middle ground. Religion must be respected in the public sector, but it is not automatically viewed as synonymous with morality. And religious "values"—depending on how the term is defined—may have a place in the public schools, but religious "teachings" may be violative of the First Amendment.

Consider the materials that follow in light of these conflicting strands of thought. To what extent have the courts succeeded in reconciling the range of perspectives that Americans express on these issues?

To what extent have the courts shown little or no interest in reconciling perspectives, given the requirements of U.S. law? What conclusions might be drawn regarding future directions in this context?

A. THE RIGHT TO ALTERNATIVE MODELS OF EDUCATION

WISCONSIN v. YODER

406 U.S. 205, 92 S.Ct. 1526 (1972).

MR. CHIEF JUSTICE BURGER delivered the opinion of the Court.

[In this case, the Court reviews the decision of the Wisconsin Supreme Court in favor of Amish families. The families contend that their rights under the Free Exercise Clause of the First Amendment were violated because the State—pursuant to compulsory school-attendance laws—required them to send their children to formal high school until the age of 16.]

* * *

In support of their position, [the Amish families] presented as expert witnesses scholars on religion and education whose testimony is uncontradicted. They expressed their opinions on the relationship of the Amish belief concerning school attendance to the more general tenets of their religion, and described the impact that compulsory high school attendance could have on the continued survival of Amish communities as they exist in the United States today. The history of the Amish sect was given in some detail, beginning with the Swiss Anabaptists of the 16th century who rejected institutionalized churches and sought to return to the early, simple, Christian life de-emphasizing material success, rejecting the competitive spirit, and seeking to insulate themselves from the modern world. As a result of their common heritage, Old Order Amish communities today are characterized by a fundamental belief that salvation requires life in a church community separate and apart from the world and worldly influence. This concept of life aloof from the world and its values is central to their faith.

A related feature of Old Order Amish communities is their devotion to a life in harmony with nature and the soil, as exemplified by the simple life of the early Christian era that continued in America during much of our early national life. Amish beliefs require members of the community to make their living by farming or closely related activities. Broadly speaking, the Old Order Amish religion pervades and determines the entire mode of life of its adherents. Their conduct is regulated in great detail by the Ordnung, or rules, of the church community. Adult baptism, which occurs in late adolescence, is the time at which Amish young people voluntarily undertake heavy obligations, not unlike the Bar Mitzvah of the Jews, to abide by the rules of the church community.

Amish objection to formal education beyond the eighth grade is firmly grounded in these central religious concepts. They object to the high school, and higher education generally, because the values they teach are in marked variance with Amish values and the Amish way of life; they view secondary school education as an impermissible exposure of their children to a "worldly" influence in conflict with their beliefs. The high school tends to emphasize intellectual and scientific accomplishments, self-distinction, competitiveness, worldly success, and social life with other students. Amish society emphasizes informal learning-through-doing; a life of "goodness," rather than a life of intellect; wisdom, rather than technical knowledge, community welfare, rather than competition; and separation from, rather than integration with, contemporary worldly society.

* * * Dr. John Hostetler, one of the experts on Amish society, testified that the modern high school is not equipped, in curriculum or social environment, to impart the values promoted by Amish society.

The Amish do not object to elementary education through the first eight grades as a general proposition because they agree that their children must have basic skills in the "three R's" in order to read the Bible, to be good farmers and citizens, and to be able to deal with non-Amish people when necessary in the course of daily affairs. They view such a basic education as acceptable because it does not significantly expose their children to worldly values or interfere with their development in the Amish community during the crucial adolescent period. * * *

On the basis of such considerations, Dr. Hostetler testified that compulsory high school attendance could not only result in great psychological harm to Amish children, because of the conflicts it would produce, but would also, in his opinion, ultimately result in the destruction of the Old Order Amish church community as it exists in the United States today. The testimony of Dr. Donald A. Erickson, an expert witness on education, also showed that the Amish succeed in preparing their high school age children to be productive members of the Amish community. He described their system of learning through doing the skills directly relevant to their adult roles in the Amish community as "ideal" and perhaps superior to ordinary high school education. The evidence also showed that the Amish have an excellent record as law-abiding and generally self-sufficient members of society.

* * *

I

There is no doubt as to the power of a State, having a high responsibility for education of its citizens, to impose reasonable regulations for the control and duration of basic education. Providing public schools ranks at the very apex of the function of a State. Yet even this paramount responsibility was, in *Pierce*, made to yield to the right of parents to provide an equivalent education in a privately operated system. There the Court held that Oregon's statute compelling attendance in a public school from age eight to age 16 unreasonably interfered with the interest of parents in directing the rearing of their off-spring, including their education in church-operated schools. As that case suggests, the values of parental direction of the religious upbringing and education of their children in their early and formative years have a high place in our society. Thus, a State's interest in universal education, however highly we rank it, is not totally free from a balancing process when it impinges on fundamental rights and interests, such as those specifically protected by the Free Exercise Clause of the First Amendment, and the traditional interest of parents with respect to the religious upbringing of their children so long as they, in the words of Pierce, "prepare (them) for additional obligations."

It follows that in order for Wisconsin to compel school attendance beyond the eighth grade against a claim that such attendance interferes with the practice of a legitimate religious belief, it must appear either that the State does not deny the free exercise of religious belief by its requirement, or that there is a state interest of sufficient magnitude to override the interest claiming protection under the Free Exercise Clause. Long before there was general acknowledgment of the need for universal formal education, the Religion Clauses had specifically and firmly fixed the right to free exercise of religious beliefs, and buttressing this fundamental right was an equally firm, even if less explicit, prohibition against the establishment of any religion by government. The values underlying these two provisions relating to religion have been zealously protected, sometimes even at the expense of other interests of admittedly high social importance.

* * *

The essence of all that has been said and written on the subject is that only those interests of the highest order and those not otherwise served can overbalance legitimate claims to the free exercise of religion. We can accept it as settled, therefore, that, however strong the State's interest in universal compulsory education, it is by no means absolute to the exclusion or subordination of all other interests.

II

* * * In evaluating [plaintiffs' claims] we must be careful to determine whether the Amish religious faith and their mode of life are, as they claim, inseparable and interdependent. A way of life, however virtuous and admirable, may not be interposed as a barrier to reasonable state regulation of education if it is based on purely secular considerations; to have the protection of the Religion Clauses, the claims must be rooted in religious belief.

* * *

[T]he record in this case abundantly supports the claim that the traditional way of life of the Amish is not merely a matter of personal preference, but one of deep religious conviction, shared by an organized group, and intimately related to daily living.

* * *

In sum, the unchallenged testimony of acknowledged experts in education and religious history, almost 300 years of consistent practice, and strong evidence of a sustained faith pervading and regulating respondents' entire mode of life support the claim that enforcement of the State's requirement of compulsory formal education after the eighth grade would gravely endanger if not destroy the free exercise of respondents' religious beliefs.

III

Neither the findings of the trial court nor the Amish claims as to the nature of their faith are challenged in this Court by the State of Wisconsin. Its position is that the State's interest in universal compulsory formal secondary education to age 16 is so great that it is paramount to the undisputed claims of respondents that their mode of preparing their youth for Amish life, after the traditional elementary education, is an essential part of their religious belief and practice. * * *

* * *

We turn, then, to the State's broader contention that its interest in its system of compulsory education is so compelling that even the established religious practices of the Amish must give way. * * *

The State advances two primary arguments in support of its system of compulsory education. It notes, as Thomas Jefferson pointed out early in our history, that some degree of education is necessary to prepare citizens to participate effectively and intelligently in our open political system if we are to preserve freedom and independence. Further, education prepares individuals to be self-reliant and self-sufficient participants in society. We accept these propositions.

However, the evidence adduced by the Amish in this case is persuasively to the effect that an additional one or two years of formal high school for Amish children in place of their long-established program of informal vocational education would do little to serve those interests.

* * *

The requirement for compulsory education beyond the eighth grade is a relatively recent development in our history. Less than 60 years ago, the educational requirements of almost all of the States were satisfied by completion of the elementary grades, at least where the child was regularly and lawfully employed. The independence and successful social functioning of the Amish community for a period approaching almost three centuries and more than 200 years in this country are strong evidence that there is at best a speculative gain, in terms of meeting the duties of citizenship, from an additional one or two years of compulsory formal education. Against this background it would require a more particularized showing from the State on this point to justify the severe interference with religious freedom such additional compulsory attendance would entail.

* * *

IV

Finally, the State * * * argues that a decision exempting Amish children from the State's requirement fails to recognize the substantive right of the Amish child to a secondary education, and fails to give due regard to the power of the State as *parens patriae* to extend the benefit of secondary education to children regardless of the wishes of their parents.

* * *

Contrary to the suggestion of the dissenting opinion of Mr. Justice DOUGLAS, our holding today in no degree depends on the assertion of the religious interest of the child as contrasted with that of the parents. It is the parents who are subject to prosecution here for failing to cause their children to attend school, and it is their right of free exercise, not that of their children, that must determine Wisconsin's power to impose criminal penalties on the parent.

* * *

[T]his case involves the fundamental interest of parents, as contrasted with that of the State, to guide the religious future and education of their children. The history and culture of Western civilization reflect a strong tradition of parental concern for the nurture and upbringing of their children. This primary role of the parents in the upbringing of their children is now established beyond debate as an enduring American tradition. If not the first, perhaps the most significant statements of the Court in this area are found in *Pierce v. Society of Sisters*, in which the Court observed:

'Under the doctrine of *Meyer v. Nebraska*, we think it entirely plain that the Act of 1922 unreasonably interferes with the liberty of parents and guardians to direct the upbringing and education of children under their control. * * * The fundamental theory of liberty upon which all governments in this Union repose excludes any general power of the State to standardize its children by forcing them to accept instruction from public teachers only. The child is not the mere creature of the State; those who nurture him and direct his destiny have the right, coupled with the high duty, to recognize and prepare him for additional obligations.'

The duty to prepare the child for 'additional obligations,' referred to by the Court, must be read to include the inculcation of moral standards, religious beliefs, and elements of good citizenship. * * *

[T]he Court's holding in Pierce stands as a charter of the rights of parents to direct the religious upbringing of their children. And, when the interests of parenthood are combined with a free exercise claim of the nature revealed by this record, more than merely a "reasonable relation to some purpose within the competency of the State" is required to sustain the validity of the State's requirement under the First Amendment. To be sure, the power of the parent, even when linked to a free exercise claim, may be subject to limitation * * * if it appears that parental decisions will jeopardize the health or safety of the child, or have a potential for significant social burdens. But in this case, the Amish have introduced persuasive evidence undermining the arguments the State has advanced to support its claims in terms of the welfare of the child and society as a whole. The record strongly indicates that accommodating the religious objections of the Amish by forgoing one, or at most two, additional years of compulsory education will not impair the physical or mental health of the child, or result in an inability to be self-supporting or to discharge the duties and responsibilities of citizenship, or in any other way materially detract from the welfare of society.

    * * *

V

For the reasons stated we hold, with the Supreme Court of Wisconsin, that the First and Fourteenth Amendments prevent the State from compelling respondents to cause their children to attend formal high school to age 16.

    * * *

Mr. Justice Douglas, dissenting in part.

I

I agree with the Court that the religious scruples of the Amish are opposed to the education of their children beyond the grade schools, yet I disagree with the Court's conclusion that the matter is within the dispensation of parents alone. The Court's analysis assumes that the only interests at stake in the case are those of the Amish parents on the one hand, and those of the State on the other. The difficulty with this approach is that, despite the Court's claim, the parents are seeking to vindicate not only their own free exercise claims, but also those of their high-school-age children.

It is argued that the right of the Amish children to religious freedom is not presented by the facts of the case, as the issue before the Court involves only the Amish parents' religious freedom to defy a state criminal statute imposing upon them an affirmative duty to cause their children to attend high school. * * *

[However,] no analysis of religious-liberty claims can take place in a vacuum. If the parents in this case are allowed a religious exemption, the inevitable effect is to impose the parents' notions of religious duty upon their children. Where the child is mature enough to express potentially conflicting desires, it would be an invasion of the child's rights to permit such an imposition without canvassing his views. * * * And, if an Amish child desires to attend high school, and is mature enough to have that desire respected, the State may well be able to override the parents' religiously motivated objections.

* * *

II

This issue has never been squarely presented before today. Our opinions are full of talk about the power of the parents over the child's education. And we have in the past analyzed similar conflicts between parent and State with little regard for the views of the child. Recent cases, however, have clearly held that the children themselves have constitutionally protectible interests.

* * *

In *Tinker v. Des Moines Independent Community School District*, we dealt with 13–year-old, 15–year-old, and 16–year-old students who wore armbands to public schools and were disciplined for doing so. We gave them relief, saying that their First Amendment rights had been abridged. * * *

In *West Virginia State Board of Education v. Barnette*, we held that school-children, whose religious beliefs collided with a school rule requiring them to salute the flag, could not be required to do so. * * *

It is the future of the student, not the future of the parents, that is imperiled by today's decision. If a parent keeps his child out of school beyond the grade school, then the child will be forever barred from entry into the new and amazing world of diversity that we have today. The child may decide that that is the preferred course, or he may rebel. It is the student's judgment, not his parents', that is essential if we are to give full meaning to what we have said about the Bill of Rights and of the right of students to be masters of their own destiny.[3] If he is harnessed to the Amish way of life by those in authority over him and if his education is truncated, his entire life may be stunted and deformed. The child, therefore, should be given an opportunity to be heard before the State gives the exemption which we honor today.

The views of the two children in question were not canvassed by the Wisconsin courts. The matter should be explicitly reserved so that new hearings can be held on remand of the case.[4]

* * *

3. The court below brushed aside the students' interests with the offhand comment that '(w)hen a child reaches the age of judgment, he can choose for himself his religion.' But there is nothing in this record to indicate that the moral and intellectual judgment demanded of the student by the question in this case is beyond his capacity. Children far younger than the 14 and 15 year olds involved here are regularly permitted to testify in custody and other proceedings. Indeed, the failure to call the af-

fected child in a custody hearing is often reversible error. Moreover, there is substantial agreement among child psychologists and sociologists that the moral and intellectual maturity of the 14 year old approaches that of the adult. The maturity of Amish youth, who identify with and assume adult roles from early childhood, is certainly not less than that of children in the general population.

4. Canvassing the views of all school age Amish children in the State of Wisconsin

Notes

1. *Pierce v. Society of Sisters*, referenced in the *Yoder* decision, is generally viewed as a paradigmatic case in the development of the law relating to parental rights in the public sector. Indeed, *Pierce* and *Yoder* together stand for a broad parental right to direct the upbringing of children. How far the right extends, however, is the subject of ongoing controversy.

2. Issues of conflicting values are at the heart of the controversy in *Yoder*, and it is important to note that the word *values* appears in the opinions many times. In this regard, how applicable might the *Yoder* decision be to the range of controversies that are discussed throughout this chapter? Does *Yoder* provide a workable rule whereby courts can determine who prevails when values are in conflict, or is it—in the end—a very narrow and fact-specific decision?

3. Consider the Court's language to the effect that "the activities of individuals, even when religiously based, are often subject to regulation by the States in the exercise of their undoubted power to promote the health, safety, and general welfare." Indeed, the Court emphasizes that "the power of the parent, even when linked to a free exercise claim, may be subject to limitation . . . if it appears that parental decisions will jeopardize the health or safety of the child, or have a potential for significant social burdens." Under this language, might a public school district be able to restrict parental ability to "opt out" of HIV-related education on the grounds that the policy imperative of seeking to eradicate the disease would outweigh any competing religious claims under the Free Exercise Clause? *See infra*, Section E of this chapter.

4. The area of home schooling is directly relevant to the inquiry in this sub-section. *See, e.g.*, Brad Colwell & Brian D. Schwartz, *Implications for Public Schools: Legal Aspects of Home Schools*, 173 Ed. Law Rep. 381 (2003); *see also* David W. Fuller, Note, *Public School Access: The Constitutional Right of Home–Schoolers to "Opt In" to Public Education on a Part–Time Basis*, 82 Minn. L. Rev. 1599 (1998).

B. PATRIOTISM, RELIGION, AND FREEDOM OF EXPRESSION: THE FLAG SALUTE CONTROVERSIES

WEST VIRGINIA STATE BD. OF EDUC. v. BARNETTE

319 U.S. 624, 63 S.Ct. 1178 (1943).

Mr. Justice Jackson delivered the opinion of the Court.

* * *

The Board of Education on January 9, 1942, adopted a resolution . . . ordering that the salute to the flag become "a regular part of the

would not present insurmountable difficulties. A 1968 survey indicated that there were at that time only 256 such children in the entire State.

program of activities in the public schools," that all teachers and pupils "shall be required to participate in the salute honoring the Nation represented by the Flag; provided, however, that refusal to salute the Flag be regarded as an Act of insubordination, and shall be dealt with accordingly."

The resolution originally required the "commonly accepted salute to the Flag" which it defined. Objections to the salute as "being too much like Hitler's" were raised by the Parent and Teachers Association, the Boy and Girl Scouts, the Red Cross, and the Federation of Women's Clubs. Some modification appears to have been made in deference to these objections, but no concession was made to Jehovah's Witnesses.[4] What is now required is the "stiff-arm" salute, the saluter to keep the right hand raised with palm turned up while the following is repeated: "I pledge allegiance to the Flag of the United States of America and to the Republic for which it stands; one Nation, indivisible, with liberty and justice for all."

Failure to conform is "insubordination" dealt with by expulsion. Readmission is denied by statute until compliance. Meanwhile the expelled child is "unlawfully absent" and may be proceeded against as a delinquent. His parents or guardians are liable to prosecution, and if convicted are subject to fine not exceeding $50 and jail term not exceeding thirty days.

Appellees, citizens of the United States and of West Virginia, brought suit in the United States District Court for themselves and others similarly situated asking its injunction to restrain enforcement of these laws and regulations against Jehovah's Witnesses. The Witnesses are an unincorporated body teaching that the obligation imposed by law of God is superior to that of laws enacted by temporal government. Their religious beliefs include a literal version of Exodus, Chapter 20, verses 4 and 5, which says: "Thou shalt not make unto thee any graven image, or any likeness of anything that is in heaven above, or that is in the earth beneath, or that is in the water under the earth; thou shalt not bow down thyself to them nor serve them." They consider that the flag is an "image" within this command. For this reason they refuse to salute it.

Children of this faith have been expelled from school and are threatened with exclusion for no other cause. Officials threaten to send them to reformatories maintained for criminally inclined juveniles. Parents of such children have been prosecuted and are threatened with prosecutions for causing delinquency.

* * *

4. They have offered in lieu of participating in the flag salute ceremony "periodically and publicly" to give the following pledge:

I have pledged my unqualified allegiance and devotion to Jehovah, the Almighty God, and to His Kingdom, for which Jesus commands all Christians to pray.

I respect the flag of the United States and acknowledge it as a symbol of freedom and justice to all.

I pledge allegiance and obedience to all the laws of the United States that are consistent with God's law, as set forth in the Bible.

[T]he refusal of these persons to participate in the ceremony does not interfere with or deny rights of others to do so. Nor is there any question in this case that their behavior is peaceable and orderly. The sole conflict is between authority and rights of the individual. The State asserts power to condition access to public education on making a prescribed sign and profession and at the same time to coerce attendance by punishing both parent and child. The latter stand on a right of self-determination in matters that touch individual opinion and personal attitude.

* * *

There is no doubt that, in connection with the pledges, the flag salute is a form of utterance. Symbolism is a primitive but effective way of communicating ideas. The use of an emblem or flag to symbolize some system, idea, institution, or personality, is a short cut from mind to mind. Causes and nations, political parties, lodges and ecclesiastical groups seek to knit the loyalty of their followings to a flag or banner, a color or design. The State announces rank, function, and authority through crowns and maces, uniforms and black robes; the church speaks through the Cross, the Crucifix, the altar and shrine, and clerical reiment. Symbols of State often convey political ideas just as religious symbols come to convey theological ones. Associated with many of these symbols are appropriate gestures of acceptance or respect: a salute, a bowed or bared head, a bended knee. A person gets from a symbol the meaning he puts into it, and what is one man's comfort and inspiration is another's jest and scorn.

* * *

Whether the First Amendment to the Constitution will permit officials to order observance of ritual of this nature does not depend upon whether as a voluntary exercise we would think it to be good, bad or merely innocuous. Any credo of nationalism is likely to include what some disapprove or to omit what others think essential, and to give off different overtones as it takes on different accents or interpretations. If official power exists to coerce acceptance of any patriotic creed, what it shall contain cannot be decided by courts, but must be largely discretionary with the ordaining authority, whose power to prescribe would no doubt include power to amend. Hence validity of the asserted power to force an American citizen publicly to profess any statement of belief or to engage in any ceremony of assent to one presents questions of power that must be considered independently of any idea we may have as to the utility of the ceremony in question.

Nor does the issue as we see it turn on one's possession of particular religious views or the sincerity with which they are held. While religion supplies appellees' motive for enduring the discomforts of making the issue in this case, many citizens who do not share these religious views hold such a compulsory rite to infringe constitutional liberty of the individual. It is not necessary to inquire whether non-conformist beliefs will exempt from the duty to salute unless we first find power to make the salute a legal duty.

* * *

The Fourteenth Amendment, as now applied to the States, protects the citizen against the State itself and all of its creatures—Boards of Education not excepted. These have, of course, important, delicate, and highly discretionary functions, but none that they may not perform within the limits of the Bill of Rights. That they are educating the young for citizenship is reason for scrupulous protection of Constitutional freedoms of the individual, if we are not to strangle the free mind at its source and teach youth to discount important principles of our government as mere platitudes.

* * *

Struggles to coerce uniformity of sentiment in support of some end thought essential to their time and country have been waged by many good as well as by evil men. Nationalism is a relatively recent phenomenon but at other times and places the ends have been racial or territorial security, support of a dynasty or regime, and particular plans for saving souls. As first and moderate methods to attain unity have failed, those bent on its accomplishment must resort to an ever-increasing severity. As governmental pressure toward unity becomes greater, so strife becomes more bitter as to whose unity it shall be. Probably no deeper division of our people could proceed from any provocation than from finding it necessary to choose what doctrine and whose program public educational officials shall compel youth to unite in embracing. Ultimate futility of such attempts to compel coherence is the lesson of every such effort from the Roman drive to stamp out Christianity as a disturber of its pagan unity, the Inquisition, as a means to religious and dynastic unity, the Siberian exiles as a means to Russian unity, down to the fast failing efforts of our present totalitarian enemies. Those who begin coercive elimination of dissent soon find themselves exterminating dissenters. Compulsory unification of opinion achieves only the unanimity of the graveyard.

It seems trite but necessary to say that the First Amendment to our Constitution was designed to avoid these ends by avoiding these beginnings. There is no mysticism in the American concept of the State or of the nature or origin of its authority. We set up government by consent of the governed, and the Bill of Rights denies those in power any legal opportunity to coerce that consent. Authority here is to be controlled by public opinion, not public opinion by authority.

The case is made difficult not because the principles of its decision are obscure but because the flag involved is our own. Nevertheless, we apply the limitations of the Constitution with no fear that freedom to be intellectually and spiritually diverse or even contrary will disintegrate the social organization. To believe that patriotism will not flourish if patriotic ceremonies are voluntary and spontaneous instead of a compulsory routine is to make an unflattering estimate of the appeal of our institutions to free minds. We can have intellectual individualism and the rich cultural diversities that we owe to exceptional minds only at the price of occasional eccentricity and abnormal attitudes. When they are so harmless to others or to the State as those we deal with here, the price is not too great. But freedom to differ is not limited to things that do not matter much. That would be a mere shadow of freedom. The test of its substance is the right to differ as to things that touch the heart of the existing order.

If there is any fixed star in our constitutional constellation, it is that no official, high or petty, can prescribe what shall be orthodox in politics, nationalism, religion, or other matters of opinion or force citizens to confess by word or act their faith therein. If there are any circumstances which permit an exception, they do not now occur to us.

We think the action of the local authorities in compelling the flag salute and pledge transcends constitutional limitations on their power and invades the sphere of intellect and spirit which it is the purpose of the First Amendment to our Constitution to reserve from all official control.

* * *

Affirmed.

PROBLEM 39: Deciding *Newdow* Under the Establishment Clause

Newdow v. U.S. Congress, 292 F.3d 597 (9th Cir. 2002);
Elk Grove Unified Sch. Dist. v. Newdow, 542 U.S. 1, 124 S.Ct. 2301 (2004).

On June 14, 2004, the U.S. Supreme Court decided *Elk Grove Unified School District v. Newdow.* In that case, Michael Newdow had challenged the constitutionality of the school district's requirement that the pledge of allegiance be recited every day in all its elementary school classes. Newdow contended that because the Pledge contains the words "under God," the policy amounted to a religious indoctrination of his child in violation of the First Amendment.

A divided Ninth Circuit panel agreed with Newdow. In a 5–4 decision, the U.S. Supreme Court reversed, but the majority did not reach the Establishment Clause question, ruling instead that Newdow did not have standing because he did not have legal custody of his biological child.

Consider the following excerpts and overviews from various selected opinions at both the Ninth Circuit and the Supreme Court level. Had a majority of the Supreme Court reached the Establishment Clause question, how should the case have been decided? Why?

ELK GROVE UNIFIED SCHOOL DIST. v. NEWDOW
542 U.S. 1, 124 S.Ct. 2301 (2004).

STEVENS, J., delivered the opinion of the Court, in which KENNEDY, SOUTER, GINSBURG, and BREYER, JJ., joined. REHNQUIST, C.J., filed an opinion concurring in the judgment, in which O'CONNOR, J., joined, and in which THOMAS, J., joined as to Part I. O'CONNOR, J., and THOMAS, J., filed opinions concurring in the judgment. SCALIA, J., took no part in the consideration or decision of the case.

● **Facts of the Case (from the majority opinion by Justice Stevens)**

Each day elementary school teachers in the Elk Grove Unified School District (School District) lead their classes in a group recitation of the Pledge of Allegiance. Respondent, Michael A. Newdow, is an atheist whose daughter participates in that daily exercise. Because the Pledge contains the words "under God," he views the School District's policy as a religious indoctrination of his child that violates the First Amendment. A divided panel of the Court of Appeals for the Ninth Circuit agreed with Newdow. In light of the obvious importance of that decision, we granted certiorari to review the First Amendment issue and, preliminarily, the question whether Newdow has standing to invoke the jurisdiction of the federal courts. We conclude that Newdow lacks standing and therefore reverse the Court of Appeals' decision.

I

"The very purpose of a national flag is to serve as a symbol of our country," and of its proud traditions "of freedom, of equal opportunity, of religious tolerance, and of good will for other peoples who share our aspirations." As its history illustrates, the Pledge of Allegiance evolved as a common public acknowledgement of the ideals that our flag symbolizes. Its recitation is a patriotic exercise designed to foster national unity and pride in those principles.

The Pledge of Allegiance was initially conceived more than a century ago. As part of the nationwide interest in commemorating the 400th anniversary of Christopher Columbus' discovery of America, a widely circulated national magazine for youth proposed in 1892 that pupils recite the following affirmation: 'I pledge allegiance to my Flag and the Republic for which it stands: one Nation indivisible, with Liberty and Justice for all.' In the 1920's, the National Flag Conferences replaced the phrase 'my Flag' with 'the flag of the United States of America.'

In 1942, in the midst of World War II, Congress adopted, and the President signed, a Joint Resolution codifying a detailed set of "rules and customs pertaining to the display and use of the flag of the United States of America." Section 7 of this codification provided in full:

> That the pledge of allegiance to the flag, "I pledge allegiance to the flag of the United States of America and to the Republic for which it stands, one Nation indivisible, with liberty and justice for all", be rendered by standing with the right hand over the heart; extending the right hand, palm upward, toward the flag at the words "to the flag" and holding this position until the end, when the hand drops to the side. However, civilians will always show full respect to the flag when the pledge is given by merely standing at attention, men

removing the headdress. Persons in uniform shall render the military salute.

This resolution, which marked the first appearance of the Pledge of Allegiance in positive law, confirmed the importance of the flag as a symbol of our Nation's indivisibility and commitment to the concept of liberty.

Congress revisited the Pledge of Allegiance 12 years later when it amended the text to add the words "under God." The House Report that accompanied the legislation observed that, "[f]rom the time of our earliest history our peoples and our institutions have reflected the traditional concept that our Nation was founded on a fundamental belief in God." The resulting text is the Pledge as we know it today: "I pledge allegiance to the Flag of the United States of America, and to the Republic for which it stands, one Nation under God, indivisible, with liberty and justice for all."

II

Under California law, "every public elementary school" must begin each day with "appropriate patriotic exercises." The statute provides that "[t]he giving of the Pledge of Allegiance to the Flag of the United States of America shall satisfy" this requirement. The Elk Grove Unified School District has implemented the state law by requiring that "[e]ach elementary school class recite the pledge of allegiance to the flag once each day." Consistent with our case law, the School District permits students who object on religious grounds to abstain from the recitation. See *West Virginia Bd. of Ed. v. Barnette,* 319 U.S. 624 (1943).

In March 2000, Newdow filed suit in the United States District Court for the Eastern District of California against the United States Congress, the President of the United States, the State of California, and the Elk Grove Unified School District and its superintendent. At the time of filing, Newdow's daughter was enrolled in kindergarten in the Elk Grove Unified School District and participated in the daily recitation of the Pledge.... [T]he complaint explains that Newdow is an atheist who was ordained more than 20 years ago in a ministry that "espouses the religious philosophy that the true and eternal bonds of righteousness and virtue stem from reason rather than mythology." The complaint seeks a declaration that the 1954 Act's addition of the words "under God" violated the Establishment and Free Exercise Clauses of the United States Constitution, as well as an injunction against the School District's policy requiring daily recitation of the Pledge. It alleges that Newdow has standing to sue on his own behalf and on behalf of his daughter as "next friend."

... We granted the School District's petition for a writ of certiorari to consider two questions: (1) whether Newdow has standing as a noncustodial parent to challenge the School District's policy, and (2) if so, whether the policy offends the First Amendment.

* * *

• **Highlights of the Various Opinions at the Supreme Court Level**

1.   It was the "liberal" wing, plus Justice Kennedy, that held that Newdow did not have "standing."

2.   The conservative wing (minus Justice Scalia, who had recused himself), plus Justice O'Connor, held that Newdow *did* have standing.

3.   Both Chief Justice Rehnquist and Justice O'Connor wrote separately to argue that under Establishment Clause principles, as they saw them, the pledge as it stood *was* constitutional.

4.   Justice O'Connor asserted that under an endorsement analysis, history, character, and context prevent certain instances of "ceremonial deism" from being constitutional violations. She argued that this was the case here, relying on four key points: history and ubiquity, absence of worship or prayer, absence of reference to particular religion, and minimal religious content. No one else joined her opinion, in the end.

5.   Justice Thomas wrote separately to say: "I conclude that, as a matter of our precedent, the Pledge policy is unconstitutional." He therefore wrote that "I would take this opportunity to begin the process of rethinking the Establishment Clause."

* * *

• **Excerpts from the Amended Majority Opinion by Judge Goodwin, 328 F.3d 466 (9th Cir. 2003)**

The Establishment Clause of the First Amendment states that "Congress shall make no law respecting an establishment of religion," U.S. CONST. amend. I, a provision that "the Fourteenth Amendment makes applicable with full force to the States and their school districts." * * *

The Court formulated the "coercion test" when it held unconstitutional the practice of including invocations and benedictions in the form of "nonsectarian" prayers at public school graduation ceremonies. *Lee*, 505 U.S. at 599, 112 S.Ct. 2649. [I]t relied on the principle that "at a minimum, the Constitution guarantees that government may not coerce anyone to support or participate in religion or its exercise, or otherwise to act in a way which establishes a state religion or religious faith, or tends to do so." *Id.* (citations and internal quotation marks omitted). The Court first examined the degree of school involvement in the prayer, and found that "the graduation prayers bore the imprint of the State and thus put school-age children who objected in an untenable position." *Id.* at 590, 112 S.Ct. 2649. The next issue the Court considered was "the position of the students, both those who desired the prayer and she who did not." *Id.* Noting that "there are heightened concerns with protecting freedom of conscience from subtle coercive pressure in the elementary and secondary public schools," *id.* at 592, 112 S.Ct. 2649, the Court held that the school district's supervision and control of the graduation ceremony put impermissible pressure on students to participate in, or at least show respect during, the prayer, *id.* at 593, 112 S.Ct. 2649. The

Court concluded that primary and secondary school children may not be placed in the dilemma of either participating in a religious ceremony or protesting. *Id.* at 594, 112 S.Ct. 2649.

Finally, in its most recent school prayer case, the Supreme Court applied the ... coercion test to strike down a school district's policy of permitting student-led "invocations" before high school football games. *See Santa Fe Independent School Dist. v. Doe,* 530 U.S. 290, 310–16, 120 S.Ct. 2266. Citing *Lee,* the Court held that "the delivery of a pregame prayer has the improper effect of coercing those present to participate in an act of religious worship." *Id.* at 312, 120 S.Ct. 2266. * * *

[W]e conclude that the school district policy impermissibly coerces a religious act and accordingly hold the policy unconstitutional....

In the context of the Pledge, the statement that the United States is a nation "under God" is a profession of a religious belief, namely, a belief in monotheism. The recitation that ours is a nation "under God" is not a mere acknowledgment that many Americans believe in a deity. Nor is it merely descriptive of the undeniable historical significance of religion in the founding of the Republic. Rather, the phrase "one nation under God" in the context of the Pledge is normative. To recite the Pledge is not to describe the United States; instead, it is to swear allegiance to the values for which the flag stands: unity, indivisibility, liberty, justice, and—since 1954—monotheism. A profession that we are a nation "under God" is identical, for Establishment Clause purposes, to a profession that we are a nation "under Jesus," a nation "under Vishnu," a nation "under Zeus," or a nation "under no god," because none of these professions can be neutral with respect to religion. The school district's practice of teacher-led recitation of the Pledge aims to inculcate in students a respect for the ideals set forth in the Pledge, including the religious values it incorporates.

The Supreme Court recognized the normative and ideological nature of the Pledge in *Barnette,* 319 U.S. 624, 63 S.Ct. 1178. There, the Court held unconstitutional a school district's wartime policy of punishing students who refused to recite the Pledge and salute the flag. *Id.* at 642, 63 S.Ct. 1178. The Court noted that the school district was compelling the students "to declare a belief," *id.* at 631, 63 S.Ct. 1178, and "requir[ing] the individual to communicate by word and sign his acceptance of the political ideas [the flag] ... bespeaks," *id.* at 633, 63 S.Ct. 1178. "[T]he compulsory flag salute and pledge requires affirmation of a belief and an attitude of mind." *Id.* The Court emphasized that the political concepts articulated in the Pledge[4] were idealistic, not descriptive: " '[L]iberty and justice for all,' if it must be accepted as descriptive of the present order rather than an ideal, might to some seem an overstatement." *Id.* at 634 n. 14, 63 S.Ct. 1178. The Court concluded that: "If there is any fixed star in our constitutional constellation, it is that no official, high or petty, can prescribe what shall be orthodox in

---

4. *Barnette* was decided before "under God" was added, and thus the Court's discussion was limited to the political ideals contained in the Pledge.

politics, nationalism, religion, or other matters of opinion or force citizens to confess by word or act their faith therein." *Id.* at 642, 63 S.Ct. 1178.

The school district's policy here, like the school's action in *Lee,* places students in the untenable position of choosing between participating in an exercise with religious content or protesting. The defendants argue that the religious content of "one nation under God" is minimal. To an atheist or a believer in non-Judeo–Christian religions or philosophies, however, this phrase may reasonably appear to be an attempt to enforce a "religious orthodoxy" of monotheism, and is therefore impermissible. As the Court observed with respect to the graduation prayer in *Lee:* "What to most believers may seem nothing more than a reasonable request that the nonbeliever respect their religious practices, in a school context may appear to the nonbeliever or dissenter to be an attempt to employ the machinery of the State to enforce a religious orthodoxy." *Lee,* 505 U.S. at 592, 112 S.Ct. 2649.

The coercive effect of the policy here is particularly pronounced in the school setting given the age and impressionability of schoolchildren, and their understanding that they are required to adhere to the norms set by their school, their teacher and their fellow students.[5] Furthermore, under *Lee,* non-compulsory participation is no basis for distinguishing *Barnette* from the case at bar because, even without a recitation requirement for each child, the mere presence in the classroom every day as peers recite the statement "one nation under God" has a coercive effect.[6] The coercive effect of the Pledge is also made even more apparent when we consider the legislative history of the Act that introduced the phrase "under God." These words were designed to be recited daily in school classrooms. President Eisenhower, during the Act's signing ceremony, stated: "From this day forward, the millions of our school children will daily proclaim in every city and town, every village and rural schoolhouse, the dedication of our Nation and our people to the Almighty."[7] All in all, there can be little doubt that under the controlling Supreme Court cases the school district's policy fails the coercion test.

5. The "subtle and indirect" social pressure which permeates the classroom also renders more acute the message sent to non-believing school-children that they are outsiders. *See Lee,* 505 U.S. at 592–93, 112 S.Ct. 2649 (stating that "the risk of indirect coercion" from prayer exercises is particularly "pronounced" in elementary and secondary public school because students are subjected to peer pressure and public pressure which is "as real as any overt compulsion").

6. The objection to the Pledge in *Barnette,* like in the case at bar, was based upon a religious ground. The Pledge in the classroom context imposes upon schoolchildren the constitutionally unacceptable choice between participating and protest-

ing. Recognizing the severity of the effect of this form of coercion on children, the Supreme Court in *Lee* stated, "the State may not, consistent with the Establishment Clause, place primary and secondary school children in this position." 505 U.S. at 593, 112 S.Ct. 2649.

7. In addition, the legislative history of the 1954 Act makes it plain that the sponsors of the amendment knew about and capitalized on the state laws and school district rules that mandate recitation of the Pledge. The legislation's House sponsor, Representative Louis C. Rabaut, testified at the Congressional hearing that "the children of our land, in the daily recitation of the pledge in school, will be daily impressed with a true understanding of our way of life

● **Excerpts from the opinions of Chief Justice Rehnquist and Justice O'Connor, who would have both found the District policy constitutional.**

CHIEF JUSTICE REHNQUIST

The Court today erects a novel prudential standing principle in order to avoid reaching the merits of the constitutional claim. I dissent from that ruling. On the merits, I conclude that the Elk Grove Unified School District (School District) policy that requires teachers to lead willing students in reciting the Pledge of Allegiance, which includes the words 'under God,' does not violate the Establishment Clause of the First Amendment.

* * *

II

The Pledge of Allegiance reads:

> I pledge allegiance to the Flag of the United States of America, and to the Republic for which it stands, one Nation under God, indivisible, with liberty and justice for all.

As part of an overall effort to "codify and emphasize existing rules and customs pertaining to the display and use of the flag of the United States of America," Congress enacted the Pledge on June 22, 1942. Congress amended the Pledge to include the phrase "under God" in 1954. The amendment's sponsor, Representative Rabaut, said its purpose was to contrast this country's belief in God with the Soviet Union's embrace of atheism. We do not know what other Members of Congress thought about the purpose of the amendment. Following the decision of the Court of Appeals in this case, Congress passed legislation that made extensive findings about the historic role of religion in the political development of the Nation and reaffirmed the text of the Pledge. To the millions of people who regularly recite the Pledge, and who have no access to, or concern with, such legislation or legislative history, "under God" might mean several different things: that God has guided the destiny of the United States, for example, or that the United States exists under God's authority. How much consideration anyone gives to the phrase probably varies, since the Pledge itself is a patriotic observance focused primarily on the flag and the Nation, and only secondarily on the description of the Nation.

The phrase 'under God' in the Pledge seems, as a historical matter, to sum up the attitude of the Nation's leaders, and to manifest itself in many of our public observances. Examples of patriotic invocations of God and official acknowledgments of religion's role in our Nation's history abound.

* * *

and its origins." This statement was incorporated into the report of the House Judiciary Committee.

The motto "In God We Trust" first appeared on the country's coins during the Civil War. Secretary of the Treasury Salmon P. Chase, acting under the authority of an Act of Congress passed in 1864, prescribed that the motto should appear on the two cent coin. The motto was placed on more and more denominations, and since 1938 all United States coins bear the motto. Paper currency followed suit at a slower pace; Federal Reserve notes were so inscribed during the decade of the 1960s. Meanwhile, in 1956, Congress declared that the motto of the United States would be "In God We Trust."

Our Court Marshal's opening proclamation concludes with the words "God save the United States and this honorable Court." The language goes back at least as far as 1827.

All of these events strongly suggest that our national culture allows public recognition of our Nation's religious history and character. In the words of the House Report that accompanied the insertion of the phrase "under God" in the Pledge: "From the time of our earliest history our peoples and our institutions have reflected the traditional concept that our Nation was founded on a fundamental belief in God." Giving additional support to this idea is our national anthem "The Star–Spangled Banner," adopted as such by Congress in 1931. The last verse ends with these words:

> Then conquer we must, when our cause it is just,
> And this be our motto: "In God is our trust."
> And the star-spangled banner in triumph shall wave
> O'er the land of the free and the home of the brave!

As pointed out by the Court, California law requires public elementary schools to "conduc[t] ... appropriate patriotic exercises" at the beginning of the schoolday, and notes that the "giving of the Pledge of Allegiance to the Flag of the United States of America shall satisfy the requirements of this section." The School District complies with this requirement by instructing that "[e]ach elementary school class recite the [P]ledge of [A]llegiance to the [F]lag once each day." Students who object on religious (or other) grounds may abstain from the recitation. *West Virginia Bd. of Ed. v. Barnette,* 319 U.S. 624, 642 (1943) (holding that the government may not compel school students to recite the Pledge).

Notwithstanding the voluntary nature of the School District policy, the Court of Appeals, by a divided vote, held that the policy violates the Establishment Clause of the First Amendment because it "impermissibly coerces a religious act." *Newdow v. United States Congress,* 328 F. 3d 466, 487 (9th Cir. 2003). To reach this result, the court relied primarily on our decision in *Lee v. Weisman,* 505 U.S. 577 (1992). That case arose out of a graduation ceremony for a public high school in Providence, Rhode Island. The ceremony was begun with an invocation, and ended with a benediction, given by a local rabbi. The Court held that even though attendance at the ceremony was voluntary, students who objected to the prayers would nonetheless feel coerced to attend and to stand during each prayer. But the Court throughout its opinion referred to the prayer as 'an explicit religious exercise,' *id.* at 598, and "a formal religious exercise," *id.* at 589.

As the Court notes in its opinion, "the Pledge of Allegiance evolved as a common public acknowledgement of the ideals that our flag symbolizes. Its recitation is a patriotic exercise designed to foster national unity and pride in those principles."

I do not believe that the phrase "under God" in the Pledge converts its recital into a "religious exercise" of the sort described in *Lee*. Instead, it is a declaration of belief in allegiance and loyalty to the United States flag and the Republic that it represents. The phrase "under God" is in no sense a prayer, nor an endorsement of any religion, but a simple recognition of the fact noted in H.R. Rep. No. 1693, at 2: "From the time of our earliest history our peoples and our institutions have reflected the traditional concept that our Nation was founded on a fundamental belief in God." Reciting the Pledge, or listening to others recite it, is a patriotic exercise, not a religious one; participants promise fidelity to our flag and our Nation, not to any particular God, faith, or church.

There is no doubt that respondent is sincere in his atheism and rejection of a belief in God. But the mere fact that he disagrees with this part of the Pledge does not give him a veto power over the decision of the public schools that willing participants should pledge allegiance to the flag in the manner prescribed by Congress. There may be others who disagree, not with the phrase "under God," but with the phrase "with liberty and justice for all." But surely that would not give such objectors the right to veto the holding of such a ceremony by those willing to participate. Only if it can be said that the phrase "under God" somehow tends to the establishment of a religion in violation of the First Amendment can respondent's claim succeed, where one based on objections to "with liberty and justice for all" fails. Our cases have broadly interpreted this phrase, but none have gone anywhere near as far as the decision of the Court of Appeals in this case. The recital, in a patriotic ceremony pledging allegiance to the flag and to the Nation, of the descriptive phrase "under God" cannot possibly lead to the establishment of a religion, or anything like it.

When courts extend constitutional prohibitions beyond their previously recognized limit, they may restrict democratic choices made by public bodies. Here, Congress prescribed a Pledge of Allegiance, the State of California required patriotic observances in its schools, and the School District chose to comply by requiring teacher-led recital of the Pledge of Allegiance by willing students. Thus, we have three levels of popular government—the national, the state, and the local—collaborating to produce the Elk Grove ceremony. The Constitution only requires that schoolchildren be entitled to abstain from the ceremony if they chose to do so. To give the parent of such a child a sort of "heckler's veto" over a patriotic ceremony willingly participated in by other students, simply because the Pledge of Allegiance contains the descriptive phrase "under

God,'' is an unwarranted extension of the Establishment Clause, an extension which would have the unfortunate effect of prohibiting a commendable patriotic observance.

JUSTICE O'CONNOR

I join the concurrence of THE CHIEF JUSTICE in full.... But while the history presented by THE CHIEF JUSTICE illuminates the constitutional problems this case presents, I write separately to explain the principles that guide my own analysis of the constitutionality of that policy.

As I have said before, the Establishment Clause "cannot easily be reduced to a single test. There are different categories of Establishment Clause cases, which may call for different approaches." When a court confronts a challenge to government-sponsored speech or displays, I continue to believe that the endorsement test "captures the essential command of the Establishment Clause, namely, that government must not make a person's religious beliefs relevant to his or her standing in the political community by conveying a message 'that religion or a particular religious belief is favored or preferred.' " In that context, I repeatedly have applied the endorsement test, *Wallace* [*v. Jaffree*, 472 U.S. 38, 69 (1985)] (statute authorizing a meditative moment of silence in classrooms), and I would do so again here.

Endorsement, I have explained, "sends a message to nonadherents that they are outsiders, not full members of the political community, and an accompanying message to adherents that they are insiders, favored members of the political community." In order to decide whether endorsement has occurred, a reviewing court must keep in mind two crucial and related principles.

First, because the endorsement test seeks "to identify those situations in which government makes adherence to a religion relevant ... to a person's standing in the political community," it assumes the viewpoint of a reasonable observer. Given the dizzying religious heterogeneity of our Nation, adopting a subjective approach would reduce the test to an absurdity. Nearly any government action could be overturned as a violation of the Establishment Clause if a "heckler's veto" sufficed to show that its message was one of endorsement. Second, because the "reasonable observer" must embody a community ideal of social judgment, as well as rational judgment, the test does not evaluate a practice in isolation from its origins and context. Instead, the reasonable observer must be deemed aware of the history of the conduct in question, and must understand its place in our Nation's cultural landscape.

The Court has permitted government, in some instances, to refer to or commemorate religion in public life. While the Court's explicit rationales have varied, my own has been consistent; I believe that although these references speak in the language of religious belief, they are more properly understood as employing the idiom for essentially secular purposes. One such purpose is to commemorate the role of religion in our history. In my view, some references to religion in public life and government are the inevitable consequence of our Nation's origins. Just as the Court has refused to ignore changes in the religious composition of our Nation in explaining the modern scope of the Religion Clauses, *see, e.g., Wallace, supra*, at 52–54 (even if the Religion Clauses were originally meant only to forestall intolerance between Christian sects, they now encompass all forms of religious conscience), it should not deny that our history has left its mark on our national traditions. It is unsurprising that a Nation founded by religious refugees and dedicated to religious freedom should find references to divinity in its symbols, songs, mottoes, and oaths. Eradicating such references would sever ties to a history that sustains this Nation even today.

Facially religious references can serve other valuable purposes in public life as well. Twenty years ago, I wrote that such references "serve, in the only ways reasonably possible in our culture, the legitimate secular purposes of solemnizing public occasions, expressing confidence in the future, and encouraging the recognition of what is worthy of appreciation in society." For centuries, we have marked important occasions or pronouncements with references to God and invocations of divine assistance. Such references can serve to solemnize an occasion instead of to invoke divine provenance. The reasonable observer discussed above, fully aware of our national history and the origins of such practices, would not perceive these acknowledgments as signifying a government endorsement of any specific religion, or even of religion over non-religion.

There are no *de minimis* violations of the Constitution—no constitutional harms so slight that the courts are obliged to ignore them. Given the values that the Establishment Clause was meant to serve, however, I believe that government can, in a discrete category of cases, acknowledge or refer to the divine without offending the Constitution. This category of "ceremonial deism" most clearly encompasses such things as the national motto ("In God We Trust"), religious references in traditional patriotic songs such as the Star–Spangled Banner, and the words with which the Marshal of this Court opens each of its sessions ("God save the United States and this honorable Court"). These references are not minor trespasses upon the Establishment Clause to which I turn a blind eye. Instead, their history, character, and context prevent them from being constitutional violations at all.

This case requires us to determine whether the appearance of the phrase "under God" in the Pledge of Allegiance constitutes an instance of such ceremonial deism. Although it is a close question, I conclude that it does, based on my evaluation of the following four factors.

History and Ubiquity

The constitutional value of ceremonial deism turns on a shared understanding of its legitimate nonreligious purposes. That sort of understanding can exist only when a given practice has been in place for a significant portion of the Nation's history, and when it is observed by enough persons that it can fairly be called ubiquitous. By contrast, novel or uncommon references to religion can more easily be perceived as government endorsements because the reasonable observer cannot be presumed to be fully familiar with their origins. As a result, in examining whether a given practice constitutes an instance of ceremonial deism, its 'history and ubiquity' will be of great importance. As I explained in *Allegheny*:

> Under the endorsement test, the "history and ubiquity" of a practice is relevant not because it creates an "artificial exception" from that test. On the contrary, the "history and ubiquity" of a practice is relevant because it provides part of the context in which a reasonable observer evaluates whether a challenged governmental practice conveys a message of endorsement of religion.

Fifty years have passed since the words "under God" were added, a span of time that is not inconsiderable given the relative youth of our Nation. In that time, the Pledge has become, alongside the singing of the Star–Spangled Banner, our most routine ceremonial act of patriotism; countless schoolchildren recite it daily, and their religious heterogeneity reflects that of the Nation as a whole. As a result, the Pledge and the context in which it is employed are familiar and nearly inseparable in the public mind. No reasonable observer could have been surprised to learn the words of the Pledge, or that petitioner school district has a policy of leading its students in daily recitation of the Pledge.

It cannot be doubted that "no one acquires a vested or protected right in violation of the Constitution by long use, even when that span of time covers our entire national existence and indeed predates it. Yet an unbroken practice . . . is not something to be lightly cast aside." And the history of a given practice is all the more relevant when the practice has been employed pervasively without engendering significant controversy. In *Lynch*, where we evaluated the constitutionality of a town Christmas display that included a crèche, we found relevant to the endorsement question the fact that the display had "apparently caused no political divisiveness prior to the filing of this lawsuit" despite its use for over 40 years. Similarly, in the 50 years that the Pledge has been recited as it is now, by millions of children, this was, at the time of its filing, only the third reported case of which I am aware to challenge it as an impermissible establishment of religion. The citizens of this Nation have been neither timid nor unimaginative in challenging government practices as forbidden "establishments" of religion. Given the vigor and creativity of such challenges, I find it telling that so little ire has been directed at the Pledge.

Absence of worship or prayer

"[O]ne of the greatest dangers to the freedom of the individual to worship in his own way [lies] in the Government's placing its official stamp of approval upon one particular kind of prayer or one particular form of religious services." *Engel v. Vitale,* 370 U.S. 421, 429 (1962). Because of this principle, only in the most extraordinary circumstances could actual worship or prayer be defended as ceremonial deism. We have upheld only one such prayer against Establishment Clause challenge, and it was supported by an extremely long and unambiguous history. Any statement that has as its purpose placing the speaker or listener in a penitent state of mind, or that is intended to create a spiritual communion or invoke divine aid, strays from the legitimate secular purposes of solemnizing an event and recognizing a shared religious history. *Santa Fe Independent School Dist. v. Doe*, 530 U.S. 290, 309 (2000) ("[T]he use of an invocation to foster ... solemnity is impermissible when, in actuality, it constitutes [state-sponsored] prayer").

Of course, any statement *can* be imbued by a speaker or listener with the qualities of prayer. But, as I have explained, the relevant viewpoint is that of a reasonable observer, fully cognizant of the history, ubiquity, and context of the practice in question. Such an observer could not conclude that reciting the Pledge, including the phrase "under God," constitutes an instance of worship. I know of no religion that incorporates the Pledge into its canon, nor one that would count the Pledge as a meaningful expression of religious faith. Even if taken literally, the phrase is merely descriptive; it purports only to identify the United States as a Nation subject to divine authority. That cannot be seen as a serious invocation of God or as an expression of individual submission to divine authority. *Cf. Engel, supra*, at 424 (describing prayer as "a solemn avowal of faith and supplication for the blessing of the Almighty"). A reasonable observer would note that petitioner school district's policy of Pledge recitation appears under the heading of "Patriotic Observances," and the California law which it implements refers to "appropriate patriotic exercises." Petitioner school district also employs teachers, not chaplains or religious instructors, to lead its students' exercise; this serves as a further indication that it does not treat the Pledge as a prayer. *Cf. Lee v. Weisman*, 505 U.S. 577, 594 (1992) (reasoning that a graduation benediction could not be construed as a *de minimis* religious exercise without offending the rabbi who offered it).

It is true that some of the legislators who voted to add the phrase "under God" to the Pledge may have done so in an attempt to attach to it an overtly religious message. But their intentions cannot, on their own, decide our inquiry. First of all, those legislators also had permissible secular objectives in mind—they meant, for example, to acknowledge the religious origins of our Nation's belief in the "individuality and the dignity of the human being." Second—and more critically—the *subsequent* social and cultural history of the Pledge shows that its original secular character was not transformed by its amendment. In *School Dist. of Abington Township v. Schempp*, we explained that a government may initiate a practice "for the impermissible purpose of supporting religion" but nevertheless "retai[n] the la[w] for the permissible purpose of furthering overwhelmingly secular ends." Whatever the sectarian ends its authors may have had in mind, our continued repetition of the reference to "one Nation under God" in an exclusively patriotic context has shaped the cultural significance of that phrase to conform to that context. Any religious freight the words may have been meant to carry originally has long since been lost. See *Lynch* (Brennan, J., dissenting) (suggesting that the reference to God in the Pledge might be permissible because it has "lost through rote repetition any significant religious content").

Absence of reference to particular religion

"The clearest command of the Establishment Clause is that one religious denomination cannot be officially preferred over another." While general acknowledgments of religion need not be viewed by reasonable observers as denigrating the nonreligious, the same cannot be said of instances "where the endorsement is sectarian, in the sense of specifying details upon which men and women who believe in a benevolent, omnipotent Creator and Ruler of the world are known to differ." *Weisman, supra,* at 641 (SCALIA, J., dissenting). As a result, no religious acknowledgment could claim to be an instance of ceremonial deism if it explicitly favored one particular religious belief system over another.

The Pledge complies with this requirement. It does not refer to a nation "under Jesus" or "under Vishnu," but instead acknowledges religion in a general way: a simple reference to a generic "God." Of course, some religions—Buddhism, for instance—are not based upon a belief in a separate Supreme Being. But one would be hard pressed to imagine a brief solemnizing reference to religion that would adequately encompass every religious belief expressed by any citizen of this Nation. The phrase "under God," conceived and added at a time when our national religious diversity was neither as robust nor as well recognized as it is now, represents a tolerable attempt to acknowledge religion and to invoke its solemnizing power without favoring any individual religious sect or belief system.

Minimal religious content

A final factor that makes the Pledge an instance of ceremonial deism, in my view, is its highly circumscribed reference to God. In most of the cases in which we have struck down government speech or displays under the Establishment Clause, the offending religious content has been much more pervasive. *See, e.g., Weisman, supra,* at 581–582 (prayers involving repeated thanks to God and requests for blessings). Of course, a ceremony cannot avoid Establishment Clause scrutiny simply by avoiding an explicit mention of God. See *Wallace v. Jaffree,* 472 U.S. 38 (1985) (invalidating Alabama statute providing moment of silence for meditation or voluntary prayer). But the brevity of a reference to religion or to God in a ceremonial exercise can be important for several reasons. First, it tends to confirm that the reference is being used to acknowledge religion or to solemnize an event rather than to endorse religion in any way. Second, it makes it easier for those participants who wish to "opt out" of language they find offensive to do so without having to reject the ceremony entirely. And third, it tends to limit the ability of government to express a preference for one religious sect over another.

The reference to "God" in the Pledge of Allegiance qualifies as a minimal reference to religion; respondent's challenge focuses on only two of the Pledge's 31 words. Moreover, the presence of those words is not absolutely essential to the Pledge, as demonstrated by the fact that it existed without them for over 50 years. As a result, students who wish to avoid saying the words 'under God' still can consider themselves meaningful participants in the exercise if they join in reciting the remainder of the Pledge.

I have framed my inquiry as a specific application of the endorsement test by examining whether the ceremony or representation would convey a message to a reasonable observer, familiar with its history, origins, and context, that those who do not adhere to its literal message are political outsiders. But consideration of these factors would lead me to the same result even if I were to apply the 'coercion' test that has featured in several opinions of this Court. *Santa Fe Independent School Dist. v. Doe,* 530 U.S. 290 (2000); *Lee v. Weisman,* 505 U.S. 577 (1992).

The coercion test provides that, "at a minimum ... government may not coerce anyone to support or participate in religion or its exercise, or otherwise act in a way which 'establishes a [state] religion or religious faith, or tends to do so.' " Any coercion that persuades an onlooker to participate in an act of ceremonial deism is inconsequential, as an Establishment Clause matter, because such acts are simply not religious in character. As a result, symbolic references to religion that qualify as instances of ceremonial deism will pass the coercion test as well as the endorsement test. This is not to say, however, that government could *overtly* coerce a person to participate in an act of ceremonial deism. Our cardinal freedom is one of belief; leaders in this Nation cannot force us to proclaim our allegiance to *any* creed, whether it be religious, philosophic, or political. That principle found eloquent expression in a case involving the Pledge itself, even before it contained the words to which respondent now objects. See *West Virginia Bd. of Ed. v. Barnette,* 319 U.S. 624, 642 (1943) (Jackson, J.). The compulsion of which Justice Jackson was concerned, however, was of the direct sort—the Constitution does not guarantee citizens a right entirely to avoid ideas with which they disagree. It would betray its own principles if it did; no robust democracy insulates its citizens from views that they might find novel or even inflammatory.

* * *

Michael Newdow's challenge to petitioner school district's policy is a well-intentioned one, but his distaste for the reference to "one Nation under God," however sincere, cannot be the yardstick of our Establishment Clause inquiry. Certain ceremonial references to God and religion in our Nation are the inevitable consequence of the religious history that gave birth to our founding principles of liberty. It would be ironic indeed if this Court were to wield our constitutional commitment to religious freedom so as to sever our ties to the traditions developed to honor it.

Note

1.   On September 14, 2005, the U.S. District Court, Eastern District of California, found in a lawsuit almost identical in nature to the case addressed above, that the inclusion of the words "under God" in the pledge violated the Establishment Clause. The case was essentially re-filed by Dr. Newdow, and now included as plaintiffs a group of parents who indeed had legal custody of their children. *See Newdow v. Congress of the U.S.*, 383 F.Supp.2d 1229 (E.D. Cal. 2005).

C.   DISPUTED ACCESS TO CAMPUS FORUMS AND FACILITIES

1.   ACCESS TO FORUMS

ROSENBERGER v. UNIVERSITY OF VIRGINIA
515 U.S. 819, 115 S.Ct. 2510 (1995).

[The facts of this case are set forth in Chapter 3, *supra,* where the Free Speech Clause aspects of the opinion are included.

Plaintiffs had relied upon the First Amendment in challenging the university's denial of funds to a registered student group, Wide Awake Productions. The group had requested money from the Student Activities Fund to help cover the cost of publication for an on-campus newspaper with "a Christian perspective on both personal and community issues." But the request was denied by a student committee on the grounds that the newspaper "promote[d] or manifest[ed] a particular belie[f] in or about a deity or an ultimate reality."

Analyzing the Free Speech Clause issue under the viewpoint discrimination doctrine, the Court ruled in favor of the students.[a] The Court then turned to the Establishment Clause component of the case.]

KENNEDY, J.

* * *

III

Before its brief on the merits in this Court, the University had argued at all stages of the litigation that inclusion of WAP's contractors in SAF funding authorization would violate the Establishment Clause.

* * *

a. *See* 515 U.S. at 829: "Once it has opened a limited forum, . . . the State must respect the lawful boundaries it has itself set. The State may not exclude speech where its distinction is not "reasonable in light of the purpose served by the forum," nor may it discriminate against speech on the basis of its viewpoint. . . . The SAF is a forum more in a metaphysical than in a spatial or geographic sense, but the same principles are applicable."

While on its most basic level the free speech component of *Rosenberger* stands for the proposition that regulating religious speech on campus constitutes viewpoint discrimination, the language of the decision is very broad and sweeping. Commentators have thus viewed the case as not only strengthening the viewpoint discrimination doctrine in general, but as significantly expanding its scope.

The Court of Appeals ruled that withholding SAF support from Wide Awake contravened the Speech Clause of the First Amendment, but proceeded to hold that the University's action was justified by the necessity of avoiding a violation of the Establishment Clause, an interest it found compelling.

* * *

If there is to be assurance that the Establishment Clause retains its force in guarding against those governmental actions it was intended to prohibit, we must in each case inquire first into the purpose and object of the governmental action in question and then into the practical details of the program's operation. Before turning to these matters, however, we can set forth certain general principles that must bear upon our determination.

A central lesson of our decisions is that a significant factor in upholding governmental programs in the face of Establishment Clause attack is their neutrality towards religion.... We have held that the guarantee of neutrality is respected, not offended, when the government, following neutral criteria and evenhanded policies, extends benefits to recipients whose ideologies and viewpoints, including religious ones, are broad and diverse. More than once have we rejected the position that the Establishment Clause even justifies, much less requires, a refusal to extend free speech rights to religious speakers who participate in broad-reaching government programs neutral in design.

The governmental program here is neutral toward religion. There is no suggestion that the University created it to advance religion or adopted some ingenious device with the purpose of aiding a religious cause. The object of the SAF is to open a forum for speech and to support various student enterprises, including the publication of newspapers, in recognition of the diversity and creativity of student life. The University's SAF Guidelines have a separate classification for, and do not make third-party payments on behalf of, "religious organizations," which are those "whose purpose is to practice a devotion to an acknowledged ultimate reality or deity." The category of support here is for "student news, information, opinion, entertainment, or academic communications media groups," of which Wide Awake was 1 of 15 in the 1990 school year. WAP did not seek a subsidy because of its Christian editorial viewpoint; it sought funding as a student journal, which it was.

The neutrality of the program distinguishes the student fees from a tax levied for the direct support of a church or group of churches. A tax of that sort, of course, would run contrary to Establishment Clause concerns dating from the earliest days of the Republic. The apprehensions of our predecessors involved the levying of taxes upon the public for the sole and exclusive purpose of establishing and supporting specific sects. The exaction here, by contrast, is a student activity fee designed to reflect the reality that student life in its many dimensions includes the necessity of wide-ranging speech and inquiry and that student expression is an integral part of the University's educational mission. The fee is mandatory, and we do not have before us the question whether an objecting student has the First Amendment right to demand a pro rata return to the extent the fee is expended for speech to which he or she does not subscribe. We must treat it, then, as an exaction upon the students. But the $14 paid each semester by the students is not a general tax designed to raise revenue for the University. The SAF cannot be used for unlimited purposes, much less the illegitimate purpose of supporting one religion. * * * [T]he money goes to a special fund from which any group of students with CIO status can draw for purposes consistent with the University's educational mission; and to the extent the student is interested in speech, withdrawal is permitted to cover the whole spectrum of speech, whether it manifests a religious view, an antireligious view, or neither. Our decision, then, cannot be read as addressing an expenditure from a general tax fund. Here, the disbursements from the fund go to private contractors for the cost of printing that which is protected under the Speech Clause of the First Amendment. This is a far cry from a general public assessment designed and effected to provide financial support for a church.

Government neutrality is apparent in the State's overall scheme in a further meaningful respect. The program respects the critical difference "between *government* speech endorsing religion, which the Establishment Clause forbids, and *private* speech endorsing religion, which the Free Speech and Free Exercise Clauses protect."

* * *

It does not violate the Establishment Clause for a public university to grant access to its facilities on a religion-neutral basis to a wide spectrum of student groups, including groups that use meeting rooms for sectarian activities, accompanied by some devotional exercises. See *Widmar*, 454 U.S. at 269, 102 S.Ct. at 274; *Mergens*, 496 U.S. at 252, 110 S.Ct. at 2373. This is so even where the upkeep, maintenance, and repair of the facilities attributed to those uses are paid from a student activities fund to which students are required to contribute.

* * *

By paying outside printers, the University in fact attains a further degree of separation from the student publication, for it avoids the duties of supervision, escapes the costs of upkeep, repair, and replacement attributable to student use, and has a clear record of costs. As a result, and as in *Widmar*, the University can charge the SAF, and not the taxpayers as a whole, for the discrete activity in question. It would be formalistic for us to say that the University must forfeit these advantages and provide the services itself in order to comply with the Establishment Clause. It is, of course, true that if the State pays a church's bills it is subsidizing it, and we must guard against this abuse. That is not a danger here, based on the considerations we have advanced and for the additional reason that the student publication is not a religious institution, at least in the usual sense of that term as used in our case law, and it is not a religious organization as used in the University's own regulations. It is instead a publication involved in a pure forum for the expression of ideas, ideas that would be both incomplete and chilled were the Constitution to be interpreted to require that state officials and courts scan the publication to ferret out views that principally manifest a belief in a divine being.

* * *

To obey the Establishment Clause, it was not necessary for the University to deny eligibility to student publications because of their viewpoint. The neutrality commanded of the State by the separate Clauses of the First Amendment was compromised by the University's course of action. The viewpoint discrimination inherent in the University's regulation required public officials to scan and interpret student publications to discern their underlying philosophic assumptions respecting religious theory and belief. That course of action was a denial of the right of free speech and would risk fostering a pervasive bias or hostility to religion, which could undermine the very neutrality the Establishment Clause requires. There is no Establishment Clause violation in the University's honoring its duties under the Free Speech Clause.

The judgment of the Court of Appeals must be, and is, reversed.

It is so ordered.

DOWNS v. LOS ANGELES UNIFIED SCH. DIST.
228 F.3d 1003 (9th Cir. 2000).

TROTT, Circuit Judge:

The narrow question we must answer is whether the First Amendment compels a public high school to share the podium with a teacher with antagonistic and contrary views when the school speaks to its own constituents on the subject of how students should behave towards each other while in school. The answer to this question clearly is no.

Appellant Robert Downs is a teacher at Doris S. Leichman High School ("Leichman High"), a school within appellee Los Angeles Unified School District ("LAUSD"). Downs filed suit against LAUSD pursuant to 42 U.S.C. § 1983 and the United States and California Constitutions, seeking a permanent injunction, declaratory judgment, compensatory damages and attorneys' fees. In his lawsuit, Downs alleged that LAUSD, through its officers and employees, violated his constitutional right to freedom of speech by removing, and by asking Downs to remove, competing material that Downs had posted in the school in response to materials posted on bulletin boards set up by Leichman High staff members for the purpose of recognizing Gay and Lesbian Awareness Month.

* * *

Factual Background

* * * [O]n April 11, 1997, LAUSD issued "Memorandum No. 111," titled "Gay and Lesbian Awareness Month," to all schools and offices in the school district. Memorandum No. 111 referred to a May 18, 1992, formal Board of Education resolution designating June of each year as "a time to focus on gay and lesbian issues." The Memorandum noted that the Board of Education's resolution was passed to support "Educating for Diversity." The Memorandum also specified that

> the District's multicultural and human relations education policy includes the expectations that: "Each student has equal access to a quality education and an opportunity to participate fully in the academic and social activities of the school," and "School policies and practices act to foster a climate that reduces fears related to difference and deters name-calling and acts of violence or threats motivated by hate and bigotry."

The Memorandum informed the schools and offices that the "Office of Intergroup Relations and the Multicultural Unit, Division of Instructional Services, and the Gay and Lesbian Education Commission" would provide posters and materials in support of Gay and Lesbian Awareness Month.

The posters and materials to be provided to the schools were designed to aid in "the elimination of hate and the creation of a safe school environment for all students." "In recognition that some of the materials can be controversial in nature," the Memorandum provided that "the representations on the posters" were reviewed by, among other groups, the "Parent Community Services Branch." The Memorandum also "recognize[d] that schools are part of a community and must respect the sentiments held by the local community."

Pursuant to Memorandum No. 111 and the policies described therein, at some time in late May or early June 1997, some Leichman High staff members created a bulletin board inside the school building on which faculty and staff could post materials related to Gay and Lesbian Awareness Month in addition to the materials provided by the district office. Staff members created a similar board the following year. Materials did not need approval before posting on the Gay and Lesbian Awareness bulletin boards, but were subject to the oversight of the school principal, who had ultimate authority within the school over the content of the boards. This was the actual practice and policy at Leichman High. During the time period at issue in this case, there were two different principals at Leichman High: Donna Olmsted from January 1993 to June 1997, and Joseph Marino from July 1997 through at least the beginning of this litigation. As school principals, Olmsted and Marino were accountable to the school board, which itself is made up of publicly elected officials.

Materials posted by faculty and staff that Olmsted and Marino allowed to remain on the school's Gay and Lesbian Awareness bulletin boards covered a wide range of topics. They included a poster titled "The Civil Rights Movement;" a poster titled "Diversity is Beautiful;" a poster on Name Calling; a poster titled "What is a Family;" a bar/pie chart reflecting Statistics on Hate Crimes; a sheet of paper on "The Rainbow

Flag;" a sheet of paper explaining the gay and lesbian symbols; a laminated felt rainbow flag with the Greek letter Lambda; a newspaper article regarding LAUSD Board approval of domestic partner benefits; a Board resolution regarding discrimination; a Los Angeles County Human Relations Commission brochure regarding anti-gay and lesbian bashing; a statement that June is Gay and Lesbian Awareness/Pride month; a sheet of paper identifying famous gays and lesbians in history; a sheet of paper discussing the history of the pink triangle symbol; and a sheet of paper discussing the Lamda symbol. There is no evidence in the record that individuals other than faculty and staff at Leichman High posted these or any other materials on the school's Gay and Lesbian Awareness bulletin boards.

Downs objected to the recognition of Gay and Lesbian Awareness Month at Leichman High. In June of 1997, Downs created his own bulletin board across the hall from his classroom titled "Testing Tolerance." In June of 1998, in response to postings on other Gay and Lesbian Awareness bulletin boards within the school, Downs created a competing bulletin board titled "Redefining the Family." Included among the materials posted by Downs were a portion of the Declaration of Independence, newspaper articles, various school district memoranda, and the following four separate excerpts:

> According to lesbian activist Tories Osborn, 60% of Americans hold the belief that homosexuality is immoral. Most mainline religions in America . . . condemn homosexual behavior.

> Do not lie with a man as one lies with a woman; that is detestable. Do not have sexual relations with an animal and defile yourself with it. A woman must not present herself to an animal to have sexual relations with it; that is a perversion. Do not defile yourselves in any of these ways because this is how the nations that I am going to drive out before you become defiled. Leviticus 18:22–24.

> Obviously and without contention the simultaneous stimulation and mutual satisfaction which the complementary anatomical structures and functioning of the procreative organs of the man and woman produce indicate that they are purposefully intended for one another. Procreation and thereby the proliferation of the human species are further confirmation that such unions are appropriate and natural. Beyond this, the various organs of the digestive and excretory systems can and have been used for similar gratification, but obviously these acts are different and can be objectively evaluated as such.

> Anti-sodomy laws in many states stand to prevent or at least complicate homosexual marriage and adoption . . . because . . . the United States Supreme Court upheld state authority to maintain laws prohibiting homosexual sodomy.

* * *

In both 1997 and 1998, after other faculty members complained, Olmsted and Marino either removed Downs's materials or ordered Downs to remove them himself. The record clearly demonstrates that Downs's materials were ordered to be removed in part because members of the school community deemed them "disrespectful," "offensive," "upsetting," "objectionable," and "derogatory." Marino testified that he considered Downs's material inconsistent with the purposes of the Gay and Lesbian Awareness month because he "did not see [Downs's] activity supporting tolerance [and] did not see [Downs's] material supporting diversity."

* * *

[T]he district court granted LAUSD's second motion for summary judgment, filed on July 1, 1999.

* * *

The court ... held that "[j]ust as a school could prohibit a teacher from posting racist material on a bulletin board designated for Black History Month, [LAUSD] may prohibit [Downs] from posting intolerant materials during 'Gay and Lesbian Awareness Month.' " Finally, the court indicated, in dicta, its belief that even if viewpoint-neutrality principles were implicated in the case, LAUSD had not "advanced" the gay and lesbian lifestyle, but had instead engaged in the legitimate pedagogical interest of teaching tolerance.

Discussion

We review a grant of summary judgment de novo. We must determine, viewing the evidence in the light most favorable to Downs, whether there are any genuine issues of material fact and whether the district court correctly applied the relevant substantive law.

In order to decide whether the district court applied the substantive law to Downs's claim correctly, we must decide whether his postings on Leichman High's bulletin boards warranted any First Amendment protection. If so, we would have to assess what type of protection the First Amendment provides and whether LAUSD deprived Downs of that protection. Premised on our conclusion that the bulletin boards contained only "government speech," we conclude that Downs had no First Amendment right to dictate or to contribute to the content of that speech. Thus, LAUSD did not act unconstitutionally in removing Downs's materials or in ordering that the materials be removed. In summary, the district court's analysis of the issue it addressed was correct.

A.   Whose Speech Was It?

* * *

Viewpoint neutrality ... does not apply to LAUSD's actions in this case. This ... is a case of the government itself speaking, whether the government is characterized as Leichman High, LAUSD, or the school board.

* * *

Only school faculty and staff had access to post materials on these boards. While these faculty and staff members may have received materials from outside organizations, the faculty and staff members alone posted material on the bulletin boards, and at all times their postings were subject to the oversight of the school principals.

* * *

Because the school district and the school board were in fact responsible for 1) the recognition of Gay and Lesbian Awareness month and 2) the content of the bulletin boards through school principals' oversight, this case is clearly distinguishable from cases involving student-written articles in a school-sponsored newspaper or an outside organization's advertisements in school-sponsored student newspapers, yearbooks, and athletic programs.

* * *

We do not face an example of the government opening up a forum for either unlimited or limited public discussion. Instead, we face an example of the government opening up its own mouth: LAUSD, by issuing Memorandum No. 111, and Leichman High, by setting up the Gay and Lesbian Awareness bulletin boards. The bulletin boards served as an expressive vehicle for the school board's policy of "Educating for Diversity."

* * *

B.   To What Extent Can the Government Control Its Own Speech?

Now that we have concluded that this case involves government speech in a nonpublic forum, we must decide to what extent the First Amendment allows others to interfere with it.... We conclude that when a public high school is the speaker, its control of its own speech is not subject to the constraints of constitutional safeguards and forum analysis, but instead is measured by practical considerations applicable to any individual's choice of how to convey oneself: among other things, content, timing, and purpose. Simply because the government opens its mouth to speak does not give every outside individual or group a First Amendment right to play ventriloquist. As applied here, the First Amendment allows LAUSD to decide that Downs may not speak as its representative. This power is certainly so if his message is one with which the district disagrees.

Although "[i]t is axiomatic that the government may not *regulate* speech based on its substantive content or the message it conveys," "when the State is the speaker, it may make content-based choices."

* * *

When the government is formulating and conveying its message, "it may take legitimate and appropriate steps to ensure that its message is neither garbled nor distorted" by its individual messengers. *Rosenberger,* 515 U.S. at 833, 115 S.Ct. 2510. For example, a government's administration will not just make a decision to talk about taxes. It will have a viewpoint on the utility of taxes, and there is no constitutional reason why it should not be able to convey that message with clarity. * * *

An arm of local government—such as a school board—may decide not only to talk about gay and lesbian awareness and tolerance in general, but also to advocate such tolerance if it so decides, and restrict the contrary speech of one of its representatives. . . . *Rosenberger* supports this notion. . . .

At oral argument, Downs asserted that his case is indistinguishable from *Rosenberger* because, he alleges, LAUSD invited a variety of viewpoints on gay and lesbian issues. Downs, of course, is correct in his argument that his postings "focused on gay and lesbian issues," as contemplated by Memorandum No. 111. If we myopically limited Memorandum No. 111's message to that phrase, we might agree with Downs that this case would be indistinguishable from *Rosenberger* as inviting a myriad of viewpoints on a single topic of discussion, and thus requiring forum analysis. . . . However, that Downs's postings did indeed "focus on gay and lesbian issues" does not mean that they satisfied all aspects of LAUSD's policy as announced in Memorandum No. 111.

In addition to inviting a "focus on gay and lesbian issues," Memorandum No. 111 made clear that it was "the District's multicultural and human relations education policy" to "Educat[e] for Diversity," and that this included the expectation that all students would be given equal access to a quality education and the academic and social activities of the school. The policy also made clear a focus on "foster[ing] a climate that reduces fears related to difference and deters name-calling and acts of violence or threats motivated by hate and bigotry." In LAUSD's view, Downs's contributions to the bulletin boards harmed, rather than helped, the promotion of tolerance for and appreciation of diversity.

Moreover, Downs had notice that he was not dealing with a situation in which the government had opened up a forum inviting private speech and debate. In fact, Downs had continuous notice that he was violating district policy, even if he could successfully argue that Memorandum No. 111 was ambiguous regarding what it allowed him to contribute to Gay and Lesbian Awareness month in the school. Olmsted and Marino, as representatives of the elected school board, informed him that he was not conveying the government's chosen message, and that as long as he was employed by LAUSD, he was expected to adhere to the district's policy. Estrada–Melendez, LAUSD's legal counsel, informed Downs that the bulletin boards were not "free speech zones."

    * * *

Downs's citation to passages from the Bible might [also] present Establishment Clause problems.

    * * *

Whether or not the bulletin boards by themselves may be characterized as part of the school district's "curriculum" is unimportant, because curriculum is only one outlet of a school district's expression of its policy. Nevertheless, our decision is consistent with cases holding that school teachers have no First Amendment right to influence curriculum as they so choose.

* * *

In order for the speaker to have the opportunity to speak as the government, the speaker must gain favor with the populace and survive the electoral process.... The LAUSD school board is elected by the public, and until its current members are voted out of office, they "speak" for the school district through the policies they adopt. Furthermore, in the case of the typical school board, influence from the community does not end at the ballot box, but continues through publicly-held school board meetings at which parents and other interested parties may express satisfaction or dissatisfaction with the school board's policies or "speech." This is reflected in this case by Memorandum No. 111's acknowledgment that community groups had participated in a review of the posters and materials LAUSD sent to each of the schools for Gay and Lesbian Awareness month.

The district court in this case noted that "[j]ust as a school could prohibit a teacher from posting racist material on a bulletin board designated for Black History Month, [LAUSD] may prohibit [Downs] from posting intolerant materials during 'Gay and Lesbian Awareness Month.'" The Supreme Court has recognized a similar principle in the context of the government's ability to regulate its employees' speech and discipline those employees for that speech. * * *

Our holding, however, does not prevent Downs from propounding his own opinion on the morality of homosexuality. Subject to any applicable forum analysis, he may do so on the sidewalks, in the parks, through the chat-rooms, at his dinner table, and in countless other locations.... He may not do so, however, when he is speaking as the government, unless the government allows him to be its voice.

Conclusion

We hold that when the school district speaks through bulletin boards that are not "free speech zones," but instead are vehicles for conveying a message from the school district, the school district may formulate that message without the constraint of viewpoint neutrality. Here, LAUSD, an arm of local government, is firmly policing the boundaries of its own message. As such, LAUSD did not violate Downs's First Amendment free speech rights. Because we determine that Downs has no First Amendment right to speak for the government, his equal protection claim based upon the deprivation of this asserted right also fails to withstand summary judgment.

The district court's grant of summary judgment in favor of LAUSD is AFFIRMED.

HARPER v. POWAY UNIFIED SCH. DIST.

345 F.Supp.2d 1096 (S.D. Cal. 2004).

HOUSTON, District Judge.

INTRODUCTION

Now before the Court are defendants' motion to dismiss the complaint pursuant to Federal Rule of Civil Procedure 12(b)(6) and plaintiff's motion for preliminary injunction. After careful consideration of the pleadings and relevant exhibits submitted, and for the reasons set forth below, this Court GRANTS IN PART and DENIES IN PART defendants' motion to dismiss and DENIES plaintiff's motion for preliminary injunction in its entirety.

BACKGROUND

I. Factual Background[1]

Plaintiff Tyler Chase Harper ("plaintiff") is a minor and enrolled at Poway High School ("the School") in the Poway Unified School District. Plaintiff is a Christian with the firmly held religious belief that homosexuality is immoral. In the weeks prior to April 21, 2004, plaintiff became aware that the School planned to observe a "Day of Silence" that he believed "endorsed, encouraged, subsidized and promoted" homosexual activity. Plaintiff felt compelled to communicate his "sincerely-held religious beliefs" regarding "the Biblical condemnation of homosexual behavior to others in his school and his community." Therefore, on April 21, 2004 (the "Day of Silence"), plaintiff wore a T-shirt to the School on which the words "I WILL NOT ACCEPT WHAT GOD HAS CONDEMNED" had been placed on the front and the words "HOMOSEXUALITY IS SHAMEFUL 'Romans 1:27'" had been placed on the back.

In addition, on April 22, 2004, plaintiff wore a different T-shirt to school with the words "BE ASHAMED" "OUR SCHOOL EMBRACED WHAT GOD HAS CONDEMNED" placed on the front and the words "HOMOSEXUALITY IS SHAMEFUL Romans 1:27" placed on the back. During Plaintiff's second period class on April 22, 2004, the classroom teacher, defendant David LeMaster ("LeMaster"), informed plaintiff that he "was in violation of the school's dress code" and told plaintiff to remove the shirt "or leave class and report directly to the school office." Plaintiff apparently decided not to remove the T-shirt but, instead, met with the School's Vice Principal, defendant Lynell Antrim ("Antrim"). Antrim informed plaintiff that the T-shirt was "clearly in violation of the dress code because it had a 'homemade' message, as opposed to a printed or more permanent message on the garment." Antrim further informed plaintiff that "the words on the T-shirt were 'inflammatory,'"

---

1. These background facts are taken directly from plaintiffs' complaint and are accepted as true for purposes of defendants' motion to dismiss pursuant to Fed. R. Civ. P. § 12(b)(6).

and that plaintiff should replace the shirt if he wished to return to class. Plaintiff "politely" refused to change the shirt and was directed to wait to discuss the matter with the principal.

The School's Principal, defendant Scott Fisher ("Fisher"), then interviewed plaintiff, during which Fisher "repeatedly" inquired as to why plaintiff wore the T-shirt on both days. Fisher also informed plaintiff that the T-shirt was "too 'aggressive' and that wearing it would not be tolerated at [the School]." In addition, Fisher further informed plaintiff that any punishment meted out would be the same whether the T-shirt had been homemade or pre-manufactured "because the content was inflammatory." Finally, Fisher told plaintiff that, due to his courteousness and respect toward school authorities, plaintiff would be required to remain in an office during the rest of the school day, not be allowed to leave the office without an escort, and be required to depart the school grounds immediately thereafter "by the most direct route." Plaintiff remained in an office as directed.

Plaintiff received visits from "various school security personnel" while he remained in the office. In particular, a former coach of plaintiff's, questioned him as to whether wearing the T-shirt "was worth it." A deputy sheriff also questioned plaintiff while he was in the School's office. The deputy sheriff, wearing a badge and carrying sidearm, informed plaintiff he was "there to determine if [plaintiff] was a dangerous student, to find out why he wore the particular T-shirt, and to determine if he was going to engage in similar behavior in the future." The deputy sheriff suggested plaintiff should "not be offensive to others" because the Christian faith is not based on hate and further informed plaintiff that the T-shirt was " 'inflammatory' and 'could encourage uprising and violence against homosexuals.' "

At the end of the school day, plaintiff was directed to defendant Vice Principal Ed Giles' ("Giles") office. Giles explained to plaintiff that Giles knew plaintiff's family and youth pastor and that Giles was a Christian believer. Giles further explained to plaintiff that when Giles came to school "he had to leave his faith 'in the car' " and "advised [plaintiff] that when he comes to [the School] ... he too must 'leave his faith in the car.' " Plaintiff informed Giles he could not do so. Plaintiff was then informed to leave school directly without stopping at his locker for any homework assignments, to which he complied.

Just prior to the end of the school day, Giles telephoned plaintiff's father, Ron Harper ("Ron Harper"), and informed him of plaintiff's detention and suspension for the day due to the T-shirt. Ron Harper was initially given the reason for the suspension as being due to the homemade nature of the T-shirt but, after further inquiry, Giles explained that, based on his view, the message on the T-shirt was "negative" and "only positive community messages were allowed." The next day, Ron Harper went to the School to discuss the previous day's suspension and was told that plaintiff conducted himself respectfully and honorably and that "no disruptions, altercations or other incidents among students at the school" had occurred due to his son's T-shirt.

II.   Procedural History

The instant complaint was filed on June 2, 2004. Plaintiff's complaint, filed pursuant to 42 U.S.C. § 1983, alleges that defendants' actions violated plaintiff's rights: (1) to freedom of speech under the First Amendment to the United States Constitution; (2) to free exercise of religion under the First Amendment; (3) to equal protection under the Fourteenth Amendment; (4) to due process under the Fourteenth Amendment; (5) under the Establishment Clause of the First Amendment; and (6) pursuant to California Civil Code § 52.1. Plaintiff seeks declaratory and injunctive relief as well as nominal and punitive damages.

* * *

II.   Plaintiff's Motion for Preliminary Injunction

* * *

B.   Analysis

1.   Likelihood of Success on the Merits

Plaintiff contends that there is a high probability he will succeed on the merits of his claims. Defendants disagree. This Court, after a thorough review of the pleadings, declarations, and relevant exhibits submitted by the parties, finds that plaintiff has failed to demonstrate he will succeed on the merits of his claims.

* * *

Three of plaintiff's constitutional claims have survived defendants' motion to dismiss: (1) the violation of plaintiff's right to free speech; (2) the violation of plaintiff's right to free exercise of religion; and (3) the violation of plaintiff's rights under the Establishment Clause. The Court addresses each of the remaining claims in turn.

a.   Freedom of Speech Claim

Defendants have not provided any additional evidence to aid this Court's determination of whether the speech at issue is "plainly offensive" thereby rendering the speech suppressible under *Fraser.* However, student speech will not offend the Constitution's free speech prohibitions if it "materially disrupts classwork or involves substantial disorder or invasion of the rights of others." *Tinker,* 393 U.S. at 513, 89 S.Ct. 733. "*Tinker* does not require certainty that disruption will occur, 'but rather the existence of facts which might reasonably lead school officials to forecast substantial disruption.' " *LaVine,* 257 F.3d at 989 (quoting *Tinker,* 393 U.S. at 514, 89 S.Ct. 733). Thus, a showing that the suppressed speech might reasonably be forecasted as a material disruption at school negates plaintiff's claims.

Defendants have presented such a showing. The declaration of Lynell Antrim, Assistant Principal, indicates that the previous year's

"Day of Silence" conducted at the school had resulted in "volatile behavior," including altercations between students. David LeMaster, a History and English teacher at the School, testifies in his declaration that he observed a disruption in the class that plaintiff attended while wearing the T-shirt at issue here. LeMaster also stated that he recalled that the events from the previous year's "Day of Silence" had resulted in "tensions between students." Scott Fisher, Principal at the School, stated that plaintiff told him a "tense verbal conversation with a group of students" had already taken place due to the T-shirt's message and was mindful of altercations that had occurred during the previous year's "Day of Silence."

This evidence, along with the allegations contained in the complaint espousing the concerns of Principal Giles, Assistant Principal Antrim and the deputy sheriff, and reciting the school policies, is sufficient, in this Court's view, to permit that the school officials to "reasonably ... forecast substantial disruption of or material interference with school activities." *Tinker,* 393 U.S. at 514, 89 S.Ct. 733. Therefore, this Court finds that plaintiff has failed to demonstrate a likelihood of success on the merits of his free speech claim.

b.   Free Exercise Claim

Plaintiff bases his free exercise claim, in part, on it being a "hybrid" claim which requires strict scrutiny analysis. As plaintiff correctly points out, without the free speech claim, plaintiff's free exercise claim does not require strict scrutiny. Plaintiff concedes that the School's prohibition on speech is "arguably" a neutral law requiring scrutiny pursuant to a rational basis test. This Court finds the School's policies are clearly based on a legitimate pedagogical concern—avoidance of disruption based on intolerance of others—which provides a rational basis for the School's suppression of plaintiff's expression. *See Tinker,* 393 U.S. at 514, 89 S.Ct. 733. Plaintiff's right to free exercise does not relieve him of his obligation to comply with valid and neutral policies having general application to all students. *Smith,* 494 U.S. at 879, 110 S.Ct. 1595. Therefore, in light of the allegations in the complaint and the evidence presented in defendants' declarations, as detailed above, this Court finds that, without the free speech claim, plaintiff has failed to demonstrate that defendants' actions were irrational or wholly arbitrary. Accordingly, plaintiff has failed to demonstrate a likelihood of success on the merits of his free exercise claim.

c.   Establishment Clause Claim

Plaintiff's Establishment Clause claim is similarly devoid of support. Plaintiff alleges that the statements made by the deputy sheriff and defendant Giles were attempts by school authorities to coerce plaintiff to change his religious views. This Court denied defendants' motion to dismiss this claim because the allegations could possibly be proven. However, this Court's decision rested on the fact that, on motion to dismiss, the facts and allegations, along with all inferences construed from those facts, must be viewed in the light most favorable to plaintiff.

The requirement of deference to plaintiff's allegations is not present in determining whether plaintiff can demonstrate a likelihood of success on the merits. From the standpoint of plaintiff's motion for injunctive relief, the Court finds it unlikely that the statements in the complaint relating to Giles and the deputy sheriff were given to coerce plaintiff into changing his religious beliefs. As previously stated, the complaint avers that the deputy sheriff "*proposed* to [plaintiff] that as a member of the Christian faith, he *should* understand that Christianity was based on love not hate, and that [plaintiff] *should* not be offensive to others." Defendant Giles, similarly, merely "*advised* [plaintiff] that when he comes to Poway High, *if* his religious beliefs are offensive, he too must 'leave his faith in the car.' " Plaintiff's deliberate use of the words "proposed," "should," and "advised" signifies that the speaker did not specifically order plaintiff to cease and desist in expressing his religious views. Further, the use of the word "if" signifies that the speaker left the decision as to whether to "leave his faith in the car" to Plaintiff "if" it was plaintiff's belief that the expressive message would be offensive. This Court finds it unlikely that the statements alleged to be made by the school officials could be proven to be attempts to coerce plaintiff to change his religious views. It appears more reasonable that the trier of fact would infer that the officials' statements relied upon by plaintiff to depict coercion were no more than options presented to and left with plaintiff.

In addition, the policies and statements made had a secular purpose, *i.e.,* promoting tolerance, and not advancing or inhibiting religion. Moreover, there are no facts to suggest that defendants approved one religious message over another or approved "irreligion over religion." Indeed, plaintiff has not presented any further evidence to persuade this Court that the claim will succeed. Therefore, this Court finds that plaintiff has failed to demonstrate a likelihood of success on the merits of his Establishment Clause claim.

2.   Balance of Hardships

In determining whether the balance of hardships tip sharply in plaintiff's favor, plaintiff's "sincerely held religious beliefs" regarding the Biblical condemnation of homosexual behavior and his assertion that the First Amendment permits him to express his beliefs in a school setting must be balanced against the School's responsibility to act *in loco parentis* on behalf of the students, promote tolerance, and protect the rights of other students. The Supreme Court has recognized that school officials have a responsibility to discipline students where there "is reason to believe the student's expression 'intrudes upon the work of the schools or on the rights of other students.' " *Tinker,* 393 U.S. at 508, 89 S.Ct. 733. School officials are in a better position, based upon their familiarity with the pulse and culture of the school setting, to decide whether restrictions on expression are appropriate. Here, the School's policies implement State of California rules to prohibit discrimination, intimidation, harassment and hate based upon, among other classifications, sexual orientation. This Court notes that there is nothing in the record to suggest plaintiff would not be free to proselytize any religious view or any other viewpoint in a manner that does not violate neutral and valid school policies. On the other hand, requiring the School to allow plaintiff to express this particular viewpoint could result in disruption of the work of the schools or the violation of the rights of other students.

Defendants, in their opposition, contend that the public interest would not be served by allowing plaintiff's expression in school. Defendants point out that the School has an obligation to keep their students "safe regardless of sexual orientation." According to defendants, "the safety and well-being of gay and lesbian students, and the ability of school administrators to regulate anti-gay speech, outweighs [p]laintiff's competing interest." This Court agrees with defendants. Moreover, in this Court's view, balancing the needs of the School to keep all their students safe coupled with the foreseeable vision that other students may feel free to exhibit these types of expressions that would interfere with the work of the school and violate the rights of others against plaintiff's interests does not tip the scales sharply in plaintiff's favor.

C. Conclusion

Because this Court finds that plaintiff has failed to demonstrate a likelihood of success on the merits of any of the claims that survived defendants' motion to dismiss and that the balance of hardships do not tip sharply in plaintiff's favor, plaintiff's motion for preliminary injunction is DENIED.

* * *

Note

1. Plaintiff appealed this decision to the Ninth Circuit, which proceeded to hear oral argument regarding the case in June 2005.

2. ACCESS TO CAMPUS FACILITIES

GOOD NEWS CLUB v. MILFORD CENTRAL SCH.
533 U.S. 98, 121 S.Ct. 2093 (2001).

JUSTICE THOMAS delivered the opinion of the Court.

This case presents two questions. The first question is whether Milford Central School violated the free speech rights of the Good News Club when it excluded the Club from meeting after hours at the school. The second question is whether any such violation is justified by Milford's concern that permitting the Club's activities would violate the Establishment Clause. We conclude that Milford's restriction violates the Club's free speech rights and that no Establishment Clause concern justifies that violation.

I.

* * * Stephen and Darleen Fournier reside within Milford's district and therefore are eligible [under school district policy] to use the school's facilities as long as their proposed use is approved by the school. Together they are sponsors of the local Good News Club, a private Christian organization for children ages 6 to 12. Pursuant to Milford's policy, in September 1996 the Fourniers submitted a request to Dr. Robert McGruder, interim superintendent of the district, in which they sought permission to hold the Club's weekly afterschool meetings in the school cafeteria. * * * The next month, McGruder formally denied the Fourniers' request on the ground that the proposed use—to have "a fun time of singing songs, hearing a Bible lesson and memorizing scripture,"—was "the equivalent of religious worship." According to McGruder, the community use policy, which prohibits use "by any individual or organization for religious purposes," foreclosed the Club's activities.

In response to a letter submitted by the Club's counsel, Milford's attorney requested information to clarify the nature of the Club's activities. The Club sent a set of materials used or distributed at the meetings and the following description of its meeting:

> The Club opens its session with Ms. Fournier taking attendance. As she calls a child's name, if the child recites a Bible verse the child receives a treat. After attendance, the Club sings songs. Next Club members engage in games that involve, *inter alia,* learning Bible verses. Ms. Fournier then relates a Bible story and explains how it applies to Club members' lives. The Club closes with prayer. Finally, Ms. Fournier distributes treats and the Bible verses for memorization.

McGruder and Milford's attorney reviewed the materials and concluded that "the kinds of activities proposed to be engaged in by the Good News Club were not a discussion of secular subjects such as child rearing, development of character and development of morals from a religious perspective, but were in fact the equivalent of religious instruction itself." In February 1997, the Milford Board of Education adopted a resolution rejecting the Club's request to use Milford's facilities "for the purpose of conducting religious instruction and Bible study."

In March 1997, petitioners * * * filed an action under Rev. Stat. § 1979, 42 U.S.C. § 1983, against Milford in the United States District Court for the Northern District of New York. The Club alleged that Milford's denial of its application violated its free speech rights under the First and Fourteenth Amendments, its right to equal protection under the Fourteenth Amendment, and its right to religious freedom under the Religious Freedom Restoration Act of 1993. * * *

II.

The standards that we apply to determine whether a State has unconstitutionally excluded a private speaker from use of a public forum depend on the nature of the forum. If the forum is a traditional or open public forum, the State's restrictions on speech are subject to stricter scrutiny than are restrictions in a limited public forum. We have previously declined to decide whether a school district's opening of its facilities pursuant to N.Y. Educ. Law § 414 creates a limited or a traditional public forum. See *Lamb's Chapel, supra,* at 391–392, 113 S.Ct. 2141. Because the parties have agreed that Milford created a limited public forum when it opened its facilities in 1992 * * * we need not resolve the issue here. Instead, we simply will assume that Milford operates a limited public forum.

When the State establishes a limited public forum, the State is not required to and does not allow persons to engage in every type of speech. The State may be justified "in reserving [its forum] for certain groups or for the discussion of certain topics." *Rosenberger v. Rector and Visitors of Univ. of Va.,* 515 U.S. 819 (1995). The State's power to restrict speech, however, is not without limits. The restriction must not discriminate against speech on the basis of viewpoint, *Rosenberger,* and the restriction must be "reasonable in light of the purpose served by the forum."

III.

Applying this test, we first address whether the exclusion constituted viewpoint discrimination. We are guided in our analysis by two of our prior opinions, *Lamb's Chapel* and *Rosenberger.* In *Lamb's Chapel,* we held that a school district violated the Free Speech Clause of the First Amendment when it excluded a private group from presenting films at the school based solely on the films' discussions of family values from a religious perspective. Likewise, in *Rosenberger,* we held that a university's refusal to fund a student publication because the publication addressed issues from a religious perspective violated the Free Speech Clause. Concluding that Milford's exclusion of the Good News Club based on its religious nature is indistinguishable from the exclusions in these cases, we hold that the exclusion constitutes viewpoint discrimination. Because the restriction is viewpoint discriminatory, we need not decide whether it is unreasonable in light of the purposes served by the forum. * * *

Just as there is no question that teaching morals and character development to children is a permissible purpose under Milford's policy, it is clear that the Club teaches morals and character development to children. For example, no one disputes that the Club instructs children to overcome feelings of jealousy, to treat others well regardless of how they treat the children, and to be obedient, even if it does so in a nonsecular way. * * *

Applying *Lamb's Chapel,* we find it quite clear that Milford engaged in viewpoint discrimination when it excluded the Club from the after-school forum. In *Lamb's Chapel,* the local New York school district similarly had ... prohibited use "by any group for religious purposes." Citing this prohibition, the school district excluded a church that wanted to present films teaching family values from a Christian perspective. We held that, because the films "no doubt dealt with a subject otherwise permissible" under the rule, the teaching of family values, the district's exclusion of the church was unconstitutional viewpoint discrimination.

Like the church in *Lamb's Chapel,* the Club seeks to address a subject otherwise permitted under the rule, the teaching of morals and character, from a religious standpoint. Certainly, one could have characterized the film presentations in *Lamb's Chapel* as a religious use, as the Court of Appeals did. And one easily could conclude that the films' purpose to instruct that "society's slide toward humanism ... can only be counterbalanced by a loving home where Christian values are instilled from an early age," was "quintessentially religious." The only apparent difference between the activity of Lamb's Chapel and the activities of the Good News Club is that the Club chooses to teach moral lessons from a Christian perspective through live storytelling and prayer, whereas Lamb's Chapel taught lessons through films. This distinction is inconsequential. Both modes of speech use a religious viewpoint. Thus, the exclusion of the Good News Club's activities, like the exclusion of Lamb's Chapel's films, constitutes unconstitutional viewpoint discrimination.

Our opinion in *Rosenberger* also is dispositive. In *Rosenberger,* a student organization at the University of Virginia was denied funding for printing expenses because its publication, *Wide Awake,* offered a Christian viewpoint. Just as the Club emphasizes the role of Christianity in students' morals and character, *Wide Awake* "challenge[d] Christians to live, in word and deed, according to the faith they proclaim and ... encourage[d] students to consider what a personal relationship with Jesus Christ means." Because the university "select[ed] for disfavored treatment those student journalistic efforts with religious editorial viewpoints," we held that the denial of funding was unconstitutional. Although in *Rosenberger* there was no prohibition on religion as a subject matter, our holding did not rely on this factor. Instead, we concluded simply that the university's denial of funding to print *Wide Awake* was viewpoint discrimination, just as the school district's refusal to allow Lamb's Chapel to show its films was viewpoint discrimination. Given the obvious religious content of *Wide Awake,* we cannot say that the Club's activities are any more "religious" or deserve any less First Amendment protection than did the publication of *Wide Awake* in *Rosenberger.*

Despite our holdings in *Lamb's Chapel* and *Rosenberger,* the Court of Appeals, like *Milford,* believed that its characterization of the Club's activities as religious in nature warranted treating the Club's activities as different in kind from the other activities permitted by the school. The "Christian viewpoint" is unique, according to the court, because it contains an "additional layer" that other kinds of viewpoints do not. That is, the Club "is focused on teaching children how to cultivate their relationship with God through Jesus Christ," which it characterized as "quintessentially religious." With these observations, the court concluded that, because the Club's activities "fall outside the bounds of pure 'moral and character development,'" the exclusion did not constitute viewpoint discrimination.

We disagree that something that is "quintessentially religious" or "decidedly religious in nature" cannot also be characterized properly as the teaching of morals and character development from a particular viewpoint. What matters for purposes of the Free Speech Clause is that we can see no logical difference in kind between the invocation of Christianity by the Club and the invocation of teamwork, loyalty, or patriotism by other associations to provide a foundation for their lessons. It is apparent that the unstated principle of the Court of Appeals' reasoning is its conclusion that any time religious instruction and prayer are used to discuss morals and character, the discussion is simply not a "pure" discussion of those issues. According to the Court of Appeals, reliance on Christian principles taints moral and character instruction in a way that other foundations for thought or viewpoints do not. We, however, have never reached such a conclusion. Instead, we reaffirm our holdings in *Lamb's Chapel* and *Rosenberger* that speech discussing otherwise permissible subjects cannot be excluded from a limited public forum on the ground that the subject is discussed from a religious viewpoint. Thus, we conclude that Milford's exclusion of the Club from use of the school, pursuant to its community use policy, constitutes impermissible viewpoint discrimination. * * *

V.

When Milford denied the Good News Club access to the school's limited public forum on the ground that the Club was religious in nature, it discriminated against the Club because of its religious viewpoint in violation of the Free Speech Clause of the First Amendment. Because Milford has not raised a valid Establishment Clause claim, we do not address the question whether such a claim could excuse Milford's viewpoint discrimination. * * *

The judgment of the Court of Appeals is reversed, and the case is remanded for further proceedings consistent with this opinion.

It is so ordered.

JUSTICE STEVENS, dissenting.

The Milford Central School has invited the public to use its facilities for educational and recreational purposes, but not for "religious purposes." Speech for "religious purposes" may reasonably be understood to encompass three different categories. First, there is religious speech that is simply speech about a particular topic from a religious point of view. The film in *Lamb's Chapel v. Center Moriches Union Free School District* illustrates this category. Second, there is religious speech that amounts to worship, or its equivalent. Our decision in *Widmar v. Vincent* concerned such speech. Third, there is an intermediate category that is aimed principally at proselytizing or inculcating belief in a particular religious faith.

A public entity may not generally exclude even religious worship from an open public forum. Similarly, a public entity that creates a limited public forum for the discussion of certain specified topics may not exclude a speaker simply because she approaches those topics from a religious point of view. Thus, in *Lamb's Chapel* we held that a public school that permitted its facilities to be used for the discussion of family issues and child rearing could not deny access to speakers presenting a religious point of view on those issues.

But, while a public entity may not censor speech about an authorized topic based on the point of view expressed by the speaker, it has broad discretion to "preserve the property under its control for the use to which it is lawfully dedicated." * * * Accordingly, "control over access to a nonpublic forum can be based on subject matter and speaker identity so long as the distinctions drawn are reasonable in light of the purpose served by the forum and are viewpoint neutral." The novel question that this case presents concerns the constitutionality of a public school's attempt to limit the scope of a public forum it has created. More specifically, the question is whether a school can, consistently with the First Amendment, create a limited public forum that admits the first type of religious speech without allowing the other two.

Distinguishing speech from a religious viewpoint, on the one hand, from religious proselytizing, on the other, is comparable to distinguishing meetings to discuss political issues from meetings whose principal purpose is to recruit new members to join a political organization. If a school decides to authorize after-school discussions of current events in its classrooms, it may not exclude people from expressing their views simply because it dislikes their particular political opinions. But must it therefore allow organized political groups—for example, the Democratic Party, the Libertarian Party, or the Ku Klux Klan—to hold meetings, the principal purpose of which is not to discuss the current-events topic from their own unique point of view but rather to recruit others to join their respective groups? I think not. Such recruiting meetings may introduce divisiveness and tend to separate young children into cliques that undermine the school's educational mission. * * *

This case is undoubtedly close. Nonetheless, regardless of whether the Good News Club's activities amount to "worship," it does seem clear, based on the facts in the record, that the school district correctly classified those activities as falling within the third category of religious speech and therefore beyond the scope of the school's limited public forum. In short, I am persuaded that the school district could (and did) permissibly exclude from its limited public forum proselytizing religious speech that does not rise to the level of actual worship. I would therefore affirm the judgment of the Court of Appeals.

Accordingly, I respectfully dissent.

JUSTICE SOUTER, with whom JUSTICE GINSBURG joins, dissenting.

* * * It is beyond question that Good News intends to use the public school premises not for the mere discussion of a subject from a particular, Christian point of view, but for an evangelical service of worship calling children to commit themselves in an act of Christian conversion. The majority avoids this reality only by resorting to the bland and general characterization of Good News's activity as "teaching of morals and character, from a religious standpoint." If the majority's

statement ignores reality, as it surely does, then today's holding may be understood only in equally generic terms. Otherwise, indeed, this case would stand for the remarkable proposition that any public school opened for civic meetings must be opened for use as a church, synagogue, or mosque, * * *

Notes

1. While the *Milford* dispute concerned only access to campus facilities after school, how applicable might the decision be in subsequent disputes regarding what might be allowable in the public school classroom on school time? Assume, for example, that students in an eleventh grade English class are assigned to write essays on a hero or heroine of their choice, but that when a student indicates that she wishes to write about Jesus, she is told by her teacher that she must keep to secular figures. If the student challenges the decision as violative of her First Amendment rights, can the *Milford* decision be the basis of a successful argument? How might such an argument be structured?

2. In *Child Evangelism Fellowship of New Jersey v. Stafford*, 386 F.3d 514 (3d Cir. 2004), the Third Circuit provided the fellowship, which sponsors Good News Clubs, with another victory in a disputed access case. The decision applied *Milford* to uphold the legality of the organization's posting and distribution of religious materials and its participation in so-called "Back-to-School" nights.

EQUAL ACCESS TO PUBLIC SCHOOL FACILITIES UNDER THE "NO CHILD LEFT BEHIND" ACT

20 U.S.C. § 7905 (2005).

(a) Short title

This section may be cited as the "Boy Scouts of America Equal Access Act".

(b) In general

(1) Equal access

Notwithstanding any other provision of law, no public elementary school, public secondary school, local educational agency, or State educational agency that has a designated open forum or a limited public forum and that receives funds made available through the Department shall deny equal access or a fair opportunity to meet to, or discriminate against, any group officially affiliated with the Boy Scouts of America, or any other youth group listed in Title 36 of the United States Code (as a patriotic society), that wishes to conduct a meeting within that designated open forum or limited public forum, including denying such access or opportunity or discriminating for reasons based on the membership or leadership criteria or oath of allegiance to God and country of the Boy Scouts of America or of the youth group listed in Title 36 of the United States Code (as a patriotic society).

(d) Definition and rule

(1) Definition

In this section, the term "youth group" means any group or organization intended to serve young people under the age of 21.

(2) Rule

For the purpose of this section, an elementary school or secondary school has a limited public forum whenever the school involved grants an offering to, or opportunity for, one or more outside youth or community groups to meet on school premises or in school facilities before or after the hours during which attendance at the school is compulsory.

ACCESS OF THE MILITARY TO EDUCATIONAL INSTITUTIONS

Two federal statutes providing the military with access to students for purposes of recruiting have been the subject of considerable debate in recent years. At the K–12 level, the U.S. "No Child Left Behind" Act, 20 U.S.C. Section 7908, provides military recruiters with "access to students and student recruiting information." At the higher education level, the Solomon Amendment, 10 U.S.C. Section 983, requires the U.S. Department of Defense to deny federal funding to institutions that prohibit military representatives access to and assistance for recruiting purposes.

By 2006, the NCLB provision had generated extensive debate, with widespread accusations of alleged improprieties by military recruiters being set forth. At the same time, the constitutionality of the Solomon Amendment was being challenged in *Rumsfeld v. FAIR,* a case that reached the U.S. Supreme Court in December 2005.

Armed Forces Recruiter Access to Students and Student Recruiting Information
Under the U.S. "No Child Left Behind" Act

20 U.S.C. § 7908 provides, in pertinent part:

(a) Policy

(1) Access to student recruiting information

* * * [E]ach local educational agency receiving assistance under this chapter shall provide, on a request made by military recruiters or an institution of higher education, access to secondary school students names, addresses, and telephone listings.

(2) Consent

A secondary school student or the parent of the student may request that the student's name, address, and telephone listing described in paragraph (1) not be released without prior written parental consent, and the local educational agency or private school shall notify parents of the option to make a request and shall comply with any request.

(3) Same access to students

Each local educational agency receiving assistance under this chapter shall provide military recruiters the same access to secondary school students as is provided generally to post secondary educational institutions or to prospective employers of those students.

* * *

Rumsfeld v. FAIR

On December 6, 2005, the U.S. Supreme Court heard oral argument in *Rumsfeld v. FAIR*, the constitutional challenge to the Solomon Amendment. The U.S. government was appealing the decision by the Third Circuit, which had ruled in favor of the plaintiffs. *See* 390 F.3d 219 (3rd Cir. 2004):

[The Forum for Academic and Institutional Rights, Inc. ("FAIR"), an association of law schools and law faculty, had sought to enjoin enforcement of the Solomon Amendment in 2003. Two of the three judges on the Third Circuit panel determined "that FAIR [had] demonstrated a likelihood of success on the merits of its First Amendment claims and that it [was] entitled to preliminary injunctive relief."]

A.   Law Schools' Nondiscrimination Policies

Law schools have long maintained formal policies of nondiscrimination that withhold career placement services from employers who exclude employees and applicants based on such factors as race, gender, and religion. In the 1970s law schools began expanding these policies to prohibit discrimination based on sexual orientation as well. In response to this trend the American Association of Law Schools ("AALS") voted unanimously in 1990 to include sexual orientation as a protected category. As a result, virtually every law school now has a comprehensive policy like the following:

[The] School of Law is committed to a policy of equal opportunity for all students and graduates. The Career Services facilities of this school shall not be available to those employers who discriminate on the grounds of race, color, religion, national origin, sex, handicap or disability, age, or sexual orientation. . . . Before using any of the Career Services interviewing facilities of this school, an employer shall be required to submit a signed statement certifying that its practices conform to this policy.

B.   Congress Passes the Solomon Amendment

The United States military excludes service members based on evidence of homosexual conduct and/or orientation. Citing their nondiscrimination policies, some law schools began in the 1980s refusing to provide access and assistance to military recruiters. This caught the attention of members of Congress. In 1994, Representative Gerald Solomon of New York sponsored an amendment to the annual defense appropriation bill that proposed to withhold DOD funding from any educational institution with a policy of denying or effectively preventing the military from obtaining entry to campuses (or access to students on campuses) for recruiting purposes.

During debate in the House of Representatives, Representative Solomon urged the passage of his amendment "on behalf of military preparedness" because "recruiting is the key to an all-volunteer military." He argued that it was hypocritical for schools to receive federal money while at the same time denying the military access to their campuses: "[T]ell[ ] recipients of Federal money at colleges and universities that if you do not like the Armed Forces, if you do not like its policies, that is fine. That is your [F]irst [A]mendment right[ ]. But do not expect Federal dollars to support your interference with our military recruiters." The amendment's co-sponsor, Representative Richard Pombo of California, said Congress needed to target "policies of ambivalence or hostility to our Nation's armed services" that are "nothing less than a backhanded slap at the honor and dignity of service in our Nation's Armed Forces." He urged his colleagues to "send a message over the wall of the ivory tower of higher education" that colleges' and universities' "starry-eyed idealism comes with a price. If they are too good—or too righteous—to treat our Nation's military with the respect it deserves[,] then they may also be too good to receive the generous level of taxpayer dollars presently enjoyed by many institutions of higher education in America."

Other Representatives opposed the amendment, alleging violations of academic freedom and civil rights. *See, e.g., [140 Cong. Rec. H3861,]* H3862 (Rep. Dellums) ("We should not ... chill or abridge privacy, speech, or conscience by threatening a college with a Federal funds termination because it chose for whatever reason to deny access to military recruiters.... We should not browbeat them ... into becoming involuntary agents of Federal policy."). In light of Vietnam War-era legislation, rarely invoked, that already granted the DOD discretion to withhold funding from colleges and universities that barred military recruiters, the DOD itself objected to the proposed amendment as "unnecessary" and "duplicative." The DOD also feared that withholding funds from universities could be potentially harmful to defense research initiatives. But the House voted for the amendment by a vote of 271 to 126. Several months later the Senate approved the defense spending appropriations bill, including Representative Solomon's amendment, and the "Solomon Amendment" ultimately became law.

C. Subsequent Amendments and Regulatory Interpretations

In 1997 Congress amended the Solomon Amendment by expanding its penalty to include, in addition to DOD funds, funds administered by other federal agencies, including the Departments of Transportation, Labor, Health and Human Services, and Education.

* * *

Following the 1999 amendment, the DOD enforced the Solomon Amendment consistent with its terms. Only schools whose policies or practices "prohibit[ed], or in effect prevent[ed]," military representatives "from gaining entry to campuses, or access to students . . . on campuses for purposes of military recruiting," were penalized. Thus, by merely allowing military recruiters to gain access to campuses, many law schools avoided the Solomon Amendment's penalty while reaffirming their opposition to the military's exclusionary employment policy by not providing them affirmative assistance in the manner provided to other recruiters. Harvard Law School, for example, allowed military recruiters on campus to recruit at the offices of its Veterans Association but did not volunteer its placement personnel to arrange interviews. Boston College Law School allowed military recruiters to conduct on-campus interviews, but kept their literature in the library rather than in the career services office. Until the fall of 2001, the DOD did not consider these and other similar "ameliorative measures" to violate the Solomon Amendment and expressed enthusiasm for the law schools' cooperation with what it described as successful recruiting efforts.

But following the terrorist attacks in the United States in September 2001, the DOD began applying an informal policy of requiring not only access to campuses, but treatment equal to that accorded other recruiters. As evidence of this informal policy, a letter from the DOD's Acting Deputy Undersecretary William J. Carr to Richard Levin, the President of Yale University, stated that universities are required "to provide military recruiters access to students equal in quality and scope to that provided to other recruiters." The same letter stated that the "DOD requires that there not be a substantial disparity in the treatment of military recruiters as compared to other potential employers." This changed context meant that Yale's willingness to let military recruiters use a room in Yale Law School's building for interviews would not pass muster unless it also provided military recruiters with the same level of assistance from its career development office (arranging interviews, posting notices, *etc.*) provided to other recruiters. Furthermore, the DOD intimated that failure to comply would result in a loss to Yale University not only of DOD funds, but of all federal funds (a penalty that is not consistent with the DOD's existing regulations, under which the offending subelement's parent institution is penalized with the loss of only DOD funds.

* * *

Congress [subsequently] amended the Solomon Amendment to codify the DOD's informal policy. Now, under the terms of the statute itself, law schools and their parent institutions are penalized for preventing military representatives from gaining entry to campuses for the purpose of military recruiting "in a manner that is at least equal in quality and scope to the [degree of] access to campuses and to students that is provided to any other employer."

D.   Current Litigation

In September 2003, FAIR sued the DOD and the other federal departments whose funds are restricted under the Solomon Amendment, seeking on constitutional grounds a preliminary injunction enjoining enforcement of the statute and the then-existing (now codified) informal policy. * * *

Judge Ambro, writing for the majority in the Third Circuit, found that the Solomon Amendment violated FAIR's First Amendment rights. He determined that not only were the law schools "expressive associations" whose First Amendment right to disseminate their chosen message had been "impaired by the inclusion of military recruiters on their campuses," but that the law schools were "insulated by free speech protections from being compelled to assist military recruiters in the expressive act of recruiting."

Judge Aldisert, dissenting, would hold "that Congress' use of the spending power and fulfillment of the requirements to maintain the military under Articles I and II do not unreasonably burden speech and, therefore, do not offend the First Amendment":

> I apply the balance-of-interests test and decide that the interest of protecting the national security of the United States outweighs the indirect and attenuated interest in the law schools' speech, expressive association and academic freedom rights. The Solomon Amendment survives the constitutional attack because its provisions, the 2004 amendments thereto and related regulations, govern conduct while only incidentally affecting speech. In serving its compelling interest in recruiting military lawyers, the statute does not require the government to engage in unconstitutional conduct.

At oral argument, a majority of the justices appeared very sympathetic to the government's position. *See, e.g.,* Linda Greenhouse, *Justices Weigh Military's Access to Law Schools,* N.Y. Times, December 7, 2005.

Given the clear need to recruit "volunteers" for the armed forces, a compelling argument can be made that the military must have access to campuses for this purpose. However, in light of the controversies that have emerged–fueled during this era by an increasingly unpopular war in Iraq–are there viable alternatives to the current legal mandates that can be identified as a matter of policy?

D.   THE PARAMETERS OF THE RIGHT TO RECEIVE INFORMATION & IDEAS

PROBLEM 40: Montoya v. Gold Coast Unified School District

The following problem takes place in the fictional city of Gold Coast, Eldorado. Gold Coast Unified is a large urban public school district with over 250,000 pupils.

As a result of the June elections, the political and philosophical makeup of the Gold Coast school board changed dramatically. Two new members with ties to the Millennium Institute were elected, and they immediately joined together with two other members to enact a series of curricular and structural reforms.

The Millennium Institute, formed in 1999, includes members of all the world's major religions and is "committed to peace and understanding through the promotion of good will between and among all nations, cultures, and religions."

One of the key reforms enacted by the new school board majority was the establishment of three new magnet schools focusing on "philosophy and culture." In Gold Coast, as in other urban districts nationwide, magnet schools had long been the most popular method of desegregating students via parental choice. The magnet schools provide distinct educational programs designed to attract students of different races or ethnic backgrounds. As Professor Amy Stuart Wells explains, "The idea is to create schools that offer an enhanced and engaging educational program that parents of all races prefer to their neighborhood school." *See* Amy Stuart Wells, Time to Choose: America at the Crossroads of School Choice Policy (1993).

The curriculum mandated by the school board for the new philosophy and culture magnets included the following controversial requirements:

A. An intensive twenty-week focus on the Book of Genesis. Students will attempt to make sense out of the book's recurring patterns: the violent conflicts between siblings, the eventual victory—against all custom—of latter-born sons, the fragility of inheritance. They will address the question of how covenants such as the one set forth in Genesis can continue in a world ruled by covetousness, murder, lust and disorder.

B. A twenty-week exploration into the nature of Zen, as reflected in such diverse sources as the writings of Lao Tzu, the formulas of Chinese herbalists, the teachings of the Dalai Lama, and the "beat" literature of 20th Century America. Students will learn a value system based on Zen's way of looking at the world: where the best moment is now, where things *are* what they seem to be, where we see with the refreshing directness of a child, and not through eyes grown stale from routine.

In addition, the following books were among those added to the school library as resources:

1. Bill Moyers, *Genesis: A Living Conversation* (based on the PBS series)

2. Karen Armstrong, *In the Beginning: A New Interpretation of Genesis*

3. A.G. Zornberg, *The Beginning of Desire: Reflections on Genesis*

4. Alan Watts, *The Way of Zen*

5. *Tao Te Ching* (writings of Lao Tzu)

6. *The City Lights Pocket Poets Anthology* (edited by Lawrence Ferlinghetti)

* * *

A group of angry Gold Coast parents consults you for the purpose of filing a wide-ranging lawsuit against the district. In their conversations with you, it becomes clear that they oppose the recent actions of the school board for three basic reasons: (1) the new magnet schools were formed without any input from parent groups, and they feel that accountability to the community seems to be lacking; (2) religious teachings have been introduced into the public school curriculum; and (3) they believe that the value-laden education mandated by the new curriculum is completely inappropriate in a public school setting.

What arguments might you set forth on behalf of the plaintiffs? What result? Discuss.

* * *

Assume, instead, that you are counsel for the school district, and that you were consulted before all these changes were made. Would you have advised the district to do anything differently from a legal perspective? From a policy perspective? Explain.

PROBLEM 41: The Columbia Education Initiatives

This question is based on the following hypothetical, which takes place in the fictional State of Columbia.

In order to pursue the goals set forth by the U.S. "No Child Left Behind" Act, the Columbia State Board of Education adopts a new statewide curriculum geared to basic skills. However, consistent with the perceived will of the people as reflected in the election of political leaders who openly espouse religious values, the curriculum also contains values-based lessons on the importance of spirituality. These lessons include instruction based on primary religious texts (or edited children's versions, as appropriate). Each semester, students are expected to spend two weeks reading from a different primary religious text, until they have been exposed to the holy books of Judaism, Christianity, Islam, Hinduism and Buddhism.

Consistent with this new curriculum, the State Board encourages local boards of education to remove from their school libraries all books containing rock music lyrics and to replace them with at least 25 copies of primary religious texts per library. Most school boards follow this advice within the next three months.

* * *

As a result of these events, the following legal action takes place:

A. An Establishment Clause challenge to the new curriculum. Plaintiffs, the United Coalition for Religious Freedom, are prepared to argue that whether the court analyzes this curriculum under purpose and effects, endorsement, coercion, or even a neutrality inquiry as applied in *Simmons-Harris,* the curriculum will ultimately be found unconstitutional.

B. A "right not to receive information & ideas" lawsuit, filed by parents who do not want their children exposed to primary texts of religions other than their own.

C. A lawsuit challenging the removal of the library books under the "right to receive information & ideas" set forth in *Pico*.

What arguments will be set forth by plaintiffs? What result? Discuss.

1. THE RIGHT TO RECEIVE INFORMATION

BOARD OF EDUC., ISLAND TREES UNION FREE SCH. DIST. NO. 26 v. PICO

457 U.S. 853, 102 S.Ct. 2799 (1982).

JUSTICE BRENNAN announced the judgment of the Court and delivered an opinion, in which JUSTICE MARSHALL and JUSTICE STEVENS joined, and in which JUSTICE BLACKMUN joined except for Part II–A–(1).

The principal question presented is whether the First Amendment imposes limitations upon the exercise by a local school board of its discretion to remove library books from high school and junior high school libraries.

I

Petitioners are [current and former members of] the Board of Education of the Island Trees Union Free School District No. 26, in New York.... The Board is a state agency charged with responsibility for the operation and administration of the public schools within the Island Trees School District, including the Island Trees High School and Island Trees Memorial Junior High School. Respondents are [former students of the District's junior and senior high schools].

In September 1975, [three school board members] attended a conference sponsored by Parents of New York United (PONYU), a politically conservative organization of parents concerned about education legislation in the State of New York. At the conference these petitioners obtained lists of books described by [Board President] Ahrens as "objectionable," and by [Board Vice–President] Martin as "improper fare for school students."[2] It was later determined that the High School library contained nine of the listed books, and that another listed book was in the Junior High School library.[3] In February 1976, at a meeting with the Superintendent of Schools and the Principals of the High School and Junior High School, the Board gave an "unofficial direction" that the listed books be removed from the library shelves and delivered to the

2. The District Court noted, however, that petitioners "concede that the books are not obscene."

3. The nine books in the High School library were: Slaughter House Five, by Kurt Vonnegut, Jr.; The Naked Ape, by Desmond Morris; Down These Mean Streets, by Piri Thomas; Best Short Stories of Negro Writers, edited by Langston Hughes; Go Ask Alice, of anonymous authorship; Laughing Boy, by Oliver LaFarge; Black Boy, by Rich-

ard Wright; A Hero Ain't Nothin' But A Sandwich, by Alice Childress; and Soul On Ice, by Eldridge Cleaver. The book in the Junior High School library was A Reader for Writers, edited by Jerome Archer. Still another listed book, The Fixer, by Bernard Malamud, was found to be included in the curriculum of a twelfth-grade literature course.

Board's offices, so that Board members could read them.[4] When this directive was carried out, it became publicized, and the Board issued a press release justifying its action. It characterized the removed books as "anti-American, anti-Christian, anti-Sem[i]tic, and just plain filthy," and concluded that "[i]t is our duty, our moral obligation, to protect the children in our schools from this moral danger as surely as from physical and medical dangers."

A short time later, the Board appointed a "Book Review Committee," consisting of four Island Trees parents and four members of the Island Trees schools staff, to read the listed books and to recommend to the Board whether the books should be retained, taking into account the books' "educational suitability," "good taste," "relevance," and "appropriateness to age and grade level." In July, the Committee made its final report to the Board, recommending that five of the listed books be retained and that two others be removed from the school libraries. As for the remaining four books, the Committee could not agree on two, took no position on one, and recommended that the last book be made available to students only with parental approval. The Board substantially rejected the Committee's report later that month, deciding that only one book should be returned to the High School library without restriction, that another should be made available subject to parental approval, but that the remaining nine books should "be removed from elementary and secondary libraries and [from] use in the curriculum."[12] The Board gave no reasons for rejecting the recommendations of the Committee that it had appointed.

Respondents reacted to the Board's decision by bringing the present action under 42 U.S.C. § 1983 in the United States District Court for the Eastern District of New York. They alleged that petitioners had

> ordered the removal of the books from school libraries and proscribed their use in the curriculum because particular passages in the books offended their social, political and moral tastes and not because the books, taken as a whole, were lacking in educational value.

Respondents claimed that the Board's actions denied them their rights under the First Amendment. They asked the court for a declaration that the Board's actions were unconstitutional, and for preliminary

---

4. The Superintendent of Schools objected to the Board's informal directive, noting:

[W]e already have a policy ... designed expressly to handle such problems. It calls for the Superintendent, upon receiving an objection to a book or books, to appoint a committee to study them and make recommendations. I feel it is a good policy—and it is Board policy—and that it should be followed in this instance. Furthermore, I think it can be followed quietly and in such a way as to reduce,

perhaps avoid, the public furor which has always attended such issues in the past.

The Board responded to the Superintendent's objection by repeating its directive "that *all copies* of the library books in question be removed from the libraries to the Board's office."

12. As a result, the nine removed books could not be assigned or suggested to students in connection with school work. However, teachers were not instructed to refrain from discussing the removed books or the ideas and positions expressed in them.

and permanent injunctive relief ordering the Board to return the nine books to the school libraries and to refrain from interfering with the use of those books in the schools' curricula.

* * *

II

We emphasize at the outset the limited nature of the substantive question presented by the case before us. Our precedents have long recognized certain constitutional limits upon the power of the State to control even the curriculum and classroom. For example, *Meyer v. Nebraska* struck down a state law that forbade the teaching of modern foreign languages in public and private schools, and *Epperson v. Arkansas* declared unconstitutional a state law that prohibited the teaching of the Darwinian theory of evolution in any state-supported school. But the current action does not require us to re-enter this difficult terrain, which *Meyer* and *Epperson* traversed without apparent misgiving. For as this case is presented to us, it does not involve textbooks, or indeed any books that Island Trees students would be required to read. Respondents do not seek in this Court to impose limitations upon their school Board's discretion to prescribe the curricula of the Island Trees schools. On the contrary, the only books at issue in this case are *library* books, books that by their nature are optional rather than required reading. Our adjudication of the present case thus does not intrude into the classroom, or into the compulsory courses taught there. Furthermore, even as to library books, the action before us does not involve the *acquisition* of books. Respondents have not sought to compel their school Board to add to the school library shelves any books that students desire to read. Rather, the only action challenged in this case is the *removal* from school libraries of books originally placed there by the school authorities, or without objection from them.

* * *

[D]oes the First Amendment impose *any* limitations upon the discretion of petitioners to remove library books from the Island Trees High School and Junior High School?

* * *

A

(1)

The Court has long recognized that local school boards have broad discretion in the management of school affairs. *Epperson v. Arkansas* reaffirmed that, by and large, "public education in our Nation is committed to the control of state and local authorities," and that federal courts should not ordinarily "intervene in the resolution of conflicts which arise in the daily operation of school systems." *Tinker v. Des Moines School Dist.*, 393 U.S. 503, 507, 89 S.Ct. 733, 736 (1969), noted that we have "repeatedly emphasized ... the comprehensive authority of the States and of school officials ... to prescribe and control conduct in the schools." We have also acknowledged that public schools are vitally important "in the preparation of individuals for participation as citizens," and as vehicles for "inculcating fundamental values necessary to the maintenance of a democratic political system." We are therefore in full agreement with petitioners that local school boards must be permitted "to establish and apply their curriculum in such a way as to transmit community values," and that "there is a legitimate and substantial community interest in promoting respect for authority and traditional values be they social, moral, or political."

At the same time, however, we have necessarily recognized that the discretion of the States and local school boards in matters of education must be exercised in a manner that comports with the transcendent imperatives of the First Amendment. In *West Virginia Board of Education v. Barnette*, 319 U.S. 624, 63 S.Ct. 1178 (1943), we held that under the First Amendment a student in a public school could not be compelled to salute the flag. We reasoned:

> Boards of Education ... have, of course, important, delicate, and highly discretionary functions, but none that they may not perform within the limits of the Bill of Rights. That they are educating the young for citizenship is reason for scrupulous protection of Constitutional freedoms of the individual, if we are not to strangle the free mind at its source and teach youth to discount important principles of our government as mere platitudes. *Id.* at 637, 63 S.Ct. at 1185.

Later cases have consistently followed this rationale. Thus *Epperson v. Arkansas*, invalidated a State's anti-evolution statute as violative of the Establishment Clause, and reaffirmed the duty of federal courts "to apply the First Amendment's mandate in our educational system where essential to safeguard the fundamental values of freedom of speech and inquiry." And *Tinker v. Des Moines School Dist., supra*, held that a local school board had infringed the free speech rights of high school and junior high school students by suspending them from school for wearing black armbands in class as a protest against the Government's policy in Vietnam; we stated there that the "comprehensive authority ... of school officials" must be exercised "consistent with fundamental constitutional safeguards." 393 U.S. at 507, 89 S.Ct. at 736. In sum, students do not "shed their constitutional rights to freedom of speech or expression at the schoolhouse gate," *id.* at 506, 89 S.Ct. at 736, and therefore local school boards must discharge their "important, delicate, and highly discretionary functions" within the limits and constraints of the First Amendment.

The nature of students' First Amendment rights in the context of this case requires further examination. *West Virginia Board of Education v. Barnette, supra*, is instructive. There the Court held that students' liberty of conscience could not be infringed in the name of "national unity" or "patriotism." 319 U.S. at 640–41, 63 S.Ct. at 1186. We explained that the action of the local authorities in compelling the flag salute and pledge transcends constitutional limitations on their power and invades the sphere of intellect and spirit which it is the purpose of the First Amendment to our Constitution to reserve from all official control. *Id.* at 642, 63 S.Ct. at 1187.

Similarly, *Tinker v. Des Moines School Dist.*, held that students' rights to freedom of expression of their political views could not be abridged by reliance upon an "undifferentiated fear or apprehension of disturbance" arising from such expression:

> Any departure from absolute regimentation may cause trouble. Any variation from the majority's opinion may inspire fear. Any word spoken, in class, in the lunchroom, or on the campus, that deviates from the views of another person may start an argument or cause a disturbance. But our Constitution says we must take this risk, and our history says that it is this sort of hazardous freedom—this kind of openness—that is the basis of our national strength and of the independence and vigor of Americans who grow up and live in this ... often disputatious society. 393 U.S. at 508–09, 89 S.Ct. at 737.

In short, "First Amendment rights, applied in light of the special characteristics of the school environment, are available to ... students." *Id.* at 506, 89 S.Ct. at 736.

Of course, courts should not "intervene in the resolution of conflicts which arise in the daily operation of school systems" unless "basic constitutional values" are "directly and sharply implicate[d]" in those conflicts. But we think that the First Amendment rights of students may be directly and sharply implicated by the removal of books from the shelves of a school library. Our precedents have focused "not only on the role of the First Amendment in fostering individual self-expression but also on its role in affording the public access to discussion, debate, and the dissemination of information and ideas." And we have recognized that "the State may not, consistently with the spirit of the First Amendment, contract the spectrum of available knowledge." In keeping with this principle, we have held that in a variety of contexts "the Constitution protects the right to receive information and ideas." This right is an inherent corollary of the rights of free speech and press that are explicitly guaranteed by the Constitution, in two senses. First, the right to receive ideas follows ineluctably from the *sender's* First Amendment right to send them: "The right of freedom of speech and press ... embraces the right to distribute literature, and necessarily protects the right to receive it." "The dissemination of ideas can accomplish nothing if otherwise willing addressees are not free to receive and consider them. It would be a barren marketplace of ideas that had only sellers and no buyers."

More importantly, the right to receive ideas is a necessary predicate to the *recipient's* meaningful exercise of his own rights of speech, press, and political freedom. Madison admonished us:

> A popular Government, without popular information, or the means of acquiring it, is but a Prologue to a Farce or a Tragedy; or, perhaps both. Knowledge will forever govern ignorance: And a people who mean to be their own Governors, must arm themselves with the power which knowledge gives.[20]

As we recognized in *Tinker*, students too are beneficiaries of this principle:

> In our system, students may not be regarded as closed-circuit recipients of only that which the State chooses to communicate.... [S]chool officials cannot suppress "expressions of feeling with which they do not wish to contend." 393 U.S. at 511, 89 S.Ct. at 739 (quoting *Burnside v. Byars*, 363 F.2d 744, 749 (5th Cir. 1966)).

In sum, just as access to ideas makes it possible for citizens generally to exercise their rights of free speech and press in a meaningful manner, such access prepares students for active and effective participation in the pluralistic, often contentious society in which they will soon be adult members. Of course all First Amendment rights accorded to students must be construed "in light of the special characteristics of the school environment." *Tinker v. Des Moines School Dist.*, 393 U.S. at 506, 89 S.Ct. at 736. But the special characteristics of the school *library* make that environment especially appropriate for the recognition of the First Amendment rights of students.

A school library, no less than any other public library, is "a place dedicated to quiet, to knowledge, and to beauty." *Keyishian v. Board of Regents* observed that " 'students must always remain free to inquire, to study and to evaluate, to gain new maturity and understanding.' " The school library is the principal locus of such freedom. As one District Court has well put it, in the school library

> a student can literally explore the unknown, and discover areas of interest and thought not covered by the prescribed curriculum.... Th[e] student learns that a library is a place to test or expand upon ideas presented to him, in or out of the classroom.

Petitioners emphasize the inculcative function of secondary education, and argue that they must be allowed *unfettered* discretion to "transmit community values" through the Island Trees schools. But that sweeping claim overlooks the unique role of the school library. It appears from the record that use of the Island Trees school libraries is completely

---

20. For a modern version of this observation, see A. MEIKLEJOHN, FREE SPEECH AND ITS RELATION TO SELF-GOVERNMENT 26 (1948):

> Just so far as ... the citizens who are to decide an issue are denied acquaintance with information or opinion or doubt or disbelief or criticism which is relevant to that issue, just so far the result must be ill-considered, ill-balanced planning, for the general good.

See also Butler v. Michigan; *Procunier v. Martinez*; *Houchins v. KQED, Inc.* (STEVENS,

J., dissenting) ("[T]he First Amendment protects not only the dissemination but also the receipt of information and ideas"); *Saxbe v. Washington Post Co.* (POWELL, J., dissenting) ("[P]ublic debate must not only be unfettered; it must be informed. For that reason this Court has repeatedly stated that First Amendment concerns encompass the receipt of information and ideas as well as the right of free expression").

voluntary on the part of students. Their selection of books from these libraries is entirely a matter of free choice; the libraries afford them an opportunity at self-education and individual enrichment that is wholly optional. Petitioners might well defend their claim of absolute discretion in matters of *curriculum* by reliance upon their duty to inculcate community values. But we think that petitioners' reliance upon that duty is misplaced where, as here, they attempt to extend their claim of absolute discretion beyond the compulsory environment of the class-room, into the school library and the regime of voluntary inquiry that there holds sway.

(2)

In rejecting petitioners' claim of absolute discretion to remove books from their school libraries, we do not deny that local school boards have a substantial legitimate role to play in the determination of school library content. We thus must turn to the question of the extent to which the First Amendment places limitations upon the discretion of petitioners to remove books from their libraries. In this inquiry we enjoy the guidance of several precedents. *West Virginia Board of Education v. Barnette*, stated:

> If there is any fixed star in our constitutional constellation, it is that no official, high or petty, can prescribe what shall be orthodox in politics, nationalism, religion, or other matters of opinion.... If there are any circumstances which permit an exception, they do not now occur to us. 319 U.S. at 642, 63 S.Ct. at 1187.

This doctrine has been reaffirmed in later cases involving education. For example, *Keyishian v. Board of Regents* noted that "the First Amendment ... does not tolerate laws that cast a pall of orthodoxy over the classroom." And *Mt. Healthy City Board of Ed. v. Doyle* recognized First Amendment limitations upon the discretion of a local school board to refuse to rehire a nontenured teacher. The school board in *Mt. Healthy* had declined to renew respondent Doyle's employment contract, in part because he had exercised his First Amendment rights. Although Doyle did not have tenure, and thus "could have been discharged for no reason whatever," *Mt. Healthy* held that he could "nonetheless establish a claim to reinstatement if the decision not to rehire him was made by reason of his exercise of constitutionally protected First Amendment freedoms." We held further that once Doyle had shown "that his conduct was constitutionally protected, and that this conduct was a 'substantial factor' ... in the Board's decision not to rehire him," the school board was obliged to show "by a preponderance of the evidence that it would have reached the same decision as to respondent's reemployment even in the absence of the protected conduct."

With respect to the present case, the message of these precedents is clear. Petitioners rightly possess significant discretion to determine the content of their school libraries. But that discretion may not be exercised in a narrowly partisan or political manner. If a Democratic school board, motivated by party affiliation, ordered the removal of all books written by or in favor of Republicans, few would doubt that the order violated the constitutional rights of the students denied access to those books. The same conclusion would surely apply if an all-white school board, motivated by racial animus, decided to remove all books authored by blacks or advocating racial equality and integration. Our Constitution does not permit the official suppression of *ideas*. Thus whether petitioners' removal of books from their school libraries denied respondents their First Amendment rights depends upon the motivation behind petitioners' actions. If petitioners *intended* by their removal decision to deny respondents access to ideas with which petitioners disagreed, and if this intent was the decisive factor in petitioners' decision,[22] then petitioners have exercised their discretion in violation of the Constitution. To permit such intentions to control official actions would be to encourage the precise sort of officially prescribed orthodoxy unequivocally condemned in *Barnette*. On the other hand, respondents implicitly concede that an unconstitutional motivation would *not* be demonstrated if it were shown that petitioners had decided to remove the books at issue because those books were pervasively vulgar. And again, respondents concede that if it were demonstrated that the removal decision was based solely upon the "educational suitability" of the books in question, then their removal would be "perfectly permissible." In other words, in respondents' view such motivations, if decisive of petitioners' actions, would not carry the danger of an official suppression of ideas, and thus would not violate respondents' First Amendment rights.

As noted earlier, nothing in our decision today affects in any way the discretion of a local school board to choose books to *add* to the libraries of their schools. Because we are concerned in this case with the suppression of ideas, our holding today affects only the discretion to *remove* books. In brief, we hold that local school boards may not remove books from school library shelves simply because they dislike the ideas contained in those books and seek by their removal to "prescribe what shall be orthodox in politics, nationalism, religion, or other matters of opinion." *West Virginia Board of Education v. Barnette*, 319 U.S. at 642, 63 S.Ct. at 1187. Such purposes stand inescapably condemned by our precedents.

* * *

Affirmed.

JUSTICE BLACKMUN, concurring in part and concurring in the judgment.

While I agree with much in today's plurality opinion, and while I accept the standard laid down by the plurality to guide proceedings on remand, I write separately because I have a somewhat different perspective on the nature of the First Amendment right involved.

---

22. By "decisive factor" we mean a "substantial factor" in the absence of which the opposite decision would have been reached.

I

To my mind, this case presents a particularly complex problem because it involves two competing principles of constitutional stature. On the one hand, as the dissenting opinions demonstrate, and as we all can agree, the Court has acknowledged the importance of the public schools "in the preparation of individuals for participation as citizens, and in the preservation of the values on which our society rests." Because of the essential socializing function of schools, local education officials may attempt "to promote civic virtues," and to "awake[n] the child to cultural values." *Brown v. Board of Education*, 347 U.S. 483, 493, 74 S.Ct. 686, 691 (1954). Indeed, the Constitution presupposes the existence of an informed citizenry prepared to participate in governmental affairs, and these democratic principles obviously are constitutionally incorporated into the structure of our government. It therefore seems entirely appropriate that the State use "public schools [to] . . . inculcat[e] fundamental values necessary to the maintenance of a democratic political system."

On the other hand, as the plurality demonstrates, it is beyond dispute that schools and school boards must operate within the confines of the First Amendment. In a variety of academic settings the Court therefore has acknowledged the force of the principle that schools, like other enterprises operated by the State, may not be run in such a manner as to "prescribe what shall be orthodox in politics, nationalism, religion, or other matters of opinion." *West Virginia Board of Education v. Barnette*, 319 U.S. 624, 642, 63 S.Ct. 1178, 1187 (1943). While none of these cases define the limits of a school board's authority to choose a curriculum and academic materials, they are based on the general proposition that "state-operated schools may not be enclaves of totalitarianism. . . . In our system, students may not be regarded as closed-circuit recipients of only that which the State chooses to communicate." *Tinker v. Des Moines School Dist.*, 393 U.S. 503, 511, 89 S.Ct. 733, 739 (1969).

The Court in *Tinker* thus rejected the view that "a State might so conduct its schools as to 'foster a homogeneous people.' " *Id.* at 511, 89 S.Ct. at 739, quoting *Meyer v. Nebraska*. Similarly, *Keyishian v. Board of Regents*—a case that involved the State's attempt to remove "subversives" from academic positions at its universities, but that addressed itself more broadly to public education in general—held that "[t]he classroom is peculiarly the 'marketplace of ideas' "; the First Amendment therefore "does not tolerate laws that cast a pall of orthodoxy over the classroom." And *Barnette* is most clearly applicable here: its holding was based squarely on the view that "[f]ree public education, if faithful to the ideal of secular instruction and political neutrality, will not be partisan or enemy of any class, creed, party, or faction." 319 U.S. at 637, 63 S. Ct. at 1185. The Court therefore made it clear that imposition of "ideological discipline" was not a proper undertaking for school authorities.

In combination with more generally applicable First Amendment rules, most particularly the central proscription of content-based regulations of speech, see *Police Department of Chicago v. Mosley*, the cases outlined above yield a general principle: the State may not suppress exposure to ideas—for the sole *purpose* of suppressing exposure to those ideas—absent sufficiently compelling reasons. Because the school board must perform all its functions "within the limits of the Bill of Rights," *Barnette*, 319 U.S. at 637, 63 S. Ct. at 1185, this principle necessarily applies in at least a limited way to public education. Surely this is true in an extreme case: as the plurality notes, it is difficult to see how a school board, consistent with the First Amendment, could refuse for political reasons to buy books written by Democrats or by Negroes, or books that are "anti-American" in the broadest sense of that term. Indeed, Justice REHNQUIST appears "cheerfully [to] concede" this point.

In my view, then, the principle involved here is both narrower and more basic than the "right to receive information" identified by the plurality. I do not suggest that the State has any affirmative obligation to provide students with information or ideas, something that may well be associated with a "right to receive." And I do not believe, as the plurality suggests, that the right at issue here is somehow associated with the peculiar nature of the school library; if schools may be used to inculcate ideas, surely libraries may play a role in that process. Instead, I suggest that certain forms of state discrimination *between* ideas are improper. In particular, our precedents command the conclusion that the State may not act to deny access to an idea simply because state officials disapprove of that idea for partisan or political reasons.

* * *

II

In my view, we strike a proper balance here by holding that school officials may not remove books for the *purpose* of restricting access to the political ideas or social perspectives discussed in them, when that action is motivated simply by the officials' disapproval of the ideas involved. It does not seem radical to suggest that state action calculated to suppress novel ideas or concepts is fundamentally antithetical to the values of the First Amendment. At a minimum, allowing a school board to engage in such conduct hardly teaches children to respect the diversity of ideas that is fundamental to the American system. In this context, then, the school board must "be able to show that its action was caused by something more than a mere desire to avoid the discomfort and unpleasantness that always accompany an unpopular viewpoint," *Tinker v. Des Moines School Dist.*, 393 U.S. at 509, 89 S.Ct. at 737, and that the board had something in mind in addition to the suppression of partisan or political views it did not share.

As I view it, this is a narrow principle. School officials must be able to choose one book over another, without outside interference, when the first book is deemed more relevant to the curriculum, or better written, or when one of a host of other politically neutral reasons is present. These decisions obviously will not implicate First Amendment values. And even absent space or financial limitations, First Amendment principles would allow a school board to refuse to make a book available to students because it contains offensive language, or because it is psychologically or intellectually inappropriate for the age group, or even, perhaps, because the ideas it advances are "manifestly inimical to the public welfare." And, of course, school officials may choose one book over another because they believe that one subject is more important, or is more deserving of emphasis.

As is evident from this discussion, I do not share Justice REHNQUIST's view that the notion of "suppression of ideas" is not a useful analytical concept. Indeed, Justice REHNQUIST's discussion itself demonstrates that "access to ideas" has been given meaningful application in a variety of contexts. And I believe that tying the First Amendment right to the *purposeful* suppression of ideas makes the concept more manageable than Justice REHNQUIST acknowledges. Most people would recognize that refusing to allow discussion of current events in Latin class is a policy designed to "inculcate" Latin, not to suppress ideas. Similarly, removing a learned treatise criticizing American foreign policy from an elementary school library because the students would not understand it is an action unrelated to the *purpose* of suppressing ideas. In my view, however, removing the same treatise because it is "anti-American" raises a far more difficult issue.

It is not a sufficient answer to this problem that a State operates a school in its role as "educator," rather than its role as "sovereign," for the First Amendment has application to all the State's activities. While the State may act as "property owner" when it prevents certain types of expressive activity from taking place on public lands, for example, few would suggest that the State may base such restrictions on the content of the speaker's message, or may take its action for the purpose of suppressing access to the ideas involved. And while it is not clear to me from Justice REHNQUIST's discussion whether a State operates its public libraries in its "role as sovereign," surely difficult constitutional problems would arise if a State chose to exclude "anti-American" books from its public libraries—even if those books remained available at local bookstores.

Concededly, a tension exists between the properly inculcative purposes of public education and any limitation on the school board's absolute discretion to choose academic materials. But that tension demonstrates only that the problem here is a difficult one, not that the problem should be resolved by choosing one principle over another. As the Court has recognized, school officials must have the authority to make educationally appropriate choices in designing a curriculum: "the State may 'require teaching by instruction and study of all in our history and in the structure and organization of our government, including the guaranties of civil liberty, which tend to inspire patriotism and love of country.'" *Barnette*, 319 U.S. at 631, 63 S.Ct. at 1181, quoting *Miners-*

ville School District v. Gobitis. Thus school officials may seek to instill certain values "by persuasion and example," 319 U.S. at 640, 63 S.Ct. at 1186, or by choice of emphasis. That sort of positive educational action, however, is the converse of an intentional attempt to shield students from certain ideas that officials find politically distasteful. Arguing that the majority in the community rejects the ideas involved does not refute this principle: "The very purpose of a Bill of Rights was to withdraw certain subjects from the vicissitudes of political controversy, to place them beyond the reach of majorities and officials.... " *Barnette*, 319 U.S. at 638, 63 S.Ct. at 1185.

As THE CHIEF JUSTICE notes, the principle involved here may be difficult to apply in an individual case. But on a record as sparse as the one before us, the plurality can hardly be faulted for failing to explore every possible ramification of its decision. And while the absence of a record "underscore[s] the views of those of us who originally felt that the cas[e] should not be taken," the case is here, and must be decided.

Because I believe that the plurality has derived a standard similar to the one compelled by my analysis, I join all but Part II–A(1) of the plurality opinion.

EDWARDS v. AGUILLARD
482 U.S. 578, 107 S.Ct. 2573 (1987).

JUSTICE BRENNAN delivered the opinion of the Court.

The question for decision is whether Louisiana's "Balanced Treatment for Creation–Science and Evolution–Science in Public School Instruction" Act (Creationism Act) is facially invalid as violative of the Establishment Clause of the First Amendment.

I

The Creationism Act forbids the teaching of the theory of evolution in public schools unless accompanied by instruction in "creation science." No school is required to teach evolution or creation science. If either is taught, however, the other must also be taught. The theories of evolution and creation science are statutorily defined as "the scientific evidences for [creation or evolution] and inferences from those scientific evidences."

Appellees, who include parents of children attending Louisiana public schools, Louisiana teachers, and religious leaders, challenged the constitutionality of the Act in District Court, seeking an injunction and declaratory relief.

* * *

II

The Establishment Clause forbids the enactment of any law "respecting an establishment of religion." The Court has applied a three-pronged test to determine whether legislation comports with the Establishment Clause. First, the legislature must have adopted the law with a secular purpose. Second, the statute's principal or primary effect must be one that neither advances nor inhibits religion. Third, the statute must not result in an excessive entanglement of government with religion. *Lemon v. Kurtzman*.[4] State action violates the Establishment Clause if it fails to satisfy any of these prongs.

* * *

The Court has been particularly vigilant in monitoring compliance with the Establishment Clause in elementary and secondary schools.[5] Families entrust public schools with the education of their children, but condition their trust on the understanding that the classroom will not purposely be used to advance religious views that may conflict with the private beliefs of the student and his or her family. Students in such institutions are impressionable and their attendance is involuntary.... Furthermore, "[t]he public school is at once the symbol of our democracy and the most pervasive means for promoting our common destiny. In no activity of the State is it more vital to keep out divisive forces than in its schools...."

* * *

III

Lemon's first prong focuses on the purpose that animated adoption of the Act. "The purpose prong of the *Lemon* test asks whether government's actual purpose is to endorse or disapprove of religion." A governmental intention to promote religion is clear when the State enacts a law to serve a religious purpose. This intention may be evidenced by promotion of religion in general, see *Wallace v. Jaffree*, 472 U.S. [38,] 52–53, 105 S.Ct. [2479,] 2487 [(1985)] (Establishment Clause protects individual freedom of conscience "to select any religious faith or none at all"), or by advancement of a particular religious belief, *e.g., Stone v. Graham* (invalidating requirement to post Ten Commandments, which are "undeniably a sacred text in the Jewish and Christian faiths"); *Epperson v. Arkansas* (holding that banning the teaching of evolution in public schools violates the First Amendment since "teaching and learning" must not "be tailored to the principles or prohibitions of any religious

---

4. The *Lemon* test has been applied in all cases since its adoption in 1971, except in *Marsh v. Chambers*, where the Court held that the Nebraska Legislature's practice of opening a session with a prayer by a chaplain paid by the State did not violate the Establishment Clause. The Court based its conclusion in that case on the historical acceptance of the practice. Such a historical approach is not useful in determining the proper roles of church and state in public schools, since free public education was virtually nonexistent at the time the Constitution was adopted. * * *

5. The potential for undue influence is far less significant with regard to college students who voluntarily enroll in courses. "This distinction warrants a difference in constitutional results." *Abington School Dist. v. Schempp* (BRENNAN, J., concurring). Thus, for instance, the Court has not questioned the authority of state colleges and universities to offer courses on religion or theology. See *Widmar v. Vincent*, 454 U.S. 263, 271, 102 S.Ct. 269, 275; *id.,* at 281, 102 S.Ct., at 280 (STEVENS, J., concurring in judgment). *(footnote moved)* sect or dogma"). If the law was enacted for the purpose of endorsing religion, "no consideration of the second or third criteria [of *Lemon*] is necessary." *Wallace v. Jaffree, supra,* 472 U.S. at 56, 105 S.Ct. at 2489. In this case, appellants have identified no clear secular purpose for the Louisiana Act.

True, the Act's stated purpose is to protect academic freedom. This phrase might, in common parlance, be understood as referring to enhancing the freedom of teachers to teach what they will. The Court of Appeals, however, correctly concluded that the Act was not designed to further that goal. We find no merit in the State's argument that the "legislature may not [have] use[d] the terms 'academic freedom' in the correct legal sense. They might have [had] in mind, instead, a basic concept of fairness; teaching all of the evidence." Even if "academic freedom" is read to mean "teaching all of the evidence" with respect to the origin of human beings, the Act does not further this purpose. The goal of providing a more comprehensive science curriculum is not furthered either by outlawing the teaching of evolution or by requiring the teaching of creation science.

A

While the Court is normally deferential to a State's articulation of a secular purpose, it is required that the statement of such purpose be sincere and not a sham. See *Wallace v. Jaffree,* 472 U.S. at 64, 105 S.Ct. at 2494 (POWELL, J., concurring); *id.* at 75, 105 S.Ct. at 2499 (O'CONNOR, J., concurring in judgment); *Abington School Dist. v. Schempp,* 374 U.S. at 223–24, 83 S.Ct. at 1572–73. As JUSTICE O'CONNOR stated in *Wallace*: "It is not a trivial matter, however, to require that the legislature manifest a secular purpose and omit all sectarian endorsements from its laws. That requirement is precisely tailored to the Establishment Clause's purpose of assuring that Government not intentionally endorse religion or a religious practice." 472 U.S. at 75, 105 S.Ct. at 2499–500 (concurring in judgment).

It is clear from the legislative history that the purpose of the legislative sponsor, Senator Bill Keith, was to narrow the science curriculum. During the legislative hearings, Senator Keith stated: "My preference would be that neither [creationism nor evolution] be taught." Such a ban on teaching does not promote—indeed, it undermines—the provision of a comprehensive scientific education.

It is equally clear that requiring schools to teach creation science with evolution does not advance academic freedom. The Act does not grant teachers a flexibility that they did not already possess to supplant the present science curriculum with the presentation of theories, besides evolution, about the origin of life. Indeed, the Court of Appeals found that no law prohibited Louisiana public school teachers from teaching any scientific theory. As the president of the Louisiana Science Teachers Association testified, "[a]ny scientific concept that's based on established fact can be included in our curriculum already, and no legislation allowing this is necessary." The Act provides Louisiana school teachers with no new authority. Thus the stated purpose is not furthered by it.

The Alabama statute held unconstitutional in *Wallace v. Jaffree* is analogous. In *Wallace*, the State characterized its new law as one designed to provide a 1–minute period for meditation. We rejected that stated purpose as insufficient, because a previously adopted Alabama law already provided for such a 1–minute period. Thus, in this case, as in *Wallace*, "[a]ppellants have not identified any secular purpose that was not fully served by [existing state law] before the enactment of [the statute in question]." 472 U.S. at 59, 105 S.Ct. at 2491.

Furthermore, the goal of basic "fairness" is hardly furthered by the Act's discriminatory preference for the teaching of creation science and against the teaching of evolution. While requiring that curriculum guides be developed for creation science, the Act says nothing of comparable guides for evolution. Similarly, resource services are supplied for creation science but not for evolution. Only "creation scientists" can serve on the panel that supplies the resource services. The Act forbids school boards to discriminate against anyone who "chooses to be a creation-scientist" or to teach "creationism," but fails to protect those who choose to teach evolution or any other non-creation science theory, or who refuse to teach creation science.

If the Louisiana Legislature's purpose was solely to maximize the comprehensiveness and effectiveness of science instruction, it would have encouraged the teaching of all scientific theories about the origins of humankind. But under the Act's requirements, teachers who were once free to teach any and all facets of this subject are now unable to do so. Moreover, the Act fails even to ensure that creation science will be taught, but instead requires the teaching of this theory only when the theory of evolution is taught. Thus we agree with the Court of Appeals' conclusion that the Act does not serve to protect academic freedom, but has the distinctly different purpose of discrediting "evolution by counter-balancing its teaching at every turn with the teaching of creationism...."

* * *

In this case, the purpose of the Creationism Act was to restructure the science curriculum to conform with a particular religious viewpoint. Out of many possible science subjects taught in the public schools, the legislature chose to affect the teaching of the one scientific theory that historically has been opposed by certain religious sects. As in *Epperson*, the legislature passed the Act to give preference to those religious groups which have as one of their tenets the creation of humankind by a divine creator. The "overriding fact" that confronted the Court in *Epperson* was "that Arkansas' law selects from the body of knowledge a particular segment which it proscribes for the sole reason that it is deemed to conflict with ... a particular interpretation of the Book of Genesis by a particular religious group." Similarly, the Creationism Act is designed *either* to promote the theory of creation science which embodies a particular religious tenet by requiring that creation science be taught whenever evolution is taught *or* to prohibit the teaching of a scientific theory disfavored by certain religious sects by forbidding the teaching of evolution when creation science is not also taught. The Establishment Clause, however, "forbids *alike* the preference of a religious doctrine *or* the prohibition of theory which is deemed antagonistic to a particular dogma." Because the primary purpose of the Creationism Act is to advance a particular religious belief, the Act endorses religion in violation of the First Amendment.

We do not imply that a legislature could never require that scientific critiques of prevailing scientific theories be taught. Indeed, the Court acknowledged in *Stone* that its decision forbidding the posting of the Ten Commandments did not mean that no use could ever be made of the Ten Commandments, or that the Ten Commandments played an exclusively religious role in the history of Western Civilization. In a similar way, teaching a variety of scientific theories about the origins of humankind to schoolchildren might be validly done with the clear secular intent of enhancing the effectiveness of science instruction. But because the primary purpose of the Creationism Act is to endorse a particular religious doctrine, the Act furthers religion in violation of the Establishment Clause.

     * * *

Notes

1. In August 2005, the *New York Times* reported the results of a recent national poll, which found that "nearly two-thirds of Americans say that creationism should be taught alongside evolution in public schools.":

> The poll found that 42 percent of respondents held strict creationist views, agreeing that "living things have existed in their present form since the beginning of time."

> In contrast, 48 percent said they believed that humans had evolved over time. But of those, 18 percent said that evolution was "guided by a supreme being," and 26 percent said that evolution occurred through natural selection. In all, 64 percent said they were open to the idea of teaching creationism in addition to evolution, while 38 percent favored replacing evolution with creationism.

> The poll was conducted July 7–17 by the Pew Forum on Religion and Public Life and the Pew Research Center for the People and the Press. The questions about evolution were asked of 2,000 people. The margin of error was 2.5 percentage points. Laurie Goodstein, *Teaching of Creationism Is Endorsed in New Survey*, N.Y. TIMES, Aug. 31, 2005

2. In September 2005, the U.S. District Court held a bench trial in the case of *Kitzmiller v. Dover Area Sch. Dist.*, 2005 WL 3465563 (M.D. Pa. 2005). In *Kitzmiller,* parents challenged the constitutionality of a decision by the Dover Area School Board to require science teachers—in addition to teaching evolution—to read the following statement to their students:

The Pennsylvania Academic Standards require students to learn about Darwin's theory of evolution and eventually to take a standardized test of which evolution is a part.

Because Darwin's theory is a theory, it continues to be tested as new evidence is discovered. The theory is not a fact. Gaps in the theory exist for which there is no evidence. A theory is defined as a well-tested explanation that unifies a broad range of observations.

Intelligent design is an explanation of the origin of life that differs from Darwin's view. The reference book, "Of Pandas and People," is available for students who might be interested in gaining an understanding of what intelligent design actually involves.

With respect to any theory, students are encouraged to keep an open mind. The school leaves the discussion of the origins of life to individual students and their families. As a standards-driven district, class instruction focuses upon preparing students to achieve proficiency on standards-based assessments.

Applying Establishment Clause principles as reflected primarily in the endorsement inquiry, the Court ruled in favor of the plaintiffs:

First, we will consider "the message conveyed by the disclaimer to the students who are its intended audience," from the perspective of an objective Dover Area High School student. At a minimum, the pertinent inquiry is whether an "objective observer" in the position of a student of the relevant age would "perceive official school support" for the religious activity in question. * * *

A "hypothetical reasonable observer," adult or child, who is "aware of the history and context of the community and forum" is also presumed to know that [intelligent design (ID)] is a form of creationism. The evidence at trial demonstrates that ID is nothing less than the progeny of creationism. What is likely the strongest evidence supporting the finding of ID's creationist nature is the history and historical pedigree of the book to which students in Dover's ninth grade biology class are referred, *Pandas*. *Pandas* is published by an organization called FTE, as noted, whose articles of incorporation and filings with the Internal Revenue Service describe it as a religious, Christian organization. *Pandas* was written by Dean Kenyon and Percival Davis, both acknowledged creationists, and Nancy Pearcey, a Young Earth Creationist, contributed to the work.

As Plaintiffs meticulously and effectively presented to the Court, *Pandas* went through many drafts, several of which were completed prior to and some after the Supreme Court's decision in *Edwards*, which held that the Constitution forbids teaching creationism as science. By comparing the pre and post *Edwards* drafts of *Pandas*, three astonishing points emerge: (1) the definition for creation science in early drafts is identical to the definition of ID; (2) cognates of the word creation (creationism and creationist), which appeared approximately 150 times were deliberately and systematically replaced with the phrase ID; and (3) the changes occurred shortly after the Supreme Court held that creation science is religious and cannot be taught in public school science classes in

Edwards. This word substitution is telling, significant, and reveals that a purposeful change of *words* was effected without any corresponding change in *content,* which directly refutes FTE's argument that by merely disregarding the words "creation" and "creationism," FTE expressly rejected creationism in *Pandas.* * * *

This compelling evidence strongly supports Plaintiffs' assertion that ID is creationism re-labeled. Importantly, the objective observer, whether adult or child, would conclude from the fact that *Pandas* posits a master intellect that the intelligent designer is God. * * *

After a careful review of the record, we find that an objective student would view the [four-paragraph statement] as a strong official endorsement of religion. * * *

In summary, the disclaimer singles out the theory of evolution for special treatment, misrepresents its status in the scientific community, causes students to doubt its validity without scientific justification, presents students with a religious alternative masquerading as a scientific theory, directs them to consult a creationist text as though it were a science resource, and instructs students to forego scientific inquiry in the public school classroom and instead to seek out religious instruction elsewhere. * * *

As a result of the foregoing analysis, we conclude that an informed, objective adult member of the Dover community aware of the social context in which the ID Policy arose would view [also] Defendants' conduct and the challenged Policy to be a strong endorsement of a religious view.

* * *

After a searching review of the record and applicable case law, we find that while ID arguments may be true, a proposition on which the Court takes no position, ID is not science. We find that ID fails on three different levels, any one of which is sufficient to preclude a determination that ID is science. They are: (1) ID violates the centuries-old ground rules of science by invoking and permitting supernatural causation; (2) the argument of irreducible complexity, central to ID, employs the same flawed and illogical contrived dualism that doomed creation science in the 1980's; and (3) ID's negative attacks on evolution have been refuted by the scientific community. [I]t is additionally important to note that ID has failed to gain acceptance in the scientific community, it has not generated peer-reviewed publications, nor has it been the subject of testing and research.

* * *

Although Defendants attempt to persuade this Court that each Board member who voted for the biology curriculum change did so for the secular purpose of improving science education and to exercise critical thinking skills, their contentions are simply irreconcilable with the record evidence. Their asserted purposes are a sham, and they are accordingly unavailing.

* * *

To briefly reiterate, we first note that since ID is not science, the conclusion is inescapable that the only real effect of the ID Policy is the advancement of religion. Second, the disclaimer read to students "has the effect of implicitly bolstering alternative religious theories of origin by suggesting that evolution is a problematic theory even in the field of science." Third, reading the disclaimer not only disavows endorsement of educational materials but also "juxtaposes that disavowal with an urging to contemplate alternative religious concepts implies School Board approval of religious principles."

The effect of Defendants' actions in adopting the curriculum change was to impose a religious view of biological origins into the biology course, in violation of the Establishment Clause. * * *

Before the decision was handed down, the school board majority that had introduced intelligent design into the science curriculum was voted out of office. After the decision, the new majority announced that it would not appeal. *See Board Rescinds 'Intelligent Design Policy,* AP Online, January 4, 2006.

If a school board decided to introduce the same four-paragraph statement into a history class, pursuant to an effort to comply with a state law that mandates the teaching of values, and this decision were challenged under the Establishment Clause, would the result be the same? Should the result be the same?

THE BIBLE & PUBLIC SCHOOLS: A FIRST AMENDMENT GUIDE (1999)

Published by the National Bible Association
and the First Amendment Center[a]

* * *

The Bible and the Religious—Liberty Rights of Students

Many Americans continue to hold the mistaken view that the Supreme Court decisions in the 1960s concerning prayer and devotional

---

a. The guide has been endorsed by the following organizations:

American Association of School Administrators

American Federation of Teachers

American Jewish Committee

American Jewish Congress

Anti-Defamation League

Association for Supervision and Curriculum Development

Baptist Joint Committee on Public Affairs

Christian Educators Association International

Christian Legal Society

Council on Islamic Education

National Association of Evangelicals

National Association of Secondary School Principals

National Council of Churches of Christ in the U.S.A.

National Council for the Social Studies

National Education Association

National School Boards Association

People for the American Way Foundation

Union of American Hebrew Congregations

Bible-reading prohibited students from expressing their faith in a public school. Actually, the Court did not eliminate prayer or the Bible from public schools; it barred state-sponsored religious practices, including devotional use of the Bible by public-school officials.

Student Religious Expression

In "Religion in the Public Schools: A Joint Statement of Current Law," 35 religious and civil liberties organizations give the following summary of the rights of students to express their faith in a public school:

> Students have the right to pray individually or in groups or to discuss their religious views with their peers so long as they are not disruptive. Because the Establishment Clause does not apply to purely private speech, students enjoy the right to read their Bibles or other scriptures, say grace before meals, pray before tests, and discuss religion with other willing student listeners. In the classroom students have the right to pray quietly except when required to be actively engaged in school activities (e.g., students may not decide to pray just as a teacher calls on them). In informal settings, such as the cafeteria or in the halls, students may pray either audibly or silently, subject to the same rules of order as apply to other speech in these locations. However, the right to engage in voluntary prayer does not include, for example, the right to have a captive audience listen or to compel other students to participate.

* * *

The Bible and the Public–School Curriculum

Educators widely agree that study about religion, where appropriate, is an important part of a complete education. Part of that study includes learning about the Bible in courses such as literature and history. Knowledge of biblical stories and concepts contributes to our understanding of literature, history, law, art, and contemporary society.

What do the courts say?

The Supreme Court has held that public schools may teach students about the Bible as long as such teaching is "presented objectively as part of a secular program of education."[6]

The Court has also held that religious groups may not teach religious courses on school premises during the school day.[7] The U.S. Department of Education guidelines reiterate that public schools "may not provide religious instruction, but they may teach about religion, including the Bible or other scripture."[8] In keeping with the First

---

6. School District of Abington Twp. v. Schempp, 374 U.S. 203, 225 (1963), *see* Stone v. Graham, 449 U.S. 39, 42 (1980) (per curiam).

7. People ex rel. McCollum v. Board of Education, 333 U.S. 203 (1948).

8. "Religious Expression in Public Schools," Department of Education, Letter

Amendment's mandate of governmental neutrality toward religion, any study of religion in a public school must be educational, not devotional. This principle holds true whether teaching about the Bible occurs in literature, history or any other class and whether the course is required or an elective.

A relatively small number of lower court decisions have dealt directly with the constitutionality of Bible classes in public schools.[9] These rulings show that the constitutionality of such classes is highly dependent on such factors as how the class is taught, who teaches it, and which instructional materials and lessons are used.

How the class is taught: Any class about the Bible must be taught in an objective, academic manner.[10] The class should neither promote nor disparage religion, nor should it be taught from a particular sectarian point of view.[11]

Who teaches the class: A superintendent or school board should select teachers for a class about the Bible in the same manner all other teachers are selected.[12] School districts should not delegate the employment of such teachers to an outside committee that selects teachers based upon their religious beliefs or perspectives.[13] Teachers should be selected based upon their academic qualifications, rather than their religious beliefs or nonbeliefs.[14] Teachers should not be disqualified, however, simply because they have received religious training.[15]

Funding for an elective course in religion may be provided by outside sources as long as the funds are contributed with "no strings attached."[16]

Which instructional materials are used: Decisions concerning instructional materials, including which translation of the Bible may be

from Secretary Richard Riley (Aug. 10, 1995) (original emphasis).

9. *See* Hall v. Board of Commissioners of Conecuh County, 656 F.2d 999 (5th Cir. 1981); Gibson v. Lee County School Board, 1 F.Supp.2d 1426 (M.D. Fla. 1998); Chandler v. James, 985 F.Supp. 1062 (M.D. Ala. 1997); Herdahl v. Pontotoc County School District, 933 F.Supp. 582 (N.D. Miss. 1996); Doe v. Human, 725 F.Supp. 1503 (W.D. Ark. 1989), *aff'd without opinion*, 923 F.2d 857 (8th Cir. 1990), *cert. denied*, 499 U.S. 922 (1991); Crockett v. Sorenson, 568 F.Supp. 1422 (W.D. Va. 1983); Wiley v. Franklin, 468 F.Supp. 133 (E.D. Tenn. 1979), supp. op., 474 F.Supp. 525 (E.D. Tenn. 1979), supp. op., 497 F.Supp. 390 (E.D. Tenn. 1980); Vaughn v. Reed, 313 F.Supp. 431 (W.D. Va. 1970). *Cf.* Malnak v. Yogi, 592 F.2d 197 (3d Cir. 1979) (holding unconstitutional a school course in which students participated in transcendental meditation ceremonies).

10. *Schempp*, 374 U.S. at 225; *Graham*, 449 U.S. at 42; *Hall*, 656 F.2d at 1002; *Gibson*, 1 F.Supp.2d at 1432; *Chandler*, 985

F.Supp. at 1063; *Herdahl*, 933 F.Supp. at 592; *Human*, 725 F.Supp. at 1508; *Crockett*, 568 F.Supp. at 1427; *Wiley*, 497 F.Supp. at 392, 394; *Vaughn*, 313 F.Supp. at 433; *Malnak*, 592 F.2d at 197 (holding unconstitutional a school course in which students participated in transcendental meditation ceremonies).

11. *Wiley*, 497 F.Supp. at 394, *see also Gibson*, 1 F.Supp.2d at 1433–34; *Herdahl*, 933 F.Supp. at 595.

12. *Crockett*, 568 F.Supp. at 1431, *see also Gibson*, 1 F.Supp.2d at 1433; *Vaughn*, 313 F.Supp. at 434.

13. *Herdahl*, 933 F.Supp. at 593–94; *Wiley*, 468 F.Supp. at 152.

14. *Wiley*, 468 F.Supp. at 152.

15. *Id.* at 393.

16. *Crockett*, 568 F.Supp. at 1431, *see also Gibson*, 1 F.Supp.2d at 1433; *Herdahl*, 933 F.Supp. at 598–99.

used, should remain under the control of the board of education.[17] The Bible may be used as a primary text, although it probably should not be the only text for a course.[18] Schools should avoid the use of instructional materials and lessons that are of a devotional nature, such as those used in a Sunday school. Supernatural occurrences and divine action described in the Bible may not be taught as historical fact in a public school.[19] The historicity of many persons and events described in the Bible may or may not be confirmed by evidence outside of biblical literature. * * *

Teaching *about* the Bible

If teachers are to understand clearly how to teach about the Bible—and to feel safe doing so—then local school boards should adopt policies on the role of study about religion in the curriculum. The policy should reflect constitutional principles and current law, and should be developed with the full involvement of parents and other community members. Parents need to be assured that the goals of the school in teaching about religion, including teaching about the Bible, are academic and not devotional, and that academic teaching about the Bible is not intended to either undermine or reinforce the beliefs of those who accept the Bible as sacred scripture or of those who do not. Faith formation is the responsibility of parents and religious communities, not the public schools.

In recent years, a consensus has emerged among many religious and educational groups about the appropriate role for religion in the public-school curriculum. In 1989, a coalition of 17 religious and educational organizations issued the following statements to distinguish between teaching about religion in public schools and religious indoctrination:

- The school's approach to religion is academic, not devotional.

- The school may strive for student awareness of religions, but should not press for student acceptance of any religion.

- The school may sponsor study about religion, but may not sponsor the practice of religion.

- The school may expose students to a diversity of religious views, but may not impose, discourage, or encourage any particular view.

- The school may educate about all religions, but may not promote or denigrate any religion.

- The school may inform the student about various beliefs, but should not seek to conform him or her to any particular belief.[20]

17. *Crockett*, 568 F.Supp. at 1431, *see also Gibson*, 1 F.Supp.2d at 1433.

18. *Herdahl*, 933 F.Supp. at 595 & n.9, 600, *see also Hall*, 656 F.2d at 1002–03; *Wiley*, 468 F.Supp. at 151; *Chandler*, 985 F.Supp. at 1063.

19. *Gibson*, 1 F.Supp.2d at 1434; *Herdahl*, 933 F.Supp. at 596, 600; *Wiley*, 474 F.Supp. at 531.

20. This consensus statement, as well as extensive guidelines and resources for teaching about religion in public schools, can be found in *Finding Common Ground: A First Amendment Guide to Religion and Public Education* by Charles C. Haynes and Oliver Thomas. *Finding Common Ground* is available at cost from the First Amendment Center.

When teaching about the Bible in a public school, teachers must understand the important distinction between advocacy, indoctrination, proselytizing, and the practice of religion—which is unconstitutional—and teaching about religion that is objective, nonjudgmental, academic, neutral, balanced, and fair—which is constitutional.

Which Bible?

Selecting a Bible for use in literature, history, or elective Bible courses is important, since there is no single Bible. There is a Jewish Bible (the Hebrew Scriptures, or Tanakh), and there are various Christian Bibles—such as Catholic, Protestant, and Orthodox—some with additional books, arranged in a different order. These differences are significant. For example, Judaism does not include the Christian New Testament in its Bible, and the Catholic Old Testament has 46 books while the Protestant has 39. There are also various English translations within each of these traditions.

To adopt any particular Bible—or translation—is likely to suggest to students that it is normative, the best Bible. One solution is to use a biblical sourcebook that includes the key texts of each of the major Bibles or an anthology of various translations.

At the outset and at crucial points in the course, teachers should remind students about the differences between the various Bibles and discuss some of the major views concerning authorship and compilation of the books of the Bible. Students should also understand the differences in translations, read from several translations, and reflect on the significance of these differences for the various traditions.

Which interpretation?

The Bible is interpreted in many different ways, religious and secular. For example: In Judaism, the Hebrew Bible is typically read through the eyes of various rabbinic commentators. For Roman Catholics, the authoritative interpretation of the church is crucial for understanding the Bible. Some Christians and Jews use the findings of modern secular scholarship to interpret the Bible, while others reject some or all of modern scholarship.

Because there are many ways to interpret the Bible—religious and secular—public-school teachers should expose students to a variety of interpretations. Teachers should allow students to encounter the text directly (like any primary source), and then draw on the resources of different religious and secular interpretative traditions for understanding it. To do this effectively requires the use of secondary sources that provide a discussion of the various religious and secular approaches to the Bible.

* * *

The Bible and literature

Academic study of the Bible in a public secondary school may appropriately take place in literature courses. Students might study the

Bible as literature. They would examine the Bible as they would other literature in terms of aesthetic categories, as an anthology of narratives and poetry, exploring its language, symbolism, and motifs. Students might also study the Bible in literature, the ways in which later writers have used Bible literature, language, and symbols. Much drama, poetry, and fiction contains material from the Bible.

* * *

Bible electives in history

An elective history course that focuses on the Bible is a difficult undertaking for public schools because of the complex scholarly and religious debates about the historicity of the Bible. Such a course would need to include non-biblical sources from a variety of scholarly perspectives. Students would study archeological findings and other historical evidence in order to understand the history and cultures of the ancient world. Teachers who may be assigned to teach a history course focused on the Bible need a great deal of preparation and sophistication.

Unless schools are prepared to design a course that meets the above requirements, they will face legal and educational challenges. In view of these requirements, most public schools that have offered a Bible elective have found it safer and more age-appropriate to use the Bible literature approach discussed earlier in this guide.

Schools must keep in mind that the Bible is seen by millions of Jews and Christians as scripture. For adherents of these faiths, the Bible makes sense of events in terms of God's purposes and actions. This means that the Bible may not be treated as a history textbook by public-school teachers but must be studied by examining a variety of perspectives—religious and non-religious—on the meaning and significance of the biblical account.

As we have already noted, sorting out what is historical in the Bible is complicated and potentially controversial. Teachers who teach a history course focused on the Bible need to be sensitive to the differences between conventional secular history and the varieties of sacred history. Students must learn something about the contending ways of assessing the historicity of the Bible. They cannot be uncritically taught to accept the Bible as literally true, as history. Nor should they be uncritically taught to accept as historical only what secular historians find verifiable in the Bible.

Sometimes, in an attempt to make study about the Bible more "acceptable" in public schools, educators are willing to jettison accounts of miraculous events. But this too is problematic, for it radically distorts the meaning of the Bible. For those who accept the Bible as scripture, God is at work in history, and there is a religious meaning in the patterns of history. A Bible elective in a public school may examine all parts of the Bible, as long as the teacher understands how to teach about the religious content of the Bible from a variety of perspectives.

The Bible and world religions

* * * [A] course that includes study about the Bible and its influence will not educate students about religion generally. Just as there is more to history than American history, so there is more to religion than the Bible, Judaism, and Christianity.

Public schools should also include study about other religious faiths in the core curriculum and offer electives in world religions. Because religion plays a significant role in history and society, study about religion is essential to understanding both the nation and the world. Moreover, knowledge of the roles of religion in the past and present promotes cross-cultural understanding in our increasingly diverse society.

Some school districts require that high schools offering a Bible elective also offer an elective in world religions. There is considerable merit in this approach. This gives students an opportunity to learn about a variety of religions and conveys to students from faiths other than the biblical traditions that their religions are also worthy of study. It is important for public schools to convey the message that the curriculum is designed to offer a good education, and not to prefer any religious faith or group.

Elementary education

The study of family, community, various cultures, the nation, and other themes and topics important in elementary education may involve some discussion of religion. Elementary students are introduced to the basic ideas and practices of the world's major religions in a number of textbooks and curriculums used in public schools. These discussions of religion focus on the generally agreed-upon meanings of religious faiths—the core beliefs and symbols, as well as important figures and events. Such discussions may include an introduction to biblical literature as students learn something about the various biblical faiths.

This early exposure to study about religion builds a foundation for later, more complex discussions in secondary school literature and history courses. Such teaching is introductory in nature; elementary education is not the place for in-depth treatment of religion. Stories drawn from various religious faiths may be included among the wide variety of stories read by students. But the material selected must always be presented in the context of learning about religion.

One court has permitted elective Bible courses at the elementary level.[21] But if such instruction is undertaken, it must be done academically and objectively by a qualified teacher. Children would need to understand that they are studying about what the people of a particular religious tradition believe and practice. Devotional books intended for faith formation or religious education may not be used in a public-school classroom.

21. Wiley v. Franklin, 468 F.Supp. 133 (E.D. Tenn. 1979).

As in secondary schools, a balanced and fair curriculum in the elementary grades would not limit study about religion to Judaism and Christianity, but would include a variety of the world's major religious faiths.

CALIFORNIA EDUCATION CODE SECTION 233.5
(Values Instruction)

(a) Each teacher shall endeavor to impress upon the minds of the pupils the principles of morality, truth, justice, patriotism, and a true comprehension of the rights, duties, and dignity of American citizenship, and the meaning of equality and human dignity, including the promotion of harmonious relations, kindness toward domestic pets and the humane treatment of living creatures, to teach them to avoid idleness, profanity, and falsehood, and to instruct them in manners and morals and the principles of a free government.

(b) Each teacher is also encouraged to create and foster an environment that encourages pupils to realize their full potential and that is free from discriminatory attitudes, practices, events, or activities, in order to prevent acts of hate violence, as defined in subdivision (e) of Section 233.

2. THE RIGHT NOT TO RECEIVE INFORMATION

MOZERT v. HAWKINS COUNTY BD. OF EDUC.

827 F.2d 1058 (6th Cir. 1987).

LIVELY, CHIEF JUDGE.

This case arose under the Free Exercise Clause of the First Amendment, made applicable to the states by the Fourteenth Amendment. * * *

I.

A.

Early in 1983 the Hawkins County, Tennessee Board of Education adopted the Holt, Rinehart and Winston basic reading series (the Holt series) for use in grades 1–8 of the public schools of the county. In grades 1–4, reading is not taught as a separate subject at a designated time in the school day. Instead, the teachers in these grades use the reading texts throughout the day in conjunction with other subjects. In grades 5–8, reading is taught as a separate subject at a designated time in each class. However, the schools maintain an integrated curriculum which requires that ideas appearing in the reading programs reoccur in other courses. By statute public schools in Tennessee are required to include "character education" in their curricula. The purpose of this requirement is "to help each student develop positive values and to improve student conduct as students learn to act in harmony with their positive values and learn to become good citizens in their school, community, and society."

Like many school systems, Hawkins County schools teach "critical reading" as opposed to reading exercises that teach only word and sound recognition. "Critical reading" requires the development of higher order cognitive skills that enable students to evaluate the material they read, to contrast the ideas presented, and to understand complex characters that appear in reading material. Plaintiffs do not dispute that critical reading is an essential skill which their children must develop in order to succeed in other subjects and to function as effective participants in modern society. Nor do the defendants dispute the fact that any reading book will do more than teach a child how to read, since reading is instrumental in a child's total development as an educated person.

The plaintiff Vicki Frost is the mother of four children, three of whom were students in Hawkins County public schools in 1983. At the beginning of the 1983–84 school year Mrs. Frost read a story in a daughter's sixth grade reader that involved mental telepathy. Mrs. Frost, who describes herself as a "born again Christian," has a religious objection to any teaching about mental telepathy. Reading further, she found additional themes in the reader to which she had religious objections. After discussing her objections with other parents, Mrs. Frost talked with the principal of Church Hill Middle School and obtained an agreement for an alternative reading program for students whose parents objected to the assigned Holt reader. The students who elected the alternative program left their classrooms during the reading sessions and worked on assignments from an older textbook series in available office or library areas. Other students in two elementary schools were excused from reading the Holt books.

B.

In November 1983 the Hawkins County School Board voted unanimously to eliminate all alternative reading programs and require every student in the public schools to attend classes using the Holt series. Thereafter the plaintiff students refused to read the Holt series or attend reading classes where the series was being used. The children of several of the plaintiffs were suspended for brief periods for this refusal. Most of the plaintiff students were ultimately taught at home, or attended religious schools, or transferred to public schools outside Hawkins County. One student returned to school because his family was unable to afford alternate schooling. Even after the board's order, two students were allowed some accommodation, in that the teacher either excused them from reading the Holt stories, or specifically noted on worksheets that the student was not required to believe the stories.

On December 2, 1983, the plaintiffs, consisting of seven families—14 parents and 17 children—filed this action pursuant to 42 U.S.C. § 1983. In their complaint the plaintiffs asserted that they have sincere religious beliefs which are contrary to the values taught or inculcated by the reading textbooks and that it is a violation of the religious beliefs and convictions of the plaintiff students to be required to read the books and a violation of the religious beliefs of the plaintiff parents to permit their children to read the books. The plaintiffs sought to hold the defendants liable because "forcing the student-plaintiffs to read school books which teach or inculcate values in violation of their religious beliefs and convictions is a clear violation of their rights to the free exercise of religion protected by the First and Fourteenth Amendments to the United States Constitution."

* * *

B.

[At trial,] Vicki Frost ... presented the most complete explanation of the plaintiffs' position. The plaintiffs do not belong to a single church or denomination, but all consider themselves born again Christians. Mrs. Frost testified that the word of God as found in the Christian Bible "is the totality of my beliefs." There was evidence that other members of their churches, and even their pastors, do not agree with their position in this case.

Mrs. Frost testified that she had spent more than 200 hours reviewing the Holt series and had found numerous passages that offended her religious beliefs. She stated that the offending materials fell into seventeen categories which she listed. These ranged from such familiar concerns of fundamentalist Christians as evolution and "secular humanism" to less familiar themes such as "futuristic supernaturalism," pacifism, magic and false views of death.

In her lengthy testimony Mrs. Frost identified passages from stories and poems used in the Holt series that fell into each category. Illustrative is her first category, futuristic supernaturalism, which she defined as teaching "Man As God." Passages that she found offensive described Leonardo da Vinci as the human with a creative mind that "came closest to the divine touch." Similarly, she felt that a passage entitled "Seeing Beneath the Surface" related to an occult theme, by describing the use of imagination as a vehicle for seeing things not discernible through our physical eyes. She interpreted a poem, "Look at Anything," as presenting the idea that by using imagination a child can become part of anything and thus understand it better. Mrs. Frost testified that it is an "occult practice" for children to use imagination beyond the limitation of scriptural authority. She testified that the story that alerted her to the problem with the reading series fell into the category of futuristic supernaturalism. Entitled "A Visit to Mars," the story portrays thought transfer and telepathy in such a way that "it could be considered a scientific concept," according to this witness. This theme appears in the testimony of several witnesses, *i.e.*, the materials objected to "could" be interpreted in a manner repugnant to their religious beliefs.

Mrs. Frost described objectionable passages from other categories in much the same way. Describing evolution as a teaching that there is no

God, she identified 24 passages that she considered to have evolution as a theme. She admitted that the textbooks contained a disclaimer that evolution is a theory, not a proven scientific fact. Nevertheless, she felt that references to evolution were so pervasive and presented in such a factual manner as to render the disclaimer meaningless. After describing her objection to passages that encourage children to make moral judgments about whether it is right or wrong to kill animals, the witness stated, "I thought they would be learning to read, to have good English and grammar, and to be able to do other subject work." * * *

Another witness for the plaintiffs was Bob Mozert, father of a middle school and an elementary school student in the Hawkins County system. . . . He also found objectionable passages in the readers that dealt with magic, role reversal or role elimination, particularly biographical material about women who have been recognized for achievements outside their homes, and emphasis on one world or a planetary society. Both witnesses testified under cross-examination that the plaintiff parents objected to passages that expose their children to other forms of religion and to the feelings, attitudes and values of other students that contradict the plaintiffs' religious views without a statement that the other views are incorrect and that the plaintiffs' views are the correct ones.

C.

The district court held that the plaintiffs' free exercise rights have been burdened[.]

* * *

The court entered an injunction prohibiting the defendants "from requiring the student-plaintiffs to read from the Holt series," and ordering the defendants to excuse the student plaintiffs from their classrooms "[d]uring the normal reading period" and to provide them with suitable space in the library or elsewhere for a study hall. * * *

III.

A.

The first question to be decided is whether a governmental requirement that a person be exposed to ideas he or she finds objectionable on religious grounds constitutes a burden on the free exercise of that person's religion as forbidden by the First Amendment. This is precisely the way the superintendent of the Hawkins County schools framed the issue in an affidavit filed early in this litigation. In his affidavit the superintendent set forth the school system's interest in a uniformity of reading texts. The affidavit also countered the claims of the plaintiffs that the schools were inculcating values and religious doctrines contrary to their religious beliefs, stating: "Without expressing an opinion as to the plaintiffs' religious beliefs, I am of the opinion that plaintiffs misunderstand the fact that exposure to something does not constitute teaching, indoctrination, opposition or promotion of the things exposed. While it is true that these textbooks expose the student to varying values and religious backgrounds, neither the textbooks nor the teachers teach, indoctrinate, oppose or promote any particular value or religion." That the district court accepted the issue as thus framed is clear from its reference to "exposure to the Holt series."

It is also clear that exposure to objectionable material is what the plaintiffs objected to albeit they emphasize the repeated nature of the exposure. The complaint mentioned only the textbooks that the students were required to read. It did not seek relief from any method of teaching the material and did not mention the teachers' editions. The plaintiffs did not produce a single student or teacher to testify that any student was ever required to affirm his or her belief or disbelief in any idea or practice mentioned in the various stories and passages contained in the Holt series. However, the plaintiffs appeared to assume that materials clearly presented as poetry, fiction and even "make-believe" in the Holt series were presented as facts which the students were required to believe. Nothing in the record supports this assumption.

At numerous places in her testimony Vicki Frost referred to various exercises and suggestions in the teachers' manuals as support for her view that objectionable ideas were being inculcated as truth rather than being offered as examples of the variety of approaches possible to a particular question. However, the students were not required to read the teachers' materials. While these materials suggested various ways of presenting the lessons, including "acting out" and round table discussions, there was no proof that any plaintiff student was ever called upon to say or do anything that required the student to affirm or deny a religious belief or to engage or refrain from engaging in any act either required or forbidden by the student's religious convictions. Mrs. Frost seemed to assume that each teacher used every suggested exercise or teaching tool in the teachers' editions. There was evidence that reading aloud and acting out the themes encountered in school lessons help young people learn. One of the teachers stated that students read some of the stories aloud. Proof that an objecting student was *required* to participate beyond reading and discussing assigned materials, or was disciplined for disputing assigned materials, might well implicate the Free Exercise Clause because the element of compulsion would then be present. But this was not the case either as pled or proved. The record leaves no doubt that the district court correctly viewed this case as one involving exposure to repugnant ideas and themes as presented by the Holt series.

* * *

The only way to avoid conflict with the plaintiffs' beliefs in these sensitive areas would be to eliminate all references to the subjects so identified. However, the Supreme Court has clearly held that it violates the Establishment Clause to tailor a public school's curriculum to satisfy the principles or prohibitions of any religion.

* * *

C.

* * * [P]laintiffs, in this court, have relied particularly upon [certain] Supreme Court decisions. We find them all distinguishable.

* * *

Board of Education v. Barnette, 319 U.S. 624, 63 S.Ct. 1178 (1943), grew out of a school board rule that required all schools to make a salute to the flag and a pledge of allegiance a regular part of their daily program. All teachers and students were required to participate in the exercise and refusal to engage in the salute was considered an act of insubordination which could lead to expulsion and possible delinquency charges for being unlawfully absent. The plaintiff was a Jehovah's Witness who considered the flag an "image" which the Bible forbids worshiping in any way. Justice Jackson, writing for the Court, stated:

> Here, . . . we are dealing with a compulsion of students to declare a belief. They are not merely made acquainted with the flag salute so that they may be informed as to what it is or even what it means.

* * *

It is abundantly clear that the exposure to materials in the Holt series did not compel the plaintiffs to "declare a belief," "communicate by word and sign [their] acceptance" of the ideas presented, or make an "affirmation of a belief and an attitude of mind." In *Barnette* the unconstitutional burden consisted of compulsion either to do an act that violated the plaintiff's religious convictions or communicate an acceptance of a particular idea or affirm a belief. No similar compulsion exists in the present case.

It is clear that governmental compulsion either to do or refrain from doing an act forbidden or required by one's religion, or to affirm or disavow a belief forbidden or required by one's religion, is the evil prohibited by the Free Exercise Clause. * * *

The plaintiffs appear to contend that the element of compulsion was supplied by the requirement of class participation in the reading exercises. As we have pointed out earlier, there is no proof in the record that any plaintiff student was required to engage in role play, make up magic chants, read aloud or engage in the activity of haggling. In fact, the Director of Education for the State of Tennessee testified that most teachers do not adhere to the suggestions in the teachers' manuals and a teacher for 11 years in the Hawkins County system stated that she looks at the lesson plans in the teachers' editions, but "does her own thing." Being exposed to other students performing these acts might be offensive to the plaintiffs, but it does not constitute the compulsion described in the Supreme Court cases, where the objector was required to affirm or deny a religious belief or engage or refrain from engaging in a practice contrary to sincerely held religious beliefs.

D.

The third Supreme Court decision relied upon by the plaintiffs is the only one that might be read to support the proposition that requiring mere exposure to materials that offend one's religious beliefs creates an unconstitutional burden on the free exercise of religion. *Wisconsin v. Yoder,* 406 U.S. 205, 92 S.Ct. 1526 (1972). However, *Yoder* rested on such a singular set of facts that we do not believe it can be held to announce a general rule that exposure without compulsion to act, believe, affirm or deny creates an unconstitutional burden. The plaintiff parents in *Yoder* were Old Order Amish and members of the Conservative Amish Mennonite Church, who objected to their children being required to attend either public or private schools beyond the eighth grade. Wisconsin school attendance law required them to cause their children to attend school until they reached the age of 16. Unlike the plaintiffs in the present case, the parents in *Yoder* did not want their children to attend any high school or be exposed to any part of a high school curriculum. The Old Order Amish and the Conservative Amish Mennonites separate themselves from the world and avoid assimilation into society, and attempt to shield their children from all worldly influences. The Supreme Court found from the record that—

> [C]ompulsory school attendance to age 16 for Amish children carries with it a very real threat to undermining the Amish community and religious practice as they exist today; they must either abandon belief and be assimilated into society at large, or be forced to migrate to some other and more tolerant region. *Id.* at 218, 92 S.Ct. at 1534 (footnote omitted).

As if to emphasize the narrowness of its holding because of the unique 300 year history of the Old Amish Order, the Court wrote:

> It is one thing to say that compulsory education for a year or two beyond the eighth grade may be necessary when its goal is the preparation of the child for life in modern society as the majority live, but it is quite another if the goal of education be viewed as the preparation of the child for life in the separated agrarian community that is the keystone of the Amish faith. *Id.* at 222, 92 S.Ct. at 1536 (citation omitted).

This statement points up dramatically the difference between *Yoder* and the present case. The parents in *Yoder* were required to send their children to some school that prepared them for life in the outside world, or face official sanctions. The parents in the present case want their children to acquire all the skills required to live in modern society. They also want to have them excused from exposure to some ideas they find offensive. Tennessee offers two options to accommodate this latter desire. The plaintiff parents can either send their children to church schools or private schools, as many of them have done, or teach them at home. Tennessee law prohibits any state interference in the education process of church schools:

> The state board of education and local boards of education are prohibited from regulating the selection of faculty or textbooks or the establishment of a curriculum in church-related schools.

Similarly the statute permitting home schooling by parents or other teachers prescribes nothing with respect to curriculum or the content of class work.

Yoder was decided in large part on the impossibility of reconciling the goals of public education with the religious requirement of the Amish that their children be prepared for life in a separated community. As the Court noted, the requirement of school attendance to age 16 posed a "very real threat of undermining the Amish community and religious practice as they exist today...." 406 U.S. at 218, 92 S.Ct. at 1534. No such threat exists in the present case, and Tennessee's school attendance laws offer several options to those parents who want their children to have the benefit of an education which prepares for life in the modern world without being exposed to ideas which offend their religious beliefs.

E.

At oral argument plaintiffs' counsel identified [a concurring opinion in] *Grove v. Mead School Dist. No. 354* as [one] which strongly supports the plaintiffs' position.... [But] the plaintiffs failed to note other ... statements in the same concurring opinion that, while addressing a different issue, are at odds with their theories:

> Were the free exercise clause violated whenever governmental activity is offensive to or at variance with sincerely held religious precepts, virtually no governmental program would be constitutionally possible. *Id.* at 1542.

> The lesson is clear: governmental actions that merely offend or cast doubt on religious beliefs do not on that account violate free exercise. An actual burden on the profession or exercise of religion is required.

> In short, distinctions must be drawn between those governmental actions that actually interfere with the exercise of religion, and those that merely require or result in exposure to attitudes and outlooks at odds with perspectives prompted by religion. *Id.* at 1543 (citation omitted).

These statements echo similar ones in the majority opinion, *e.g.,*

> To establish a violation of that clause [Free Exercise], a litigant must show that challenged state action has a coercive effect that operates against a litigant's *practice* of his or her religion. *Id.* at 1533 (emphasis added).

IV.

A.

The Supreme Court has recently affirmed that public schools serve the purpose of teaching fundamental values "essential to a democratic society." These values "include tolerance of divergent political and religious views" while taking into account "consideration of the sensibilities of others." *Bethel School Dist. No. 403 v. Fraser,* 478 U.S. 675, 106

S.Ct. 3159, 3164 (1986). The Court has noted with apparent approval the view of some educators who see public schools as an "assimilative force" that brings together "diverse and conflicting elements" in our society "on a broad but common ground." The critical reading approach furthers these goals. Mrs. Frost stated specifically that she objected to stories that develop "a religious tolerance that all religions are merely different roads to God." Stating that the plaintiffs reject this concept, presented as a recipe for an ideal world citizen, Mrs. Frost said, "We cannot be tolerant in that we accept other religious views on an equal basis with ours." While probably not an uncommon view of true believers in any religion, this statement graphically illustrates what is lacking in the plaintiffs' case.

The "tolerance of divergent ... religious views" referred to by the Supreme Court is a civil tolerance, not a religious one. It does not require a person to accept any other religion as the equal of the one to which that person adheres. It merely requires a recognition that in a pluralistic society we must "live and let live." If the Hawkins County schools had required the plaintiff students either to believe or say they believe that "all religions are merely different roads to God," this would be a different case. No instrument of government can, consistent with the Free Exercise Clause, require such a belief or affirmation. However, there was absolutely no showing that the defendant school board sought to do this; indeed, the school board agreed at oral argument that it could not constitutionally do so. Instead, the record in this case discloses an effort by the school board to offer a reading curriculum designed to acquaint students with a multitude of ideas and concepts, though not in proportions the plaintiffs would like. While many of the passages deal with ethical issues, on the surface at least, they appear to us to contain no religious or anti-religious messages. Because the plaintiffs perceive every teaching that goes beyond the "three Rs" as inculcating religious ideas, they admit that any value-laden reading curriculum that did not affirm the truth of their beliefs would offend their religious convictions.

Although it is not clear that the plaintiffs object to all critical reading, Mrs. Frost did testify that she did not want her children to make critical judgments and exercise choices in areas where the Bible provides the answer. There is no evidence that any child in the Hawkins County schools was required to make such judgments. It was a goal of the school system to encourage this exercise, but nowhere was it shown that it was required. When asked to comment on a reading assignment, a student would be free to give the Biblical interpretation of the material or to interpret it from a different value base. The only conduct compelled by the defendants was reading and discussing the material in the Holt series, and hearing other students' interpretations of those materials. This is the exposure to which the plaintiffs objected. What is absent from this case is the critical element of compulsion to affirm or deny a religious belief or to engage or refrain from engaging in a practice forbidden or required in the exercise of a plaintiff's religion.

B.

* * *

Since we have found none of the prohibited forms of governmental compulsion in this case, we conclude that the plaintiffs failed to establish the existence of an unconstitutional burden. * * *

The judgment of the district court granting injunctive relief and damages is reversed, and the case is remanded with directions to dismiss the complaint. * * *

E. SEX EDUCATION

PROBLEM 42: The Riverview Lawsuits

The following hypothetical takes place in the fictional state of Riverview.

The state legislature, determined to bring religion, morality, and values back into public education, revises its sex education statutes and implementing regulations. As now set forth, the following key guidelines apply:

1. Public school campuses shall forbid any discussion of sexual activity and birth control other than abstinence.

2. The words *abortion* and *condom* shall not appear in any of the instructional materials, nor are they to be used in any classroom lesson.

    * * *

A. A group of angry Riverview parents file a lawsuit challenging the new instructional framework. What arguments might be set forth under the right to an education generally? Under the right to receive information and ideas? What result? Discuss.

B. Assume that, some time during the second year of implementation, an eleventh grader at Riverview High is diagnosed as HIV positive. It soon becomes clear that this student had been infected by a fellow student after the two had engaged in consensual sexual activity over a period of several months in a variety of secluded locations on the way home from school. If the parents of the student who had become infected seek to file a negligence lawsuit against the school district, what arguments might be set forth under the duty to supervise/protect? Under the duty to warn? What result? Discuss.

C. Assume, instead, that the state legislature—under a different leadership—adopts an exact version of California Senate Bill 71. A group of parents, infuriated with the new law, file a lawsuit under the right not to receive information and ideas, and are prepared to contend that the statutory scheme is not only *not* educationally suitable (under *Pico*), but is violative of the Free Exercise Clause. What arguments will be set forth? What result? Discuss.

D. Same facts as C, except that the opt-out provisions of SB 71 have been deleted. Under this new version of SB 71, which supersedes any inconsistent policies established by individual school districts, no family may opt out of the mandatory instruction. What arguments might then be set forth by the parents under the First Amendment? Under the Fourteenth Amendment right to direct the upbringing of their children? What result? Discuss.

E.   Same facts as C, except that several members of the community are prepared to challenge the statutory scheme as not going far enough. Specifically, plaintiffs want the state to mandate (1) an objective discussion of abortion as a viable form of birth control; (2) objective instruction documenting the growing number of states, provinces, and countries where same-sex marriage is already legal, and (3) an objective inquiry into what every young person can do to help stop the HIV/AIDS epidemic, both in his/her own community and across the globe. Assuming that plaintiffs can establish standing, what arguments might be set forth under the legal theories relied upon by the Riverview parents in lawsuit A above? Will these arguments be more effective or less effective in this context? Why? What result? Discuss.

BROWN v. HOT, SEXY AND SAFER PROD., INC.

68 F.3d 525 (1st Cir. 1995).

TORRUELLA, CHIEF JUDGE.

* * *

On April 8, 1992, [Plaintiffs] Mesiti and Silva attended a mandatory, school-wide "assembly" at Chelmsford High School. Both students were fifteen years old at the time. The assembly consisted of a ninety-minute presentation characterized by the defendants as an AIDS awareness program (the "Program"). The Program was staged by defendant Suzi Landolphi ("Landolphi"), contracting through defendant Hot, Sexy, and Safer, Inc., a corporation wholly owned by Landolphi.

Plaintiffs allege that Landolphi gave sexually explicit monologues and participated in sexually suggestive skits with several minors chosen from the audience. Specifically, the complaint alleges that Landolphi: 1) told the students that they were going to have a "group sexual experience, with audience participation"; 2) used profane, lewd, and lascivious language to describe body parts and excretory functions; 3) advocated and approved oral sex, masturbation, homosexual sexual activity, and condom use during promiscuous premarital sex; 4) simulated masturbation; 5) characterized the loose pants worn by one minor as "erection wear"; 6) referred to being in "deep sh—" after anal sex; 7) had a male minor lick an oversized condom with her, after which she had a female minor pull it over the male minor's entire head and blow it up; 8) encouraged a male minor to display his "orgasm face" with her for the camera; 9) informed a male minor that he was not having enough orgasms; 10) closely inspected a minor and told him he had a "nice butt"; and 11) made eighteen references to orgasms, six references to male genitals, and eight references to female genitals.

Plaintiffs maintain that the sexually explicit nature of Landolphi's speech and behavior humiliated and intimidated Mesiti and Silva. Moreover, many students copied Landolphi's routines and generally displayed overtly sexual behavior in the weeks following the Program, allegedly exacerbating the minors' harassment. The complaint does not allege that either of the minor plaintiffs actually participated in any of the skits, or were the direct objects of any of Landolphi's comments.

The complaint names eight co-defendants along with Hot, Sexy, and Safer, and Landolphi, alleging that each played some role in planning, sponsoring, producing, and compelling the minor plaintiffs' attendance at the Program.... All the defendants were physically present during the Program.

A school policy adopted by the School Committee required "[p]ositive subscription, with written parental permission" as a prerequisite to "instruction in human sexuality." The plaintiffs allege, however, that the parents were not given advance notice of the content of the Program or an opportunity to excuse their children from attendance at the assembly.

* * *

DISCUSSION

The plaintiffs seek both declaratory and monetary relief, alleging that the school sponsored program deprived the minor plaintiffs of: (1) their privacy rights under the First and Fourteenth Amendments; (2) their substantive due process rights under the First and Fourteenth Amendments; (3) their procedural due process rights under the Fourteenth Amendment; and (4) their First Amendment rights under the Free Exercise Clause (in conjunction with a deprivation of the parent plaintiffs' right to direct and control the upbringing of their children). Plaintiffs also allege that the Program created a sexually hostile educational environment in violation of Title IX of the Education Amendments of 1972, 20 U.S.C. § 1681 *et seq.*

* * *

I. *Privacy Rights and Substantive Due Process*

The Fourteenth Amendment provides that "[n]o State shall ... deprive any person of life liberty or property without due process of law." The substantive component of due process protects against "certain government actions regardless of the fairness of the procedures used to implement them." * * * There are two theories under which a plaintiff may bring a substantive due process claim. Under the first, a plaintiff must demonstrate a deprivation of an identified liberty or property interest protected by the Fourteenth Amendment. Under the second, a plaintiff is not required to prove the deprivation of a specific liberty or property interest, but, rather, he must prove that the state's conduct "shocks the conscience." Plaintiffs contend that compelling the minors' attendance at the Program constitutes a substantive due process violation under both tests.

A. *Conscience Shocking Behavior*

Plaintiffs' claim that the defendants engaged in conscience shocking behavior when they compelled the minor plaintiffs to attend the Program. The Supreme Court set the standard for analyzing claims of conscience shocking behavior in *Rochin.* In that case, the Court held that the government could not use evidence obtained by pumping a defendant's stomach against his will because the state actor's conduct was so egregious that it "shock[ed] the conscience" and offended even "hardened sensibilities." The Court explained that the stomach pumping employed by the state was "too close to the rack and screw to permit of constitutional differentiation."

Similarly, we have found "conscience shocking" conduct only where the state actors engaged in "extreme or intrusive physical conduct."

* * *

Although we have not foreclosed the possibility that words or verbal harassment may constitute "conscious shocking" behavior in violation of substantive due process rights, our review of the caselaw indicates that the threshold for alleging such claims is high and that the facts alleged here do not rise to that level.

In *Souza,* the plaintiff alleged that the prosecutor had caused the suicide of her son by conducting press conferences in which he encouraged the media to link the son to a string of serial murders. The plaintiff further alleged that the prosecutor knew of her son's suicidal tendencies and should have known that he would take his own life as a result of the accusations. Although we "pause[d] to make clear that we do not condone the conduct alleged by Souza," we nevertheless found that the conduct was not "conscience shocking."

In *Pittsley,* police officers told two young children—ages four and ten—that "if we ever see your father on the street again, you'll never see him again." When the police subsequently arrested the children's father, they "use[d] vulgar language" and refused to let the children give their father a hug and kiss goodbye. In affirming the directed verdicts for defendants, we explained: "As despicable and wrongful as it may have been, the single threat made by the officers is not sufficient to 'shock the conscience.'"

The facts alleged at bar are less severe than those found insufficient in *Souza* and *Pittsley.* The minor teenagers in this case were compelled to attend a sexually explicit AIDS awareness assembly without prior parent approval. While the defendants' failure to provide opt-out procedures may have displayed a certain callousness towards the sensibilities of the minors, their acts do not approach the mean-spirited brutality evinced by the defendants in *Souza* and *Pittsley.* We accordingly hold that the acts alleged here, taken as true, do not constitute conscience shocking and thus fail to state a claim under *Rochin.*

B. *Protected Liberty Interests*

The Supreme Court has held that the Fourteenth Amendment encompasses a privacy right that protects against significant government intrusions into certain personal decisions. This right of privacy "has some extension to activities relating to marriage, procreation, contraception, family relationships, and child rearing and education." Nevertheless, the Supreme Court has explained that only those rights that "can be deemed 'fundamental' or 'implicit in the concept of ordered liberty' are included in this guarantee of personal privacy." Regulations limiting these "fundamental rights" may be justified "only by a 'compelling state interest' ... [and] must be narrowly drawn to express only the legitimate interests at stake."

1. *Right to Rear Children*

Parent-plaintiffs allege that the defendants violated their privacy right to direct the upbringing of their children and educate them in accord with their own views. This, they maintain, is a constitutionally protected "fundamental right" and thus can only be infringed upon a showing of a "compelling state interest" that cannot be achieved by any less restrictive means.

The genesis of the right claimed here can be found in *Meyer v. Nebraska* and *Pierce v. Society of Sisters.* In *Meyer,* the Court struck down a state law forbidding instruction in certain foreign languages in part because it arbitrarily interfered with the "right of parents" to procure such instruction for their children. * * *

Two years later the Court in *Pierce* struck down a state statute requiring public school attendance—and thus precluding attendance at parochial schools—because it "unreasonably interfere[d] with the liberty of parents or guardians to direct the upbringing and education of children under their control." The *Meyer* and *Pierce* decisions have since been interpreted by the Court as recognizing that, under our Constitutional scheme, "the custody, care and nurture of the child reside first in the parents." [S]ee *Wisconsin v. Yoder,* 406 U.S. 205, 232–33, 92 S.Ct. 1526, 1541–42 (1972).

Nevertheless, the *Meyer* and *Pierce* cases were decided well before the current "right to privacy" jurisprudence was developed, and the Supreme Court has yet to decide whether the right to direct the upbringing and education of one's children is among those fundamental rights whose infringement merits heightened scrutiny. We need not decide here whether the right to rear one's children is fundamental because we find that, even if it were, the plaintiffs have failed to demonstrate an intrusion of constitutional magnitude on this right.

The *Meyer* and *Pierce* cases, we think, evince the principle that the state cannot prevent parents from choosing a specific educational program—whether it be religious instruction at a private school or instruction in a foreign language. That is, the state does not have the power to "standardize its children" or "foster a homogenous people" by completely foreclosing the opportunity of individuals and groups to choose a different path of education. We do not think, however, that this freedom encompasses a fundamental constitutional right to dictate the curriculum at the public school to which they have chosen to send their children. We think it is fundamentally different for the state to say to a parent, "You can't teach your child German or send him to a parochial school," than for the parent to say to the state, "You can't teach my child subjects that are morally offensive to me." The first instance involves the state proscribing parents from educating their children, while the second involves parents prescribing what the state shall teach their children. If all parents had a fundamental constitutional right to dictate individually what the schools teach their children, the schools would be forced to cater a curriculum for each student whose parents had genuine moral disagreements with the school's choice of subject matter. We cannot see that the Constitution imposes such a burden on state educational systems, and accordingly find that the rights of parents as described by *Meyer* and *Pierce* do not encompass a broad-based right to restrict the flow of information in the public schools.

2.   *Right to be Free from Offensive Speech*

The minor plaintiffs maintain that the defendants' conduct violated their privacy right to be free from "exposure to vulgar and offensive language and obnoxiously debasing portrayals of human sexuality." Plaintiffs cite no cases—and we have found none—indicating that such a fundamental privacy right exists. Rather, they attempt to extract the claimed privacy right from the Supreme Court's First Amendment cases which uphold the *state's* limited power to regulate or discipline speech to protect minors from offensive or vulgar speech. *See Bethel Sch. Dist. No. 403 v. Fraser,* 478 U.S. 675, 685, 106 S.Ct. 3159, 3165 (1986) (cited for the proposition that "[a] high school assembly or classroom is no place for a sexually explicit monologue directed towards an unsuspecting audience of teenage students"). We agree with the district court that these cases "do not create a private cause of action against state officials for exposure" to patently offensive language.[7]

II.   *Procedural Due Process*

The plaintiffs' third claim alleges that their procedural due process rights under the Fourteenth Amendment were violated when the defendants compelled the minor plaintiffs to attend the Program without giving the parents advance notice and an opportunity to opt out of attending.

* * *

---

7. The Supreme Court has explained that a special situation pertains where a free exercise challenge is brought in conjunction with a substantive due process challenge involving the right of parents to direct the upbringing of their children. *See Wisconsin v. Yoder,* 406 U.S. 205, 233–34, 92 S.Ct. 1526, 1542–43 (1972). We therefore analyze this "hybrid right" along with their free exercise challenge.

[We] find that the plaintiffs have failed to state a procedural due process claim.

III. *Free Exercise Clause*

Plaintiffs' fourth claim seeks both monetary and declaratory relief, alleging that the defendants' endorsement and encouragement of sexual promiscuity at a mandatory assembly "imping[ed] on their sincerely held religious values regarding chastity and morality," and thereby violated the Free Exercise Clause of the First Amendment.

In *Employment Div., Oregon Dep't of Human Resources v. Smith*, the Supreme Court addressed a free exercise challenge to a facially neutral and generally applicable criminal statute. The Court held that the compelling interest test did not apply to free exercise challenges to "generally applicable prohibitions of socially harmful conduct." The Court explained that the First Amendment was not offended by neutral, generally applicable laws, unless burdening religion was the object of the law.

In 1994, Congress enacted the Religious Freedom Restoration Act ("RFRA"), in response to the Supreme Court's decision in *Smith*. RFRA states, in relevant part:

(a) In General—Government shall not substantially burden a person's exercise of religion even if the burden results from a rule of general applicability, except as provided in subsection (b) of this section.

(b) Exception—Government may substantially burden a person's exercise of religion only if it demonstrates that application of the burden to the person—

(1) is in furtherance of a compelling governmental interest; and

(2) is the least restrictive means of furthering that compelling governmental interest.

Id. RFRA states that it was enacted to bring the law back to its pre-*Smith* state.

The plaintiffs' Free Exercise challenge raises two complex constitutional issues. The threshold issue is whether the Free Exercise Clause even applies to public education.[11] If indeed the Free Exercise Clause applies to the plaintiffs' claim, the question would then be whether their free exercise rights were violated by the compulsory attendance at the Program. Because the Program was staged in 1992, and RFRA was enacted in 1994, however, a cause of action under RFRA exists only if

---

11. At least one federal judge has argued that the Free Exercise Clause does not restrict the "prerogative of school boards to set curricula," concluding that school boards' authority in such matters is bound-ed only by the Establishment Clause. *Mozert v. Hawkins County Board of Education*, 827 F.2d 1058, 1078–81 (6th Cir.1987) (Boggs, J., concurring).

the statute applies retroactively. . . . [W]e conclude that RFRA does not apply retroactively to plaintiffs' claim for monetary damages.

* * *

[P]laintiffs allege that their case falls within the "hybrid" exception recognized by *Smith* for cases that involve "the Free Exercise Clause in conjunction with other constitutional protections." The most relevant of the so-called hybrid cases is *Wisconsin v. Yoder,* 406 U.S. 205, 232–33, 92 S.Ct. 1526, 1541–42 (1972), in which the Court invalidated a compulsory school attendance law as applied to Amish parents who refused on religious grounds to send their children to school. . . . We find that the plaintiffs allegations do not bring them within the sweep of *Yoder* for two distinct reasons.

First, as we explained, the plaintiffs' allegations of interference with family relations and parental prerogatives do not state a privacy or substantive due process claim. Their free exercise challenge is thus not conjoined with an independently protected constitutional protection. Second, their free exercise claim is qualitatively distinguishable from that alleged in *Yoder*. . . . Here, the plaintiffs do not allege that the one-time compulsory attendance at the Program threatened their entire way of life. Accordingly, the plaintiffs' free exercise claim for damages was properly dismissed.

* * *

IV.   *Sexual Harassment*

The plaintiffs' fifth claim alleges that the defendants engaged in sexual harassment by creating a sexually hostile environment, in violation of Title IX of the Education Amendments of 1972.

* * *

[W]e find that the facts alleged here are insufficient to state a claim for sexual harassment under a hostile environment theory. The plaintiffs' allegations * * * when considered in sum, are clearly insufficient to establish the existence of an objectively hostile or abusive environment.

* * *

CONCLUSION

We have considered the other claims of the plaintiffs and find them similarly without merit.

Affirmed.

Notes

1.   In light of case decisions and other related developments since 1995, would this First Circuit case be decided any differently today? Why or why not?

2.   In a related matter, several courts have considered challenges to the distribution of condoms by school districts on school grounds. *See, e.g.,*

Parents United for Better Schools, Inc. v. School Dist. of Philadelphia Bd. of Ed., *148 F.3d 260 (3d Cir. 1998), ruling in favor of the District*. But see *the U.S. "No Child Left Behind" Act, 20 U.S.C. Section 7906, which provides, in pertinent part:*

None of the funds authorized under this chapter shall be used—

(1) to develop or distribute materials, or operate programs or courses of instruction directed at youth, that are designed to promote or encourage sexual activity;

* * *

(3) to provide sex education or HIV-prevention education in schools unless that instruction is age appropriate and includes the health benefits of abstinence; or

(4) to operate a program of contraceptive distribution in schools.

2. In *Leebaert v. Harrington,* 332 F.3d 134 (2d Cir. 2003), the Court considered the question of whether a school district was obligated to excuse a child—upon the request of the parent—from attending health education classes. Finding in favor of the District, the Court ruled that the parental right to direct the upbringing and education of a child does not require the District to comply with such a request.

3. In *Fields v. Palmdale Sch. Dist.,* 427 F.3d 1197 (9th Cir. 2005), the Court found that the administration of a psychological questionnaire to elementary school students—containing some questions involving sexual topics and with the announced goal "of establishing a community baseline measure of children's exposure to early trauma"—was neither a violation of "the due process right to control a child's upbringing" nor a violation of "the constitutional right to privacy." The Court declared that "there is no fundamental right of parents to be the exclusive provider of information regarding sexual matters to their children, either independent of their right to direct the upbringing and education of their children or encompassed by it." It also found "that parents have no due process or privacy right to override the determination of public schools as to the information to which their children will be exposed while enrolled as students."

4. Consider the following excerpts from the 2003 California Sex Education Statutes, which are generally viewed as among the most progressive of the era. What changes might you recommend, as a matter of policy, in light of recent and ongoing developments in this area?

THE CALIFORNIA SEX EDUCATION STATUTES

California Education Code
From SB 71 (Kuehl) (2003)

CHAPTER 5.6. CALIFORNIA COMPREHENSIVE SEXUAL HEALTH AND HIV/AIDS PREVENTION EDUCATION ACT

Article 1. General Provisions

51930. (a) This chapter shall be known and may be cited as the California Comprehensive Sexual Health and HIV/AIDS Prevention Education Act.

(b) The purposes of this chapter are as follows:

    (1) To provide a pupil with the knowledge and skills necessary to protect his or her sexual and reproductive health from unintended pregnancy and sexually transmitted diseases.

    (2) To encourage a pupil to develop healthy attitudes concerning adolescent growth and development, body image, gender roles, sexual orientation, dating, marriage, and family.

51931. For the purposes of this chapter, the following definitions apply:

(a) "Age appropriate" refers to topics, messages, and teaching methods suitable to particular ages or age groups of children and adolescents, based on developing cognitive, emotional, and behavioral capacity typical for the age or age group.

(b) "Comprehensive sexual health education" means education regarding human development and sexuality, including education on pregnancy, family planning, and sexually transmitted diseases.

* * *

(d) "HIV/AIDS prevention education" means instruction on the nature of HIV/AIDS, methods of transmission, strategies to reduce the risk of human immunodeficiency virus (HIV) infection, and social and public health issues related to HIV/AIDS. For the purposes of this chapter, "HIV/AIDS prevention education" is not comprehensive sexual health education.

(e) "Instructors trained in the appropriate courses" means instructors with knowledge of the most recent medically accurate research on human sexuality, pregnancy, and sexually transmitted diseases.

(f) "Medically accurate" means verified or supported by research conducted in compliance with scientific methods and published in peer-reviewed journals, where appropriate, and recognized as accurate and objective by professional organizations and agencies with expertise in the relevant field, such as the federal Centers for Disease Control and Prevention, the American Public Health Association, the American Academy of Pediatrics, and the American College of Obstetricians and Gynecologists.

* * *

51932. (a) This chapter does not apply to description or illustration of human reproductive organs that may appear in a textbook, adopted pursuant to law, on physiology, biology, zoology, general science, personal hygiene, or health.

(b) This chapter does not apply to instruction or materials that discuss gender, sexual orientation, or family life and do not discuss human reproductive organs and their functions.

Article 2. Authorized Comprehensive Sexual Health Education

51933.   (a) School districts may provide comprehensive sexual health education, consisting of age-appropriate instruction, in any kindergarten to grade 12, inclusive, using instructors trained in the appropriate courses.

(b) A school district that elects to offer comprehensive sexual health education pursuant to subdivision (a), whether taught by school district personnel or outside consultants, shall satisfy all of the following criteria:

(1) Instruction and materials shall be age appropriate.

(2) All factual information presented shall be medically accurate and objective.

(3) Instruction shall be made available on an equal basis to a pupil who is an English learner, consistent with the existing curriculum and alternative options for an English learner pupil as otherwise provided in this code.

(4) Instruction and materials shall be appropriate for use with pupils of all races, genders, sexual orientations, ethnic and cultural backgrounds, and pupils with disabilities.

(5) Instruction and materials shall be accessible to pupils with disabilities, including, but not limited to, the provision of a modified curriculum, materials and instruction in alternative formats, and auxiliary aids.

(6) Instruction and materials shall encourage a pupil to communicate with his or her parents or guardians about human sexuality.

(7) Instruction and materials shall teach respect for marriage and committed relationships.[2]

(8) Commencing in grade 7, instruction and materials shall teach that abstinence from sexual intercourse is the only certain way to prevent unintended pregnancy, teach that abstinence from sexual activity is the only certain way to prevent sexually transmitted diseases, and provide information about the value of abstinence while also providing medically accurate information on other methods of preventing pregnancy and sexually transmitted diseases.

2. This language replaced the following language in former Cal. Educ. Code Section 51553: "(6) Course material and instruction shall teach honor and respect for monogamous heterosexual marriage."

(9) Commencing in grade 7, instruction and materials shall provide information about sexually transmitted diseases. This instruction shall include how sexually transmitted diseases are and are not transmitted, the effectiveness and safety of all federal Food and Drug Administration (FDA) approved methods of reducing the risk of contracting sexually transmitted diseases, and information on local resources for testing and medical care for sexually transmitted diseases.

(10) Commencing in grade 7, instruction and materials shall provide information about the effectiveness and safety of all FDA-approved contraceptive methods in preventing pregnancy, including, but not limited to, emergency contraception.

(11) Commencing in grade 7, instruction and materials shall provide pupils with skills for making and implementing responsible decisions about sexuality.

(12) Commencing in grade 7, instruction and materials shall provide pupils with information on the law on surrendering physical custody of a minor child 72 hours or younger, pursuant to Section 1255.7 of the Health and Safety Code and Section 271.5 of the Penal Code.

(c) A school district that elects to offer comprehensive sexual health education pursuant to subdivision (a) earlier than grade 7 may provide age appropriate and medically accurate information on any of the general topics contained in paragraphs (8) to (12), inclusive, of subdivision (b).

(d) If a school district elects to offer comprehensive sexual health education pursuant to subdivision (a), whether taught by school district personnel or outside consultants, the school district shall comply with the following:

(1) Instruction and materials may not teach or promote religious doctrine.

(2) Instruction and materials may not reflect or promote bias against any person on the basis of any category protected by Section 220.

Article 3. Required HIV/AIDS Prevention Education

51934.   (a) A school district shall ensure that all pupils in grades 7 to 12, inclusive, receive HIV/AIDS prevention education from instructors trained in the appropriate courses. Each pupil shall receive this instruction at least once in junior high or middle school and at least once in high school.

(b) HIV/AIDS prevention education, whether taught by school district personnel or outside consultants, shall satisfy all of the criteria set forth in paragraphs (1) to (6), inclusive, of subdivision (b) and paragraphs (1) and (2) of subdivision (d) of Section 51933, shall accurately reflect the latest information and recommendations from the United States Surgeon General, the federal Centers for Disease Control and Prevention, and the National Academy of Sciences, and shall include the following:

(1) Information on the nature of HIV/AIDS and its effects on the human body.

(2) Information on the manner in which HIV is and is not transmitted, including information on activities that present the highest risk of HIV infection.

(3) Discussion of methods to reduce the risk of HIV infection. This instruction shall emphasize that sexual abstinence, monogamy, the avoidance of multiple sexual partners, and abstinence from intravenous drug use are the most effective means for HIV/AIDS prevention, but shall also include statistics based upon the latest medical information citing the success and failure rates of condoms and other contraceptives in preventing sexually transmitted HIV infection, as well as information on other methods that may reduce the risk of HIV transmission from intravenous drug use.

(4) Discussion of the public health issues associated with HIV/AIDS.

(5) Information on local resources for HIV testing and medical care.

(6) Development of refusal skills to assist pupils in overcoming peer pressure and using effective decisionmaking skills to avoid high-risk activities.

(7) Discussion about societal views on HIV/AIDS, including stereotypes and myths regarding persons with HIV/AIDS. This instruction shall emphasize compassion for persons living with HIV/AIDS.

* * *

Article 5. Notice and Parental Excuse

51937. It is the intent of the Legislature to encourage pupils to communicate with their parents or guardians about human sexuality and HIV/AIDS and to respect the rights of parents or guardians to supervise their children's education on these subjects. The Legislature intends to create a streamlined process to make it easier for parents and guardians to review materials and evaluation tools related to comprehensive sexual health education and HIV/AIDS prevention education, and, if they wish, to excuse their children from participation in all or part of that instruction or evaluation.

The Legislature recognizes that while parents and guardians overwhelmingly support medically accurate, comprehensive sex education, parents and guardians have the ultimate responsibility for imparting values regarding human sexuality to their children.

51938. A parent or guardian of a pupil has the right to excuse their child from all or part of comprehensive sexual health education, HIV/AIDS prevention education, and assessments related to that education, as follows:

(a) At the beginning of each school year, or, for a pupil who enrolls in a school after the beginning of the school year, at the time of that pupil's enrollment, each school district shall notify the parent or guardian of each pupil about instruction in comprehensive sexual health education and HIV/AIDS prevention education and research on pupil health behaviors and risks planned for the coming year. The notice shall include all of the following:

(1) Advise the parent or guardian that written and audio visual educational materials used in comprehensive sexual health education and HIV/AIDS prevention education are available for inspection.

(2) Advise the parent or guardian whether the comprehensive sexual health education or HIV/AIDS prevention education will be taught by school district personnel or by outside consultants.

(3) Information explaining the parent's or guardian's right to request a copy of this chapter.

(4) Advise the parent or guardian that the parent or guardian may request in writing that his or her child not receive comprehensive sexual health education or HIV/AIDS prevention education.

* * *

F. INTERNET FILTERING AND THE SAFETY OF CHILDREN IN CYBERSPACE

JUST HOW DIFFERENT IS CYBERSPACE?

From Beyond Our Control? Confronting the Limits
of Our Legal System in the Age of Cyberspace
Stuart Biegel.
MIT Press (2001).

For those who seek to regulate cyberspace, the question of how different it is becomes a central component of the inquiry. If the Internet is simply another high-tech method of sending and receiving information, then arguably the same legal and policy principles that apply to other forms of communication are applicable here. If the differences are only a matter of degree, then minor adjustments can be made in the law and the task still remains relatively straightforward. But if the online world is different enough to be distinguishable from the offline world in significant ways—and noted commentators have argued as much—then the task of would-be regulators becomes much more complicated indeed.

At the most basic level, everyone agrees. The 1990s version of the Internet has become a new, widely used form of communication with three distinguishing features. It has provided the means for instantaneous global transmission of written messages, which may also be accompanied by graphic and audio-visual material. It has expanded the ability of individuals to communicate easily with large numbers of people. And it has emerged as a vehicle for unprecedented access to information. While fax machines and various other forms of telephone, radio, and satellite transmission may provide many similar benefits, the scope of Internet communication via e-mail, newsgroups, and the World Wide Web—combined with the relatively low cost for those who already have the hardware—makes it at least somewhat different from anything that has come before.

For the majority of people, however, the Internet is more than just a bit different. Most would concede that it is different enough to merit a level of attention that very few other modes of communication have received. And many see the Internet as something more than simply another communication tool, although just how one might classify this new medium has been the subject of debate at the highest levels of government and industry.

The controversy regarding the correct classification—or perhaps the most appropriate analogy—for the Internet came to the forefront during the *Reno v. ACLU* litigation of 1996–1997.[3] At the oral arguments for the first Internet-related case to reach the U.S. Supreme Court, both the attorneys and the justices focused extensively on the nature of cyberspace and sought to identify the most relevant analogy.

Deputy Solicitor General Seth P. Waxman, representing the government, argued that the Internet might be viewed as analogous to a library. Building on the fact that many people do indeed use the Internet as a research tool, he argued that the Communications Decency Act (CDA) simply required that certain indecent material be put in "a different room" of this library.[4] Plaintiffs also liked the library analogy, but for different reasons. Judith Krug of the American Library Association noted with pleasure that during the oral arguments in the *Reno* case "the justices paid special attention to the threat that the CDA would

---

3. 521 U.S. 844 (1997).

4. See Oral Argument of Seth P. Waxman, Esq. On Behalf of the Appellants, *Cyber-Liberties: American Civil Liberties*

Union, at http://www.aclu.org/issues/cyber/trial/sctran.html#waxman (last visited May 17, 2000) [hereinafter *Reno v. ACLU Oral Argument*].

pose to libraries around the country seeking to use the Internet to provide greater public access to information."[5]

Justice Stephen Breyer wondered aloud at the oral argument whether the Internet might simply be more like a telephone. With a great percentage of online users at the time communicating via modems over telephone lines, the analogy seemed quite appropriate. Breyer asked whether a group of high school students discussing their sexual experiences online might appropriately be characterized as simply teenagers talking on the telephone, and he appeared genuinely concerned about the prospect of criminalizing such behavior.[6]

Justices Sandra Day O'Connor and Anthony Kennedy suggested in their questions to Mr. Waxman that the Internet might be considered analogous to "a street corner or a park," raising the question of whether the online world could be viewed as a traditional public forum for purposes of First Amendment analysis.[7] Commentators have wrestled extensively with this issue, seeking to determine whether the Internet might best be characterized as a public street corner or more akin to a private shopping mall.[8]

The government, however, appeared at other times to prefer that the Internet be viewed as more akin to broadcast media. The Justice Department's brief in *Reno* relied heavily on *FCC v. Pacifica*,[9] the case that considered the complaints of a father who heard the broadcast of George Carlin's "Seven Dirty Words" monologue with his young son. In *Pacifica*, the Court found that "broadcasting . . . has received the most limited First Amendment protection" . . . both because of its pervasiveness and because of child accessibility.[10] Building on *Pacifica* in its brief, the government argued that it should be able to regulate online speech because there is a "danger of inadvertent exposure to indecent material on the Internet as well."[11] Plaintiffs countered, however, with the argument that if the Internet is analogous to any form of media, the most appropriate analogy would be newspapers and magazines—which are afforded much greater First Amendment protection under constitutional law.[12]

While in the end the Court found that the Internet—at least for purposes of deciding the *Reno* case—is more analogous to both a library *and* a shopping mall, it can be argued that every one of the analogies raised in the oral arguments might apply at some point depending on the circumstances. Indeed, at the turn of the century, the Internet can probably be viewed as all of the above, and more: a library, a telephone,

---

5. Stuart Biegel, Reno v. ACLU in the Supreme Court: Justices Hear Oral Argument in Communication Decency Act Case, *UCLA Online Institute for Cyberspace Law and Policy*, March 27, 1997, *at* http://www.gseis.ucla.edu/iclp/mar97.html (last visited August 28, 2000).

6. *See Reno v. ACLU Oral Argument, supra* note 2.

7. *See id.*

8. *See, e.g., PruneYard Shopping Center v. Robins*, 447 U.S. 74 (1980).

9. 438 U.S. 726 (1978).

10. *Id.* at 748.

11. *See Reno v. ACLU Oral Argument, supra* note 2.

12. *See* Biegel, *supra* note 3.

a public park, a local bar, a shopping mall, a broadcast medium, a print medium, a medical clinic, a private living room, and a public educational institution. No previous mode of communication in the history of mankind has served so many purposes all at once.

* * *

In cyberspace, one can achieve a level of anonymity that is generally just not possible in our day-to-day affairs. While on some level there is less privacy in cyberspace, on another level a person can change his/her age, gender, race, and/or socioeconomic status and present a completely different persona to others in online chat rooms and discussion forums. People become less inhibited and feel more free to act in ways that they might not think of acting in the actual physical presence of others. Countless stories have emerged of people with minimal social skills who have raised havoc in cyberspace, relying implicitly or explicitly on the apparent lack of accountability for ones actions that has often become part of this picture. A certain level of anarchy has in fact been tolerated in many parts of the online world, reflecting a libertarian Net culture that insists on freedom of expression at all times and in all contexts.

* * * [The] level of openness that has emerged as a result of both the nature of the online world and the still-prevalent Net culture can also lead to some very extreme and unsettling experiences. Laws are broken with impunity, unsubstantiated rumors take on an inappropriate level of credibility, young people have unprecedented access to adult information, and people witness things they may not have chosen to witness.

* * *

[In this context,] most people are concerned on at least some level that young people may encounter obscenity years before they have the emotional maturity to sort out the relevant issues that may be involved. As the Internet becomes a central component of innovative education programs, more and more young people have been accessing the online world. When they do, they can easily find some of the most extreme pornography ever available to the average person of any age.

* * *

[T]he only viable option for the average online user who [does] not want to encounter obscenity in cyberspace [is] to try [an] architectural solution of some sort. Internet filtering, for example, ... proliferated in the aftermath of the U.S. Supreme Court's Reno decision, bolstered by the majority opinion's clear suggestion that the control of obscenity would be up to individual users.

Filtering software [has] improved significantly, and many [see] it as a viable option. But typical filtering systems [continue] to block many sites that could be important to access depending on the nature of one's online use.

PROBLEM 43: The Marbury Student
Council Community Web Site

Over a twenty-year period, Marbury Middle School—a fictional urban campus located in Southern California—developed a unique relationship with the Fred Korematsu Public Library. Both the school's main office & classroom facility and the public library were situated in the same complex, and when a combination of overcrowding and budget cutbacks led to the dismantling and closing down of the school's own library collection, a close working arrangement was established between the two separate institutions. Under this informal arrangement, all Marbury students received automatic borrowing privileges, later expanded to include free and unlimited use of the fifteen computer terminals. Teachers brought their classes to the library on a regular basis pursuant to a schedule worked out by Korematsu librarians. And when the library installed unrestricted Internet access on all the terminals students were able to benefit from this additional service as well.

Several years later the Marbury Student Council voted to set up several "community service" subcommittees, with the express goal of identifying key problems in the community and investigating possible solutions. One day in late February, while visiting the American College Health Association Web site via a Korematsu library terminal, s.t.d./teen pregnancy subcommittee member Bill Jones discovered a page entitled "Making Sex Safer." The page contained an overview of various sexually transmitted diseases, and discussed explicit ways that men and women could protect themselves. It concluded by classifying fifteen different sexual "acts" into four categories: safe, less risky, risky, and dangerous. Believing that the entire school community could benefit from this information, Bill decided to include a link to the page on the new Student Council Community Service Web Site.

A. Assume that the Student Council goes ahead with these plans, and that Principal Janet Morrison receives several complaints from parents regarding the link. Morrison subsequently appears at the next student council meeting, and informs the students that under no circumstances are they to be conducting their own sex education program at Marbury Middle School. The entire Web site is taken down, and a new Student Council Faculty Advisor is appointed. The students, represented by the ACLU, file a lawsuit, arguing that their rights have been violated. What arguments might the respective parties set forth? What result? Discuss.

B. Assume instead that no parents complain, but that a major controversy develops regarding the unrestricted access to the Internet that had been available to Marbury students in the Fred Korematsu library. In response, the school district and the library announce at a joint press conference that because some Internet content is not "educationally suitable," they have arranged with familyclick.com to implement server-based content filtering on all library computers. And while familyclick.com enables adults with proper passwords to override the filtering system, passwords would not be distributed to patrons here because so many young students walked around the library throughout the day and could conceivably view unsuitable material as they passed by computer screens.

After the content filtering system is finally installed, Albert Hall, Editor of *The Marbury Street Sheet* (a newspaper published by the city's homeless population), files a lawsuit challenging the new system as violative of his right to receive information and ideas. What arguments would Hall set forth under *Pico* and *Loudoun*? What result? Discuss.

C.   Assume that instead of agreeing to install a content filtering system, the library breaks with the school district and refuses to make any changes. Assume that a lawsuit is then filed by a group of Marbury families who are highly religious and object to the unfiltered Internet access at the library. According to the families' religious precepts, mere exposure to graphic pictorial sexual content is considered an abomination. What arguments might the parents set forth? What result? Discuss.

MAINSTREAM LOUDOUN v. BOARD OF TRUSTEES OF THE LOUDOUN COUNTY LIBRARY

2 F.Supp.2d 783 (E.D. Va. 1998).

BRINKEMA, DISTRICT JUDGE.

Before the Court . . . [is] a case of first impression, involving the applicability of the First Amendment's free speech clause to public libraries' content-based restrictions on Internet access.

I.   Background

The plaintiffs in this case are an association, Mainstream Loudoun, and ten individual plaintiffs, all of whom are both members of Mainstream Loudoun and adult patrons of Loudoun County public libraries. * * *

On October 20, 1997, the Library Board voted to adopt a "Policy on Internet Sexual Harassment" (the "Policy"), which requires that "[s]ite-blocking software . . . be installed on all [library] computers" so as to: "a. block child pornography and obscene material (hard core pornography)"; and "b. block material deemed Harmful to Juveniles under applicable Virginia statutes and legal precedents (soft core pornography)." To implement the Policy, the Library Board chose "X–Stop," a commercial software product intended to limit access to sites deemed to violate the Policy.

Plaintiffs allege that the Policy impermissibly blocks their access to protected speech such as the Quaker Home Page, the Zero Population Growth Web site, and the site for the American Association of University Women–Maryland. They also claim that there are no clear criteria for blocking decisions and that defendants maintain an unblocking policy that unconstitutionally chills plaintiffs' receipt of constitutionally protected materials.

* * *

IV. Plaintiffs' First Amendment Claim

* * *

[D]efendants concede that the Policy prohibits access to speech on the basis of its content. However, defendants argue that the "First Amendment does not in any way limit the decisions of a public library on whether to provide access to information on the Internet." . . . Thus, the central question before this Court is whether a public library may, without violating the First Amendment, enforce content-based restrictions on access to Internet speech.

No cases directly address this issue. However, the parties agree that the most analogous authority on this issue is *Board of Education v. Pico,* 457 U.S. 853, 102 S.Ct. 2799 (1982), in which the Supreme Court reviewed the decision of a local board of education to remove certain books from a high school library based on the board's belief that the books were "anti-American, anti-Christian, anti-Sem[i]tic, and just plain filthy." *Id.* 457 U.S. at 856. . . . A sharply-divided Court voted to affirm the Court of Appeal's decision to remand the case for a determination of the school board's motives. However, the Court did not render a majority opinion. Justice Brennan, joined by three Justices, wrote what is commonly referred to as the "plurality" opinion. Justice Brennan held that the First Amendment necessarily limits the government's right to remove materials on the basis of their content from a high school library. *See id.* at 864–69 (plurality op.). Justice Brennan reasoned that the right to receive information is inherent in the right to speak and that "the State may not, consistently with the spirit of the First Amendment, contract the spectrum of available knowledge." [S]ee also Stanley v. Georgia, 394 U.S. 557, 564, 89 S.Ct. 1243 (1969)("the Constitution protects the right to receive information and ideas"). Justice Brennan explained that this principle was particularly important given the special role of the school's library as a locus for free and independent inquiry. *See* [Pico] 457 U.S. at 869. At the same time, Justice Brennan recognized that public high schools play a crucial inculcative role in "the preparation of individuals for participation as citizens" and are therefore entitled to great discretion "to establish and apply their curriculum in such a way as to transmit community values." *Id.* at 863–64. Accordingly, Justice Brennan held that the school board members could not remove books "simply because they dislike the ideas contained [in them]," thereby "prescrib[ing] what shall be orthodox in politics, nationalism, religion, or other matters of opinion," but that the board might remove books for reasons of educational suitability, for example pervasive vulgarity.

* * *

Defendants contend that the *Pico* plurality opinion has no application to this case because it addressed only decisions to remove materials from libraries and specifically declined to address library decisions to acquire materials. *See id.* at 861–63, 871–72 (plurality op.). Defendants liken the Internet to a vast Interlibrary Loan system, and contend that restricting Internet access to selected materials is merely a decision not to acquire such materials rather than a decision to remove them from a library's collection. As such, defendants argue, the instant case is outside the scope of the *Pico* plurality.

In response, plaintiffs argue that, unlike a library's collection of individual books, the Internet is a "single, integrated system." As plaintiffs explain, "[t]hough information on the Web is contained in individual computers, the fact that each of these computers is connected to the Internet through [World Wide Web] protocols allows all of the information to become part of a single body of knowledge." Accordingly, plaintiffs analogize the Internet to a set of encyclopedias, and the Library Board's enactment of the Policy to a decision to "black out" selected articles considered inappropriate for adult and juvenile patrons.

After considering both arguments, we conclude that defendants have misconstrued the nature of the Internet. By purchasing Internet access, each Loudoun library has made all Internet publications instantly accessible to its patrons. Unlike an Interlibrary loan or outright book purchase, no appreciable expenditure of library time or resources is required to make a particular Internet publication available to a library patron. In contrast, a library must actually expend resources to restrict Internet access to a publication that is otherwise immediately available. In effect, by purchasing one such publication, the library has purchased them all. The Internet therefore more closely resembles plaintiffs' analogy of a collection of encyclopedias from which defendants have laboriously redacted portions deemed unfit for library patrons. As such, the Library Board's action is more appropriately characterized as a removal decision. We therefore conclude that the principles discussed in the *Pico* plurality are relevant and apply to the Library Board's decision to promulgate and enforce the Policy.

* * *

To the extent that *Pico* applies to this case, we conclude that it stands for the proposition that the First Amendment applies to, and limits, the discretion of a public library to place content-based restrictions on access to constitutionally protected materials within its collection. Consistent with the mandate of the First Amendment, a public library, "like other enterprises operated by the State, may not be run in such a manner as to 'prescribe what shall be orthodox in politics, nationalism, religion, or other matters of opinion.'" *Id.* at 876 (Blackmun, J., concurring) (quoting *Barnette*, 319 U.S. at 642).

Furthermore, the factors which justified giving high school libraries broad discretion to remove materials in *Pico* are not present in this case. The plaintiffs in this case are adults rather than children. Children, whose minds and values are still developing, have traditionally been afforded less First Amendment protection, particularly within the context of public high schools. *See Tinker v. Des Moines Sch. Dist.*, 393 U.S. 503, 506, 89 S.Ct. 733 (1969). In contrast, adults are deemed to have acquired the maturity needed to participate fully in a democratic society, and their right to speak and receive speech is entitled to full First Amendment protection. Accordingly, adults are entitled to receive categories of speech, for example "pervasively vulgar" speech, which may be inappropriate for children. *See Reno v. ACLU,* 521 U.S. 844, 117 S.Ct. 2329, 2346 (1997).

More importantly, the tension Justice Blackmun recognized between the inculcative role of high schools and the First Amendment's prohibition on content-based regulation of speech does not exist here. *See Pico,* 457 U.S. at 876–80 (Blackmun, J., concurring). Public libraries lack the inculcative mission that is the guiding purpose of public high schools. Instead, public libraries are places of freewheeling and independent inquiry. *See id.* at 914 (Rehnquist, J., dissenting). Adult library patrons are presumed to have acquired already the "fundamental values" needed to act as citizens, and have come to the library to pursue their personal intellectual interests rather than the curriculum of a high school classroom. As such, no curricular motive justifies a public library's decision to restrict access to Internet materials on the basis of their content.

Finally, the unique advantages of Internet speech eliminate any resource-related rationale libraries might otherwise have for engaging in content-based discrimination. The Supreme Court has analogized the Internet to a "vast library including millions of readily available and indexed publications," the content of which "is as diverse as human thought." *Reno,* 117 S.Ct. at 2335. Unlike more traditional libraries, however, there is no marginal cost associated with acquiring Internet publications. Instead, all, or nearly all, Internet publications are jointly available for a single price. Indeed, it costs a library more to restrict the content of its collection by means of blocking software than it does for the library to offer unrestricted access to all Internet publications. Nor do Internet publications, which exist only in "cyberspace," take up shelf space or require physical maintenance of any kind. Accordingly, considerations of cost or physical resources cannot justify a public library's decision to restrict access to Internet materials. *Cf. Pico,* 457 U.S. at 909 (Rehnquist, J., dissenting) (budgetary considerations force schools to choose some books over others); 879 n. 1 (Blackmun, J., concurring)(same).

In sum, there is "no basis for qualifying the level of First Amendment scrutiny" that must be applied to a public library's decision to restrict access to Internet publications. *Reno,* 117 S.Ct. at 2344. We are therefore left with the First Amendment's central tenet that content-based restrictions on speech must be justified by a compelling governmental interest and must be narrowly tailored to achieve that end. This principle was recently affirmed within the context of Internet speech. *See Reno,* 117 S.Ct. at 2343–48. Accordingly, we hold that the Library Board may not adopt and enforce content-based restrictions on access to protected Internet speech absent a compelling state interest and means narrowly drawn to achieve that end.

This holding does not obligate defendants to act as unwilling conduits of information, because the Library Board need not provide access to the Internet at all. Having chosen to provide access, however, the Library Board may not thereafter selectively restrict certain categories of Internet speech because it disfavors their content. * * *

A. *Obscenity, Child Pornography, and Speech "Harmful to Juveniles"*

Having determined that a public library must satisfy strict scrutiny before it may engage in content-based regulation of protected speech, we now consider the speech regulated by the Policy. The Policy prohibits access to three types of speech: obscenity, child pornography, and materials deemed "[h]armful to [j]uveniles." Obscenity and child pornography are not entitled to the protections of the First Amendment, and the government may legitimately restrict access to such materials. *See New York v. Ferber* (child pornography); *Miller v. California* (obscenity). Indeed, "[t]ransmitting obscenity and child pornography, whether via the Internet or other means, is already illegal under federal law for both adults and juveniles." *Reno,* 117 S.Ct. at 2348 n.44. In the instant case, however, plaintiffs allege that the X–Stop filtering software chosen by defendants restricts many publications which are not obscene or pornographic, including materials unrelated to sex altogether, such as the Quaker's Web site. Moreover, plaintiffs allege that X–Stop fails to block access to pornographic materials arguably covered by the Policy. Most importantly, plaintiffs allege that the decision as to which materials to block is made by a California corporation based on secret criteria not disclosed even to defendants, criteria which may or may not bear any relation to legal definitions of obscenity or child pornography. As such, plaintiffs argue that the means called for by the Policy are not narrowly tailored to any legitimate interest defendants may have in regulating obscenity and child pornography.

The Policy also prohibits access to materials which are "deemed Harmful to Juveniles under applicable Virginia statutes and legal precedents." ... Plaintiffs allege that the Policy improperly limits adult Internet speech to what is fit for children. In support, plaintiffs cite *Reno,* 117 S.Ct. at 2329. In *Reno,* the Supreme Court held that a content-based Internet regulation intended to prevent the transmission of material harmful to minors was unconstitutional because it suppressed speech adults were constitutionally entitled to send and receive. The Court stated:

> It is true that we have repeatedly recognized the governmental interest in protecting children from harmful materials. But that interest does not justify an unnecessarily broad suppression of speech addressed to adults. As we have explained, the Government may not "reduc[e] the adult population ... to ... only what is fit for children."

* * *

As plaintiffs point out, even when government regulation of content is undertaken for a legitimate purpose, whether it be to prevent the communication of obscene speech or materials harmful to children, the means it uses must be a "reasonable response to the threat" which will alleviate the harm "in a direct and material way." Plaintiffs have adequately alleged a lack of such reasonable means here. As such, plaintiffs have stated a valid First Amendment claim which may go forward.

B. *The Unblocking Policy*

Defendants contend that, even if the First Amendment limits the Library Board's discretion to remove materials, the unblocking procedure ensures the constitutionality of the Policy because it allows library staff to make certain that only constitutionally unprotected materials are blocked. Under the unblocking policy, library patrons who have been denied access to a site may submit a written request which must include their name, telephone number, and a detailed explanation of why they desire access to the blocked site. The library staff then "decide[s] whether the request should be granted."

Plaintiffs argue that the unblocking procedure constitutes an unconstitutional burden on the right of library patrons to access protected speech, citing *Lamont*. The statute at issue in *Lamont* directed the Postmaster General not to deliver "communist propaganda" to postal patrons unless they first returned to the Post Office a card bearing their names and addresses and specifically requesting that such materials be sent to them. The Supreme Court held the statute to be "unconstitutional because it require[d] an official act (viz., returning the reply card) as a limitation on the unfettered exercise of the addressees' First Amendment rights." In particular, the Court noted the severe chilling effect of forcing citizens to publicly petition the Government for access to speech it clearly disfavored.

Here, as in *Lamont,* the unblocking policy forces adult patrons to petition the Government for access to otherwise protected speech, for example speech "Harmful to Juveniles." Indeed, the Loudoun County unblocking policy appears more chilling than the restriction at issue in *Lamont,* because it grants library staff standardless discretion to refuse access to protected speech, whereas the statute at issue in *Lamont* required postal employees to grant access requests automatically. As such, defendants' alleged unblocking procedure does not in any way undercut plaintiffs' First Amendment claim.

Notes

1. Neither *Loudoun* nor the *U.S. v. ALA* case that follows are school-related per se, but of course public libraries provide a very important educative function to many members of the community . . . and particularly to those with fewer economic resources at their disposal.

2. In November 1998, Judge Brinkema issued a new decision in this case following a trial on the merits. While somewhat different in its focus,

the ultimate result was consistent with the earlier determination by the Court that the filtering policy violated the First Amendment. *See* Mainstream Loudoun v. Board of Trustees of the Loudoun County Public Library, 24 F.Supp.2d 552 (E.D. Va. 1998).

UNITED STATES v. AMERICAN LIBRARY ASS'N, INC.

539 U.S. 194, 123 S.Ct. 2297 (2003).

Chief JUSTICE REHNQUIST announced the judgment of the Court.

To address the problems associated with the availability of Internet pornography in public libraries, Congress enacted the Children's Internet Protection Act (CIPA). Under CIPA, a public library may not receive federal assistance to provide Internet access unless it installs software to block images that constitute obscenity or child pornography, and to prevent minors from obtaining access to material that is harmful to them. The District Court held these provisions facially invalid on the ground that they induce public libraries to violate patrons' First Amendment rights. We now reverse.

To help public libraries provide their patrons with Internet access, Congress offers two forms of federal assistance. First, the E-rate program established by the Telecommunications Act of 1996 entitles qualifying libraries to buy Internet access at a discount. In the year ending June 30, 2002, libraries received $58.5 million in such discounts. Second, pursuant to the Library Services and Technology Act (LSTA), the Institute of Museum and Library Services makes grants to state library administrative agencies to "electronically lin[k] libraries with educational, social, or information services," "assis[t] libraries in accessing information through electronic networks," and "pa[y] costs for libraries to acquire or share computer systems and telecommunications technologies." In fiscal year 2002, Congress appropriated more than $149 million in LSTA grants. These programs have succeeded greatly in bringing Internet access to public libraries: By 2000, 95% of the Nation's libraries provided public Internet access.

* * *

By connecting to the Internet, public libraries provide patrons with a vast amount of valuable information. But there is also an enormous amount of pornography on the Internet, much of which is easily obtained. The accessibility of this material has created serious problems for libraries, which have found that patrons of all ages, including minors, regularly search for online pornography. Some patrons also expose others to pornographic images by leaving them displayed on Internet terminals or printed at library printers.

Upon discovering these problems, Congress became concerned that the E-rate and LSTA programs were facilitating access to illegal and harmful pornography. Congress learned that adults "us[e] library computers to access pornography that is then exposed to staff, passersby, and children," and that "minors acces[s] child and adult pornography in libraries."

But Congress also learned that filtering software that blocks access to pornographic Web sites could provide a reasonably effective way to prevent such uses of library resources. By 2000, before Congress enacted CIPA, almost 17% of public libraries used such software on at least some of their Internet terminals, and 7% had filters on all of them. A library can set such software to block categories of material, such as "Pornography" or "Violence." When a patron tries to view a site that falls within such a category, a screen appears indicating that the site is blocked. But a filter set to block pornography may sometimes block other sites that present neither obscene nor pornographic material, but that nevertheless trigger the filter. To minimize this problem, a library can set its software to prevent the blocking of material that falls into categories like "Education," "History," and "Medical." A library may also add or delete specific sites from a blocking category, and anyone can ask companies that furnish filtering software to unblock particular sites.

Responding to this information, Congress enacted CIPA. It provides that a library may not receive E-rate or LSTA assistance unless it has "a policy of Internet safety for minors that includes the operation of a technology protection measure ... that protects against access" by all persons to "visual depictions" that constitute "obscen[ity]" or "child pornography," and that protects against access by minors to "visual depictions" that are "harmful to minors." The statute defines a "[t]echnology protection measure" as "a specific technology that blocks or filters Internet access to material covered by" CIPA. CIPA also permits the library to "disable" the filter "to enable access for bona fide research or other lawful purposes." 20 U.S.C. § 9134(f)(3); 47 U.S.C. § 254(h)(6)(D). Under the E-rate program, disabling is permitted "during use by an adult." Under the LSTA program, disabling is permitted during use by any person.

Appellees are a group of libraries, library associations, library patrons, and Web site publishers, including the American Library Association (ALA) and the Multnomah County Public Library in Portland, Oregon (Multnomah). They sued the United States and the Government agencies and officials responsible for administering the E-rate and LSTA programs in District Court, challenging the constitutionality of CIPA's filtering provisions. A three-judge District Court convened pursuant to § 1741(a) of CIPA.

        * * *

Congress has wide latitude to attach conditions to the receipt of federal assistance in order to further its policy objectives. But Congress may not "induce" the recipient "to engage in activities that would themselves be unconstitutional." To determine whether libraries would violate the First Amendment by employing the filtering software that CIPA requires, we must first examine the role of libraries in our society.

Public libraries pursue the worthy missions of facilitating learning and cultural enrichment. Appellee ALA's Library Bill of Rights states that libraries should provide "[b]ooks and other . . . resources . . . for the interest, information, and enlightenment of all people of the community the library serves." To fulfill their traditional missions, public libraries must have broad discretion to decide what material to provide to their patrons. Although they seek to provide a wide array of information, their goal has never been to provide "universal coverage." Instead, public libraries seek to provide materials "that would be of the greatest direct benefit or interest to the community." To this end, libraries collect only those materials deemed to have "requisite and appropriate quality." See W. Katz, Collection Development: The Selection of Materials for Libraries ("The librarian's responsibility . . . is to separate out the gold from the garbage, not to preserve everything"); F. Drury, Book Selection xi ("[I]t is the aim of the selector to give the public, not everything it wants, but the best that it will read or use to advantage"); Rebuttal Expert Report of Donald G. Davis, Jr. ("A hypothetical collection of everything that has been produced is not only of dubious value, but actually detrimental to users trying to find what they want to find and really need").

We have held in two analogous contexts that the government has broad discretion to make content-based judgments in deciding what private speech to make available to the public. In *Arkansas Ed. Television Comm'n v. Forbes*, we held that public forum principles do not generally apply to a public television station's editorial judgments regarding the private speech it presents to its viewers. "[B]road rights of access for outside speakers would be antithetical, as a general rule, to the discretion that stations and their editorial staff must exercise to fulfill their journalistic purpose and statutory obligations." Recognizing a broad right of public access "would [also] risk implicating the courts in judgments that should be left to the exercise of journalistic discretion."

Similarly, in *National Endowment for Arts v. Finley*, we upheld an art funding program that required the National Endowment for the Arts (NEA) to use content-based criteria in making funding decisions. We explained that "[a]ny content-based considerations that may be taken into account in the grant-making process are a consequence of the nature of arts funding." In particular, "[t]he very assumption of the NEA is that grants will be awarded according to the 'artistic worth of competing applicants,' and absolute neutrality is simply inconceivable." We expressly declined to apply forum analysis, reasoning that it would conflict with "NEA's mandate . . . to make esthetic judgments, and the inherently content-based 'excellence' threshold for NEA support."

The principles underlying *Forbes* and *Finley* also apply to a public library's exercise of judgment in selecting the material it provides to its patrons. Just as forum analysis and heightened judicial scrutiny are incompatible with the role of public television stations and the role of the NEA, they are also incompatible with the discretion that public libraries must have to fulfill their traditional missions. Public library staffs necessarily consider content in making collection decisions and enjoy broad discretion in making them.

The public forum principles on which the District Court relied are out of place in the context of this case. Internet access in public libraries is neither a "traditional" nor a "designated" public forum. First, this resource—which did not exist until quite recently—has not "immemorially been held in trust for the use of the public and, time out of mind, . . . been used for purposes of assembly, communication of thoughts between citizens, and discussing public questions." We have "rejected the view that traditional public forum status extends beyond its historic confines." The doctrines surrounding traditional public forums may not be extended to situations where such history is lacking.

Nor does Internet access in a public library satisfy our definition of a "designated public forum." To create such a forum, the government must make an affirmative choice to open up its property for use as a public forum. "The government does not create a public forum by inaction or by permitting limited discourse, but only by intentionally opening a non-traditional forum for public discourse." The District Court likened public libraries' Internet terminals to the forum at issue in *Rosenberger v. Rector and Visitors of Univ. of Va.*, 515 U.S. 819, 115 S.Ct. 2510 (1995). In *Rosenberger,* we considered the "Student Activity Fund" established by the University of Virginia that subsidized all manner of student publications except those based on religion. We held that the fund had created a limited public forum by giving public money to student groups who wished to publish, and therefore could not discriminate on the basis of viewpoint.

The situation here is very different. A public library does not acquire Internet terminals in order to create a public forum for Web publishers to express themselves, any more than it collects books in order to provide a public forum for the authors of books to speak. It provides Internet access, not to "encourage a diversity of views from private speakers," *Rosenberger*, 515 U.S. at 834, 115 S.Ct. 2510, but for the same reasons it offers other library resources: to facilitate research, learning, and recreational pursuits by furnishing materials of requisite and appropriate quality. As Congress recognized, "[t]he Internet is simply another method for making information available in a school or library." It is "no more than a technological extension of the book stack."

* * *

Because public libraries' use of Internet filtering software does not violate their patrons' First Amendment rights, CIPA does not induce libraries to violate the Constitution, and is a valid exercise of Congress' spending power. Nor does CIPA impose an unconstitutional condition on public libraries. Therefore, the judgment of the District Court for the Eastern District of Pennsylvania is

Reversed.

JUSTICE KENNEDY, concurring in the judgment.

If, on the request of an adult user, a librarian will unblock filtered material or disable the Internet software filter without significant delay, there is little to this case.

* * *

There are, of course, substantial Government interests at stake here. The interest in protecting young library users from material inappropriate for minors is legitimate, and even compelling, as all Members of the Court appear to agree. Given this interest, and the failure to show that the ability of adult library users to have access to the material is burdened in any significant degree, the statute is not unconstitutional on its face. For these reasons, I concur in the judgment of the Court.

JUSTICE BREYER, concurring in the judgment.

The Children's Internet Protection Act (Act) sets conditions for the receipt of certain Government subsidies by public libraries. Those conditions require the libraries to install on their Internet-accessible computers technology, say, filtering software, that will help prevent computer users from gaining Internet access to child pornography, obscenity, or material comparably harmful to minors. The technology, in its current form, does not function perfectly, for to some extent it also screens out constitutionally protected materials that fall outside the scope of the statute (*i.e.,* "overblocks") and fails to prevent access to some materials that the statute deems harmful (*i.e.,* "underblocks"). In determining whether the statute's conditions consequently violate the First Amendment, the plurality first finds the "public forum" doctrine inapplicable, and then holds that the statutory provisions are constitutional. I agree with both determinations. But I reach the plurality's ultimate conclusion in a different way.

In ascertaining whether the statutory provisions are constitutional, I would apply a form of heightened scrutiny, examining the statutory requirements in question with special care. The Act directly restricts the public's receipt of information. And it does so through limitations imposed by outside bodies (here Congress) upon two critically important sources of information—the Internet as accessed via public libraries. See *Board of Ed., Island Trees Union Free School Dist. No. 26 v. Pico,* 457 U.S. 853, 915, 102 S.Ct. 2799 (1982) (REHNQUIST, J., dissenting)(describing public libraries as places "designed for freewheeling inquiry"). For that reason, we should not examine the statute's constitutionality as if it raised no special First Amendment concern—as if, like tax or economic regulation, the First Amendment demanded only a "rational basis" for imposing a restriction. Nor should we accept the Government's suggestion that a presumption in favor of the statute's constitutionality applies.

* * *

In [heightened scrutiny] cases the Court has asked whether the harm to speech-related interests is disproportionate in light of both the justifications and the potential alternatives. It has considered the legitimacy of the statute's objective, the extent to which the statute will tend to achieve that objective, whether there are other, less restrictive ways of achieving that objective, and ultimately whether the statute works speech-related harm that, in relation to that objective, is out of proportion. * * *

The Act's restrictions satisfy these constitutional demands. The Act seeks to restrict access to obscenity, child pornography, and, in respect to access by minors, material that is comparably harmful. These objectives are "legitimate," and indeed often "compelling." ... As the District Court found, software filters "provide a relatively cheap and effective" means of furthering these goals. Due to present technological limitations, however, the software filters both "overblock," screening out some perfectly legitimate material, and "underblock," allowing some obscene material to escape detection by the filter. But no one has presented any clearly superior or better fitting alternatives.

At the same time, the Act contains an important exception that limits the speech-related harm that "overblocking" might cause. As the plurality points out, the Act allows libraries to permit any adult patron access to an "overblocked" Web site; the adult patron need only ask a librarian to unblock the specific Web site or, alternatively, ask the librarian, "Please disable the entire filter."

The Act does impose upon the patron the burden of making this request. But it is difficult to see how that burden (or any delay associated with compliance) could prove more onerous than traditional library practices associated with segregating library materials in, say, closed stacks, or with interlibrary lending practices that require patrons to make requests that are not anonymous and to wait while the librarian obtains the desired materials from elsewhere. Perhaps local library rules or practices could further restrict the ability of patrons to obtain "overblocked" Internet material.... But we are not now considering any such local practices. We here consider only a facial challenge to the Act itself.

Given the comparatively small burden that the Act imposes upon the library patron seeking legitimate Internet materials, I cannot say that any speech-related harm that the Act may cause is disproportionate when considered in relation to the Act's legitimate objectives. I therefore agree with the plurality that the statute does not violate the First Amendment, and I concur in the judgment.

Justice Stevens, dissenting.

"To fulfill their traditional missions, public libraries must have broad discretion to decide what material to provide their patrons." Accordingly, I agree with the plurality that it is neither inappropriate nor unconstitutional for a local library to experiment with filtering software as a means of curtailing children's access to Internet Web sites displaying sexually explicit images. I also agree with the plurality that the 7% of public libraries that decided to use such software on *all* of their Internet terminals in 2000 did not act unlawfully. Whether it is constitutional for the Congress of the United States to impose that requirement on the other 93%, however, raises a vastly different question. Rather than allowing local decisionmakers to tailor their responses to local problems, the Children's Internet Protection Act (CIPA) operates as a blunt nationwide restraint on adult access to "an enormous amount of valuable information" that individual librarians cannot possibly review. Most of that information is constitutionally protected speech. In my view, this restraint is unconstitutional.

Notes

1.   The Children's Internet Protection Act (CIPA) is one of four major pieces of federal legislation passed during the years that the Internet emerged as a central feature of daily life for most Americans. All were designed to "protect our children" in cyberspace, and all faced major challenges in court. In the end, the "decency provisions" of the Communications Decency Act (CDA) were struck down by the U.S. Supreme Court in Reno v. ACLU, 521 U.S. 844, 117 S.Ct. 2329 (1997), the Child Online Protection Act (COPA) was held up in the courts for many years (*cf.* Ashcroft v. ACLU, 542 U.S. 656, 124 S.Ct. 2783 (2004)), and portions of the Child Pornography Prevention Act (CPPA) were struck down in *Ashcroft v. The Free Speech Coalition,* 535 U.S. 234, 122 S.Ct. 1389 (2002). Only the CIPA appears to have withstood a legal challenge. But even so, in upholding the constitutionality of the CIPA, the justices could muster only a plurality opinion.

2.   Note that CIPA also applied to public schools, but that school districts did not ultimately contest it.

3.   Is *Loudoun* no longer good law after *U.S. v. ALA,* or are the two decisions reconcilable? Why?

Chapter X

COPYRIGHT ISSUES
IN EDUCATION

This chapter provides an overview of intellectual property issues in the area of copyright that have confronted educators and educational institutions. Intellectual property law is comprised primarily of copyright, trademark, and patent; and while issues arise in education settings under all three of these areas, copyright disputes are far-and-away the most prominent and the most complex. These disputes include, but are not limited to, litigation addressing fair use and disagreements over the applicability of traditional principles to Internet-related activities.

Controversies regarding intellectual property have emerged at all levels of the educational system, but it is at colleges and universities that the issues are particularly compelling. With most research taking place primarily in a digital environment, traditional questions regarding protection for academic work have become more intricate. In addition, major efforts by the entertainment industry to limit online copyright infringement have led to increased pressure on the higher education community to intervene, both legally and as a matter of a policy.

It is important to note, at the outset, the basic distinctions between copyright, trademark, and patent. Copyright law only protects the expression of ideas; a person's ideas themselves are protected by patent law. And copyright law does not generally protect names, titles, or short phrases. Such protection is relegated to trademark law, which has been designed to provide rights in distinctive words, phrases, logos, symbols, slogans and any other devices used to identify and distinguish products or services in the marketplace.

While copyright issues predominate in education, trademark questions involving the unauthorized use of university names and symbols have been widespread, and the changing nature of patent law has led to novel issues in recent years. Most trademark disputes are not education specific, and very few trademark cases are actually situated in education settings. Patent-related questions, however, are being raised with much greater frequency at the higher education level, and it is anticipated that this area of intellectual property will expand over time.[a]

The chapter begins by providing an overview of basic copyright law principles. It then addresses copyright ownership disputes, the parameters of the fair use doctrine and its applicability, the "No Electronic Theft" Act, and the Digital Millennium Copyright Act. It concludes by highlighting ongoing issues regarding peer-to-peer file sharing.

A. BASIC PRINCIPLES OF U.S. COPYRIGHT LAW

U.S. copyright law grants certain exclusive rights to the creator of an original work that has been "fixed in a tangible medium of expression." As a general rule, the protection is automatic, and creators do not typically need to register a copyright or even indicate on the work itself that it has been "copyrighted" as of a particular date. The basic term of copyright protection for works completed on or after January 1, 1978 is "the life of the author plus 70 years."

Most copyright disputes are pursued in civil proceedings, but certain egregious copyright violations may also be considered crimes. Persons and entities who are not themselves infringers can be held responsible for violations of copyright law if they help facilitate the infringement under either a contributory copyright infringement theory or a vicarious liability theory.

a. In 1980, the federal government passed two laws allowing universities to patent ideas that resulted from government-funded research. *See* Bayh–Dole Act, 96 Pub. L. No. 517, 94 Stat. 3015 (1980) (codified as amended in scattered sections of 35 U.S.C.); Stevenson–Wydler Technology Innovation Act of 1980, 96 Pub. L. No. 480, 94 Stat. 2311 (codified as amended in 15 U.S.C. §§ 3710–3714). That same year, the Supreme Court stated that "anything under the sun that is made by man" is patentable. *Diamond v. Chakrabarty*, 447 U.S. 303, 309, 100 S.Ct. 2204 (1980).

University technology transfer offices sprang into existence to take advantage of this newfound source of possible wealth. But, while universities were able to negotiate profitable deals, there were costs as well. The requirement that patents not be issued for ideas that have been "described in a printed publication . . . more than one year prior to the date of the application for patent" (35 U.S.C.A. § 102(b) (2005)) has resulted in a trend of less peer review and more secrecy among university scientists. Consequently, many ideas are not shared until they are in their final stages and virtually ready for publication. This has several deleterious effects, influencing everything from the overall spirit of collegiality and collaboration to the requirement of "publish or perish." For a fuller discussion of the problems, see Jeremy M. Grushcow, *Measuring Secrecy: A Cost of the Patent System Revealed*, 33 J. LEGAL STUD. 59 (2004).

Additionally, with "anything under the sun" being patentable, research in new and exciting fields is stagnating under the weight of a "patent anticommons." For example, because the law requires permission to use a patented idea even for experimental or research purposes (as long as the proposed research has any possible commercial implication), university scientists may find it increasingly difficult to conduct any nanotechnology-related research at all. For a greater overview of the problem of a patent anticommons, see Terry Tullis, *Application of the Government License Defense to Federally Funded Nanotechnology Research: The Case for a Limited Patent Compulsory Licensing Regime*, 53 UCLA L. REV. 279 (2005).

The five exclusive rights of the copyright owner include (1) the reproduction right, (2) the modification right, (3) the distribution right, (4) the public performance right, and (5) the public display right. Each of these rights embody complex rules and various exceptions, but the basic principle is that a creator is granted a "monopoly" interest in his or her work. The creator may, of course, convey an interest in these rights to others. In addition, persons may be entitled to share these rights through implied licenses that may emerge over time.

Several explicit exceptions to the five exclusive rights have been included in the specific text of the law. The First Sale Doctrine, for example, allows a person who has legally obtained a copy to sell or dispose of it without authorization from the copyright holder. Under section 109 of the U.S. Copyright Act, once a copy of a work is sold, the owner has no further right to control the distribution of *that particular copy*. Thus an individual, a library, or another entity is free to give away, lend, rent, or sell its copies of books and many other materials. But the distribution of "phonorecords" and computer programs is subject to certain detailed restrictions.

There is no copyright protection for works that are in the public domain. Some works, such as government documents, are automatically in the public domain. Others move into the public domain when their term of protection has expired. As a general rule, for example, the basic texts of the bible and Shakespeare are both in the public domain. Works in the public domain may be freely copied and distributed by anyone at any time.

In addition, even if a work is protected under one or more of the five exclusive rights, it may be copied, modified, distributed, performed, or displayed without permission if the fair use doctrine applies. Particularly with the advent of the Internet, many believe that the fair use doctrine has become the single most important set of legal principles under U.S. copyright law. This doctrine exemplifies the balance of interests contemplated by Article I, Section 8, Clause 8 of the U.S. Constitution, which states that Congress shall have the power

> To promote the Progress of Science and useful Arts, by securing for limited Times to Authors and Inventors the exclusive Right to their respective Writings and Discoveries.

Indeed, the U.S. Supreme Court has repeatedly emphasized that the copyright protections granted to creators constitute a "monopoly privilege," and it has explained that this privilege is "neither unlimited nor primarily designed to provide a special private benefit." It is, the Court determined, "a means by which an important public purpose may be achieved." Thus, unlike the laws of many other countries, copyright law in the U.S. is not—as many people incorrectly believe—an absolute protection of the creator's work. In fact, the law "makes reward to the owner a secondary consideration," and the "granting of such exclusive rights" to the creator has been viewed as conferring "a benefit upon the public that outweighs the evils of the temporary monopoly." *Sony Corp.*

v. Universal City Studios, Inc., 464 U.S. 417, 429, 104 S.Ct. 774 (1984) (quoting H.R. Rep. No. 2222, 60th Cong., 2d Sess. 7 (1909)).

Copyright law thus embodies a tension between the interests of an individual creator and the interests of the public as a whole. Creators may have individual property rights in their works, but only for the ultimate purpose of benefiting the public by encouraging the creation of more works. And these principles are particularly compelling in an education setting, since the entire enterprise of education is geared toward the public good.

The following sections highlight the range of copyright disputes that arise in such settings.

B. OWNERSHIP OF COPYRIGHT AND RELATED MATTERS

WILLIAMS v. WEISSER

273 Cal.App.2d 726, 78 Cal.Rptr. 542 (1969).

KAUS, P. J.

Defendant Weisser, who does business under the fictitious name of Class Notes, appeals from a judgment which enjoins him from copying, publishing and selling notes of lectures delivered by plaintiff in his capacity as an Assistant Professor of Anthropology at the University of California at Los Angeles ("UCLA"). The judgment also awards plaintiff $1,000 in compensatory and $500 in exemplary damages.

A joint pretrial statement described the nature of the case as follows: "Plaintiff is Assistant Professor at UCLA in the Anthropology Department. Defendant does business in Westwood, California as Class Notes selling outlines for various courses given at UCLA. In 1965, defendant paid Karen Allen, a UCLA student, to attend plaintiff's class in Anthropology 1 to take notes from the lectures, and to type up the notes. Allen delivered the typed notes to defendant and defendant placed a copyright notice thereon in defendant's name, reproduced the typed notes, and sold and offered them for sale. Plaintiff objected. Defendant did not cease these activities until served with summons, complaint and temporary restraining order. Plaintiff seeks a permanent injunction, general damages, and punitive damages."

At the pretrial it was agreed that: "Defendant has used plaintiff's name in selling the publications here in question."

The judgment in plaintiff's favor was based on two grounds: 1. defendant infringed plaintiff's common law copyright in his lectures; and 2. defendant invaded plaintiff's privacy by the use of plaintiff's name.

* * *

1. The product of the mind in which the plaintiff claims a copyright consists of the extensive notes which he had compiled before the beginning of the course, together with the oral expression at the time of

delivery of the lectures, based on the notes, which delivery included charts and diagrams placed on the classroom blackboard. This is, therefore, not a case where the concrete expression of the "composition" consists solely of an intangible oral presentation. As far as this litigation is concerned, the chief importance of the oral presentation is that it provided defendant with access to plaintiff's work and with an argument that there had been a divestive publication.

* * *

Ownership of Copyright

Plaintiff became employed by UCLA starting in July 1965. Defendant's relations with the university started in 1948 when he began to publish and sell to students what purported to be notes of various courses. In 1963 defendant and the university authorities agreed on certain ground rules as a condition to advertising in the Daily Bruin, the student newspaper. Friction arose between defendant and the administration. The matter culminated in a memorandum dated November 19, 1964, addressed to all members of the faculty.

* * *

We are * * * convinced that in the absence of evidence the teacher, rather than the university, owns the common law copyright to his lectures. [T]here was no evidence that plaintiff had assigned his copyright to the university[.] * * *

Defendant claims that the opposite is the law. His sole statutory authority is section 2860 of the Labor Code which reads as follows: "Everything which an employee acquires by virtue of his employment, except the compensation which is due to him from his employer, belongs to the employer, whether acquired lawfully or unlawfully, or during or after the expiration of the term of his employment."

It is obvious that a literal application of that section does not cover the present situation. The code speaks of things which the employee "acquires," not matters which he creates. * * * [And] the section has been applied principally, though not exclusively, to unfair competition carried on by former employees with the use of trade secrets and the like. Even so it has been narrowly employed. We do not believe it applies here.

Defendant also claims that plaintiff is in the position of an employee for hire whose employment calls for the creation of a copyrightable work or, perhaps, of an independent contractor who has been so commissioned. In such cases it is usually presumed that, unless a different intention is shown, the employer or commissioner is the owner of the copyright.

This contention calls for some understanding of the purpose for which a university hires a professor and what rights it may reasonably expect to retain after the services have been rendered. A university's obligation to its students is to make the subject matter covered by a course available for study by various methods, including classroom presentation. It is not obligated to present the subject by means of any particular expression. As far as the teacher is concerned, neither the record in this case nor any custom known to us suggests that the university can prescribe his way of expressing the ideas he puts before his students. Yet expression is what this lawsuit is all about. No reason has been suggested why a university would want to retain the ownership in a professor's expression. Such retention would be useless except possibly for making a little profit from a publication and for making it difficult for the teacher to give the same lectures, should he change jobs.

Indeed the undesirable consequences which would follow from a holding that a university owns the copyright to the lectures of its professors are such as to compel a holding that it does not. Professors are a peripatetic lot, moving from campus to campus. The courses they teach begin to take shape at one institution and are developed and embellished at another. That, as a matter of fact, was the case here. Plaintiff testified that the notes on which his lectures were based were derived from a similar course which he had given at another university. If defendant is correct, there must be some rights of that school which were infringed at UCLA. Further, should plaintiff leave UCLA and give a substantially similar course at his next post, UCLA would be able to enjoin him from using the material which, according to defendant, it owns.

No one but defendant, an outsider as far as the relationship between plaintiff and UCLA is concerned, suggests that such a state of the law is desirable.

Another strange consequence which would follow from equating university lectures with other products of the mind which an employee is hired to create, is, that in order to determine just what it is getting, the university would have to find out the precise extent to which a professor's lectures have taken concrete shape when he first comes to work. Not even defendant suggests that a contract for employment implies an assignment to the university of any common law copyright which the professor already owns.

The many cases cited by defendant for the general rule probably reach desirable results that are in accord with common understanding in their respective areas, but a rule of law developed in one context should not be blindly applied in another where it violates the intention of the parties and creates undesirable consequences. (8) University lectures are *sui generis*. Absent compulsion by statute or precedent, they should not be blindly thrown into the same legal hopper with valve designs, motion picture background music, commercial drawings, mosaics designed for the Congressional Library in Washington, D.C., high school murals, song stylings, radio scripts, commercial jingles, lists of courses taught by a correspondence school, and treatises on the use of ozone or on larceny and homicide.

* * *

[N]o authority supports the argument that the copyright to plaintiff's notes is in the university. The indications from the authorities are the other way and so is common sense.

* * *

Taking the evidence as a whole, the trial court was amply justified in concluding that defendant was not an innocent layman, caught in the complexities of the law, but a businessman who, for personal profit, was determined to pursue a certain course of action even if it meant riding roughshod over the rights of others.

The judgment is affirmed.

WEINSTEIN v. UNIVERSITY OF ILLINOIS

811 F.2d 1091 (7th Cir. 1987).

EASTERBROOK, CIRCUIT JUDGE.

[This dispute] ... is about the order in which the names of an article's authors will be listed. The article is D.J. Belsheim, R.A. Hutchinson & M.M. Weinstein, *The Design and Evaluation of a Clinical Clerkship for Hospital Pharmacists*, 50 Am. J. Pharmaceutical Education 139–45 (1986). Weinstein believes that it should have been published as M.M. Weinstein, D.J. Belsheim & R.A. Hutchinson, *Etc.* According to Weinstein, the publication of the article with the names in the wrong order violated the due process clause of the fourteenth amendment.

I

Weinstein was an Assistant Professor of Pharmacy Administration in the College of Pharmacy of the University of Illinois at Chicago. According to his complaint, from which we take these facts, he proposed a clinical program for practicing pharmacists, who would operate for two weeks in a "clerkship" under the guidance of professors. * * * Although Weinstein asserts that he supplied most of the ideas and did most of the work, he concedes that the three [professors] agreed to write jointly on the results. Weinstein believes that he had an agreement with Belsheim under which Weinstein would be the first-listed author of a paper describing the clerkship and the data obtained from questionnaires, while Belsheim would be lead author of a paper to be called "Teaching Problem Solving in a Post–Graduate Clinical Pharmacy Clerkship."

In January 1984 Weinstein gave Belsheim a draft. Belsheim was dissatisfied. The two disagreed about the subjects to be covered and the conclusions to be drawn. By January 1985 Weinstein had completed another draft. One day he found the draft in Belsheim's wastebasket, with many editorial marks and sections snipped out. Belsheim denied doing more than making "notes" but shortly produced a new draft, revising both the text and the order of listing of authors. Weinstein did not like either the new order or the new text. * * * [O]n July 19, 1985, Belsheim submitted the article to the American Journal of Pharmaceutical Education. It was published in the Journal's Summer 1986 issue.

* * * [Weinstein's lawsuit contends that the others] mutilated his work and stole the credit, denying him due process of law. * * *

Weinstein says that the listing of names is no small matter. He is seeking a topic on which to write a dissertation and believes that the clerkship program would have been suitable, but that Belsheim's being listed as first author precludes it. * * * He also believes that because the principal author is listed first, the appearance of his name in third place will diminish his accomplishments in the eyes of other professors—a significant problem because, as we discuss below, he is looking for a job. His attorney adds the point that academic departments sometimes use the number of citations to a scholar's work as one indication of the importance of that work in the profession. The principal citation services list articles by first author only, so that any citations to the Belsheim, Hutchinson & Weinstein article would be collected under Belsheim's name.

We shall assume, given the posture of the case, that Weinstein could make good his claims of injury-in-fact. We shall also assume that the acts of Belsheim, an employee of a state university, were taken "under color of state law".... None of these assumptions assists Weinstein unless the acts to which he objects have deprived him of "property", for the due process clause applies only to deprivations of "life, liberty or property", and Weinstein does not invoke the first two.

II

The district court concluded that the article was the University's property rather than Weinstein's because it was a "work for hire". The copyright law gives an employer the full rights in an employee's "work for hire", 17 U.S.C. § 201(b), unless a contract provides otherwise. The statute is general enough to make every academic article a "work for hire" and therefore vest exclusive control in universities rather than scholars. The University of Illinois, like many other academic institutions, responded to the 1978 revision of the copyright laws by adopting a policy defining "work for hire" for purposes of its employees, including its professors. According to the policy, which is a part of each professor's contract with the University, a professor retains the copyright unless the work falls into one of three categories:

    (1) The terms of a University agreement with an external party require the University to hold or transfer ownership in the copyrightable work, or

    (2) Works expressly commissioned in writing by the University, or

    (3) Works created as a specific requirement of employment or as an assigned University duty. Such requirements or duties may be contained in a job description or an employment agreement which designates the content of the employee's University work. If such requirements or duties are not so specified, such works will be those for which the topic or content is determined by the author's employment duties and/or which are prepared at the

University's instance and expense, that is, when the University is the motivating factor in the preparation of the work.

The district court held that Weinstein's work is covered by paragraph (3) because the University funded the clerkship program and because, as a clinical professor, Weinstein was required to conduct and write about clinical programs.

This interpretation of the University's policy collides with the role of the three categories as exceptions to a rule that faculty members own the copyrights in their academic work. A university "requires" all of its scholars to write. Its demands—especially the demands of departments deciding whether to award tenure—will be "the motivating factor in the preparation of" many a scholarly work. When Dean Manasse told Weinstein to publish or perish, he was not simultaneously claiming for the University a copyright on the ground that the work had become a "requirement or duty" within the meaning of paragraph (3). The University concedes in this court that a professor of mathematics who proves a new theorem in the course of his employment will own the copyright to his article containing that proof. This has been the academic tradition since copyright law began, a tradition the University's policy purports to retain. The tradition covers scholarly articles and other intellectual property. When Saul Bellow, a professor at the University of Chicago, writes a novel, he may keep the royalties.

The University's copyright policy reads more naturally when applied to administrative duties. Perhaps the University forms a committee to study the appropriate use of small computers and conscripts professors as members. The committee may publish a report, in which the University will claim copyright. We do not say that a broader reading is impossible, but such a reading should be established by evidence about the deliberations underlying the policy and the course of practice— material that is neither in the record nor an appropriate basis on which to dismiss the complaint for failure to state a claim. We would be surprised if any member of the faculty of the College of Pharmacy treats his academic work as the property of the University. Dean Manasse, for example, has not submitted an affidavit stating that the faculty regularly obtains consent (or a transfer of copyright) from the University before publishing articles. The record does not contain the contracts between the American Journal of Pharmaceutical Education and Professors Belsheim, Hutchinson, and Weinstein, but we venture a guess that each represented to the Journal that he owned the copyright and was empowered to transfer the copyright to the Journal. (The article as published carries the Journal's copyright notice rather than that of the authors or the University of Illinois.) Dean Manasse told Weinstein to *publish* the article, not to ask the University for permission to publish—permission that would have been essential if the University owned the copyright.

If the members of the University's faculty own the copyright interest in their scholarly articles, Weinstein has some "property". But did the University "deprive" him of this property without "due process"?

Both "deprivation" and "due process" are problematic. If the University does not own the copyright, the article is covered by 17 U.S.C. § 201(a), which states that "[t]he authors of a joint work are coowners of copyright in the work." This provision applies to all works of joint authorship, and Weinstein concedes that the article in question is (and was supposed to be) a jointly written work. Each coowner of a copyright may revise the work (that is, make a derivative work) and publish the original or the revision. So far as copyright law is concerned, Belsheim was entitled to do what he did. Belsheim is answerable to Weinstein for Weinstein's share of any royalties, but Weinstein does not claim that Belsheim made off with the profits. Belsheim did not diminish any of Weinstein's property rights; neither did the University. The University did not make Belsheim's acts possible. It therefore did not "deprive" Weinstein of any property interest. Indeed it could not have done so. No amount of academic deliberation or hearings before the College Executive Committee could have diminished Belsheim's entitlement to revise the article. Perhaps the University could have threatened Belsheim with sanctions, such as a duty to teach boring subjects, to induce him to desist, but the due process clause does not require a state to impose penalties on those who exercise legal entitlements.

Perhaps Weinstein, Belsheim, and the University could have agreed by contract to give the University the power to make binding decisions concerning disputes over academic papers, but Weinstein does not identify any such agreement. The University therefore had no more power over this manuscript than it did over the title to Belsheim's car or Weinstein's family heirlooms. The potential use of contracts does identify the essence of this dispute, however. It is really a contract dispute between Belsheim and Weinstein about their contributions to the article. Authors may make contracts as they please about their endeavors. These derive their force from private agreement, and disputes about them arise under state law rather than copyright law.

The courts of Illinois are open to Weinstein if he claims that the state "deprived" him of any rights established by contract with Belsheim. Contractual rights are a kind of property. * * *

III

If war is the extension of diplomacy by other means, this suit—like other litigation a form of warfare—is the extension of academic politics by other means. Weinstein and Belsheim were unable to compromise, and Weinstein has dragged his fellow scholars and the University into the contest. His willingness, even eagerness, to sue his colleagues may be explained by the fact that the University has fired him.

     * * *

Weinstein is litigating a defunct claim. He hasn't a chance; he never did; but he has put the University to some expense. This is frivolous litigation. * * * The defendants are entitled to attorneys' fees for the time necessary to reply to Weinstein's attack in this court on his discharge. They have 15 days to file an appropriate statement with the clerk of this court.

AFFIRMED.

CUDAHY, CIRCUIT JUDGE, concurring in part and dissenting in part.

I agree that Weinstein must lose in all branches of his case, although I believe that the majority inaccurately diminishes Weinstein's complaint by saying that it involves only the order of authors' names. Weinstein also alleges that the procedure employed by the university to evaluate him for a tenured position denied him due process, that the publication of his article in a revised form denied him his property interest in the writing without due process and that the university violated his first amendment rights. Although Weinstein does not win on any of these claims, his suit is not as meritless as the majority's brief description of the dispute implies.

* * *

SHAUL v. CHERRY VALLEY–SPRINGFIELD CENT. SCH. DIST.

218 F.Supp.2d 266 (N.D.N.Y. 2002).

HURD, DISTRICT JUDGE.

I. *INTRODUCTION*

On May 8, 2000, plaintiff William R. Shaul ("Shaul" or "plaintiff") commenced the instant action, pursuant to 42 U.S.C. § 1983 alleging that the defendants violated his Fourth Amendment rights. * * *

II. *FACTS*

Shaul was and is a tenured teacher at the School District, since 1969. In a 1990 administrative hearing, he was found guilty of having an inappropriate relationship with a female student. In November of 1998, as a result of an investigation performed by the School District into alleged improprieties toward another young female student, plaintiff was suspended with pay on January 15, 1999 to March 10, 2000, and ordered to remain off school property.

* * *

Plaintiff * * * claims that Principals Strange and Culbert conducted an unconstitutional search of his assigned room, and during this search unconstitutionally seized property belonging to him in violation of his Fourth Amendment rights. * * *

As to the plaintiff's illegal search claim, the defendants assert that Shaul did not have an expectation of privacy in anything within his assigned classroom and accordingly there was no illegal search. With respect to the illegal seizure claim, the defendants contend that plaintiff abandoned his property, and in the alternative, the School District owned the educational materials found in plaintiff's former classroom under the work for hire doctrine in copyright law.

* * *

2. *The Illegal Seizure Claim*

* * *

The defendants' second argument claims that the tests, quizzes, and other educational material found in plaintiff's former classroom belong to the School District under the work for hire doctrine found in the Copyright Act of 1976. Copyright ownership usually "vests initially in the author or authors of the work." However, "work made for hire" is defined as "a work prepared by an employee within the scope of his or her employment."[2] "In the case of work made for hire, the employer ... is considered the author ... and, unless the parties have expressly agreed otherwise in a written instrument signed by them, owns all the rights comprised in the copyright."

In determining whether copyrighted work is work made for hire, the hired party that created the work has to be an employee under the common law of agency. The Supreme Court has identified thirteen factors to consider in determining if one is an employee.[3] It is well established that tenured public teachers are employees who have a constitutionally protected property interest in their employment. Accordingly, the work made for hire doctrine applies in this case to Shaul's tests, quizzes, and other educational materials produced in furtherance of his employment duties as a public teacher.

Plaintiff's illegal seizure claim fails. A seizure of property "occurs when 'there is some meaningful interference with an individual's possessory interests in that property.'" Shaul does not have a possessory

---

2. There is a second definition under "work made for hire" stating that the author retains ownership when,

a work [is] specially ordered or commissioned for use as a contribution to a collective work, as a part of a motion picture or other audiovisual work, as a translation, as a supplementary work, as a compilation, as an instructional text, as a test, as answer material for a test, or as an atlas, if the parties expressly agree in a written instrument signed by them that the work shall be considered a work made for hire.

17 U.S.C.A. § 101 (West Supp. 2002). This second definition is not applicable to this case because there has been no express written agreement between the parties designating plaintiff's work product as work made for hire and plaintiff's work was not specially ordered or commissioned.

3. The factors are,

the hiring party's right to control the manner and means by which the product is accomplished ... the skill required; the source of the instrumentalities and tools; the location of the work; the duration of the relationship between the parties; whether the hiring party has the right to assign additional projects to the hired party; the extent of the hired party's discretion over when and how long to work; the method of payment; the hired party's role in hiring and paying assistants; whether the work is part of the regular business of the hiring party; whether the hiring party is in business; the provision of employee benefits; and the tax treatment of the hired party.

interest in the educational materials he used to teach his students, which makes up the bulk of his illegal seizure complaint.

* * *

Accordingly, the defendants are entitled to summary judgment as to plaintiff's first claim, because no reasonable jury could return a verdict for the plaintiff.

* * *

IV. *CONCLUSION*

There is no genuine issue for trial on the issue of an illegal search and seizure of the contents in plaintiff's former classroom. Thus, no award for punitive damages can be granted. Shaul's cause of action against the municipality fails to state a claim.

Note

1. In *Foraste v. Brown University,* 290 F.Supp.2d 234 (D. R.I. 2003), the Court noted—in finding against the plaintiff (a former photographer for the university)—that:

> the traditional "faculty exception" to the work made for hire doctrine, "whereby academic writing [is] presumed not to be work made for hire," is inapposite here. That exception is meant to protect the "scholarly articles and other intellectual property" created by university professors while in the employ of an academic institution. *Weinstein v. University of Illinois,* 811 F.2d 1091, 1094 (7th Cir.1987). Various equitable considerations often mandate that a scholar retain the copyrights in his work, notwithstanding the work made for hire doctrine. *See, e.g., id.* at 1094–95 (for example, the requirement that a scholar "publish or perish"). These equitable policy concepts do not apply here because Foraste was not working under an implicit or explicit "publish or perish" directive, and because he was usually directed by Brown officials to photograph specific scenes.

C. THE PARAMETERS OF THE FAIR USE DOCTRINE

The language of the fair use doctrine can be found in Section 107 of the U.S. Copyright Act. The statute begins with an introduction, which establishes the scope of the doctrine and has set the tone for its application by courts of law. Indeed, many judges have quoted from this introduction when faced with difficult questions of interpretation in this area:

> the fair use of a copyrighted work . . . for purposes such as criticism, comment, news reporting, teaching (including multiple copies for classroom use), scholarship, or research, is not an infringement of copyright.

While the use of copyrighted materials without permission for these specified purposes is not automatically a "fair use," it is clear from numerous subsequent court decisions as well as from the discussions in Congress that copying for purposes of criticism, comment, news reporting, teaching, scholarship, or research has achieved favored status under the law.

No matter what the use, however, the four "statutory factors" described in Section 107 must be considered when an alleged copyright infringer raises the fair use defense:

In determining whether the use made of a work in any particular case is a fair use the factors to be considered shall include—

(1) the purpose and character of the use, including whether such use is of a commercial nature or is for nonprofit educational purposes;

(2) the nature of the copyrighted work;

(3) the amount and substantiality of the portion used in relation to the copyrighted work as a whole; and

(4) the effect of the use upon the potential market for or value of the copyrighted work.

No one formula exists for weighing the four factors. Thus it may be the case that only one of the factors may be decided in favor of a defendant, but that this one factor—under the circumstances—may be sufficient to decide the case ... even if the other three factors tilt the other way.

In addition, it must be noted that a court's analysis is not limited to the four statutory factors, but can also include additional factors relevant to the particular case.

Fair use disputes engender great emotion. Copyright owners, for example, chafe at the possibility that their work can be freely copied, at times, without permission. In the education community, professors may become very upset when persons in charge of copying in their department tell them that their copy requests cannot be fulfilled because of written or unwritten policy guidelines. And K–12 teachers can become incredulous when they are told that they may not show an educational video that they themselves may have recorded at home.

Online issues have brought the debate over the parameters of fair use to the forefront. Copyright disputes are consistently viewed as reflecting the most unique aspects of cyberspace ... including speed, scale, and the ability to make perfect digital copies. The PC is a versatile copy machine, and so much of what the typical online user does from day to day constitutes copying under traditional legal doctrine. A new reality has thus emerged that simply did not exist before. Although there were copyright enforcement problems in the offline world before the 1990s, and although many parallels to the current situation can be discerned in some of the issues raised by the introduction of xerox machines, audiotaping, and videotaping, the speed, scale, and perfect quality of the digital reproduction has generated a set of circumstances that can truly be described as unique. Further complicating the debate is the extent to which some form of reproduction, distribution, or modification of copyrighted material actually occurs online from day-to-day.

The dramatic power and easy availability of digital technology, combined with the libertarian online culture of the early and mid 1990s that encouraged the widespread sharing of information, led to intensive efforts by content owners to strengthen copyright laws at the federal level. Three major statutes were passed by Congress and signed into law as a result of these efforts: the "No Electronic Theft" (NET) Act, the Digital Millennium Copyright Act (DMCA), and the Sonny Bono Copyright Term Extension Act. Many who opposed these statutes argued that the balance of interests contemplated by the U.S. Constitution had been disrupted by the changes. But perhaps the most vehement criticism was reserved for the drafters of the DMCA, which arguably represented a significant departure from federal copyright law in that it foreclosed the possibility of a fair use defense for a violation of its terms. Indeed, commentators and activists continue to raise questions regarding the future of the fair use doctrine, focusing in particular on education.

The materials that follow begin with a dispute between two public school teachers over the copying of material from a cake-decorating manual, continue with two decisions addressing fair use issues in standardized testing, and conclude with two high profile cases involving the duplication of material for course readers. Consider the opinions in these diverse cases. What consistent principles can be discerned that would be applicable to future education-related disputes in this context?

MARCUS v. ROWLEY

695 F.2d 1171 (9th Cir. 1983).

PFAELZER, DISTRICT JUDGE:

This is an appeal from a dismissal on the merits of a suit for copyright infringement brought by a public school teacher who is the owner of a registered copyright to a booklet on cake decorating. The defendant, also a public school teacher, incorporated a substantial portion of the copyrighted work into a booklet which she prepared for use in her classes. * * * The district court * * * dismissed the action on the merits on the ground that defendant's copying of plaintiff's material constituted fair use. We reverse.

I. FACTUAL BACKGROUND

From September 1972 to June 1974, plaintiff, Eloise Toby Marcus was employed by the defendant, San Diego Unified School District ("District") as a teacher of home economics. Plaintiff resigned from the District's employ in 1974 and taught adult education classes intermittently from 1975 to 1980. Shortly after leaving her teaching position with the District, she wrote a booklet entitled "Cake Decorating Made Easy". Plaintiff's booklet consisted of thirty-five pages of which twenty-nine were her original creation. The remaining six pages consisted of material incorporated with the permission of the authors of the materials for which the authors were given appropriate credit.

Plaintiff properly registered the copyright for "Cake Decorating Made Easy" with the Register of Copyrights, and one hundred and twenty-five copies of the booklet were published in the spring of 1975. All of the copies of plaintiff's booklet contained a designation of copyright as evidenced by an encircled "c" followed by "1975 Eloise Marcus." This designation appeared on the table of contents page, the first page, and the page following the cover-title sheet.

Plaintiff sold all but six of the copies of her booklet for $2.00 each to the students in the adult education cake decorating classes which she taught. Plaintiff's profit was $1.00 on the sale of each booklet. Copies of plaintiff's booklet were never distributed to or sold by a bookstore or other outlet. Plaintiff never authorized anyone to copy or reproduce her booklet or any part of it.

Defendant, Shirley Rowley ("Rowley"), teaches food service career classes in the District. In the spring of 1975, she enrolled in one of plaintiff's cake decorating classes and purchased a copy of plaintiff's book. During the following summer, Rowley prepared a booklet entitled "Cake Decorating Learning Activity Package" ("LAP") for use in her food service career classes. The LAP consisted of twenty-four pages and was designed to be used by students who wished to study an optional section of her course devoted to cake decorating. Defendant had fifteen copies of the LAP made and put them in a file so that they would be available to her students. She used the LAP during the 1975, 1976 and 1977 school years. The trial court found that sixty of Rowley's two hundred twenty-five students elected to study cake decorating. The trial court further found that neither Rowley nor the District derived any profit from the LAP.

Rowley admits copying eleven of the twenty-four pages in her LAP from plaintiff's booklet. The eleven pages copied consisted of the supply list, icing recipes, three sheets dealing with color flow and mixing colors, four pages showing how to make and use a decorating bag, and two pages explaining how to make flowers and sugar molds. * * * Twenty pages of plaintiff's booklet were not included in Rowley's LAP. Rowley did not give plaintiff credit for the eleven pages she copied, nor did she acknowledge plaintiff as the owner of a copyright with respect to those pages.

Plaintiff learned of Rowley's LAP in the summer of 1977 when a student in plaintiff's adult education class refused to purchase plaintiff's book. The student's son had obtained a copy of the LAP from Rowley's class. After examining Rowley's booklet, the student accused plaintiff of plagiarizing Rowley's work. Following these events, plaintiff made a claim of infringement against Rowley and the District. Both denied infringement and the plaintiff filed suit.

* * * The trial court * * * dismissed the case on the merits. The ground for dismissal was that the defendant's copying of the plaintiff's material for nonprofit educational purposes constituted fair use.

II. THE APPLICABLE COPYRIGHT ACT

* * * [T]he outcome of this case * * * turns entirely on the application of the doctrine of fair use[,] * * * a judicially articulated concept until Congress recognized its importance and incorporated it into section 107 of the revised Copyright Act. The legislative history states that "section 107 is a restatement of this judicially developed doctrine—it neither enlarges nor changes it in any way." Section 107 codifies the factors developed under the prior case law.

III. THE DOCTRINE OF FAIR USE

Fair use is most often defined as the "privilege in others than the owner of a copyright to use the copyrighted material in a reasonable manner without his consent, notwithstanding the monopoly granted to the owner...." This doctrine was judicially created to "avoid rigid application" of the copyright laws when that application would defeat the law's original purpose which was the fostering of creativity. Because the doctrine was developed with a view to the introduction of flexibility and equity into the copyright laws, it has evolved in such a manner as to elude precise definition. It is clear, however, that "assuming the applicable criteria are met, fair use can extend to the reproduction of copyrighted material for purposes of classroom teaching." * * *

A. *The Purpose and Character of the Use*

The first factor to be considered in determining the applicability of the doctrine of fair use is the purpose and character of the use, and specifically whether the use is of a commercial nature or is for a nonprofit educational purpose. It is uncontroverted that Rowley's use of the LAP was for a nonprofit educational purpose and that the LAP was distributed to students at no charge. These facts necessarily weigh in Rowley's favor. Nevertheless, a finding of a nonprofit educational purpose does not automatically compel a finding of fair use.

This court has often articulated the principle that a finding that the alleged infringers copied the material to use it for the same intrinsic purpose for which the copyright owner intended it to be used is strong indicia of no fair use.

In this case, both plaintiff's and defendant's booklets were prepared for the purpose of teaching cake decorating, a fact which weighs against a finding of fair use.[6]

---

6. Of course, this finding is not decisive on the issue of fair use. The fact that both works were used for the same intrinsic purpose carries less weight in a case such as this, because plainly the doctrine of fair use permits some copying of educational materials for classroom use. The critical issues here are the nature and the extent of defendant's copying.

Because fair use presupposes that the defendant has acted fairly and in good faith, the propriety of the defendant's conduct should also be weighed in analyzing the purpose and character of the use.

Here, there was no attempt by defendant to secure plaintiff's permission to copy the contents of her booklet or to credit plaintiff for the use of her material even though Rowley's copying was for the most part verbatim.[8] Rowley's conduct in this respect weighs against a finding of fair use.

B. *The Nature of the Copyrighted Work*

The second factor to be weighed is the nature of the copyrighted work. * * * [T]his court stated that analysis of this factor requires consideration of whether the work is "informational" or "creative." The court stated that "the scope of fair use is greater when informational type works, as opposed to more creative products, are involved." Here, plaintiff's booklet involved both informational and creative aspects. Some pages in her booklet undoubtedly contained information available in other cake decorating books or in recipe books. Other parts of her booklet contained creative hints she derived from her own experiences or ideas; certainly the manner in which plaintiff assembled her book represented a creative expression. Thus, on balance, it does not appear that analysis of this factor is of any real assistance in reaching a conclusion as to applicability of fair use.

C. *The Amount and Substantiality of the Portion Used*

The third factor to be considered is the amount and substantiality of the portion used in relation to the copyrighted work as a whole. Any conclusion with respect to this factor requires analysis of both the quantity and quality of the alleged infringement.

With respect to this factor, this court has long maintained the view that wholesale copying of copyrighted material precludes application of the fair use doctrine. Other courts are in accord with this principle, and two courts have specifically addressed the issue in relation to copying for educational purposes.

Wihtol v. Crow involved alleged infringement by the defendant, a school teacher and church choir director, of a hymn entitled "My God and I". The defendant Crow incorporated plaintiff's original piano and solo voice composition into an arrangement for his choirs. He made forty-eight copies of his arrangement and had the piece performed on two occasions: once by the high school choir at the school chapel, and once in church on Sunday. The music was identified as "arranged Nelson E. Crow", but no reference was made to plaintiff as the original composer. The Eighth Circuit affirmed the trial court's finding that Crow had infringed plaintiff's copyright and in addressing the issue of whether Crow's copying constituted fair use, the court stated that

---

8. Attribution is, of course, but one factor. Moreover, acknowledgment of a source does not excuse infringement when the other factors listed in section 107 are present.

"whatever may be the breadth of the doctrine of 'fair use', it is not conceivable to us that the copying of all, or substantially all, of a copyrighted song can be held to be a 'fair use' merely because the infringer had no intent to infringe."

The court in *Encyclopaedia Britannica Educational Corp. v. Crooks* also considered the issue of fair use in the educational context. In that case, three corporations which produced educational motion picture films sued the Board of Cooperative Educational Services of Erie County ("BOCES") for videotaping several of plaintiffs' copyrighted films without permission. BOCES distributed the copied films to schools for delayed student viewing. Defendants' fair use defense was rejected on the ground that although defendants were involved in non-commercial copying to promote science and education, the taping of entire copyrighted films was too excessive for the fair use defense to apply.[9]

In this case, almost 50% of defendant's LAP was a verbatim copy of plaintiff's booklet and that 50% contained virtually all of the substance of defendant's book. Defendant copied the explanations of how to make the decorating bag, how to mix colors, and how to make various decorations as well as the icing recipes. In fact, the only substantive pages of plaintiff's booklet which defendant did not put into her booklet were hints on how to ice a cake and an explanation of how to make leaves. Defendant argues that it was fair to copy plaintiff's booklet because the booklet contained only facts which were in the public domain. Even if it were true that plaintiff's book contained only facts, this argument fails because defendant engaged in virtually verbatim copying. Defendant's LAP could have been a photocopy of plaintiff's booklet but for the fact that defendant retyped plaintiff's material. This case presents a clear example of both substantial quantitative and qualitative copying.

D.   *The Effect of the Use Upon the Potential Market for or Value of the Copyrighted Work*

The final factor to be considered with respect to the fair use defense is the effect which the allegedly infringing use had on the potential market for or value of the copyrighted work. * * * Here, despite the fact that at least one of plaintiff's students refused to purchase her booklet as a result of defendant's copying, the trial court found that it was unable to conclude that the defendant's copying had any effect on the market for the plaintiff's booklet. Even assuming that the trial court's finding was not erroneous, and that that finding must be accepted and weighed in Rowley's favor, it does not alter our conclusion. The mere absence of measurable pecuniary damage does not require a finding of fair use. Fair use is to be determined by a consideration of all of the evidence in the case. Thus, despite the trial court's finding, we conclude that the factors

---

9. *Contra, Williams & Wilkins Co. v. United States*, 487 F.2d 1345, 1352–54 (Ct. Cl. 1973), aff'd, 420 U.S. 376, 95 S. Ct. 1344 (1975) (the existence of verbatim copying was not dispositive when the conduct encouraged scientific progress and did not cause plaintiff substantial monetary harm).

analyzed weigh decisively in favor of the conclusion of no fair use. This conclusion is [also] in harmony with the Congressional guidelines[.]

* * *

We conclude that the fair use doctrine does not apply to these facts[.] * * * Rowley's LAP work, which was used for the same purpose as plaintiff's booklet, was quantitatively and qualitatively a substantial copy of plaintiff's booklet with no credit given to plaintiff. Under these circumstances, neither the fact that the defendant used the plaintiff's booklet for nonprofit educational purposes nor the fact that plaintiff suffered no pecuniary damage as a result of Rowley's copying supports a finding of fair use.

The order of the district court is reversed, summary judgment is entered for the plaintiff, and the case is remanded for a determination of damages pursuant to the provisions of the Copyright Act.

PROBLEM 44: Cadillac University

After some deliberation, the President of Cadillac University (CU)—a small, private, liberal arts college in the fictional state of Eldorado—decides to create a new, updated, and glitzy high-tech web site to replace the school's old plain vanilla Internet presence. There are many motivating factors behind this decision, but the three main reasons are as follows: (1) to provide additional resources for its students; (2) to attract additional corporate funding; and (3) because every other college and university seems to be doing the same thing. A Web site committee is set up, chaired by Maria Orneles, an adjunct professor and a local librarian. Maria is particularly interested in putting together a library of resources for the Cadillac students, and she becomes actively involved in this portion of the project.

In the process of putting together the online library, the following events transpire:

A. Maria wishes to post several recent newspaper and magazine articles about Cadillac University. She obtains electronic copies of these from the Fleetwood Times Web site. However, because she is told by a member of the committee that she does not need permission to post these on CU's site, she does not contact any of these publications.

B. Coming across an elaborate spread on the history of automobiles on the General Motors Web site, Maria believes that this would be perfect for the CU students. At first she thinks it would be appropriate to simply set up a link to the GM site, but then she realizes that this particular display would not stay on the Internet forever. She then copies the entire article along with all the accompanying pictures and prepares to post the entire spread on CU's Web site. Since she believes she is doing this for educational purposes only, she does not seek permission.

C. One of Maria's favorite books is *Cadillac University: A Memoir* by Charles Osgood III, a famous graduate of CU. Believing this would be a perfect book to place on the site, she has the entire volume scanned, and she directs her administrative assistant to contact Osgood and obtain permission to post the book on the new CU site. However, the administrative assistant is unsuccessful in tracking down either Osgood or any members of his family. As the time grows closer to the day the new site will be launched, Maria decides to post three chapters (95 pages) of the five-chapter book.

Soon after the new CU site is posted on the Internet, both The Fleetwood Times and GM file copyright infringement lawsuits against the university. And Dr. Osgood—who had been out of the country for some time but returned soon after the Web site was posted—also chooses to file a lawsuit. What legal and policy arguments would CU set forth under the Federal Copyright Act generally? Under the Fair Use Doctrine of Section 107? What result?

PROBLEM 45: ETS v. Wong

Betty Wong, a student activist at Golden Valley High and op-ed editor of her student newspaper, is so offended by a new standardized testing program which requires all 10th graders to take a 10th grade version of the SAT (the TSAT) that she decides to organize a boycott of the test. In a scathing op-ed piece, she denounces the governor and the state legislature, and calls for a student boycott. She urges all the tenth graders at Golden Valley High to either stay home on the day the test is administered or to come in and refuse to take it. As a back-up position, for students who fear retribution from the administration or faculty, she calls on the tenth graders to fill in answer D for each question.

Betty is suspended for ten days to make sure that she is not anywhere near the classrooms on the day of the test, and she is also removed from her position as editor. But she decides to continue her activism online, and creates a Web site via her off-campus Comcast account that is devoted to criticism of ETS, standardized testing, and the TSAT. Taking advantage of the fact that her older brother—who recently took the regular SAT—has a remarkable memory, she asks him to type up the exact wording of 15 actual questions from the test and then posts them on the site ... along with a caption that derides the usefulness of such questions in a 21st century educational setting.

ETS files a lawsuit against Betty, and is prepared to argue that her posting of test questions without permission constitutes copyright infringement and is not fair use. What arguments will be set forth? What result? Discuss.

EDUCATIONAL TESTING SERVS. v. KATZMAN

739 F.2d 533 (3d Cir. 1986).

SLOVITER, CIRCUIT JUDGE:

Educational Testing Service (ETS), a non-profit educational organization that prepares and administers numerous standardized tests, sought and was granted a preliminary injunction that enjoined defendants Princeton Review and John Katzman, its sole shareholder and president (collectively referred to as Review unless otherwise noted), from a wide range of activities involving ETS' tests and information therefrom. * * *

I. INTRODUCTORY FACTS

ETS develops and administers testing programs, among them the Scholastic Aptitude Test (SAT) and Achievement Tests in specific subjects, which are both multiple-choice tests given to high school students for college admission purposes. ETS regards the tests as secret until they have been released by it and attempts to maintain strict secrecy with respect to these tests. It registers them for copyright under "secure test" registration. It makes the tests that it has "retired" available to the public.

Review is a company which charges a fee for preparing students to take the SAT and Achievement Tests offered by ETS. * * *

The present dispute has its genesis in events occurring a number of years ago. In 1982, ETS learned that Review had given to its enrollees copies of a "Math Level I" and of an "English Composition" Achievement test that ETS subsequently administered on November 6, 1982. Although this test was stolen from ETS, ETS does not allege that Katzman or his agents were responsible for the theft. ETS cancelled the scores of those Review students who had been given access to the stolen test.

Following these events, ETS, Katzman, and an associate not involved in this litigation entered into a written agreement in 1983 under which Katzman and his associate promised to return all copies of the purloined tests, to refrain from copying or distributing any ETS copyrighted or copyrightable materials or registering for or attending any test administered by ETS unless it was for bona fide purposes, and to notify ETS if any unlawfully obtained ETS tests came into their possession and provide ETS with information as to their source.

In its complaint in this action, ETS claims that in May 1985 (1) Katzman distributed to Review enrollees a "facsimile" "Math Level I" practice test which was "copied or paraphrased" from the same stolen test book that Review had given its students prior to the November 1982 test, and that Katzman had promised to return, which forced ETS to provide another examination for a June 1985 exam and to retire the exam in question from use; (2) Review handed out a "facsimile" English Composition Achievement Test that contained 53 questions "obviously ... adapted directly" from the test booklet Katzman supposedly had returned earlier, forcing ETS to make a last minute substitution for an English Composition Test scheduled to be administered on June 2, 1985; and (3) Katzman and Review distributed "facsimile" SATs that contained "verbatim or nearly verbatim" SAT questions, forcing ETS to retire numerous SAT questions. ETS suggests that Review obtained these questions by having its employees register and take the SAT in violation of the 1983 agreement. ETS contends in its brief that defendants' actions have compelled it to retire from use in "secure" testing at least 289 questions, consisting of 51 Math Achievement questions, 90 English Composition Achievement Test questions, and 148 SAT questions.

ETS contends that defendants' actions constituted infringement of ETS' copyrights, breach of the 1983 agreement, and interference with "ETS' common law right to preserve the integrity of its testing program and the confidentiality of its secure tests and secure test questions." * * *

[The Court then discussed various procedural issues, as well as other copyright issues, finding that they cut in favor of ETS.]

* * *

We are also unpersuaded by defendants' argument that the teaching instruction offered by Review makes "fair use" of ETS' questions. The Copyright Act protects "fair use ... for purposes such as criticism, comment, news reporting, teaching (including multiple copies for classroom use), scholarship, or research...." * * *

In *Association of American Medical Colleges v. Mikaelian*, Judge Broderick rejected the argument that the defendant, who operated a course very much like Review's, fit into the category of teaching for purposes of the fair use defense. The court reasoned:

> To be sure, Mikaelian and Multiprep give test preparation courses, and provide instruction in test preparation as part of these courses. However, Multiprep students do not receive a degree, do not become qualified or certified in anything after taking the course, and may not use the course as a prerequisite for further education and training in any educational or vocational endeavor.

Even assuming that Review's courses qualify as teaching within the meaning of the statute, after consideration of the statutory factors, we cannot find that its showing on the issue of fair use in this record is so strong as to require us to overturn the trial court's finding of likelihood of success on the merits. The first factor of "the purpose and character of the use" is intended to favor noncommercial and productive uses. Review's use is highly commercial.

With respect to the second factor, "the nature of the copyrighted work", the unique nature of secure tests means that any use is destructive of ETS's rights. As stated in *Mikaelian*, "The very purpose of copyrighting the ... questions is to prevent their use as teaching aids, since such use would confer an unfair advantage to those taking a test preparation course."

In its interpretation of the third factor, "the amount and substantiality of the portion used," the Supreme Court in *Harper & Row* upheld the district court's finding that copying of 300 words from a book-length manuscript was substantial because defendant copied "the heart" of the book. While the copying shown on the record to date in this case cannot be so characterized, neither can we regard it as insubstantial.

Finally, the fourth factor, "effect * * * upon the potential market," seems dispositively in favor of ETS. Although Review asserts that it is not in competition with ETS, use of ETS' materials by Review renders the materials worthless to ETS.

Thus * * * we believe that the record before us is sufficient for the purpose of concluding that there was some copying by defendants of ETS' copyrighted material, and that defendants have not shown that such copying was permissible under the doctrines they invoke. We will not disturb the district court's finding that there was a likelihood of success on the merits in the copyright infringement claim.

    * * *

CHICAGO BD. OF EDUC. v. SUBSTANCE, INC.

354 F.3d 624 (7th Cir. 2003).

Posner, Circuit Judge:

In 1999 the Chicago Board of Education brought this suit for copyright infringement against a Chicago public school teacher named Schmidt and a corporation that owns a local newspaper called Substance, aimed at such teachers, which Schmidt edits.

    * * *

The following facts are either undisputed or indisputable. At some considerable expense (more than $1 million, according to Schmidt, though the actual figure is not in the record), the school board created and copyrighted a series of standardized tests that it called the "Chicago Academic Standards Exams" (CASE). These were, in copyright lingo, "secure tests." "A secure test is a nonmarketed test administered under supervision at specified centers on specific dates, all copies of which are accounted for and either destroyed or returned to restricted locked storage following each administration. For these purposes a test is not marketed if copies are not sold but it is distributed and used in such a manner that ownership and control of copies remain with the test sponsor or publisher." To maintain secrecy, the Library of Congress does not retain a copy of such a test.

The first step in making the CASE tests was to create a pool of questions—the record does not indicate how many—that would be drawn on to create the individual exams, each consisting of between three and 30 questions. The teachers who administered the exams were instructed not to make copies of them and to collect the test papers at the end of each exam so that the tests could be reused. Reuse of questions in standardized testing is not a sign of laziness but a way of validating a test, since if performance on the same questions is inconsistent from year to year this may indicate that the questions are not well designed and are therefore eliciting random answers. Such validation is of particular importance for a new battery of standardized tests, such as CASE, the subject of a three-year pilot program. And publication of standardized tests would not only prevent validation by precluding reuse of any of the questions in them, but also require the school board to create many new questions, at additional expense; and they might not be as good as the original questions, in which event there would be diminished quality as well as added cost. Hence the copyright category "secure tests."

It may seem paradoxical to allow copyright to be obtained in secret documents, but it is not. For one thing, the tests are not secret from the students taking them. For another, federal copyright is now available for unpublished works that the author intends never to see the light of day. Most important, tests are expressive works that are not costlessly created, and the costs are greater and so the incentive to create the tests diminished if the tests cannot be reused. There is no analytical difference between destroying the market for a copyrighted work by producing and selling cheap copies and destroying the subsequent years' market for a standardized test by blowing its cover.

In the newspaper that he edits, Schmidt published six of the tests given in January 1999. He did this because he thought them bad tests and that he could best demonstrate this by publishing them in full. His answer to the school board's complaint asserted that the unauthorized copying and publication of the tests were a fair use and therefore not a copyright infringement. The district court dismissed the fair use defense * * *.

Each side of this case has a one-sided view of the law. The school board contends that the case is governed by *Harper & Row Publishers, Inc. v. Nation Enterprises*, a case in which a magazine published unauthorized excerpts from Gerald Ford's copyrighted memoirs before the memoirs were published, thus jumping the gun and by doing so reducing the value of the copyright. The school board points out that Schmidt impaired the value of the exams by publishing them prematurely. (Presumably the school board will not complain if they are published * * * a century from now.) But the board overlooks the fact that the *Nation* was not publishing the excerpts from Ford's memoirs in order to be able to criticize Ford, or anyone or anything else, and the further fact that Schmidt was not trying to steal the school board's market, because unlike Harper & Row the school board did not intend ever to publish the copyrighted work that the alleged infringer published first. The second point has little force, as we'll see; but the first is important. As Schmidt points out, one office of the fair use defense is to facilitate criticism of copyrighted works by enabling the critic to quote enough of the criticized work to make his criticisms intelligible. Copyright should not be a means by which criticism is stifled with the backing of the courts. And since doubts that fair use could ever be a defense to infringement of a copyright on an unpublished work have now been stilled, the fact that the CASE tests were quasi-secret does not exclude the possibility of a fair use defense.

But Schmidt overreads our decision in *Ty, Inc. v. Publications Int'l Ltd.* to hold that a purpose of criticizing creates a privilege of unlimited copying regardless of the harm to the copyright owner's legitimate interests. Ty was trying to enjoin the publication of Beanie Babies collectors' guides that contained criticisms of some of the Beanie Babies, with accompanying photographs that constituted derivative works of the soft-sculpture Beanie Babies and hence prima facie infringements of Ty's copyrights. There was no danger that if Ty failed to enjoin the publication of the collectors' guides the value of its copyrights would be impaired, because collectors' guides are not substitutes for the Beanie Babies themselves. More precisely, the only harm that could come to Ty from the unauthorized publication of the guides would be caused by the criticisms of particular Beanie Babies, whereas a harm to the school board from Schmidt's copying and publication that is independent of any criticisms is the cost of creating substitutes for the questions that Schmidt published and of extending the period of the pilot program because his publishing the six tests prevented the board from asking any of the questions in those tests in subsequent years.

The board thus is correct that Schmidt did it harm going beyond the force of his criticisms. Yet he was entitled to criticize the tests and to do that effectively he had to be able to quote from them, just as a parodist has to be able to quote, sometimes very extensively, from the parodied work in order to make the criticism of it that is implicit in parodying it comprehensible. Indeed, there is no per se rule against copying in the name of fair use an entire copyrighted work if necessary. This would be obvious if the school board had copyrighted each question separately, as it might well have done, since it wants to reuse questions without necessarily reusing an entire test.

So where to draw the line? The question cannot be answered precisely. The fair use defense defies codification. As we said in *Ty*, the four factors that Congress listed when it wrote a fair use defense (a judicial creation) into the *Copyright Act in 1976* are not exhaustive and do not constitute an algorithm that enables decisions to be ground out mechanically. The general standard, however, is clear enough: the fair use copier must copy no more than is reasonably necessary (not strictly necessary—room must be allowed for judgment, and judges must not police criticism with a heavy hand) to enable him to pursue an aim that the law recognizes as proper, in this case the aim of criticizing the copyrighted work effectively.

The burden of proof is on the copier because fair use is an affirmative defense and Schmidt has presented no evidence sufficient to withstand summary judgment. He insists that he had to copy six tests out of the 22 to 44 tests given in January 1999 (it is unclear from the record which number is correct, so we will give Schmidt the benefit of the doubt and assume that it is the higher number) in order to drive his criticisms home. * * * Granted that he had to quote some of the test questions in order to substantiate his criticisms, why entire tests? Does he think all the questions in all six tests bad? * * * What purpose is served by quoting the good questions?

* * *

[Schmidt] argues that the school board does not intend to sell the tests, and so Schmidt isn't eating into their market by publishing the tests. This is true, but irrelevant, because he is destroying the value of the tests and the fact that it's not a *market* value has no significance once the right to copyright unpublished works is conceded, as it must be. [Schmidt] argues that expert testimony would establish that there is no educational value in publishing the exact same exam year after year. No one supposes there is; the argument rather is that *some* questions must be carried over to future years in order to validate the exam. [Schmidt] argues that if [he] quoted only a few of the questions, the school board would respond that he was cherry-picking the worst. But if the board did that without a solid grounding, it would open the door for him to quote additional questions; it would be a pro tanto waiver of confidentiality. [Schmidt]'s remaining argument is that expert witnesses can be found to testify that the CASE tests are "dramatically inadequate." No doubt. But in so arguing [Schmidt] misunderstands the fair use privilege of criticism. It is not a privilege to criticize just bad works, and there is no right to copy copyrighted works promiscuously merely upon a showing that they are bad.

There is more than a suspicion that Schmidt simply does not like standardized tests. That is his right. But he does not have the right, as he believes he does (he claims a right to copy any test that an expert will testify is no good), to destroy the tests by publishing them indiscriminately, any more than a person who dislikes Michelangelo's statue of David has a right to take a sledgehammer to it. From the amicus curiae briefs filed in this case, moreover, it is apparent that many other teachers share Schmidt's unfavorable opinion of standardized tests. (A cynic might say that this is because such tests can make teachers look bad if their students don't do well on them.) So if Schmidt can publish six tests, other dissenters can each publish six other tests, and in no time all 44 will be published. The board will never be able to use the same question twice, and after a few years of Schmidtian tactics there will be such difficulty in inventing new questions without restructuring the curriculum that the board will have to abandon standardized testing. Which is Schmidt's goal.

If ever a "floodgates" argument had persuasive force, therefore, it is in this case. And this suggests another fair use factor that supports the school board: the aspect of academic freedom that consists of the autonomy of educational institutions, including their authority here gravely threatened to employ standardized tests in support of their conception of their educational mission. If Schmidt wins this case, it is goodbye to standardized tests in the Chicago public school system;

Schmidt, his allies, and the federal courts will have wrested control of educational policy from the Chicago public school authorities.

* * *

BASIC BOOKS, INC. v. KINKO'S GRAPHICS CORP.

758 F.Supp. 1522 (S.D.N.Y. 1991).

MOTLEY, DISTRICT JUDGE:

Plaintiffs, all major publishing houses in New York City, brought this suit against Kinko's alleging copyright infringement pursuant to the Copyright Act of 1976. More specifically, plaintiffs allege that Kinko's infringed their copyrights when Kinko's copied excerpts from books, whose rights are held by the plaintiffs, without permission and without payment of required fees and sold the copies for a profit. Plaintiffs request relief in the form of statutory damages, injunction, declaratory judgment and attorney's fees and costs.

Kinko's admits that it copied the excerpts in suit without permission, compiled them into course "packets," and sold them to college students. It defends on four grounds. First, Kinko's claims their use of the excerpts was a "fair use," specifically provided for in § 107 of the Copyright Act. * * *

This court finds and concludes that defendant did violate the Copyright Act. * * * Kinko's has not convincingly shown that the excerpts it appropriated without seeking permission were a fair use of the works in question. This court hereby awards plaintiffs injunctive relief, as well as statutory damages in the amount of $510,000, attorneys fees and costs.

FINDINGS OF FACT

There are 12 instances of copyright infringement alleged in this case. The 12 excerpts, which vary in length from 14 to 110 pages, were copied from books previously published by the plaintiffs, compiled in five numbered packets ("anthologies") with excerpts from other books and distributed by Kinko's. Kinko's neither sought nor obtained permission to copy any of these works. * * * Below is a list of the 5 packets, by number and title, and a list of the titles of the works copied. Next to the latter title is the total number of pages copied, the approximate percentage of the entire book that was copied and whether the work was in-or out-of print.

PACKET #1: "WORK AND COMMUNITY".

This packet included 388 pages of copied work[1] taken from 25 books. This course was taught at the New School for Social Research by

---

1. Kinko's uses double-sided pages. This means that, in this instance, Kinko's used 194 pages of copy paper to reproduce 388 pages of material. In this instance, as well as most others involved, Kinko's was also able to copy 2 pages of copyrighted material per side of paper. Therefore, for example, 10 pages of copy paper could potentially infringe 40 pages of copyrighted material.

Professor Hoffman; 3 students were enrolled. This packet was sold for $24.00: $21.75 for copying and $2.25 for binding.

1. *Understanding Capitalism* 22 pp. [5%], in-print, by Samuel Bowles & Richard Edwards.

Pages 62–83 (all of chapter 4) of this 15–chapter book was copied. The book has 419 pages of text in addition to 11 pages of introductory material. It was published in 1985. The amount copied which encompasses an entire chapter of Bowles and Edwards' relatively recent book weighs against defendant.

2. *Community: A Critical Response* 23pp. [18–21%], out-of-print, by Joseph Gusfield.

Pages 1–22 (all of chapter 1) of this 4–chapter book was copied. The book is 120 pages. The soft-cover version exhibited at trial has a price of $3.95. The book was published in 1975. This book was out-of-print and is relatively old, however, the amount copied weighs heavily against defendant.

3. *Work and Community in the West* 34pp. [22–24%], out-of-print. An anthology with contributions from six authors, edited by Edward Shorter.

Pages 1–33 (chapter 1) of this 6–chapter book was copied. The book totals 146 pages. The soft-cover version exhibited at trial has a price of $2.95. It was published in 1973. This book was out-of-print and is relatively old, however, the amount copied weighs heavily against defendant.

4. *The Deindustrialization of America* 53pp. [16–20%], in-print, by Barry Bluestone & Bennett Harrison.

Pages 3–21 (chapter 1) and pages 231–64 (chapter 8) were copied from this 8–chapter book. The book is 323 pages. The book was published in 1982. The amount copied weighs against defendant.

5. *All Our Kin: Strategies for Survival in a Black Community*; 14pp. [8–11%], in-print, by Carol Stack.

This book has 175 pages in addition to 21 pages of introductory material. The pages copied were pages 32–45, one of the 8 chapters in the book. The exhibited copy of the hardcover book has a price of $7.95. It was published in 1974. The amount copied weighs against defendant.

6. *A Lesser Life* 37pp. [8–9%], in-print, by Sylvia Ann Hewlett.

Pages 11–47 of this book were copied; they include the Introduction and one additional chapter. The book has 461 pages. The exhibited hardcopy has a price of $17.95. It was published in 1986. The amount copied weighs against defendant.

[The court then went on to list the four other packets, finding that the amount copied weighed against the defendant for each part of each packet.]

Each packet has a cover page, printed with the Kinko's logo, "Kinko's Copies: Professor Publishing," the name of the course and professor, the designated packet number, and a price listing. There is a space on the price listing to designate the royalty charges included. Only one packet lists a charge for royalty fees. On the inside cover of three of the five packets is a sheet entitled "Education and Fair Use: The Federal Copyright Law." It lists the § 107 fair use factors and displays the Professor Publishing logo and course information. None of the excerpts carries a copyright creditline as required by copyright law.

It is undisputed that Kinko's markets and provides its copying services directly to university professors and students. At trial, Kinko's presented marketing brochures produced by the company which are distributed by their marketing representatives to university professors and used as the subject of follow-up visits. These brochures openly solicit from the professors lists of readings they plan to use in their courses. Kinko's then copies excerpts, some quite large, and sells them in bound form with excerpts copied from other books as well. Unaudited financial statements of Kinko's Graphics Corporation for the years 1988 and 1989 show revenue of $42 million and $54 million, respectively, and net profit of $200,000 and $3 million, respectively. Its assets totalled $12 million in 1988 and $15 million in 1989. Appropriately, plaintiffs refer to this bound packet as an "anthology." Plaintiffs derive a significant part of their income from textbook sales and permissions fees. Kinko's has conducted its Professor Publishing business at least since the mid–1980's.

DISCUSSION

I. FAIR USE.

Coined as an "equitable rule of reason," the fair use doctrine has existed for as long as the copyright law.

* * *

The codification was intended to "restate the present judicial doctrine of fair use, not to change, narrow, or enlarge it in any way." Therefore, thorough analysis of the case law is necessary.

For almost 300 years, American law has protected intellectual property rights through the copyright law. * * * Section 106 of the 1976 Copyright Act provides that "subject to Section[] 107 ... the owner of copyright under this title has the exclusive rights ... to reproduce the copyrighted work." In *Folsom v. Marsh*, Justice Story set forth the meaning of fair use to which we adhere today. "In short, we must often ... look to the nature and objects of the selections made, the quantity and value of the materials used, and the degree in which the use may prejudice the sale, or diminish the profits, or supersede the objects, of the original work."

Fair use more currently has been defined as the "privilege in others than the owner of a copyright to use the copyrighted material in a reasonable manner without his consent, notwithstanding the monopoly granted to the owner.... " The copyright law, through the fair use doctrine, has promoted the goal of encouraging creative expression and integrity by ensuring that those who produce intellectual works may benefit from them.

Courts and commentators disagree on the interpretation and application of the four factors, topics of current debate. The search for a coherent, predictable interpretation applicable to all cases remains elusive. This is so particularly because any common law interpretation proceeds on a case-by-case basis. The two Supreme Court precedents on the issue of fair use, *Sony Corp. v. Universal City Studios, Inc.* and *Harper & Row v. Nation Enterprises*, were both overturned at each level of review.

This case is distinctive in many respects from those which have come before it. It involves multiple copying. The copying was conducted by a commercial enterprise which claims an educational purpose for the materials. The copying was just that—copying—and did not "transform" the works in suit, that is, interpret them or add any value to the material copied, as would a biographer's or critic's use of a copyrighted quotation or excerpt. [T]his court has the task of evaluating the copying under fair use doctrine. * * *

A.   The 4 Factors of Fair Use.

1.   *Purpose and Character of the Use.*

Section 107 specifically provides that under this factor we consider "whether [the] use is of a commercial nature or is for *nonprofit* educational purposes." The Supreme Court has held that "commercial use of copyrighted material is presumptively an unfair exploitation of the monopoly privilege that belongs to the owner of the copyright." Additionally, the Supreme Court has found that "the distinction between 'productive' and 'unproductive' uses may be helpful in calibrating the balance [of interests]." While both are significant considerations, neither of these is determinative.

Transformative use.

It has been argued that the essence of "character and purpose" is the transformative value, that is, productive use, of the secondary work compared to the original. District Court Judge Leval has noted that, "the use ... must employ the quoted matter in a different manner or for a different purpose from the original. A quotation of copyrighted material that merely repackages or republishes the original is unlikely to pass the test." Kinko's work cannot be categorized as anything other than a mere repackaging.

Most contested instances of copyright infringement are those in which the infringer has copied small portions, quotations or excerpts of works and represents them in another form, for example, a biography, criticism, news article or other commentary. In this case, there was absolutely no literary effort made by Kinko's to expand upon or contextualize the materials copied. The excerpts in suit were merely copied, bound into a new form, and sold. The plaintiffs refer to this process as "anthologizing." The copying in suit had productive value only to the extent that it put an entire semester's resources in one bound volume for students. It required the judgment of the professors to compile it, though none of Kinko's.

Commercial use.

The use of the Kinko's packets, in the hands of the students, was no doubt educational. However, the use in the hands of Kinko's employees is commercial. Kinko's claims that its copying was educational and, therefore, qualifies as a fair use. Kinko's fails to persuade us of this distinction.

Kinko's has not disputed that it receives a profit component from the revenue it collects for its anthologies. The amount of that profit is unclear; however, we need only find that Kinko's had the intention of making profits. Its Professor Publishing promotional materials clearly indicate that Kinko's recognized and sought a segment of a profitable market, admitting that "tremendous sales and profit potential arise from this program."

Although Kinko's tries to impress this court with its purportedly altruistic motives, the facts show that Kinko's copying had "the *intended purpose* of supplanting the copyright holder's commercially valuable right." Kinko's promotional literature compares its "prompt" service to the "ineffectiveness of traditional publishing to meet the changing needs of faculty and students."

In *Pacific & Southern Co. v. Duncan*, the Eleventh Circuit denied the fair use defense to a company which videotaped and sold copyrighted portions of a television news show to the featured subject. Noting that "every commercial exchange of goods and services involves both the giving of the good or service and the taking of the purchase price," the court found character and use against the defendant since "the fact that TV News Clips focuses on the giving rather than the taking cannot hide the fact that profit is its primary motive for making the exchange." The same holds true for Kinko's.

Kinko's offers a 10% discount if professors get in their orders early, emphasizes student savings, convenience, and service—all "at no cost to your department." Kinko's shows that it is keenly aware of students' and professors' preoccupation with educational costs and provides additional services to get their business: offering campus pick-up and delivery and free copyright permission assistance. The extent of its insistence that theirs are educational concerns and not profitmaking ones boggles the mind.

Kinko's has periodically asserted that it acted at the instruction of the educational institution, that is, as the agent of the colleges and is without responsibility. Yet, Kinko's promotional materials belie this contention particularly because Kinko's takes responsibility for obtaining copyright permission while touting the expertise of its copyright permissions staff (a "service [which] is provided at no charge to all Kinko's customers.").

Kinko's is paid directly by students who come into its stores to purchase the packets. Professors do not pay a fee; in fact, Kinko's provides incentives to professors for choosing their copy center over others.

While financial gain "will not preclude [the] use from being a fair use," consideration of the commercial use is an important one.

"The crux of the profit/nonprofit distinction is not whether the sole motive of the use is monetary gain but whether the user stands to profit from exploitation of the copyrighted material without paying the customary price." This is precisely the concern here and why this factor weighs so strongly in favor of plaintiffs.

Courts' consideration of the profit factor usually arises because the alleged infringing work competes in the same market as the copyrighted work, thus making the "commerciality" more harmful to the copyright holder. In cases in which a defendant is claiming fair use for a criticism, commentary or other scholarly research, the courts are more likely to find fair use under this factor. In *New Era Publications v. Carol Publishing*, the Second Circuit found fair use under the character and use factor since the publication in suit was not an economic exploitation of the original work but a legitimate critical biography. In that case, a critic and biographer of L. Ron Hubbard and the Church of Scientology defended his use of quotes from 48 of Hubbard's works.

A potentially widespread use which was notably non-commercial has been held to be a fair use. In *Sony Corp. v. Universal City Studios*, television viewers taped plaintiffs' television programs on home video recorders, doing nothing to enhance the program—simply copying them in order to view them later. The Court decided this "time-shifting" was fair use and placed emphasis on the fact that the viewers were not selling their copies of these programs for profit.

2. *The Nature of the Copyrighted Work.*

The second factor concerns the nature of the copyrighted work. Courts generally hold that "the scope of fair use is greater with respect to factual than non-factual works." Factual works, such as biographies, reviews, criticism and commentary, are believed to have a greater public value and, therefore, uses of them may be better tolerated by the copyright law. Works containing information in the public interest may require less protection. Fictional works, on the other hand, are often based closely on the author's subjective impressions and, therefore, require more protection. These are general rules of thumb. The books infringed in suit were factual in nature. This factor weighs in favor of defendant.

3. *The Amount and Substantiality of the Portion Used.*

"There are no absolute rules as to how much of a copyrighted work may be copied and still be considered a fair use." This third factor considers not only the percentage of the original used but also the "substantiality" of that portion to the whole of the work; that is, courts must evaluate the qualitative aspects as well as the quantity of material copied. A short piece which is "the heart of" a work may not be fair use and a longer piece which is pedestrian in nature may be fair use. The balancing of the four factors must be complete, relying solely upon no one factor. The purpose of the use may be balanced against the amount and substantiality of the use. For example, "even substantial quotations might qualify as fair use in a review of a published work."

Courts have found relatively small quantitative uses to be fair use.

Additionally, "reference to a work's availability is appropriate." Therefore, longer portions copied from an out-of-print book may be fair use because the book is no longer available. (This has been thought to be true because, presumably, there is little market effect produced by the copying. However, plaintiffs in this case convincingly argue that damage to out-of-print works may in fact be greater since permissions fees may be the only income for authors and copyright owners.)

This court finds and concludes that the portions copied were critical parts of the books copied, since that is the likely reason the college professors used them in their classes. While it may be impossible to determine, as the Court did in *Harper & Row*, that the quoted material was "essentially the heart of" the copyrighted material, it may be inferred that they were important parts.

This factor, amount and substantiality of the portions appropriated, weighs against defendant. In this case, the passages copied ranged from 14 to 110 pages, representing 5.2% to 25.1% of the works. In one case Kinko's copied 110 pages of someone's work and sold it to 132 students. Even for an out-of-print book, this amount is grossly out of line with accepted fair use principles.

In almost every case, defendant copied at least an entire chapter of a plaintiff's book. This is substantial because they are obviously meant to stand alone, that is, as a complete representation of the concept explored in the chapter. This indicates that these excerpts are not material supplemental to the assigned course material but the assignment. Therefore, the excerpts, in addition to being quantitatively substantial, are qualitatively significant.

4. *The Effect of the Use on Potential Markets for or Value of the Copyrighted Work.*

The fourth factor, market effect, also fails the defendant. This factor has been held to be "undoubtedly the single most important element of fair use." "To negate fair use one need only show that if the challenged use 'should become widespread, it would adversely affect the *potential* market for the copyrighted work.' "

Kinko's confirms that it has 200 stores nationwide, servicing hundreds of colleges and universities which enroll thousands of students. The potential for widespread copyright infringement by defendant and other commercial copiers is great. In this case, Kinko's has admitted that its market for these anthologies or packets is college students. The packets were compiled as a result of orders placed by professors at Columbia University, New York University and the New School for Social Research as to what readings they needed to supply their courses. In this case, the competition for "student dollars" is easily won by Kinko's which produced 300 to 400–page packets including substantial portions of copyrighted books at a cost of $24 to the student. Packet #34 contained excerpts from 20 different books, totalled 324 pages, and cost $21.50. While it is possible that reading the packets whets the appetite of students for more information from the authors, it is more likely that purchase of the packets obviates purchase of the full texts. This court has found that plaintiffs derive a significant part of their income from textbook sales and permissions. This court further finds that Kinko's copying unfavorably impacts upon plaintiffs' sales of their books and collections of permissions fees. This impact is more powerfully felt by authors and copyright owners of the out-of-print books, for whom permissions fees constitute a significant source of income. This factor weighs heavily against defendant.

5. *Other Factors.*

In this case an important additional factor is the fact that defendant has effectively created a new nationwide business allied to the publishing industry by usurping plaintiffs' copyrights and profits. This cannot be sustained by this court as its result is complete frustration of the intent of the copyright law which has been the protection of intellectual property and, more importantly, the encouragement of creative expression. Because of the vastness and transitory nature of its business (Kinko's has 200 stores nationwide which are typically located near colleges), it has become difficult for plaintiffs to challenge defendant.

Additionally, the Classroom Guidelines express a specific prohibition of anthologies. The fact that these excerpts were compiled and sold in anthologies weighs against defendant.

Kinko's claims that "the evidence shows that course packets are of tremendous importance to teaching and learning, and are the subject of widespread and extensive use in schools throughout the country" and that "an injunction against the educational photocopying at issue would pose a serious threat to teaching and the welfare of education." This appears to be a "fair use by reason of necessity" argument. Kinko's has failed to prove this central contention which is that enjoining them from pirating plaintiffs' copyrights would halt the educational process.

Kinko's did not produce any professor to testify that he or she uses course packets and would be disabled from teaching effectively if Kinko's could not copy without paying permissions fees. Defendant did produce a witness, Dr. Bruce Johnson, who testified to the results of a survey he conducted which showed the widespread use of course packets by college professors and the reasons for this use. Notwithstanding professors' complaints of costly original materials, rapid change in course subject matter, and inadequate current offerings—which are all good reasons for desiring anthologies—defendant's witnesses did not produce evidence which would explain why they could not seek and pay for permission to create these anthologies. Dr. Johnson's survey fails to do so. This argument also fails.

B. The Classroom Guidelines.

The Classroom Guidelines, entitled the "Agreement on Guidelines for Classroom Copying in Not–For–Profit Educational Institutions," are a part of the legislative history of the Copyright Act of 1976. These Guidelines were the result of negotiation and agreement among the Ad Hoc Committee of Educational Institutions and Organizations on Copyright Law Revision, the Authors League of America, Inc., and the Association of American Publishers. One commentator confirms the Guidelines as an act of compromise which "was necessitated by the widespread availability of reprographic technology which eliminated much of the copyright owner's control over the reproduction of his work." The legislative history acknowledges "the long controversy over the related problems of fair use and the reproduction (mostly by photocopying) of copyrighted material for educational and scholarly purposes." This indicates that Congress saw the maelstrom beginning to churn and sought to clarify, through broad mandate, its intentions.

For a proper analysis, there must be initial consideration given to the issue of what comprises educational copying and whether Kinko's status as a for-profit corporation, and its profitmaking intent, renders it outside of a Guidelines review. We believe that it does.

Kinko's contends that it serves an important function in the educational process—providing prompt, cost-effective service to educational institutions. If they did not provide this service to colleges and universities, they claim, these institutions and their students would suffer educationally and financially. However, Kinko's is *in the business* of providing copying services for whomever is willing to pay for them and, as evidenced in this case, students of colleges and universities are willing to pay for them.

This commercial copying can be contrasted to library copying. In *Williams & Wilkins Co. v. United States*, the court found library copying to be a fair use. In that case, the Department of Health, Education and Welfare, through the National Institutes of Health (NIH) and the National Library of Medicine (NLM) copied articles from medical journals and disseminated them to researchers and personnel who requested them. The libraries established rules regarding page limitations, frequency and number of copies, and they did not charge a copying fee. The NLM reproduced each copy with a statement saying: "This is a single photostatic copy made by the National Library of Medicine for purposes of study or research in lieu of lending the original." Classroom and library copying are viewed more sympathetically "since they generally involve no commercial exploitation and ... [have] socially useful objectives. * * * This is not true of photocopy shops, which reproduce for profit."

This court finds and concludes that even if Kinko's copying warranted review under the Classroom Guidelines, it is excessive and in violation of the Guidelines requirements.

There is dispute as to whether the Guidelines represent a maximum or minimum of allowable copying. The Guidelines assert its intended meaning thusly: "the purpose of the following guidelines is to state the minimum and not the maximum standards of educational fair use under Section 107 of H.R. 2223." The Guidelines clearly state that notwithstanding their promulgation, fair use standards may be more or less permissive—depending upon the circumstances and based upon equitable considerations. This court finds that the copying in suit clearly deviates from the letter and spirit of the Guidelines.

Under the section "Multiple Copies for Classroom Use," the stated premise is that "multiple copies (not to exceed in any event more than one copy per pupil in a course) may be made by *or for* the teacher giving the course for classroom use or discussion...."[13] The Guidelines provide that a teacher may make multiple copies of copyrighted material if the copying meets the tests of brevity, spontaneity, and cumulative effect and so long as "each copy includes a notice of copyright." It has already been found that Kinko's failed to include copyright notices on any of the works in suit.

Brevity, in prose, is defined as "a complete article, story or essay of less than 2,500 words," or an excerpt of "not more than 1,000 words or 10% of the work, whichever is less." Defendant does not meet this requirement.

Spontaneity requires that "the inspiration and decision to use the work and the moment of its use for maximum teaching effectiveness [be] so close in time that it would be unreasonable to expect a timely reply to a request for permission." Because Kinko's copying coincided with the start of each semester and was prompted by Kinko's obtaining a list of course materials from professors, we find that the copying in suit cannot be considered spontaneous. The anthologies were created to last the full semester, or at least for several weeks, since they averaged 200 to 400 pages per course packet.

Additionally, while it is true that modern teaching methods present copyright dilemmas by requiring frequent updating of information from varied sources, the excerpts in suit were not copied from current publications. The most recent publication date among the books in suit was 1985.

13.   Expressly, the decision of this court does not consider copying performed by students, libraries, nor on-campus copyshops, whether conducted for-profit or not.

Cumulative effect proscribes any more than "nine instances of multiple copying for one course during one class term," limits the copied material to one course only, and to no more than one piece of work per author. Defendants fail this requirement. Of the five course packets containing 7, 22, 23, 25, and 43 instances of multiple copying, four of them clearly exceed the nine permissible instances.

Anthologies. In addition to these tests, most of which defendant has failed, Kinko's conduct appears to violate a specific mandate of the Classroom Guidelines:

> III. *Prohibitions as to I and II Above.* Notwithstanding any of the above, the following shall be prohibited:
>
> > (A) *Copying shall not be used to create or to replace or substitute for anthologies, compilations or collective works* . * * *
> >
> > (C) Copying shall not: (a) substitute for the purchase of books, publishers' reprints or periodicals.
> >
> > (D) No charge shall be made to the student beyond the actual cost of the photocopying.

(emphasis added)

Plaintiffs argue that, notwithstanding the "safe harbor" provided in the spontaneity, brevity and cumulative effect requirements of Parts I and II, Part III of the Guidelines "flatly and unequivocally prohibit[s]" copying of the sort in suit. Defendant urges the court to seek a less rigid view of the meaning of the Guidelines. We are convinced that this is the more prudent path than a bright line pronouncement and refuse to hold that all unconsented anthologies are prohibited without a fair use analysis. However, the fact that these excerpts were placed in anthologies weighs significantly against defendant.

Lastly, plaintiffs argue that "even without examining the Classroom Guidelines, § 107, itself, read in the light of the legislative history, clearly renders unauthorized anthologizing (especially when undertaken for profit) outside the bounds of fair use." This court is not prepared to so hold. While we agree that Congress did manifest a specific apprehension of the use of anthologies, it is not clear that Congress intended strict application of this prohibition without fair use balancing.

* * *

V. RELIEF.

A. Injunction.

* * *

[T]his court thinks it prudent and equitable to grant plaintiffs' request for injunction and will enjoin defendant from future anthologizing and copying of plaintiffs' works without permission and prepayment of fees in the manner shown violative of the concept of fair use as proved in this case, and including similar works not currently existing but which may in the future be owned by plaintiffs and as to which plaintiffs have not consented.

Plaintiffs request an injunction against all unconsented anthologizing. This court refuses to do so for the simple reason that some anthologizing may fall within fair use requirements. This court is not in the position, for example, to enjoin uses which are fair as determined by the Guidelines and set out in the Copyright Act.

B.   Declaratory Judgment.

* * *

For declaratory judgment, a controversy must be "of a justiciable nature, thus excluding an advisory decree upon a hypothetical state of facts."

Plaintiffs say they are entitled to declaratory judgment as to *any and all* instances of copying or "anthologizing" without the author's permission. This is not so. The fact that Congress has set forth a statement in its Classroom Guidelines that anthologizing is prohibited does not require this court to paint with the broad brush plaintiffs suggest. Declaring that all anthologies published without permission is infringement would preclude fair use analysis of any excerpt included in an anthology. If Congress meant for anthologizing to nullify a fair use analysis, it would have expressly said so. The Guidelines state that some instances of copying which exceed its boundaries may in fact "be permitted under the criteria of fair use." Declaratory judgment is denied.

* * *

CONCLUSION

This court finds the excerpts copied by defendant Kinko's are not a fair use of plaintiffs' copyrights and, therefore, constitute infringement.

* * *

SO ORDERED

PRINCETON UNIV. PRESS v. MICHIGAN DOCUMENT SERVS.

99 F.3d 1381 (6th Cir. 1996).

DAVID A. NELSON, CIRCUIT JUDGE:

This is a copyright infringement case. The corporate defendant, Michigan Document Services, Inc., is a commercial copyshop that reproduced substantial segments of copyrighted works of scholarship, bound the copies into "coursepacks," and sold the coursepacks to students for use in fulfilling reading assignments given by professors at the University of Michigan. The copyshop acted without permission from the copyright holders, and the main question presented is whether the "fair use" doctrine codified at *17 U.S.C. § 107* obviated the need to obtain such permission.

Answering this question "no," and finding the infringement willful, the district court entered a summary judgment order in which the copyright holders were granted equitable relief and were awarded damages that may have been enhanced for willfulness. A three-judge panel of this court reversed the judgment on appeal, but a majority of the active judges of the court subsequently voted to rehear the case *en banc*. The appeal has now been argued before the full court.

We agree with the district court that the defendants' commercial exploitation of the copyrighted materials did not constitute fair use, and we shall affirm that branch of the district court's judgment. We believe that the district court erred in its finding of willfulness, however, and we shall vacate the damages award because of its possible linkage to that finding.

I.

* * *

The plaintiffs allege infringement of the copyrights on six different works that were excerpted without permission. The works in question, and the statistics on the magnitude of the excerpts, are as follows: Nancy J. Weiss, *Farewell to the Party of Lincoln: Black Politics in the Age of FDR* (95 pages copied, representing 30 percent of the entire book); Walter Lippmann, *Public Opinion* (45 pages copied, representing 18 percent of the whole); Robert E. Layne, *Political Ideology: Why the American Common Man Believes What He Does* (78 pages, 16 percent); Roger Brown, *Social Psychology* (52 pages, 8 percent); Milton Rokeach, *The Nature of Human Values* (77 pages, 18 percent); James S. Olson and Randy Roberts, *Where the Domino Fell, America and Vietnam, 1945–1950* (17 pages, 5 percent). The extent of the copying is undisputed, and the questions presented by the case appear to be purely legal in nature.

II.

* * *

[The fair use doctrine] does not provide blanket immunity for "multiple copies for classroom use." Rather, "whether a use referred to in the first sentence of Section 107 is a fair use in a particular case . . . depends upon the application of the determinative factors."

The four statutory factors may not have been created equal. In determining whether a use is "fair," the Supreme Court has said that the most important factor is the fourth, the one contained in *17 U.S.C. § 107*(4). We take it that this factor, "the effect of the use upon the potential market for or value of the copyrighted work," is at least *primus inter pares*, figuratively speaking, and we shall turn to it first.

The burden of proof as to market effect rests with the copyright holder if the challenged use is of a "noncommercial" nature. The alleged infringer has the burden, on the other hand, if the challenged use is "commercial" in nature. In the case at bar the defendants argue that the burden of proof rests with the publishers because the use being challenged is "noncommercial." We disagree.

It is true that the use to which the materials are put by the students who purchase the coursepacks is noncommercial in nature. But the use of the materials by the students is not the use that the publishers are challenging. What the publishers are challenging is the duplication of copyrighted materials for sale by a for-profit corporation that has decided to maximize its profits—and give itself a competitive edge over other copyshops—by declining to pay the royalties requested by the holders of the copyrights.[2]

The defendants' use of excerpts from the books at issue here was no less commercial in character than was *The Nation* magazine's use of copyrighted material in *Harper & Row*, where publication of a short article containing excerpts from the still unpublished manuscript of a book by President Ford was held to be an unfair use. Like the students who purchased unauthorized coursepacks, the purchasers of *The Nation* did not put the contents of the magazine to commercial use—but that did not stop the Supreme Court from characterizing the defendant's use of the excerpts as "a publication [that] was commercial as opposed to nonprofit. . . ." And like the use that is being challenged in the case now before us, the use challenged in *Harper & Row* was "presumptively an unfair exploitation of the monopoly privilege that belongs to the owner of the copyright."

* * *

If we are wrong about the existence of the presumption—if the challenged use is not commercial, in other words, and if the plaintiff publishers have the burden of proving an adverse effect upon either the potential market for the copyrighted work or the potential value of the work—we believe that the publishers have carried the burden of proving a diminution in potential market value.

One test for determining market harm—a test endorsed by the Supreme Court in *Sony, Harper & Row*, and *Campbell*—is evocative of Kant's categorical imperative. "To negate fair use," the Supreme Court has said, "one need only show that *if the challenged use 'should become widespread, it would adversely affect the potential market* for the copyrighted work.'" *Harper & Row* (emphasis supplied in part). Under this test, we believe, it is reasonably clear that the plaintiff publishers have succeeded in negating fair use.

---

2. Two of the dissents suggest that a copyshop merely stands in the shoes of its customers and makes no "use" of copyrighted materials that differs materially from the use to which the copies are put by the ultimate consumer. But subject to the fair use exception, *17 U.S.C. § 106* gives the copyright owner the "exclusive" right "to reproduce the copyrighted work in copies. . . ." And if the fairness of making copies depends on what the ultimate consumer does with the copies, it is hard to see how the manufacture of pirated editions of any copyrighted work of scholarship could ever be an unfair use. As discussed in Part III A, infra, the dissenters' suggestion—which proposes no limiting principle—runs counter to the legislative history of the Copyright Act and has properly been rejected by the courts.

As noted above, most of the copyshops that compete with MDS in the sale of coursepacks pay permission fees for the privilege of duplicating and selling excerpts from copyrighted works. The three plaintiffs together have been collecting permission fees at a rate approaching $500,000 a year. If copyshops across the nation were to start doing what the defendants have been doing here, this revenue stream would shrivel and the potential value of the copyrighted works of scholarship published by the plaintiffs would be diminished accordingly.

* * *

The potential uses of the copyrighted works at issue in the case before us clearly include the selling of permission to reproduce portions of the works for inclusion in coursepacks—and the likelihood that publishers actually will license such reproduction is a demonstrated fact.

* * *

III.

In the context of nontransformative uses, at least, and except insofar as they touch on the fourth factor, the other statutory factors seem considerably less important. We shall deal with them relatively briefly.

A.

As to "the purpose and character of the use, including whether such use is of a commercial nature or is for nonprofit educational purposes," we have already explained our reasons for concluding that the challenged use is of a commercial nature.

The defendants argue that the copying at issue here would be considered "nonprofit educational" if done by the students or professors themselves. The defendants also note that they can profitably produce multiple copies for less than it would cost the professors or the students to make the same number of copies. Most of the copyshops with which the defendants compete have been paying permission fees, however, and we assume that these shops too can perform the copying on a more cost-effective basis than the professors or students can. This strikes us as a more significant datum than the ability of a black market copyshop to beat the do-it-yourself cost.

As to the proposition that it would be fair use for the students or professors to make their own copies, the issue is by no means free from doubt. We need not decide this question, however, for the fact is that the copying complained of here was performed on a profit-making basis by a commercial enterprise. And "the courts have ... properly rejected attempts by for-profit users to stand in the shoes of their customers making nonprofit or noncommercial uses." As the House Judiciary Committee stated in its report on the 1976 legislation,

It would not be possible for a non-profit institution, by means of contractual arrangements with a commercial copying enterprise, to authorize the enterprise to carry out copying and distribution functions that would be exempt if conducted by the non-profit institution itself.

It should be noted, finally, that the degree to which the challenged use has transformed the original copyrighted works—another element in the first statutory factor—is virtually indiscernible. If you make verbatim copies of 95 pages of a 316–page book, you have not transformed the 95 pages very much—even if you juxtapose them to excerpts from other works and package everything conveniently. This kind of mechanical "transformation" bears little resemblance to the creative metamorphosis accomplished by the parodists in the *Campbell* case.

B.

The second statutory factor, "the nature of the copyrighted work," is not in dispute here. The defendants acknowledge that the excerpts copied for the coursepacks contained creative material, or "expression;" it was certainly not telephone book listings that the defendants were reproducing. This factor too cuts against a finding of fair use.

C.

The third statutory factor requires us to assess "the amount and substantiality of the portion used in relation to the copyrighted work as a whole." Generally speaking, at least, "the larger the volume (or the greater the importance) of what is taken, the greater the affront to the interests of the copyright owner, and the less likely that a taking will qualify as a fair use."

The amounts used in the case at bar—8,000 words in the shortest excerpt—far exceed the 1,000–word safe harbor that we shall discuss in the next part of this opinion. The defendants were using as much as 30 percent of one copyrighted work, and in no case did they use less than 5 percent of the copyrighted work as a whole. These percentages are not insubstantial. And to the extent that the third factor requires some type of assessment of the "value" of the excerpted material in relation to the entire work, the fact that the professors thought the excerpts sufficiently important to make them required reading strikes us as fairly convincing "evidence of the qualitative value of the copied material." We have no reason to suppose that in choosing the excerpts to be copied, the professors passed over material that was more representative of the major ideas of the work as a whole in preference to material that was less representative.

The third factor may have more significance for the 95–page excerpt from the black politics book than for the 17–page excerpt from the Vietnam book. In each instance, however, the defendants have failed to carry their burden of proof with respect to "amount and substantiality."[5]

---

5. "Fair use serves as an affirmative defense to a claim of copyright infringement, and thus the party claiming that its secondary use of the original copyrighted work constitutes a fair use typically carries

IV.

We turn now to the pertinent legislative history. The general revision of the copyright law enacted in 1976 was developed through a somewhat unusual process. Congress and the Register of Copyrights initiated and supervised negotiations among interested groups—groups that included authors, publishers, and educators—over specific legislative language. Most of the language that emerged was enacted into law or was made a part of the committee reports. The statutory fair use provisions are a direct result of this process. So too is the "Agreement on Guidelines for Classroom Copying in Not-for-Profit Educational Institutions With Respect to Books and Periodicals"—commonly called the "Classroom Guidelines"—set out in H.R. Rep. No. 1476 at 68–71, 94th Cong., 2d Sess. (1976). The House and Senate conferees explicitly accepted the Classroom Guidelines "as part of their understanding of fair use," and the Second Circuit has characterized the guidelines as "persuasive authority. . . ."

There are strong reasons to consider this legislative history. The statutory factors are not models of clarity, and the fair use issue has long been a particularly troublesome one. Not surprisingly, courts have often turned to the legislative history when considering fair use questions.

Although the Classroom Guidelines purport to "state the minimum and not the maximum standards of educational fair use," they do evoke a general idea, at least, of the type of educational copying Congress had in mind. The guidelines allow multiple copies for classroom use provided that (1) the copying meets the test of brevity (1,000 words, in the present context); (2) the copying meets the test of spontaneity, under which "the inspiration and decision to use the work and the moment of its use for maximum teaching effectiveness [must be] so close in time that it would be unreasonable to expect a timely reply to a request for permission;" (3) no more than nine instances of multiple copying take place during a term, and only a limited number of copies are made from the works of any one author or from any one collective work; (4) each copy contains a notice of copyright; (5) the copying does not substitute for the purchase of "books, publishers' reprints or periodicals;" and (6) the student is not charged any more than the actual cost of copying. The Classroom Guidelines also make clear that unauthorized copying to create "anthologies, compilations or collective works" is prohibited.

In its systematic and premeditated character, its magnitude, its anthological content, and its commercial motivation, the copying done by MDS goes well beyond anything envisioned by the Congress that chose to incorporate the guidelines in the legislative history. Although the guidelines do not purport to be a complete and definitive statement of fair use law for educational copying, and although they do not have the force of law, they do provide us general guidance. The fact that the MDS copying is light years away from the safe harbor of the guidelines weighs against a finding of fair use.

the burden of proof as to all issues in the dispute."

Although the Congress that passed the Copyright Act in 1976 would pretty clearly have thought it unfair for a commercial copyshop to appropriate as much as 30 percent of a copyrighted work without paying the license fee demanded by the copyright holder, the changes in technology and teaching practices that have occurred over the last two decades might conceivably make Congress more sympathetic to the defendants' position today. If the law on this point is to be changed, however, we think the change should be made by Congress and not by the courts.

* * *

VIII.

The grant of summary judgment on the fair use issue is **AFFIRMED**. * * *

BOYCE F. MARTIN, JR., CHIEF JUDGE, dissenting:

This case presents for me one of the more obvious examples of how laudable societal objectives, recognized by both the Constitution and statute, have been thwarted by a decided lack of judicial prudence. Copyright protection as embodied in the Copyright Act of 1976 is intended as a public service to both the creator and the consumer of published works. Although the Act grants to individuals limited control over their original works, it was drafted to stimulate the production of those original works for the benefit of the whole nation. The fair use doctrine, which requires unlimited public access to published works in educational settings, is one of the essential checks on the otherwise exclusive property rights given to copyright holders under the Copyright Act.

Ironically, the majority's rigid statutory construction of the Copyright Act grants publishers the kind of power that Article I, Section 8 of the Constitution is designed to guard against. The Copyright Clause grants Congress the power to create copyright interests that are *limited* in scope. Consequently, the Copyright Act adopted the fair use doctrine to protect society's vested interest in the sharing of ideas and information against pursuits of illegitimate or excessive private proprietary claims. While it may seem unjust that publishers must share, in certain situations, their work-product with others, free of charge, that is not some "unforeseen byproduct of a statutory scheme;" rather, it is the "essence of copyright" and a "constitutional requirement."

Michigan Document Services provided a service to the University of Michigan that promoted scholarship and higher education. Michigan Document Services was paid for its services; however, that fact does not obviate a fair use claim under these facts. Requiring Michigan Document Services to pay permission fees in this instance is inconsistent with the primary mission of the Copyright Act. The individual rights granted by the Act are subservient to the Act's primary objective, which is the promotion of creativity generally. We must therefore consider the fair use provision of Section 107 of the Act in light of the sum total of public benefits intended by copyright law. In this instance, there is no adverse economic impact on Princeton University Press that can outweigh the benefits provided by Michigan Document Services. Indeed, to presume adverse economic impact, as has the majority, is to presume that the $50,000 in fees currently earned by plaintiff is mandated by the Act in every instance—something I hesitate to presume.

That the majority lends significance to the identity of the person operating the photocopier is a profound indication that its approach is misguided. Given the focus of the Copyright Act, the only practical difference between this case and that of a student making his or her own copies is that commercial photocopying is faster and more cost-effective. Censuring incidental private sector profit reflects little of the essence of copyright law. Would the majority require permission fees of the Professor's teaching assistant who at times must copy, at the Professor's behest, copyrighted materials for dissemination to a class, merely because such assistant is paid an hourly wage by the Professor for this work?

The majority's strict reading of the fair use doctrine promises to hinder scholastic progress nationwide. By charging permission fees on this kind of job, publishers will pass on expenses to colleges and universities that will, of course, pass such fees on to students. Students may also be harmed if added expenses and delays cause professors to opt against creating such specialized anthologies for their courses. Even if professors attempt to reproduce the benefits of such a customized education, the added textbook cost to students is likely to be prohibitive.

The Copyright Act does not suggest such a result. Rather, the fair use doctrine contemplates the creation and free flow of information; the unhindered flow of such information through, among other things, education in turn spawns the creation and free flow of new information.

In limiting the right to copy published works in the Copyright Act, Congress created an exception for cases like the one before us. When I was in school, you bought your books and you went to the library for supplemental information. To record this supplemental information, in order to learn and benefit from it, you wrote it out long-hand or typed out what you needed—not easy, but effective. Today, with the help of free enterprise and technology, this fundamental means of obtaining information for study has been made easier. Students may now routinely acquire inexpensive copies of the information they need without all of the hassle. The trend of an instructor giving information to a copying service to make a single set of copies for each student for a small fee is just a modern approach to the classic process of education. To otherwise enforce this statute is nonsensical. I therefore dissent.

MERRITT, CIRCUIT JUDGE, dissenting.

The copying done in this case is permissible under the plain language of the copyright statute that allows "multiple copies for classroom use:" "The fair use of a copyrighted work ... for purposes such as ...

teaching (*including multiple copies for classroom use*), ... is not an infringement of copyright." (emphasis added). * * *

I.

This is a case of first impression with broad consequences. Neither the Supreme Court nor any other court of appeals has interpreted the exception allowing "multiple copies for classroom use" found in § 107 of the copyright statute. There is no legal precedent and no legal history that supports our Court's reading of this phrase in a way that outlaws the widespread practice of copying for classroom use by teachers and students.

For academic institutions, the practical consequences of the Court's decision in this case are highly unsatisfactory, to say the least. Anyone who makes multiple copies for classroom use for a fee is guilty of copyright infringement unless the portion copied is just a few paragraphs long. Chapters from a book or articles from a journal are verboten. No longer may Kinko's and other corner copyshops, or school bookstores, libraries and student-run booths and kiosks copy anything for a fee except a small passage. I do not see why we should so construe plain statutory language that on its face permits "multiple copies for classroom use." The custom of making copies for classroom use for a fee began during my college and law school days forty years ago and is now well-established. I see no justification for overturning this long-established practice.

I disagree with the Court's method of analyzing and explaining the statutory language of § 107 providing a fair use exception.[1] Except for "teaching," the statute is cast in general, abstract language that allows fair use for "criticism," "comment," "news reporting" and "research." The scope or extent of copying allowed for these uses is left undefined. Not so for "teaching." This purpose, and this purpose alone, is immediately followed by a definition. The definition allows "multiple copies for classroom use" of copyrighted material. The four factors to be considered, *e.g.*, market effect and the portion of the work used, are of limited assistance when the teaching use at issue fits squarely within the specific language of the statute, *i.e.*, "multiple copies for classroom use." In the present case that is all we have—"multiple copies for classroom use."

There is nothing in the statute that distinguishes between copies made for students by a third person who charges a fee for their labor and copies made by students themselves who pay a fee only for use of the

1. Both the majority opinion and Judge Ryan's dissent approach the determination of whether the use at issue here is infringing solely by use of the four statutory factors set out in § 107. Neither the plain language of the statute nor the case law requires that determination to be made solely on the narrow grounds of those four factors. Because the plain language of the statute is clear concerning "multiple copies for classroom use" and because determinations of infringement are to be made on a case-by-case basis taking into consideration the reasonableness of the copying from an equitable perspective, I do not believe that the four factors are controlling. The specific plain language should be given much more weight in this case than the four abstract considerations of little relevance to copying for classroom use.

copy machine. Our political economy generally encourages the division and specialization of labor. There is no reason why in this instance the law should discourage high schools, colleges, students and professors from hiring the labor of others to make their copies any more than there is a reason to discourage lawyers from hiring paralegals to make copies for clients and courts. The Court's distinction in this case based on the division of labor—who does the copying—is short sighted and unsound economically.

Our Court cites no authority for the proposition that the intervention of the copyshop changes the outcome of the case. The Court errs by focusing on the "use" of the materials made by the copyshop in making the copies rather than upon the real user of the materials—the students. Neither the District Court nor our Court provides a rationale as to why the copyshops cannot "stand in the shoes" of their customers in making copies for noncommercial, educational purposes where the copying would be fair use if undertaken by the professor or the student personally.

Rights of copyright owners are tempered by the rights of the public. The copyright owner has never been accorded complete control over all possible uses of a work. Generally, "the monopoly privileges [of copyright] that Congress may authorize are neither unlimited nor primarily designed to provide a special private benefit," a statement the Court more fully explained as follows:

The limited scope of the copyright holder's statutory monopoly, like the limited copyright duration required by the Constitution, reflects a balance of competing claims upon the public interest: Creative work is to be encouraged and rewarded, but private motivation must ultimately serve the cause of promoting broad public availability of literature, music, and the other arts.... When technological change has rendered its literal terms ambiguous, the Copyright Act must be construed in light of its basic purpose.

The public has the right to make fair use of a copyrighted work and to exercise that right without requesting permission from, or paying any fee to, the copyright holder. The essence of copyright is the promotion of learning—not the enrichment of publishers.

* * *

RYAN, CIRCUIT JUDGE, dissenting:

It is clear from the application of the four fair use factors of *17 U.S.C. § 107* that MDS's copying of the publishers' copyrighted works in this case is fair use and, thus, no infringement of the publishers' rights. Indeed, it is a use which is merely an aspect of the professors' and students' classroom use, and, only in the narrowest and most technical sense, a use of a separate genre under section 107. And, so, I must dissent from the majority's contrary view and, in expressing my understanding of the matter, I shall identify three important subissues on which I think my colleagues' analysis has led them to mistakenly conclude that MDS's activity is not a fair use of the publishers' materials.

In my judgment, my colleagues have erred in

1. focusing on the loss of permission fees in evaluating "market effect" under section 107(4);

2. finding that the evidence supports the conclusion that permission fees provide an important incentive to authors to create new works or to publishers to publish new works; and

3. using legislative history, specifically the "Classroom Guidelines," to decide the issue of classroom use.

* * *

[After a lengthy analysis of the first two items on the above list, Judge Ryan turned to the third, focusing on the "Classroom Guidelines."]

Finally, a word about the majority's argument that the unenacted legislative history of the Copyright Act instructs us that the MDS's copying function is not a fair use under the enacted provisions of sections 106 and 107.

The majority opinion stresses the fact that Congress "initiated and supervised negotiations among interested groups—groups that included authors, publishers, and educators—over specific legislative language [and that m]ost of the language that emerged was enacted into law or was made a part of the committee reports." However, what were not "enacted into law," but only made a part of the conference committee reports, are the Classroom Guidelines upon which the majority so heavily relies to decide how the language enacted into law applies. Indisputably, the Classroom Guidelines assure educators that nonprofit copying for educational purposes of "not more than 1,000 words" is fair use when "the inspiration and decision to use the work and the moment of its use for maximum teaching effectiveness are so close in time that it would be unreasonable to expect a timely reply to a request for permission." The Classroom Guidelines "prohibit[] ... copying ... used to create ... anthologies, compilations or collective works." But, as the majority opinion acknowledges, that language did not survive congressional debate and was not enacted into law.

Despite the well-settled rule that legislative history is irrelevant and inappropriate to consider except to clarify an ambiguity in the text of a statute, the majority relies upon the legislative history without identifying any ambiguity in the statute, but only because "the statutory factors are not models of clarity, ... the fair use issue has long been a particularly troublesome one ... , [and other] courts have often turned to the legislative history when considering fair use questions." I wish to emphasize in the strongest terms that it is entirely inappropriate to rely on the Copyright Act's legislative history at all.

* * * The Classroom Guidelines do not become more authoritative by their adoption into a Committee Report. "It is the statute, and not the Committee Report, which is the authoritative expression of the law." We may not permit the statutory text enacted by both Houses of Congress and signed by the President "to be expanded or contracted by the statements of individual legislators or committees during the course of the enactment process." That the Classroom Guidelines are not law should be reason enough for this court to refrain from using them to find infringement, but this is not the only reason to reject out of hand arguments based on legislative history. Committee Reports are unreliable "as a genuine indicator of congressional intent" *and* "as a safe predictor of judicial construction." Committee Reports do not accurately indicate congressional intent because they do not "necessarily say anything about what Congress as a whole thought," *even if* all the members of the Committee "actually adverted to the interpretive point at issue . . . [and] were in unanimous agreement on the point." The members of Congress who voted for the statutory language of section 107 could have had any variety of understandings about the application of the fair use factors; all we know for certain is that the full House, the full Senate, and the President, pursuant to the procedures prescribed by the Constitution, enacted into law the text of section 107, and did not enact the standards of the Classroom Guidelines. Committee Reports do not reliably further consistent judicial construction. I subscribe wholeheartedly to Judge Harold Leventhal's observation that "the use of legislative history [is] the equivalent of entering a crowded cocktail party and looking over the heads of the guests for one's friends." "We use [Committee Reports] when it is convenient, and ignore them when it is not."

The statutory language of section 107, like most statutory language, may not be a "model of clarity," and the fair use issue, like many issues of law we face, may be a difficult or "troublesome" one, but neither of these inconveniences is a substitute for the requisite ambiguity that, alone, justifies recourse to legislative history.

Our duty in this case, as in all cases that require application of a statute, is to apply the broad dictates of the statute to the unique factual situations presented by the evidence. The fact that the Supreme Court has indulged in explanatory side-references to the Classroom Guidelines does not diminish in any measure the *rule* that legislative history is not a proper source of authority for this court when the language of the statute is not analogous. It is particularly inappropriate to rely on the specific language of the Classroom Guidelines as an interpretive tool when we know that members of Congress actually considered the language and rejected it in favor of the very language now claimed to lack clarity. The majority substitutes language contained only in pre-enactment political maneuvering of Congress for our obligation to rely, as we are required to do, on the rich body of case law that properly guides our application of the statutory factors to the specific facts of a case. In *Campbell*, the Court noted that "the task is not to be simplified with bright-line rules, for the statute, like the doctrine it recognizes, calls for case-by-case analysis."

The case for copyright infringement is very weak indeed if the court must rely on the unenacted theater of Committee Reports to find infringement. The fact that Congress saw fit, very likely in the interests of political expediency, to pay unusual deference to the "agreement" of interested parties about what *they* would like the law to be, even to the point of declaring (but not in the statute) that the parties' agreement was part of the committee's "understanding" of fair use, does not affect the rule of construction that binds this court.

In sum, even if the four statutory factors of section 107 are not "models of clarity" and their application to the facts of this case is "troublesome"—a challenge of the kind federal appellate judges are paid to face every day—the four factors are not ambiguous. Therefore, we may not properly resort to legislative history. I am satisfied to rely exclusively upon the evidence and lack of evidence on the record before us and the plain language of the Copyright Act and its construction in the case law; and they lead me to conclude that MDS's compilation into coursepacks of excerpts selected by professors is a "fair use" of the copyrighted materials.

IV.

For all the foregoing reasons, I conclude that MDS did not infringe upon the copyrights of the publishers.

Note

1. Taking advantage of ongoing improvements in digital technology, a growing number of academics are working to develop new ways of packaging and distributing course materials. Some have focused only on their own courses for their own students, but others have participated in high-profile projects—funded by sizable grants—that seek to create innovative models which can then be used in other places. Many of these models contemplate the online publishing of extensive sets of course materials—such as syllabi, lecture notes, and quizzes—which could then be used freely by anyone. Some have also developed state-of-the-art software that can facilitate both the dissemination of materials and student interaction around these materials.

One such effort is MIT's Open Courseware. As the *Chronicle of Higher Education* reported in March 2005:

> * * * MIT officials are spending $6–million per year on the project, much of which is coming from grants from the William and Flora Hewlett Foundation and the Andrew W. Mellon Foundation. The project, which has already published more than 900 of MIT's 1,800 courses, is being touted as a success, as it has drawn downloaders from around the world who are using the materials as models for their own teaching or to learn on their own.
>
> Proponents say the main beneficiaries are in the developing world, where students cannot afford textbooks and universities are looking for

help setting up courses. MIT officials say that the materials are also inspiring more people to apply to the institute, as well as helping students at MIT decide which courses to sign up for.

Though many professors at other colleges already create course Web sites, the majority do so haphazardly, or in a way that is designed to be used only by their students. Open courseware seeks to make sure each course's materials are far more complete, and are presented in a way that makes them easy for others to use.

The growth of these giveaways marks a major philosophical shift from the mid–1990s, when many colleges and professors thought they could rake in profits selling course materials online. * * *

Of course, copyright issues inevitably arise in this context. As *The Chronicle* reported * * *

Copyright is another challenge in running open-courseware projects * * *[.] Many professors regularly use charts, graphs, or other illustrations they've culled from textbooks or other copyrighted works in slide presentations or handouts. Although using those illustrations in a classroom is allowed under fair-use provisions of copyright law, universities must get permission before putting the same materials online where anyone can see them. That can take time and money because officials must track down who owns the copyright and often must pay a fee to post the materials. One college decided not to convert a popular course to an open format because it included so many copyrighted items that it would have been unmanageable. Jeffrey R. Young, *'Open Courseware' Idea Spreads,* CHRONICLE OF HIGHER ED., Mar. 4, 2005.

D. PROSECUTIONS UNDER THE "NO ELECTRONIC THEFT" ACT

PROBLEM 46: Fighting "Electronic Theft"

Assume that Al and Joanne maintain a Web site on Earthlink as part of an independent study project for their History of American Film class. On this site, they have been able to post excerpts of classic films and complete versions of *The Godfather* Saga in fifteen minute segments for easier access/viewing. In a separate section on DVD technology, they post links to sites where software and other resources are available for working with DVD files, including but not limited to file-sharing guides and technologies.

Under pressure from the entertainment industry to make examples of college students who may be violating the law, the U.S. Attorneys Office prosecutes Al and Joanne under the 'No Electronic Theft' (NET) Act.

A. What arguments might Al & Joanne set forth in support of their assertion that they have not violated the terms of the Act? What result?

B. Might there be a law that could address this sort of activity in a better way?

C. Consider the efficacy of the following relevant legislation, introduced in the California State Legislature in 2005. In light of your analysis of the regulatory design and whether the plan is likely to achieve its purpose, would you recommend passage of such a bill? Why? Alternatively, could you support a modified version of this bill? If so, what modifications might be appropriate?

California Senate Bill 96
(amended Aug. 15, 2005)

Section 653.15 is added to the Penal Code, to read:

(a)(1) Any person or entity that sells, offers for sale, advertises, distributes, disseminates, provides, or otherwise makes available peer-to-peer file sharing software that enables its user to electronically disseminate commercial recordings or audiovisual works via the Internet or any other digital network, and who fails to incorporate available filtering technology into that software to prevent use of that software to commit an unlawful act with respect to a commercial recording or audiovisual work * * * is punishable, in addition to any other penalty or fine imposed, by a fine not exceeding two thousand five hundred dollars ($2,500), imprisonment in a county jail for a period not to exceed one year, or by both that fine and imprisonment.

(2) This section shall not apply to the following:

(A) Computer operating system or Internet browser software.

(B) An electronic mail service or Internet service provider.

(C) Transmissions via a personal network or local area network (LAN).

(b) As used in this section, 'peer-to-peer file sharing software' means software that contains a sequence of instructions written in any programming language that is executed on a computer the primary purpose of which, once installed and launched, is to enable the user to connect his or her computer to a network of other computers on which the users of these computers have made available recordings or audiovisual works for electronic dissemination to other users who are connected to the network. When a transaction is complete, the user has an identical copy of the file on his or her computer and may also then disseminate the file to other users connected to the network. * * *

A ROAD TO NO WAREZ: THE NO ELECTRONIC THEFT ACT AND CRIMINAL COPYRIGHT INFRINGEMENT

Eric Goldman.
82 OR. L. REV. 369 (2003).

The [No Electronic Theft] Act represents a significant change to copyright law because it subtly shifts the paradigm underlying criminal copyright infringement. For 100 years, criminal infringement punished infringers who derived a commercial benefit based on someone else's copyrighted work. However, through the Act, Congress adopted a paradigm that criminal copyright infringement is like physical-space theft, specifically shoplifting. As a result, the Act significantly extends the boundaries of criminal copyright infringement.

* * *

I.

Development of the Act.

Prior to the Act, criminal copyright infringement required willful infringement committed for commercial advantage or private financial gain. A case involving David LaMacchia highlighted the limits of this statute.

David LaMacchia was a twenty-one-year-old student at the Massachusetts Institute of Technology ("MIT"). From late 1993 to early 1994, he used MIT's equipment to operate Cynosure, a bulletin board system ("BBS") that allowed users to upload and download infringing software applications and videogames. LaMacchia was not accused of uploading or downloading any infringing programs himself. However, prosecutors asserted that he maintained the BBS (including deleting files and transferring files between servers) and asked BBS users to upload specific software programs. Judge Stearns described LaMacchia's behavior as, at best, "heedlessly irresponsible, and at worst as nihilistic, self-indulgent, and lacking in any fundamental sense of values." Although the term was not widely used at the time, LaMacchia was an early warez trader.

Like a typical warez trader, LaMacchia operated the BBS for fun and without any commercial advantage or private financial gain. Therefore, prosecutors could not charge him with criminal copyright infringement. Instead, prosecutors charged him with one count of conspiracy to commit wire fraud. Judge Stearns applied the U.S. Supreme Court case of Dowling v. United States, which had ruled that intangible intellectual property was not capable of being stolen, converted or taken by fraud. That case, he concluded, "precludes LaMacchia's prosecution for criminal copyright infringement under the wire fraud statute," and he dismissed the indictment.

Despite the dismissal, Judge Stearns issued a challenge to Congress:

> Criminal as well as civil penalties should probably attach to willful, multiple infringements of copyrighted software even absent a commercial motive on the part of the infringer. One can envision ways that the copyright law could be modified to permit such prosecution. But, it is the legislature, not the Court, which is to define a crime, and ordain its punishment.

B. A Legislative Response to LaMacchia

Copyright owners seized upon Judge Stearns's challenge and lobbied Congress for just such a law. * * * [T]he NET Act * * * was enacted in 1997.

The Act effected six principal changes to criminal copyright law. First, the NET Act expanded the Copyright Act's definition of "financial gain" to include the receipt (or expectation of receipt) of anything of value, including other copyrighted works. Second, in addition to willful infringement for commercial advantage or private financial gain, the Act criminalized the reproduction or distribution, in any 180 day period, of copyrighted works with a total retail value of more than $1,000. Third, the Act said that evidence of reproducing and distributing copyrighted works does not, by itself, establish willfulness. Fourth, the Act changed the punishments for criminal infringement. For infringements of more than $1,000, the punishment includes imprisonment of up to one year and a fine. For infringements of $2,500 or more, the punishment includes imprisonment of up to three years and a fine. For second or subsequent offenses involving commercial advantage or private financial gain, the punishment includes imprisonment of up to six years. Fifth, the Act permits copyright infringement victims to submit victim impact statements. Finally, the Act instructed the United States Sentencing Commission (the "Sentencing Commission") to adjust the United States Sentencing Guidelines (the "Sentencing Guidelines") for criminal copyright infringement to make the punishments sufficiently stringent to deter the crimes and to reflect the infringed items' retail value and quantity.

C. The Act's Goals

Because the LaMacchia case directly instigated the Act, the law is often characterized as being intended to close the LaMacchia loophole. Indeed, the House Report said it desired to "reverse the practical consequences of" the LaMacchia case, and several legislators reiterated this goal. However, accepting these statements on their face still leaves open a central question: Exactly what aspects of LaMacchia did Congress intend to reverse?

Some legislators specifically targeted LaMacchia's warez trading, referencing targets such as "commercial scale" piracy and self-aggrandizing infringers.

LaMacchia's BBS primarily traded software (as opposed to other copyrighted works), and the legislative history also extensively discussed software piracy. As the House Report says, "copyright piracy flourishes in the software world" despite existing sanctions. The report cited industry estimates that software counterfeiting and piracy cost copyright owners $11 billion in 1996, resulting in "130,000 lost U.S. jobs, $5.6 billion in corresponding lost wages, $1 billion in lower tax revenue, and higher prices for honest purchasers of copyrighted software." Individual legislators also expressed a desire to target software pirates and to protect the software industry.

Finally, even though the Act criminalizes infringements regardless of distribution media, several legislators specifically targeted Internet-based piracy. Of course, the Act's title ("No Electronic Theft," with the acronym "NET") reinforces that objective.

Therefore, the legislative history suggests Congress targeted La-Macchia's use of the Internet to distribute infringing software on a commercial scale but without a profit motive. In other words, Congress specifically targeted warez trading.

* * *

II

Developments After the Act's Enactment

A.   Congressional Oversight of Implementation and Use

No convictions under the Act were announced in the first eighteen months following the Act's passage. This perceived lack of action prompted Rep. Howard Coble, one of the Act's co-sponsors, to convene hearings of the House Judiciary Committee's Subcommittee on Courts and Intellectual Property in May 1999 (the "Oversight Hearings"). * * *

Kevin DiGregory of the United States Department of Justice (the "DOJ") responded by enumerating several general challenges to prosecuting digital piracy, including: (1) Internet pirates do not have sizable or easily-located manufacturing operations; (2) calculating damages and losses is difficult because it is hard to count the number of illegitimate copies made over the Internet; (3) no government agency has primary responsibility for enforcing Internet-based crimes, and prosecutions often cut across prosecutors' territories; and (4) Internet-savvy law enforcement officials are hard to retain and often asked to help with other computer crime enforcements.

Mr. DiGregory also identified specific difficulties with enforcing the Act against pirate Web site operators: (1) for-profit criminals are a higher priority; (2) operators are often juveniles; (3) Web sites move overseas, complicating investigation and enforcement; (4) establishing an operator's identity can be challenging; (5) prosecutors cannot prove willfulness; (6) young not-for-profit operators are sympathetic defendants; (7) the Sentencing Commission had not established the mandated changes to the Sentencing Guidelines; and (8) the Sentencing Guideline's computation of retail value leads to low penalties. He concluded that "although there are many Web sites on the Internet offering illegal software and other copyrighted materials, investigating and prosecuting the offenders is hardly shooting fish in a barrel."

Despite the dozen challenges mentioned by Mr. DiGregory, the DOJ also quickly responded to the Oversight Hearings, delivering the first criminal conviction under the Act just three months later. Since then, the prosecution machine has ramped up significantly, and nearly eighty defendants have been convicted under the Act.

* * *

C.   Prosecutions under the Act

As mentioned above, nearly eighty defendants have been convicted under the Act. This subsection discusses some of the publicized convictions.

* * *

In August 1999, Jeffrey Levy, a twenty-two-year old University of Oregon senior, became the first individual convicted under the Act. He operated a Web site that allowed third parties to download thousands of software and game programs, songs, and movies, at least some of which Levy uploaded himself. After Levy was arrested and an information was filed against him, he was given a choice: he could remain in prison six months while the FBI analyzed his computers to determine the value of the infringing works, or he could plead guilty. Levy chose the latter and pleaded guilty to distributing software with a retail value of at least $5,000 (although a "conservative[] estimate" of the actual retail value was $70,000). He was sentenced to two years probation.

* * *

Eric Thornton, a twenty-four-year old Navy avionics technician, operated a Web site called "No Patience" permitting users to download software such as Adobe Premiere and Adobe Illustrator. In one specific instance, a third party downloaded twenty software programs with a retail value of $9,638. Thornton used the third party software to attract traffic to his Web site. However, when his Internet access provider noticed the traffic spike, his provider shut down the Web site and notified the FBI.

In December 1999, Thornton pleaded guilty to a misdemeanor violation of the Act. He received five years probation and had to pay restitution of $9,600. In addition, for eighteen months Thornton's Web site described his arrest and conviction.

* * *

In October 2000, twenty-one-year-old Brian Baltutat pleaded guilty to violating the Act. He operated a Web site called "Hacker Hurricane," visited by 65,000 people, that offered 142 software programs for downloading. Baltutat received three years probation, 180 days home confinement (including a tether), restitution, and forty hours of community service.

* * *

Pirates With Attitude (PWA) was [a] major warez group, characterized as "the 'oldest and most sophisticated' band of software pirates in Internet history." PWA operated thirteen FTP servers for software uploading and downloading. Its flagship site was Sentinel, located at the University of Sherbrooke in Quebec, which operated from late 1995 to January 2000. Sentinel users obtained the right to download software by uploading pirated software or by performing other services to the group. During Sentinel's operation, over 30,000 software programs (including games, MP3 files, operating systems, utilities, and applications from vendors such as Microsoft, Adobe, Norton, Oracle, IBM, Lotus, and Novell, some of which were pre-release versions) were uploaded to Sentinel and downloaded by more than 100 individuals. The FBI cracked the case when a confidential informant helped them gain access to Sentinel. PWA members claimed their activities were "for fun and entertainment, not to try to make ourselves rich."

Seventeen defendants were indicted in 2000. Twelve defendants were PWA members, and five were Intel Corporation employees who provided computer hardware to PWA for access rights to the warez library.

Following the indictments, many defendants negotiated plea agreements. After the plea agreements were entered into, the government contended that the infringements had a retail value over $10 million. A group of defendants jointly moved to limit the retail value based on expectations defendants formed while negotiating their plea agreements. The judge denied the motion but permitted defendants to rescind their plea agreements (and thus withdraw their guilty pleas) if they wanted. None chose to rescind.

A group of defendants then petitioned the court for a lower retail value, and the court agreed, setting the retail value at $1,424,640. With the retail value set, individual defendants were sentenced.

Robin Rothberg, the PWA leader, entered a blind guilty plea but requested downward departure from the Sentencing Guidelines. The court granted him some relief, and he was sentenced to eighteen months in prison.

Another PWA member, Christian Morley, did not negotiate a plea agreement and instead took his case to trial. A jury found him guilty, and he received two years in prison. Two other defendants, Jason Slater and Justin Robbins, received jail sentences of eight months and seven months, respectively. Nine defendants received five years probation (and most of these defendants also received a $5,000 fine), and two defendants, Thomas Oliver and Steven Ahnen, each received three years probation. Two defendants, Mark Veerboken and Kaj Bjorlin, are fugitives. In November 2003, two defendants, Jason Slater and Christian Morley, appealed the case to the Seventh Circuit Court of Appeals. The Seventh Circuit upheld the district court's refusal to instruct the jury on fair use and its calculation of retail value.

* * *

IV.

What Exactly Does the Act Criminalize?

A. Criminalization of Everyday Activities

* * *

The everyday activities potentially covered by the Act are breathtaking in scope and ubiquity. Our digital society requires us to make copies—lots of copies—to function productively, and all of those copies infringe if they involve third-party copyrighted works. Thus, the Act makes every file uploaded to the Internet or email forwarded to a friend the potential basis of criminal prosecution. The process of committing little acts of infringement is endemic in our lives, and all of those are, in theory, subject to scrutiny should we ever be prosecuted.

But perhaps the most problematic everyday infringing activity is P2P file-sharing. * * * [F]ifty-seven million Americans use P2P file-sharing services, and the P2P file-sharing software programs KaZaA and Morpheus—the market leaders after Napster's shutdown—have collectively been downloaded over 360 million times.

Yet, P2P file-sharers likely violate the Act. Some users download enough files to clear the Act's financial thresholds. But even lower-activity users automatically store files in a shared directory where other users can download the files, and some users altruistically choose to share infringing files. In either of those cases, any actual downloads made could also count toward the financial threshold. If enough files are uploaded or downloaded, the user may clear the criminal financial thresholds.

Alternatively, irrespective of a user's quantity of downloads or uploads, every file-sharer may be criminally infringing due to the expanded definition of "financial gain," which could apply to the sharer's receipt of other copyrighted works through the file-sharing system.

There is little debate that P2P file-sharing could be criminal, and Congress certainly has made it clear that it wants P2P file-sharing prosecuted. In Summer 2002, nineteen members of Congress, led by Sen. Joseph Biden, wrote to U.S. Attorney General John Ashcroft requesting that the DOJ make a priority of using criminal copyright laws to curtail infringement via P2P networks. The letter specifically requested that the DOJ prosecute P2P network operators "who intentionally facilitate mass piracy" and individuals who "intentionally allow mass copying from their computer" over P2P networks. In response, the DOJ pledged to bring criminal prosecutions against individual file-sharers, but no timetable has been set.

* * *

Despite Congress's exhortations, no P2P file-sharer has been prosecuted yet. More generally, there are a number of reasons why prosecutors may choose not to prosecute average Americans for everyday and common activities: the activity could be fair use, the activity may not clear the financial thresholds, evidence may be too difficult to collect, or the infringement may not be committed "willfully."

Specifically, the willfulness standard plays a critical role in distinguishing between legal and criminal activity and thus warrants more discussion. The U.S. Supreme Court has characterized willfulness as " 'a word of many meanings' whose construction is often dependent on the context in which it appears." Yet, Congress did not define willfulness in the Act.

This omission was not an oversight. The word's definition was discussed extensively in the legislative history, and some legislators wanted to define it explicitly.

* * *

[T]he House Report says merely that the Act "will not change the current interpretation of the word as developed by case law and as applied by the Department of Justice." In floor debates, Sen. Leahy repeated those words and continued, "nor does [the Act] change the definition of 'willful' as it is used elsewhere in the Copyright Act."

Accepting these statements at face value, this legislative history still does not clarify matters because, as discussed below, the existing case law was inconsistent. Further, where the legislators did explain their views on the word, the articulations were also inconsistent and suggest a split of opinion between the House and Senate.

In the Senate discussions, Sen. Hatch articulated a traditional definition of willfulness as "the intent to violate a known legal duty." In contrast, in the House discussions, Rep. Coble articulated a more lax definition of willfulness:

> It should be emphasized that proof of the defendant's state of mind is not required. The Government should not be required to prove that the defendant was familiar with the criminal copyright statute or violated it intentionally. Particularly in cases of clear infringement, the willfulness standard should be satisfied if there is adequate proof that the defendant acted with reckless disregard of the rights of the copyright holder. In such circumstances, a proclaimed ignorance of the law should not allow the infringer to escape conviction. Willfulness is often established by circumstantial evidence, and may be inferred from the facts and circumstances of each case.

The willfulness definition has not gotten any clearer since the Act's passage. The academic commentary remains confused about the implications of the willfulness standard, and while many cases have interpreted the term willfulness in a civil infringement context, relatively few cases have done so in criminal copyright cases. As a consequence, the case law continues to create "uncertainty in an area already filled with vagueness, gray areas, and doctrines with no bright line rules."

* * * The majority view is that willfulness requires the government to prove that the defendant specifically intended to infringe such that the infringement was a voluntary, intentional violation of a known legal duty. The minority view is that willfulness requires the government to prove only that the defendant had the intent to copy.

For purposes of understanding how the Act impacts our everyday activities, the difference between the views is critical. Under the majority view, defenses to willfulness include the infringer's ignorance of the law, an infringer's subjective good-faith belief that the use was fair, and the infringer's subjective good-faith belief that the infringing work was not actually infringing, because the new work was not substantially similar to the preexisting work or a defense such as the First Sale doctrine applied.

If ignorance of the law is a defense, then many otherwise infringing activities would escape punishment. Only in rare cases can prosecutors overcome that defense. Similarly, a defense that the infringer had a good faith belief that the use was fair would significantly narrow the Act's scope. With the fair use defense's inherent unpredictability and inconsistency, defendants can legitimately believe that most de minimis infringements committed during everyday activity constitute fair use. However, case law has already said that P2P file-sharing and warez trading are not fair use, so defendants may lack a good faith belief in those situations.

Thus, under the majority view, the Act only criminalizes commercial-scale infringers who have no hope of claiming ignorance of the law or fair use. Indeed, some commentators criticize the majority view for this very reason. However, whether one agrees or disagrees with the policy implications of the majority view, there is some chance that the majority view will not apply in a particular case. In those cases, the minority view should apply, and defenses like ignorance of the law and a good faith but erroneous belief in fair use may not be available.

* * *

B.   Criminalization of Facilitators

The Act's coverage also leaves open the degree to which "facilitation" is criminalized. This ambiguity can be traced to the Act's inception, because arguably LaMacchia did not commit copyright infringement at all. While LaMacchia created and maintained Cynosure, which others used to commit copyright infringement, the government did not allege that LaMacchia uploaded or downloaded any copyrighted material himself. While the Act should apply easily to Cynosure users for the files those users personally uploaded and downloaded, it is less clear why LaMacchia's facilitation role should be criminalized.

Unfortunately, Congress did not specifically address why LaMacchia's actions were criminal or how the statute distinguishes between infringers and facilitators. As with the willfulness definition, when this issue was raised to Congress, a number of legislators made strong remarks that they did not want the Act to cover Internet access providers, and Nimmer even proposed language to correct this deficiency.

However, Congress ultimately acknowledged this issue only through the weak clarifying language regarding willfulness discussed above. How does this language distinguish Internet access providers from LaMacchia? In other words, exactly what did LaMacchia do beyond operating a Web site that reproduced and distributed copyrighted works?

Two facts might distinguish LaMacchia from Internet access providers. First, LaMacchia encouraged infringement because he allegedly requested his users to upload specific software to Cynosure, and second, he knew Cynosure users would exchange pirated software and wanted them to do so. While superficially these differences may distinguish LaMacchia from an Internet access provider who passively transmits packets across its network, these factors do little to distinguish other types of online service providers like web hosts that host infringing content or directories or search engines that link to infringing content.

Indeed, any individual or entity who commits contributory civil infringement probably has criminal willfulness under either the majority or minority view. Contributory civil copyright infringement occurs when an individual with "knowledge of the infringing activity, induces, causes or materially contributes to the infringing conduct of another." Certainly anyone who meets this standard will satisfy the minority view, but the combination of scienter and involvement should satisfy the majority view as well. In the DMCA, Congress putatively provided some facilitators a safe harbor from civil liability for user-caused infringement, but this safe harbor has proved largely illusory because it does not appear to apply when an online service provider meets the standard for contributory copyright liability. So, anyone who contributes to civil copyright infringement may also be a criminal infringer (assuming, if applicable, the financial thresholds are met).

Specifically, to the extent the provider otherwise meets the definition of contributory infringement, any of the following activities could lead to criminal prosecution: allowing artists to upload MP3 files for others to enjoy, providing access to USENET newsgroups where some postings contain infringing content, establishing web links to infringing content (either directly or by allowing a user to do so), operating P2P file-sharing services, allowing users to conduct auctions of infringing items, operating swap meets, and operating a marketing network for web sites that host infringing content.

* * *

Notes

1. In order to obtain a felony conviction under the "No Electronic Theft" Act, 17 U.S.C. § 506(a) and 18 U.S.C. § 2319, the government must demonstrate that the defendant infringed at least ten copies of one or more copyrighted works with a total retail value of more than $2,500 within a 180–day period. [For a misdemeanor,] the government must demonstrate that the infringement was done either (a) for purposes of commercial advantage or private financial gain, or (b) by reproduction or distribution of one or more copyrighted works with a total retail value of more than $1,000 within a 180–day period. U.S. Dep't of Justice, Prosecuting Intellectual Property Crimes (2001), http://www.usdoj.gov/criminal/cybercrime/ipmanual/03ipma.htm.

2. As referenced above in the Goldman piece, the Court in *United States v. Rothberg*, 2002 WL 171963 (N.D. Ill. 2002), addressed the question

of how to determine value of infringing items under the NET Act. In *Rothberg*, at issue were 3,947 software titles found to be on a File Transfer Protocol (FTP) site called Sentinel.

> * * * The government obtained the retail prices for 2,200 of the 3,947 software titles found to be on the site at the time of the seizure. After some revisions and corrections, it derived an average price of $384 per program. * * * [W]e are satisfied that the estimate is reasonably accurate such that we can rely upon it for purposes of the Sentencing Guidelines calculation.

> Defendants argue that because [Pirates with Attitude (PWA)] did not sell the infringing software, the value for Guidelines purposes is zero. The Court disagrees. First of all, the Guideline does not direct the Court to determine the retail *price*; rather it requires us to determine the retail *value*. * * * [T]he pirated software had value, even if those who downloaded it were not charged a fee.

> The question, however, is what the value is. We cannot simply adopt the retail price of the legitimate software items without considering other factors; the 1998 version of Guideline § 2B5.3 and Application Note 1 clearly do not permit this. * * *

> In this case we lack any solid evidence of the value of the infringing items other than the retail price of the genuine articles. Defendants have offered evidence garnered from reports of other cases in which counterfeit software was sold on the black market. But even assuming some figure, or range of figures, from those cases properly could be applied in this one, black market pricing is not always a proper surrogate for actual value. In this case the programs were fully-functioning versions of the products sold at retail, and they were mass-distributed, or at least made available for mass distribution, by PWA. The only significant differences between PWA's programs and the genuine articles were the unavailability of a manual, technical support, and a warranty. There is no basis to believe, however, that these affected the value of the programs to PWA's downloaders, particularly in view of the availability of "help" files on the programs themselves.

> The law is clear that when there is an absence of other reliable evidence concerning the value of the infringing item, and the item is materially indistinguishable from the genuine article, the Court may adopt the retail price of the genuine item as the value of the infringing item. That is the case here. For these reasons, the Court will use the $384 average price determined by the government for the 2,200 programs that it reviewed as the average price for the full set of the infringing items. We therefore find that the value of the infringing items for purposes of Guideline § 2B5.3 is $1,424,640 (3,710 times $384). *Id.* at *4.

E. ASSESSING THE PARAMETERS OF THE DIGITAL MILLENNIUM COPYRIGHT ACT

PROBLEM 47: Fighting "Electronic Burglary"

Al and Joanne (the main characters in Problem 46) continue to maintain their Web site on Earthlink as part of an independent study project for their History of American Film class. On this site, they have been able to post excerpts of classic films and complete versions of *The Godfather* Saga in fifteen minute segments for easier access/viewing. In a separate section on DVD technology, they post links to sites where software and other resources are available for working with DVD files, including but not limited to file-sharing FAQ's and DeCSS guides.[1]

Assume that the U.S. Attorneys office prosecutes Al and Joanne under the Anti–Circumvention Provisions of the Digital Millennium Copyright Act (DMCA), 17 U.S.C. §§ 1201(a)(1)-(2), (b), 1202(a)-(b). The relevant provisions of the Act prohibit circumvention of both access controls and copy controls in copy protection systems.[2] Also prohibited is "trafficking" in technologies that are primarily designed for the circumvention of technological measures. Any person who violates Section 1201 or 1202 willfully and for purposes of commercial advantage or private financial gain faces a maximum of 5 years' imprisonment and a $500,000 fine (first offense).

A. What arguments might Al & Joanne set forth in support of their assertion that they have not violated the terms of the Act? What additional facts might need to be identified before the result can be predicted? What might be the likely result, in the end?

B. Might there be laws that could address this type of activity in a better way?

C. Alternatively, might there be another way for educational institutions to address this area as a matter of policy?

THE DIGITAL MILLENNIUM COPYRIGHT ACT: PROVISIONS ON CIRCUMVENTING PROTECTION SYSTEMS AND LIMITING LIABILITY OF SERVICE PROVIDERS

Francisco Castro.
4 J. Intell. Prop. 3 (2004).

* * * [O]n October 28, 1998, Congress passed the Digital Millennium Copyright Act (DMCA). This comprehensive piece of legislation was

---

1. DeCSS is a decryption computer program designed to circumvent "CSS," the encryption technology that studios place on DVDs to prevent unauthorized viewing and copying.

2. Access controls prevent usage, not copying. Copy controls can be thought of as measures which actually prevent copying. Examples of access controls include encryption, passwords, usage restrictions. Examples of copy controls include serial copy protection for digital works and old floppy protection schemes.

intended to implement the [World Intellectual Property Organization (WIPO)] treaties and to respond to a variety of pressing copyright issues affecting the entertainment industry, especially the increased ease of music and video piracy on the Internet. * * *

Among the vast number of issues addressed by the DMCA, two key sets of provisions have particular importance in the protection and access to artistic material on the Internet: the prohibition of unauthorized access to copyrighted works by technologies that circumvent protection systems and the limitation of copyright infringement liability of online service providers.

I. CIRCUMVENTION OF COPYRIGHT PROTECTION SYSTEMS

* * * Under the DMCA, protection is given to technological measures used to limit access of copyrighted works by prohibiting the use and distribution of techniques, tools, or devices that can circumvent security controls in order to gain access to copyrighted material. It is a federal offense to bypass security measures even when done as a part of a research project or in order to use copyrighted work in a manner permitted by law.

The following paragraphs provide a brief summary of the most important prohibitions, rights, limitations, defenses, and exemptions described in Section 1201:

A. *Prohibition of Technologies to Circumvent Access Controls*

The basic prohibition of circumvention states that no person shall circumvent a technological measure that effectively controls access to copyrighted material. The law does not impose any standards or requirements on the manner or purpose of technical measures used to control access. *17 U.S.C. § 1201*(a)(1)(A).

B. *Prohibition of Use or Distribution of Technologies to Circumvent Access Controls*

The manufacture, import, or traffic of any technology, service, or device for the purpose of circumventing access controls to copyrighted works is prohibited. This provision limits access to permitted copyrighted material if a device is needed to get around access controls. *17 U.S.C. § 1201*(a)(2).

C. *Prohibition of Use or Distribution of Technologies to Circumvent Protection of Copyrighted Works*

There are additional prohibitions on the use or distribution of technologies, products, services, or devices primarily intended to circumvent measures that protect the rights of a copyright owner. This section pertains to the copyrighted works or materials themselves rather than access controls. *17 U.S.C. § 1201*(b).

D. Rights, Limitations, and Defenses

* * * [D]efenses to copyright violations do not serve as defenses to violations of Section 1201. *17 U.S.C. § 1201*(c).

E. Recognized Exemptions

Congress provided for a number of exceptions since it recognized that there are several legitimate reasons for circumventing technical measures used to control access to copyrighted works. [These exceptions include * * *]

(a) Nonprofit Libraries, Archives, and Educational Institutions. Nonprofit libraries, archives, or educational institutions are allowed to gain access to a commercially exploited copyrighted work to decide whether to purchase it for a legal purpose. This exception is only available when a copy of an identical work cannot be obtained by other means and does not preclude restrictions to circumventing access controls previously discussed. In order [for] libraries or archives to qualify for this exemption, their collections must be available to the public and also to persons doing research in the field covered by the protected work. *17 U.S.C. § 1201*(d).

(b) Law Enforcement and Intelligence Activities. * * * *17 U.S.C. § 1201*(e).

(c) Reverse Engineering. * * * *17 U.S.C. § 1201*(f).

(d) Encryption Research. * * * *17 U.S.C. § 1201*(g) [and]

(e) Exception Regarding Minors. Parents would not be in violation of the DMCA when attempting to protect their children from harmful material on the Internet. This section permits a component or part to be incorporated in a technology, product, service or device which has the sole purpose to prevent the access of minors to material on the Internet. *17 U.S.C. § 1201*(h).

* * *

II. LIMITATIONS ON LIABILITY RELATING TO ONLINE MATERIALS

Title II of the DMCA limits monetary liability of online service providers (OSPs) for copyright infringement in the event that others place infringing material on web sites hosted by the OSP or in the case that the OSP provides a link or networking connection to a web site containing infringing material. These new provisions were implemented in *17 U.S.C. § 512* and provide legal protection to an OSP as long as it follows certain guidelines. These guidelines define various "safe harbors" or exemptions based upon the type of OSP activity. The exemptions offered by the DMCA are in addition to any defense that an OSP might have under copyright law or any other applicable law.

* * *

The following paragraphs provide a brief summary of the requirements for eligibility, definitions of a service provider, safe harbor requirements, and limitations described in Section 1201:

A.   *Requirements for Eligibility*

The OSP must establish several requirements in order to qualify for the exemptions provided by the DMCA.

(a) Termination Policy. An OSP must adopt, reasonably implement, and inform its subscribers and account holders of the service provider's system or network of, a policy that provides for the termination of those who are repeat infringers. *17 U.S.C. § 512* (i)(1)(A).

(b) Accommodation of Technical Measures. An OSP cannot interfere with standard technical measures. "Standard technical measures" is defined in Section 512(i)(2) as measures used by copyright owners to protect and identify copyrighted works. * * * *17 U.S.C. § 512*(i)(1)(B).

(c) Monitoring or Access. For an OSP to qualify for the exemptions offered by the DMCA, it is not required to monitor its service or affirmatively search for facts that show infringing activity. Moreover, the OSP does not have to gain access, remove, or disable access to material in cases where such actions are prohibited by law. *17 U.S.C. § 512*(m).

B.   *Definition of Service Provider*

[In most cases,] * * * "Service Provider" is defined as a provider of online services or network access, or the operator of facilities therefor. *17 U.S.C. § 512*(k).

C.   *Safe Harbor When OSP Acts as a Transitory Digital Network* * * * *17 U.S.C. § 512*(a). * * *

D.   *Safe Harbor When OSP Temporarily Stores Material* * * * *17 U.S.C. § 512*(b). * * *

E.   *Safe Harbor When Information Resides on System at Direction of Users*

An OSP is not liable for monetary relief, and it is subject to only injunctive or equitable relief, for infringing by reason of the storage at the direction of a user of material that resides on a system or network controlled or operated by the OSP. *17 U.S.C. § 512*(c)(1). To qualify for this exemption the OSP must:

(i)   not have knowledge that the material is infringing;

(ii) not be aware of facts or circumstances from which infringing activity is apparent;

(iii) upon obtaining knowledge or awareness, acts expeditiously to remove or disable access to the material; and

(iv) does not receive financial benefit directly attributable to any infringing activity, if it has the right and ability to control such activity.

Under Section 512(c)(2), the limitation on liability established by this safe harbor applies only if the OSP has designated an agent to receive notifications of claimed infringement. The OSP must make this agent available through its service, including on its Web site in a location accessible to the public, and by providing the Copyright Office with the person's name, address, phone number, electronic mail address, and any other contact information that the Register of Copyrights may deem appropriate.

Elements of proper notification of infringement are specified in Section 5129(c)(3) and include identification of the copyrighted work, identification of the infringing material in sufficient detail to allow the OSP to locate it, complaining party contact information, a statement signed electronically or physically by the complaining party which shows it has the authority to enforce the rights that are claimed to be infringed, and a good faith belief that the use of the material in the manner complained of is not authorized by the copyright owner, its agent, or the law. If a notice complies with at least the first three elements of proper notification, the OSP is required to promptly contact the complaining party in order to take advantage of the safe harbor provisions of the DMCA.

F. Safe Harbor When OSP Provides Information Location Tools * * * *17 U.S.C. § 512*(d).

G. Limitation on Liability of Nonprofit Educational Institutions

Section 512(e) contains an additional liability limitation for public or other institutions of higher education that act as an OSP. This Section provides that online infringement activities by faculty members or graduate students that take place when performing teaching or research functions will not be attributed to the institution if:

(i) the infringing activities do not involve the provision of online access to instructional material that are or were required or recommended within the preceding three-year period, for a course taught at the institution by a faculty member or graduate student;

(ii) the institution has not, within the three-year period, received more than two notifications of claimed infringement by such faculty member or graduate student; and

(iii) the institution provides all users of its system with informational materials that accurately describe and promote compliance with, the laws of the United States relating to copyright.

Note

1. In *Universal v. Reimerdes,* 111 F.Supp.2d 294 (S.D.N.Y. 2000), Judge Kaplan construed the DMCA as mandating "a limited prohibition against linking to web sites containing DeCSS. He required clear and

convincing evidence that those responsible for the link (a) know at the relevant time that the offending material is on the linked-to site, (b) know that it is circumvention technology that may not lawfully be offered, and (c) create or maintain the link for the purpose of disseminating that technology." *Universal v. Corley,* 273 F.3d 429, 456 (2d Cir. 2001).

> The anti-trafficking provision of the DMCA is implicated where one presents, holds out or makes a circumvention technology or device available, knowing its nature, for the purpose of allowing others to acquire it.

> To the extent that defendants have linked to sites that automatically commence the process of downloading DeCSS upon a user being transferred by defendants' hyperlinks, there can be no serious question. Defendants are engaged in the functional equivalent of transferring the DeCSS code to the user themselves.

> Substantially the same is true of defendants' hyperlinks to web pages that display nothing more than the DeCSS code or present the user only with the choice of commencing a download of DeCSS and no other content. The only distinction is that the entity extending to the user the option of downloading the program is the transferee site rather than defendants, a distinction without a difference.

> Potentially more troublesome might be links to pages that offer a good deal of content other than DeCSS but that offer a hyperlink for downloading, or transferring to a page for downloading, DeCSS. If one assumed, for the purposes of argument, that the *Los Angeles Times* web site somewhere contained the DeCSS code, it would be wrong to say that anyone who linked to the *Los Angeles Times* web site, regardless of purpose or the manner in which the link was described, thereby offered, provided or otherwise trafficked in DeCSS merely because DeCSS happened to be available on a site to which one linked. *Id.* at 325.

PROBLEM 48: Linking and Related Activities at Educational Institutions

Assume that all of the protagonists in the following hypotheticals are either employees or students at public educational institutions. Assume, also, that the activities take place on the institutions' servers. Under current legal doctrine and emerging trends, would any of the following activities be illegal? Why?

A. Cyberspace commentator, visiting scholar, and ultimate libertarian John Perry Barlow—noted for his view that copyright law is irrelevant on the Net and that all information should be free—links to an overseas site that features and encourages the dissemination of DeCSS code.

B. Adjunct Professor Delaine McGriff, herself an outspoken cyberspace libertarian, writes an overview of John Perry Barlow's legal troubles as a result of his linking activities and posts it on her course Web page. In the document, she includes a link to the same overseas site that features and encourages the dissemination of DeCSS code.

C. Professor Valdez requires all students in her Technology and the Law class to present online examples that reflect the class readings for the day, and posts an updated list of links to these examples for the students on the law school course page. After a student presents a Web site that features downloads of pirated software, Valdez updates the list of links on the course page by adding a link to that site.

D. Professor Tran, during a class presentation, goes to the blog of an Idaho militia member who is dedicated to bringing the U.S. government down. On the blog is a link to a hacker site that features instructions for hacking into the Pentagon Web site. In response to a student request, Tran e-mails a link to the blog to the whole class.

E. Law student Ryan LaFleur, in his *Journal of Law & Technology* article on the First Amendment, includes a link to an undergraduate student's blog that contains examples of alleged online obscenity. The journal publishes the article and also posts it online.

F. PEER-TO-PEER FILE SHARING AND OTHER INTERNET– RELATED DISPUTES

The longstanding battle between the entertainment industry and the large number of persons who download and share digital copies of multimedia files without permission has impacted colleges and universities legally and as a matter of policy. While no one disputes the fact that peer-to-peer technology can and does have many legitimate uses in the higher education community, it is also true that a significant percentage of those who have used this technology are students who have done so for the sole purpose of obtaining free music, software, and other copyright protected products. And many have taken advantage of high-speed connections on campus to facilitate these activities.

A central question as a matter of law is whether and to what extent educational institutions can be held liable for copyright infringement taking place on their watch. If direct copyright infringement can be shown, one or more of two theories may be invoked, criminal copyright infringement and vicarious liability for infringement.

Major court decisions addressing file sharing have strengthened these doctrines. In *A&M Records v. Napster,* 239 F.3d 1004 (9th Cir. 2001), the Court found the highly popular service liable under both contributory infringement and vicarious liability for infringement, and the ruling eventually put the company out of business. In *MGM v. Grokster,* ___ U.S. ___, 125 S.Ct. 2764 (2005), the U.S. Supreme Court bolstered the ability of plaintiffs to prevail under a contributory copyright theory by finding that if a company distributed file sharing software pursuant to a business model that relied on *inducement,* such activity could result in liability as well.

Educational institutions, however, can take advantage of the afore-mentioned Digital Millennium Copyright Act (DMCA) to insulate themselves from liability. Section 512 provides a safe harbor, as long as its terms and conditions are satisfied. Yet the DMCA is far from the end of the story. Many academics have criticized the statutory scheme, both for its apparent sublimation of fair use principles and for its "guilty until proven innocent" take-down provisions. And as a matter of policy colleges and universities are still faced with the dilemma of how to address prospective illegal activity on the part of members of the campus community every day.

Thus, even in spite of major victories by the entertainment industry in the nation's highest courts, the problem has not gone away. Indeed, peer-to-peer technology is only becoming stronger and more efficient.

Consider these issues in light of the materials that follow. What should the role of colleges and universities be in this context? Is an aggressive, interventionist stance warranted, or is a laissez-faire approach—albeit accompanied by compliance with the DMCA—the one that still makes the most sense under the circumstances?

What predictions would you make regarding how these issues might play out over the next 5–10 years?

SCHOOL HOUSES ROCK: UNIVERSITY RESPONSE TO THE THREAT OF CONTRIBUTORY COPYRIGHT INFRINGEMENT AND FORCED COMPLIANCE OF THE DIGITAL MILLENNIUM COPYRIGHT ACT: THE ENTERTAINMENT INDUSTRY MAY HAVE WON THE BATTLE AGAINST NAPSTER, BUT CAN IT WIN THE WAR AGAINST UNIVERSITIES?

Elizabeth M. Harris.
31 Rutgers Computer & Tech. L.J. 187 (2004).

Introduction

With the advent of the Internet, digital technologies have become a necessity in the classroom. In response, schools struggle to provide students with the tools and skills necessary to create their own ideas, as opposed to borrowing those readily available with the click of a mouse. As a result, universities have found themselves in dual roles: providing their students with intellectual stimulation, as well as the more daunting task of functioning as a service provider. Inadvertently, academia has also played an instrumental role in the illegal downloading of digital music.

Perhaps the single largest demographic responsible for music piracy on the Internet is young people between the ages of 18 and 29. This also means that students, at both the graduate and college levels, have become the safe haven that harbors the media industry's most wanted criminals.

* * * To date, the Recording Industry Association of America ("RIAA") has sent more than 1,000 subpoenas to American colleges and universities, warning schools that they must prevent their students from engaging in illegal activity on their networks. Laws such as the Digital Millennium Copyright Act ("DMCA") have provided the RIAA with some legal remedy. However, there remains a clear and present danger of music piracy continuing. It seems no matter how hard copyright holders and the legal community try, savvy computer users and avid entertainment fans are too bold to be frightened by the industry's admonishments. Fear that strict enforcement of the DMCA could stifle free thought on college campuses has been a pressing concern of the education and legal communities for some time. * * * [T]he recording industry has boldly instituted a policy of suing college students, as well as fiercely threatening the academic institutions themselves with civil lawsuits. * * *

Part I

* * *

[T]he RIAA has resorted to seeking legal recourse against universities for their failure to adequately monitor and prevent the illegal activities of their students. The media industry is hoping the threat of contributory copyright infringement litigation will scare universities into compliance and force them to take adequate steps to ensure students are not violating the law on university servers. In some cases, the threat of litigation has provided remedial relief for copyright holders. In 2000, Metallica filed a lawsuit against Yale University for the copyright infringement of its students on Yale computer systems. In response, the school promptly banned Napster. Metallica subsequently dropped its suit against the school.

A. The RIAA Strikes Back

The entertainment industry has stated that it only intends to go after egregious copyright infringers. Unfortunately, this makes college students the prime target, as they happen to be among the worst offenders of illegal file sharing. Thus, it was only a matter of time before the media industry turned its attention from the schools to the perpetrators they harbor.

In spring 2003, the RIAA sent shockwaves throughout the academic community when it filed suit against four college students: Joseph Nievelt of Michigan Technological University ("Michigan Tech"), Aaron Sherman and Jesse Jordan of Rensselaer Polytechnic Institute, and Daniel Peng of Princeton University ("Princeton"), for maintaining sites on their campus networks that facilitated P2P file sharing. The defendants later settled their cases by paying fines between $12,500 and $17,500.

What is alarming about this case is that the RIAA bypassed administrators at all three universities, taking matters into its own hands. Since the advent of the DMCA, a university's incentive to cooperate with the Motion Picture Association of America ("MPAA") and the RIAA has arisen from Section 512(a), which grants an internet service provider ("ISP" or "service provider") protection from liability for vicarious copyright infringement if it complies with certain conditions.

First, the service provider must adopt and implement a policy of terminating the accounts of subscribers who are repeat infringers. Virtually every institution of higher education has published such a policy. As a preemptive measure, even schools that have yet to receive a single notice of infringing activity have developed policies that make compliance with federal copyright laws explicit.

Second, the service provider must accommodate and not interfere with "standard technical measures." "Standard technical measures" are defined as those measures typically used by copyright holders that enable them to identify copyright infringers. Thus, a school cannot install a firewall that may block access to its internet protocol ("IP") addresses by copyright owners such as the RIAA.

Typically, universities and colleges are alerted of copyright infringement on their servers from a notification by the RIAA or the MPAA, pursuant to sections 512(c) and (d) of the DMCA. The notification may be sent via e-mail or paper, and must include the identification of the infringed material. This identification tells the university "the specific . . . computer address" where the violation occurred. This notification by the copyright holder triggers an investigation by the university. The university then enforces its own policy, hopefully resulting in the student's abstention from the activity. In 2002, both Princeton and Cornell Universities received more than 200 notifications about infringing activity on their networks through this procedure.

The RIAA claims it deviated from this protocol with the four students because of the seriousness of their offenses. Nievelt, for example, "shared at least 200 songs" by major recording artists on Michigan Tech's network. However, the RIAA's blatant failure to provide the universities with fair warning about alleged infringing activity occurring on their systems by their own students has clearly changed the rules of engagement between universities and copyright holders. The RIAA carried its ambush against the four students in military-like fashion, providing university administrators with no warning whatsoever as to its impending attack. More importantly, however, a message was sent to the P2P world: the entertainment industry is not afraid to pursue legal action against college kids. As a result, anyone is fair game. Under this theory, it is safe to assume that the RIAA was hoping to make an example of the four students.

This tactic by the RIAA of thwarting university officials may discourage schools from cooperating with copyright holders in preventing further illegal activity. In a scornful letter to the RIAA, Michigan Tech

President Curtis Tompkins admonished the Association for its poor handling of the situation, stating that "had [the RIAA] followed the previous methods established in notification of a violation, [the school] would have shut off the student and not allowed the problem to grow to the size and scope that it is today." Furthermore, Princeton has had a long-standing policy against illegal downloading, and in the past has effectively ensured cooperation from infringing students when they are apprehended.

Conflict between copyright holders and universities over how to handle illegal downloading may prove inevitable. If the goal of the university is to prevent copyright infringement in an effort to protect the student, while the goal of the RIAA is to simply prosecute e-piracy with little concern for the welfare of the student, then the problem of illegal downloading on university campuses may never be resolved. * * *

B. Universities Respond

Arguably, section 512 of the DMCA provides universities some relief from accountability. However, those who seek to protect copyrighted works believe a large part of the problem is that university culture itself perpetuates piracy of music on the Internet. Historically, colleges have acted as protectors of intellectual freedom. Ironically, it is for this same reason that a recent study squarely places the blame for copyright infringement at college campuses on university culture itself. Providing high speed internet access, posting course materials on the web, and requiring students to constantly check their email for announcements from faculty and administration, "makes people more likely to download . . . " Furthermore, the study cites university failure to make policies explicit as a leading cause of student defiance.

However, the entertainment industry's cries have not fallen on deaf ears, as universities and colleges across the country have instituted a wide range of anti-infringement measures intended to deter their students from conducting illegal activity. At Colorado University, for example, students are subject to a "three strikes" policy. The first strike consists of a warning to the copyright violator. The second strike results in a suspension of network privileges to be reinstated upon completion of an educational requirement. Upon a third violation, a student or faculty administrator finds herself in a judicial hearing with university officials.

Another method many universities employ is to educate incoming students about appropriate Internet use from the moment they arrive on campus. At Pennsylvania State University ("Penn State"), students are required "to take an online tutorial" about appropriate Internet usage, as well as agree to refrain from downloading copyrighted material before gaining access to the university's system. The University of California, Berkeley ("Berkeley") instituted a similar policy, where freshmen and transfer students must "sit through a three-part program on the school's computer policy." At the University of Minnesota, students are explicitly warned during summer orientation about the school's policy against "using programs such as Kazaa and Morpheus."

Another, far more draconian, method has been the confiscation of student hardware. In the spring of 2003, a Penn State student was stripped of his computer privileges for allegedly engaging in illegal activity on the school's server. In November 2003, Massachusetts Institute of Technology ("M.I.T.") shut down a student-run, student-created alternative to Internet file-swapping: a system that allowed music to travel via cable connections into students' television sets. Although M.I.T. acted preemptively, pressure by record label Vivendi Universal precluded the students from obtaining a licensing agreement to operate the system.

Anyone doubting the veracity of a school's policy against illegal Internet use need only consider Northwestern University, which enforces its policy equally as to employees and students. In the summer of 2002, the school fired a secretary after she downloaded and stored approximately 2,000 music files on her work computer. The school claimed the secretary violated its policy barring personal use of the school's computer by employees.

Schools with sufficient capital are finding innovative ways to protect the legal rights of copyright holders while quenching the musical thirst of their students. In the spirit of innovation, or perhaps as a result of its frustration with policies that failed to act as a deterrent, Penn State became the first university in the country to announce that it would pay for its students to legally download music. In a revolutionary deal, the school has partnered with Napster to provide the service "at no cost to its students," who in turn have access to more than 500,000 music files in Napster's library. Acting as a test group, students living on campus were the first to exploit this service. Following Penn State's footsteps, universities such as Vanderbilt and Cornell have already signed partnership agreements with Napster.

* * *

Part II

A. Subpoena Power Under the DMCA

* * *

On July 24, 2002, Verizon was served with a subpoena by the RIAA to compel disclosure of the identity of a Verizon subscriber "whom the RIAA believed to be engaging in infringing activity." Although the RIAA may trace an infringer to her ISP via the infringer's IP address, only the ISP has access to information that reveals the identity of the infringer. In the instant case, the RIAA used section 512(h) of the DMCA to compel Verizon to reveal the infringer's identity by providing her name and address. This would have enabled the RIAA to sue the infringer directly.

Verizon, however, flatly refused to reveal the identity of their subscriber. It argued that section 512(h) "[did] not apply to an ISP acting merely as a conduit for an individual using a P2P file sharing program to exchange files."

* * *

[T]he RIAA asked the court to accept a broadly construed definition of an ISP in section 512(k)(1)(B). Essentially, the RIAA argued that the subpoena provision was applicable to any ISP, regardless of whether it acts as merely a conduit of information or engages in the caching of infringing material. The court found this argument laughable, noting that even if one defined "all the world as an ISP," any entity acting as a conduit rather than storing infringing material would not fit the specific condition of section 512(c)(3)(A). As a result, the court held that a subpoena under the DMCA may only be issued to an ISP engaged in storing infringing material on its server.

The Verizon decision has important implications for universities and colleges. Prior to the decision, schools such as the University of California at Los Angeles, Northeastern University, and M.I.T. complied with subpoenas issued under section 512(h) of the DMCA. As a result, several lawsuits were filed by the RIAA against the infringers, all of whom were college students. * * * [T]he scope of section 512(h) was never addressed.

Nonetheless, Verizon remains a tremendous victory for universities. Pursuant to the court's reasoning, schools that have only acted as a conduit between students and infringing activities are not required to comply with subpoenas issued under the DMCA. Thus, schools may protect the identity of their students. However, universities must comply with a subpoena if they store infringing material on their server. Because most schools offer their students significant storage space on their servers, liability only arises for universities who store any infringing material their students download. Otherwise, the school is merely a "conduit" between the infringer and the infringing material.

B. Contributory Copyright Infringement

Schools that fail to comply with the DMCA expose themselves to liability for contributory and vicarious copyright infringement. A contributory infringement claim arises when a defendant knowingly contributes to the pirating of copyright-protected material.

* * *

To prevail on a claim of contributory infringement, a copyright holder must first prove that the defendant had knowledge of the infringing activity, but did nothing to prevent it. This first prong is particularly problematic for copyright holders such as the RIAA and the MPAA who intend to sue schools under this claim. To satisfy the knowledge element of a contributory infringement claim, the copyright holder must have "evidence of actual knowledge [by the defendant] of specific acts of infringement." However, historically, courts have found that constructive, rather than actual knowledge may fulfill this first prong. At first glance, the notice requirement of section 512(d) of the DMCA provides universities and ISPs with a duty requirement that may bring them one step closer to liability for contributory infringement. This is ironic because the DMCA is also intended to give ISPs immunity from contributory infringement.

However, there is an important difference between, for example, Napster's constructive knowledge of infringing activity and a university's constructive knowledge by way of a 512(d) notification. Namely, Napster had a general awareness that its site was accessed primarily for the purpose of illegally downloading MP3s. More precisely put, illegal downloading was the very purpose for Napster's existence. Thus, Napster had both constructive and actual knowledge of the infringing activity.

Academic institutions, on the other hand, do not have this general awareness, as the server space and the Internet connection they provide their students with is primarily for educational purposes. The mere existence of a server that happens to be used by students to engage in infringing activity is not dispositive of a school's constructive knowledge of that infringing use. Consequently, the less stringent evidentiary standard of constructive notice is inapplicable to colleges and universities whose students illegally download copyright-protected works. As a result, a copyright holder who intends to bring a contributory infringement claim against a university must show that the school had actual notice of the infringement.

Part III

A. Traffic Shaping: An Answer?

* * *

At college, students have the luxury of accessing a much quicker Internet connection than they do at home, and with infinitely more storage space. In response, schools must purchase more bandwidth to accommodate the amount of traffic their servers are subjected to, much of which is devoted to e-piracy. For example, in early fall 2001, Binghamton University's T–3 connection, which is "roughly 1000 times faster than a phone line," was completely exhausted. In Napster's heyday, it was banned by many universities because it "clogged campus networks."

In response to this network crunch, many universities have engaged in "traffic shaping," a way of preventing music from being downloaded through their systems. Currently, more than 700 universities around the country use "Packeteer," a hardware appliance with multiple software options that enable large institutions to manage computer network traffic by focusing on how they can increase visibility, control bandwidth, and compress network traffic. * * *

Other universities have created their own traffic shaping software. Because more than 90 percent of its network traffic consisted of P2P file sharing, the University of Florida unveiled Integrated Computer Application for Recognizing User Services, or "Icarus," in the summer of 2003.

That summer, Icarus caught 769 P2P users and an additional 300 in the fall. Impressively, "bandwidth usage [subsequently] dropped 85 percent." Icarus works by immediately sending an e-mail and a pop-up message to a student who attempts to engage in file sharing. The student is subsequently disconnected from the network.

Among the disadvantages of traffic shaping systems like Packeteer, Radware, and Icarus are that the hardware sifts through downloads by file type, failing to differentiate between legally downloaded music and illegal P2P sharing. Nonetheless, schools like network traffic management systems because they help them avoid contributory infringement liability and comply with the DMCA. Perhaps most importantly though, the very presence of traffic shaping software acts as a deterrent for some students.

* * *

Notes

1.   Additional details regarding ongoing tensions and noteworthy developments in this area have been documented extensively in relevant legal and public policy literature. For example, Peter K. Yu wrote the following in 2005 regarding the RIAA's automated web crawlers and their prospective implications:

> To seek out information about infringing material, the RIAA has used automated Web crawlers and other computer programs to scour the Internet for what it believed to be illegally traded songs. Although these automated Web crawlers drastically reduced the costs of policing copyrights, they also yielded false positives that caused the industry public embarrassment. For example, during the second week of May 2003, the RIAA issued an erroneous take-down notice to Speakeasy, a national broadband provider, alleging that the FTP site of one of its subscribers illegally offered copyrighted sound files for download. According to the form letter, many of the "approximately 0" files on the Web site "contain recordings owned by our member companies, including songs by such artists as Creed." * * *

> That same week, the RIAA's crawlers confused Peter Usher, a retired professor of astronomy and astrophysics at Pennsylvania State University, with Usher Raymond, the best-selling rhythm-and-blues performer. After the crawler located on the university's departmental server a directory named "usher" that contained a sound file in MP3 format, the RIAA sent Professor Usher a cease-and-desist letter. The suspect file, it turned out, was a recording by The Chromatics, an a cappella group of Penn State astronomers and astrophysicists, of a song about the Swift gamma ray satellite that Penn State had helped to design. The RIAA later withdrew the notice and apologized to Professor Usher, offering to send him a compact disc and T-shirt "in appreciation of his understanding." According to the RIAA, the dozens of faulty copyright infringement notices that went out during that week were sent by a temporary

worker who failed to follow regular protocol to confirm the content of the suspect files.

* * *

The Penn State incident demonstrates the chilling effect of the take-down provision. When the university's central computing office received the RIAA's letter on May 8, it notified the Department of Astronomy and Astrophysics that it would shut down the department's Internet connection, right in the middle of spring-semester final examinations, unless the infringing material was removed within forty-eight hours. Fortunately, the manager of the departmental server was able to locate Professor Usher's a cappella MP3 and convince the central computing office not to shut down the connection. Had he failed, some students in the department would have been unable to take finals or complete other end-of-term assignments. Research would have come to a halt, and grant applications for some cutting-edge projects may have been fatally de-layed. Unfortunately, the DMCA would not have provided any legal redress in any of these scenarios unless the victims could show that the RIAA had knowingly materially misrepresented information in the take-down notice. Peter K. Yu, *P2P and the Future of Private Copying,* 76 U. Colo. L. Rev. 653 (2005)

2. Analyzing how college and university policies have changed during this era, Kristina Groennings wrote:

Specific university policies exemplary of those spawned by the recent litigation are those of the University of Colorado, Colorado State Univer-sity, Pennsylvania State University, Iowa State University, and Indiana University. At these schools, repercussions for illegal activity conducted using university networks range from Internet disconnection to expul-sion from the school. For example, students at Colorado State University and the University of Colorado at Colorado Springs must sign an agreement that states they will not conduct illegal activity on the university network. The university monitors the network for high vol-umes of activity, and notifies a potential infringer that she must either stop or be disconnected. Pennsylvania State University limits the amount of data students can download to 1.5 gigabytes. If a student exceeds this limit, the university slows down the Internet connection to dial-up speed. The university sent a warning of the ramifications of file-sharing to 110,000 students in March 2003. In April 2003, it suspended Internet access of 220 students. At Iowa State University, first-time offenders are only required to remove infringing copyrighted material. However, the university is threatening greater repercussions in the future, including disciplinary actions, probation, and even deferred expulsion for illegal file-sharing. Repeat offender cases are turned over to the federal legal system.

Indiana University's program has been reported by the U.S. House Judiciary Committee's Subcommittee on Courts, the Internet, and Intel-lectual Property to be particularly effective in preventing illegal file-sharing. The university implemented an online file-sharing tutorial and quiz to educate students about copyright laws. Students who receive an illegal file-sharing notice must pass an online quiz and agree to delete infringing files. If they refuse, network access is terminated. For second-time offenders, termination is immediate and the individual's name is forwarded to the dean of students. The number of illegal file-sharing notices received by the university from the RIAA dropped by over fifty percent between the 2003 and 2004 academic years.

A number of schools are also resorting to limitations on per-student bandwidth, due to the potential of high traffic to overburden school servers, a measure which increases downloading time. In addition, almost forty universities and colleges now use "CopySense Network Appliance," a product created by Audible Magic that prevents the transfer of copyrighted files to students' computers. The University of Florida uses another program, ICARUS, to prevent file-sharing altogether.

Colleges and universities also made major changes in the way students can access digital entertainment content from 2003 to 2004. Negotiations with legitimate music services, coupled with disincentives for illegal P2P use, may work to both immediately reduce file-sharing among university students and ultimately reduce illegal downloading by encouraging legal habits at an early age. Pennsylvania State University was the first to enter negotiations with the newly legitimate Napster. University students are given access to Napster's database of 500,000 songs. Tethered downloading is offered free of charge, and students are able to download each song on up to three personal computers. In addition, students may purchase a song for 99 cents for permanent use. On the fourth day that the service was provided, over 2,600 students had registered for the service and over 100,000 songs had been downloaded. As of fall 2004, Napster, MusicNet, Rhapsody, and iTunes have all negotiated deals with multiple universities. Duke University distributed over 1,500 iPods to freshmen, along with ten free downloads from iTunes. * * * Kristina Groennings, *Costs and Benefits of the Recording Industry's Litigation Against Individuals,* 20 BERKELEY TECH. L.J. 571 (2005).

3. Consider the U.S. Supreme Court's decision in the *Grokster* case, which follows. Although not an education-related decision per se, many believe that it will have a wide-ranging impact throughout the higher education community over time. What are some of the prospective changes that might be anticipated as a result of this decision?

METRO–GOLDWYN–MAYER STUDIOS v. GROKSTER

___ U.S. ___, 125 S.Ct. 2764 (2005).

SOUTER, J., delivered the opinion for a unanimous Court.

The question is under what circumstances the distributor of a product capable of both lawful and unlawful use is liable for acts of copyright infringement by third parties using the product. We hold that one who distributes a device with the object of promoting its use to infringe copyright, as shown by clear expression or other affirmative steps taken to foster infringement, is liable for the resulting acts of infringement by third parties.

I

A

Respondents, Grokster, Ltd., and StreamCast Networks, Inc., defendants in the trial court, distribute free software products that allow computer users to share electronic files through peer-to-peer networks, so called because users' computers communicate directly with each other, not through central servers. The advantage of peer-to-peer networks over information networks of other types shows up in their substantial and growing popularity. Because they need no central computer server to mediate the exchange of information or files among users, the high-bandwidth communications capacity for a server may be dispensed with, and the need for costly server storage space is eliminated. Since copies of a file (particularly a popular one) are available on many users' computers, file requests and retrievals may be faster than on other types of networks, and since file exchanges do not travel through a server, communications can take place between any computers that remain connected to the network without risk that a glitch in the server will disable the network in its entirety. Given these benefits in security, cost, and efficiency, peer-to-peer networks are employed to store and distribute electronic files by universities, government agencies, corporations, and libraries, among others.

Other users of peer-to-peer networks include individual recipients of Grokster's and StreamCast's software, and although the networks that they enjoy through using the software can be used to share any type of digital file, they have prominently employed those networks in sharing copyrighted music and video files without authorization. A group of copyright holders (MGM for short, but including motion picture studios, recording companies, songwriters, and music publishers) sued Grokster and StreamCast for their users' copyright infringements, alleging that they knowingly and intentionally distributed their software to enable users to reproduce and distribute the copyrighted works in violation of the Copyright Act, MGM sought damages and an injunction.

* * *

In addition to * * * evidence of express promotion, marketing, and intent to promote further, the business models employed by Grokster and StreamCast confirm that their principal object was use of their software to download copyrighted works. Grokster and StreamCast receive no revenue from users, who obtain the software itself for nothing. Instead, both companies generate income by selling advertising space, and they stream the advertising to Grokster and Morpheus users while they are employing the programs. As the number of users of each program increases, advertising opportunities become worth more. While there is doubtless some demand for free Shakespeare, the evidence shows that substantive volume is a function of free access to copyrighted work. Users seeking Top 40 songs, for example, or the latest release by Modest Mouse, are certain to be far more numerous than those seeking a free Decameron, and Grokster and StreamCast translated that demand into dollars.

Finally, there is no evidence that either company made an effort to filter copyrighted material from users' downloads or otherwise impede the sharing of copyrighted files. Although Grokster appears to have sent e-mails warning users about infringing content when it received threatening notice from the copyright holders, it never blocked anyone from continuing to use its software to share copyrighted files. StreamCast not only rejected another company's offer of help to monitor infringement, but blocked the Internet Protocol addresses of entities it believed were trying to engage in such monitoring on its networks.

* * *

The Court of Appeals affirmed [the U.S. District Court's ruling in favor of Grokster]. In the court's analysis, a defendant was liable as a contributory infringer when it had knowledge of direct infringement and materially contributed to the infringement. But the court read *Sony Corp. of America v. Universal City Studios, Inc.,* 464 U.S. 417, 104 S. Ct. 774 (1984), as holding that distribution of a commercial product capable of substantial noninfringing uses could not give rise to contributory liability for infringement unless the distributor had actual knowledge of specific instances of infringement and failed to act on that knowledge. The fact that the software was capable of substantial noninfringing uses in the Ninth Circuit's view meant that Grokster and StreamCast were not liable, because they had no such actual knowledge, owing to the decentralized architecture of their software. The court also held that Grokster and StreamCast did not materially contribute to their users' infringement because it was the users themselves who searched for, retrieved, and stored the infringing files, with no involvement by the defendants beyond providing the software in the first place.

The Ninth Circuit also considered whether Grokster and StreamCast could be liable under a theory of vicarious infringement. The court held against liability because the defendants did not monitor or control the use of the software, had no agreed-upon right or current ability to supervise its use, and had no independent duty to police infringement. We granted certiorari.

II

A

MGM and many of the *amici* fault the Court of Appeals's holding for upsetting a sound balance between the respective values of supporting creative pursuits through copyright protection and promoting innovation in new communication technologies by limiting the incidence of liability for copyright infringement. The more artistic protection is favored, the more technological innovation may be discouraged; the administration of copyright law is an exercise in managing the trade-off.

The tension between the two values is the subject of this case, with its claim that digital distribution of copyrighted material threatens copyright holders as never before, because every copy is identical to the original, copying is easy, and many people (especially the young) use file-sharing software to download copyrighted works. This very breadth of the software's use may well draw the public directly into the debate over copyright policy, and the indications are that the ease of copying songs or movies using software like Grokster's and Napster's is fostering disdain for copyright protection. As the case has been presented to us, these fears are said to be offset by the different concern that imposing liability, not only on infringers but on distributors of software based on its potential for unlawful use, could limit further development of beneficial technologies.[8]

The argument for imposing indirect liability in this case is, however, a powerful one, given the number of infringing downloads that occur every day using StreamCast's and Grokster's software. When a widely shared service or product is used to commit infringement, it may be impossible to enforce rights in the protected work effectively against all direct infringers, the only practical alternative being to go against the distributor of the copying device for secondary liability on a theory of contributory or vicarious infringement.

One infringes contributorily by intentionally inducing or encouraging direct infringement, and infringes vicariously by profiting from direct infringement while declining to exercise a right to stop or limit it.[9] Although "[t]he Copyright Act does not expressly render anyone liable for infringement committed by another," these doctrines of secondary

---

8. The mutual exclusivity of these values should not be overstated, however. On the one hand technological innovators, including those writing file-sharing computer programs, may wish for effective copyright protections for their work. *See, e.g.,* Tim Wu, *When Code Isn't Law*, 89 Va. L .Rev. 679, 750 (2003). (StreamCast itself was urged by an associate to "get [its] technology written down and [its intellectual property] protected."). On the other hand the widespread distribution of creative works through improved technologies may enable the synthesis of new works or generate audiences for emerging artists. *See Eldred v. Ashcroft*, 537 U.S. 186, 223–26, 537 U.S. 186, 123 S. Ct. 769 (2003) (STEVENS, J., dissenting); Molly Van Houweling, *Distributive Values in Copyright*, 83 Texas L. Rev. 1535, 1539–40, 1562–64 (2005); Brief for Sovereign Artists et al. as Amici Curiae 11.

9. We stated in *Sony Corp. of America v. Universal City Studios, Inc.*, 464 U.S. 417, 104 S. Ct. 774 (1984), that " 'the lines between direct infringement, contributory infringement and vicarious liability are not clearly drawn'.... [R]easoned analysis of

[the Sony plaintiffs' contributory infringement claim] necessarily entails consideration of arguments and case law which may also be forwarded under the other labels, and indeed the parties ... rely upon such arguments and authority in support of their respective positions on the issue of contributory infringement," *id.* at 435 n.17, 104 S. Ct. 774 (quoting Universal City Studios, Inc. v. Sony Corp., 480 F.Supp. 429, 457–58 (C.D.Cal. 1979)). In the present case MGM has argued a vicarious liability theory, which allows imposition of liability when the defendant profits directly from the infringement and has a right and ability to supervise the direct infringer, even if the defendant initially lacks knowledge of the infringement. *See, e.g.,* Shapiro, Bernstein & Co. v. H.L. Green Co., 316 F.2d 304, 308 (2d Cir. 1963); Dreamland Ball Room, Inc. v. Shapiro, Bernstein & Co., 36 F.2d 354, 355 (7th Cir. 1929). Because we resolve the case based on an inducement theory, there is no need to analyze separately MGM's vicarious liability theory.

liability emerged from common law principles and are well established in the law.

B

Despite the currency of these principles of secondary liability, this Court has dealt with secondary copyright infringement in only one recent case, and because MGM has tailored its principal claim to our opinion there, a look at our earlier holding is in order. In *Sony Corp. v. Universal City Studios,* this Court addressed a claim that secondary liability for infringement can arise from the very distribution of a commercial product. There, the product, novel at the time, was what we know today as the videocassette recorder or VCR. Copyright holders sued Sony as the manufacturer, claiming it was contributorily liable for infringement that occurred when VCR owners taped copyrighted programs because it supplied the means used to infringe, and it had constructive knowledge that infringement would occur. At the trial on the merits, the evidence showed that the principal use of the VCR was for "time-shifting," or taping a program for later viewing at a more convenient time, which the Court found to be a fair, not an infringing, use. There was no evidence that Sony had expressed an object of bringing about taping in violation of copyright or had taken active steps to increase its profits from unlawful taping. Although Sony's advertisements urged consumers to buy the VCR to "record favorite shows" or "build a library" of recorded programs, neither of these uses was necessarily infringing.

On those facts, with no evidence of stated or indicated intent to promote infringing uses, the only conceivable basis for imposing liability was on a theory of contributory infringement arising from its sale of VCRs to consumers with knowledge that some would use them to infringe. But because the VCR was "capable of commercially significant noninfringing uses," we held the manufacturer could not be faulted solely on the basis of its distribution.

* * *

In sum, where an article is "good for nothing else" but infringement, there is no legitimate public interest in its unlicensed availability, and there is no injustice in presuming or imputing an intent to infringe. Conversely, the doctrine absolves the equivocal conduct of selling an item with substantial lawful as well as unlawful uses, and limits liability to instances of more acute fault than the mere understanding that some of one's products will be misused. It leaves breathing room for innovation and a vigorous commerce.

* * *

We agree with MGM that the Court of Appeals misapplied *Sony,* which it read as limiting secondary liability quite beyond the circumstances to which the case applied. * * * The Ninth Circuit has read *Sony's* limitation to mean that whenever a product is capable of substantial lawful use, the producer can never be held contributorily liable for third parties' infringing use of it; it read the rule as being this broad, even when an actual purpose to cause infringing use is shown by evidence independent of design and distribution of the product, unless the distributors had "specific knowledge of infringement at a time at which they contributed to the infringement, and failed to act upon that information." Because the Circuit found the StreamCast and Grokster software capable of substantial lawful use, it concluded on the basis of its reading of *Sony* that neither company could be held liable, since there was no showing that their software, being without any central server, afforded them knowledge of specific unlawful uses.

This view of *Sony,* however, was error.

* * *

C

Sony's rule limits imputing culpable intent as a matter of law from the characteristics or uses of a distributed product. But nothing in *Sony* requires courts to ignore evidence of intent if there is such evidence, and the case was never meant to foreclose rules of fault-based liability derived from the common law. * * * Thus, where evidence goes beyond a product's characteristics or the knowledge that it may be put to infringing uses, and shows statements or actions directed to promoting infringement, *Sony's* staple-article rule will not preclude liability.

The classic case of direct evidence of unlawful purpose occurs when one induces commission of infringement by another, or "entic[es] or persuad[es] another" to infringe, as by advertising. Thus at common law a copyright or patent defendant who "not only expected but invoked [infringing use] by advertisement" was liable for infringement "on principles recognized in every part of the law." * * *

The rule on inducement of infringement as developed in the early cases is no different today. Evidence of "active steps ... taken to encourage direct infringement," such as advertising an infringing use or instructing how to engage in an infringing use, show an affirmative intent that the product be used to infringe, and a showing that infringement was encouraged overcomes the law's reluctance to find liability when a defendant merely sells a commercial product suitable for some lawful use[.] * * *

For the same reasons that *Sony* took the staple-article doctrine of patent law as a model for its copyright safe-harbor rule, the inducement rule, too, is a sensible one for copyright. We adopt it here, holding that one who distributes a device with the object of promoting its use to infringe copyright, as shown by clear expression or other affirmative steps taken to foster infringement, is liable for the resulting acts of infringement by third parties. We are, of course, mindful of the need to keep from trenching on regular commerce or discouraging the development of technologies with lawful and unlawful potential. Accordingly, just as *Sony* did not find intentional inducement despite the knowledge of the VCR manufacturer that its device could be used to infringe, mere knowledge of infringing potential or of actual infringing uses would not be enough here to subject a distributor to liability. Nor would ordinary acts incident to product distribution, such as offering customers technical support or product updates, support liability in themselves. The inducement rule, instead, premises liability on purposeful, culpable expression and conduct, and thus does nothing to compromise legitimate commerce or discourage innovation having a lawful promise.

    * * *

In sum, this case is significantly different from *Sony* and reliance on that case to rule in favor of StreamCast and Grokster was error. *Sony* dealt with a claim of liability based solely on distributing a product with alternative lawful and unlawful uses, with knowledge that some users would follow the unlawful course. The case struck a balance between the interests of protection and innovation by holding that the product's capability of substantial lawful employment should bar the imputation of fault and consequent secondary liability for the unlawful acts of others.

MGM's evidence in this case most obviously addresses a different basis of liability for distributing a product open to alternative uses. Here, evidence of the distributors' words and deeds going beyond distribution as such shows a purpose to cause and profit from third-party acts of copyright infringement. If liability for inducing infringement is ultimately found, it will not be on the basis of presuming or imputing fault, but from inferring a patently illegal objective from statements and actions showing what that objective was.

There is substantial evidence in MGM's favor on all elements of inducement, and summary judgment in favor of Grokster and StreamCast was error. On remand, reconsideration of MGM's motion for summary judgment will be in order.

The judgment of the Court of Appeals is vacated, and the case is remanded for further proceedings consistent with this opinion.

It is so ordered.

Note

1. After the unanimous decision was announced in the *Grokster* case, commentators and educational policy makers engaged in widespread speculation regarding its prospective impact on the higher education community. Consider the following overview from the *Chronicle of Higher Education*, as set forth immediately after the decision. In retrospect, how many of these predictions have come true? How have things changed since 2005?

> College officials are divided over the impact of the U.S. Supreme Court's ruling last week that commercial producers of file-sharing software can be sued for copyright infringement. The software has been wildly popular among college students, who use it to download songs and movies—usually in violation of copyright law.
>
> Some college officials say the decision will have little impact, either on colleges' policies regarding music and movie downloading or on whether

they decide to sign deals with companies that offer legal downloading services. But other officials say the court's ruling could lead to an increase in such deals, through which colleges hope to lure students away from illegal file sharing.

The court's decision was a disappointment to scholars and technology developers who had tried to persuade the justices that a decision in favor of the entertainment industry could stifle technological innovation and prevent scholars from legally trading data, video, music, and literature using peer-to-peer networks.

As for students, many are expected to continue swapping songs and movies online—and to go on violating copyright—even if subsequent court rulings force the file-sharing companies to shut down. Students may be able to continue using existing versions of file-sharing software even if the companies have to close their doors. * * *

Sheldon E. Steinbach, vice president and general counsel at the American Council on Education, said the decision would encourage colleges to sign contracts with online services that allow students to download music legally. At least 20 institutions now provide students with free access to online music libraries like Napster and Cdigix. * * *

He also predicted that colleges would step up efforts to educate students about the liability they face when downloading copyrighted music and movies. The Recording Industry Association of America and, to a lesser extent, the Motion Picture Association of America have filed thousands of lawsuits against individuals who swap music online. Many of the suits filed by the recording-industry group are directed at college students. * * *

Charles E. Phelps, provost of the University of Rochester, agreed that colleges probably would increase efforts to educate students about copyright. He also said colleges will become much more active in trying to block the file-sharing services from campus networks.

Rochester has signed deals with Napster and Cflix that allow students to download songs and films legally from those services. * * *

William M. Mahon III, a spokesman for Pennsylvania State University, said the court's ruling would have no impact there. Penn State was one of the first universities to sign a deal with Napster, enabling students to listen to a large selection of music legally and at no cost. They must pay per-song fees, however, to download music permanently. * * *

Georgia K. Harper, a lawyer for the University of Texas System, said the court's decision was unlikely to affect the behavior of colleges toward illegal file sharing. "We are already doing pretty much everything we should do," she said.

Little will change at the Catholic University of America, which requires students to view a video about copyright infringement and then take a quiz about it, said Margaret L. O'Donnell, assistant general counsel. The university will probably not try to increase efforts to stop file sharing on the campus, she said. "Colleges are already maxed out on their resources they can expend policing students." * * * Andrea L. Foster, *Colleges Split Over Effects of Court Ruling on File Sharing*, CHRONICLE OF HIGHER ED., July 8, 2005.

Chapter XI

THE RIGHTS OF EDUCATORS

This chapter highlights the range of issues that may arise in disputes between educators and their employers. Part A begins with a broad overview of perspectives on labor relations in public education. Part B addresses the right to acquire and retain tenure, and Part C follows by examining the related area of dismissal. Part D focuses on freedom of expression, first exploring the scope of constitutional protection generally and then turning to the surprisingly complex topic of academic freedom. Part E concludes by documenting the types of employment discrimination cases that have been litigated in the education community over time.

A. PERSPECTIVES ON LABOR RELATIONS IN PUBLIC EDUCATION

1. COLLECTIVE BARGAINING AND THE EDUCATION PROCESS

From **4 UCLA Journal of Education (1990)**
Special Symposium Edition

● **Craig Becker,** *Governing the Schools: Teachers' Unions and Public Education*, 4 UCLA J. Ed. 49 (1990)

Teachers' unions are an enigma. Although less than a fifth of workers in all industries were organized in 1988, over four fifths of public school teachers now carry union cards. In the last decade, membership in public employee unions has grown dramatically: thirty six percent of all government workers are now organized. Even so, the proportion of union members in schools is more than double this figure. And while just over a tenth of female employees are organized, in the teaching profession—one long dominated by women—two unions, the National Education Association (NEA) and American Federation of Teachers (AFT), together comprise a membership of over two and one-half million.

Not only have teachers organized, they have vigorously asserted their collective right to join in setting the terms and conditions of their employment. Teachers make up roughly a third of the nation's public employees; however, they call some two thirds of the strikes among government workers. And even after agreement is reached, teachers are more likely than other public employees to press grievances to arbitration.

The new tenacity of teachers in organizing and adopting traditional trade union practices has provoked a rising tide of reaction. Critics of teachers' unions typically contrast the alleged selfishness of organized labor to the selflessness deemed essential in schools. A century ago the *Chicago Times–Herald* decried the formation of the Chicago Federation of Teachers, the predecessor of the AFT, charging that the union sprang from "a spirit not creditable to the high standards of professional ethics" Recently, a school superintendent echoed this critique, declaring: "Teachers have lost their image as being public servants and are relegating themselves to being comparable to the dinner bucket, hard-hat union member." * * *

The ideal of the teacher implied in the term "public servant" has been held up to schoolmarms since the early nineteenth century. Since the Civil War, in fact, most teachers have been women. Until the advances brought by the contemporary feminist movement, there were few other secure or relatively high status occupations open to women. In 1963, the National Opinion Research Center ranked teaching thirty fifth in its scale of all occupations by social status, but first among jobs dominated by women. As late as 1981, over two thirds of all teachers were women, yet virtually all were supervised by male principals who reported to school boards composed almost entirely of men. Traditionally, too, teaching has figured as an act of dedication—even self sacrifice—on women's part. The figures of the mother and teacher have appeared as one. As Catharine Beecher, one of the earliest advocates of teaching as a female profession, affirmed in 1829, "It is to *mothers*, and to *teachers*, that the world is to look for the character which is be enstamped on each succeeding generation." "What is *the profession of a Woman*," Beecher asked. "Is it not to form immortal minds?"

Yet teaching often proved difficult for women to reconcile with their family roles. Through the first third of this century, many schools fired women who married. And until 1974, when the United States Supreme Court struck down the policy, school boards routinely kept pregnant women out of the classroom: requiring them to go on unpaid maternity leave several months before giving birth and to remain out for several months thereafter. These constraints reflected a culture that consecrated the female role of motherhood, but which, ironically, taught women teachers that students were the only proper object of their supposedly innate maternal instincts.

For generations, custom, policy, and economic circumstances combined to channel women into teaching, but also to confine them in the classroom and inhibit union organization. However, the past two decades have witnessed striking parallel transformations both in the teaching profession itself and in legal and cultural constructions of women's status: the dynamic growth of teachers' unions is systematically linked to the dismantling of occupational sex segregation and other discriminatory policies against women.

In part, the attack on teachers' unions rests on socially constructed gender categories, the image of the nurturing female teacher—an image shattered by her audacious agency in organizing collectively, like men in industrial trades. Early efforts to organize teachers evoked especially vehement opposition precisely because they were undertaken by women. In 1915, a member of the Chicago Board of Education successfully promoted a rule prohibiting teachers from joining unions, condemning the Chicago Federation of Teachers as a "curse to the school system." He went on to explain, "in a large municipality . . . there is no need for lady labor sluggers. All labor sluggers are bad but I maintain that the female of the species is more deadly than the male." In the early NEA, Nicholas Murray Butler, the president of Columbia University, denounced Margaret Haley, an elementary school teacher and the president of the Chicago Teachers, as "a fiend in petticoats."

But today's attack on teachers' unions goes far beyond nostalgia for the spinster school teacher who, with few other options, devoted herself to teaching and adopted her pupils as children. Some critics go so far as to contend that unions are at the root of all the problems in public education. * * *

● **Lisa Mendel, *Collective Bargaining in California Under the Rodda Act*, 4 UCLA J. Ed. 3 (1990)**

* * * The Rodda Act of 1975, [CAL. GOV'T CODE § 3540 (West 1988)] introduced by State Senator Albert Rodda, [sought] "to promote the improvement of personnel management and employer-employee relations within the public school systems" in California by recognizing the employees' right to exclusive representation by the organization of their choice and affording them a voice in the formulation of school policy. The Act limits the scope of negotiations to "matters relating to wages, hours of employment, and other terms and conditions of employment." Parties are required to negotiate in good faith, but the Act does not require them to reach an agreement. Other significant provisions of this Act provide for exclusive representation of employees, impasse resolution procedures, and the establishment of the Public Employee Relations Board.

The Rodda Act provides for exclusive representation for all teachers within a bargaining unit. Certification of an organization as representative is granted after submission of support by a majority of all teachers within a bargaining unit. This section grants teachers the power to negotiate and enter into a written agreement with the school district through a single group representing the teachers.

The Act also mandates impasse resolution procedures to break deadlocks between negotiating parties. If either party declares an impasse, a mediator is appointed within five days. If the mediator, after attempting to resolve the problem, agrees with the requesting party that fact-finding is needed, the issue is submitted to a three-person fact-finding panel. The fact finders' recommendations must be made public, but are only advisory to the school board.

Finally, the Rodda Act established the Public Employees Relations Board (PERB) to govern all public labor relations. The duties of PERB include the conducting of representational elections, the appointment of mediators and the resolution of unfair labor practice charges filed with the board. When an unfair labor practice is committed by a school district or an employee organization, PERB may investigate, hold hearings, and prescribe appropriate remedial action. Examples of unfair labor practices include refusal to meet and negotiate in good faith, and breach of duty of fair representation.

The Effect of the Rodda Act on Teacher Strikes

Arguably, the most obvious indication to the public of whether the Rodda Act has served its purpose by improving the quality of employment relations is the absence or occurrence of teacher strikes. One would hope that the requirement that parties attempt to negotiate in good faith and the classification of refusal to negotiate as a punishable unfair labor practice would discourage such disruptions. Yet, as early as 1977, a study suggested that the Rodda Act had been ineffective in preventing strikes. In a period of fourteen months, beginning late 1987, there were major strikes in Los Angeles, Beverly Hills, Sacramento, Stockton and Santa Maria. This continuing large number of strikes since the passage of the Act indicates deterioration rather than improvement of labor relations.

In May 1989, for example, anger and frustration led to a nine-day strike in Los Angeles, the nation's second largest school district. Throughout the strike, the number of teachers on the picket line never dropped below 20,000. Although the district and teachers finally settled, the benefits to each side are inconclusive and many issues remained unsolved. The district agreed to give the teachers a 24% raise, but this was only 2.5% above what was offered before the strike; and teachers who struck for nine days lost 4.5% of that year's salary. The strike cost the United Teachers–Los Angeles (UTLA) $750,000, and the new contract will require a cut of at least $120,000 from existing programs. The agreement did mandate a restructuring of the district to provide for more community control of the schools, but it is not clear whether community school councils can make better administrative decisions than current administrators. Also, many union demands were postponed, and other issues remained unsettled.

Further complicating the debate over whether strikes are valuable is the controversy regarding the legality of strikes under the Rodda Act. The California Labor Code expressly allows concerted activities by employees against employers. The Rodda Act—while specifically granting a right to organize, choose representatives, and be free from employer interference—does not expressly allow or prohibit concerted activities. However, according to some commentators, judicial precedent indicates that strikes are illegal. Former Senator Rodda also contends that he did not intend the statute to grant teachers the right to strike.

* * *

• **Kelvin Lee, *Collective Bargaining and Faculty Governance at the Higher Education Level: Lessons for the K–12 Community?*, 4 UCLA J. Ed. (1990)**

* * * [W]hen examining possible reforms in labor relations within the K–12 educational system, it may be instructive to turn to the higher education model of collective bargaining and faculty governance. The higher education model appears to offer a number of advantages over the K–12 system. Not only are there fewer labor disputes at the college level, college faculty have greater control over their work circumstances and more autonomy in the classroom. Furthermore, college faculty enjoy greater professional recognition and higher salaries than K–12 teachers.

However, differences between the higher education and K–12 systems will undoubtedly limit both the implementation and effectiveness of higher education models of collective bargaining and faculty governance in the K–12 system. The higher education model also has drawbacks of its own, such as a relative lack of job security for instructors, large inequities in both pay and recognition among faculty members, and methods of evaluating teacher performance which are often criticized as arbitrary, unfair and ineffectual. Thus while it is certainly instructive to compare the higher education and K–12 models, adoption of higher education "reforms" in the primary and secondary school levels should certainly be approached with caution.

Comparisons Between Higher Education and K–12 Models of Collective Bargaining and Faculty Governance

Compared to K–12 teachers, higher education instructors generally have much greater control over their work circumstances. There exist several different higher education models of faculty governance, including those employed in the University of California (UC), California State University (CSU) and community college systems; however, all allow greater autonomy and freedom to faculty members than K–12 educators enjoy.

The UC model involves faculty in many areas of governance, particularly those involving personnel matters, which include the hiring of new instructors and decisions regarding tenure. The Higher Education Act places UC employees in four different categories: (1) Academic Senate, (2) Researchers, (3) Lecturers, (4) Librarians. The Higher Education Act mandates that tenure-track faculty be placed in a separate unit[.] [T]herefore, within the UC system, lecturers and librarians are covered by collective bargaining agreements. * * *

While there is only minimal unionization among faculty in the UC system, working conditions and the general environment of the faculty in the CSU system have led to significant collective bargaining among faculty members. The CSU's make fewer distinctions between full-time and part-time faculty within their system, and the CSU administration has created a large pool of part-time faculty, largely because of a great need for flexibility in staffing within their system. In the CSU system, part-time and full-time instructors are placed in the same collective bargaining unit. Therefore long term employment is often extended to part-time CSU instructors.

Many California community colleges began as small adjuncts to public secondary schools, and their organizational forms resembled the K–12 level, with a largely credential-oriented system. During the early 1970's, the Legislature enacted AB 1725, which purported to be a comprehensive reform of the community college system designed to move it closer to models of governance in four-year institutions. AB 1725 thus allowed each of the 71 different community colleges in California to define their own requirements for faculty in different academic and service areas. Furthermore, faculty unions at the community college level are organized around each individual community college district, as opposed to faculty unions in the UC and CSU system, which operate on a systemwide basis. * * *

While higher education may be broadly described to employ a "merit-based" system in hiring and retention of instructors, primary and secondary education may be said to employ "credential-based" systems of faculty governance. In contrast to the higher education model, entry and advancement within the K–12 system still involves obtaining an initial credential and then advancing through the system by obtaining additional credentials through continuing education and accumulating seniority. K–12 instructors are initially placed in a probationary status for a number of years; however, the vast majority of teachers (85–95%) eventually advance to become licensed, certificated staff. In fact, most of those instructors who do not complete this step leave the teaching profession for personal or other reasons, rather than because of non-advancement.

Introduction of a "merit-based" rather than "credential" or "seniority-based" model in the K–12 system would certainly face considerable resistance. For a number of reasons, K–12 educators feel strongly about maintaining the current system. The principle of advancement based on seniority is firmly entrenched within the K–12 system, and there is a strong and pervasive feeling that those teachers who "last through the process" of credentialing, licensing, and classroom teaching over a number of years are entitled to claim professional advancement and pay increases based on seniority. In addition, teachers hesitate to base promotions, which are currently obtained through relatively well-defined criteria, on the more subjective evaluation procedure that a merit system would inevitably entail.

The Role of Student and Peer Teaching Evaluations in Instructor Performance Assessment

One prominent feature of the higher education model is that periodic assessments of an instructor's performance occur through student and peer evaluations. These evaluations are also employed to distinguish competent from incompetent instructors. However, student and peer teaching evaluations are only partially effective at achieving their objectives, and create several problems. In the university system, student evaluations often undermine the effectiveness of part-time and/or new instructors, who may soften their demands on students for fear of provoking poor teaching evaluations from the students. On the other hand, student evaluations are often meaningless with respect to tenured professors. While negative evaluations may affect a professor's ego and personal emotions, they usually provide professors with little constructive input, and the fact remains that few tenured professors are removed for being poor classroom instructors. Within the UC and CSU systems, there are provisions in theory for the removal of the more incompetent professors, but they are rarely, if ever, employed.

The universities also have extensive peer review concerning the merit of colleagues. In both the UC and CSU systems, faculty committees regularly review the work of faculty members at both the departmental and university wide level. Although faculty recommendations on personnel decisions are generally accepted by the administration, administrators may overrule the faculty, and in exceptional cases the chancellor or university president may make the ultimate decision.

While community colleges are striving to implement more procedures allowing peer and student evaluation of faculty members, their efforts have been largely ineffectual. Community colleges were previously based on a credential-oriented system, and teaching contracts reflect this structure. Once community college instructors enter the system, their advancement continues according to a pre-determined schedule. Only an exceptionally strong offense such as a felony conviction or serious moral turpitude may slow the promotion of a community college instructor through the system, and an even more serious offense must be found to justify firing a faculty member.

In keeping with an effort to move closer toward the higher education model of faculty governance, community colleges attempted to widen the use of peer review and student evaluations. Yet both are relatively impotent in influencing personnel decisions. Instructors who receive negative evaluations may immediately "appeal to their contracts," which give them many job rights. Those who seek to remove an instructor have the burden of proof, and therefore community college administrators only take action against faculty in the most extreme cases.

By contrast, teacher performance evaluations have a much less important role in the K–12 system. No student evaluations are conducted in the K–12 system; the nearly unanimous consensus is that students in these grade levels lack the maturity to answer such questionnaires responsibly. There are also few situations in the K–12 system where teachers have the responsibility to evaluate each other as in the higher education system. Resistance to such evaluations exists for two major reasons. First, K–12 teachers, who have more contact with each other than higher education instructors, often are hesitant to evaluate their peers. Second, teachers are quite concerned that assessments of teaching performance, particularly those of administrators, could be affected by the biases of the evaluators. Presently, more outside pressure is being brought to bear to create a more "merit-based" system, and some suggest that unless K–12 teachers allow for more serious peer evaluation, their efforts towards achieving greater professional status will be forestalled.

* * *

Greater professional status and recognition attach to teaching positions in higher education, and college faculty have greater flexibility and control over their working conditions than K–12 teachers do. Although college faculty generally receive greater pay than K–12 teachers, salary inequities exist in higher education to a much greater extent than in the K–12 system. * * *

[On the other hand,] [t]he K–12 system has * * * historically faced a exodus of quality classroom instructors as many of the best teachers become administrators. This trend has slowed in recent years as administrator's higher salaries and greater professional status are offset by longer work hours and responsibilities. Nonetheless, many of the best classroom teachers are left performing bureaucratic work, shuffling papers and dealing with red tape, while a shortage of qualified classroom teachers persists.

* * *

Three prominent aspects of the higher education model of faculty governance may potentially be adopted in the K–12 system: (1) more extensive peer review, (2) differentiated teaching levels, and (3) merit pay based on teaching evaluations. However, each of these mechanisms employed in the higher education system also create a number of disadvantages, and barriers exist to their implementation in the K–12 system.

While the K–12 system continues to search for much-needed reforms, adopting the features of the higher education model will not be a panacea. The K–12 and higher education systems will most likely retain their largely separate identities in the area of faculty governance. Nonetheless it is instructive to compare the models, and see how the successes of the higher education model in various areas of labor relations may be translated into meaningful reforms within the K–12 system.

PUBLIC EMPLOYEES' RIGHT TO STRIKE: LAW AND EXPERIENCE

Martin H. Malin.
26 U. Mich. J.L. Reform 313 (1993).

* * *

I. PUBLIC POLICY AND PUBLIC EMPLOYEE STRIKES

Although arguments have been made to the contrary, this Article begins with the assumption that public policy favors collective bargaining by public employees when a majority of employees in an appropriate bargaining unit opt for union representation. Impasses in collective bargaining are inevitable. Accordingly, jurisdictions that provide for public employee collective bargaining have developed three approaches to resolving such impasses. The first approach relies on the threat or actual use of economic weapons, primarily the strike or lockout, to motivate the parties to reach agreement. The second approach prohibits strikes, but provides for fact-finding in the event of impasse. Under this approach, the parties present their positions to a neutral fact finder who makes findings and recommends a settlement, which the parties are free to accept or reject as they see fit. The third approach provides that the parties submit unresolved impasses to binding arbitration.

* * *

II. THE LAW OF STRIKES WHERE STRIKES ARE LEGAL

Although it may be trite to speak of the states as laboratories experimenting with different approaches to problems, that characterization aptly applies to public sector impasse resolution. Not only are the states divided over which impasse resolution device (strike, fact-finding, or interest arbitration) should be provided, but they also display considerable diversity of approach to each device. Those states which recognize a right to strike in public employment vary considerably in how they implement that right.

Illinois, Ohio, Oregon, and Pennsylvania provide a manageable sample of the different approaches to legalizing the public employee strike. These jurisdictions differ with respect to the type of prestrike impasse resolution procedures that they mandate. Illinois requires only mediation. Ohio and Oregon mandate prestrike fact-finding, while Pennsylvania, until a recent amendment governing teacher strikes, gave its labor board discretion to require prestrike fact-finding.

The laws of these jurisdictions also differ with respect to the standards that courts must employ when deciding whether to enjoin a lawful strike. Illinois and Ohio limit the issuance of injunctions to strikes that pose a clear and present danger to public health and safety. Oregon and Pennsylvania provide for the enjoining of strikes which pose a clear and present danger to the public welfare.

* * *

III.   THE LESSONS OF EXPERIENCE

State legislatures that legalize strikes by public employees do not intend to encourage work stoppages. Rather, they believe that once strikes are legal, they can be regulated and procedures can be required which will reduce the incidence of strikes and shorten those strikes that do occur. * * *

2. THE PERCEIVED TENSION BETWEEN REFORM EFFORTS AND THE RIGHTS OF EDUCATORS

FROM THE STATEHOUSE TO THE SCHOOLHOUSE: HOW LEGISLATURES AND COURTS SHAPED LABOR RELATIONS FOR PUBLIC EDUCATION EMPLOYEES DURING THE LAST DECADE

David J. Strom, Stephanie S. Baxter.
30 J.L. & EDUC. 275 (2001).

I.   INTRODUCTION

During the last decade, * * * courts and legislatures across the country increasingly have turned to more drastic measures under the guise of education reform. Regardless of one's opinion on the "reform" in question, it is clear that these measures are having a substantial impact on the rights of public school employees. Moreover, several trends are evident throughout the varied approaches states and localities have taken in the name of reform. * * * While there have been some victories on behalf of education employees in the last decade, many have lost rights and even more have had to wage a battle to retain the rights most believed were well settled.

In this paper, we examine six areas that have shaped the rights of education employees. In section two, we discuss the labor ramifications of disestablishing local schools through reconstitution and school take-overs. In section three, we assess the movement toward privatizing education through the use of voucher and tuition tax credit programs. In section four, we examine the charter school movement and the question of whether teachers have retained their bargaining rights. In section five, we recount various measures across the country to restrict the scope of bargaining for public sector employees, and in section six we discuss various attacks on teacher tenure. Last, we examine the trend to challenge the means by which unions and their members participate in the political system.

II.   DISESTABLISHING LOCAL SCHOOLS: SCHOOL TAKEOVERS AND RECONSTITUTION

In the past decade, there has been an increase in the use of existing law, as well as a proliferation of new laws on the state and local level to "takeover" or "reconstitute" schools that repeatedly failed to properly educate students. * * *

The legal authority that allows for school takeovers or reconstitution varies. In some instances, the authority derives from a court order or consent decree in ongoing desegregation litigation. Alternatively, federal, state, or local laws may provide for intervention. In other situations, the power to reconstitute schools may arise from negotiations between school and union officials. Although the words "reconstitution" and "takeover" are often used interchangeably, they describe different situations in both a legal and labor relations context. However, as described below, reconstitution and its concomitant effects may closely follow the takeover of a district.

Generally, in a state takeover situation, either the state board of education, the state legislature, or a federal court chooses a designated entity, such as the mayor or the state department of education, to manage the affairs of a local school district for a limited period of time. State takeovers are generally triggered when a school amasses a history of problems in various prescribed areas, which differ depending on the law in question. State takeover decisions may be based on a variety of factors, including inadequate student performance, low test scores, high dropout rates, fiscal mismanagement, failing infrastructure, or indications of poor administration and management. States often put school districts on a "watch" list as a warning that in the absence of improvement, a state takeover is likely. At least 23 states have some form of legislation to allow for the takeover of deficient districts. During the last decade, various states used these laws, although the extent to which the local school board was divested of control varied. The extent to which the takeovers adversely affected staff and/or labor relations in general further varied from state-to-state.

School takeovers differ from reconstitution in several respects, not the least of which is the greater impact reconstitution generally has on staff. Reconstitution is a process by which some or all of the school staff, including administrators, teachers, custodial and cafeteria workers are replaced by new personnel. In some instances, staff may reapply for their old jobs, while in other situations, staff simply have the option to apply for positions elsewhere in the district. Reconstitution is usually the last step in a process designed to improve schools. Generally, a school will first be warned that it is eligible for reconstitution because it has been identified as a low performing school. Usually there is a second step in which a school is put on notice that it must improve or it will face reconstitution. If the school shows little or no improvement, reconstitution is the step of last resort. From a labor relations perspective, reconstitution often yields unfair outcomes.

School Takeovers

In New Jersey, school takeovers took hold in the 1980s and continued in the 1990s. At least two urban districts, Paterson and Newark, were taken over in 1992 and 1995 respectively. The New Jersey Department of Education found that students in both cities were not receiving the minimum education and had histories of poor performance on state reviews and assessments. According to New Jersey law, if the state determines that it should take over a district, local school board members and high-ranking administrators are replaced with new managers. Importantly, in the context of takeovers, the New Jersey statute requires that "collective bargaining agreements entered into by the school district shall remain in force" and "all teaching staff members and other employees of a State-operated district shall retain and continue to acquire all rights and privileges accorded by Title 18A of the New Jersey Statutes."

Connecticut also ventured into the arena of school takeovers in 1997, when the state Legislature enacted a law to abolish the locally elected school board in the city of Hartford. The school board was replaced by a board of trustees appointed by the governor in conjunction with House and Senate majority and minority leadership. With regard to labor relations, the Act provides: "All contracts and agreements, including collective bargaining agreements, made in the name of the Hartford Board of Education shall be assigned to the State Board of Trustees for the Hartford Public Schools which shall be deemed the successor party in interest and deemed to be in privity of contract for all lawful purposes." The Act also provides various procedures to reopen negotiations, negotiate, and arbitrate with the exclusive representative of the employees. Interestingly, the new law also changes the criteria that interest arbitrators are to apply in resolving a dispute between the parties. Arbitrators shall not apply any presumption in favor of prior contract terms or arbitrator awards, but rather should give the highest priority to the educational interests of the students. Thus, while the Hartford law maintains collective bargaining, it adds an interesting new twist to the relationship of the parties by placing the needs of the students above the needs of labor and management.

A similar bill was passed in Michigan; it transferred the powers of the Detroit school board to the mayor. The mayor is empowered to appoint a reform board, which ultimately will control the Detroit public schools. This bill allows elected school board members to continue to serve in an advisory capacity without compensation or staff support until their terms expire. The Michigan law permits the reform board to terminate any contract entered into by the elected school board, except for collective bargaining agreements. Individual employment contracts, however, may be terminated. Interestingly, the law provides that five years after the appointment of the reform board, the question of whether to retain the board will be placed on the ballot in the district.

Reconstitution

Perhaps the first school district to experience reconstitution, the San Francisco Unified School District (SFUSD), has reconstituted more than 10 schools since 1984. The legal authority for reconstitution in San Francisco was * * * a consent decree entered into between the parties to the [SFNAACP v. SFUSD] lawsuit. * * * Local union affiliates of the American Federation of Teachers and the National Education Association petitioned the court to be recognized as interested parties so that they would be able to participate in the discussions of school improvement, but their petitions were denied. * * *

[During the 1990s,] the original parties to the lawsuit entered into another [agreement] when it became apparent that the schools identified as "needing help" were not achieving the same levels of academic excellence as those schools that had been reconstituted.

San Francisco created a Comprehensive School Improvement Program (CSIP) to identify low-performing schools. CSIP schools receive a central office administrator to help create and implement a school improvement plan, additional resources, and increased budget flexibility. The program also includes a management consultation process. Participating schools are periodically assessed using such factors as, student grades and writing samples, average daily attendance rates, student suspension and dropout rates, and the effective implementation of the school's improvement plan.

San Francisco teachers and their representatives were barred from participating in discussions at the critical stages of reconstitution policy development. For more than ten years, the union's only role in the process was an attempt to negotiate transfer policies for the staff that were affected by reconstitution. However, the union finally negotiated an agreement with the SFUSD on a new school improvement process in 1997. The agreement declared the mutual commitment of the district and the union to "improving teaching and learning in the schools of San Francisco and to creating alternatives which are intended to lead to the elimination of the need for reconstitution." * * *

New York City handled reconstitution in a wholly different manner. Reconstitution procedures were negotiated with the teachers union, the United Federation of Teachers. When the state determines that a school is unacceptable, it may be subject to the school redesign process. Under the process, at least half of the positions in the redesigned school can be reserved for existing qualified staff. A personnel committee, which includes two union representatives, chooses the staff for the redesigned school. Teachers that leave the school are given "priority transfers," which provide them with the first choice of other available positions in the district for which they are qualified.

Hybrid Takeover and Reconstitution Examples

In 1994, a court-enforced desegregation consent decree granted the Cleveland (Ohio) school district the power to reconstitute schools. In 1995, a United States federal judge mandated that the state take over the Cleveland public school system. Two years later, control of the school system was transferred to the mayor. The Ohio Legislature followed suit by passing legislation to identify and correct educationally deficient schools. The legislation provides for the use of corrective action plans at deficient schools, monitoring programs, and the use of experts to assist in plan implementation. It is important to note that the legislation also provides that no action taken under the statute may abrogate any term of a collective bargaining agreement and requires that where a union is in place, the union must consent to the corrective action plan in writing.

Despite the fact that the law protects collective bargaining agreements, Cleveland's early reconstitution efforts did not take union contracts into consideration. Instead, the school district took the position that it could circumvent the collective bargaining agreements based on the 1994 desegregation order. The Cleveland Teachers Union filed unfair labor practice charges and grievances claiming that the reconstitution violated transfer and reassignment provisions of the collective bargaining agreement. The district and the union ultimately reached a contractual agreement governing the transformation of the city's schools. The agreement provides that bargaining unit members receive adequate notice of reconstitution and a list of other available positions in the district, the ability to return a list of preferences, and a statement that reconstituted staff will not experience reprisals.

Similarly, the Illinois Legislature shifted control of the Chicago Public Schools to the mayor, who was charged with the power to appoint the school board and the district's chief executive officer. The chief executive officer, in turn, was empowered to fill a variety of high-ranking positions, such as chief fiscal officer, chief educational officer, and chief purchasing officer. Beyond takeover, the Legislature provided procedures for school reconstitution.

In an apparent effort to ease school reform, the Illinois Legislature also determined that a variety of traditionally accepted subjects of bargaining would be prohibited subjects of bargaining. This change left employees with little say in the process and only limited ability to negotiate regarding subjects integral to teachers employment in the system. The statute prohibits bargaining on decision-making and the impact of decisions: (1) to layoff employees or reduce staff; (2) determinations regarding class size, class staffing, assignments, scheduling, academic calendars, and pupil assignment; (3) relating to the use of technology and pilot programs; and (4) decisions regarding charter schools or the use of third-party providers.

In Illinois, reconstitution is the last step after other reform processes have failed. Once it is determined that a school will be reconstituted, the principal is generally removed and all staff members must reapply for their jobs. Staff who are not rehired at the reconstituted school can apply for other employment in the district and will receive full pay for 10 months while they attempt to find another placement. Displaced teachers are expected to substitute teach during this 10 month period. However, teachers who do not find a placement within this time frame may be dismissed.

Maryland also has experience with both takeovers and reconstitution. In 1997, the state and the city of Baltimore forged a partnership to run the Baltimore City Schools. A new nine member school board was created, with members appointed jointly by the mayor and the governor. In 1997, the Legislature also enacted a law and promulgated regulations to provide for reconstitution when a school continually fails to meet academic standards.

In January 2000, the Maryland Board of Education announced that three schools of the original 40 placed on the state's list as being eligible for reconstitution in 1994 will indeed be reconstituted. However, in an unprecedented move, the state entered into a contract with a for-profit company, Edison, Inc., to operate these schools. Unlike other reconstitutions, employees who apply for positions at the newly reconstituted schools will be employed by the private contractor, not the school system. The schools no longer will be subject to union contracts and employees no longer will be able to participate in the Teachers' Retirement System or state health plans. Teachers will also lose the tenure protections provided to public school teachers.

The Baltimore Teachers Union filed a lawsuit in Baltimore Circuit Court seeking a declaration that the city and state may not delegate their authority under various statutes to a private business. Further, the suit requests that the court void the contract with Edison and order Edison to refund any monies it was paid under the contract. On July 20, 2000, Circuit Judge Stuart Berger held that the Maryland State Board of Education acted within its statutory power when it contracted with Edison, Inc. to operate three failing schools. This case is currently on appeal before the Maryland Court of Appeals.

While both school takeovers and reconstitution inevitably effect employees in a variety of ways, from a labor relations perspective, employees enjoyed greater protection in takeover situations in the last decade. Takeover legislation generally recognized and left intact the collective bargaining relationship, which at the very least, allows the employees to retain the rights provided by contract. On the other hand, reconstitution efforts yielded varied results for the affected employees. In some instances, the union was simply ignored in the process. In others, the legislature eased reconstitution by altering the subjects over which employees are able to bargain. In Maryland, reconstitution is now being employed as a bridge to privatization. Thus, while takeovers shook up the top levels of power, reconstitution seemed to more directly affect the day to day lives of educational employees.

* * *

IV. CHARTER SCHOOLS

* * * Although the specifics of the laws vary, the general theory behind charter school legislation is to allow individuals or companies to create schools that are public, but which operate outside the traditional public school scheme. * * *

State statutes generally provide two avenues for chartering schools: (1) an existing public school converts to a charter school; or (2) an individual or group applies to charter a new school. In either case, from a labor relations perspective it is very important how employees will be treated with regard to unionization and bargaining.

Charter school laws vary in the extent to which they deal, if at all, with employee relations issues. In Alaska, Connecticut, Hawaii, Michigan, Nevada, and Wisconsin public charter school employees enjoy the same rights to organize and bargain collectively as other public employees in the respective states. These states automatically consider charter school employees a part of the existing district bargaining unit and subject to the current collective bargaining agreement. In Louisiana, charter school employees are subject to terms of existing collective bargaining agreements, unless otherwise specified in the charter.

In some states, such as Delaware, Florida, Idaho, Illinois, New Hampshire, Pennsylvania, and the District of Columbia, employees have the right to bargain, but the law requires the charter school to be a separate bargaining unit. In Minnesota, charter school employees can bargain as part of a separate unit, unless all parties agree that the employees should be part of the district unit. Interestingly, charter school employees in Oklahoma may bargain as separate units, subject to the rules of the National Labor Relations Board, as opposed to a state labor relations board.

Other states draw bargaining lines depending on how the charter school began. For instance, in New Jersey, when a public school converts to a charter school, the charter school employees must remain part of the district bargaining unit. However, start-up charter schools in New Jersey "may choose whether or not to offer the terms of any collective bargaining already established by the school district for its employees, but the board shall adopt any health and safety provisions of the agreement." Similarly, in Ohio, conversion school staff remain part of the district bargaining unit unless they vote to form a separate unit. In Rhode Island employees in district charter schools remain part of the district bargaining unit, but if the charter school is started by an outside group, the employees must secure recognition as a separate unit. In Michigan and Kansas, employees may remain in the district unit if they work in a school chartered by the district.

In New York, employees of a conversion charter school are included in the school district bargaining unit and are subject to the same collective bargaining agreement. However, a majority of members within a charter school may modify the collective bargaining agreement, with the approval of the charter school trustees, to address an issue specific to charter school employment. The New York also provides that employees of a newly created charter school, with at least 250 students, "shall be deemed to be represented in a separate negotiating unit at the charter school by the same employee organization, if any, that represents like employees in the school district in which the charter is located."

Ten states do not allow charter school employees to bargain, however, these states generally do not allow bargaining for public sector employees. These states are Arizona, Arkansas, Georgia, Mississippi, North Carolina, South Carolina, Texas, Utah, Virginia, and Wyoming.

V. LEGISLATIVE EFFORTS TO RESTRICT THE SCOPE OF BARGAINING FOR PUBLIC SECTOR EDUCATION EMPLOYEES

In a number of states with mature public sector collective bargaining statutes, legislatures have enacted new laws that restrict the scope of bargaining for education employees. This legislation is notable for at least two reasons. First, it singles out education employees for different treatment under the state's public sector collective bargaining law. Second, the legislation does not track similar developments in the private sector under the National Labor Relations Act. Indeed, in circumstances where the parties have a well-developed collective bargaining relationship, the tradition has been to expand the scope of bargaining, even if that is accomplished informally.

* * *

Overall, the 1990s redefined collective bargaining for education employees in the public sector as a fragile right that can be threatened by an unfriendly state legislature and/or governor. Once public education employees have gained collective bargaining rights through law there are no guarantees that these rights cannot be taken away, as was the case in New Mexico, or severely eroded, as in Illinois and Michigan. * * *

VI. ATTACKS ON TEACHER TENURE

In the last several years, there has been a growing wave of criticism about teacher tenure laws. Critics claim that schools are full of incompetent or ineffectual teachers who cannot be fired because of tenure laws. Although these critics misunderstand the purposes and rights granted by most tenure systems, states and localities have responded to these attacks in a variety of ways. Some states have repealed tenure and several states have eliminated the term "tenure," while maintaining the system's basic due process components. Other states have responded by streamlining procedural aspects of the tenure system in an effort to speed the process of dismissing a teacher. In one state, tenure policies became a collective bargaining matter to be negotiated at the local level. Further, without changing the law, some school districts attempted to circumvent the state tenure system by offering jobs contingent upon applicants waiving their rights under the tenure system.

Although tenure requirements and protections vary widely from state to state, tenure is generally achieved after a teacher successfully completes a multi-year probationary period. Tenure does not mean that a teacher cannot lose his or her job, rather, tenure provides due process when teachers are threatened with dismissal. The general purpose of tenure laws is to protect competent teachers from arbitrary employment actions, including dismissal based on personal or political beliefs, school board politics, anti-union animus, or nepotism.

In 1997, Oregon radically changed its teacher tenure law. The Oregon Fair Dismissal Law eliminated the tenure system, which had provided that employees who passed a three-year probation became permanent employees who could only be removed for several specified reasons. Although new law provides for two-year renewable contracts, it retains a variety of protections that teachers enjoyed under the previous law. Even though the new law was touted as a means to dismiss poor teachers more quickly and efficiently, it emphasizes teacher rehabilitation as opposed to dismissal by requiring districts to work with a teacher for at least one year after a teacher's contract is not renewed. Further, once the law went into effect, districts generally retained the same percentage of teachers, even though it would have been easier to dismiss poor teachers.

Colorado, Florida, Massachusetts, New Mexico, and South Dakota are among the state that have eliminated the term "tenure," replacing it with terms such as "nonrenewal of contract" and "continuing contract." However, these states generally retained the protections that were previously available for teachers, including an entitlement to re-employment based on good performance and conduct and due process provisions in the context of discipline and dismissal.

Other states, such as Connecticut, Michigan, and New York, have simply streamlined the time lines within due process procedures in an attempt to ensure a timely outcome. Interestingly, in streamlining the process teachers may benefit from the fact that changes often result in a hearing before an impartial hearing officer at an earlier time, rather than having to go multiple levels of hearings, often before bodies and individuals who may not be truly impartial. Moreover, although there is not much data available on outcomes at this stage, assuming the process is fair, a shorter process also benefits the teacher who is wrongfully terminated by returning him/her to work more quickly.

In 1995, Wisconsin also passed radical changes, eliminating the tenure system as part of state law, but allowing parties to negotiate tenure type systems pursuant to collective bargaining agreements. Although teachers in large cities and counties who obtained tenure prior to Dec. 1995, retain tenure protections, contract renewal and due process issues for all other teachers are based on the applicable collective bargaining agreement.

Several New York school districts attempted to get around the state's tenure scheme by passing resolutions requiring new teachers to waive the tenure protections provided by Section 3012 of the Education Law. Teachers in these districts were expected to work outside the tenure scheme pursuant to contracts that were renewable annually. Fortunately, at least two New York courts held that the school boards in question exceeded their authority and contravened public policy by attempting to eliminate the tenure system.

* * *

VIII.   A PEEK AT THE FUTURE

Teachers and school employees are among the most highly organized groups in the country. In the 1960's and 1970's education employees gained enormous power in the labor relations context as over 30 states passed laws that allowed collective bargaining. In the 1980's wages and employment benefits continued to improve for education employees. The 1990's, however, proved to be a challenging decade for educational labor relations.

As we look ahead * * *, it appears probable that the climate for education reform will continue and this * * * will have a definite impact on education employees. * * *

Notes

1. Consider the accountability provisions of the "No Child Left Behind" (NCLB) Act in light of the materials in this section. Will it be possible to harmonize the NCLB mandates with legal and policy imperatives of collective bargaining law? Once corrective action must be taken, can conflict be avoided? Or is conflict inevitable?

2. The history of reconstitution in San Francisco provides an important case study in this context. As referenced above, reconstitution began in 1983 pursuant to the requirements of the *SFNAACP* Consent Decree, and was included in the "No Child Left Behind" Act as one of the options for corrective action under the accountability provisions. Pursuant to the San Francisco Decree, all the adults at persistently low performing schools were removed, and a new group of adults were brought in. People could reapply for their former jobs if they were willing to commit to a different operating structure, but they were not guaranteed reappointment. However, those with tenure or other types of job protection were guaranteed positions somewhere in the District

By 2005, over twenty SFUSD schools had been reconstituted, albeit in very different ways. One set of schools was reconstituted in 1983, pursuant to "Phase One" reforms mandated by the Decree. A second group was reconstituted from 1993–1997, under the highly structured Comprehensive School Improvement Program (CSIP). A third group, designated as "Dream Schools," was reconstituted from 2003–2005 in the shadow of the "No Child Left Behind" Act, with both the methods of reconstitution and the mandated reforms varying greatly from campus to campus. The United Educators of San Francisco (UESF) consistently attempted to resist reconstitution, seeking instead to implement a more collaborative process. *See generally* Kelly C. Rozmus, *Education Reform and Education Quality: Is Reconstitution the Answer?*, 1998 BYU EDUC. & L.J. 103.

The jury is still out on the efficacy of reconstitution as a viable education reform. In certain instances, in San Francisco, there was clear evidence that reconstitution had worked. In other instances, reconstituted schools improved, but it was not clear how much the improvement had to do with reconstitution itself and how much it had to do with other factors, such as the additional resources and restructured programs that sometimes accompanied the changes. In other cases, reconstitution clearly did not work. One thing is certain, reconstitution by itself was never sufficient. For the strategy to work, it necessarily had to be accompanied by a vision and a detailed education plan.

For an overview and analysis of reconstitution in San Francisco, see generally The Independent Reports of the Consent Decree Monitoring Team (1997–2005), http://www.gseis.ucla.edu/courses/edlaw/sfrepts.htm (last visited Oct. 23, 2005). In particular, see Report #14 (September 1997) at pages 90–107 and Report #16 (July 1999) at pages 140–170, both available on that site.

Finally, it is important to note that even schools that had turned around under this Consent Decree were not always able to sustain their gains. As the independent Monitoring Team found:

> [T]here is no magic formula in the world of education reform. No one silver bullet has yet been found in this context. Research has shown that turning around a low performing school requires—among other things—the right combination of people, interpersonal communication, programs, funding, and relationships. It requires a great deal of hard, day-to-day work over time ... establishing partnerships between and among the District's educators, the school's students, and the local community. Such efforts—even if successful—do not continue automatically. People change, students change, circumstances change, and new relationships must be built. Turning around a low performing school is thus an ongoing process, not a one-time operation that can then be expected to last indefinitely. *See* Report #17 at page 172 (July 2000).

B. THE RIGHT TO ACQUIRE & RETAIN TENURE

At the K–12 level, most states have enacted legislation granting tenure protection for teachers. At the higher education level, tenure is sometimes governed by statute, sometimes by campus policy, and sometimes by a combination of the two.

While debates regarding the efficacy of prospective tenure reform continue unabated, legal disputes in this area do not generally focus on changes in tenure structures. Instead, the controversies often reflect bitter disagreements over denial of tenure, dismissal of tenured employees, and related matters.

One of the most unique and arguably far-reaching cases in this context is *Perry v. Sindermann,* where the U.S. Supreme Court considered the question of when de facto tenure might arise.

PERRY v. SINDERMANN
408 U.S. 593, 92 S.Ct. 2694 (1972).

Mr. Justice Stewart delivered the opinion of the Court.

From 1959 to 1969 the respondent, Robert Sindermann, was a teacher in the state college system of the State of Texas. After teaching for two years at the University of Texas and for four years at San Antonio Junior College, he became a professor of Government and Social Science at Odessa Junior College in 1965. He was employed at the college for four successive years, under a series of one-year contracts. He was successful enough to be appointed, for a time, the cochairman of his department.

During the 1968–1969 academic year, however, controversy arose between the respondent and the college administration. The respondent was elected president of the Texas Junior College Teachers Association. In this capacity, he left his teaching duties on several occasions to testify before committees of the Texas Legislature, and he became involved in public disagreements with the policies of the college's Board of Regents. In particular, he aligned himself with a group advocating the elevation of the college to four-year status—a change opposed by the Regents. And, on one occasion, a newspaper advertisement appeared over his name that was highly critical of the Regents.

Finally, in May 1969, the respondent's one-year employment contract terminated and the Board of Regents voted not to offer him a new contract for the next academic year. The Regents issued a press release setting forth allegations of the respondent's insubordination. But they provided him no official statement of the reasons for the nonrenewal of his contract. And they allowed him no opportunity for a hearing to challenge the basis of the nonrenewal.

The respondent then brought this action in Federal District Court. He alleged primarily that the Regents' decision not to rehire him was based on his public criticism of the policies of the college administration and thus infringed his right to freedom of speech. He also alleged that their failure to provide him an opportunity for a hearing violated the Fourteenth Amendment's guarantee of procedural due process. The petitioners—members of the Board of Regents and the president of the college—denied that their decision was made in retaliation for the respondent's public criticism and argued that they had no obligation to provide a hearing. * * * We granted a writ of certiorari and we have considered this case along with *Board of Regents v. Roth*.

I

The first question presented is whether the respondent's lack of a contractual or tenure right to re-employment, taken alone, defeats his claim that the nonrenewal of his contract violated the First and Fourteenth Amendments. We hold that it does not.

For at least a quarter-century, this Court has made clear that even though a person has no "right" to a valuable governmental benefit and even though the government may deny him the benefit for any number of reasons, there are some reasons upon which the government may not rely. It may not deny a benefit to a person on a basis that infringes his constitutionally protected interests—especially, his interest in freedom of speech. For if the government could deny a benefit to a person because of his constitutionally protected speech or associations, his exercise of those freedoms would in effect be penalized and inhibited. This would allow the government to "produce a result which (it) could not command directly." Such interference with constitutional rights is impermissible.

We have applied this general principle to denials of tax exemptions, unemployment benefits, and welfare payments. But, most often, we have applied the principle to denials of public employment. We have applied the principle regardless of the public employee's contractual or other claim to a job. * * *

Thus, the respondent's lack of a contractual or tenure "right" to re-employment for the 1969–1970 academic year is immaterial to his free speech claim. Indeed, twice before, this Court has specifically held that the nonrenewal of a nontenured public school teacher's one-year contract may not be predicated on his exercise of First and Fourteenth Amendment rights.

* * *

[W]e hold that the grant of summary judgment against the respondent, without full exploration of this issue, was improper.

II

The respondent's lack of formal contractual or tenure security in continued employment at Odessa Junior College, though irrelevant to his free speech claim, is highly relevant to his procedural due process claim. But it may not be entirely dispositive.

We have held today in *Board of Regents v. Roth* that the Constitution does not require opportunity for a hearing before the nonrenewal of a nontenured teacher's contract, unless he can show that the decision not to rehire him somehow deprived him of an interest in "liberty" or that he had a "property" interest in continued employment, despite the lack of tenure or a formal contract. In *Roth* the teacher had not made a showing on either point to justify summary judgment in his favor.

Similarly, the respondent here has yet to show that he has been deprived of an interest that could invoke procedural due process protection. As in *Roth*, the mere showing that he was not rehired in one particular job, without more, did not amount to a showing of a loss of liberty. Nor did it amount to a showing of a loss of property.

But the respondent's allegations—which we must construe most favorably to the respondent at this stage of the litigation—do raise a genuine issue as to his interest in continued employment at Odessa Junior College. He alleged that this interest, though not secured by a formal contractual tenure provision, was secured by a no less binding understanding fostered by the college administration. In particular, the respondent alleged that the college had a de facto tenure program, and that he had tenure under that program. He claimed that he and others legitimately relied upon an unusual provision that had been in the college's official Faculty Guide for many years:

"Teacher Tenure: Odessa College has no tenure system. The Administration of the College wishes the faculty member to feel that he has permanent tenure as long as his teaching services are satisfactory and as long as he displays a cooperative attitude toward his co-workers and his superiors, and as long as he is happy in his work."

Moreover, the respondent claimed legitimate reliance upon guidelines promulgated by the Coordinating Board of the Texas College and University System that provided that a person, like himself, who had been employed as a teacher in the state college and university system for seven years or more has some form of job tenure.[6] Thus, the respondent offered to prove that a teacher with his long period of service at this particular State College had no less a "property" interest in continued employment than a formally tenured teacher at other colleges, and had no less a procedural due process right to a statement of reasons and a hearing before college officials upon their decision not to retain him.

We have made clear in Roth that "property" interests subject to procedural due process protection are not limited by a few rigid, technical forms. Rather, "property" denotes a broad range of interests that are secured by "existing rules or understandings." A person's interest in a benefit is a "property" interest for due process purposes if there are such rules or mutually explicit understandings that support his claim of entitlement to the benefit and that he may invoke at a hearing.

A written contract with an explicit tenure provision clearly is evidence of a formal understanding that supports a teacher's claim of entitlement to continued employment unless sufficient "cause" is shown. Yet absence of such an explicit contractual provision may not always foreclose the possibility that a teacher has a "property" interest in reemployment. For example, the law of contracts in most, if not all, jurisdictions long has employed a process by which agreements, though not formalized in writing, may be "implied." Explicit contractual provi-

---

6. The relevant portion of the guidelines, adopted as "Policy Paper 1" by the Coordinating Board on October 16, 1967, reads:

"A. Tenure

"Tenure means assurance to an experienced faculty member that he may expect to continue in his academic position unless adequate cause for dismissal is demonstrated in a fair hearing, following established procedures of due process.

"A specific system of faculty tenure undergirds the integrity of each academic institution. In the Texas public colleges and universities, this tenure system should have these components:

"(1) Beginning with appointment to the rank of full-time instructor or a higher rank, the probationary period for a faculty member shall not exceed seven years, including within this period appropriate full-time service in all institutions of higher education. This is subject to the

provision that when, after a term of probationary service of more than three years in one or more institutions, a faculty member is employed by another institution, it may be agreed in writing that his new appointment is for a probationary period of not more than four years (even though thereby the person's total probationary period in the academic profession is extended beyond the normal maximum of seven years).

* * *

"(3) Adequate cause for dismissal for a faculty member with tenure may be established by demonstrating professional incompetence, moral turpitude, or gross neglect of professional responsibilities." The respondent alleges that, because he has been employed as a "full-time instructor" or professor within the Texas College and University System for 10 years, he should have 'tenure' under these provisions.

sions may be supplemented by other agreements implied from "the promisor's words and conduct in the light of the surrounding circumstances." And, "(t)he meaning of (the promisor's) words and acts is found by relating them to the usage of the past."

A teacher, like the respondent, who has held his position for a number of years, might be able to show from the circumstances of this service—and from other relevant facts—that he has a legitimate claim of entitlement to job tenure. Just as this Court has found there to be a "common law of a particular industry or of a particular plant" that may supplement a collective-bargaining agreement, so there may be an unwritten "common law" in a particular university that certain employees shall have the equivalent of tenure. This is particularly likely in a college or university, like Odessa Junior College, that has no explicit tenure system even for senior members of its faculty, but that nonetheless may have created such a system in practice.[7]

In this case, the respondent has alleged the existence of rules and understandings, promulgated and fostered by state officials, that may justify his legitimate claim of entitlement to continued employment absent "sufficient cause." We disagree with the Court of Appeals insofar as it held that a mere subjective "expectancy" is protected by procedural due process, but we agree that the respondent must be given an opportunity to prove the legitimacy of his claim of such entitlement in light of "the policies and practices of the institution." Proof of such a property interest would not, of course, entitle him to reinstatement. But such proof would obligate college officials to grant a hearing at his request, where he could be informed of the grounds for his nonretention and challenge their sufficiency.

Therefore, while we do not wholly agree with the opinion of the Court of Appeals, its judgment remanding this case to the District Court is affirmed.

Affirmed.

C.   DISPUTES REGARDING THE DISMISSAL PROCESS GENERALLY

This section examines two representative K–12 dismissal cases, one involving a teacher and the other involving a principal. It is important to note that dismissal controversies often involve most, if not all, of the areas addressed in this chapter. Indeed, many landmark decisions in the areas of tenure, freedom of expression, and employment discrimination often stem from disputes regarding dismissal. Problem 49 highlights some of the issues that may arise in this context.

7. We do not now hold that the respondent has any such legitimate claim of entitlement to job tenure. For "(p)roperty interests ... are not created by the Constitution. Rather, they are created and their dimensions are defined by existing rules or understandings that stem from an independent source such as state law...." If it is the law of Texas that a teacher in the respondent's position has no contractual or other claim to job tenure, the respondent's claim would be defeated.

PROBLEM 49: Teacher Dismissal at the K–12 Level

The following hypothetical takes place in the Topanga Creek Unified School District.

Sal Marcos was a longtime Filipino community activist, Green Party member, faculty sponsor of the school's large and vibrant Filipino Student Association, and outspoken union rep at Oakridge Road High School. A superior teacher and debate coach whose students "swore by him," Marcos' ten years in the District had been marred by several disputes with administrators and fellow faculty members. Finally, at the end of his tenth year, Marcos was suspended from his teaching position, and District officials began dismissal proceedings.

Four specific incidents during the most recent school year were specified by the District in these proceedings:

A. *Statements Regarding District Issues and Personnel*—Marcos occasionally debated members of his team who were in his social studies classes, during class time, in order to strengthen their debating skills. (There was no separate class for debate.) On one occasion, in late April, a debate was held on a resolution recently passed by the Topanga Creek School Board in support of the Bush administration's war effort in Iraq. Marcos' words were recorded on tape by one of the students, and included the following declaration: "All of us ultimately lose in this battle. If only the school board members realized this . . . if only we all opened our eyes we could see how evil this war effort is . . . we need to fight it at every level, starting with this campus, this principal, and this faculty."

B. *Film (shown without permission)*—In the fall, during a unit on the years 1865–1900 in his eleventh grade U.S. History class, Marcos showed a film that members of the school's Filipino Student Association had put together under his supervision. The film presented in vivid detail the argument that the U.S. not only caused significant damage to the Philippines and its inhabitants over time, but that discrimination and disparate treatment continue in this country today.

C. *Events Occurring During Student Visits to Teacher's Home*—Members of the debate team, and their friends, often visited Marcos' home. On one occasion in December, Marcos' wife recruited several of the students to help plan an anti-war demonstration.

D. *Comments Regarding Controversial Topics*—In May, during another recorded practice debate (this one on the draft), Marcos said the following: "If this administration reinstituted the draft, and I was of draft age, I would leave the country before I would become part of this madness."

It was after this last incident that Mr. Marcos was suspended. He admits that these four incidents occurred exactly as described above.

Mr. Sal Marcos, upon his dismissal, sued for reinstatement. What legal and policy arguments would the plaintiff be likely to advance? How should the court rule? Why?

Assume that Marcos was also the baseball coach, that he was 53–years-old, that he had recently been in an accident which required the use of a wheelchair from time to time, and that the baseball coach who replaced him was 16 years younger. In addition, assume that the principal was quoted by the school newspaper as saying that she felt it was important for a baseball coach to be able to demonstrate certain skills such as batting, pitching, and fielding, and that she was happy that the new coach would be able to do that. What additional arguments might the teacher set forth? What result?

* * *

Assume instead that Mr. Marcos was a middle school teacher. How much of an impact, if any, would this change in grade level have on the outcome of the case? How much of an impact, if any, should it have? Why?

* * *

Relevant provisions of the State Education Code provide, in pertinent part:

(a) No permanent employee shall be dismissed except for one or more of the following causes:

    (1) Immoral or unprofessional conduct.

    * * *

    (3) Dishonesty.

    (4) Unsatisfactory performance.

    (5) Evident unfitness for service.

    (6) Physical or mental condition unfitting him or her to instruct or associate with children.

    (7) Persistent violation of or refusal to obey the school laws of the state or reasonable regulations prescribed for the government of the public schools by the State Board of Education or by the governing board of the school district employing him or her.

    (8) Conviction of a felony or of any crime involving moral turpitude.

    * * *

    (10) Knowing membership by the employee in the Communist Party.

    (11) Alcoholism or other drug abuse which makes the employee unfit to instruct or associate with children.

MORRISON v. STATE BD. OF EDUC.

1 Cal.3d 214, 461 P.2d 375, 82 Cal.Rptr. 175 (1969).

Tobriner, Justice.

For a number of years prior to 1965 petitioner held a General Secondary Life Diploma and a Life Diploma to Teach Exceptional Children, issued by the State Board of Education, which qualified petitioner for employment as a teacher in the public secondary schools of California. On August 5, 1965, an accusation was filed with the State Board of Education charging that petitioner's life diplomas should be revoked for cause. On March 11, 1966, following a hearing, and pursuant to the recommendations of a hearing examiner, the board revoked petitioner's life diplomas because of immoral and unprofessional conduct and acts involving moral turpitude as authorized by section 13202 of the Education Code.[1] This revocation rendered petitioner ineligible for employment as a teacher in any public school in the state. On February 14, 1967, petitioner sought a writ of mandate from the Superior Court of Los Angeles County to compel the board to set aside its decision and restore his life diplomas. After a hearing the superior court denied the writ, and this appeal followed.

For the reasons hereinafter set forth we conclude (a) that section 13202 authorizes disciplinary measures only for conduct indicating unfitness to teach, (b) that properly interpreted to this effect section 13202 is constitutional on its face and as here applied, and (c) that the record contains no evidence to support the conclusion that petitioner's conduct indicated his unfitness to teach. The judgment of the superior court must therefore be reversed.

I. *The Facts*

For a number of years prior to 1964 petitioner worked as a teacher for the Lowell Joint School District. During this period, so far as appears from the record, no one complained about, or so much as criticized, his performance as a teacher. Moreover, with the exception of a single incident, no one suggested that his conduct outside the classroom was other than beyond reproach.

Sometime before the spring of 1963 petitioner became friends with Mr. and Mrs. Fred Schneringer. Mr. Schneringer also worked as a teacher in the public school system. To the Schneringers, who were involved in grave marital and financial difficulties at the time, petitioner gave counsel and advice. In the course of such counseling Mr. Schneringer frequently visited petitioner's apartment to discuss his problems. For a one-week period in April, during which petitioner and Mr. Schneringer experienced severe emotional stress, the two men engaged in a limited, non-criminal[4] physical relationship which petitioner described as being of

---

1. Section 13202 provides: "The State Board of Education shall revoke or suspend for immoral or unprofessional conduct, or for persistent defiance of, and refusal to obey, the laws regulating the duties of persons serving in the Public School System, or for any cause which would have warranted the denial of an application for a certification document or the renewal thereof, or for evident unfitness for service, life diplomas, documents, or credentials issued pursuant to this code." Among the causes warranting denial of such documents is the commission of "any act involving moral turpitude."

4. Neither sodomy (Pen. Code, § 286), oral copulation (Pen. Code, § 288a), public solicitation of lewd acts (Pen. Code § 647, subd. (a)), loitering near public toilets (Pen. Code, § 647, subd. (d)), nor exhibitionism (Pen. Code, § 314) were involved.

Conviction of such offenses would have resulted in the mandatory revocation of all diplomas and life certificates issued by the State Board of Education.

a homosexual nature. Petitioner has never been accused or convicted of any criminal activity whatever, and the record contains no evidence of any abnormal activities or desires by petitioner since the Schneringer incident some six years in the past. Petitioner and Schneringer met on numerous occasions in the spring and summer after the incident and nothing untoward occurred. When Schneringer later obtained a separation from his wife, petitioner suggested a number of women whom Schneringer might consider dating.

Approximately one year after the April 1963 incident, Schneringer reported it to the Superintendent of the Lowell Joint School District. As a result of that report petitioner resigned his teaching position on May 4, 1964.

Some 19 months after the incident became known to the superintendent, the State Board of Education conducted a hearing concerning possible revocation of petitioner's life diplomas. * * * Mr. Cavalier, an investigator testifying for the board, stated that the Schneringer incident "was the only time that [petitioner] ever engaged in a homosexual act with anyone." No evidence was presented that petitioner had ever committed any act of misconduct whatsoever while teaching.

The Board of Education finally revoked petitioner's life diplomas some three years after the Schneringer incident. The board concluded that that incident constituted immoral and unprofessional conduct, and an act involving moral turpitude, all of which warrant revocation of life diplomas under section 13202 of the Education Code.

II.   *Petitioner's actions cannot constitute immoral or unprofessional conduct or conduct involving moral turpitude within the meaning of section 13202 unless those actions indicate his unfitness to teach.*

Section 13202 of the Education Code authorizes revocation of life diplomas for "immoral conduct," "unprofessional conduct," and "acts involving moral turpitude." Legislation authorizing disciplinary action against the holders of a variety of certificates, licenses and government jobs other than teaching also contain these rather general terms. This court has not attempted to formulate explicit definitions of those terms which would apply to all the statutes in which they are used. Rather, we have given those terms more precise meaning by referring in each case to the particular profession or the specific governmental position to which they were applicable.

In *Hallinan v. Committee of Bar Examiners* for example, we considered the meaning of "acts of moral turpitude" as applied to an applicant for admission to practice law. In that case the applicant had been arrested and convicted of a number of minor offenses in connection with

The Education Code thus draws an important distinction between different types of sexual indiscretions by teachers, dealing with such conduct in two different parts of the code. Conviction of certain sex crimes entails automatic dismissal. But other sexual misconduct results in discipline only if it is "immoral," "unprofessional" or involves "moral turpitude." * * *

peace demonstrations and civil rights "sit ins"; he had likewise been involved in a number of fistfights. We held that the applicant could not be denied admission to the bar. The nature of these acts, we ruled, "does not bear a direct relationship to petitioner's fitness to practice law. Virtually all of the admission and disciplinary cases in which we have upheld decisions of the State Bar to refuse to admit applicants or to disbar, suspend, or otherwise censure members of the bar have involved acts which bear upon the individual's manifest dishonesty and thereby provide a reasonable basis for the conclusion that the applicant or attorney cannot be relied upon to fulfill the moral obligations incumbent upon members of the legal profession. * * * Although petitioner's past behavior may not be praiseworthy it does not reflect upon his honesty and veracity *nor does it show him unfit for the proper discharge of the duties of an attorney.*" (Italics added.)

In *Yakov v. Board of Medical Examiners*, we were also concerned with moral turpitude. In that case a doctor had been convicted of nine counts of violation of section 4227 of the Business and Professions Code (furnishing dangerous drugs without prescription), and the Board of Medical Examiners had revoked his medical certificate. The superior court reversed the board's action; we upheld that court's disposition of the matter, stating, inter alia, "The purpose of an action seeking revocation of a doctor's certificate is not to punish the doctor but rather to protect the public. * * * While revocation of a certificate certainly works an unavoidable punitive effect, the board can seek to achieve a legitimate punitive purpose only through criminal prosecution. *Thus, in this proceeding the inquiry must be limited to the effect of Dr. Yakov's actions upon the quality of his service to his patients.*" (Italics added.)

Board of Education v. Swan and *Board of Trustees v. Owens* dealt with the term "unprofessional conduct" as applied to teachers. In *Swan* we stressed: "One employed in public service does not have a constitutional right to such employment and is subject to reasonable supervision and restriction by the authorized governmental body or officer *to the end that proper discipline may be maintained, and that activities among the employees may not be allowed to disrupt or impair the public service.*" (Italics added.) In *Owens* the Court of Appeal held that in deciding whether certain conduct by a teacher constituted unprofessional conduct which warranted discipline, a trial court must inquire whether that conduct had produced "any disruption or impairment of discipline or the teaching process * * *."

In *Orloff v. Los Angeles Turf Club, Inc.*, we dealt with a statute authorizing the exclusion from theaters, museums, and race courses of persons of "immoral character." We reasoned that the objective of the statute was "the protection of others on the premises." Accordingly we held that a person might be excluded if, for example, he committed a lewd act or an act inimical to the public safety or welfare after gaining admittance to the place of entertainment. But we stressed that no sweeping inquiry could be made into the background and reputation of each person seeking admission. "[T]he private business, the personal relations with others, the past conduct not on the premises, of a person applying for or admitted to the [race] course, whether or not relevant to indicate his character, are immaterial in the application of the statutory standards. * * * "

In *Jarvella v. Willoughby–Eastlake City School Dist.*, the court faced the issue of whether a teacher could be dismissed for "immorality" merely because he had written a private letter to a friend containing language which some adults might find vulgar and offensive. The court held that Ohio Revised Code Section 3319.16, authorizing dismissal for "immorality," did not cover the teacher's actions, and that he could not therefore be dismissed. The court explained, "Whatever else the term 'Immorality' may mean to many, it is clear that when used in a statute it is inseparable from 'conduct' * * * But it is not 'immoral conduct' considered in the abstract. It must be considered in the context in which the Legislature considered it, as conduct which is hostile to the welfare of the general public; more specifically in this case, conduct which is hostile to the welfare of the school community. * * * In providing standards to guide school boards in placing restraints on conduct of teachers, the Legislature is concerned with the welfare of the school community. Its objective is the protection of students from corruption. This is a proper exercise of the power of a state to abridge personal liberty and to protect larger interests. But reasonableness must be the governing criterion. * * * The private conduct of a man, who is also a teacher, is a proper concern to those who employ him only to the extent it mars him as a teacher * * * . Where his professional achievement is unaffected, where the school community is placed in no jeopardy, his private acts are his own business and may not be the basis of discipline."

By interpreting these broad terms to apply to the employee's performance on the job, the decisions in *Hallinan, Yakov, Swan, Owens, Orloff* and *Jarvella* give content to language which otherwise would be too sweeping to be meaningful. Terms such as "immoral or unprofessional conduct" or "moral turpitude" stretch over so wide a range that they embrace an unlimited area of conduct. In using them the Legislature surely did not mean to endow the employing agency with the power to dismiss any employee whose personal, private conduct incurred its disapproval. Hence the courts have consistently related the terms to the issue of whether, when applied to the performance of the employee on the job, the employee has disqualified himself.

In the instant case the terms denote immoral or unprofessional conduct or moral turpitude of the teacher which indicates unfitness to teach. Without such a reasonable interpretation the terms would be susceptible to so broad an application as possibly to subject to discipline virtually every teacher in the state.[15] In the opinion of many people

15. A sweeping provision purporting to penalize or sanction so large a group of people as to be incapable of effective enforcement against all or even most of them necessarily might offend due process. Such a statute, unless narrowed by clear and well-known standards, affords too great a potential for arbitrary and discriminatory laziness, gluttony, vanity, selfishness, avarice, and cowardice constitute immoral conduct. A recent study by the State Assembly reported that educators differed among themselves as to whether "unprofessional conduct" might include "imbibing alcoholic beverages, use of tobacco, signing petitions, revealing contents of school documents to legislative committees, appealing directly to one's legislative representative, and opposing majority opinions * * * ." We cannot believe that the Legislature intended to compel disciplinary measures against teachers who committed such peccadillos if such passing conduct did not affect students or fellow teachers. Surely incidents of extramarital heterosexual conduct against a background of years of satisfactory teaching would not constitute "immoral conduct" sufficient justify revocation of a life diploma without any showing of an adverse effect on fitness to teach.

Nor is it likely that the Legislature intended by section 13202 to establish a standard for the conduct of teachers that might vary widely with time, location, and the popular mood. One could expect a reasonably stable consensus within the teaching profession as to what conduct adversely affects students and fellow teachers. No such consensus can be presumed about "morality." "Today's morals may be tomorrow's ancient and absurd customs." And conversely, conduct socially acceptable today may be anathema tomorrow. Local boards of education, moreover, are authorized to revoke their own certificates and dismiss permanent teachers for immoral and unprofessional conduct; an overly broad interpretation of that authorization could result in disciplinary action in one county for conduct treated as permissible in another. A more, constricted interpretation of "immoral," "unprofessional," and "moral turpitude" avoids these difficulties, enabling the State Board of Education to utilize its expertise in educational matters rather than having to act "as the prophet to which is revealed the state of morals of the people or the common conscience."[19]

application and administration. (See United States v. Reese ("It would certainly be dangerous if the Legislature could set a net large enough to catch all possible offenders, and leave it to the courts to step inside and say who could be rightfully detained, and who should be set at large.") In *Norton v. Macy*, the United States Civil Service Commission defined "immorality" as a violation of "the prevailing mores of our society." The court commented, "So construed, 'immorality' covers a multitude of sins. Indeed, it may be doubted whether there are in the entire Civil Service many persons so saintly as never to have done any act disapproved by the 'prevailing mores of our society.'" With regard to the feasibility of a ban on all persons with any sort of homosexual background, the court argued, "The most widely accepted study of American sexual practices estimates that 'at least 37 per cent' of the American male population have at least one homosexual experience during their lifetime. If this is so, a policy excluding all persons who have engaged in homosexual conduct from government employ would disqualify for public service over one-third of the male population. This result would be both inherently absurd and devastating to the public service."

19. The problem of ascertaining the appropriate standard of "morality" was aptly put in Robert N. Harris, Jr., *Private Consensual Adult Behavior: The Requirement of Harm to Others in the Enforcement of Morality*, 14 UCLA L. Rev. 581, 582 & n.4. "[I]n a secular society—America today—there may be a plurality of moralities. Whose morals shall be enforced? * * * There is a tendency to say that public morals should be enforced. But that just begs the question. Whose morals are the public morals?"

That the meaning of "immoral," "unprofessional," and "moral turpitude" must depend upon, and thus relate to, the occupation involved finds further confirmation in the fact that those terms are used in a wide variety of contexts. Along with public school teachers, all state college employees, all state civil service workers, and all barbers can be disciplined for "immoral conduct." The prohibition against "acts involving moral turpitude" applies to attorneys and to technicians, bioanalysts and trainees employed in clinical laboratories, as well as to teachers. The ban on "unprofessional conduct" is particularly common, covering not only teachers, but also dentists, physicians, vocational nurses, optometrists, pharmacists, psychiatric technicians, employment agency officials, state college employees, certified shorthand reporters, and funeral directors and embalmers. Surely the Legislature did not intend that identical standards of probity should apply to more than half a million professionals and government employees in widely varying fields without regard to their differing duties, responsibilities, and degree of contact with the public.

We therefore conclude that the Board of Education cannot abstractly characterize the conduct in this case as "immoral," "unprofessional," or "involving moral turpitude" within the meaning of section 13202 of the Education Code unless that conduct indicates that the petitioner is unfit to teach. In determining whether the teacher's conduct thus indicates unfitness to teach the board may consider such matters as the likelihood that the conduct may have adversely affected students or fellow teachers, the degree of such adversity anticipated, the proximity or remoteness in time of the conduct, the type of teaching certificate held by the party involved, the extenuating or aggravating circumstances, if any, surrounding the conduct, the praiseworthiness or blameworthiness of the motives resulting in the conduct, the likelihood of the recurrence of the questioned conduct, and the extent to which disciplinary action may inflict an adverse impact or chilling effect upon the constitutional rights of the teacher involved or other teachers. These factors are relevant to the extent that they assist the board in determining whether the teacher's fitness to teach, i.e., in determining whether the teacher's future classroom performance and overall impact on his students are likely to meet the board's standards.

* * *

IV. *The record contains no evidence that petitioner's conduct indicated his unfitness to teach.*

As we have stated above, the statutes, properly interpreted, provide that the State Board of Education can revoke a life diploma or other document of certification and thus prohibit local school officials from hiring a particular teacher only if that individual has in some manner indicated that he is unfit to teach. Thus an individual can be removed from the teaching profession only upon a showing that his retention in the profession poses a significant danger of harm to either students, school employees, or others who might be affected by his actions as a teacher. * * * Petitioner's conduct in this case is not disputed. Accordingly, we must inquire whether any adverse inferences can be drawn from that past conduct as to petitioner's teaching ability, or as to the possibility that publicity surrounding past conduct may in and of itself substantially impair his function as a teacher.

As to this crucial issue, the record before the board and before this court contains no evidence whatsoever. The board called no medical, psychological, or psychiatric experts to testify as to whether a man who had had a single, isolated, and limited homosexual contact would be likely to repeat such conduct in the future. The board offered no evidence that a man of petitioner's background was any more likely than the average adult male to engage in any untoward conduct with a student. The board produced no testimony from school officials or others to indicate whether a man such as petitioner might publicly advocate improper conduct. The board did not attempt to invoke the provisions of the Government Code authorizing official notice of matters within the special competence of the board.

This lack of evidence is particularly significant because the board failed to show that petitioner's conduct in any manner affected his performance as a teacher. There was not the slightest suggestion that petitioner had ever attempted, sought, or even considered any form of physical or otherwise improper relationship with any student. There was no evidence that petitioner had failed to impress upon the minds of his pupils the principles of morality as required by section 13556.5 of the Education Code. There is no reason to believe that the Schneringer incident affected petitioner's apparently satisfactory relationship with his co-workers.

The board revoked petitioner's license three years after the Schneringer incident; that incident has now receded six years into the past. Petitioner's motives at the time of the incident involved neither dishonesty nor viciousness, and the emotional pressures on both petitioner and Schneringer suggest the presence of extenuating circumstances. Finally, the record contains no evidence that the events of April 1963 have become so notorious as to impair petitioner's ability to command the respect and confidence of students and fellow teachers in schools within or without the Lowell Joint School District.

Before the board can conclude that a teacher's continued retention in the profession presents a significant danger of harm to students or fellow teachers, essential factual premises in its reasoning should be supported by evidence or official notice. In this case, despite the quantity and quality of information available about human sexual behaviour, the record contains no such evidence as to the significance and implications of the Schneringer incident. Neither this court nor the superior court is authorized to rectify this failure by uninformed speculation or conjecture as to petitioner's future conduct.

* * *

V. *Conclusion*

In deciding this case we are not unmindful of the public interest in the elimination of unfit elementary and secondary school teachers. But petitioner is entitled to a careful and reasoned inquiry into his fitness to teach by the Board of Education before he is deprived of his right to pursue his profession. "The right to practice one's profession is sufficiently precious to surround it with a panoply of legal protection" and terms such as "immoral," "unprofessional," and "moral turpitude" constitute only lingual abstractions until applied to a specific occupation and given content by reference to fitness for the performance of that vocation.

The power of the state to regulate professions and conditions of government employment must not arbitrarily impair the right of the individual to live his private life, apart from his job, as he deems fit. Moreover, since modern hiring practices purport to rest on scientific judgments of fitness for the job involved, a government decision clothed in such terms can seriously inhibit the possibility of the dismissed employee thereafter successfully seeking non-government positions. That danger becomes especially acute under circumstances such as the present case in which loss of certification will impose upon petitioner "a 'badge of infamy,' * * * fixing upon him the stigma of an official defamation of character."

* * *

The judgment of the superior court denying the writ of mandate is reversed, and the cause is remanded to the superior court for proceedings consistent with this opinion.

HEAD v. CHICAGO SCH. REFORM BD. OF TRUSTEES

225 F.3d 794 (7th Cir. 2000).

WILLIAMS, CIRCUIT JUDGE.

* * *

I

In March of 1994, the Chicago Board of Education, acting through the Local School Council, hired Head as the principal for Nathaniel Pope Elementary School ("Pope Elementary") and gave him a four-year contract ending June 30, 1998. By its own terms, the contract could be terminated only on certain limited grounds.[2] Similarly, under the Illinois

---

2. The contract provides:

This Agreement may be terminated for any one of the following reasons or by any one of the following methods:

　(a) written agreement of the Local School Council, Board of Education and the Principal;

　(b) discharge of the Principal for cause pursuant to Ill.Rev.Stat. Ch. 122, sec. 34–85;

　(c) closure of the attendance center;

　(d) death, resignation or retirement of the Principal;

School Code, Head could be discharged during the term of his contract only for cause following an extensive and detailed notice and hearing process.

Beginning in 1995, the Board, aided by newly enacted state laws granting it greater powers, began to step up its efforts to remedy deficient performance in Chicago's public schools. Pursuant to these efforts, in October 1996, Pope Elementary was identified as a poorly performing school and was placed on probation. A school on probation is subject to greater Board oversight and must take certain steps to improve performance. In particular, Head, as Pope Elementary's principal, had primary responsibility for implementing a Corrective Action Plan to raise student test scores.

During the 1996–97 school year, the Board came to the conclusion that Head was not fulfilling his responsibility in this regard. Therefore, in early June of 1997, Hazel Stewart, the Education Officer for the region encompassing Pope Elementary, advised Head that the Board would seek to remove him as Pope Elementary's principal at the end of that school year. A letter signed by Chicago Public Schools CEO Paul Vallas and dated July 2, notified Head that pursuant to 105 Ill. Comp. Stat. 5/34–8.3(d), which governs schools under probation, a principal removal hearing would be scheduled for Pope Elementary. Head received a second letter signed by Vallas, dated July 3, scheduling the removal hearing for July 14 and detailing the criteria the Board used in deciding to seek his removal.[3] A separate letter also notified the school community of the principal removal hearing.

Margaret Fitzpatrick presided over the July 14 hearing. During the hearing, eight witnesses presented evidence supporting Head's removal while seven witnesses testified on Head's behalf. After the hearing, Head, through his attorney, submitted a brief arguing against his removal. About a week after the hearing, Fitzpatrick issued a written decision recommending that Head be removed as principal of Pope Elementary. That same week, a Chicago Public Schools official, Phillip Hansen, criticized Head's performance on a cable access program. Then, on July 28, the Board adopted Fitzpatrick's recommendation and removed Head as principal of Pope Elementary.

* * *

(e) misrepresentation referred to in section IX of this Agreement [which requires certain truthful representations to be made].

3. Specifically, the criteria detailed were:

A. Failure of the Principal to effectively and/or sufficiently implement the Corrective Action Plan, which has resulted in deficiencies in any of the following:

* School leadership;

* Parent/community partnerships;

* Student centered learning climate;

* Professional development and collaboration;

* Quality instruction plan; and

* School management.

B. Failure of the school to show sufficient increase in student scores on the TAP achievement test.

C. Failure of the Principal to effectively and/or sufficiently follow the recommendation(s) of the Probation Manager.

D. Failure to improve student attendance and/or drop-out rate in the school.

Eventually, Head filed suit against the Board based on the Board's actions in removing him as principal of Pope Elementary. He raised essentially four claims: (1) that, without due process, the Board had deprived him of a liberty interest in pursuing his occupation; (2) that, without due process, the Board had deprived him of a property interest in employment beyond the term of his contract; (3) that, without due process, the Board had deprived him of a property interest in employment through the end of his contract; and (4) that the Board had breached its contract with him.

* * *

III

A.   Claims Resolved in Motion to Dismiss Decision

We consider first the two claims the district court dismissed under Rule 12(b)(6)—that, without due process, the Board deprived Head of a liberty interest in pursuing the occupation of his choice and that, without due process, the Board deprived Head of a property interest in employment beyond the term of his contract. We review such dismissals *de novo*, taking a plaintiff's factual allegations as true and drawing all reasonable inferences in his or her favor. * * *

1.   Liberty Interest Claim

In setting out the basis for his due process liberty interest claim in his complaint, Head alleged that the Board (or at least certain persons associated with the Board) deprived him of a liberty interest in pursuing the occupation of his choice by disseminating false allegations regarding his performance as Pope Elementary's principal. * * *

A claim that a government employer has infringed an employee's liberty to pursue the occupation of his or her choice requires that (1) the employee be stigmatized by the employer's actions; (2) the stigmatizing information be publicly disclosed; and (3) the employee suffer a tangible loss of other employment opportunities as a result of the public disclosure. However, simply labeling an employee as being incompetent or otherwise unable to meet an employer's expectations does not infringe the employee's liberty. The employee's good name, reputation, honor, or integrity must be called into question in such a way as to make it virtually impossible for the employee to find new employment in his chosen field.

* * *

[However,] [s]imple charges of professional incompetence do not impose the sort of stigma that actually infringes an employee's liberty to pursue an occupation. Only if the circumstances of an employee's discharge so sully the employee's reputation or character that the employee will essentially be blacklisted in his or her chosen profession will it be possible to pursue a due process liberty interest claim. *Lashbrook* [*v. Oerkfitz*] (listing charges of immorality, dishonesty, alcoholism, disloyalty, Communism, or subversive acts as the sort of charges that infringe an employee's liberty); *Ratliff v. City of Milwaukee* (concluding that charges of untruthfulness, neglect of duty, and insubordination against a police officer impose sufficient stigma). As Head's allegations of stigma fall short of this threshold, he has failed to state a due process liberty interest claim.

2. Property Interest Claim

Head claims that a requirement, found both in his contract and in a 1996 Board publication, that he be given notice five months before the end of the contract term regarding whether his contract would be renewed, grants him a property interest in employment beyond the term of his contract, which the Board could not deprive him of without due process. After reviewing Head's entire contract (which Head attached to his complaint), the district court concluded that Head had no property interest in future employment with the Board and therefore could not state a due process claim. We agree.

Property interests are enforceable entitlements to a benefit or right. They can arise directly from state or federal law (as with a statute granting a benefit) or indirectly through the operation of state or federal law on certain conduct (as with a contract). A mere opportunity to acquire property, however, does not itself qualify as a property interest protected by the Constitution.

Head's contract with the Board makes it plain that Head has no enforceable entitlement to employment beyond the term of the contract. It provides, "This Agreement, including and not withstanding the procedures set forth herein, shall expire at the end of its stated term and shall not grant or create any contractual rights or other expectancy of continued employment beyond the term of this Agreement." This provision conclusively dispels any confusion regarding the possibility of a property interest in future employment created by the requirement that Head be given five months notice of whether his contract would be renewed. And, there is nothing in the Illinois School Code that overrides (or is even inconsistent with) this aspect of the contract. Accordingly, the district court properly dismissed Head's claim that the Board unconstitutionally deprived him of a protected property interest in employment beyond the term of his contract.

B. Claims Resolved in Summary Judgment Decision

We turn next to the two claims on which the district court granted summary judgment—that, without due process, the Board deprived Head of a property interest in remaining the principal of Pope Elementary through the end of his contractual term of employment, and that the Board breached its contract with him. * * *

1. Due Process Claim

In support of his remaining due process claim, Head contends that by removing him from his position as principal of Pope Elementary before the end of his contract, the Board deprived him of a property interest in continuing in that position for the term of his contract. There can be no doubt that, as a public employee who by contract and statute could be removed only on limited grounds, Head had a property interest in completing his contract in accordance with the terms of his contract, one of which specifically made him principal of Pope Elementary. The question the Board raises, which the district court never adequately addressed, is whether the deprivation Head suffered is more than *de minimis*, as it must be to be actionable.

The Board suggests that because Head received the same salary and benefits after his removal that he did when he was principal, he, at most, suffered a *de minimis* deprivation of property. The Board's suggestion is flawed, however. To begin with, the relevant question is whether Head received all the salary and benefits he would have received if he had remained Pope Elementary's principal. Head opposed the Board's summary judgment motion on the ground that he did not receive all he would have been due. If he is right, he suffered an injury that is plainly more than *de minimis*. See *Swick* [*v. City of Chicago*] (pecuniary losses qualify as actionable deprivations of property). Moreover, even if Head did receive all he would have been due had he remained Pope Elementary's principal, he might still have had a constitutionally protected property interest in remaining in that position. We have recognized that a loss of position that impedes future job opportunities or has other indirect effects on future income can inflict an actionable deprivation of property. We need not definitively answer whether Head has adequately established that he possessed a protected property interest in remaining Pope Elementary's principal through the end of his contract, however, since we agree with the district court that Head's challenges to the adequacy of the procedures afforded him prior to his removal are without merit.

A public employer who removes an employee from a job in which the employee has a constitutionally protected interest must provide certain limited pre-termination procedures, including, at a minimum: (1) oral or written notice of the charges; (2) an explanation of the employer's evidence; and (3) an opportunity for the employee to tell his or her side of the story. Also, the chosen decisionmaker must be impartial. Head contends that the procedures he was afforded did not satisfy these minimum requirements in two respects.

Head first complains that he did not receive adequate notice of the charges that led to his removal. We cannot accept this argument, however. Notice is constitutionally adequate if it is reasonably calculated to apprise interested parties of the proceeding and afford them an opportunity to present their objections. In a pair of letters sent over one week prior to the removal hearing, the Board informed Head that a principal removal hearing had been scheduled for Pope Elementary and detailed four particular grounds on which his removal was being sought. Clearly, Head was apprised of the removal proceedings, and, while the charges against him may not have been as specific as Head would have liked, they were certainly sufficient to allow him to defend himself. In any event, Head admits that he was fully apprised of the charges at the hearing and that afterwards he was able to submit a brief in response to the evidence presented at the hearing. For both of these reasons, we find it impossible to conclude that Head did not receive adequate notice of the charges that led to his removal.

Head also complains that Margaret Fitzpatrick, the hearing officer who presided over his removal hearing, was not an impartial decision-maker. Specifically, Head contends that Fitzpatrick cannot be considered an impartial decisionmaker because she was employed by the Board, he had no input on her selection, she had previously represented him and the Board, and she had on a prior occasion presented evidence regarding an earlier controversy at Pope Elementary. Those serving as adjudicators are presumed to act in good faith, honestly, and with integrity. To overcome this presumption, a plaintiff must come forward with substantial evidence of actual or potential bias, such as evidence of a pecuniary interest in the proceeding, personal animosity toward the plaintiff, or actual prejudgment of the plaintiff's case. Evidence of prior familiarity with the plaintiff or his or her situation, or even of involvement in the particular matter under consideration, is not adequate by itself to overcome the presumption. Viewed in the light most favorable to Head, the evidence he relies on amounts to nothing more than evidence of Fitzpatrick's prior familiarity with him and Pope Elementary. As such, it does not overcome the presumption of good faith that is afforded adjudicators. Accordingly, Head's claim that Fitzpatrick was biased must fail.

As there appears to be no reason to doubt that the Board afforded Head constitutionally adequate procedures before removing him as principal of Pope Elementary, the Board was entitled to summary judgment on Head's due process property interest claim relating to his removal before the end of his contractual term of employment.

2.   Breach of Contract Claim

Head claims that by removing him from his position as principal of Pope Elementary before the end of his four-year contractual term of employment, the Board breached its contract with him. The district court concluded that no breach occurred because the Illinois School Code governs Head's contract and, in removing Head, the Board complied with the provisions of the Illinois School Code regarding the removal of a principal from a school on probation (specifically 105 Ill. Comp. Stat. 5/34–8.3(d)). Head argues that the district court misinterpreted the contract. We agree.

As the contract between Head and the Board specifically makes Head principal of Pope Elementary, there can be no doubt that the Board terminated the contract by removing Head from that position. The question is whether it had grounds for terminating the contract. As noted above, the contract provides five grounds for termination. Removal of the principal pursuant to 105 Ill. Comp. Stat. 5/34–8.3(d) is not one of them, nor has the Board ever suggested that any of the grounds for termination has been satisfied. The only ground with any connection to the reasons for Head's removal is, "discharge of the Principal for cause pursuant to Ill.Rev.Stat. Ch. 122, sec. 34–85." But, the Board concedes that it did not follow the procedures or afford Head the rights provided by § 34–85.

The district court did not consider whether the Board had established any of the contractual grounds for terminating its contract with Head. Instead, the court concluded that the contract is governed by, and therefore apparently incorporates, the Illinois School Code, and that if Head was properly removed under any provision of the Illinois School Code, there could not be a breach of the contract. This interpretation reads too much into the contract. The contract does provide that Head must fulfill the obligations placed on him by the Illinois School Code, but the contract says nothing about incorporating, wholesale, the various provisions of the Illinois School Code relating to the removal of a principal. There is, for instance, no term allowing for termination of the contract upon "discharge of the principal pursuant to the Illinois School Code." To the contrary, the contract specifically identifies a single provision, § 34–85, that must be used in discharging a principal for cause. As we read the Board's contract with Head, the contract may be terminated only if one of the five contractual grounds for termination is satisfied.

Whether by mistake or design, Head's contract grants him greater rights than the Illinois School Code appears to grant him. The Board was obligated to honor those contractual rights by satisfying one of the five contractual grounds for termination of the contract. It did not do so. Accordingly, we conclude that the district court erred in ruling that the Board did not breach its contract with Head.

IV

For the foregoing reasons, we conclude that there is no merit to Head's due process claims, but that his breach of contract claim should have survived summary judgment. Accordingly, we AFFIRM in part and REVERSE in part the judgment of the district court, and we REMAND the case for further proceedings.

D.   FIRST AMENDMENT RIGHTS OF EDUCATORS

Freedom of expression for educators is a surprisingly complex area of inquiry. At the K–12 level, for example, educators may actually have fewer rights than students. And interpretations of First Amendment principles in this context not only vary from jurisdiction to jurisdiction, but sometimes prove quite difficult to pinpoint with any great degree of certainty.

At the higher education level, there are ongoing disputes over the parameters of academic freedom. Many people assume the existence of academic freedom as a matter of course, but in reality the courts have recognized some fairly substantial limitations.

Notable recent scholarship has pinpointed the depth and breadth of the complexities in this area. *See, e.g.,* Ailsa W. Chang, *Resuscitating the Constitutional "Theory" of Academic Freedom: A Search for a Standard Beyond Pickering and Connick,* 53 STAN. L. REV. 915 (2001); R. Weston Donehower, *Boring Lessons: Defining the Limits of a Teacher's First Amendment Right to Speak Through the Curriculum,* 102 MICH. L. REV. 517 (2003); Kevin G. Welner, *Locking Up the Marketplace of Ideas and Locking Out School Reform: Courts' Imprudent Treatment of Controversial Teaching in America's Public Schools,* 50 UCLA L. REV. 959 (2003).

This section begins with *Pickering* and *Connick,* the two U.S. Supreme Court cases that together comprise foundational doctrine in the area. It then follows with representative academic freedom disputes at both the K–12 and the higher education levels. Taken together, do these decisions reflect any discernible trend, or are the courts left with conflicting strands and little apparent consistency? How might current realities shift in the future? What types of controversies might engender such a shift?

a. U.S. Supreme Court Doctrine Generally

PICKERING v. BOARD OF EDUC. OF TOWNSHIP HIGH SCH. DIST. 205

391 U.S. 563, 88 S.Ct. 1731 (1968).

MR. JUSTICE MARSHALL delivered the opinion of the Court.

Appellant Marvin L. Pickering, a teacher in Township High School District 205, Will County, Illinois, was dismissed from his position by the appellee Board of Education for sending a letter to a local newspaper in connection with a recently proposed tax increase that was critical of the way in which the Board and the district superintendent of schools had handled past proposals to raise new revenue for the schools. Appellant's dismissal resulted from a determination by the Board, after a full hearing, that the publication of the letter was "detrimental to the efficient operation and administration of the schools of the district" and hence, under the relevant Illinois statute, that "interests of the schools require(d) (his dismissal)."

* * *

I.

* * *

[Pickering's] letter constituted, basically, an attack on the School Board's handling of the 1961 bond issue proposals and its subsequent allocation of financial resources between the schools' educational and athletic programs. It also charged the superintendent of schools with attempting to prevent teachers in the district from opposing or criticizing the proposed bond issue.

The Board dismissed Pickering for writing and publishing the letter. Pursuant to Illinois law, the Board was then required to hold a hearing on the dismissal. At the hearing the Board charged that numerous statements in the letter were false and that the publication of the statements unjustifiably impugned the "motives, honesty, integrity, truthfulness, responsibility and competence" of both the Board and the school administration. The Board also charged that the false statements damaged the professional reputations of its members and of the school administrators, would be disruptive of faculty discipline, and would tend to foment "controversy, conflict and dissension" among teachers, administrators, the Board of Education, and the residents of the district. * * * The Board found the statements to be false as charged. No evidence was introduced at any point in the proceedings as to the effect of the publication of the letter on the community as a whole or on the administration of the school system in particular, and no specific findings along these lines were made.

* * *

III.

The Board contends that "the teacher by virtue of his public employment has a duty of loyalty to support his superiors in attaining the generally accepted goals of education and that, if he must speak out publicly, he should do so factually and accurately, commensurate with his education and experience." Appellant, on the other hand, argues that the test applicable to defamatory statements directed against public officials by persons having no occupational relationship with them, namely, that statements to be legally actionable must be made "with knowledge that [they were] * * * false or with reckless disregard of whether [they were] * * * false or not," should also be applied to public statements made by teachers. Because of the enormous variety of fact situations in which critical statements by teachers and other public employees may be thought by their superiors, against whom the statements are directed to furnish grounds for dismissal, we do not deem it either appropriate or feasible to attempt to lay down a general standard against which all such statements may be judged. However, in the course of evaluating the conflicting claims of First Amendment protection and the need for orderly school administration in the context of this case, we shall indicate some of the general lines along which an analysis of the controlling interests should run.

An examination of the statements in appellant's letter objected to by the Board reveals that they, like the letter as a whole, consist essentially of criticism of the Board's allocation of school funds between educational and athletic programs, and of both the Board's and the superintendent's methods of informing, or preventing the informing of, the district's taxpayers of the real reasons why additional tax revenues were being sought for the schools. The statements are in no way directed towards any person with whom appellant would normally be in contact in the course of his daily work as a teacher. Thus no question of maintaining either discipline by immediate superiors or harmony among coworkers is presented here. Appellant's employment relationships with the Board and, to a somewhat lesser extent, with the superintendent are not the kind of close working relationships for which it can persuasively be claimed that personal loyalty and confidence are necessary to their proper functioning. Accordingly, to the extent that the Board's position here can be taken to suggest that even comments on matters of public concern that are substantially correct, such as statements (1)–(4) of appellant's letter, may furnish grounds for dismissal if they are sufficiently critical in tone, we unequivocally reject it.

We next consider the statements in appellant's letter which we agree to be false. The Board's original charges included allegations that the publication of the letter damaged the professional reputations of the Board and the superintendent and would foment controversy and conflict among the Board, teachers, administrators, and the residents of the district. However, no evidence to support these allegations was introduced at the hearing. So far as the record reveals, Pickering's letter was greeted by everyone but its main target, the Board, with massive apathy and total disbelief. The Board must, therefore, have decided, perhaps by analogy with the law of libel, that the statements were per se harmful to the operation of the schools.

However, the only way in which the Board could conclude, absent any evidence of the actual effect of the letter, that the statements contained therein were per se detrimental to the interest of the schools was to equate the Board members' own interests with that of the schools. Certainly an accusation that too much money is being spent on athletics by the administrators of the school system (which is precisely the import of that portion of appellant's letter containing the statements that we have found to be false) cannot reasonably be regarded as per se detrimental to the district's schools. Such an accusation reflects rather a difference of opinion between Pickering and the Board as to the preferable manner of operating the school system, a difference of opinion that clearly concerns an issue of general public interest.

                              * * *

More importantly, the question whether a school system requires additional funds is a matter of legitimate public concern on which the judgment of the school administration, including the School Board, cannot, in a society that leaves such questions to popular vote, be taken as conclusive. On such a question free and open debate is vital to informed decision-making by the electorate. Teachers are, as a class, the members of a community most likely to have informed and definite opinions as to how funds allotted to the operations of the schools should be spent. Accordingly, it is essential that they be able to speak out freely on such questions without fear of retaliatory dismissal.

                              * * *

What we do have before us is a case in which a teacher has made erroneous public statements upon issues then currently the subject of public attention, which are critical of his ultimate employer but which are neither shown nor can be presumed to have in any way either impeded the teacher's proper performance of his daily duties in the classroom[5] or to have interfered with the regular operation of the schools generally. In these circumstances we conclude that the interest of the school administration in limiting teachers' opportunities to contribute to public debate is not significantly greater than its interest in limiting a similar contribution by any member of the general public.

IV.

The public interest in having free and unhindered debate on matters of public importance—the core value of the Free Speech Clause of the First Amendment—is so great that it has been held that a State cannot authorize the recovery of damages by a public official for defamatory statements directed at him except when such statements are shown to have been made either with knowledge of their falsity or with reckless disregard for their truth or falsity. The same test has been applied to suits for invasion of privacy based on false statements where a "matter of public interest" is involved. It is therefore perfectly clear that, were appellant a member of the general public, the State's power to afford the appellee Board of Education or its members any legal right to sue him for writing the letter at issue here would be limited by the requirement that the letter be judged by the standard laid down in New York Times.

This Court has also indicated, in more general terms, that statements by public officials on matters of public concern must be accorded First Amendment protection despite the fact that the statements are directed at their nominal superiors. In Garrison, the New York Times test was specifically applied to a case involving a criminal defamation conviction stemming from statements made by a district attorney about the judges before whom he regularly appeared.

While criminal sanctions and damage awards have a somewhat different impact on the exercise of the right to freedom of speech from dismissal from employment, it is apparent that the threat of dismissal from public employment is nonetheless a potent means of inhibiting speech. We have already noted our disinclination to make an across-the-board equation of dismissal from public employment for remarks critical of superiors with awarding damages in a libel suit by a public official for similar criticism. However, in a case such as the present one, in which the fact of employment is only tangentially and insubstantially involved in the subject matter of the public communication made by a teacher, we conclude that it is necessary to regard the teacher as the member of the general public he seeks to be.

5. We also note that this case does not present a situation in which a teacher's public statements are so without foundation as to call into question his fitness to perform his duties in the classroom. In such a case, of course, the statements would merely be evidence of the teacher's general competence, or lack thereof, and not an independent basis for dismissal.

In sum, we hold that, in a case such as this, absent proof of false statements knowingly or recklessly made by him, a teacher's exercise of his right to speak on issues of public importance may not furnish the basis for his dismissal from public employment. Since no such showing has been made in this case regarding appellant's letter, his dismissal for writing it cannot be upheld and the judgment of the Illinois Supreme Court must, accordingly, be reversed and the case remanded for further proceedings not inconsistent with this opinion. It is so ordered.

Judgment reversed and case remanded with directions.

CONNICK v. MYERS

461 U.S. 138, 103 S.Ct. 1684 (1983).

JUSTICE WHITE delivered the opinion of the Court.

In *Pickering v. Board of Education,* 391 U.S. 563, 88 S. Ct. 1731 (1968), we stated that a public employee does not relinquish First Amendment rights to comment on matters of public interest by virtue of government employment. We also recognized that the State's interests as an employer in regulating the speech of its employees "differ significantly from those it possesses in connection with regulation of the speech of the citizenry in general." *Id,* at 568, 88 S. Ct. at 1734. The problem, we thought, was arriving "at a balance between the interests of the [employee], as a citizen, in commenting upon matters of public concern and the interest of the State, as an employer, in promoting the efficiency of the public services it performs through its employees." *Ibid.* We return to this problem today and consider whether the First and Fourteenth Amendments prevent the discharge of a state employee for circulating a questionnaire concerning internal office affairs.

I

The respondent, Sheila Myers, was employed as an Assistant District Attorney in New Orleans for five and a half years. She served at the pleasure of petitioner Harry Connick, the District Attorney for Orleans Parish. During this period Myers competently performed her responsibilities of trying criminal cases.

In the early part of October, 1980, Myers was informed that she would be transferred to prosecute cases in a different section of the criminal court. Myers was strongly opposed to the proposed transfer[1] and expressed her view to several of her supervisors, including Connick. Despite her objections, on October 6 Myers was notified that she was being transferred. Myers again spoke with Dennis Waldron, one of the first assistant district attorneys, expressing her reluctance to accept the transfer. A number of other office matters were discussed and Myers

---

1. Myers' opposition was at least partially attributable to her concern that a conflict of interest would have been created by the transfer because of her participation in a counseling program for convicted defendants released on probation in the section of the criminal court to which she was to be assigned.

later testified that, in response to Waldron's suggestion that her concerns were not shared by others in the office, she informed him that she would do some research on the matter.

That night Myers prepared a questionnaire soliciting the views of her fellow staff members concerning office transfer policy, office morale, the need for a grievance committee, the level of confidence in supervisors, and whether employees felt pressured to work in political campaigns. Early the following morning, Myers typed and copied the questionnaire. She also met with Connick who urged her to accept the transfer. She said she would "consider" it. Connick then left the office. Myers then distributed the questionnaire to 15 assistant district attorneys. Shortly after noon, Dennis Waldron learned that Myers was distributing the survey. He immediately phoned Connick and informed him that Myers was creating a "mini-insurrection" within the office. Connick returned to the office and told Myers that she was being terminated because of her refusal to accept the transfer. She was also told that her distribution of the questionnaire was considered an act of insubordination. Connick particularly objected to the question which inquired whether employees "had confidence in and would rely on the word" of various superiors in the office, and to a question concerning pressure to work in political campaigns which he felt would be damaging if discovered by the press.

Myers filed suit under 42 U.S.C. § 1983, contending that her employment was wrongfully terminated because she had exercised her constitutionally-protected right of free speech.

     * * *

II

For at least 15 years, it has been settled that a state cannot condition public employment on a basis that infringes the employee's constitutionally protected interest in freedom of expression. Our task, as we defined it in *Pickering,* is to seek "a balance between the interests of the [employee], as a citizen, in commenting upon matters of public concern and the interest of the State, as an employer, in promoting the efficiency of the public services it performs through its employees." 391 U.S. at 568, 88 S. Ct. at 1734. The District Court, and thus the Court of Appeals as well, misapplied our decision in *Pickering* and consequently, in our view, erred in striking the balance for respondent.

A

The District Court got off on the wrong foot in this case by initially finding that, "[t]aken as a whole, the issues presented in the questionnaire relate to the effective functioning of the District Attorney's Office and are matters of public importance and concern." Connick contends at the outset that no balancing of interests is required in this case because Myers' questionnaire concerned only internal office matters and that such speech is not upon a matter of "public concern," as the term was used in *Pickering*. Although we do not agree that Myers' communication in this case was wholly without First Amendment protection, there is much force to Connick's submission. The repeated emphasis in *Pickering* on the right of a public employee "as a citizen, in commenting upon matters of public concern," was not accidental. This language, reiterated in all of *Pickering's* progeny, reflects both the historical evolvement of the rights of public employees, and the common sense realization that government offices could not function if every employment decision became a constitutional matter.

For most of this century, the unchallenged dogma was that a public employee had no right to object to conditions placed upon the terms of employment—including those which restricted the exercise of constitutional rights. The classic formulation of this position was Justice Holmes', who, when sitting on the Supreme Judicial Court of Massachusetts, observed: "A policeman may have a constitutional right to talk politics, but he has no constitutional right to be a policeman." For many years, Holmes' epigram expressed this Court's law.

The Court cast new light on the matter in a series of cases arising from the widespread efforts in the 1950s and early 1960s to require public employees, particularly teachers, to swear oaths of loyalty to the state and reveal the groups with which they associated. * * * [By 1963,] it was already "too late in the day to doubt that the liberties of religion and expression may be infringed by the denial of or placing of conditions upon a benefit or privilege." It was therefore no surprise when in *Keyishian v. Board of Regents*, the Court invalidated New York statutes barring employment on the basis of membership in "subversive" organizations, observing that the theory that public employment which may be denied altogether may be subjected to any conditions, regardless of how unreasonable, had been uniformly rejected.

In all of these cases, the precedents in which *Pickering* is rooted, the invalidated statutes and actions sought to suppress the rights of public employees to participate in public affairs. The issue was whether government employees could be prevented or "chilled" by the fear of discharge from joining political parties and other associations that certain public officials might find "subversive." The explanation for the Constitution's special concern with threats to the right of citizens to participate in political affairs is no mystery. The First Amendment "was fashioned to assure unfettered interchange of ideas for the bringing about of political and social changes desired by the people." "[S]peech concerning public affairs is more than self-expression; it is the essence of self-government." Accordingly, the Court has frequently reaffirmed that speech on public issues occupies the "highest rung of the hierarchy of First Amendment values," and is entitled to special protection.

　　　* * *

Our cases following *Pickering* also involved safeguarding speech on matters of public concern. The controversy in *Perry v. Sindermann,* 408 U.S. 593, 92 S. Ct. 2694 (1972), arose from the failure to rehire a teacher in the state college system who had testified before committees of the Texas legislature and had become involved in public disagreement over whether the college should be elevated to four-year status—a change opposed by the Regents. In *Mt. Healthy City Board of Ed. v. Doyle*, a public school teacher was not rehired because, allegedly, he had relayed to a radio station the substance of a memorandum relating to teacher dress and appearance that the school principal had circulated to various teachers. The memorandum was apparently prompted by the view of some in the administration that there was a relationship between teacher appearance and public support for bond issues, and indeed, the radio station promptly announced the adoption of the dress code as a news item. Most recently, in *Givhan v. Western Line Consolidated School District*, we held that First Amendment protection applies when a public employee arranges to communicate privately with his employer rather than to express his views publicly. Although the subject-matter of Mrs. Givhan's statements were not the issue before the Court, it is clear that her statements concerning the school district's allegedly racially discriminatory policies involved a matter of public concern.

Pickering, its antecedents and progeny, lead us to conclude that if Myers' questionnaire cannot be fairly characterized as constituting speech on a matter of public concern, it is unnecessary for us to scrutinize the reasons for her discharge. When employee expression cannot be fairly considered as relating to any matter of political, social, or other concern to the community, government officials should enjoy wide latitude in managing their offices, without intrusive oversight by the judiciary in the name of the First Amendment. Perhaps the government employer's dismissal of the worker may not be fair, but ordinary dismissals from government service which violate no fixed tenure or applicable statute or regulation are not subject to judicial review even if the reasons for the dismissal are alleged to be mistaken or unreasonable.

We do not suggest, however, that Myers' speech, even if not touching upon a matter of public concern, is totally beyond the protection of the First Amendment. "The First Amendment does not protect speech and assembly only to the extent it can be characterized as political. 'Great secular causes, with smaller ones, are guarded.'" We in no sense suggest that speech on private matters falls into one of the narrow and well-defined classes of expression which carries so little social value, such as obscenity, that the State can prohibit and punish such expression by all persons in its jurisdiction. For example, an employee's false criticism of his employer on grounds not of public concern may be cause for his discharge but would be entitled to the same protection in a libel action accorded an identical statement made by a man on the street. We hold only that when a public employee speaks not as a citizen upon matters of public concern, but instead as an employee upon matters only of personal interest, absent the most unusual circumstances, a federal court is not the appropriate forum in which to review the wisdom of a personnel decision taken by a public agency allegedly in reaction to the employee's behavior. Our responsibility is to ensure that citizens are not deprived of fundamental rights by virtue of working for the government; this does not require a grant of immunity for employee grievances not afforded by the First Amendment to those who do not work for the state.

Whether an employee's speech addresses a matter of public concern must be determined by the content, form, and context of a given statement, as revealed by the whole record. In this case, with but one exception, the questions posed by Myers to her coworkers do not fall under the rubric of matters of "public concern." We view the questions pertaining to the confidence and trust that Myers' coworkers possess in various supervisors, the level of office morale, and the need for a grievance committee as mere extensions of Myers' dispute over her transfer to another section of the criminal court.

* * *

One question in Myers' questionnaire, however, does touch upon a matter of public concern. Question 11 inquires if assistant district attorneys "ever feel pressured to work in political campaigns on behalf of office supported candidates." * * *

B

Because one of the questions in Myers' survey touched upon a matter of public concern, and contributed to her discharge we must determine whether Connick was justified in discharging Myers. Here the District Court again erred in imposing an unduly onerous burden on the state to justify Myers' discharge. The District Court viewed the issue of whether Myers' speech was upon a matter of "public concern" as a threshold inquiry, after which it became the government's burden to "clearly demonstrate" that the speech involved "substantially interfered" with official responsibilities. Yet *Pickering* unmistakably states, and respondent agrees, that the state's burden in justifying a particular discharge varies depending upon the nature of the employee's expression. Although such particularized balancing is difficult, the courts must reach the most appropriate possible balance of the competing interests.

C

The *Pickering* balance requires full consideration of the government's interest in the effective and efficient fulfillment of its responsibilities to the public.

* * *

Also relevant is the manner, time, and place in which the questionnaire was distributed. As noted in *Givhan v. Western Line Consolidated School Dist.*, "Private expression ... may in some situations bring additional factors to the *Pickering* calculus. When a government employee personally confronts his immediate superior, the employing agency's institutional efficiency may be threatened not only by the content of the employee's message but also by the manner, time, and place in which it is delivered." Here the questionnaire was prepared, and distributed at the office; the manner of distribution required not only Myers to leave her work but for others to do the same in order that the questionnaire be completed. Although some latitude in when official work is performed is to be allowed when professional employees are involved, and Myers did not violate announced office policy, the fact that Myers, unlike Pickering, exercised her rights to speech at the office supports Connick's fears that the functioning of his office was endangered.

Finally, the context in which the dispute arose is also significant. This is not a case where an employee, out of purely academic interest, circulated a questionnaire so as to obtain useful research. Myers acknowledges that it is no coincidence that the questionnaire followed upon the heels of the transfer notice. When employee speech concerning office policy arises from an employment dispute concerning the very application of that policy to the speaker, additional weight must be given to the supervisor's view that the employee has threatened the authority of the employer to run the office. * * *

III

Myers' questionnaire touched upon matters of public concern in only a most limited sense; her survey, in our view, is most accurately characterized as an employee grievance concerning internal office policy. The limited First Amendment interest involved here does not require that Connick tolerate action which he reasonably believed would disrupt the office, undermine his authority, and destroy close working relationships. Myers' discharge therefore did not offend the First Amendment. We reiterate, however, the caveat we expressed in *Pickering, supra* at 569, 88 S. Ct. at 1735: "Because of the enormous variety of fact situations in which critical statements by . . . public employees may be thought by their superiors . . . to furnish grounds for dismissal, we do not deem it either appropriate or feasible to lay down a general standard against which all such statements may be judged."

Our holding today is grounded in our long-standing recognition that the First Amendment's primary aim is the full protection of speech upon issues of public concern, as well as the practical realities involved in the administration of a government office. Although today the balance is struck for the government, this is no defeat for the First Amendment. For it would indeed be a Pyrrhic victory for the great principles of free expression if the Amendment's safeguarding of a public employee's right, as a citizen, to participate in discussions concerning public affairs were confused with the attempt to constitutionalize the employee grievance that we see presented here. The judgment of the Court of Appeals is

Reversed.

JUSTICE BRENNAN, with whom JUSTICE MARSHALL, JUSTICE BLACKMUN, and JUSTICE STEVENS join, dissenting.

Sheila Myers was discharged for circulating a questionnaire to her fellow Assistant District Attorneys seeking information about the effect of petitioner's personnel policies on employee morale and the overall work performance of the District Attorney's Office. The Court concludes that her dismissal does not violate the First Amendment, primarily because the questionnaire addresses matters that, in the Court's view, are not of public concern. It is hornbook law, however, that speech about "the manner in which government is operated or should be operated" is an essential part of the communications necessary for self-governance the protection of which was a central purpose of the First Amendment. Because the questionnaire addressed such matters and its distribution did not adversely affect the operations of the District Attorney's Office or interfere with Myers' working relationship with her fellow employees, I dissent.

I

The Court correctly reaffirms the long established principle that the government may not constitutionally compel persons to relinquish their First Amendment rights as a condition of public employment. *Pickering* held that the First Amendment protects the rights of public employees "as citizens to comment on matters of public interest" in connection with the operation of the government agencies for which they work. 391 U.S. at 568, 88 S. Ct. at 1734. We recognized, however, that the government has legitimate interests in regulating the speech of its employees that differ significantly from its interests in regulating the speech of people generally. *Ibid.* We therefore held that the scope of public employees' First Amendment rights must be determined by balancing "the interests of the [employee], as a citizen, in commenting upon matters of public concern and the interest of the State, as an employer, in promoting the efficiency of the public services it performs through its employees." *Ibid.*

The balancing test articulated in *Pickering* comes into play only when a public employee's speech implicates the government's interests as an employer. When public employees engage in expression unrelated to their employment while away from the work place, their First Amendment rights are, of course, no different from those of the general public. See *id,* at 574, 88 S. Ct. at 1737. Thus, whether a public employee's speech addresses a matter of public concern is relevant to the constitutional inquiry only when the statements at issue—by virtue of their content or the context in which they were made—may have an adverse impact on the government's ability to perform its duties efficiently.[1]

The Court's decision today is flawed in three respects. First, the Court distorts the balancing analysis required under *Pickering* by sug-

---

1. Although the Court's opinion states that "if Myers' questionnaire cannot be fairly characterized as constituting speech on a matter of public concern, it is unnecessary for us to scrutinize the reasons for her discharge," I do not understand it to imply that a governmental employee's First Amendment rights outside the employment context are limited to speech on matters of public concern. To the extent that the Court's opinion may be read to suggest that the dismissal of a public employee for speech unrelated to a subject of public interest does not implicate First Amendment interests, I disagree, because our cases establish that public employees enjoy the full range of First Amendment rights guaranteed to members of the general public. Under the balancing test articulated in *Pickering*, however, the government's burden to justify such a dismissal may be lighter.

gesting that one factor, the context in which a statement is made, is to be weighed *twice*—first in determining whether an employee's speech addresses a matter of public concern and then in deciding whether the statement adversely affected the government's interest as an employer. Second, in concluding that the effect of respondent's personnel policies on employee morale and the work performance of the District Attorney's Office is not a matter of public concern, the Court impermissibly narrows the class of subjects on which public employees may speak out without fear of retaliatory dismissal. Third, the Court misapplies the *Pickering* balancing test in holding that Myers could constitutionally be dismissed for circulating a questionnaire addressed to at least one subject that *was* "a matter of interest to the community," in the absence of evidence that her conduct disrupted the efficient functioning of the District Attorney's Office.

II

* * *

We have long recognized that one of the central purposes of the First Amendment's guarantee of freedom of expression is to protect the dissemination of information on the basis of which members of our society may make reasoned decisions about the government.

* * *

The constitutionally protected right to speak out on governmental affairs would be meaningless if it did not extend to statements expressing criticism of governmental officials.

* * *

In *Pickering* we held that the First Amendment affords similar protection to critical statements by a public school teacher directed at the Board of Education for whom he worked. 391 U.S. at 574, 88 S. Ct. at 1737. In so doing, we recognized that "free and open debate" about the operation of public schools "is vital to informed decision-making by the electorate." *Id.* at 571–572, 88 S. Ct. at 1736. We also acknowledged the importance of allowing teachers to speak out on school matters.

* * *

Applying these principles, I would hold that Myers' questionnaire addressed matters of public concern because it discussed subjects that could reasonably be expected to be of interest to persons seeking to develop informed opinions about the manner in which the Orleans Parish District Attorney, an elected official charged with managing a vital governmental agency, discharges his responsibilities. The questionnaire sought primarily to obtain information about the impact of the recent transfers on morale in the District Attorney's Office. It is beyond doubt that personnel decisions that adversely affect discipline and morale may ultimately impair an agency's efficient performance of its duties. Because I believe the First Amendment protects the right of public employees to discuss such matters so that the public may be better informed about how their elected officials fulfill their responsibilities, I would affirm the District Court's conclusion that the questionnaire related to matters of public importance and concern.

The Court's adoption of a far narrower conception of what subjects are of public concern seems prompted by its fears that a broader view "would mean that virtually every remark—and certainly every criticism directed at a public official—would plant the seed of a constitutional case." Obviously, not every remark directed at a public official by a public employee is protected by the First Amendment. But deciding whether a particular matter is of public concern is an inquiry that, by its very nature, is a sensitive one for judges charged with interpreting a constitutional provision intended to put "the decision as to what views shall be voiced largely into the hands of each of us...." The Court recognized the sensitive nature of this determination in *Gertz v. Robert Welch, Inc.*, which held that the scope of the constitutional privilege in defamation cases turns on whether or not the plaintiff is a public figure, not on whether the statements at issue address a subject of public concern. In so doing, the Court referred to the "difficulty of forcing state and federal judges to decide on an *ad hoc* basis which publications address issues of 'general or public interest' and which do not," and expressed "doubt [about] the wisdom of committing this task to the conscience of judges." In making such a delicate inquiry, we must bear in mind that "the citizenry is the final judge of the proper conduct of public business."

The Court's decision ignores these precepts. Based on its own narrow conception of which matters are of public concern, the Court implicitly determines that information concerning employee morale at an important government office will not inform public debate. To the contrary, the First Amendment protects the dissemination of such information so that the people, not the courts, may evaluate its usefulness. The proper means to ensure that the courts are not swamped with routine employee grievances mischaracterized as First Amendment cases is not to restrict artificially the concept of "public concern," but to require that adequate weight be given to the public's important interests in the efficient performance of governmental functions and in preserving employee discipline and harmony sufficient to achieve that end.

III

* * *

Pickering recognized the difficulty of articulating "a general standard against which all ... statements may be judged," 391 U.S. at 569, 88 S. Ct. at 1735; it did, however, identify a number of factors that may affect the balance in particular cases. Those relevant here are whether the statements are directed to persons with whom the speaker "would normally be in contact in the course of his daily work"; whether they had an adverse effect on "discipline by intermediate supervisors or harmony among coworkers"; whether the employment relationship in question is "the kind ... for which it can persuasively be claimed that personal loyalty and confidence are necessary to their proper functioning"; and whether the statements "have in any way impeded [the employee's] proper performance of his daily duties ... or ... interfered with the regular operations of the [office]." *Id.* at 568–573, 88 S. Ct. at 1734–1737. In addition, in *Givhan,* we recognized that when the statements in question are made in private to an employee's immediate supervisor, "the employing agency's institutional efficiency may be threatened not only by the content of the ... message but also by the manner, time, and place in which it is delivered."

The District Court weighed all of the relevant factors identified by our cases. It found that petitioner failed to establish that Myers violated either a duty of confidentiality or an office policy. Noting that most of the questionnaires were distributed during lunch, it rejected the contention that the distribution of the questionnaire impeded Myers' performance of her duties, and it concluded that "Connick has not shown *any* evidence to indicate that the plaintiff's work performance was adversely affected by her expression."

The Court accepts all of these findings. It concludes, however, that the District Court failed to give adequate weight to the context in which the questionnaires were distributed and to the need to maintain close working relationships in the District Attorney's Office.

    * * *

Such extreme deference to the employer's judgment is not appropriate when public employees voice critical views concerning the operations of the agency for which they work. * * *

In this regard, our decision in *Tinker v. Des Moines Independent Community School District,* 393 U.S. 503, 89 S. Ct. 733 (1969), is controlling. *Tinker* arose in a public school, a context similar to the one in which the present case arose in that the determination of the scope of the Constitution's guarantee of freedom of speech required consideration of the "special characteristics of the ... environment" in which the expression took place. See *id.* at 506, 89 S. Ct. at 736. At issue was whether public high school students could constitutionally be prohibited from wearing black armbands in school to express their opposition to the Vietnam conflict. The District Court had ruled that such a ban "was reasonable because it was based on [school officials'] fear of a disturbance from the wearing of armbands." *Id.* at 508, 89 S.Ct. at 737. We found that justification inadequate, because "in our system, undifferentiated fear or apprehension of a disturbance is not enough to overcome the right to freedom of expression." *Ibid.* We concluded:

> "In order for the State ... to justify prohibition of a particular expression of opinion, it must be able to show that its action was caused by something more than a mere desire to avoid the discomfort and unpleasantness that always accompany an unpopular viewpoint. *Certainly where there is no finding and no showing that engaging in the forbidden conduct would "materially and substan-*

tially interfere with the requirements of appropriate discipline in the operation of the school," the prohibition cannot be sustained." Id. at 509, 89 S.Ct. at 738 (emphasis supplied).

Because the speech at issue addressed matters of public importance, a similar standard should be applied here. After reviewing the evidence, the District Court found that "it cannot be said that the defendant's interest in promoting the efficiency of the public services performed through his employees was either adversely affected or substantially impeded by plaintiff's distribution of the questionnaire." Based on these findings the District Court concluded that the circulation of the questionnaire was protected by the First Amendment. The District Court applied the proper legal standard and reached an acceptable accommodation between the competing interests. I would affirm its decision and the judgment of the Court of Appeals.

IV

The Court's decision today inevitably will deter public employees from making critical statements about the manner in which government agencies are operated for fear that doing so will provoke their dismissal. As a result, the public will be deprived of valuable information with which to evaluate the performance of elected officials. Because protecting the dissemination of such information is an essential function of the First Amendment, I dissent.

b. *"Academic Freedom" at the K–12 Level*

COCKREL v. SHELBY COUNTY SCH. DIST.

270 F.3d 1036 (6th Cir. 2001).

MOORE, CIRCUIT JUDGE.

* * *

I. BACKGROUND

Plaintiff Donna Cockrel, a tenured fifth-grade teacher at Simpsonville Elementary School in the Shelby County, Kentucky School District was terminated on July 15, 1997 by the District's superintendent, Dr. Leon Mooneyhan. The School District's proffered grounds for Cockrel's termination were insubordination, conduct unbecoming a teacher, inefficiency, incompetency, and neglect of duty. As the basis for these charges, the School District detailed seventeen specific instances of misconduct engaged in by Cockrel, including: failing to teach and disparaging the school's "Just Think" curriculum; calling Principal Harry Slate names in front of staff members and students; and failing to cooperate with the Title I program and the Title I aides in her class, as well as with other faculty members and staff of Simpsonville Elementary School.

While the School District alleged numerous reasons for its decision to terminate Cockrel, she claims that the District fired her due to her decision to invite Woody Harrelson, the television and film actor most famous for his role as "Woody" on the network television show "Cheers," and others to her classroom to give presentations on the environmental benefits of industrial hemp. Hemp, an illegal substance in Kentucky, is a plant from which both marijuana and a valuable fiber can be harvested. There are two varieties of the hemp plant. One is the marijuana plant itself, with approximately four to seven percent of its weight comprised of tetrahydrocannabinol ("THC"), the active chemical in the marijuana drug; the other is industrial hemp, a plant which grows in stalks and from which fibers can be taken to make various goods such as paper and clothes. Unlike marijuana, the industrial hemp plant is only comprised of between 0.1 and 0.4 percent THC, an insufficient amount to have any narcotic effect. Nevertheless, Kentucky law prohibits possession of both varieties of the hemp plant, including "its seeds or resin or any compound, mixture, or preparation which contains any quantity of these substances."

Cockrel claims that on at least three occasions during her seven-year tenure at Simpsonville Elementary she organized outside speakers to come to her class to speak about industrial hemp. Cockrel further claims that both Principal Slate and Superintendent Mooneyhan knew that she organized industrial hemp presentations. While Principal Slate alleges that he never knew industrial hemp was being discussed in Cockrel's class, he does admit that Cockrel's lesson plans, on at least one occasion, specifically mentioned that hemp was to be discussed.

On or about April 9, 1996, following Cockrel's decision to end the 1995–96 school year with a project entitled "Saving the Trees," in which the use of industrial hemp fibers as a possible alternative to wood pulp was to be discussed, Cockrel was contacted by a representative of the Cable News Network ("CNN") and asked if she would permit CNN's cameras to film her class presentation for use in a larger program on tree conservation. Cockrel claims that she then immediately informed Slate of CNN's potential visit to their school, though Slate does not recall this conversation.

In early May 1996, Joe Hickey, president of the Kentucky Hemp Growers Association, informed Cockrel that Woody Harrelson might visit Kentucky with CNN, and that Harrelson might also visit her classroom. Cockrel claims that she was given no specific information as to when Harrelson might visit her classroom, and that it was not until the morning of May 30, 1996, the last day of the school year, that she was notified that Harrelson would be visiting Simpsonville Elementary School that day. Cockrel informed Principal Slate of the impending visit, and he agreed to allow it, though Slate claims that he was only told that the presentation to be given was about agriculture.

Harrelson arrived at the school later that morning with an "entourage, including representatives of the Kentucky Hemp Museum and Kentucky Hemp Growers Cooperative Association, several hemp growers from foreign countries, CNN, and various Kentucky news media representatives." As stated in Cockrel's complaint, Harrelson spoke with the children about his opposition to marijuana use, yet he distinguished marijuana from industrial hemp and advocated the use of industrial hemp as an alternative to increased logging efforts. As part of the presentation, products made from hemp were shown to the children, as were hemp seeds, a banned substance in the state of Kentucky. Harrelson's visit received both local and national media attention. One student who did not have parental permission to be videotaped or photographed by the news media was included by the press in a class photograph with Harrelson.

Following Harrelson's visit and the media attention it garnered, parents and teachers wrote numerous letters to members of the Shelby County School District voicing their concern and dismay regarding the industrial hemp presentation. Several of the letters noted the mixed message the school was sending on drug use as Harrelson's presentation occurred on the same day that many Simpsonville Elementary School students were graduating from the Drug Abuse Resistance Education ("D.A.R.E.") program offered in the school.

Based on the complaints expressed in the letters, Superintendent Mooneyhan decided to initiate an investigation into Cockrel's conduct. Following the investigation, Mooneyhan advised the Kentucky Education Professional Standards Board ("EPSB") that Cockrel had allowed hemp seeds, an illegal substance, to be passed around to students in her class during Harrelson's class visit. The Standards Board, after investigating the matter, ultimately dismissed Mooneyhan's complaint without prejudice, stating that there was an "insufficient basis to warrant [a] certificate revocation action."

In the months following Harrelson's visit, Simpsonville Elementary School adopted a new visitors policy for "controversial" topics that required advance approval by school administration and written consent by students' parents. This policy was put to use when, during the next school year, Cockrel informed Slate that Harrelson would be making a second visit to her classroom to discuss industrial hemp. Cockrel met all of the requirements of the new visitors policy, including providing the requisite advance notice to Principal Slate and obtaining permission from the parents of her students for their children to attend the presentation.[2] Slate did not attempt to discourage Cockrel from having another class presentation on industrial hemp, nor did he tell her that Harrelson should not be invited back to the school. According to Cockrel, however, Superintendent Mooneyhan did tell her earlier in the school year that it would not be in her best interests if Harrelson made any more visits to her class. While Harrelson was unable to attend on the day of his scheduled visit, a small group of parents, unaware that Harrelson was not coming, went to the school and "loudly voiced their

---

2. All but one of her students was given permission to attend the Harrelson presentation.

objections" to Slate about his permitting Harrelson to visit the school a second time.

Harrelson rescheduled the visit for the following week, January 29, 1997, and Cockrel again fully complied with the school's visitors policy. Principal Slate again approved Harrelson's visit. This time Harrelson did make an appearance. Harrelson was met by a group of parents outside the school who were protesting his visit. Due to school scheduling problems, Harrelson was only able to speak to the students for a few minutes before the students had to leave for lunch. Harrelson's visit again garnered national media attention from CNN.

* * *

The termination letter informing Cockrel of her discharge detailed numerous instances of misconduct, all of which allegedly served as the basis for her discharge. Several of these charges detailed misconduct that occurred well before Harrelson made his initial visit to Simpsonville Elementary. There is no evidence in the record, however, that Cockrel had been reprimanded for such activity prior to Harrelson's visits to her classroom.

* * *

On June 4, 1998, Cockrel filed suit in the United States District Court for the Eastern District of Kentucky. Cockrel brought a claim pursuant to 42 U.S.C. § 1983 in which she alleged that she was terminated in retaliation for exercising her First Amendment right of free speech when discussing the potential environmental benefits of industrial hemp. * * *

II.   ANALYSIS

* * *

C.   Cockrel's First Amendment Retaliation Claim

* * *

2.   The Elements of a First Amendment Retaliation Claim

Donna Cockrel, a teacher in the Shelby County Public School District, is a public employee. For a public employee to establish a claim of First Amendment retaliation, this court has held that she must demonstrate:

> (1) that [she] was engaged in a constitutionally protected activity; (2) that the defendant's adverse action caused [her] to suffer an injury that would likely chill a person of ordinary firmness from continuing to engage in that activity; and (3) that the adverse action was motivated at least in part as a response to the exercise of [her] constitutional rights.

To demonstrate that she was engaging in constitutionally protected speech, Cockrel must show that her speech touched on matters of public concern, and that her "interest in commenting upon matters of public concern ... outweigh[s] the interest of the State, as an employer, in promoting the efficiency of the public services it performs through its employees." If the plaintiff can establish the three elements of her First Amendment retaliation claim, the burden of persuasion then shifts to the defendants, who must show, by a preponderance of the evidence, that they "would have taken the same action even in the absence of the protected conduct."

a. Was This Speech?

Before deciding whether Cockrel's speech was constitutionally protected, this court must first address the question of whether Cockrel's activity can be considered speech at all. The district court's decision disposing of Cockrel's First Amendment claims appears to be based on two separate theories that the court uses interchangeably. First, the district court stated that Cockrel's decision to bring in a speaker who would give a presentation on industrial hemp should not be considered speech. The district court further held that a teacher's decisions regarding the content of the curriculum she will teach to her class, even if considered speech, is still not protected by the First Amendment. We put the second holding aside for a moment and turn to the first.

The district court held that, because Cockrel simply chose to bring in speakers who would talk about industrial hemp, rather than speaking on the matter herself, "[h]er free speech claim is based solely on conduct." Also influential in the district court's decision was its notion that, in staging an industrial hemp presentation, Cockrel was not intending to convey a "particularized message," nor was she advocating or speaking against hemp's use as an environmental alternative to cutting down trees.

Regardless of the reasoning upon which it relied, the district court erred in holding Cockrel's conduct not to be speech. First, to the extent the district court was persuaded that Cockrel's actions did not constitute speech because Woody Harrelson, rather than Cockrel, was doing the speaking, this was error. As the Supreme Court stated in *Hurley v. Irish–American Gay, Lesbian & Bisexual Group*, to receive First Amendment protection, a speaker does not have "to generate, as an original matter, each item featured in the communication." For example, cable operators, even though they only broadcast material written, spoken, and produced by others, are still considered to be engaged in protected speech. The same First Amendment protections exist for newspapers, which in their opinion pages simply collect and present the speech of others. We see no reason, nor have the defendants explained to this court, why a teacher's selection of a speaker for an in-class presentation is less a form of speech than a cable operator's decision as to which programs it chooses to present to its viewing audience.

To the extent that the district court relied on the argument that Cockrel's conduct was not speech because she had no advocative purpose when bringing industrial hemp enthusiasts to her class, this was also error. The Supreme Court has held that films, radio programs, and live entertainment are all protected by the First Amendment. Moreover, to have constitutional protection, those who choose to show the film or stage the play need not show that they intended to convey a particularized message in doing so, nor that they approved or disapproved of its content, for such activities are inherently expressive and entitled to constitutional protection.

The district court points to Judge Milburn's concurring opinion in *Fowler v. Board of Education*, in support of its argument that Cockrel's conduct should not be considered speech. In *Fowler*, a high school teacher, at the request of her students, showed them *Pink Floyd—The Wall*, an "R"-rated film containing nudity and a great deal of violence, on the last day of school while she completed grade cards. The teacher was later terminated for showing the film. The teacher then brought suit, claiming that she was terminated in retaliation for exercising her First Amendment rights.

Judge Milburn, writing only for himself on the issue of whether the conduct of showing the film to the class constituted protected speech, stated that, because the teacher had never seen the movie before and had no idea of its content, her decision to show the film could not be considered "expressive or communicative" in nature. Thus, Judge Milburn concluded, the teacher's conduct in showing the film was not entitled to First Amendment protection.

Judges Peck and Merritt disagreed with Judge Milburn's analysis of whether the teacher's showing of a film could be considered speech. Judge Peck, while concurring in the outcome of the case, stated that the expressive conduct cases used by Judge Milburn to analyze the teacher's showing of the film were "inapposite." Judge Merritt, noting that books, movies, and music that are purely for entertainment value still receive First Amendment protection, argued that the teacher's decision to show the film clearly was protected speech.

While Judge Milburn's analysis in *Fowler* is not binding on this court, even if it were, the facts of this case are clearly distinguishable from *Fowler*. Unlike the teacher's showing of a film the content of which she knew nothing about, Cockrel's decision to bring in industrial hemp advocates did have an intent to convey a particularized message. Cockrel, who in her complaint states that "[s]he was a teacher trainer in the state sponsored Kentucky Agriculture and Environment in the Classroom project from 1993 to 1997[,]" worked at designing methods to integrate agricultural topics into her fifth-grade curriculum. She had, on at least three occasions before the Harrelson visit, brought in speakers who advocated the use of industrial hemp to conserve trees and other natural resources. Viewing the facts in the light most favorable to Cockrel, we cannot state, as the district court did, that it was not until "some point during or after the presentation [that] Plaintiff may have developed an approval or disapproval of the use of industrial hemp[.]" Instead, the evidence shows that Cockrel was well aware of the arguments for industrial hemp, and that this was a message she wanted delivered to her students.

Thus, while we believe that Cockrel had an advocative purpose in bringing in speakers who presented her students with information on the environmental benefits of industrial hemp, even if Cockrel did not have such a purpose when organizing these presentations, her decision to present these speakers to her class still constitutes speech.

b. Is Cockrel's Speech Constitutionally Protected?

Given our determination that Cockrel's decision to bring industrial hemp advocates into her class is speech, the next question we must ask is whether that speech is constitutionally protected. As stated earlier, speech of a public employee is protected by the First Amendment only if it touches on matters of public concern, and only if "the employee's interest in commenting upon matters of public concern ... outweigh[s] the interest of the State, as an employer, in promoting the efficiency of the public services it performs through its employees." If Cockrel's speech cannot meet both of these standards, then her First Amendment retaliation claim cannot go forward.

i. Does Cockrel's Speech Touch on a Matter of Public Concern?

In determining whether Cockrel's speech touched on a matter of public concern, we turn to *Connick v. Myers,* 461 U.S. 138, 103 S. Ct. 1684 (1983), the Supreme Court's most instructive case on this issue. In *Connick,* the Court stated that matters of public concern are those that can "be fairly considered as relating to any matter of political, social, or other concern to the community[.]" *Id.* at 146, 103 S. Ct. 1684. There is no question that the issue of industrial hemp is a matter of great political and social concern to many citizens of Kentucky, and we believe that Cockrel's presentations clearly come within the Supreme Court's understanding of speech touching on matters of public concern.

In support of this conclusion, we first turn to the district court's opinion, which unequivocally stated "that the issue of industrial hemp is politically charged and of great concern to certain citizens." Second, in the past year alone, industrial hemp advocacy in Kentucky has made news on several occasions, revealing the significant extent to which industrial hemp has become an important and publicly debated issue in the State. In October, presidential candidate Ralph Nader, in a campaign stop in Kentucky, spoke out in favor of the legalization of industrial hemp and of the benefits it would have for small family farmers. In December, after the Drug Enforcement Agency confiscated industrial hemp being grown on the Pine Ridge, South Dakota Indian Reservation, members of the Kentucky Hemp Growers Association, including former Kentucky governor Louie B. Nunn, traveled to South Dakota and, in a ceremony at the base of Mount Rushmore, delivered legally imported industrial hemp to the tribe as a sign of its solidarity. These examples only scratch the surface of the extent to which industrial hemp has become an issue of contentious political and economic debate in Kentucky.

While discussion of industrial hemp plainly meets the broad concept of "public concern" as defined by the Supreme Court, some courts have focused on other portions of the Supreme Court's *Connick* decision in concluding that a teacher's classroom speech does not touch on matters of public concern. These cases pay particular attention to the following portion of the *Connick* Court's holding:

> [W]hen a public employee speaks not as a citizen upon matters of public concern, but instead as an employee upon matters only of personal interest, absent the most unusual circumstances, a federal court is not the appropriate forum in which to review the wisdom of a personnel decision taken by a public agency allegedly in reaction to the employee's behavior. *Connick,* 461 U.S. at 147, 103 S.Ct. 1684.

Based upon this language, the Fourth and Fifth Circuits have determined that a teacher, in choosing what he will teach his students, is not speaking as a citizen, but rather as an employee on matters of private interest.

We believe that the Fourth and Fifth Circuits have extended the holding of *Connick* beyond what the Supreme Court intended. Under the courts' analyses in *Boring* and *Kirkland,* a teacher, regardless of what he decides to include in his curriculum, is speaking as an employee on a private matter. This essentially gives a teacher no right to freedom of speech when teaching students in a classroom, for the very act of teaching is what the employee is paid to do. Thus, when teaching, even if about an upcoming presidential election or the importance of our Bill of Rights, the Fourth and Fifth Circuits' reasoning would leave such speech without constitutional protection, for the teacher is speaking as an employee, and not as a citizen.

The facts in *Connick* indicate that the Fourth and Fifth Circuits have read the Supreme Court's language too broadly. In *Connick,* an assistant district attorney, following a disagreement with a supervisor, prepared a questionnaire seeking the opinions of her co-workers on issues such as "office transfer policy, office morale, the need for a grievance committee, the level of confidence in supervisors, and whether employees felt pressured to work in political campaigns." *Connick,* 461 U.S. at 141, 103 S.Ct. 1684. Connick was later fired for circulating the questionnaire on the grounds of insubordination. *Id.* The Court held that, while many of the questions simply reflected the plaintiff's efforts to gather information to use against her supervisors in her private employment dispute, Myers's question regarding the pressure to work on political campaigns *did* touch on a matter of public concern. *Id.* at 149, 103 S.Ct. 1684. Thus, the Court held that, even though Myers was speaking as an employee out of her private interest in combating her supervisors' decision to transfer her, the fact that one of her questions dealt with the fundamental constitutional right not to be coerced into campaigning for a political candidate was enough to make this particular issue touch on a matter of public concern. *Id.*

If the Fourth and Fifth Circuits' interpretation of *Connick* were correct, then any time a public employee was speaking as an employee, like Myers was when she asked her question about employees being pressured to campaign, the speech at issue would not be protected. As the Supreme Court made clear in its analysis, however, the key question is not whether a person is speaking in his role as an employee or a citizen, but whether the employee's speech in fact touches on matters of public concern. *Id.* 148–49, 103 S.Ct. 1684. Thus, even if a public employee were acting out of a private motive with no intent to air her speech publicly, as was the case with Myers, so long as the speech relates to matters of "political, social, or other concern to the community," as opposed to matters "only of personal interest," it shall be considered as touching upon matters of public concern. *Id.* at 146–49, 103 S.Ct. 1684.

In Cockrel's case, although she was speaking in her role as an employee when presenting information on the environmental benefits of industrial hemp, the content of her speech, as discussed *supra,* most certainly involved matters related to the political and social concern of the community, as opposed to mere matters of private interest. Thus, contrary to the analyses in *Boring* and *Kirkland,* we hold that Cockrel's speech does touch on matters of public concern.[5]

ii. *Pickering* Balancing

Having held that Cockrel's speech touches on matters of public concern, we must now weigh the employee's interest in speaking against the employer's interest in regulating the speech to determine if the speech is constitutionally protected. In *Pickering v. Board of Education,* 391 U.S. 563, 88 S. Ct. 1731 (1968), the Supreme Court endeavored to strike a balance between a public employee's speech rights on matters of public interest (in that case a public school teacher's speech outside of school) and the State's interest as an employer in maintaining a productive workplace. In accordance with the balancing test created in *Pickering,* public employee speech, even if touching on matters of public

---

5. While Cockrel, in teaching her students about the environmental benefits of industrial hemp, was arguably speaking both as an employee and as a citizen, we do not believe that this case is best analyzed as a "mixed speech" case. In mixed speech cases, the employee at issue speaks not only as both a citizen and an employee, but the content of her speech involves matters of both public and private concern. In this case, while the very nature of Cockrel's profession entails that her speech on matters of political and social interest is likely to be made both as an employee and a citizen, the content of her speech is not mixed. Instead, rather than concerning, in part, an employee grievance or some other private dispute, as was the case with the professor's speech in *Bonnell,* Cockrel's speech relates to matters particularly of public concern. Even if we were to apply the mixed speech analysis, so long as "any part of an employee's speech, which contributes to the discharge, relates to matters of public concern, the court must conduct a balancing of interests test as set forth in *Pickering v. Board of Education,* 391 U.S. 563, 88 S.Ct. 1731 (1968)." As we will discuss in more detail later, because Cockrel's speech does relate to matters of public concern, and because this speech, at least in part, contributed to her discharge, a balancing of interests under *Pickering* is in order.

concern, will not be constitutionally protected unless the employee's interest in speaking on these issues "outweigh[s] 'the interest of the State, as an employer, in promoting the efficiency of the public services it performs through its employees.' " In striking the balance between the State's and the employee's respective interests, this court has stated that it will "consider whether an employee's comments meaningfully interfere with the performance of her duties, undermine a legitimate goal or mission of the employer, create disharmony among co-workers, impair discipline by superiors, or destroy the relationship of loyalty and trust required of confidential employees."

Before engaging in a "particularized balancing" of the competing interests at stake in this case, *Connick,* 461 U.S. at 150, 103 S.Ct. 1684, it is important to note that "if an employee's speech substantially involve[s] matters of public concern, an employer may be required to make a particularly strong showing that the employee's speech interfered with workplace functioning before taking action." In this case, it is clear that Cockrel's speech did substantially involve matters of public concern, and thus the defendants will have to make a stronger showing that their interests in regulating plaintiff's speech outweighed Cockrel's interests in speaking.

Weighing in plaintiff's favor in this analysis is the fact that her speech substantially involved matters of significant public concern in Kentucky. Defendants claim, however, that their "interest in maintaining loyalty, efficient operation of the schools, and workplace harmony" outweighs the plaintiff's interest in speaking about industrial hemp. We first note that the defendants do not claim that Cockrel's presentations on industrial hemp meaningfully interfered with the performance of her teaching duties. Defendants would have a difficult time making this argument, however, considering they openly acknowledged in a public statement to CNN that there was "educational value" in teaching students about industrial hemp as an alternative crop. We further note that defendants' purported interest in "maintaining loyalty" is inapposite in this case. While this circuit has stated that it would consider in its balancing whether employee speech operated to "destroy the relationship of loyalty and trust required of confidential employees[,]"a public school teacher, we believe, is hardly the type of confidential employee the court had in mind. Thus, any loyalty concerns that the defendants may have will not be taken into consideration in our weighing of the competing interests at stake.

Turning to the defendants' proffered interests in an efficient operation of the school and a harmonious work environment, there is evidence that plaintiff's speech has led to problems in both of these areas. For example, following Harrelson's first visit to Simpsonville, numerous members of the school's faculty and staff circulated and or signed letters addressed to school officials criticizing Cockrel's actions in advocating the use of industrial hemp to her students. Cockrel thereafter expressed her displeasure with her co-workers' sentiments on several occasions. As discussed earlier, following D.A.R.E. officer Yeager's criticism of the

Harrelson visits, Cockrel no longer wanted the officer in her classroom instructing her students. Cockrel asked Slate to find a replacement for Yeager as well. Cockrel's termination letter detailed several instances of disputes Cockrel had with co-workers, including an instance in which Cockrel jerked a phone away from a co-worker who had signed one of the letters speaking out against the Harrelson visit, and an incident in which Cockrel told two co-workers "not to waste their breath after they said 'good morning' to [her.]" At least one of these co-workers had also signed a letter critical of Cockrel's decision to speak about industrial hemp.

Many parents and members of the school community also expressed great concern over Cockrel's decision to invite speakers to her class who advocated the use of industrial hemp. Parents wrote letters to Principal Slate and Superintendent Mooneyhan in opposition to Cockrel's industrial hemp presentations, and a small number came to Simpsonville Elementary to protest on the final two occasions Harrelson was scheduled to visit. In addition, the PTA passed a position statement recommending that Cockrel no longer teach in the Shelby County School District.

Although this evidence of a contentious and periodically disrupted work environment weighs in favor of the defendants, the amount of weight we should give this evidence is an entirely different question. We are troubled by the fact that, whereas school officials gave plaintiff prior approval to host all three of the industrial hemp presentations at issue in this case, defendants now forward concerns of school efficiency and harmony as reasons supporting their decision to discharge Cockrel. Principal Slate approved all of Harrelson's scheduled visits in advance, and Slate openly stated that he had no problem with Cockrel teaching her students about industrial hemp. Cockrel also met the conditions of the new visitors policy implemented after the initial Harrelson visit, including obtaining the permission of each student's parents before a child could participate in the presentation. We do not believe that defendants can use the outcry within the school community protesting Cockrel's speech, speech that was approved by school officials in advance, as a shield for their decision to discharge her. While ordinarily we would give substantial weight to the government employer's concerns of workplace efficiency, harmony, and discipline in conducting our balancing of the employee's and employer's competing interests, we cannot allow these concerns to tilt the *Pickering* scale in favor of the government, absent other evidence, when the disruptive consequences of the employee speech can be traced back to the government's express decision permitting the employee to engage in that speech.[6]

Accordingly, we hold that, on balance, the defendants' interests in an efficient operation of the school and a harmonious workplace do not outweigh the plaintiff's interests in speaking about the benefits of

---

6. This circuit has noted, with minimal explanation, that an unconstitutional dilemma may exist for a teacher whose controversial speech is approved ex ante by school officials, but used ex post, in the wake of parental and or community dismay with that speech, as the reason for the teacher's discharge.

industrial hemp, an issue of substantial political and economic concern in Kentucky. Thus, because Cockrel's speech touches on matters of public concern and because the balancing of interests under *Pickering* weighs in her favor, her speech is constitutionally protected.[7] We now proceed with an examination of the remainder of the elements of plaintiff's First Amendment retaliation claim.

c.   Did the Plaintiff Suffer an Injury as a Result of Her Speech That Would Chill an Ordinary Person From Continuing to Engage in Such Speech?

For the next element of Cockrel's retaliation claim, she must show "that the defendant[s'] adverse action caused [her] to suffer an injury that would likely chill a person of ordinary firmness from continuing to engage in that activity[.]" There is no question that, by being terminated, Cockrel has suffered an injury that would chill an ordinary person from continuing to engage in speech on the environmental benefits of industrial hemp.

d.   Was the Decision to Terminate Cockrel Motivated, at Least in Part, by Plaintiff's Decision to Speak About Industrial Hemp?

* * *

Although there certainly is significant evidence that Cockrel's behavior at school, apart from the industrial hemp presentations, was often inappropriate, we believe that Cockrel has presented enough evidence such that a reasonable jury could find that the defendants, in terminating her, were at least partially motivated by her decision to speak on industrial hemp. * * *

After examining this evidence, we conclude that a jury could find, by a preponderance of the evidence, that the defendants' decision to discharge Cockrel was motivated, at least in part, by her decision to teach her students about industrial hemp. The temporal proximity between the Harrelson visits and Cockrel's series of unscheduled evaluations, as well as the influence the parent and teacher complaints appeared to have on the defendants in the wake of the Harrelson visits, constitute sufficient evidence for Cockrel to establish the causation element of her First Amendment retaliation claim.

* * *

7. Rather than apply *Pickering*, several circuits have chosen to apply the Supreme Court's analysis of students' in-class speech rights in *Hazelwood School District v. Kuhlmeier*, 484 U.S. 260, 108 S.Ct. 562 (1988), to cases in which teachers' in-class speech rights are at issue. The *Pickering* balancing analysis has been consistently applied to cases of teacher speech in this circuit. *See, e.g., Bonnell* [*v. Lorenzo*] (applying *Pickering* to a college professor's speech); *Leary* [*v. Daeschner*] (applying *Pickering* to elementary school teachers' speech). We see no reason to part from *Pickering* when deciding cases involving a teacher's in-class speech, nor have either of the parties in this case argued that *Pickering* should not apply.

We are well aware that Cockrel's decision to speak cannot immunize her from an adverse employment decision arising out of inappropriate workplace behavior unrelated to her protected speech. * * * [However,] [i]n this case, the defendants have not met this burden, and we believe that a genuine issue of material facts exists from which a reasonable jury could conclude that Cockrel would not have been terminated had she not engaged in constitutionally protected activity. Thus, this matter should be resolved at trial rather than at the summary judgment stage.

III. SUMMARY

For the foregoing reasons, we REVERSE the district court's decision granting defendants' motion for summary judgment, and REMAND to that court for further proceedings.

NICHOL v. ARIN INTERMEDIATE UNIT 28

268 F.Supp.2d 536 (W.D. Pa. 2003).

SCHWAB, DISTRICT JUDGE.

I. Introduction

* * *

On April 8, 2003, Brenda Nichol was suspended pursuant to the Garb Statute and ARIN's Religious Affiliations policy from her job as an instructional assistant at the Penns Manor Area Elementary School ("Penns Manor"), a school within Intermediate Unit 28, for refusing to comply with her supervisor's request that she remove or conceal a small cross she regularly wore on a necklace.

Because this Court finds that ARIN's Religious Affiliations policy violates the Free Exercise of Religion and Free Speech Clauses of the First Amendment to the United States Constitution, that Ms. Nichol will suffer irreparable injury in the event the Court does not grant her request for injunctive relief, and that the balance of equities (i.e., the harm to plaintiff if the Court does not grant a preliminary injunction versus any harm to other parties and to the public if such relief is granted) weighs in her favor, the Court finds the ARIN's Religious Affiliations policy unconstitutional, and will direct defendants to reinstate Ms. Nichol to her former position pending disposition of plaintiff's request for a permanent injunction.

* * *

III. Stipulation of Undisputed Facts

* * *

B. Background

* * *

11. As an instructional assistant in an emotional support classroom, Ms. Nichol's duties include assisting students in mainstream

classroom activities, monitoring and recording behavior of those students, and implementing the behavior and educational plan for those students. At the time relevant to this lawsuit, she spent most of her time with one particular fourth grade student who is considered emotionally disabled and who has difficulties especially with transitions. However, there are other fourth, fifth and sixth grade students in the classroom.

12. In 1997, Ms. Nichol received a notice with her paycheck, dated October 16, 1997 and addressed to Intermediate Unit Staff, that explained the "Pennsylvania Public School Code (24 Pa. Stat. Ann. § 11–1112)" did not allow wearing religious jewelry, giving "Crosses or Stars of David" as examples. The notice included an explanation of consequences—a one-year suspension, and a permanent suspension in the event of a second infraction.

C. The Suspension

13. On March 11, 2003, Mr. Truscello approached the teacher in Ms. Nichol's classroom, as well as Ms. Nichol and other co-workers of Ms. Nichol, reminding them to comply with the Pennsylvania School Code that prohibits wearing any religious symbol, or not to display any religious symbol openly if they chose to wear one, while at work. He explained that this prohibition included a cross or any other religious symbol. They were asked either not to wear their crosses or to tuck them in.

14. The Policy that restricts plaintiff Nichol's ability to openly display her cross necklace was promulgated under the authority of, and is controlled by, ARIN, which cites to the Pennsylvania School Code, 24 Pa. Stat. Ann. § 11–1112 as its authority.

15. On April 4, 2003, Mr. Truscello approached Ms. Nichol regarding the matter, and Ms. Nichol explained to him that she believed that his request was like asking her to remove or hide her wedding rings. Ms. Nichol also explained that the cross was a symbol of freedom for her, and that she could not deny Christ in such a way as she was being asked to do. Mr. Truscello responded to Ms. Nichol's explanation by saying that he was not buying the wedding ring rationale, and that Ms. Nichol's religion is in her heart, not in what she wears.

16. Later in the day on April 4, 2003, Mr. Truscello returned to Ms. Nichol's classroom, specifically to give Ms. Nichol a copy of the ARIN Intermediate Unit 28 handbook, and he cited to it, explaining that she could not wear her cross. Mr. Truscello again asked Ms. Nichol to tuck in her cross, and he gave her until April 8, 2003 to decide whether she would comply. He warned that if Ms. Nichol wore her cross on April 8, 2003, he would suspend her for one year, as the Pennsylvania School Code required.

17. On April 8, 2003, Ms. Nichol visibly wore her cross to work and was suspended.

18. Ms. Nichol later received an official letter of suspension, dated April 8, 2003, from John T. Smith, Jr. notifying her that she was

suspended from employment as of April 7, 2003, with pay, until further notice.

* * *

20.   On May 9, 2003, the parties filed a supplement to their joint stipulation of facts, which provides that Ms. Nichol does not have a teaching or other professional certificate from the Pennsylvania State Board of Education or from ARIN.

21.   Following the evidentiary hearing, the parties filed a second supplemental stipulation accompanied by Plaintiff's Exhibit 3, which is an actual sized photograph of the cross alongside a ruler taken in natural lighting. The cross has white stones embedded on it and no other symbols or figures. Exhibit 3 supports the parties' oral stipulation that Ms. Nichol's cross is 1 & 7/16 inches in height and 15/16 inches in width.

IV.   Additional Fact Findings and Credibility Determinations by the Court

22.   Ms. Nichol testified, inter alia, that her mother gave her the cross as a gift after her mother's stroke in 1996, and she began wearing the cross to school shortly after that; plaintiff wore the cross on average three times a week in the classroom and throughout the school, and in the presence of the teacher she worked with, Debbie Dudt, who saw her wearing the cross; other employees at Penns Manor saw her wear the cross at work; plaintiff never tucked in the cross when she wore it; no one said anything to her about the cross until March 20, 2003, when Ms. Dudt reminded her of Mr. Truscello's request that her cross be tucked in, and then on April 4, 2003, when Mr. Truscello approached her about it; plaintiff had received a memo or notice about the religious dress policy in 1997 but she continued to wear her cross, as other school district employees were wearing similar jewelry. Ms. Nichol also stated the following reason she wore her cross and refused to take it off upon request: "I believe in Jesus Christ as my Lord and Savior. And I believe that this would be denying him in a sense of tucking this cross in because I am not ashamed of my Lord and Savior Jesus. I will do nothing to deny my faith and belief in him."

* * *

27.   * * * [T]he Court observed Ms. Nichol wearing the cross in court in the manner she usually wore it at work. The Court finds that plaintiff's cross is unobtrusive.

28.   There was no evidence introduced or offered that plaintiff's cross wearing caused any disturbances or disruptions to classes or school activities, or any harm to the school environment.

29.   There was no evidence introduced or offered that plaintiff's cross wearing caused any dissension, problems or controversy between her and Ms. Dudt or any other teacher or employee with ARIN or Penns Manor.

30. There was no evidence introduced or offered that plaintiff's cross wearing caused any dissension, problems or controversy between her and the student she primarily worked with, or with any other student.

31. To the contrary, Ms. Nichol and Mr. Truscello both testified as to the close and very successful relationship plaintiff had with the fourth grade boy she was primarily assisting with his emotional problems, especially with transition issues, and that this student has almost made a complete transition to the mainstream, with her valuable assistance.

32. There was no evidence introduced or offered that any student, parent, teacher, supervisor or other employee of ARIN or Penns Manor complained about plaintiff's cross.

33. There was no evidence introduced or offered that plaintiff proselytized, preached or taught her religious beliefs to students, faculty or others while at school.

34. Mr. Truscello testified that on March 27, 2003, Dr. Smith informed him that he had received a report from someone in the teachers union that one of the instructional assistants Mr. Truscello supervised had been observed wearing a cross on her necklace while at work.

35. ARIN permits the wearing of decorative jewelry with no religious symbolism by teachers and employees under its authority if it has no message or the message is secular. In fact, Mr. Truscello wore a lapel pin to court on May 12, 2003, which he sometimes wears to school, which consists of the word "DAD."

* * *

V. Statutory and Regulatory Framework

The Pennsylvania School Code's Garb Statute provides as follows:

Religious garb, insignia, etc., prohibited; penalty

(a) That no teacher in any public school shall wear in said school or while engaged in the performance of his duty as such teacher any dress, mark, emblem or insignia indicating the fact that such teacher is a member or adherent of any religious order, sect or denomination.

(b) Any teacher employed in any of the public schools of this Commonwealth, who violates the provisions of this section, shall be suspended from employment in such school for the term of one year, and in case of a second offense by the same teacher he shall be permanently disqualified from teaching in said school. Any public school director who after notice of any such violation fails to comply with the provisions of this section shall be guilty of a misdemeanor, and upon conviction of the first offense, shall be sentenced to pay a fine not exceeding one hundred dollars ($100), and on conviction of a second offense, the offending school director shall be sentenced to pay a fine not exceeding one hundred dollars ($100) and shall be deprived of his office as a public school director. A person thus twice convicted shall not be eligible to appointment or election as a director of any public school in this Commonwealth within a period of five (5) years from the date of his second conviction.

* * *

VII. Likelihood of Success

A. Pennsylvania Garb Statute

Preliminarily, the Court concludes that the Pennsylvania Garb Statute does not apply to plaintiff who, although she probably devotes 50% or more of her time at teaching and educational activities, is not one of the enumerated professional employees designated by section 11–1141 of the School Code, 24 Pa. Stat. Ann. § 11–1141, nor has she been "certificated in accordance with the qualifications established by the State Board of Education."

* * *

Nevertheless, defendants suspended plaintiff pursuant to ARIN's Religious Affiliations policy, which references and was adopted to implement the Garb Statute, and that policy must be measured against the constitutional protections afforded by the First Amendment.

* * *

E. Free Speech

* * * [T]here is significant overlap between the analysis of the Free Exercise of Religion and Free Speech Clauses of the First Amendment where, as here, the speech expresses a religious viewpoint. * * *

The familiar *Pickering* balance of public employer and employee interests is well established[.] * * *

1. Threshold Questions

As *Connick* held, a threshold inquiry is whether the employee's speech can fairly be considered to have been on a matter of public concern.

* * *

3. Matter of Public Concern

* * * The Supreme Court of the United States has held that "First Amendment rights are implicated *only* when a public employee's speech relates to matters of public concern." Before a *Pickering* balance may be conducted, therefore, it is incumbent upon the Court to determine if the employee's speech may be "fairly characterized as constituting speech on a matter of public concern."

A public employer is relatively (although not absolutely) unrestrained in regulating speech of its public employees unless that speech crosses the "public concern" threshold. The determination of whether a public employee's speech fairly relates to "any matter of political, social, or other concern to the community," *Connick,* 461 U.S. at 146, 103 S. Ct. 1684, is a legal one, "to be determined by the content, form and context of a given statement, as revealed by the whole record." * * *

(a) Content

"Public concern" is a term of art as employed at the *Pickering* threshold, and more often than not, the subset of public concern speech is measured more by what it is not than by what it is. Examination of public concern cases, starting with *Connick,* reveals a judicial pattern: speech tends to be deemed "fairly related to a matter of public concern" so long as the public employee's speech is not merely about "mundane employment grievances" exclusively of interest to the affected employee, or nearly so.

* * *

In *Tucker,* the United States Court of Appeals for the Ninth Circuit performed the threshold analysis where a computer analyst for the California Department of Education sued to enjoin it from enforcing its ban against any religious advocacy at the workplace. In rejecting the state's contention that private religious advocacy by an employee is not public concern speech, the Court reasoned as follows:

> This circuit and other courts have defined public concern speech broadly to include almost any matter other than speech that relates to internal power struggles within the workplace.... In *National Treasury Employees Union v. United States*, the D.C. Circuit [Court of Appeals] wrote:
>
> > The contrast, [between public concern speech and non-public concern speech], then was between issues of external interest as opposed to ones of internal office management. Accordingly, we read the "public concern" criterion as referring not to the number of interested listeners or readers but to whether the expression relates to some issue of interest beyond the employee's bureaucratic niche.
>
> The Supreme Court has also made it clear that an employee need not address the public at large, for his speech to be deemed to be on a matter of public concern. *See Rankin v. McPherson* (employee statement made only to co-worker concerning President Reagan was speech on a matter of public concern). *Here, the speech is religious expression and it is obviously of public concern.* 97 F.3d at 1210 (emphasis added; parallel and certain other citations omitted).

There is no doubt that the religious content or viewpoint of plaintiff's symbolic speech makes it a matter of public concern relating to social or community interests, as contrasted with speech about "mundane employment grievances" expressing personal employment complaints and office critiques important only (or primarily) to the speaker, as discussed in *Connick* and its public concern progeny. Plaintiff's symbolic non-verbal speech is an expression of her personal religious convictions and viewpoint, which is a matter of social and community concern entitled to the full protection of the First Amendment. The content of plaintiff's symbolic speech, therefore, inclines it toward a finding of public concern speech.

(b) Form

As previously discussed, plaintiff's wearing a cross on a necklace is symbolic speech commonly perceived as expressing a Christian faith or viewpoint. This symbolic expression is not advanced in a public forum for speech (like an auditorium), but neither is it merely a shared communication between plaintiff and other like-minded co-workers. The form of plaintiff's speech does not appear to be a significant factor in the public concern equation.

(c) Context

Placing plaintiff's symbolic speech in context also tilts the determination toward public concern speech. Plaintiff was not simply disciplined after an administrative adjudication or executive decision finding that her speech was disruptive of the workplace or caused some other problem for the employer, as most of the *Pickering* cases seem to be, but rather, she was suspended pursuant to ARIN's categorical, content-based, Religious Affiliations regulation prohibiting religious symbolic speech but not other kinds of symbolic speech. Such categorical and content-driven regulation of speech is inherently suspect because it applies to a broad range of employees and impacts (i.e., chills) more than one employee's expression of beliefs.

Moreover, plaintiff's symbolic expression is not made in the context of an employment grievance, either mundane and personal or of more general interest in the workplace. Instead, this expression is a long-standing practice by plaintiff of her religious beliefs. This has nothing to do with the employment environment or the terms or conditions of employment, except indirectly to the extent the public employer now has prevented plaintiff from expressing her religious beliefs while at work. Nor does the private nature of plaintiff's expression of beliefs to co-workers, visitors, administrators and students who may notice and appreciate the significance of her cross wearing disqualify it from the protection afforded by the First Amendment to matters of public concern.

(d) Determination

While the form of plaintiff's speech is neutral, its content and its context strongly indicate that this symbolic expression goes to a matter of public concern, and the Court so finds. Having crossed the last threshold, therefore, the Court proceeds to the *Pickering* balance of interests.

4. The *Pickering* Balance

The discussion in Section VII. D. effectively resolves the *Pickering* balance in plaintiff's favor. A public employer must make a "substantial showing that the [public employee's] speech is, in fact, likely to be disruptive." Pertinent considerations on the employer's side of the scale include speech which impairs discipline by superiors or harmony among co-workers, detrimentally impacts close working relationships, or impedes the performance of the speaker's duties or interferes with the regular operation of the employer's business.

There are no valid government interests served by enforcing the Religious Affiliations policy to ban the wearing of small items of jewelry expressing a religious viewpoint, in the absence of any direct or indirect attempted coercion or indicia of endorsement of such viewpoint by ARIN. Plaintiff's wearing her cross has not been disruptive, controversial (until banned by ARIN), distracting or confusing to students, nor has it caused any dissension or problems in the working or school environment. There is no evidence—nor even an allegation—that it causes any interference with ARIN's operations. Further, there is no danger that permitting an ARIN employee to wear a cross while working at school will encroach upon the Establishment Clause.

On the other hand, employees are prevented from quietly expressing their personal religious views or beliefs by wearing items of jewelry imbued with religious meaning. This is a broad category of content and viewpoint based discrimination. Such categorical restrictions on public employees' speech are presumptively invalid. Defendants have not overcome the presumption in this case.

It is apparent that plaintiff has a strong likelihood of success on the merits of her Free Speech claim * * * .

c. *"Academic Freedom" at the Higher Education Level*

UROFSKY v. GILMORE

216 F.3d 401 (4th Cir. 2000).

WILKINS, CIRCUIT JUDGE:

Appellees, six professors employed by various public colleges and universities in Virginia, brought this action challenging the constitutionality of a Virginia law restricting state employees from accessing sexually explicit material on computers that are owned or leased by the state. * * *

I.

The central provision of the Act states:

> Except to the extent required in conjunction with a bona fide, agency-approved research project or other agency-approved undertaking, no agency employee shall utilize agency-owned or agency-leased computer equipment to access, download, print or store any information infrastructure files or services having sexually explicit content. Such agency approvals shall be given in writing by agency heads, and any such approvals shall be available to the public under

the provisions of the Virginia Freedom of Information Act. Va.Code Ann. § 2.1–805.

Another section of the Act defines "sexually explicit content." When the district court ruled, and when the panel initially considered this appeal, the Act defined "sexually explicit content" to include:

(i) any description of or (ii) any picture, photograph, drawing, motion picture film, digital image or similar visual representation depicting sexual bestiality, a lewd exhibition of nudity, as nudity is defined in § 18.2–390, sexual excitement, sexual conduct or sadomasochistic abuse, as also defined in § 18.2–390, coprophilia, urophilia, or fetishism. Va.Code Ann. § 2.1–804.

Following our panel decision, the Virginia General Assembly amended the definition of "sexually explicit content" to add the italicized language:

content having as a dominant theme (i) any *lascivious* description of or (ii) any *lascivious* picture, photograph, drawing, motion picture film, digital image or similar visual representation depicting sexual bestiality, a lewd exhibition of nudity, as nudity is defined in § 18.2–390, sexual excitement, sexual conduct or sadomasochistic abuse, as also defined in § 18.2–390, coprophilia, urophilia, or fetishism. Va. Code Ann. § 2.1–804 (emphasis added).[3]

As its language makes plain, the Act restricts access by state employees to lascivious sexually explicit material on computers owned or leased by the state. But, the Act does not prohibit all access by state employees to such materials, for a state agency head may give permission for a state employee to access such information on computers owned or leased by the state if the agency head deems such access to be required in connection with a bona fide research project or other undertaking. Further, state employees remain free to access sexually explicit materials from their personal or other computers not owned or leased by the state. Thus, the Act prohibits state employees from accessing sexually explicit materials only when the employees are using

---

3. Section 18.2–390 provides in pertinent part:

(2) "Nudity" means a state of undress so as to expose the human male or female genitals, pubic area or buttocks with less than a full opaque covering, or the showing of the female breast with less than a fully opaque covering of any portion thereof below the top of the nipple, or the depiction of covered or uncovered male genitals in a discernibly turgid state.

(3) "Sexual conduct" means actual or explicitly simulated acts of masturbation, homosexuality, sexual intercourse, or physical contact in an act of apparent sexual stimulation or gratification with a persons clothed or unclothed genitals, pu-

bic area, buttocks or, if such be female, breast.

(4) "Sexual excitement" means the condition of human male or female genitals when in a state of sexual stimulation or arousal.

(5) "Sadomasochistic abuse" means actual or explicitly simulated flagellation or torture by or upon a person who is nude or clad in undergarments, a mask or bizarre costume, or the condition of being fettered, bound or otherwise physically restrained on the part of one so clothed.

Va.Code Ann. § 18.2–390(2) to–390(5) (Michie 1996) (emphasis omitted).

computers that are owned or leased by the state and permission to access the material has not been given by the appropriate agency head.

None of the Appellees has requested or been denied permission to access sexually explicit materials pursuant to the Act. Indeed, the record indicates that no request for access to sexually explicit materials on computers owned or leased by the state has been declined.

Appellees maintain that the restriction imposed by the Act violates the First Amendment rights of state employees. Appellees do not assert that state employees possess a First Amendment right to access sexually explicit materials on state-owned or leased computers for their personal use; rather, Appellees confine their challenge to the restriction of access to sexually explicit materials for work-related purposes. Appellees' challenge to the Act is twofold: They first maintain that the Act is unconstitutional as to all state employees; failing this, they argue more particularly that the Act violates academic employees' right to academic freedom.

II.

It is well settled that citizens do not relinquish all of their First Amendment rights by virtue of accepting public employment. *See United States v. National Treasury Employees Union* [hereinafter *NTEU*]; *Connick v. Myers*, 461 U.S. 138, 142, 103 S. Ct. 1684 (1983); *Pickering v. Board of Educ.*, 391 U.S. 563, 568, 88 S. Ct. 1731 (1968). Nevertheless, the state, as an employer, undoubtedly possesses greater authority to restrict the speech of its employees than it has as sovereign to restrict the speech of the citizenry as a whole. * * *

The threshold inquiry thus is whether the Act regulates speech by state employees in their capacity as citizens upon matters of public concern. If a public employee's speech made in his capacity as a private citizen does not touch upon a matter of public concern, the state, as employer, may regulate it without infringing any First Amendment protection.

    * * *

To determine whether speech involves a matter of public concern, we examine the content, context, and form of the speech at issue in light of the entire record. *See Connick*, 461 U.S. at 147–48, 103 S.Ct. 1684. Speech involves a matter of public concern when it involves an issue of social, political, or other interest to a community. *See id.* at 146, 103 S.Ct. 1684. An inquiry into whether a matter is of public concern does not involve a determination of how interesting or important the subject of an employee's speech is. Further, the place where the speech occurs is irrelevant: An employee may speak as a citizen on a matter of public concern at the workplace, and may speak as an employee away from the workplace. *Compare Rankin v. McPherson* (holding public employee's discharge was violative of First Amendment when based on comment by employee as a private citizen on a matter of public concern made at work), *with DiMeglio v. Haines* (recognizing that speech by a public employee outside the workplace was made in the employee's official capacity).

The Supreme Court has made clear that the concern is to maintain for the government employee the same right enjoyed by his privately employed counterpart. To this end, in its decisions determining speech to be entitled to First Amendment protection the Court has emphasized the unrelatedness of the speech at issue to the speaker's employment duties.

* * *

The speech at issue here—access to certain materials using computers owned or leased by the state for the purpose of carrying out employment duties—is clearly made in the employee's role as employee. Therefore, the challenged aspect of the Act does not regulate the speech of the citizenry in general, but rather the speech of state employees in their capacity as employees. It cannot be doubted that in order to pursue its legitimate goals effectively, the state must retain the ability to control the manner in which its employees discharge their duties and to direct its employees to undertake the responsibilities of their positions in a specified way. * * * The essence of Appellees' claim is that they are entitled to access sexually explicit material in their capacity as state employees by using equipment owned or leased by the state. Because, as Appellees acknowledge, the challenged aspect of the Act does not affect speech by Appellees in their capacity as private citizens speaking on matters of public concern, it does not infringe the First Amendment rights of state employees.

III.

Alternatively, Appellees maintain that even if the Act is valid as to the majority of state employees it violates the First Amendment academic freedom rights of professors at state colleges and universities, and thus is invalid as to them.[9] In essence, Appellees contend that a university professor possesses a constitutional right to determine for himself, without the input of the university (and perhaps even contrary to the university's desires), the subjects of his research, writing, and teaching. Appellees maintain that by requiring professors to obtain university approval before accessing sexually explicit materials on the Internet in connection with their research, the Act infringes this individual right of academic freedom. Our review of the law, however, leads us to conclude that to the extent the Constitution recognizes any right of "academic

---

9. Appellees assert that the Act infringes on academic freedom by hindering professors' ability to perform their employment duties, particularly teaching and research. The facts alleged in the complaint illustrate the type of restrictions with which Appellees are primarily concerned. Melvin I. Urofsky, the lead plaintiff in the district court, alleged that he had declined to assign an online research project on indecency law because he feared he would be unable to verify his students' work without violating the Act. Appellee Terry L. Meyers contended that he is affected by the Act because his ability to access Virginia's database to research sexually explicit poetry in connection with his study of Victorian poets is restricted by the policy. Appellee Paul Smith's Web site has been censored as a result of the Act. And, appellees Dana Heller, Bernard H. Levin, and Brian J. Delaney maintained that they were hesitant to continue their Internet research of various aspects of human sexuality.

freedom" above and beyond the First Amendment rights to which every citizen is entitled, the right inheres in the University, not in individual professors, and is not violated by the terms of the Act.

"Academic freedom" is a term that is often used, but little explained, by federal courts. As a result, decisions invoking academic freedom are lacking in consistency, and courts invoke the doctrine in circumstances where it arguably has no application. Accordingly, we begin with a brief review of the history of the concept of academic freedom in the United States.

Prior to the late nineteenth century, institutions of higher education in this country were not considered centers of research and scholarship, but rather were viewed as a means of passing received wisdom on to the next generation. "Faculty performed essentially fixed if learned operations within a traditional curriculum under the sanction of established truth.... [A]cademic freedom as we know it simply had no meaning." Additionally, American universities during this period were characterized by "legal control by non-academic trustees; effective governance by administrators set apart from the faculty by political allegiance and professional orientation; [and] dependent and insecure faculty." This began to change, however, as Americans who had studied at German universities sought to remodel American universities in the German image.

The German notion of academic freedom was composed primarily of two concepts: *Lehrfreiheit* and *Lernfreiheit. Lehrfreiheit,* or freedom to teach, embodied the notion that professors should be free to conduct research and publish findings without fear of reproof from the church or state; it further denoted the authority to determine the content of courses and lectures. *Lernfreiheit* was essentially a corollary right of students to determine the course of their studies for themselves.

In 1915, a committee of the American Association of University Professors (AAUP) issued a report on academic freedom that adapted the concept of *Lehrfreiheit* to the American university. In large part, the AAUP was concerned with obtaining for professors a measure of professional autonomy from lay administrators and trustees. The AAUP defined academic freedom as "a right claimed by the accredited educator, as teacher and investigator, to interpret his findings and to communicate his conclusions without being subjected to any interference, molestation, or penalization because the conclusions are unacceptable to some constituted authority within or beyond the institution." Significantly, the AAUP conceived academic freedom as a professional norm, not a legal one: The AAUP justified academic freedom on the basis of its social utility as a means of advancing the search for truth, rather than its status as a manifestation of First Amendment rights. The principles adopted in the 1915 report were later codified in a 1940 Statement of Principles on Academic Freedom and Tenure promulgated by the AAUP and the Association of American Colleges. The 1940 Statement since "has been endorsed by every major higher education organization in the nation," "through its adoption into bylaws, faculty contracts, and collective bargaining agreements."[12]

Appellees' insistence that the Act violates their rights of academic freedom amounts to a claim that the academic freedom of professors is not only a professional norm, but also a constitutional right. We disagree. It is true, of course, that homage has been paid to the ideal of academic freedom in a number of Supreme Court opinions, often with reference to the First Amendment. *See, e.g., Regents of the Univ. of Mich. v. Ewing*; *Regents of the Univ. of Cal. v. Bakke* (opinion of Powell, J.); *Keyishian v. Board of Regents*; *Sweezy v. New Hampshire* (plurality opinion); *id.* (Frankfurter, J., concurring in the result). Despite these accolades, the Supreme Court has never set aside a state regulation on the basis that it infringed a First Amendment right to academic freedom. *Cf. Minnesota State Bd. for Community Colleges v. Knight* (stating that the Court has not recognized a First Amendment right of faculty to participate in academic policymaking).

Moreover, a close examination of the cases indicates that the right praised by the Court is not the right Appellees seek to establish here. Appellees ask us to recognize a First Amendment right of academic freedom that belongs to the professor as an individual. The Supreme Court, to the extent it has constitutionalized a right of academic freedom at all, appears to have recognized only an institutional right of self-governance in academic affairs.

* * *

This emphasis on institutional rights is particularly evident in more recent Supreme Court jurisprudence. For example, in *Bakke* Justice Powell discussed academic freedom as it related to a program of admissions quotas established by a medical school. Relying on *Keyishian* and on Justice Frankfurter's concurrence in *Sweezy,* Justice Powell characterized academic freedom as "[t]he freedom of a university to make its own judgments as to education." Similarly, in *Ewing* the Court described academic freedom as a concern of the institution.

---

12. In view of this history, we do not doubt that, as a matter of professional practice, university professors in fact possess the type of academic freedom asserted by Appellees. Indeed, the claim of an academic institution to status as a "university" may fairly be said to depend upon the extent to which its faculty members are allowed to pursue knowledge free of external constraints. *See* [Richard Hofstadter & Walter P.] Metzger[, *The Development of Academic Freedom in United States*] (explaining that the authors of the 1915 AAUP report believed "that any academic institution that restrict[ed] the intellectual freedom of its professors . . . cease[d] to be a true university"). Were it not so, advances in learning surely would be hindered in a manner harmful to the university as an institution and to society at large. However, Appellees fail to appreciate that the wisdom of a given practice as a matter of policy does not give the practice constitutional status. *See Minnesota State Bd. for Community Colleges v. Knight* (concluding that "[f]aculty involvement in academic governance has much to recommend it as a matter of academic policy, but it finds no basis in the Constitution").

Additionally, we note that we are not here called upon to decide the wisdom of the Act as a matter of policy. That an enactment may be utterly unnecessary, or even profoundly unwise, does not affect its validity as a matter of constitutional law.

Significantly, the Court has never recognized that professors possess a First Amendment right of academic freedom to determine for themselves the content of their courses and scholarship, despite opportunities to do so. * * *

Taking all of the cases together, the best that can be said for Appellees' claim that the Constitution protects the academic freedom of an individual professor is that teachers were the first public employees to be afforded the now-universal protection against dismissal for the exercise of First Amendment rights. Nothing in Supreme Court jurisprudence suggests that the "right" claimed by Appellees extends any further. Rather, since declaring that public employees, including teachers, do not forfeit First Amendment rights upon accepting public employment, the Court has focused its discussions of academic freedom solely on issues of institutional autonomy. We therefore conclude that because the Act does not infringe the constitutional rights of public employees in general, it also does not violate the rights of professors.

* * *

MURNAGHAN, CIRCUIT JUDGE, dissenting:

The majority's interpretation of the "public concern" doctrine makes the role of the speaker dispositive of the analysis. Specifically, the majority states that "critical to a determination of whether employee speech is entitled to First Amendment protection is whether the speech is 'made primarily in the [employee's] role as citizen or primarily in his role as employee.' " The majority then rejects the plaintiffs' First Amendment claim because "[t]he speech at issue here . . . is clearly made in the employee's role as employee." Because an analysis of *Connick v. Myers,* 461 U.S. 138, 103 S.Ct. 1684 (1983), and its progeny reveals that the majority has adopted an unduly restrictive interpretation of the "public concern" doctrine, I respectfully dissent.

I.

A.

In *Connick,* the Supreme Court held that, as a threshold matter, if a public employee's speech "cannot be fairly characterized as constituting speech on a matter of public concern," then a court does not balance the employer's interests with those of the employee. *Connick,* 461 U.S. at 146, 103 S.Ct. 1684. The Court broadly defined speech of public concern as speech "relating to any matter of political, social, or other concern to the community." *Id.* The Court also stated that "[w]hether an employee's speech addresses a matter of public concern must be determined by the content, form, and context of a given statement, as revealed by the whole record." *Id.* at 147–48, 103 S. Ct. 1684. Nowhere in *Connick,* however, did the Court state that the role of the speaker, standing alone, would be dispositive of the public concern analysis.

Indeed, the facts of *Connick* belie this suggestion. Sheila Myers, an Assistant District Attorney, was discharged for distributing a questionnaire to the other attorneys in her office. In general, Myers' questionnaire asked her peers what they thought of the trustworthiness of certain attorneys in the office, the morale of the office, and the office's transfer policy. *See id.* at 141, 103 S.Ct. 1684.

The Court held that these questions "do not fall under the rubric of matters of 'public concern,'" because they were "mere extensions of Myers' dispute over her transfer to another section of the criminal court." *Id.* at 148, 103 S.Ct. 1684. Myers' questionnaire, however, also asked whether her fellow attorneys "ever feel pressured to work in political campaigns on behalf of office supported candidates." *Id.* at 149, 103 S.Ct. 1684. This question was in the same form and context as Myers' other questions—an internal questionnaire distributed by an employee complaining about on-the-job conditions. The question thus was *speech by an employee in her role as an employee.* The Court nevertheless held that this question did "touch upon a matter of public concern." *Id.* The majority's formalistic focus on the "role of the speaker" in employee speech cases therefore runs directly contrary to Supreme Court precedent.

B.

Post-*Connick* decisions of this court also make it clear that the role of the speaker does not control the public concern analysis. In *Piver v. Pender County Bd. of Educ.*, the plaintiff, a high school teacher, circulated a petition to his students during class urging retention of the school's principal. The plaintiff undoubtedly was speaking in his role as an employee, as he was being paid by the State and using State facilities (classrooms) to carry out his employment duties (instructing students). The court nevertheless held that the plaintiff's speech was on a matter of public concern because it was a "matter in which the community ... was vitally interested." The court also stressed that the speech was "of much wider importance than a mere 'private personnel grievance,'" that would not be of public concern.

In *Piver,* the court relied on the "public concern" analysis set out by this court in *Berger v. Battaglia.* In *Berger,* the court interpreted the public concern doctrine as excluding from First Amendment protection only those matters of purely personal interest to the employee.

> *Pickering,* its antecedents, and its progeny—particularly *Connick*—make it plain that the "public concern" or "community interest" inquiry is better designed—and more concerned—to identify a narrow spectrum of employee speech that is not entitled even to qualified protection than it is to set outer limits on all that is. The principle that emerges is that *all* public employee speech that by content is within the general protection of the first amendment is entitled to at least qualified protection against public employer chilling action except that which, realistically viewed, is of purely "personal concern" to the employee—most typically, a private personnel grievance.

Furthermore, the court stated that when analyzing whether speech is upon "any matter of political, social, or other concern to the community," *see Connick*, 461 U.S. at 146, 103 S.Ct. 1684, "[t]he focus is . . . upon whether the 'public' or the 'community' is likely to be truly concerned with or interested in the particular expression, or whether it is more properly viewed as essentially a 'private' matter between employer and employee."

Berger's broad approach to the public concern doctrine, focusing on the public importance of the speech, stands in stark contrast to the majority's singular focus on the role of the speaker—regardless of the public import of the speaker's message. *See also Arvinger v. Mayor and City Council of Baltimore* ("Although the *Connick* court did not elaborate on the relative weight to be accorded these three factors, this court has held that 'content, subject-matter, is always the central aspect.' ").

C.

The majority justifies its singular focus on the role of the speaker by citing to language from *United States v. National Treasury Employees Union* ("*NTEU*"). In *NTEU,* the plaintiffs were executive branch employees challenging a law prohibiting federal employees from accepting any compensation for making speeches or writing articles, even when the speeches or articles did not have any connection to the employees' official duties. The Supreme Court held that the plaintiffs' speech was on a matter of public concern. In doing so, the Court stated that "[t]hey seek compensation for their expressive activities in their capacity as citizens, not as Government employees. . . . With few exceptions, the content of respondents' messages has nothing to do with their jobs and does not even arguably have any adverse impact on the efficiency of the offices in which they work."

The majority's analysis of this language attempts to push *NTEU* where it did not go. The Court in *NTEU* stated that the plaintiffs' speech was on a matter of public concern in part because it was unrelated to the plaintiffs' employment; however, nowhere in *NTEU* did the Court state the converse: namely, that *if* the plaintiffs' speech was in their role as employees, then it automatically would not qualify as speech on a matter of public concern. Therefore, at best, *NTEU* suggests that the role of the speaker is a *factor* in a public concern analysis. But even a broad reading of *NTEU* does not suggest that the role of the speaker is the *only* factor to consider in a public concern analysis, despite the majority's claims to the contrary.

The majority also relies on our decision in *Boring v. Buncombe County Bd. of Educ.* In *Boring,* the plaintiff, a high school teacher, was transferred by her principal for producing a student-acted play that addressed controversial topics such as lesbianism and teen pregnancy. The plaintiff alleged that the County violated her First Amendment rights by transferring her in retaliation for producing the play.

A majority of this court framed the issue in *Boring* as only "whether a public high school teacher has a First Amendment right to participate in the makeup of the school curriculum through the selection and production of a play." The majority held that the plaintiff's selection of the play was not a matter of public concern and was merely an "ordinary employment dispute." As their framing of the issue shows, however, the majority's reasoning was not based on the fact that the plaintiff's production of the play was in her role as a school district employee. Rather, the majority answered the narrower question of whether a teacher has a First Amendment right to participate in the makeup of the curriculum.

Judge Luttig's concurring opinion in *Boring* also illustrates that the majority's holding did not deal with the broader issue of whether speech by an employee in her role as an employee can qualify as speech on a matter of public concern. Judge Luttig stated that

> [the dissent] fails to recognize the elementary difference between teacher in-class speech which is curricular, and teacher in-class speech which is noncurricular, because it assumes that every word uttered by a teacher in a classroom is curriculum. *In the latter context of teacher in-class noncurricular speech, the teacher assuredly enjoys some First Amendment protection.* (emphasis added)

Presumably, Judge Luttig meant that teacher in-class noncurricular speech could be speech on a matter of public concern. As stated previously, however, a teacher's in-class speech is speech in her role as an employee, whether the speech is curricular or noncurricular. While students are under her care and supervision in the classroom, a teacher surely cannot be regarded as a "citizen" rather than an "employee" merely because she is discussing something other than trigonometry. Thus, *Boring* must rest on something other than the principle that speech by an employee in her role as an employee never qualifies as speech on a matter of public concern. *See Boring* (Motz, J., dissenting) ("Because the majority does not attempt to explicitly hold that the role in which an employee speaks is determinative [or overrule prior precedent], this reasoning must not be the basis for its conclusion that Boring's speech does not relate to a matter of public concern."). *Boring* therefore does not compel a finding that the plaintiffs' speech is not on a matter of public concern, merely because the plaintiffs' speech occurs in their role as employees.[1]

D.

Because speech by an employee in her role as an employee can qualify as speech on a matter of public concern, the issue thus becomes whether, in the instant case, the plaintiffs' speech is on a "matter of political, social, or other concern to the community." *Connick,* 461 U.S.

---

1. In any event, to the extent that *Boring* controls the public concern analysis in the instant case, and I do not agree that it does, I would revisit that holding. Judge Motz persuasively argued in her dissent in *Boring* why the majority's approach to public employees is at odds with *Connick* and its progeny.

at 146, 103 S.Ct. 1684. The plaintiffs' speech easily meets this test. The Supreme Court has stated that "[s]ex, a great and mysterious motive force in human life, has indisputably been a subject of absorbing interest to mankind through the ages; *it is one of the vital problems of human interest and public concern.*" (emphasis added).

The Act restricts over 101,000 state employees, including university professors, librarians, museum workers, and physicians and social workers at state hospitals, from researching, discussing, and writing about sexually explicit material. As the district court noted, "the Act's broad definition of 'sexually explicit' content would include research and debate on sexual themes in art, literature, history and the law, speech and research by medical and mental health professionals concerning sexual disease, sexual dysfunction, and sexually related mental disorders, and the routine exchange of information among social workers on sexual assault and child abuse." These topics undeniably touch on matters of public concern.

The Commonwealth's recent revision to the Act limiting the definition of "sexually explicit content" to materials and descriptions that are "lascivious" does not change the analysis. Many works of public import could be classified as lascivious; in fact, many were specifically intended to have such an effect. For instance, the works of Toni Morrison and many themes found in Victorian poetry, including the material researched online by one of the plaintiffs, Professor Myers, could be classified as lascivious. Also, the application of the Act to "lascivious" e-mail discussions by psychologists and social workers implicates topics of public import, because the public has an interest in unfettered discussions by State professionals concerning the abnormal sexual behaviors of their patients, in order to better diagnose and understand sexual deviancy.

Finally, the form of the plaintiffs' speech, Internet and e-mail communications, makes the speech of special public significance. In the information age, electronic communications may be the most important forum for accessing and discussing topics of concern to the community. This court should be wary of allowing the State to regulate this important medium of communication without requiring a legitimate justification for the regulation.

* * *

PROBLEM 50: Disciplinary Sanctions
at the Higher Education Level

A.   Assume the same set of facts as set forth in Problem 49, above, except that the setting is a public college or university. Is it conceivable that Professor Marcos would have been sanctioned for similar behavior? If so, why? If not, what modifications in the existing fact pattern would be required before the professor might have been disciplined?

B.   If the professor were indeed disciplined in some fashion under the same or a similar scenario, and subsequently filed a lawsuit, would he prevail? Under what theory or theories?

Assume that the institution's faculty code of conduct contains the following pertinent provisions:

- The types of discipline that may be imposed on a member of the faculty are as follows, in order of increasing severity: written censure, reduction in salary, demotion, suspension, denial or curtailment of emeritus status, and dismissal from the employ of the University.

- The *Types of Unacceptable Conduct* listed below are examples of types of conduct which are presumptively subject to University discipline.

Teaching and Students: Types of unacceptable conduct

1.   Failure to meet the responsibilities of instruction, including:

*   *   *

(b) significant intrusion of material unrelated to the course;

2.   Discrimination, including harassment, against a student on political grounds, or for reasons of race, religion, sex, sexual orientation, ethnic origin, national origin, ancestry, marital status, medical condition, status as a covered veteran, or, within the limits imposed by law or University regulations, because of age or citizenship or for other arbitrary or personal reasons.

*   *   *

4.   Use of the position or powers of a faculty member to coerce the judgment or conscience of a student or to cause harm to a student for arbitrary or personal reasons.

5.   Participating in or deliberately abetting disruption, interference, or intimidation in the classroom.

The University

*   *   *

7.   Serious violation of University policies governing the professional conduct of faculty, including but not limited to policies applying to research, outside professional activities, conflicts of commitment, clinical practices, violence in the workplace, and whistleblower protections.

E.   EMPLOYMENT DISCRIMINATION

In general, the area of public sector employment discrimination includes a very large number of cases, statutes, regulations, and relevant policies. Many of the issues that arise in an education context are not necessarily education-specific, and these issues are often resolved by the application of broad overarching principles contained in employment discrimination law.

There are, however, a significant number of employment discrimination cases exemplifying disputes that are uniquely linked to education settings, and these cases raise very specific education-related questions. This section provides an overview of notable decisions in this regard, highlighting litigation that alleged discrimination on the basis of race, gender, LGBT status, religion, age, and disability.

1. RACE/ETHNICITY

In *Wygant v. Jackson Board of Education*, 476 U.S. 267, 106 S.Ct. 1842 (1986), the Court addressed the question of "whether a school board, consistent with the Equal Protection Clause, may extend preferential protection against layoffs to some of its employees because of their race or national origin."

> In 1972 the Jackson Board of Education, because of racial tension in the community that extended to its schools, * * * [added] a layoff provision to the Collective Bargaining Agreement (CBA) between the Board and the Jackson Education Association (Union) that would protect employees who were members of certain minority groups against layoffs. * * *

> * * * After [subsequent federal and state litigation], the Board adhered to [the layoff provision,] Article XII. As a result, during the 1976–1977 and 1981–1982 school years, nonminority teachers were laid off, while minority teachers with less seniority were retained. The displaced nonminority teachers * * * brought suit in Federal District Court, alleging violations of the Equal Protection Clause, Title VII, 42 U.S.C. § 1983, and other federal and state statutes. *Id.* at 270–72.

Unable to muster a majority, Justice Powell announced the judgment of the Court and delivered an opinion in which The Chief Justice and Justice Rehnquist joins, and in all but Part IV of which Justice O'Connor joined. In the decision, the Court ruled in favor the plaintiff:

> Petitioners' central claim is that they were laid off because of their race in violation of the Equal Protection Clause of the Fourteenth Amendment. * * * This Court has "consistently repudiated '[d]istinctions between citizens solely because of their ancestry' as being 'odious to a free people whose institutions are founded upon the doctrine of equality.'" "Racial and ethnic distinctions of any sort are inherently suspect and thus call for the most exacting judicial examination." * * *

> The Court of Appeals, relying on the reasoning and language of the District Court's opinion, held that the Board's interest in providing minority role models for its minority students, as an attempt to alleviate the effects of societal discrimination, was sufficiently important to justify the racial classification embodied in the layoff provision. The court discerned a need for more minority faculty role models by finding that the percentage of minority teachers was less than the percentage of minority students. * * *

[T]he role model theory employed by the District Court has no logical stopping point. The role model theory allows the Board to engage in discriminatory hiring and layoff practices long past the point required by any legitimate remedial purpose. Indeed, by tying the required percentage of minority teachers to the percentage of minority students, it requires just the sort of year-to-year calibration the Court stated was unnecessary * * * .

Moreover, because the role model theory does not necessarily bear a relationship to the harm caused by prior discriminatory hiring practices, it actually could be used to escape the obligation to remedy such practices by justifying the small percentage of black teachers by reference to the small percentage of black students. Carried to its logical extreme, the idea that black students are better off with black teachers could lead to the very system the Court rejected in *Brown v. Board of Education,* 347 U.S. 483, 74 S.Ct. 686 (1954) (*Brown I*).

Societal discrimination, without more, is too amorphous a basis for imposing a racially classified remedy. The role model theory announced by the District Court and the resultant holding typify this indefiniteness. * * * *Id.* at 273–76.

It is important to note that not even four justices joined all parts of Justice Powell's opinion. What is the precedential value of *Wygant* in the aftermath of *Grutter* (*supra,* Chapter 5)? Can an argument be made that *Grutter* limited the scope and impact of the *Wygant* ruling? Why or why not?

2. GENDER

In *Cleveland Board of Education v. LaFleur,* 414 U.S. 632, 94 S.Ct. 791 (1974), the Court was asked to rule on the lawsuit brought by Jo Carol LaFleur and Ann Elizabeth Nelson, junior high school teachers employed by the Board of Education of Cleveland, Ohio:

Pursuant to a rule first adopted in 1952, the school board requires every pregnant school teacher to take maternity leave without pay, beginning five months before the expected birth of her child. * * * A teacher on maternity leave is not allowed to return to work until the beginning of the next regular school semester which follows the date when her child attains the age of three months. A doctor's certificate attesting to the health of the teacher is a prerequisite to return; an additional physical examination may be required. The teacher or maternity leave is not promised re-employment after the birth of the child; she is merely given priority in reassignment to a position for which she is qualified. Failure to comply with the mandatory maternity leave provisions is ground for dismissal.

Neither Mrs. LaFleur nor Mrs. Nelson wished to take an unpaid maternity leave; each wanted to continue teaching until the end of the school year. Because of the mandatory maternity leave rule, however, each was required to leave her job in March 1971.[3] The two women then filed separate suits in the United States District Court for the Northern District of Ohio under 42 U.S.C. § 1983, challenging the constitutionality of the maternity leave rule. * * *

Susan Cohen, was employed by the School Board of Chesterfield County, Virginia. That school board's maternity leave regulation requires that a pregnant teacher leave work at least four months prior to the expected birth of her child. Notice in writing must be given to the school board at least six months prior to the expected birth date. * * *

Mrs. Cohen * * * filed this suit under 42 U.S.C. § 1983 in the United States District Court for the Eastern District of Virginia. * * *

We granted certiorari in both cases in order to resolve the conflict between the Courts of Appeals regarding the constitutionality of such mandatory maternity leave rules for public school teachers. *Id.* at 634–38.

Justice Stewart, writing on behalf of the majority, explained that the Court "has long recognized that freedom of personal choice in matters of marriage and family life is one of the liberties protected by the Due Process Clause of the Fourteenth Amendment":

> By acting to penalize the pregnant teacher for deciding to bear a child, overly restrictive maternity leave regulations can constitute a heavy burden on the exercise of these protected freedoms. Because public school maternity leave rules directly affect 'one of the basic civil rights of man,' the Due Process Clause of the Fourteenth Amendment requires that such rules must not needlessly, arbitrarily, or capriciously impinge upon this vital area of a teacher's constitutional liberty. The question before us in these cases is whether the interests advanced in support of the rules of the Cleveland and Chesterfield County School Boards can justify the particular procedures they have adopted.

> The school boards in these cases have offered two essentially overlapping explanations for their mandatory maternity leave rules. First, they contend that the firm cutoff dates are necessary to maintain continuity of classroom instruction, since advance knowledge of when a pregnant teacher must leave facilitates the finding and hiring of a qualified substitute. Secondly, the school boards seek to justify their maternity rules by arguing that at least some teachers become physically incapable of adequately performing certain of their duties during the latter part of pregnancy. By keeping the pregnant teacher out of the classroom during these final months, the maternity leave rules are said to protect the health of

3. Effective February 1, 1971, the Cleveland regulation was amended to provide that only teachers with one year of continuous service qualified for maternity leave; teachers with less than one year were required to resign at the beginning of the fifth month of pregnancy. * * *

the teacher and her unborn child, while at the same time assuring that students have a physically capable instructor in the classroom at all times.

* * * But * * * while the advance-notice provisions in the Cleveland and Chesterfield County rules are wholly rational and may well be necessary to serve the objective of continuity of instruction, the absolute requirements of termination at the end of the fourth or fifth month of pregnancy are not. Were continuity the only goal, cutoff dates much later during pregnancy would serve as well as or better than the challenged rules, providing that ample advance notice requirements were retained. Indeed, continuity would seem just as well attained if the teacher herself were allowed to choose the date upon which to commence her leave, at least so long as the decision were required to be made and notice given of it well in advance of the date selected. * * *

We * * * conclude that the arbitrary cutoff dates embodied in the mandatory leave rules before us have no rational relationship to the valid state interest of preserving continuity of instruction. As long as the teachers are required to give substantial advance notice of their condition, the choice of firm dates later in pregnancy would serve the boards' objectives just as well, while imposing a far lesser burden on the women's exercise of constitutionally protected freedom.

The question remains as to whether the cutoff dates at the beginning of the fifth and sixth months can be justified on the other ground advanced by the school boards—the necessity of keeping physically unfit teachers out of the classroom. There can be no doubt that such an objective is perfectly legitimate, both on educational and safety grounds. And, despite the plethora of conflicting medical testimony in these cases, we can assume, arguendo, that at least some teachers become physically disabled from effectively performing their duties during the latter stages of pregnancy. * * *

While the medical experts in these cases differed on many points, they unanimously agreed on one—the ability of any particular pregnant woman to continue at work past any fixed time in her pregnancy is very much an individual matter. Even assuming, arguendo, that there are some women who would be physically unable to work past the particular cutoff dates embodied in the challenged rules, it is evident that there are large numbers of teachers who are fully capable of continuing work for longer than the Cleveland and Chesterfield County regulations will allow. * * *

We conclude * * * that neither the necessity for continuity of instruction nor the state interest in keeping physically unfit teachers out of the classroom can justify the sweeping mandatory leave regulations that the Cleveland and Chesterfield County School Boards have adopted. While the regulations no doubt represent a good-faith attempt to achieve a laudable goal, they cannot pass muster under the Due Process Clause of the Fourteenth Amendment. * * * *Id.* at 639–48.

3. LGBT STATUS

No education cases addressing alleged discrimination on the basis of LGBT status have reached the U.S. Supreme Court, but the Court did address LGBT-related discrimination in *Lawrence v. Texas,* 539 U.S. 558, 123 S.Ct. 2472 (2003). This broad victory for plaintiffs is bound to have an impact on subsequent education-related discrimination claims in this context.

At its most basic level, *Lawrence* focused on the Fourteenth Amendment rights of LGBT persons. Justice Kennedy's majority opinion relied primarily on the fundamental right to privacy at the intersection of the Due Process Clause and the Equal Protection Clause. Justice O'Connor, in her concurrence, focused entirely on the discrimination claim under equal protection. Both opinions strongly backed the claims of the plaintiffs in this context. "[P]etitioners," Kennedy wrote, "are entitled to respect for their private lives. The State cannot demean their existence or control their destiny by making their private conduct a crime." *Id.* at 578, 123 S. Ct. at 2484.

The Court included language reminiscent of the analogous discussion of stigma in *Brown v. Board of Education,* addressing the dignity of individuals within the context of equal treatment and "equal worth." Kennedy explained that:

> When homosexual conduct is made criminal by the law of the State, that declaration in and of itself is an invitation to subject homosexual persons to discrimination both in the public and in the private spheres. * * * [It] demeans the lives of homosexual persons.

> The stigma this statute imposes, moreover, is not trivial. * * * [I]t remains a criminal offense with all that imports for the dignity of the persons charged. *Id.* at 575, 123 S. Ct. at 2482.

Such language is consistent with principles articulated in noteworthy Fourteenth Amendment scholarship over time. Kenneth Karst, for example, has written that the Fourteenth Amendment "resonates ... strongly against the stigmatic harm and group subordination that are the main targets of the equal citizenship principle." And Ronald Dworkin has explained that "the fundamental moral principle embodied by the Equal Protection Clause is the equal intrinsic worth of all humans."

Many recent legal disputes at the K–12 level have focused on circumstances where these principles have not been followed and LGBT persons have not been treated equally. In most cases, the courts have ruled in favor of the plaintiffs. These decisions are certain to be strengthened and reinforced by the ruling in *Lawrence.*

For example, in the Fourteenth Amendment Equal Protection Clause case of *Glover v. Williamsburg Local School District,* 20 F.Supp.2d 1160 (S.D. Ohio 1998), the Court considered the allegations by openly gay teacher Bruce Glover that the decision not to renew his teaching contract at the Williamsburg Local School District was discriminatory "based on his sexual orientation, his gender, and the race of his partner." *Id.* at 1162. Defendants denied these allegations and claimed that "Glover was not renewed because of deficiencies in his teaching skills." *Id.*

The Court determined that "[h]omosexuals, while not a 'suspect class' for equal protection analysis, are entitled to at least the same protection as any other identifiable group which is subject to disparate treatment by the state." *Id.* at 1169. The Court explained:

[T]he principle would be the same if [plaintiff] had been arrested discriminatorily based on [his] hair color, [his] college bumper sticker ... or [his] affiliation with a disfavored * * * company. Furthermore, a state action which discriminates against homosexuals and is motivated solely by animus towards that group necessarily violates the Equal Protection Clause, because a "desire to effectuate one's animus against homosexuals can never be a legitimate governmental purpose."; *Romer* [*v. Evans*] ("If the constitutional conception of 'equal protection of the laws' means anything, it must at the very least mean that a bare ... desire to harm a politically unpopular group cannot constitute a legitimate governmental interest.").

* * *

The Court finds that the evidence, taken together, demonstrates that the Board's purported reason for Glover's nonrenewal was pretextual, and in fact the Board discriminated against Glover on the basis of his sexual orientation. The Court can only speculate as to exactly why the Board acted as it did. Perhaps the Board feared that a gay teacher would act inappropriately or somehow be a trouble-maker. Or perhaps the Board was responding to perceived disapproval in the community of having a gay teacher at Williamsburg. Regardless of the Board's reasoning, Glover had established that he was an above average first-year teacher who was more qualified than the woman chosen by the Board to replace him. This fact was evident to the Board from the evaluation and observation material they were given in the decision-making process. In fact, this material revealed that Glover performed better than Whiteman in managing student behavior, the purported reason for his nonrenewal. Glover's successful showing of pretext, together with the other evidence introduced at trial, supports a finding that the Board's decision was motivated by animus towards him as a homosexual. * * *

* * *

The Court finds that reinstatement and compensatory damages are appropriate in this case. The Board's wrongful decision denied Glover the opportunity to teach at Williamsburg Elementary School in 1996–97 and 1997–98, and Glover has been unable to secure a permanent teaching job since the nonrenewal of his contract. Therefore, the Court hereby orders the Board to reinstate Glover as a full-time teacher at Williamsburg Elementary School with a two-year contract, beginning with the 1998–99 school year.

Glover is also hereby awarded compensatory damages for back pay as well as emotional distress. * * * [A]s a result of the Board's wrongful actions, he has suffered considerable anguish as well as humiliation in the community. Glover's psychological injuries also had physical effects, including anxiety, sleeplessness, and digestive problems for which Glover has been receiving treatment since the Fall of 1996. * * *

Therefore, the Court hereby ORDERS the Board to provide the following relief to Glover: (1) reinstatement as a full-time teacher at Williamsburg Elementary School with a two-year teaching contract, beginning in the 1998–99 school year; (2) compensatory damages in the amount of $71,492.00, which includes back pay and emotional distress; and (3) attorneys fees and costs. * * * *Id.* at 1169–76.

In *Weaver v. Nebo School District*, 29 F.Supp.2d 1279 (D. Utah 1998), the Court considered the case of 19–year veteran teacher and volleyball coach Wendy Weaver—a person with an "unblemished" record and a reputation as "an effective and capable teacher"—who acknowledged that she was gay when asked by a senior team member. *Id.* at 1280. She was subsequently admonished "not to make any comments, announcements or statements to students, staff members, or parents of students regarding [her] homosexual orientation or lifestyle." *Id.* at 1281. In addition, she was removed from her position as volleyball coach.

Ms. Weaver brought this action challenging the school district's decisions under both the First Amendment and the Fourteenth Amendment. The Court found that Plaintiff's acknowledgement of her sexual orientation outside the classroom would not, and indeed did not, result in a material or substantial disruption in the school," and "to the extent [that the letters to her] limit her speech in this area, they violate the First Amendment." *Id.* at 1285.

Turning to the Equal Protection Clause claim, the Court also found in favor of the plaintiff:

Despite mounting evidence that gay males and lesbians suffer from employment discrimination and, as recent events in Wyoming remind us, other more life-threatening expressions of bias, courts, including the Supreme Court, have not yet recognized a person's sexual orientation as a status that deserves heightened protection. To date, Congress has expressly prohibited employment discrimination on the basis of race, religion, national origin, gender, age, and disability, but not sexual orientation. As of this year, eleven states and the District of Columbia offer statutory protection against discrimination on the basis of sexual orientation; thirty-nine states, including Utah, do not.

Nevertheless, the Fourteenth Amendment of the United States Constitution entitles all persons to equal protection under the law. It appears that the plain language of the Fourteenth Amendment's Equal Protection Clause prohibits a state government or agency from engaging in intentional discrimination—even on the basis of sexual orientation—absent some rational basis for so doing.

The Supreme Court has recognized that an "irrational prejudice" cannot provide the rational basis to support a state action against an equal protection challenge. * * *

The question then is whether bias concerning Ms. Weaver's sexual orientation furnishes a rational basis for the defendants' decision not to assign her as volleyball coach. The "negative reaction" some members of the community may have to homosexuals is not a proper basis for discriminating against them. So reasoned the Supreme Court in the context of race. *See, e.g., Brown v. Board of Educ.,* 347 U.S. 483, 495, 74 S.Ct. 686 (1954) (declaring that racial school segregation is unconstitutional despite the widespread acceptance of the practice in the community and in the country). If the community's perception is based on nothing more than unsupported assumptions, outdated stereotypes, and animosity, it is necessarily irrational and under *Romer* and other Supreme Court precedent, it provides no legitimate support for the School District's decisions.

The record now before the court contains no job-related justification for not assigning Ms. Weaver as volleyball coach. Nor have the defendants demonstrated how Ms. Weaver's sexual orientation bears any rational relationship to her competency as teacher or coach, or her job performance as coach—a position she has held for many years with distinction. As mentioned earlier, it is undisputed that she was an excellent coach and apparently, up until the time her sexual orientation was revealed, the likely candidate for the position. Principal Wadley's decision not to assign Ms. Weaver (a decision reached after consulting with the other defendants) was based solely on her sexual orientation. Absent some rational relationship to job performance, a decision not to assign Ms. Weaver as coach because of her sexual orientation runs afoul of the Fourteenth Amendment's equal protection guarantee.

Although the Constitution cannot control prejudices, neither this court nor any other court should, directly or indirectly, legitimize them. * * * *Id.* at 1287–89.

4. RELIGION

While protections against discrimination on the basis of religion have been clearly established at public colleges and universities, the situation at the K–12 level has been much more uneven. Many school districts and school site administrators continue to express concerns that openly religious educators may have an undue influence on their younger, more impressionable students.

The Supreme Court has not directly addressed this question in an education setting, but lower courts have been wrestling with these issues for some time. The question of whether and to what extent teachers can wear religious clothing or accessories has often served as a focal point of this controversy.

In *Nichol v. Arin Intermediate Unit 28*, 268 F.Supp.2d 536 (W.D. Pa. 2003), the Court addressed the discrimination claim of Instructional Assistant Nichol, who was suspended for refusing to comply with her supervisor's request that she remove or conceal a small cross she regularly wore on a necklace.[a] Plaintiff argued that the Religious Affiliations policy under which she was suspended violated the Free Exercise Clause. The Court found in favor of the plaintiff, distinguishing prior inconsistent decisions by other federal judges:

> ARIN's Religious Affiliations policy is openly and overtly averse to religion because it singles out and punishes *only* symbolic speech by its employees having religious content or viewpoint, while permitting its employees to wear jewelry containing secular messages or no messages at all.

> ARIN's Religious Affiliations policy thus displays, in purpose and effect, decided hostility toward religion, without any important or compelling state interests served, and violates the Free Exercise Clause of the First Amendment. * * *

> * * * [The] policy is decidedly not neutral, and has both the effect and the express purpose of discriminating against religion. * * *

> Elementary school children as a group are more impressionable than high school or college students, to be sure. However, the impressionability of elementary school students is not a sufficient reason for discriminating against the First Amendment rights of ARIN employees unless the employees are doing something that is likely to influence the students by exploiting their impressionability. * * *

> Given the inconspicuous nature of plaintiff's expression of her religious beliefs by wearing a small cross on a necklace, and the fact that other jewelry with secular messages or no messages is permitted to be worn at school, it is extremely unlikely that even elementary students would perceive Penns Manor or ARIN to be *endorsing* her otherwise unvoiced Christian viewpoint, and defendants certainly presented no evidence to support such a perception. Merely employing an individual, such as plaintiff, who unobstrusively displays her religious adherence is not tantamount to government endorsement of that religion, absent any evidence of endorsement or coercion.

> * * *

Defendants' strongest argument is that the Garb Statute, pursuant to which its Religious Affiliations policy was promulgated, was

---

a. Plaintiff raised both free speech and free exercise claims, and the free speech claim is addressed above, in the academic freedom section of this chapter.

upheld in *United States v. Bd. of Educ. for the School District of Philadelphia (Philadelphia Bd. of Educ.)*, 911 F.2d 882 (3d Cir. 1990), which found that the preservation of an atmosphere of religious neutrality was a compelling state interest. The Garb Statute was enforced in that case to prohibit Alima Reardon, a Muslim teacher, upon pain of prosecution, from wearing identifiable Muslim garb which fully covered her entire body save face and hands. Pursuant to her belief, Amilia Reardon regularly wore a head scarf covering her head, neck and bosom, leaving only her face visible, and a long loose dress which covered her arms to her wrists.

Ms. Reardon mounted a Title VII employment discrimination challenge on the basis of religion, [but the challenge failed]. * * *

Moreover, in the course of discussing a First Amendment challenge to Oregon's garb statute, the Court of Appeals in *Philadelphia Bd. of Educ.* specifically and approvingly highlighted the Oregon Supreme Court's observation that *"offending dress ... would not include dress that communicates an ambiguous message, such as, for example, the occasional wearing of jewelry that incorporates common decorations like a cross or a Star of David."*

Thus, *Philadelphia Bd. of Educ.* is factually and legally distinguishable, and does not constrain this Court from engaging in an unrestricted Establishment and Free Exercise Clause analysis. Moreover, the Court's analysis today is supported by "subsequent doctrinal developments" in the First Amendment precedent of the Supreme Court, as explicitly recognized explained by the United States Court of Appeals for the Third Circuit only last year.... In the current legal landscape of the Establishment Clause, it is unlikely that the Garb Statute would withstand the heightened scrutiny and endorsement analysis to which it now must be subjected.

For all of the foregoing reasons, the Court holds that ARIN's Religious Affiliations policy violates the Free Exercise Clause of the First Amendment, and that its suspension of Ms. Nichol pursuant to that policy cannot stand. *Id.* at 548–55.

5. AGE

Employment discrimination claims on the basis of age are generally brought under the Age Discrimination in Employment Act (ADEA). In *EEOC v. Board of Regents of the University of Wisconsin System*, 288 F.3d 296 (7th Cir. 2002), the Court considered the allegations of the Equal Employment Opportunity Commission (EEOC) under section 7 of the Age Discrimination in Employment Act (ADEA), 29 U.S.C. § 626:

The University of Wisconsin Press is a nonprofit organization associated with the UW Graduate School and under the direction of the UW Board of Regents. * * * The EEOC's case is based on claims by four "charging" parties: Rosalie Robertson, who was 50 years old at the relevant time; Mary Braun, who was 46; Joan Strasbaugh, age

47; and Charles Evenson, who was 54. * * * Finding evidence of "ageism" in the terminations, the EEOC filed this action. * * *

In an age discrimination case, we evaluate whether there is evidence that the employer discriminated against the employees "because of" age. Our task, then, is to examine the record to see whether there was evidence from which a reasonable jury could conclude that the "charging" parties were terminated "because of" their ages.

A claim of discrimination can be proven by the direct or indirect methods of proof. * * *

* * * [U]ltimately * * * what we are looking for is proof of intentional discrimination based on an examination of all the evidence in the record viewed in the light favorable to the nonmoving party. * * *

* * * The unavoidable fact is that the four oldest employees were the only ones terminated, and the terminations occurred under circumstances from which one could, in fact, draw an inference that they were chosen because of their ages. These workers were terminated and the responsibilities were taken over either by other employees or by replacements brought in from the outside, which supports an inference of discrimination. Robertson was terminated from the acquisitions department, and 2 weeks later the Press hired Sheila McMahon, who was in her mid-twenties, to work in acquisitions. Strasbaugh was 47 when she was terminated as assistant marketing manager. Her duties were assumed by a woman in her twenties or thirties, whose contract was renewed and extended shortly after Strasbaugh's termination. Evenson was 54 years old when he was terminated from his position as a senior marketing specialist, while 23–year-old Rebecca Gimenez was retained. Other people in their twenties and thirties were brought into the acquisitions and marketing departments as well. * * *

Although the "Justification" was said to be an assessment of the skills and experience of the various people working at the Press, neither Bethea nor Salemson spoke with the charging parties about their skills. The two men did not solicit the opinions of managers regarding who should be let go. There were no formal employee evaluations. Documents they did look at included out-of-date resumes which had been on file at the Press, and these were not looked at until April, after the termination decisions had already been made.

The "Justification" can be read to show that they held the charging parties to a higher standard than the younger workers. It claims that Evenson would have to take courses to get "up to speed" on "Webpage programming or the electronic transfer of data and images." In the document there is no indication whether Gimenez, the preferred younger employee, herself had taken such courses. The facts show she had not. Gimenez also received credit in the "Justification" for things she had not done. It says she created the Webpage, but, in fact, it had been created before she began working at the Press.

A reasonable jury could believe that the "Justification" uses code words which reflect an age bias. It refers to Evenson as having skills suited to the "pre-electronic" era and that he would have to be brought "up to speed" on "new trends of advertising via electronic means."

The UW also justifies the termination decisions by saying that the job titles of the newly hired younger people were different from those of the charging parties. Some of the people were hired as "limited term employees." We do not think that hiring individuals under less desirable terms can necessarily overcome the inference that the persons being replaced were replaced because of their ages.

* * *

In addition to finding discrimination, the jury also found that the discrimination was willful. Under the ADEA, an employer's violation of the statute is willful if the "employer knew or showed reckless disregard for the matter of whether its conduct was prohibited by the ADEA." A plaintiff does not need to show that the employer's conduct was "outrageous," nor does he need to provide direct evidence of the employer's motives. An employer who truly violates the ADEA without knowing it and whose ignorance is not reckless is protected from a finding of recklessness. As one might imagine, given the length of time the ADEA has been with us, a finding of nonreckless ignorance is rare.

* * *

* * * We have previously said that "leaving managers with hiring authority in ignorance of the basic features of the discrimination laws is an 'extraordinary mistake' " from which a jury can infer reckless indifference.

* * *

The judgment of the district court is AFFIRMED. *Id.* at 299–305.

6. DISABILITY

In *School Board of Nassau County v. Arline*, 480 U.S. 273, 107 S.Ct. 1123 (1987), the Court reached a landmark decision construing Section 504 of the Rehabilitation Act of 1973, which prohibits a federally funded state program from discriminating against an individual with disabilities solely by reason of his or her disability.[a] On behalf of the majority, Justice Brennan wrote:

This case presents the questions whether a person afflicted with tuberculosis, a contagious disease, may be considered a "handi-

---

a. It should be noted that the decision uses the now outmoded terms "handicap" and "handicapped," which were employed in that era. Today the terms "disability," "disabled," and "persons with disabilities" are more routinely and appropriately used.

capped individual" within the meaning of § 504 of the Act, and, if so, whether such an individual is "otherwise qualified" to teach elementary school.

From 1966 until 1979, respondent Gene Arline taught elementary school in Nassau County, Florida. She was discharged in 1979 after suffering a third relapse of tuberculosis within two years. After she was denied relief in state administrative proceedings, she brought suit in federal court, alleging that the school board's decision to dismiss her because of her tuberculosis violated § 504 of the Act.

* * * Arline was hospitalized for tuberculosis in 1957. For the next 20 years, Arline's disease was in remission. Then, in 1977, a culture revealed that tuberculosis was again active in her system; cultures taken in March 1978 and in November 1978 were also positive.

* * * After * * * her third relapse in November 1978, the school board suspended Arline with pay for the remainder of the school year. At the end of the 1978–1979 school year, the school board held a hearing, after which it discharged Arline, "not because she had done anything wrong," but because of the "continued reoccurence [*sic*] of tuberculosis." * * *

Id. at 275–76. Documenting the history and the parameters of Section 504, the Court explained:

In enacting and amending the Act, Congress enlisted all programs receiving federal funds in an effort "to share with handicapped Americans the opportunities for an education, transportation, housing, health care, and jobs that other Americans take for granted." To that end, Congress not only increased federal support for vocational rehabilitation, but also addressed the broader problem of discrimination against the handicapped by including § 504, an antidiscrimination provision patterned after Title VI of the Civil Rights Act of 1964. Section 504 of the Rehabilitation Act reads in pertinent part:

> No otherwise qualified handicapped individual in the United States, as defined in section 706(7) of this title, shall, solely by reason of his handicap, be excluded from participation in, be denied the benefits of, or be subjected to discrimination under any program or activity receiving Federal financial assistance. . . .

In 1974 Congress expanded the definition of "handicapped individual" for use in § 504 to read as follows:

> [A]ny person who (i) has a physical or mental impairment which substantially limits one or more of such person's major life activities, (ii) has a record of such an impairment, or (iii) is regarded as having such an impairment.

The amended definition reflected Congress' concern with protecting the handicapped against discrimination stemming not only from simple prejudice, but also from "archaic attitudes and laws" and from "the fact that the American people are simply unfamiliar with and insensitive to the difficulties confront[ing] individuals with handicaps." To combat the effects of erroneous but nevertheless prevalent perceptions about the handicapped, Congress expanded the definition of "handicapped individual" so as to preclude discrimination against "[a] person who has a record of, or is regarded as having, an impairment [but who] may at present have no actual incapacity at all." *Southeastern Community College v. Davis,* 442 U.S. 397, 405–406, n.6, 99 S.Ct. 2361, 2366–2367, n.6 (1979).[4]

In determining whether a particular individual is handicapped as defined by the Act, the regulations promulgated by the Department of Health and Human Services * * * are particularly significant here because they define two critical terms used in the statutory definition of handicapped individual. "Physical impairment" is defined as follows:

[A]ny physiological disorder or condition, cosmetic disfigurement, or anatomical loss affecting one or more of the following body systems: neurological; musculoskeletal; special sense organs; respiratory, including speech organs; cardiovascular; reproductive, digestive, genitor-urinary; hemic and lymphatic; skin; and endocrine.

In addition, the regulations define "major life activities" as

functions such as caring for one's self, performing manual tasks, walking, seeing, hearing, speaking, breathing, learning, and working. *Id.* at 277–80.

The Court then went on to analyze Arline's claim within this statutory and regulatory framework:

[W]e must consider whether Arline can be considered a handicapped individual. According to the testimony of Dr. McEuen, Arline suffered tuberculosis "in an acute form in such a degree that it affected her respiratory system," and was hospitalized for this condition. Arline thus had a physical impairment as that term is defined by the regulations, since she had a "physiological disorder or condition . . . affecting [her] . . . respiratory [system]." This impairment was serious enough to require hospitalization, a fact more than sufficient to establish that one or more of her major life activities were substantially limited by her impairment. Thus, Arline's hospitalization for tuberculosis in 1957 suffices to establish that she has a "record of . . . impairment" within the meaning of 29 U.S.C. § 706(7)(B)(ii), and is therefore a handicapped individual.

4. See *id.,* at 39 ("This subsection includes within the protection of sections 503 and 504 those persons who do not in fact have the condition which they are perceived as having, as well as those persons whose mental or physical condition does not substantially limit their life activities and who thus are not technically within clause (A) in the new definition. Members of both of these groups may be subjected to discrimination on the basis of their being regarded as handicapped"); *id.,* at 37–39, 63–64.

Petitioners concede that a contagious disease may constitute a handicapping condition to the extent that it leaves a person with "diminished physical or mental capabilities," and concede that Arline's hospitalization for tuberculosis in 1957 demonstrates that she has a record of a physical impairment. Petitioners maintain, however, that Arline's record of impairment is irrelevant in this case, since the school board dismissed Arline not because of her diminished physical capabilities, but because of the threat that her relapses of tuberculosis posed to the health of others.

We do not agree with petitioners that, in defining a handicapped individual under § 504, the contagious effects of a disease can be meaningfully distinguished from the disease's physical effects on a claimant in a case such as this. Arline's contagiousness and her physical impairment each resulted from the same underlying condition, tuberculosis. It would be unfair to allow an employer to seize upon the distinction between the effects of a disease on others and the effects of a disease on a patient and use that distinction to justify discriminatory treatment.

Nothing in the legislative history of § 504 suggests that Congress intended such a result. That history demonstrates that Congress was as concerned about the effect of an impairment on others as it was about its effect on the individual. * * *

Allowing discrimination based on the contagious effects of a physical impairment would be inconsistent with the basic purpose of § 504, which is to ensure that handicapped individuals are not denied jobs or other benefits because of the prejudiced attitudes or the ignorance of others. By amending the definition of "handicapped individual" to include not only those who are actually physically impaired, but also those who are regarded as impaired and who, as a result, are substantially limited in a major life activity, Congress acknowledged that society's accumulated myths and fears about disability and disease are as handicapping as are the physical limitations that flow from actual impairment. Few aspects of a handicap give rise to the same level of public fear and misapprehension as contagiousness. Even those who suffer or have recovered from such noninfectious diseases as epilepsy or cancer have faced discrimination based on the irrational fear that they might be contagious. The Act is carefully structured to replace such reflexive reactions to actual or perceived handicaps with actions based on reasoned and medically sound judgments: the definition of "handicapped individual" is broad, but only those individuals who are both handicapped *and* otherwise qualified are eligible for relief. The fact that *some* persons who have contagious diseases may pose a serious health threat to others under certain circumstances does not justify excluding from the coverage of the Act *all* persons with actual or perceived contagious diseases. Such exclusion would mean that those accused of being contagious would never have the opportunity to have their condition evaluated in light of medical evidence and a determination made as to whether they were "otherwise qualified." Rather, they would be vulnerable to discrimination on the basis of mythology—precisely the type of injury Congress sought to prevent. We conclude that the fact that a person with a record of a physical impairment is also contagious does not suffice to remove that person from coverage under § 504. *Id.* at 280–86.

Finally, the Court considered the remaining question of whether Arline was "otherwise qualified for the job of elementary schoolteacher":

> To answer this question in most cases, the district court will need to conduct an individualized inquiry and make appropriate findings of fact. Such an inquiry is essential if § 504 is to achieve its goal of protecting handicapped individuals from deprivations based on prejudice, stereotypes, or unfounded fear, while giving appropriate weight to such legitimate concerns of grantees as avoiding exposing others to significant health and safety risks. The basic factors to be considered in conducting this inquiry are well established. In the context of the employment of a person handicapped with a contagious disease, we agree with *amicus* American Medical Association that this inquiry should include
>
>> [findings of] facts, based on reasonable medical judgments given the state of medical knowledge, about (a) the nature of the risk (how the disease is transmitted), (b) the duration of the risk (how long is the carrier infectious), (c) the severity of the risk (what is the potential harm to third parties) and (d) the probabilities the disease will be transmitted and will cause varying degrees of harm.
>
> In making these findings, courts normally should defer to the reasonable medical judgments of public health officials. The next step in the "otherwise-qualified" inquiry is for the court to evaluate, in light of these medical findings, whether the employer could reasonably accommodate the employee under the established standards for that inquiry.
>
> Because of the paucity of factual findings by the District Court, we, like the Court of Appeals, are unable at this stage of the proceedings to resolve whether Arline is "otherwise qualified" for her job. * * * Accordingly, the resolution of whether Arline was otherwise qualified requires further findings of fact.
>
> We hold that a person suffering from the contagious disease of tuberculosis can be a handicapped person within the meaning of § 504 of the Rehabilitation Act of 1973, and that respondent Arline is such a person. We remand the case to the District Court to determine whether Arline is otherwise qualified for her position. The judgment of the Court of Appeals is *Affirmed. Id.* at 287–89.

Index

†